RECENT TRENDS IN COMPUTATIONAL INTELLIGENCE ENABLED RESEARCH

RECENT TRENDS IN COMPUTATIONAL INTELLIGENCE ENABLED RESEARCH

Theoretical Foundations and Applications

Edited by

SIDDHARTHA BHATTACHARYYA
Rajnagar Mahavidyalaya, Birbhum, India

PARAMARTHA DUTTA
Visva Bharati University, Santiniketan, India

DEBABRATA SAMANTA
CHRIST University, Bangalore, India

ANIRBAN MUKHERJEE
RCC Institute of Information Technology, Kolkata, India

INDRAJIT PAN
RCC Institute of Information Technology, Kolkata, India

Academic Press is an imprint of Elsevier
125 London Wall, London EC2Y 5AS, United Kingdom
525 B Street, Suite 1650, San Diego, CA 92101, United States
50 Hampshire Street, 5th Floor, Cambridge, MA 02139, United States
The Boulevard, Langford Lane, Kidlington, Oxford OX5 1GB, United Kingdom

British Library Cataloguing-in-Publication Data
A catalogue record for this book is available from the British Library

Library of Congress Cataloging-in-Publication Data
A catalog record for this book is available from the Library of Congress

ISBN: 978-0-12-822844-9

For Information on all Academic Press publications
visit our website at https://www.elsevier.com/books-and-journals

Publisher: Mara Conner
Editorial Project Manager: Michelle Fisher
Production Project Manager: Swapna Srinivasan
Cover Designer: Mark Rogers

Typeset by MPS Limited, Chennai, India

Dedication

Siddhartha Bhattacharyya would like to dedicate this book to his beloved wife Rashni, his brother-in-law Rishi, and his nieces Rajrupa and Rishika.

Paramartha Dutta would like to dedicate this book to his father Late Arun Kanti Dutta, and his mother Late Bandana Dutta.

Debabrata Samanta would like to dedicate this book to his parents Mr. Dulal Chandra Samanta, Mrs. Ambujini Samanta, his elder sister Mrs. Tanusree Samanta, and his daughter Ms. Aditri Samanta.

Anirban Mukherjee would like to dedicate this book to his colleagues of RCCIIT.

Indrajit Pan would like to dedicate this book in the profound memory of his beloved father Late Prof. (Dr.) Sitansu Kumar Pan.

Contents

List of contributors

Sriyankar Acharyya Department of Computer Science and Engineering, Maulana Abul Kalam Azad University of Technology, Kolkata, India

Joy Adhikary Department of Computer Science and Engineering, Maulana Abul Kalam Azad University of Technology, Kolkata, India

Basavaraj M. Angadi Department of Electronics and Communication Engineering, Basaveshwar Engineering College, Bagalkot, India

V.N. Manjunath Aradhya Department of Computer Applications, JSS Science and Technology University, Mysuru, India

Anjan Bandyopadhyay Department of Computer Science & Engineering, Amity University, Kolkata, India

Jyoti Sekhar Banerjee Department of ECE, Bengal Institute of Technology, Kolkata, India

Antara Banik Department of Computer Science & Engineering, Amity University, Kolkata, India

Arup Kumar Bhattacharjee RCC Institute of Information Technology, Kolkata, India

Joy Bhattacharjee Department of Electronic Science, Acharya Prafulla Chandra College, New Barrackpore, India

Himadri Biswas Department of Computer Science and Engineering, University of Kalyani, Kalyani, India

Pratyay Biswas Department of Computer Science & Engineering, Amity University, Kolkata, India

Sagnick Biswas Department of ECE, Bengal Institute of Technology, Kolkata, India

Suparna Biswas Computer Science and Engineering, Maulana Abul Kalam Azad University of Technology, Kolkata, India

Fernando Cervantes-Sanchez Math Research Center (CIMAT), Guanajuato México

Arpita Chakraborty Department of ECE, Bengal Institute of Technology, Kolkata, India

Poornima M. Chanal Department of Electronics and Communication Engineering, Basaveshwar Engineering College, Bagalkot, India

Ayan Chatterjee Department of Information and Communication Technology, Centre for e-Health, University of Agder, Kristiansand, Norway

Rohit Kamal Chatterjee Birla Institute of Technology, Mesra, Ranchi, India

Sreeja Cherillath Sukumaran Department of Computer Science CHRIST (deemed to be University), Bengaluru, India

Ivan Cruz-Aceves CONACYT—Math Research Center (CIMAT), Guanajuato México

Abhishek Das Department of Computer Science and Engineering, Aliah University, Kolkata, India; Aliah University, Kolkata, India

Utsav Datta Department of Computer Science & Engineering, Amity University, Kolkata, India

Joydeep Dey Department of Computer Science, M.U.C. Women's College, Burdwan, India

Arpan Deyasi RCC Institute of Information Technology, Kolkata, India; Department of Electronics and Communication Engineering, RCC Institute of Information Technology, Kolkata, India

Om Prakash Dhakal Department of Medicine, Sikkim Manipal Institute of Medical Sciences, Gangtok, India

Rajarshi Dhar IIEST Shibpur, Howrah, India

Soumyadip Dhar Department of Information Technology, RCC Institute of Information Technology, Kolkata, India

Martin W. Gerdes Department of Information and Communication Technology, Centre for e-Health, University of Agder, Kristiansand, Norway

Miguel-Angel Gil-Rios Department of Sciences and Engineering (DICIS), University of Guanajuato, Guanajuato México

Amlan Gupta Department of Pathology, Sikkim Manipal Institute of Medical Sciences, Gangtok, India

Mousumi Gupta Department of Computer Applications, Sikkim Manipal Institute of Technology, Majitar, India

D.S. Guru Department of Studies in Computer Science, University of Mysore, Mysuru, India

Igor Guryev Department of Sciences and Engineering (DICIS), University of Guanajuato, Guanajuato México

Khondekar Lutful Hassan Aliah University, Kolkata, India

Daneshwari I. Hatti Department of ECE, BLDEA's V.P. Dr. P. G. Halakatti College of Engineering & Technology (Affiliated to VTU Belagavi), Vijayapur, India; Department of ECE, Basveshwar Engineering College, Bagalkot, India

Mayurakshi Jana Department of Computer Science, Bijoy Krishna Girls' College, Howrah, India

Mahabaleshwar S. Kakkasageri Department of Electronics and Communication Engineering, Basaveshwar Engineering College, Bagalkot, India

Sunil Karforma Department of Computer Science, The University of Burdwan, Burdwan, India

Pankaj Khatiwada Department of Information and Communication Technology, Centre for e-Health, University of Agder, Kristiansand, Norway

Subhadeep Koley Department of Electronics and Communication Engineering, RCC Institute of Information Technology, Kolkata, India

Gururaj S. Kori Department of Electronics and Communication Engineering, Biluru Gurubasava Mahaswamiji Institute of Technology, Mudhol, India

Nimrita Koul School of Computing & Information Technology, REVA University, Bangalore, India

B.H. Lohithashva Department of Computer Applications, JSS Science and Technology University, Mysuru, India

Juan-Manuel López-Hernández Department of Sciences and Engineering (DICIS), University of Guanajuato, Guanajuato México

Sunil Kumar S. Manvi School of Computing and Information Technology, REVA University, Bangalore, India

Santiago Martinez Department of Health and Nursing Science, Centre for e-Health, University of Agder, Kristiansand, Norway

Kaniz Fatima Mian Department of Computer Science and Engineering, Aliah University, Kolkata, India

Priyanjana Mitra University of Calcutta, Kolkata, India

Sanjoy Mondal University of Calcutta, Kolkata, India

Shukla Mondal Department of Computer Science and Engineering, Aliah University, Kolkata, India

Soumen Mukherjee RCC Institute of Information Technology, Kolkata, India

Rajat Suvra Nandy Aliah University, Kolkata, India

Ravi Ranjan Department of CSE, Bengal Institute of Technology, Kolkata, India

Hiranmoy Roy Department of Information Technology, RCC Institute of Information Technology, Kolkata, India

Sayak Saha Department of CSE, Bengal Institute of Technology, Kolkata, India

Prashant Sangulagi Bheemanna Khandre Institute of Technology, Bhalki, India

Soumen Santra Department of Computer Application, Techno International Newtown, Kolkata, India

Debabrata Sarddar Department of Computer Science and Engineering, University of Kalyani, Kalyani, India

Arindam Sarkar Department of Computer Science & Electronics, Ramakrishna Mission Vidyamandira, Belur Math, India

Vaskar Sarkar Department of Mathematics, School of Science, Adamas University, Kolkata, India

Priyajit Sen Department of Computer Science, Directorate of Distance Education, Vidyasagar University, Midnapore, India

Ali Shahaab Cardiff School of Technologies, Cardiff Metropolitan University, Cardiff, United Kingdom

Labhvam Kumar Sharma Department of CSE, Bengal Institute of Technology, Kolkata, India

Ashok V. Sutagundar Department of ECE, Basveshwar Engineering College, Bagalkot, India

Preface

The field of computational intelligence (CI) has assumed importance of late, thanks to the evolving soft computing and artificial intelligence methodologies, tools, and techniques for envisaging the essence of intelligence embedded in real-life observations. As a consequence, scientists have been able to explain and understand real-life processes and practices which previously often remained unexplored by dint of their underlying imprecision, uncertainties, and redundancies owing to the nonavailability of appropriate methods for describing the inexactness, incompleteness, and vagueness of information representation. This understanding has been made possible to a greater extent by the advent of the field of CI, which attempts to explore and unearth the intelligence, otherwise insurmountable, embedded in the system under consideration. To be specific, imparting intelligence has become the thrust of various computational paradigms irrespective of the nature of application domains. With the advent and development of CI, almost every technological innovation currently is being driven by intelligence in one form or the other. Of late, CI has made its presence felt in every nook and corner of the world, thanks to the rapid exploration of research in this direction. CI is now not limited to only specific computational fields, but has made inroads into signal processing, smart manufacturing, predictive control, robot navigation, smart cities, and sensor design to name but a few. Thus, the use of this computational paradigm is no longer limited to the fields of computing or computing-related disciplines and the present scenario demands a wider perspective of the application of CI to virtually every sphere of human civilization which handles meaningful information. Keeping this broader spectrum of the application of CI across different platforms/disciplines in mind, this treatise is targeted to inculcate a knowledge base of various research initiatives in this direction.

This volume aims to bring together researchers, engineers, developers, and practitioners from academia and industry working in all major areas and interdisciplinary areas of CI, communication systems, computer networks, and soft computing to share their experience, and exchange and cross-fertilize their ideas. It is expected that the present endeavor will entice researchers to bring up new prospects for collaboration across disciplines and gain ideas facilitating novel breakthroughs.

The volume comprises 23 excellent chapters covering multidisciplinary applications of CI.

In recent years, the integration of wireless sensor networks (WSNs) and cloud computing has played an important role in fast and reliable computation and also communication. The integration, also called the sensor cloud, is very specific and the use of simulations is necessary in its architecture, implementation, and operational characteristics. There are several issues which need attention in order to optimize the sensor cloud in a more intelligent and efficient manner. Chapter 1, Optimization in the Sensor Cloud: Taxonomy, Challenges, and Survey, focuses on providing a review of the challenges, survey, and taxonomy of an intelligent sensor cloud optimization which is a new methodology that is still evolving. The key objectives of this chapter are new insights into sensor cloud optimization such as increasing network lifetime, which is achieved by addressing critical parameters including load balancing, classification, processing, and transmission of information.

A WSN is deployed normally in harsh environments for collecting and delivering data to a remotely located base station (BS). In a sensor network it is very important to know the position of the sensor node and data collected by that node as it has a strong impact on the overall performance of the WSN. Grouping of SNs to form clusters has been adopted widely to overcome the scalability problem. It has been proved that for organizing the network into a connected hierarchy, clustering is an effective approach. In Chapter 2, Computational Intelligence Techniques for Localization and Clustering in Wireless Sensor Networks, the authors address the localization and clustering techniques in WSN, challenges/issues to provide localization and clustering for WSN, and usage of computational techniques for localization and clustering algorithms. The chapter also outlines the recent research works on the use of CI techniques and future challenges that need to be addressed in providing CI techniques for localization and clustering.

A WSN contributes significantly to emerging areas such as ubiquitous computing, smart systems, and the Internet of Things (IoT). WSNs, being highly distributed networks of tiny sensors that are self-conscious, are deployed in different locations around the globe for various applications. These tiny sensors face resource problems in terms of power consumption, processing speed, communication range, and available bandwidth, etc. To extend the lifetime of a WSN, efficient and smart use of available resources is very important. Therefore intelligent/effective resource management (RM) is a complex job which includes resource discovery/identification, resource scheduling, resource allocation, resource provisioning, resource sharing, resource utilization, and resource monitoring in the networks. Chapter 3, Computational Intelligent Techniques for Resource Management Schemes in Wireless Sensor Networks, provides an insight into different CI techniques to address the critical issues and challenges of WSNs.

In the era of the IoT, most devices communicate without human intervention through the Internet, however heterogeneous devices possess varied resource capability and require additional resources for processing. Management of resources becomes a crucial aspect, imposing some challenges, namely RM for the processing of tasks with reduced response time, energy consumption, authenticity, and bandwidth utilization. Therefore computing and communication resources through the fog computing paradigm, and the enhancement of intelligence through agents are offered. Chapter 4, Swarm Intelligence Based MSMOPSO for Optimization of Resource Provisioning in Internet of Things, presents an MSMOPSO technique with agent technology for managing diverse devices and dynamic changing of resources of fog device to optimize the provisioning of resources for end users. The presented method authenticates devices, provision resources based on fitness value, and schedules by time-shared and cloudlet-shared scheduling policies.

Data security and privacy are always considered as critical aspects, especially in healthcare. The advent of technologies such as the IoT has gathered a great deal of attention in this digital era and helped to improve e-health services. IoT-based services in healthcare and its applications have led to the potential growth of quality services in healthcare. However, the sensitive nature of healthcare data and IoT devices which store and collect real-time data makes it even more vulnerable to various attacks. With the development of digitalized data and IoT-based e-health systems, authentication mechanisms are essential to ensure both usability and security. Considering these aspects, a novel, secure user authentication scheme is presented in Chapter 5, DNA-based Authentication to Access Internet of Things-Based Healthcare Data, that uses user ID, unique ID (AADHAAR), password, DNA steganography, and hash function. An OTP method is also illustrated to strengthen the device authentication.

CI techniques follow a pragmatic approach to learning and decision-making rather than a hard approach, as in expert systems or rule-based systems. In Chapter 6, Computational Intelligence Techniques for Cancer Diagnosis, the authors discuss the applications of important techniques under CI that have been applied to computational diagnosis of cancers. These include fuzzy logic, artificial neural networks, evolutionary computation based on principles of natural selection, learning theory which is the study of learning mechanisms of natural organisms, and probabilistic or random methods which inherently account for uncertainty in input or the events. Fuzzy logic is applied in the identification of tumors in medical imaging reports where approximate reasoning is helpful. Neural networks like convolutional neural networks (CNNs) have been demonstrated to accurately identify and classify various type of tumors. Evolutionary computation or natural computation methods apply the principle of natural selection to solve multiobjective optimization problems. These methods, including swarm intelligence etc., have wide application in the areas of genomic data analysis.

IoT devices (nodes) are capable of capturing, preserving, analyzing, and sharing data about themselves and their physical world. Security and privacy are the major challenges in the implementation of IoT technology. Major privacy aspects in the IoT are stealing data, monitoring, and tracking, etc. Authentication, integrity, and confidentiality are major concerns for privacy and security preservation in the IoT. Chapter 7, Security and Privacy in the Internet of Things: Computational Intelligent Techniques-based Approaches, focuses on privacy and security in the IoT, including quantum cryptography.

In Chapter 8, Automatic Enhancement of Coronary Arteries Using Convolutional Gray-level Templates and Path-based Metaheuristics, a novel method for coronary vessel imaging enhancement is presented. Its effectiveness relies on the use of metaheuristics for the automatic generation of convolutional gray-level templates. Instead of having an image filter in the form of a convolutional template with predefined values, it is generated automatically in a training stage using a set of 100 X-ray images. After the template is generated, its performance is evaluated using a test set of 30 images. In order to ensure the effectiveness of the method, four different strategies have been implemented, which include iterated local search, tabu search, simulated annealing (which are single-solution based), and univariate marginal distribution algorithm (which is population-based). The image database contains the corresponding ground-truth images delineated by a professional cardiologist specialist and is publicly available. To measure the performance of the proposed method, the area under the receiver operating characteristic curve is used, showing that the iterated local search strategy achieves the highest performance in the training and test stages with 0:9581 and 0:9610, respectively.

Car theft is one of the most common worldwide crimes currently, and so protection of cars is important. Thieves generally steal vehicles by breaking a window to gain access. As a solution to this problem, Chapter 9, Smart City Development: Theft Handling of Public Vehicles Using Image Analysis and Cloud Network, presents a camera sensor mounted within the car's steering column whereby the driver needs to confirm his/her identity, thereby enabling only the owner to use the key to unlock and/or start the vehicle. Once the camera takes the driver's photo, the photo is compared with all existing drivers by checking the number of the particular car in a city center (a cloud data center holds all of a city's cars and their registered drivers in detail).

In Chapter 10, Novel Detection of Cancerous Cell Through Image Segmentation Approach Using Principle Component Analysis, the principal component analysis (PCA) technique, along with confusion matrix formation using K-means clustering algorithm is applied for sensitive medical images for segmentation of cancerous portions through a threshold detection procedure. Tumors present in the cancerous image with respect to the percentage of occupied portions by tumors cell is predicted based on a predefined threshold level (cut-off level), where simulated findings show better performance than those obtained by Otsu's threshold method. This is established by comparison of the peak signal-to-noise ratio, and for better comparison, an edge detection operation is carried out on the image based upon Canny's algorithm.

Chapter 11, Classification of Operating Spectrum for RAMAN Amplifier embedded Optical Communication System Using Soft Computing Techniques, to obtain the influential parameters in a RAMAN amplifier embedded optical communication system designed at both 1310 and 1550 nm spectra, where only five and four variables, respectively, have been identified as the governing factor for performance of the system through the PCA technique. Weight factors of those attributes are statistically evaluated using the relief technique. Excellent correlation coefficient is obtained for both multilayer perceptron-based analysis and also using the bagging classifier for both windows for three combinations of training–testing pairs, and design at 1310 nm outperforms the conventional 1550 nm wavelength system. Five-, 10-, and 20-fold cross-validations are used to obtain the results. The forest of random tree method is also applied for the same purpose, and eventually confirms the previous findings obtained using PCA. Simulated observations yield key parameters which are critical for designing the system with optimum outcome.

Chapter 12, Random Walk Elephant Swarm Water Search Algorithm (RW-ESWSA) for Identifying Order Preserving Sub-Matrices in Gene Expression Data: A New Approach Using ESWSA, presents a new variant of the Elephant Swarm Water Search Algorithm (ESWSA), namely, the Random Walk ESWSA (RW-ESWSA) to find order-preserving submatrices (OPSM) from gene expression data sets expressed in a matrix form. The OPSM is a submatrix where a subset of genes changes their expression rate in approximately similar manner in the different conditions of a disease. This is the first attempt to identify OPSMs using metaheuristic approaches. In this chapter, the presented variant RW-ESWSA, which has better exploration in the search strategy incorporating randomized walk or movements, proves its efficacy in the performance of benchmark functions and statistical analysis. Having better exploration capability, it performs better than other metaheuristic algorithms in convergence analysis. Apart from benchmark functions, all these algorithms have been executed on two gene expression data sets: yeast and leukemia. The significant OPSMs have been retrieved using each of the algorithms.

Fog computing is a relatively new paradigm which uses distributed fog nodes to overcome the limitations and drawbacks of the centralized cloud computing paradigm. In Chapter 13, Geopositioning of Fog Nodes Based on User Device Location and Framework for Game Theoretic Applications in an Fog to Cloud Network, the authors present a method to compute the positions for installation of fog nodes in a two-fog layer fog to cloud (F2C) architecture based on user device density in a particular area. The motivation for making the position of fog nodes a function of end user device density comes from the fact that localization of a distributed fog network improves the network's overall effectiveness and, by reducing the geographical displacement between end users and the fog servers, the latency can be reduced, resulting in better performance. The application and working of the created F2C network is also demonstrated using game theoretic approaches.

The ever-emanating sector of computer vision and image processing demand real-time enhancement techniques to properly restore hazy images. Although dark channel prior is most notable for single-image haze removal, the major drawback is its long processing time. In Chapter 14, A Wavelet-based Low Frequency Prior for Single Image Dehazing, the authors present a time-efficient wavelet-based prior, namely, low-frequency prior, which assumes that the majority of the haze is contained in the low-frequency components of a hazy image. The authors have transformed the hazy image into the wavelet domain using discrete wavelet transform, to segregate the low- and high-frequency components. Only the spatial low-frequency components are subjected to the dark channel prior dehazing. The obtained dehazed image with low contrast is then subjected to a novel fuzzy contrast enhancement framework. Qualitative and quantitative comparison with other state-of-the-art methods proves the primacy of the framework.

The accurate vessel structure segmentation from the ophthalmoscopic image of the retina is a major task of early computer-aided diagnosis (CADx) of diabetic retinopathy. Chapter 15, Segmentation of Retinal Blood Vessel Structure Based on Statistical Distribution of Area of Isolated Objects, presents an unsupervised segmentation technique by discriminating the statistical distribution of the area of the isolated objects. An adaptive mathematical morphology-based algorithm is used for the initial segmentation, followed by a locally adaptive threshold to extract the vessel structure from the background. Unfortunately, along with the vessel structure, an enumerable number of noisy artifacts are introduced by this process. To discriminate the vessels from the artifacts, the statistical distribution of the area of isolated objects is computed. Since noise and vessels assume different statistical distributions, depending on the shape and monotonicity of the histogram a threshold is determined to separate the noisy objects and the blood vessel structure. This method extracts the vessel structure from the background with an accuracy of 96.38%.

A pivotal research problem in the field of WSN-assisted IoTs (WSN-IoT) is to enhance the network lifetime. One of the primary concerns is to reduce the energy consumption of IoT devices. A traditional approach to this solution is clustering the IoT devices and, within each cluster, a leader node called the cluster head (CH) is responsible for gathering data from member nodes and transmitting them to the BS. Direct communication from the CH to the BS produces long edges that may lead to a significant amount of energy depletion. In Chapter 16, Energy Efficient Rendezvous Point Based Routing in Wireless Sensor Network With Mobile Sink, the authors present a rendezvous point (RP)-based routing algorithm using the Multiobjective Genetic Algorithm to enhance the network lifetime. RPs collect data from the CH nodes and transmit them to the BS. Experimental results reveal that the presented algorithm outperforms the state-of-the-art in respect to scalability and energy efficiency. From the simulation results, it can also be concluded that the presented technique not only enhances the network lifetime of the IoT system but also uniformly distributes the energy load in the IoT network.

Activity recognition is a prominent and difficult research problem, and it is a branch of machine learning. Currently, there is increased interest in ensuring safety in private and public sectors. Therefore surveillance cameras have been deployed to monitor suspicious activity. Consequently, many researchers have worked on developing an automatic surveillance system to detect violent events. However, violent events remain difficult to detect because of illumination, complex background, and scale variation in surveillance cameras. In Chapter 17, An Integration of Handcrafted Features for Violent Event Detection in Videos, the authors use GHOG (global histograms of oriented gradients), HOFO (histogram of optical flow orientation), GIST handcrafted feature descriptors, and integration of GHOG + HOFO + GIST descriptors to improve the performance of the presented method. Finally, prominent features are used with support vector machine classifier for violent event detection. Experimentation is conducted on the Hockey Fight data set and Violent-Flows data set with the feature integration descriptors showing promising results.

Diabetic retinopathy (DR) is an important disease that causes loss of sight, and it is one of the most serious issues of diabetes. Automated diagnosis for DR detection is very effective in the case of clinical usage as well as to assist doctors efficiently. Various approaches have been proposed by the researchers to detect DR automatically from retina images. In Chapter 18, Deep Learning-based Diabetic Retinopathy Detection for Multiclass Imbalanced Data, a deep learning approach is presented to recognize DR automatically for five different imbalanced classes of DR images. The model is trained using various pretrained CNN architectures coupled with hyperparameter tuning and transfer learning. The results demonstrate better accuracy to deal with data imbalances by using CNN architectures and transfer learning for classifying DR images.

In this generation of advanced IoTs-based e-health systems, medical data communication is a significant area of concern. Dementia, anxiety, schizophrenia, depression, and major depressive disorder are among the most common mental complications. In Chapter 19, Internet of Things E-Health Revolution: Secured Transmission of Homeopathic E-Medicines Through Chaotic Key Formation, a chaotic symmetric key of 128 bits has been generated by the key distribution center (KDC). Homeopathy physicians issue e-prescriptions to treat patients after online symptoms analysis. This e-prescription may be encrypted through that session key which has been received from the KDC. Secret sharing on the predefined number of users in the homeopathy telemedicine system has been incorporated. The reverse operation may be done to decrypt the e-prescription after mixing the threshold shares. Several statistics-related tests have been performed on the proposed technique for its validation.

In Chapter 20, Smart Farming and Water Saving Based Intelligent Irrigation System Implementation using the Internet of Things, the authors deploy an array of sensors to measure the temperature, soil moisture, humidity, and water usage to automate a traditional agricultural system more smartly as agriculture is one of the most important factors contributing to a nation's GDP. The significant contribution of this chapter is in identifying the predicted amount of water required for a particular field for a particular length of time, as all the water consumption details of the field are stored in the cloud. Hence, it is possible to find out using the Artificial Intelligence-Machine Learning tool which can be accessed through the Web and a mobile application for daily, monthly, or seasonal water consumption requirements.

The IoTs has gained popularity in recent years in various research domains for applications in real-life problems such as healthcare, precision farming, and surveillance. The IoT, in combination with machine learning (ML) techniques, can predict better results. Further, metaheuristic techniques are used to handle heterogeneous data and can solve complex problems. In Chapter 21, Intelligent and Smart Enabling Technologies in Advanced Applications: Recent Trends, an exhaustive study has been made on intelligent and smart enabling technologies.

Health data are a sensitive category of personal data. Their misuse can result in a high risk to the individual and health information handling rights and opportunities unless there is adequate protection. Reasonable security standards are needed to protect electronic health records (EHRs). Maintaining access to medical data, even in the developing world, would help health and well-being across the world. Unfortunately, there are still countries that hinder the portability of medical records. Numerous occurrences have shown that it still takes weeks for medical data to be ported from one general physician to another. Cross-border portability is almost impossible due to the lack of technical infrastructure and standardization. The authors demonstrate the difficulty of ensuring the portability of medical records with some example case studies in Chapter 22, Leveraging Technology for Healthcare and Retaining Access to Personal Health Data to Enhance Personal Health and Well-being, as a collaborative engagement exercise through a data mapping process to describe how different people and data points interact and evaluate EHR portability techniques. A blockchain-based EHR system is also proposed that allows secure and cross-border sharing of medical data.

Histopathology provides for the morphological diagnosis of many diseases including cancer. It is done by visualizing sections of tissue under a microscope and determining the arrangements of cells. Automation in microscopic images is still in its infancy because of difficulty in microscopic image segmentation. Chapter 23, Enhancement of Foveolar Architectural Changes in Gastric Endoscopic Biopsies, deals with the segmentation and highlighting of one of the most common small tissue in endoscopic biopsy of stomach. Dysplastic epithelium is sometimes difficult to diagnose. Pathologists used dysplasia as a marker for stomach cancer diagnosis. Early-stage diagnosis of gastric cancer is dependent on endoscopy and biopsy followed by histopathology. During endoscopy margins of gastric folds are identified. The biopsy sample is stained with hematoxylin & eosin (H&E) stain and the pathologist observes the unnatural haphazard branching of gastric foveolar and pits. Survival rates may be prolonging through early diagnosis and treatment. One of the early evidences of cancer is dysplasia. Foveolar type dysplasia is seen in histology in many cases. Foveolar inflammation or hyperplasia occurs in case of loss of mucous folds. Subtle features make detection of the foveolar architectural changes are highly variable. Such changes often result in the discrepancy of interpretation among pathologists. This chapter presents an approach that segments and highlights the foveolar architectural lesions from gastric histopathology images. Watershed transformation is used to segment the normal gastric biopsy image into several different regions. Foveolar lesions are highlighted by evaluating the boundaries for adjacent catchment basins. Growing regional minima help to identify the inflammation regions.

This volume is aimed to serve as a treatise for undergraduate students of computer engineering, information science, and electrical and electronics engineering for some parts of their curriculum. The editors feel that this attempt will be worthwhile, if the book benefits the end users.

Siddhartha Bhattacharyya,
Paramartha Dutta,
Debabrata Samanta,
Anirban Mukherjee and
Indrajit Pan

CHAPTER

1

Optimization in the sensor cloud: Taxonomy, challenges, and survey

Prashant Sangulagi[1] *and Ashok Sutagundar*[2]

[1]**Bheemanna Khandre Institute of Technology, Bhalki, India** [2]**Basaveshwar Engineering College, Bagalkot, India**

1.1 Introduction

The sensor cloud (SC) is a new representation of cloud computing (CC), which collects information from physical sensors and transmits all sensory information to a CC infrastructure. Wireless sensor network (WSN) information may be stored over the cloud so that it can be correctly utilized by numerous programs and via this integration the cloud services can provide sensors as a service. In SC, there is more than one physical sensor network that is mapped with the virtual sensor networks (VSNs) using the cloud to provide efficient aid to users. Users are recommended to carry out more than one application of WSNs via VSNs (Khan, Dwivedi, & Kumar, 2019a). The CC is responsible for storing unrestricted amounts of information. The CC monitors the status of the WSN remotely (Glitho, Morrow, & Polakos, 2013) and makes logical clusters to provide seamless service to the end-user. Due to the WSN issues, the CC is integrated with the WSN to provide seamless service to end-users without any obstacles. SC is a well-designed information storage, visualization, and remote management platform that supports powerful CC technologies to deliver high scalability, visualization, and user-programmable analysis (Lan, 2010; Shea, Liu, Ngai, & Cui, 2013). Further, SC can be defined as "an infrastructure that allows truthfully invasive computation utilizing sensors as an interface among physical and cyber worlds, the information-compute clusters as the cyber spine and the internet as the communication medium" (Intellisys, 2020; Irwin, Sharma, Shenoy, & Zink, 2010). An SC gathers and integrates information through various sensing nodes, which enables large-scale processing of information, and collaborates with cloud applications. The SC integrates multiple networks with numerous sensing applications and CC platforms by enabling cross-disciplinary applications that can be traversed across organizational diversity. SC allows users to quickly capture, access, process, display, analyze, store, share, and search large amounts of sensor information from multiple applications. These enormous amounts of information are stored, processed, analyzed, and then viewed using the cloud's computer information technology and storage resources (Doukas & Maglogiannis, 2011).

The general SC architecture is as presented in Fig. 1.1. The SC consists of three main layers, the physical layer, also called the physical sensor network, the gateway, which is the middle connecting layer between the physical sensor network and the SC server, and finally the SC layer (Yujin & Park, 2014).

The SC's architecture includes the following specifications.

Physical sensor network: This consists of sensor nodes deployed in a predefined area, either random or manually, depending upon the scenario of the environment. The nodes deployed are of the same or different sensing properties depending upon the interest. All the nodes in the sensing field use one of the optimal routing techniques to send the sensed information to the cluster head (CH) or directly to the sink node (SN). There is a need for optimization to save battery energy and to send only the required information to the SN, prolonging the network lifetime of the physical network.

Sink node: Eventually, all the nodes in the sensor network send their data to the SN. The SN manages all the nodes in the sensing network. The SN stores the entire sensor node details in its range and is updated frequently.

Recent Trends in Computational Intelligence Enabled Research.
DOI: https://doi.org/10.1016/B978-0-12-822844-9.00036-0

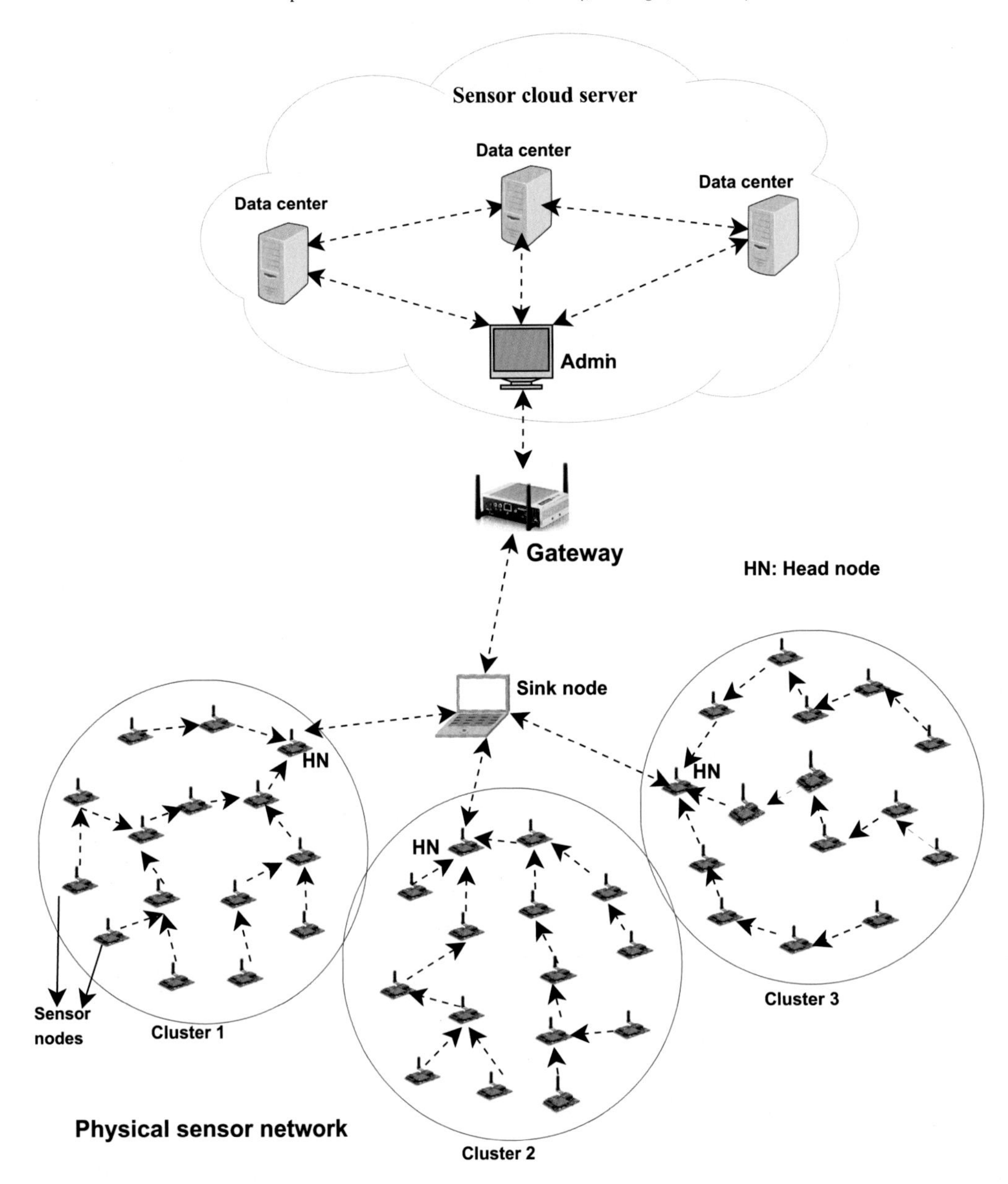

FIGURE 1.1 General architecture of the sensor cloud.

Gateway: The gateway acts as a middle part between the CC and WSN. Sensor information is stored in a cloud server using traditional wired or wireless technologies. Preferably wireless networking is used for the transmission of information from the physical sensor network to a SC server.

Sensor cloud server: The sensor cloud server (SCS) has a huge database and is used to save the information coming from different networks. The SCS is the endpoint where all the sensed information is stored. Diverse users can access the information anywhere at any point in time, irrespective of where the actual sensors/information is stored.

Users: Users are the end-users who use the SC services. Additionally, users can insert the request into the network and wait for the results. Users can access information of any kind with conditions, such as, if the information is open then there will be no cost of viewing/accessing it and if the information is encrypted then the user needs a password to access it.

Virtual sensors group: This is the logical network of the physical WSN created at the SCS. This offers the real physical network condition and is persistently updating the SCS. If any node runs out of battery power or there is a concern it may expire, then the virtual network eliminates the node from the network virtually and updates the routing table.

The CC is an entirely motivating solution for SC infrastructure for many reasons, including agility, dependability, accessibility, real-time, adaptability, etc. Monitoring based on organizational health and environment requires extremely sensitive information, so implementations of this nature cannot be managed by standard information tools existing in terms of scalability, accuracy, programmability, or availability. Hence there is a need for improved infrastructure and capabilities to manage such extremely susceptible applications in real time. There are many advantages to the SC and they are listed as analysis, scalability, multitenancy, collaboration, visualization, response time, automation, flexibility, and dynamic provision (Ansari, Alamri, Hassan, & Shoaib, 2013). Due to the attractive features of the SC, nowadays it has many applications. The SC applications include military, agriculture, healthcare, weather forecasting, disaster monitoring, traffic analysis, vehicle monitoring, educational department, etc. (Sindhanaiselvan & Mekala, 2014). The creation, processing, and storage of every bit of information, however, adds to the energy costs, increases delay, and then further significantly affects the system environment. As can be seen in Fig. 1.2 the amount of energy used by the SC data centers is growing annually and is predicted to reach 7500 terawatt hours (TWh) by 2028–2030 (Andrae & Edler, 2015). Various SC systems are available currently and they are being used for various applications. Various SC systems have different components to fulfill the requirements. A comparative study of different SC systems is depicted in Table 1.1.

This chapter presents a detailed study on SC optimization, introduces the concept of intelligent optimization, and explains problems that are either triggered or enhanced by heterogeneity. The taxonomy of origins of heterogeneity in optimization is conceived through differentiation of SC conditions. Optimization heterogeneity is identified and classified into vertical and horizontal facets based on the heterogeneity of physical WSN and CC. Brief details are given below.

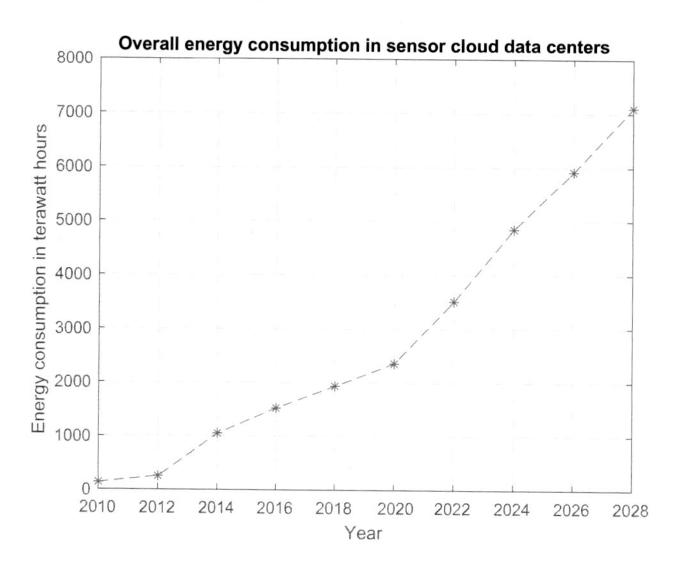

FIGURE 1.2 Overall annual energy usage in sensor cloud systems.

In general, optimization can be characterized as a method with the most cost-effective or viable benefit under prescribed conditions by maximizing desired variables and reducing unnecessary ones. Maximization, on the other hand, means attempting to produce the optimal or maximum outcome or consequence, irrespective of the expense of gain. Optimization is an integral aspect of the computer system design phase. By constantly exploring alternative solutions, thus following resource and expense constraints, it focuses on seeking optimal approaches to a design problem. Optimization is usually accomplished by the usage of linear programming techniques in computer-based simulation challenges.

The optimization model design phases include (1) collection of information, (2) problem description and formulation, (3) development of model, (4) validation of model with performance evaluation, and finally, (5) interpretation of results. Optimization techniques have become essential and widespread in various technical applications in the light of advancements in computing devices (Tsai, Carlsson, Ge, Hu, & Shi, 2014). Methods of optimization have been generally classified as first-order and second-order optimization. Optimization algorithms for first order are simple to evaluate, and require less time to converge on broad knowledge sets. Second-order strategies are quicker when the second-order derivative is otherwise established; such strategies are always slower and time-consuming computational processes along with memory. Several intelligent optimization techniques like neural network, fuzzy logic, genetic algorithm, ant colony optimization, simulated annealing, etc. have been considered in this chapter.

Usually, a classification method utilizes divisions in a hierarchical structure in which each group is associated with procedures on how information is treated and what protection precautions it requires (Darwazeh, Al-Qassas, & Al Dosari, 2015). Classification of information can be classified as private, hybrid, and public information. Consistent usage of information classification would encourage more effective management processes and reduce the expense of holding protected information. A standard classification of information has four key stages: (1) designing the information classification scheme, (2) finding information sensitivity, (3) applying the label, and (4) utilizing the results.

Load balancing is a way of reallocating the overall load to the specific data center of the virtual machine system to utilize the resource efficiently and to maximize the reaction time. Load balancing of activities is essential in all CC and WSN systems for distributing the load equally to boost the life span of the SC system. The load-balancing algorithm for the cloud/WSN can check the situations under which some of the nodes are overloaded and others underloaded. Load balancing is a key goal of network traffic control. By

TABLE 1.1 Comparative study of different sensor cloud systems.

Reference	Layers	Major components	Applications
Nimbits Data Logging Cloud Sever	IoT, sensors, cloud	Data processing, IoT platform, data points	Social network and alert system
Pachube Feed Cloud Service	Web service, cloud server, IoT, sensors, real-time	Database service, sensor data, web	Real-time, social network
Guezguez, Jacem, Rekhis, and Boudriga (2018)	WSN, cloud computing, quality of service, security	Physical sensors, virtual sensors, cloud computing	Healthcare applications
Zhang, Yan, and Sun (2013)	Internet, virtual sink, sensor zone	Sink point, cloud nodes, sensor zone, and scheduler	Decentralized computing and data transmission for any network
Das, Das, Mishra, and Mohapatra (2017)	Cloud computing, sensor network, physical network, end-users	R_{prof} prediction scheme, logistic activation function, sensor data	Expanded toward application of any kind
ThingSpeak IoT−ThingSpeak	Application, sensor-cloud, physical WSNs	SC sensing as a service, request aggregator, and virtual and physical sensor manager	Expanded toward applications of any kind
Dinh and Kim (2016)	IoT, Internet	Cloud computing, data management, IoT applications	Modern environmental tracking or electronic healthcare systems
Kansal, Nath, Liu, and Zhao (2007)	Sensors, web	Sensor nodes, sensor map, web API	Expanded toward applications of any kind

utilizing the approach of hardware or software, or by combining both, load balancing may be achieved by delivering a fast response to every user. Load balancing is usually a reaction to SC server grouping behaviors. Load balancing can balance some types of information on each processor to improve overall efficiency, such as the number of jobs waiting in a ready queue, work delivery time, CPU loading rate, and so on (Beaumont, Eyraud-Dubois, & Larchevêque, 2013). There are two different forms of load balancing: static load balancing and dynamic load balancing (Ahmed et al., 2019; Pawar & Wagh, 2012).

The organization of this chapter is as follows, Section 1.1 presented an introduction to sensor cloud-like architecture of SC, working of SC, advantages of SC, and applications of SC, Section 1.2 describes the challenges/issues of using optimized SC systems, Section 1.3 depicts the taxonomical representation of the optimization in SC, design issues of SC systems, and energy-optimized SC systems, Section 1.4 discuss the methodology used along with future research in the term intelligent optimization technique for SC systems, and finally Section 1.5 concludes the chapter.

1.2 Background and challenges in the sensor cloud

The CC and WSN are integrated into SC. Both WSN operators and cloud providers profit from this collaboration. WSN information can be processed in the cloud and can be utilized effectively by multiple apps and with this combination the cloud hosting can offer sensors as a service (Khan, Dwivedi, & Kumar, 2019c). There can be various sensor networks in the SC that are linked only with the VSN using a cloud to deliver application management. End-users are supported by utilizing these VSNs to perform several WSN applications. Various approaches and techniques have been introduced in the SC for the optimization process. This section explains the terminology used and their optimization techniques in the SC. This section also outlines the main issues that the current research has addressed.

1.2.1 Key definitions

This section describes some of the key concepts and perceptions that would be discussed all through due to the diversity of methods developed in the intelligent SC optimization process.

Sensor cloud: An architecture that makes truly omnipresent computation utilizing sensors as an intermediary between the physical and digital realms, the data-computing clusters as the network backend, and the Internet as a means of interaction. An SC receives and analyzes information from multiple sensors that allows large-scale information processing and collaborates between users on cloud services.

Optimization: This can be defined as searching for a solution to the most economical or feasible results under the limitations provided, by maximizing desirable variables and reducing undesirable considerations. Maximization, by contrast, involves aiming to obtain the best or optimum effect or consequence without reference to risk or expense. Optimization research is confined by the lack of proper knowledge and the lack of time to determine what data are accessible.

Load balancing: This is the technique of optimizing device efficiency by transferring the workload between the processors/nodes. It is a method of reallocating the overall load to the cumulative system's network entities to allow resource usage efficiency and to enhance the reaction time while eliminating a situation through which a few nodes are overwhelmed while others are underloaded. The load balancing attempts to improve the performance of the system, maintains stability in the system, and prepares for possible system changes (Alakeel, 2010).

Information classification: Classification of information is a method wherein organizations evaluate the information they hold as well as the degree of security it should provide. Organizations typically classify the information as sensitive, insensitive, and restricted. In particular, information that would be impacted by higher consequences must be assigned a greater degree of confidentiality. Classification includes labeling information to make it easy to find and also to record. It also removes various information duplications that can lower the amount of storage and management while accelerating the searching.

Information processing: Information processing is the technology involved in the selection, interpretation, storage, retrieval, and classification of stored information. This process describes all changes that occur in the systems. The information should be processed in such a way that the information is small in size, covering all the information which is intended by the systems. The information should be processed promptly to reach the goals of the systems along with maintaining its accuracy. The computing facilities should meet to achieve better quality of service (QoS) while considering the information-processing concepts (Lin & Wang, 2015). The hypothesis of information processing is a valuable tool to guide the preparation of organizations.

Information transmission: Information transmission relates to transferring information between multiple digital devices in terms of bytes. Information transmission is the act of transmitting processed information coherently via a means of communication from one individual to another. Information transmission should always be energy efficient, and minimum information with greater accuracy should be transmitted from end to end. The information transmission can be defined as parallel transmission and serial transmission.

1.2.2 Challenges/issues

There are many challenges/issues in SC such as design issues, energy issues, engineering issues, efficient communication, and continuous data transfer that need to be addressed before designing the architecture for SC which can be operable for particular applications or other general applications (Rolim, Koch, Sekkaki, & Westphall, 2008). Some of the major design issues and challenges in SC are as follows.

Fault tolerance and reliable data transfer: Several things need to be monitored when implementing a network in actual environments, such as education, healthcare, and hospitals, and those should be fault-tolerant, with stable continuous information transmission from sensors to the cloud server (Jit et al., 2010).

Real-time multimedia processing: Using huge amounts of information in real time as well as its extraction has become a significant challenge in integrating diverse and huge cloud storage sources. It is also a major challenge to classify multimedia information and content in real time, so that it can activate the appropriate facilities and help the user in his/her present location.

Power: Using the handset as a gateway power is the greatest problem that needs to be addressed as the continuing processing and wireless communication will exhaust the handset battery within a few days or weeks. It is therefore important to connect the phones directly to the system operating within the handset to monitor the proper functioning of power management.

Authorization: For doctors, patients, assistants, caretakers, etc., a web-based interface can be used for remotely examining and evaluating the health-relevant conditions of the patient, therefore the system must offer various authorization roles for different user kinds and verify them through this web app. This will provide some level of privacy by encouraging nurses to limit themselves to just one patient that they can take good care of.

Service level agreement violation: Consumers' reliance on cloud providers for their computer-related applications like processing, storing, and analysis of sensory data on demand may require the quality of the service to be sustained for the stability of user applications and to achieve its objectives. However, if cloud service providers (CSPs) are unable to provide such quality of services on demand by the client in the case of handling large sensor data in crucial situations, this would lead in a violation of service level agreement (SLA) and the service provider has to be accountable. Therefore, there is a need for reliable, dynamic collaborative work between CSPs.

Storage: Several engineering issues, such as information stored on the server, need to be taken into account when moving information from mobile to server. To combat such timestamps, every data packet is sent to aid in the server for information reconstruction. Most information analysis is done at the end of the application, therefore a system needs to be designed to prevent busty operation because of several devices linked to the network concurrently.

Network access management: In SC design applications, there are different and multiple networks to handle. For such different networks, there is a need for proper and effective access management strategies as this will optimize bandwidth utilization and enhance performance links.

Bandwidth limitation: Bandwidth constraint is also one of the major challenges currently facing cloud-sensor networks because the frequency of sensor nodes and their cloud applications is significantly increased. To handle the allocation of bandwidth with such a massive infrastructure comprised of the enormous amount of device and cloud clients, the objective of distributing bandwidth to all systems and clients becomes challenging (Xu, Helal, Thai, & Scmalz, 2011).

Security and privacy: Due to authorized transactions, there are lower standards required to ensure data security in response to reform. Users have to understand if their data are well encrypted at the cloud or who is monitoring the encryption/decryption keys. Private information may become public due to error or inaccuracy, that is, the privacy of the customer may be compromised in the cloud, and sensor information or information submitted to the cloud may not be adequately monitored by the user. Annually, many documents have been leaked and become widely available online.

Event processing and management: The SC has to handle complicated computation and management of events such as how to synchronize the information from different sources at different times, how the rules should be adapted and how they can be changed without affecting the system, how the messages of various event systems are synchronized and managed at one place, and how to organize the context according to the events. These are some of the event processing and management issues which need to be addressed.

Interfacing issue: Currently, web services provide communication for SC customers and server users. However, web interfaces can provoke payload since web interfaces are not designed specifically for smart phones. There would also be web interface compatibility issues between devices, and so in this scenario typical protocol and interface to communicate with SC clients with the cloud would necessitate fast and efficient implementation utilities.

Information classification: Seamless information is generated from the sensor devices, with most of them having the most redundant information, and processing such redundant information consumes a lot of time and energy. The SC should provide such a provision to select minimum information that has enough about the event or task to be executed.

Pricing issues: Sensor-service providers (SSPs) and CSPs are active in accessing SC infrastructure. Nevertheless, all SSPs and CSPs have the administration, systems integration, payment options, and prices of different clients. Altogether this can cause a variety of problems (Dinh, Lee, Niyato, & Wang, 2011) such as how to set the prices, how to make the payment, and how a price is distributed among different items. All these problems need to be taken care of and better solutions obtained for SC systems.

In particular, the issues with respect to optimization, classification, and load balancing have problems as shown in Fig. 1.3.

The problems related to optimization, classification, and load balancing need to be addressed before they are used for SC systems. Optimization considers factors such as energy, computation, bandwidth, latency, cost, user demand, and overall throughput to check the efficiency of a particular system. Similarly, classification and load balancing have certain criteria such as the number of nodes considered, node types, type of information, latency, classification accuracy, bandwidth, and energy. A taxonomical representation of the intelligent optimization of the sensor cloud is presented in Section 1.3.

1.3 Taxonomy for optimization in the sensor cloud

The taxonomy impacts how efficiently an SC system can be used to send the sensed information from the physical sensor network to the SC server. Care should be taken that information generated from the group of sensors is redundant free, precisely classified, and should reach the server in a timely manner for providing services to users in a more classified way. The taxonomy briefs some of the major techniques used to optimize the SC systems to make them reliable for all conditions. We propose taxonomy to represent different performance management perceptions in the SC addressing all aspects of information collection, classification, processing, interpretation, balance load, transmission, and reduced capital solutions. The taxonomy consists of four main factors, namely: load balancing, information classification, information transmission techniques, and information processing, as shown in Fig. 1.4.

All optimization methods have unique ways to optimize the SC system to make it reliable for all applications and also improve the lifetime of the system in a more accurate and better way. In recent years the work

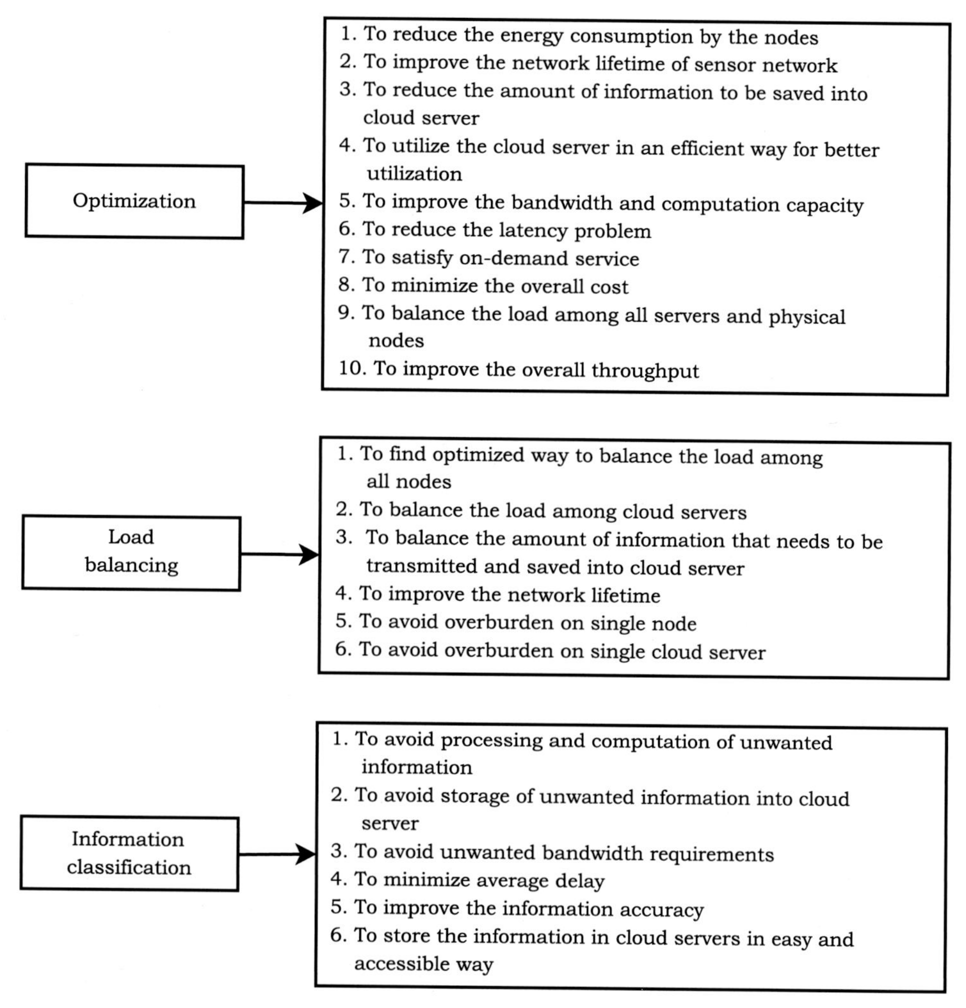

FIGURE 1.3 Issues in the sensor cloud.

carried out for optimization of the SC with respect to performance parameters is depicted in Fig. 1.5.

The performance parameters like energy, load balancing, classification, bandwidth, packet delivery ratio (PDR), accuracy, QoS, response time, delay, and lifetime play important roles in optimizing SC systems.

1.3.1 Load balancing

Load balancing performs a significant part in optimizing SC systems. Load balancing involves the selection of the head node (HN), the path from the source node to the HN or directly to the SN, and information transmission. Information transmission is further divided into various factors that are depicted in the section on information processing. Load balancing is among the main challenges for SC as many resources arrive from multiple places and handling these resources is one of the challenging tasks. A generalized load-balancing concept is depicted in Fig. 1.6.

The load balancing can be applied at three possible situations; first, it can be used at the cluster to find the optimal route. Instead of considering one intermediate node for most of the information transmission process, it is better to find the optimal path which uses the nodes which have sufficient energy as well as residual energy. Second, the load balancing can also be applied to the information which is being sent from nodes to HN/SN. Most of the nodes sense the same information about the event and instead of sending multiple copies of the same information it is better to select the node with good residual energy with distance to HN/SN and similar information should be merged into a single copy and sent to the HN/SN, thereby minimizing the energy consumption and balancing the load as well. Finally, at the SC server if user requests for the service and server memory are low, then the neighbor service provides the required memory to fulfill the user's requirements. Usually, based on the availability of the servers, one of the servers is assigned to the user and if all servers are busy then the load balancer assigns the waiting time to

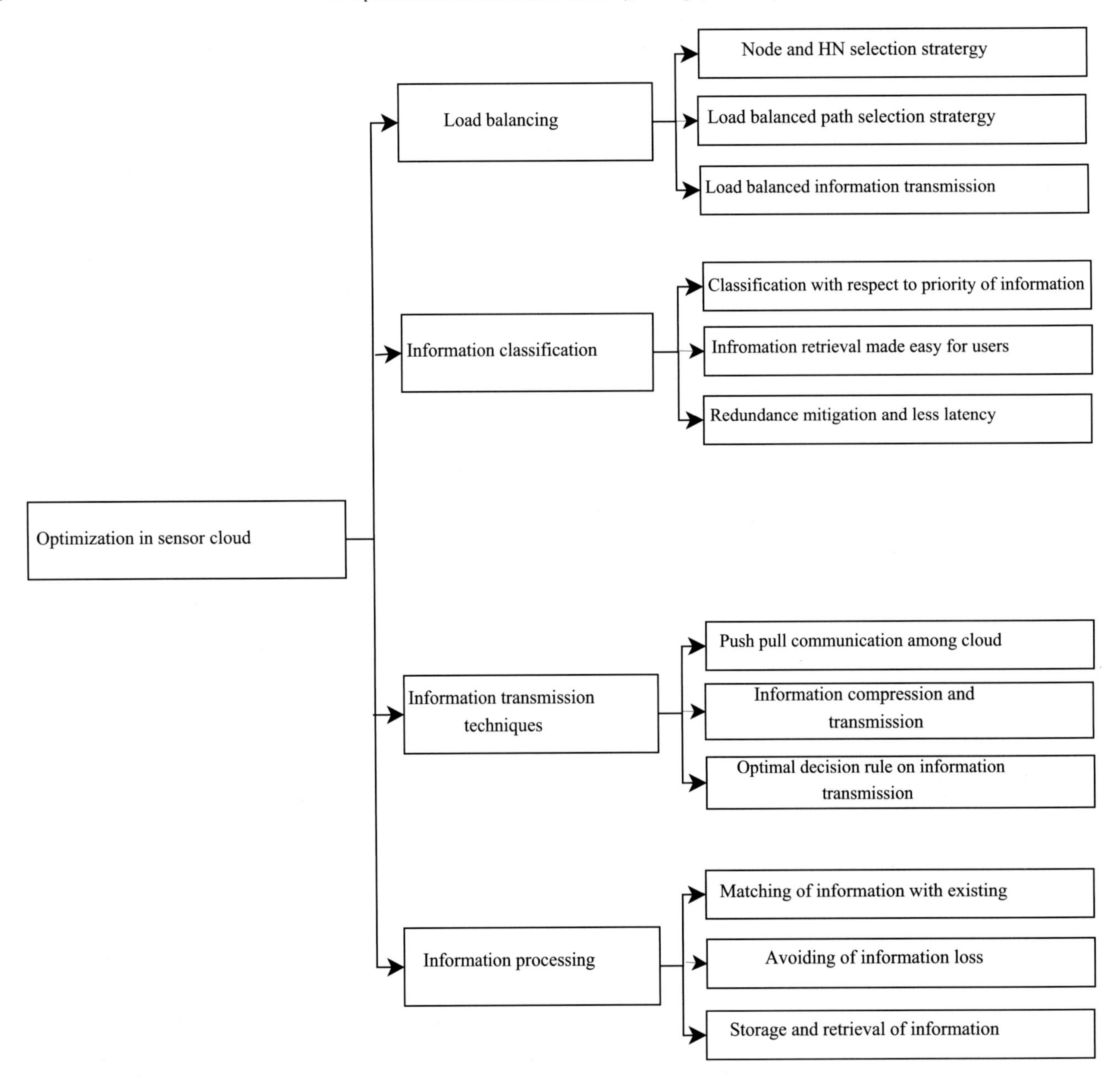

FIGURE 1.4 Taxonomy of optimization in the sensor cloud.

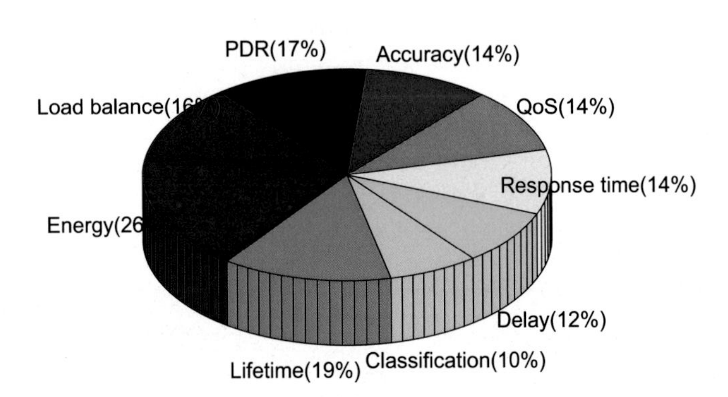

FIGURE 1.5 Parameter-wise optimization in the sector cloud.

the requested user. The dynamic load balancing is also possible and it also works efficiently in solving the user request in a timely manner by communicating with other servers belonging to another group.

The work carried out on load balancing in the fields of the WSN, CC, and SC is depicted here.

Baviskar, Patil, and Govind (2015) proposed an energy-efficient load balancing in cloud-based WSN. Load balancing is used for dividing the processing tasks and providing quicker liberation of services. For load balancing, the virtual servers have been assigned. The ant optimization is used for the selection of virtual servers scheduling and which intern improves the system stability and increases performance. Node stabilization

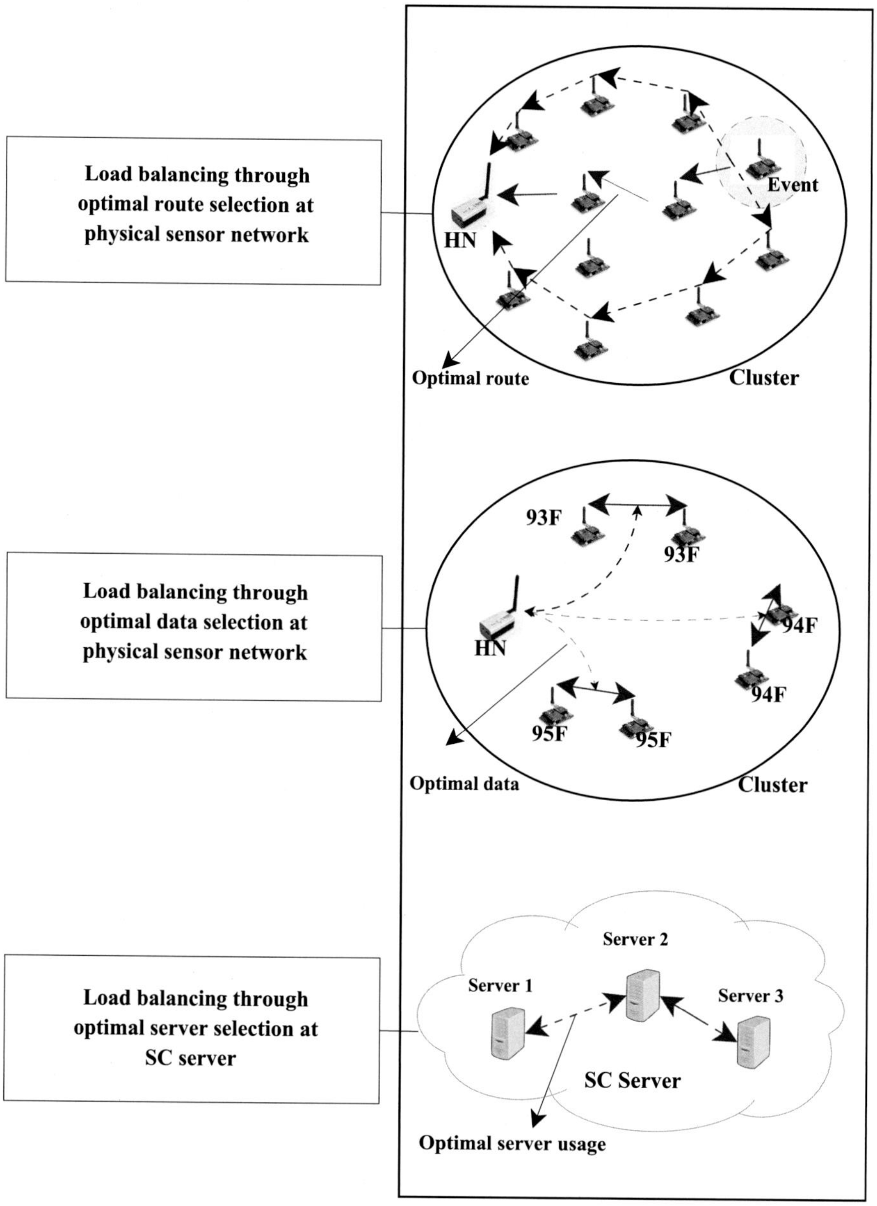

FIGURE 1.6 Example scenario of load balancing at various stages. *HN*, head node; *SC*, sensor cloud.

is not addressed in the paper and a scheme for next node selection is also not given by the authors.

Yousif, Badlishah, Yaakob, & Amir (2018) mentioned that in most of the clustering approaches the CH is selected either randomly or using a centralized approach. Also, most of the energy is consumed due to single-hop communication. A load-balancing clustering scheme based on a distributed approach is used to select the CH using residual energy and the number of neighbor nodes covered parameters along with relay cost parameters for multihop communication between CHs. The proposed work improves the network lifetime by properly balancing the node's residual energy. Only path selection was considered in the paper and it did not address redundant data.

Load unbalancing occurs in CC due to dynamics and complexity (Dasoriya, Kotadiya, Arya, Nayak, & Mistry, 2017). To reduce unbalancing, the map-reduce programming model is used, which provides a multi-task scheduling algorithm. Compared to the min-min algorithm, the improved genetic algorithm holds well and properly balances the load with good accuracy. Here the population and fitness function are designed according to requirements, then selection, crossover, and mutation operators are defined but the main drawback of the genetic algorithm, maximum selection criteria along with the latency factor, is not addressed.

The load can also be balanced by incorporating edge computing along with SC systems. The addition of edge with the SC improves the overall optimization, affecting parameters such as latency, energy consumption, and throughput. The edge computing, also called fog computing, is located in the middle of the SC systems. The sensor information is computed, processed, compressed, and made redundant free at this system stage (Singh, 2017).

An optimization of information in SC through mutual virtual sensors has been described in El Rachkidi, Agoulmine, Chendeb, and Belaid (2017). When clients require the same content, it will be assigned several real-time devices and many resources would be lost alongside time consumption. The article aims to improve the network and device infrastructure using a common virtual sensor approach to concurrently supply the client with the required information from multiple platforms. The developed system decreases the traffic, that is, the responsibility on the WSN, lowers the use of the network and resources, reduces the cost of implementation, and attains the QoS.

Mahendran and Priya (2016) mentioned that the mobile cloud with WSNs is an experimental system that attracts magnetism as they accumulated the power of sensor nodes to an information fraternity with CC efficiency. Most of the sensor network fails to locate mobile users, has high energy consumption, and no proper load-balancing technique. The article describes the load-balancing approach with a location-based sleep approach to improve the system efficiency. Various models have been proposed to attain the load balancing, positioning recognition, and sleep/wake up approaches. The system complexity increases alongside the energy parameter which is not suitably added for network lifetime improvement.

Table 1.2 shows the major contributions and their achievements and research gaps.

1.3.2 Information classification

The points which need to be considered in information classification for SC intelligent optimization are monitoring the type of information and its emergency level, extraction of the information and making it suitable for further processes, along with the elimination of redundant information and reducing the size of the information while maintaining the accuracy as well as submitting into servers on time. The simple information classification approach is described in Fig. 1.7. The SC server comprises of logical physical network where all the corresponding nodes and their cluster formation appears same as physical network. The information coming from the nodes is continuously monitored and saved into the servers depending upon the type of information. The information herein is classified as public and private, and further classified as low, medium, and high. Depending on the information type and its urgency, it is saved into the respective subservers. This process gives more accuracy to the information and also provides accurate information to the users requiring it. Depending upon the requirement and traffic, the numbers of servers is enhanced with the same functionality.

Next, information classification in the WSN, CC, and SC fields is described.

Various classification algorithms such as naïve Bayes, K-NN (K-nearest neighbors), iterative dichotomizer-3 (ID3), and decision trees are used as the most suitable intelligent classification techniques for networking-related research. ID3 is one of the simplest decision tree type classifiers and requires discrete values and should have relevant attributes. Naïve Bayes assumes there is no dependency among the attributes selected, and such a type of classification is fast at making decisions but returns probability output. K-NN classifies objects based on the majority of neighbors available. K-NN functions locally and most of the time used a Euclidian distance formula to know its neighbors. With respect to performance parameters accuracy, precision, recall, and AUC, the naïve Bayes performs well compared to K-NN, however the accuracy can be improved (Ahmad, Paryudi, & Tjoa, 2013).

Saha (2015a) investigated SC data management in a secure manner by integrating with the nearby environment with the use of routing techniques. With an efficient routing protocol, high-speed communication is achieved securely. The work defined is suitable for high traffic in the defined network and is more useful for practical applications. Only routing was considered and no technique has been defined to classify the data as well as the energy-saving methodology not up to the mark.

Yang, Chen, Lee, Liou, & Wang (2007) described that the neuro-fuzzy classifier utilizes one tri-axial accelerometer and signature reduction techniques. The tri-axial accelerometer is used to collect acceleration records of subjects and to train the neuron-fuzzy classifier to identify excellent sports/actions. A revised mapping-restricted agglomerative clustering set of guidelines is built to expose a portable data structure from the acceleration metrics to configure the neuron-fuzzy classifier.

Rahman, Salan, Shuva, and Khan (2017) developed an effective SC connectivity solution that reduces the excessive bandwidth and timing demand by utilizing machine-based statistical classification and compression using a deflated algorithm with limited data loss. Transactions among the WSN and CC are done by integrating the principle of machine learning methodology with compression and information-processing methods. The results depict minimization in data loss along with a delay. The proposed work is 4.7 times better than the

TABLE 1.2 Load-balancing methods and research gaps

Reference	Methods used	Problem highlighted	Achievement	Limitations
Xin, Huang, Ma, and Meng (2019)	Software-defined WSN (SDWSN)	Load balancing in WSN is not adaptable and flexible	Improved SDSNLB routing performs far better than LEACH in balancing the traffic load and improves throughput	Route optimization is carried out and information optimization is yet to be addressed
Vamsi, Mohan, and Shantharajah (2016)	Load-balancing approach and fuzzy logic	Load-balancing requirement for public cloud computing	Load balancing focused on adaptive neuro-fuzzy is applied to increase the total reliability of cloud infrastructure in the resource utilization and affordability region	The data can be saved in a particular server with the priority not being addressed. Accuracy and latency are still an issue
Velde and Rama (2017)	Load balancing and fuzzy logic	Efficient load-balancing algorithm for cloud computing	Fuzzy logic allows offering of adequate cloud storage. Processing speed coupled with a virtual compute included to handle the load simultaneously	Reaction time and overall stability of the system is still an issue
Zenon, Mahadevan, Aslanzadeh, and Mcdermid (2011)	Load balancing, improving availability	Network availability and load balancing	With clouds, load balancing is used as a technique through different networks to enhance network performance by minimizing laptop usage, technological failures, and avoiding recovery hurdles	Device load balancing is carried out, simultaneously data load balancing is required to optimize the whole network
Kapoor and Dabas (2015)	Load balance min-min scheduling algorithm	Load balancing, response time	Load balance min-min (LBMM) scheduling algorithm is proposed which minimizes task completion time and balances load	Energy constraints were not considered and it is complex
Shen et al. (2015)	Access point identification algorithm	Measuring complicated happenings	Efficient, with little reaction time, appropriate coverage, and cost-effective	Does not endorse QoS when viewing videos
Zhao and Chen (2014)	Routing approach	Balances energy among all the nodes	Improved network lifespan	Does not endorse scalability and QoS
Alonso–Calvo, Crespo, Garc'ia-Remesal, Anguita, and Maojo (2010)	Cloud-based storage and analysis	Handling wide picture sets is a significant concern for businesses and organizations	Region-based information storage and analysis are proposed using low-level descriptors. Image is divided into various subimages and stored, thereby decreasing processing time and balancing the load	Time- and bandwidth-consuming tasks

existing methods. It did not concentrate on the energy factor and heterogeneous network.

A hybrid classification method was introduced in Xiao, Su, Zhang, Zhu, & Wang (2017) employing RFRS (Relief F Rough Set) methodology. The RFRS unit, Relief-F, is used for feature mining, whereby a heuristic rough approach for dimensionality reduction is generated. A C4.5-based community classification model is incorporated into the identifying feature set for cardiovascular disease. A cumulative classification precision of 92% was obtained to support the superiority of the classifier but difficulty was somewhat more delayed.

Table 1.3 shows the major contributions and with their achievements and research gaps.

1.3.3 Information transmission

In this type of intelligent optimization method, optimization can be achieved by adapting the methods such as push-pull communication, compression of information to reduce the size of the information for minimizing the latency issues, and taking an optimum decision on information for applying the best possible processing method and storing outcomes more efficiently.

Further, information transmission in the WSN, CC, and SC fields is described here.

Madria, Kumar, and Dalvi (2014) described the integral works of WSN and mobile CC for reliable data transfer. The WSN is used to sense the environmental parameters and sensed data are stored in the cloud server, which has powerful storage and processing capability. The combinational work is defined in two phases, first selective data are transmitted in a timely fashion with priority through the gateway to the cloud server as requested by the mobile user and, secondly, the nodes are given instructions as to when they should move in the wake up mode and sleep mode. This can efficiently save more energy.

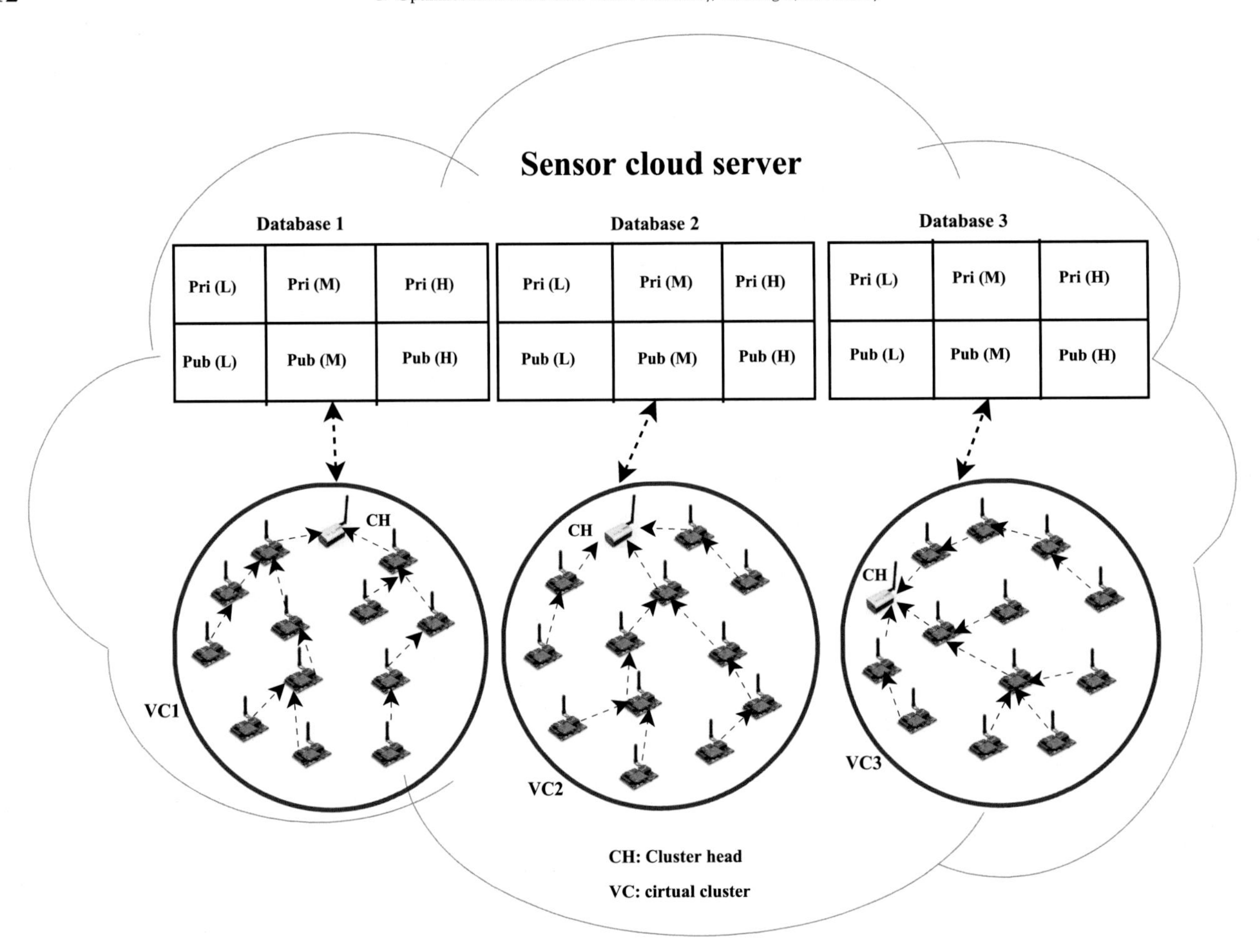

FIGURE 1.7 Example scenario of information classification at the sensor cloud server.

Das, Das, Mishra, and Mohapatra (2017) described an energy-efficient data prediction model for the SC. Whenever a user requests for data it is always redirected to physical sensors for data collection and submitted back to the cloud server consuming more energy. The Rprof algorithm using a logistic activation function to improve the accuracy of the system with less delay. Using the depicted algorithm the future sensor data are predicted and user requests are solved at the cloud server itself, without utilizing the service of physical sensors all the time. The data transmission and energy consumption are reduced and the network lifetime is improved.

dos Santos et al. (2018) described the architecture for the cloud for sensor networks. The cloud of sensors is built on the virtualization concept and has the main challenge of energy consumption by the sensor networks. It has a three-tier architecture, namely sensor nodes, edge network, and cloud server. The architecture was implemented using the FIWARE platform. FIWARE offers basic foundations for Future Online services and supports the three-tiered design of the edge network. The work described needs improvement and experimental results are yet to be implemented and analyzed to prove energy consumption is less.

Jiang, Sun, Sun, and Xu (2013) has presented a methodology to send data to the next-hop node instead of sending it in a multihop forwarding method. The method has three different parameters to find the next-hop node for data transmission, that is, energy, closeness to the next node, and closeness to the SN. For all three requirements, a fuzzy membership function is defined to find the optimal route and the result shows there is an improvement in the lifetime of the sensor network. The authors concentrated on physical parameters and need to address multimedia content as well.

Chatterjee, Sarkar, and Misra (2015) described that the information transmission into the cloud from sensor nodes is promising and challenging task for the researchers. The conventional WSN for a VSN transmits information to the cloud via any intermediate nodes, that is, the bridge nodes. This research aims to make an acceptable judgment law for picking a bridge node on a VSN's behalf. Earlier there were possibilities that some nodes produced unpredictable information which was not defined by the system specification and

TABLE 1.3 Information classification methods and research gaps.

References	Methods used	Problem highlighted	Achievement	Limitations
Darwazeh et al. (2015)	Data classification and security	Increased data in cloud computing with less security	The cloud model mitigates latency and processing time required to secure data using various security methods and different key sizes to maintain the adequate level of privacy necessary for the data	Redundant data were not mitigated and overall optimization remains an issue
L. P. D. Kumar et al. (2012)	Data filtering in WSN using a neural network	Storage of sensory data in cloud	Improved congestion control and effective use of bandwidth	The proposed work for heterogeneous networks is not addressed. Accuracy remains an issue
Chen, Wu, Liu, Yang, and Zheng (2011)	Query execution model	Data integration and analysis	Data flow style query execution model is implemented where each query is divided into subqueries. Obtain results of subqueries and finally, they are reconstructed to obtain a better integrity value along with greater analysis results	The proposed work has complexity and data selection is not described
Rahulamathavan, Phan, Veluru, Cumanan, and Rajarajan (2014)	Classification of data and privacy	To provide customer satisfaction it is located at different locations where there is a need for data classification to be performed at various servers	The proposed protocol carries out PP classification to two and multiclass issues. The scheme exhibits Pailler homomorphic encryption features and secured computing for two parties	QoS and accuracy remain an issue

passed the information to other hop nodes, degrading the overall performance. In VSNs where those actions include the participating nodes of the network, each participant node communicates its decision in the form of packets consolidated to imply the network's action. Selecting the optimal bridge node is the key factor to saving energy and ensuring efficient transmission.

The study depicted in Saha (2015b) analyzed SC information processing including security through the use of routing strategies to connect with the surrounding locality. The WSN and CC are integrated to give fast and reliable transmission to users. The high-speed interaction is safely accomplished via an effective routing algorithm. The specified research fits the established network for heavy traffic and is, therefore, more valuable for realistic applications. Only routing has been suggested, and no methodology is specified for classifying the information, and also an energy-saving approach that might not be up to standard. The framework provided helps to effectively control and manage the sensor information for communication and coordination of protection.

Table 1.4 shows the major contributions and their achievements and research gaps.

1.3.4 Information processing

In this SC optimization method, information processing is carried out in many ways, such as matching of information, avoiding loss of important information, and storing the information in cloud servers for better usage in the future. These optimization types play an important role in boosting the SC performance and also making it reliable for all applications.

Finally, information processing in the WSN, CC, and SC fields is described.

Jacem, Rekhis, and Boudriga (2018) described how reliability, extensibility, and availability can be improved by integrating the WSN with the CC. They investigated health applications by combining sensor networks and the CC to help a medical representative to take the appropriate action remotely during a high-risk situation. The authentication protocol is presented to authenticate high-risk patients and involvement of the WSN for data collection, and it also improves the quality by using flow control and traffic scheduling features. The virtual sensor is associated with physical sensors concerning time and location to monitor the patient's activity along with the surrounding activity. The presented method also manages a virtual sensor at the cloud server.

Nimbits (Nimbits Data Logging Cloud Sever) is an information-processing tool that can be used to record and share data from sensors in the cloud. It is a secure, collaborative, and open-source IoT platform. Users can create data points in the cloud with Nimbits and fed them with modifying binary, text-dependent, GPS, and XML values. Customizing data points to conduct

TABLE 1.4 Information transmission methods and research gaps.

References	Methods used	Problem highlighted	Achievement	Limitations
Doukas & Maglogiannis (2011)	Wearable textile platform based on hardware and software	Data collection and maintenance, interconnectivity and heterogeneous resource quality, standard and all-time accessibility	Acquire and wirelessly store activity and pulse information on an open cloud environment for tracking and analysis	Raw data are saved, leading to instability in the overall network. The system is not completely energy efficient
Dwivedi and Kumar (2018)	WSN and cloud computing	WSN issues like processing, storage, memory, scalability, security, availability	Integration of WSN and cloud computing creates virtualization possibilities to execute various applications using the same physical node	Data preserving, storage, and classifications in sensor cloud are not addressed
Khan, Dwivedi, and Kumar (2019b)	Optimal decision rule and Bayesian classifier	Efficient transfer of information at the SC	Surveyed on achieving energy-efficient data transmission in SC considering energy efficiency, QoS, and security parameters	Classification and load-balancing approaches need to be examined to describe the system as energy efficient
Zhu, Sheng, Leung, Shu, and Yang (2015)	TPSS scheme consisting of TPSDT and PSS	Time- and priority-based transmission of data from WSN to cloud for better reliability	TPSS is used for improving the worth sensory information and the consistency of WSN	The system reliability which is required for overall optimization can be achieved by considering classification algorithms and a load-balancing approach
Suto, Nishiyama, Kato, and Huang (2015)	E2DAWCS	Network connectivity and sleep scheduling	Node energy consumption is minimized	Scalability is not addressed and optimization is not up to the mark
Sheng, Mahapatra, Leung, Chen, and Sahu (2018)	Node selection procedure	Optimal use of nodes, energy efficient	Minimum energy consumption	Issues relating to multihop transmission with resource restriction situations are not dealt with
Shakena Grace and Sumalatha (2014)	Senud compression algorithm	Information replication and compression	An energy-efficient connectivity is described in the sensor cloud	Only data were compressed and there remain many factors which are playing a pivotal role in energy consumption

calculations, create warnings, transmit data to social media, and link to scalable vector graphics process control charts, laptops, portals, and much more can be done using Nimbits. Nimbits uses mathematical equations to offer a compression scheme, system for controlling warnings, and analysis of sensory information.

Kalyan, Das, Darji, and Mishra (2018) examined some of the energy-efficient network management technologies used by cloud sensor combinations. The integration provides better scalability and an efficient computing environment. The survey report shows that much research is pending for enhancing the quality of service, scalability, and network lifetime. Some of the energy-efficient techniques are classified based on scheduling strategies, sensing procedures, techniques for data transfer, sophisticated system design, data analysis, and load balancing. The techniques have been analyzed using some of the well-known parameters like bandwidth, data size, computation energy, throughput, delay, packet loss, and network lifetime.

Dash, Sahoo, Mohapatra, and Pati (2012) mentioned that quantities of data generated from sensor nodes are very high and it is necessary to save them in a web-based portal called a virtual community. Combinational technology can be used in a wide variety of applications. The sharing and assessment of real-time sensor data are made simpler if the cloud is integrated with WSNs. Through the CC, a large amount of data coming from the WSN can be analyzed, processed, and stored in the servers for further use. Users can run a particular application and gather the required type of sensor data during a specific period by obtaining a subset of sensors.

A key challenge in SC is the transfer of replicated information from a cloud to sensor applications, a cycle that typically increases the demands on resources, bandwidth, and energy (Zhu, Leung, Wang, Yang, & Zhang, 2017). A further problem occurs when several clients of the SC concurrently demand similar information. Here, large volumes of information have to be transmitted simultaneously from the cloud to clients, resulting in greater energy and bandwidth usage. A multimethod information provision strategy for SC clients was suggested to solve these challenges. The outcomes of the proposed system are doing well as per the delivery time, but system complexity remains an issue.

Zhu et al. (2015) described that the sensory information was acquired through sensor nodes dependent on the trust factor related to the node of the system. If the confidence value of the sensor node meets a desired threshold, which describes the confidence level of the sensor node, the information is then later transmitted to servers. The broad information center computing resources require effective storing and processing of huge volumes of collected data while retaining confidence level. While this model allows confidence-based information collection on SCs, the confidence parameters are expressed related to negative and positive views of sensor nodes and storage systems that are not completely justified and may not even be realistic.

Sukanya, Priya, Paul, and Sankaranarayanan (2015) described a data-processing approach that intends to quickly and reliably transfer requested information to users while protected. The structure lowers the storage capacity for sensor nodes and gateway. It also reduces the need for traffic and throughput for sensor networks. Furthermore, the approach could also anticipate the outcome pattern of the sensory information. The system ensures that mobile users get their information quickly. The proposed method ensures data processing, compression, along with encryption and is applicable to mobile users as well. The energy consumed and complexity of the system are not addressed here.

Misra, Chatterjee, & Obaidat (2017) described theoretical modeling of the SC. The authors mentioned that very few articles dealt with theoretical specification and studies that can be utilized to construct systems to solve various SC issues. They presented the mathematical representation for the SC. The results show there has been an improvement in the lifetime of the SC system by 3.25% and energy consumption is reduced by 36.68%. There is a need to address the complexity reduction methodology along with further improvement in the lifespan of the whole SC system.

Kumar et al. (2012) developed a method for moving high quantities of sensed information from the sensor node database to the CC. The authors proposed transferring information-processing responsibilities to the cloud gateways, thus attaining better energy throughput. The proposed algorithm was used to perform information filtering for the backpropagation systems inside the cloud gateways. The activities mainly enlisted and explored the advantages of SC and the problems connected with the same. Some of the work concentrated on developing an application-specific system and the methods for transmitting information.

Table 1.5 shows the major contributions and their achievements and research gaps.

1.3.5 Limitations of existing work

We have investigated many research articles along with their research proposals, methodology, simulation, and results, and it has been observed that most of the research is carried out in designing a better architecture for SC systems, the transmission of raw information to cloud server from the physical sensor network and applications-oriented architectures (like healthcare applications), but very few have concentrated on energy, latency, and security parameters. Also, very rare research was conducted on optimizing the SC system by considering the parameters like network lifetime, energy consumption, load balancing, information classification, information accessibility, information accuracy, priority-based information classification, latency, and user-friendliness. To make the SC system more reliable it is necessary to go through the

TABLE 1.5 Information processing methods and research gaps.

References	Methods used	Problem highlighted	Achievement	Limitations
Sneha (2016)	Data compression and data encryption	Node energy and location	Enhanced sensor battery life and a lightweight position-verification system which executes location verification both on-site and in-region	Overall system optimization was not addressed
Kalyan et al. (2018)	Energy-efficient techniques for sensor-cloud integration	Optimum decision policy, flexible sensory information platform, wireless power transmission, pull-push connectivity, and compression method	Various energy-efficient sensor cloud methods are described	System optimization concerning classification was not addressed
Dalvi and Madria (2015)	TDMA-based scheduling	Scheduling for fine-granularity tasks	Offers a lower reaction time, high performance, and energy efficiency	Scalability and performance need to be confronted

following points before using SC for a wide variety of applications:

1. Minimum energy should be utilized for transmitting information from the physical sensor network to the SC server in the SC system.
2. Minimum information size with great accuracy should be stored in the cloud server.
3. All nodes in the network should be operated so that equal energy is consumed to avoid energy deficiency on a particular node and this in turn improves the lifetime of the network.
4. Minimizing the end–end delay to make the SC system more reliable.
5. Optimizing the SC systems so that they can be used in multiple applications.

It is necessary to consider the above points to make the SC more prominent and usable for numerous applications. To achieve this, it is necessary to find better optimization techniques along with load balancing and information classification techniques for better utilization of nodes in the physical network and also classifying the information according to its importance.

To carry out operations in a more fast and timely manner, agents can be deployed at the physical network and the cloud server for fast processing and lower energy consumption. Various research papers have been referred to find their research gap and also the parameters required for getting the optimized SC systems.

The performances of WSN, CC, and SC are also verified from recent research using the various performance parameters like load balancing, QoS, classification, delay, network lifetime, response time, energy consumption, and optimization. To achieve a better optimization result it is necessary to have good outcomes from the performance considered. Table 1.6 shows the performance parameter analyses of different systems.

1.4 Discussion and future research

This section describes the issues highlighted to optimize the SC system in a better way than the existing versions. Further, this section reveals the future directions of optimization of the SC, explaining other opportunities which are not covered in this chapter to optimize the SC system.

1.4.1 Discussion

This chapter distinguishes optimization into four main factors, namely information processing, transmission, classification, and load balancing. It reviewed the state of

TABLE 1.6 Various WSN, cloud computing, and sensor cloud systems along with their performance parameter analysis.

References	Load balancing	QoS	Information classification	End–end delay	Network lifetime	Response time	Energy consumption	Overall optimization
Darwazeh et al. (2015)	X	✓	✓	Medium	No	Medium	Medium	No
Das, Das, Darji, and Mishra (2017)	✓	✓	X	Medium	Medium	High	Medium	Medium
Mostefa and Feham (2018)	X	✓	X	Medium	Medium	Low	Medium	Medium
Kumar Kashyap, Kumar, Dohare, Kumar, and Kharel (2019)	✓	✓	X	Medium	Medium	High	Less	Medium
Dasgupta, Mandal, Dutta, Mandal, and Dam (2013)	✓	✓	X	High	Medium	Low	Not defined	Less
Song (2017)	✓	✓	X	Medium	Medium	High	More	Less
Kumar and Sharma (2017)	✓	X	X	Low	No	Low	Not defined	Less
Zegrari, Idrissi, and Rehioui (2016)	✓	✓	X	Medium	No	Low	Less	Medium
Naranjo, Pooranian, Shojafar, Conti, and Buyya (2019)	✓	✓	X	Low	Medium	Low	Less	Medium
Mohamed, Beni-Hssane, and Saadi (2018)	✓	✓	X	Medium	Medium	Low	Less	Medium
Deif and Gadallah (2014)	X	✓	✓	Not defined	No	No	Medium	Medium
Mohamed et al. (2018)	X	X	X	Medium	Medium	Low	Medium	Medium
Baranidharan and Balachandran (2017)	X	X	X	Medium	Medium	Medium	Medium	Less

the art of current technologies which are used for the sensing of environmental parameters as well as storing them in a place where users can access them without any problems, along with it being irrespective of where they are located. The process identified the major challenges and issues in SC systems. Currently available techniques are categorized based on the flow of the process starting from sensing of information (physical sensor nodes) to the storing of information on SC servers. Current approaches used different methods to improve the performance of SC systems and considered multiple performance parameters to check their efficiency. Many approaches have suggested that information extraction and storage are made easy using SC systems: huge information processing is possible, lower end–end delay, and large storage capacity. Network lifetime, system reliability, latency, information compression, and energy consumption are some of the parameters which highlight/improve the optimization of systems that are doing well in the SC.

The four important aspects which are major requirements for optimization in the SC play a crucial role in deciding the system stability in making an optimized system. Different load balancing is already highlighted by the research into WSN, CC, and SC systems. The correct selection of an optimized load-balancing technique is a major concern. The information which is initially available at the physical sensor node must be sent to the SC server and care should be taken that all nodes equally contribute in transferring the information into the SC server and overburdening of a few sets of nodes is avoided. The virtual network created at the SC server regularly monitors and updates the energy status of each the physical nodes and likewise the SC server sends an energy-efficient path link from the source to the HN/SN, hence balancing the load among all nodes.

Next is information classification in SC. Equivalent to load balancing, information classification also plays a major role in optimizing the SC system in a better way. The WSN generates lots of information regularly and storing such huge amounts of information is again a challenging and time-consuming process. Most of the information is redundant and saving such huge information makes no sense, and hence it should be eliminated and only a little information with better accuracy can be saved into SC servers, savings time, information accuracy, and overall system efficiency. Many classification techniques are being used for the classification of information in the WSN, CC, and SC. Some of the popular classification techniques are K-NN, ID3, naïve Bayes, decision tree, etc., which are used for the classification of information sensed. All have good classification accuracy and, depending upon the type of information, any of the information techniques can be used to classify information for improving system stability.

Further, optimization of the SC can be made possible by concentrating on one more important factor, which is information transmission. Information transmission equally plays an important role in deciding the optimized system by considering important factors such as finding the shortest path from the source to the destination, as well as sending the information to an authenticated device. A delay occurs if the link used for transmission is not optimal or has a block hole issue that can cause the system to lose its stability. There is a need for better transmission methodology which should give enhanced opportunities for selecting the optimal path and should have the required amount of bandwidth as well as energy to transmit the information in a very efficient and timely manner. Many research articles related to information transmission in both WSN and SC systems have been published. Some methods have fast transmission approaches and also consume less time and energy to reach the destination. In the next phase of information transmission, edge computing or fog computing is used along with the SC system to further reduce the latency issue and provide a seamless service to users.

Finally, the discussion now is on information processing in SC systems. Different organizations have different requirements; some want less bandwidth and others require a larger bandwidth. Different organizations run different applications; some operate on static content and some on multimedia content. There is a necessity for preparing an SC model which runs on both types of information. Currently, there are various types of models that are available and have SC functionally with them. The models have multifunctionality function and work better on both static and multimedia content. The models have the functionality to process the incoming information better and perform the required task so that only the important information is sent to the cloud server. Processing of information before transmission improves the accuracy of the information and consumes less power and bandwidth for further transmission. It also helps to optimize the overall system by allowing only valid information for further process and utilizes less power and energy. Redundant information can also be eliminated at this stage, and hence the delay factor can be improved. There are only a few articles that highlight the information-processing functionalities in SC systems. Still, there is a requirement for more research in SC to make it efficient for all applications. Greater effort is needed for load balancing, classification of information, transmission of processing, and finally processing of information. Many other parameters also needed attention, such as resource management and fault tolerance, and proper routing in SC.

1.4.2 Future research

Future research directions in the context of intelligent optimization in the SC are described in this section. The SC technology is a new approach that aims to expand on previous WSN and CC systems. It is under aggressive research and SC optimization is in its infant stages, primarily because of the nevertheless developing applications for real-world SC. By looking at the findings of this study, we may say that certain SC properties exist in some implementations, thus we have to be conscious of recent developments in all fields to develop improved SC strategies. We have shown the challenges, taxonomy, and simulators used in SC with a detailed survey on intelligent optimization.

Research can be further extended by considering many other factors that are not covered in this chapter. The factors which are not highlighted in this survey include fault tolerance, routing, security, node deployment, and information maintenance. Further research can be carried out on these factors to improve the SC.

1.4.2.1 Fault tolerance

Fault tolerance is the factor that tries to improve the SC by collecting information about the status of the nodes and the information they are injecting into the network. Device authentication and authorization plays an important role in every networking system. It is necessary to check the faulty nodes available in the physical network at regular instances. Faulty nodes inject false information into the network and can degrade the overall efficiency. Alongside fault detection, it is important to check the errors coming with the information as it impacts the accuracy of the information at a higher level. There are different types of errors and faults that occur at the physical network as well as at the cloud environment, and a suitable fault tolerance technique must be used to provide better network optimization.

1.4.2.2 Node routing

Maximum energy is consumed when the information is routed from the source to the destination. Proper routing approaches need to be included when there is information to be transmitted from the source node to the HN/SN. The routing approach should consume less energy and time along with a good PDR. New and energy-efficient routing techniques need to be implemented to make the SC system more optimal and efficient. In the present context, many routing approaches for WSNs are available and, depending upon the application scenario, existing energy-efficient routing techniques can also be used for information transmission.

1.4.2.3 Node deployment

Information needs to be submitted to the SC server as it is retrieved from sensors. A difficulty in information gathering occurs where sensors should be positioned in a sensing area to allow an effective information collection operation. Sensors installed near the cloud gather information more rapidly than sensors installed far from the SC server. When transferring information to the server, this condition causes an information dependence issue. In the context of hostile environments where sensors are far removed from others, the issue is exacerbated. SC systems need to introduce WSN and CC best practices to address this challenge.

1.4.2.4 Security

Research can be extended by providing security to information. Securing information is an important aspect of the SC. The information moves from the physical network to the SC server and it comes across many stages where a third party has the opportunity to access the information. Security can be given to each node, gateway, and/or SC server or it can be given to the links which are connecting all nodes with the HN/SN, gateway, and SC server. Advanced 128 bit advanced encryption techniques can be used to provide security to the information. The future security system, blockchain, can also be used to provide end–end security at both physical networks and cloud servers. Research could also be carried out to find an intelligent optimal security algorithm for SC applications that run without any complexities and should place fewer burdens on the system.

1.4.2.5 Information maintenance

Information maintenance/control are an important factor in the intelligent optimization of SC systems. Management of information is a necessary step in the SC system as it requires continuous monitoring of the type of information received, eliminating duplicate information, and saving information into defined servers without any errors or delays. Very little research has been carried out so far on resource management in the SC. Overall information management should be carried out starting from the source node to saving in the SC servers.

Many open challenges arise when optimizing the SC system in an intelligent manner and this chapter highlights some of them which play an effectual role in making the SC system more reliable and efficient.

1.5 Conclusion

It has been noticed over the last decade, how well the recent new technologies have molded distributed applications and contributed to the introduction of the WSN and CC. Cloud providers must store, process, and analyze the information generated by sensor nodes to ensure robustness and stability. SC is a new-era technology which combines both WSN and CC technology to meet the market requirements and also to boost the networking system to new heights. There is always a need for intelligent optimization in SCs to make them a more profitable technology for most applications. The purpose of the research was to react to such major issues; hence this chapter performs an intelligent optimization of the SC through surveys and taxonomy. The contribution of this work resides in the perspectives applicable when performing the categorizations. The taxonomy of SCs has identified four major aspects for intelligent optimization: load balancing, information classification, processing, and transmission. The chapter has also discussed the importance of intelligence optimization in SCs for multiple applications. The research exposes the work carried out so far in SCs and future directives. Our key suggestion for further work is to pursue concept extensions by taking into consideration areas such as routing, fault tolerance, security, control, and management of resources.

References

Ahmad, A., Paryudi, I., & Tjoa, A. M. (2013). Performance comparison between Naïve Bayes, decision tree and k-nearest neighbor in searching alternative design in an energy simulation tool. *International Journal of Advanced Computer Science and Applications (IJACSA)*, *4*(11).

Ahmed, A., Arkian, H.R., Battulga, D., Fahs, A.J., Farhadi, M., Giouroukis, D., Gougeon, A. (2019). Fog computing applications: Taxonomy and requirements, arXiv preprint arXiv:1907.11621.

Alakeel, A. M. (2010). A guide to dynamic load balancing in distributed computer systems. *IJCSNS International Journal of Computer Science and Network Security*, *10*(6).

Alonso–Calvo, R., Crespo, J., Garc'ia–Remesal, M., Anguita, A., & Maojo, V. (2010). On distributing load in cloud computing: A real application for very-large image datasets. *Procedia Computer Science*, *1*(1), 2669–2677. Available from https://doi.org/10.1016/j.procs.2010.04.300.

Andrae, A. S. G., & Edler, T. (2015). On global electricity usage of communication technology: Trends to 2030. *Challenges*, *6*(1), 117–157.

Ansari, W. S., Alamri, A. M., Hassan, M. M., & Shoaib, M. (2013). A survey on sensor-cloud: Architecture, applications and approaches. *International Journal of Distributed Sensor Networks*, *2013*, 1–18, Saudi Arabia.

Baranidharan, B., & Balachandran, S. (2017). FLECH: Fuzzy logic based energy efficient clustering hierarchy for non uniform wireless sensor networks. *Wireless Communications and Mobile Computing*, *2017*.

Baviskar, Y.S., Patil, S.C., & Govind, S.B. (2015). Energy efficient load balancing algorithm in cloud based wireless sensor network. *2015 International conference on information processing (ICIP)* (pp. 464–467). Pune.

Beaumont, O., Eyraud-Dubois, L., & Larchevêque, H. (2013). Reliable service allocation in clouds. *2013 IEEE 27th international symposium on parallel and distributed processing* (pp. 55–66). Boston, MA.

Chatterjee, S., Sarkar, S., & Misra, S. (2015). Energy-efficient data transmission in sensor-cloud. *2015 Applications and innovations in mobile computing (AIMoC)* (pp. 68–73). Kolkata. doi: 10.1109/AIMOC.2015.7083832.

Chen, G., Wu, Y., Liu, J., Yang, G., & Zheng, W. (2011). Optimization of sub-query processing in distributed data integration systems. *Journal of Network and Computer Applications*, *34*(4), 1035–1042. Available from https://doi.org/10.1016/j.jnca.2010.06.007.

Dalvi, R., & Madria, S.K. (2015). Energy efficient scheduling of fine granularity tasks in a sensor cloud. In *International conference on database systems for advanced applications (DASFAA)* (pp. 498–513). Hanoi, Vietnam.

Darwazeh, N. S., Al-Qassas, R. S., & Al Dosari, F. (2015). "A secure cloud computing model based on data classification". *Procedia Computer Science*, *52*, 1153–1158.

Das, K., Das, S., Darji, R.K., & Mishra, A. (2017). Energy efficient model for the sensor cloud systems. *2017 2nd IEEE international conference on recent trends in electronics, information & communication technology (RTEICT)* (pp. 373–375). Bangalore.

Das, K., Das, S., Mishra, A., & Mohapatra, A. (2017). Energy efficient data prediction model for the sensor cloud environment. *2017 International conference on IoT and application (ICIOT)* (pp. 1–3). Nagapattinam.

Dasgupta, K., Mandal, B., Dutta, P., Mandal, J. K., & Dam, S. (2013). A genetic algorithm (GA) based load balancing strategy for cloud computing. *Procedia Technology*, *10*, 340–347.

Dash, S.K., Sahoo, J.P., Mohapatra, S., & Pati, S.P. (2012). Sensor-cloud: Assimilation of wireless sensor network and the cloud. In *International conference on computer science and information technology* (pp. 455–464). Springer, Berlin, Heidelberg.

Dasoriya, R., Kotadiya, P., Arya, G., Nayak, P. and Mistry, K. (2017). Dynamic load balancing in cloud a data-centric approach. *2017 International conference on networks & advances in computational technologies (NetACT)* (pp. 162–166). Thiruvanthapuram. 10.1109/NETACT.2017.8076760.

Deif, D. S., & Gadallah, Y. (2014). Classification of wireless sensor networks deployment techniques. *IEEE Communications Surveys & Tutorials*, *16*(2), 834–855, Second Quarter.

Dinh, T., & Kim, Y. (2016). An efficient interactive model for on-demand sensing-as-a-services of sensor-cloud. *Sensors*, *16*(7).

Dinh, H. T., Lee, C., Niyato, D., & Wang, P. (2011). A survey of mobile cloud computing: Architecture, applications, and approaches. *Wireless Communications and Mobile Computing*, 1–38, Wiley Online Library.

dos Santos, I. L., Alves, M. P., Delicato, F. C., Pires, P. F., Pirmez, L., Li, W., & Khan, S. U. (2018). A system architecture for cloud of sensors. In *2018 IEEE 16th Intl Conf on Dependable, Autonomic and Secure Computing, 16th Intl Conf on Pervasive Intelligence and Computing, 4th Intl Conf on Big Data Intelligence and Computing and Cyber Science and Technology Congress (DASC/PiCom/DataCom/CyberSciTech)*, (pp. 666–672). IEEE.

Doukas, C., & Maglogiannis, I. (2011). Managing wearable sensor data through cloud computing. In *Third IEEE international conference on cloud computing technology and science*, (pp. 440–445). IEEE.

Dwivedi, R.K. & Kumar, R. (2018). Sensor cloud: Integrating wireless sensor networks with cloud computing. *2018 5th IEEE Uttar Pradesh section international conference on electrical, electronics and computer engineering (UPCON)* (pp. 1–6). Gorakhpur.

El Rachkidi, E., Agoulmine, N., Chendeb, N., & Belaid, D. (2017). Resources optimization and efficient distribution of shared virtual sensors in sensor-cloud. *2017 IEEE international conference on com-*

munications (ICC) (pp. 1–6). Paris. doi: 10.1109/ICC.2017.7996643.

Glitho, R., Morrow, M., & Polakos, P. (2013). A cloud based architecture for cost efficient applications and services provisioning in wireless sensor networks. *IFIP WMNC, IEEE*, 1–4.

S. Shakena Grace, & M.R. Sumalatha (2014). SCA–An energy efficient transmission in sensor cloud. In *IEEE 2014 international conference on recent trends in information technology* (pp. 1–5).

Guezguez., Jacem, M., Rekhis, S., & Boudriga, N. (2018). "A sensor cloud for the provision of secure and QoS-aware healthcare services,". *Arabian Journal for Science and Engineering, 43*(12), 7059–7082.

Intellisys. Available at <http://www.ntu.edu.sg/intellisys> Accessed 5.02.20.

Irwin, D., Sharma, N., Shenoy, P., & Zink, M. (2010). Towards a virtualized sensing environment. In *Proceedings of the 6th international conference on test beds and research infrastructures for the development of networks and communities*.

Jacem, G. M., Rekhis, S., & Boudriga, N. (2018). A sensor cloud for the provision of secure and QoS-aware healthcare services. *Arabian Journal for Science and Engineering, 43*(12), 7059–7082.

Jiang, H., Sun, Y., Sun, R., & Xu, H. (2013). Fuzzy-logic-based energy optimized routing for wireless sensor networks. *International Journal of Distributed Sensor Networks*, 1–8.

Jit, B., Maniyeri, J., Gopalakrishnan, K., Louis, S., Eugene, P.J., Palit, H.N., ... & Xiaorong, L. (2010). Processing of wearable sensor data on the cloud – A step towards scaling of continuous monitoring of health and well-being. *32 Annual intl conference* (pp. 3860–3863). IEEE EMBS.

Kalyan, D., Das, S., Darji, R. K., & Mishra, A. (2018). Survey of energy-efficient techniques for the cloud-integrated sensor network. *Journal of Sensors*.

Kansal, A., Nath, S., Liu, J., & Zhao, F. (2007). SenseWeb: An infrastructure for shared sensing. *IEEE MultiMedia, 14*, 8–13.

Kapoor, S., & Dabas, C. (2015). Cluster based load balancing in cloud computing. *2015 Eighth international conference on contemporary computing (IC3)* (pp. 76–81). Noida.

Khan, M.F., Dwivedi, R.K., & Kumar, R. (2019a). Energy efficient data transmission in sensor cloud: A review. In *2019 3rd international conference on trends in electronics and informatics (ICOEI)* (pp. 308–313). IEEE.

Khan, M.F., Dwivedi, R.K., & Kumar, R. (2019b). Energy efficient data transmission in sensor cloud: A review. *2019 3rd International conference on trends in electronics and informatics (ICOEI)* (pp. 308–313). Tirunelveli, India.

Khan, M.F., Dwivedi, R.K., & Kumar, R. (2019c). Towards power aware data transmission in sensor cloud: A survey. In *International conference on computer networks and inventive communication technologies* (pp. 317–325). Springer, Cham.

Kumar, L. D., Grace, S. S., Krishnan, A., Manikandan, V. M., Chinraj, R., & Sumalatha, M. R. (2012). Data filtering in wireless sensor networks using neural networks for storage in cloud. In *2012 International Conference on Recent Trends in Information Technology*, (pp. 202–205). IEEE.

Kumar, L.P.D., Shakena Grace, S., Krishnan, A., Manikandan, V.M., Chinraj, R. & Sumalatha, M.R. (2012). Data filtering in wireless sensor networks using neural networks for storage in cloud. In *Proceedings of the International Conference on Recent Trends In Information Technology (ICRTIT)* (pp. 202–205).

Kumar, M., & Sharma, S. C. (2017). Dynamic load balancing algorithm for balancing the workload among virtual machine in cloud computing. *Procedia Computer Science, 115*, 322–329.

Kumar Kashyap, P., Kumar, S., Dohare, U., Kumar, V., & Kharel, R. (2019). Green computing in sensors-enabled internet of things: Neuro fuzzy logic-based load balancing. *Electronics, 8*(4), 1–21, 384.

Lan, K.T. (2010). What's next? sensor + cloud?. In *Proceeding of 7th international workshop on data management for sensor networks* (pp. 1–1). ISBN: 978-1-4503-0416-0, ACM Digital Library.

Lin, C., & Wang, L. (2015). Signal and information processing in mobile cloud computing: Trends and challenges. *2015 International conference on computing, networking and communications (ICNC)* (pp. 625–629). Garden Grove, CA. DOI: 10.1109/ICCNC.2015.7069417.

Madria, S., Kumar, V., & Dalvi, R. (2014). Sensor cloud: A cloud of virtual sensors. *IEEE Software, 31*(2), 70–77.

Mahendran, N., & Priya, R. (2016). Sleep scheduling schemes based on location of mobile user in sensor-cloud. *International Journal of Computer and Information Engineering, 10*(3), 637–642.

Misra, S., Chatterjee, S., & Obaidat, M. S. (2017). On theoretical modeling of sensor cloud: A paradigm shift from wireless sensor network. *In IEEE Systems Journal, 11*(2), 1084–1093. Available from https://doi.org/10.1109/JSYST.2014.2362617.

Mohamed, E. F., Beni-Hssane, A., & Saadi, M. (2018). Multi-mobile agent itinerary planning-based energy and fault aware data aggregation in wireless sensor networks. *EURASIP Journal on Wireless Communications and Networking, 2018*(1), 92.

Mostefa, B., & Feham, M. (2018). Intelligent communication in wireless sensor networks. *Future Internet, 10*(9), 1–19.

Naranjo, P. G. V., Pooranian, Z., Shojafar, M., Conti, M., & Buyya, R. (2019). FOCAN: A fog-supported smart city network architecture for management of applications in the Internet of Everything environments. *Journal of Parallel and Distributed Computing, 132*, 274–283.

Nimbits Data Logging Cloud Sever. <http://www.nimbits.com> Accessed 15.02.20.

Pachube Feed Cloud Service.<http://www.pachube.com> Accessed 15.02.20.

Pawar, C.S. & Wagh, R.B. (2012). Priority based dynamic resource allocation in cloud computing. *2012 International symposium on cloud and services computing* (pp. 1–6).

Rahman, M. T., Salan, M. S. A., Shuva, T. F., & Khan, R. T. (2017). Efficient sensor-cloud communication using data classification and compression. *International Journal of Information Technology and Computer Science, 9*(6), 9–17. Available from https://doi.org/10.5815/ijitcs.2017.06.02.

Rahulamathavan, Y., Phan, R. C.-, Veluru, S., Cumanan, K., & Rajarajan, M. (2014). Privacy-preserving multi-class support vector machine for outsourcing the data classification in cloud. *IEEE Transactions on Dependable and Secure Computing, 11*(5), 467–479. Available from https://doi.org/10.1109/TDSC.2013.51.

Rolim, C. O., Koch, F. L., Sekkaki, A., & Westphall, C. B. (2008). Telemedicine with grids and wireless sensors networks. In *Proceedings of e-Medisys'08, International Conference on E-medical Systems*, IEEE Tunisia Section.

Saha, S. (2015a). Secure sensor data management model in a sensor – Cloud integration environment. *Proceedings – International conference on 2015 applications and innovations in mobile computing, AIMoC*. 10.1109/AIMOC.2015.7083846.

Saha, S. (2015b). Secure sensor data management model in a sensor-cloud integration environment. In *2015 Applications and innovations in mobile computing (AIMoC)* (pp. 158–163). IEEE.

Shea, R., Liu, J., Ngai, E.-H., & Cui, Y. (2013). Cloud gaming: Architecture and performance. *IEEE Network, 27*(4), 16–21.

Shen, H., Bai, G., Ma, D., Zhao, L., & Tang, Z. (2015). C2EM: Cloud assisted complex event monitoring in wireless multimedia sensor networks. *EURASIP Journal on Wireless Communications and Networking, 2015*(1), 124.

Sheng, Z., Mahapatra, C., Leung, V. C. M., Chen, M., & Sahu, P. K. (2018). Energy efficient cooperative computing in mobile wireless sensor networks. *IEEE Transactions on Cloud Computing, 6*(1), 114–126.

Sindhanaiselvan, K., & Mekala, T. (2014). A survey on sensor cloud: Architecture and applications. *International Journal of P2P Network Trends and Technology, 6*, 49–53.

Singh, S. (2017). Optimize cloud computations using edge computing. *2017 International conference on big data, IoT and data science (BID)* (pp. 49–53). Pune. 10.1109/BID.2017.8336572.

Sneha, N. P. (2016). Analysis of energy efficient sensor cloud. *International Journal of Innovative Research in Computer and Communication Engineering, 4*(7), 13157–13163.

Song, C. (2017). A novel wireless sensor network architecture based on cloud computing and big data". *International Journal of Online and Biomedical Engineering, 13*(12), 18–25.

Sukanya, C., Priya, K., Paul, V., & Sankaranarayanan, P. (2015). Integration of wireless sensor networks and mobile cloud-a survey. *International Journal of Computer Science and Information Technologies, 6*, 159–163.

Suto, K., Nishiyama, H., Kato, N., & Huang, C. (2015). An energy-efficient and delay-aware wireless computing system for industrial wireless sensor networks. *IEEE Access, 3*, 1026–1035.

Thing Speak IoT–ThingSpeak. <http://www.thingspeak.com> Accessed 15.02.20.

Tsai, J.-F., Carlsson, J. G., Ge, D., Hu, Y.-C., & Shi, J. (2014). Optimization theory, methods, and applications in engineering 2013. *Mathematical Problems in Engineering, 2014*, Article ID 319418, 5 pages.

Vamsi, M., Mohan., & Shantharajah, S. P. (2016). "Adaptive neural fuzzy interface system for cloud computing". *International Journal, 6*(10).

Velde, V. & Rama, B. (2017). An advanced algorithm for load balancing in cloud computing using fuzzy technique. *2017 International conference on intelligent computing and control systems (ICICCS)* (pp. 1042–1047). Madurai.

Xiao, L., Su, Q., Zhang, M., Zhu, Y., & Wang, Q. (2017). A hybrid classification system for heart disease diagnosis based on the RFRS method. *Computational and Mathematical Methods in Medicine, 2017.*

Xin, C., Huang, X., Ma, Y., & Meng, Q. (2019). A load balancing routing mechanism based on SDWSN in smart city. *Electronics, 8* (3), 273.

Xu, Y., Helal, S., Thai, M., & Scmalz, M. (2011). Optimizing push/pull envelopes for energy-efficient cloud-sensor systems. In *Proceedings of the 14th ACM international conference on Modeling, analysis and simulation of wireless and mobile systems*, (pp. 17–26). ACM.

Yang, J. Y., Chen, Y. P., Lee, G. Y., Liou, S. N., & Wang, J. S. (2007). Activity recognition using one triaxial accelerometer: A neuro-fuzzy classifier with feature reduction. In *International Conference on Entertainment Computing*, (pp. 395–400). Berlin, Heidelberg: Springer.

Yousif, Y. K., Badlishah, R., Yaakob, N., & Amir, A. (2018). An energy efficient and load balancing clustering scheme for wireless sensor network (WSN) based on distributed approach. *Journal of Physics: Conference Series, 1019*(1), IOP Publishing.

Yujin, L., & Park, J. (2014). Sensor resource sharing approaches in sensor-cloud infrastructure. *International Journal of Distributed Sensor Networks, 10*(4), 1–8.

Zegrari, F., Idrissi, A., & Rehioui, H. (2016). Resource allocation with efficient load balancing in cloud environment. In *Proceedings of the international conference on big data and advanced wireless technologies (BDAW '16)* (pp. 1–7). New York, NY, USA: Association for Computing Machinery. Article 46.

Zenon, C., Mahadevan, V., Aslanzadeh, S., and Mcdermid, C. (2011). Availability and load balancing in cloud computing. In *International conference on computer and software modeling, vol. 14* (pp. 134–140). Singapore.

Zhang, P., Yan, Z., & Sun, H. (2013, Jan). A novel architecture based on cloud computing for wireless sensor network. *Proceedings of the 2nd international conference on computer science and electronics engineering* (pp. 472–475). ISBN 978-90-78677-61-1.

Zhao, S., & Chen, Y. (2014). Development of cloud computing system based on wireless sensor network protocol and routing. *Journal of Chemical and Pharmaceutical Research, 6*(7), 1680–1684.

Zhu, C., Leung, V. C., Yang, L. T., Shu, L., Rodrigues, J. J., & Li, X. (2015). Trust assistance in sensor-cloud. In *2015 IEEE Conference on Computer Communications Workshops (INFOCOM WKSHPS)*, (pp. 342–347). IEEE.

Zhu, C., Leung, V. C., Wang, K., Yang, L. T., & Zhang, Y. (2017). Multi-method data delivery for green sensor-cloud. *IEEE Communications Magazine, 55*(5), 176–182.

Zhu, C., Sheng, Z., Leung, V. C. M., Shu, L., & Yang, L. T. (2015). Toward offering more useful data reliably to mobile cloud from wireless sensor network. *IEEE Transactions on Emerging Topics in Computing, 3*(1), 84–94.

CHAPTER

2

Computational intelligence techniques for localization and clustering in wireless sensor networks

Basavaraj M. Angadi[1], *Mahabaleshwar S. Kakkasageri*[1] *and Sunilkumar S. Manvi*[2]

[1]Department of Electronics and Communication Engineering, Basaveshwar Engineering College (Autonomous), Bagalkot, India [2]School of Computing and Information Technology, REVA University, Bangalore, India

2.1 Introduction

Wireless sensor networks (WSNs) are used to simplify and manage complex problems in most applications. Energy conservation in WSNs is a prime concern. It is important as the lifetime of the network depends mainly on the WSN energy consumption. Hence the highest priority is given to balancing and preserving the consumption of energy. Therefore the design and development of algorithms with minimum energy expenditure is a main challenge in WSNs. To achieve this, new protocols and schemes have to be designed using emerging computational techniques (Primeau, Falcon, Abielmona, & Petriu, 2018).

In a sensor network, it is very important to know about the location of the sensor node (SN) and data collected by that node which can be obtained using localization techniques. Accurate position estimation of target nodes in WSNs is highly desirable as it has a significant impact on the overall network performance. Normally, information regarding location is useful for deployment, coverage, location service, routing, target tracking, and rescue. In some industries, SNs are used to identify minute changes such as gas leaks, pressure, and temperature, and in military applications for the detection of landmines. Location information plays a key role in both of these cases.

In general, clustering means the process of grouping SNs into clusters to overcome the scalability problem. Clustering of SNs also helps in achieving high energy efficiency and extends the network lifetime, especially in large-scale WSN environments. It has been proved that for organizing a network into a connected hierarchy, clustering is an effective topology control approach (Angadi, Kakkasageri, & Kori, 2016). Hierarchical routing and data collection protocols include cluster-based organization of SNs for data fusion and aggregation purposes (Kakkasageri & Manvi, 2014), which leads to a substantial decrease in energy consumption.

Most computational intelligent technologies are interdisciplinary in nature, such as the integration of artificial intelligence (AI) with computer science and information systems with decision support systems. Some of the intelligent techniques include natural computation, bio-inspired computational techniques, game theory, AI, neural systems/networks, fuzzy logic techniques, genetic algorithms (GAs), intelligent multiagent systems, policy-based multiagent systems, machine learning, and so on (Alomari, Phillips, Aslam, & Comeau, 2018; Baranidharan & Santhi, 2016; Mann & Singh, 2017b; Singh, Khosla, & Kumar, 2018).

The chapter is organized as follows. Section 2.2 describes WSNs. Localization and clustering are explained in Section 2.3. Computational intelligence (CI) techniques for localization and clustering are discussed in Section 2.4, and finally, Section 2.5 presents further research challenges that need to be addressed.

Recent Trends in Computational Intelligence Enabled Research.
DOI: https://doi.org/10.1016/B978-0-12-822844-9.00011-6

2.2 Wireless sensor networks

A WSN is a collection of thousands of randomly deployed spatially scattered SNs for the collection of information or data in the node's sensing range and communicates this to the user via the sink, gateway, or base station (BS), as shown in Fig. 2.1. The BS serves as a bridge between WSNs and wired infrastructure that links the end user to where sensed data can be collected, processed, and analyzed (Sharma & Kumar, 2018). These nodes sense changes in the network environment, such as pressure, temperature, and sound, and transmit that sensed information to the real world (Sarobin & Ganesan, 2015).

Traditional SNs are homogeneous in nature and single-task performers. They consist of a sensing unit, computational unit, communication unit, power unit, and memory unit. These nodes have built-in self-organizing and self-communication protocols (Akyildiz, Su, Sankarasubramaniam, & Cayirci, 2002), whereas modern SNs are designed and developed with heterogeneity in nature, ability to manage multitasking with built in global positioning systems (GPSs), and enhanced on-chip memory. These nodes are gaining popularity due to their fast computation and accurate results. The main aim of using these SNs is to get high-quality, automatic, and accurate results from the network (Akyildiz, Melodia, & Chowdury, 2007).

2.2.1 Characteristics

In some applications, replacement of the battery or energy source is a very difficult task, especially when the SNs are deployed in harsh and unattended regions. In most cases the lifetime of the WSN can be extended by minimizing energy consumption, which results in a reduction of the cost of the network. WSNs must be energy efficient, scalable, intelligent, reliable, programmable, and accurate for long periods of time, with low purchase cost and installation, and low maintenance requirement. Some of the characteristics of the WSN (Ahmed, Huang, Sharma, & Cui, 2012) are depicted in Fig. 2.2.

- *Low cost*: Usually, WSNs consist of a high number, that is in range of hundreds or thousands, of SNs, which are randomly deployed for measuring or sensing physical environment. Therefore the

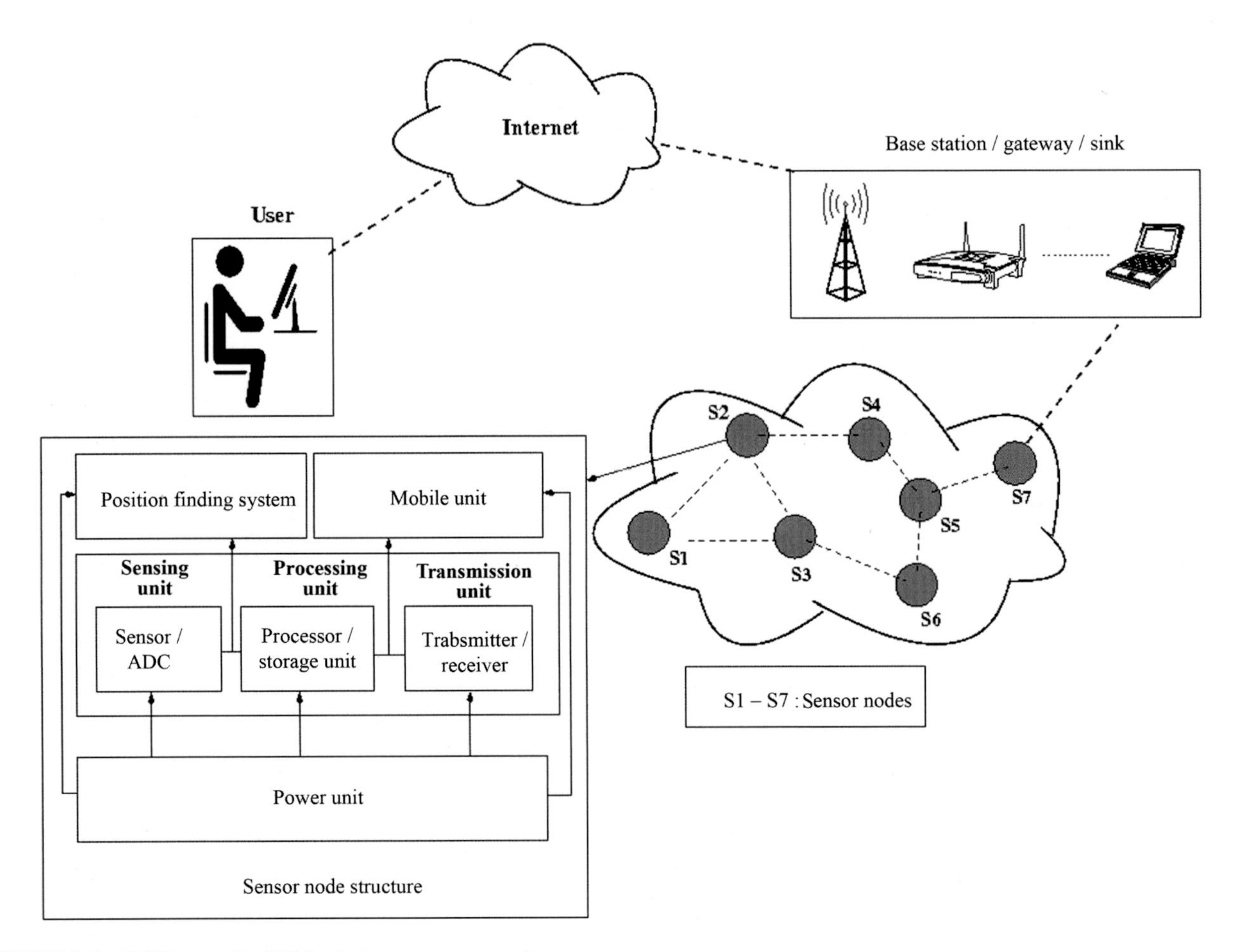

FIGURE 2.1 WSN scenario. *WSN*, wireless sensor network.

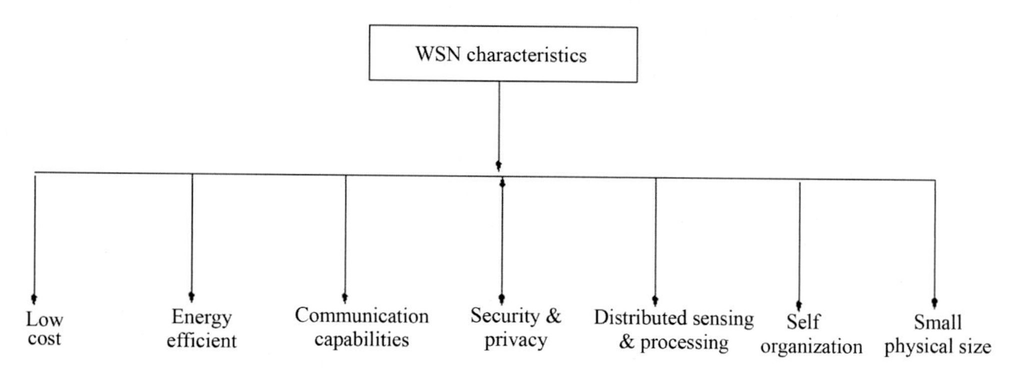

FIGURE 2.2 WSN characteristics. *WSN*, wireless sensor network.

development of a cost-effective network is necessary and can be achieved by minimizing SN cost.

- *Energy efficient*: Energy is necessary for communication, computation, storage, etc., and in some harsh environments, it is not possible to recharge the SNs. Hence the development of the algorithms and protocols must take power consumption as an important factor.
- *Communication capabilities*: WSNs normally communicate over a wireless channel by means of radio waves and also have the property of short-range communication along with dynamic and narrow bandwidth. The medium of communication may be either one-way or two-way. If a WSN is to be operated in a hostile and unattended environment, it is necessary to consider resiliency, security, and robustness for communication.
- *Security and privacy*: In order to avoid unauthorized access and attacks, security mechanisms should be incorporated into every SN.
- *Distributed sensing and processing*: Normally SNs are distributed randomly or uniformly in huge numbers. Every SN has the capability to collect, process, aggregate, and send information to the BS. Hence distributed sensing gives the system robustness.
- *Self-organization*: SNs need to be deployed in a harsh and unattended environment. Therefore for proper functioning, they should be capable of organizing themselves and automatically forming a network by working collaboratively.
- *Small physical size*: Usually SNs are tiny in size and have a limited communication range.

2.2.2 Research issues/challenges

To develop successful applications for a WSN, it is necessary to understand important sensor network factors. A WSN has many open issues/challenges, as described in Fig. 2.3, such as localization, network lifetime, clustering, node deployment, node scheduling, connectivity, data gathering, and coverage.

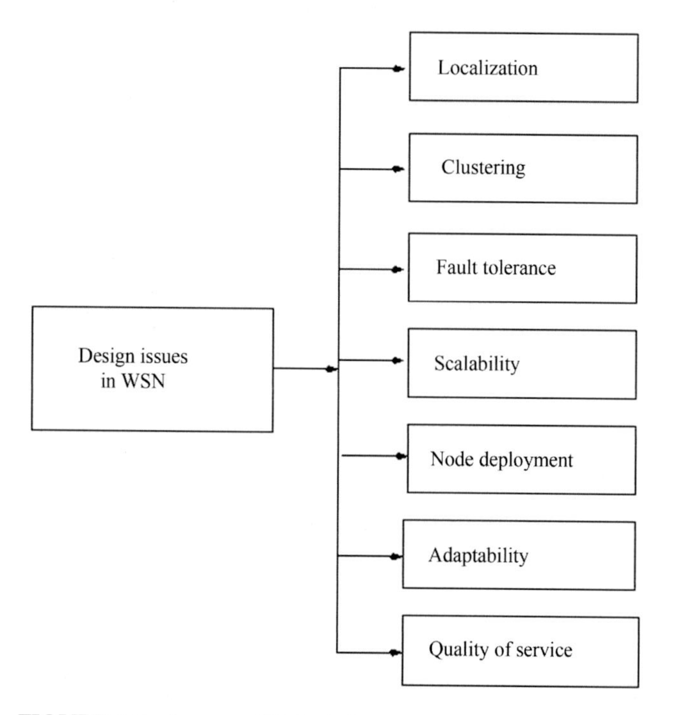

FIGURE 2.3 Issues in WSNs. *WSN*, wireless sensor network.

- *Localization*: Most of the applications like target tracking, coverage, node deployment routing, rescues, and location service require location information. GPS is used to obtain location information which becomes costly, especially for large-scale networks. It is considered as one of the important research issues in WSN.
- *Clustering*: In a large-scale network, direct communication is not feasible as it consumes more energy. Therefore grouping of the SNs into clusters and the process of grouping called clustering helps in achieving high energy efficiency and prolongs the network lifetime. It also helps to overcome the scalability problem.

- *Fault tolerance*: Due to a hardware problem or shortage of power, SNs may fail. Usually failure of nodes occurs in a WSN rather than a wired network. Hence it is necessary to develop protocols capable of detecting node failures that are robust enough to handle these failures without disturbing the network functionality.
- *Scalability*: Some of the applications need high-resolution data, which requires increasing numbers of nodes to be deployed. As the number of nodes varies in a large number, the protocols used in sensor network should be scalable and maintain desirable performance.
- *Node deployment*: Nodes are usually deployed either manually (deterministic) or randomly scattered (self-organizing). When nodes are placed manually, the data routing path is predetermined, in other cases it is done in an ad hoc manner.
- *Adaptability*: During operation of the WSN system, some changes may happen due to node failure, environmental conditions, or application requirements. A WSN should be adoptable or able to handle these changes without altering the functionality and lifetime of the network.
- *Quality of service (QoS)*: Since the topology of the network is dynamic in nature, it is very difficult to provide a good-quality service. It is necessary to develop a QoS mechanism to provide better quality service, irrespective of the constraints.

2.3 Localization and clustering in wireless sensor networks

Determining the localization of nodes in a WSN involves collaboration between SNs. Localization is an essential service since it is applicable to many applications and key functions of the network, such as routing, formation of cluster, communication, and network coverage. Clustering is one of WSN's essential strategies for extending the lifetime of the network. It includes grouping of SNs into clusters, with cluster head (CH) selection for all the clusters. CHs collect the information from nodes of the respective clusters and forward the gathered information to the BS.

2.3.1 Localization

Localization is one of the most important issues in WSNs, because location information is needed for deployment, target tracking, coverage, routing, rescues, and location services (Alrajeh, Bashir, & Shams, 2013; Angadi & Kakkasageri, 2020; as shown in Fig. 2.4). For example, SNs sense the occurrence of an event in the sensing region and the information sensed is disseminated via satellite/Internet and BS/sink/gateway to the end user. If the event location is not in association with the sensed data, then the user cannot take immediate action. Therefore the users need to know not only the occurrence of the event but also where the interested event is occurring. For this reason, node localization is considered as a critical issue for WSN.

The goal of localization is to assign geographic coordinates to every node with an unknown position in the deployment region (Paul & Sato, 2017). Location information of the SN can be obtained either by recording the location while deploying or using built-in GPS for the nodes (Pescaru & Curiac, 2014). It is not possible to record the location information manually, especially for large-scale networks. Because of these drawbacks, various localization strategies/schemes have been developed. Localization schemes are classified based on various criteria, as shown in Table 2.1.

2.3.2 Clustering

The main goal of the clustering algorithms in WSN is grouping of sensors to form clusters and CH selection for every cluster. It is known that direct communication of the SNs with the BS consumes more energy, resulting in early expiration of the WSN. In particular, the adoption of direct communication is practically very difficult for a large-scale network. For efficient utilization of the energy in a WSN, data from cluster members are aggregated by CH and sent to the BS/gateway/sink (as depicted in Fig. 2.5). In a two-layered clustering protocol, the decision of the optimal CH set is dealt by the first layer of protocol, whereas the second layer of protocol takes the responsibility for transmitting data to the BS (Jan, Farman, Khan, Javed, & Montrucchio, 2017).

Clustering protocols not only should facilitate data transmission in WSNs but also should consider the limitations of the SNs. That is, they should meet the WSN requirements, which include reliability in data delivery, energy efficiency, and scalability requirements. In clustering, a sleep scheduling mechanism can be used to reduce energy consumption by making the SN sleep when not in use and wake up or activate intermittently to check the necessity, which improves network lifespan. In clustering protocols, the formation and number of clusters are considered as important factors. Clusters are formed in such a way that load balancing is maintained and a minimum number of messages are exchanged during cluster formation process.

As the network grows, there is a linear increment in the complexity of the clustering algorithm. Another important challenge which affects directly the performance of the network is the selection of the CH. Some

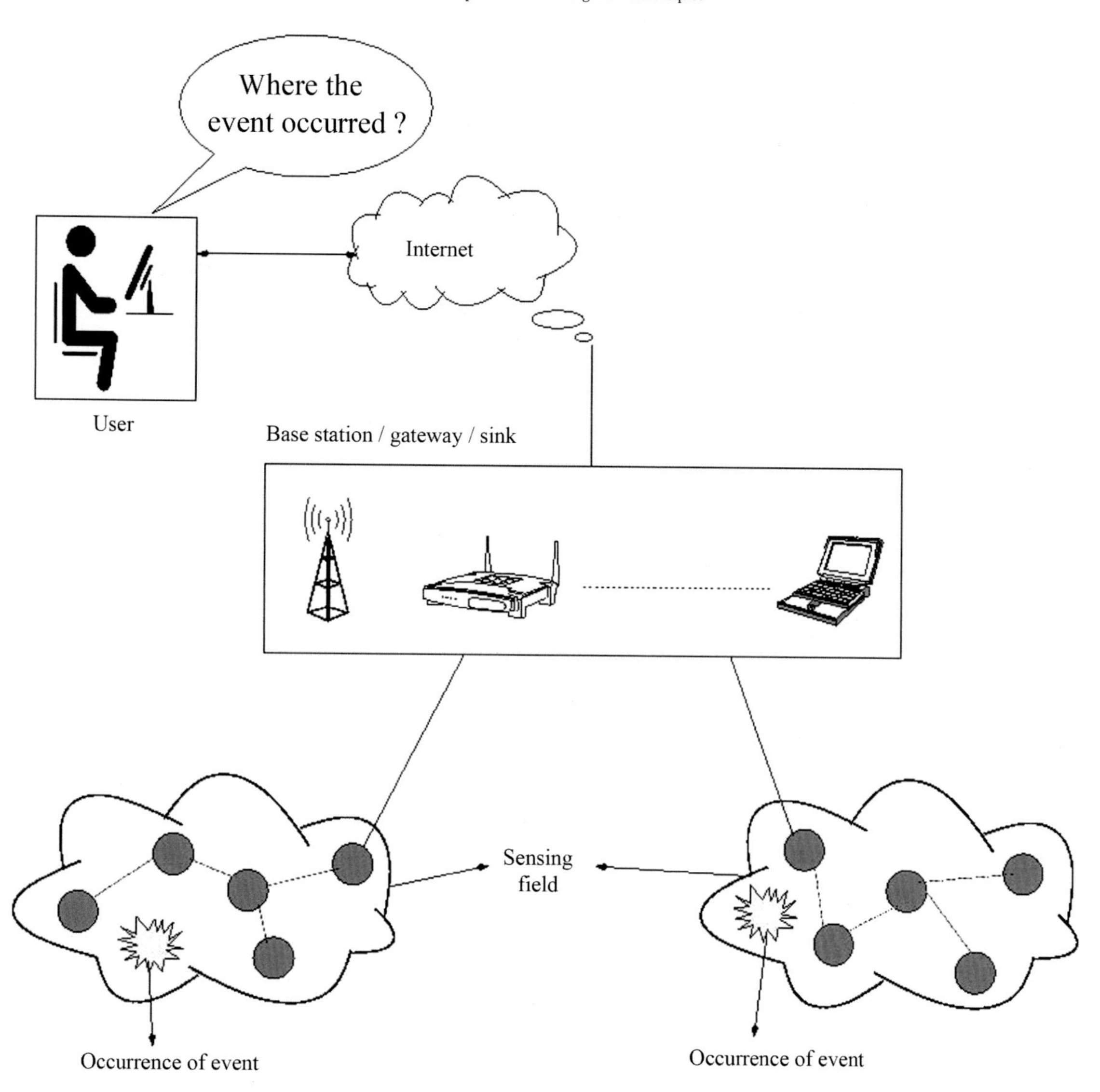

FIGURE 2.4 Necessity of localization for WSNs. *WSN*, wireless sensor network.

of the parameters that affect the cluster formation process, either directly or indirectly, are cluster count which varies depending upon network size, cluster formation which is either centralized or distributed, and intracluster communication which may be one-hop for a small-scale network or multihop for a large-scale network. The introduction of new technologies and emerging developments in applications challenge the research findings for the performance in WSNs, particularly from an energy point of view.

It is essential to develop efficient clustering algorithms for controlling the topology of the network and to overcome issues such as selection of CH, load balancing in the cluster, reducing the control messages for clustering, and hence reducing energy consumption by eliminating redundant energy consumption. Classification of the clustering algorithms is shown in Table 2.2.

2.4 Computational intelligence techniques

CI is a dynamic research area comprised of a number of methodologies that motivate the use of various natural and social practices to model and resolve a variety of real-world challenging problems (Primeau et al., 2018; Serpen, Li, & Liu, 2013). The term CI is not an indication of a single methodology but it is like a description of a large umbrella under which numerous socially and biologically inspired techniques have emerged, as shown in Table 2.3. The CI field has expanded its classical foundations focused on all-around fuzzy systems, artificial neural networks (ANNs), and evolutionary algorithms (EAs) to introduce other associated methodologies such as game theory, swarm intelligence, deep learning, granular computation, artificial immune systems, and hybrids of the above-mentioned

TABLE 2.1 Classification of localization schemes.

Mechanisms	Localization techniques used	Advantages/disadvantages
Localization precision (Niewiadomska-Szynkiewicz, 2012)	• Coarse-grained localization	• Approximate coordinates • Lower precision
	• Fine-grained localization	• Accurate coordinates • Higher precision
Fitting with GPS (anchor) (Niewiadomska-Szynkiewicz, 2012)	• GPS-free or anchor-free localization schemes	• Use of only connectivity between nodes • Dedicated hardware not required
	• Anchor-based localization schemes	• Use of GPS or dedicated hardware • Use of available knowledge
Internode distance measurement (Nazir, Arshad, Shahid, & Raza, 2012)	• Range-based (distance-based) methods	• Fine-grained accuracy • Expensive due to additional hardware
	• Range-free (connectivity-based) methods	• Coarse-grained accuracy • Cost effective and simple
Calculation methods (Mekelleche & Haffaf, 2017; Saeed, Nam, Haq, & Bhatti, 2018)	• Geometrical techniques	• These are usually range-free • Uses various geometric shapes such as circle, triangle, rectangle
	• Multidimensional scaling	• Depends on experimental measurement or estimated ranges between the nodes • Set of techniques used for reducing the dimensionality of the data
Distribution of the calculation process (Li, Li, Wei, & Pei, 2010)	• Centralized localization schemes	• Central unit calculates the position of nodes • Achieves efficiency through local • Optimization
	• Distributed localization schemes	• Each node estimates its own position • Achieves efficiency through global optimization
Environment (Saeed, Nam, Al-Naffouri, & Alouini, 2019; Yassin et al., 2017)	• Outdoor positioning system (PS)	• Normally PS equipped with GPS • Accuracy ranges between 5 m and 10 m
	• Indoor PS	• Normally PS equipped with Bluetooth, Wi-Fi, Zig-bee modules • Complexity is more due to obstacles, nonline of sight, noise, etc.
	• Underwater PS	• Uses acoustic distance for positioning • PS are equipped with baseline stations such as LBL, USBL

GPS, global positioning system.

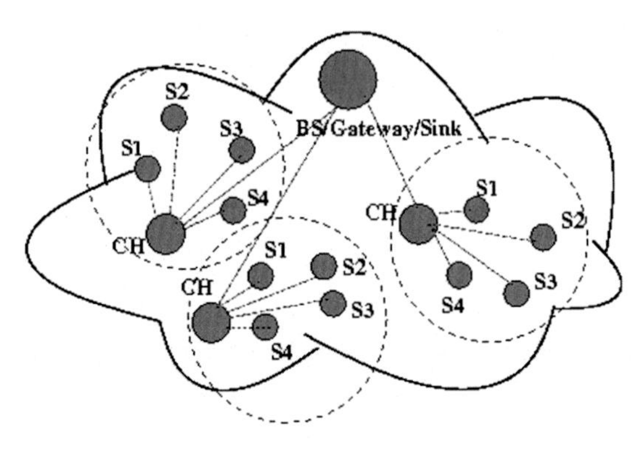

FIGURE 2.5 Communication between cluster head and base station.

systems (Kulkarni, Forster, & Venayagamoorthy, 2011; Parulpreet, Arun, Anil, & Mamta, 2019).

EAs are well suited for multiobjective optimization and for solving non-deterministic polynomial-time (NP) hard problems effectively (Slowik & Kwasnicka, 2020) in which the necessity of mathematical-related knowledge is reduced. However, EA schemes do not guarantee the ideal solutions in finite time and also require the addition of domain-specific knowledge using external processes. The systems with a Swarm Intelligence Algorithm (SIA) are scalable as similar control architecture can be applied to a couple of agents or a large number of agents, and they are flexible due to the

TABLE 2.2 Classification of clustering algorithms.

Clustering mechanisms	Characteristics	Algorithms used
Partitioning method (Xu, Wunsch, 2020; Wang et al., 2018; Yun et al., 2019)	• Find mainly spherical-shaped clusters • Distance based • Single-level partitioning • Effective for small or medium-sized data sets	• K-means—Iterative algorithm that divides dataset into K predefined dissimilar nonoverlapping subgroups • K-MEDOIDS—Robust alternative to K-means • CLARANS—A scheme to cluster objects for spatial data mining
Hierarchical methods (Jan et al., 2017; Wang et al., 2018)	• Hierarchical decomposition (i.e., multiple levels) • Incorporates techniques like microclustering • Merges the objects or groups until all the groups are merged into one	• BIRCH—Stands for Balanced Iterative Reducing and Clustering using Hierarchies • CHAMELEON—Hierarchical clustering algorithm using dynamic modeling • CURE—An effective clustering scheme for large databases
Density-based methods (Yang, Liu, Zhang, & Yang, 2012)	• Discovers arbitrarily shaped clusters • Needs density parameters specified • One scan	• DBSCAN—based on intuitive notion of clusters and noise • OPTICS—Stands for ordering points to Identify the Clustering Structure • DENCLU—Based on kernel density estimation
Grid-based methods (Serpen et al., 2013)	• Use of multiresolution grid data structure • Fast processing time • Divides space into finite number of cells	• STING—Statistical Information Grid approach • CLIQUE—A dimension-growth subspace clustering method • Wave-Cluster—multiresolution clustering approach

TABLE 2.3 Brief classification of computational intelligence (CI) techniques.

CI techniques	Algorithms	Characteristics
Evolutionary algorithms (EA) (Du, Pan, Chu, Luo, & Hu, 2020; Kulkarni et al., 2011)	Genetic Algorithms (GAs), Artificial Immune System (AIS), Differential Evolution (DE), Multiobjective Evolutionary Algorithms (MOEAs), Quasiaffine Transformation Evolutionary algorithm (QUATRE)	• Finding approximate solutions to challenging optimization problems • Uses random probability transition rule rather than deterministic transition rule
Swarm intelligence algorithms (SIAs) (Daneshvar, Alikhah Ahari Mohajer, & Mazinani, 2019; Maruthi & Panigrahi, 2020; Ramesh, Divya, Rekha, Kulkarni, & Swarm, 2012)	Particle Swarm Optimization (PSO), Artificial Bee Colony (ABC), Ant Colony Optimization (ACO), Glowworm Search Optimization (GSO), Firefly Algorithm (FA), Whale Optimization Algorithm (WOA), Grey Wolf optimization (GWO)	• Motivated by nature and based on the interactions among living organisms • Enhancement of fitness functions in combinatorial and numerical optimization problems by discovering different combinations of value
Fuzzy logic (FL) (Cheng, Hang, Wang, Bi, & Fuzzy, 2019; Kulkarni et al., 2011)	Fuzzy sets, Fuzzy Inference System (FIS), Fuzzy C-Means (FCM)	• Suits undefined or approximate reasoning • Allows decision taking under partial or uncertain knowledge with estimated values • Deteriorates nonline of sight error
Learning systems (machine learning) (Kulkarni et al., 2011)	Artificial neural network (ANN), support vector machine (SVM), reinforcement learning (RL), import vector machine (IVM)	• Learning relationships among objects • Capable of capturing complex, nonlinear relationships

addition or deletion of agents without influencing the structure.

In general, SIAs are unpredictable (complexity of the swarm system leads to unforeseeable results), nonimmediate (complex swarm systems take time), nonoptimal (highly redundant and no central control), and uncontrollable (Sun, Tang, Zhang, Huo, & Shu, 2020).

Fuzzy logic enables the modeling and inclusion of inconsistencies in the knowledge base and also enhances the anatomy of the system because rules in the knowledge base function are independent of each other. Using fuzzy logic, it is convenient to express expert and common sense knowledge and also eliminate borderline cases.

The limitation of fuzzy logic is that determination of the exact fuzzy rules and membership functions is a difficult task. It also becomes an obstacle in a highly complex system due to verification of the system reliability and fuzzy reasoning mechanisms that cannot learn from their mistakes. Therefore it is necessary to develop a system that can learn or learn to forget. A key benefit of a learning system is the ability of this technology to review vast volumes of data and identify patterns and trends that might not be evident to a human. Usually this technology improves its performance and accuracy over time as the volume of data being processed is increased.

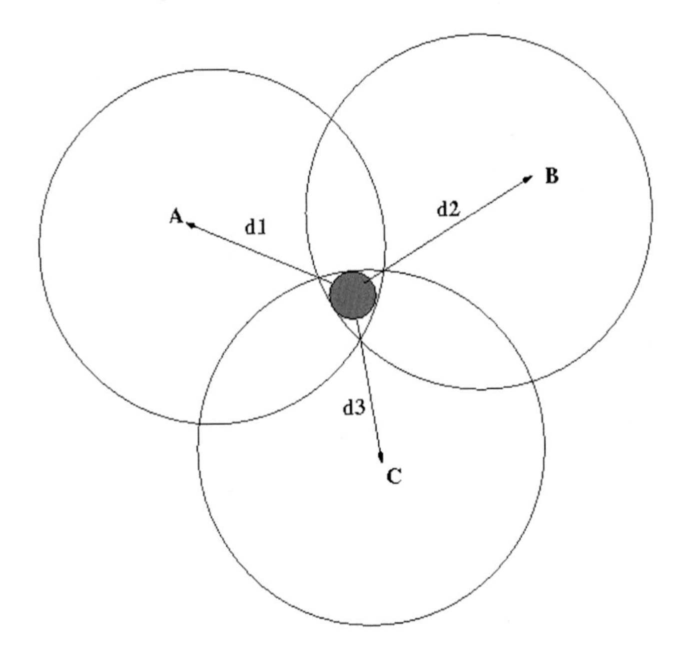

FIGURE 2.6 Intersection of circles in trilateration method.

2.4.1 Computational intelligence techniques for localization

This section reviews CI mechanisms that are used to help localization in WSNs.

2.4.1.1 *Evolutionary algorithms*

Many of the present localization techniques emphasize the use of various heuristic-based or mathematical-oriented techniques for precise location. A recent research study shows that several algorithms are inspired by nature, for example GAs or ant-based algorithms can efficiently overcome various challenging issues in optimization. GAs belong to the EAs category. Basically, GAs are used in localization to solve problems related to optimization.

The GAs are adopted in the localization techniques to effectively search the appropriate and more efficient anchor nodes that are used for estimation of the position of an unknown node (Kulkarni et al., 2011). As an example, if we use the trilateration method for estimating the location of an unknown node, a minimum of three anchor nodes are required, as shown in Fig. 2.6. A, B, and C are the anchor nodes whose distances from the unknown node are d1, d2, and d3, respectively. These distances are measured using the RSSI (received signal strength indicator) values. After calculating the distance between an unknown node and anchor node using the trilateration method the location is estimated by determining the intersection of three circles.

Consider the network consists of 200 nodes and that we use 10% of the anchor nodes of the total number of nodes. To get the best three anchor nodes among 20 anchors, the possible number of anchor combinations required by considering all remaining 180 unknown (nonanchor) nodes is approximately 205,200 ($180 \times {}^{20}C_3$) in every iteration. Therefore it is very difficult to search the best anchors using the traditional method which requires more time and it may not even be possible to improve the localization accuracy. In optimization, a gene is considered as the variable and all the genes together are considered as a chromosome which denotes the evaluation of all variables.

With inspiration from nature, a GA or EA effectively accomplishes a local parallel search in several parts of the search space by preserving a chromosome population to iteratively improve consecutive generations. This algorithm explains the selection of a natural mechanism in which the fittest or strongest individuals are preferred for reproduction to yield offspring for consecutive generations.

In general, for GA the population is initialized by a number of randomly generated solutions or by some simple heuristics such as dispatch rules. The values of decision variables must be within their defined range or domain. The initial solutions are then evaluated by calculating their fitness functions. A further iteration process is repeated with the help of mutation or crossover operators in order to generate new solutions. Newly generated solutions are tested and updated in the population based on a certain predefined set of rules. At the same time, the fitness function is also updated with corresponding values. The process is as shown in Fig. 2.7, and it is repeated until the occurrence of desired values and the fitness function.

In general, the fitness function is represented mathematically as shown in Eq. (2.1).

$$ftnss(X', Y') = \sum_{j=1}^{3}\left(\sqrt{(X' - X_j) - (Y' - Y_j)} - pdst_j\right) \tag{2.1}$$

In Eq. (2.1), (X', Y') denotes present estimated position and (X_j, Y_j) is the anchor nodes absolute location with

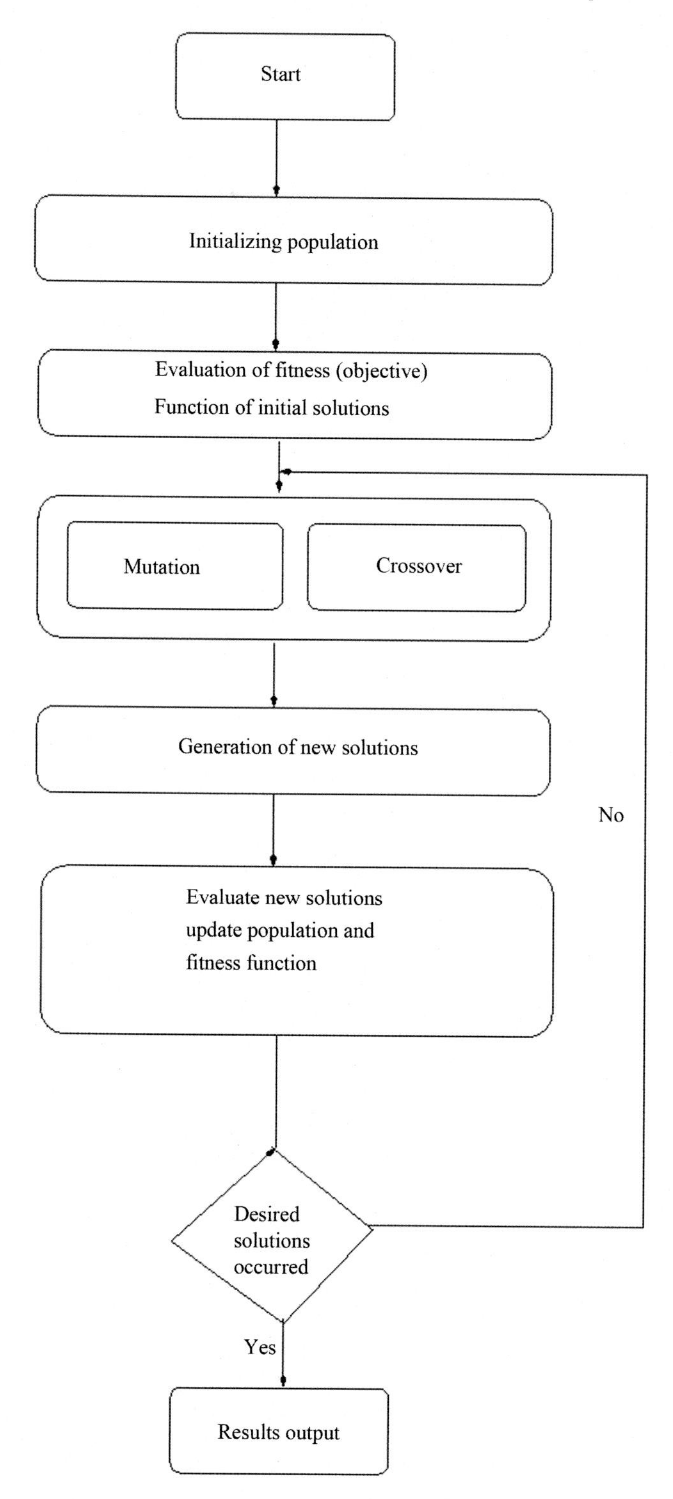

FIGURE 2.7 Procedure for a genetic algorithm.

j varying from 1 to 3 for three nearest and best anchors. The relative distance between the anchor node j and estimated current position is represented by $pdst_j$. It is clear that, the fitness function provides the average squared error of the present estimated position pertaining to the three adjacent anchor nodes position and the measured relative distance.

A Micro-Genetic Algorithm (MGA) (Tam, Cheng, & Lui, 2006) based on evolutionary approach is presented as an optimization technique for the localization mechanisms such as an ad hoc positioning system to increase the location precision. In MGA, two operators named the descend-based mutation and descend-based crossovers are used for the production of the best values (offspring) for fitness function. EA belongs to the current search method set based on heuristics and is also a subset of evolutionary computations (EC). It is an effective method of problem solving for commonly used global optimization problems due to the versatile existence and robust behavior inherited from EC. It can be used effectively in several high-complexity applications (Slowik & Kwasnicka, 2020; Vikhar, 2016).

2.4.1.2 *Swarm intelligence algorithms*

In general, swarm intelligence algorithms are nature-inspired algorithms developed based on the interactions between living organisms such as flocks of birds, ants, and fish. These algorithms help in the enhancement of fitness functions in combinatorial and numerical optimization problems by discovering different combinations of values. Particle swarm optimization (PSO) was proposed in Kennedy and Eberhart (1995). It is one of the popular bio-inspired stochastic global search algorithms which models the social behavior of a flock of birds. Basically, PSO comprises a set of population (swarm) that is "S" number of particles. Every particle represents a solution for every candidate. Particles discover "n" dimensional search space to obtain a global solution, where n represents the number of parameters considered for optimization.

Let us consider every particle j is going to occupy the position P_{jd} and move with velocity V_{jd}. Initially the position and velocities to the particles are assigned randomly with some fixed limits or boundaries, that is, $P_{\min} < P_{jd} < P_{\max}$ and $V_{\min} < V_{jd} < V_{\max}$. The position of the particles determines the fitness of particles, which has a higher value if the particle is closer to the solution than a far away particle. In every iteration particle locations and velocities are updated to encourage them to accomplish better fitness. This updating process is iteratively repeated either until a global solution is met by a particle within acceptable tolerance limits or until it completes an adequately huge number of iterations.

In the modified versions of the PSO, every particle has some memory for storing the best location information in which it has the highest fitness. Let *gbest* be the modified version of PSO and $pbest_{jd}$ be the best position with high fitness. In addition, every particle can also access the position $gbest_d$ which is the maximum fitness position of the particle. For every iteration

m, PSO is going to add V_{jd} (velocity) to each X_{jd} (position) and directs the particles towards its $pbest_{jd}$ and $gbest_d$ using Eqs. (2.2) and (2.3).

$$V_{jd}(m+1) = w \cdot V_{jd}(m) + k_1 \cdot rnd_1 \cdot (pbest_{jd} - x_{jd}) + k_2 \cdot rnd_2 \cdot (gbest_d - x_{jd}) \quad (2.2)$$

$$x_{jd}(m+1) = x_{jd}(m) + V_{jd}(m+1) \quad (2.3)$$

The velocity update in Eq. (2.2) indicates that three components related to acceleration influence a particle. The term w involves the inertia coefficient ranging between 0.2 and 1.2, and denotes the particle inertia (Shi & Eberhart, 1998). Random variables rnd_1 and rnd_2 are used which have uniform range (0, 1) distribution. In the second term, constant k_1 implicates cognitive acceleration, which makes the particle move in the direction of the position where it has maximum fitness. Similarly, the third term contains constant k^2, which indicates social acceleration and propels the particle toward the presently highest valued fitness particle.

Several variants of the PSO are developed to solve the optimization problem in the localization technique. A distributed two-phase PSO algorithm (Li & Wen, 2015), Comprehensive Learning Particle Swarm Optimization (CLPSO) (Ramesh, Divya, Rekha, & Kulkarni, 2012) and metric-based hop localization algorithm (Prasha & Kumar, 2020) is presented to overcome the difficulty in flip and to increase the localization efficiency. The traditional PSO algorithm works on the basis of a set of some possible solutions within the search space, that is, a swarm of particles with randomly initialized locations.

In Li and Wen (2015), the initial search space is minimized with the use of a bounding box method. In this method, the communication range of SN is represented by the squares with $2r$ side length instead of circles with radius r. Therefore the initial space to be searched is described by the overlapping portion of the squares, as shown in Fig. 2.8.

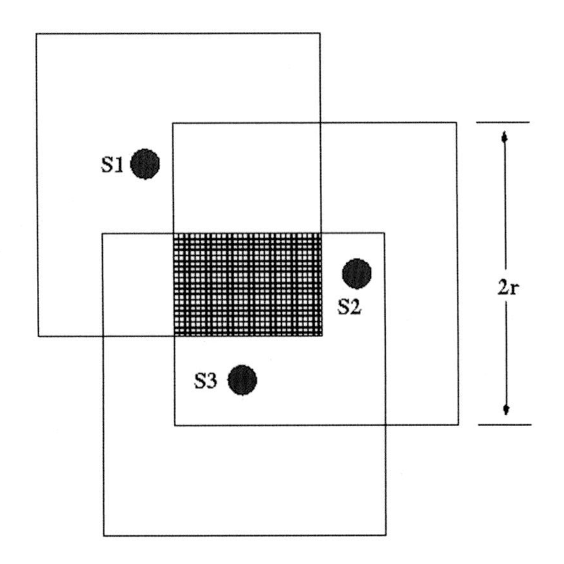

FIGURE 2.8 Bounding box method.

Therefore compared with the traditional PSO where it considers complete solution space as the initial search space for the targeted nodes, the proposed protocol will reduce the time for computation as well as flip ambiguity problem. To improve the localization accuracy, a hybrid protocol based on the Firefly Algorithm (FA) is proposed in SrideviPonmalar, Senthil Kumar, and Harikrishnan (2017) and Sun et al. (2020), which optimizes error along with variations in the number of fireflies, iteration requirements, and time complexity.

2.4.1.3 *Fuzzy logic*

Human reasoning usually comprises some linguistic variables, such as frequently, most, many, and rarely, to quantify imprecision or uncertainty. This type of approximation in reasoning is modeled by fuzzy logic, which is a multivalued logic allowing to define some intermediate values between threshold and conventional values. For making some decisions or conclusions, fuzzy systems allow the use of fuzzy sets which are different from traditional sets and an object may be allowed to be a partial member of a set (Marwan, Mourad, Mousa, & 2020, 2020; Sangeetha, Vijayalakshmi, Ganapathy, & Kannan, 2020). Let us consider a person as a member of a set short to some degree. The dynamic behavior of a system in fuzzy systems is considered using some linguistic fuzzy rules depend upon the human expert knowledge.

In general, fuzzy rules are of the form "if antecedent(s) then consequent(s)," where both antecedent(s) and consequent(s) are propositions comprised of linguistic variables. Incorporation of fuzzy sets with logical operations results in the formation of a fuzzy rule. Hence, the knowledge base of a rule-based fuzzy inference system (FIS) is formed collectively by fuzzy rules and sets, as shown in Fig. 2.9.

A fuzzy logic-based mechanism is proposed in Amri et al. (2019), based on a weighted centroid localization method, in which the positions of unknown nodes are estimated using a fuzzy logic method. In the scheme, FIS with RSSI value as input and weight value as output were modeled by Mamdani and Sugeno methods. Estimation of unknown node position using a fuzzy Mamdani and Sugeno inference system is adopted to improve localization accuracy and also effectively selects the next CH to minimize the energy dissipation that leads to an extended lifetime of WSN. An advantage of this scheme is that since the RSSI value is used, it does not require any additional hardware. A novel distributed range-free algorithm for mobility-assisted localization in WSNs (Alomari, Phillips, Aslam, & Comeau, 2017) is introduced with

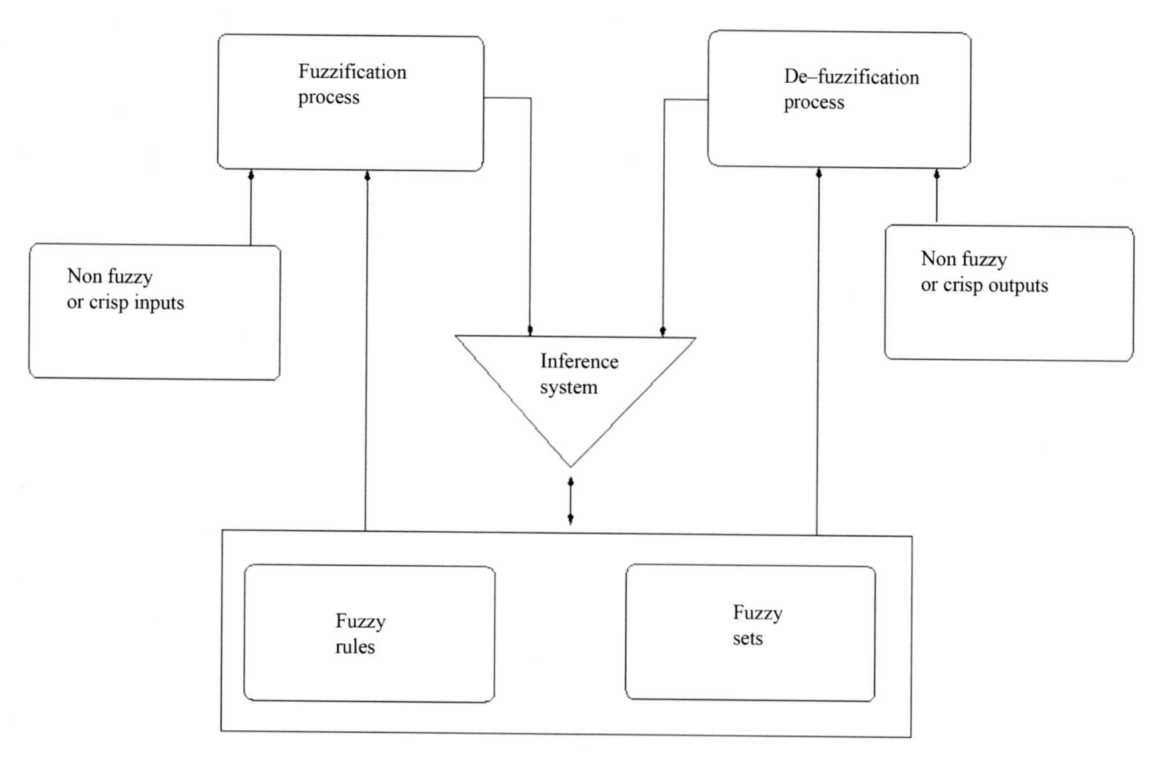

FIGURE 2.9 Fuzzy inference system.

limited movement of the mobile anchor. The path model is designed in a fuzzy-logic approach dependent upon a number of inputs which help in developing a superior optimized path when the MA's movement is restricted.

2.4.1.4 *Learning systems*

An ANN and neural fuzzy inference system (ANFIS) based on a range and localization methods are proposed in Gharghan, Nordin, Ismail, and Wireless (2016) for tracking a bicycle in a field. These two techniques are based on a range-based scheme of position that relies on measuring the RSSI from three Zig-Bee anchor nodes placed over the track cycling field. A novel nonline of sight identification mechanism with a feature selection approach and import vector machine (IVM)-based localization algorithm is presented in Yang, Zhao, and Chen (2018), which has high accuracy and less complexity. The localization algorithm uses the probability outputs of IVM and produces higher positioning accuracy than its counterpart method the support vector machine (SVM).

An improved SVM-based parameter optimization scheme is proposed in Fang and Junfang (2017), which uses the Immune Memory Clone Algorithm. This algorithm has better optimization ability than PSO- and GA-based optimization techniques. Compared to existing SVM-based localization techniques, it has better accuracy and effectively addressed coverage hole and border problems. A node localization algorithm based on the nature-inspired meta-heuristic algorithm, namely Butterfly Optimization Algorithm (Arora & Singh, 2017), determines more reliable and precise position of SNs as compared to the existing node localization schemes based on PSO and FA mechanisms.

Another metaheuristic method (Zhao, Meng, & Multidimensional, 2013), called Bat Algorithm (BA), has a working principle based on echolocation behavior of bats and is considerably superior to other existing protocols in terms of efficiency and accuracy. Since a bat is unable to explore all directions in search space, its success rate is much reduced. In order to resolve this problem, the existing BA is modified with the use of bacterial foraging strategies of a bacterial foraging optimization algorithm (Goyal & Patterh, 2016). The modified bat algorithm performance is consistently better, not only in improving localization success ratios but also in enhancing its robustness.

To reduce the localization error, a feed-forward ANN-based node localization scheme for WSNs in a 2D environment is proposed in Kumar, Jeon, and Lee (2014) and Madhumathi and Suresh (2018). For estimation of the location of the mobile node, three anchor nodes' RSSI values are fed as input for the above ANN. Since the SNs have built-in radio frequency modules it is advantageous to use RSSI values for location estimation as it avoids additional hardware requirement. A Trust-based Secure Sensor Localization

Scheme is presented in Angadi, Balavalad, Katageri, Patil, and Privacy-Preserving (2014) and Zhang, He and Zhang (2012) to overcome the security and privacy issue in localization that depends on trust evaluation of beacon nodes and considers the behaviors and identities of the beacon nodes closely following the principles of neural network.

Some of the CI techniques for localization are compared with respect to the error in location estimation, time taken for the computation, energy consumed, and the number of node locations identified, as shown in Table 2.4. From the survey it is clear that the modified and hybrid computational intelligent techniques are more efficient than the original. For example, the CLPSO technique is more efficient than PSO.

2.4.2 Computational intelligence techniques for clustering

Clustering is considered to be one of the key methods for extending the network lifetime in WSNs. This section reviews the computational intelligent techniques that are suitable for clustering wireless SNs in WSN.

2.4.2.1 *Evolutionary algorithms*

Several energy-efficient clustering algorithms for WSNs have been designed and developed with the application of CI. Especially for low-power, multifunctional WSNs, energy-efficient clustering algorithms are greatly needed. Since hierarchical clustering in WSN has the ability to reduce the energy consumption demands, it is necessary to investigate intelligent cluster creation and management techniques. A GA introduced in Hussain, Matin, and Islam (2007) is used to build energy-efficient clusters to disseminate the data in WSNs. Energy-efficient CH selection techniques based on GA are used as a CH selection method to take ensure optimization of the selection process, whereas heads are selected based on their residual energy and considering the mutual cooperation of inter- and intracluster distance. The Krill Herd (KH) algorithm presented in Karthick and Palanisamy (2019) falls under the bio-mimic algorithms category, whereas the source of the algorithm is the creation of different classes of nonrandom and underdispersed oceanic species. This can be found in WSN clustering as the KH algorithm is executed.

A spatial clustering algorithm based on a path-searching mechanism is proposed in Sun, Luo, Ding, Zhang, and Novel (2014) for spatial data clustering with the existence of obstacles and facilitators. In this work, obstacle distance is embedded into an affinity function for calculating the immune clonal optimization and to update the center of the cluster dependent on selected antibodies to overcome the limitations of the classical methods effectively. A hybrid clustering approach based on an artificial immune system is proposed in Abdi, Fathian, Safari, and Novel (2012). Integrating simulated annealing and immune-based algorithms and incorporating the benefits of both methods is used to build an effective method of clustering. The authors employed iterations of mutation, cloning, and enrichment operators, along with consideration of interactions with antibodies. A multiobjective, membrane-based EA is analyzed and proposed in Ju, Zhang, and Ding (2016) to solve the problem of network clustering. The average population is divided into various membrane structures and within membrane systems the evolutionary process is carried out in which the membrane vector reduces the population.

2.4.2.2 *Swarm intelligence algorithms*

A metaheuristic-based approach is one of the applications of CI. Artificial Bee Colony (ABC) is one of the

TABLE 2.4 Comparison of computational intelligence techniques for localization.

Computational intelligence	Localization error	Computation time	Power consumption	Number of localized nodes
EA (Tam et al., 2006)	Medium	Less	Less	Average
SIA (Kennedy & Eberhart, 1995)	Medium	Medium	High	Average
CLPSO (Ramesh et al., 2012)	Less	Less	Less	More
ANN (Gharghan et al., 2016; Kumar et al., 2014)	Less	Medium	Medium	Average
BOA (Arora & Singh, 2017)	Much Less	Much Less	Less	More
BA (Zhao et al., 2013)	Medium	High	High	Average
MBA (Goyal & Patterh, 2016)	Less	Less	Medium	More
FA (SrideviPonmalar et al., 2017)	Less	Less	Medium	Average

ANN, artificial neural network; *BA*, Bat algorithm; *BOA*, Butterfly Optimization Algorithm; *CLPSO*, Comprehensive Learning Particle Swarm Optimization; *EA*, evolutionary algorithm; *FA*, Firefly Algorithm; *SIA*, Swarm Intelligence Algorithm.

metaheuristic-based approaches which has increased interest over other population-based metaheuristics to overcome optimization problems in WSNs. ABC is given greater preference than other metaheuristics because of its adaptive nature and simplicity in implementation (Karaboga, Okdem, & Ozturk, 2012; Mann & Singh, 2017a, b). In ABC, three types of bees are considered, namely employed, onlookers, and scout bees. Initially, partial information such as the direction and availability of the food source is carried by the employed bees and then shared with onlooker bees. After getting the information, selection of the food source will be decided by the onlooker bees depending upon the probability function associated with the availability of the food source, whereas new sources of food are randomly explored by the scout bees around the hive.

If an onlooker or scout bee discovers any the new food source, they again start to play the employed bee role. When a food source is completely exploited, all employed bees will become scouts. This principle of the operation of bees is adopted in clustering to solve the optimization problems. Representation of the possible solution for the optimization problem is food source position and the amount of the availability of the food source will resemble the fitness (quality) of the related solution. The ABC proposed in Karaboga et al. (2012) has been widely used in clustering techniques by simulating intelligent foraging activity of honey bee swarms and to find the cluster-heads it employs a population of bees. An improved ABC is proposed in Mann and Singh (2017a) with an improved sampling technique by using compact probability density function (Students' *t*-distribution) which is going to require storage of only one control parameter in memory. The capabilities of the proposed work are utilized and an improved ABC-based clustering algorithm called bee-cluster is presented for selection of the optimal CH which is one of the optimization problems identified in WSNs.

Based on the derivation of an efficient particle-encoding scheme and fitness function for balancing the consumption of energy of the CHs, a PSO approach clustering algorithm is proposed in Blas and Tolic (2016) and Kuila and Jana (2014). Ant Colony Optimization (ACO) does not suit heterogeneous WSNs (Inkaya, Kayalıgil, & Ozdemirel, 2015). There is still a coverage issue in WSNs, even after ACO is applied. This problem can be solved with the use of PSO, but there is a problem in PSO due to its greedy approach to finding the optimal solution, and so the Cuckoo Search Optimization technique (Kumar & Singh, 2018) has been modified to overcome the problem for heterogeneous WSNs.

2.4.2.3 *Fuzzy logic*

For managing the discrepancies in the estimation of CH radius, several fuzzy logic-based energy-aware unequal clustering algorithms have been discussed (Bagci and Yazici, 2013; Baranidharan & Santhi, 2016; Logambigai & Kannan, 2016; Shamshirband et al., 2014; Singh, Purohit, & Varma, 2013) to address the hot spot problem. It also decreases the intracluster work of the CHs for the nodes that are close to the BS or remain with reduced battery power. The fuzzy approach-based Energy Aware Unequal Clustering Algorithm (EAUCF) has been proposed (Bagci and Yazici, 2013) mainly to overcome the hot spot problem. In this technique, adjustment of radius mechanism is used to overcome the problem, which reduces the intracluster work of the CHs closer to the BS.

Using some probabilistic model, EAUCF elects the tentative CHs. With consideration of the distance from these elected CHs to the BS and left-out energy, it determines the values of competition radius which is changing dynamically. When the residual energy of CH is decreasing, it is necessary to reduce the service area otherwise it leads to a rapid decrease in the battery power of the SN. Taking this situation into consideration, EAUCF minimizes the competition radius and computation of this radius is accomplished using some predefined if−then fuzzy mapping rules for handling the uncertainty.

Distributed unequal clustering (DUCF) based on fuzzy logic is introduced in Baranidharan and Santhi (2016) using one parameter, that is, node degree along with residual energy and distance from BS as inputs for selection of CH. The DUCF performs well in balancing the load among clusters, which improves the network lifetime as compared to the EAUCF. A density-based clustering algorithm presented in Shamshirband et al. (2014) aims to develop the imperialist competitive algorithm for the creation and handling of arbitrary cluster shapes. The fuzzy logic controller adapts imperialist competition by modifying the fuzzy rules to prevent potential mistakes in the worst imperialist selection technique.

In order to pick an appropriate CH for data aggregation and routing, load balancing was accomplished by selecting the best parameters for fuzzy-based clustering (Lata, Mehfuz, Urooj, & Alrowais, 2020; Rajaram & Kumaratharan, 2020). Energy-efficient clustering based on fuzzy logic for hierarchical routing protocols is proposed in Hamzah, Shurman, Al-Jarrah, and Taqieddin (2019). As it is known that many factors will influence selection of the CH, to get the best results, it is necessary to combine all influencing factors appropriately. A FIS is one effective mechanism which allows combining influencing factors (parameters) to achieve effectiveness in selection of the CH.

To accomplish maximum benefits from fuzzy logic for selection of the CH, five descriptors are used, such as Energy (remaining energy), BS_Distance (distance

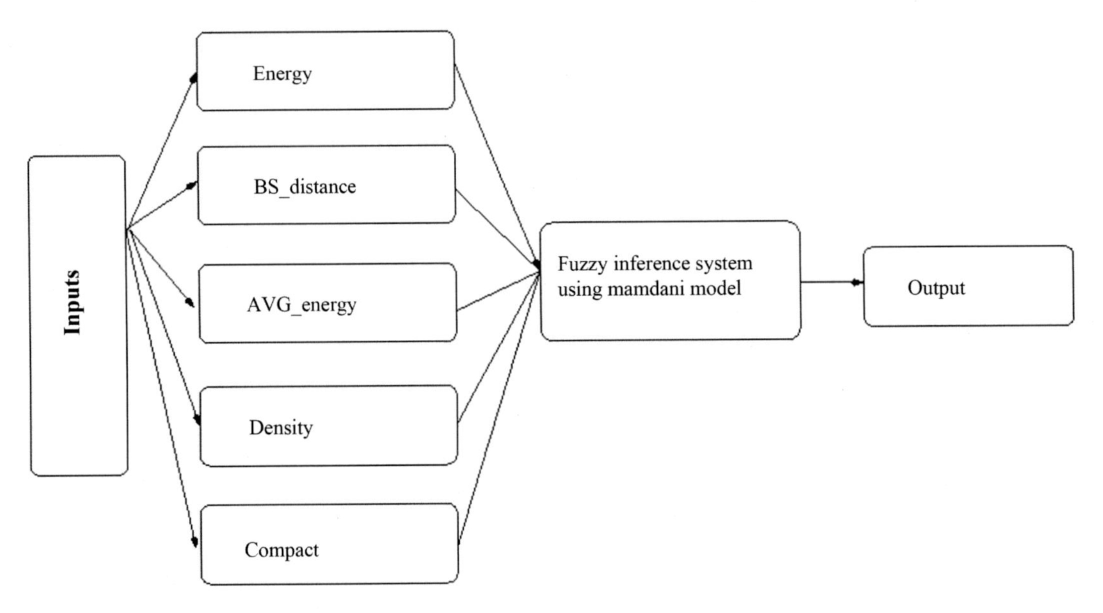

FIGURE 2.10 Fuzzy model.

from BS), AVG_Energy (average energy consumed), Density (density of surrounding nodes), and Compact (compaction of surrounding nodes), as shown in Fig. 2.10, to evaluate the probability of each node being the CH. Another strategy to decrease communication distances is multisink deployment proposed in Rajput and Kumaravelu (2020), which also helps in resolving the problems associated with congestion and hot spot. To estimate the optimal number of sinks, an iterative filtering model is suggested, while positions of sink are calculated based on the fuzzy logic inference system. The suggested scheme decreases the system's deployment cost and propagation delay, thus improving the lifespan of the network.

2.4.2.4 *Learning systems*

With the advancements in 5G and AI, there has been a rapid development of different emerging technologies introduced in wireless communication. Especially, AI plays an important role in exposing the potential of the IoT and some future technologies. Therefore for effective data transmission and allocation of resources (Kambalimath & Kakkasageri, 2020) between the physical, network, and application layer, it is necessary to embed intelligence with an IoT environment which results in automation and information ionization.

A power demand approach deep neural network-based clustering technique for secure Industrial IoT was discussed in Mukherjee, Goswami, and Yang (2020) for maintaining data information security. The work depends on the device model multiple-input single-output and is constructed using beam forming and artificial noise. Initially, the system's security capacity is determined by considering the mutual information of the primary and eavesdropping channel. Later, the optimal transmit power is initiated under the maximum transmit power constraint based on deep learning in order to improve the security capacity of the system. Lastly, based on the determined power, the demand network is clustered.

In the two-stage clustering techniques, the ANN has the capability of noise removal and reducing data complexity, which was seen as one of the outstanding intermediaries (Ching & Chen, 2015). In the medical field, for practitioners, information regarding tongue color is very important for the diagnosis of tongue-related problems and its correlation with internal organs. Sometimes it is not possible to judge the exact color due to unstable lighting and the naked eye's capability to catch specific color distribution when as tongue is a multicolored substance. Therefore to solve this uncertainty a SVM-based two-stage tongue multicolor classification using K-means clustering identifiers is proposed in Kamarudin et al. (2017). The proposed automated color diagnostic technique is helpful for early detection of conditions causing imbalances within the body.

It is very important to identify the unusual changes in mental workload (MWL) to prevent accidents and inattentiveness of human operators in safety-critical human–machine systems. For identification of the variations in MWL, several neuroimaging technologies are available. A novel electroencephalogram (EEG) based approach by integrating local linear embedding (LLE), supporting vector clustering, and supporting vector data definition techniques is proposed in Yin and Zhang (2014). In this work, with the combination of supervised and unsupervised learning, a MWL

TABLE 2.5 Comparison of computational intelligence techniques for clustering.

Parameters considered	Computational intelligence techniques						
	ABC (Mann & Singh, 2017a, b)	FL (Baranidharan & Santhi, 2016)	PSO (Kuila & Jana, 2014)	ACO (Inkaya et al., 2015)	CSO (Ju et al., 2016)	GA (Mann & Singh, 2017a, b)	KH (Karthick & Palanisamy, 2019)
Network lifetime	High	Less	Medium	Less	More	Less	Much less
Packet delivery ratio	High	Medium	Medium	Less	More	High	Very high
Latency	Less	—	More	—	—	Average	Less

ABC, Artificial Bee Colony; *ACO*, Ant Colony Optimization; *CSO*, Cuckoo Search Optimization; *FL*, Fuzzy logic; *GA*, genetic algorithm; *KH*, Krill Herd; *PSO*, Particle swarm optimization.

detection framework based on EEG-data is proposed and validated depending on the most typical EEG markers (MWL indicators) extracted using an LLE algorithm. A critical problem affecting the reliability of the monitoring system is sensor data drift. Therefore to track and calibrate the sensor data drift, a machine learning-based scheme is presented in Wu and Li (2020), which uses a Kalman filter for tracking and correcting the data drift of the target sensor.

Various CI techniques for clustering are presented and compared in Table 2.5. From the comparison table it is clear that no single intelligence technique can be adopted in clustering to fulfill all the parameters. Most of the CI techniques concentrate on energy efficiency, which helps in improving the network life time, packet delivery ratio, and latency. Therefore there is a need to combine the various techniques to develop hybrid CI techniques to improve the efficiency of the clustering algorithms in all perspectives.

2.5 Future research directions

WSNs are significantly different from other wireless networks due to their unique design, numerous limitations, and high-level implementation, which enable their contributions to many research challenges. The motivation behind localization and clustering in WSNs is to minimize the network communication overhead, overcome scalability problem, provide location services, and handle the dynamic changes in the network topology due to node mobility. Therefore the overall performance of the network can be improved by extending the network lifetime. This section addresses the emerging research problems which need to establish a new paradigm for SN localization and clustering in WSNs:

- Due to the complexity of most of the techniques, additional hardware may be required, which affects cost. Most methods require high processing that is high cost to determine the reference nodes and most of the algorithms are useful in 2D space only. Therefore the implementation of 3D space algorithms remains a good topic for future research.
- A set of beacon nodes with known locations is required for approaches based on anchors. It is necessary to have a lower number of anchors or beacons in a region for an optimal and robust scheme. Further research work is needed to determine the minimum number of locations where beacons are to be placed so that the entire network may be localized with more accuracy and overall performance can be improved.
- Most of the applications require a network with the ability to grow or expand and operate continuously without intervention of humans or central dependence. Therefore it is necessary to design and develop a system which should be scalable and autonomous.
- Privacy preservation is necessary in localization to protect user location privacy on wearable devices, which is becoming increasingly important with the emergence of new location-based services. Therefore it needs the development of low complexity for privacy-preserving device-centric location solutions to provide the location-based services.
- Implementation of robust methods for positioning mobile nodes is very difficult due to the network coverage area and node movement. However, node mobility is needed to improve connectivity, compromising with mobile node coverage is an issue for localization algorithms. Therefore it needs to handle the dynamic changes in the network topology due to node mobility.
- Clustering algorithms need to overcome the challenges such as optimal selection of the group of SNs as cluster, optimum CH selection, balanced energy scheme for assigning the role of the CH in a cluster on a rotation basis, effective energy

utilization at the CH, and maintaining intra- and intercluster.
- In WSNs, data collection is one of the most energy-intensive processes. In a hierarchical system sensed information is sent to a CH node, and then all the data collected by the CH are aggregated and compressed to make a single chunk of data. Then the compressed data are forwarded to the sink or BS for further analysis. To increase the protocol's efficiency, it is necessary to design and develop a protocol that can aggregate a nondiscrete object without changing the information.
- To maintain the confidentiality of the data, it is essential to modify the existing research work by including security features in data transmission, fault detection and tolerant capabilities, and mobility features.

Wireless sensors networks have become an interesting and attractive research area for the past few years due to their widespread applications in our daily lives, which is expected to be continued in future years. Localization has become one of the difficulties faced by researchers in expanding the use of wireless sensors due to indoor problems and the high cost of GPSs. Clustering also becomes a very critical process in a variety of WSN applications, and since it is not the main work of WSN, it must ensure lifetime extension and minimal energy consumption.

This chapter has focused on localization and clustering in WSNs, which provides the concept and importance of CI to overcome localization and clustering issues. We have addressed a general view of the present status of CI in localization and clustering for WSNs. We have also identified several research challenges that need further improvement in the efficiency and accuracy of the localization and clustering algorithms.

References

Abdi, K., Fathian, M., Safari, E., & Novel, A. (2012). Algorithm based on hybridization of artificial immune system and simulated annealing for clustering problem. *The International Journal of Advanced Manufacturing Technology*, *60*(8), 723–732.

Ahmed, M. R., Huang, X., Sharma, D., & Cui, H. (2012). Wireless sensor network: Characteristics and architectures. *International Journal of Information and Communication Engineering*, *6*(12), 1398–1401.

Akyildiz, I. F., Melodia, T., & Chowdury, K. R. (2007). Wireless multimedia sensor networks: A survey. *IEEE Wireless Communications*, *14*(6), 32–39.

Akyildiz, I. F., Su, W., Sankarasubramaniam, Y., & Cayirci, E. (2002). Wireless sensor networks: A survey. *Computer Networks*, *38*(4), 393–422.

Alomari, A., Phillips, W., Aslam, N., & Comeau, F. (2017). Dynamic fuzzy-logic based path planning for mobility-assisted localization in wireless sensor networks. *Sensors*, *17*(8), 1–26.

Alomari, A., Phillips, W., Aslam, N., & Comeau, F. (2018). Swarm intelligence optimization techniques for obstacle-avoidance mobility-assisted localization in wireless sensor networks. *IEEE Access*, *6*, 22368–22385.

Alrajeh, N. A., Bashir, M., & Shams, B. (2013). Localization techniques in wireless sensor networks. *International Journal of Distributed Sensor Networks*, *2013*, 1–9.

Amri, S., Khelifi, F., Bradai, A., Rachedi, A., Kaddachi, M. L., Atri, M., & New, A. (2019). Fuzzy logic based node localization mechanism for wireless sensor networks. *Future Generation Computer Systems*, *93*, 799–813.

Angadi, B. M., Balavalad, K. B., Katageri, A. C., Patil, P. S., & Privacy-Preserving, A. (2014). Location monitoring system for WSNs with blocking misbehaving users in anonymity networks. *Journal of Advances in Computer Networks*, 2(4), 248–253.

Angadi, B.M., & Kakkasageri, M.S. (2020). Anchor based effective node localization algorithm for wireless sensor networks. International Conference on Recent Trends in Machine Learning, IOT, Smart Cities & Applications, 1245, pp. 473–479.

Angadi, B.M., Kakkasageri, M.S., & Kori, G.S. (2016). Topology control scheme for fault tolerance in wireless sensor network. Proceedings of the IEEE International conference on Signal Processing, Communication, Power and Embedded System (SCOPES-2016), 3, pp. 245–250.

Arora, S., & Singh, S. (2017). Node localization in wireless sensor networks using butterfly optimization algorithm. *Arabian Journal for Science and Engineering*, *42*(8), 3325–3335.

Bagci, H. H., & Yazici, A. (2013). An energy aware fuzzy approach to unequal clustering in wireless sensor networks. *Applied Soft Computing*, *13*, 1741–1749.

Baranidharan, B. B., & Santhi, B. (2016). DUCF: Distributed load balancing unequal clustering in wireless sensor networks using fuzzy approach. *Applied Soft Computing*, *40*, 495–506.

Blas, N. N. G., & Tolic, O. L. (2016). Clustering using particle swarm optimization. *International Journal Information Theories and Applications*, *23*(1), 24–33.

Cheng, L., Hang, J., Wang, Y., Bi, Y., & Fuzzy, A. (2019). C-means and hierarchical voting based RSSI quantify localization method for wireless sensor network. *IEEE Access*, *7*, 47411–47422.

Ching, C. C. C., & Chen, S. H. (2015). A comparative analysis on artificial neural network-based two-stage clustering. *Cogent Engineering*, *2*(1).

Daneshvar, S. M. M. H., Alikhah Ahari Mohajer, P., & Mazinani, S. M. (2019). Energy-efficient routing in WSN: A centralized cluster-based approach via Grey Wolf optimizer. *IEEE Access*, *7*, 170019–170031.

Du, Z., Pan, J., Chu, S., Luo, H., & Hu, P. (2020). Quasi-affine transformation evolutionary algorithm with communication schemes for application of RSSI in wireless sensor networks. *IEEE Access*, *8*, 8583–8594.

Fang, Z., & Junfang, W. (2017). Localization algorithm in wireless sensor networks based on improved support vector machine. *Journal of Nanoelectronics and Optoelectronics*, *12*(5), 452–459.

Gharghan, S. K., Nordin, R., Ismail, M., & Wireless, A. (2016). Sensor network with soft computing localization techniques for track cycling applications. *Sensors*, *16*(8), 1–29.

Goyal, S., & Patterh, M. S. (2016). Modified bat algorithm for localization of wireless sensor network. *Wireless Personal Communication*, *86*(2), 657–670.

Hamzah, A. A., Shurman, M., Al-Jarrah, O., & Taqieddin, E. (2019). Energy-efficient fuzzy-logic-based clustering technique for hierarchical routing protocols in wireless sensor networks. *Sensors*, *19*(3), 561.

Hussain, S., Matin, A. W., & Islam, O. (2007). Genetic algorithm for hierarchical wireless sensor networks. *Journal of Networks*, *2*(5), 87–97.

Inkaya, T. T., Kayalıgil, S., & Ozdemirel, N. E. (2015). Ant colony optimization based clustering methodology. *Applied Soft Computing*, *28*, 301–311.

Jan, B., Farman, H., Khan, M., Javed, S. A., & Montrucchio, B. (2017). Energy efficient hierarchical clustering approaches in wireless sensor networks: A survey. *Wireless Communications and Mobile Computing, 2017*, 1–14.

Ju, Y., Zhang, S., Ding, N., et al. (2016). Complex network clustering by a multi-objective evolutionary algorithm based on decomposition and membrane structure. *Scientific Reports, 6*(1), 1–13.

Kakkasageri, M. S., & Manvi, S. S. (2014). Regression based critical information aggregation and dissemination in VANETs: A cognitive agent approach. *Journal of Vehicular Communications, Elsevier, 1*(4), 168–180.

Kamarudin, N. N. D., Ooi, C. Y., Kawanabe, T., Odaguchi, H., Kobayashi, F., & Fast, A. (2017). SVM-based tongue's colour classification aided by k-means clustering identifiers and colour attributes as computer-assisted tool for tongue diagnosis. *Journal of Healthcare Engineering, 2017*, 1–13.

Kambalimath, M. M. G., & Kakkasageri, M. S. (2020). Cost optimization based resource allocation for vehicular cloud networks. *International Journal of Computer Network and Information Security, 2*, 22–31.

Karaboga, D. D., Okdem, S., & Ozturk, C. (2012). Cluster based wireless sensor network routing using artificial bee colony algorithm. *Wireless Networks, 18*, 847–860.

Karthick, P. T., & Palanisamy, C. (2019). Optimized cluster head selection using Krill Herd algorithm for wireless sensor network. *Automatika, 60*(3), 340–348, Taylor and Francis.

Kennedy, J., & Eberhart, R. (1995). Particle swarm optimization. Proceedings of the IEEE International Conference on Neural Networks, pp. 1942–1948.

Kuila, P. P., & Jana, P. K. (2014). Energy efficient clustering and routing algorithms for wireless sensor networks: Particle swarm optimization approach. *Engineering Applications of Artificial Intelligence, 33*, 127–140.

Kulkarni, R. V., Forster, A., & Venayagamoorthy, G. K. (2011). Computational intelligence in wireless sensor networks: A survey. *IEEE Communications Surveys and Tutorials, 13*(1), 68–96.

Kumar, H. H., & Singh, P. K. (2018). Comparison and analysis on artificial intelligence based data aggregation techniques in wireless sensor networks. *Procedia Computer Science, 132*, 498–506.

Kumar, S., Jeon, S. M., & Lee, S. R. (2014). Localization estimation using artificial intelligence technique in wireless sensor networks. *The Journal of Korea Information and Communications Society, 39*(9), 820–827.

Lata, S. S., Mehfuz, S., Urooj, S., & Alrowais, F. (2020). Fuzzy clustering algorithm for enhancing reliability and network lifetime of wireless sensor networks. *IEEE Access, 8*, 66013–66024.

Li, D., & Wen, X. (2015). An improved PSO algorithm for distributed localization in wireless sensor networks. *International Journal of Distributed Sensor Networks, 2015*, 1–8.

Li, Z., Li, R., Wei, Y., & Pei, T. (2010). Survey of localization techniques in wireless sensor networks. *Information Technology Journal, 9* (8), 1754–1757.

Logambigai, R. R., & Kannan, A. (2016). Fuzzy logic based unequal clustering for wireless sensor networks. *Wireless Networks, 22*(3), 945–957.

Madhumathi, K., & Suresh, T. (2018). A study on localization in wireless sensor network using neural network. *Asian Journal of Computer Science and Technology, 7*(1), 50–53.

Mann, P. S., & Singh, S. (2017a). Improved metaheuristic based energy-efficient clustering protocol for wireless sensor networks. *Engineering Applications of Artificial Intelligence, 57*, 142–152.

Mann, P. S., & Singh, S. (2017b). Energy efficient clustering protocol based on improved metaheuristic in wireless sensor networks. *Journal of Network and Computer Applications, 83*, 40–52.

Maruthi, S. P., & Panigrahi, T. (2020). Robust mixed source localization in WSN using swarm intelligence algorithms. *Digital Signal Processing, 98*, 1–12.

Marwan, A., Mourad, O., & Mousa, H. (2020). A survey of fuzzy logic in wireless localization. *EURASIP Journal on Wireless Communications and Networking, 2020*(1), 1–45.

Mekelleche, F., & Haffaf, H. (2017). Classification and comparison of range-based localization techniques in wireless sensor networks. *Journal of Communications, 12*(4), 221–227.

Mukherjee, A. A., Goswami, P., Yang, L., et al. (2020). Deep neural network-based clustering technique for secure IIoT. *Neural Computing and Applications*, 1–9.

Nazir, U., Arshad, M.A., Shahid, N., & Raza, S.H. (2012). Classification of localization algorithms for wireless sensor network: A survey. 2012 International Conference on Open Source Systems and Technologies, pp. 1–5.

Niewiadomska-Szynkiewicz, E. (2012). Localization in wireless sensor networks: Classification and evaluation of techniques. *International Journal of Applied Mathematics and Computer Science, 22*(2), 281–297.

Parulpreet, S., Arun, K., Anil, K., & Mamta, K. (2019). Computational intelligence techniques for localization in static and dynamic wireless sensor networks—A review. *Computational Intelligence in Sensor Networks, 776*, 25–54.

Paul, A. K., & Sato, T. (2017). Localization in wireless sensor networks: A survey on algorithms, measurement techniques, applications and challenges. *Journal of Sensor and Actuator Networks, 6* (24), 1–23.

Pescaru, D., & Curiac, D. (2014). Anchor node localization for wireless sensor networks using video and compass information fusion. *Sensors, 14*(3), 4211–4224.

Prasha, D., & Kumar, D. (2020). Performance evaluation of the optimized error correction based hop localization approach in a wireless sensor network. *Wireless Personal Communications, 111*, 2517–2543.

Primeau, N., Falcon, R., Abielmona, R., & Petriu, E. M. (2018). A review of computational intelligence techniques in wireless sensor and actuator networks. *IEEE Communications Surveys & Tutorials, 20*(4), 2822–2854.

Rajaram, V. V., & Kumaratharan, N. (2020). Multi-hop optimized routing algorithm and load balanced fuzzy clustering in wireless sensor networks. *Journal of Ambient Intelligence and Humanized Computing*, 1–9.

Rajput, A. A., & Kumaravelu, V. B. (2020). Fuzzy-based clustering scheme with sink selection algorithm for monitoring applications of wireless sensor networks. *Journal of Ambient Intelligence and Humanized Computing, 45*, 6601–6623.

Ramesh, M.V., Divya, P.L., Rekha, P., Kulkarni, R.V., & Swarm, A. (2012). Intelligence based distributed localization technique for wireless sensor network. Proceedings of the International Conference on Advances in Computing, Communications and Informatics, pp. 367–373.

Ramesh, M.V., Divya, P.L., Rekha, P., & Kulkarni, R.V. (2012). Performance enhancement in distributed sensor localization using swarm intelligence. 2012 International Conference on Advances in Mobile Network, Communication and Its Applications, pp. 103–106.

Saeed, N., Nam, H., Haq, M. I. U., & Bhatti, D. M. S. (2018). A survey on multidimensional scaling. *ACM Computing Surveys, 51*(3), 1–25.

Saeed, N., Nam, H., Al-Naffouri, T. Y., & Alouini, M. (2019). A state-of-the-art survey on multidimensional scaling-based localization techniques. *IEEE Communications Surveys and Tutorials, 21*(4), 3565–3583.

Sangeetha, G., Vijayalakshmi, M., Ganapathy, S., & Kannan, A. (2020). An improved congestion-aware routing mechanism in sensor networks using fuzzy rule sets. *Peer-to-Peer Networking and Applications, 13*, 890–904.

Sarobin, M. V. R., & Ganesan, R. (2015). Swarm intelligence in wireless sensor networks: A survey. *International Journal of Pure and Applied Mathematics*, *101*(5), 773–807.

Serpen, G., Li, J., & Liu, L. (2013). Adaptive and intelligent wireless sensor. *Network, Procedia Computer Science*, *20*, 406–413.

Shamshirband, S. S., Amini, A., Anuar, N. B., Kiah, L. M., The, Y. W., & Furnell, S. (2014). D-FICCA: A density-based fuzzy imperialist competitive clustering algorithm for intrusion detection in wireless sensor networks. *Measurement*, *55*, 212–226.

Sharma, G., & Kumar, A. (2018). Improved range-free localization for three-dimensional wireless sensor networks using genetic algorithm. *Computers & Electrical Engineering*, *72*, 808–827.

Shi, Y., & Eberhart, R.C. (1998). Parameter selection in particle swarm optimization. 7th International Conference on Evolutionary Programming, pp. 591–600.

Singh, A. A. K., Purohit, N., & Varma, S. (2013). Fuzzy logic based clustering in wireless sensor networks: A survey. *International Journal of Electronics*, *100*(1), 126–141.

Singh, P., Khosla, A., & Kumar, A. (2018). Computational intelligence based localization of moving target nodes using single anchor node in wireless sensor networks. *Telecommunication Systems*, *69*, 397–411.

Slowik, A., & Kwasnicka, H. (2020). Evolutionary algorithms and their applications to engineering problems. *Neural Computing and Applications*, *32*, 12363–12379.

SrideviPonmalar, P., Senthil Kumar, V. J., & Harikrishnan, R. (2017). Hybrid firefly variants algorithm for localization optimization in WSN. *International Journal of Computational Intelligence Systems*, *10* (1), 1263–1271.

Sun, L., Luo, Y., Ding, X., Zhang, J., & Novel, A. (2014). Artificial immune algorithm for spatial clustering with obstacle constraint and its applications. *Computational Intelligence and Neuroscience*, *2014*, 1–11.

Sun, W., Tang, M., Zhang, L., Huo, Z., & Shu, L. (2020). A survey of using swarm intelligence algorithms in IoT. *Sensors*, *20*(5), 1420–1447.

Tam, V., Cheng, K. Y., & Lui, K. S. (2006). Using micro-genetic algorithms to improve localization in wireless sensor networks. *Journal of Communications*, *1*(4), 1–10.

Vikhar, P.A. (2016). Evolutionary algorithms: A critical review and its future prospects. International Conference on Global Trends in Signal Processing, Information Computing and Communication, pp. 261–265.

Wang, J., Zhu, C., Zhou, Y., Zhu, X., Wang, Y., & Zhang, W. (2018). From partition-based clustering to density-based clustering: Fast find clusters with diverse shapes and densities in spatial databases. *IEEE Access*, *6*, 1718–1729.

Wu, J., & Li, G. (2020). Drift calibration using constrained extreme learning machine and Kalman filter in clustered wireless sensor networks. *IEEE Access*, *8*, 13078–13085.

Xu, R., & Wunsch, D. (2020). Survey of clustering algorithms. *IEEE Transactions on Neural Networks*, *16*(3), 645–678.

Yang, X., Zhao, F., & Chen, T. (2018). NLOS identification for UWB localization based on import vector machine. *International Journal of Electronics and Communications*, *87*, 128–133.

Yang, Y., Liu, Z., Zhang, J., & Yang, J. (2012). Dynamic density-based clustering algorithm over uncertain data streams. 2012 9th International Conference on Fuzzy Systems and Knowledge Discovery, pp. 2664–2670.

Yassin, A., et al. (2017). Recent advances in indoor localization: A survey on theoretical approaches and applications. *IEEE Communications Surveys and Tutorials*, *19*(2), 1327–1346.

Yin, Z., & Zhang, J. (2014). Identification of temporal variations in mental workload using locally-linear-embedding-based EEG feature reduction and support-vector-machine-based clustering and classification techniques. *Computer Methods and Programs in Biomedicine*, *115*(3), 119–134.

Yun, D., Jung, I. I., Jung, H., Kang, H., Yang, W., & Park, I. Y. (2019). Improvement in computation time of the finite multipole method by using K-means clustering. *IEEE Antennas and Wireless Propagation Letters*, *18*(9), 1814–1817.

Zhang, T., He, J., & Zhang, Y. (2012). Secure sensor localization in wireless sensor networks based on neural network. *International Journal of Computational Intelligence Systems*, *5*(5), 914–923.

Zhao, Q. S., Meng, G. Y., & Multidimensional, A. (2013). Scaling localization algorithm based on bacterial foraging algorithm. *International Journal Wireless and Mobile Computing*, *6*(1), 58–65.

C H A P T E R

3

Computational intelligent techniques for resource management schemes in wireless sensor networks

Gururaj S. Kori[1], *Mahabaleshwar S. Kakkasageri*[2] *and Sunil Kumar S. Manvi*[3]

[1]Department of Electronics and Communication Engineering, Biluru Gurubasava Mahaswamiji Institute of Technology, Mudhol, India [2]Department of Electronics and Communication Engineering, Basaveshwar Engineering College, Bagalkot, India [3]School of Computing and Information Technology, REVA University, Bangalore, India

3.1 Introduction

The wireless sensor network (WSN) is a highly distributed network of tiny sensors that are self-conscious and are distributed in diverse geographical regions for various applications. Sensors or motes communicate the sensed information (Akyildiz, Su, Sankarasubramaniam, & Cayirci, 2002; Akyildiz, Melodia, & Chowdhury, 2007a, 2007b). Wireless sensor motes are constrained with resources in terms of power, computational speed, memory, bandwidth, communication range, etc. For WSNs, when shared for multiple tasks, sensor resources management becomes a challenging task. Effective utilization of available resources is a critical issue to prolong the life span of WSNs (Khan & Belqasmi et al., 2015; Yick, Mukherjee, & Ghosal, 2008; Akyildiz, Su, Sankarasubramaniam, & Cayirci, 2013; Rawat, Singh, Chaouchi, & Bonnin, 2014). Resource management (RM) is a process of computing methods that are used to acquire and store the resources, and provide the best service from the perspective of Quality of Service (QoS) parameters. RM includes resource identification/discovery, resource provisioning (pooling), resource sharing, resource scheduling, resource allocation, resource utilization, and resource monitoring in WSNs (Lin, Kwok, & Wang, 2009; Regini, Lim, & Rosing, 2011).

The process of discovering a suitable network resource is called resource identification. Resource scheduling defines the order in which the access requests must be executed for the specific applications. Resource allocation releases specific resources to carry out a specific job. Resource provisioning involves choosing, deploying, and controlling the run-time of software/hardware resources of the network to ensure assured efficiency. Resource sharing refers to the joint or alternating use of inherently finite resources available in the network. Resource utilization refers to the method of making the resources available to sensor nodes to achieve a specific task. Resource monitoring gives information about network resources in real time (Shakshuki & Isiuwe, 2018; Rakshe, Prasad, Akshay, & Channaveer, 2016; Modieginyane, Letswamotse, Malekian, & Mahfouz, 2018).

Computational intelligent techniques are efficient mechanisms to address the issues and challenges of WSNs. These techniques include artificial intelligence (AI), bioinspired computational techniques, blockchain mechanisms, machine learning (ML), game theory (GT), artificial neural networks (ANNs), fuzzy logic (FL), deep learning (DL), genetic algorithms (GA), intelligent multiagent systems, cognitive agents, norm aware multiagent systems, etc. The integration of computational intelligence (CI) and RM enhances the WSN lifetime under a resource-constrained situation. Intelligent algorithms for RM include uninterrupted services, less use of resources, reliability, consistency, and accountability (Kakkasageri & Manvi, 2014; Kumar & Sharma, 2012; Moura & Hutchison, 2019; Kulkarni, Förster, & Venayagamoorthy, 2011; Primeau, Falcon, Abielmona, & Petriu, 2018; Praveen Kumar, Amgoth, & Annavarapu, 2019; Cao, Cai,

Recent Trends in Computational Intelligence Enabled Research.
DOI: https://doi.org/10.1016/B978-0-12-822844-9.00023-2

& Yue, 2019; Fernandez, Herrera, Cordon, Jesus, & Marcelloni, 2019; Jabbar, Iram, Minhas, Shafi, & Khalid, 2013; Kaur, Goyal, & Luthra, 2014).

The chapter is organized as follows. Section 3.2 explains the concept of WSN architecture, application, characteristics, and issues. RM mechanisms in WSNs and CI schemes and applications of these schemes in solving RM are explained in Section 3.3. Section 3.4 explains the future research directions.

3.2 Wireless sensor networks

WSNs integrate basic wireless networking with limited processing facilities. Typical sensing activities in WSN may be temperature, illumination, vibration, echo, radiation, etc. The sensor node comprises of a radio antenna in-front end, a microcontroller with a memory chip, power supply, sensors, and actuators. While all WSNs are presumed to have similar functionality in several environments, some applications exhibit a heterogeneous environment. Modern sensor motes are gaining popularity over traditional nodes due to their fast computation and accurate results (Karray, Jmal, Ortiz, Abid, Obeid, 2018; Mancilla, Mellado, & Siller, 2016).

As shown in Fig. 3.1, the cluster consists of a cluster member (CM) and a cluster head (CH). The CH gathers the information from CMs and then transfers it to the base station (BS). The CH transmits information in two ways; inter- and intracommunication in the clusters. The communication between nodes and the sink node may be via a single hop or multihops. The position of the BS is fixed in such a way that it is connected to the entire network so that less power is consumed in data transmission from CH to BS or CM to BS (Ketshabetswe, Zungeru, Mangwala, Chuma, & Sigweni, 2019; Sulaiman, Saleh, Saida, Kacem, & Abid, 2020). The information aggregated by the nodes is transmitted via the multihop approach to the BS and the external world is linked through the Internet.

3.2.1 Characteristics

Sensor motes are tiny in size but powerful in terms of computation. They have plug-and-play capability and the results acquired from WSNs are accurate (Ari, Gueroui, Labraoui, & Yenke, 2015; Gupta & Sinha, 2014; Fortino, Bal, Li, & Shen, 2015). Some of the important WSN characteristics are presented in Fig. 3.2.

1. Independence: WSN is capable of working without any central control point.
2. Self-organizing: Allowing devices to cooperate in the formation of topologies for monitoring and

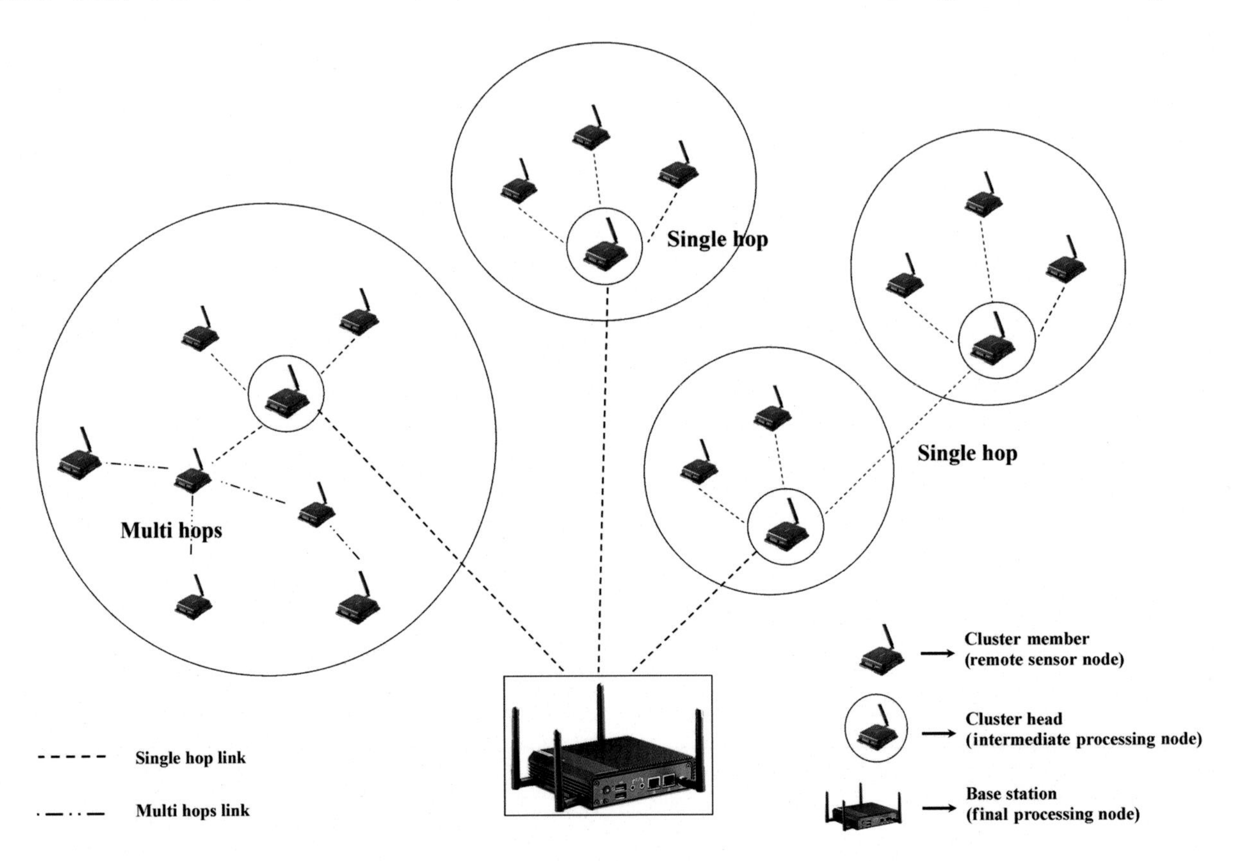

FIGURE 3.1 Wireless sensor network architecture.

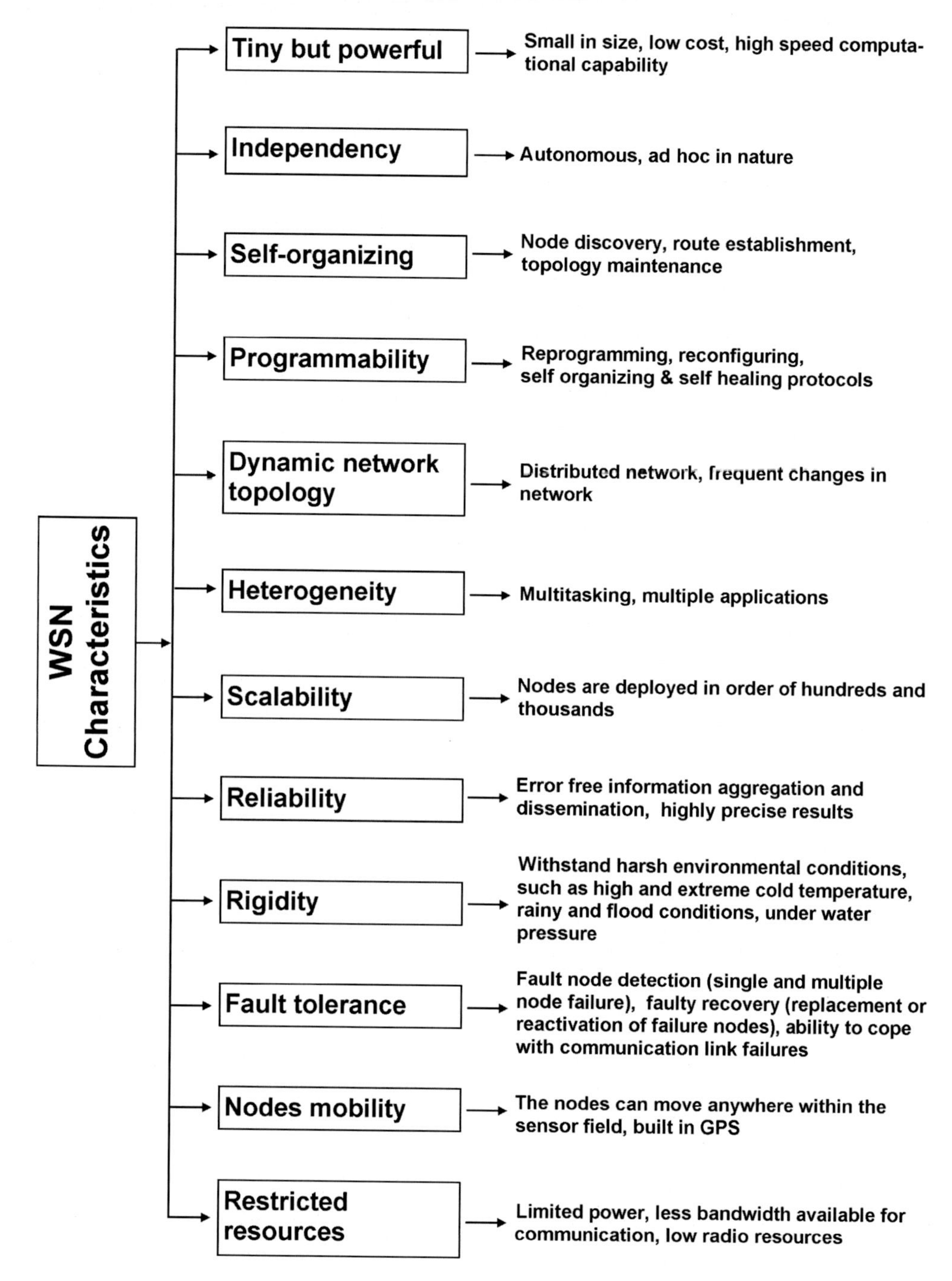

FIGURE 3.2 Wireless sensor network characteristics.

adaptation to environmental issues. Resilience to deal with harsh environmental conditions.
3. Programmability: To respond to any unpredictable changes in the WSN, the sensor node should be capable of reprogramming or reconfiguring instantaneously.
4. Dynamic network topology: Connection of sensor motes follows a certain basic topology. The motes must be smart enough to work in dynamic topology.
5. Heterogeneity of nodes: Sensor motes distributed in networks are of different types and need to operate cooperatively. Nodes with various technologies with unique multitasking abilities, different processing, computational capability, and sensing multiple parameters need to work for a specific application.
6. Scalability: The capacity of the network to expand in terms of the number of sensor nodes connected should not create unnecessary overheads in terms of data.

7. Reliability: The data must be transmitted without error. WSN promises reliability by ensuring that information is transmitted to the destination using an unreliable wireless medium which is achieved by acknowledgments. Reliable protocols are used to recover data from those errors caused during transmission.
8. Rigidity: Capacity to survive severe weather surroundings such as hot and intense cold temperatures, thick vegetation, rainforest, flood situations, under the ocean, water pressure, and other changing environmental conditions.
9. Fault tolerance: Fault tolerance is the ability to maintain WSN functionality without any failure in the network.
10. Mobility of nodes: To improve communication efficiency and network performance, nodes may move anywhere in the sensor network area depending upon the type of application.
11. Restricted resources: Various resource limitations are the prominent characteristics of a WSN which poses a significant challenge for researchers. Many limitations such as poor processing capacity, insufficient memory, restricted energy supplies, and inadequate radio resources in networks (bandwidth and communication range) may create difficulties in utilizing security and safety in WSNs.

3.2.2 Applications

Applications of WSN include military observation, personal access, traffic control, manufacturing, industrial automation, process control, inventory management, decentralized robotics, weather/environmental monitoring, and the monitoring of buildings and structures (Ali, Ming, Chakraborty, & Iram, 2017; Dener, 2017; Ramson & Moni, 2017; Rashid & Rehmani, 2016). A shortlist of WSN applications is given in Fig. 3.3.

1. Military applications: As WSNs can be distributed rapidly and are self-organized, they are very useful for detecting and tracking friendly or aggressive movements in military operations. WSNs are capable of battlefield surveillance, missiles management, survey of enemy forces, border monitoring, and battle damage assessment.
2. Medical and health applications: In health/medical applications some sensor devices are embedded or implanted in the body and other sensor devices are wearable on the body surface. Sensor motes perform functions such as tracking and monitoring of patients' activities, recording of patients' physiological data, and past patient medical reports and drug administrations.
3. Environmental applications: Sensor nodes are used to track the movement of animals and birds using mobile nodes (drones). Monitoring of the Earth and its atmosphere, and recording the physiological changes can be done through these sensors. They can also be used for the detection of fires, floods, earthquakes, forest fire detection, chemical/biological outbreaks, disaster relief operations, etc.
4. Retailer and consumer applications: WSNs create new possibilities for both retailer and consumer applications. There are several retailer and consumer applications for WSN technology, such as home appliances, security and monitoring systems,

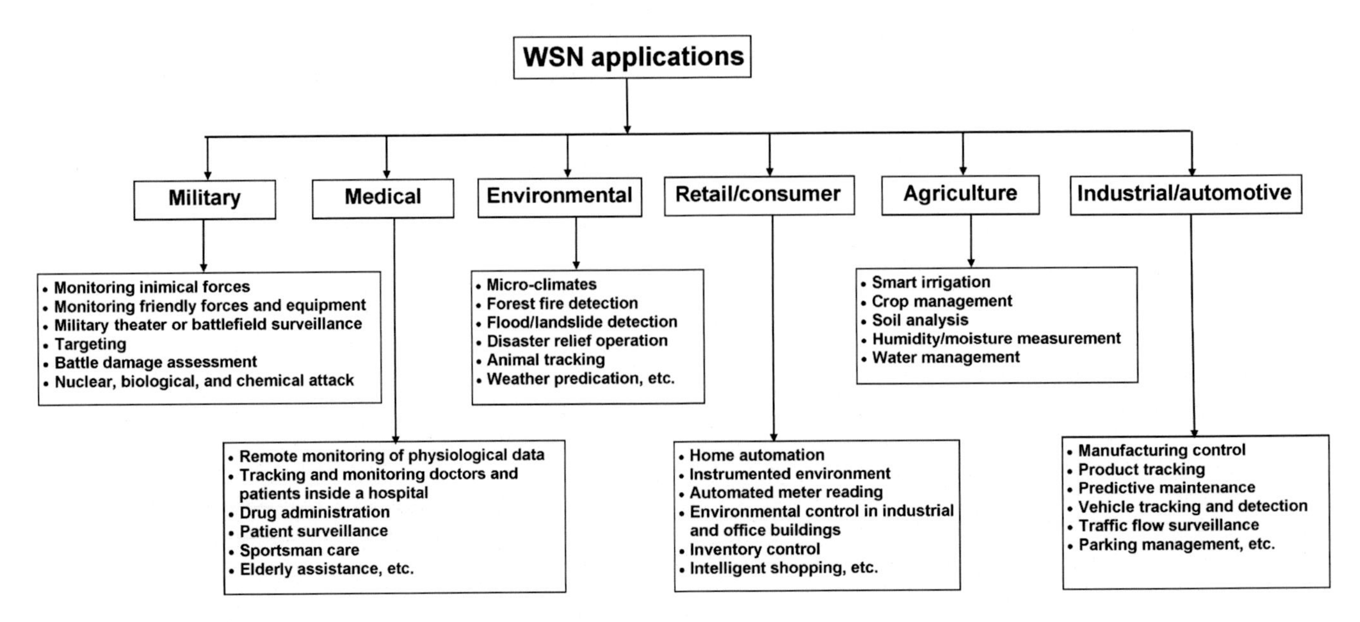

FIGURE 3.3 Wireless sensor network applications.

consumer applications, monitoring, inventory management, smart offices, interactive museums, and interactive robots.

5. Agriculture applications: WSN technologies in smart farming will empower farmers to reduce waste and upgrade efficiency, ranging from the amount of fertilizer used to the number of journeys farm vehicles are required to make. WSN is also used for temperature control, monitoring moisture levels in commercial greenhouses and soil analysis, sustainable agriculture, agricultural drones, insect monitoring, intelligent/smart greenhouses, etc.
6. Industrial and automotive applications: Wireless sensor nodes navigate hazardous and forbidden areas. Common WSN applications encompass machine diagnosis, transport, factory instrumentation, actuator control, semiconductor processing chambers, and wind tunnels. The goal of intelligent transport systems is to reduce traffic congestion, free parking, prevent accidents, and detect drunk drivers via sensor networks. Modern smart sensors are used in position tracking using GPS sensors, speed-monitoring accelerometers, heading gyrators, vehicle identification using RFID tags, traveler and vehicle tallying using infrared sensors, automatic toll payments, traffic recording cameras, etc.

3.2.3 Issues/challenges

Many technical challenges need to be addressed for advanced services in WSNs. These problems encompass architecture levels, hardware/software, communication range, and application design. Various research issues in WSN are listed in Fig. 3.4 (Chawla, 2014; Kobo, Mahfouz, & Hancke, 2017; Shahdad, Sabahath, & Parveez, 2016; Sharma, Bansal, & Bansal, 2013).

1. Architecture: The design of WSN architecture should consider a series of rules for integrating various functional components with protocols to make a sensor node robust, flexible, and scalable.
2. Hardware and software issues: Large amounts of microcontrollers, microprocessors, memories, and field programmable gate arrays (FPGA) are required to provide flexibility for CPU implementation. Multiple-input and multiple-output antennas should be used to increase the receiving and transmitting range. WSN software should be hardware-independent and protocols should be structured to be less complicated and helpful in reducing power consumption and computational latency.
3. Power consumption: Sensors require power for sensing any change in network, aggregation, dissemination of data, processing the sensed data, storing the results, and during the active state. Even during the sleep state, nodes constantly listen to the medium for faithful service. Hence a large amount of energy is consumed both during active and idle states.
4. Self-organization: The WSN should operate without human intervention once it is deployed in the environment. Nodes should be able to configure, maintain, and repair themselves, which is called as self-management.
5. Node deployment: Deployment of nodes depends on the geographical area of the application. Node deployment is a laborious and cumbersome activity, and if locations are out of human reach sensors are dropped by drones/helicopters.
6. Routing: Transmitting of information from source to sink is an essential function of any distributed, large ad hoc networks. Routing should be done with limited overheads and with minimum bandwidth. During routing, challenges such as privacy and security, multicast, energy efficiency, and QoS should be considered.
7. Mobility and flow control: If the sensor motes are mobile, the WSN becomes dynamic and the network becomes unpredictable, therefore the network should adapt accordingly. Mobile sensor motes in the network should dynamically reestablish routes among themselves according to the network changes.
8. QoS: To provide good QoS is difficult in wireless networks due to dynamic network topology, and routing is inherently imprecise in such networks. Therefore QoS schemes should be well designed for considering the available resources and should support network scalability.

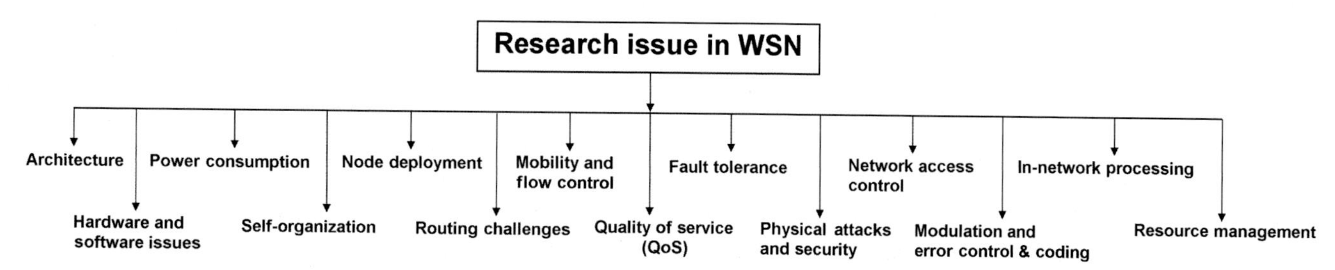

FIGURE 3.4 Wireless sensor network research issues.

9. Fault tolerance: Fault tolerance in WSNs is the ability that makes a system continue its smooth functioning if node failure occurs. In the case of network failure, sensor motes should be capable of adapting dynamically according to the changes in the network.
10. Physical attacks and security: The deployment of sensor nodes in the open environment leads to physical attacks and security threats. Physical attackers may alter node hardware/software or may replace the mote with a malicious one. Various security and privacy challenges in WSNs include changing the routing information, hacking the data, active and passive attacks, and jamming.
11. Network access control: Network access control uses medium access control algorithms on how sensors access a shared radio channel to communicate with other nodes and BSs.
12. Modulation and error control coding: A simple and low-power narrowband and wideband communications modulation scheme is used in the WSN model to conserve energy. Error control coding is a classic approach used to establish the accuracy of the data, communication link, and reduce the transmission energy needed. Use of automatic repeat request protocols in WSNs is used for retransmission of data in rare cases to reduce costs and overheads.
13. In-network processing: WSN protocols should reduce communication costs, redundant data, and congestion in WSNs by preventing duplicate copies of the data and aggregation of disseminated data.
14. RM: This is a process used to present the status of available resources, storing their information, providing their availability at the right time to achieve the goal considering QoS parameters and is critically required for WSNs.

3.3 Resource management in wireless sensor networks

To protract the life span of WSNs and speed up the response time, intelligent utilization of available resources is necessary. Techniques that are used to notify about the available resources, storing their information, providing their availability, and selecting the best considering QoS parameters are referred to as RM. RM in WSNs includes resource identification, resource scheduling, resource allocation, resource sharing, resource provisioning (pooling), resource sharing, resource utilization, and resource monitoring in the networks (Kim & Kim, 2011; Shelke et al., 2013). A RM scheme classification is as shown in Fig. 3.5.

RM techniques must address the following issues of WSNs:

1. Resource discovery/identification relates to the process of detecting or identifying the available network resources such as the number of active nodes, battery life, radio resources, bandwidth, path information (routing table), etc. (Galluzzi & Heman, 2012; Helmy, 2005; Tilak, Chiu, Ghazaleh, & Fountain, 2005).
2. Resource scheduling refers to a set of user actions used to execute a specific application by efficiently assigning the available resources of the network. The order in which requests are processed impacts heavily on the overall system response time (Mahidhar & Raut, 2015; Wang et al., 2019).
3. Resource allocation refers to the process of assigning and managing resources effectively in a sensor network that is used to execute a strategic goal. Allocation refers to the selection of specific resources (sensor nodes) from the network to perform the specified task (Fulkar & Kapgate, 2014; Li et al., 2013).
4. Resource sharing provides the cooperating libraries with an opportunity to access available resource materials from other libraries, which should result in cost savings (Cid, Michiels, Joosen, & W Hughes, 2010; Maerien, Michiels, Hughes, & Joosen, 2014; Ramanathan et al., 2006).
5. Resource provisioning refers to the steps required to manage the resources for deployment and execution management for an assigned task (Padmavathi, Soniha, Soundarya, & Srimathi, 2017; Yu, Song, Du, Huang, & Jia, 2017).
6. Resource utilization refers to providing the most available resources to the nodes in the network to achieve the goal or to perform the application. As

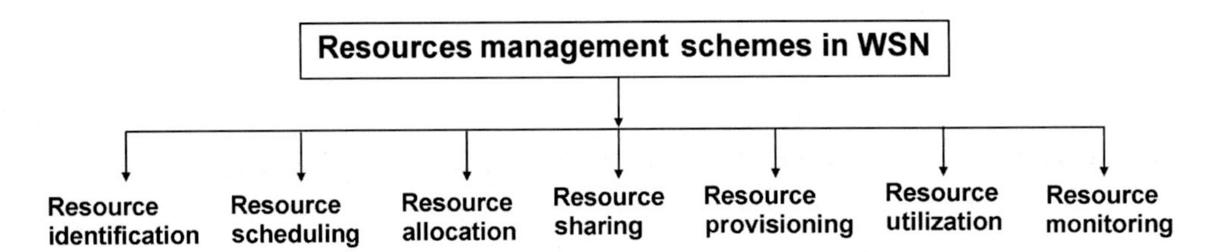

FIGURE 3.5 Wireless sensor network resource management schemes.

long as resources are limited in the network, efficient utilization of resources never stops due to increasing demand for computation (Ni, Zhang, & Li, 2019; Surendran & Tamilvizhi, 2018).
7. Resource monitoring gives complete information about the use of hardware, software, and resources of networks in real time (Christopher, Hauser, & Wesner, 2018; Du & Li, 2017).

3.3.1 Computational intelligence techniques

CI is the concept for the design, deployment, creation of computer-based, linguistically, biologically driven computational paradigms to execute a particular set of data or experimental observations. CI is typically a collection of bioinspired and other intelligent computational methods and strategies to solve challenging real-world problems (Leszek, 2008; Nazmul & Hojjat, 2013).

There are two forms of CI: hard computing and soft computing. CI and AI aim to serve the same goal; they are the two ways of performing any assigned task to machines just like human beings. CI includes bio-nature-inspired algorithms based on animal and plant behavior, GA, artificial immune systems, AI, ML, GT, ANNs, fuzzy logic techniques, DL, intelligent multiagent systems, cognitive agents, etc. (Artificial Intelligence, 2015; IEEE Computational Intelligence Society History, 2015; Lu et al., 2018).

3.3.2 Literature survey

Natural computation is also referred to as a bioinspired computation which is dependent on three different types of computation methods: (1) algorithms inspired by nature (behavior of animals/plants); (2) intelligent techniques using computers/machines, data sets, and special software; and (3) some protocols which use natural materials (e.g., molecular/DNA/genetics structures and behaviors) to solve a real-time problem (Adnan, Razzaque, Ahmed, & Isnin, 2013; Khan, Loret, & Lopez, 2015).

A genetic algorithm (GA) is motivated by the principle of natural evolution as described by Charles Darwin. GA demonstrates the natural selection strategy where the fittest entities (individuals) are opted to reproduce progenies of the next generation. GA is a type of ML algorithm that derives its actions from a description of the evolutionary processes in nature (Kaur et al., 2014; Njini & Ekabua, 2014).

AI is a competent and skilled application-based computer that imitates human knowledge for making decisions. AI algorithms are used to solve complicated real-time problems. AI is divided into two subsystems: (1) inference engine and (2) knowledge base. Inference engines include debugging capacities using a set of rules and the knowledge base represents numerous facts from data previous bases (Khedikar, Kapur, & Survanshi, 2012; Paladina, Biundo, Scarpa, & Puliafito, 2009).

ANNs are a class of computational learning models influenced by biological neural networks of humans/animals and used for approximating functions that may rely on a large number of inputs and are highly unpredictable. ANNs are widely described as interconnected "neuron" structures that transmit signals to one another. The connections have numerical weights and can be modified based on practice, rendering neural networks adaptable to inputs (Enami, Moghadam, Dadashtabar, & Hoseini, 2010).

Fuzzy logic systems are applied to a situation with the concept of partial truth. The value of truth ranges between absolute truth and complete false (truth value that ranges between 0 and 1) (Sharma, Gupta, & Comprehensive, 2013; Tahmasebi & Hezarkhani, 2012).

GT is the science of strategy or at least the optimum decision making of independent and competing players in a strategic context. GTs are mathematical models comprised of cooperative decision making. GT concepts apply whenever the actions of several agents are interdependent (Kori & Kakkasageri, 2020; Shi, Wang, Kwok, & Chen, 2012).

Agent technology is a smart and intelligent computational software platform used for the compilation of interactions of individual agent entities to meet a common goal. Agent technology combines elements of software agents, cognitive agents, and multiagent systems (both static and mobile agents) (Kakkasageri, Manvi, & Soragavi, 2006; Kori & Kakkasageri, 2019; Wei & Blake, 2012).

ML is a subset of AI technology, which can design and develop algorithms from data sets. These ML algorithms access other data sets and use them to learn on their own. DL is a branch of AI and a subset of ML that has networks capable of learning from unstructured or unlabeled data without oversight. ML is often known as computational cognitive learning or a deep neural network (Alsheikh, Lin, Niyato, & Tan, 2014; Kim, Stankovi, Johansson, & Kim, 2015; Zappone, Renzo, & Debbah, 2019).

A lot of research work has been done in the area of CI techniques. Figs. 3.6 and 3.7 depict the detailed taxonomy of CI and its application in the area of WSNs, respectively (Adnan et al., 2013; Alsheikh et al., 2014; Artificial Intelligence, 2015; Cao et al., 2019; Enami et al., 2010; Fernandez et al., 2019; IEEE Computational Intelligence Society History, 2015; Jabbar et al., 2013; Kakkasageri & Manvi, 2014; Kakkasageri et al., 2006; Kaur et al., 2014; Khan & Belqasmi et al., 2015; Khedikar et al., 2012; Kim et al., 2015; Kori & Kakkasageri, 2019;

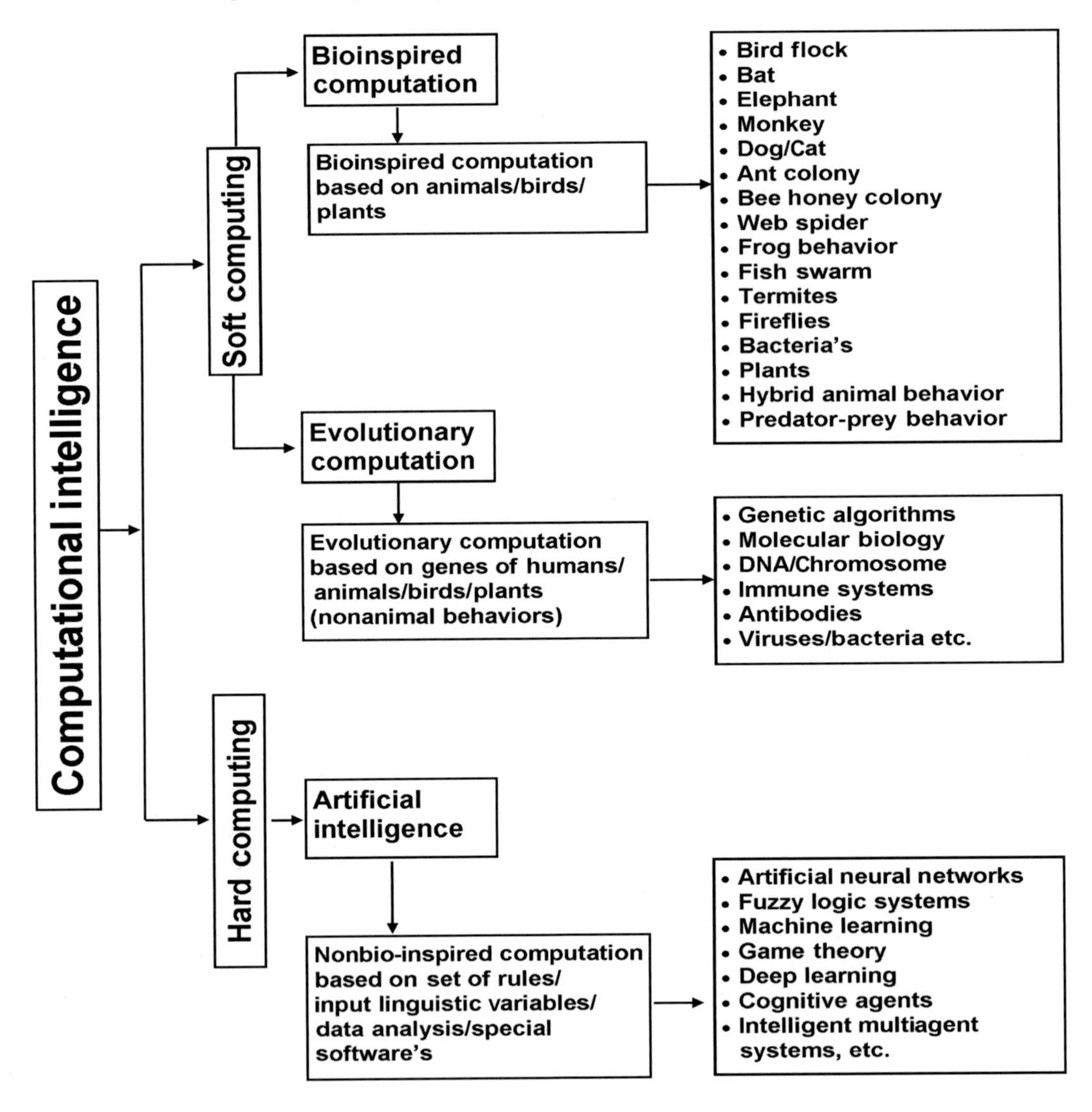

FIGURE 3.6 Computational intelligence.

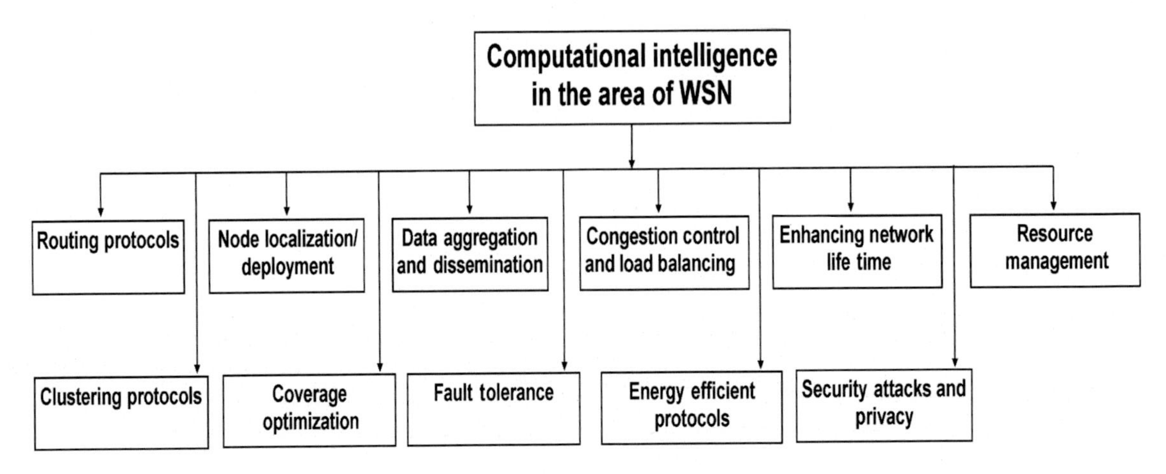

FIGURE 3.7 Computational intelligence in wireless sensor network.

Kori & Kakkasageri, 2020; Kulkarni et al., 2011; Kumar & Sharma, 2012; Leszek, 2008; Lu et al., 2018; Moura & Hutchison, 2019; Nazmul & Hojjat, 2013; Njini & Ekabua, 2014; Paladina et al., 2009; Praveen Kumar et al., 2019; Primeau et al., 2018; Sharma et al., 2013; Shi et al., 2012; Tahmasebi & Hezarkhani, 2012; Zappone et al., 2019).

3.3.2.1 Resource management scheme in wireless sensor networks using computational intelligence: ongoing research works

Fig. 3.8 shows the taxonomy for RM schemes for WSNs. Some of the issues related to RM using CI are as follows.

3.3.2.1.1 Resource identification scheme

Resources discovery/identification in a grid and distributed computation environment is complicated due to the heterogeneous, dynamic nature of the network with the RM policies (Murugan & Lopez, 2011). Authors have explored resource discovery mechanisms such as an agent-based, knowledge-driven approach, Gnutella protocol, and broker-based schemes. Resource discovery in wireless dynamic sensors that improve the operation level of sensor motes in sensing and transmitting information to the BS based on multilayer perceptron, that is, ANNs is presented in Manaf, Porker, and Gheisari (2015).

In Kambalimath and Kakkasageri (2019), a resource discovery scheme for vehicular cloud systems using the Honey bee optimization (HBO) technique integrated using an agent platform is discussed. The mobile agent aggregates the vehicular cloud information and the static agent intelligently identifies the required resources by the vehicle. A hybrid resource identification scheme based on soft set symbiotic organisms search (SSSOS) is proposed in Ezugwu and Adewumi (2017). Uncertainty problems that arise in static and dynamic systems are very well handled by the SSSOS algorithm. The scheme provides strength for tackling dynamic environments in search of optimal solutions and provides efficient management of available resources in the cloud.

Table 3.1 shows a comparison of the existing resource identification protocols using different CI mechanisms. The advantages and limitations of existing schemes are shown in the table and summarizes

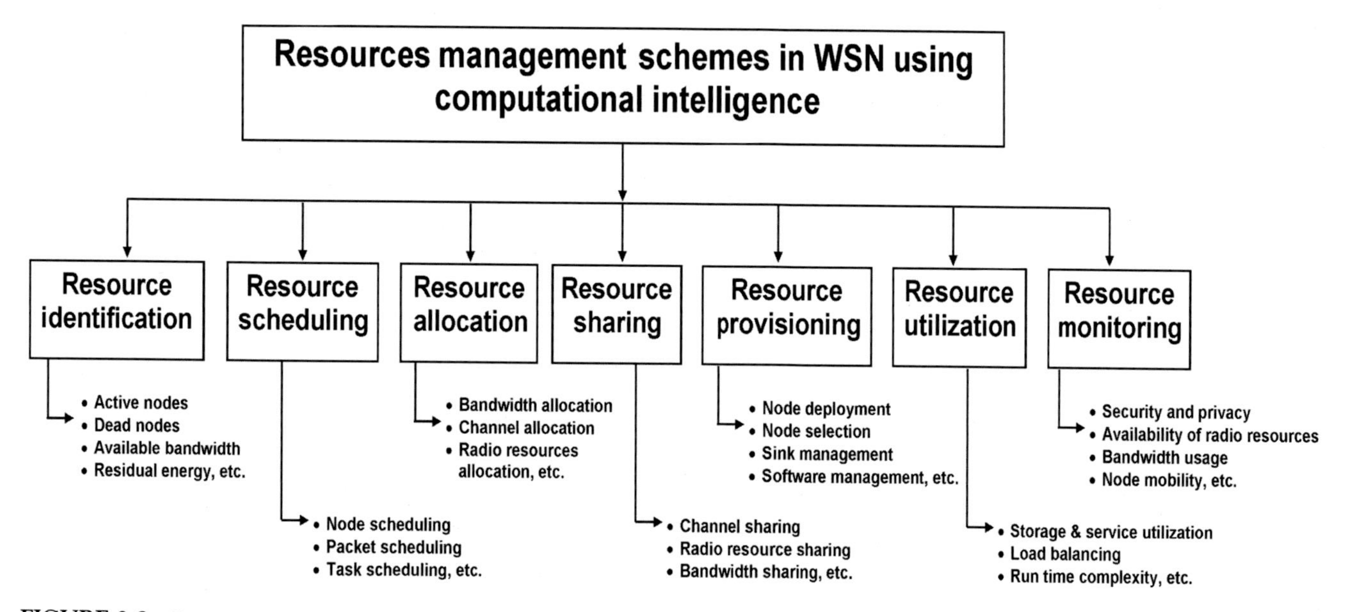

FIGURE 3.8 Resource management schemes in wireless sensor network using computational intelligence.

TABLE 3.1 Summary of resource-identification schemes in wireless sensor network.

Computational intelligence	No. of resources identified	Resource identification computational delay	Total end-to-end delay	Accuracy test
Artificial neural network (Manaf et al., 2015)	High	Low	Low	High
Soft set symbiotic organisms search (Ezugwu & Adewumi, 2017)	Medium	Medium	Low	High
Honey bee optimization (Kambalimath & Kakkasageri, 2019)	Medium	High	High	Low

that an ANNs is a suitable computational technique to solve the problems of resource identification in WSNs.

3.3.2.1.2 Resource scheduling

The convergence of biocomputing and scheduling algorithms for WSN is discussed in Musilek, Kromer, and Barton (2015). It depicts the best in these fields and provides a cutting-edge survey of the latest advancements in this interdisciplinary research area. An ant colony optimization (ACO) algorithm based on the three constraint conditions to determine the issue of resource scheduling in edge/fog and cloud computing is discussed. The ant colony algorithm is involved in three phases: information elicitation factor, expect inspiration factor, and pheromone update strategy (Yuan, Li, & Du, 2012). The efficient energy coverage (EEC) problem is solved by ant colony-based scheduling algorithm (ACB-SA) and is proposed in Lee and Lee (2012). To deal with the EEC issue more practically, a probability sensor detection scheme along with ACB-SA is more effective. A task scheduling scheme based on ant colony algorithm and bee colony optimization (BCO) algorithm for trusted applications in WSN is presented in Zhang, Song, & Bai (2016).

Biologically inspired models have received extensive consideration for data transmission, routing, and broadcasting and uses epidemic theory (Zhaofeng & Aiwan, 2016). Multiple access channels layer issues are very efficiently solved by fuzzy Hopfield neural network (FHNN) (Byun & So, 2016) using the broadcasting scheduling process. Discrete energy optimization is used by FHNN and TDMA is used to schedule nodes in a wireless network.

In Shen and Wang (2008), exploitation and exploration techniques in a hybridized whale optimization (HWO) scheme for handling the resource scheduling problem in cloud environments are discussed. The productivity and performance of an HWO scheme are dependent on the remaining resources of the network. The use of ML to ease decision making during radio resource scheduling in wireless networks is discussed in Strumberger, Bacanin, Tuba, and Tuba (2019). The optimization problem in wireless communication is solved using the transmission time intervals technique in combination with enforcement ML.

Table 3.2 shows the evaluation of existing resource scheduling schemes using different intelligence techniques. The advantages and limitations of existing schemes shown in the table summarize that ANN and FL are identified as a better solution for solving resource scheduling problems in WSNs.

3.3.2.1.3 Resource allocation

A DL scheme for resource allocation in distributed, dynamic, and multimedia wireless networks is highlighted in Comşa, Zhang, Aydin, and Kuonen (2019). The deep reinforcement learning approach is used to solve the problems of resource allocation.

The multiagent platform-based adaptive distributed artificial intelligence technique is used to address resource allocation issues in WSN (Liang, Ye, Yu, & Li, 2020). Resource allocation for intracluster WSN topology using adaptive particle swarm optimization is discussed based on node parameters. Intercloud resource allocation using an intelligent agent-based approach is presented in Mukherjee, Goswami, Yan, Yang, and Rodrigues (2019). The agent platform interacts, coordinates, and negotiates with each cloud for efficient allocations of available resources. In Sim (2019), the author proposed a GT model for effective resource allocation in vehicular cloud networks using the Hungarian model which provides the available resources to the vehicle by considering the less expensive method by achieving a reduction in the cost.

A fuzzy logic-based power allocation scheme for a dynamic, distributed, and cooperative WSN using opportunistic relaying is proposed in Kambalimath and Kakkasageri (2020). Table 3.3 summarizes resource allocation techniques using various intelligence mechanisms. Agent-based artificial intelligence is good in terms of latency and the number of resources allocated.

3.3.2.1.4 Resource sharing

Every node connected to the Internet announces through some standard algorithm messages (Yousaf,

TABLE 3.2 Summary of resource-scheduling schemes in wireless sensor network.

Computational intelligence	No. of resources scheduled	Resource scheduling computational delay	Scheduled sensor rate	Total end-to-end delay
Artificial neural network using machine learning (Byun & So, 2016; Strumberger et al., 2019)	High	Low	High	Low
FL with agent (Kori & Kakkasageri, 2019)	High	Medium	Very high	Low
Honey bee optimization (Shen & Wang, 2008)	Medium	High	Low	Medium
ACO, BCO (Lee & Lee, 2012; Zhang et al., 2016)	Less	High	Very low	High

Ahmad, Ahmed, & Haseeb, 2017), and the ML model is used to share some commonly available resources in the network. Collaborating the resources of all clouds and cooperatively sharing the resources is an emerging technology. Based on weights and reputation as input, the neural networks of the service required by the resources are shared (Ramirez, Taha, Lloret, & Tomas, 2019). A ML scheme based on Q-learning (reinforcement policy) used for deciding an opportunistic resource sharing in long-term evolution and wireless fidelity is presented in Saranyadevi and Vijayanand (2014).

A software-based semiautonomous agent in first virtual WSN is used to solve the problem of resource sharing (Rastegardoost & Jabbari, 2018). These agents address more queries with a much shorter reaction time. Decentralized spectrum sharing in cognitive radio networks using a GT noncooperative game, that is, a pricing-based spectrum-sharing concept is used for negotiation between the primary and secondary users (Yıldırım & Tata, 2018).

Table 3.4 shows existing resource-sharing mechanisms using different CI mechanisms. ML algorithm performance is better than the agent and GT techniques.

3.3.2.1.5 Resource provisioning

ML methods are the best solutions for resource provisioning issues in diverse and heterogeneous joint edge-cloud networks. The authors categorized the problem into three groups: (1) load prediction and balancing, (2) system consideration and node placement, (3) heterogeneous and multitasking (Handouf, Sabir, & Sadik, 2018; Duc, Leiva, Casari, & Ostberg, 2019). ML algorithms minimize the overhead of resource provisioning and dynamic demand of resources, and maintain the QoS parameters of data during resource provisioning in vehicular clouds (Trivedi & Somani, 2016).

A cooperative GT based on a matching game model and mood values is presented in Salahuddin, Fuqaha, and Guizani (2016). The authors proposed an effective and dynamic resource provisioning scheme for data centers for efficient and fair operation in the network. A GT model to manage on-demand resource provision in wireless networks is presented in Kim and New (2018). GT fairly optimizes the uses of resources, minimizes latency, and security and thrust level are increased. Fuzzy C Means (FCM) and Possibilities C Means (PCM) techniques are used to addressing the resource provisioning challenge in data management (Aloqaily, Kantarci, & Mouftah, 2016). In the FCM scheme, available resources are well utilized compared to PCM. A monitoring agent with fuzzy logic is used for resource provisioning in cloud computation (Agarkhed & Kodli, 2018).

Table 3.5 exhibits resource provisioning using various CI mechanisms. The ML algorithms are better in terms of performance and security levels compared with GT and fuzzy logic.

3.3.2.1.6 Resource utilization

Resource utilization algorithms based on localization, deployment, congestion control techniques, and

TABLE 3.3 Summary of resource-allocation schemes in wireless sensor network.

Computational intelligence	Resource allocation computational delay	Successfully resources allocated	Error rate	Latency
Deep learning (Comşa et al., 2019)	Low	Medium	Moderate	Medium
Agent-based adaptive distributed artificial intelligence (Liang et al., 2020; Mukherjee et al., 2019)	Very low	High	Less	Low
Game theory (Sim, 2019)	Medium	Medium	Moderate	Medium
FL (Kambalimath & Kakkasageri, 2020)	High	Less	High	High

TABLE 3.4 Summary of resource-sharing schemes in wireless sensor network.

Computational intelligence	Total no. of resources shared	Computational complexity	Latency
Machine learning (Ramirez et al., 2019; Saranyadevi & Vijayanand, 2014; Yousaf et al., 2017)	More	Less complex	Low
Agent-based (Rastegardoost & Jabbari, 2018)	Less	Complex	High
Game theory (Yıldırım & Tata, 2018)	Few	Complex	Medium

spectrum utilization are surveyed in Padmavathi, Soniha, Soundarya, and Srimathi (2017) and Rana and Kamboj (2016). Channel utilization and bandwidth utilization to improve the performance and throughput based on the Fuzzy Logic Decision Support System in cognitive radio networks are presented in Luo, Huang, and Zhu (2015).

Suppot vector regression techinque can be used for resource utilization in wireless networks and cloud computing for future heterogrnrous applications. (Ali, Abbas, Shafiq, Bashir, & Afzal, 2019). Radial basis function at kernel levels and sequential minimal optimization protocol, training, and regression estimation are used for heterogeneous and distributed networks. In dynamic resource usage among shared networks, efficient resource prediction and allocation are done using ML for better resource utilization (Abdullah, Li, Jamali, Badwi, & Ruan, 2020). A feed-forward neural network based on a continuous-time Markov decision model is used for efficient resource utilization in cloud-based data centers (Mehmood, Latif, & Malik, 2018).

Table 3.6 shows many resource utilization protocols using DL, policy-based, and fuzzy logic. Neural networks based on intelligent algorithms are more efficient than other algorithms.

3.3.2.1.7 Resource monitoring

A GT concept used for dynamic behavior monitoring of sensor nodes is proposed in Ni et al. (2019). Balance is maintained between the security aspect, energy conversation, and cluster-based routing protocol. A negotiation GT model is used to monitor packet collision and to identify a group of malicious/selfish nodes in MANETs (Yang, Lu, Liu, Guo, & Liang, 2018). Cloud computing, IoT, and WSN face major problems in resource monitoring, and Njilla, Ouete, and Doungwa (2016) provide an intelligent architecture for wireless networks using DL. Reinforcement learning schemes make wireless networks automatic and negotiate the best configuration for efficient management of available resources.

A Long-Short Term Memory scheme used to reduce the computational complexity and execution time in WSNs based on cloud data storage is a challenging task due to the nonlinear nature of the data size and storage capacity, as presented in Zhang, Yao, and Guan (2017). An agent and fuzzy logic-based mechanism integrates different resources and services for RFID, WSN, and Internet of Things with cloud storage to handle the dynamic service operations; also, an adaptive monitoring protocol is discussed to update service status information (Shah et al., 2017). Table 3.7 compares various parameters of resource

TABLE 3.5 Summary of resource-provisioning schemes in wireless sensor network.

Computational intelligence	Resource provision computational delay	No. of resources supplied	Latency	Security level
Machine learning (Duc et al., 2019; Handouf et al., 2018; Trivedi & Somani, 2016)	Less	More	Low	High
Game theory (Kim & New, 2018; Salahuddin et al., 2016)	Medium	Few	High	Medium
FL (Agarkhed & Kodli, 2018; Aloqaily et al., 2016)	High	Less	Medium	Low

TABLE 3.6 Summary of resource-utilization schemes in wireless sensor network.

Computational intelligence	Resource utilization	Throughput	Runtime
FL	Average	Medium	High
Machine learning (Njilla et al., 2016)	Very high	High	Low
Neural network (Zhang et al., 2017)	High	High	High

TABLE 3.7 Summary of resource-monitoring schemes in wireless sensor network.

Computational intelligence	Resource-monitoring accuracy	Computational complexity	Security and privacy
Game theory (Ni et al., 2019; Yang et al., 2018)	High	Medium	Medium
Deep learning (Njilla et al., 2016)	High	Low	High
Neural networks (Zhang et al., 2017)	Medium	High	Medium
FL (Shah et al., 2017)	Low	Medium	Less

monitoring in WSN. GT and artificial intelligent schemes are better in terms of accuracy and security levels.

3.3.2.2 *Analytical study of ongoing research works in computational intelligence*

After reviewing the behavior of animals and plants, evolutionary biology, natural behavior, and AI, it can be concluded that the system can be made more stable and efficient by using these techniques.

A new improved system can be designed and developed by using these CI techniques. A statistical analysis of the usage of CI techniques is shown in Figs. 3.9–3.13. The graphical representation shows the

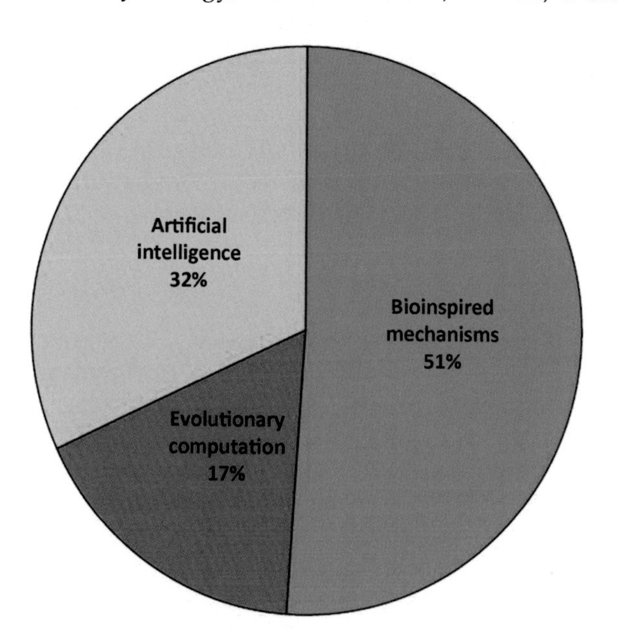

FIGURE 3.9 Percentage of computational intelligence used in wireless sensor network.

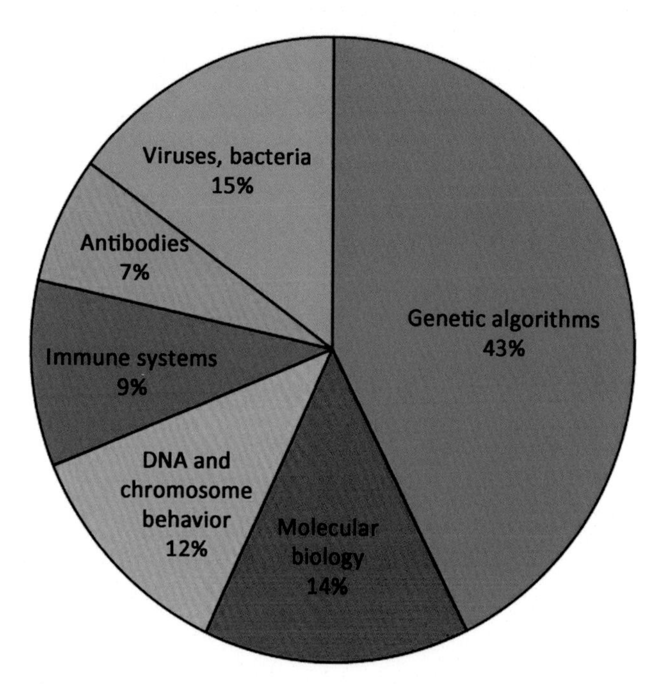

FIGURE 3.11 Evolutionary computation used in wireless sensor network.

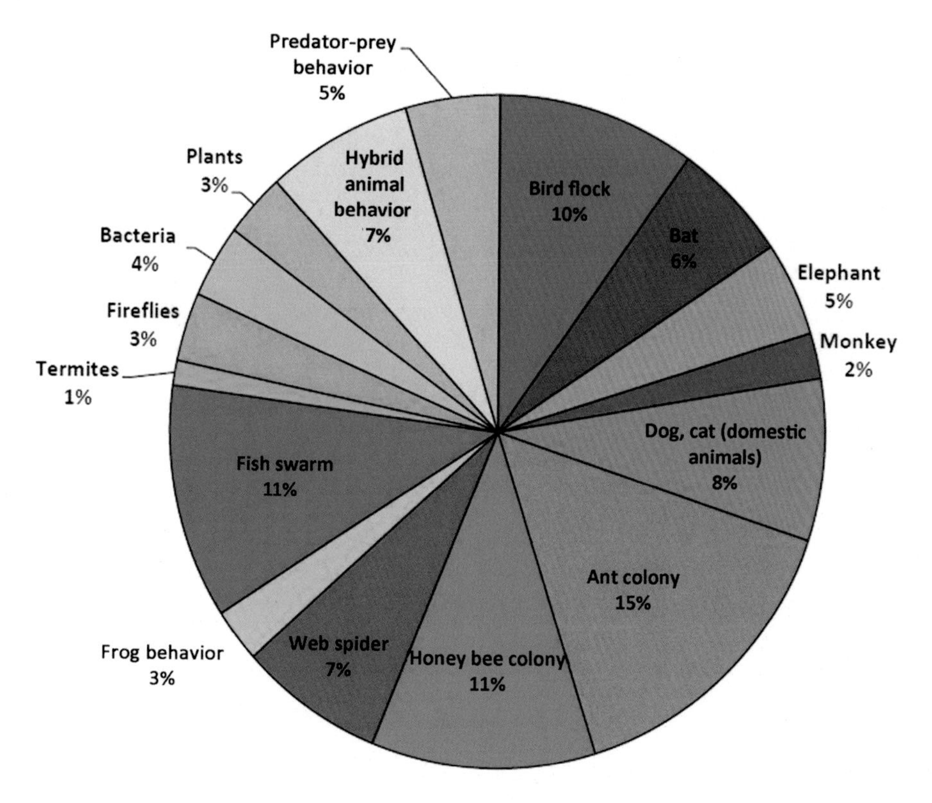

FIGURE 3.10 Bioinspired mechanisms used in wireless sensor network.

type of mechanism used, that is, animal and/or other natural behaviors, and AI along the behavior type they imitate. On the other side, understanding what sort of application the programs and solutions are intended for is critical (Abdullah et al., 2020; Adnan et al., 2013; Agarkhed & Kodli, 2018; Ali et al., 2019; Aloqaily et al., 2016; Alsheikh et al., 2014; Artificial Intelligence, 2015; Byun & So, 2016; Cao et al., 2019; Comşa et al., 2019; Duc et al., 2019; Enami et al., 2010; Ezugwu & Adewumi, 2017; Fernandez et al., 2019; Handouf et al., 2018; IEEE Computational Intelligence Society History, 2015; Jabbar et al., 2013; Kakkasageri & Manvi, 2014; Kakkasageri et al., 2006; Kambalimath & Kakkasageri, 2019; Kambalimath & Kakkasageri, 2020; Kaur et al., 2014; Khan & Belqasmi et al., 2015; Khedikar et al., 2012; Kim & New, 2018; Kim et al., 2015; Kori & Kakkasageri, 2019; Kori & Kakkasageri, 2020; Kulkarni et al., 2011; Kumar & Sharma, 2012; Lee & Lee, 2012; Leszek, 2008; Liang et al., 2020; Lu et al., 2018; Luo et al., 2015; Manaf et al., 2015; Mehmood et al., 2018; Moura & Hutchison, 2019; Mukherjee et al., 2019; Murugan & Lopez, 2011; Musilek et al., 2015; Nazmul & Hojjat, 2013; Ni et al., 2019; Njilla et al., 2016; Njini & Ekabua, 2014; Padmavathi et al., 2017; Paladina et al., 2009; Praveen Kumar et al., 2019; Primeau et al., 2018; Ramirez et al., 2019; Rana & Kamboj, 2016; Rastegardoost & Jabbari, 2018; Salahuddin et al., 2016; Saranyadevi & Vijayanand, 2014; Shah et al., 2017; Sharma et al., 2013; Shen & Wang, 2008; Shi et al., 2012; Sim, 2019; Strumberger et al., 2019; Tahmasebi & Hezarkhani, 2012; Trivedi & Somani, 2016; Yang et al., 2018; Yıldırım & Tata, 2018; Yousaf et al., 2017; Yuan et al., 2012; Zappone et al., 2019; Zhang et al., 2016; Zhang et al., 2017; Zhaofeng & Aiwan, 2016).

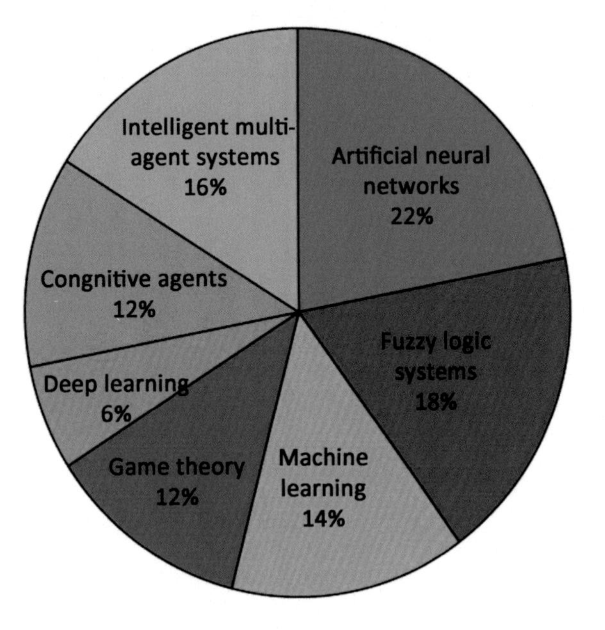

FIGURE 3.12 Artificial intelligence used in wireless sensor network.

Fig. 3.9 depicts the percentage of CI used in WSNs, where more than 50% of the research is done using bioinspired computational techniques (animal behaviors), followed by AI at approximately 32%, and evolutionary computations are used for only 17%, which is the same as for physiological functions.

Fig. 3.10 shows different bioinspired mechanisms used in WSN. The behavior of animals and birds is

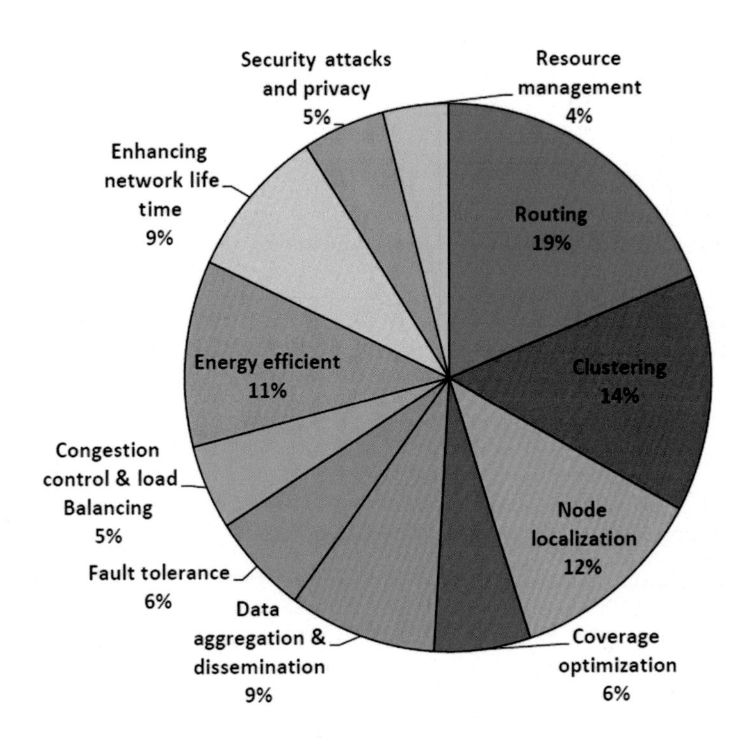

FIGURE 3.13 Use of computational intelligence in wireless sensor network.

considered for solving many issues in WSN, followed by plant and virus/bacterium behaviors with the fewest employed. The most commonly used techniques are those which are based on a colony, flock, or swarm of animals. With less than 10%, we can find some animal behavior that lives in a natural habitat within human society, may also be used to solve few issues in WSN.

Bioinspired systems groups include GA, imitation of bacteria, virus behavior followed by antibiotics, and the immune system and are presented in Fig. 3.11. Fig. 3.12 shows the second type of CI technique, called hard computing, which is based on nonbioinspired mechanisms with input linguistic variables, sets of rules, data analysis, and special software. Neural networks and fuzzy sets are used to solve most WSN issues, followed by ML, DL, agent platform, and GT.

Issues related to routing, clustering and node localization protocols, network lifetime, data aggregation, and dissemination followed by congestion control, load balancing, fault tolerance, providing security, and privacy of WSNs are presented in Fig. 3.13. A variety of bioinspired and AI techniques are available to solve the problem of RM in WSNs. These CI algorithms will create new contributions not only in WSN but also in IoT, vehicular adhoc networks (VANET), and cloud computing.

3.3.2.3 *Resource management scheme for wireless sensor network using an artificial neural network*

In this section, we discuss the usage of ANN (ANN for RM in WSNs. A computational machine consisting of several processing layers/nodes that make the dynamic decision based on external inputs is defined as an ANN. ANNs consist of multiple nodes that work the same as the neurons of the human brain. These nodes/neurons are interconnected and communicate with each other via linkages. The nodes can take data from external inputs, perform basic computer operations, and produce the required accurate output known as a node value. Each linkage has predefined weights. ANNs are capable of training by changing the weight values that control the signal between two neurons/nodes. ANNs are able to learn and need to be educated; there are several strategies for learning, including ML, DL, etc.

The input layer explicitly transfers the data to the first hidden layer, where the results are compounded by the weights. No computation is performed at the input layer/nodes; they just pass on the information to the hidden layer/nodes through active functions. In the hidden layer, artificial neurons accumulate a series of weighted inputs and generate output via an activation function. The final layer is the output layer which produces the desired output for a set of given inputs.

Neural networks are used to solve complex problems of WSNs in real-time situations. ANNs are used to improve the decision-making process to solve RM issues. These networks can learn, train, and model the relationships between inputs and outputs which are complex and nonlinear for better performance of WSNs with the minimum use of resources.

Agents are self-serving, autonomous, purposeful, and intellectually directed to achieve one or more goals; they use their cognitive notions to accomplish that common goal. Agent technology [a group of static agents (SAs) and mobile agents (MAs)] is a type of computational technique that incorporates intelligent techniques such as ML, AI, GT, bioinspired techniques, and evolutionary programming.

Software agent technology has influenced the design of future WSNs and their applications. Agent technology is an "add-on" to existing technology that makes it more versatile, more adaptable, and customized for future applications in the next generation of WSNs.

Fig. 3.14 shows the integration of agent technology and ANN to solve various RM issues in WSNs. Two agents, that is, group of MA and SA, are used, where a mobile agency is fitted to the sensor nodes that collect the network and node resource information periodically and update it to the knowledge base and feed as an ANN input layer. The static agency is present in the BS where ANN intelligence is present with different learning, training, and decision-making models that are used to make RM decisions. The output layer produces the output (resource scheduling, resource allocation, etc.,) according to the input given by MA and activation functions or weights of the hidden layers. The output decision is highly accurate, error-free, and fast based on the CI used by the hidden layer.

3.4 Future research directions and conclusion

Some of the future research challenges for RM in WSNs are presented in this section.

1. All the network parameters such as network size, type of nodes used, deployment techniques, applications, and resources available should be considered in the WSN for designing the holistic solutions in RM schemes.
2. The main challenge of RM lies in effectively discovering, allocating, and utilizing the WSN resources.
3. WSN is highly dynamic and it is difficult to maintain resources. Therefore RM is a major problem that has to be addressed intelligently.
4. For maintaining available resources versus consumption trade-offs, the resources should be allocated, shared, and utilized to the application based on the required performance level.

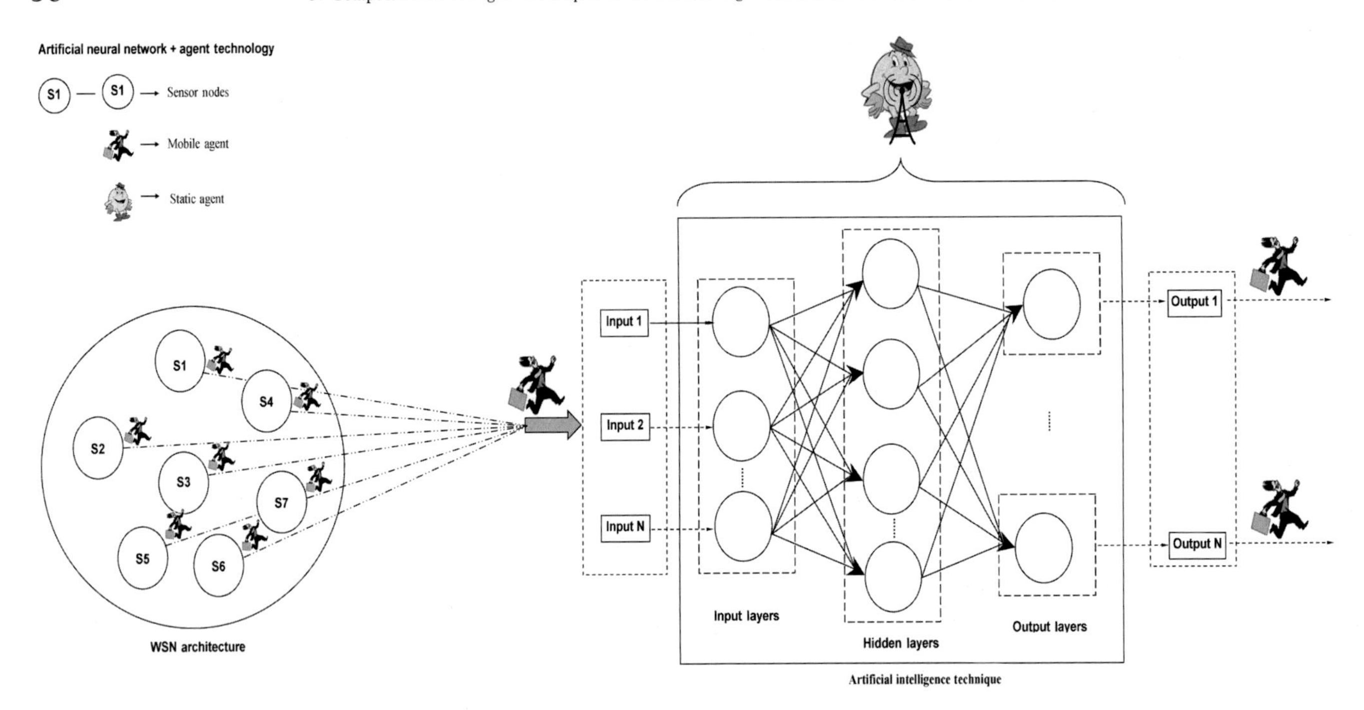

FIGURE 3.14 Artificial neural networks model for resource management scheme in wireless sensor network.

5. Guaranteeing enhanced security and privacy to the widespread applications of WSNs is to be assured by the RM techniques.
6. Heterogeneity should be approached in different levels of WSNs, including node level, gateway level, network level, and fog/cloud level using a RM scheme.

Remotely distributed WSNs have been an active research topic, and thus attracted the attention of many researchers. If there are intelligent RM schemes in WSNs, then there is a promising future for applications of WSNs in many areas from defense to agriculture and from space to classroom laboratories.

This chapter has focused on RM in WSNs that reflects the concept and importance of CI to solve RM issues. We have presented a holistic view of the current status of CI in the area of RM for WSNs. Based on this analysis, we have identified some research challenges that need further investigation in the area of RM.

The scope of the study can be extended to global scheduling of resources when WSNs are integrated with fog/edge computing; local scheduling of WSNs with cloud resources; resource estimation and utilization in real-time applications; resource demand profiling; resource pricing and profit maximization, etc. Further to this, comparative studies can be initiated amongst various RM techniques in WSNs using future intelligent computational algorithms.

References

Abdullah, L., Li, H., Jamali, S. A., Badwi, A. A., & Ruan, C. (2020). Predicting multi-attribute host resource utilization using support vector regression technique. *IEEE Access*, *8*, 66048–66067.

Adnan, Md. A., Razzaque, M. A., Ahmed, I., & Isnin, I. F. (2013). Bio-mimic optimization strategies in wireless sensor networks: A survey. *Sensors Journal Publishing Corporation*, *14*, 299–345.

Agarkhed, J. & Kodli, S. (2018). Fuzzy logic based data provisioning using cloud computing, In *Proceedings of the international conference on information, communication, engineering and technology*.

Akyildiz, I. F., Melodia, T., & Chowdhury, K. R. (2007a). A survey on wireless multimedia sensor networks. *Journal of Computer and Telecommunication Networking*, *51*(4), 921–960, Elsevier.

Akyildiz, I. F., Melodia, T., & Chowdhury, K. R. (2007b). A survey on wireless multimedia sensor networks. *IEEE Wireless Communications*, *14*(16), 32–39.

Akyildiz, I. F., Su, W., Sankarasubramaniam, Y., & Cayirci, E. (2002). Wireless sensor networks: A survey. *Journal of Computer Networks*, *38*(4), 393–422, Elsevier.

Akyildiz, I. F., Su, W., Sankarasubramaniam, Y., & Cayirci, E. (2013). Wireless sensor networks: A survey. *Journal of Computer Networks*, 393–422, Elsevier.

Ali, A., Abbas, L., Shafiq, M., Bashir, A. K., & Afzal, M. K. (2019). Hybrid fuzzy logic scheme for efficient channel utilization in cognitive radio networks. *IEEE Access*, *7*, 24463–24476.

Ali, A., Ming, Y., Chakraborty, S., & Iram, S. (2017). A comprehensive survey on real-time applications of WSN,. *Journal for Future Internet*, *7*, 1–22, MDPI.

Aloqaily, M., Kantarci, B., & Mouftah, H. T. (2016). Multiagent/multiobjective interaction game system for service provisioning in vehicular cloud. *IEEE Access*, *4*, 3153–3168.

Alsheikh, M. A., Lin, S., Niyato, D., & Tan, H. P. (2014). Machine learning in wireless sensor networks: Algorithms, strategies, and applications. *IEEE Communications Surveys and Tutorials*, *16*(4), 1996–2018.

Ari, A. A., Gueroui, A., Labraoui, N., & Yenke, B. O. (2015). Concepts and evolution of research in the field of wireless sensor networks. *International Journal of Computer Networks and Communications*, *7*(1), 82–98.

Artificial Intelligence. (2015). Computational intelligence, soft computing, natural computation - What's the difference? <www.andata.at>.

Byun, H., & So, J. (2016). Node scheduling control inspired by epidemic theory for data dissemination in wireless sensor-actuator networks with delay constraints. *IEEE Transactions on Wireless Communications*, *15*(3), 1794–1807.

Cao, L., Cai, Y., & Yue, Y. (2019). Swarm intelligence-based performance optimization for mobile wireless sensor networks: Survey, challenges, and future directions. *IEEE Access*, *7*, 161524–161553.

Chawla, H. (2014). Some issues and challenges of wireless sensor networks. *International Journal of Advanced Research in Computer Science and Software Engineering*, *4*(7), 236–239.

Christopher, B., Hauser, C.B., Wesner, S. (2018). Reviewing cloud monitoring: Towards cloud resource profiling. In *Proceedings of the eleventh IEEE international conference on cloud computing*.

Cid, D., Michiels, P.J., Joosen, S., Hughes, W D. (2010). Middleware for resource sharing in multi-purpose wireless sensor networks. In *Proceedings of the IEEE international conference on networked embedded systems for enterprise applications* (pp. 1–8).

Comşa, I.S., Zhang, S., Aydin, M.E., & Kuonen, P. (2019). *Machine learning in radio resource scheduling*, Chapter 02, IGI Global Publisher, (pp. 24–48).

Dener, M. (2017). WiSeN: A new sensor node for smart applications with wireless sensor networks. *Journal of Computers and Electrical Engineering*, *64*, 380–394, Elsevier.

Du, M., & Li, F. (2017). ATOM: Efficient tracking, monitoring, and orchestration of cloud resources. *IEEE Transactions on Parallel and Distributed Systems*, *28*(8), 2172–2189.

Duc, T. L., Leiva, R. G., Casari, P., & Ostberg, P. O. (2019). Machine learning methods for reliable resource provisioning in edge-cloud computing: A survey. *ACM Computational Survey*, *52*(5), 1–15.

Enami, N., Moghadam, R. A., Dadashtabar, K., & Hoseini, M. (2010). Neural network based energy efficiency in wireless sensor networks: A survey. *International Journal of Computer Science & Engineering Survey*, *1*(1), 39–55.

Ezugwu, A. E., & Adewumi, A. O. (2017). Soft sets based symbiotic organisms search algorithm for resource discovery in cloud computing environment. *Future Generation Computer Systems*, *76*, 33–50, Elsevier.

Fernandez, A., Herrera, F., Cordon, O., Jesus, M. J., & Marcelloni, F. (2019). Evolutionary fuzzy systems for explainable artificial intelligence: Why, when, what for, and where to? *IEEE Computational Intelligence Magazine*, *14*(01), 69–81.

Fortino, G., Bal, M., Li, W., & Shen, W. (2015). Collaborative wireless sensor networks: Architectures, algorithms and applications. *Journal of Information Fusion*, *22*, 1–2, Elsevier.

Fulkar, S., & Kapgate, D. (2014). Energy efficient resource allocation in wireless sensor networks. *International Journal of Computer Science and Mobile Computing*, *3*(5), 887–892.

Galluzzi, V., & Heman, T. (2012). Survey: Discovery in wireless sensor networks. *International Journal of Distributed Sensor Networks*, *8*(1), 12–24.

Gupta, S., & Sinha, P. (2014). Overview of wireless sensor networks: A survey. *International Journal of Advanced Research in Computer and Communication Engineering*, *3*(1).

Handouf, S., Sabir, E., & Sadik, M. (2018). A leasing-based spectrum sharing framework for cognitive radio networks. In *Proceeding of the IEEE sixth international conference on wireless networks and mobile communications*.

Helmy, A. (2005). *Efficient resource discovery in wireless ad hoc networks: Contacts do help, resource management in wireless networking* (16). Springer.

IEEE Computational Intelligence Society History, Engineering and technology (2015).

Jabbar, S., Iram, R., Minhas, A. A., Shafi, I., & Khalid, S. (2013). Intelligent optimization of wireless sensor networks through bio-inspired computing: Survey and future directions. *International Journal of Distributed Sensor Networks*, *10*, 13–25.

Kakkasageri, M. S., & Manvi, S. S. (2014). Regression based critical information aggregation and dissemination in VANETs: A cognitive agent approach. *Journal of Vehicular Communications*, *1*(4), 168–180, Elsevier.

Kakkasageri, M. S., Manvi, S. S., & Soragavi, G. D. (2006). Agent-based information access in wireless sensor networks. *WSEAS Transactions on Information Science and Applications Journal*, *3*(7), 1369–1374.

Kambalimath, M. G., & Kakkasageri, M. S. (2019). Dynamic resource discovery scheme for vehicular cloud networks. *International Journal of Information Technology and Computer Science*, *11*(12), 38–49, MECS Press.

Kambalimath, M. G., & Kakkasageri, M. S. (2020). Cost optimization based resource allocation for vehicular cloud networks. *International Journal of Computer Network and Information Security*, *2*, 22–31, MECS Press.

Karray, F., Jmal, M. W., Ortiz, A. G., Abid, M., & Obeid, A. M. (2018). A comprehensive survey on wireless sensor node hardware platforms. *Journal of Computer Networks*, *144*, 89–110, Elsevier.

Kaur, S., Goyal, V., & Luthra, P. (2014). A survey on applications of genetic algorithm in wireless sensor networks. *International Journal of Advanced Research in Computer Science and Software Engineering*, *4*(8), 664–668.

Ketshabetswe, L. K., Zungeru, A. M., Mangwala, M., Chuma, J. M., & Sigweni, B. (2019). Communication protocols for wireless sensor networks: A survey and comparison. *Journal of Heliyon*, *5*(5), e01591, Elsevier.

Khan, I., Belqasmi, F., Glitho, R., Crespi, N., Morrow, M., & Polakos, P. (2015). Wireless sensor network virtualization: A survey. *IEEE Communications Surveys and Tutorials*, *18*(1), 553–576.

Khan, S., Loret, J., & Lopez, E. M. (2015). Bio-inspired mechanisms in wireless sensor networks. *International Journal of Distributed Sensor Networks*, *10*, 2–12.

Khedikar, R.S., Kapur, A.R., & Survanshi, Y. (2012). Wireless sensor network simulation by artificial intelligent. In *Proceedings of the second IEEE international conference on power, control and embedded systems*, (pp. 9–12).

Kim, H. & Kim, J. (2011). Energy-efficient resource management in wireless sensor network. In *Proceedings of the IEEE topical conference on wireless sensors and sensor networks*, (pp. 69–72).

Kim, S., & New, A. (2018). Adaptive data centre resource provisioning scheme based on the dual-level cooperative game approach. *IEEE Access*, *6*, 52047–52057.

Kim, W., Stankovi, M. S., Johansson, K. H., & Kim, H. J. (2015). A distributed support vector machine learning over wireless sensor networks. *IEEE Transactions on Cybernetics*, *45*(11), 2599–2611.

Kobo, H. I., Mahfouz, A. M., & Hancke, G. P. (2017). A survey on software-defined wireless sensor networks: Challenges and design requirements. *IEEE Journals and Magazines*, *5*, 1872–1899.

Kori, G.S. & Kakkasageri, M.S. (2019). Intelligent agent based resource scheduling in wireless sensor networks. In *Proceedings of the tenth IEEE international conference on computing, communication and networking technologies*, India, (pp. 72–85).

Kori, G.S. & Kakkasageri, M.S. (2020). Intelligent resource identification scheme for wireless sensor networks. In *Proceedings of the international conference on recent trends in machine learning, IOT, smart cities & applications.*

Kulkarni, R. V., Förster, A., & Venayagamoorthy, G. (2011). Computational intelligence in wireless sensor networks: A survey. *IEEE Communications Surveys and Tutorials*, *13*(1), 68–96.

Kumar, S., & Sharma, M. (2012). Convergence of artificial intelligence, emotional intelligence, neural network and evolutionary computing. *International Journal of Advanced Research in Computer Science and Software Engineering*, *2*(3).

Lee, J. W., & Lee, J. J. (2012). Ant-colony-based scheduling algorithm for energy-efficient coverage of WSN. *IEEE Sensors Journal*, *12*(10), 3036–3046.

Leszek, R. (2008). *Computational intelligence: Methods and techniques*. Springer.

Li, W., Delicato, F. C., Pires, P. F., Lee, Y. C., Zomaya, A. Y., Miceli, C., & Pirmez, L. (2013). Efficient allocation of resources in multiple heterogeneous wireless sensor networks. *Journal of Parallel and Distributed Computing*, *74*(1), 1775–1788.

Liang, L., Ye, H., Yu, G., & Li, G. Y. (2020). Deep learning based wireless resource allocation with application to vehicular networks. *IEEE Access*, *108*(2), 341–356.

Lin, X. H., Kwok, Y. K., & Wang, H. (2009). *Energy-efficient resource management techniques in wireless sensor networks. Guide to wireless sensor networks computer communications and networks* (pp. 439–468). Springer.

Lu, J., Behbood, V., Hao, P., Zuo, H., Xue, S., & Zhang, G. (2018). Transfer learning using computational intelligence: A survey. *Journal of Knowledge Based Systems*, *80*, 14–23, Elsevier.

Luo, H., Huang, Z., & Zhu, T. (2015). A survey on spectrum utilization in wireless sensor networks. *Journal of Sensors*, *15*, 1–13.

Maerien, J., Michiels, S., Hughes, D., & Joosen, W. (2014). Enabling resource sharing in heterogeneous wireless sensor networks. In *Proceedings of the first ACM workshop on middleware for context-aware applications in the IoT*. (pp. 7–12).

Mahidhar, R. & Raut, A. (2015). A survey on scheduling schemes with security in wireless sensor networks. In *Proceedings of the international conference on information security and privacy*, (pp. 756–762).

Manaf, S., Porker, P., & Gheisari, M. (2015). New algorithm for resource discovery in sensor networks based on neural network. *International Journal of Biology, Pharmacy and Allied Sciences*, *4*(12), 125–140.

Mancilla, M. C., Mellado, E. L., & Siller, M. (2016). Wireless sensor networks formation: Approaches and techniques. *Journal of Sensors*, *16*, 01–18, Hindwai.

Mehmood, T., Latif, S., & Malik, S. (2018). Prediction of cloud computing resource utilization. In *Proceedings of the IEEE international conference on smart cities improving quality of life using ICT and IoT (HONET-ICT)*, (pp. 38–42).

Modieginyane, K. M., Letswamotse, B. B., Malekian, R., & Mahfouz, A. M. A. (2018). Software defined wireless sensor networks application opportunities for efficient network management: A survey. *Journal of Computers and Electrical Engineering*, *66*, 274–287, Elsevier.

Moura, J., & Hutchison, D. (2019). Game theory for multi-access edge computing: Survey, use cases, and future trends. *IEEE Communications Surveys and Tutorials*, *21*(01), 260–288.

Mukherjee, A., Goswami, P., Yan, Z., Yang, L., & Rodrigues, J. J. P. C. (2019). ADAI and adaptive PSO based resource allocation for wireless sensor networks. *IEEE Access*, *7*, 1–9.

Murugan, B. S., & Lopez, D. (2011). A survey of resource discovery approaches in distributed computing environment. *International Journal of Computer Applications*, *22*(9), 44–46.

Musilek, P., Kromer, P., & Barton, T. (2015). Review of nature-inspired methods for wake-up scheduling in wireless sensor networks. *Journal of Computer Networks Swarm and Evolutionary Computation*, *25*, 100–118, Elsevier.

Nazmul, S., & Hojjat, A. (2013). *Computational intelligence: Synergies of fuzzy logic, neural networks and evolutionary computing*. John Wiley and Sons.

Ni, W., Zhang, Y., & Li, W. W. (2019). An optimal strategy for resource utilization in cloud data centres. *IEEE Access*, *7*, 158095–158112.

Njilla, L.L., Ouete, H.N., & Doungwa, K. (2016). Monitoring colluding behaviour in MANETs using game theory. In *Proceedings of the IEEE international workshop on computer aided modelling and design of communication links and networks (CAMAD)*. (pp. 152–153).

Njini, I., & Ekabua, O. O. (2014). Genetic algorithm based energy efficient optimization strategies in wireless sensor networks: A survey. *Advances in Computer Science: An International Journal*, *3*(5), 1–9.

Padmavathi, S., Soniha, P.K., Soundarya, N., & Srimathi, S. (2017). Dynamic resource provisioning and monitoring for cloud computing. In *Proceedings of the IEEE international conference on intelligent techniques in control, optimization and signal processing* (pp. 978–983).

Paladina, L., Biundo, A., Scarpa, M., & Puliafito, A. (2009). Artificial intelligence and synchronization in wireless sensor networks. *Journal of Networks*, *4*(6), 382–391, Academy Publisher.

Praveen Kumar, D., Amgoth, T., & Annavarapu, C. S. R. (2019). Machine learning algorithms for wireless sensor networks: A survey. *Journal of Information Fusion*, *49*, 1–25, Elsevier.

Primeau, N., Falcon, R., Abielmona, R., & Petriu, E. M. (2018). A review of computational intelligence techniques in wireless sensor and actuator networks. *IEEE Communications Surveys and Tutorials*, *20*(04), 2822–2854.

Rakshe, A., Prasad, B., Akshay, V., & Channaveer, C. (2016). Resource management in wireless sensor network. *International Journal on Emerging Technologies*, *7*(2), 293–298.

Ramanathan, N., Balzano, L., Estrin, D., Hansen, M., Harmon, T., Jay, J., ... Gaurav. (2006). Designing wireless sensor networks as a shared resource for sustainable development. In *Proceedings of the IEEE international conference on information and communication technologies and development* (pp. 256–265).

Ramirez, P. L. G., Taha, M., Lloret, J., & Tomas, J. (2019). An intelligent algorithm for resource sharing and self-management of wireless IoT-gateway. *IEEE Access*, *8*, 3159–3170.

Ramson, S.R.J. & Moni, D.J. (2017). Applications of wireless sensor networks—A survey. In *Proceedings of the IEEE international conference on innovations in electrical, electronics, instrumentation and media technology* (pp. 325–329).

Rana, S.N. & Kamboj, P. (2016). Resource utilization based congestion control for wireless sensor network: A review. In *Proceedings of the IEEE international conference on computing for sustainable global development (INDIACom)*.

Rashid, B., & Rehmani, M. H. (2016). Applications of wireless sensor networks for urban areas: A survey. *Journal of Network and Computer Applications*, *60*, 192–219, Elsevier.

Rastegardoost, N. & Jabbari, B. (2018). A machine learning algorithm for unlicensed LTE and WiFi spectrum sharing. In *Proceedings of the IEEE international symposium on dynamic spectrum access networks*.

Rawat, P., Singh, K., Chaouchi, H., & Bonnin, J. M. (2014). Wireless sensor networks: A survey on recent developments and potential synergies. *The Journal of Supercomputing*, *68*(01), 1–48, Springer.

Regini, E., Lim, D., & Rosing, T. S. (2011). Resource management in heterogeneous wireless sensor networks. *Journal of Low Power Electronics*, *7*, 1–18, American Scientific Publishers.

Salahuddin, M. A., Fuqaha, A. A., & Guizani, M. (2016). Reinforcement learning for resource provisioning in vehicular cloud. *IEEE Wireless Communications Journal*, *23*(4), 128–135.

Saranyadevi, C., & Vijayanand, G. (2014). Efficient resource sharing in cloud using neural network. *International Journal of Engineering Research and Applications*, *4*(11), 36–39.

Shah, S.Y., Yuan, Z., Lu, S., & Zerfos, P. (2017). Dependency analysis of cloud applications for performance monitoring using recurrent neural networks. In *Proceedings of the IEEE international conference on big data* (pp. 1534–1543).

Shahdad, S.Y., Sabahath, A., & Parveez, R. (2016). Architecture, issues and challenges of wireless mesh network. In *Proceedings of the IEEE international conference on communication and signal processing* (pp. 0557–0560).

Shakshuki, E.M. & Isiuwe, S. (2018). Resource management approach to an efficient wireless sensor network. In *Proceedings of the ninth international conference on emerging ubiquitous systems and pervasive networks*, Elsevier, Procedia Computer Science (pp.190–198).

Sharma, S., Bansal, R., & Bansal, S. (2013). Issues and challenges in wireless sensor networks. In *Proceedings of the IEEE international conference on machine intelligence research and advancement* (pp. 58–62).

Sharma, V., Gupta, A. K., & Comprehensive, A. (2013). Study of fuzzy logic. *International Journal of Advanced Research in Computer Science and Software Engineering*, *3*(2).

Shelke, R., Kulkarni, G., Sutar, R., Bhore, P., Nilesh, D., & Belsare, S., (2013) Energy management in wireless sensor network. In *Proceedings of the fifteenth IEEE international conference on computer modelling and simulation* (pp. 668–671).

Shen, Y. J., & Wang, M. S. (2008). Broadcast scheduling in wireless sensor networks using fuzzy Hopfield neural network. *Journal of Expert Systems with Applications*, *34*(2), 900–907.

Shi, H. Y., Wang, W. L., Kwok, N. M., & Chen, S. Y. (2012). Game theory for wireless sensor networks: A survey. *Sensors Journal Publishing Corporation*, *12*, 9055–9097.

Sim, K. M. (2019). Agent-based approaches for intelligent intercloud resource allocation. *IEEE Transactions on Cloud Computing*, *7*(2), 1–14.

Strumberger, I., Bacanin, N., Tuba, M., & Tuba, E. (2019). Resource scheduling in cloud computing based on a hybridized whale optimization algorithm. *Journal for Applied Sciences*, *9*, 1–40, MDPI Publisher.

Sulaiman, M., Saleh, B., Saida, R., Kacem, Y. H., & Abid, M. (2020). Wireless sensor network design methodologies: A survey. *Journal of Sensors*, *20*, 01–12, Hindwai.

Surendran, R. & Tamilvizhi, T., (2018). How to improve the resource utilization in cloud data center? In *Proceedings of the IEEE international conference on innovation and intelligence for informatics, computing, and technologies*.

Tahmasebi, P., & Hezarkhani, A. (2012). A hybrid neural networks-fuzzy logic-genetic algorithm for grade estimation. *Journal of Computers and Geosciences*, *42*, 18–27, Elsevier.

Tilak, S., Chiu, K., Ghazaleh, N.B.A., & Fountain, T. (2005). Dynamic resource discovery for wireless sensor networks. In *Proceedings of the international conference embedded and ubiquitous computing* (pp. 785–796).

Trivedi, M., & Somani, H. (2016). A survey on resource provisioning using machine learning in cloud computing. *International Journal of Engineering Development and Research*, *4*(4), 546–549.

Wang, Z., Chen, Y., Liu, B., Yang, H., Su, Z., & Zh, Y. (2019). A sensor node scheduling algorithm for heterogeneous wireless sensor networks. *International Journal of Distributed Sensor Networks*, *15*(1), 1–11, Sage Publisher.

Wei, Y. & Blake, M. (2012). An agent-based services framework with adaptive monitoring in cloud environments. In *Proceedings of the IEEE international workshop on enabling technologies: infrastructure for collaborative enterprises*.

Yang, L., Lu, Y., Liu, S., Guo, T., & Liang, Z. (2018). A dynamic behaviour monitoring game-based trust evaluation scheme for clustering in wireless sensor networks. *IEEE Access*, *6*, 71404–71412.

Yick, J., Mukherjee, B., & Ghosal, D. (2008). Wireless sensor network survey. *Journal of Computer and Telecommunications Networking*, *52*(12), 2292–2330, Elsevier.

Yıldırım, G., & Tata, Y. (2018). Simplified agent-based resource sharing approach for WSN and WSN interaction in IoT/CPS projects. *IEEE Access*, *6*, 78077–78091.

Yousaf, R., Ahmad, R., Ahmed, W., & Haseeb, A. (2017). Fuzzy power allocation for opportunistic relay in energy harvesting wireless sensor networks. *IEEE Access*, *5*, 17165–17176.

Yu, N., Song, Z., Du, H., Huang, H., & Jia, X. (2017). Dynamic resource provisioning for energy efficient cloud radio access networks. *IEEE Transactions on Cloud Computing*, *7*(4).

Yuan, H., Li, C., & Du, M. (2012). Resource scheduling of cloud computing for node of wireless sensor network based on ant colony algorithm. *Information Technology Journal*, *11*, 1638–1643.

Zappone, A., Renzo, M. D., & Debbah, M. (2019). Wireless networks design in the era of deep learning: Model-based, AI-based, or both? *IEEE Transactions on Communications*, *67*(10), 7331–7376.

Zhang, W., Song, B., & Bai, E. (2016). A trusted real-time scheduling model for wireless sensor networks. *Journal of Sensors*, *16*, 01–08, Hindawi Publishing Corporation.

Zhang, Y., Yao, J., & Guan, H. (2017). Intelligent cloud resource management with deep reinforcement learning. *IEEE Cloud Computing*, *4*(6), 60–69.

Zhaofeng, Y., & Aiwan, F. (2016). Application of ant colony algorithm in cloud resource scheduling based on three constraint conditions. *Advanced Science and Technology Letters*, *123*, 215–219.

CHAPTER

4

Swarm intelligence based MSMOPSO for optimization of resource provisioning in Internet of Things

Daneshwari I. Hatti[1,2] and *Ashok V. Sutagundar*[2]

[1]Department of ECE, BLDEA's V.P. Dr. P. G. Halakatti College of Engineering & Technology (Affiliated to VTU Belagavi), Vijayapur, India [2]Department of ECE, Basveshwar Engineering College, Bagalkot, India

4.1 Introduction

In the present context, Internet of Things (IoT) applications are increasing with an increase in demand from users. IoT possessing constraint resource devices processes the sensed data at the cloud. The increased number of devices degrades the performance, leading to communication latency and data traffic. Cloud resources are shared and reallocated by adhering to user demand with the best resource provisioning approach. IoT applications are latency sensitive, and offloading the tasks onto the cloud with reduced latency is challenging. Edge computing and fog computing (FC) paradigms are preferred to reduce the latency and traffic.

FC (Wang, Varghese, Matthaiou, & Nikolopoulos, 2017), as an intermediate layer used for computation, processes the device requests at the edge. Due to resource the limitations and unpredictable behavior of fog devices, resource management at the fog layer has become a challenging issue. Optimization of resources is performed prior to allocation for effective utilization of computational and communication resources.

Due to the billions of devices/things (Ketel, 2017) connected over the network, managing with less service failure is difficult. Intelligence similar to human intelligence among devices is necessary to manage the scarce resources. The strong resemblance of the behavior of devices/things in the IoT network with the behavior of particles in a swarm led to utilization of the working principle of swarm intelligence (SI) in some IoT circumstances. Groups including fish, birds, ants, and other creatures are described as swarms. A swarm is considered as a single network consisting of a population, that is, bees, ants, birds, etc., working in a group that is mapped to the behavior of devices existing in the IoT network. The population of a swarm is assumed to be IoT devices and a few individuals are grouped into one swarm or multiple swarms based on the type of application. Each individual is built in with intelligence and can take decisions by seeking advice from its neighborhood without disturbing the network, before reaches its destination.

Resources are provisioned by employing particle swarm optimization (PSO) without violating service level agreement (SLA) and achieve better quality of service (QoS). Provisioning includes reactive, proactive, and hybrid approaches. Reactive mechanisms involve provisioning of resources based on present workload, whereas proactive refers to the prediction of workload and provisioning.

The proposed work prefers reactive resource provisioning based on cost, energy consumption, bandwidth, and workload.

The objectives of this work are:

1. To minimize the response time: The fog manager searches appropriate fog instance to provision resources for the requested devices based on priority while ensuring a reduced response time.
2. Minimize energy consumption: The service provider manages to provision with reduced energy consumption.
3. To manage bandwidth: The fog manager manages the available bandwidth by balancing workload at the device and offloading to the cloud.

Recent Trends in Computational Intelligence Enabled Research.
DOI: https://doi.org/10.1016/B978-0-12-822844-9.00028-1

4. To maximize resource utilization: The manager has to discover, authenticate, and provision the resources with reduced resource cost and increased resource utilization.

For efficient and optimized provision of resources from the available resources, the proposed scheme is applied. The proposed work plans to share resources and dynamic updates of resources for allocating diverse requests at the fog layer. In view of overcoming the problems that occur during traditional methods of resource provisioning, the proposed work applies the Multi-Swarm-Multi-Objective-Particle-Swarm-Optimization (MSMOPSO) algorithm.

In this work, Multi Objective Particle Swarm Optimization (MOPSO) finds the Pareto optimal solution taking into account multiple objectives such as the response time, energy consumption, and resource cost. To increase the efficiency of system-distributed resource provisioning, authentication and scaling of resources for managing numerous requests is employed. It is evaluated for multiple criteria with effective resource management in the IoT.

4.1.1 Related work

Some works related to resource management in cloud computing, IoT, and FC are as follows. Challenges in resource management, workload management by preprocessing the tasks, and SI-based algorithms for efficient management of resources are surveyed in this section.

Cloud computing is the delivery of extremely scalable IT-related facilities as a service through the Internet to multiple clients (Birje, Challagidad, Goudar, & Tapale, 2017). FC bridges the gap between the cloud and end devices (e.g., IoT nodes) by enabling computing, storage, networking, and data management on network nodes within the close vicinity of IoT devices (Yousefpour et al., 2019). The IoT aims to control the physical real world using a global network constituting heterogeneous smart objects, connected through the Internet (Pico-Valencia & Holgado-Terriza, 2018). Due to the increased demand of IoT devices the processing is not afforded at the IoT tier, hence processing is done at the fog tier and cloud.

Cloud-based resource allocation for the IoT environment is proposed by Ali, Ansari, and Alam (2020) to ensure increased resource utilization by reducing operational cost and energy consumption. Edge computing (Samie, 2018) is proposed for allocating resources using gateways to process the data sensed by IoT devices. Mobile edge computing for dynamic task scheduling and resource management for specific IoT applications with the objective of achieving profit to the service provider is dealt with (Huang, Li, & Chen, 2020). Edge computing is employed for managing the resources at the devices level for reduced latency (Toczé & Nadjm-Tehrani, 2018).

FC is an extension of the cloud computing paradigm ensuring services by virtualized cloud services to the IoT devices at the edge (Ketel, 2017). Prior to the FC paradigm, applications processed at the cloud resulted in huge latency and traffic, and so to overcome this problem applications are processed in the fog layer. The fog layer is comprised of heterogeneous fog devices, namely routers, switches, access points etc. Issues in resource management, task placement, offloading, and balancing at the FC paradigm (Ghobaei-Arani, Souri, & Rahmanian, 2020) are reviewed.

Puranikmath (2017) proposed various resource allocation techniques in IoT. The resource management and routing approaches, QoS, and security approaches are reviewed by the authors (Zahoor & Mir, 2018). In Rahbari and Nickray (2019) the scheduling strategies and Greedy Knapsack-based Scheduling algorithm for allocating resources in wireless sensor networks as IoT applications processed in fog environment are proposed. Resource allocation by decentralized architecture is performed to reduce latency (Avasalcai & Dustdar, 2018). The pervasive IoT applications are managed by resource virtualization through fog, cloud, and mobile computing. Resource virtualization is dealt with by cloud computing and brings some challenging tasks related to resource management.

Resource management imposes challenges in terms of metrics such as energy efficiency, SLA violations, load balancing, network load, and profit maximization. Mustafa, Nazir, Hayat, Khan, and Madani (2015) have addressed works regarding the performance metrics and provided solutions for solving the problems related to SLA violations, load balancing, and network load. Yao and Ansari (2018) proposed a resource provisioning problem in FC with integer linear programming model and Weighted Best Fit Decreasing algorithm for providing services to latency-sensitive applications with minimized cost and failures of services.

Resource scheduling is carried out to manage resources for handling disaster circumstances (Kumar & Zaveri, 2019). Scheduling of servers to provide services to heterogeneous users is done by dynamically adapting to the request of users based on priorities (Narman, Hossain, Atiquzzaman, & Shen, 2017) and implemented with homogeneous/heterogeneous environment considering system performance metrics dropout, throughput, and resource utilization.

The devices in the IoT are distinct in nature. Devices require services, processing elements, and communication bandwidth. The maintenance of devices plays a crucial role in establishing connectivity, and resisting faults and link failures. IoT applications are categorized as hard real time and soft real time, hence scheduling tasks and processing at edge devices taking into consideration restraint resources is essential. Ullah and Youn (2020) proposed a K-means algorithm for classifying the tasks and scheduling based on resource requirements of CPU, I/O, and memory in an edge computing environment. The tasks are scheduled to process at the edge devices with an increased resource utilization of edge devices and nodes execution time. FC leverages the computation and storage facility toward the edge of devices. In addition, the tasks of the devices are preprocessed in view of managing the resources efficiently. Suarez and Salcedo (2017) have classified the devices based on their characteristics using a rule-based decision tree and implemented with an ID3 algorithm. López, Brintrup, Isenberg, and Mansfeld (2011) have argued about clustering of objects to reduce energy consumption and usage of software agents to manage the resources of IoT devices.

SI plays a vital role in regulating the resources in this context as it employs PSO for optimizing the resource usage and meets the criteria of all devices. Naturally, a swarm possesses some features that are comparable to IoT devices features contributing to achieving efficiency in resource management. Some of the features include decentralized, self-adaptation, and searching mechanisms, optimization, and flexibility. Each particle in a swarm collaborates and make decisions based on the fitness value (Sun, Tang, Zhang, Huo, & Shu, 2020). SI-based algorithms and their applications have been reviewed by Hatti and Sutagundar (2019). Particles in a swarm cooperate and take decisions to achieve optimal solution similarly, in the IoT, devices are grouped into a swarm for proper utilization of resources.

Some works related to resource provisioning, task scheduling, and resource allocation using SI have been surveyed. However, the traditional method of resource management in fog, cloud, and at the IoT device layer has been surveyed and the IoT is gaining demand in various applications requiring devices with intelligence inbuilt for decision-making. Ramirez, Taha, Lloret, and Tomas (2020) managed an IoT network with centralized architecture, controlled by artificial intelligence to discover and allocate the resources. Optimization of multiple objectives with constraint PSO-based virtual machine (VM) resource scheduling for cloud computing was proposed by Kumar and Raza (2015) in the allocation of VM to a host or physical machine to minimize resource wastage and the number of servers. They compared the results with best-fit and worst-fit algorithms. Mani and Krishnan (2017) proposed an effective provisioning of resources for minimizing the cost, maximizing the quality parameters, and improving resource utilization. As the device computing requirement is increased, it offers services in less time and has led to an evolution of FC paradigm.

Resource allocation in IoT applications with adaptive distributed artificial intelligence and adaptive particle swarm optimization with objective function as node distance between intercluster and intraclustered sensor nodes and their respective energy loads has been proposed by Mukherjee, Goswami, Yan, Yang, and Rodrigues (2019). Swarm intelligence algorithm Ant Colony Optimization was adopted by Feki, Masmoudi, Belghith, Zarai, and Obaidat (2019) for exploiting available resources among users and meeting the required quality of parameters to reduce the computational complexity in device-to-device communication. For efficient resource utilization, PSO was employed by Sharif, Mercelis, Marquez-Barja, and Hellinckx (2018) to allocate resources in order to improve network performance and cost effectiveness. The data collected from IoT devices have to be processed in the fog or cloud due to insufficient resources at the devices end.

Yadav, Natesha, & Guddeti (2019) proposed genetic algorithms, including PSO for allocating services considering minimal total makespan and energy consumption for IoT applications processed at fog layer. Dynamical Particle Swarm Optimization (ID-PSO) algorithm was used to optimize the allocation of resources in fog-enabled cloud for smart home IoT devices (*Fog Enabled Cloud Based Intelligent Resource Management Approach Using Improved Dynamical Particle Swarm Optimization Model for Smart Home IoT Devices R*, Sudha. Pdf, n.d.). A cloudlet scheduling model has been proposed with the objective of reducing makespan by employing original monarch butterfly optimization (MBO) metaheuristic algorithm and hybrid combination of MBO and Artificial Bee Colony algorithm (Strumberger, Tuba, Bacanin, & Tuba, 2019). Resource management in FC used Novel Bioinspired Hybrid Algorithm for task scheduling, resource allocation in FC to optimize the resource utilization and to minimize the response time and processing cost and results to verify the effectiveness of the proposed approach in terms of energy consumption, processing cost, and response time (Rafique et al., 2019).

Delay-constrained Regional IoT Service Provisioning to assign resources of devices was based on the demand of the regional IoT services in order to maximize users' quality of experience. In situ task scheduling based on a tabu search using first come first serve (FCFS) was employed (Nakamura et al., 2018). FC affords the storage, processing, and analysis of data from cloud computing to a network edge to reduce high latency.

Reduced latency for healthcare application in the IoT using hybrid fuzzy-based reinforcement learning algorithm in a fog computing environment (Shukla, Hassan, Khan, Jung, & Awang, 2019) has been proposed. Resource allocation is performed using a game theoretic approach and ant colony optimization algorithm to search for space for managing emergency services (Wang, Xu, Yang, & Peng, 2009). The processing is carried out using an agent approach for ensuring quality service to the devices in reduced time as devices are enabled with intelligence using an agent embedded as a software program. An agent approach for resource brokering in wireless grids was proposed by Birje, Manvi, and Das (2014).

Several existing works have addressed the agent approach, scheduling the clustered devices, authentication and SI-based provision considering the cost and several other factors. It is imperative to govern the resources for fulfillment of user requests using the SLA with applied intelligence. Some of the limitations of existing resource management in IoT are as follows: lack of intelligence in preprocessing the tasks, distributed provision of resources, periodic updating of resources, provisioning of resources to multiple swarms, and lack of intelligence in authenticating devices.

This work proposes the composite of preprocessing the tasks, authentication, distributed management, and scaling of resources and provision resources taking into account resource utilization, cost, response time, energy consumption, and throughput using agent technology.

4.1.2 Our contributions

Resource scheduling, allocation, provisioning, task placement, and offloading based on traditional methods and a meta-heuristics algorithm are employed for providing the services to heterogeneous and homogeneous devices in IoT. The proposed work differs from others in the following ways: (1) preprocessing of tasks, (2) scaling of resources, and (3) distributed provision of resources using an SI approach and agent technology. In this work the MOMSPSO algorithm using static and dynamic agents is proposed to address the resource provisioning and allocation of tasks to specific resources with a reduction of cost, maximal resource utilization, and reduced energy consumption and latency.

The chapter is organized as follows. The proposed MSMOPSO algorithm for resource provisioning is highlighted in Section 4.2. Section 4.3 discusses the agencies. The simulation procedure and results are discussed in Section 4.4. Finally, Section 4.5 presents the conclusion and future directions.

4.2 Proposed method

Resource provisioning allows users to access the specified resources as per their availability. It includes reactive, proactive, and hybrid provisioning strategies. In this work, a reactive method of resource provisioning is employed ensuring reduced latency and increased resource utilization. To overcome the problem of under- and over-provisioning, the proposed work is applied for allocating tasks and authenticating devices to reduce wastage of valuable resources. FC leverages the enactment of IoT devices close to the user's location and reduces latency. An SI approach is employed for managing the resources in a distributed way because a centralized approach consumes extra time. The algorithm processes multiple swarms and fog colonies paralleling the provision of resources based on cost, energy consumption, resource utilization, and response time.

The proposed algorithm addresses multiobjective optimization with decentralized management of devices by embedding intelligence. This model includes (1) swarms and fog colonies formation using K-means, (2) applying MOPSO for multiple swarms, (3) resource provisioning based on fitness matrix, (4) applying a modified best-fit algorithm to allocate new tasks in suitable fog instances, and (5) estimated resource cost, energy consumption, and resource utilization. In this section on the network environment, agencies at the device and fog for processing the tasks, authentication, and provisioning the resources are described.

4.2.1 Network environment

The network model consists of three tiers at the bottom, the IoT layer, at the middle the fog layer, and at the top the cloud layer. IoT devices include sensors, vehicles, smart phones, human beings, etc. The fog layer constitutes fog devices such as routers, access points, and surveillance cameras. The cloud is comprised of high computing servers, storage units, etc. The devices in the IoT layer sense the environment, and data sensed are collected at the fog layer for processing. The resources required for processing, if not available at the fog, are forwarded to the cloud. Processing of data and required services are provided by the fog and cloud using the proposed algorithm. The proposed MSMOPSO for provisioning resources at the fog layer includes (1) at the bottom layer, devices with heterogeneous capacity and clustered using K-means algorithm (Suarez & Salcedo, 2017) by initializing the nearest device as centroid, (2) multiple swarms constituting devices are created to work in parallel and efficiency is increased as discussed by authors (Röhler, Chen, & 2011, 2011). Similar to swarms, fog devices with varied capacity are clustered to form a fog colony. (3) The distance is computed between each swarm and fog colony. (4) The nearest fog colony is selected to provide the resources based on response time, CPU, memory requirement, and bandwidth. Taking into account the above objectives, MOPSO is applied to compute the best fitness value. (5) In the intervening time, the nearest fog instance with maximum resources is allocated to the tasks

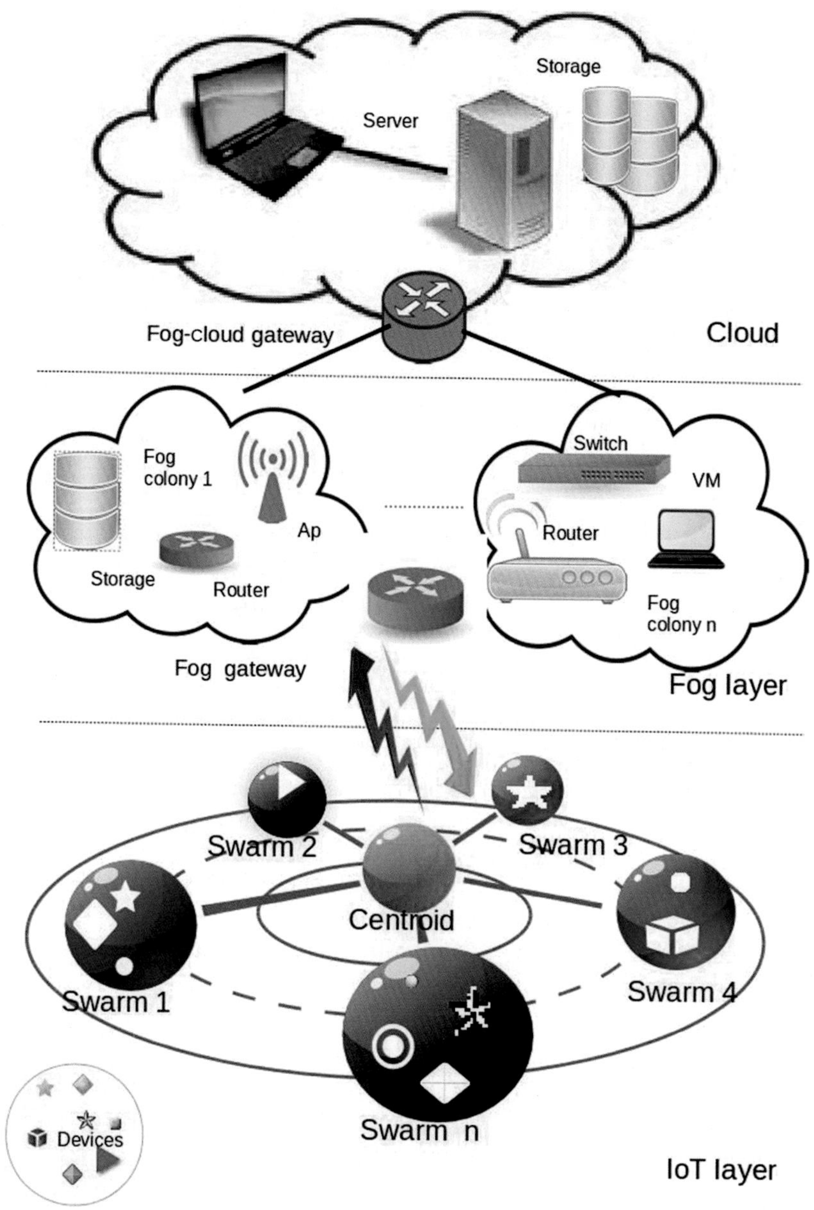

FIGURE 4.1 Illustration of resource provision in the network environment.

attaining maximal resource utilization and reduced resource cost. The network environment is shown in Fig. 4.1.

The sequence of steps employed is detailed in the flowchart shown in Fig. 4.2.

4.2.1.1 *Creation of swarms*

The authentication of devices is performed by a software token approach. Authenticated devices id and their positions are updated in DKB. Swarms are formed by clustering the devices located in the area of $x \times x$ (m^2). The centroid is initialized randomly, the devices near to the centroid limited to boundary region of $n \times n$ (m^2) are grouped into a swarm. The Euclidean distance using Eq. (4.7) is used for finding the nearest device position. All the distances are computed and updated in the matrix of $[n \times m]$. Rows in the matrix refer to swarm and columns depict fog colonies. Algorithm 4.1 is used for clustering diverse devices and fog instances. Fog devices existing in the area of $m \times m$ (m^2) are clustered to form fog colonies. Fog colonies constitute diverse resource capacity fog instances for provisioning the requests. This leads to a combination of distinct resources in every fog colony for providing the services to any type of request. Devices in a swarm bind to the fog colony by taking reference of the matrix and fitness value obtained by considering multiobjectives such as response time, CPU, memory, and bandwidth.

Fig. 4.3 shows the cluster of devices represented as a swarm and Fig. 4.4 shows the grouping of fog instances

ALGORITHM 4.1 Formation of swarms using K-means

{Si, Fi} = K-means {no of tasks, no of fog instances}

Begin
Step 1: Consider no. of tasks = {T1, T2...Tn} area of [n n] to form swarm Si = {S1,S2,...Sn no. of fog instances = {f1, f2,...fn} area of [m m] to form fog colony Fci = {Fc1,Fc2,...Fcn}
Step 2: SMA randomly select "n" clusters centers for creating swarm of tasks
Si = {S1, S2,...Sn} and fog colonies Fci = {Fcl, Fc2...Fcn} using Euclidean distance [Eq. (4.7)]
Step 3: Calculate distance between each swarm and fog colony using Eq. (4.7)
Step 4: Assign the swarm to fog colonies
Step 5: Update the swarm based on arrival tasks with new centroid
Step 6: Repeat step 5 at the scheduled interval by fetching information from DMA
End

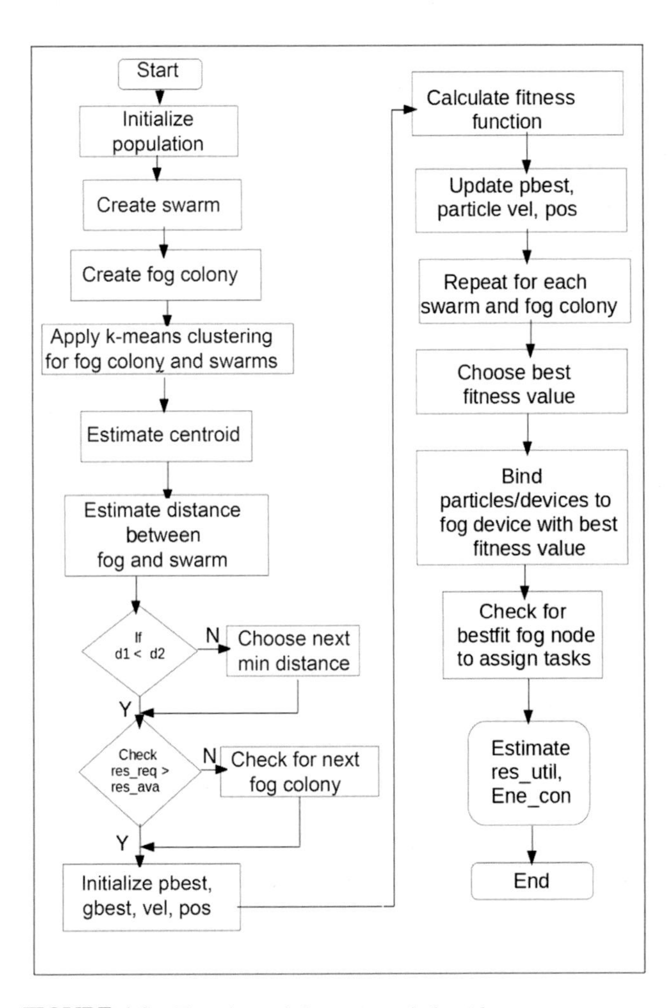

FIGURE 4.2 Flowchart of the proposed algorithm.

forming a fog colony. The number of fog instances is limited to 15 for each fog colony comprising "i" fog instance with diverse resources capacity in area of $m \times m$. The number of device tasks in a swarm is varied from 30 to 100, with varied resource requirement in area $n \times n$. Fig. 4.5 shows the clustered fog instance in fog colonies and swarms with devices in area $x \times x$ (m^2). After clustering, the MOPSO is applied for providing resources with optimization of the performance parameters.

4.2.1.2 *Multi-swarm multi-objective particle swarm optimization*

Swarm intelligence-based particle swarm optimization is applied in many applications listed Sun et al. (2020), and is applied for the proposed work to optimize the performance parameters. In this work additionally multiple swarms are formed to process the tasks in parallel along with MOPSO and modified best-fit algorithm. PSO consists of "i" particles with velocity "vi," and position "Pp^i," has memory for storing previous best, inertia factor, social, cognitive acceleration coefficient in range [0 1] and helps in converging to obtain the best solution with few iterations. A swarm of ants, bees, or birds moves in search of good-quality food, with every individual in the swarm searching and finally following the global best solution obtained together with a swarm. Every individual searches for a food and saves it as the local best "p_best," and updates its position by traversing to a new position "Pp^{i+1}" with velocity "vi^{t+1}." The particles are updated with new velocity and position and continue to reach g_best. Optimization of this searching process is performed by varying inertia and coefficients to reach g_best in less iterations. Using Eq. (4.1), the particle position is updated and velocity is updated by Eq. (4.2) (Talukder, 2011). Fig. 4.6 shows the particle velocity and position updating to reach p_best and g_best. In this context, the particle position is expressed as the device position, it searches the search space to find the appropriate fog instance recorded as p_best, and updates the velocity to reach g_best. g_best is the nearest fog instance possessing resources greater than or equal to the resource required.

$$Pp^{i+1} = Pp^i + vi^{t+1}; \forall Pp^i \in R\{\min, \max\} \quad (4.1)$$

where Pp^{i+1} is a new position obtained by Eq. 4.1 using present position and velocity vi^{t+1} at $t+1$ subject to a condition that the particle should be in the range of a particular swarm.

$$vi_j^{t+1} = vi_j^t + a_1 r_{1j}^t (p\_best_i^t - Pp_{ij}^t) + a_2 r_{2j}^t (g\_best - Pp_{ij}^t) \quad (4.2)$$

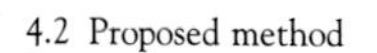

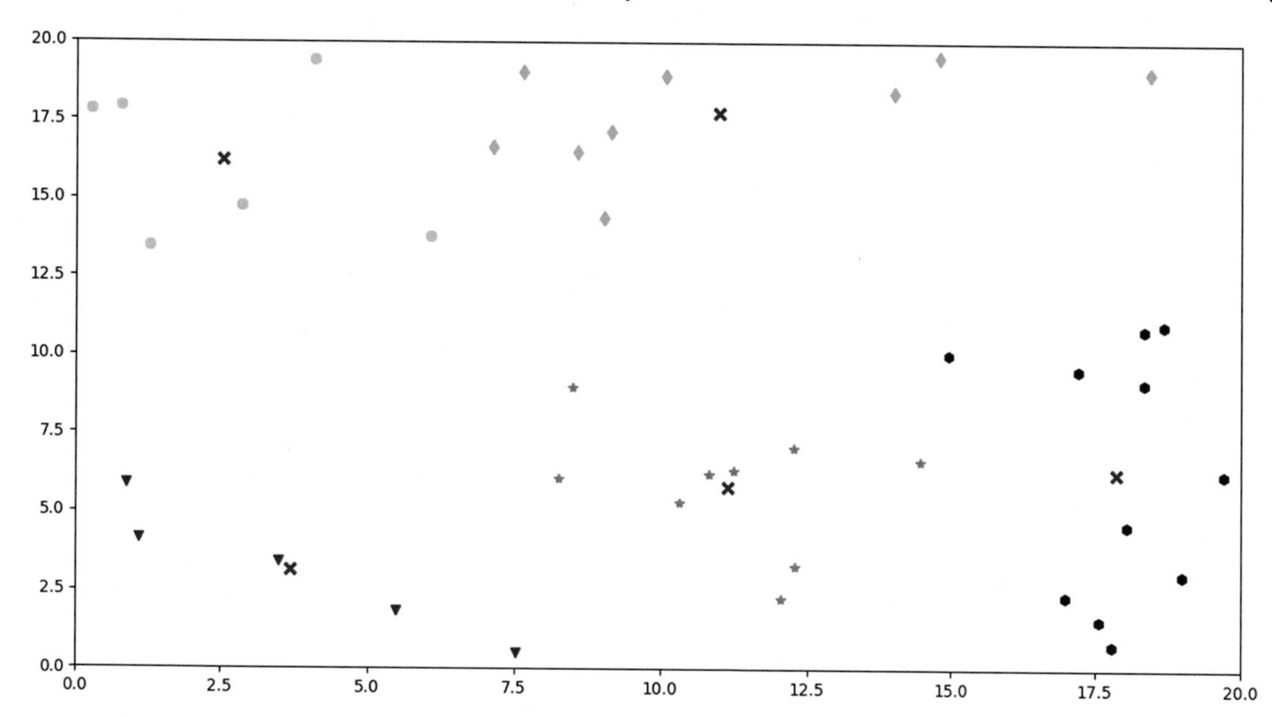

FIGURE 4.3 Clustered tasks using K-means clustering.

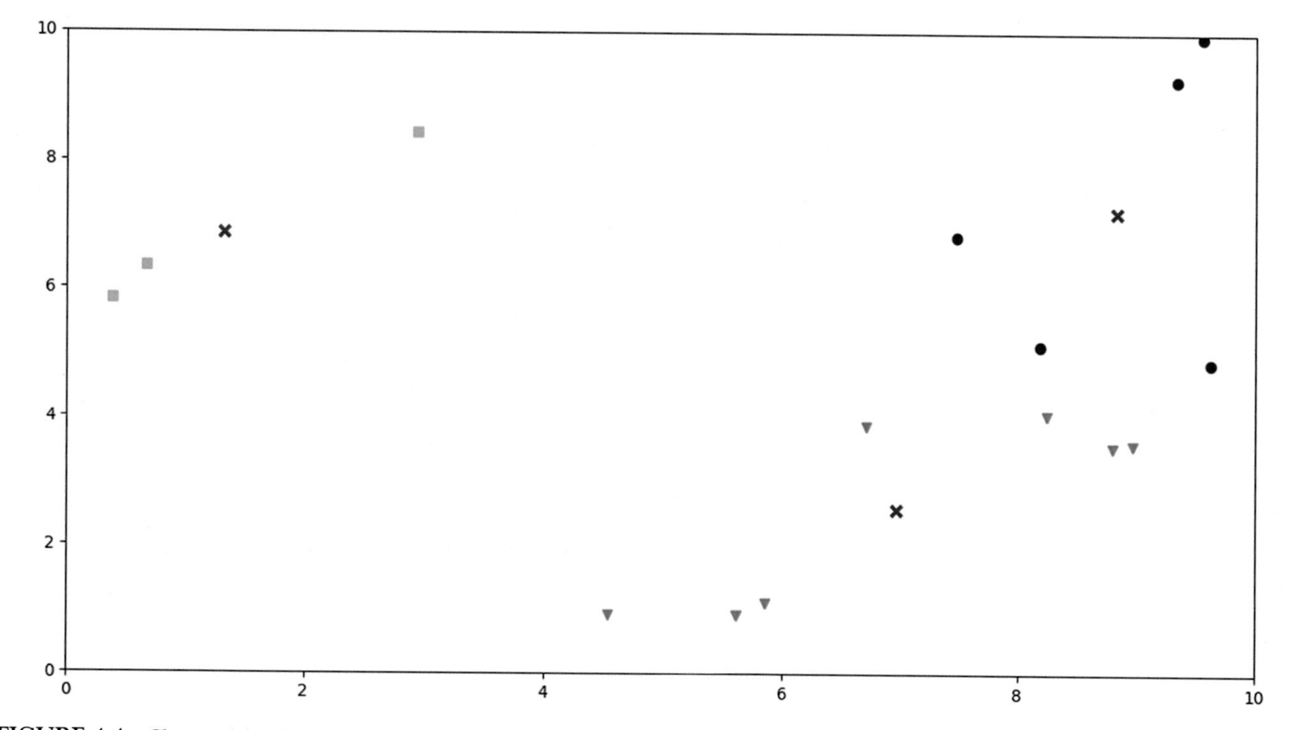

FIGURE 4.4 Clustered fog devices using K-means clustering.

where

vi_j^{t+1} is the pdated velocity in dimension j at time $t+1$;

vi_j^t is the present velocity of particle in dimension j at current time t;

$a_1 r_{1j}^t$, $a_2 r_{2j}^t$ are the product of acceleration coefficients and random distribution in range [0 1];

$p\_best_i^t$ is the particle best solution;

Pp_{ij}^t is the particle position at current time "t";

and $g_best$is the global best solution of a swarm.

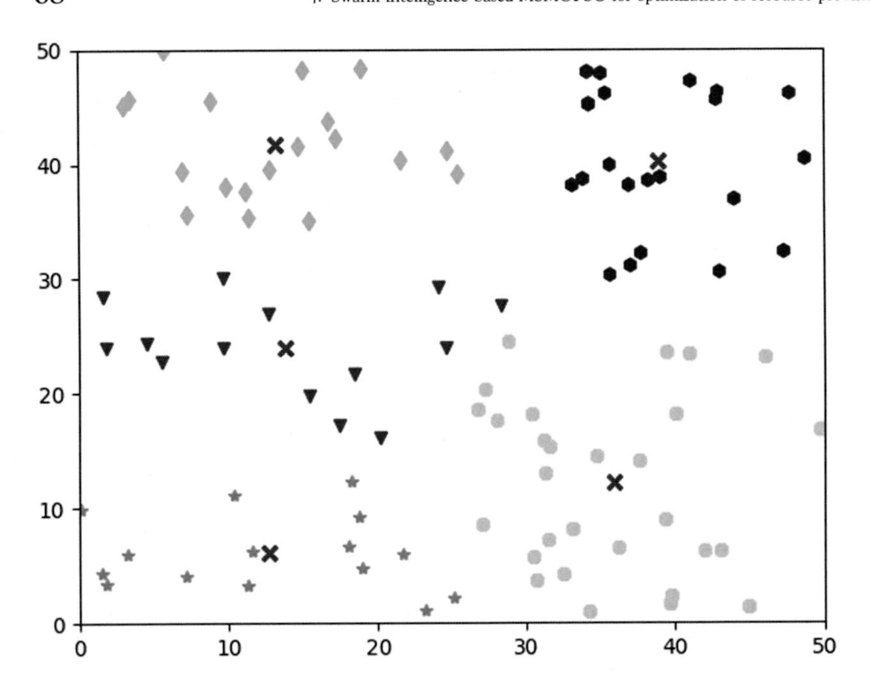

FIGURE 4.5 Clustered tasks and fog devices using K-means clustering.

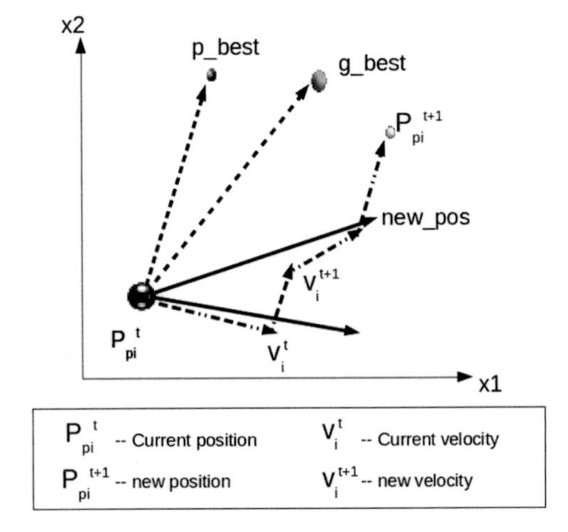

FIGURE 4.6 Illustration of particle velocity and position update.

In this work, PSO is applied to provision the resources based on resp_time (α), resource requirement CPU (β), and bandwidth (γ) usage with reduced energy consumption and resource cost. PSO is applied for single objective optimization but a compromise between other objectives is intolerant. For minimizing this problem PSO is used for multi-objectives with few constraints. MOPSO is comprised of several methods surveyed by authors (Talukder, 2011).

The provisioning of resources is done by estimating the fitness value using the weighted PSO method. The weights are varied based on the type of applications. For example, the applications are computational sensitive and then processing capacity is assigned as high priority and optimization of CPU is dealt with for data processing and storage is prioritized. Priority of all sorts of applications is handled by weighted PSO (Talukder, 2011). In the proposed work weighted PSO is applied at the fog agency for provisioning of resources to the tasks based on the best fitness value calculated taking into consideration the multiobjectives represented in Eq. (4.8).

$$pi = \{\alpha, \beta, \gamma\} \tag{4.3}$$

where pi = {res_tim, MI, BW} for each task of a device in a swarm.

$$\text{fog\_}i = \{\delta, \varepsilon, \lambda\} \tag{4.4}$$

Fog_i = {proc_time, MIPS, BW} of fog instance in each fog colony.

$$\delta = \frac{\beta}{\varepsilon} \tag{4.5}$$

Proc_time = pi_MI/fog_i_MIPS

$$x\text{\_del} = \delta + d_{ij} \tag{4.6}$$

where x_del is the total delay calculated by summation of processing time estimated at particular fog instance and propagation delay calculated by applying Euclidean distance measurement shown in Eq. (4.7).

$$d_{ij} = \sqrt{(f\_ix - t\_ix)^2 (f\_iy - t\_iy)^2} \tag{4.7}$$

where d_{ij} is the distance between fog instance and swarm, (f_ix, f_iy) is the coordinates of the i-th fog instance and (t_ix, t_iy) is the coordinates of the i-th devices in the j dimension.

The fitness function represented in Eq. (4.8) is used for computation of the best solution taking into account multiobjectives for minimizing energy consumption, resource cost, and maximal resource utilization by optimizing CPU usage, BW usage, and provision resources with reduced response time.

$$\text{fit\_fun} = A * \left[\frac{\text{x\_del}}{\alpha}\right] + B * \left[\frac{\beta/\alpha}{\varepsilon}\right] + C * \left[\frac{\gamma}{\lambda}\right] \quad (4.8)$$

A, B, and C are the weights assigned according to the priority of the tasks. If the task priority is response time, then the A value is set to 0.5 and B decides the processing factor and C is for the bandwidth factor. If the tasks are hard real time then priority is given to A then B, and finally C. Here $A = 0.5$, $B = 0.4$, and $C = 0.3$ are chosen to evaluate the performance of various tasks with heterogeneous requirements. The particle velocity and position are updated according to Eqs. (4.1)and (4.2). The proposed work is represented in Algorithm 4.2.

ALGORITHM 4.2 Proposed work (MSMOPSO)

Input: *Tasks of devices T = {T1, T2,. . .Tn}; Swarm Si = {S1,S2. . .Sn};*
Res_req = {MI, BW, RAM}; Fog colonies Fi = {F1, F2. . .Fn}; Fog_inst$_i$ = {f1,f2. . .fi1};
f1 = {MIPS, BW, RAM}
Output: *p_best, g_best, fitness value (index)*

Begin
Step 1: Randomly generate devices with heterogeneous resource capacity and requirement in area of $x \times x$ m^2
Step 2: **{Si, Fi} = K-means** {no of tasks, no of fog instances}
Step 3: Tasks from the devices are clustered in to swarms *Si = {S1{T11, T21,. Ti1}},{S2{{T12, T22,. Ti2}}, {S3{ T13, T23,. Ti3}}, {S4{ T14, T24,. Ti4}}*
Step 4: Cluster fog virtual instances in to fog colonies
Fi = {F1{f11,f21. . .fi1};{F2{f12,f22. . .fi2};{F3{f13,f23. . .fi3};
For Si, i 1 to n
Calculate the distance between Si and Fi using Eq. (4.7)
Construct a matrix mat_Si_Fi = {row = swarms and columns = fog colonies}
Collect resource requirement through DMA and store in DKB
Update resource availability of fog colonies in FKB
for mat_Si_Fi i 1 to n
for mat_Si_Si j 1 to n
If res_req < res_aval
For Si {Ti1} i 1 to n
p_best_i = **MOPSO** *(res_req, res_ava, dij)*
g_best = min{p_best_1,p_best_2. . .p_best_n}
if Fi_res < req_res
[Ti,fi] = **bestfit***{res_req,res_ava$_t$, dij}*
end
end loop
end
end loop
end loop
Step 5: Get the fitness value from MOPSO and bind virtual instances to tasks of devices
Step 6: Set cloudlet/task scheduler as space shared and fog virtual instance scheduler as time shared
Step 7: Apply power linear model for evaluating energy consumption
Step 8: Initialize costperbw, costperproc, costperram
Step 9: Start the simulation, at scheduled intervals, get resource utilization summary, energy consumption, resource cost, and execution time
END

In Algorithm 4.2, fog colonies $F_i = \{F_1, F_2 ... F_n\}$ and tasks/cloudlets in swarm $S_i = \{S_1, S_2, ... S_n\}$ are represented. The minimum distance between each fog colony and swarm is calculated and referred to as p_best. All fog colony and swarm minimum distances are recorded at fog knowledge base (FKB) and among those the minimum it is assigned as g_best. After choosing g_best corresponding matrix $m \times n$ is framed. Here "m" is jobs/tasks and "n" refers to fog colonies. The corresponding swarm and fog colony is mapped with the least minimum distance. Each task of swarms is allocated to a specific fog instance of fog colony by obtaining the g_best obtained through Algorithm 4.2. The p_best is calculated as the minimum distance and maximum resource utilization meeting criteria obtained by Eq. (4.8). All requested devices and mapped fog colony, distances, and resource capacity are updated in FKB. Every fit_fun is p_best and accordingly the position and velocity are updated. If previous p_best is less than the current p_best, then the position and velocity are not updated and they are retained with the previous values. To find g_best, the lowest of all p_best is obtained. The requests sent to individual fog instance is not processed then the request is scheduled among nearest fog instances of fog colonies. If the request does not have sufficient resources at allocated fog instance then it is forwarded to the cloud. Resources are provisioned to the tasks meeting the resource requirement with the best fitness value. If the resources required and availability matching is more than 50% the tasks are subdivided and scheduled among the nearest fog instances in the same fog colony, and if matching is less than 50% between the resource requirement and what is available, the request is sent to the cloud for processing that incurs a high resource cost and energy consumption.

ALGORITHM 4.3 Illustration of the estimation of best solution using MOPSO in each swarm.

g_best = MOPSO (res_req, res_ava, dij)

Begin
Step 1: Initialize (S_i,v_i, Pp_i, p_best, g_best)
Step 2: *for pi in T*
Step 3: *for fi in Fi*
Step 4: fit_fun = Compute fitness (Ti,fi) using Eq. (4.8)
Step 5: p_best = (fit_fun(Ti))
Step 6: Update velocity (vi) using Eq. (4.1)
Step 7: Update position (Pp_i) using Eq. (4.2)
Step 8: *End*
Step 9: *End*
Step 10: g_best = min (p_best1, p_best2...p_besti)
End

After provisioning the resources from fog colonies the remaining resources are updated in FKB. Device-tracking agent (DTA) sends the request of newly arrived tasks to fog manager agent (FMA). FMA adapts to the available resources and provisions by applying MSMOPSO. Resources left after provisioning to the arrived request are handled by a modified best-fit algorithm. Algorithm 4.4 is modified best-fit searched for the best nearest fog instance with maximum resources required for executing the newly arrived tasks.

4.2.1.3 *Best-fit approach*

This approach benefits in allocating the best fog instance to new incoming tasks. Utilization is increased by allocating the available resources among devices in the next iteration. The best-fit approach for finding the nearest best fog instance to process the incoming tasks is illustrated in Algorithm 4.4.

ALGORITHM 4.4 Best-fit approach for allocation of resources to the newly arrived tasks

***[Ti,fi]* = bestfit** *{res_req,res_ava$_t$, dij}*

Begin
Step 1: DMA updates DKB
Step 2: DTA checks DKB and FKB
Step 3: *for* **Ti_req < fi_ava**
Step 4: dij = min (d11, d12,...d1n)
Step 5: Allocates Ti to fi with min dij
Step 6: Repeat for all unallocated tasks
End
Step 7: *if res_req > res_av(fi)*
Step 8: send request to Cloud
End
End

4.3 Agency

The proposed work includes agencies in the devices and at the fog comprising static and mobile agents. The processing is performed by added intelligence among the devices at the IoT and fog. Decisions are taken by agents embedded in the devices. This section describes the agencies and agent communication for provisioning of resources.

4.3.1 Device agency

This includes the device manager agent (DMA), device knowledge base (DKB), and swarm manager agent (SMA). DMA and DKB are static agents, and SMA is a mobile agent. The interaction among agents is depicted in Fig. 4.7.

Device manager agent: The DMA is a static agent that exits the devices. It creates a static agent DKB and mobile agent SMA. The arrival of devices, their characteristics, and types of tasks requested are collected by the DMA. The DMA fetches the information regarding the registration of the devices, its id, position and capacity of devices, and resource requirement. After fetching it updates DKB. The incoming device identity is authenticated by the DMA and keeps it in track in a queue at the time of processing by the swarm. At every scheduled interval, the devices are updated in the DKB.

Device knowledge base: This is a static agent created by the DMA. This agent gets updates from the DMA agent. The agents in fog can access this DKB for reading and writing the resource configuration of tasks using the DTA. The DKB is updated at every

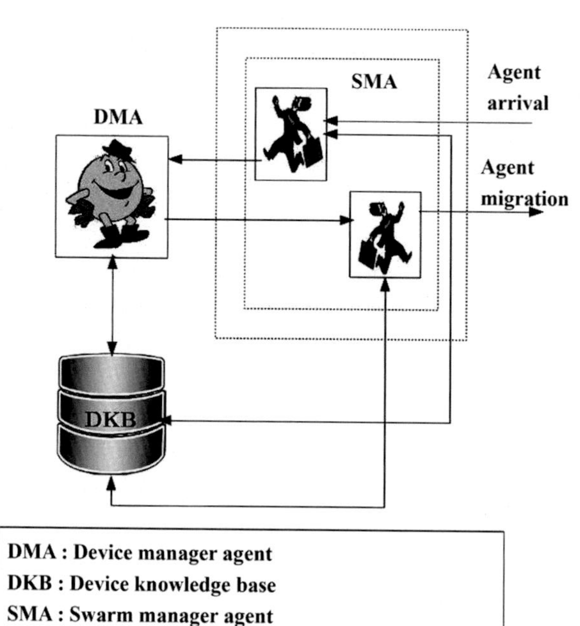

FIGURE 4.7 Device agency.

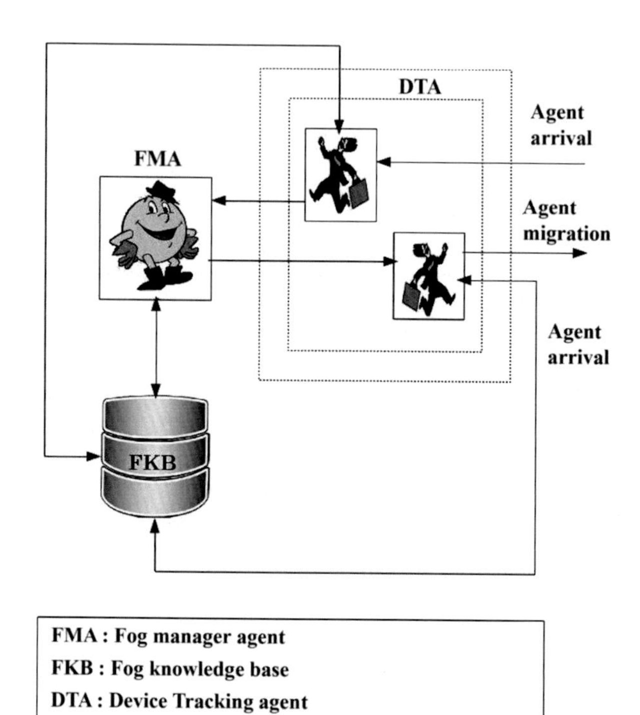

FIGURE 4.8 Fog agency.

scheduled interval by DMA. The requirement for task execution, resource utilization history, task failure and success, and execution time of particular device tasks is updated in the DKB and can be used by other agents to provision the resources to the incoming tasks.

Swarm manager agent: This is a mobile agent that adapts to the dynamic variation of incoming devices. Once the devices are authenticated by the DMA it stores in the DKB. The SMA clusters these devices into swarms. The number of devices is limited to 30–40 for converging in less iteration. If particles have more or less convergence they should be attained with a proper count of iterations. The SMA decides the number of clusters to be framed for efficient implementation of the proposed work. The number of swarms to be framed is done by fetching the information of devices from the DKB. The SMA employs K-means clustering. Consider "n" as number of swarms and deployed devices possessing heterogeneous resources randomly in the area of $n \times n$ (m^2). The swarm is updated based on incoming devices. It estimates the distance between the swarm center and all devices, updates to the DKB, and recenters if new devices are registered by the DMA. The SMA collects information of newly entered devices from the DKB at every scheduled interval. The devices in a swarm store their resource requirement information in the DKB, with device ids and requirements tracked by the DTA with updates to the FKB for processing.

4.3.2 Fog agency

This consists of two static and one mobile agent. These include the FMA, DTA, and FKB. The FMA and FKB are static agents and the DTA is a mobile agent. This section describes the agent approach and agent communication at the fog layer to supervise the resources. Fig. 4.8 depicts the fog agency.

Fog manager agent: The static agent FMA resides in fog instances, and manages the device requests and provision resources based on the solution obtained through MSMOPSO. The FMA creates the DTA and FKB for tracking incoming requests and stores resource usage of devices. The FMA receives information of device requests for resources and Algorithm 4.1 is employed for provisioning resources based on multiobjectives to achieve lower energy consumption and resource cost. The FMA assigns the best fog instance to deliver resources for the requested devices and computes available resources after first iteration, and the same is updated to the FKB. The DTA gets information from the DKB and updates the FKB. The FKB can be read by the FMA and fetches information from the swarm and its requirements.

Fog knowledge base: This is a static agent that holds particulars of the swarm and fog instance. The resource capacity of a fog instance in a fog colony is updated in the FKB by the FMA. At completion of iteration resources are estimated and stored in the FKB. This includes the information of distance matrix calculated between fog colonies to swarms, and the relevant resource characteristics of a fog instance. It aggregates the resource configuration of a fog instance in the FKB at scheduled intervals. Likely resources are utilized in completion of tasks for assuring demand of users is met efficiently.

Device-tracking agent: This is a mobile agent created by the FMA. The DTA tracks information of arrival tasks from the DKB and forwards it to the FKB. It moves between the fog agency and device agency. This agent helps to communicate between multiagents by updating the DKB and FKB. It tracks recent requests, updates the FKB and DKB, and allocates and provides resources according to the solution obtained by the proposed algorithm.

4.3.3 Example scenario

In this section, the IoT–fog–cloud environment for processing the IoT applications is illustrated by a sequence diagram. The operation of the proposed MSMOPSO algorithm is shown in Fig. 4.9.

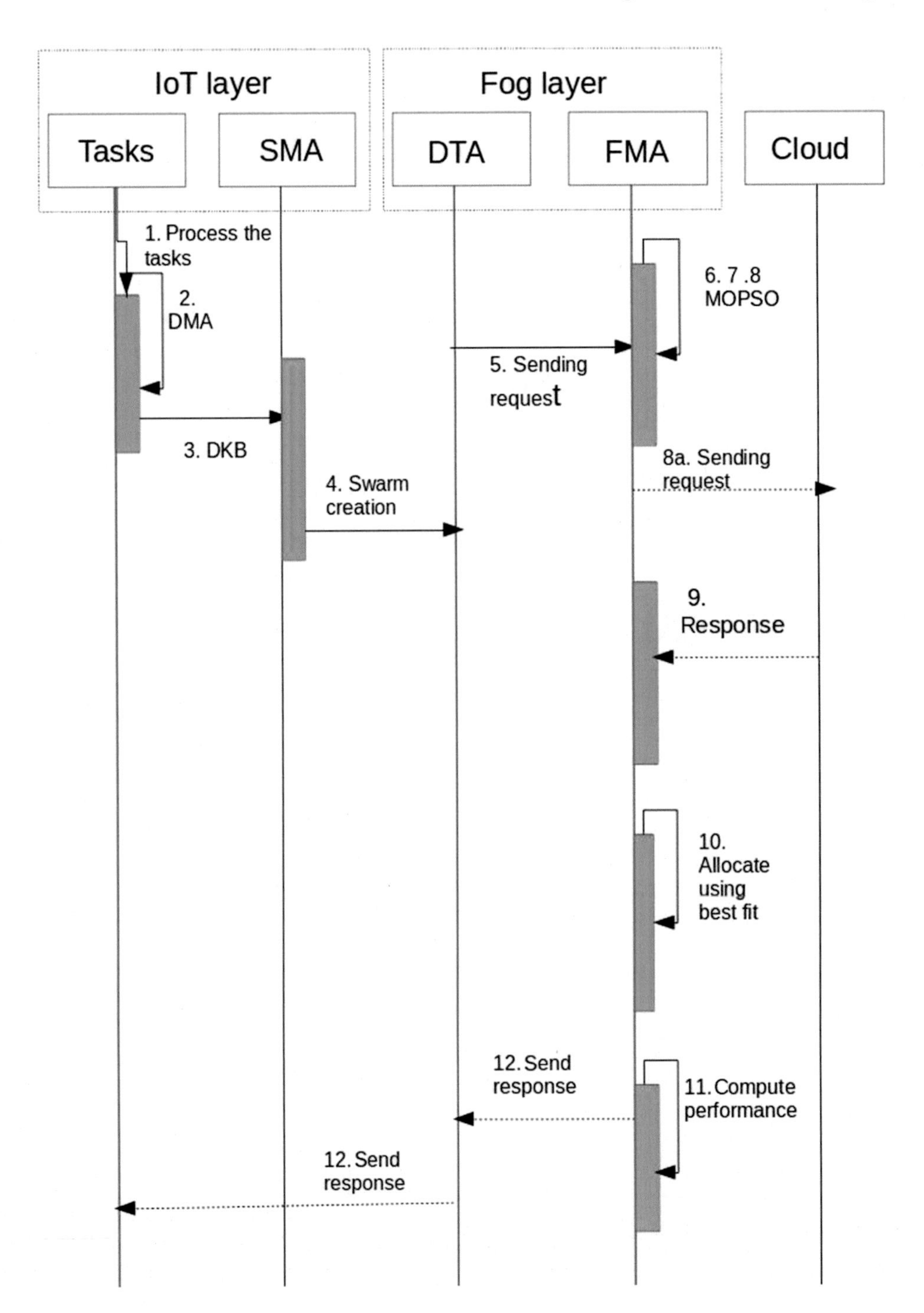

FIGURE 4.9 Sequence diagram.

An example scenario is shown in Fig. 4.9, where the numbering indicates the sequence steps involved for operation of the proposed MSMOPSO algorithm. It comprises of devices in IoT, fog devices, and cloud nodes.

1. Processing of users/devices at the device level.
2. The requests are monitored by the DMA and it authenticates the entered devices into the network.
3. The DKB is created by the DMA; after authentication the characteristics and requirements of devices are updated in the DKB.
4. The SMA is created by the DMA and explores new devices in the search space of $x \times x$ (m^2) and adapts to form appropriate swarms of jobs/tasks.
5. The DMA creates the DTA for tracking the devices and sends requests to the FMA for processing.
6. The FKB is created by the FMA to store the requests. The FMA at the fog layer fetches the information from the FKB to compute the distance between each swarm and fog colony.
7. The FMA maps the nearest fog colony with maximal capability to swarm.
8. MOPSO is applied by the FMA to the best fog instances in the fog colony to provision the resources to tasks present in a swarm.
   a. If adequate resources are extinct at the fog instance then the request is forwarded to the cloud.
9. Responses are forwarded to the FMA.
10. A modified best-fit algorithm is applied to allocate recently added tasks with suitable fog instance.
11. Compute energy consumption (Joules), execution time (ms), and resource cost, resource utilization (step 10) using Eqs. (4.9)–(4.12).
12. The response is sent to the users.

To evaluate the proposed algorithm various characteristics are varied and performance measures are presented in next section.

4.4 Simulation

To simulate the proposed model, CloudSim Plus is used for simulating. CloudSim Plus (Silva Filho, Oliveira, Monteiro, Inácio, & Freire, 2017) is a simulation framework that offers the dynamic creation of cloudlets and virtual machines during runtime, and scaling of resources as per user requirements. In comparison to CloudSim, CloudSim Plus includes extended features and executes in a shorter time. The proposed algorithm is applied, simulated for various scenarios to evaluate the performance measures, and performs better than existing algorithms. This section discusses the simulation procedure, performance metrics, and results.

4.4.1 Simulation inputs

Simulation is performed using CloudSim Plus, Eclipse, and PyCharm editor tool. The parameters for simulating the environment are listed in Tables 4.1 and 4.2.

Table 4.3 lists the characteristics of various applications. The network environment is simulated with the proposed algorithm by setting the fog server configurations and hardware requirements as shown in Table 4.4. Resource provisioning is performed using MSMOPSO for varied capacity and number of fog instances by employing cloudlet time shared and space-shared scheduling policies. The allocation of tasks is performed through a modified best-fit approach. The proposed work is compared with different scheduling and allocation mechanisms such as best-fit, first-fit, and worst-fit algorithms. The proposed work performs better in terms of resource cost, energy consumption, and number of executed cloudlets/tasks.

The simulation results are evaluated and monitor the resource utilization of each fog instance,

TABLE 4.1 Fog layer parameters.

Parameter	Fog	Cloud
No. of fog nodes	5–15	3
CPU MIPS	500–2500	4000–10000
BW cost ($)	0.05	1.0
Processing cost ($)	0.1	1.0

TABLE 4.2 Properties of tasks/cloudlets.

No. of tasks/cloudlets	30–100
Cloudlets MI	500–1000
Memory	256–1024 MB
Input/output file size	600 MB

TABLE 4.3 Types of application.

Application	Cloudlet length (MI)
Sensed data	200
Audio	500
Healthcare data (images)	1000

TABLE 4.4 Configuration and characteristics of hardware units.

System configuration	
System	Intel core i5, 2.3 GHz
Memory	6 GB
Operating system	Ubuntu 16.04
Fog servers and cloud characteristics	
Software	CloudSim Plus
IDE	Eclipse, PyCharm
Architecture	X86
VM	Xen
Datacenter configuration and hardware requirements	
Hosts	3
No. of processing units	8
Processing capability (MIPS)	1000
Storage (MB)	1 TB
Memory size (MB)	20,480,000
Bandwidth (Mbps)	200,000

TABLE 4.5 Simulation parameters.

Parameter	Value
Inertia factor (w)	0.4
Acceleration coefficient (a1)	0.9
Social cognitive factor (a2)	0.9
Target error	0.00001
Swarm area in "$n \times n$"	20×20
Fog colony area "$m \times m$"	10×10
Number of swarm	5
Number of fog colony	3
Fog instance capacity (vmsmall)	500–600 MIPS, 400–600 Mbps
Fog instance capacity (vmmed)	1500–1600 MIPS, 600–800 Mbps
Fog instance capacity (vmhigh)	2400–2500 MIPS, 800–1024 Mbps
Response time	10–40 ms

resource cost, and energy consumption by setting the parameters listed in Table 4.5. The performance measures and results are discussed in the preceding sections.

4.4.2 Simulation procedure

Algorithm 4.5 presents the simulation steps for evaluating the proposed work using the CloudSim Plus framework. The MSMOPSO algorithm is applied for varied capacity of fog instances and diverse requirement by the cloudlets/tasks.

ALGORITHM 4.5 Simulation algorithm

Begin
Step 1: Deploy randomly heterogeneous devices with diverse resource capacity
Step 2: Authenticate the incoming devices
Step 3: Apply Algorithm 4.1 for forming swarms.
Step 4: Apply Algorithms 4.2 and 4.3
Step 5: Track the new devices for scheduled interval and apply Algorithm 4.4
Step 6: Estimate the performance of the system using Eqs. (4.9)–(4.14)
Step 7: Repeat for a few iterations to execute more cloudlets/tasks to optimize resource utilization and minimize resource cost
End

4.4.3 Performance measures

This section depicts the performance measures that are used to evaluate the proposed model. The estimation of resource cost, resource utilization, energy consumption, and execution time is discussed in this section.

4.4.3.1 Cost

The tasks are executed in fog instances with reduced resource cost and maximum resource utilization. The total cost is estimated by considering the bandwidth and processing cost. Tasks/jobs processed at the fog layer require less cost and latency compared to the cloud. Total cost incurred by the cloudlet is estimated by Eq. (4.9). The processing cost and bandwidth cost at the fog layer are considered as 0.1$ and 0.05$ for each unit, respectively. The processing cost and bandwidth cost at the cloud layer are considered as 1.0$ and 1.0$, respectively, for each unit.

$$\begin{aligned} C_P &= t \times \text{cpu\_usage} \times c_p \\ C_B &= t \times \text{bw\_usage} \times c_b \\ C &= C_P + C_B + C_{pre} \end{aligned} \tag{4.9}$$

where C_P is the cost for processing each task and c_p is the cost per unit, C_B is the cost for bandwidth usage by each task and c_b is the cost per unit, C_{pre} is the cost incurred by agent interaction and processing across several agents, t is the time duration for which resources are used, and C is the total cost incurred by each task execution. Cost C_s for the proposed network environment is obtained by summing the cost of n

cloudlets costing Ci in i number of swarms using Eq. (4.10).

$$C_s = \sum_{i=1}^{5} \sum_{i=1}^{n} Ci \tag{4.10}$$

The proposed algorithm is evaluated by varying the number of cloudlets and task length, and also varying fog instance capacity and numbers.

4.4.3.2 Resource utilization

Uniform utilization of fog instance resources is achieved by the proposed algorithm. The resource utilization of fog instances is calculated by Eq. (4.11).

$$\text{rs\_util} = \sum_{\forall j\_fcol} \sum_{j=1}^{n} \frac{c\_\text{req}}{f\_\text{ava}} \tag{4.11}$$

where rs_util is resource utilization (%) of the network environment, j_fcol is the number of fog colonies, c_req is the requested resource requirement, and f_ava is the available resources at fog instance of the j-th fog colony. The fog instances are allocated to the users at the first round based on fit_fun, and in the next round the available resources are updated in the FKB that provisions the unallocated tasks and to meet the future demand of users. Tasks are provisioned with resources without waiting for a longer time as the tasks present in a swarm ensure parallelism and distributed approach of managing the resources and requests. Over-provisioning and under-provisioning are overcome by the proposed work with maximum utilization of resources and reduced resource cost. Tasks are subdivided for processing if sufficient resources are not available at the fog instance in a particular fog colony. If the requirement is not fulfilled after subdividing then a request is sent to the cloud for processing, but this increases resource cost compared to computation at the fog layer. It does not affect the performance of other tasks in various fog colonies.

4.4.3.3 Energy consumption

Energy is consumed during the processing of tasks, exploring the search space, transmitting the request, and responding to the request. The fitness function (fit_fun) computed by the MOPSO decides the best mapping of fog instances to arrive at tasks. the energy component is considered as the objective in PSO to find the best solution among the available fog instances to process the requests. A weighted MOPSO method is applied for evaluating multiple objectives with second priority allotted to energy consumption. CPU and BW usage, and rate of usage by task per unit are summed to estimate the power consumption using Eq. (4.12).

Energy consumption for the scheduled interval is obtained by integrating the power consumption of fog instances for the network environment using Eq. (4.13).

$$P_{total} = \text{idle} + \sum_{\forall i \in S} [\text{CPU}_i, \text{BW}_i, \text{RAM}_i, A\_\text{int}_i] * \begin{bmatrix} R\_cpu \\ R\_bw \\ R\_ram \\ R\_aint \end{bmatrix} \tag{4.12}$$

$$E = \int_0^{c\_exe} P_{total}(t)\mathrm{d}t \tag{4.13}$$

Network resources consume power in static and dynamic modes. In the idle case the power consumption assumed is 70 J. If tasks do not exist the instances are kept in the sleep mode to reduce power usage. Energy consumption is dependent on CPU usage and bandwidth usage for the stipulated time interval. After execution of all cloudlets existing in a swarms, the enery consumption is measured. The rate of energy consumption assumed in this work is 1 W s^{-1} (1 J) for CPU, bandwidth, RAM, and for agent interaction between the IoT–fog–cloud layers.

4.4.3.4 Execution time

The time required for executing tasks in a swarm on fog instances is computed by Eq. (4.14). The total time required for execution is estimated by several factors which are preprocessing time for forming clusters/swarms/fog colonies, evaluating distances, and updating the distance matrix. Resource discovery and mapping of tasks to fog instances, in particular fog colony by MOPSO, allocating future tasks based on best-fit algorithm, and time required to send the request to the fog/cloud and provision the services. Execution time (ms) is calculated by varying the resource capacity of fog instances and tasks using Eq. (4.14).

$$E_{time} = C_t + \sum_{\forall tasks \in swarm} D_t + t_{MOPSO} + t_{bestfit} + P_t + l \tag{4.14}$$

where C_t refers to the time for forming swarms, D_t is the time required to estimate the distance matrix for each swarm, fog colony, and resource discovery, t_{MOPSO} is the time required to process the tasks with the proposed algorithm, $t_{bestfit}$ is the time required to allocate the unallocated tasks and new arrived tasks, P_t is the processing time required for execution of tasks at the fog instances, and l is the time required to send the request to the FMA and deliver the services to users/tasks. The results are discussed in the next section.

4.4.4 Results

This section presents the results obtained by simulating the proposed work. The results are compared with best-fit and first-fit algorithms in terms of resource utilization, resource cost, energy consumption, execution time, and throughput.

Fig. 4.10 shows the number of cloudlets executed versus the number of cloudlets submitted. Here fog colonies possess fog instances of small, medium, high, and mixed capacity. The result obtained is for the first iteration. Cloudlet execution varies in small, medium, high, and mixed fog colony capacities. The graph shows that heterogeneous fog colonies perform better than others.

Fig. 4.11 shows the energy consumption in Joules for varying fog devices and 30 incoming requests/cloudlets with a cloudlet length of 1000 MI. Fog colonies are assumed to be three and the number of fog devices in fog colonies varies from three to seven. The total number of fog devices in the fog layer is assumed to be 5, 7, 10, and 15. The fog devices have diverse resource capacity with small, medium, or high resources. The energy consumption is calculated using the equations given in Section 4.4.3. Fog colonies with diverse resources provide the resources with less energy consumption compared to other fog colonies. For some tasks, resources are not available at fog colonies and those are forwarded to the cloud for processing, leading to high energy consumption.

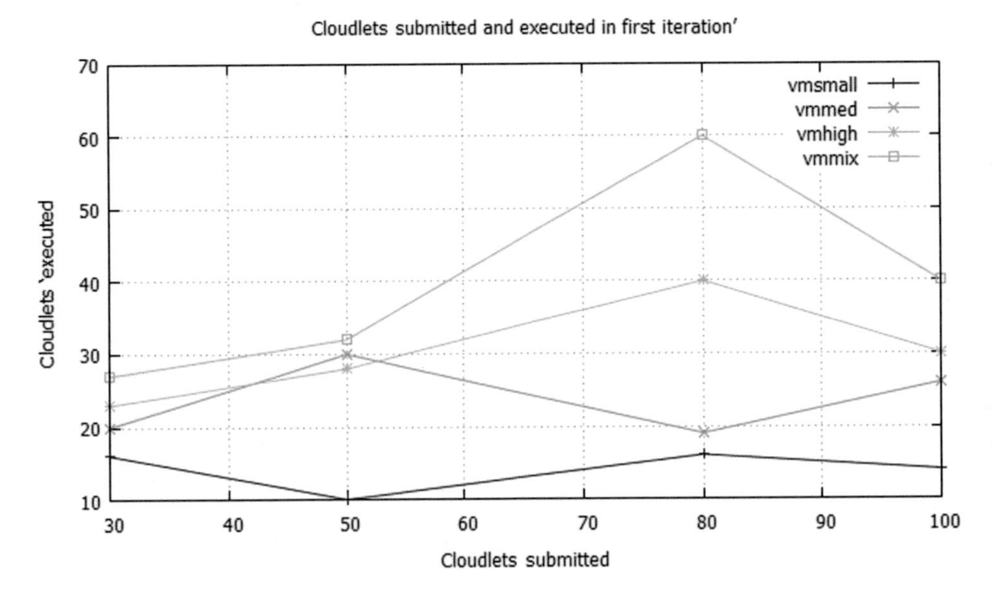

FIGURE 4.10 Cloudlet submitted versus number executed.

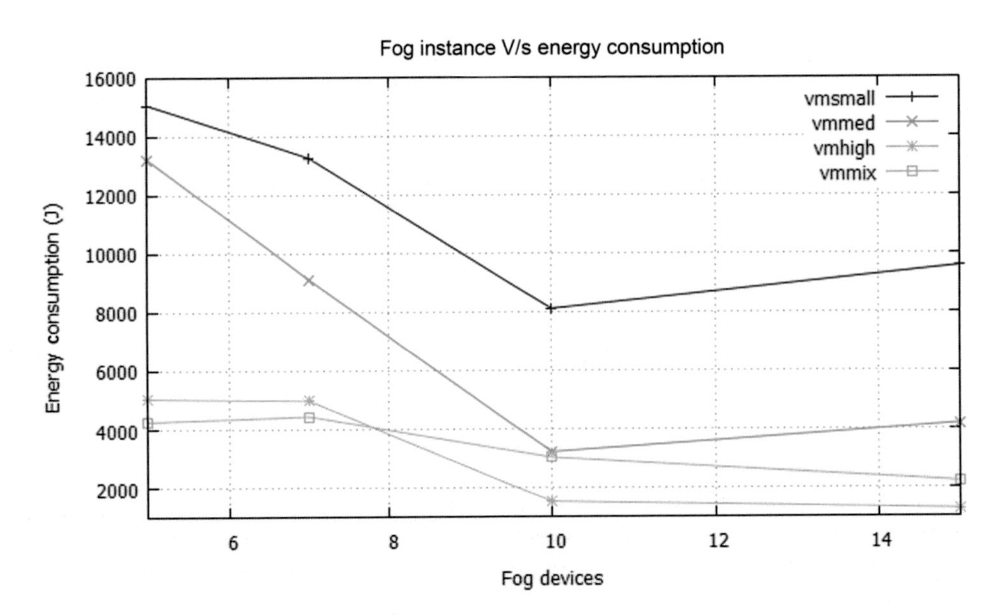

FIGURE 4.11 Fog instances versus energy consumption for 30 cloudlets/tasks.

Fig. 4.12 presents the energy consumption (*j*) for varying fog devices and 50 incoming requests/cloudlets with a cloudlet length of 1000 MI. Fig. 4.13 represents the energy consumption for varying fog devices and 80 incoming requests/cloudlets with a cloudlet length of 1000 MI. Fig. 4.14 presents the energy consumption (*j*) for varying fog devices and 100 incoming requests/cloudlets with a cloudlet length of 1000 MI.

As the number of cloudlets increases, energy consumption is increased due to insufficient resources at the fog and the requests are forwarded to the cloud for processing. In all cases, vmmix provisions resources efficiently with minimization of energy consumption as compared to other fog colonies.

Fig. 4.15 depicts that energy consumption is reduced for each case with a higher number of iterations.

Fig. 4.16 shows the resource cost obtained for cloudlets 50 with *n* number of iterations. The resource cost is estimated as discussed in Section 4.4.3.

Fig. 4.17 shows the resource cost obtained from varying fog instances in fog colonies and their capacities as vmsmall, medium, high, and mix (heterogeneous). The cost obtained is less in vmmix which is a heterogeneous fog colony compared to other types of fog instances in fog colonies.

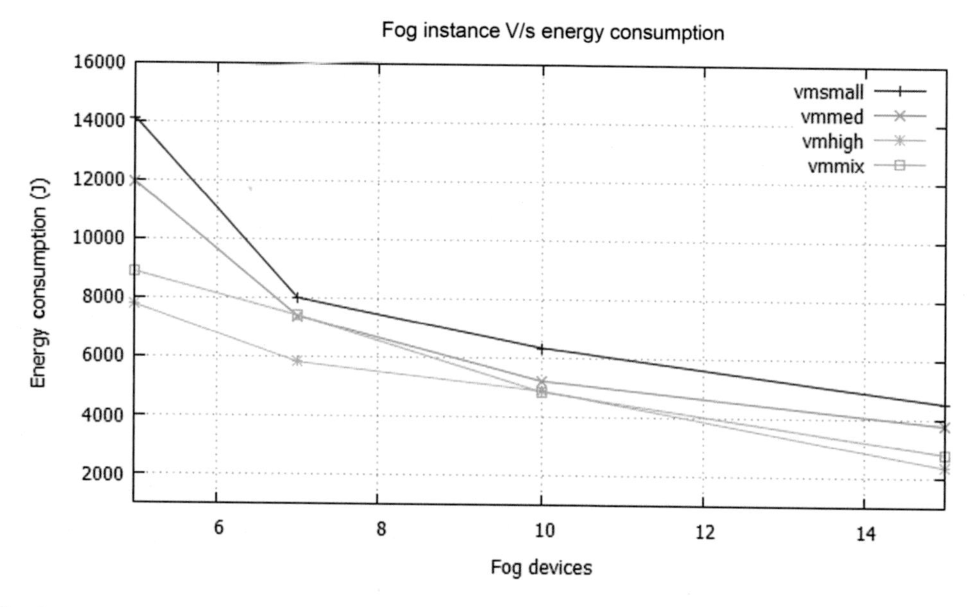

FIGURE 4.12 Fog instances versus energy consumption for 50 cloudlets/tasks.

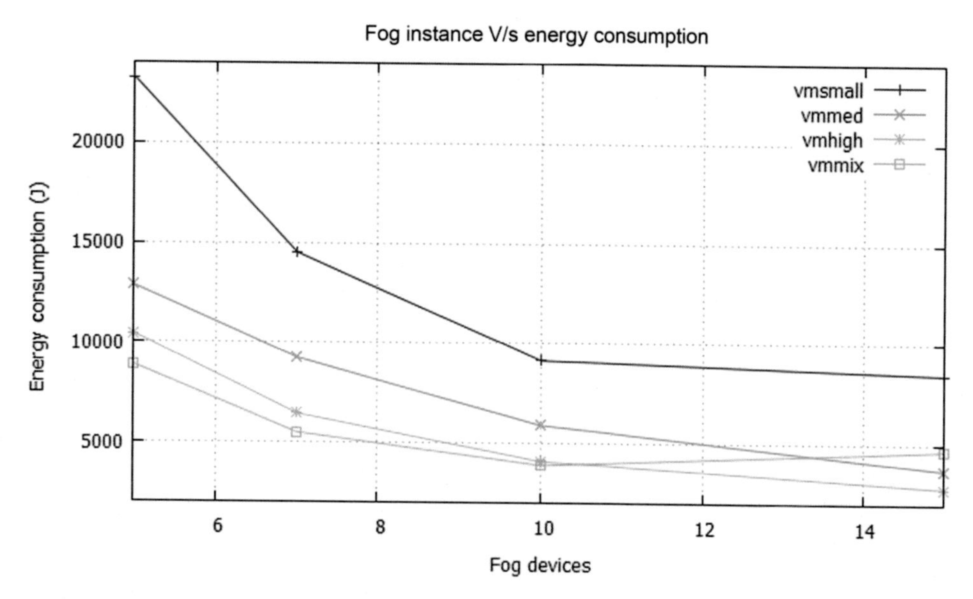

FIGURE 4.13 Fog instances versus energy consumption for 80 cloudlets/tasks.

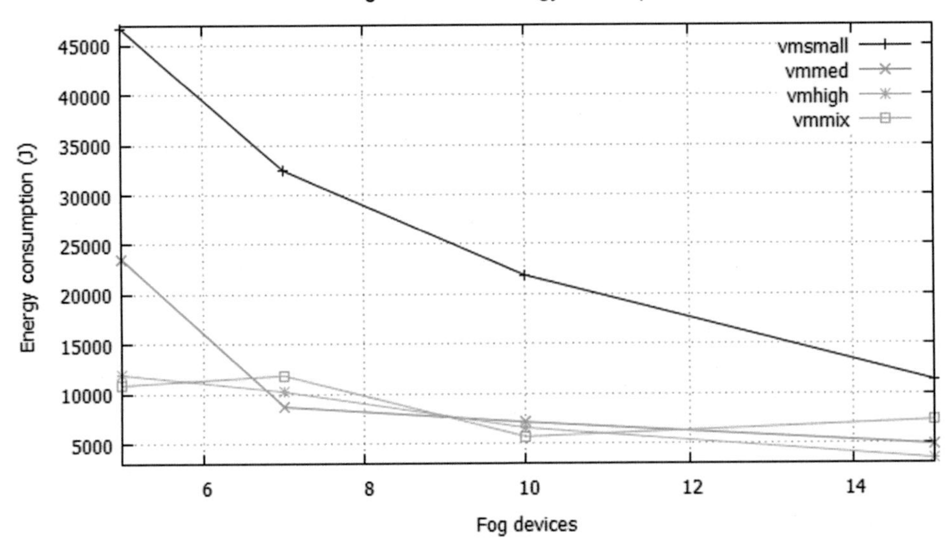

FIGURE 4.14 Fog instances versus energy consumption for 100 cloudlets/tasks.

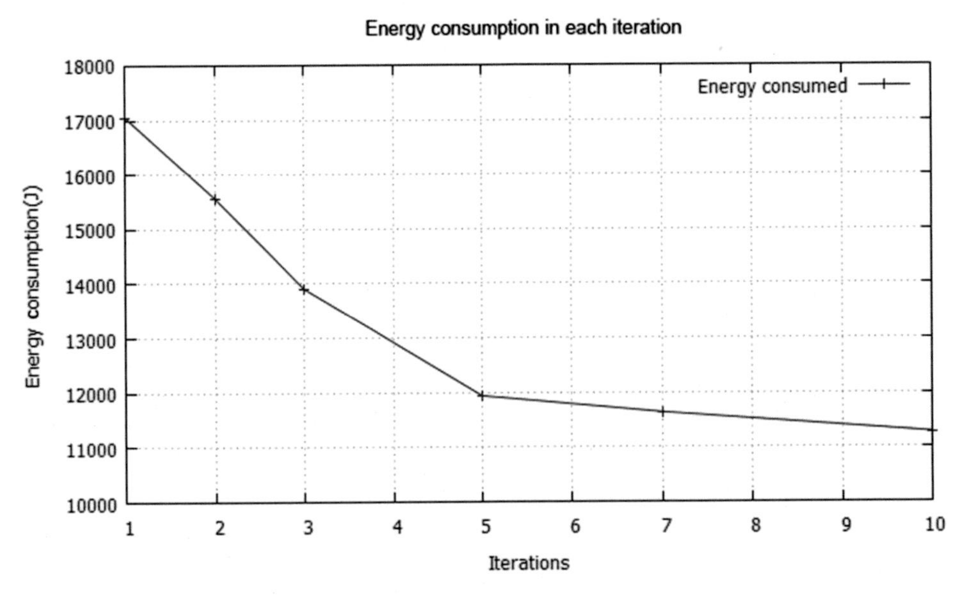

FIGURE 4.15 Number of iterations versus energy consumption for cloudlets 50.

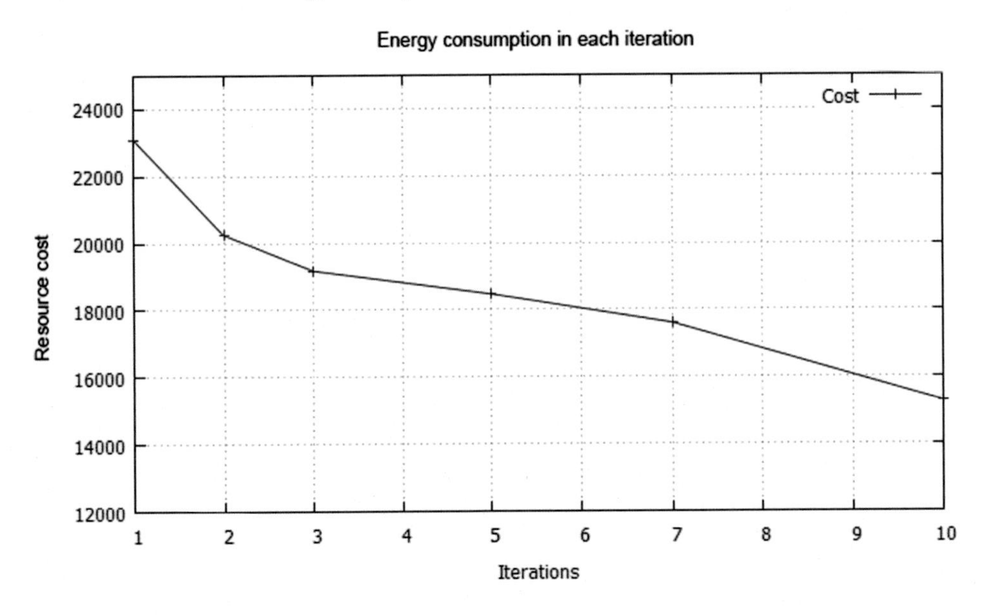

FIGURE 4.16 Number of iterations versus resource cost.

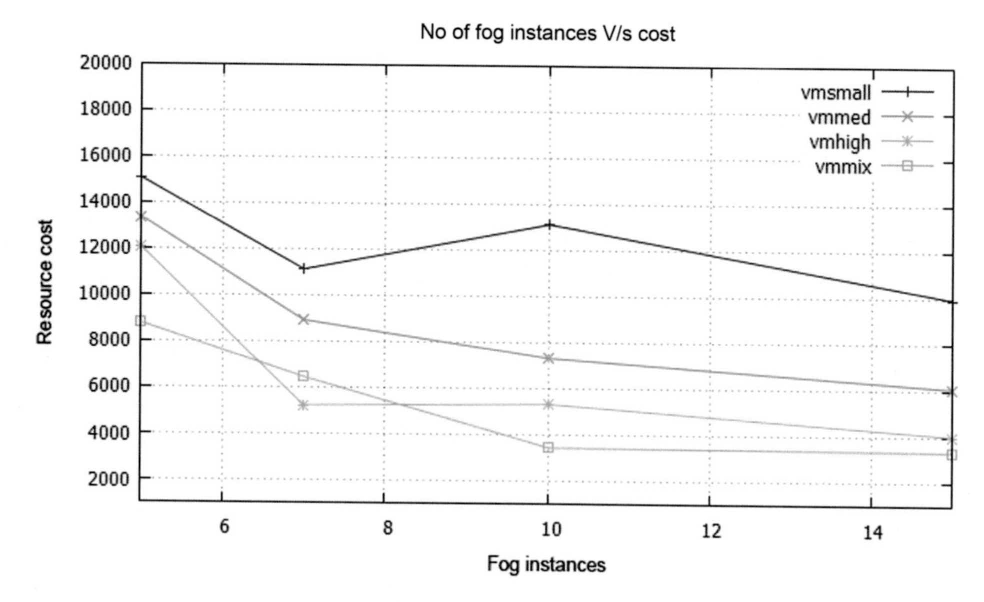

FIGURE 4.17 Fog instances versus resource cost for 50 cloudlets/tasks.

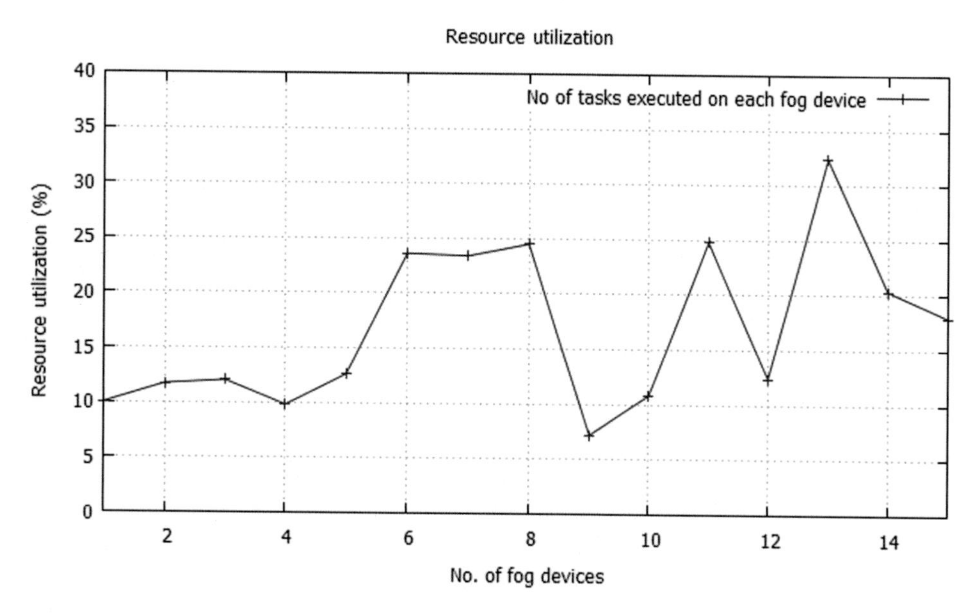

FIGURE 4.18 Resource utilization (%) of fog devices/instances.

Fig. 4.18 shows the resource utilization of fog instance with 50 incoming requests. The utilization of each fog colony is 70%, 85%, and 93%. The resources are available after allocating 50 cloudlets, hence new tasks are allocated to the least utilized fog colony. The fog instances are not overloaded or underloaded but they are uniformly distributed with load based on the MOPSO fitness function (fit_fun).

Scheduling of tasks is evaluated for time shared and space shared. In time shared each task is scheduled to execute in a specific time interval and in space shared the tasks are allocated to execute by sharing resources in fog instances for the complete duration of execution. Table 4.6 shows the performance measures obtained by applying two scheduling policies for executing a set of cloudlets.

Cloudlet time shared exhibits better results than space shared in terms of cost, execution time, energy consumption, and throughput.

Fig. 4.19A and B shows the comparative analysis of the proposed work, first-fit and best-fit algorithms in terms of the number of executed cloudlets, resource cost, and energy consumption with 30 and 40 cloudlets as incoming requests. The proposed work exhibits

TABLE 4.6 Comparison of cloudlet time shared and space shared scheduling.

Cloudlet time shared					Cloudlet space shared				
No. of cloudlets	Executed	Cost ($)	Execution time (ms)	Mean energy consumption (J)	No. of cloudlets	Executed	Cost ($)	Execution time (ms)	Mean energy consumption (J)
40	30	1289	1436	34.23	40	30	2204	1377	34.10
50	45	1323	2380	35.01	50	47	2363	2067	34.77
60	55	1410	3408	37.78	60	59	2714	2425	36.12
70	60	2406	3648	38.99	70	65	3166	2841	37.46
90	70	3553	7690	39.67	90	79	4235	3447	37.99

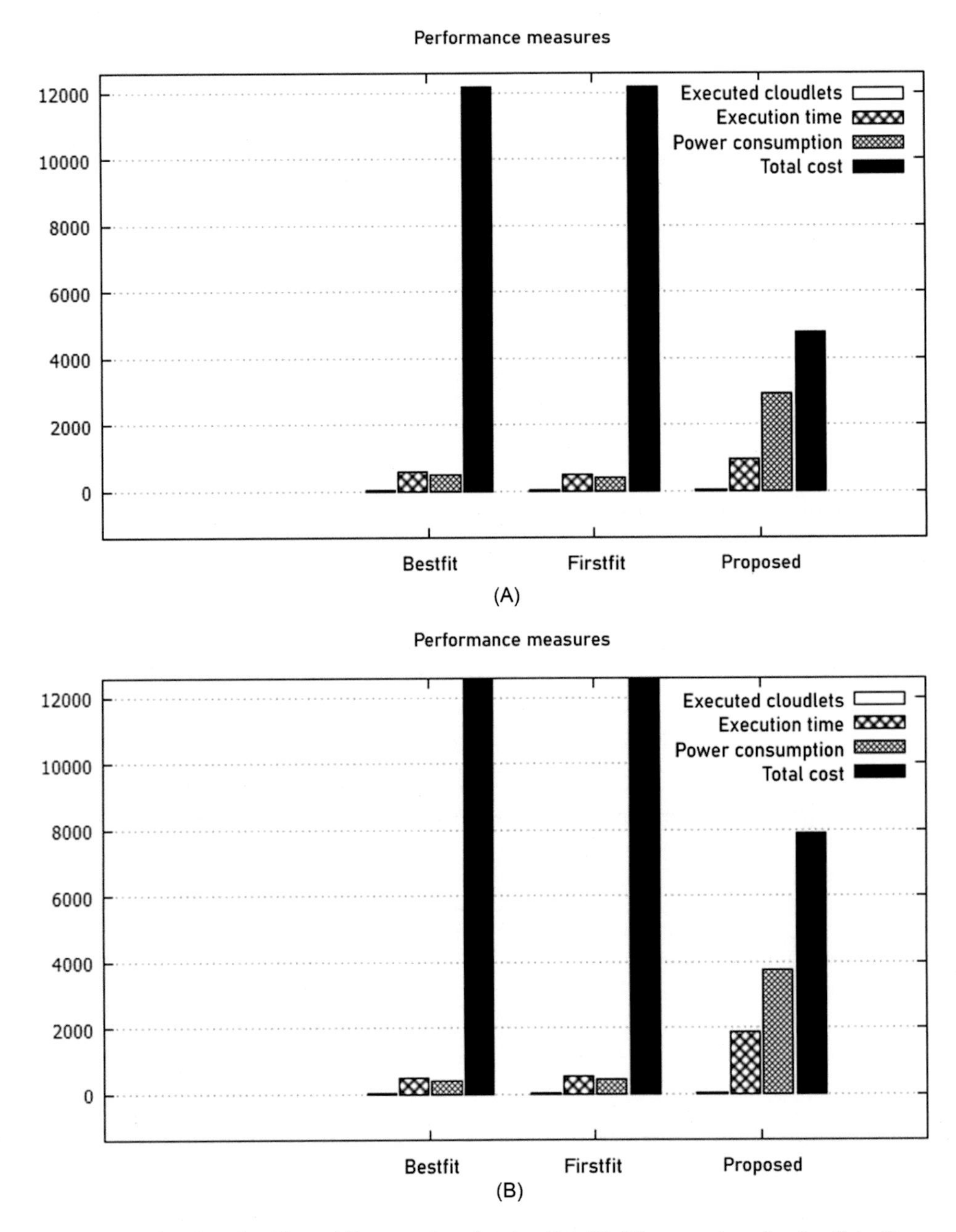

FIGURE 4.19 Comparison with other algorithms: (A) comparison for cloudlets 30; (B) comparison for cloudlets 40.

better results than the other two algorithms with reduced energy consumption and cost, and increased resource utilization and throughput.

Resource provisioning is performed in a reactive way for executing the tasks by choosing appropriate fog instances to meet the QoS. Additionally, authentication, adapting, and allocating are achieved in the proposed work. The advantage of using MOPSO is to achieve the optimal solution by meeting several criteria in view of reducing the wastage of resources.

4.5 Conclusion

This work overcomes the problem of a centralized approach for managing the diverse and constraint resources at the fog layer. Due to an increase in demand from users, seeking appropriate services with reduced waiting time and distributing the available resources for processing the request has become a challenge in the context of the IoT and fog environment. Edge devices possess resources but are inadequate to address all the requests arriving in the system. All these requests are served by the cloud with increased latency and huge traffic, to overcome this drawback the fog environment offers services to the edge devices constituting CPU, bandwidth, storage, and memory. The proposed work provides the resources by fog instances to the swarms in parallel, without violating SLA and performing better for heterogeneous requests. This approach assures diverse request handling by reducing the waiting time and allocates all types of tasks in available fog instances efficiently. The results shows that the proposed work performs better than best-fit, first-fit, and worst-fit algorithms in terms of energy consumption (J), resource cost, resource utilization, execution time, and throughput. Rather than searching the relevant resources at every instant of time, executing and calculating the performance metrics, the proposed work provisions for the nearest fog instances to all tasks, irrespective of priorities as the tasks are clustered in various swarms at scheduled intervals. Randomness in the creation of swarms and fog colonies might result in increased energy consumption and cost, but to achieve consistent results they simulate a few iterations employing the proposed MSOPSO. User requests declined by any fog instances are reiterated and other fog instances are mapped to complete the tasks without violating SLA. The reactive provisioning approach is employed in this work by authenticating the devices prior to allocation and scheduling. At regular intervals, based on the demand, resources are planned to provide for the users retaining QoS. Provisioning by a proactive mechanism that predicts the resources requirement and modeling for dynamic update of the inertia factor, acceleration, and cognitive factors in MOPSO will be part of future work.

Acknowledgment

The authors are thankful to the All India Council for Technical Education (AICTE) and Basveshwar Engineering College for providing the required facilities. The work was funded by an AICTE grant for carrying out this work under the project "Resource Management in Internet of Things" with Reference File Number 8-40/RIFD/RPS/POLICY-1/2016-17 sanctioned on August 2, 2017.

References

Ali, S. A., Ansari, M., & Alam, M. (2020). Resource management techniques for cloud-based IoT environment. In Internet of Things (IoT) (pp. 63–87). Springer.

Avasalcai, C. & Dustdar, S. (2018). Latency-aware decentralized resource management for IoT applications. In *Proceedings of the 8th international conference on the Internet of Things* (pp. 1–4). Available from: https://doi.org/10.1145/3277593.3277637.

Birje, M. N., Challagidad, P. S., Goudar, R. H., & Tapale, M. T. (2017). Cloud computing review: Concepts, technology, challenges and security. *International Journal of Cloud Computing, 6*(1), 32–57.

Birje, M. N., Manvi, S. S., & Das, S. K. (2014). Reliable resources brokering scheme in wireless grids based on non-cooperative bargaining game. *Journal of Network and Computer Applications, 39*, 266–279. Available from: https://doi.org/10.1016/j.jnca.2013.07.007.

Feki, S., Masmoudi, A., Belghith, A., Zarai, F., & Obaidat, M. S. (2019). Swarm intelligence-based radio resource management for V2V-based D2D communication. *International Journal of Communication Systems, 32*(17), e3817. Available from: https://doi.org/10.1002/dac.3817.

Ghobaei-Arani, M., Souri, A., & Rahmanian, A. A. (2020). Resource management approaches in fog computing: A comprehensive review. *Journal of Grid Computing, 18*(1), 1–42. Available from:: https://doi.org/10.1007/s10723-019-09491-1.

Hatti, D. I., & Sutagundar, A. V. (2019). Nature inspired computing for wireless networks applications: A survey. *International Journal of Applied Evolutionary Computation, 10*(1), 1–29. Available from: https://doi.org/10.4018/IJAEC.2019010101.

Huang, J., Li, S., & Chen, Y. (2020). Revenue-optimal task scheduling and resource management for IoT batch jobs in mobile edge computing. *Peer-to-Peer Networking and Applications*. Available from: https://doi.org/10.1007/s12083-020-00880-y.

Ketel, M. (2017). Fog-cloud services for IoT. *Proceedings of the SouthEast Conference*, 262–264. Available from: https://doi.org/10.1145/3077286.3077314.

Kumar, D. & Raza, Z. (2015). A PSO based VM resource scheduling model for cloud computing. In *Proceedings of the 2015 IEEE international conference on computational intelligence & communication technology* (pp. 213–219). Available from: https://doi.org/10.1109/CICT.2015.35.

Kumar, J. S., & Zaveri, M. A. (2019). Resource Scheduling for Postdisaster Management in IoT Environment. *Wireless Communications and Mobile Computing, 2019*, 1–19. Available from: https://doi.org/10.1155/2019/7802843.

López, T. S., Brintrup, A., Isenberg, M.-A., & Mansfeld, J. (2011). Resource management in the Internet of Things: Clustering, synchronisation and software agents. In D. Uckelmann, M. Harrison, & F. Michahelles (Eds.), *Architecting the Internet of Things* (pp. 159–193). Springer Berlin Heidelberg. Available from: https://doi.org/10.1007/978-3-642-19157-2_7.

Mani, K., & Krishnan, R. M. (2017). Flexible cost based cloud resource provisioning using enhanced PSO. *International Journal of Computational Intelligence Research, 13*(6), 1441–1453.

Mukherjee, A., Goswami, P., Yan, Z., Yang, L., & Rodrigues, J. J. P. C. (2019). ADAI and adaptive PSO-based resource allocation for wireless sensor networks. *IEEE Access, 7*, 131163–131171. Available from:: https://doi.org/10.1109/ACCESS.2019.2940821.

Mustafa, S., Nazir, B., Hayat, A., Khan, A. ur R., & Madani, S. A. (2015). Resource management in cloud computing: Taxonomy, prospects, and challenges. *Computers & Electrical Engineering, 47*, 186–203. Available from: https://doi.org/10.1016/j.compeleceng.2015.07.021.

Nakamura, Y., Mizumoto, T., Suwa, H., Arakawa, Y., Yamaguchi, H., & Yasumoto, K. (2018). In-situ resource provisioning with adaptive scale-out for regional IoT services. In *Proceedings of the 2018 IEEE/ACM Symposium on Edge Computing (SEC)* (pp. 203–213). Available from: https://doi.org/10.1109/SEC.2018.00022

Narman, H. S., Hossain, Md. S., Atiquzzaman, M., & Shen, H. (2017). Scheduling internet of things applications in cloud computing. *Annals of Telecommunications, 72*(1–2), 79–93. Available from:: https://doi.org/10.1007/s12243-016-0527-6.

Pico-Valencia, P., & Holgado-Terriza, J. A. (2018). Agentification of the Internet of Things: A systematic literature review. *International Journal of Distributed Sensor Networks, 14*(10). Available from: https://doi.org/10.1177/1550147718805945, 155014771880594.

Puranikmath, J. (2017). A review on resource allocation techniques for Internet of Things. *International Journal of Engineering Science*, 14786.

Rafique, H., Shah, M. A., Islam, S. U., Maqsood, T., Khan, S., & Maple, C. (2019). A novel bio-inspired hybrid algorithm (NBIHA) for efficient resource management in fog computing. *IEEE Access, 7*, 115760–115773. Available from: https://doi.org/10.1109/ACCESS.2019.2924958, In this issue.

Rahbari, D., & Nickray, M. (2019). Low-latency and energy-efficient scheduling in fog-based IoT applications. *Turkish Journal of Electrical Engineering & Computer Sciences*, 1406–1427. Available from: https://doi.org/10.3906/elk-1810-47.

Ramirez, P. L. G., Taha, M., Lloret, J., & Tomas, J. (2020). An intelligent algorithm for resource sharing and self-management of wireless-IoT-gateway. *IEEE Access, 8*, 3159–3170. Available from:: https://doi.org/10.1109/ACCESS.2019.2960508.

Röhler, A. B., & Chen, S. (2011). An analysis of sub-swarms in multi-swarm systems. In D. Wang, & M. Reynolds (Eds.), *Advances in artificial intelligence* (7106, pp. 271–280). Springer Berlin Heidelberg. Available from: https://doi.org/10.1007/978-3-642-25832-9_28.

R. Sudha.pdf. (n.d.). *Fog enabled cloud based intelligent resource management approach using improved dynamical particle swarm optimization model for smart home IoT devices.*

Samie, F. (2018). *Resource management for edge computing in Internet of Things (IoT).* (2018) Farzad: Samie. Available from: doi.org/10.5445/IR/1000081031.

Sharif, M., Mercelis, S., Marquez-Barja, J., & Hellinckx, P. (2018). A particle swarm optimization-based heuristic for optimal cost estimation in Internet of Things environment. In *Proceedings of the 2018 2nd international conference on big data and Internet of Things - BDIOT 2018* (pp. 136–142). Available from: https://doi.org/10.1145/3289430.3289433.

Shukla, S., Hassan, M. F., Khan, M. K., Jung, L. T., & Awang, A. (2019). An analytical model to minimize the latency in healthcare internet-of-things in fog computing environment. *PLoS One, 14* (11), e0224934.

Silva Filho, M.C., Oliveira, R.L., Monteiro, C.C., Inácio, P.R., & Freire, M.M. (2017). CloudSim plus: A cloud computing simulation framework pursuing software engineering principles for improved modularity, extensibility and correctness. In *Proceedings of the 2017 IFIP/IEEE symposium on integrated network and service management (IM)* (pp. 400–406).

Strumberger, I., Tuba, M., Bacanin, N., & Tuba, E. (2019). Cloudlet scheduling by hybridized Monarch butterfly optimization algorithm. *Journal of Sensor and Actuator Networks, 8*(3), 44. Available from: https://doi.org/10.3390/jsan8030044.

Suarez, J.N. & Salcedo, A. (2017). ID3 and k-means based methodology for Internet of Things device classification. In *Proceedings of the 2017 international conference on mechatronics, electronics and automotive engineering (ICMEAE)* (pp. 129–133). Available from: https://doi.org/10.1109/ICMEAE.2017.10.

Sun, W., Tang, M., Zhang, L., Huo, Z., & Shu, L. (2020). A survey of using swarm intelligence algorithms in IoT. *Sensors, 20*(5), 1420. Available from: https://doi.org/10.3390/s20051420.

Talukder, S. (2011). *Mathematicle modelling and applications of particle swarm optimization.*

Toczé, K., & Nadjm-Tehrani, S. (2018). A taxonomy for management and optimization of multiple resources in edge computing. *Wireless Communications and Mobile Computing, 2018*, 1–23. Available from: https://doi.org/10.1155/2018/7476201.

Ullah, I., & Youn, H. Y. (2020). Task classification and scheduling based on K-means clustering for edge computing. *Wireless Personal Communications*. Available from: https://doi.org/10.1007/s11277-020-07343-w.

Wang, N., Varghese, B., Matthaiou, M., & Nikolopoulos, D. S. (2017). ENORM: A framework for edge NOde resource management. *IEEE Transactions on Services Computing*, 1–1. Available from: https://doi.org/10.1109/TSC.2017.2753775.

Wang, Z., Xu, W., Yang, J., & Peng, J. (2009). A game theoretic approach for resource allocation based on ant colony optimization in emergency management. In *Proceedings of the 2009 International Conference on Information Engineering and Computer Science* (pp. 1–4). Available from: https://doi.org/10.1109/ICIECS.2009.5365328.

Yadav, V., Natesha, B.V., & Guddeti, R.M.R. (2019). GA-PSO: Service allocation in fog computing environment using hybrid bio-inspired algorithm. In *TENCON 2019-2019 IEEE Region 10 Conference (TENCON)* (pp. 1280–1285).

Yao, J. & Ansari, N. (2018). Reliability-aware fog resource provisioning for deadline-driven IoT services. In *Proceedings of the* 2018 IEEE Global Communications Conference (GLOBECOM) (pp. 1–6).

Yousefpour, A., Fung, C., Nguyen, T., Kadiyala, K., Jalali, F., Niakanlahiji, A., ... Jue, J. P. (2019). All one needs to know about fog computing and related edge computing paradigms: A complete survey. *Journal of Systems Architecture, 98*, 289–330. Available from: https://doi.org/10.1016/j.sysarc.2019.02.009.

Zahoor, S., & Mir, R. N. (2018). Resource management in pervasive Internet of Things: A survey. *Journal of King Saud University - Computer and Information Sciences*. Available from: https://doi.org/10.1016/j.jksuci.2018.08.014.

CHAPTER

5

DNA-based authentication to access internet of things-based healthcare data

Sreeja Cherillath Sukumaran

Department of Computer Science CHRIST (deemed to be University), Bengaluru, India

5.1 Introduction

Authentication is considered a critical aspect to ensure one's identity in a network. Taking account of the degree of electronic services a user has to access daily, recollecting countless ID–password pairs will lead to memorability issues. These usability issues inspire users to reuse the same credentials across multiple platforms, which often results in vulnerability of the credentials and the system itself. Considering these aspects to ensure security, many schemes for user authentication have been proposed including two-factor and multifactor authentication schemes. Nevertheless, while designing a secure user authentication scheme the trade-off amid usability and security remains a key concern for researchers.

The security concerns in the Internet of Things (IoT) are not limited to authentication, but also include concerns related to other critical aspects such as integrity, confidentiality, nonrepudiation, privacy, and availability. With the development of digitalized data and IoT-based e-health systems, proper authentication mechanisms are essential to ensure both usability and security. Considering these aspects and based on a literature review, a novel authentication mechanism is proposed based on DNA encoding. This chapter proposes a novel secure authentication scheme using ID, password unique ID, which can be used for national ID, DNA steganography, and hash function for user authentication. The proposed system uses AADHAAR, which is a 12-digit identification number issued by the UIDAI to residents of India and is verifiable (Aadhar Card, n.d.). The proposed model can be used globally, in any country where a unique national ID is used. The authentication scheme can be integrated with healthcare ID also. Connecting DNA with healthcare data has numerous health benefits, with the futures of healthcare and medicine are based on genomics (Robinson, 2016).

The organization of this starts with a literature review on the related areas that is provided in Section 5.2, including concepts and challenges in using the IoT, DNA cryptography, and DNA authentication techniques, followed by inferences. The proposed authentication scheme is explained in Section 5.3, followed by security analysis in Section 5.4. A further discussion on Scyther analysis and the conclusions are given in Sections 5.5 and 5.6, respectively.

5.2 Literature survey

Authentication is the process of giving a user access to a system based on their credentials. It is considered as one of the critical aspects of information security and turns out to be life-threatening in the case of medical devices connected to the IoT environment. This section explores a literature review based on the IoT environment, security mechanisms used in the IoT, the challenges, and attacks on IoT devices. The section also explores the literature on DNA in information security authentication techniques, and the uses and benefits of using DNA encoding for authentication.

The IoT emerged as one of the most prominent technologies that have applications in all domains. The variability of applications and its usage has resulted in information diffusion of a huge number of users that demand the utmost security concerns. In an IoT

Recent Trends in Computational Intelligence Enabled Research.
DOI: https://doi.org/10.1016/B978-0-12-822844-9.00008-6

environment, authentication of users plays a significant factor as the system permits the user to connect securely with the device. Authentication techniques when integrated through the IoT establish a secure connection and data retrieval. Authentication of the IoT is a field of wide research activities. The methods used in authentication for the IoT are important to secure IoT devices, and there have been several methods proposed (Kavianpour et al., 2019; Xue et al., 2019).

The IoT is a large network with connected smart devices such as sensors that are used extensively in many fields including, but not limited to, healthcare, smart transportation, smart homes, smart cities, and agriculture. The IoT has many challenges and the main one is in connecting numerous devices to communicate with each other and another concern is the security challenges involved, specifically attacks related to IoT networks. These challenges are increased because of the resource-limited nature of IoT devices, which results in the infeasibility of applying conventional communication protocols and security schemes to it. The challenges related to security issues are exponentially growing in the IoT, which is so critical that a security breach may even lead to mortality. The security requirement in the IoT network largely depends on the domain and the security requirements of the application.

The key requirement for the IoT is authentication and to ensure that the devices participating in the network are trustworthy and efficient in the network. A security attack on a node connected to the IoT network may result in the failure of the entire network and also may lead to critical issues. These critical aspects also include confidentiality and integrity.

5.2.1 Internet of things generic architecture

The IoT has a different approach compared to conventional networks and connects to and supports a variety of applications. However, this type of connection results in heavy traffic, demanding the requirement of big data storage. In an IoT environment, the TCP/IP architecture may not address all the requirements including quality of service, security aspects, and interoperability, though it has been used widely for network connectivity for a long time. For the IoT, although many architectures have been proposed, a reference architecture is essential. The model proposed is a three-layer architecture which includes perception, network, and application layers (El-hajj, Fadlallah, Chamoun, & Serhrouchni, 2019).

1. *Perception layer*: The physical layer that senses the environment to discern the physical properties using end-nodes by using the various technologies related to senses.
2. *Network layer*: This layer performs the role of fetching and transmitting the data from the perception layer to the application layer by means of different network technologies.
3. *Application layer*: This layer has the responsibility of delivering application-specific services to the user. The significance is based on the fact that this layer has applications in numerous areas including healthcare, building automation, etc.

An architecture which has five-layer has been also proposed, with these listed below in order of top to bottom (El-hajj et al., 2019).

The functions performed by the perception, transport, and application layers are identical to the basic model, whereas the five-layer model has the two layers mentioned below:

1. *Processing layer*: This layer has responsibilities of ensuring numerous services such as storing, analyzing, and data processing with reference to the results based on computations.
2. *Business layer*: This layer provides complete IoT system activities and functionalities. It receives data from the application layer and analyzes the data by generating models and graphs to aid in decision-making.

5.2.2 Challenges in the internet of things

Dealing with connected devices, every day may have a critical impact and lead to life-threatening security issues. The integration of smart technologies into vehicles and healthcare devices will lead to detrimental situations when exploited by attackers. The progress and acceptance of IoT applications had grown exponentially at the same time that security breaches related to these are high, especially with IoT applications that deal with sensitive data such as healthcare and data related to government agencies. Similar to other network-related applications, IoT applications also have security concerns which include but are not limited to authentication, integrity, nonrepudiation, confidentiality, availability, authorization, and privacy (Burhan, Rehman, Khan, & Kim, 2018).

1. Authentication: This is the procedure of ensuring user identity based on the credentials. All the connected nodes in an IoT environment must be

capable of identifying and authenticating all other nodes connected to the network.
2. Authorization: This is the method in which an object receives permission to access the system after successful verification.
3. Integrity: Any changes or modifications to the existing information in the system by unauthorized entities may lead to critical issues in the IoT.
4. Confidentiality: This is one of the critical aspects which includes protecting information from unauthorized access. Confidentiality and managing data are major concerns in the IoT environment.
5. Nonrepudiation: This aspect ensures that the ability to prove that an event has occurred and cannot be denied at a later point in time.
6. Availability: This ensures that the service required is accessible irrespective of the place and time for authorized users.
7. Privacy: This aspect ensures that confidential data are not accessible by attackers.

5.2.3 Security challenges in internet of things layers

5.2.3.1 Challenges related to perception layer

The perception layer is comprised of sensors that are categorized based on their capacity related to storage, and the processing power is limited. These confinements result in various security attacks (Rao and Haq, 2018) with some of these attacks listed below:

1. Node capture: The attackers will be able to observe the nodes without great difficulty. Node capture permits the attackers to easily capture information related to the keys (the keys themselves) and information related to the protocols. It also allows the attacker to realign the malicious node across the network, which will critically affect the whole network security.
2. Denial of service (DoS) attack: This is another critical issue as this attack denies access to valid users who are authorized to access the system. The attackers perform this by overloading the network, which results in failure of the network and thereby denying services to the user.
3. Denial of sleep attack: This attack deals with the node's power supply. The attacker attains this by reducing the period of services of the node by rising the power consumption.
4. Distributed denial of service attack: This is considered as the most critical issue in the IoT environment, as the connected nodes are utilized toward the victim server.
5. Fake node attack: This attack is attained by using fake identities, which the attacker can deploy by using fake nodes. These nodes can be used to send information, which is spam, across the nodes resulting in utilizing the energy of the nodes and adversely affecting the services.
6. Replay attack: This attack is usually listed as one of the security attacks related to the authentication protocol in which the data transmitted are stored and the same is used for unauthorized communication later by retransmitting the stored data.

5.2.3.2 Challenges related to the network layer security

The network layer plays a significant role in routing and analysis of the information and numerous technologies are used to perform the same.

Some of the attacks related to the network layer are detailed here:

1. DoS: This attack can be attained by congestion during transmission of radio signals, which can be achieved by using a fake node and also by disturbing the routing process.
2. Eavesdropping: In this attack the intruder is capable of eavesdropping on a private communication link that enables the intruder to retrieve vital information including user login credentials. It also enables retrieving of information related to nodes which might be helpful for the intruder to perform various attacks.
3. Routing attacks: These attacks are related to the transmission of information where the attacker tries to disturb the normal processes in the layer.
    a. Black hole: This is a denial of service attack using a fake node that declares the shortest path and creates traffic, and the node has the capacity to transmit the packets or to drop it.
    b. Gray hole: This attack is comparable to a black hole attack, however in this attack only selected packets are dropped.
    c. Worm hole: The attacker controls two nodes and establishes a connection in the network after setting up that gathers information and use these collected details to retransmit the information.
    d. Hello flood: In this attack the attacker aims at the power consumption of the nodes by using fake nodes to send request messages which will result in enormous traffic in the system.
    e. Sybil: This attack is performed using fake nodes which show many identities, this is used to regulate and send information across the network thereby rejecting access to the network by the normal nodes.

5.2.3.3 Authentication schemes in the internet of things

This layer is in charge, as it provides services. It acts as a user interface and the application layer protocols are the message-passing protocols which include but are not limited to Constrained Application Protocol and Message Queuing Telemetry Transport. The conventional protocols in this layer do not execute well for the IoT environment and there is no standard defined for the IoT which makes it susceptible to various attacks, and the same is applicable to the application layer.

A. Data accessibility and authentication: User authentication is always a major concern in most network-related concepts. In the IoT, it is a critical concept as the number of devices connected are numerous and there are many connected users. Unauthorized users attempting to access the network is a major concern.

B. Data privacy and identity: In the IoT, this is another critical concept considering the number of devices and users connected to the IoT network. Different applications may use different schemes which make the integration process highly difficult and this makes ensuring identities and privacy even more difficult.

C. Data management: In the IoT environment, managing data is a major aspect as this network involves many connected devices and users. The amount of data that needs to be managed is too high, and so are the security issues related to it. Authentication plays a major role here in ensuring continuous accessibility of the application layer services.

1. Authentication factor, identity: This is the credentials presented by an entity to another one for authenticating itself to the system. Identity-based authentication schemes can be used including hash, symmetric, or asymmetric schemes. It can be done through multifactor authentication which also uses one of the physical characteristics of an individual, such as face recognition, iris detection, and DNA-based schemes.
2. Token-based: This deals with user or device authentication by means of a token for identification generated by the server.
3. Nontoken-based: This deals with the credentials which have to be exchanged every time.
4. Schemes for authentication
   - **a.** One-way authentication method: In a one-way authentication, one entity will authenticate itself to the other involved in the communication, while the second entity remains unauthenticated.
   - **b.** Two-way authentication: This authentication method is also called mutual authentication as both entities involved in the communication will authenticate each other.
   - **c.** Three-way authentication: In this process authentication and mutual authentication of the entities involved in the communication will occur through a central authority.
5. Authentication architecture
   - **a.** Distributed: The communication amid the parties is established by means of a distributed method for authentication.
   - **b.** Centralized: In this scenario, a trusted third party is involved in the distribution and management of the user credentials. Either centralized or distributed, the architecture involved in the authentication process can be:
     - **i.** Hierarchical: For the authentication process the architecture involved is multilevel;
     - **ii.** Flat: For the authentication process the architecture in this method does not use the hierarchical method.
   - **c.** IoT layer: Techniques for authentication are used in this layer.
   - **d.** Perception layer: In the IoT environment, the perception layer is accountable for data management related to the end nodes.
   - **e.** Network layer: This is accountable for getting the perceived data from the perception layer and processing the data.
   - **f.** Application layer: This provides services to the user as per the request received and also based on the data received from the network layer.
   - **g.** Based on hardware: The authentication procedure sometimes may include the involvement of the hardware or characteristics of it.
   - **h.** Based on implicit hardware: To improve the authentication using the physical features of the device.
   - **i.** Based on explicit hardware: This depends on the use of a trusted platform module, a hardware that has the secret values/keys used for authentication.

5.2.4 Authentication schemes in the internet of things

The review is given based on the multicriteria classification. The literature review is described based on the application domain in IoT research.

Due to its efficiency and effectiveness, the smart grid is dominant over traditional power grids, nevertheless, this domain has a threat due to the vulnerability issues and securing the domain remains challenging. An authentication scheme has been proposed (Li, Lu, Zhou, Yang, & Shen, 2014) which depends on a Merkle-hash tree. To assemble the usage of power, each household is set up with a smart meter that will send the collected information using a radio-based communication to the neighborhood gateway (NG). The NG directs this information to the control sensors center, which in turn gathers the details such as the bill and shares it with the client. The two-way authentication amongst the smart meter and NG is performed by means of a lightweight method, which is effective in terms of computation and communication overhead. The main features to be considered while developing a smart grid depend on the information that is shared to the control unit or gateway, and it must be directed from a valid smart meter and related to the customer privacy such as the methods should not learn the pattern of energy consumption of the customer as it will affect the consumer privacy.

Considering those features as a methodology for authentication (Chim, Yiu, Hui, & Li, 2011) is proposed for smart grids using a Hash-based Message Authentication Code (HMAC). This method guarantees the privacy of the consumer. The authentication is attained by means of a lightweight Diffie–Hellman method and HMAC ensures the integrity of data.

An authentication scheme for radio frequency identification (RFID) tags using physical unclonable function (PUF) has been proposed. The method includes three stages: recognition of tag, followed by verification and update. As the name indicates in the first transaction, the tag reader recognizes the tag. The next stage involves the verification process, in which the authenticity is verified between the reader and the tag. In the update transaction, the most recently used key should be held up for the next verification (Xu, Ding, Li, Zhu, & Wang, 2018). An RFID-based solution was used to shield the devices that are connected to the management of the supply chain. The authentication process involves (1) examining the connectivity amongst the tag and the IoT device involved, followed by (2) approving the perceptibility of the tag. In the scheme which has an IoT and RFID, the reader for the RFID will be an Internet-coupled one to act as an end device and that will be connected to the tagged objects using the protocols.

The tagged item is portable, hence it can move from a reader to the other one and due to this, there is a necessity of verification by means of mutual authentication. As cryptographic features are not available in RFID, the scheme is highly susceptible to security attacks (Lee, Lin, & Huang, 2014; Yang, Forte, & Tehranipoor, 2015).

A two-way authentication scheme was proposed for applications that use IoT-RFID with a focus on mobile-based networks by giving the reader a cache that will store the keys for authentication; in terms of cost of computation this reduces the cost and in security terms it is increased. A two-way authentication scheme was also proposed for IoT near field communication (NFC) based applications for mobile networks (Fan, Gong, Liang, Li, & Yang, 2016).

Cloud-based IoT authentication is another research area. Cloud is appropriate for data management for devices connected to the IoT. Integration of the IoT into the cloud environment has a remarkable effect on day-to-day activities. Compared to the generic IoT architecture, cloud-based IoT procedures are better as the cost related to query processing will be less than with generic architecture. A user has to validate himself to the network environment and the process needs a proper authentication procedure.

IoT data management is a tedious process, and a platform based on the cloud is a better option. In IoT-based applications, users should be authenticated properly to access data from sensors and the related storage. Wazid et al. discussed methods for authentication of IoT devices connected to the cloud environment and proposed a lightweight authentication scheme (Wazid, Das, Bhat, & Vasilakos, 2020).

Feng, Qin, Zhao, and Feng (2018) proposed a lightweight methodology for Attestation and Authentication of Things (AAoT), which ensures the integrity of software, two-way authentications, and a feature to resist tampering for smart devices. The method relies on PUFs. This protocol uses two variants: strong and weak PUFs. PUF-based memory random filling is responsible for lessening the utilization of resources related to memory. The scheme ensures effective ways for all AAoT parts/blocks involved, such as optimization, and also ensures two-way authentication.

Authenticating centralized systems in the IoT is difficult and not very efficient. A decentralized authentication mechanism called bubbles of trust has been proposed (Hammi, Hammi, Bellot, & Serhrouchni, 2018). Here bubbles are created in which an identification and trusting mechanism for the entities is performed by means of blockchain technology—Ethereum that uses smart contracts. The master sends a transaction that contains its identifier and the identifier of the group. The blockchain checks the uniqueness of both. For all the transactions involved, if it is valid the bubble will be created. The objects which are followers direct transactions to the appropriate bubbles. Each follower involved will have a ticket that consists of a related ID, address, and a signature that uses the elliptic curve digital signature algorithm. The smart contract verifies the uniqueness of the involved credentials. If the initial transaction is successful then there is no need for further authentication by the object.

Extensive researches have been done on the integration of the IoT and blockchains, however the research on security challenges involved in the application of blockchain and the IoT remains minimal. Although mechanisms ensure complete secrecy, there is no guarantee related to the identification process involved. To ensure identification, applying blockchain methods can be used. These methods have disadvantages including the trouble of introducing a new device. In the IoT, checking the identity of a device entering the system is the fundamental security aspect. Authentication is a process that governs and ensures the user has entry to the specified system. The process is divided into three categories: knowledge based, possession based, and ownership based.

The applications connected to the network are prone to various attacks, including but not limited to password guessing/dictionary attack, replay attack, server spoofing attack, remote server attack, stolen verifier attack, and server spoofing attack. Though various techniques have been proposed so far to address the attacks there remains a need for novel techniques. DNA cryptography is one of the recent research areas in the field of information security.

5.2.5 DNA cryptography

DNA computing is an evolving model for information security using the computational features of DNA. DNA computing was initially proposed by Adleman (Adleman, 1994) A proof of concept was illustrated using DNA for computation to solve the seven-point Hamiltonian path problem, which is a nondeterministic algorithm. That marked the beginning of a new field in cryptography, DNA cryptography.

DNA-based cryptography depends on the dominant concepts of modern molecular biology and related concepts. DNA computing concepts not only laid the foundation of modern molecular biology but also promoted DNA computing-based encryption techniques. DNA computing is an exciting and fast-developing interdisciplinary area of research that includes theoretical approaches, experiments, and applications.

Various DNA-based methodologies are proposed for authentication (Mohammed and Sreeja, 2015) and confidentiality (Sukumaran and Mohammed, 2018a; Sukumaran and Mohammed, 2018b), and the research specifies on achieving security aspects using DNA encryption techniques. DNA coding rules are used in most DNA encryption techniques and the DNA coding method is depicted in Table 5.1. The DNA sequence consists of four nucleic acid bases that are adenine (A), cytosine (C), guanine (G), and thymine (T), where A and T are complementary, and G and C are complementary. The literature review indicates that DNA encryption techniques are broadly categorized into:

TABLE 5.1 Coding used in DNA.

Bases	Gray coding
A	01
G	10
C	11
T	00

- DNA-based symmetric cryptography;
- DNA-based asymmetric encryption that uses bioconcepts in combination with conventional cryptographic techniques; and
- Pseudo-DNA cryptography.
  DNA encryption techniques play a vital role in ensuring security aspects and have many applications. However, this research area requires extensive research to explore more applications. Fig. 5.1 depicts the base pairing in DNA.

5.3 Methodology

This section proposes a secure user authentication procedure that uses DNA-based encoding and steganography in view of both security and usability. This authentication protocol uses a text-based password, DNA encoding, steganography, and hash function. The proposed system also uses a unique ID as a healthcare ID which can be a national identification number in this scheme. Aadhaar, a unique identification number, is proposed for UID which is allotted by the Unique Identification Authority of India. A two-factor method, One Time Password (OTP) is also proposed to strengthen the device authentication. The notations used in the proposed algorithm are depicted in Table 5.2. Fig. 5.2 represents the user registration phase.

5.4 Security analysis

This section details and discusses the theoretical security analysis of the proposed scheme for authentication.

5.4.1 Password file compromise attack

In the proposed method, computing the hash value of passphrase along with other additional credentials

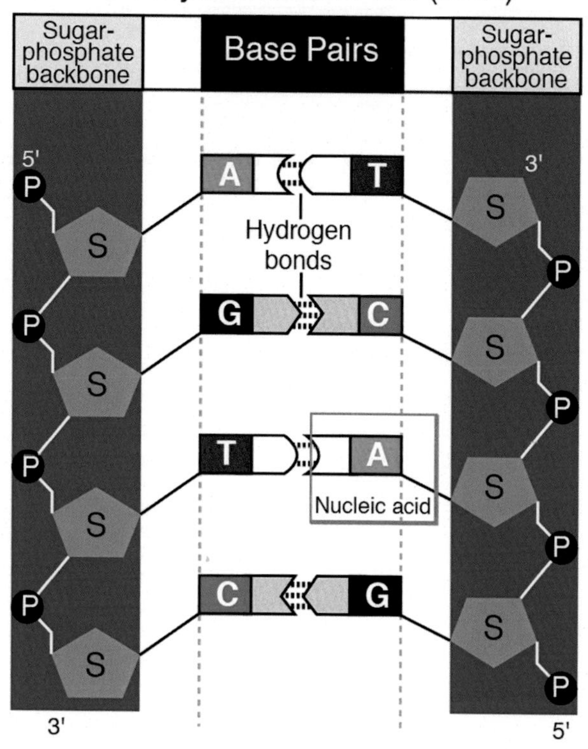

FIGURE 5.1 Base pairing in DNA (Pray, 2008). *Source: https://www.genome.gov/genetics-glossary/Double-Helix.*

TABLE 5.2 Notations used in the algorithm.

Notations	Description
U, AS	User, authentication server
ID_U	Username or ID of user
pwd_U	Passphrase nominated by U in the course of registration
UID	Unique ID, healthcare ID of user U
MI_U	The ID number of the medical device
h()	Hash function
DNA Seq_U	AGCT sequence alloted for the user in the course of registration

Algorithm 1A: Registration Phase for the User

UR1: Registration request to the AS by the U.

UR2: AS displays the registration interface to U.

UR3: U has to set the information for registration including user ID (ID_U), mobile number UID, a healthcare ID which is a unique ID such as National ID of the user.

UR4: U selects Password, pwd_U.

UR5: Applying DNA coding method for DNA sequence enhances security. AS selects the DNA coding as the default method given in Table 5.1. U can customize the sequence values for additional security. However, in this case, U should recollect the assigned values as an additional credential. U can also select the option for receiving OTP during authentication.

UR6: For U, AS selects a DNA Seq_U from the digital database.

UR7: Depending on the credentials U has nominated throughout the registration, AS computes the key:

Key = HASH [Stego DNA [$_U$]] where,

Steg DNA [$_U$] = [Encoded [binary [pwd_U + DNA seq_U]]] injected into the DNA Seq_U.

UR8: U completes the registration and AS notifies U regarding the same.

Algorithm 1B: Registration Phase for the Medical Device

MDR1: The medical device (MD_U) for the user U should be registered with the AS using the electronic product code of the device MD_{EPC}

MDR2: AS computes $h(MD_{EPC}) || h(UID)$ and stores the value in the device details table and the registration of MD_U is successful.

Algorithm 2A: Authentication Phase

L1: U enters username—ID_U.

L2: If ID_U is valid, the system displays an interface to enter UID.

L3: If it is valid, U can enter the pwd_U else go to L1.

L4: If U had selected UR5 during registration. U has to enter the binary code sequence for DNA after entering pwd_U otherwise U can proceed to L5.

L5: Based on the ID_U, UID, and pwd_U. AS picks the DNA seq_U from the database and performs DNA steganography.

L6: DNA steganography(DNA_s) = Encodes[code[pwd_U → DNA] → DNA seq_U].

L7: Computes h(DNA_s), using a secure hash algorithm (SHA-256) and hash value will be collated against the hash value generated in the registration process. If both values match, then the authentication is granted for the user U, otherwise access will be denied.

Algorithm 2B: Authentication Phase of Medical Device (MD_U)

L1: After successful user authentication AS sends an OTP to the U.

L2: Ur enters the OTP into the MD_U and the AS validates the OTP and upon successful authentication, the session is established.

Algorithm 3: Password Change Phase

PC1: U enters—ID_U.

PC2: If ID_U is valid, one system produces an interface for UID.

PC3: If UID is effective, correct U can enter the pwd_U else go to P1. If the user forgets pwd_U, it can be recovered using the registered mobile number or email ID.

PC4: Depending on ID_U, UID, and pwd_U. AS preferences the DNA seq_U from the database and performs DNA steganography.

PC5: DNA steganography (DNA_s) = Encodes[code [pwd_U → DNA] → DNA seq_U].

PC6: Computes h(DNA_s). Computes using a secure hash algorithm. The hash value will be compared against the hash value generated and stored during registration. If both values match, then the authentication is granted for the user U otherwise access will be denied.

PC7: After a successful process, the user can generate a new password pwd_{U1}.

PC8: After setting pwd_{U1}, AS performs operations defined as per PC5 and P6 and stores the newly generated hash value (Fig. 5.3).

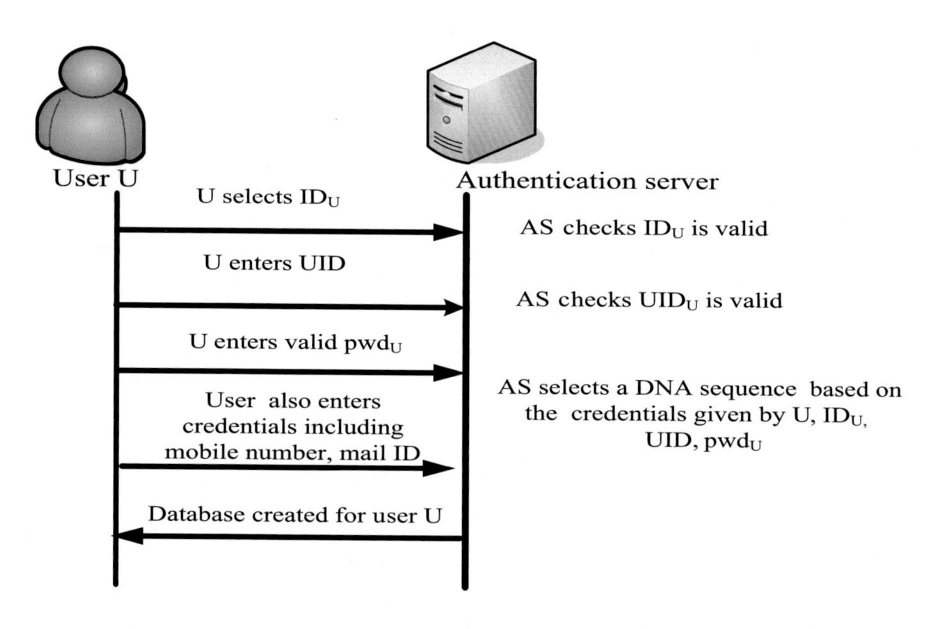

FIGURE 5.2 Registration phase for the user.

ensures protection from password file compromise attack as the attacker will not be able to retrieve the password from the hash value. OTP generated for device authentication also enhances security. The DNA sequence method for stegonagraphy also plays a vital role in resisting password file compromise attacks.

5.4.2 Dictionary attack

A dictionary attack is a method used to attack an authentication system by trying to determine the password with the probability of all possible words in a dictionary. The proposed scheme is resistant to this attack since the attacker cannot calculate the pwd, as the knowledge of pwd is not sufficient to access the account should the attacker insert the proper binary code of base pairs. The nonce generated for the device also makes the attacker resistant to performing the dictionary attack.

5.4.3 Replay attack

The proposed system uses a nonce value which will resist the possibility of this attack, where an adversary

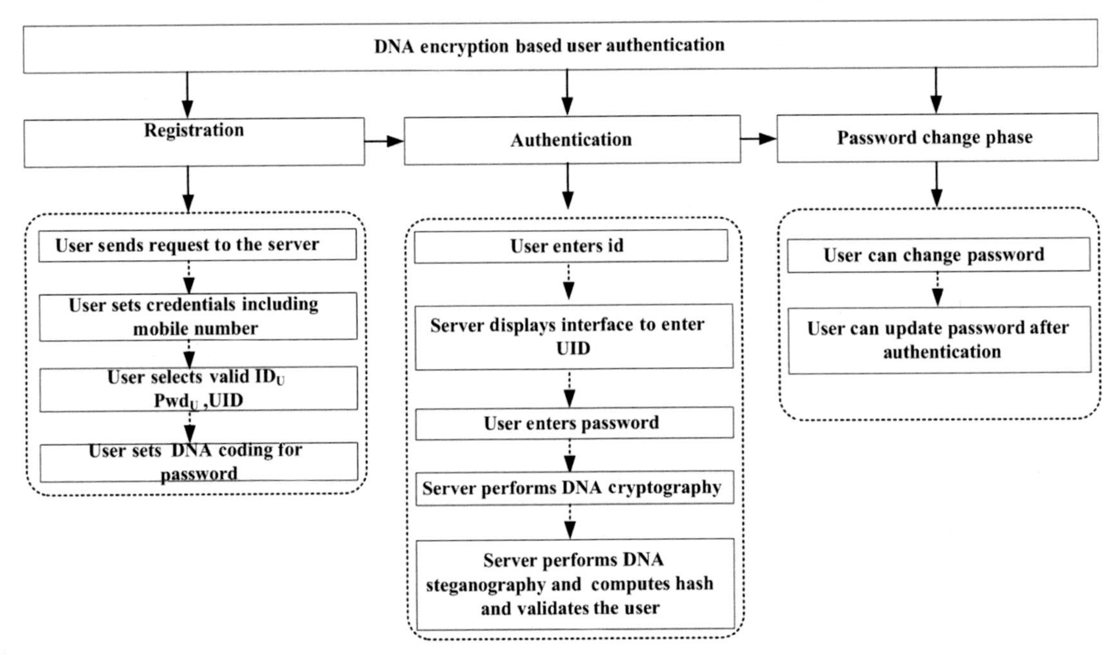

FIGURE 5.3 Proposed architecture.

Scyther results : verify

Claim				Status	Comments
authlogin	I	authlogin,i1	Secret IDu	Ok	No attacks within bounds.
		authlogin,i2	Alive	Ok	No attacks within bounds.
		authlogin,i3	Niagree	Ok	No attacks within bounds.
		authlogin,i4	Nisynch	Ok	No attacks within bounds.
		authlogin,i5	Secret o	Ok	No attacks within bounds.
		authlogin,i6	Secret k	Ok	No attacks within bounds.
		authlogin,i7	Secret PW	Ok	No attacks within bounds.
		authlogin,i8	Weakagree	Ok	No attacks within bounds.
	R	authlogin,r1	Secret IDu	Ok	No attacks within bounds.
		authlogin,r2	Secret o	Ok	No attacks within bounds.
		authlogin,3r	Alive	Ok	No attacks within bounds.
		authlogin,r4	Niagree	Ok	No attacks within bounds.
		authlogin,r5	Nisynch	Ok	No attacks within bounds.

FIGURE 5.4 Proposed authentication protocol.

tries to record a communication session and attempts to replay the entire session. The nonce value generated for every session ensures security from this type of attack.

5.5 Scyther analysis

Analysis of the proposed protocol is completed by means of the Scyther tool, an automated tool for the verification, falsification, and formal analysis of protocols defined for security. The protocol verification and the validated claims are depicted in Fig. 5.4.

5.6 Conclusion

Authentication in the IoT is a major concern. This chapter reviews existing methodologies used by the IoT and reviews the security challenges involved and identifies authentication as a major concern. To address the issues of user authentication, especially considering the security issues in healthcare and IoT-connected medical devices, a DNA-based authentication scheme is proposed which ensures both usability and security. Security analysis of the proposed method is also analyzed using Scyther and validated with no attacks.

References

Aadharcard Kendra Organization. (n.d.). What is Aadhar Card—Its Uses, Benefits and Why You Should Have it! http://www.aadharcardkendra.org.in/what-is-aadhar-card-benefits-uses-1424/.

Adleman, L.M. (1994). Molecular computation of solutions to combinatorial problems, Science-AAAS-Weekly Paper Edition 266.5187, vol., no 266, pp. 1021–1023, Nov. 1994.

Burhan, M., Rehman, R. A., Khan, B., & Kim, B.-S. (2018). IoT elements, layered architectures and security issues: A comprehensive survey. *Sensors*, *18*(9).

Chim, T., Yiu, S., Hui, L.C., & Li, V.O. (2011). PASS: Privacy-preserving authentication scheme for smart grid network. In Proceedings of the 2011 IEEE International Conference on Smart Grid Communications (SmartGridComm).

El-hajj, M., Fadlallah, A., Chamoun, M., & Serhrouchni, A. (2019). A survey of internet of things (IoT) authentication schemes. *Sensors*, *19*(5), 1141.

Fan, K., Gong, Y., Liang, C., Li, H., & Yang, Y. (2016). Lightweight and ultralightweight RFID mutual authentication protocol with cache in the reader for IoT in 5G. *Security and Communication Networks*.

Feng, W., Qin, Y., Zhao, S., & Feng, D. (2018). AAoT: Lightweight attestation and authentication of low-resource things in IoT and CPS. *Computer Networks*, *134*.

Hammi, M. T., Hammi, B., Bellot, P., & Serhrouchni, A. (2018). Bubbles of Trust: A decentralized blockchain-based authentication system for IoT. *Computers & Security*, *78*, 126–142.

Kavianpour, S., Shanmugam, B., Azam, S., Zamani, M., Narayana Samy, G., & De Boer, F. (2019). A Systematic Literature Review of Authentication in Internet of Things for Heterogeneous Devices. *Journal of Computer Networks and Communications*, 2019.

Lee, J.Y., Lin, W.C., & Huang, Y.H. (2014). A lightweight authentication protocol for Internet of Things. In Proceedings of the 2014 International Symposium on Next-Generation Electronics (ISNE), Kwei-Shan, Taiwan, 7–10 May 2014.

Li, H., Lu, R., Zhou, L., Yang, B., & Shen, X. (2014). An efficient Merkle-tree-based authentication scheme for smart grid. *IEEE Systems Journal*, *8*, 655–663.

Mohammed, M., & C.S. Sreeja. (2015). "A secure image-based authentication scheme employing DNA crypto and steganography." In Proceedings of the Third International Symposium on Women in Computing and Informatics, pp. 595–601.

Pray, L. (2008). Discovery of DNA structure and function: Watson and Crick. *Nature Education*.

Rao, T. A., & Haq, E. U. (2018). Security challenges facing IoT layers and its protective measures. *International Journal of Computer Applications*, *975*, 8887.

Robinson, A. (2016). Genomics–the future of healthcare and medicine. *Prescriber*, *27*(4), 51–55.

Sukumaran, S. C., & Mohammed, M. (2018a). PCR and Bio-signature for data confidentiality and integrity in mobile cloud computing. *Journal of King Saud University-Computer and Information Sciences*, in press.

Sukumaran, S. C., & Mohammed, M. (2018b). DNA cryptography for secure data storage in Cloud. *IJ Network Security*, *20*, 447–454.

Wazid, M., Das, A. K., Bhat, V., & Vasilakos, A. V. (2020). LAM-CIoT: Lightweight authentication mechanism in cloud-based IoT environment. *Journal of Network and Computer Applications*, *150*, 102496.

Xu, H., Ding, J., Li, P., Zhu, F., & Wang, R. (2018). A lightweight RFID mutual authentication protocol based on physical unclonable function. *Sensors*, *18*, 760.

Xue, Q., Ju, X., Zhu, H., Zhu, H., Li, F., & Zheng, X. (2019). A biometric-based IoT device identity authentication scheme. In S. Han, L. Ye, & W. Meng (Eds.), *Artificial Intelligence for Communications and Networks. AICON 2019. Lecture Notes of the Institute for Computer Sciences, Social Informatics and Telecommunications Engineering* (vol. 287). Cham: Springer.

Yang, K., Forte, D., & Tehranipoor, M.M. (2015). Protecting endpoint devices in IoT supply chain. In Proceedings of the 2015 IEEE/ACM International Conference on Computer-Aided Design (ICCAD), Austin, TX, USA, 2–6 November 2015.

CHAPTER

6

Computational intelligence techniques for cancer diagnosis

Nimrita Koul and Sunil Kumar S. Manvi

School of Computing and Information Technology, REVA University, Bangalore, India

6.1 Introduction

Cancer is a condition in which the body's natural cycle of cell division (Nordling, 2017), growth, and death is disturbed in certain tissues. This leads to a build-up of abnormal cell mass that interferes with the natural processes of the human body and leads to serious sickness. This disease can occur due to various causes including genetic mutations, can originate at different tissues in the body, and can metastasize to other parts. Even in the same tissue, cancer tumors may have varying molecular signatures. There are around 200 known subtypes of cancer, each one requiring a different line of treatment. Therefore no single medicine can control the tumors of varying types and subtypes. Tumors progress with evolution at somatic levels within the cell populations, and there is selective mutation and cloning among cancer cells that continuously increase their numbers. All of these factors make cancer research one of the most challenging and important biomedical challenges for humanity. With the advent of next-generation sequencing (NGS) technologies, genetic mutations and abnormalities can be computationally analyzed and personalized treatment approaches prescribed for the patients. This will prevent damage to healthy cells and tissues, which is a side effect of generalized chemotherapy and radiotherapy. Methods in computational intelligence (CI) can be used to discriminate tumor types based on molecular signatures, mathematical modeling can help with understanding evolutionary patterns (Armitage & Doll, 1954) in cancer progression, and these computational techniques can also be used to develop appropriate drugs suited to particular tumor types. Computational methods like artificial intelligence, machine learning, and evolutionary computing have effectively advanced healthcare research in diseases like cancer. The use of computational methods for data processing and analysis has led to early and improved accuracy of diagnosis. With the use of advanced techniques like probabilistic methods and deep learning, we are now ushering in the era of personalized therapy, custom treatment approaches, and targeted drug discovery and delivery. These are aimed at improving the effectiveness of treatment and quality of life for patients. The availability of a massive volume of healthcare data in the form of genomic (Shendure & Lieberman Aiden, 2012; Vidyasagar, 2017) and imaging data (Nahar, Imam, Tickle, Ali, & Chen, 2012; Fogel, 2008) from magnetic resonance imaging (MRI) technology, computed tomography (CT) scans, medical records, laboratory reports, etc. along with the development of several machine learning-based tools and databases has enabled scientists and researchers to gain better insights into various biological mechanisms related to diseases and to develop better drugs. Both clinical oncology and CI fields have seen huge technological advances in terms of medical data generation, high-performance computational platforms, and deep machine learning models in the recent past, therefore a strong collaboration between artificial intelligence along with its subset technologies, clinical oncology, and cancer researchers will greatly benefit patients by improving their quality of life.

6.2 Background

6.2.1 Cancer research data

Cancer research is an umbrella term involving research at the epidemiological, clinical, molecular, mathematical, and computational levels. Computational

Recent Trends in Computational Intelligence Enabled Research.
DOI: https://doi.org/10.1016/B978-0-12-822844-9.00032-3

research in cancer uses data generated by various techniques for analysis. The prominent types of data include genomic or molecular data produced by genomic technologies like NGS, DNA microarrays, mass spectrometry, imaging data produced by technologies like CT scanning, radiology data like MRI, X-rays, etc., clinical data, pathological data produced as a result of blood and tissue pathological examination, relapse, quality of life and survival data generated by clinical trials and cohort studies, demographics data, medical prescriptions or notes by oncologists, etc. (Menze et al., 2015; Li, Liang, & Yao, 2018; Gillies, Kinahan, & Hricak, 2016; Jha & Topol, 2016). Before making use of data for decision making in cancer research we need to ensure the reliability, validity, quality, and completeness of data, and in addition we also need to ensure that our data satisfy all legal and regulatory requirements. The efficiency and reliability of computational techniques applied to derive meaningful and actionable insights from cancer data depend on the quality of input data and their completeness. Though some CI techniques have been developed to handle missing data or class imbalances in data, still the use of bad data results in bad predictions and decisions. Cancer research to provide precision oncology uses genomic data to prescribe targeted and specific drug combinations that are thought to be most suitable for the specific types of cancer the patient has. This is aimed at improving the outcomes of the treatment. Data from molecular imaging have shown promising results, providing very accurate diagnostic markers in precision oncology.

6.2.2 Genomic data for cancers

In the 1950s, Nordling (Nordling, 2017) and Armitage (Armitage & Doll, 1954) analyzed cancer incidence data and inferred that cancer is a multistage process with an accumulation of genomic alterations. NGS technologies (Chaudhary, Poirion, Lu, & Garmire, 2018) have produced huge volumes of high-dimensional cancer genomic data from a sampling of tumors and individual tumor cells at molecular levels. Genes within cells contain the information about what proteins to make and when, they regulate the production of these building blocks of the body. Since direct measurement of these proteins is difficult, we measure the messenger RNA levels through cDNA microarray experiments. These experiments give us log values of expression values as there often is a huge difference in the value of expression of different genes of the same sample. Cancer genomes, epigenomes, transcriptomes, proteomes, and other molecular profiles are available to assess intertumor and intratumor heterogeneity. These data have been hosted on several publicly available data repositories like The Cancer Genome Atlas (Armitage & Doll, 1954). Efficient analysis of these data using computational techniques can significantly help with the development of more effective drugs, diagnostics, and treatment approaches, which can help evaluate the response of tumors to drugs. The aim is to successfully translate advances in technology to clinical benefits to patients and society at large. Typically, the data corresponding to tumors are in the form of a matrix (x_i, y_i), where $i = 1, 2, m$ and m is the number of tumors or samples. For each tuple, the element x_i is the vector consisting of real numbers corresponding to molecular measurement like DNA methylation data, gene expression levels, copy number variations, etc. Each row in this matrix corresponds to data measurements for one sample and it can consist of thousands of features. Here y_i is the label or the clinical decision parameter, for example, diagnosis, survival result, etc., for the sample. The parameter y_i can be the real type or categorical. The number of features in each row of the input matrix is much larger than the number of rows or samples in the matrix. One of the important challenges in computational cancer research is to reduce the number of features in input data. This is done by feature subset identification methods (Hsieh et al., 2011; Scrobotă et al., 2017; Zhang et al., 2018; Kovalerchuk, Triantaphyllou, Ruiz, & Clayton, 1997) that search for a small subset of features S which provide a good approximation for each y_i. Therefore two important steps in the computational diagnosis of cancers are:

1. To find the smallest subset S, from the original set of input features $(x_1, x_2 \ldots x_i)$, of most relevant features of the outcome indicated by y_i. These features are also referred to as biomarkers of the disease.
2. To build a computational model that can predict the value of label y_i from the set of selected features in step 1 above.

In case, y_i takes continuous values, the computational model is a regression model, in the case that y_i takes categorical values, it is a classification model. When the number of samples is more than features, the least-squares regression is helpful, but in the case of cancer research, the number of samples is much less than the number of samples, therefore we have to apply sparse methods. When y has just two possibilities, it is sparse binary classification, for more than two possibilities in y, we need to apply multiclass classification procedures.

Fig. 6.1 shows the generation of molecular data including genomics data such as microarray data and NGS data and proteomics data. These data have been used by various computational studies for the automated classification of cancer profiles. Gillies et al. (2016) applied gene expression data of noncoding RNAs for the successful diagnosis of gastric cancers.

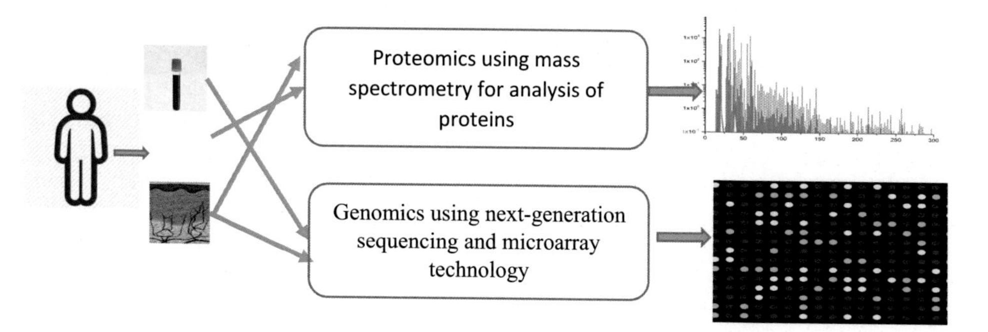

FIGURE 6.1 Molecular cancer diagnostics.

6.2.3 Imaging data for cancers

Prominent imaging techniques used for diagnosis and staging of human cancers include CT scans and plain film X-rays, ultrasound images, MRI (Hsieh et al., 2011; Scrobotă et al., 2017; Szilágyi, Lefkovits, & Benyó, 2015), single-photon emission computed tomography (SPECT), positron emission tomography (PET) (Fogel, 2008), and optical imaging. Of these, CT, MRI, SPECT, and PET technologies return three-dimensional images of any part of the human body, however these techniques lack resolution. A typical human cell is around 10 μm in diameter, that is, each 1 cm^3 of tissue has approximately one billion cells. These imaging techniques can detect abnormal tumor growths only at later stages when the size of the tumor falls within their resolution. This may be too late for certain patients and tumors. The concept of signal-to-background ratio, or tumor-to-background ratio is used to detect cancer cells against the backdrop of normal cells. The accurate detection needs signals produced by contrast mechanisms to be higher than the background signal. There are many barriers to accurate capturing of tumors at initial stages by imaging including the finite achievable concentration for receptor-targeted agents, inherent limitations of imaging technology, voluntary and physiologic motion artifacts at low levels near tumors, and high hydrostatic pressure impeding homogeneous infiltration of diagnostic agents. Several corrective techniques are employed to capture accurate images of the area around the suspect tumorous sites. However, recently, genomic data have been primarily used for early and more accurate diagnosis and staging of cancers by researchers worldwide. Dynamic contrast enhanced-MRI (Cheng, 2017) also has been used for complementary diagnosis of breast cancer through computer-aided diagnosis systems. Deep neural network approaches like convolutional neural networks (CNNs) and U-net architecture have been successfully applied to analyze MRI images for segmentation and detection of tumorous areas in these images.

Fig. 6.2 shows the weighted contrast MRI pictures of three kinds of brain tumors: pituitary gland tumor, glioma, and meningioma. The data set (Cheng, 2017) consists of 3064 high-contrast MRI images of the brain. This data set can be used to train a classifier for the automatic identification of brain tumors.

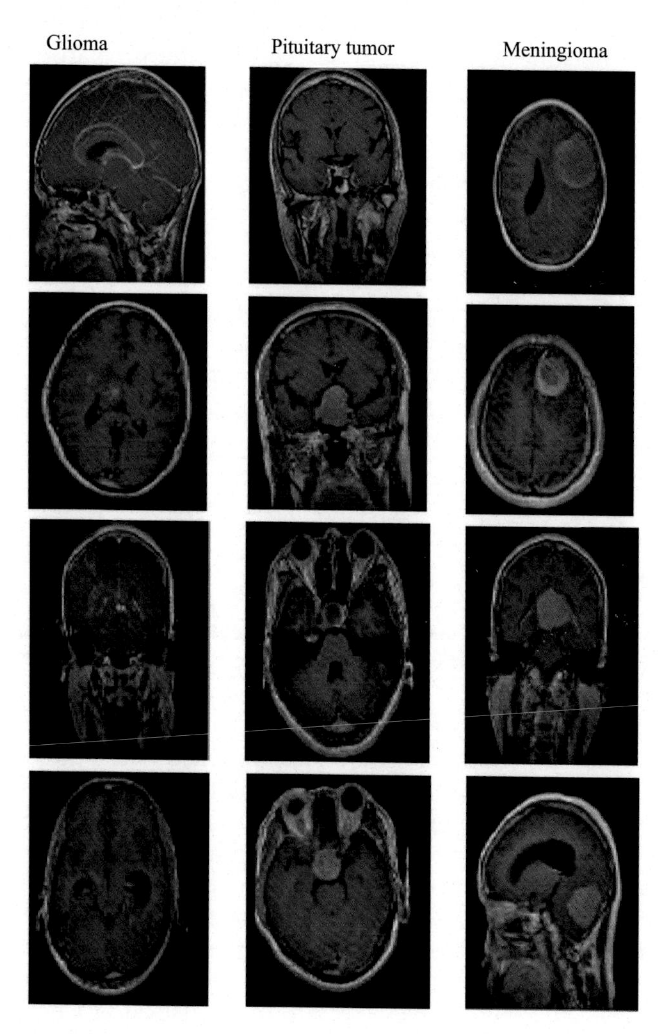

FIGURE 6.2 Weighted contrast magnetic resonance imaging images for three types of brain tumors: glioma, pituitary gland tumor, and meningioma.

6.3 Approaches to computational intelligence

CI refers to the theory, design, application, and development of biologically inspired computing paradigms. It has three main components: artificial neural networks (ANNs), fuzzy systems, and evolutionary computation. Minor components also include ambient intelligence, artificial life, cultural learning, artificial endocrine networks, social reasoning, and artificial hormone networks. It includes many models and techniques using fuzzy sets, neurocomputing, and bio- and nature-inspired evolutionary computing. While we can manage complex reasoning systems using fuzzy logic, the neural networks help us with the learning patterns in inputs, evolutionary algorithms help in single and multiobjective optimization in machine learning and search algorithms. Nature-inspired techniques like bee colony optimization and ant colony optimization help us in identifying the best solutions heuristically. CI has been used for the development of very intelligent computing systems used in disease diagnosis, like cancer diagnosis (Kalantari et al., 2018; Arasi, El-Horbaty, Salem, & El-Dahshan, 2017; Hassanien, Al-Shammari, & Ghali, 2013; Yang, Niemierko, Yang, Luo, & Li, 2007; Hassanien, Milanova, Smolinski, & Abraham, 2018; Dheeba, Singh, & Selvi, 2014; Abbass, 2002), gaming, medicine, computer vision, natural language processing, etc. Five main approaches used in CI are described in the following sections.

6.3.1 Evolutionary computation

Evolutionary computation (Abbass, 2002; Tan, Quek, Ng, & Razvi, 2008; Peña-Reyes & Sipper, 1999; Cosma, Brown, Archer, Khan, & Pockley, 2017) involves the use of algorithms that can evolve with the availability of more data and experience. These algorithms derive from the natural evolutionary processes as observed in organisms and processes in nature. Evolutionary computation begins with a possible set of solutions to a problem, then evaluates and modifies the possible set to arrive at the most suitable solution. These approaches include evolutionary strategies, genetic programming, swarm intelligence (Cosma et al., 2017; Nahar, Shawkat Ali, Imam, Tickle, & Chen, 2016), genetic algorithms (Peña-Reyes & Sipper, 1999), evolutionary programming, differential evolution (Anter & Hassenian, 2018), evolvable hardware, and algorithms used for multiobjective optimization tasks (Anter & Hassenian, 2018; Alzubaidi, Cosma, Brown, & Pockley, 2016; Wang, Ma, Wong, & Li, 2019). Since evolutionary computation simulates natural evolution, it involves optimization algorithms that iteratively enhance the quality of the solution set until an optimal solution is obtained. The ability of a solution to survive and reproduce in a particular environment is known as its evolutionary fitness.

Genetic algorithms (Wang et al., 2019) are a subfield of evolutionary computation. A genetic algorithm represents the variables in the problem domain in the form of chromosomes of fixed length. We have to choose the parameters like the initial size of the chromosome population, probability of crossover, and mutation, also a fitness function is decided on to select the chromosomes that will get the opportunity to mate during the phase of reproduction. The individuals which result from the mating of the parent chromosomes form the next generation of solutions and the process is repeated. Genetic algorithms are often used in cancer diagnosis for optimal feature selection from gene expression sets.

6.3.2 Learning theory

Learning theory involves combining cognitive, emotional, and environmental experiences for acquisition, enhancement, and change in knowledge, skills, values, and world views. Learning theory helps understand the processing of experiences and effects and making predictions using experience.

6.3.3 Artificial neural networks

ANNs are computational models inspired by the structure of natural neurons in the brain. They involve distributed information-processing systems which help in learning from experience. An ANN is a computing system constituted of several simple, highly interconnected processing elements, called neurons. A neuron processes information in parallel and responds dynamically to inputs. A neuron takes in one or more inputs, X_i, each input is assigned with a weight W_i. The neuron calculates the product of each input with corresponding weight and then sums all the products. The sum is passed through an activation function which is a nonlinear function. The activation function acts as a thresholding function on the weighted sum of inputs. Commonly used activation functions include sigmoid function, step function, rectified linear unit, leaky rectified linear unit, etc. Fig. 6.3 shows various parts of an artificial neuron.

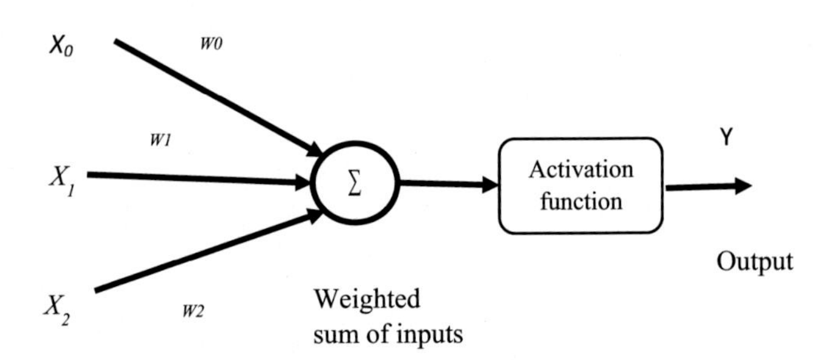

FIGURE 6.3 An artificial neuron.

When these neurons are connected such that the output of one neuron can be fed an input to the next neuron, we get an ANN. While a single neuron can compute a weighted sum, an ANN can compute a complex function. In ANNs neurons are arranged in layers and these layers have connections among them. Input is fed to the very first layer of neurons called the input layer, and each subsequent layer can perform a different transformation on input data (Fig. 6.4).

ANNs learn from data. Depending on whether the data are labeled or not, the training of ANNs is classified as supervised learning in the case that you have labeled data available, semisupervised learning in the case that some labeled data are available, and unsupervised learning in the case that there are no labeled data available. Reinforcement learning is a method for training a neural network that involves the use of reward and feedback systems to reinforce the correct response by the network. We can see that a neural network is an extended linear regression that can capture more complex nonlinear relations in data through its hidden layers. The value of parameters, that is, weights, is learned during the training of a neural network using algorithms like backpropagation. Backpropagation helps in adjusting the weights of all features in the network to minimize the output error. Neural network classifiers have been applied to the diagnosis of cancers by many researchers. Khan, Wei, and Ringnér (2001) used ANNs for the diagnosis of tumors. The input data set consisted of gene expression profiles of 6567 genes. Dheeba et al. (2014) applied an ANN classifier for the prediction of cancer of the breast, where the input data consisted of mammography images.

6.3.4 Probabilistic methods

Probabilistic methods leverage randomness in algorithms, this helps to bring out possible solutions using prior knowledge. Fuzzy systems model the imprecision and uncertainty to solve problems using approximate reasoning. This includes fuzzy controllers, fuzzy summarization, fuzzy neural networks, fuzzy clustering, and classification, etc. Bayesian networks use the probabilistic relationship between a set of random variables with some propositions. In cancer diagnosis, the node in a Bayesian network can represent the proposition about the presence of cancer. Edges account for probabilistic dependencies between variables. Bayesian networks are directed acyclic graphs and they can handle multivalued variables.

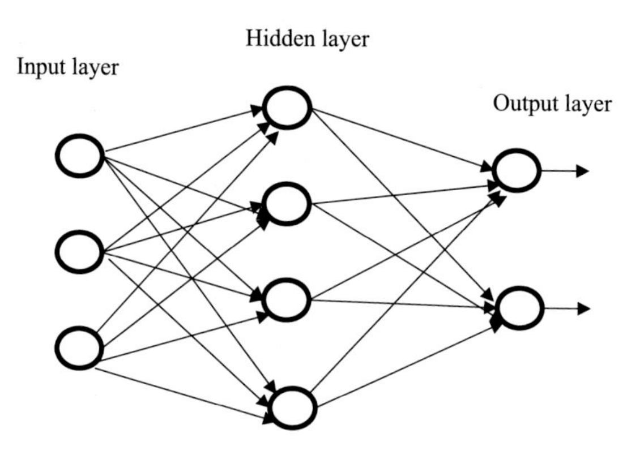

FIGURE 6.4 Basic structure of an artificial neural network consisting of one input, one output, and one hidden layer.

Since malignant tumors differ widely among themselves, therefore cancer treatments can benefit hugely from personalized medicine with customized therapy to patients. This needs a further understanding of the way subcellular components and processes work. However, with patient stratification the cancers are classified according to similarities, and therapies are directed at cancers belonging to the same class. This classification of tumors can be based on the location of origin of the tumor, microscopic anatomy of cells in the tumor, histological considerations, physical properties like color, texture, size of the tumor, etc. For example, there are two forms of lung cancer—small cell lung cancer and nonsmall cell lung cancer—nonsmall cell lunch cancer is further divided into three subclasses based on histology: adenocarcinoma, squamous cell carcinoma, and large cell carcinoma. There are four subtypes of breast cancer based on expression levels of three genes—estrogen receptor gene, progesterone receptor gene, and HER2 (Tan, Ung, Cheng, & Greene, 2018). Treatment and prognosis of cancers depend on their type. Therefore it is very important to accurately determine the type of tumor and prescribe the appropriate therapy for the same. This is where CI techniques play an important part. These techniques are aimed at enabling precision medicine. Precision medicine refers to medicine that has been customized for the genotype and phenotype of a person and their disease if present. Through CI methods, we can reach precision medicine in cancer treatment that targets genes, gene transcripts, proteins, and metabolites of an individual using a systems biology approach.

6.4 Computational intelligence techniques for feature selection in cancer diagnosis

Feature selection is the task of selecting a subset of features from the set of original features that are most informative and most relevant for the task under consideration. An effective technique for feature selection can discriminate relevant features from noisy and irrelevant features. Generally, feature selection techniques consider the relevance and redundancy of each feature during feature selection. A relevant feature has a higher predictive power toward the classification task. A redundant feature has a high correlation with other features and hence does not add significant new information to the decision-making process and can be dropped. In some data sets, the features may not be relevant when taken individually but are significantly relevant to predictive accuracy when taken in combination with other features.

6.4.1 Advantages of feature selection

Feature selection (Zhang et al., 2018) plays an important role during computational diagnosis (Tan et al., 2018; Zhang et al., 2018) of cancer. Feature selection improves the performance of classification models in case of both image data as well as genomic data. These advantages are listed below:

1. The reduction is the time taken to train the learning models for classification—Training of a smaller number of highly relevant features improves the prediction accuracy of diagnosis tasks during both training and testing phases. This can also reduce the complexity of the learning algorithm.
2. Increase in the predictive accuracy of the diagnosis systems—With the application of the most relevant features, the prediction accuracy of the diagnosis algorithm improves, and at the same time the computational complexity is reduced.
3. Convenient and easy to comprehend visualization—With a lower number of features, it is easier to visualize the impact of each feature on the outcome variable.
4. Lower storage requirement—Since the number of relevant features is less, we need to store fewer data.

Evolutionary computation-based methods like genetic algorithms, fuzzy rough sets, art colony optimization, particle swarm optimization (PSO), simulated annealing, whale optimization, gravitational search algorithm, etc. have been used for optimization of the search procedure in the feature selection task.

6.4.2 Rough sets for feature selection

Rough sets find a minimal representation of the original data set, thereby reducing its dimensionality. A rough set-based feature selection method can be combined with a classifier based on a neural network or fuzzy system. Under the rough set theory, the rough set attribute reduction approach is a filter method for feature selection that selects the minimal-sized most informative, nonredundant subset of features.

The algorithm QuickReduct in Fig. 6.5 computes dependency of all features, until the dependency of the resulting reduct is equal to the consistency of the data set. Conditional attributes that do not appear in the set are eliminated. The search can be terminated when dependency stabilizes. QuickReduct used forward selection for searching the features, a modification to quickly reduce the algorithm is the ReverseReduct algorithm, which uses backward elimination. QuickReduct in this form provides no guarantees concerning the minimal size of the resulting subset. The following search techniques (Hsieh et al., 2011) have been used with QuickReduct algorithm:

1. Greedy hill climbing—In this search method, the dependency function is used to identify the locally best features. The reaching of maximum dependency is the stopping criteria for the search procedure.
2. Breadth-first search—In this search method, all features are represented as nodes of a graph, and each node is visited exhaustively level by level to

Algorithm:	QuickReduct
Input:	C - Set of conditional features, D set of decision features
Output:	R -Subset of most relevant features
Step 1	R = { }
Step 2	Repeat until gR(D) = gc(D)
Step 3	T=R
Step 4	For all x in (C-R)
Step 5	If gRU{x} (D) > gr(D) where gR(D) = Card(POSR(D))/Card(U)
Step 6	T = RU{x}
Step 7	R = T
Step 8	Return R

FIGURE 6.5 Algorithm QuickReduct.

consider its suitability. The search can stop when a subset with maximum dependency is found.

3. Depth-first search—Like breadth-first search, depth-first search also arranges features as nodes of a graph and searches the graph branch by branch going from root to leaf in one branch at a time. Backtracking is used to go back to the previous node in case the current branch is not found to be giving the optimal solution subset and then the search continues at the next node.
4. Best-first search—In this search technique, the nodes are expanded greedily using a cost function. The nature of the cost function determines the suitability of this search technique.
5. A* search—In this method also, the features are arranged as nodes of the graph and the solution involves the search for the most suitable features. However, this search method minimizes the cost involved in searching the optimal solution path in the graph. This method finds the shortest path first just like breadth-first search.
6. Iterative deepening—In this method, the graph nodes are visited in depth-first manner, at each level the maximum depth limit of the search is increased and the search is repeated until the solution is found with minimum depth in the graph. Both A* and iterative deepening search are complete and give optimal solutions.

6.4.2.1 *Fuzzy-rough set-based feature selection*

To handle uncertainty in information, the fuzzy rough sets help to catch the vagueness as well as indiscernibility. A fuzzy rough set uses two approximations, one for lower and the other for upper limits. The elements can have a membership in the range [0, 1]. Fuzzy rough feature selection can be applied to both real-valued data, both continuous and nominal, as well as discrete data, and can handle noise in data well. Both the classification and regression tasks can be performed using this feature selection method. All fuzzy (Szilágyi et al., 2015) sets can be derived from input data and fuzzy partitions can be computed, however the inputs from genome experts and oncologists can help in deciding the partitions. An object x belongs to the positive or negative region only if its corresponding equivalence class belongs to the positive or negative region. To be effective in feature selection, the fuzzy rough feature reduction process has to handle dependency among subsets of the original feature set through evaluation of the degree of dependency in the decision features. Various reformulations can be applied to speed up the calculation of reducts using a fuzzy rough set-based feature selection procedure.

6.4.3 Genetic algorithms for feature selection

Genetic algorithms are evolutionary algorithms based on the principle of natural evolution and survival of the fittest. These algorithms use operators like selection, crossover, and mutation. These algorithms are used for the optimization of the search procedure involved in the feature selection process, they return a Pareto front of the optimal solution. These have been often used for the task of feature selection in the case of disease classification and diagnosis. In combination with classifiers like neural networks, support vector machines, or decision trees, the genetic algorithms and their modifications have been proved to give very good diagnosis accuracies for various types of cancer.

The components of a genetic algorithm are:

1. Chromosome—A chromosome is a representation of the search space as well as a potential solution to the problem. These are represented as strings of bits and are made up of gene sequences.
2. The population is a set of chromosomes where each chromosome represents a possible solution.
3. Fitness function—This is a function that is used to evaluate the suitability of an individual chromosome toward the desired outcome of the problem being solved. This function usually returns a nonnegative value for suitable individuals.
4. Selection operator—The selection operator is a function that selects some chromosomes from the current generation, based on their fitness, to participate in the reproduction process.
5. Crossover operator—This is a function that takes in a pair of chromosomes of the current generation and produces a new pair of chromosomes by applying them to mix. The mixing can be at a single point or two points. In single-point mixing, the mixing of chromosome bit values occurs at a randomly chosen place. In two-point mixing, the mixing happens at two points.
6. Mutation operator—The mutation operator introduces diversity in the chromosomes after the cross-over operator has worked on them. The mutation operator randomly selects a gene from a chromosome and introduces a random mutation in it.

To decide when the iterations of the genetic algorithm-based feature selection should stop, we have to continuously apply fitness function to the new generation and when the fitness values are best as compared to all other iterations since the beginning of the genetic algorithm iterations we can stop. If the current fitness is less than that in previous generations, we may have obtained the best solution. In some cases, the stopping criteria are also when a maximum number of iterations have been reached. It helps to plot fitness values of the current population since the start of the algorithm with the generation number to keep track of the growth of the fitness of a population. The mutation rate has to be decided with caution as too high a rate results in nonconvergence of the algorithm. When we reach a generation with equal fitness levels of individuals, the algorithm should be terminated. The algorithm for feature selection using a genetic algorithm is presented in Fig. 6.6.

Many variants of the basic genetic algorithm also are used in practice. Koul and Manvi (2020b) applied a genetic algorithm-based pipeline of feature selection methods for the identification of the most important genes for the classification of small round blue cell tumor (SRBCT). This tumor occurs in four subtypes, all appearing round in shape and bluish in color: Ewing's family of tumors, neuroblastoma, non-Hodgkin lymphoma, and rhabdomyosarcoma. The original gene expression data set consists of 2308 genes, the authors identified the 50 most important genes using the genetic algorithm pipeline, and using these genes they were able to classify the four subtypes of SBCTS with 97% accuracy. Fig. 6.7 shows the classification accuracy and cross-validation accuracy for the SRBCT gene expression dataset using 10, 20, 30, 40, and 50 selected genes. We can see that the maximum value of the cross-validation score is reached with 50 features.

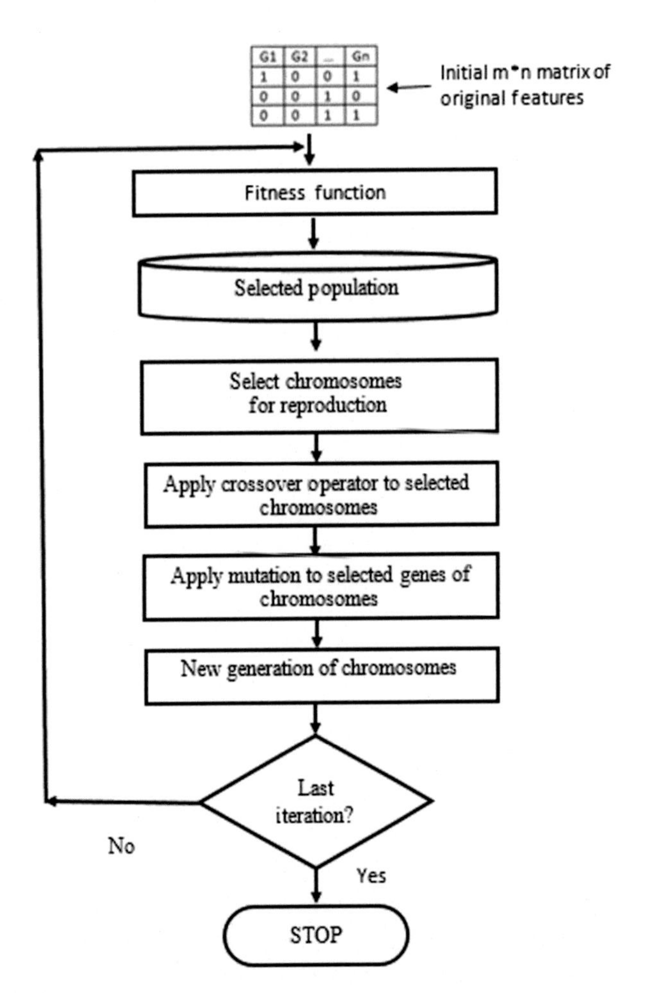

FIGURE 6.6 Flowchart of feature selection using a genetic algorithm.

6.4.4 Adaptive network fuzzy inference system

An adaptive network fuzzy inference system (ANFIS) is an ANN with a fuzzification layer. The inference system in ANFIS has a set of fuzzy "if-then" rules that approximate nonlinear functions. The parameters for ANFIS can be obtained using genetic algorithms. The network structure of an ANFIS system has two parts—the premise and the consequence. These are divided into five layers. The input layer is responsible for computing membership functions and deciding the membership degrees of input by applying premise parameters. This layer acts as the fuzzification layer. The second layer is the rule layer which generates the firing strengths for rules. The third layer normalizes the firing strengths. The fourth layer is the defuzzification layer which uses normalized values and consequence parameters. The fifth layer is the output layer. Unlike neural networks, ANFIS neural networks do not need the sigmoid function, they instead need a fuzzier function that applies membership function. The membership function associates

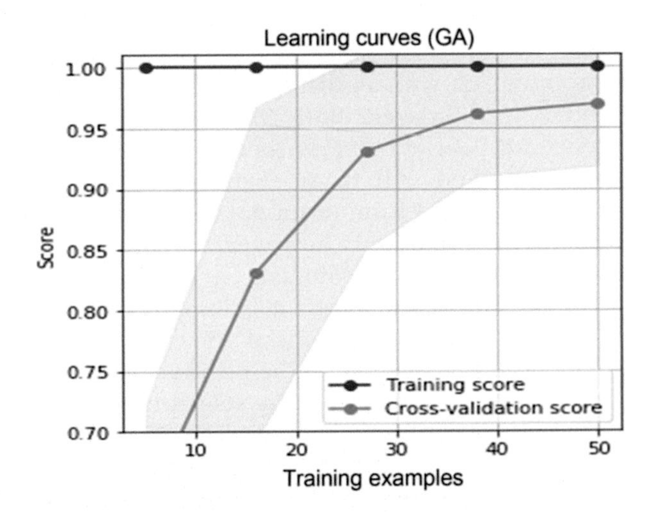

FIGURE 6.7 Classification performance on small round blue cell tumor data set using the genetic algorithm pipeline.

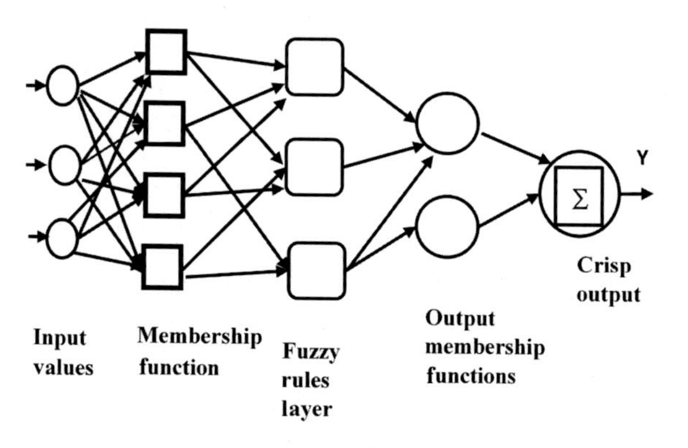

FIGURE 6.8 Neurofuzzy inference system.

categorical descriptions like tumor or nontumor to the numerical inputs based on some threshold value. Fig. 6.8 shows the arrangement of layers in the adaptive neurofuzzy inference system. The first layer is where the crisp inputs are fed into the system, layer two applies membership functions to the inputs and converts then inputs into fuzzy values, the next layer is a layer containing fuzzy rule about the type of cancer that is being diagnosed through this system, next is the output membership layer which converts fuzzy values back into the crisp output. The outputs are then passed through an activation function to generate the final output of the system.

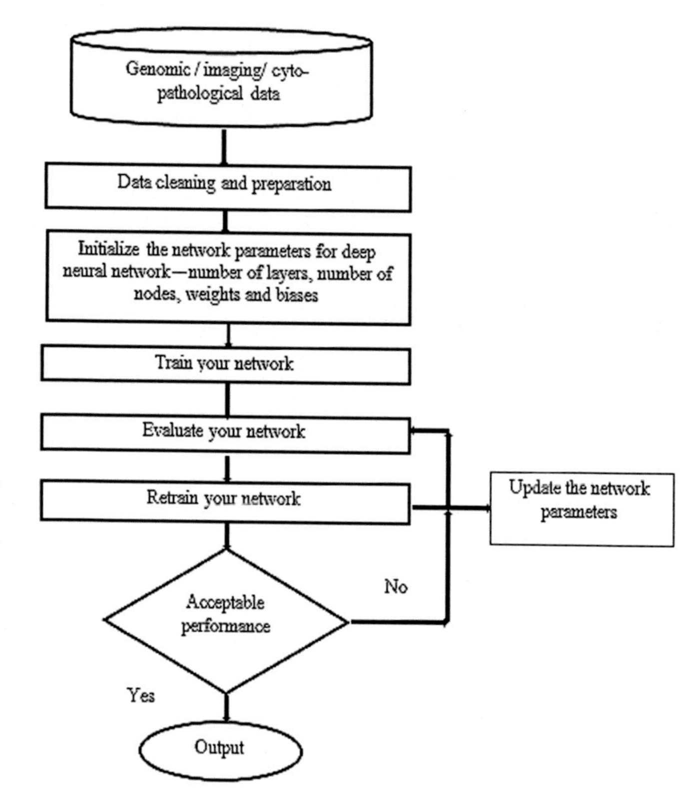

FIGURE 6.9 Flowchart for using a deep neural network for a classification task.

6.4.5 Deep learning for cancer diagnosis

Deep learning refers to the use of many-layered ANNs. It is a commonly accepted convention that if the number of layers in a neural network, including input and output layers, exceeds three, the corresponding network is called a deep neural network.

Fig. 6.9 shows the step-by-step flowchart of various tasks involved in the use of a deep neural network for classification tasks. The first few hidden layers learn the representative features of the data and the later layers are used for classification or regression.

6.4.5.1 *Deep neural networks as feature extractors*

A deep neural network uses the first few hidden layers for learning the features or representations of input data. Therefore the need for manual feature selection or feature engineering is reduced. Having more layers also enabled a deep neural network to work with features in data having complex nonlinear relationships among themselves. The most common deep learning models that have been used in cancer research are CNNs (Lecun, Bottou, & Bengio, 1998) that have shown very good accuracies for classification using cancer imaging data, recurrent neural networks, and deep belief networks or Boltzmann machines. Sometimes CNNs (Feng et al., 2019; Wang et al., 2018; Wang et al., 2020; Firoozbakht, Rezaeian, Ngom, Rueda, & Porter, 2015; Karim, Wicaksono, Costa, Decker, & Beyan, 2019; Cai, Long, Dai, & Huang, 2020) and their variants have shown very good results for computer vision problems. The CNNs have been applied to cancer medical images for automatic and accurate detection and localization of various types of tumors. This sometimes needs user-drawn boxes as regions of interest for the neural network to classify as tumors or nontumors. Esteva, Kuprel, and Novoa (2017) applied CNNs for the diagnosis of skin cancer using imaging data with 90% accuracy.

As shown in Fig. 6.10, a CNN uses filters to automatically extract important features from cancer images. The positional information of the pixels is kept intact even in the extracted features. In mathematics, convolution is a matrix operation involving a matrix multiplication between a larger and a smaller matrix in a revolving fashion. The images from which we need to extract features are represented as matrices, and the mathematical operations that extract required features are represented as filters. The number of trainable parameters increases with the increase in the size of input images. With CNNs, the spatial features are retained (Cai et al., 2020).

Variations of CNN implementations like VGGnet20 have been used for prostate cancer diagnosis (Cosma et al., 2017; Feng et al., 2019; Kwak & Hewitt, 2017)

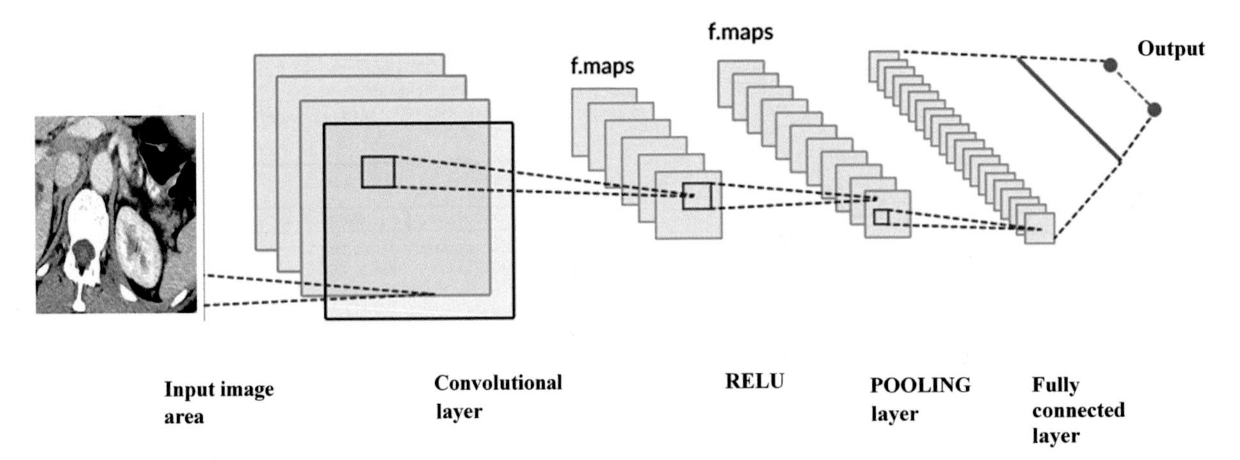

FIGURE 6.10 A convolutional neural network for feature selection and classification of cancer images.

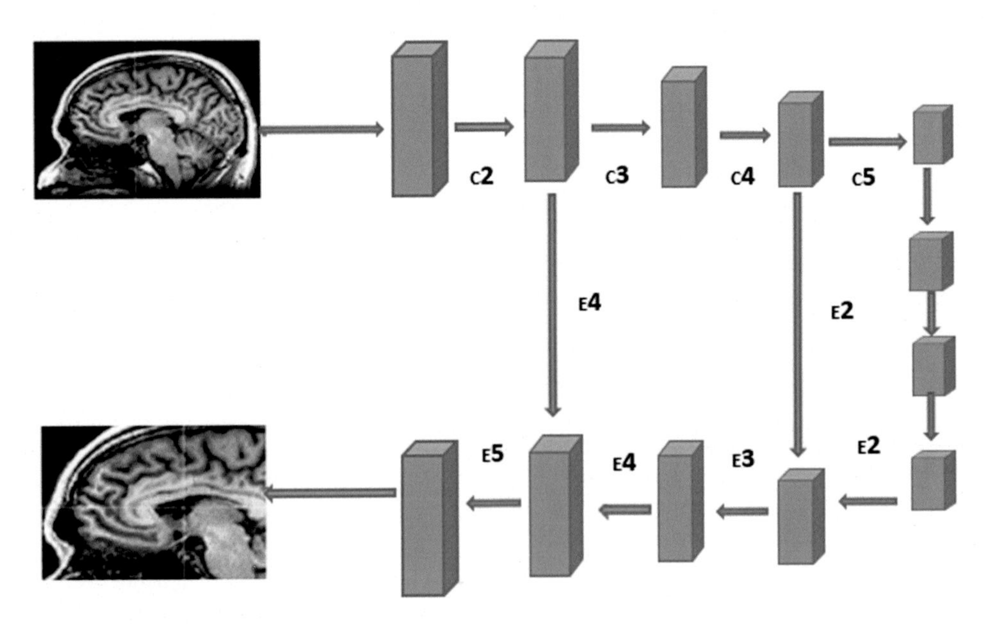

FIGURE 6.11 U-Net architecture for segmentation of magnetic resonance imaging images.

from MRI images; this network has nine convolutional layers and provided an Area under the Receiver Operating Characteristic (ROC) Curve (AUC) value of 0.84 on the test data set. AUC is a measure of a classifier's performance ability to differentiate between different classes. Li, Wang, Tang, Fan, and Yu (2019) applied U-Net28 architecture with ResNet for slice-level analysis of prostate cancer images with an AUC of 0.79. These deep neural network-based approaches do not need manual feature selection. Clustering, which is an unsupervised learning approach, has also been used for the segmentation of brain tumors in MRI images by many researchers. Clustering uses a similarity measure like Euclidean distance for grouping together tumorous and nontumorous images. Fuzzification and other procedures can also be combined with clustering for segmentation of cancer images. For example, Singh, Verma, and Cui (2019) have combined fuzzy based clustering with region-growing procedure in T1-weighted and T2-weighted images for the purpose of brain tumor segmentation. Karim et al. (2019) and Szilágyi et al. (2015) have used a fuzzy c-means algorithm to segment multimodal MRI brain tumor images.

Fig. 6.11 shows the architecture of the U-Net deep neural network for the segmentation of images. This network uses a fully connected architecture and is specially designed to carry out the task of image segmentation efficiently and very fast with the need for fewer training images. On modern graphical processing units, the U-Net architecture can precisely segment a 512×512 image in a fraction of a second. The U-Net architecture consists of two paths of neuron layers—a contracting path that does dimensionality reduction, and an expansive path that does the expansion. It is because of this arrangement that the architecture is known as "U" net architecture. Contracting layers consist of convolutional layers, RELU, and pooling layers just like CNN, expansive layers consist of up-convolutions which expand the data size, and representations are concatenated with features of high resolutions which have been obtained in the contracting path. U-Net architecture has been successfully used for the segmentation of images in the case of brain and liver cancers. There are three important variants of U-Net architecture:

1. U-Net with pixel-wise regression;
2. U-Net to learn 3D dense volumetric representations from sparse inputs;
3. pretrained U-Net, for example, TernausNet—This U-Net combines a VGG11 encoder for better image segmentation.

6.4.6 Autoencoders for feature extraction

Autoencoders are deep neural networks that apply representational learning. These networks impose a bottleneck on the layers such that a compressed representation of the input data is created.

This compression helps eliminate the mutually dependent features, it learns the dependencies like correlation among input data, and leverages these structures during the compressed representation of data through the bottleneck of the network. An autoencoder model has to be sensitive enough to catch structure in data for building accurate representations yet it has to avoid overfitting on training data. Autoencoders can also be used for denoising of data, in addition to dimensionality reduction. In cancer classification, they can be used to combine data at different scales to identify features of various cancers like liver cancer, breast cancer, and neuroblastomas (Scrobotă et al., 2017; Tan et al., 2018; Zhang et al., 2018). Fig. 6.12 shows the architecture of an autoencoder neural network. This network can learn the representations of input data in an unsupervised way. These representations are the compressed forms of original data, as the network is trained to ignore the unnecessary part of the input. The reconstruction part of the network is responsible for the generation of output data which are as similar to input data as possible by using the compressed representations. Denoising autoencoders, sparse autoencoders, and contractive autoencoders are effective in creating reduced dimensional representations for the classification of various types of cancers.

6.4.7 Particle swarm optimization for feature selection

The main principle behind PSO (Arasi et al., 2017; Srisukkham, Zhang, Neoh, Todryk, & Lim, 2017; Abdulrahman, Khalifa, Roushdy, & Salem, 2020) is the use of individual and group experiences of a population

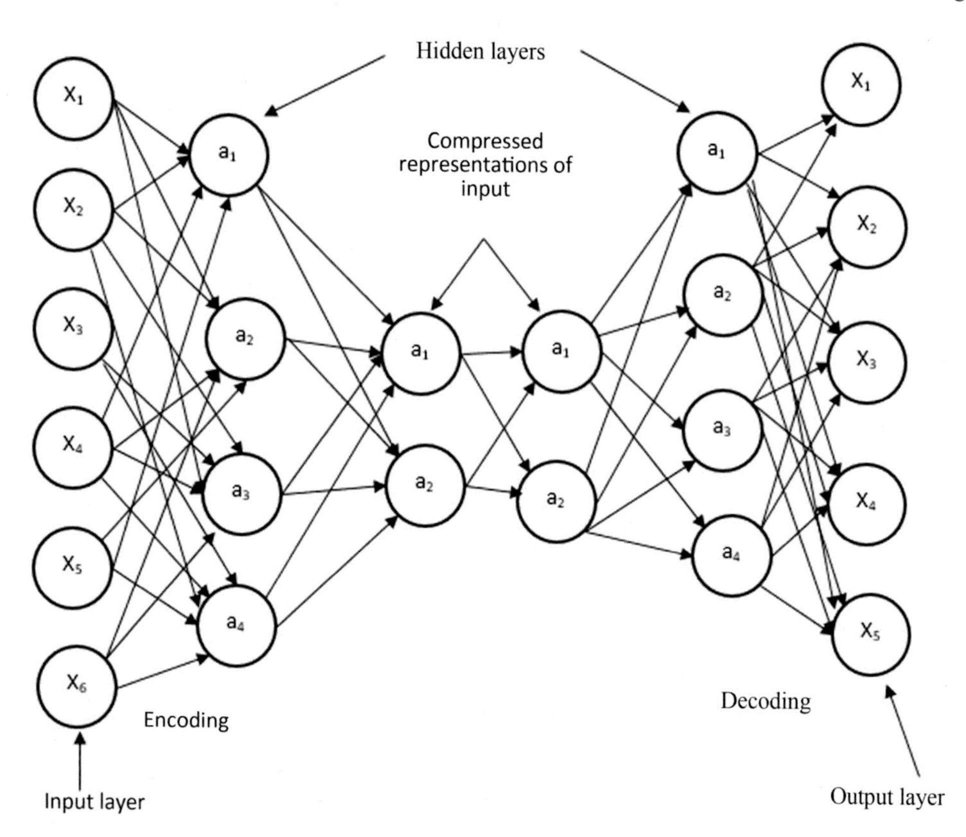

FIGURE 6.12 Autoencoder architecture for feature selection.

```
Algorithm    PSO
:
Initializ    Let the initial swarm contain all features of the
ation:       dataset, size of this swarm is P
             For each particle i in the swarm:
             Randomly initialize Xi
             Randomly initialize Vi
             Compute the fitness of each Xi
             Initialize pbesti from Xi
             Initialize gbest
Step 1:      Repeat till stopping criteria is met:
Step 2:         For each particle i:
Step 3:            Update the velocity vector Vi^t and Xi^t
Step 4:            Evaluate the fitness f(Xi^t)
Step 5:            pbesti = Xi^t  if f(pbesti) < f(Xi^t)
Step 6:            gbesti = Xi^t  if f(gbesti) < f(Xi^t)
```

FIGURE 6.13 Algorithm for PSO. *PSO*, particle swarm optimization.

to explore a decision space to find optimal solutions. The procedure begins with a random set of solutions and this set is updated with time. Each candidate solution is called a particle, the particles share some pieces of information during the course of the algorithm like their current position and best position. The best position is the position with minimum prediction error. The particles are displaced to reduce the prediction error. The particle can change the direction of the motion as well. Every particle has current position X and current velocity V_i. Each particle maintains the information about its best value so far, known as Pbest, and the group best known as Gbest. The general flow of PSO algorithms is as follows:

1. evaluate the fitness of each particle;
2. update local best position;
3. update global best position;
4. update velocity of each particle;
5. update the position of each particle.

These steps are repeated until some stopping condition is met. The complete algorithm for the PSO procedure is given in Fig. 6.13.

PSO algorithms can be combined with deterministic methods for better performance. While deterministic methods use a gradient and aim at minimizing it, the heuristic methods like PSO mimic natural processes to find the points that give an optimum value of the objective function. Hybrid methods combine the advantages of both approaches. The heuristic method is used to localize the position of the global optimum, then the deterministic method can locate the local best solution. PSO (Srisukkham et al., 2017) has been successfully applied to the diagnosis of leukemia from images. Koul and Manvi (2020a) applied binary PSO along with a logistic regression classifier for the classification of colon cancers. This is a two-class classification problem where the gene expression profiles of 2000 patients were differentiated into cancerous and noncancerous. Fig. 6.14 shows the feature selection procedure used by Koul and Manvi (2020a) on colon cancer data.

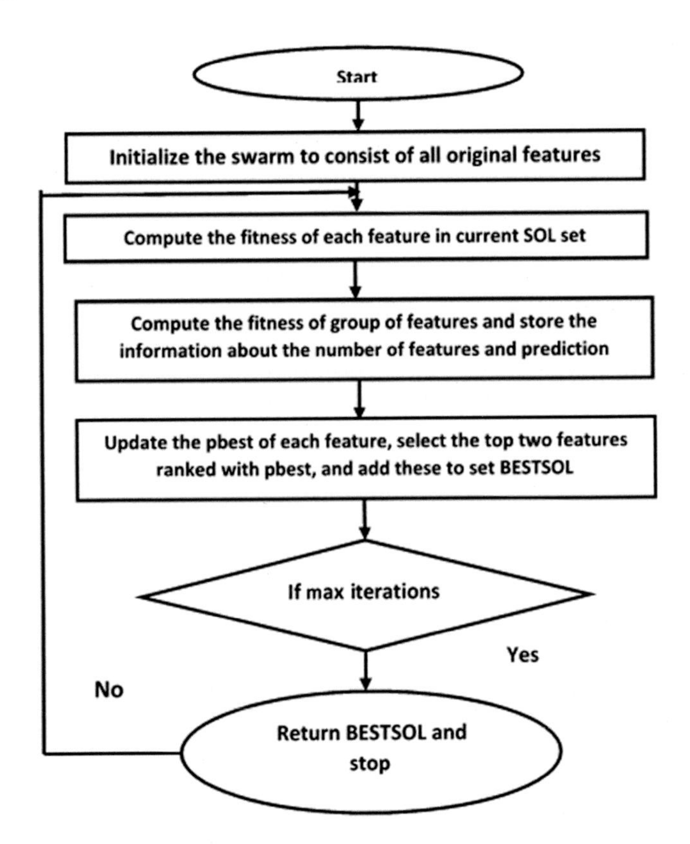

FIGURE 6.14 The procedure of feature selection using particle swarm optimization.

6.5 Computational intelligence methods for cancer classification

Classification algorithms, neural networks, support vector machines, decision trees, logistic regression, and combinations of these have been successfully applied for the classification of samples of images or genomic data as cancerous or noncancerous. They can also be applied to subclassify the same type of tumors according to stages of growth and metastasis. Many of these methods use fuzzy logic, genetic algorithms, and other heuristic and evolutionary search optimization techniques described in the previous section for the selection of a minimal set of most relevant features before the classification step. These classification methods use testing to reduce overfitting. Overfitting is the bias toward training samples and a lack of generalization to test data. This calls for the use of cross-validation methods to ensure good performance of a classification algorithm on test data also. A common cross-validation method is K-fold validation. The input data are partitioned into subsets called folds. One fold is excluded at a time from the training set and used to evaluate the performance of the classifier trained on the training set. Cross-validation is performed multiple times, each time excluding one fold from training. A common convention is to use 5 or 10 folds for cross-validation. The performance of a classification algorithm is measured through parameters of confusion matrix, that is, accuracy, precision, recall, and f-score.

6.5.1 Classification methods

6.5.1.1 *Fuzzy multilayer perceptron*

Mathematically, a fuzzy set (Wang et al., 2018), A, is a set of ordered pairs (U,m), that is, $A = (U,m)$, where U is a set and "m" is a membership function. The set U is also known as a universe of discourse, "m" is a mapping from U -> [0, 1]. Each element x in U has an associated membership grade represented as $m(x)$. Fig. 6.15 shows the membership function for a fuzzy set and Fig. 6.16 shows an example of a fuzzy membership function that is trapezoidal in shape.

Fuzzy logic is defined as the logic of fuzzy sets. Fuzzy logic uses a multivalued truth space inside the binary truth space of [0, 1] values. Using fuzzy logic,

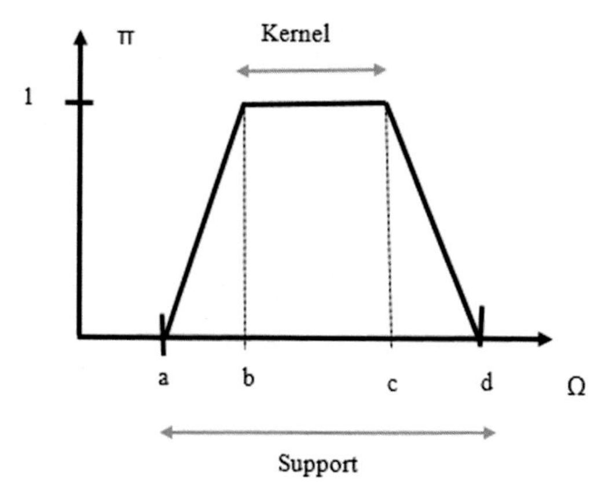

FIGURE 6.16 A trapezoidal membership function for oral cancer diagnosis using fuzzy logic.

For a set U = {x1, x2, .. ,xn},
the fuzzy set (U,m) is represented as {m(x1)/x1, ..., m(xn)/xn}

For each element x in U,

1. If m(x) ==0, x is not a member of fuzzy set (U,m)
2. If m(x) ==1, x is a full member of fuzzy set (U,m)
3. If 0<m(x)<1, x is a fuzzy member of a fuzzy set (U,m) with a membership grade equal to m.

For any fuzzy set A=(U,m), the corresponding crisp set can be defined are follows -

1. α-level set or α -cut when $A^{>\alpha} = A_{\alpha}$ ={x ∈ U | m(x) >= α}
2. Strong α -level set or strong α -cut when $A^{>\alpha} = A_{\alpha}'$ ={x ∈ U | m(x) >= α}
3. Support - Support(A) = $A^{>0}$ ={x ∈ U | m(x) >= α}
4. Core- Core (A)= $A^{=1}$ ={x ∈ U | m(x) =1}.

Core (A) is also known as the kernel of A.

FIGURE 6.15 Membership function in a fuzzy set.

we can generate inferences even with the partial match between the antecedents and data, unlike in propositional logic which needs a total match.

A fuzzy multilayer perceptron contains a fuzzy layer that assigns fuzzy output membership values to input data, thus enabling the neural network to perform better classification in case the data have overlapping class boundaries. Backtracking can be used to produce sets of positive and negative rules in networks. A fuzzy multilayer perceptron network can be used as a soft classifier for both cancer imaging data and radiomics data (Chouhan, Kaul, & Singh, 2019; Gillies et al., 2016). Scrobotă et al. (2017) applied fuzzy logic for the diagnosis of oral cancers using clinical and histopathological data of patients. Fuzzy logic is used to create interpretations of input data (concentration of blood serum parameters in this case) using a set of rules and fuzzy, categorical values are assigned to real-valued inputs based on the degree of membership of each value. These fuzzy classes were very small, small, medium, high, and very high and the classification results were based on the class most inputs belonged to. A trapezoidal membership function was used to decide the classes of input data. Kovalerchuk et al. (1997) applied fuzzy logic for the diagnosis of breast cancer. They used mammographic images as input and fuzzy logic was used for automatic detection of lobulation and microlobulation (Mario, 2020; Ali Hossain, Asa, Huq, Quinn, & Moni, 2020) of nodules. Fuzzy logic is feasible as well as effective for early diagnosis of multiple cancer types.

6.5.1.2 Artificial neural network classifier and deep neural networks

An ANN classifier can be used for both binary and multiclass classification problems. ANNs are built from simple computational functions called "neurons." Each neuron can take as input one or more real-valued signals, multiplying these inputs by a weight. The products of weight and input are summed up and a nonlinear activation function is applied to it. The neuron is said to fire or pass on its output to the next neuron or output if the sum of products is above a threshold set by the activation function. Multiple neurons can be organized in a neural network and multiple neural networks can be arranged in multiple layers to construct a deep neural network architecture. Thus an ANN can learn a complex function with more neurons. An ANN classifier with a sigmoid activation function has been successfully used for the classification of cancers like breast cancer, leukemia, and colorectal cancer. Colorectal cancer consists of colon cancer and rectal cancer resulting from mutation and overexpression of the *p53* gene. Using gene expression data as input and ANN as a classifier the cancerous and noncancerous samples have been successfully discriminated. Fig. 6.15 shows the typical architecture of an ANN.

Many nature-inspired optimization functions such as gradient descent, simulated annealing, cuckoo search, ant colony optimization, PSO, whale optimization, and gravitational algorithm have been used for training deep neural networks through backpropagation. Cuckoo search is an optimization algorithm inspired by the behavior of the cuckoo bird searching for its eggs which it lets them hatch in the nests of other birds. This method has been applied in many optimizations and CI techniques. Cuckoo search is applied during feature selection to gene expression profile data to select the subset of most relevant genes for the training of the classifier.

6.6 Conclusion

Advanced CI techniques along with enormous advancements in computing hardware and availability of large volumes of single-cell genomics and spatiotemporal data have led to significant progress in computational cancer research. Many statistical, mathematical, and computational methods help computational biologists tackle the problems in modeling and understanding various aspects of cancer incidence and progression. Supervised and unsupervised, linear and nonlinear machine learning algorithms like linear discriminant analysis, regression, support vector machines, decision trees, neural networks, fuzzy systems, deep neural network architectures like autoencoders, CNNs, deep belief networks, and principal component analysis have been successfully applied for improving the diagnosis, survival analysis, and treatment approaches for various cancer types. However, the challenges like predictive modeling of the evolution of cancer tumors, mathematical interpretation of mutations in genes, modeling of the response of patients to various drugs, and treatment approaches remain important research areas for clinical and computational cancer researchers. Breakthroughs in these areas can help realize the possibility of personalized cancer treatment in the near future.

Acknowledgment

The authors would like to thank the Department of Science and Technology (DST), Government of India, for supporting this research work under the grant scheme DST-ICPS-2018.

References

Abbass, H. A. (2002). An evolutionary artificial neural networks approach for breast cancer diagnosis. *Artificial Intelligence in Medicine*, *25*(3), 265–281.

Abdulrahman, S. A., Khalifa, W., Roushdy, M., & Salem, A.-B. M. (2020). Comparative study for 8 computational intelligence algorithms for human identification. *Computer Science Review, 36*(100237).

Ali Hossain, M., Asa, T. A., Huq, F., Quinn, J. M. W., & Moni, M. A. (2020). A network-based approach to identify molecular signatures and comorbidities of thyroid cancer. In Uddin M., Bansal J. (Eds.) *Proceedings of international joint conference on computational intelligence. algorithms for intelligent systems. springer, Singapore.*

Alzubaidi, A., Cosma, G., Brown, D., & Pockley, A. G. (2016). A new hybrid global optimization approach for selecting clinical and biological features that are relevant to the effective diagnosis of ovarian cancer. In: *Proceedings of the IEEE symposium series on computational intelligence (SSCI)*, (pp. 1–8), Athens.

Anter, A. M., & Hassenian, A. E. (2018). Computational intelligence optimization approach based on particle swarm optimizer and neutrosophic set for abdominal CT liver tumor segmentation. *Journal of Computational Science, 25*, 376–387.

Arasi, M. A., El-Horbaty, E. M., Salem, A. M., & El-Dahshan, E. A. (2017). Computational intelligence approaches for malignant melanoma detection and diagnosis. In: *Proceedings of the eighth international conference on information technology (ICIT)*, (pp. 55–61). Amman, https://doi.org/10.1109/ICITECH.2017.8079915.

Armitage, P., & Doll, R. (1954). The age distribution of cancer and a multi-stage theory of carcinogenesis. *British Journal of Cancer, 8*, 1–12.

Cai, L., Long, T., Dai, Y., & Huang, Y. (2020). Mask R-CNN-based detection and segmentation for pulmonary nodule 3D visualization diagnosis. *IEEE Access, 8*, 44400–44409.

Chaudhary, K., Poirion, O. B., Lu, L., & Garmire, L. X. (2018). Deep learning-based multi-omics integration robustly predicts survival in liver cancer. *Clinical Cancer Research Official Journal of American Association for Cancer Research, 24*, 1248–1259.

Cheng J., (2017). *Brain tumor dataset*, <https://figshare.com/articles/brain_tumor_dataset/1512427>

Chouhan, S. S., Kaul, A., & Singh, U. P. (2019). Image segmentation using computational intelligence techniques: Review. *Archives of Computational Methods in Engineering, 26*, 533–596.

Cosma, G., Brown, D., Archer, M., Khan, M., & Pockley, A. G. (2017). A survey on computational intelligence approaches for predictive modeling in prostate cancer. *Expert Systems with Applications, 70*, 1–19.

Dheeba, J., Singh, N. A., & Selvi, S. T. (2014). Computer-aided detection of breast cancer on mammograms: A swarm intelligence optimized wavelet neural network approach. *Journal of Biomedical Informatics, 49*, 45–52.

Esteva, A., Kuprel, B., Novoa, R. A., et al. (2017). Dermatologist-level classification of skin cancer with deep neural networks. *Nature, 542*, 115–118.

Feng, Y., et al. (2019). A deep learning approach for targeted contrast-enhanced ultrasound based prostate cancer detection. *IEEE/ACM Transactions on Computational Biology and Bioinformatics, 16*(6), 1794–1801.

Firoozbakht, F., Rezaeian, I., Ngom, A., Rueda, L., & Porter, L. (2015). A novel approach for finding informative genes in ten subtypes of breast cancer. In: *Proceedings of the IEEE conference on computational intelligence in bioinformatics and computational biology (CIBCB)*, (pp. 1–6). Niagara Falls.

Fogel, G. B. (2008). Computational intelligence approaches for pattern discovery in biological systems. *Briefings in Bioinformatics, 9*(4), 307–316.

Gillies, R. J., Kinahan, P. E., & Hricak, H. (2016). Radiomics: images are more than pictures, they are data. *Radiology, 278*, 563–577.

Hassanien, A. E., Al-Shammari, E. T., & Ghali, N. I. (2013). Computational intelligence techniques in bioinformatics. *Computational Biology and Chemistry, 47*, 37–47.

Hassanien, A. E., Milanova, M. G., Smolinski, T. G., & Abraham, A. (2018). Computational intelligence in solving bioinformatics problems: Reviews, perspectives, and challenges. In T. G. Smolinski, M. G. Milanova, & A. E. Hassanien (Eds.), *Computational intelligence in biomedicine and bioinformatics. studies in computational intelligence* (151).

Hsieh, T. M., Liu, Y.-M., Liao, C.-C., Xiao, F., Chiang, I.-J., & Wong, J.-M. (2011). Automatic segmentation of meningioma from non-contracted brain MRI integrating fuzzy clustering and region growing. *BMC Medical Informatics and Decision Making, 11*(54).

Jha, S., & Topol, E. J. (2016). Adapting to artificial intelligence: Radiologists and pathologists as information specialists. *The Journal of the American Medical Association, 316*, 2353–2354.

Kalantari, A., Kamsin, A., Shamshirband, S., Gani, A., Alinejad-Rokny, H., & Chronopoulos, A. T. (2018). Computational intelligence approaches for classification of medical data: State-of-the-art, future challenges, and research directions. *Neurocomputing, 276*, 2–22.

Karim, M. R., Wicaksono, G., Costa, I. G., Decker, S., & Beyan, O. (2019). Prognostically relevant subtypes and survival prediction for breast cancer based on multimodal genomics data. *IEEE Access, 7*, 133850–133864.

Khan, J., Wei, J. S., Ringnér, M., et al. (2001). Classification and diagnostic prediction of cancers using gene expression profiling and artificial neural networks. *Nature Medicine, 7*, 673–679.

Koul, N., & Manvi, S. S. (2020a). Colon cancer classification using binary particle swarm optimization and logistic regression. In *Proceedings of the international conference on emerging technologies in data mining and information security*, India, July 2–3.

Koul, N., & Manvi, S. S. (2020b). Small round blue cell tumor classification using pipeline genetic algorithm. *Test Engineering and Management, 83*.

Kovalerchuk, B., Triantaphyllou, E., Ruiz, J. F., & Clayton, J. (1997). Fuzzy logic in computer-aided breast cancer diagnosis: Analysis of lobulation. *Artificial Intelligence in Medicine, 11* (1), 75–85.

Kwak, J. T., & Hewitt, S. M. (2017). Nuclear architecture analysis of prostate cancer via convolutional neural networks. *IEEE Access, 5*, 18526–18533.

Lecun, Y., Bottou, L., Bengio, Y., et al. (1998). Gradient-based learning applied to document recognition. *Proceedings of the IEEE Institution of Electrical Engineers, 86*, 2278–2324.

Li, C. Y., Liang, G. Y., Yao, W. Z., et al. (2018). Integrated analysis of long non-coding RNA competing interactions reveal the potential role in the progression of human gastric cancer: Based on public database. *Molecular Medicine Reports, 17*, 7845–7858.

Li, X., Wang, Y., Tang, Q., Fan, Z., & Yu, J. (2019). Dual U-Net for the segmentation of overlapping glioma nucle. *IEEE Access, 7*, 84040–84052.

Mario, C. (2020). Deep learning technology for improving cancer care in society: New directions in cancer imaging driven by artificial intelligence. *Technology in Society, 60*, 101198.

Menze, B. H., et al. (2015). The multimodal brain tumor image segmentation benchmark (BRATS). *IEEE Transactions on Medical Imaging, 34*, 1993–2024.

Nahar, J., Imam, T., Tickle, K. S., Ali, A. B. M. S., & Chen, Y.-P. P. (2012). Computational intelligence for microarray data and biomedical image analysis for the early diagnosis of breast cancer. *Expert Systems with Applications, 39*(no.16), 12371–12377.

Nahar, J., Shawkat Ali, A.B.M., Imam, T., Tickle, K., & Chen, P., (2016). Brain cancer diagnosis-association rule-based computational intelligence approach, In *Proceedings of the IEEE international conference on computer and information technology (CIT)*. (pp. 89–95).

Nordling, C. O. (2017). A new theory on cancer-inducing mechanism. *British Journal of Cancer, 7*, 68–72, pmid:13051507.

Peña-Reyes, C. A., & Sipper, M. (1999). A fuzzy-genetic approach to breast cancer diagnosis. *Artificial Intelligence in Medicine, 17*(no.2), 131–155.

Scrobotă, I., et al. (2017). Application of fuzzy logic in oral cancer risk assessment. *Iranian Journal of Public Health, 46*(5), 612–619.

Shendure, J., & Lieberman Aiden, E. (2012). The expanding scope of DNA sequencing. *Nature Biotechnology, 30*, 1084–1094.

Singh, V., Verma, N. K., & Cui, Y. (2019). Type-2 fuzzy PCA approach in extracting salient features for molecular cancer diagnostics and prognostics. *IEEE Transactions on Nanobioscience, 18*(3), 482–489.

Srisukkham, W., Zhang, L., Neoh, S. C., Todryk, S., & Lim, C. P. (2017). Intelligent leukemia diagnosis with bare-bones PSO based feature optimization. *Applied Soft Computing, 56*, 405–419.

Szilágyi, L., Lefkovits, L., & Benyó, B. (2015). Automatic brain tumor segmentation in multispectral MRI volumes using a fuzzy c-means cascade algorithm *In Proceedings of the 12th international conference on fuzzy systems and knowledge discovery (FSKD)* (pp. 285–291).

Tan, J., Ung, M., Cheng, C., & Greene, C. (2018) Unsupervised feature construction and knowledge extraction from genome-wide assays of breast cancer with denoising autoencoders. In *Proceedings of the Pacific symposium on biocomputing*. 20, (pp. 132–143).

Tan, T. Z., Quek, C., Ng, G. S., & Razvi, K. (2008). Ovarian cancer diagnosis with complementary learning fuzzy neural network. *Artificial Intelligence in Medicine, 43*(no.2), 207–222.

Vidyasagar, M. (2017). Machine learning methods in computational cancer biology. *Annual Reviews in Control, 43*, 107–127.

Wang, J. L., Ibrahim, A. K., Zhuang, H., Muhamed Ali, A., Li, A. Y., & Wu, A. (2018). A study on automatic detection of IDC breast cancer with convolutional neural networks. In *Proceedings of the international conference on computational science and computational intelligence (CSCI)*, (pp. 703–708), Las Vegas, NV, USA.

Wang, Y., et al. (2020). Comparison study of radiomics and deep learning-based methods for thyroid nodules classification using ultrasound images. *IEEE Access, 8*, 52010–52017.

Wang, Y., Ma, Z., Wong, K., & Li, X. (2019). Evolving multiobjective cancer subtype diagnosis from cancer gene expression data. *IEEE/ACM Transactions on Computational Biology and Bioinformatics, 23*(10).

Yang, J. Y., Niemierko, A., Yang, M. Q., Luo, Z., & Li, J. (2007). Predicting tumor malignancies using combined computational intelligence, bioinformatics and laboratory molecular biology approaches. In *Proceedings of the IEEE symposium on computational intelligence and bioinformatics and computational biology*, (pp. 46–53). Honolulu, HI.

Zhang, L., Lv, C., Jin, Y., Cheng, G., Fu, Y., Yuan, D., et al. (2018). Deep learning-based multi-omics data integration reveals two prognostic subtypes in high-risk neuroblastoma. *Frontiers in Genetics, 9*, 477.

CHAPTER

7

Security and privacy in the internet of things: computational intelligent techniques-based approaches

Poornima M. Chanal[1], *Mahabaleshwar S. Kakkasageri*[1] *and Sunil Kumar S. Manvi*[2]

[1]Department of Electronics and Communication Engineering, Basaveshwar Engineering College, Bagalkot, India
[2]School of Computing and Information Technology, REVA University, Bangalore, India

7.1 Introduction

The Internet of Things (IoT) is an interconnection of objects/things which are capable of processing, transceiving, and storing data through a wired or wireless network. Modern applications with embedded systems consisting of radio-frequency identifications (RFIDs), wireless sensor networks, and others contribute to empower the IoT. IoT devices are ad hoc, mobile, self-organizing, interoperability, network connectivity, which can aggregate and disseminate data at any time and anywhere. The main aim of the IoT is to create intelligent environments used in the construction of smart cities, smart homes, smart transport systems, and so on (Ahanger & Aljumah, 2018; Shen, Tang, Zhu, Du, & Guizani, 2019; Yan, Pei, & Li, 2019; Jayasinghe, Lee, Um, & Shi, 2019; Alepis & Patsakis, 2017; Gubbi, Buyya, Marusic, & Palaniswami, 2013).

Millions and trillions of IoT devices are interconnected with each other. A large amount of information is generated, aggregated, and disseminated periodically where privacy and security challenges are detected (Atzori, Iera, & Morabito, 2010; Bandyopadhyay & Sen, 2011; Miorandi, Sicari, Pellegrini, & Chlamtac, 2012; Yang, Liu, & Liang, 2010). The lack of security, privacy, threats, and malfunctions in the IoT can overwhelm its strengths, benefits, and applications (Covington & Carskadden, 2013; Vermesan & Friess, 2013; Okkonen et al., 2013; Friess, Guillemin, & Sundmaeker, 2010). Traditional security and privacy techniques are inefficient. The security and protection platform should be scalable, reliable, and robust, etc. When dealing with a huge number of things, particular aspects will be involved in security features (Binti, Noor, & Hassan, 2019; Vermesan, 2011; Yang, Xu, Chen, Qi, & Wang, 2010; Roman, Najera, & Lopez, 2011; Suo, Wan, Zou, & Liu, 2012).

The IoT is growing very fast and has become common in people's lives. IoT devices are limited by size, the life of batteries, and some computational methods, so that they may not support old devices (Pan, Paul, & Jain, 2011; Tewari & Gupta, 2020; Farooq, Waseem, Mazhar, Khairi, & Kamal, 2015; Sonar & Upadhyay, 2014). The Internet-connected number of current IoT nodes and new nodes may produce new challenges and they need new methods to give solutions to issues of privacy and security.

Computational intelligent techniques are an efficient tool to address the critical issues and challenges of the IoT. These techniques include quantum cryptography, blockchain models, game theory, artificial intelligence (AI), neural networks, natural computational techniques, bio-inspired computational techniques, fuzzy logic techniques, genetic algorithms, intelligent multiagents, and policy-based multiagent systems, etc. The rapid development in technology requires intelligent techniques to manage high levels of security and privacy in the IoT to achieve good performance. Intelligent techniques must manage the security of data, and control and manage congestion in the network by improving the overall privacy in the network (Cao, Cai, & Yue, 2019; Fernandez, Herrera, Cordon, Jesus,

Recent Trends in Computational Intelligence Enabled Research.
DOI: https://doi.org/10.1016/B978-0-12-822844-9.00009-8

& Marcelloni, 2019; Jabbar, Iram, Minhas, Shafi, & Khalid, 2013; Kakkasageri & Manvi, 2014; Kumar & Sharma, 2012; Moura & Hutchison, 2019; Primeau, Falcon, Abielmona, & Petriu, 2018).

The chapter is organized as follows. Section 7.2 explains the concept of the IoT (architecture, application, characteristics, and issues). The concept of security and privacy in IoT is explained in Section 7.3. Section 7.4 presents the various computational intelligence techniques for security and privacy in the IoT, and Section 7.5 presents further research challenges that need to be addressed.

7.2 Internet of things

IoT devices are embedded with sensors, RFID, and other intelligent devices that sense, process, and interact with other devices over the Internet. The IoT enables smart technologies in all areas of our everyday communications and enhances the quality of life. All devices in the network can gather, analyze, and make decisions without any human communication (Goyal, Sahoo, Sharma, & Singh, 2020). Hence privacy and security is a major constraint in such conditions. IoT security and privacy will be a key issue that needs to be addressed to allow several applications. The IoT has three main features, such as normal things that are instrumented, autonomic terminals that are connected, and ubiquitous facilities that are intelligent. The IoT is comprehensive interdisciplinary technology, for example, including various areas such as sensor technology, computer science, communications, AI, and microelectronics.

7.2.1 Architecture

The IoT architecture is a fundamental way to design the various elements of the IoT so that it can deliver services over the networks. In essence, IoT architecture is the system of numerous elements: sensors, protocols, actuators, cloud services, and layers. There is no single architecture to match different IoT applications. IoT architecture can be classified as three-layer, four-layer, five-layer, and service-oriented architecture (SoA).

7.2.1.1 Three-layer architecture

The most basic IoT architecture is three-layer architecture as shown in Fig. 7.1. It was introduced in the early stages of research in this area. It has three layers, namely, the perception, network, and application layers.

- Perception layer: This is also called the sensor layer. This layer's task is to recognize objects and gather the data from sensors. The sensors are preferred based upon the requirement of applications. Data collected by these sensors may include position, variations in the air, surroundings, vibration, etc.
- Network layer: This layer is also known as the transmission layer. It carries data collected from physical objects and transmits them via sensors. It is highly sensitive to privacy and security attacks.
- Application layer: The main task of this layer is to transmit information from IoT application services to individuals. The services can vary for each application since they depend on the data gathered by the sensors.

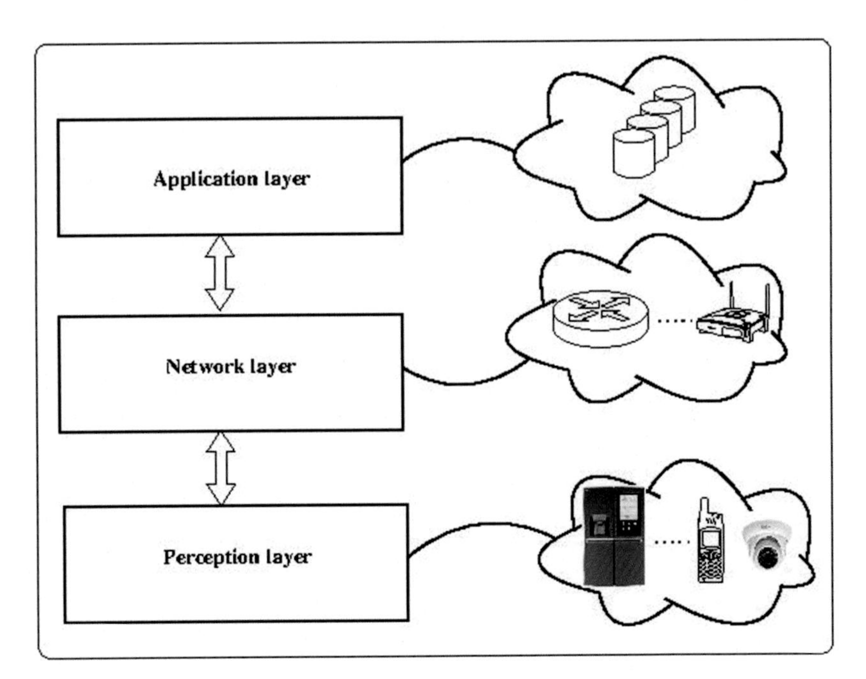

FIGURE 7.1 Three-layer architecture.

7.2.1.2 *Four-layer architecture*

The three-layer architecture defines the basic requirements of IoT, but it is not sufficient for a larger scale of IoT applications. Therefore, four layers of IoT architecture may be used for finer aspects of IoT as shown in Fig. 7.2.

- Perception layer: This layer has physical things required to sense or control the physical world and acquire data. The task of the perception layer is to know each node in the network.
- Network layer: The network layer job is to connect all devices and servers to transfer and process the data in the IoT system. While transmitting the data, this layer is more prone to security attacks.
- Data processing layer: The reason for creating the data processing layer is to provide security in the IoT network. This layer ensures that the data are submitted to authorize customers and secured from attacks. This layer verifies the users and data using authentication techniques.
- Application layer: This layer is responsible for the integration of IoT system resources with the customer. This describes many areas where IoT can be implemented, like smart houses, smart cities, smart transport systems, etc.

7.2.1.3 *Five-layer architecture*

This architecture is designed to meet the requirements of different industries, companies, institutes, and governments, etc. It has data collection from the physical layer to the top of the business layer (Kraijak & Tuwanut, 2015). The five-layered IoT architecture is as shown in Fig. 7.3.

- Perception layer: This layer manages overall devices and collects the data by different types of sensor devices. This collected information transmits to the data processing system via a transmission/network layer for safe communication.
- Network layer: This layer plays a vital function in safe communication and keeps critical data confidential from sensors to the data processing system. This layer's task is to transfer the data from the physical layer to the top business layer.
- Middleware layer: Service management and storing the bottom layer data into the database are two features of the middleware layer. This layer is used to restore and process the information in the IoT network.
- Application layer: This layer is responsible for transmitting information from applications of the IoT to individuals. The IoT applications can be

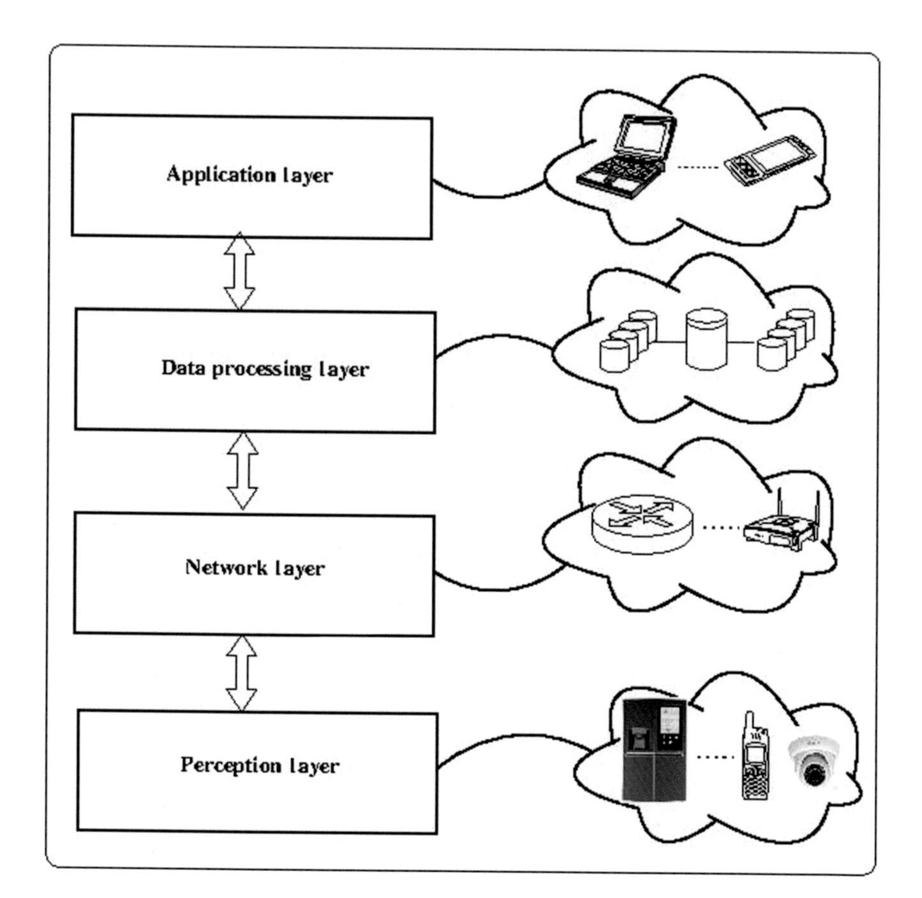

FIGURE 7.2 Four-layer architecture.

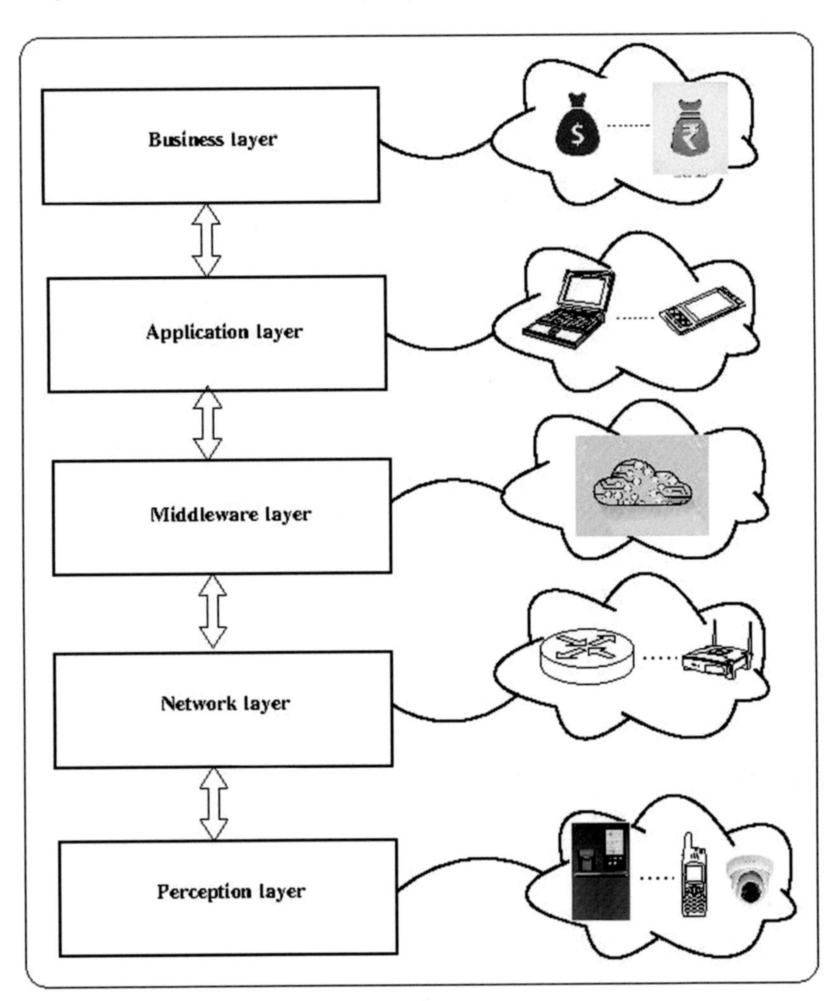

FIGURE 7.3 Five-layer architecture.

smart postal, medical applications, smart independent living, etc.
- Business layer: In the IoT, the business layer contains various services and applications. This layer collects and analyzes the correct data and generates graphs, executive reports, etc. It introduces new data sharing, information integration, and facilities with new criteria and challenges.

7.2.1.4 SoA-based architecture

A SoA is as shown in Fig. 7.4. The transferring system functions to the end customer from the various applications from the top layer of the architecture. These IoT devices consist of a heterogeneous collection of objects and each entity has one unique language feature. The abstraction layer can provide access to the many nodes with a common language. The service management framework includes significant features that are required for each entity and enable their supervision in the network. The functions for the composition of the single service provided by nodes to construct different applications are described in the service management and composition layer.

7.3 Characteristics

The IoT system has various characteristics compared to other networks (Patel & Patel, 2016). General characteristics of the IoT are as follows.

- Intelligence: The IoT is a smart system because it uses a combination of various algorithms and computation techniques, software, and hardware. Intelligence in the IoT increases its capacities, which make it easy for nodes to react intelligently in all conditions and supports for different functions. IoT intelligence achieves communication among users and nodes through standard approaches.
- Connectivity: Connectivity is the main characteristic of the IoT because it connects millions of things/nodes anywhere, anytime, which makes the IoT network intelligent. This increases system availability and compatibility in the network.

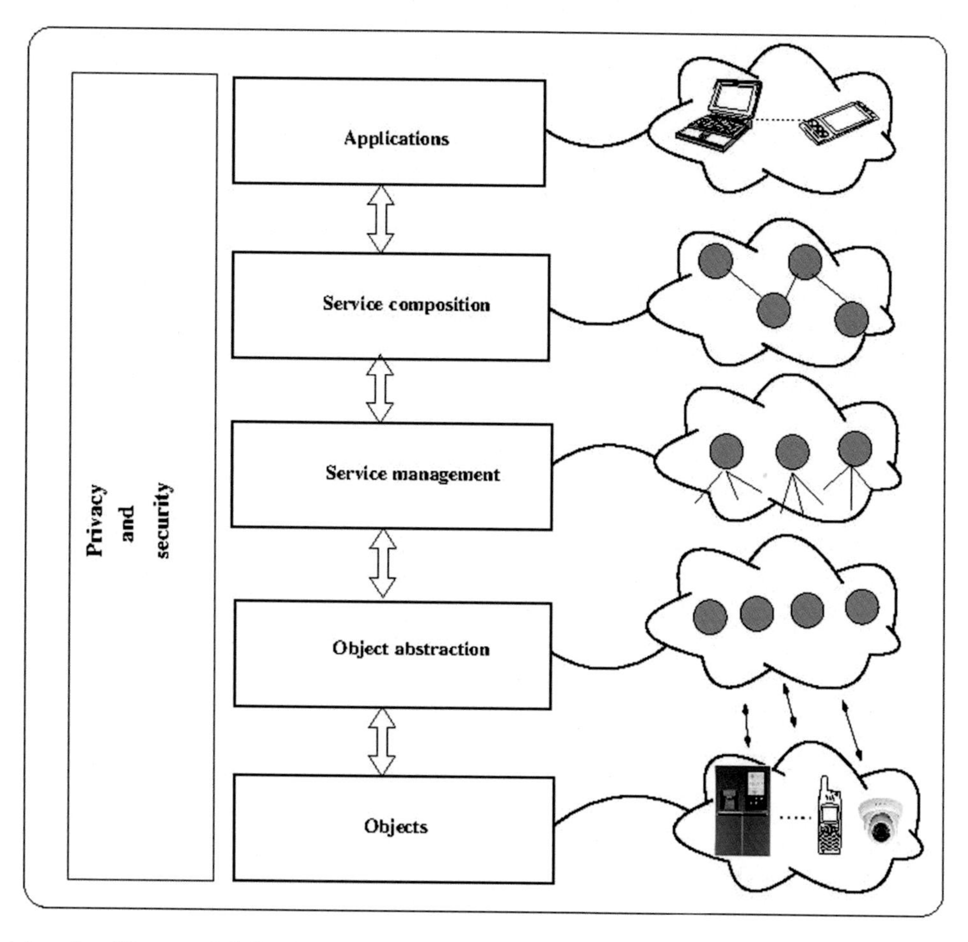

FIGURE 7.4 SoA-based architecture. *SoA*, Service-oriented architecture.

- Dynamic nature: The purpose of IoT devices is to gather data and this is accomplished by complex adjustments taking place across the units. The status of such devices varies continuously, for example, sleeping and waking, attached and/or detached, and devices including temperature, position, and distance. The number of devices also changes vigorously with respect to time, place, and user.
- Enormous scale: The management and interpretation of the data produced from devices/things for application purposes are becoming more critical. In 2016, every day 5.6 million devices were interconnected and worldwide 6.5 billion things were connected and used. The researchers estimated that by 2021 the connectivity of nodes would be 35 billions.
- Sensing: Sensors are important devices in the IoT network to sense and measure variations in surroundings to produce data. Sensing technology gives true realization of the physical domain and the individuals within it.
- Heterogeneity: IoT devices are heterogeneous. IoT architecture supports direct communication across heterogeneous networks. Scalability, modularity, extensibility, and interoperability are core architecture criteria for heterogeneous devices in the IoT systems.
- Security and privacy: The information generated in the IoT system is very risky if the security and privacy issues in IoT are ignored. It is important to protect the data in IoT devices from security attacks in the network. Confidentiality, authorization, authentication, availability, integrity, and accessibility are major issues to provide security and privacy in the IoT.

7.4 Research issues/challenges

The IoT has enticed significant research attention since the massive connectivity brings a variety of challenges and obstacles. Some of the main challenges encountered by the IoT are as follows (Davies, 2015; Mattern & Floerkemeier, 2010):

- Scalability: The IoT has more varied key ideas than the traditional computing Internet because devices function together within an open environment. To gain an efficient scalability operation, the IoT

requires new tasks and approaches. General features such as connectivity, service detection, and other applications need to function properly in large-scale, dynamic, and distributed wireless networks.
- Self-organizing: Computers need configuration and alteration by their users in specific conditions, but IoT devices do not require any alterations because nodes in the IoT are self-organizing. To match a particular environment, nodes are used randomly to create connectivity, and arrange and configure themselves to match their specific situation.
- Data interpretation: It is important to clarify accurate data given by the sensors to support intelligent devices. Certain generalizable assumptions need to be taken from the perceived data of the sensor in the IoT.
- Interoperability: In the IoT, nodes have the ability to analyze and have interoperability of data. Smart nodes are subject to various factors such as accessibility of resources, criteria for communication bandwidth, etc. Common standards are important to promote object communication and collaboration.
- Software complexity: To handle and support nodes in the IoT, software system and background server are required. The IoT devices have to work with limited resources.
- Security and privacy: The security and privacy features are data confidentiality, authenticity, trust, and data integrity, etc., that are required for the IoT.
- Fault tolerance: IoT nodes are more dynamic, and they are changing quickly in unexpected ways. The stable and trustworthy structuring of the IoT will involve many levels and has the potential to respond dynamically to changing circumstances.

7.5 Applications

The IoT promises many human-life applications that make life simpler, healthier, and smarter. Some of the IoT applications include medical, military, industrial, automotive, environment, smart grid and smart energy, and agriculture applications.

- Medical applications: A hospitalized patient's physiological condition may be constantly tracked using IoT tracking technologies. Powerful wireless solutions with the IoT are now providing monitoring systems to these patients. IoT technologies use a variety of sensors to safely collect patient health data. Intelligent algorithms and techniques are used to study patient data and share them with medical professionals (Ahmed, Björkman, Čaušsević, Fotouhi, & Lindén, 2015).

  In the IoT network, things give important issues with respect to security and confidentiality. Major issues for IoT applications in the medical area are illegal admittance, RF congestion, tag duplicating, and cloud polling. Confidentiality and security are the main worries for patients and also for physicians. Due to sensitivity data, patients may not be prepared to reveal their health conditions to others (Zeadally, Siddiqui, Baig, & Ibrahim, 2019).

  An electrocardiogram (ECG) system-based IoT structure is discussed in Yang, Zhou, Lei, Zheng, and Xiang (2016). Wearable monitoring devices gather ECG data and directly transfer these to the IoT cloud through the Internet. To provide ECG information to patients, Message Queuing Telemetry Transport and Hypertext Transfer Protocol protocols are employed in the IoT cloud. The system is trustworthy and can assist in the primary diagnosis of some heart problems.
- Military applications: Military actions are usually carried out in difficult, multidimensional, extremely distinctive, and challenging situations with adversaries (Lamas, Carams, Albela, Castedo, & Gonzlez-Lpez, 2016). To provide an efficient application for the military, the IoT requires the following specific requirements: distributed structures, utilization of network, interoperability, trust and security, sensor and device utilization, and applications of semantic web technologies. Some military applications of the IoT include battlefield communications, tools tracking, interruption exposure, risk investigation, staff training, etc.

  In military applications, security and reliability are the main issues for IoT operation. Insufficiently secured military IoT may provide an adversary with the possibility to manipulate or disrupt information transferred between units to control or automated structures.

  Robust network cluster authentication for securing the military IoT network is discussed in Zielinski, Chudzikiewicz, and Furtak (2019). The IoT systems are furnished with a trusted module used commercially off the shelf to give secure information among sensors and gateways. Wireless ad hoc sensor networks and opportunistic sensor networks (Oppnets) give safe connectivity for military applications.
- Industrial applications: The Industrial Internet of Things (IIoT) focuses on interconnected manufacturing works devices that are inexpensive, smart, and small in size (Sisinni, Saifullah, Han, & Jennehag, 2018). These can be defined as collecting machine settings, nodes, AI, advanced analytics, etc. to boost production by improving machine health. The IIoT permits the creation of manufacturing

intelligence to communicate real-time data across the industrial network. In IIoT, Big Data, cyber-physical systems, and machine learning (ML) techniques are used to provide smooth operations in an industrial system. A combination of these techniques offers innovative strategies for tracking events in real time. Security, analysis of information and management, the convergence of data, and operating technology are the main issues handled by industry in integrating IoT.

Industrial BlockChain Tokenizer is an information-gaining method to capture information from new and old sensor-interfaced devices and is introduced in Mazzei et al. (2020). The attained information is handled by supporting the edge-filtering model on every blockchain network. The device is checked on double-chain conditions. It has been demonstrated that the device has the potential to serve as a link between industrial infrastructure and blockchain networks.

- Automotive applications: Sensors and intelligent transport systems are used to control daily traffic in urban environments. The aim of the transport scheme is a reduction of traffic jams, free parking areas, and avoidance of accidents, etc. In such applications GPS sensors are used for location finding and gyrators for heading. To verify the identity proof of vehicles RFID chips are used and an ultraviolet sensors are used for the totaling travelers and vehicles. Cameras are used for the observing vehicles information and traffic. (Rahman et al., 2020). These devices are used to measure traffic situations in various sections of a region. Some custom applications are analyzed by road traffic authorities to evaluate future traffic conditions.

  Vehicle Telematics is the main key to automotive IoT and refers to the large transmission of computer information. Vehicle holders can track vehicles even from remote places. Linked vehicles enable fast transmission of information and increase the driver's response time with improved vehicle communication and message authentication codes (MAC) system for traffic excellence services, as discussed in Rahmana et al. (2020) and Rukmini and Usha Devi (2016).
- Environmental applications: Smart environment technology is required in daily life to offer services and solutions for applications such as water pollution, air pollution, climate and energy monitoring, waste management, and many other environmental indicators all linked to individuals in the home area network. Environmental object detection, sensing and tracking, and smart environment systems integration with IoT technologies are built to achieve a green and healthy world (Li, Wang, Xu, & Zhou, 2011).

  The IoT allows environmental sensor models like airbot, waterbot, sensor drone, and air quality egg to link with smartphones through WiFi to transmit an enormous amount of information to the network. It improves the atmosphere and appropriate solutions to environmental difficulties (Ahmed & Yousef, 2019).
- Agriculture applications: Smart forming of IoT technologies will allow farmers to reduce waste and improve efficiency. Quality of soil testing, precision farming, smart greenhouses, etc. are IoT applications in the agriculture field and are discussed in (Chanal & Kakkasageri, 2020). In the initial step, products of agriculture need protection and security from insect attacks in fields. Monitoring modules for agriculture applications in an IoT network using different sensors for which data are provided from the knowledge base are discussed in Mohanraj, Ashokumar, and Naren (2016). One important technology is presented using different launchpads with interconnection sensor elements and other necessary automatic gadgets. The system reduces the problems of old agricultural procedures by using efficient water resources and labor costs.
- Smart grid and smart energy: A smart grid is an electricity supply system that employs a wide range of data technology to ensure smart energy management, which provides productive electricity and sustainability (Mohammed & Ahmed, 2017) to allow collaboration between producers and customers. Sensing and tracking methods for power flows include the elements of data and control mechanisms. Some of the smart grid and smart energy applications are an exchange of information across the grid, usage of smart meter displays in-house to inform of energy consumption, fault protection, weather data integration, advanced sensing, industrial, solar, nuclear power, etc. Smart grid technology increases reliability and transparency, and makes processes more efficient, which increases the importance of cyber security.

A case study on IoT modules and intelligent techniques integrated into a stable and low-cost sensing device that can be used for different military applications, such as smart military base actions or control of the logistics chain, is presented in Wrona, Castro, and Vasilache (2017). The Data-Centric Security (DCS) scheme is used to give security and privacy at the information object level and provided end-to-end protection between the sensor and a user. The DCS is represented by Content-based Protection and Release, and was developed by North Atlantic Treaty Organization and an information agency.

A case study of smart dairy farming in Ontario, Canada, is discussed in Vate-U-Lan and Quigley (2017).

In order to improve the milk production rate while ensuring the health of cattle and protecting the environment, a farmer in Ontario was able to implement smart farming technologies. The applications of good farming in this case included digital cow monitoring, harvest management, and data-driven dairy production. Sensor technology such as a GPS can be used by farmers to control planting, fertilizing, seed spraying, and harvesting as a result of enhanced harvest management and cost-saving activity.

The Japanese provider Kokusai Dentine Denwa International (KDDI) Technology uses smartphone IoT networking and CI technique in collaboration with the municipalities in Gotemba City and Oyama town to help climbers safely tackle Mount Fuji, Japan's highest peak (Gorman, 2019). During the climbing season, which lasts from mid-July to mid-September, KDDI uses Long Term Evolutions of Machines to monitor the number of climbers at the starting point for an ascent (the trails may become crowded), as well as temperatures and humidity levels.

7.6 Security and privacy in the internet of things

Security is one of the major challenge that needs to be overcome to push the IoT into the real world. IoT systems deal with billions of objects that communicate with one another and with other entities, such as humans or virtual entities. All these interactions should be secure somehow, protecting the data and limiting the number of incidents that will affect the entire IoT network. The security solutions should be lightweight, which means security solutions can operate with small memory, minimum power utilization, and low-cost devices (Ammar, Russello, & Crispo, 2018).

Privacy defines the rules by which data should be obtained relating to specific people. Fixed gathered information of a person can be created without the awareness of the individual. It is difficult to control and monitor such data in the present condition. The users of an IoT system need to process their details. Researchers should develop a common structure for protection in the IoT and an innovative scheme of enforcement that will maintain the scalability of the heterogeneity of IoT conditions (Sathish Kumar & Patel, 2014; Newlin Rajkumar, Chatrapathi, & Venkatesa Kumar, 2014).

7.6.1 Security

Security is a serious issue for wide-ranging implementation of technologies and applications of the IoT. Operators are unable to implement technologies of the IoT without security in terms of confidentiality, authenticity, and privacy (Yang, Wu, Yin, Li, & Zhao, 2017). Security solutions were developed mostly in an ad hoc manner. IoT has three security points: physical security, operational security, and data security. Physical security means the safety of the sensors, including sensor shielding and intercepted signal. Operational security arises in elements connected to the regular functioning of the sensor, transmission, and treatment systems. The data security is also exist in various elements that includes the sensor information and the processing system will not be stolen, manipulated, faked repudiation (Qiang, Quan, Yu, & Yang, 2013). The security difficulties raised by the sensor network are more complicated than conventional data security. Consequently, the IoT addresses general information network security problems facing IoT risks and attacks.

7.6.1.1 Issues

- Confidentiality: Data confidentiality is an important security prerequisite of the IoT network. In a network, nodes require confidentiality of data in the transmission process. Data confidentiality indicates the guarantee that data can be accessed and modified only by authorized entities. Not only users, but authorized things may also access information, which requires an access control approach and authentication process for the device (Miorandi et al., 2012; Sankaran, 2016). It can protect data from a passive attacker so that any data sent through the IoT network remain confidential. Providing confidential data is critical for IoT applications. To provide data confidentiality in networks, generally, cryptography algorithms are preferred to cipher data. This way, even if the exchanged data are overheard, the aggressor is unable to access its content.
- Integrity: IoT providers share sensitive messages with various services and even with third parties that they sensed, processed, and exchanged data must not be altered with maliciously (Atzori, Iera, & Morabito, 2017). The integrity of sensed data is important for the implementation of trustworthy and dependable applications of the IoT. This is ensured with MAC using hash functions. The selection of the MAC system is based upon the application and device abilities. For example, to provide electric billing, a smart home is linked to a smart grid network that has installed an energy usage monitoring program. The provider does not want it ever to be possible to manipulate the consumption data during transmission.

- Authentication: Authentication is needed in the IoT context because the message is used to make various decisions and actuate processes (Dabbagh & Saad, 2016). The service provider and consumer must be guaranteed that the service is retrieved by an authorized person and that the service is provided by an accurate source. Also, to prevent impersonation, a strong authentication mechanism must be deployed. Enforcement of any authentication method includes the registration of individuals and the drawback of the IoT object resources imposes tough restrictions on any authentication technique.
- Availability: The IoT environment contains sensors that provide important services. Because these IoT services are accessible at any time from any place to give continuous data, it is impossible to satisfy this property using a single safety protocol. There can be numerous strategic steps to confirm availability (Pokorni, 2019). For example, in a smart home, if the attacker learns about the owner's monitoring system, they can initiate a denial-of-service assault by merely trying to submit fake service demands, because the nodes are unable to manage a large number of requirements due to source constraints.

7.6.2 Privacy

Privacy in the IoT is a key challenge that requires the full consideration of academic and industry researchers. Privacy is the greatest concern to protect the messages of persons from disclosure in a network. It is preferred to give a unique identification, and the capability to connect individually over the Internet to give a physical or logical entity. Privacy is critically needed as objects in the IoT system transfer information independently. The interoperability of items is indeed key to the functionality of the IoT. Information exchanged by a specified endpoint is unlikely to trigger any privacy problems of its own. Hence there is a need to introduce various techniques for privacy management in the IoT (Cigdem Sengul, Privacy, 2017; Hameed, Khan, & Hameed, 2019). The IoT plays a vital role in numerous applications and individuals need the privacy of data that is related to activities with other persons. Three key axes of data privacy analysis are collection, sharing, and management (Mendez, Papapanagiotou, & Yang, 2017). Privacy in data collection requires multiple systems with different resources, networking, ability, etc.

7.6.2.1 Issues

Some important issues/challenges of privacy in the IoT (Khan & Hameed, 2016) are as follows:

- Profiling: Profiling means the threat of collecting data files related to persons to understand benefits by linking with other profiles and data. These approaches are required for personalization in e-commerce and internal optimization based on personal interests.
- Identification: Identification refers to the risk of associating an identity with a person and data about him/her, for example, a name, address, or nickname of some sort. Thus the risk lies in associating an identity with a specific context that violates privacy and also allows and worsens other risks.
- Inventory attack: This refers to an unapproved group of data related to the nature of personal items and their characteristics.
- Localization and tracking: Localization and tracking of persons is the main functionality in the IoT framework. This is an attack/threat to obtain and collect data of a person's position across time and space. A basic challenge of privacy solutions is the design of IoT interaction protocols that discourage such activity. Tracking contains some form of credentials to connect continuous localizations to a single entity. Tracking is applicable via GPS, Internet traffic, or cell phone location.
- Secure data transmission: Secure data transmission means without hiding transferring secure data from anyone through public media and thus preventing the wrong collection of data on devices and people.

7.7 Computational intelligent techniques

Computational intelligence (CI) typically relates to a computer's ability to learn a particular function from data or an experimental remark. It is a group of theoretical methods inspired by nature to solve challenging real-world problems to which mathematical or traditional forming can be unusable for some reason. For mathematical logic, the systems are complicated; some queries during the process or the method may be stochastic. Indeed, computers cannot translate many real-life issues into binary language (unique values of 0 and 1) to process it. CI offers solutions to such issues. The CI technique is a collection of computational models and methods used to solve real-life problems (Islam, Srivastava, Gupta, Zhu, & Mukherjee, 2014).

To enable intelligent operation in a complex and changing environment, CI contains learning abilities and different adaptive mechanisms. Neural networks, evolutionary computation (EC), and fuzzy systems, along with CI contain swarm intelligence, artificial immune systems (AISs), support vector machines, probabilistic approaches, etc., and a grouping of these methods. These methods are effectively used in applications in the environmental and earth sciences, for example, classes of distribution analyzed forest site quality assessment, water quality prediction, and predicting air pollution. This section presents AI (Cioffi, Travaglioni, Piscitelli, Petrillo, & Felice, 2020), neural networks, EC, AISs, fuzzy systems, blockchain, ML, and bio-inspired algorithms.

7.7.1 Artificial intelligence

AI is an instinctive mechanism that executes various tasks such as observing, learning, and reasoning (Ghosh, Chakraborty, & Law, 2018). AI is a technique of implanting intelligence in machinery that is capable of executing tasks that historically required humans. AI-based applications are developing quickly in terms of deployment, adaptation, computing speed, and capabilities. In reality, human intelligence is making a perfect decision at the right time. It can be argued that human creativity still changes the function of productive work. AI-based systems have minimized the repetition of human activities quite elegantly and may produce results in a relatively short time. AI established ML and deep learning techniques to overcome issues of IoT networks. A deep learning technique is used to solve the energy efficiency issue in IoT. With the use of ML techniques, identify patterns, anomalies, and making a guess based on a huge quantity of information are produced by IoT applications. The major challenges of AI are as follows.

- Building trustworthiness: AI is all about science, technologies, and algorithms that most people do not know about, making it difficult for them to accept.
- AI–human interface: As a modern technology, there is a scarcity of working people with data management and computer analysis skills; these, in turn, can be deputed to get the maximum performance from AI.
- Software malfunction: With AI manipulating devices and algorithms, decision-making functionality is immediately delegated to code-driven black box software. Automation makes it impossible to determine the sources of failures and malfunctions.
- Data security: ML and decision-making capabilities in AI systems are focused on vast quantities of secure information, mostly of a critical and personal nature. This makes it vulnerable to very major issues such as data loss and identity fraud.
- Algorithm bias: AI is all about data and algorithms. The consistency of AI's decision-making capacity is solely dependent on the accuracy of the testing and the use of authentic and impartial evidence.

7.7.2 Neural networks

An artificial neural network (ANN) is an important forecasting technique in almost all domains. Forecast techniques are gathered and reviewed historical information to construct a structure for capturing the underlying analysis of information. This ANN technique is a mathematical model focused on biological neural networks and its functions (Razafimandimby, Loscri, & Vegni, 2016). Data flow through an ANN has three different layers: an input layer, hidden layer, and output layer. All layers have nodes (neurons). The input and output layers have input and output nodes, respectively. Arbitrary numbers have nodes in the hidden layer. The network must be prepared and use the same system to guess unknown data when it starts to deliver accurate results (Gegovska, Koker, & Cakar, 2020). Some major issues of ANNs are as follows.

- Black box: The main issue of the ANN is in its black-box nature. A neural network is a black box in the sense that while it can approximate any function, studying its structure will not give any insights into the structure of the function being approximated.
- Amount of data: Compared to old algorithms, neural networks usually need huge data, that is, at least thousands if not millions of analyzed samples.
- Computationally expensive: ANN is computationally more expensive than old algorithms. Depending on the size of data, depth, and complexity of the network, an ANN requires computational power.

7.7.3 Evolutionary computation

EC is a class of global optimization algorithms influenced by natural growth. This method starts with the development of a community of people that respond to a problem. It is possible to construct the first population randomly using an algorithm. Individuals are evaluated with a health test and the performance of the feature indicates how well this individual addresses the problem. Then, some operators, such as convergence, mutation, selection, and replication are then extended to people that are influenced by natural evolution (Abbasi, Bin, Latiff, & Chizari, 2014). A new population is created based on the fitness values of newly developed individuals. Since the size of the population must be maintained as in the environment, some entities are removed. This method is continued until the criteria for termination are met. EC is a subfield of soft computing and AI techniques. The major challenges of ECs are as follows.

- Lack of reproducibility of experiments: EC is affected due to the lack of accepted benchmark problems, measuring performance is a tricky business, and lack of standard algorithms and implementations.
- Poor performance: Compared to other CI techniques, EC technique performance is not efficient due to long defining lengths of schemes and algorithms.
- Not suitable for real-time problems: EC techniques are not suitable for problems which are simple and for which derivative information is available. The fitness value is calculated repeatedly, which can be computationally expensive for some problems. Being stochastic, there are no guarantees on the optimality or quality of the solution.

7.7.4 Artificial immune systems

AISs are one important technique under a computationally intelligent and rules-based ML scheme stimulated by the ideas and methods of the vertebrate immune system (Pamukov, 2017). AIS is concerned with an extension of the structure and role of the immune system to computational structures and with the analysis of the usage of such methods to solve analytical problems relevant to mathematics, engineering, and information science. This methodology is a subfield of biologically inspired computation and natural computation, with developments in ML and contributing to the broader area of AI. AIS is an adaptive system based on abstract immunology and resistant purposes, with the laws and prototypes used to solve problems. The major issues of AIS are as follows.

- A combination of immune and other systems: Embedding of the AIS with machines is very complex. Therefore the mode for an understanding of the function of the immune system is to implement innovative hybrid algorithms.
- A theoretical basis for AIS: The AIS technique has been extended for different problem domains, but still effort is needed to grasp the essence of AISs and where they are best applied. Because of this, heterogeneous AIS implementations are limited.

7.7.5 Fuzzy system

Fuzzy logic is a type of multiassessed logic in which the true values of variables are a number between 0 and 1, both inclusive. It is used to deal with the concept of partial truth, where the truth value varies from fully true to false. It is focused on the fact that people make decisions focused on imprecise and non-numeric knowledge. Fuzzy models express ambiguity and imprecision of knowledge in mathematical form. These models can identify, represent, manipulate, understand, and operate data that are vague and lack certainty (Llorián et al., 2017). The challenges of a fuzzy system are as follows.

- Processing delay: Compared to ML and an ANN, fuzzy logic requires more time to process the data due to the complex fuzzy interference system.
- Unreliability: The use of fuzzy logic may become an obstacle to the verification of system reliability and requires tuning of membership functions. Fuzzy logic control may not scale well to large or complex problems due to uncertainty in fuzzy rules.

7.7.6 Machine learning

ML is a subset of AI that offers machines with the capacity to learn without programming. AI becomes practicable through ML. Computer systems perform functions through ML such as clustering, calculations, and pattern identification. The learning process is attained using various algorithms and arithmetic structures to analyze the information. This information is classified by some characteristics called features. ML is used to find a relationship between the features and some output values called labels (Li et al., 2020; Mahdavinejad et al., 2018; Schmidt, Marques, Botti, & Marques, 2019). The technique is ideal for problems like regression, classification, and collecting and association rules determination. Some important ML algorithms are K-means, naive Bayes, linear regression, canonical correlation analysis, and feed-forward neural network, etc. The challenges of ML are as follows.

- Data storage: Memory networks or memory-augmented neural networks still require large working memory to store data.
- Natural language processing: This is a massive challenge in deep networks. There remains a long way to go to achieve natural language processing and understanding of language.

7.7.7 Bio-inspired algorithm

A bio-inspired algorithm is a promising approach, which is related to ideologies and motivation of the biological growth of nature to improve new challenging techniques. This approach deals with different models, patterns, and variations among beings. Bio-inspired approaches are used in the field of security and privacy in the IoT to provide secure data using computer models that contain biological principles in nature (Riri & Sari, 2017; Sekhar, Siddesh, Tiwari, & Anand, 2020). This is a bottom-up approach and puts attention on reliability. Connectionism, emergence, and social are the main features of bio-inspired techniques. Ant colony optimization, artificial bee colony algorithm, genetic algorithm, etc., are bio-inspired algorithms. These algorithms are used to overcome issues such as resource restriction, scalability, heterogeneity, flexibility, and safety.

- Scalability: Scalability is a significant challenge for robot swarms. The scalability problem increases due to an increase in the number of IoT devices (network size) and their data.
- Heterogeneity: Bio-inspired algorithms do not support heterogeneous networks.

In the IoT network, we can track the billions of connected things and enable the process of transaction and coordination between things in a very secure manner using blockchain technology. This technique is not a CI technique. Blockchain is a progressive system behind security and protection issues in the IoT structure. It is one of the most promising techniques and has attracted interest for its clearness, security, immutability, and decentralization. It is combination of multifield structures. It includes cryptosystem and mathematics, relating peer-to-peer systems using various algorithms to solve traditional record synchronization problems. The blockchain technique gives us very reliable, accurate, and suitable services.

Blockchain is the advanced technique behind security and privacy challenges in the IoT network. The technique consists of original data, hash function blocks, and timestamp. It has a digital signature, consensus mechanism, and chain structure (Chen, Wang, & Wang, 2020). In the blockchain, a digital signature is used to protect user transactions using cryptography. The consensus mechanism gives trustworthiness to the network and protects the transaction data from being altered by unauthorized people. In a blockchain structure a block consisting of its hash and Merkle tree are broadcast to all the other nodes. By adding the hash value of the previous block into the new block's header, all subsequent blocks are chained together.

7.8 Computational intelligent techniques to provide security and privacy for the internet of things

Nowadays, many security and privacy problems cannot be optimally solved due to their complexity. The integration of CI techniques to achieve intelligent environments offers adaptive behaviors depending on the user's intentions (Zavadzki, Kleina, Drozda, & Marques, 2020). This section presents the various intelligent techniques to provide security and privacy in the IoT, such as confidentiality, integrity, authentication, and availability.

7.8.1 Confidentiality

Bio-inspired computation is a subset of a ML algorithm which deals with living organisms' biological principles used for safe data transfer and maintenance in data security of IoT architectures. Some of the bio-inspired algorithms are ant colony optimization algorithm, bee colony, genetic algorithm, etc. (Dorri, Kanhere, Jurdak, & Gauravaram, 2019) for solving real-world problems to provide confidential data in the IoT network.

Bio-inspired approaches are used to give a solution to the security problems of engineering techniques. A Lightweight Scalable Blockchain and Distributed Time-based Consensus (DTC) algorithm is used to meet IoT requirements, as presented in Ge, Liu, & Fang (2020) to provide end-to-end network security. DTC reduces delays and overheads for mining processing. The cluster heads employ a distributed trust strategy to gradually raise the overhead processing to validate new blocks. A decentralized, secure system with blockchain technique for managing important data in the IoT system is presented in Liu et al. (2020). The framework effectively addresses the data reliability, security, and privacy problems that are faced in the traditional IoT–cloud system.

Blockchain Aided Searchable Attribute-Based Encryption with effective revocation and decryption method is described in Turjman and Alturjman (2018). The decentralized blockchain network is used to generate threshold standards, given key management schemes. The blockchain performs all the revocation tasks and is required for data encryption and key update. To preserve data confidentiality and privacy, encryption is a good technique but it causes time latency and performance-related problems (Almiani, Ghazleh, Rahayfeh, Atiewi, & Razaque, 2020). Using the elliptic curve cryptography, the network allows data confidentiality, authentication, and data integrity.

A fully automated intrusion detection system for fog safety from cyber-attacks is presented in Bhattacharjee, Kwait, and Kamhoua (2017). The model utilizes multilayered neural networks implemented for fog computing security systems in the IoT. To catch particular security attacks in the IoT, a deep multilayered recursive neural network is used with a Kalman filter.

7.8.2 Integrity

For data integrity, a Bayesian model and a prospective theoretic structure are presented in Wang and Zhang (2019) to verify the reliability of collected information from nodes in the IoT network. Applied optimistic and conservative models are used to calculate the data integrity score and determine the security of the message collected from the IoT system.

Blockchain and Bilinear Mapping Scheme (BBMS) used to provide data integrity in IoT have been discussed (Pohls, 2015) and Verifiable Tags of Homomorphic are created in BBMS for sampling verifications. The integrity of data obtained from the blockchain transactions is based upon the characteristics of bilinear mapping. Performance analyses of BBMS including viability, security, dynamicity, and intricacy are presented. An elliptic curve-based signature algorithm for the generation of secret keys to protect data from unauthorized persons is presented in Altulyan, Yao, Kanhere, Wang, and Huang (2020). Digital signatures are applied to maintain the validity of end-to-end message integrity level in JavaScript Object Notation.

A comprehensive structure to maintain data security in smart cities covering the whole technology lifecycle is discussed in Aman, Sikdar, Chua, and Ali (2019). The platform is focused on three major principles, that is, secret exchange, fog computing, and blockchain. The scheme is intended to protect several attacks by utilizing a blockchain. It has much special functionality to cope with confidential data and to test this system for use as a forum for various smart city applications. An effective and easy technique to detect data manipulation in IoT systems uses random time-lapse sequences and random permutations to conceal validation details (Zhang, He, Chen, Zhang, & Xiang, 2019). The protocol efficiency review indicates that it has low numerical difficulty and is suitable for IoT applications.

7.8.3 Authentication

Compressive Sensing (CS) and Cascade Chaotic Systems (CCS) structures are discussed in Fan, Luo, Zhang, and Yang (2020). These structures confirm low overhead, confidentiality, and authentication in the network. This structure has technologies like CCS-driven CS, CCS-driven local perturbation, and authentication mechanisms that are used to introduce the data acquisition framework. The technologies use password authentication and password access to handle passive tampering attacks and active tampering attacks.

A powerful and secure RFID authentication scheme focused on the cloud is discussed in Zhang, Wang, Shang, Lu, and Ma (2020). An authentication scheme examines rotation and better permutation to encrypt data to reduce the overhead of the RFID tag. Protocols handle different threats such as threat detection, replay, and desynchronization. It also achieves mutual authentication and reverses security. The Blockchain-based Trusted Network Connection (BTNC) scheme is used for security in the IoT. Due to some features of blockchain such as devolution, trustlessness, tractability, and immutability, the BTNC scheme is used to authenticate the nodes in IoT networks, as presented in Maitra, Obaidat, Giri, Dutta, and Dahal (2019). In the IoT, the BTNC protocol performs shared user verification, device confirmation, and network trust via a cryptosystem between terminals.

An ElGamal cryptography and user credentials protection scheme for IoT applications, referred to as Secure Authentication Scheme (SAS) Cloud, are discussed in Nespoli et al. (2018). This mechanism is examined through the oracle system and it confirms the SAS scheme can protect networks from all possible attacks. The scheme provides better results than existing authentication algorithms.

IoT-enabled Continuous Authentication Framework (Rahman & Hussein, 2019) is a new scheme that can provide continuous and nonintrusive authentication and authorization solutions to users depending upon their interaction with the surrounding IoT devices.

7.8.4 Availability

Data replication for improved data quality is a dynamically disseminated hop-by-hop data replication strategy for IoT-based wireless sensor systems. The proposed scheme guarantees optimal data capacity in the case of large node data protection problems (Qaim & Ozkasap, 2018). A concept of network heterogeneity based on node deployment and uncertainty that can be used to test the node availability is presented in Wu, Cao, Jin, and Zhang (2018). The node state transition model through the Markov chain obtains complex equations for the connectivity between objects and accessibility.

A Privacy and Data Clustering (PDC) structure is designed with the help of the K-means algorithm and differential protection (Xiong et al., 2019), which select the initial node and calculate the distance between the initial node and other nodes from clusters in the network. The PDC scheme improves the availability of the clustering method. A Network Intrusion Detection System based on anomaly behavior analysis is discussed in Pacheco, Benitez, Tunc, and Grijalva (2020) to detect a fog node. The scheme identifies known and unknown anomalies due to misuse or attacks, with high-level recognition rates and low-level false apprehensions. Performance of Ultra-Reliable Energy Harvesting Cognitive Radio Internet of Things is presented in Amini and Baidas (2020). Logical sources for different IoT network metrics such as trustworthiness, accessibility, and stability, are discussed also. Some parameters such as time sensing, diversity communication, and packets in data frames are analyzed in the IoT network.

A brief summary of the existing privacy and security issues with intelligent techniques is depicted in Table 7.1.

TABLE 7.1 Security and privacy issues with intelligent techniques.

Issues	Blockchain	Machine learning	Bio-inspired algorithms	Evolutionary computation	Neural networks	Fuzzy system
Confidentiality	Very high	Very high	High	High	High	Low
Integrity	High	High	–	High	Medium	Low
Authentication	High	High	Medium	High	Very high	Very low
Availability	Medium	Medium	–	Medium	–	–

7.9 Future research direction

In this section, we address some of the emerging research issues that need to establish a new paradigm for security and privacy in the IoT, as follows:

- Analysis of information security determinants and the design of cyber protection schemes by the use of computers equipped with Internet access and IoT technology.
- Technological solutions based on convergence of IoT technology and blockchain will be one of the main developments in future years. Blockchain provides a high level of confidentiality and decentralization of information transfer on the Internet, including the execution of financial transactions through the Internet.
- In the coming years, the use of data processing and analysis approaches will be developed through Big Data database systems in combination with data processing in the cloud through the Internet from devices.
- Creating applications in risk management systems, designing Internet data storage frameworks, supporting business management systems, crisis management in metropolitan agglomerations, etc., are evolving areas of IoT technology. The IoT is growing in the context of developing network implementations that integrate the IoT with other technology, as defined by Industry 4.0.
- Providing end-to-end encryption for data is the future scope of research in the IoT. This is a challenging task due to heterogeneous IoT devices and multinetworking support.
- While manufacturing IoT products, the priority is more on their performance and less on safety. Therefore intelligent, hybrid, and secure gateways/routers must be used in IoT networks. IoT-connected devices must be safe enough to prevent the systems from being hacked. Manufacturers should also look at different systems to enhance the security of devices.
- It remains important to establish secure data management approaches, policies, or frameworks to data owners with much-needed privacy while providing this information to AI tools. Other research directions that should be explored include data storage, computer offloading, and various lightweight algorithms that can run efficiently in limited resource networks.

Advanced IoT devices connect everyone to the digital and online world through intelligent objects to make life easier and better. As a consequence, everyone can reach, link, and store their details on the network from anywhere to gain access to the IoT's smart services. The IoT has the potential to transform the world and put solutions to global problems into our hands. At the same time, security is a major concern in the IoT system for providing services. As a consequence, enhancing privacy and security protection for the IoT has become a popular research area that needs to be resolved with innovative approaches and ambitious planning strategies for preventing unpredictable attacks in the future.

In this chapter, various IoT architectures, characteristics, security and privacy issues, and applications are discussed. A comprehensive survey of existing security and privacy issues using CI techniques such as ML, AI, blockchain technology, and computational evolution is also presented.

References

Abbasi, M. J., Bin, M. S., Latiff, A., & Chizari, H. (2014). Bioinspired evolutionary algorithm based for improving network coverage in wireless sensor networks. *Journal of Recent Advances on Bioinspired Computation, 2014*, 1–9.

Ahanger, T. A., & Aljumah, A. (2018). Internet of things: A comprehensive study of security issues and defense mechanisms. *IEEE Access, 7*, 11020–11028.

Ahmed, A., & Yousef, E. (2019). Internet of things in smart environment: Concept, applications, challenges, and future directions. *International Scientific Journal, 134*, 1–51.

Ahmed M.U., Björkman M., Čaušsević A., Fotouhi H., & Lindén M. (2015). An overview on the internet of things for health monitoring systems. *Proceedings of the second international conference on IoT technologies for healthcare* (pp. 1–8). Rome, Italy.

Alepis, E., & Patsakis, C. (2017). Monkey says, monkey does: Security and privacy on voice assistants. *IEEE Access, 5*, 17841–17851.

Almiani, M., Ghazleh, A. A., Rahayfeh, A. A., Atiewi, S., & Razaque, A. (2020). Deep recurrent neural network for IoT intrusion detection system. *Journal of Simulation Modelling Practice and Theory, 101*, 1–26.

Altulyan, M., Yao, L., Kanhere, S. S., Wang, X., & Huang, C. (2020). A unified framework for data integrity protection in people-centric smart cities. *Journal of Multimedia Tools and Applications, 79*, 4989–5002.

Aman, M. N., Sikdar, B., Chua, K. C., & Ali, A. (2019). Low power data integrity in IoT systems. *Journal of IEEE Internet of Things, 5*(4), 3102–3113.

Amini, M. R., & Baidas, M. W. (2020). Availability-reliability-stability trade-offs in ultra-reliable energy-harvesting cognitive radio IoT networks. *Journal of IEEE Access, 8*, 82890–82916.

Ammar, M., Russello, G., & Crispo, B. (2018). Internet of things: A survey on the security of IoT frameworks. *Journal of Information Security and Applications, 38*, 8–27.

Atzori, L., Iera, A., & Morabito, G. (2010). The internet of things: A survey. *Journal of Computer Network, 54*(15), 2787–2805.

Atzori L., Iera A., & Morabito G. (2017). Preserving data integrity in iot networks under opportunistic data manipulation. *Proceedings of the international conference on big data intelligence and computing and cyber science and technology congress* (pp. 446–453). USA.

Bandyopadhyay, D., & Sen, J. (2011). Internet of things: Applications and challenges in technology and standardization. *Journal of Wireless Personal Communications, 58*(1), 49–69.

Bhattacharjee S., Kwait K., & Kamhoua C. (2017). Preserving data integrity in IoT networks under opportunistic data manipulation. *Proceedings of the third international conference on big data intelligence and computing and cyber science and technology congress* (pp. 446–453). USA.

Binti, M., Noor, M., & Hassan, W. H. (2019). Current research on internet of things (IoT) security: A survey. *Journal of Computer Networks, 148*, 283–294.

Cao, L., Cai, Y., & Yue, Y. (2019). Swarm intelligence-based performance optimization for mobile wireless sensor networks: Survey, challenges, and future directions. *IEEE Access, 7*, 161524–161553.

Chanal, P. M., & Kakkasageri, M. S. (2020). Security and privacy in IoT: A survey. *Journal of Wireless Personal Communication, 115*(3), 1667–1693. Available from https://doi.org/10.1007/s11277-020-07649-9.

Chen, Y. J., Wang, L. C., & Wang, S. (2020). Stochastic blockchain for iot data integrity. *Journal of IEEE Transactions on Network Science and Engineering, 7*(1), 373–384.

Cigdem Sengul Privacy (2017). Consent and authorization in IoT. *Proceedings of the twenty international conference on innovations in clouds, internet and networks* (pp. 319–321). Chicago, Illinois, USA.

Cioffi, R., Travaglioni, M., Piscitelli, G., Petrillo, A., & Felice, F. D. (2020). Artificial intelligence and machine learning applications in smart production: Progress, trends, and directions. *Journal of Sustainability*, 1–26. Available from https://doi.org/10.3390/su12020492.

Covington M., & Carskadden R. (2013). Threat implications of the internet of things. *Proceedings of the fifth international conference on cyber conflict* (1–12), Estonia.

Dabbagh Y.S., & Saad W. (2016). Authentication of devices in the internet of things. *Proceedings of the IEEE seventeeth international symposium on a world of wireless, mobile and multimedia networks*, 32 (6). Portugal.

Davies, R. (2015). The Internet of things opportunities and challenges. *European Parliamentary Research Service*, 1–8.

Dorri, A., Kanhere, S. S., Jurdak, R., & Gauravaram, P. (2019). LSB: A lightweight scalable blockchain for iot security and anonymity. *Journal of Parallel and Distributed Computing, 134*, 180–197.

Fan, K., Luo, Q., Zhang, K., & Yang, Y. (2020). Cloud-based lightweight secure RFID mutual authentication protocol in IoT. *Journal of Information Sciences, 527*, 329–340.

Farooq, U., Waseem, M., Mazhar, S., Khairi, A., & Kamal, T. (2015). A review on internet of things (IoT). *Journal of Computer Applications, 113*(1).

Fernandez, A., Herrera, F., Cordon, O., Jesus, M. J., & Marcelloni, F. (2019). Evolutionary fuzzy systems for explainable artificial intelligence: Why, when, what for, and where to? *IEEE Computational Intelligence Magazine, 14*(1), 69–81.

Friess, P., Guillemin, P., & Sundmaeker, H. (2010). *Vision and challenges for realizing the internet of things, cluster of european research projects on the internet of things*. European Commission Information Society and Media.

Gegovska, T., Koker, R., & Cakar, T. (2020). Green supplier selection using fuzzy multiple-criteria decision-making methods and artificial neural networks. *Journal of Computational Intelligence and Neuroscience*.

Ge, C., Liu, Z., & Fang, L. (2020). A blockchain-based decentralized data security mechanism for the internet of things. *Journal of Parallel and Distributed Computing, 141*, 1–9.

Ghosh, A., Chakraborty, D., & Law, A. (2018). Artificial intelligence in internet of things. *Journal of Institution Engineering and Technology (IET)*, 1–11.

Gorman, J. (2019). Mobile IoT case study: How Asia Pacific intelligently connects to IoT.

Goyal, P., Sahoo, A., Sharma, T., & Singh, P. K. (2020). Internet of things: Applications, security and privacy: A survey. *Material Today Proceedings, 34*(3), 752–759.

Gubbi, J., Buyya, R., Marusic, S., & Palaniswami, M. (2013). Internet of things (IoT): A vision, architectural elements and future directions. *ournal of Future Generation Computer Systems, 29* (7), 1645–1660.

Hameed, S., Khan, F. I., & Hameed, B. (2019). Understanding security requirements and challenges in internet of things (IoT): A review. *Journal of Computer Networks and Communications, 2019*, 1–15.

Islam, T., Srivastava, P. K., Gupta, M., Zhu, X., & Mukherjee, S. (2014). Computational intelligence techniques and applications. *Computational Intelligence Techniques in Earth and Environmental Sciences*, 3–26.

Jabbar, S., Iram, R., Minhas, A. A., Shafi, I., & Khalid, S. (2013). Intelligent optimization of wireless sensor networks through bio-inspired computing: Survey and future directions. *Journal of Distributed Sensor Networks, 10*, 13–25.

Jayasinghe, U., Lee, G. M., Um, T., & Shi, Q. (2019). Machine learning-based trust computational model for IoT services. *IEEE Transactions on Sustainable Computing, 4*(1), 39–52.

Kakkasageri, M. S., & Manvi, S. S. (2014). Regression-based critical information aggregation and dissemination in VANETs: A cognitive agent approach. *Vehicular Communications, 1*(4), 168–180.

Khan, F. I., & Hameed, S. (2016). Software defined security service provisioning framework for internet of things. *Journal of Advanced Computer Science and Applications, 7*(12), 1–12.

Kraijak, S., & Tuwanut, P. (2015). A survey on iot architectures, protocols, applications, security, privacy, real-world implementation, and future trends. *Proceedings of the eleventh international conference on wireless communications, networking and mobile computing (WiCOM 2015)* (pp. 1–6). China.

Kumar, S., & Sharma, M. (2012). Convergence of artificial intelligence, emotional intelligence, neural network, and evolutionary computing. *Journal of Advanced Research in Computer Science and Software Engineering, 2*(3).

Lamas, P. F., Carams, T., Albela, M., Castedo, L., & Gonzlez-Lpez, M. (2016). A review on internet of things for defense and public safety. *Sensors*, 2–44.

Liu, S., Yu, J., Xiao, Y., Wan, Z., Wang, S., & Yan, B. (2020). BC-SABE: Blockchain-aided searchable attribute-based encryption for cloud-IoT. *Journal of IEEE Internet of Things*, 1–17.

Li, H., Wang, H., Xu, T., & Zhou, G. (2011). Application study on internet of things in environment protection field. *Journal of Informatics in Control, Automation and Robotics, 2*, 99–106.

Li, Y., Wang, J., Gao, T., Sun, Q., Zhang, L., & Tang, M. (2020). Adoption of machine learning in intelligent terrain classification of hyperspectral remote sensing images. *Journal of Computational Intelligence and Neuroscience*. Available from https://doi.org/10.1155/2020/8886932.

Llorián, D. M., Garcia, C. G., Pelayo, B. C., BusteloJuan, G., Cueva, M., & Clime, I. (2017). The fuzzy logic and the internet of things to control indoor temperature regarding the outdoor ambient conditions. *Journal of Future Generation Computer Systems, 76*, 275–284.

Mahdavinejad, M. S., Rezvan, M., Barekatain, M., Adibi, P., Barnaghi, P., & Sheth, A. P. (2018). Machine learning for internet of things data analysis: A survey. *Journal of Digital Communications and Networks, 4*(3), 161–175.

Maitra, T., Obaidat, M. S., Giri, D., Dutta, S., & Dahal, K. (2019). ElGamal cryptosystem-based secure authentication system for cloud-based IoT applications. *Journal of Institution of Engineering and Technology Network, 8*(5), 289–298.

Mattern, F., & Floerkemeier, C. (2010). The internet of computers to the internet of things. *Active Data Management to Event-Based Systems and More, 6462*, 242–259.

Mazzei, D., Baldi, G., Fantoni, G., Montelisciani, G., Pitasi, A., Ricci, L., … Blockchain, A. (2020). Tokenizer for industrial IoT trustless applications. *Journal of Future Generation Computer Systems, 105*, 432–445.

Mendez, D., Papapanagiotou, I., & Yang, B. (2017). Internet of things: Survey on security and privacy IoT security. *Journal of IEEE Internet of Things, 4*(5), 1250–1258.

Miorandi, D., Sicari, S., Pellegrini, F. D., & Chlamtac, I. (2012). Internet of things: Vision, applications and research challenges. *Journal of Ad Hoc Networks, 10*(7), 1497–1516.

Mohammed, Z., & Ahmed, E. (2017). Internet of things applications, challenges, and related future technologies. *World Scientific News, 67*(2), 126–148.

Mohanraj, I., Ashokumar, K., & Naren, J. (2016). Field monitoring and automation using IoT in agriculture domain. *Journal of Procedia Computer Science, 93*, 931–939.

Moura, J., & Hutchison, D. (2019). Game theory for multi-access edge computing: Survey, use cases, and future trends. *IEEE Communications Surveys and Tutorials, 21*(01), 260–288.

Nespoli, P., Zago, M., Celdran, A.H., Perez, M.G., Marmol, F.G., & Clemente, F.J.G. (2018). A dynamic continuous authentication framework in iot-enabled environments. *Proceedings of the fifth international conference on internet of things: Systems, management and security (IoTSMS)* (pp. 131–138). Valencia, Spain.

Newlin Rajkumar, M., Chatrapathi, C., & Venkatesa Kumar, V. (2014). Internet of things: A vision, technical issues, applications and security. *Journal of Computer Science, 2*(8), 20–27.

Okkonen, H., Mazhelis, O., Ahokangas, P., Pussinen, P., Rajahonka, M., Siuruainen, R. … Warma, H. (2013) Internet of things market value networks and business models: State of the art report. Finland: University of Jyvaskyla.

Pacheco, J., Benitez, V.H., Tunc C., & Grijalva, C. (2020). Anomaly behavior analysis for fog nodes availability assurance in iot applications. *Proceedings of the sixteenth international conference on computer systems and applications (AICCSA)* (1–6). Abu Dhabi, UAE.

Pamukov, M.E. (2017). Application of artificial immune systems for the creation of IoT intrusion detection systems. *Proceedings of the international conference on intelligent data acquisition and advanced computing systems: Technology and applications (IDAACS)* (pp. 564–568). Bucharest, Romania.

Pan, J., Paul, S., & Jain, R. (2011). A survey of the research on future internet architectures. *IEEE Communications Magazine, 49*(7), 26–36.

Patel, K. K., & Patel, S. M. (2016). Internet of things-IoT: Definition, characteristics, architecture, enabling technologies, application, and future challenges. *Journal of International Journal of Engineering Science and Computing (IJESC), 6*(5), 6122–6131.

Pohls, H.C., (2015). JSON sensor signatures (JSS): End-to-end integrity protection from constrained device to iot application. *Proceedings of the nineth international conference on innovative mobile and internet services in ubiquitous computing*, (pp. 306–312). Brazil.

Pokorni, S. (2019). Reliability and availability of the internet of things. *Military Technical Courier*, 88–600.

Primeau, N., Falcon, R., Abielmona, R., & Petriu, E. M. (2018). A review of computational intelligence techniques in wireless sensor and actuator networks. *IEEE Communications Surveys and Tutorials, 20*(04), 2822–2854.

Qaim, W.B., & Ozkasap, O. (2018). DRAW: Data replication for enhanced data availability in IoT-based sensor systems. *Proceedings of the international conference on cyber science and technology congress* (pp. 770–775), Athens, Greece.

Qiang, C., Quan, G., Yu, B., & Yang, L. (2013). Research on security issues of the internet of things. *Journal of Future Generation Communication and Networking, 6*(6), 1–10.

Rahman, A., & Hussein, H. (2019). Internet of things (IoT): Research challenges and future applications. *Journal of Advanced Computer Science and Applications, 10*(6), 77–82.

Rahman, M. A., Asyharib, T., Kurniawan, I., Jahan Ali, M., Rahman, M. M., & Karima, M. (2020). A scalable hybrid mac strategy for traffic differentiated IoT-enabled intra vehicular networks. *Journal of Computer Communications, 157*, 320–328.

Razafimandimby, C., Loscri, V., & Vegni, A.M. (2016). A neural network and iot based scheme for performance assessment in internet of robotic things. *Proceedings of the international conference on internet-of-things design and implementation* (pp. 241–246). Berlin, Germany.

Riri, I., & Sari, F. (2017). Bioinspired algorithms for internet of things network. *Proceedings of the international conference on information technology, computer and electrical engineering* (ICITACEE) (pp. 1–7). Semarang, Indonesia.

Roman, R., Najera, P., & Lopez, J. (2011). Securing the internet of things. *Journal of Computer Network, 44*(9), 51–58.

Rukmini, M.S.S., & Usha Devi, Y. (2016). IoT in connected vehicles: Challenges and issues: A review. *Proceedings of the IEEE international conference on signal processing, communication, power and embedded system (SCOPES)* (pp. 1864–1867). Paralakhemundi, India.

Sankaran, S. (2016). Lightweight security framework for IoTs using identity-based cryptography. *Proceedings of the international conference on advances in computing, communications and informatics (ICACCI)* (pp. 880–886). Jaipur, India.

Sathish Kumar, J., & Patel, D. R. (2014). A survey on internet of things: Security and privacy issues. *Journal of Computer Applications, 90*(11), 20–26.

Schmidt, J., Marques, M. R. G., Botti, S., & Marques, M. A. L. (2019). Recent advances and applications of machine learning in solidstate materials science. *Journal of Computational Materials, 5*(83), 1–36.

Sekhar, S. R. M., Siddesh, G. M., Tiwari, A., & Anand, A. (2020). Bioinspired techniques for data security in IoT. *Internet of Things (IoT) Concepts and Applications*, 168–187.

Shen, M., Tang, X., Zhu, L., Du, X., & Guizani, M. (2019). Privacy-preserving support vector machine training over blockchain-based encrypted IoT data in smart cities. *Journal of Internet of Things, 6*(5), 7702–7712.

Sisinni, E., Saifullah, A., Han, S., & Jennehag, U. (2018). Industrial internet of things: Challenges, opportunities, and directions. *IEEE Transactions on Industrial Informatics*, 1–11.

Sonar, K., & Upadhyay, H. (2014). A survey: DDOS attack on internet of things. *Journal of Engineering Research and Development, 10*(11), 58–63.

Suo, H., Wan, J., Zou, C. & Liu, J. (2012). Security in the internet of things: A review. *Proceedings of the IEEE international conference on computer science and electronics engineering* 3 (pp. 648–651), China.

Tewari, A., & Gupta, B. B. (2020). Security, privacy and trust of different layers in internet of things (IoTs) frameworks. *Journal of Future Generation Computer Systems, 108*, 909–920.

Turjman, F. A., & Alturjman, S. (2018). Confidential smart sensing framework in the IoT era. *Journal of Supercomputing, 74*, 5187–5198.

Vate-U-Lan, P., Quigley, D. (2017). Internet of things in agriculture: A case study of smart dairy farming in Ontario, Canada. *Proceedings of the fifteenth international conference on developing real-life learning experiences* (pp. 1–9). Bangkok, Thailand.

Vermesan, O., & Friess, P. (2013). *Internet of things: Converging technologies for smart environments and integrated ecosystems*. River Publishers.

Vermesan, O., Friess, P., Guillemin, P., Gusmeroli, S., Sundmaeker, H., Bassi, A.... Doody, P. (2011) Internet of Things Strategic Research Roadmap. http://www.internet-of-things-research.eu/pdf/IoT_Cluster_Strategic_Research_Agenda_2011.pdf.

Wang, H., & Zhang, J. (2019). Blockchain-based data integrity verification for large-scale IoT data. *Journal of IEEE Access, 7*, 164996–165006.

Wrona, K., Castro, A., Vasilache, B. (2017). Data-centric security in military applications of commercial IoT technology. *IEEE world forum on internet of things (WF-IoT)* (pp. 239–244). USA.

Wu, X., Cao, Q., Jin, J., Zhang, H. (2018). Nodes availability analysis of heterogeneous wireless sensor networks based on nb-IoT under malware infection. *Proceedings of the fifth international conference on systems and informatics* (ICSAI) (pp. 429–434). China.

Xiong, J., Ren, J., Chen, L., Yao, Z., Lin, M., Wu, D., & Niu, B. (2019). Enhancing privacy and availability for data clustering in intelligent electrical service of IoT. *Journal of IEEE Internet of Things, 6* (2), 1530–1540.

Yang, D., Liu, F., Liang, Y. (2010). A survey of internet of things. *Proceedings of the international conference on e-business intelligence (ICEBI2010)* (pp. 78–99). Kunming, China.

Yang, Y., Wu, L., Yin, G., Li, L., & Zhao, H. (2017). A survey on security and privacy issues in internet of things. *Journal of IEEE Internet of Things*, 4(5), 1250–1258.

Yang, G., Xu, J., Chen, W., Qi, Z. H., & Wang, H. Y. (2010). Security characteristic and technology in the internet of things. *Journal of Nanjing University of Posts and Telecommunications, 30*(4).

Yang, Z., Zhou, Z., Lei, Q., Zheng, L., & Xiang, K. (2016). An IoT-cloud based wearable ecg monitoring system for smart health care. *Journal of Medical Systems, 40*(12), 286–296.

Yan, Y., Pei, Q., & Li, H. (2019). Privacy-preserving compressive model for enhanced deep-learning-based service provision system in edge computing. *IEEE Access, 7*, 92921–92937.

Zavadzki, S., Kleina, M., Drozda, F., & Marques, M. (2020). Computational intelligence techniques used for stock market prediction: A systematic review. *Journal of IEEE Latin America Transactions, 18*(4), 744–755.

Zeadally, S., Siddiqui, F., Baig, Z., & Ibrahim, A. (2019). Smart health care challenges and potential solutions using internet of things (IoT) and big data analytics. *PSU Research Review*, 4(2). Available from https://www.emerald.com/insight/content/doi/10.1108/PRR-08-2019-0027/.analytics.

Zhang, J., Wang, Z., Shang, L., Lu, D., & Ma, J. (2020). BTNC: A blockchain-based trusted network connection protocol in IoT. *Journal of Parallel and Distributed Computing, 143*, 1–16.

Zhang, Y., He, Q., Chen, G., Zhang, X., & Xiang, Y. (2019). A low-overhead, confidentiality assured, and authenticated data acquisition framework for IoT. *IEEE Transactions on Industrial Informatics*, 1–13.

Zielinski, Z., Chudzikiewicz, J., & Furtak, J. (2019). An approach to integrating security and fault tolerance mechanisms into the military IoT: Technology, communications and computing. *Security and Fault Tolerance in Internet of Things*, 111–128.

CHAPTER

8

Automatic enhancement of coronary arteries using convolutional gray-level templates and path-based metaheuristics

Miguel-Angel Gil-Rios[1], *Ivan Cruz-Aceves*[2], *Fernando Cervantes-Sanchez*[3], *Igor Guryev*[1] *and Juan-Manuel López-Hernández*[1]

[1]Department of Sciences and Engineering (DICIS), University of Guanajuato, Guanajuato México [2]CONACYT—Math Research Center (CIMAT), Guanajuato México [3]Math Research Center (CIMAT), Guanajuato México

8.1 Introduction

Automatic vessel imaging enhancement (also called detection) plays an important role in medical analysis and information systems. Invasive (catheter-based) X-ray coronary angiography is one of the most commonly utilized methods to assess coronary artery disease and is still considered the gold standard in clinical decision-making and therapy guidance (Mark et al., 2010). This imaging modality is based on the radiographic visualization of the coronary vessels with injection of a radiopaque contrast material (Scanlon et al., 1999). Although the X-ray procedure for coronary angiography is the most widely used strategy in clinical practice, it obtains images with different problems such as nonuniform illumination and weak contrast between the arteries and image background (Cimen, Gooya, Grass, & Frangi, 2016). In general, the specialized vessel detection methods work under the assumption that vessel-like structures can be approximated as tubular objects with different diameters and directions. However, the process to determine the parameter values of the vessel detection methods is commonly based on the empirical knowledge of an expert (Cruz-Aceves, Cervantes-Sanchez, Hernandez-Aguirre, Hernandez-Gonzalez, & Solorio-meza, 2019). For this reason, the use of predefined filters in the spatial domain is a widely explored approach where vessel-like structures are approximated as tubular and curved structures.

In recent years, several methods have been proposed for automatic vessel detection in medical images. Some methods are based on mathematical morphology. The method of Eiho and Qian (1997) is commonly used for vessel imaging segmentation because of it robustness and easy implementation. This method use the single-scale top-hat operator to enhance the shape of arteries followed by the morphological erosion, thinning and watershed operators for image segmentation of coronary arteries. This method was improved by Qian, Eiho, Sugimoto, and Fujita (1998). Maglaveras, Haris, Efstratiadis, Gourassas, and Louridas (2001) proposed a method for automatic detection of coronary arteries using the skeleton, high thresholding and connected-component operators. A fully automatic two-step method for coronary vessel detection was proposed by Bouraoui, Ronse, Baruthio, Passat, and Germain (2008). On the first step, the gray-level hit-or-miss transform is used to obtain two seed points on the arteries, and in the second step, a region-growing algorithm is used to detect coronary arteries. Lara, Faria, Araujo, and Menotti (2009) combined a region-growing algorithm with a differential-geometry approach to segment the coronary artery tree in angiograms. All these strategies have probed to achieve good results when vessels have high contrast.

Recent Trends in Computational Intelligence Enabled Research.
DOI: https://doi.org/10.1016/B978-0-12-822844-9.00005-0

However, they are very sensitive to noise, which reduces their performance significantly.

Another widely explored approach to segment vessels is the use of convolutional templates. Chaudhuri, Chatterjee, Katz, Nelson, and Goldbaum (1989) proposed Gaussian matched filters (GMF) to approximate vessels in the spatial image domain by applying a Gaussian curve as the matching template at different orientations and then, the maximum response filter from the responses bank is taken to form the final enhanced image. Chanwimaluang and Fan (2003) worked on blood vessel imaging enhancement using matched filters in a first step, followed by the use of a local entropy threshold method proposed by Pal (1989), in order to segment vessels. In the third step, the segmentation results are improved by removing isolated pixels using a length-filtering method. Kang, Wang, Chen, and Kang (2009) applied the morphological top-hat operator and a matched filter independently to the same original image. Then, a thresholding maximization method is applied to both responses. The final result is obtained applying a pixel-wise multiplication of the two maximum entropy results. Later, this method was improved by Kang, Kang, and Li (2013) using a degree segmentation instead of the entropy criterion. The method of Wang, Ji, Lin, and Trucco (2013) performed vessel recognition in retinal images making use of a wavelet kernel as a matched filter that is convolved with the original image. After, the response is treated with a hierarchical decomposition process and the final result is obtained applying a binarization method.

The use of the Hessian matrix properties for vessel recognition is another commonly used approach (Lorenz, Carlsen, Buzug, Fassnacht, & Weese, 1997; Shikata, Hoffman, & Sonka, 2004). Frangi, Niessen, Vincken, and Viergever (1998) computed the Hessian matrix by convolving the second-order derivative of a Gaussian kernel with the original image in order to obtain a set of eigenvalues. Using the obtained eigenvalues, a vesselness measure is computed to classify vessel and nonvessel pixels. Similar to the Frangi et al. method, other vesselness measures have been proposed (M'hiri, Duong, Desrosiers, & Cheriet, 2013; Salem & Nandi, 2008; Tsai, Lee, & Chen, 2013). Li, Zhou, Wu, Ma, and Peng (2012) developed a region-growing procedure using the pixels with maximum value response obtained from a vesselness measure. Wink, Niessen, and Viergever (2004) employed a vesselness measure with a minimum-cost path search that propagates a wave through the vessel map for a range of scales, and is capable to determine the central axis of vessels in angiograms. A major strength of Hessian matrix-based methods is the high capability to detect vessels at different calibers. However, due to the use of a second-order derivative, they are very sensitive to noise, significantly decreasing their performance when used with low-contrast or high-noise images.

Other approaches such as Radon transformation (Pourreza-Shahri, Tavakoli, & Kehtarnavaz, 2014), the complex continuous wavelet transform (Fathi & Naghsh-Nilchi, 2013), and Gabor filters (Ayres & Rangayyan, 2007; Gabor, 1946) have been applied for the detection of blood vessels in different clinical studies. Sang, Tang, Liu, and Weng (2004) applied multiscale Gabor filters to extract vessel centerlines in 2-D angiogram images of the brain with poor contrast and noisy background. They applied a hysteresis thresholding procedure to the maximum response map computed over several orientations and scales of the Gabor filter. Soares, Leandro, Cesar-Junior, Jelinek, and Cree (2006) used 2-D complex Gabor filters for vessel detection, followed by the application of a Bayesian classifier to discriminate vessel pixels against background pixels. Rangayyan, Ayres, Oloumi, Oloumi, and Eshghzadeh-Zanjani (2008) employed multiscale Gabor filters for the detection of blood vessels in fundus images of the retina and obtained high detection rates represented by the area (*Az*) under the receiver operating characteristic (ROC) curve. Shoujun, Jian, Yongtian, and Wufan (2010) developed a vessel-tracking framework based on multiscale Gabor filters and a vesselness measure to enhance vessel-like structures in order to extract vessel centerlines and edge points of the coronary artery tree in angiograms. Cruz-Aceves, Oloumi, Rangayyan, Aviña-Cervantes, and Hernandez-Aguirre (2015) improved the results obtained applying Gabor filters by exploring a range of values for their different parameters and adding an additional postprocessing step in which a binarizing threshold is automatically calculated by the use of multiobjective optimization.

Even when all previously mentioned techniques have been proved to have high performance and results on their respective test cases, almost all of them require the adjustment of several parameters, the values of which have an important impact on the final result. For this reason, it is required to have some problem domain knowledge in order to adjust them properly. To overcome these disadvantages, the use of metaheuristics is useful for trying to find the best initial parameters instead of predefined invariant values (Cruz-Aceves, Hernández-Aguirre, & Aviña-Cervantes, 2015). More recently, a comparative analysis between four evolutionary algorithms was introduced by Chaudhuri et al. (1989), where the strategy of differential evolution achieved the highest performance. The problem of parameter optimization is a nontrivial task that can be carried out using different strategies. The direct design of a convolutional gray-level template represents a nonpolynomial problem of $O(256^n)$ computational complexity, where n is the number of pixels in the convolutional template.

In this chapter, a novel method for the design of convolutional gray-level templates based on different optimization strategies is proposed. One of the advantages with this method relies in the use of a low quantity of adjustable parameters since the gray-level matching template is automatically designed from the information provided by the image dataset and the process is supported by the use of metaheuristics. The gray-level template is designed to be convolved in the spatial domain with the X-ray image in order to enhance coronary artery images. The detection performance is evaluated in terms of the area under the ROC curve (Az). The proposed strategies are evaluated between them since three strategies are single-solution based and one is population-based. In addition, the automatically designed gray-level convolutional templates are compared with five specialized vessel enhancement methods of the state-of-the-art. The comparison was performed in the training and testing steps, achieving the best results in both stages. For the training step, a set of 100 angiograms was used, obtaining a performance with $Az = 0.958$. After the training stage was completed, a test set of 30 angiograms was used, achieving the highest performance with $Az = 0.961$. In addition to the experimental results, the automatic design of convolutional templates represents a promising research topic for medical image processing in different areas, and based on the numerical results of the proposed method, it can be suitable for clinical decision support in cardiology.

8.2 Background

Metaheuristics are strategies applied to find solutions to problems where their domain space is significantly large, making them very difficult to be explored using traditional methods. The term metaheuristic was coined by Glover in 1989 (Glover, 1989), to refer to a set of methodologies conceptually ranked above heuristics in the sense that they guide the design of heuristics. A metaheuristic is a higher level procedure or heuristic designed to find, generate, or select a lower level procedure or heuristic (partial search algorithm) that may provide a sufficiently good solution for an optimization problem. By searching over a large set of feasible solutions, metaheuristics can often find good solutions with less computational effort than calculus-based methods, or simple heuristics, can.

Metaheuristics can be single-solution-based or population-based. Single-solution-based metaheuristics work with a single solution at any time and comprise local search-based metaheuristics such as SA, tabú search and iterated local search (ILS) (Lourenco, MArtin, & Stutzle, 2010; Martin, Otto, & Felten, 1991). In population-based metaheuristics, a number of solutions are updated iteratively until the termination condition is satisfied. Population-based metaheuristics are generally categorized into EAs and swarm-based algorithms. Single-solution-based metaheuristics are regarded to be more exploitation-oriented, whereas population-based metaheuristics are more exploration-oriented (Du & Swamy, 2016).

In this section, the single-solution-based metaheuristics of ILS, tabú search, and SA, along with the univariate marginal distribution algorithm are described in detail.

8.2.1 Iterated local search

The ILS technique was proposed in order to overcome the local minimum problem present in the local search (LS) strategy by the addition of a concept called *perturbation* (Lourenço, Martin, & Stützle, 2003). The local search was created to solve complex problems involving the combination of their solution elements. These kinds of problems are known as *combinatorial NP (nondeterministic polynomial time) problems* (Aarts & Lenstra, 1997; Papdimitriou, 1976).

One of the most representative NP combinatorial problems used to probe the efficiency and performance of heuristics and metaheuristics is the traveling salesman problem (TSP). This was the first problem where ILS was applied (Martin et al., 1991).

The basic TSP states that there exist a certain number of cities represented by their location in a 2-D plane. The objective is to visit all cities once while minimizing the total traveling distance starting off from any selected city and returning to it at the end of all travel. Also, the "basic" term indicates that all cities are connected and the traveler can visit any city with no restriction of movement. Fig. 8.1 illustrates the TSP with 10 cities connected to all of them, where a wide variety of possible solutions can be calculated. After selecting the first city to start the travel, there are nine cities that are possible to visit. When the second city was selected, there remained eight possibilities to continue visiting.

Following this method, the total number of combinations that are possible to form visiting all cities can be calculated using Eq. (8.1) as follows:

$$c = n! \therefore n! = \prod_{i=1}^{n} i, \tag{8.1}$$

where c is the total number of different combinations and n is the number of cities.

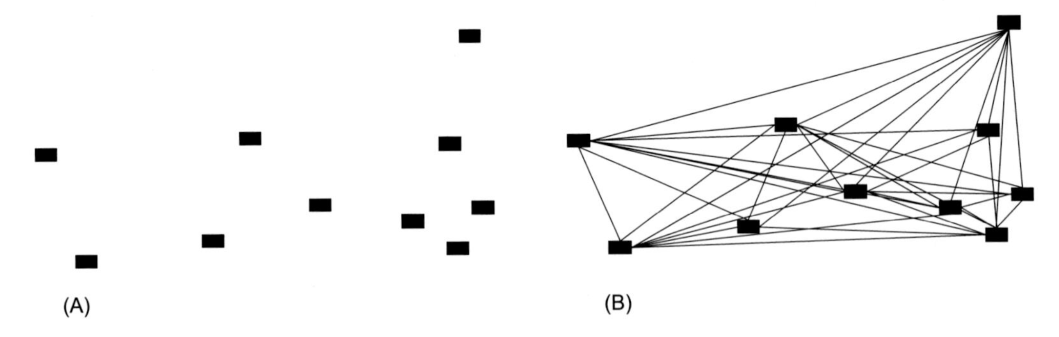

FIGURE 8.1 Cities distribution and connections for the traveling salesman problem: (A) city locations; (B) city connections.

FIGURE 8.2 Distribution of cities in the krob 100 data file.

After all traveling routes are computed (3,628,800 routes), the next step is to select the route with the lowest total traveled distance. For this TSP case with 10 cities and no constraints, using a modern computing machine the best route can be calculated evaluating all routes and selecting that with the smallest traveled distance. However, if the number of cities is augmented and new constraints are added, for instance, adding an additional cost when traveling from one city to another, the computing time can be highly demanding, making it impractical and sometimes impossible to find the best solution even with modern and powerful computing capabilities. Fig. 8.2 shows the distribution of cities from the krob100 data file (Krolak, Felts, & Marble, 1971), which contains 100 records with their corresponding (x, y) coordinates for each city. The mentioned data file is a representative data set for the TSP and is commonly used for testing and benchmarking of search and optimization strategies. For better visualization purposes, the graph edges indicating connection between all cities were removed.

8.2.1.1 Implementation details

The local search is a heuristic able to solve NP combinatorial problems finding a solution by maximizing an objective criterion (also called objective function) among a number of possible solutions. The local search algorithm explores and evaluates different solutions (search space) by applying local changes until an optimal solution is achieved or certain iterations are computed.

The pseudocode of local search can be expressed as follows:

Algorithm 1: Local Search pseudocode

```
Input:
stop_criteria /* Can be a minimal error, max number of iterations,
etc. */
1  begin
2      s = s0 /* Generate an initial random solution */
3      best = evaluate(s) /* Evaluate the generated solution */
4      while non stop_criteria is achieved do
5          s_new = s /* Make a copy of s in s_new */
6          x = random(s_new) /* Pick a random element from solution
           s_new */
7          /* Find the nearest neighbor of element x in solution s_new */
8          x_nearest = find_nearest_neighbor(s_new, x)
9          permute(s_new, x, x_nearest) /* Permute elements x and x_nearest
           in s_new */
10         current = evaluate(s_new) /* Evaluate new solution */
11         /* Check if new solution improves the best solution achieved
           */
12         if current "is better than" best then
13             s = s_new /* Save s_new in s */
Output: Solution s
```

The creation of new solutions by the local search technique is illustrated in Fig. 8.3, taking the TSP with a set of 10 cities and a supposed solution assigned to s_{new}.

Based on Fig. 8.3, the current solution starts travel in city 3 (C3) and after traveling to cities 7, 1, 9, 6, 10, 4, 5, and 2, finally visits C8. However, on the next step, local search selects city C6 randomly and the closest city to C6 is searched among all the remaining cities in s_{new}. The closest city to C6 is C2 and they are permuted. Making this movement, after traveling it arrives as C6 and will be directed to C2 instead of C10. With this search strategy, s_{new} will be evaluated and compared with the best solution achieved (s) to decide if it must be updated with the new generated solution. This process is repeated until a stop criterion is achieved.

Although the local search algorithm is very simple to implement, it has two major drawbacks:

1. The final result is very sensitive to the initial solution.

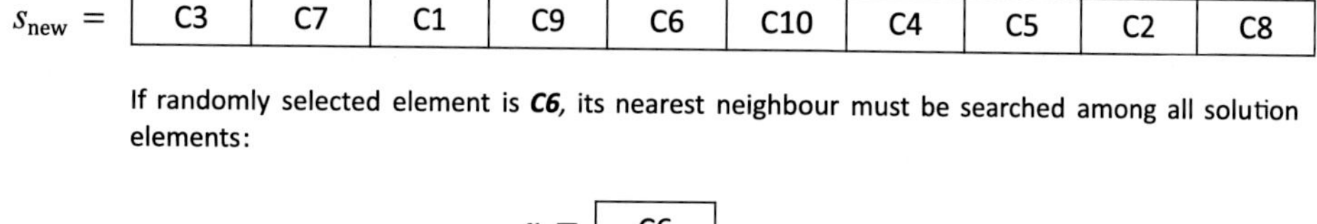

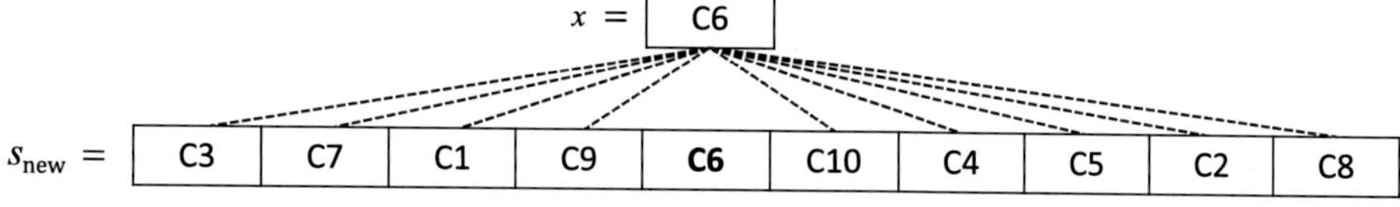

Suppose that ***C2*** is the closest element to ***C6***, in this case, ***C6*** and ***C2*** are permuted giving the new solution as:

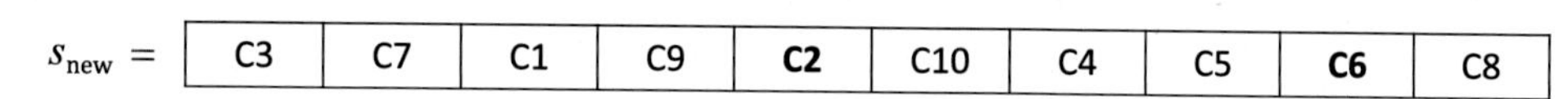

FIGURE 8.3 Procedure performed by the local search algorithm in the traveling salesman problem.

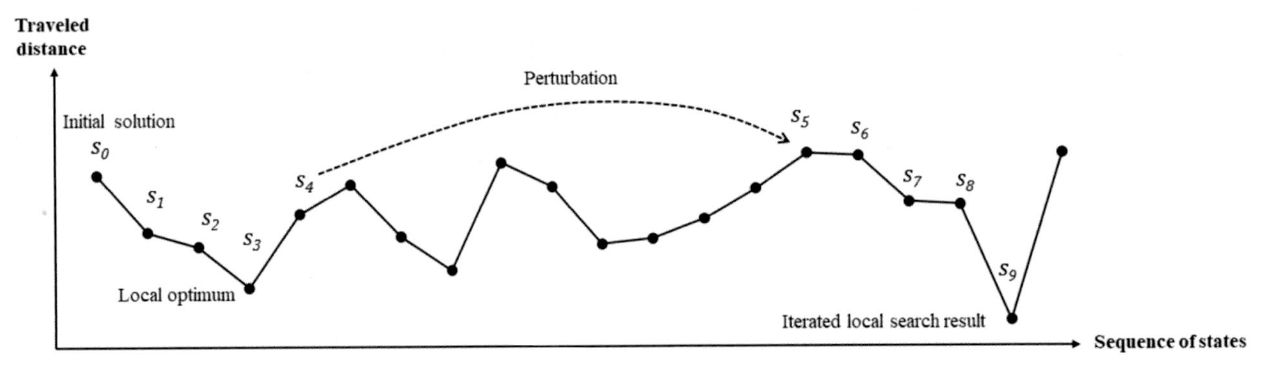

FIGURE 8.4 Illustration of how perturbation strategy is useful to escape from local optimum.

2. Since the local search depends on the initial solution, there is a high probability of getting trapped in a local optima.

To overcome the local search disadvantages, ILS makes use of a *perturbation* strategy to generate a new partial random solution. This approach is more effective than creating a full new independent random solution which is the main strength of the ILS against other similar techniques.

ILS is based on a simple principle that has been applied also in other heuristics such as the iterated Lin–Kernigham heuristic for the TSP (Johnson, 1990) and the adaptive tabú search for the quadratic assignment problem (Talbi, Hafidi, & Geib, 1998). First, a local search is applied to an initial solution. Then, at each iteration, a perturbation of the obtained local optima is carried out. Finally, a local search is applied to the perturbed solution. The generated solution is accepted as the new current solution under some conditions. This process is iteratively performed until a given stopping criterion is met. Fig. 8.4 illustrates the ILS perturbation effect to escape from a local optimum solution and explore another region in the search space.

It is important to mention that using the ILS, the perturbation length and type must be selected carefully. For instance, a strong perturbation (selecting a number of elements to be perturbed) could conduct to loss parts of a good solution and a low length perturbation might not be sufficient to escape from a local optima.

There are three strategies to deal with the perturbation length (Talbi, 2009):

1. Static: A fixed perturbation length is established a priori using some knowledge about the search space.
2. Dynamic: The length of perturbation is changed randomly on each iteration.
3. Adaptive: The length of perturbation is changed dynamically based on information provided by the search space using a deterministic procedure or some additional computational heuristic or metaheuristic method.

The ILS pseudocode can be expressed as follows:

Algorithm 2: Iterated Local Search pseudocode

```
   Input:
   stop_criteria /* Number of iterations*/
 1 begin
 2 |  s_best = s_0 /* Generate an initial random solution */
 3 |  best = evaluate(s) /* Evaluate the generated solution */
 4 |  while non stop_criteria is achieved do
 5 |  |  s_new = s_best /* Make a copy of s_best in s_new */
 6 |  |  perturb(s_new) /* Perturb the obtained local optimum */
 7 |  |  /* Perform a Local Search using s_new as the starting solution
   |  |   */
 8 |  |  s_new = localSearch(s_new)
 9 |  |  /* Evaluate s_new */
10 |  |  fitness_current = evaluateSolution(s_new)
11 |  |  if fitness_current > fitness_best then
12 |  |  |_ s_best = s_new
   |  |_
   |_
   Output: s_best /* Best solution */
```

8.2.2 Tabú search

The tabú search was proposed by F. Glover in order to overcome the local minima problem by introducing a "tabú" list of previous visited solutions (Glover, 1989). The tabú list works as a short-term memory that helps the technique to remember a set of previously found solutions. It can be used as a mechanism to reject those worst solutions generated by local search. Since the memory is a limited resource, it leads to dealing between precision and performance. Also, the tabú search can make use of an additional tabú list of moves in order to avoid the algorithm to repeat bad moves or permutations involving also the same constraints as the tabú list of solutions.

Tabú search has several similarities with SA, as both involve possible downhill movements. In fact, SA could be viewed as a special form of tabú search, where the use of an energy differential (the ΔE parameter) marks a move as tabú with a specified probability (Althofer & Koschnick, 1991).

8.2.2.1 Implementation details

The basic tabú search pseudocode algorithm is described the following:

Algorithm 3: Tabú Search pseudocode

```
Input:
stop_criteria /* Number of iterations, etc. */
max_size /* Max tabú list size */
1  begin
2    /* Create the tabú list with the specified size * /
3    tabu_list = createList(max_size)
4    s_best = s_0 /* Generate an initial random solution */
5    tabu_list.push(s_0) /* Add the initial solution at top of list */
6    best = evaluate(s) /* Evaluate the generated solution */
7    while non stop_criteria is achieved do
8      s_new = s_best /* Make a copy of s_best in s_new */
9      /* Perform a Local Search using s_new as the starting solution
         */
10     s_new = localSearch(s_new)
11     /* Check that s_new is not in tabu_list */
12     if s_new is not in tabu_list then
13       tabu_list.push(s_new) /* Add the new solution at top of
          tabú list */
14       /* Evaluate s_new */
15       s_best = evaluate(s_best, s_new)
Output: s_best /* Best solution */
```

The main difference between the TS, ILS, and LS algorithms, is the use of the tabú list that stores solutions that do not meet the acceptance criteria and then are considered as worst solutions. Also, it is important to consider that the method *push* in the tabú list puts the new elements at the top of the list and when the maximum size is reached, the last element is removed (a *pop* operation) in order to not exceed the established maximum size.

One of the main issues with the basic tabú search is that using a single tabú list with a limited size is not sufficient to prevent the generation of bad solutions. Consequently, storing all previously visited solutions could lead to efficiency issues or memory leak. To overcome this problem, the use of intensification (medium-term memory) and diversification (long-term memory) can be implemented to the basic tabú search algorithm:

1. The medium-term memory (intensification) can be used to store the best solutions during the search and they can be selected in a weighted-probabilistic manner to generate new solutions.
2. The long-term memory stores information about the visited solutions along the search. It also can contain information about valid and invalid moves in order to prevent local search to generate certain moves or solutions that could result in worse results.

Fig. 8.5 illustrates the initial solution found by an implementation of TS in Matlab, the code of which is presented in Appendix 1. The total travel distance (Euclidean) for the solution is 162, 780.00 distance units.

The best solution found by TS for the TSP is illustrated in Fig. 8.6, where the lowest distance computed

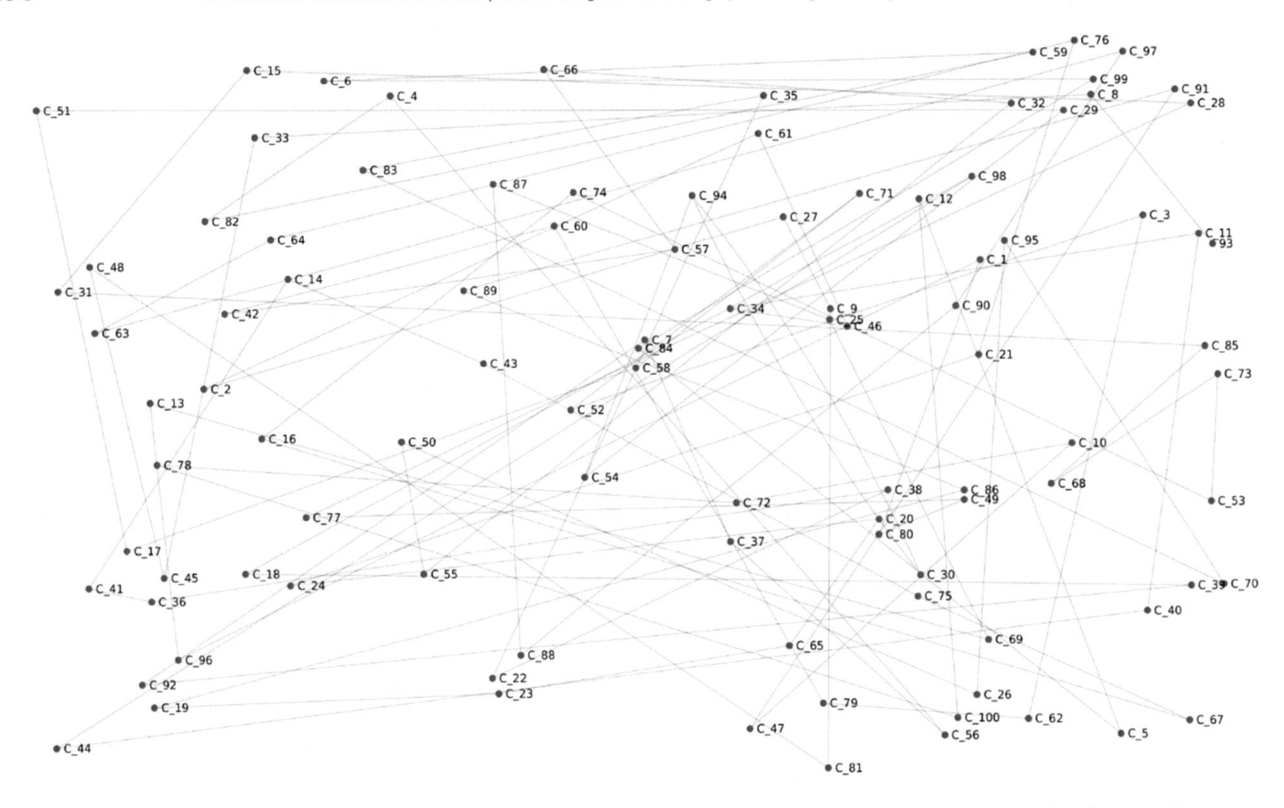

FIGURE 8.5 Initial solution calculated randomly by an implementation of the tabú search metaheuristic for the traveling salesman problem.

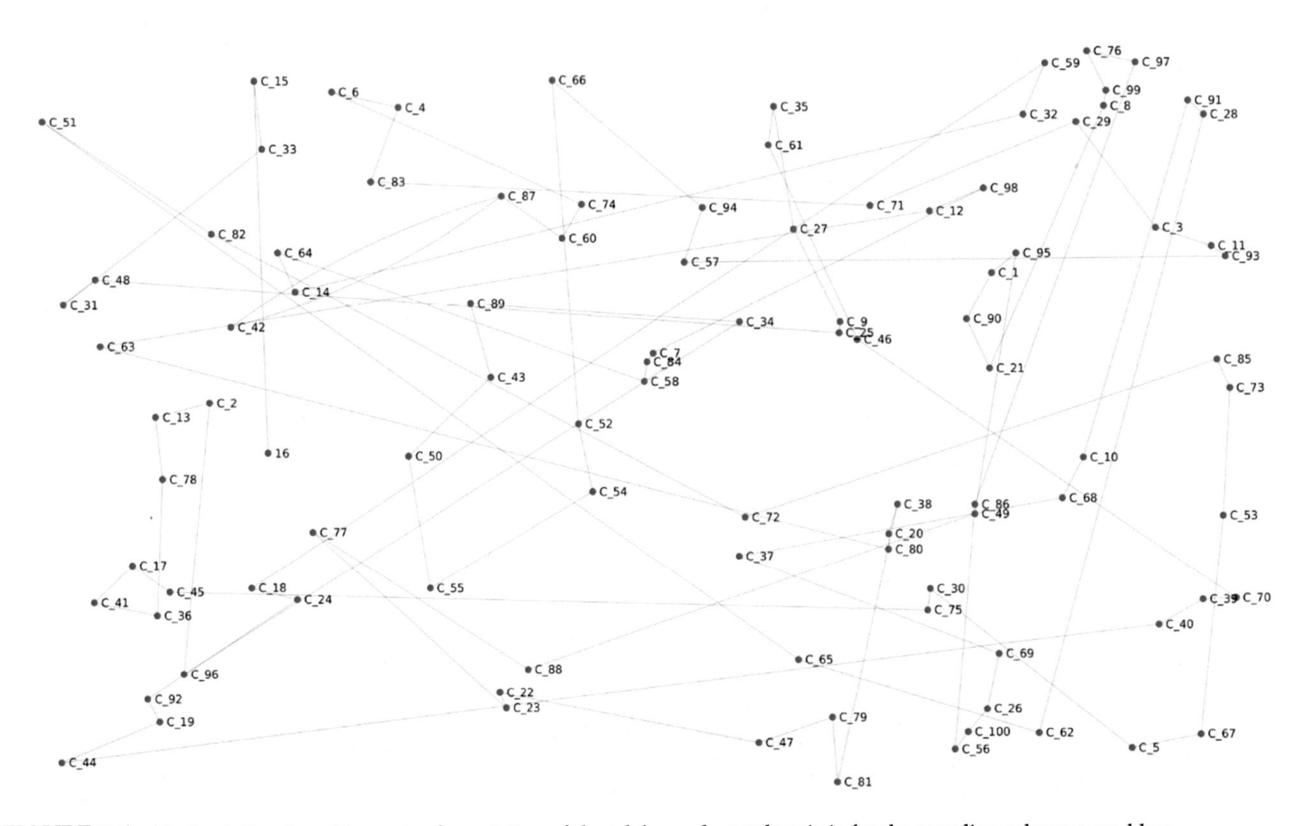

FIGURE 8.6 Final solution found by an implementation of the tabú search metaheuristic for the traveling salesman problem.

for the strategy was 79,162.00 distance units, which represents a reduction of ≈ 49% of the initial distance cost. Comparing Figs. 8.5 and 8.6, it can be appreciated that in the final solution, the number of connections between extreme location cities decreased compared with the initial solution, reducing the total traveled distance required to visit all cities.

The sequence of cities to travel in the best solution found by the TS is as follows:

C42, C87, C60, C74, C6, C4, C83, C71, C29, C3, C11, C93, C57, C94, C66, C52, C54, C55, C50, C43, C89, C34, C96, C2, C13, C78, C36, C41, C17, C45, C75, C30, C5, C67, C53, C73, C85, C72, C82, C51, C65, C62, C28, C91, C10, C68, C37, C69, C26, C100, C56, C86, C97, C76, C99, C8, C21, C90, C1, C95, C49, C88, C77, C23, C22, C47, C79, C81, C38, C20, C80, C63, C12, C98, C7, C84, C58, C64, C14, C32, C59, C18, C24, C92, C19, C44, C40, C39, C70, C46, C61, C35, C27, C9, C25, C48, C31, C33, C15, C16.

8.2.3 Simulated annealing

The SA technique was firstly proposed by Kirkpatrick, Gelatt, and Vecchi (1983). It is abstracted from the annealing process applied to the steel and ceramics in order to vary their physical properties and obtain strong structures. In the annealing process, the material is exposed to high temperatures and after the heat achieves a certain limit, the exposed material is cooled in a controlled way. When the entire annealing process ends, the material has some properties changed. Both the heating and cooling processes are decisive for the resultant structure. This means that if the initial temperature was insufficiently high or the cooling process was too slow or too fast, the resultant material will have imperfections. Also, the cooling process must be accurate in order to provide thermal equilibrium at each temperature to the annealed material. It was used first to solve combinatorial NP problems (Dekkers & Aarts, 1991; Locatelli, 2000; Ozdamar & Demirhan, 2000), such as the traveling salesman problem covered in Section 8.2.1.

SA starts building a random solution. As the algorithm performs iterations governed by the T_{max}, T_{min}, and T_{step} parameters, a new solution is created as a variant of the current by selecting a random neighbor from it with a given probability that depends on the current temperature and the decrease in the amount of ΔE based on the objective function. The probability calculation can be approximated by the Boltzmann distribution as described in:

$$P(\Delta E, T) = \frac{f(s') - f(s)}{T} \tag{8.2}$$

It uses a control parameter, called temperature, to determine the probability of accepting nonimproving solutions. At a particular level of temperature, many trials are explored. When an equilibrium state is reached, the temperature is gradually decreased according to a cooling schedule such that few nonimproving solutions are accepted at the end of the search (Talbi, 2009). Fig. 8.7 illustrates an instance of a continuous function and how temperature parameters affect the probabilities of new movements.

8.2.3.1 *Implementation details*

The SA technique applies the same concepts used in the metallurgy annealing process but adapted to a computational context (Metropolis, Rosenbluth, Rosenbluth, Teller, & Teller, 1953). The SA pseudocode algorithm can be expressed as follows:

Algorithm 4: Simulated Annealing pseudocode

```
Input:
T_max /* The maximum temperature value */
T_min /* The minimum temperature value */
T_step /* The step on how temperature will be varying from T_max to
T_min*/
1 begin
2     s = s_0 /* Generate an initial random solution */
3     T_current = T_max
4     while T_current ¿ T_min do
5         s_new = neigbour(s) /* Pick a random neighbor */
6         if P(E(s), E(s_new), T_current) ≥ random(0, 1) then
7             s = s_new
8         T_current = T_current - T_step
Output: the final state s
```

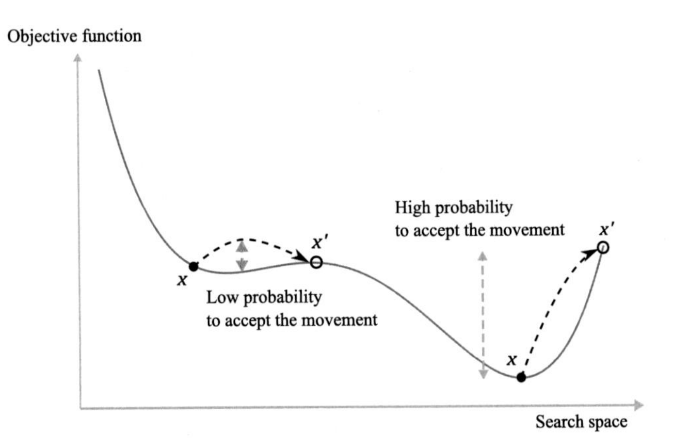

FIGURE 8.7 A continuous function and how the temperature parameter affects the probability of new movements.

Fig. 8.7 illustrates how the temperature parameter has effects in the SA strategy to search into unexplored regions in the space of a continuous problem.

8.2.4 Univariate marginal distribution algorithm

The univariate marginal distribution algorithm (UMDA) is a metaheuristic population-based technique such as genetic algorithms (Heinz & Mahnig, 2001). Instead of the population recombination and mutation concepts, UMDA uses the frequency of components in a population of candidate solutions in the construction of new ones. Each individual in the population is formed by a bit-string and is denoted as: $xi = [xi,1, xi,2, \ldots, xi,D]$ where each element xi, j is called a gene. An array of vectors $X = [x1, x2, \ldots, xn_pop]$ is called a population. In this approach, the population evolves on each generation (iteration) t and the current population is denoted as X^t. On each iteration UMDA samples a subset n_{set} with the individuals representing the best solutions. With the n_{set} sample a new population (generation) is created based on a probabilistic model using the genes in the individuals (Hashemi & Reza-Meybodi, 2011). This iterative process ends when a criterion is accomplished or a maximum value of generations is reached.

This strategy is known to achieve significant results on continuous spaces in which values can be represented as bit-strings. However, for problems where locations in the search space are unable to be discretized as bit-strings, UMDA performance is decreased significantly. To overcome this disadvantage, some strategies have been implemented (Chmielewski & Busse-Jersy, 1996; Ge-xiang, Wei-dong, & Lai-zhao, 2005; Jing, ChongZao, Bin, & DeQiang, 2011).

Compared with other population-based techniques, UMDA only requires three parameters to operate: population size, stopping criterion, and population selection ratio. The pseudocode of UMDA is described below.

Algorithm 5: UMDA pseudocode

Input:
D /* Dimensions of the problem */
n_{pop} /* Population size */
N_{gen} /* Number of maximum generations */
n_{set} /* Selected set size */
1 **begin**
2   Initialize $t = 0, X^t \sim U(0, 1)$
3   Evaluate $F^t = f(X^t)$
4   $[X_{best}, X^t] = sortX^t$ according to objective values
5   **while** *non stop_criteria is achieved* **do**
6   **for** $i = 1 \ldots D$ **do**
7       $p_i = \sum_{j=1}^{n_{set}} x_{i,j}$
8   Set $P = [p_1, p_2, ..., p_D]$
9   Sample $X^{t+1} \sim P$
10   Elitism $X^{t+1} = [X^{t+1}_{1:(n_{pop}-1)}, x_{best}]$
11     $t = t + 1$
12   Evaluate $F^t = f(X^t)$
13     $[x_{best}, X^t] = sortX^t$ according to objective values
Output: x_{best} /* The best solution achieved */

This algorithm has better performance compared to other metaheuristics in terms of speed, computational memory, and accuracy of solutions. Fig. 8.8 illustrates a case on how UMDA searches for the global optimum over a continuous function.

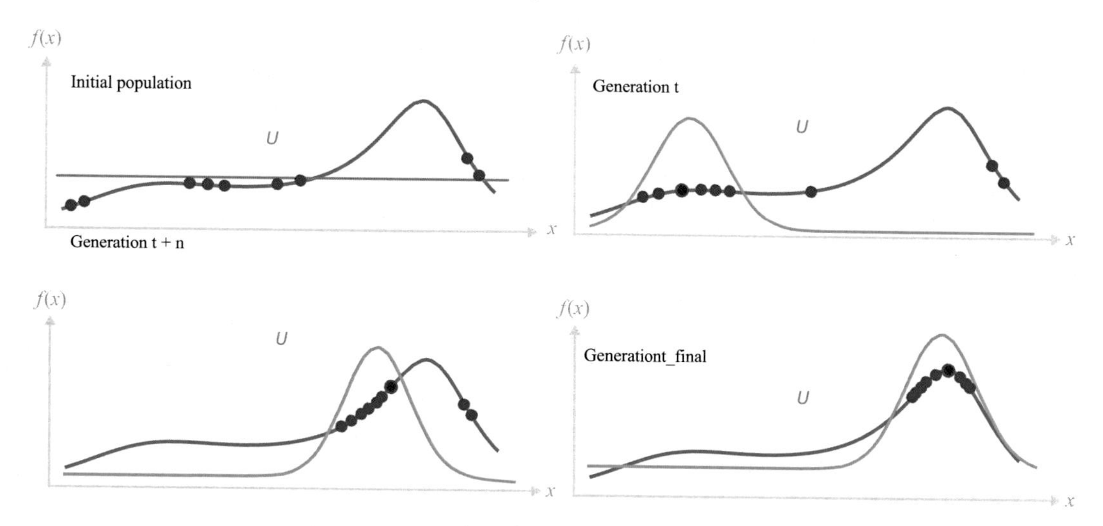

FIGURE 8.8 Univariate Marginal Distribution Algorithm behavior on a continuous function optimization.

8.3 Proposed method

Using each of the strategies presented in the previous section, the objective is to construct the best suitable convolutional gray-level template that allows enhancement of the pixels corresponding to vessels from those that are background in an X-ray coronary angiogram.

The problem of finding the most suitable convolutional gray-level template to detect vessels can be expressed as a wide search space where each template pixel represents a dimension. The total number of dimensions for a certain template size can be calculated using the following:

$$D = h * w, \tag{8.3}$$

where D represents the total number of dimensions in the problem, and h and w are the template height and width, respectively.

Moreover, each dimension is a discrete search space with values in the range [0, 255]. Considering the template size, the total number of combinations or different templates that are possible to construct can be expressed as follows:

$$C = 256^D, \tag{8.4}$$

where C represents the total number of combinations that are possible to form. According to Eqs. (8.3) and (8.4), for a template of 15 × 15 pixels, the total number of dimensions is 225 and the maximum number of templates that can be formed is 256^{225}, which represents an NP problem.

8.3.1 Automatic generation of convolutional gray-level template

Applying the above concepts, the proposed method is divided into two parts: a training stage focused on the template generation and a testing stage for the strategy performance measurement.

On the training stage, new templates are generated by the metaheuristic. Each template is convolved at different orientations (rotations) with each element in a predefined training set of images. When all rotations and convolutions have been performed for a determined image, the result is calculated taken the pixel with the highest value (intensity) across the set of previously convolved images on each position. This procedure can be generalized as follows:

$$R_i = I \circledast rot(t, i), \quad \text{for } i = 0, 15, 30, ..., 180, \tag{8.5}$$

where R_i is the response of the convolution for a certain template orientation, I is the image to be convolved, t is the template, i is the rotation angle at counterclockwise direction, and rot represents the rotation function of template t at angle i.

After the image has been convolved with the template at different orientations, the result is obtained selecting the pixels with the highest value on each position over all sets of convolution responses expressed as follows:

$$I' = \max(R), \tag{8.6}$$

where I' is the resultant response after convolution with a template at different orientations, and R is the set of convolution responses as described in Eq. (8.5).

Fig. 8.9 illustrates the convolution procedure of an image and a template at different orientations and how the result is obtained. Thus the process is applied for all training images to evaluate the overall template performance.

Based on the concepts mentioned earlier, the proposed method steps can be defined as follows:

1. Generate a new template based on the selected strategy (ILS, TS, SA or UMDA).

2. Using each image from the training set to be convolved with the template at different orientations.
3. Generate the filter response by selecting the highest intensity values across each set of convolution responses.
4. Calculate the area under the ROC curve (fitness function) using each response and their respective ground-truth image.
5. Update best global solution.
6. Repeat all previous steps until maximum iterations are reached or some other specific metaheuristic stopping criterion is not accomplished.

Fig. 8.10 presents a scheme of the training procedure explained before.

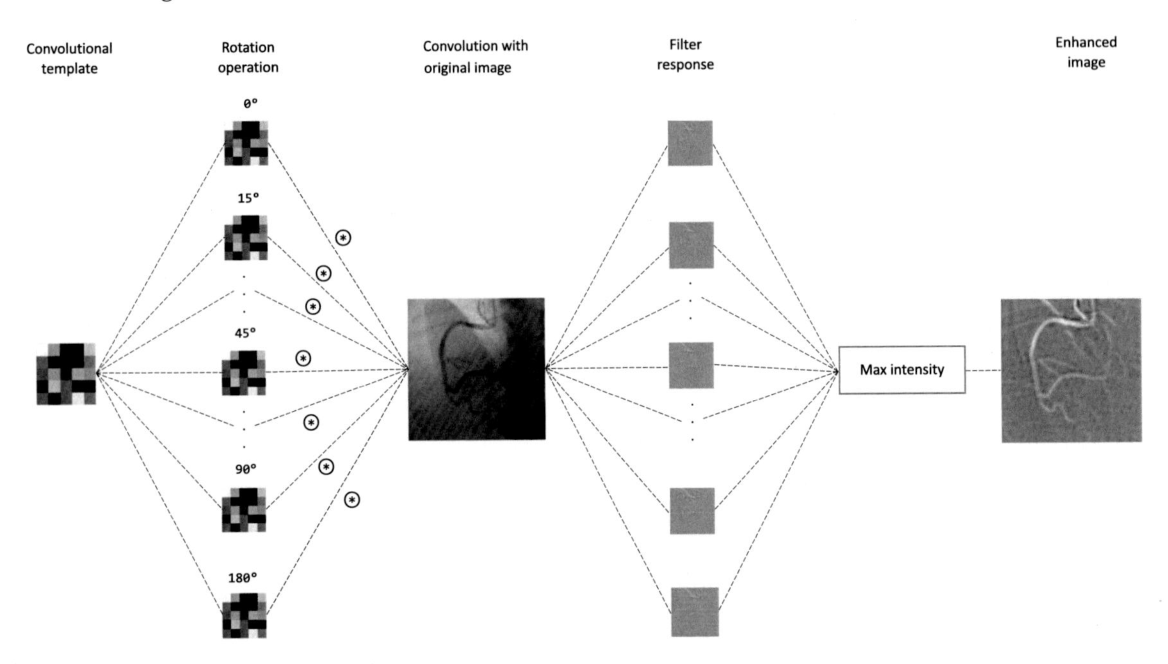

FIGURE 8.9 Convolution procedure of an image with a template at different orientations and the resulting enhanced image.

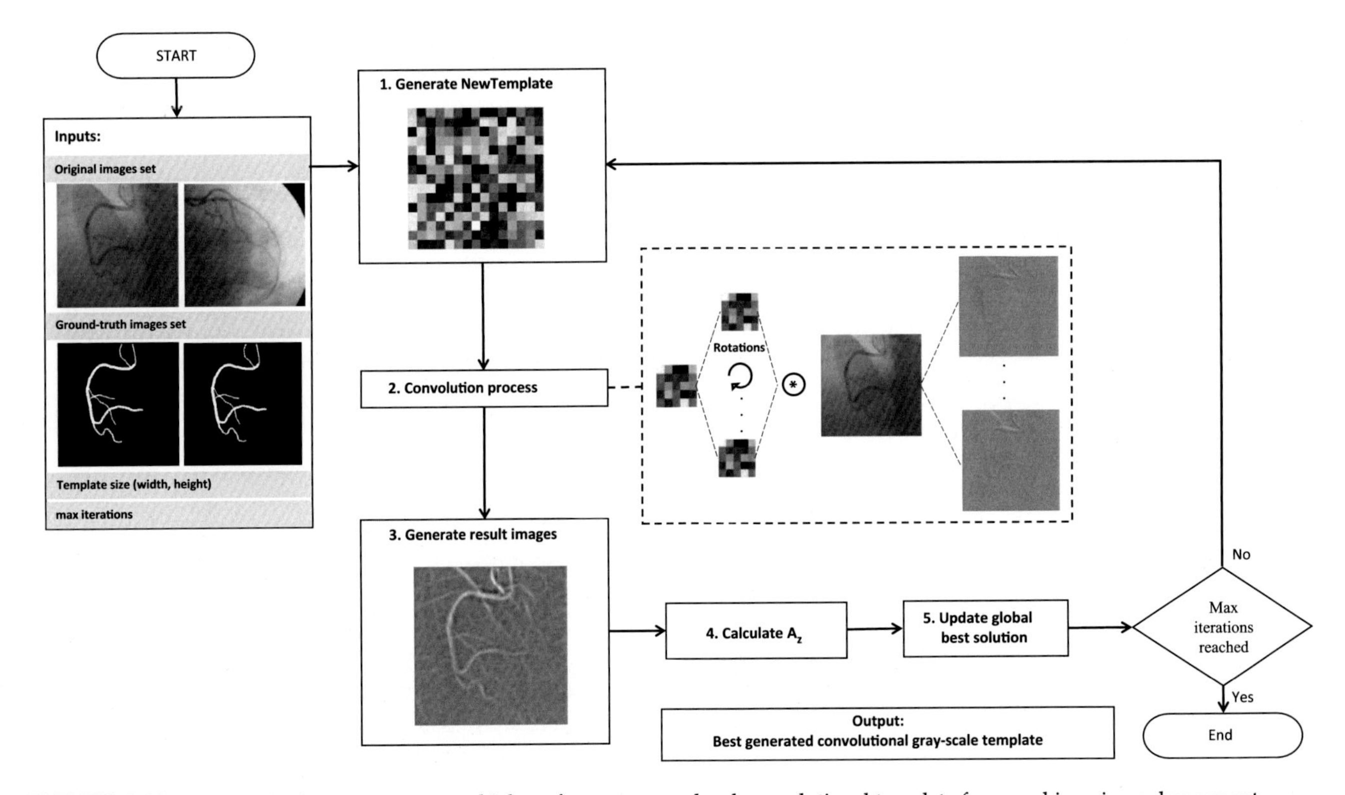

FIGURE 8.10 Proposed scheme to generate a high-performance gray-level convolutional template for vessel imaging enhancement.

It is important to mention that convolution responses contains values out of range [0, 1]. In order to adjust the response to a valid gray-scale intensity, it must be normalized. The normalization can be done using Eq. (8.7) in order to obtain a gray-level image with values in the range [0, 1].

$$I'_{i,j} = \frac{(i,j) - \min(I)}{\max(I) - \min(I)}, \quad (8.7)$$

where I is the resultant image after convolution with a template at different orientations, I' is the normalized image, max(I) is the highest value in the image I, min (I) is the lowest value in the image I, and, i, j refers to each pixel position in the image.

After training stage finishes, a testing process is performed using images not used for training. During this process, the gray-level template produced in the training stage is convolved at different orientations with each image. This process is similar to steps 2–4 of the proposed method. When the testing stage ends, the total Az is obtained and can be compared with the results produced by other strategies.

8.3.2 Binary classification of the gray-level filter response

All the previously described metaheuristics requires an *objective function* in order to achieve a result. In this research, the maximization of area under the receiver operating characteristic curve (AUC of the ROC curve) Az is used as the objective function. However, the Az measurement was designed primarily to work with binary classifiers (Metz, 1978).

Since the normalized response image has values in the range [0, 1], it must be discretized in order to contain binary values. This process involves the use of a threshold value as follows:

$$I_{\text{bin}_{(i,j)}} = \begin{cases} 0 & \text{if} I_{(i,j)} < t \\ 1 & \text{otherwise} \end{cases} \quad (8.8)$$

where I_{bin} is the binary image, I is a normalized image, t is a threshold value in range [0, 1], and i, j refers to each pixel position in the image.

To evaluate a segmented image with binary values, they are classified as vessel pixels (positive) and background pixels (negative). The ground-truth image is useful in order to determine how correct the result image is by using four measures: true-positive cases (TP), true-negative cases (TN), false-positive cases (FP), and false-negative cases (FN) as follows:

1. TP cases are pixels detected as vessel that correspond to vessel pixels in the ground-truth.
2. TN cases are pixels detected as background that correspond to background pixels in the ground-truth.
3. FP cases are pixels detected as vessel, however they correspond to background pixels in the ground-truth.
4. FN cases are pixels detected as background, however they correspond to vessel pixels in the ground-truth.

Based on TP, TN, FP, and FN metrics, other measures can be calculated such as: accuracy (ACC), sensitivity or true-positive rate (TPR); specificity or true-negative rate (TNR), and false-positive rate (FPR), which can be computed as follows:

$$\text{ACC} = \frac{\text{TP} + \text{TN}}{\text{TP} + \text{TN} + \text{FP} + \text{FN}} \quad (8.9)$$

$$\text{TPR} = \frac{\text{TP}}{\text{TP} + \text{FN}} \quad (8.10)$$

$$\text{TNR} = \frac{\text{TN}}{\text{TN} + \text{FP}} \quad (8.11)$$

$$\text{FPR} = \frac{\text{FP}}{\text{FP} + \text{TN}} \quad (8.12)$$

On the other hand, the ROC curve graph is a metric for selecting classifiers based on their performance. They have long been used in signal detection theory to depict the trade-off between hit rates and false alarm rates of classifiers (Swets, Dawes, & Monahan, 2000).

Visually, ROC curves are two-dimensional graphs in which TPR is plotted on the y-axis and the FPR rate is plotted on the x-axis. Any ROC curve depicts relative tradeoffs between benefits (true positives) and costs (false positives) (Fawcett, 2006).

To evaluate the performance of all implemented metaheuristics, the area under the ROC curve (Az) is used. ROC curve analysis can be implemented for several reasons: (1) to assess the overall performance of a classifier; (2) to compare the performance of classifiers; and (3) to determine the optimal cut-off point for a given classifier (Goksuluk, Kormaz, Zararsiz, & Ergun-Karaagaoglu, 2016). Based on the ROC curve approach, the highest area under the ROC curve (highest Az value) means a better performance for the classifier. The ROC is in range [0, 1], where 1 refers to a perfect classification performance meaning that 100% of all cases were classified correctly.

8.3.3 Image postprocessing

The image postprocessing step is an important procedure to perform if an enhanced visualization of the results from the previously processed images is required. Most image enhancement operations are applied to make the image visually more appealing. This can be accomplished by increasing contrast, optimizing brightness, and reducing the lack of sharpness and noise (White, Pharoah, & Frederiksen, 2004).

In this research, the image postprocessing involved two additional steps after the final convolution response was obtained. In first step, the resulting image is enhanced by applying a binarization process. After the binary image is acquired, a second procedure is performed in order to enhance and smooth the result by removing resultant noise from the image, giving a better visual result in order to ease their analysis.

One of the most used binarizing methods is Otsu (Otsu, 1979), which is applicable to gray-level scale images. Instead of selecting an arbitrary value or performing an exhaustive search to find the most accurate processing threshold value for a corresponding image, the Otsu method computes it automatically based on the image histogram. The algorithm is capable of acquiring a threshold value that minimizes the intraclass variance, defined as a weighted sum of variance of the two classes, expressed as follows:

$$\sigma_{\omega}^2(t) = \omega_0(t)\sigma_0^2(t) + \omega_1(t)\sigma_1^2(t), \tag{8.13}$$

where ω_0 and ω_1 weights are the probabilities of the two classes separated by a threshold t, and σ_0^2 and σ_1^2 are the statistical variances of ω_0 and ω_1, respectively.

The probabilities classes $\omega_0(t)$ and $\omega_1(t)$ are calculated as follows:

$$\begin{aligned} \omega_0(t) &= \sum_{t=0}^{t-1} p(i), \\ \omega_1(t) &= \sum_{i=t}^{L-1} p(i), \end{aligned} \tag{8.14}$$

where t is a given threshold value that is varying in range [1, 255] and L represents the maximum pixel value in the histogram (255 in a gray-scale image).

Fig. 8.11 illustrates how the Otsu threshold is used to obtain a binary classification based on a histogram.

After a binary response is acquired, the last postprocessing step performs an analysis in order to remove the remaining noise that was not eliminated with the binarization process. In this step, a searching procedure is performed in order to identify single isolated pixels or groups of them.

When the image segmentation and postprocessing procedures are finished, the resulting image shows only the vessel pixels in an enhanced manner discriminating all those elements that are classified as background pixels or noise.

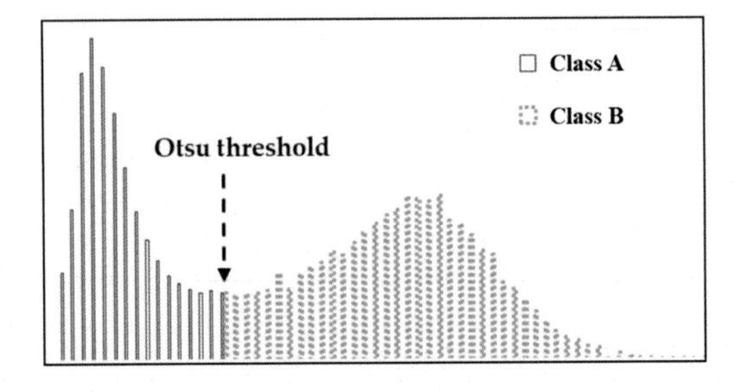

FIGURE 8.11 Otsu threshold used for binary classification based on a histogram.

8.4 Computational experiments

This section describes the different implemented strategies and how their parameters were configured to obtain significant results. All the experiments were performed using a medical database with 130 X-ray coronary angiograms including the corresponding ground-truth images, which were previously delineated by an expert cardiologist. This database of coronary angiograms is publicly available via the following web page (Cervantes-Sanchez, Cruz-Aceves, Hernandez-Aguirre, Hernandez-Gonzalez, & Solorio-Meza, 2019): http://personal.cimat.mx:8181/~ivan.cruz/DB_Angiograms.html.

The computational experiments were performed using a computer with an Intel Core i7 VPro 2.22 GHz processor, 8 GB of RAM with the Matlab software version 2018.

For the training process, a subset of 100 images was selected randomly from the database. The remaining 30 images were used as test cases.

The template size was established as 15 × 15 since it was probed to achieve better results for the involved image database (Cruz-Aceves et al., 2019).

For the ILS and tabú search strategies, the maximum number of iterations was established as 2500. The perturbation length in ILS was set to 1. For the tabú search strategy the tabúlist size was 30. Since the search space is large, the probabilities of repeated solutions are low. The maximum number of repeated solutions found during experiments with the tabú search strategy was 3. It is important to mention that after exhaustive experiments, most of the time, setting the number of iterations at a value greater than 2500 does not achieve significantly superior results. Moreover, for most tests, a better result was achieved with $\approx$ 2000 iterations.

For the univariate marginal distribution algorithm the population size was established with 30 individuals and the maximum number of iterations was 2500. Also, two versions of this strategy were implemented: normal UMDA for bit-string representation and the variant proposed by Jing et al. (2011) for nonbinary discrete features.

The directional filters (rotations) were set in the range (0, 180 degrees) with steps of 15 degrees, according to the original parameter K used by the GMF (Cervantes-Sanchez et al., 2019; Chanwimaluang & Fan, 2003; Chaudhuri et al., 1989; Cruz-Aceves et al., 2019).

8.4.1 Results of vessel imaging enhancement

In this section, the achieved vessel detection performance by each strategy is compared in both training and test steps.

TABLE 8.1 Statistical analysis with 30 runs of four single-solution metaheuristics and the evolutionary algorithm with two variants over the training set of 100 angiograms.

Method	Maximum	Minimum	Mean	Standard deviation	Median
Iterated local search	0.9581	0.9547	0.9570	0.0005	0.9570
$UMDA_{discretized}$[a]	0.9547	–	–	–	–
Simulated annealing	0.9520	0.9490	0.9470	0.0050	0.9480
Tabú search	0.9458	0.9023	0.9262	0.0137	0.9336
$UMDA_{bit\text{-}string}$[a]	0.7535	–	–	–	–

[a]*Maximum* Az *value of 1 run because of computational time* $\approx$ *10 hours.*

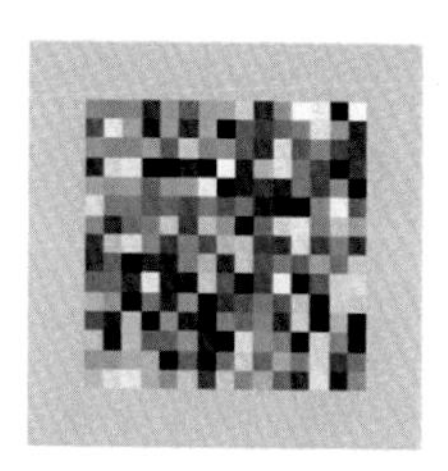
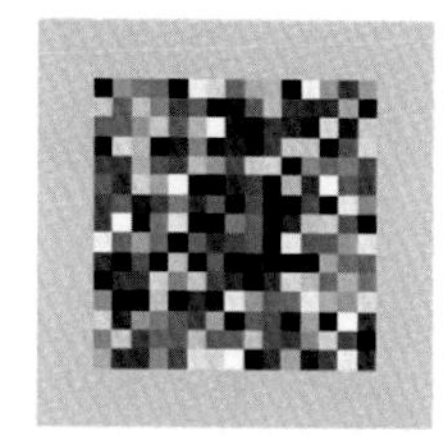

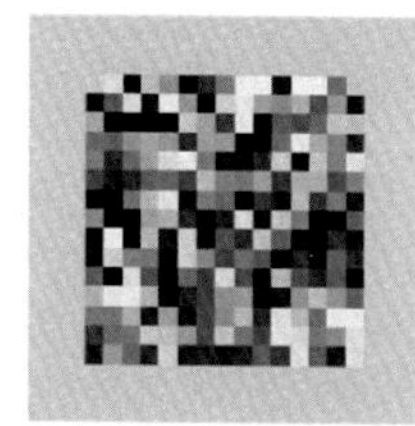
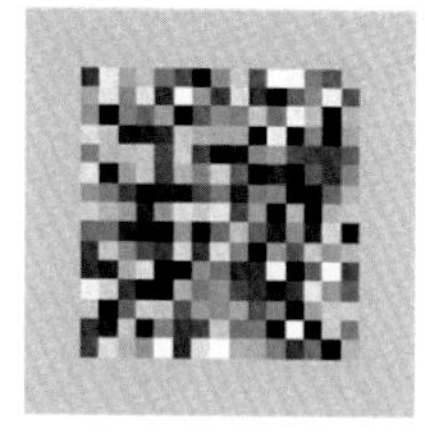

FIGURE 8.12 Best convolutional gray-level template achieved by each implemented metaheuristic. From left to right: iterated local search, $UMDA_{discretized}$, simulated annealing, tabú search, and $UMDA_{bit\text{-}string}$.

TABLE 8.2 Comparison between the proposed method and five state-of-the-art vessel detection methods of the using the test set of 30 images.

Detection method	Area under receiver operating characteristic curve (Az)
Frangi et al. (1998)	0.935
Eiho and Qian (1997)	0.944
Kang et al. (2009); Kang et al. (2013)	0.951
Chaudhuri et al. (1989)	0.953
(Cinsdikici & Aydın, 2009)	0.956
Proposed method (Iterated local search)	0.961

In Table 8.1, the performances of ILS, TS, UMDA, and SA strategies are compared in terms of the AUC of the ROC curve using the training set of 100 angiograms, where ILS achieved superior vessel detection performance.

After the training step, the best convolutional gray-level template achieved by each strategy was acquired in order to be analyzed directly with the set of 30 testing images. The obtained results are also compared with other state-of-the-art specialized vessel detection methods. In Fig. 8.12, the most suitable convolutional gray-level t"emplate achieved by each strategy is illustrated.

In Table 8.2, five different spatial-domain methods are compared with the proposed method in terms of the AUC of the ROC curve using the test set of 30 images.

From the comparative analysis, it can be seen that some strategies in the proposed method achieved an overall superior performance because the obtained convolutional gray-level template in a $O(256^n)$ search space is more suitable than the Gaussian profile with predefined values used by the traditional methods.

The TS, SA, UMDAdiscretized,and UMDAbit-string strategies also kept their respective performance rates in the testing stage. However, they were lower than that achieved by ILS. Their corresponding Az values were 0.958, 0.952, 0.928, and 0.901, respectively.

In Fig. 8.13, the vessel detection results of the different strategies implemented are illustrated. The main advantage of the proposed method is based in the generation of a convolutional template through exploring the high dimensional space, instead of the use of empirical predetermined parameter values.

8.4.2 Postprocessing procedure

The postprocessing procedure is also important in order to enhance the raw result obtained from the processing response after the convolution process is performed between the original image and the gray-level template at different orientations. The binarization process provides a binary map of values that allows for a better visualization of vessels and background from the result image. However, due to high noise levels in the original image, some entropy values remain after the binarization process, which must be removed in order to have an enhanced final image result.

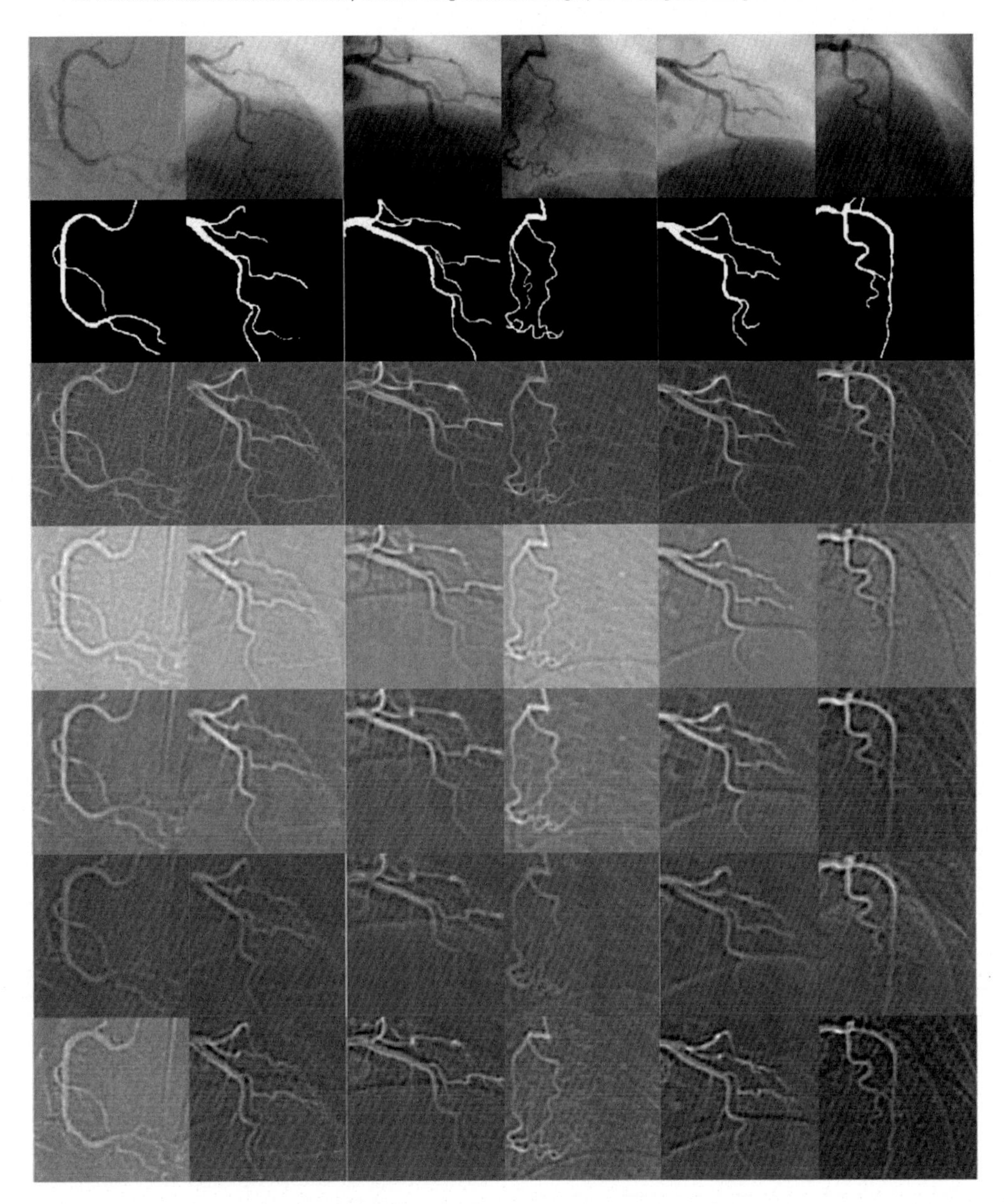

FIGURE 8.13 Visual results of vessel imaging enhancement achieved by each strategy using the test set. First and second rows: angiograms and their respective ground-truths. The remaining rows from top to bottom present the vessel detection (filter responses) of the iterated local search, tabú search, simulated annealing, $\text{UMDA}_{\text{discretized}}$, and $\text{UMDA}_{\text{bit-string}}$.

After the response images were acquired, a postprocessing procedure was applied to them in order to obtain an enhanced presentation of the results, leaving only those pixels belonging to blood vessels and removing the rest of the information in the image, which is considered as background or noise.

The postprocessing step starts with the image binarization. This process is applied directly to the image acquired as a response after the convolution operation was terminated and the result image is calculated. Fig. 8.14 illustrates the result after the Otsu method is applied.

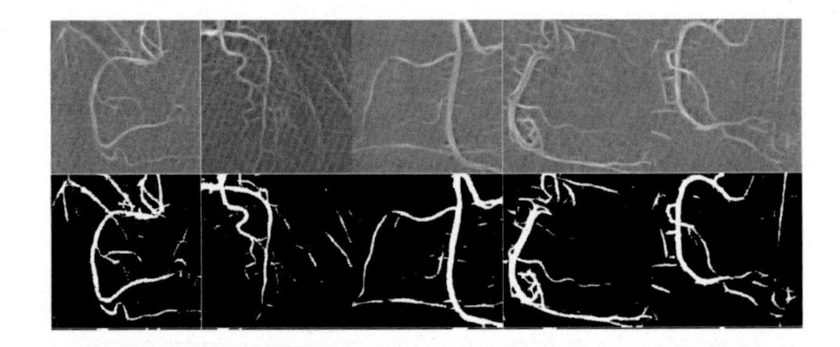

FIGURE 8.14 Binarization result with the Otsu method. The first row contains five response images obtained from the test set in the previous processing step. In the second row is their corresponding binary response when the Otsu method was applied to each of them.

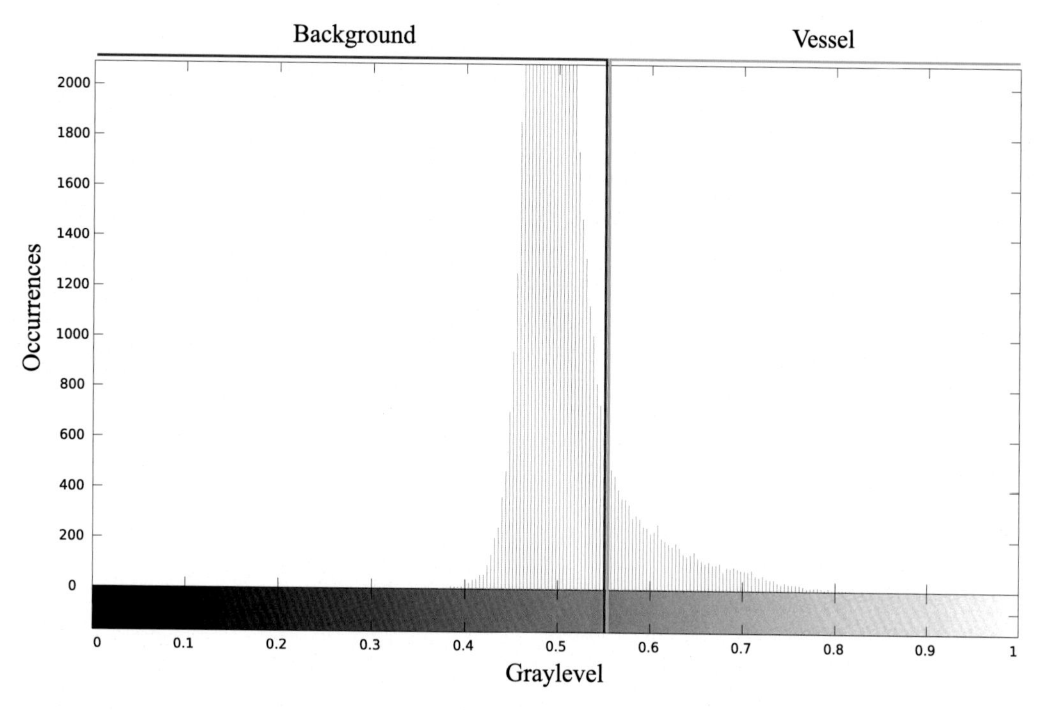

FIGURE 8.15 Image histogram corresponding to the response illustrated at the top-left corner in Fig. 8.14, from which the Otsu threshold is automatically calculated.

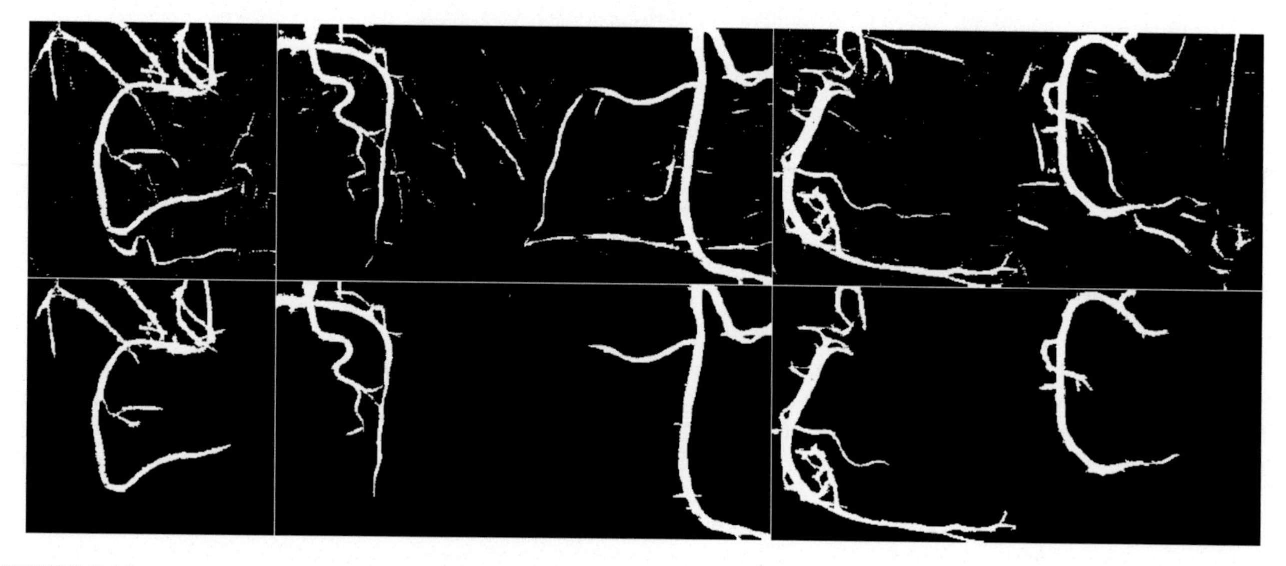

FIGURE 8.16 Final resulting image when isolated pixels are removed. The first row contains five binarized images using the Otsu method. The second row contains the corresponding images without isolated pixels.

Fig. 8.15 illustrates the histogram corresponding to the left-top corner response image presented in Fig. 8.14. The calculated threshold value by Otsu method was 0.5412.

After the binarization step, the result image contains single isolated pixels or groups of them that must be removed if a smoother image result is desired. Fig. 8.16 illustrates the result when isolated pixels groups are removed from the binary image.

Fig. 8.17 illustrates the different responses in all process steps using the gray-level convolutional template achieved by ILS. The first two rows contain the original angiogram and their corresponding ground truth. The segmentation response obtained with the convolution of the original image with a gray-level template is illustrated in the third row. The 4th and 5th rows correspond to the postprocessing results, when the response (illustrated in row 3) is binarized

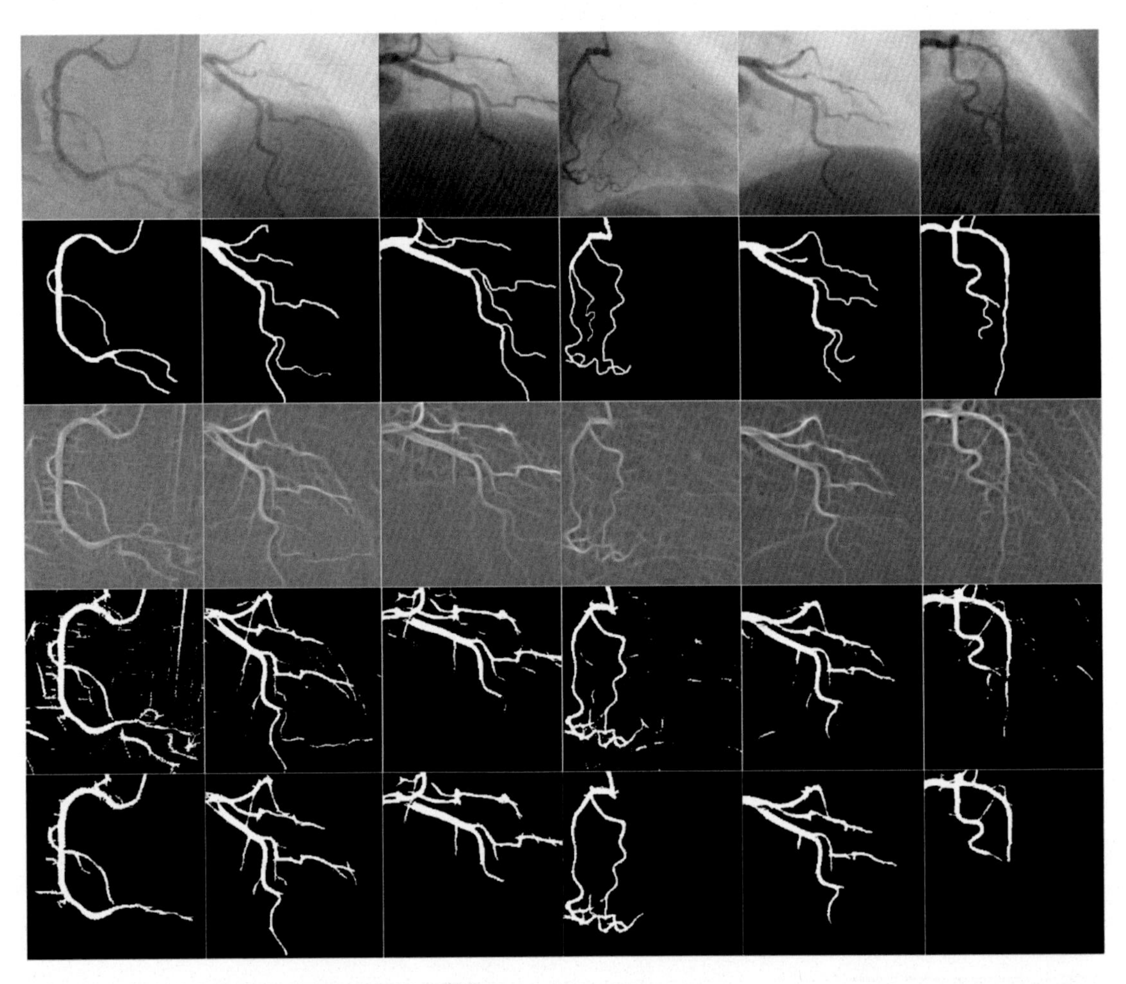

FIGURE 8.17 Map of the different responses obtained in each processing step. From left to right, six different test angiograms were selected randomly. The first two rows contain the original images and their corresponding ground-truth. The third row contains the convolution response applying the gray-level template acquired by Iterated Local Search , which was the method with the highest performance results. The fourth row contains the binarization by Otsu method of the responses illustrated in the previous row. The last row contains the final result when isolated pixel groups are removed from the binary image.

and after enhancement, respectively, in such a case, the final visual result images acquired are in the last row.

Finally, the required time for the training step was $\approx$ 6 hours for single solution-based metaheuristics (ILS, TS, and SA) and $\approx$ 10 hours for the UMDA strategy, which is population-based. Each iteration takes $\approx$ 9 seconds for single-solution-based strategies and $\approx$ 14 seconds for UMDA. However, the testing stage was performed significantly faster. Each image was segmented in $\approx$ 0.02 seconds. The total time consumed for the segmentation of all test sets with 30 images was $\approx$ 0.6 seconds.

8.5 Concluding remarks

In this chapter, a method for the automatic design of convolutional gray-level templates by the use of metaheuristics has been proposed. Because the problem of designing gray-level templates is $O(256^n)$ computational complexity, a method involving several search strategies was adopted. The proposed method was divided into two different steps. In the first step, the design of the gray-level template was performed using a training set with 100 X-ray images and applying several metaheuristics in order to explore the high-dimensional search space. The training performance results were statistically compared in terms of the area (Az) under the ROC curve. This comparative analysis reveals that automatic generation of a convolutional gray-level template obtained by ILS achieved the highest performance with Az = 0.958. In the second step, the best template achieved by each strategy was directly applied over a test set of 30 images and compared with other state-of-the-art methods for blood vessel imaging enhancement. The ILS achieved an overall highest performance with Az = 0.961. In addition to the effectiveness of the proposed method, the number of parameters to configure is fewer than with other methods and they are related only with the configuration of the used metaheuristic, without requiring a priori knowledge about the problem. Finally, in order to improve the visual results after the segmentation process was performed, a postprocessing stage in two steps was applied to the segmentation responses. In the first the postprocessing step, a binarization process over the image was performed using the Otsu method in order to obtain an auto-calculated threshold value. After this step a binary response was acquired with the classification of vessel and background pixels. In the final step, the binary response was smoothed by removing isolated pixels and groups of them, allowing the generation of an enhanced vessel image. According to the experimental results, the design of convolutional gray-level templates can be suitable for computational systems that perform vessel analysis in clinical practice.

Appendix 1 Matlab code of the tabú search for the traveler salesman problem

```
%-------------------------------------------------------------------------
%          Matlab code to solve the Traveler Salesman Problem
%-------------------------------------------------------------------------
%   Comments:   To test this code, copy and paste it into a file named
%               ts_tsp.m.
%-------------------------------------------------------------------------
% Usage:
%        [init_dist, min_dist, travel_best] = ts_tsp(matrix_coords, ...
%                                                    max_size, ...
%                                                    max_iters);
%-------------------------------------------------------------------------
% Inputs:
%            matrix_coords: A Nx2 matrix containing each city coordinates
%                           x-y pair. This matrix is conformed reading the
%                           data from the krob100.tsp file in such case,
%                           the matrix_coords will be 100x2.
%                 max_size: An integer value to indicate the max
%                           capability of the tabu list to store previous
%                           visited solutions.
%                max_iters: The maximum number of iterations to be
%                           performed by the tabu search strategy.
%
% Krob100 data file can be downloaded from:
% http://elib.zib.de/pub/mp-testdata/tsp/tsplib/tsp/kroB100.tsp
%-------------------------------------------------------------------------
% Outputs:
%            init_distance: The initial distance obtained with the first
%                           randomly generated solution.
%             min_distance: The minimum travel distance obtained by the
%                           function.
%                   travel: A vector containing the cities position in order
%                           to be visited with the lowest cost in distance
%                           terms.
%-------------------------------------------------------------------------
%   Note:
```

```
%          After download krob100 data file, remove metadata header
%          and footer. Leave only the cities data: city number,
%          x-coordinate and y-coordinate columns separated with a comma.
%------------------------------------------------------------------------
% After applied note recomendations, this function can be invoked
% with this piece of code:
%
% cities = csvread('kroB100.csv');
%
% matrix = cities(:, 2:end);
% max_size = round(sqrt(size(matrix, 1)));
% max_iterations = 2500;
%
% [init_d, min_d, travel] = ts_tsp(matrix, max_size, max_iterations);
%
% disp(sprintf('Initial distance found: %d', init_d));
% disp(sprintf('Best distance found: %d', min_d));
% disp('Best travel found: ');
% disp(travel);
% disp('Program finished');
%------------------------------------------------------------------------
function [init_distance, min_distance, travel] = ts_tsp(matrix_coords, ...
                                                         max_size, ...
                                                         max_iterations)

    %Initialize the tabu list:
    tabu_list = [];

    %Generate an initial random solution:
    travel = randperm(size(matrix_coords, 1));

    %Compute the cost of the randomly generated solution:
    min_distance = calculateCost(matrix_coords, travel);
    init_distance = min_distance;

    %Iterate up to max_iterations is reached:
    for iter = 1 : max_iterations
        disp(sprintf('Running iteration %d of %d', iter, max_iterations));
```

```
        %Generate a New Solution:
        travel_new = generateNewSolution(matrix_coords, travel);

        %Check if solution is not in Tabu List to add it and evaluate:
        pos = frindex(tabu_list, travel_new);
        if pos == 0
            %Check if tabu list is full and throw last element:
            if size(tabu_list, 1) >= max_size
                tabu_list = tabu_list(1:size(tabu_list, 1) - 1, :);
            end

            %Add the new solution at top of tabu list:
            tabu_list = [travel_new; tabu_list];

            %Evaluate new solution performance:
            current_distance = calculateCost(matrix_coords, travel_new);

            %Check if new solution improves the best current:
            if current_distance < min_distance
                min_distance = current_distance;
                travel = travel_new;
            end
        end
    end
end

%-----------------------------------------------------------------------
% This function calculates the euclidean distance between two 2-D points.
%-----------------------------------------------------------------------
function distance = getDistance(x1, y1, x2, y2)
    distance = sqrt((x2 - x1)^2 + (y2 - y1)^2);
end

%-----------------------------------------------------------------------
% This function find the nearest city to any specified.
%-----------------------------------------------------------------------
function c_index = findNearestNeighbor(matrix_coords, init_index)
    first_time = true;
```

```
    dist = 0;
    min_dist = 0;
    x1 = matrix_coords(init_index, 1);
    y1 = matrix_coords(init_index, 2);
    for i = 1 : size(matrix_coords, 1)
        if init_index ~= i
            x2 = matrix_coords(i, 1);
            y2 = matrix_coords(i, 2);
            dist = getDistance(x1, y1, x2, y2);
            if first_time
                min_dist = dist;
                c_index = i;
                first_time = false;
            elseif dist < min_dist
                min_dist = dist;
                c_index = i;
            end
        end
    end
end

%-------------------------------------------------------------------------
% This function compute the total traveled distance following the cities
% order specified in the 'travel' vector.
%-------------------------------------------------------------------------
function cost = calculateCost(matrix_coords, travel)
    cost = 0;
    for k = 1 : size(travel, 2) - 1
        x1 = matrix_coords(travel(k), 1);
        y1 = matrix_coords(travel(k), 2);
        x2 = matrix_coords(travel(k+1), 1);
        y2 = matrix_coords(travel(k+1), 2);
        cost = cost + getDistance(x1, y1, x2, y2);
    end
end

%-------------------------------------------------------------------------
% This function builds a new solution by using the Local Search
```

```
% strategy. A city is randomly selected and after, the most closest
% city is searched and permuted in the next position.
%------------------------------------------------------------------------
function new_travel = generateNewSolution(matrix_coords, travel)
    new_travel = travel;

    %Select a city randomly:
    pos = randi([1, numel(travel) - 1]);
    init_city = travel(pos);
    next_city = travel(pos + 1);

    %Find closest city to previously selected:
    closest_city = findNearestNeighbor(matrix_coords, init_city);

    %Find closest city position in travel vector:
    closest_city_pos = find(travel == closest_city);

    %Interchange next city to travel with closest city found:
    new_travel(pos + 1) = closest_city;
    new_travel(closest_city_pos) = next_city;
end

%------------------------------------------------------------------------
%Find Row Index
%   Find the index where the values of a row vector are the same
%   inside a matrix.
%------------------------------------------------------------------------
%Usage:
%   row_index = frindex(m, vector)
%
%Inputs:
%        m:  A numerical matrix.
%   vector:  The row vector with the values to be finded inside the matrix.
%
%Outputs:
%   row_index:  An Integer representing the row number where the vector
%               values were coincident inside the matrix.
%               If no coincident row vector was found, 0 is returned.


%               If there exists more than one coincidence, the first
%               occurence index is returned.
%------------------------------------------------------------------------
function row_index = frindex(m, vector)
    row_index = 0;
    for k = 1 : size(m, 1)
        if isequal(m(k, :), vector)
            row_index = k;
            k = size(m, 1) + 1;
        end
    end
end
```

References

Aarts, E., & Lenstra, J. K. (1997). *Local search in combinatorial optimization*. Wiley.

Althofer, I., & Koschnick, K.-U. (1991). On the convergence of threshold accepting. *Applied Mathematics and Optimization, 24*, 183–195.

Ayres, F., & Rangayyan, R. (2007). Design and performance analysis of oriented feature detectors. *Journal of Electronic Imaging, 16*, 023007.

Bouraoui, B., Ronse, C., Baruthio, J., Passat, N., & Germain, P. (2008). Fully automatic 3D segmentation of coronary arteries based on mathematical morphology. In: *Proceedings of the fifth IEEE international symposium on biomedical imaging (ISBI): from nano to macro*. (pp. 1059–1062).

Cervantes-Sanchez, F., Cruz-Aceves, I., Hernandez-Aguirre, A., Hernandez-Gonzalez, M., & Solorio-Meza, S. (2019). Automatic segmentation of coronary arteries in X-ray angiograms using multiscale analysis and artificial neural networks. *Applied Sciences, 9* (24), 5507.

Chanwimaluang, T. & Fan, G. (2003). An efficient blood vessel detection algorithm for retinal images using local entropy thresholding, In: *Proceedings of the international symposium on circuits and systems*. Vol. 5. (pp. 21–24).

Chaudhuri, S., Chatterjee, S., Katz, N., Nelson, M., & Goldbaum, M. (1989). Detection of blood vessels in retinal images using two-dimensional matched filters. *IEEE Transactions on Medical Imaging, 8*, 263–269.

Chmielewski, M., & Busse-Jersy, W. (1996). Global discretization of continuous attributes as preprocessing for machine learning. *International Journal of Approximate Reasoning, 15*, 319–331.

Cimen, S., Gooya, A., Grass, M., & Frangi, A. (2016). Reconstruction of coronary arteries from X-ray angiography: A review. *Medical Image Analysis, 32*, 46–68.

Cinsdikici, M., & Aydın, D. (2009). Detection of blood vessels in ophthalmoscope images using MF/ant (matched filter/ant colony) algorithm. *Computer Methods and Programs in Biomedicine, 96*(2), 85–95. Available from https://doi.org/10.1016/j.cmpb.2009.04.005, In press.

Cruz-Aceves, I., Cervantes-Sanchez, F., Hernandez-Aguirre, A., Hernandez-Gonzalez, M., & Solorio-meza, S. (2019). A novel method for the design of convolutional gray-level templates for the automatic detection of coronary arteries. In: *Proceedings of SPIE*, (pp. 1–8).

Cruz-Aceves, I., Hernández-Aguirre, A., & Aviña-Cervantes, J. (2015). Automatic segmentation of coronary arteries using a multiscale top-hat operator and multiobjective optimization. *Revista Electrónica Nova Scientia, 7*, 297–320.

Cruz-Aceves, I., Oloumi, F., Rangayyan, R., Aviña-Cervantes, J., & Hernandez-Aguirre, A. (2015). Automatic segmentation of coronary arteries using Gabor filters and thresholding based on multiobjective optimization. *Biomedical Signal Processing and Control, 25*, 76–85.

Dekkers, A., & Aarts, E. (1991). Global optimization and simulated annealing. *Mathematical Programming, 50*, 367–393.

Du, K.-L., & Swamy, M. (2016). *Search and optimization by metaheuristics*. Birkhäuser.

Eiho, S., & Qian, Y. (1997). Detection of coronary artery tree using morphological operator. *Computers in Cardiology, 24*, 525–528.

Fathi, A., & Naghsh-Nilchi, A. (2013). Automatic wavelet-based retinal blood vessels segmentation and vessel diameter estimation. *Biomedical Signal Processing and Control, 8*, 71–80.

Fawcett, T. (2006). An introduction to ROC analysis. *Pattern Recognition Letters, 27*, 861–874.

Frangi, A., Niessen, W., Vincken, K., & Viergever, M. (1998). Multiscale vessel enhancement filtering. In: *Proceedings of the international conference on medical image computing and computer-assisted intervention*. (pp. 130–137).

Gabor, D. (1946). Theory of communication. *Journal of the Institution of Electrical Engineers, 93*, 429–457.

Ge-xiang, Z., Wei-dong, J., & Lai-zhao, H. (2005). Generalized discretization of continuous attributes in rough set theory. *Control and Decision, 20*, 372–376.

Glover, F. (1989). Tabu search: Part I. *ORSA Journal on Computing, 1*, 190–206.

Goksuluk, D., Kormaz, S., Zararsiz, G., & Ergun-Karaagaoglu, A. (2016). easyROC: An interactive web-tool for ROC curve analysis using R language environment. *The R Journal, 8*, 213–230.

Hashemi, M. & Reza-Meybodi, M. (2011). Univariate marginal distribution algorithm in combination with extremal optimization (EO, GEO). In: *Proceedings of the international conference on neural information processing*, (pp. 220–227).

Heinz, M., & Mahnig, T. (2001). *Evolutionary algorithms: From recombination to search distributions. Theoretical aspects of evolutionary computing* (pp. 135–173).

Jing, Z., ChongZao, H., Bin, W., & DeQiang, H. (2011). A umda-based discretization method for continuous attributes. *Advanced Materials Research, 403–408*, 1834–1838.

Johnson, D. (1990). Local optimization and the travelling salesman problem. In: *Proceedings of the seventeenth colloquium on automata, languages and programming*. Vol. 443, 446–461.

Kang, W., Kang, W., & Li, Q.W.Y. (2013). The segmentation method of degree-based fusion algorithm for coronary angiograms. In: *Proceedings of the second international conference on measurement, information and control*. (pp. 696–699).

Kang, W., Wang, K., Chen, W., & Kang, W., (2009). Segmentation method based on fusion algorithm for coronary angiograms. In: *Proceedings of the second international congress on image and signal processing*. (pp. 1–4).

Kirkpatrick, S., Gelatt, C. D., & Vecchi, M. P. (1983). Optimization by simulated annealing. *Science (New York, N.Y.), 220*, 671–680.

Krolak, P., Felts, W., & Marble, G. (1971). Krob-100 data file, Accessed 06.04.20.

Lara, D., Faria, A., Araujo, A., & Menotti, D. (2009). A semi-automatic method for segmentation of the coronary artery tree from angiography. In: *Proceedings of the twenty-second Brazilian symposium on computer graphics and image processing*. (pp. 194–201).

Li, Y., Zhou, S., Wu, J., Ma, X., & Peng, K. (2012). A novel method of vessel seg- mentation for x-ray coronary angiography images. In: *Proceedings of the fourth international conference on computational and information sciences*. (pp. 468–471).

Locatelli, M. (2000). Simulated annealing algorithms for continuous global optimization. *Journal of Optimization Theory and Applications, 29*, 87–102.

Lorenz, C., Carlsen, I., Buzug, T., Fassnacht, C., & Weese, J. (1997). A multi-scale line filter with automatic scale selection based on the Hessian matrix for medical image segmentation. In: *Proceedings of the scale-space theories in computer-vision*. Vol. 1252. (pp. 152–163).

Lourenco, H., MArtin, O., & Stutzle, T. (2010). *Iterated local search: framework and applications*. Springer.

Lourenço, H., Martin, O., & Stützle, T. (2003). Iterated local search, Glover F., Kochenberger G.A. (Eds.) Handbook of metaheuristics. International series in operations research & management science 57, (pp. 321–353).

Maglaveras, N., Haris, K., Efstratiadis, S., Gourassas, J., & Louridas, G. (2001). Artery skeleton extraction using topographic and connected component labeling. *Computers in Cardiology, 28*, 17–20.

Mark, D., Berman, D., Budoff, M., Carr, J., Gerber, T., Hecht, H., ... Schwartz, R. (2010). ACCF/ACR/AHA/NASCI/SAIP/SCAI/SCCT 2010 expert consensus document on coronary computed tomographic angiography: A report of the American college of cardiology foundation task force on expert consensus documents. *Journal of the American College of Cardiology, 55*, 2663–2699.

Martin, O., Otto, S., & Felten, E. W. (1991). Large-step Markov chains for the traveling salesman problem. *Complex Systems, 5*, 299–326.

Metropolis, N., Rosenbluth, A., Rosenbluth, M., Teller, A., & Teller, E. (1953). Equation of state calculations by fast computing machines. *Journal of Chemical Physics, 21*, 1087–1092.

Metz, C. E. (1978). Basic principles of ROC analysis. *Seminars in Nuclear Medicine, 8*, 283–298.

M'hiri, F., Duong, L., Desrosiers, C., Cheriet, M. (2013). Vesselwalker: Coronary arteries segmentation using random walks and Hessian-based vesselness filter. In: *Proceedings of the IEEE tenth international symposium on biomedical imaging: from nano to macro*. (pp. 918–921).

Otsu, N. (1979). A threshold selection method from gray-level histograms. *IEEE Transactions on Systems, Man and Cybernetics, 9*, 62–66.

Ozdamar, L., & Demirhan, M. (2000). Experiments with new stochastic global optimization search techniques. *Computers and Operations Research, 27*, 841–865.

Pal, R. N., & Sankar, K. P. (1989). Entropic thresholding. *Signal Process*, 97–108.

Papdimitriou, C.H., (1976). The complexity of combinatorial optimization problems. (Master's thesis), Princeton University.

Pourreza-Shahri, R., Tavakoli, M., & Kehtarnavaz, N. (2014). Computationally efficient optic nerve head detection in retinal fundus images. *Biomedical Signal Processing and Control, 11*, 63–73.

Qian, Y., Eiho, S., Sugimoto, N., & Fujita, M. (1998). Automatic extraction of coronary artery tree on coronary angiograms by morphological operators. *Computers in Cardiology, 25*, 765–768.

Rangayyan, R., Ayres, F., Oloumi, F., Oloumi, F., & Eshghzadeh-Zanjani, P. (2008). Detection of blood vessels in the retina with multiscale Gabor filters. *Journal of Electronic Imaging, 17*.

Salem, N. & Nandi, A. (2008). Unsupervised segmentation of retinal blood vessels using a single parameter vesselness measure. In: *Proceedings of the IEEE sixth Indian conference on computer vision, graphics and image processing*. Vol. 34. (pp. 528–534).

Sang, N., Tang, Q., Liu, X., & Weng, W. (2004). Multiscale centerline extraction of angiogram vessels using Gabor filters. *Computational and Information Science*, 570–575.

Scanlon, P., Faxon, D., Audet, A., Carabello, B., Dehmer, G., Ea- gle, K., . . . Smith, S. (1999). *ACC/AHA guidelines for coronary angiography: Executive summary and recommendations: A report of the American college of cardiology/american heart association task force on practice guidelines (committee on coronary angiography) developed in collaboration*, . *Circulation* (99, pp. 2345–2357).

Shikata, H., Hoffman, E., & Sonka, M. (2004). Automated segmentation of pulmonary vascular tree from 3D CT images. In: *Proceedings of the SPIE international symposium medical imaging*. Vol. 5369. (pp. 107–116).

Shoujun, Z., Jian, Y., Yongtian, W., & Wufan, C. (2010). Automatic segmentation of coronary angiograms based on fuzzy inferring and probabilistic tracking. *Biomedical Engineering Online, 9*.

Soares, J., Leandro, J., Cesar-Junior, R., Jelinek, H., & Cree, M. (2006). Retinal vessel segmentation using the 2-D Gabor wavelet and supervised classification. *IEEE Transactions on Medical Imaging, 25*, 1214–1222.

Swets, J., Dawes, R., & Monahan, J. (2000). Better decisions through science. *Scientific American, 283*, 82–87.

Talbi, E.-G. (2009). *Metaheuristics, from design to implementation*. John Wiley & Sons, Inc.

Talbi, E.-G., Hafidi, Z., & Geib, J.-M. (1998). A parallel adaptive Tabu search approach. *Parallel Computing, 24*, 2003–2019.

Tsai, T., Lee, H., & Chen, M. (2013). Adaptive segmentation of vessels from coro- nary angiograms using multi-scale filtering. In: *Proceedings of the international conference on signalimage technology and internet-based systems*. (pp. 143–147).

Wang, Y., Ji, G., Lin, P., & Trucco, E. (2013). Retinal vessel segmentation using multiwavelet kernels and multiscale hierarchical decomposition. *Pattern Recognition, 46*, 2117–2133.

White, S., Pharoah, M., & Frederiksen, N. (2004). *Oral radiology: principles and interpretation* (6th ed.). St. Louis, MO: Mosby.

Wink, O., Niessen, W., & Viergever, M. (2004). Multiscale vessel tracking. *IEEE Transactions on Medical Imaging, 23*, 130–133.

CHAPTER

9

Smart city development: Theft handling of public vehicles using image analysis and cloud network

Himadri Biswas[1], *Vaskar Sarkar*[2,*], *Priyajit Sen*[3] *and Debabrata Sarddar*[1]

[1]Department of Computer Science and Engineering, University of Kalyani, Kalyani, India [2]Department of Mathematics, School of Science, Adamas University, Kolkata, India [3]Department of Computer Science, Directorate of Distance Education, Vidyasagar University, Midnapore, India

*Corresponding author.

9.1 Introduction

Car theft is the act of stealing a car or taking it to sell without the proper permission of the owner. Entry to a car to steal it can be gained by breaking a window, stealing keys, or creating duplicate keys. The theft of a car creates a number of inconveniences for the owner, including having to source another method of transport. The owner has to visit the appropriate authority to inform them of the theft and carry out any other necessary steps. The owner may also suffer from mental and economical hazards also. In order to generate an improved quality of image, image processing is used by performing specific operations the image. This is a form of signal processing during which the input is an image and the output should be a perfect image, image segment, or any extracted feature relevant to the image. Image processing is a notable area for the generation of improved graphics figures for clarity and image processing data for storage and representation for machine sensitivity. Cars and public vehicles in smart cities are relatively safe, as different methodologies are adopted to protect these vehicles using the cloud network.

9.2 Motivation scenario

In a research article, Zhang and Zhang (2010) presented a technical report on the recent advances in face detection. Using the combined features of normal, infrared, and three-dimensional images, Bowyer, Chang, Flynn, and Chen (2012) explored facial recognition "Eigen-face" and "weighted score fusion" algorithms which can increase the performance compared to multimodal techniques. In the presence of various light levels of color pictures, Hsu, Abdel-Mottaleb, and Jain (2002) suggested another algorithm for facial recognition. Dalal and Trigg (2005) presented experimentally that grids of descriptors of "Histograms of Oriented Gradient" consistently improved existing human detection feature sets. Beymer and Poggio (1995) addressed the problem of facial recognition in different postures in which only one image of each individual was visible and a solution was proposed on the concept of virtual views in which face was seen through various systems. Two algorithms (Brunelli & Poggio, 1993) are suggested, where the first is focused on the calculation of a series of geometric characteristics such as nose length and width, location of the mouth and shape of the chin, while the other was focused on matching the image with a grayish template. Tian Yinzhong et al. formulated the idea of "feature extraction elements" in the facial recognition process also using the principal component analysis (PCA) algorithm (Yinzhong, Zhixue, & Jianwei, 2010), and also summarized the PCA algorithm implementation procedures in the MATLAB program for facial recognition. Turk and Pentland (1991) suggested an approach to human facial detection and

Recent Trends in Computational Intelligence Enabled Research.
DOI: https://doi.org/10.1016/B978-0-12-822844-9.00013-X

identification and identified a functioning, near real-time facial recognition device that tracks the individual by comparing facial features with those of known individuals. Goldstein, Harmon, and Lesk (1971) gave a summary of the techniques being studied for the creation of a method of facial recognition and suggested the field's existing state-of-the-art mechanism. In biometric applications, the "emotion recognition of human face" is the most popular method, and research work (Mercy Rani & Durgadevi, 2017) has focused on recognizing the "facial emotions from the regions of the mouth." Tian, Kanade, and Cohn (2011) suggested that a sound objective of researching human behavior and expressions was the recognition of robust facial expressions. By utilizing the features of Gabor Filter, Local Binary Pattern, and Whitened PCA (LGBPWP), Zhang, Shan, Gao, Chen, and Zhang (2005) proposed a novel approach. A method was presented by Wiskott, Fellous, Krger, and Malsburg (1997) for human facial identification from single images from a wide database containing a single image per individual, where a "bunch graph" is the novel approach for extraction of the image graph that is developed from a limited collection of reference image graphs. For facial recognition, two feature extraction methods are used (Barnouti, Mahmood, & Matti, 2016), where the first is based on appearance and includes principal component analysis (**PCA**), linear discriminant analysis (**LDA**), **and** independent component analysis (**ICA**) characteristics and the other is based on models like elastic bunch graph matching (**EBGM**) and 3D Morphable. In the study by Yang and Huang (1994) another three-stage knowledge-based hierarchical method was proposed to locate human faces in a complex context, where mosaic images of different resolutions were focused on the higher two stages and an improved method of detection of edges was proposed at the lower stage. Amit, Geman, and Jedynak (1998) presented an algorithm for "shape detection" and applied it to face views with arbitrary backgrounds in still gray-level images. The identification was carried out in two phases: the first phase was focusing, and a relatively small number of regions of interest were identified, reducing computation and false negatives at the (temporary) cost of false positives; and the second was "intensive classification," during which a selected area of interest is labeled as face or context based on multiple decision trees and standardized details. Gong, McKenna, and Psarrou (2000) developed a system that faces the ability to locate and monitor through sometimes complex and dynamic scenes where the current models and algorithms in a dynamic environment are capable of performing facial recognition. To categorize and evaluate the algorithms mentioned in various articles, another detailed survey of facial detection research was provided in Yang and Ahuja (2002). Therefore considering all the scenarios, here we are suggest a new cloud-based facial recognition algorithm which may help to check the authenticity of people on a worldwide scale.

9.3 Issues and challenges of image authentication through Internet of Things-based cloud framework

Establishing credibility in the increasingly crowded cloud computing world has become extremely difficult. The need for a safe cloud authorization strategy has developed in the midst of increased concerns about security and rapid advances in cloud storage, access management, and online communication. Facial recognition, a nonintrusive method where humans use the most common biometric features to identify others, measures facial characteristics. In security areas, facial recognition-based user authentication is essential when using the cloud to access things. This will provide users with a sufficient standard of safety regarding theft. Through smart home devices, smart personal equipment, personal assistants, industrial assistance, and much more, the Internet of Things (IoT) has grown tremendously in recent years. Devices that are used in the IoT are mostly low powered, with limited computational resources, while the computing component is transferred to the cloud server back end. Here, we build a real-time facial recognition application integrated with cloud computing to demonstrate the advantages of the IoT.

9.3.1 Biometric system

To determine an individual's identity based on scientific behavioral, biological, and physical characteristics is called biometrics. In order to implement the proper authentication mechanism numerous biometric methods are currently used (Weaver, 2006).

9.3.1.1 Characteristics

Based on their unique physical and/or behavioral characteristics through the use of automation or semiautomation systems, biometrics provides a quick and effective approach to some aspects of identity management (Jain & Karthik, 2008). For automatic identification, DNA, iris, fingerprint, face, voice, retina, eye, hand, signature, keystroke, and speech including physiological and behavioral features (Fig. 9.1), are widely used currently.

In comparison, as other events are produced all the time, such as optical skin reflectance, body smell, head articulation, etc. and many more. The imaging criteria for the system differ greatly, due to the broad selection

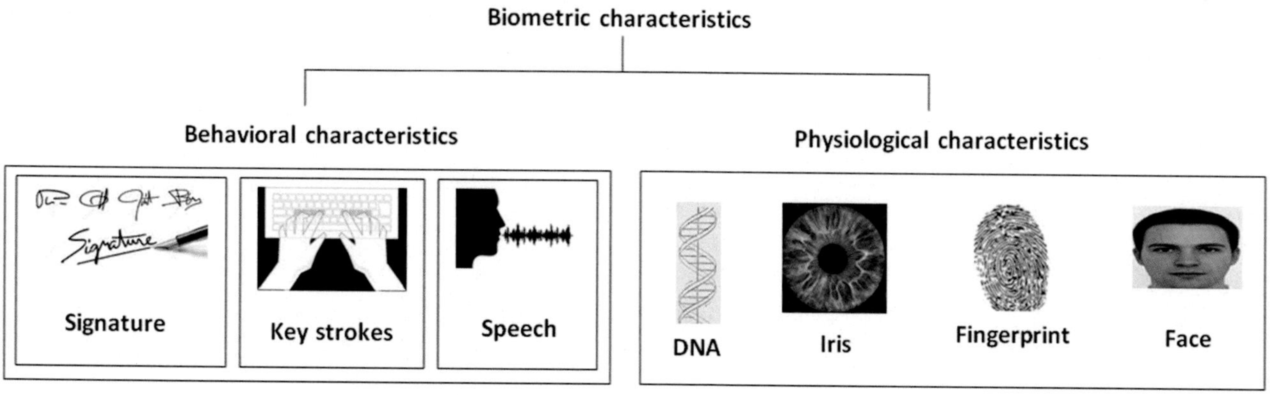

Biometric characteristics

Behavioral characteristics

Physiological characteristics

Signature

Key strokes

Speech

DNA

Iris

Fingerprint

Face

FIGURE 9.1 Physiological and behavioral characteristics of biometrics.

of features used in recognition. However the main point is that among the following biometric features the best should be identified (Wayman, 1996; Wayman, 2001)?

1. *Robustness*: This reflects "constantly and efficiently evolving over time on an individual."
2. *Evocative*: This displays great variability across the population distinctively.
3. *Available*: This indicates the population as a whole will preferably have multiples of these measurements.
4. *Accessible*: This indicates that electronic sensors are easy to photograph.
5. *Acceptable*: This illustrates that people do not object to them taking the action.

For biometric authentication, several particular elements of the features of human biology, chemistry, or behavior may be used, where it takes a weighting of several factors to pick a standard biometric for use in a specific application. Fig. 9.1 shows the biometric characteristic classification. In biometric authentication, Jain, Bolle, and Pankanti (1999) identified some specific factors being used in evaluating the ability of any biometric characteristic, such as physiological and behavioral, as listed below:

1. *Universality*: This shows that the quality will be granted to any individual user who carries out a program.
2. *Uniqueness*: The characteristic defined by uniqueness in the specific population should be sufficiently different to differentiate individuals from each other.
3. *Permanence*: Permanence is related to the way a characteristic changes over time. More precisely, with respect to the particular matching algorithm a feature with strong permanence should be fairly invariant over time.
4. *Measurability*: The ease of obtaining or calculating the attribute is represented by measurability or collectability. In addition, the data obtained should enable the relevant feature sets to be subsequently analyzed and retrieved.
5. *Performance*: This refers to the precision, velocity, and sturdiness of the technologies that are used.
6. *Acceptability*: This relates to how well people in the individual culture accept the technology and are able to capture and assess their biometric role.
7. *Circumvention*: This is the ability with which a characteristic can be imitated with the use of an object or substitute.

9.3.1.2 Biometric techniques

1. *Signature recognition*: Signature recognition is very useful in authenticating user identity based on their unique signature characteristics. In reality, it is one of the biometrics of behavior that develops over a period of time and is affected by the emotional and physical conditions of the signing.
2. *Speech recognition*: Speech is a mixture of various biometric features of the body or behavior. The anatomical features of a person's voice are based on its inner size and form, like mouth anatomy, vocal folds, and the nasal cavities and lips. To authorize the individual's identity speech recognition is used to measure the characteristics of voice tone and delivery style, but the major drawback of recognition based on voice is that the speech characteristics of people are quite sensitive to a number of factors, such as the signal strength of noise and voice, which are usually reduced by the transmission channel during performance (Khitrov, 2013).
3. *Hand geometry recognition*: The geometric form of the hand is based on biometrics in hand geometry, where human palms have ridge patterns and

valleys, such as fingerprints. Nonetheless, this method has some disadvantages as it is not suitable for children because the hand shape appears to change with increasing age, and it is also not valid for people suffering from arthritis as the hand may not be properly placed on the scanner.

4. *Retinal recognition*: This is supposed to identify individuals by the pattern of the blood vessels on the retina, however it is a procedure that is very intrusive and expensive.
5. *Iris recognition*: Iris identification is a form of recognition of individuals based on unique combinations within the iris of the eye. The speed and efficiency of the recently stationed iris-based recognition system will provide huge effectiveness for identification and, compared to other biometric characteristics, iris recognition systems are widely accepted due to the very "high false rejection rate" and "low false acceptance rate."
6. *Fingerprint recognition*: A fingerprint is a pattern of valleys and ridges on the fingertips, and within the first 7 months of fetal development, the framework is developed. As an automatic approach, recognition of fingerprints confirms that two human fingerprints have a resemblance. However, the fact that identical twins have different fingerprints has been experimentally confirmed (Jain, Flynn, & Ross, 2007). One problem is that the device can be affected by the dryness of the fingertips and dirty fingertips, with resulting errors. On the other hand, on a large scale, fingerprint recognition systems need a massive amount of computing resources. Eventually, due to aging or biological variants, fingerprints from a small amount of people may be inaccurate for automatic recognition; occupational causes, such as manual work, can cause significant numbers of fingerprint cuts and scrapes that tend to change over time (Jain et al., 2007).
7. *Palm recognition*: Identification of the palm is focused on the palm surface with ridges, main lines, and wrinkles. This strategy, however, is very costly and not suitable for children, as palm lines shift as they grow.

Any of the above strategies may be realistic and are very helpful for providing sufficient security measures in cloud storage user authentication (Yang et al., 2011).

9.3.1.3 Biometric system technology

Biometrics is a method of identification of patterns that distinguishes an individual on the basis of their biological and behavioral attributes. Fig. 9.2 represents a biometric system process flow chart for cloud computing.

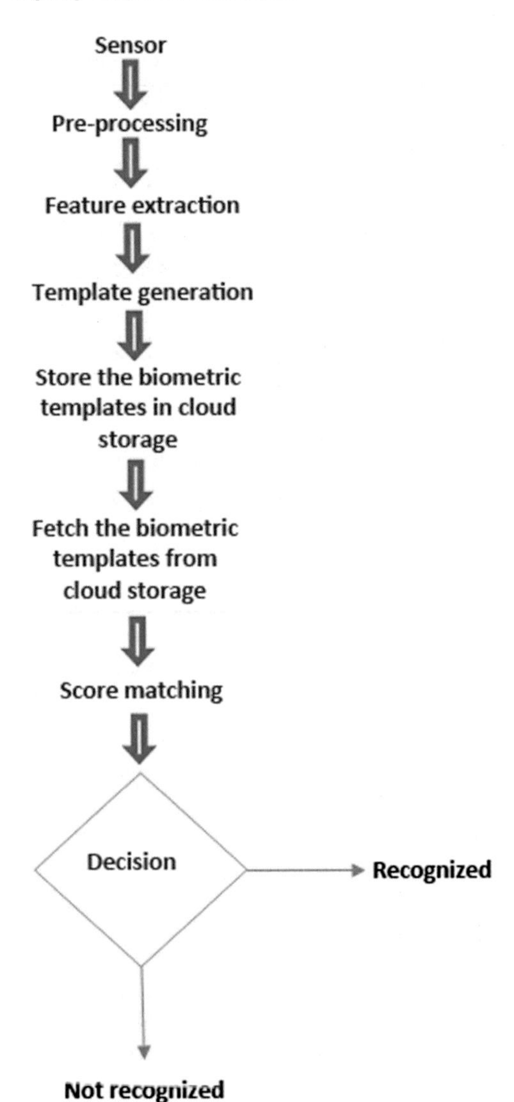

FIGURE 9.2 Biometric system process flow chart for cloud computing.

Sensor-module: An effective device, biometric scanner is required in a biometric system to extract the individuals' raw biometric data. For example, via an optical fingerprint sensor, fingerprint images can be utilized to extract individual ridges on finger, formation, and scale of ridges using an optical fingerprint sensor.

Preprocessing: Noise reduction from image capture, image segmentation, image reconstruction, edge sharpening, patterns of extraction, and misclassification are some biometrics-related preprocessing technologies. For example, Gaussian windows and resampling (Jain et al., 2007) are noise-filtering methods that are essential prior for extracting the function. Resampling is required in some systems to obtain a representation based of the shape, which consists of equivalent distance points, where resampling is immune to other approaches, as the procedure lacks such discriminatory speed characteristics.

Feature extraction: The quality and adequacy of the biometric data acquired by the sensor is determined in the efficiency assessment and extraction of features. For instance, some biometric pattern recognition systems are implemented by palm printing, fingerprinting, and iris, retina, face, hand, DNA, dental recognition, etc.

Score matching: To evaluate the identity of the biometric features of the input, it is important to compare the features extracted in the previous step with those found in the template database. By comparing the sets of features concerning two images, matching involves producing a match score in the simplest form. The score of the match shows the similarity between the two photos.

Decision process: In order to make the final decision at the decision stage, the match scores are generated in the matching module, whereas, in the identification mode of operation, the performance is a list of possible matching outcomes that can be sorted according to their match score.

9.3.1.4 Facial recognition system

Recently, facial recognition has become an attractive evolving area of study, that stresses the value of multimedia access to knowledge in the network society. It is an unobtrusive process, and the most common biometric characteristics may be facial features that people use to identify each other. From human recognition application to security of network, content indexing, content retrieval, and other applications, facial recognition technology is widely accepted because in a set of videos, the human face is always the focus of attention.

Massive, fully automated processing of human digital images has been produced in a variety of applications such as authentication of biometric systems (Gonzalez Martinez, Gonzalez Castano, Argones Rua, Alba Castro, & Rodriguez Silva, 2011), human–computer interactions, monitoring of applications, wide availability of power resources and low-cost devices, and multiple interconnected computing systems. The growing demand for quality, extensively rigorous monitoring, intelligence, fraud detection, and cloud protection has included the topic of an uncontrolled identification issue to the mainstream of computer vision and image processing applications for proper authentication by matching images as a one-to-many relationship. In the last decade, emphasis has been growing toward restricted and unrestricted verification by a one-to-one matching scheme.

9.3.1.5 Different application areas of facial recognition

Facial recognition is one of the most important image analytics technologies. It is a real challenge to create an automated device that matches the human capacity to recognize faces. While humans are very effective at identifying known faces, when dealing with a lot of unfamiliar faces, they are not as well qualified. Computers can transcend the limitations of humans with their almost unlimited memory and processing speed. Therefore facial recognition continues to be an unresolved concern and a developing requirement. The implementation areas and techniques of facial recognition are outlined in Table 9.1.

9.3.1.6 Facial recognition process flow

Facial recognition is a digital face detection and vision problem in which the human face is portrayed as a 3-D object involving the identification of objects (people) while vary the lighting, stance, expression, compression, and illumination of face, and other variables depending on the image acquired. Fig. 9.3 presents the different modules of a facial recognition system including localization of the face, standardization, detection of a feature, and matching.

Face detection automatically detects the presence of a face in an image, and separates the face from the background. The goal of facial alignment is to achieve more precise localization and standardization of faces, although rough assumptions of each identified face's position and scale are provided by facial recognition. The facial elements such as the mouth, eyes, and nose is located on the outer face and, in terms of geometric properties such as size and position, the video or image of the input face is transformed using geometric transformations or morphing, depending on the location point. The feature selection of facial images processed photometrically and geometrically is taken to provide efficient information that is useful for

TABLE 9.1 Different facial recognition application areas.

Study field	Application area
Biometrics	User authentication and reorganization (based on their biometric features, i.e., fingerprints, iris, face, retina scan, etc.)
Security of the information	Security of users and access security
Security of individuals	Recognition of facial expression, home video surveillance
Access control management	Safe access authentication, log-based database management, and authorization-based system
Enforcing the law	Video monitoring, tracking criminals, and forensic use
Entertainment or relaxation	Video gaming, applications based on a digital camera

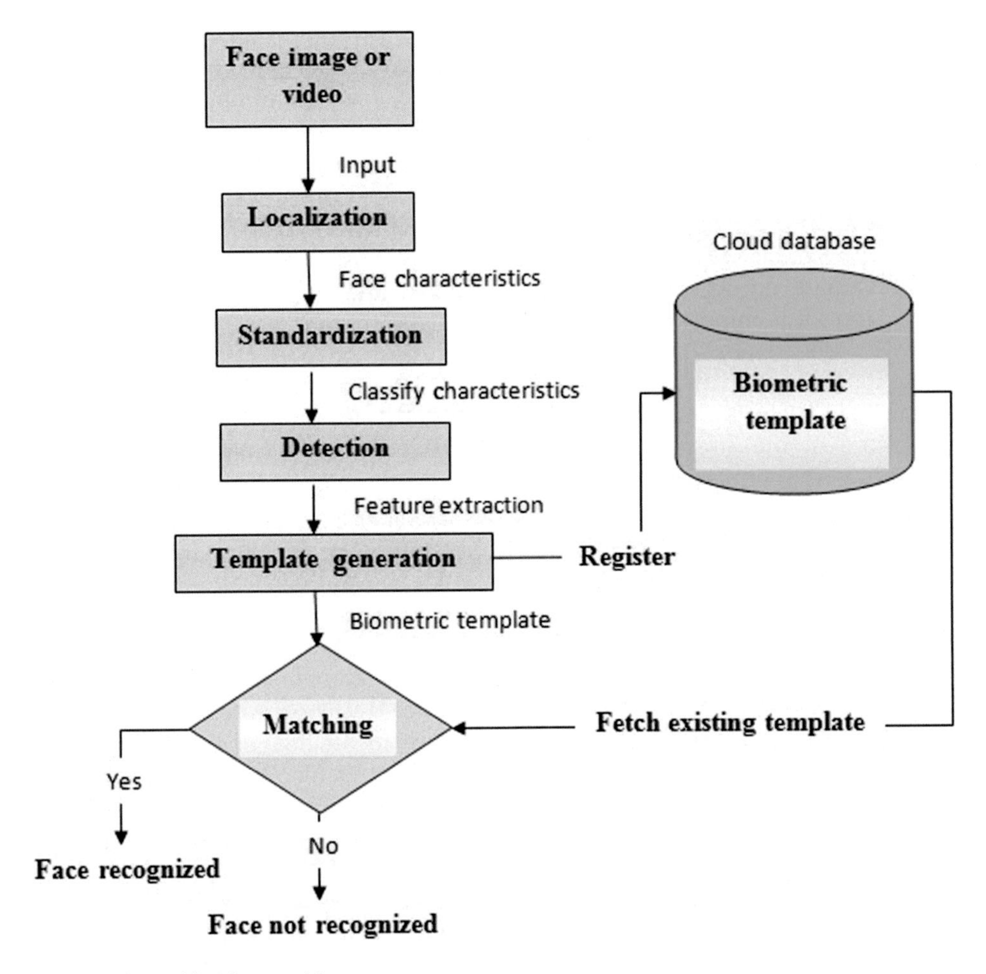

FIGURE 9.3 Process flow chart of facial recognition.

distinguishing among different people's faces and complying with photometric and geometric deviations. The function vector of the extracted input face corresponds to that of the enlisted faces in the form of a biometric template for face matching. The face is identified with a level confidence when a match is found, otherwise it indicates an unidentified face.

9.3.2 Internet of Things

In reality, it is a combination of traditional built-in systems with automated process control, small wireless microsensors, and many more that make a massive communications system. The integration of wireless connectivity and Internet-connected microelectromechanical devices has led to the development of new Internet products. It can be accessed via the Internet, and a unique identifier can identify each entity. By replacing IPV44, IPV6 plays a crucial role in the development of things on the Internet, offering a significant increase in address space. The IoT application's goal is to make things smart without user interaction. With the growing number of intelligent nodes and the amount of data provided by each node, unforeseen challenges to the integrity, privacy, compatibility, and maintenance of data etc. are expected to arise. The evolution of digital technologies and new innovations in the early 1990s introduced the idea of the Internet as a worldwide network, that is, an "Internet of computers," where services were supplied as a "world wide web" on top of the original framework. The definition of the "computer Internet" has changed over the years to the "people's Internet" with the creation of Web 2.0, where people around the world are connected through several social media sites. With the introduction of wireless networking technology and microelectromechanical machines, the Internet spectrum is expanding constantly, and computers (notebooks, laptops, cell phones, etc.) have exceeded the initial PCs, by means of improved storage capacity and processing capabilities. Once these devices, along with the actuators, are equipped with sensors, the ability to detect, compute, and communicate over an entire network can be extended to other devices.

As per Cisco, the concept of the "Internet of Things" brings people, computers, data, and things together to make interactions by network. Over the next decade, communities have collectively gained the potential to earn $1.9 trillion in revenue from the "IoT." The International Telecommunications Union (ITU) reported in a 2005 study (International Telecommunications Union, 2005) that the IoT would connect the world's objects in a perceptual and intelligent manner. In the IoT, four dimensions have been established by the ITU which integrate various technological developments such as "object recognition" (for tagging things), "sensors and wireless sensor networks" (for feeling things), "embedded systems" (for thinking things) and "nanotechnology" (for shrinking things). Thus the idea of the IoT is not focused on a specific area, and the broad concept remains fuzzy to define. As a final remark, it can be achieved through the combination of intelligent nodes communicating with other nodes, artifacts, and environments, and providing a huge amount of data. These data can be translated into effective actions that provide command and access to objects to enhance quality of life. Various IoT elements are described in Fig. 9.4.

9.3.2.1 *Internet of Things elements*

Three categories can be grouped into IoT elements: hardware, middleware, and presentation (Gubbi, Buyya, Marusic, & Palaniswani, 2013).

Hardware: Detectors, actuators, and advanced chipsets are the key physical components that play a significant part in the IoT.

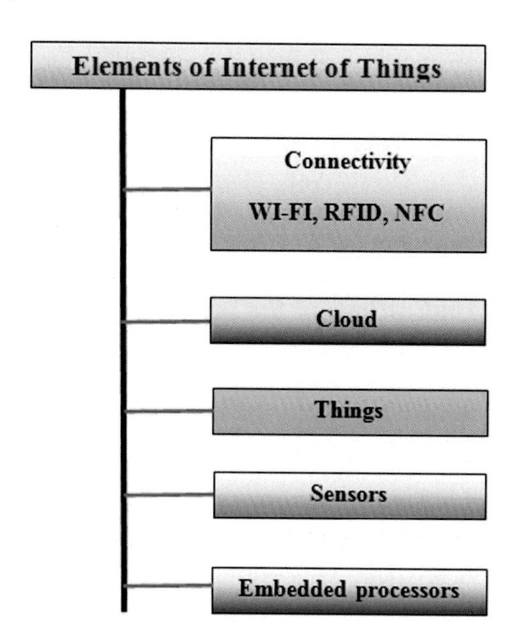

FIGURE 9.4 Elements of the IoT. *IoT*, Internet of Things.

Middleware: Storage and computing resources for on-demand data processing are available in this platform. It is a program or array of sublayers interposed between the development and assessment stages. The major characteristic is to obscure the details of the various technical difficulties and encourage the developer to develop the specific IoT-enabled device individually.

Presentation: In IoT applications, visual representation is extremely important, as it requires communication among both clients and the system. Thus visual representation for various applications needs to be user-friendly. Only realistic IoT implementation will allow the full use of smart devices with some enabling technologies to fulfill the vision of home automation, smart societies, smart cities, and smart worlds that can build up the components mentioned above in operation.

9.3.2.2 *Technologies involved in Internet of Things*

9.3.2.2.1 Wireless sensor networks

WSN hardware: The wireless sensor network (WSN) brings a modern interconnected legitimate architecture into our everyday lives with many application areas where the sensor's main node contains a transducer, tiny integrated processor, energy source, internal control, and limited space which is used only when Internet access is available to capture data from the environment and send it to the transducers or controllers. The architectural portion of a sensor node is shown in Fig. 9.5. Typically, the sensor nodes extract data with battery support from extreme energy sources, on the other hand, the actuator has higher analytical and computational capabilities. To alter the actions of the physical worlds, it then performs an operation. Although the actuator has more extended battery power support than the sensor nodes, both the actuators and sensor nodes have power sources and bandwidth restrictions. WSN systems are split into two main types for common scenarios, namely monitoring and tracking. Both the public and industry are adopting a broad

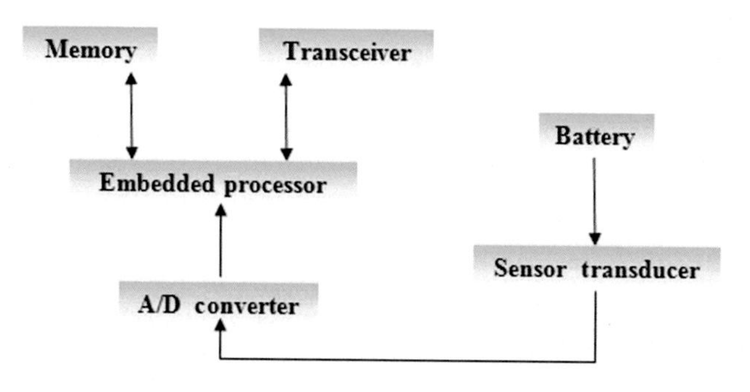

FIGURE 9.5 Structural elements of a sensor node.

selection of scanning and controlling systems. The IoT highly depends on WSNs for sensor operations.

WSN protocol layer: For any kind of applications, sensor nodes are usually deployed spontaneously in an arbitrary manner to create a network with wireless technology. Communication among the sensor nodes and, eventually, the sink node, plays a key role in WSN activities. The MAC protocols and routing are therefore essential to the construction of a topology for a sensor network. The lifespan of the network is highly dependent upon the individual node's energy consumption. Dropouts of nodes and consequent deterioration of network performance are very normal and frequent. Therefore the layering system at the sink node has to be sufficiently responsible for communicating through the Internet to the outside world.

Data aggregation/fusion: In extreme conditions, sensor networks are usually used to track events. Information about the sensor is shared between the sensor nodes and sent for analysis to distributed or centralized networks. Node failures of nodes in a wireless sensor network are often normal phenomena. However, for extended periods, each node keeps the network active due to its self-organizing ability. To increase the lifespan of the network, an efficient data collection system is therefore needed and, simultaneously, security is an important aspect for efficient data transmission at the sink node.

WSN middleware technology: "Cyber infrastructure" combined with a sensor network in a service-oriented architecture can provide a platform for all heterogeneous sensor applications, which can be accessed separately from implementation (Ghose & Das, 2008). For the creation of sensor applications, an alternative middleware system such as "Open Sensor Web Architecture" (Gubbi et al., 2013) is required.

9.3.2.2.2 Communication by radiofrequency identification

Radiofrequency identification (RFID) combines radiofrequency (RF) portions of electromagnetic waves with electromagnetic and electrostatic couplings, originally used to describe a stationary object, animal, or person, etc. The MIT auto-ID center developed (Sarma, Brock, & Ashton, 2000) an inexpensive "standardized transponder" (in 1999) that can be used to identify trillions of objects on the IoT. The creation of RFID and associated technology for retailers to potentially visualize IoT has created a variety of hurdles. RFID has been the main technology for a number of years for developing microchips for wireless data communication, with the technical advancement of embedded communication. The costs as well as standardization were lowered for passive RFID. Today, RFID is used mostly for supply chains, but also to handle library books, factory equipment, clothing products, etc. Physical objects are thus recognized by a tag as with "quick response codes" (QR) or "radiofrequency identification" (RFID). Of their many applications, active RFID tags are mainly used for tracking cargo in port containers (Bonsor & Keener, 2010).

9.3.2.2.3 IP protocol

Each person or network node should have an IP address and use the IP protocol in future Internet situations. By giving IP addresses to all intelligent objects, IPv6 can play a key role. When using the Internet infrastructure and software at any point in time all can be addressed from anywhere. However, there remains no real direction for how IPv6 can be properly classified in order to partition and distribute public IP addresses.

9.3.2.2.4 Internet of Things

Notably, the term IoT was used for "Asynchronous Javascript XML" (Ajax) using http protocol and Web 2.0 technologies. Embedded IoT processors (using Ajax in Web 2.0) require scarce resources compared to traditional Web clients, decreasing the delay in connectivity between the client and server. For example, computer or cell phone browsers and their utilities are usually addressed via URLs and treated with a simple interface. A one-way passive communication system, Web 1.0 (only for reading the content) and a two-way collaborative communication system, that is, Web 2.0, where the users may actively engage by podcasting, tweeting, tagging, social bookmarking, etc. on the web page. Web 3.0, on the other hand, is the definition of a semantic web where all information is processed in a structured way and both machines and humans can perceive it. A common platform provided by Web 3.0 is for data processing and storage of data from various sources using distributed systems, natural language processing, semantic web technologies, machine learning, etc. The latest Web 4.0 vision requires realistic implementation of the IoT. Fig. 9.5 represents the structural elements of a sensor node.

9.3.2.3 *Applications of the Internet of Things*

Though the IoT system has restricted CPU, memory, and power resources, it finds several applications in every area of human life through networking. Fig. 9.6 represents the different applications of IoT which include:

Health care: For two decades now, universal care has been visualized. Doctors may provide patients with remote access in order to reduce hospitalization costs through early diagnosis and treatment.

Camera network: This is the most frequently used application to detect unusual behaviors and widespread usage is used to track unauthorized access.

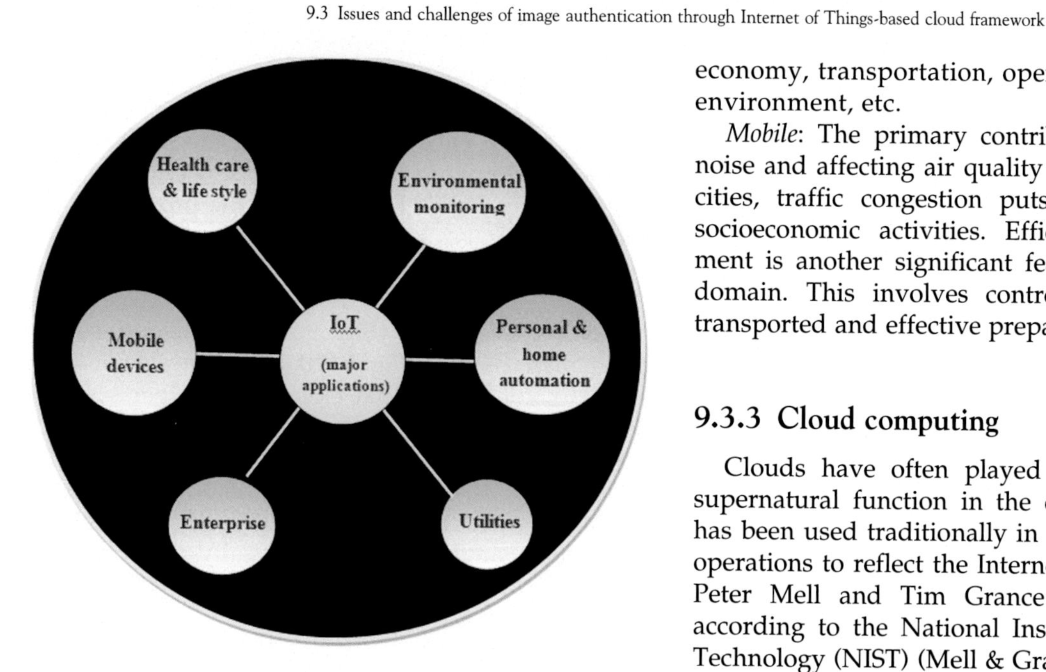

FIGURE 9.6 IoT applications. *IoT*, Internet of Things.

The study of automated behavior and identification of behavior is expected through "video-based IoT" in a few years. The most important technology dealing with the IoT is water networking control and drinking water safety. In order to achieve good quality of work and to avoid accidental modification of data, efficient sensors need to be installed in the correct locations. For instance, it may prevent unintentional mixing of the storm water drains, drinking water, and waste disposal; and it is possible to extend the same methodology to track irrigation in agricultural fields also.

Automation: personal and for the home: The IoT offers a great forum for better control and management of home electronic equipment such as TVs, micro-ovens, refrigerators, AC, etc. This will affect mostly users interested in the IoT in the same fashion as the creation of the Internet.

Utilities: Another feasible IoT technology that is used worldwide is smart metering and smart grids. For instance, effective energy usage is accomplished by installing individual meters in each house and monitoring each connection point inside the building and so altering the way power is used. This information is used to align the load at the city scale within the grid.

Enterprise: A smart environment is one of the more popular IoT applications. The first popular application that keeps a record of the number of tenants inside a building and controls the utilities is environmental monitoring. There are already enough test grounds in operation and more are expected soon which may impact human lives, such as health, economy, transportation, operation, competitiveness, environment, etc.

Mobile: The primary contributor to polluting road noise and affecting air quality is urban traffic. In most cities, traffic congestion puts a substantial cost on socioeconomic activities. Efficient logistics management is another significant feature in the mobile IoT domain. This involves control of the things being transported and effective preparation of transport.

9.3.3 Cloud computing

Clouds have often played a metaphorical almost supernatural function in the computing world. They has been used traditionally in sketching and modeling operations to reflect the Internet in a globalization era. Peter Mell and Tim Grance in the United States, according to the National Institute of Standards and Technology (NIST) (Mell & Grance, 2011) declared that cloud computing is a model for allowing omnipresent, easy, on-demand network access to a common pool of networks, servers, storage, applications, and services configurable through computing resources. Cloud computing helps customers and companies to remove different software without installation and accessing their personal data on all their Internet-accessed devices. Cloud computing includes readily accessible workstations and servers via the Internet (Senthil, Boopal, & Vanathi, 2012). Cloud offers to produce a lot of large-scale research information that is economical, less time-consuming, and presumably easier to compute and store (Menon, Anala, Trupti, & Sood, 2012). These benefits also apply to knowledge of scientific research and the tools of bioinformatics. It provides a web-based variety of demand services such as applications, hardware, server, network, and data storage (Gujar & Korade, 2013). Cloud computing, on the other hand, can be an effective platform for parallel operation of various tools, as it provides on-demand, flexible computing resources (Karlsson et al., 2012).

9.3.3.1 Features of the cloud computing model

A standard collection of various types of cloud resources in the cloud computing environment is involved in virtualization or job-scheduling strategies. Virtualization is a form of logical resource selection, usually the network, hardware, operating system, and other shared resources that are handled by software-based modules that act as physical resources. Software resources are, in particular, referred to as a hypervisor that replicates a collection of resources and enables the running of logical resources (operating system) on a virtual machine separated from the actual physical machines. The NIST definition of cloud computing describes five significant features, as described in the following subsections.

9.3.3.1.1 On-demand self-service

On-demand self-service allows customers to use cloud computing as required without human contact between consumers and service providers. Using the features of on-demand self-service, consumers can arrange various cloud resources as needed. In addition to being safe and attentive to the client, the self-service system must be user-friendly in order to access the various cloud resources and to track the service offerings effectively. The primary benefit of on-demand self-service generating efficiencies for both consumers and providers of cloud services (Mell & Grance, 2011).

9.3.3.1.2 Broad network access

With Internet connections and technologies at high bandwidth being accessible across the network and accessed via a common interface it allows simpler use to diverse customer systems to make cloud computing a successful substitute to the in-house data center. One of cloud computing's key economic benefits is reducing the expense of fast broadband transmission networks to the cloud offers access to a greater variety of mutual resources to ensure effective deployment of resources. The three-tiered configuration, on the other hand, is used by numerous organizations to provide wide-area networks with cloud computer access, printers, networking devices like mobile phones, and personal digital assistant (PDAs).

9.3.3.1.3 Resource pooling

Using a multitenant model, computer service providers are pooled to support multiple customers, with various physical and virtual resources dynamically distributed and reassigned according to customer demand. It is location independent in the sense that the user generally has little power or knowledge of the exact position of the services provided, but may assess a position at a higher level of abstraction (i.e., data center, state, or region).

9.3.3.1.4 Rapid elasticity

This is the ability to increase or decrease resource allocation to satisfy the specifications of cloud computing's self-service capabilities easily and efficiently. Capacity can be distributed and activated elastically, under certain cases automatically, to measure outward and inward proportions of demand quickly. The supply potential still seems limitless for the consumer and can be accessed at any time in any quantity.

9.3.3.1.5 Measured service

Cloud systems automatically monitor and optimize resource usage by using a metering mechanism at an abstract level unique to the specific service. To provide accountability for both clients and the provider of the cloud service used, resource usage can be tracked, managed, and recorded.

Fig. 9.7 illustrates the relationships between various delivery models (Fig. 9.7A) and cloud service deployment models (Fig. 9.7B). Cloud implementation methodologies show that cloud environments enable cloud delivery models to be made accessible to cloud clients provisioned by cloud providers. In the NIST presentation, the implementation models where the public, private, community, hybrid, and virtual private cloud can be deployed partially or wholly are summarized.

9.3.4 Different cloud management services

Fig. 9.7A represents the default cloud service models. In general, the models of cloud computing operation are:

Software as a service (SaaS): This model, along with any appropriate software, operating system, hardware, and network resources, delivers a fully prepared application.

Platform as a service (PaaS): Hardware and network resources along with operating system are supported by this model, while the user can configure or build their own software applications.

Infrastructure as a service (IaaS): Only the hardware and network resources are supported by this model, and the user produces or builds his or her own system software and applications. The various cloud deployment models are illustrated in Fig. 9.7B. Traditionally, cloud services are offered via private, public, community, or hybrid clouds.

Public cloud: Managed and operated by a cloud service provider, the public cloud offers Internet-based services (like email, online image storage services, communal networking sites, etc.) publicly.

Private cloud: The cloud platform is controlled and deeply committed to a specific company in a private cloud and is directed by the company or a mediator.

Community cloud: Here, for the provision for sharing information between various organizations and resources is not only available to those organizations, the infrastructure may be managed and controlled by the organizations themselves or by a cloud service provider.

Hybrid cloud: This is a combination of two or more private, public, or community clouds that remain as single units but are linked together and provide the

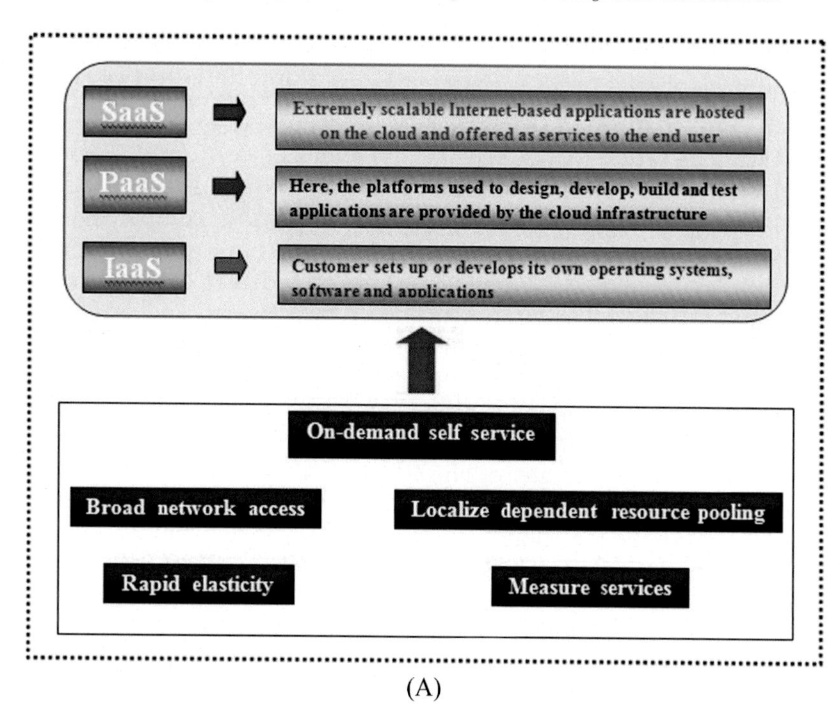

(A)

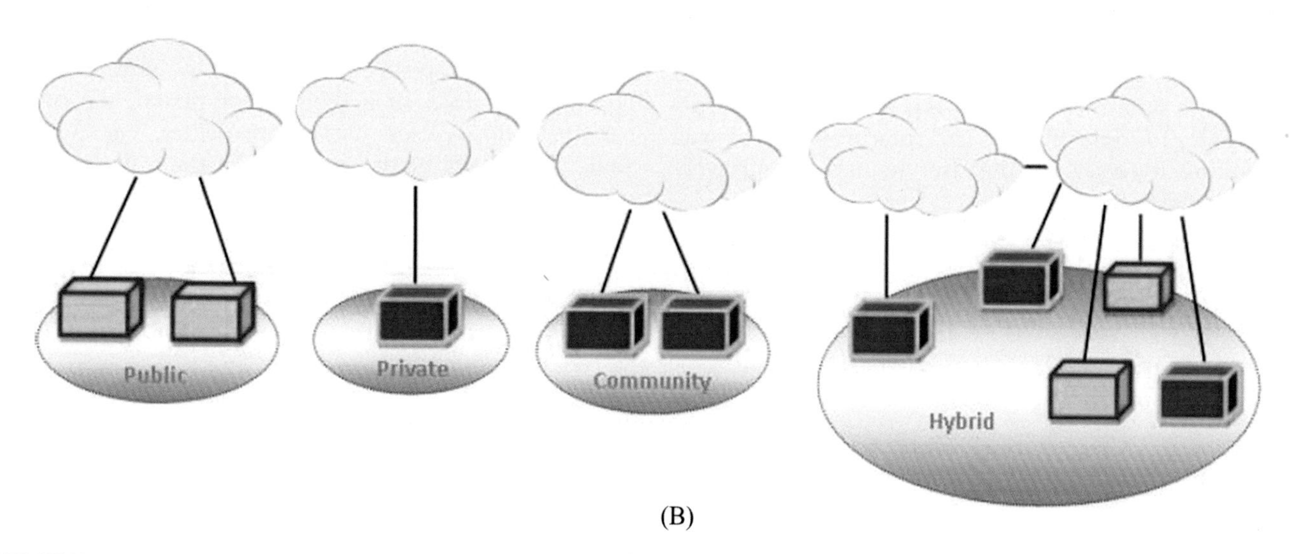

(B)

FIGURE 9.7 (A) Cloud delivery models. (B) Cloud deployment models.

benefits of scalability, reliability, quick response, and potential cost savings of public cloud storage and with the security and complete control of private cloud storage.

Based on these basic service models, different cloud management services have been presented (Biswas & Sarddar, 2018; Sarddar, Biswas, & Sen, 2017; Biswas & Sarddar, 2019; Biswas, Sarddar, & Chakraborty, 2020), where all the service models are self-regulatory models and they work as a third party between the consumers and providers of cloud services. The proposed service models (Biswas et al., 2020; Sarddar et al., 2017; Biswas & Sarddar, 2018, 2019) provide a new computing environment including "Verification as a Service" (Biswas & Sarddar, 2018), "Safety as a Service" (Sarddar et al., 2017), "Power Management as a Service" (Biswas & Sarddar, 2019), and "Environmental Viability as a Service" (Biswas et al., 2020) which not only guarantees data accountability and authentication, but also data protection, as well as lower carbon emissions with minimum power consumption, also making a balance between all clients and the CSP since user pays for their usage. Therefore safeguards are needed to avoid any unfairness.

9.3.5 Cloud-enabled Internet of Things

The term "cloud computing" refers a form of computing that depends on the sharing of computer resources to manage applications rather than a private server or system. As an Internet analogy, the phrase "cloud computing" identifies Internet-based commuting which involves various resources such as servers, storage, software, etc. It can be defined as the centralized storage of a distributed virtualized environment where a wide range of remote servers allow computer services and resources to be accessed online. Cloud computing services such as SaaS, PaaS, or IaaS can be described in three ways, where cloud computing deployment models can be classified as private, public, community or hybrid clouds that have already been addressed earlier. In order to make the IoT, cloud computing has many different perspectives. Fig. 9.8 presents the cloud-enabled IoT framework.

Fulfilling the growing demand for real-time implementations and successful IoT data transmission is the toughest problem for cloud technology. However, the latest paradigm that aims to provide satisfactory service through virtualized technologies-based next-generation data centers is emerging, and this platform serves as a data receiver from the widespread sensors as a device for data analysis and interpretation, as well as making it easier for the user to understand web-based visualization.

9.4 Proposed facial recognition system implementation for theft handling

City-Centre (Cloud Data Centre) is a new concept that can keep track of all cars in a city. Different car manufacturing companies may adopt the proposed mechanism for primary-level security of their cars. Once the driver of a car is verified only then will the lock be activated and driver able to use the key to start the car. Image comparison is required for verification of the driver. Once an owner purchases a car, he/she may add many driver information by storing their face information in the City-Centre. Primarily, a camera is installed in the steering column of the car, with the person sitting in the driver seat having his/her photo captured at that time. If the driver is a person who is previously unidentified, then they need to be introduced by the owner and a photo of that person then will be stored in the City-Centre. Otherwise it will be compared with all existing photos present in the server by matching the unique car number. The City-Centre will also help the owner or the investigating agencies detect any unauthorized access to the car and assist in identifying any person attempting to gain unauthorized access. Even if a theft is completed, the owner can track its location using City-Centre. Fig. 9.9 presents the details of the checking of the authentication of a driver by face detection analysis.

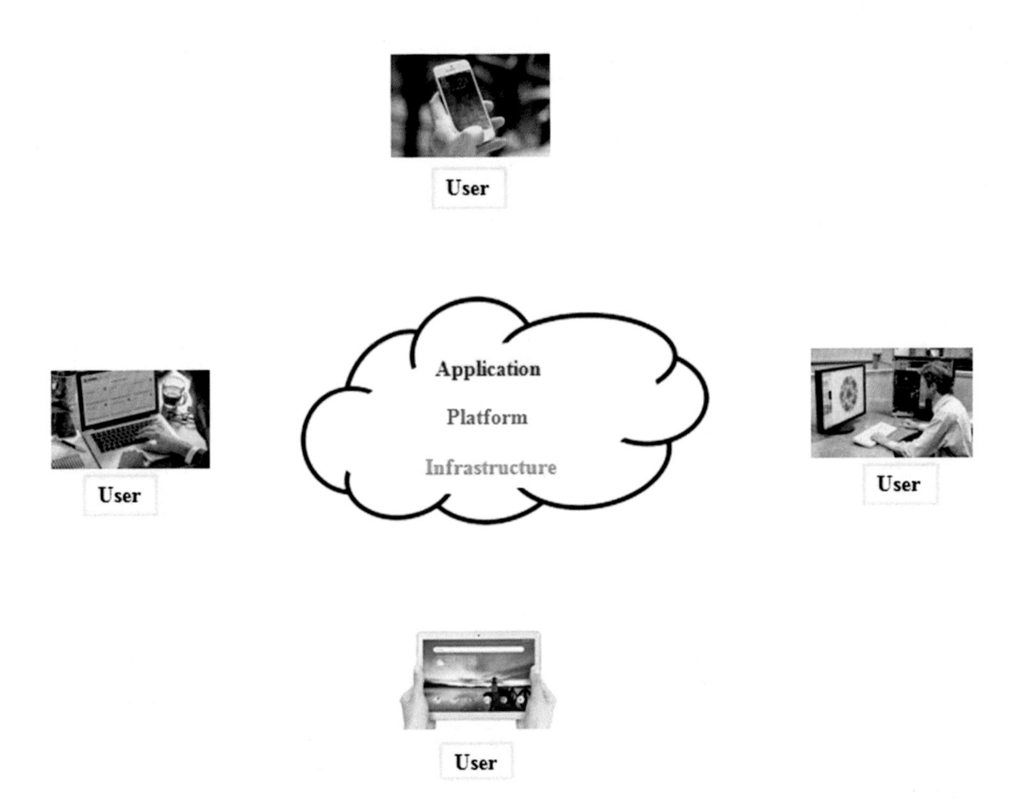

FIGURE 9.8 Cloud-enabled IoT framework. *IoT*, Internet of Things.

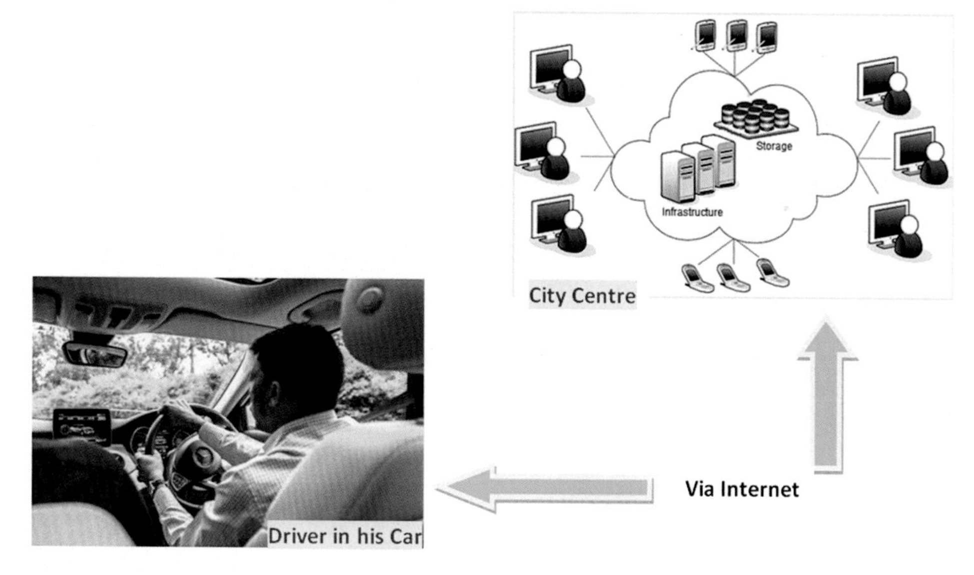

FIGURE 9.9 Authentication check of a driver.

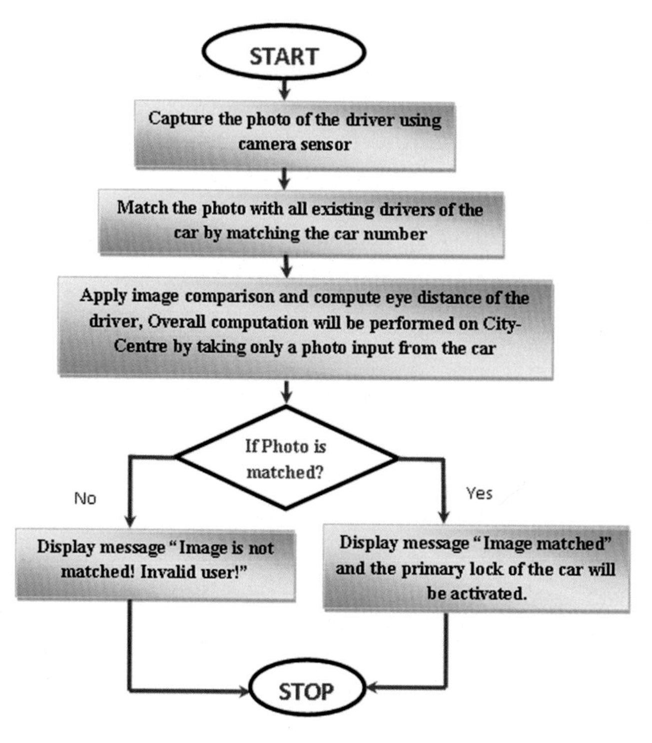

FIGURE 9.10 Flow chart of the algorithm.

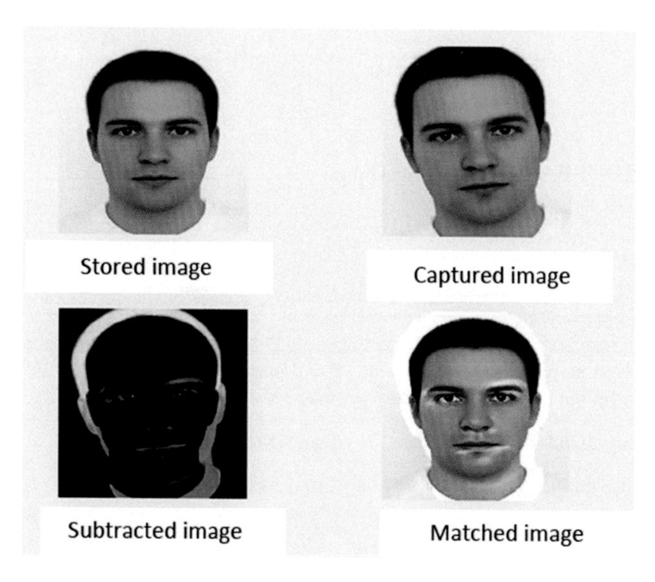

FIGURE 9.11 Image comparison.

9.4.1 Algorithm

1. The camera in the car's steering column captures a picture of the driver.
2. For all cars in a city, find the particular car from the car database by matching the car number using the cloud network (City-Centre).
3. Check all existing drivers, match the driver's photo with all existing photos enrolled for the particular car.
4. Image subtraction will be performed between the image captured and all existing images.
5. Detect parts of the face and eyes of the driver by pattern matching and store information in the server of the City-Centre. Compute the distance between the centers of the eyes, eye pairs, eye angle, and eye shapes of the driver to perform image matching.
6. If the subtraction result and eye distance are equal to a specified threshold *t*,
   a. Display message: "Image matched" and the primary lock of the car will be activated.

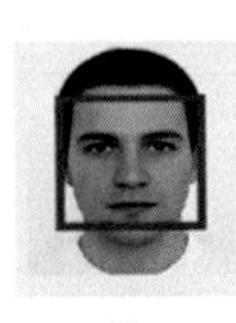
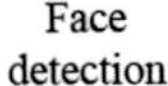

FIGURE 9.12 Face, mouth, nose, and eye detection.

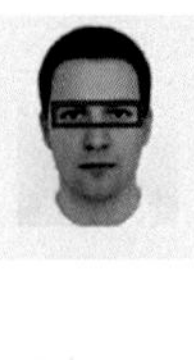

FIGURE 9.13 Image matching.

TABLE 9.2 Comparative eye distance analysis of the driver of the car.

Eye distance (in cm) in case of an image match	Eye distance (in cm) in case of an image not matching
Case 1:20.8806	Case 1:20.8806
Case 2:21.0238	Case 2:58.0775
Case 1 denotes the eye distance of the normal image	
Case 2 denotes the eye distance of a distorted or different image	

7. Else
   a. Display message: "Image is not matched! Invalid user!" and inform the owner of the car about the theft by sending a message to the owner's phone.
8. End

9.4.2 Flow chart

A flow chart of the algorithm is presented in Fig. 9.10.

9.4.3 Simulation result

Simulation work is done using MATLAB 2013a to compare images by pattern matching and also to compute the eye distance of the image of the driver of a car. An image comparison is shown in Fig. 9.11.

Face detection, parts of detected face, and eye detection are shown in Fig. 9.12 for computation purposes and pattern matching.

Computation of eye distance and matching (Fig. 9.13) is done using MATLAB.

Comparative analysis of the eye distance of the car driver is shown in Table 9.2.

9.5 Conclusion

Human face detection can be achieved using image processing. It can be used in theft handling of public or private vehicles. It is a Smart City-based IoT framework to prevent vehicle theft. The proposed work is a less expensive but secure approach for producing more secure cars. The primary-level security is achieved using this technique, whereas the secondary-level security will be the car key. The car production company can adopt the proposed mechanism so that the owners of cars can feel more comfortable about their car security. Cloud computing will help secure the framework for the safety of public vehicles and also help in Smart City development.

References

Amit, Y., Geman, D., & Jedynak, B. (1998). Efficient focusing and face detection. In H. Wechsler, P. J. Phillips, V. Bruce, F. Fogelman-Soulie, & T. S. Huang (Eds.), *Face recognition: From theory to applications* (163) pp. 124–156.

Barnouti, N. H., Mahmood, S. S., & Matti, W. E. (2016). Face recognition: A literature review. *International Journal of Applied Information Systems*, 11(4), ISSN: 2249-0868. <www.ijais.org>.

Beymer, D. & Poggio, T. (1995) Face recognition from one example view, A.I. Memo No. 1536, C.B.C.L. Paper No. 121. MIT.

Biswas, H., & Sarddar, D. (2018). Verification as a service (VaaS): A trusted multipurpose service for accounting, billing verification and approval of consumed resources at low computational overhead to enhance the cloud usability. *International Journal of Applied Engineering Research*, *13*(19), 14402–14410, ISSN 0973-4562. Available from https://doi.org/10.37622/IJAER/13.9.2018.14402-14410.

Biswas, H., & Sarddar, D. (2019). Power management as a service (PMaas) – An energy saving service by —Auto-Fit VM placement‖ algorithm in cloud computing for maximum resource utilization at minimum energy consumption without live-migrating the virtual machines by using the concept of virtual-servers. *International Journal of Innovative Technology and Exploring Engineering*, *9*(2), ISSN: 2278-3075.

Biswas, H., Sarddar, D., & Chakraborty, U. (2020). Environmental viability as a service (EVaas) – An eco-friendly cloud service for optimum use of resources at low energy consumption with less carbon emission. *International Journal of Recent Technology and Engineering*, *8*(6), 5193–5202, ISSN: 2277-3878.

Bonsor, K. & Keener, C. (2010). *How stuff works/how RFID works*. Retrieved from: http://electronics.howstuffworks.com/gadgets/high-tech-gadgets/rfid.htm.

Bowyer, K. W., Chang, K., Flynn, P. J., & Chen, X. (2012). Face recognition using 2-D, 3-D and infrared: Is it multimodal better than multisampling. *Proceedings of the IEEE, 94*(11).

Brunelli, R., & Poggio, T. (1993). Face recognition: Features versus templates. *IEEE Transactions on Pattern Analysis and Machine Intelligence, 15*(10), 1042–1052.

Dalal. N. & Trigg's N. (2005). Histograms of oriented gradients for human detection. In *Proceedings/CVPR* (886–893), Washington, DC.

Ghose, A., & Das, S. K. (2008). Coverage and connectivity issues in wireless sensor networks: A survey. *Pervasive and Mobile Computing, 4*(2008), 303–334.

Goldstein, A. J., Harmon, L. D., & Lesk, A. B. (1971). Identification of human faces. *Proceedings of the IEEE, 59*, 748–760.

Gong, S., McKenna, S. J., & Psarrou, A. (2000). *Dynamic vision: From images to face recognition*. Imperial College Press and World Scientific Publishing.

Gonzalez Martinez, D., Gonzalez Castano, F. J., Argones Rua, E., Alba Castro, J. L., & Rodriguez Silva, D. A. (2011). Secure crypto-biometric system for cloud computing. In *Proceedings of international workshop securing services on the cloud* (pp. 38–45). IWSSC.

Gubbi, J., Buyya, R., Marusic, S., & Palaniswani, M. (2013). Internet of Things (IoT): A vision, architectural elements and future directions. *Future Generation Computer Systems, 29*(7), 1645–1660. Available from https://doi.org/10.1016/j.future.2013.01.010.

Gujar, S. & Korade. (2013). STEP-2 user authentication for cloud computing. *International Journal of Engineering and Innovative Technology*.

Hsu, R. L., Abdel-Mottaleb, M., & Jain, A. K. (2002). Face detection in color images. *IEEE Transactions on Pattern Analysis and Machine Intelligence, 24*(5), 696–707.

International Telecommunications Union. (2005). ITU Internet Reports *The Internet of Things executive summary*. Geneva: Author.

Jain, A. K., Bolle, R., & Pankanti, S. (Eds.), (1999). *Biometrics: Personal identification in networked society*. Springer. Available from http://doi.org/10.1007/b117227.

Jain, A. K., Flynn, P., & Ross, A. A. (2007). *Handbook of biometrics*. Springer.

Jain, R., & Karthik. (2008). *Introduction to biometrics*. Springer.

Karlsson, J., Torreño, O., Ramet, D., Klambauer, G., Cano, M., & Trelles, O. (2012). Enabling large-scale bioinformatics data analysis with cloud computing. In *Proceedings of 10th IEEE international symposium on parallel and distributed processing with applications (ISPA)* (pp. 640–645). IEEE. Available from https://doi.org/10.1109/ISPA.2012.95

Khitrov, M. (2013). Talking passwords: Voice biometrics for data access and security. *Biometric Technology Today* (2), 9–11.

Mell, P. & Grance, T. (2011). *The NIST definition of cloud computing*. NIST.

Menon, K., Anala, K., Trupti, S. D. G., & Sood, N. (2012). Cloud computing: Applications in biological research and future prospects. In *Proceedings of cloud computing technologies, applications and management (ICCCTAM)* (pp. 102–107). ICCCTAM.

Mercy Rani, A., & Durgadevi, R. (2017). Image processing techniques to recognize facial emotions. *International Journal of Engineering and Advanced Technology, 6*(6), ISSN: 2249 – 8958.

Sarddar, D., Biswas, H., & Sen, P. (2017). Safety as a service (SFaaS) model - The new invention in cloud computing to establish a secure logical communication channel between data owner and the cloud service provider before storing, retrieving or accessing any data in the cloud. *International Journal of Grid and Distributed Computing, 10*(10), 1–20, ISSN 2005-4262.

Sarma, S., Brock, D. L., & Ashton, K. (2000). *The networked physical world*. TRMIT-AUTOIDWH-001. MIT Auto-ID Center.

Senthil, P., Boopal, N., & Vanathi, R. (2012). Improving the security of cloud computing using trusted computing technology. *International Journal of Modern Engineering Research, 2*(1), 320–325.

Tian, Y., T. Kanade, & J. F. Cohn."Facial expression recognition. In *Handbook of face recognition* (pp. 487–519). Springer London, 2011.

Turk M. & Pentland A. (1991). Face recognition using Eigenfaces. In *Proceedings of IEEE conference on computer vision and pattern recognition* (pp. 586–591), Maui, Hawaii.

Wayman, J. L. (1996). Technical testing and evaluation of biometric identification devices. *Biometrics*, 345–368.

Wayman, J. L. (2001). Fundamentals of biometric authentication technologies. *International Journal of Image and Graphics, 1*(01), 93–113. Available from https://doi.org/10.1142/S0219467801000086.

Weaver, A. C. (2006). Biometric authentication. *Computer, 39*(2), 96–97. Available from https://doi.org/10.1109/MC.2006.47.

Wiskott, L., Fellous, M., Krger, N., & Malsburg, C. (1997). Face recognition by elastic bunch graph matching. *IEEE Transactions on Pattern Analysis and Machine Intelligence, 19*, 775–779.

Yang, G., & Huang, T. S. (1994). Human face detection in complex background. *Pattern Recognition, 27*(1), 53–63.

Yang, M. H., & Ahuja, N. (2002). Detecting faces in images: A survey. *IEEE Transactions on Pattern Analysis and Machine Intelligence, 24*(1).

Yang, J., Xiong, N., Vasilakos, A. V., Fang, Z., Park, D., Xu, X., et al. (2011). A fingerprint recognition scheme based on assembling invariant moments for cloud computing communications. *IEEE Systems Journal, 5*(4), 574–583. Available from https://doi.org/10.1109/JSYST.2011.2165600.

Yinzhong, T., Zhixue, D., & Jianwei, H. (2010). Research and Implementation of face recognition algorithm based on PCA. *Inner Mongolia Science &Technology and Economy, 6*, 56–57.

Zhang B. C. & Zhang Z. (2010). A *survey of recent advances in face detection*. Technical report, Microsoft Research.

Zhang, W., Shan, S., Gao, W., Chen, X., & Zhang, H. (2005) Local gabor binary pattern histogram sequence (LGBPHS): A novel non-statistical model for face representation and recognition. In *ICCV*.

CHAPTER

10

Novel detection of cancerous cells through an image segmentation approach using principal component analysis

Joy Bhattacharjee[1], *Soumen Santra*[2] *and Arpan Deyasi*[3]

[1]Department of Electronic Science, Acharya Prafulla Chandra College, New Barrackpore, India [2]Department of Computer Application, Techno International Newtown, Kolkata, India [3]Department of Electronics and Communication Engineering, RCC Institute of Information Technology, Kolkata, India

10.1 Introduction

One of the greatest challenging and unpredictable diseases in the 20th and also in the 21st century is cancer, for which medical science still has little success, as is evident from the latest research articles (Benjamin, 2014; Biemar & Foti, 2013) and reports. Since the treatment of cancerous patients crucially depends on the diagnosis, and thereafter, analysis of the reports, researchers have centered their focus on this very specific subject; which ultimately helps medical practitioners to make the correct decisions at critical times. From here the crucial role of "image processing" has grown, and several ground-breaking reports have been released in the last decade (Jain, Jagtap, & Pise, 2015; Win et al., 2018; Wójcicka, Jędrusik, Stolarz, Kubina, & Wróbel, 2014) in this very specific subject area. However, some hidden features remain under investigation, and therefore post-image processing is critical to extract information from hidden parts (Kumar, Venkatalakshmi, & Karthikeyan, 2019). The analysis gains further importance for brain cancer detection (Nandi, 2015; Sazzad, Ahmmed, Ul-hoque, & Rahman, 2019), where inner features of X-ray or MRI images must be extracted, otherwise further analysis of the image is not possible for the medical practitioners to give accurate diagnosis and treatment of the patient.

The carcinogenic portion of the human body is a collection of malignant and benign cells, where an accurate diagnosis is necessary to avoid contamination of malignant cells into benign areas. Since malignancy enhances in terms of the exponential rate through the body, for rapid proper treatment it is most important to separate malignant and benign portions of cancerous segments. If the malignant portion is properly identified, then the segmented image of it can be converted into knowledge data from which features of image data are acquired and the prediction of contamination of disease can be assessed (Biji, Selvathi, & Panicker, 2011; Dimililer & Ilhan, 2016; Reddy, Dheeraj, Kiran, & Bhavana, 2018). This chapter is an effort to solve this prolonged problem using a machine learning (ML) technique.

ML is a learning process where machines or a model can learn from their previous experiences, just like humans (Simeone & Very, 2018). They learn from the data from their past processing techniques and build a prediction model. ML enables data to be predicted when a new set is introduced. The accuracy of prediction depends upon the size of the input matrix, and consequently, hidden features are better extracted based on the algorithm introduced (Kourou, Exarchos, Exarchos, Karamouzis, & Fotiadis, 2015). Learning can be supervised (Wu & Zhao, 2017), unsupervised (Sadoddin & Ghorbani, 2007), or reinforced (Samsuden, Diah, & Rahman, 2019), depending on the requirement. The generated model can detect features, where labels are used to train the data; here the machine knows the features of the object and the labels associated with those features. This is applicable for supervised learning. The unsupervised learning method uses unlabeled data to train the model. Based on the given data set the machine can predict those data that lie within each

Recent Trends in Computational Intelligence Enabled Research.
DOI: https://doi.org/10.1016/B978-0-12-822844-9.00035-9

category. Feedback is sometimes utilized to predict the correct output (Nasim, Rajput, & Haider, 2017). Positive feedback leads to correct output, whereas negative feedback leads to retraining of the model. In this ML method, the machine learns the model based upon its experience, which can be noted as errors. Sometimes there is a relationship between a minor dependent variable with a major independent variable (Kumar & Chong, 2018), and the latter one is hidden from the image.

10.1.1 Principal component analysis

Deep learning (DL) is a part of ML. ML inspired by the structure of the human brain which actually helps us for tracing purpose (Işın, Direkoğlu, & Şah, 2016). DL helps to extract the features of the data, which are fed into the input of the machine based on the ML method. This is an artificial neural network (Kakde et al., 2019), which can work without any human intervention, provided a very large data set is fed into the input. Analytical computation is also possible by DL when a statistical tool (SL) is incorporated. Principal component analysis (PCA) is one such technique where a SL is used to determine the probability of a selection of segmented images (Dambreville, Rathi, & Tannenbaum, 2006; Han, Feng, & Baciu, 2013; Kamencay, Jelšovka, & Zachariasova, 2011). It is a nonparametric variable reduction technique for data dependency. Maximum probability of the target image can be detected as cancerous, and not as segmented image. A set of interdependent variables can be converted into a lower number of uncorrelated variables using PCA, and these variables are linear combinations of the original variables.

10.1.2 Objective of the work

In this chapter, we have generated segmented images from the original RGB images, and a comparison is carried out between all the segmented ones. Since all the segmented images are originated from a single predicted cancerous image, a comparison is performed using the PCA method. Here two brain MRIs and two breast mammogram images are taken as input. By changing the radius of the circle multiple times, an equal number of segmented images for each input image is created. Next the image assessment parameters are calculated for each segmented image. These image assessment parameter matrices are taken as input for the PCA operation. Thereafter, the probability of being cancerous for each segmented image is calculated. By comparing those probabilities we determine which segmented image is cancerous amongst them all. For probability calculations we use values such as principal component coefficient, principal component score, and eigenvalue matrix. Here we use the centered data, which are obtained by the multiplication of principal component coefficient and principal component score data. Then we calculate the mean of the multiplicities matrix, which is the probability of selection of each of the observations, where observation means the segmented image order. Then we identify the segmented image which has the highest probability of selection, meaning that the cancerous portions covered by that image are the most accurate.

10.2 Algorithm for analysis

10.2.1 Binarized masked segmentation image

In order to obtain a segmented image from an RGB image, we have made the following algorithm, as depicted in Fig. 10.1. In this method, after initial conversion into a grayscale image, a circle of the radius is initialized along with the total number of horizontal and vertical circles. Phase-wise contour-based segmentation is carried out, and finally the masked segmented image is generated in a binary format.

For assessing the image, we first considered the confusion matrix, which is obtained through a K-means algorithm, and thereafter, PCA is applied for evaluation of the component coefficient, component score, eigenvalue matrix, etc.

10.2.2 Confusion matrix

A confusion matrix is a collection of predicted and actual classification information, which is carried out in a particular system. Data obtained for such a system are evaluated for the performance analysis. While going through predictive analysis, a confusion square matrix is created that contains positive and negative rates (both true and false). Corresponding rates for all those cases are individually computed. Also, the accuracy, sensitivity, specificity, and null error rate are evaluated from the positive and negative rates. The figure of merit is calculated by mean square error (MSE) and peak signal-to-noise ratio (PSNR).

10.2.3 Image assessment using PCA

PCA is a set of bases from views where all dimensions are orthogonal to each other. These dimensions are ranked as per the variance. Covariance matrix, which is purely the input data matrix, provides output data in the form of principal component coefficient, principal component score, principal component variance, T-squared value, etc. The centered indicator and economy indicators support the PCA operation, and are also related to the covariance matrix.

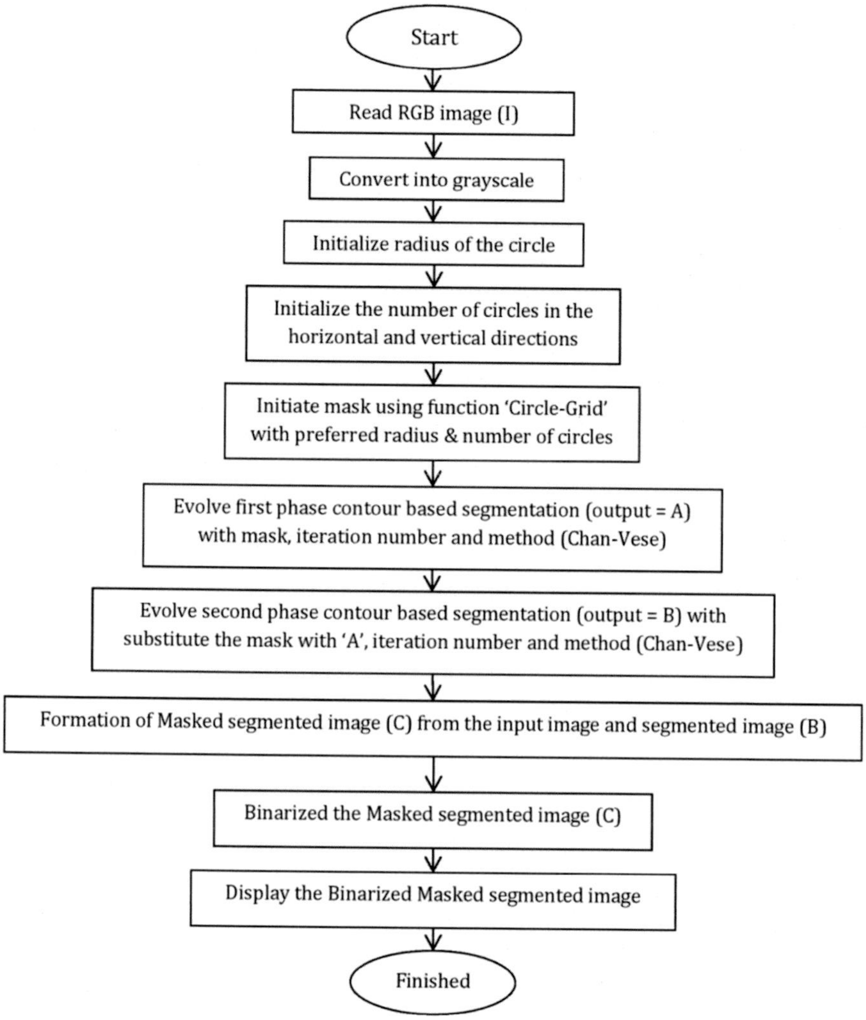

Start

Read RGB image (I)

Convert into grayscale

Initialize radius of the circle

Initialize the number of circles in the horizontal and vertical directions

Initiate mask using function 'Circle-Grid' with preferred radius & number of circles

Evolve first phase contour based segmentation (output = A) with mask, iteration number and method (Chan-Vese)

Evolve second phase contour based segmentation (output = B) with substitute the mask with 'A', iteration number and method (Chan-Vese)

Formation of Masked segmented image (C) from the input image and segmented image (B)

Binarized the Masked segmented image (C)

Display the Binarized Masked segmented image

Finished

FIGURE 10.1 Flow diagram for masked segmented image formation from an RGB image.

10.2.4 Selection of highest probability

Fig. 10.2 depicts a flow diagram which reveals how the highest probability of any arbitrary observation can be determined using PCA. After obtaining the segmented image, image assessment parameters are substituted, and principal component coefficients are calculated. After obtaining the eigenvalue of input data matrix, the mean is calculated from the total percentage variance for each component. Thereafter, the centered value matrix is calculated, and iteration is carried out between the mean and matrix size in order to compute the highest probability among all the observations.

10.3 Methodology

First, the RGB image is read and converted into grayscale using an appropriate function, as described in Fig. 10.1. Conversion takes place by eliminating the hue and saturation information while retaining the luminance. In the present segmentation process, the approach is based on the grid of circles. At first the radius of circles is initialized (let *radius* = 1). Then the circles in the x and y directions are initialized (as it is a 2D image), and termed as n_x and n_y, respectively. An illustration for $n_x = n_y = 4$ is given in Fig. 10.3.

Then segmentation is carried out using a function called "active contour." This function segments the image into the foreground and background using an active contour. Segmentation is carried out of the two-dimensional binary input image into two regions, the object and the other is the rest background region using this function called "active contour segmentation" with the binary output image of the same size as the input image.

The image segmentation is done by evolving the active contour for a maximum of N iterations. Here $N = 100$ is chosen by default. Higher values of N may be needed for a better segmentation process if the output segmented image does not satisfy the desired output image. There are many active contour methods used for segmentation. Among these, the Chan-Vese method is chosen as it may not segment all objects in

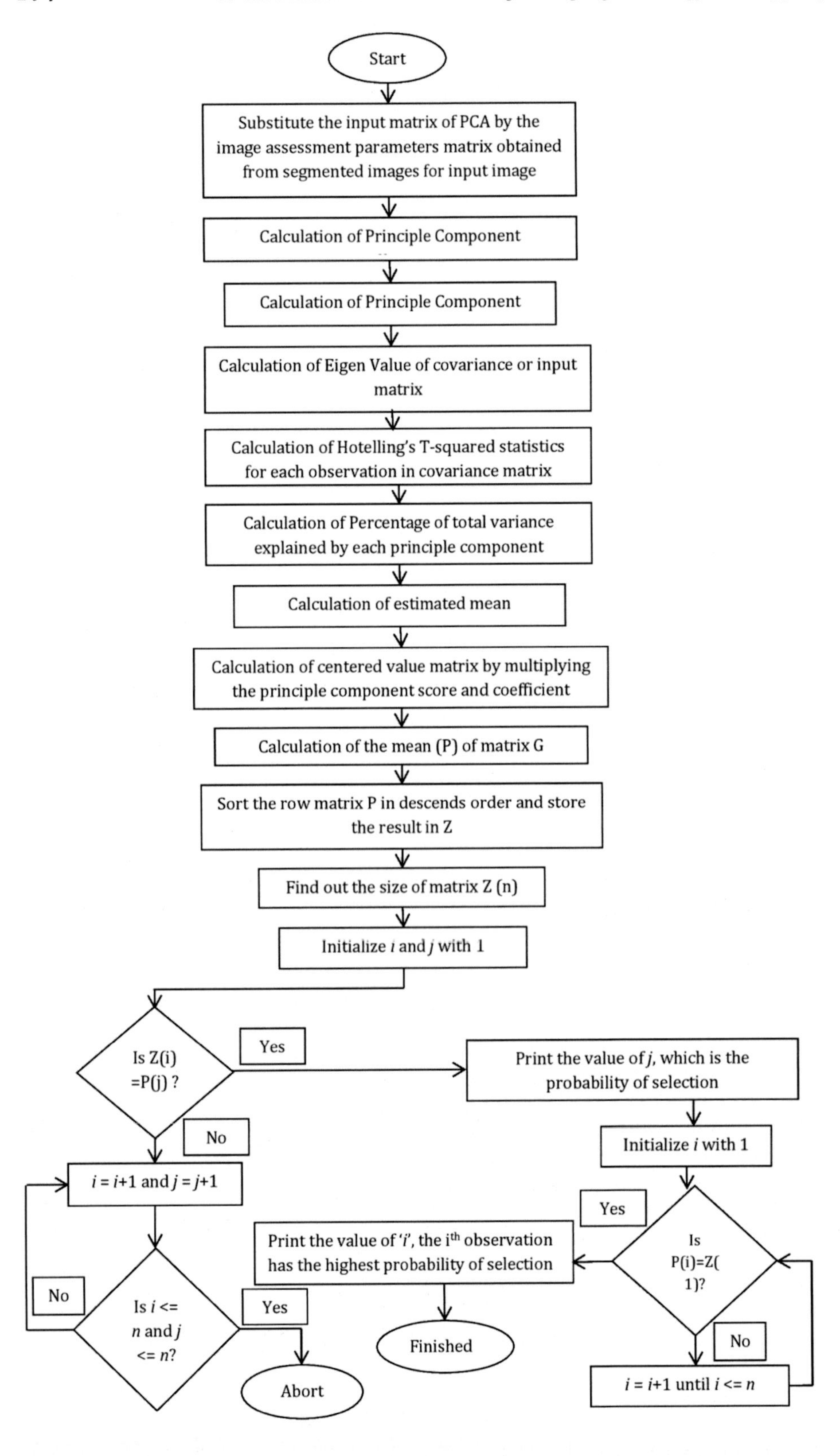

FIGURE 10.2 Highest probability calculation for any arbitrary observation.

the image, if the various object regions have significantly different grayscale intensities present.

Two-stage segmentation is carried out using the function active contour; the output of the first segmentation is the mask input in the next segmentation process. Next the masked image is formed from the segmented image. After binarization of the masked image, the segmented image of the input image is obtained. Gradually, the

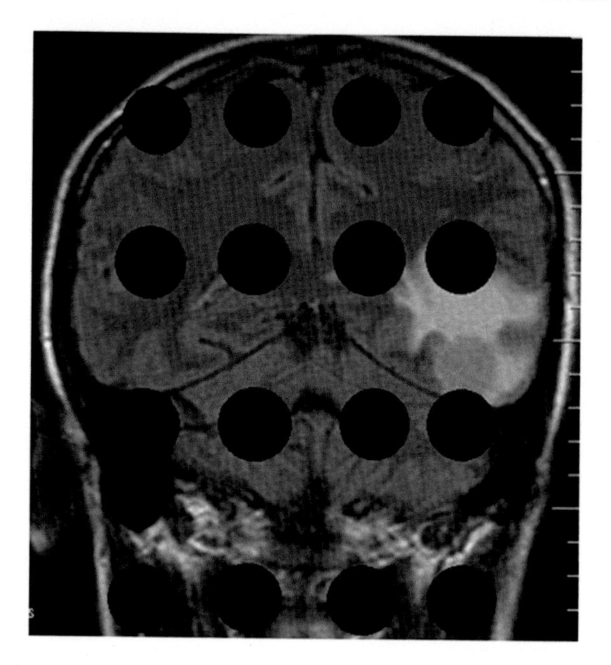

FIGURE 10.3 2D image with virtual grid circles.

radius of the circle is increased, keeping the number of circles in the vertical and horizontal position the same in every case. With an increase in the circle radius with a number in vertical and horizontal positions, the segmented portions (segmented area) from the input image are increased linearly. In this context, it may be mentioned that the objective of the work is to select a single segmented image from multiple images which have the highest probability of covering the most cancerous area. For this purpose, the following steps are taken:

1. Comparison among several segmented images, that is, the segmented images contain different portions of cancerous cells, originated from a single predicted cancerous image;
2. Comparison is done using the PCA method, which is basically a statistical ML algorithm.
3. Maybe it is the first report as per the best of knowledge of authors where cancerous cells are detected based on the probability of selection.

For probability calculation, principal component coefficient, principal component score, eigenvalue matrix, etc. are used. Here centered data are considered, which are obtained by multiplication of the principal component coefficient and principal component score data. After that, the mean of the multiplicity matrix is obtained, which is the probability of selection of each of the observations, where observation means the segmented image order. Finally, the segmented image is identified which has the highest probability of selection, meaning that the cancerous portions covered by that image are the most accurate. Fig. 10.4 contains a flowchart to describe the process.

10.4 Results and discussions

We consider two brain MRI and two breast mammogram images of suspected cancer. We discover 21 image assessment parameters corresponding to every segmented image by changing the radius of the initial circle. All image assessment parameters are given in tabular form.

10.4.1 Detection of cancerous cell from brain MRI

First we start with one brain MRI image (By © NevitDilmen), as shown in Fig. 10.5.

Corresponding segmented images with different radii are shown in:

1. Segmented image of brain MRI (Fig. 10.5) with radius 1 unit shown in Fig. 10.6.
2. Segmented image of brain MRI (Fig. 10.5) with radius 8 units shown in Fig. 10.7.
3. Segmented image of brain MRI (Fig. 10.5) with radius 15 units shown in Fig. 10.8.
4. Segmented image of brain MRI (Fig. 10.5) with radius 22 units shown in Fig. 10.9.
5. Segmented image of brain MRI (Fig. 10.5) with radius 30 units shown in Fig. 10.10.
6. Segmented image of brain MRI (Fig. 10.5) with radius 40 units shown in Fig. 10.11.

Comparisons of all segmented images of the brain MRI with different radii with the original image with respect to 21 image assessment parameters are shown in Table 10.1.

If we substitute the image assessment parameter matrix for six segmented images with the covariance matrix of PCA, then the principal component parameter values are tabulated in sequence:

1. The principal component coefficient is shown in Table 10.2.
2. The principal component score is shown in Table 10.3.
3. The eigenvalue obtained from the PCA calculation is shown in Table 10.4.
4. The percentage of total variance of each segmented image is shown in Table 10.5.
5. The centered value obtained from the PCA calculation is shown in Table 10.6.
6. The probability of selection of each segmented image is shown in Table 10.7.
7. The recalculated probability of the selection of each segmented image is shown in Table 10.8.

The coefficient matrix is shown in the Table 10.2; it is clear that the square matrix has the size of the input

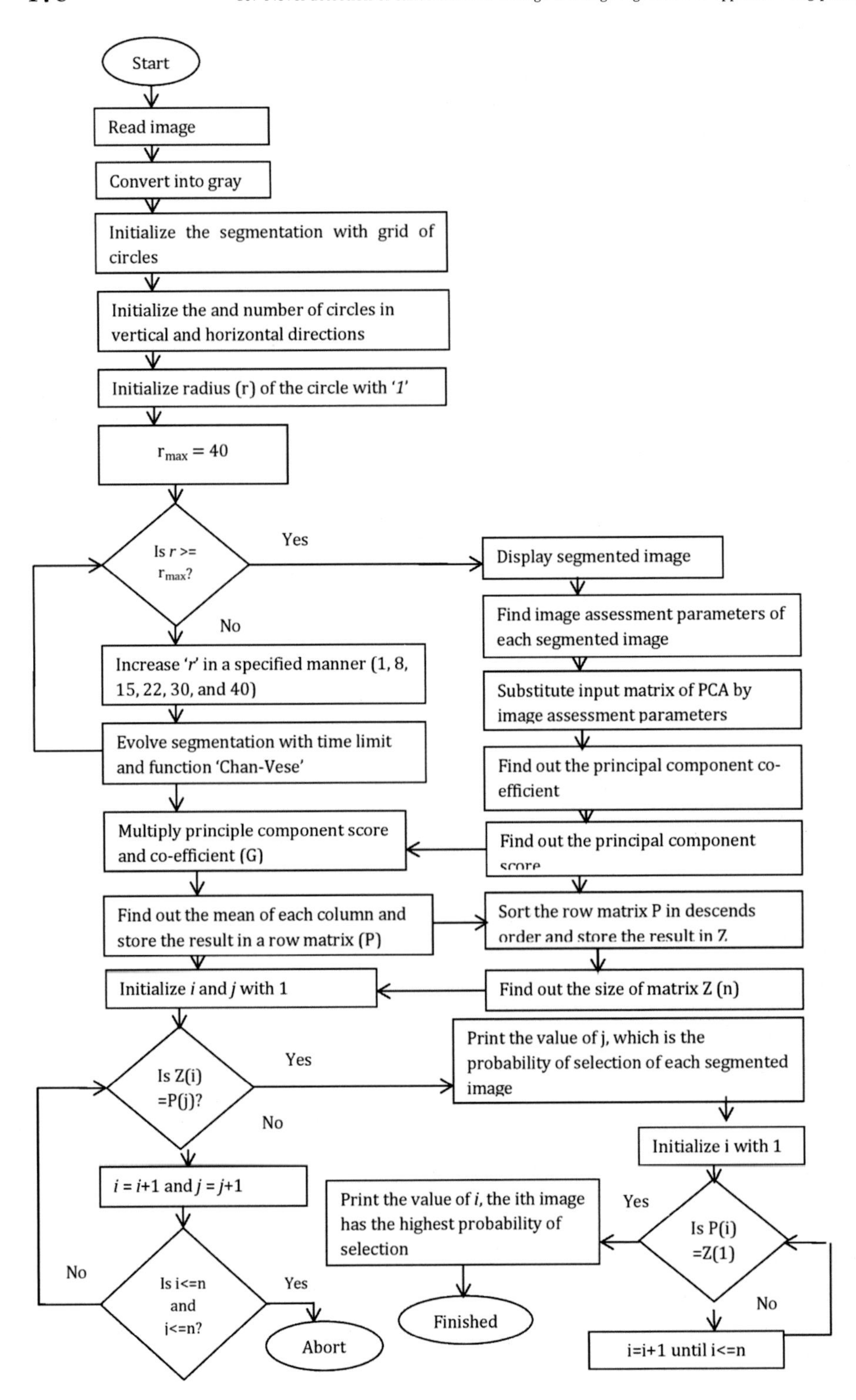

FIGURE 10.4 Choice of highest probability using PCA for different radii. *PCA*, Principal component analysis.

matrix. Each column in this table contains coefficients for one principal component; the columns are in descending order in terms of eigenvalues. Each column in the table contains eigenvectors for all eigenvalues. The principal component score is shown in Table 10.3; this is a representation of the input data matrix in principal component space. Rows of this matrix corresponding to observations, and columns are representations of

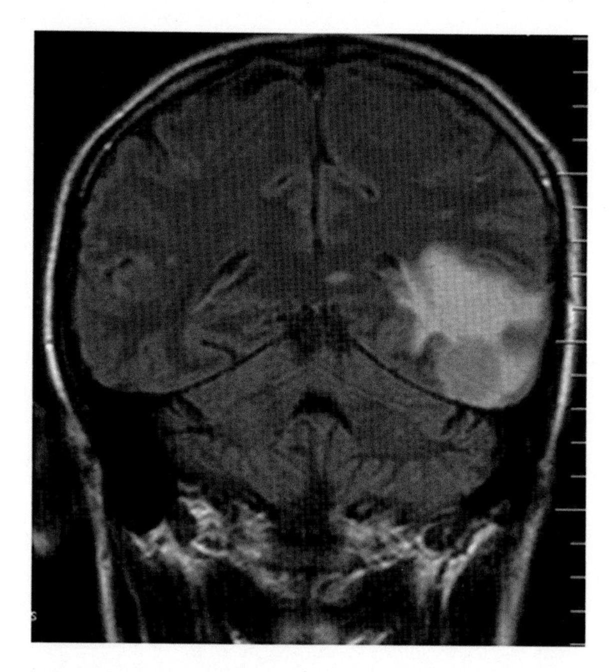

FIGURE 10.5 Brain MRI of suspected cancer. *MRI*, Magnetic resonance imaging.

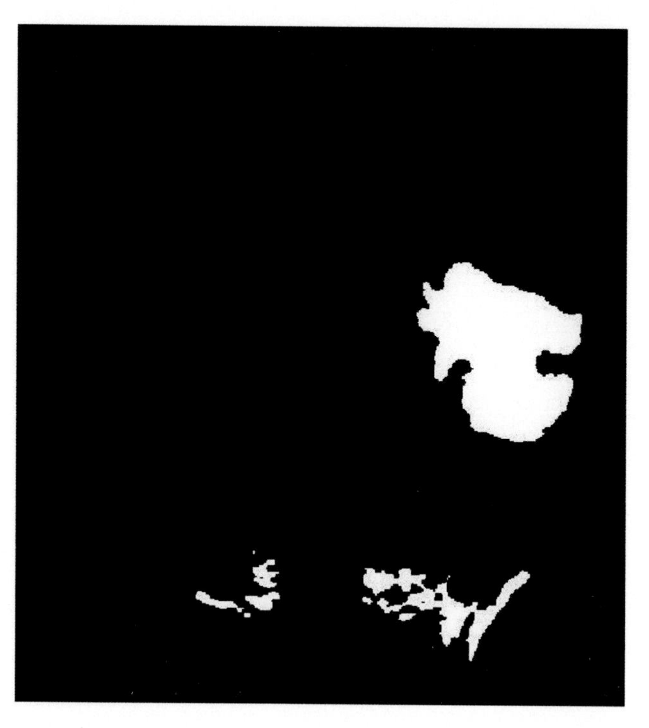

FIGURE 10.7 Segmented image of brain MRI with radius 8 units. *MRI*, Magnetic resonance imaging.

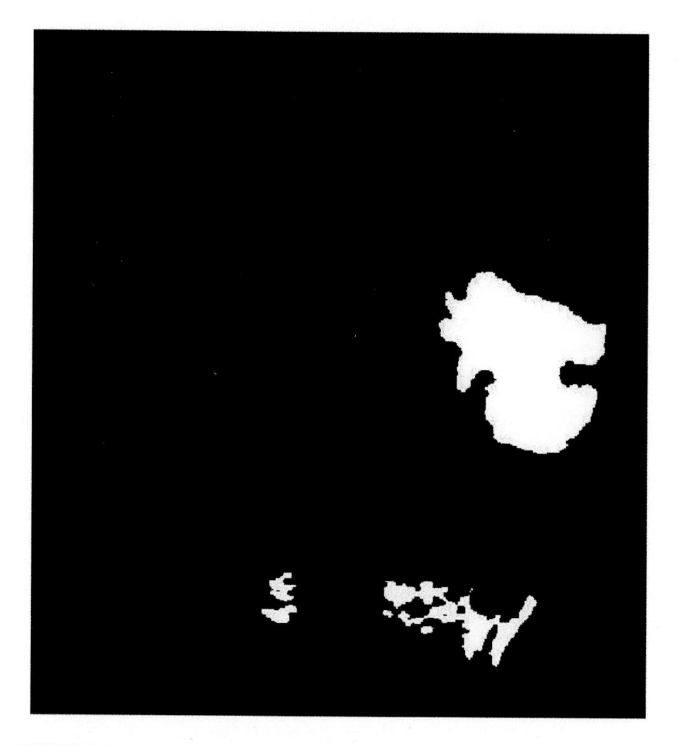

FIGURE 10.6 Segmented image of brain MRI with radius 1 unit. *MRI*, Magnetic resonance imaging.

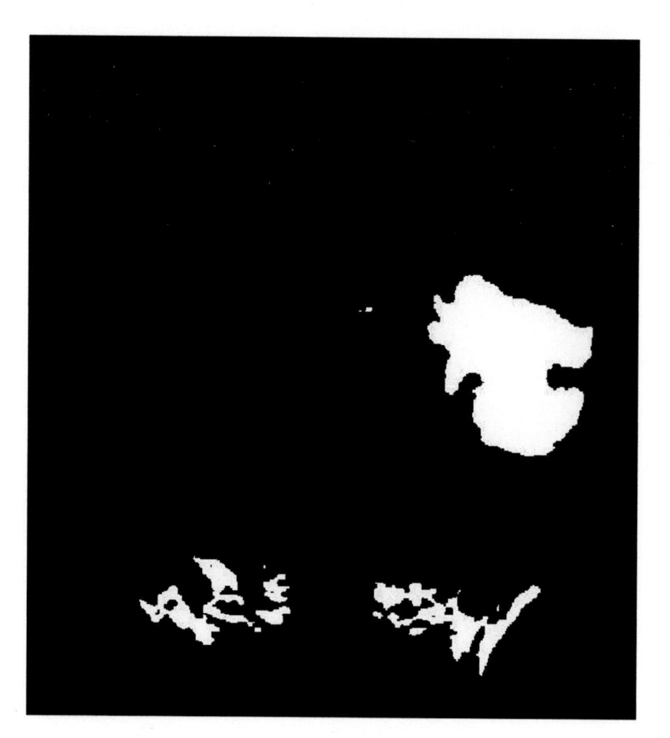

FIGURE 10.8 Segmented image of brain MRI with radius 15 units. *MRI*, Magnetic resonance imaging.

the variables that indicate how the components of the input data matrix vary in the principal component space. The eigenvalues of all observations are shown in Table 10.4; the eigenvalues are tabulated in descending order. The highest eigenvalue is 1.0613×10^4 and the lowest eigenvalue is 3.256×10^{-6}. The percentage

FIGURE 10.9 Segmented image of brain MRI with radius 22 units. *MRI*, Magnetic resonance imaging.

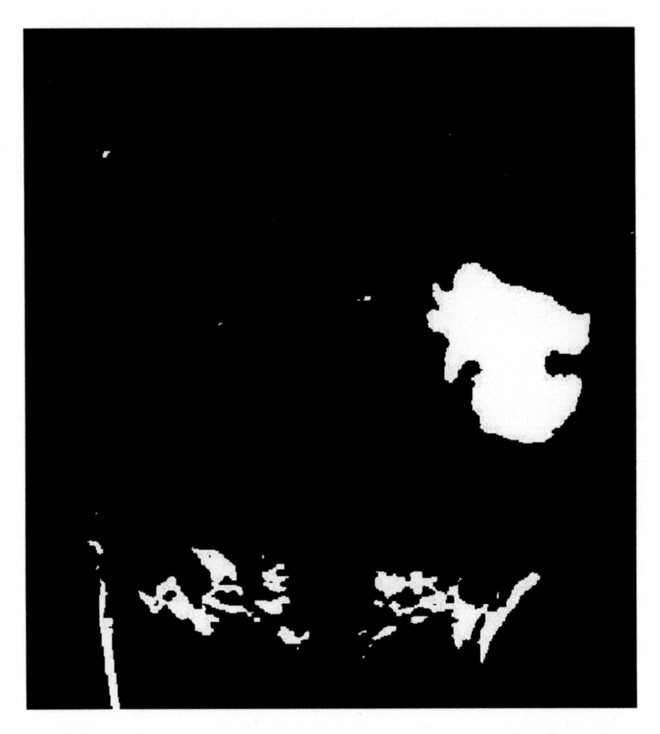

FIGURE 10.10 Segmented image of brain MRI with radius 30 units. *MRI*, Magnetic resonance imaging.

of total variance experienced by each observation is tabulated in Table 10.5; segmented image 2 has the highest percentage of all (95.6903).

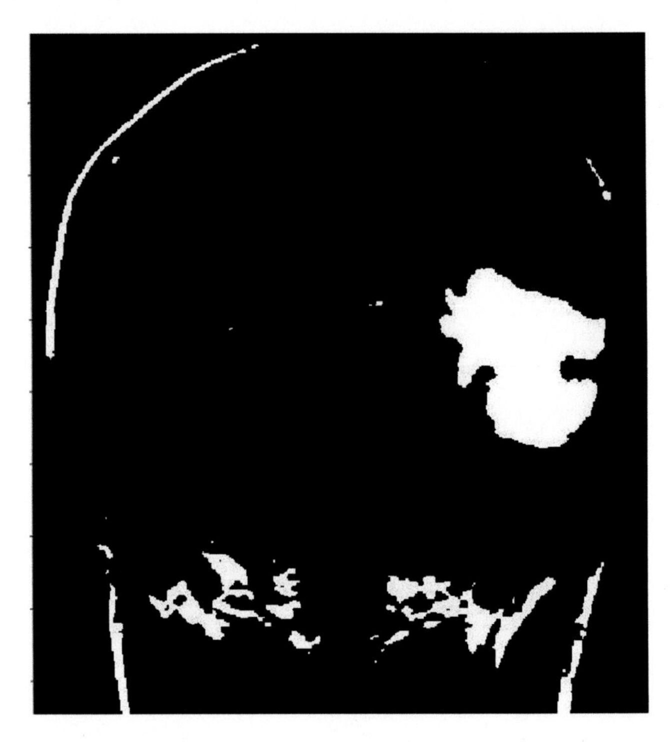

FIGURE 10.11 Segmented image of brain MRI with radius 40 units. *MRI*, Magnetic resonance imaging.

The main parameter which is taken into account for calculation of the probability of each segmented image is the centered value of each segmented MRI image of this suspected brain cancer. The centered value is obtained by multiplication of the principal component coefficient and the principal component score which are shown in Table 10.6. The mean centered value for each segmented image is tabulated in Table 10.7. A dimension-matching calculation is carried out for the mean centered value and the value is tabulated in Table 10.8.

The recalculated mean centered value, which may also be described as the probability of selection, is shown in Table 10.8. From the table it is clearly seen that segmented image 2 has the highest probability of selection (91.7726630596199) and the segmented image 3 has the lowest probability of selection (73.0741700133015). If we sequence the segmented images with respect to their probability of selection in decreasing order then the sequence is as displayed in Table 10.9.

Therefore, from the all the above results we can conclude that for this brain MRI, the segmented image with radius 8 units will be selected among all the segmented images. This means that the cancerous portion segmented by the segmented image with radius 8 units may be malignant in future.

Similar work is repeated for another brain MRI (By © NevitDilmen) shown in Fig. 10.12 and the results are tabulated in the respective tables.

TABLE 10.1 Confusion matrix for the segmented image shown in Fig. 10.5 obtained for different radii.

Image assessment parameters	Segmented image with radius 1 unit	Segmented image with radius 8 units	Segmented image with radius 15 units	Segmented image with radius 22 units	Segmented image with radius 30 units	Segmented image with radius 40 units
True positive	19	19	19	19	19	19
True negative	66	69	81	97	97	245
False negative	4	4	4	4	4	4
False positive	240	204	148	131	108	55
Confusion value	21.74943311	21.66780045	21.54081633	21.50226757	21.45011338	21.32993197
True positive rate	50.00772201	61.00896861	80.01197605	86.01333333	100.015748	169.027027
True negative rate	430.0084287	430.071333	430.1921179	430.2239076	430.2752531	430.4228072
False negative rate	42.99157125	42.92866697	42.80788209	42.77609235	42.7247469	42.57719282
False positive rate	0.992277992	0.99103139	0.988023952	0.986666667	0.984251969	0.972972973
Accuracy	0.258358663	0.297297297	0.396825397	0.462151394	0.50877193	0.817337461
Null error rate	0.741641337	0.702702703	0.603174603	0.537848606	0.49122807	0.182662539
Sensitivity	50.00772201	61.00896861	80.01197605	86.01333333	100.015748	169.027027
Specificity	430.0084287	430.071333	430.1921179	430.2239076	430.2752531	430.4228072
Probability random index	127.0190275	130.4186047	143.255814	158.4778013	158.4778013	196.6511628
Positive predicted value	0.073359073	0.085201794	0.113772455	0.126666667	0.149606299	0.256756757
Negative predicted value	0.942857143	0.945205479	0.952941176	0.96039604	0.96039604	0.983935743
False discovery rate	0.926640927	0.914798206	0.886227545	0.873333333	0.850393701	0.743243243
False omission rate	0.057142857	0.054794521	0.047058824	0.03960396	0.03960396	0.016064257
F1 score	245	209	153	136	113	60
Mean square error	0.037335865	0.035768218	0.029257933	0.028073809	0.025106307	0.015724401
Peak signal-to-noise ratio	14.27873787	14.4650269	15.3375636	15.51698662	16.00217156	18.03425886

TABLE 10.2 Principal component coefficient of the segmented images of the brain MRI shown in Fig. 10.5.

Segmented images with different radii	Principal component 1	Principal component 2	Principal component 3	Principal component 4	Principal component 5	Principal component 6
Segmented image with radius = 1	0.4194	−0.508	−0.4944	0.1286	0.3994	−0.3812
Segmented image with radius = 8	0.4141	−0.346	−0.1574	−0.2739	−0.2901	0.7242
Segmented image with radius = 15	0.4067	−0.0725	0.2978	−0.3172	−0.5771	−0.5538
Segmented image with radius = 22	0.4057	0.0391	0.3241	0.8352	−0.1277	0.1218
Segmented image with radius = 30	0.4022	0.1532	0.5415	−0.3287	0.6363	0.0916
Segmented image with radius = 40	0.4009	0.7693	−0.4936	−0.0451	−0.0414	−0.0027

TABLE 10.3 Principal component score of the segmented images of the brain MRI shown in Fig. 10.5.

Image assessment parameters	Segmented image with radius 1 unit	Segmented image with radius 8 units	Segmented image with radius 15 units	Segmented image with radius 22 units	Segmented image with radius 30 units	Segmented image with radius 40 units
True positive	−172.0311	−7.4	7.1488	0.1076	−0.3254	−0.0003
True negative	47.2317	135.7858	−49.5368	2.0775	−1.5505	−4.2581
False negative	−208.7687	−7.9247	6.8791	0.1269	−0.3117	−0.0006
False positive	145.4199	−147.3502	−26.1023	−0.4069	0.6232	−4.4833
Confusion value	−165.8047	−7.6388	7.1138	0.1036	−0.3253	−0.0003
True positive rate	3.1106	88.3338	−5.0894	−4.212	1.42327	1.3953
True negative rate	835.0615	7.3074	14.593	−0.4211	−0.6984	−0.0003
False negative rate	−113.7332	−6.894	7.5255	0.0789	−0.348	0.0065
False positive rate	−216.1506	−8.0454	6.8273	0.1312	−0.3098	−0.0005
Accuracy	−217.4526	−7.6027	6.7727	0.1397	−0.2894	−0.0028
Null error rate	−217.2289	−8.4915	6.8597	0.123	−0.3277	0.0015
Sensitivity	3.1106	88.3338	−5.0894	−4.212	1.4232	1.3953
Specificity	835.0615	7.3074	14.593	−0.4211	−0.6984	−0.0003
Probability random index	153.8715	53.6429	6.2518	6.6723	2.3307	2.1011
Positive predicted value	−218.2385	−7.9142	6.7867	0.127	−0.3008	−0.001
Negative predicted value	−216.2204	−7.9981	6.8217	0.134	−0.3082	−0.0009
False discovery rate	−216.443	−8.18	6.8456	0.1357	−0.3163	0.0001
False omission rate	−218.4611	−8.096	6.8107	0.1287	−0.3089	−0.0004
F1 score	157.6657	−147.1759	−26.0124	−0.4133	0.6187	3.6032
Mean square error	−172.0311	−7.4009	7.1488	0.1076	−0.3254	−0.0003
Peak signal-to-noise ratio	47.231748	135.7858	−49.5363	2.0775	−1.5505	−4.2584

TABLE 10.4 Eigenvalue obtained from PCA calculation of the segmented images of the brain MRI shown in Fig. 10.5.

Segmented image with different radii	Eigenvalues
Segmented image with radius = 8	106,130.0301
Segmented image with radius = 1	4504.318601
Segmented image with radius = 30	269.9826959
Segmented image with radius = 40	4.731973408
Segmented image with radius = 22	0.818508968
Segmented image with radius = 15	$3.25600909304431 \times 10^{-6}$

TABLE 10.5 Percentage of total variance of each segmented image of the brain MRI shown in Fig. 10.5.

Segmented image with different radii	Percentage of total variance
Segmented image with radius 8 units	95.69032831
Segmented image with radius 1 units	4.061241908
Segmented image with radius 30 units	0.243425285
Segmented image with radius 40 units	0.004266503
Segmented image with radius 22 units	0.000737995
Segmented image with radius 15 units	$2.93572496803479 \times 10^{-9}$

TABLE 10.6 Centered value obtained from the PCA calculation for the segmented images of the brain MRI shown in Fig. 10.5.

Image assessment parameters	Segmented image with radius 1 unit	Segmented image with radius 8 units	Segmented image with radius 15 units	Segmented image with radius 22 units	Segmented image with radius 30 units	Segmented image with radius 40 units
True positive	−72.0412	−69.7456	−67.1579	−67.643	−66.6957	−78.1805
True negative	−25.0412	−19.7456	−5.1579	10.3569	11.3042	147.8194
False negative	−87.0412	−84.7456	−82.1579	−82.6431	−81.6957	−93.1805
False positive	148.9587	115.2543	61.842	44.3569	22.3042	−42.1805
Confusion value	−69.2918	−67.0778	−64.6171	−65.1404	−64.2456	−75.8506
True positive rate	−41.0335	−27.7366	−6.1459	−0.6296	14.32	71.8464
True negative rate	338.9671	341.3257	344.0348	343.5806	344.5792	333.2423
False negative rate	−48.0497	−45.8169	−43.35	−43.8669	−42.9709	−54.6033
False positive rate	−90.049	−87.7545	−85.1699	−85.6563	−84.7114	−96.2076
Accuracy	−90.7829	−88.4483	−85.7611	−86.1808	−85.1869	−96.3632
Null error rate	−90.2996	−88.0429	−85.5547	−86.1051	−85.2045	−96.9979
Sensitivity	−41.0335	−27.7366	−6.1459	−0.6296	14.32	71.8464
Specificity	338.9671	341.3257	344.0341	343.5809	344.5792	333.2424
Probability random index	35.9777	41.6729	57.0978	71.8347	72.782	99.4705
Positive predicted value	−90.9679	−88.6604	−86.0441	−86.5163	−85.5461	−96.9238
Negative predicted value	−90.0984	−87.8004	−85.2049	−85.6826	−84.7353	−96.1966
False discovery rate	−90.1146	−87.8308	−85.2717	−85.7696	−84.8453	−96.4373
False omission rate	−90.9841	−88.6908	−86.1108	−86.6034	−85.6561	−97.1645
F1 score	153.9587	120.2543	66.842	49.3569	27.30426	−37.1805
Mean square error	−72.04129	−69.7456	−67.1579	−67.643	−66.6957	−78.1805
Peak signal-to-noise ratio	−25.0412	−19.7456	−5.1579	10.3569	11.30426	147.8194

TABLE 10.7 Probability of selection of each segmented image of the brain MRI shown in Fig. 10.5.

Segmented image with different radii	Probability of selection
Segmented image with radius = 1	$-1.3462914993349 \times 10^{-14}$
Segmented image with radius = 8	$-8.22733694038011 \times 10^{-15}$
Segmented image with radius = 15	$-2.69258299866985 \times 10^{-14}$
Segmented image with radius = 22	$-2.46820108211403 \times 10^{-14}$
Segmented image with radius = 30	$-1.7202613602613 \times 10^{-14}$
Segmented image with radius = 40	$-2.09423122118766 \times 10^{-14}$

TABLE 10.8 Recalculated probability of the selection of each segmented image of the brain MRI shown in Fig. 10.5.

Segmented image with different radii	Probability of selection (recalculated)
Segmented image with radius = 1	86.53708501
Segmented image with radius = 8	91.77266306
Segmented image with radius = 15	73.07417001
Segmented image with radius = 22	75.31798918
Segmented image with radius = 30	82.7973864
Segmented image with radius = 40	79.05768779

TABLE 10.9 Segmented images sequence order to probability of selection.

Segmented image with different radii	Probability of selection sequentially
Segmented image with radius = 8	91.77266306
Segmented image with radius = 1	86.53708501
Segmented image with radius = 30	82.7973864
Segmented image with radius = 40	79.05768779
Segmented image with radius = 22	75.31798918
Segmented image with radius = 15	73.07417001

Corresponding segmented images with different radii shown in this sequence:

1. Segmented image of brain MRI (Fig. 10.12) with radius 1 unit is shown in Fig. 10.13.
2. Segmented image of brain MRI (Fig. 10.12) with radius 8 units is shown in Fig. 10.14.
3. Segmented image of brain MRI (Fig. 10.12) with radius 15 units is shown in Fig. 10.15.
4. Segmented image of brain MRI (Fig. 10.12) with radius 22 units is shown in Fig. 10.16.
5. Segmented image of brain MRI (Fig. 10.12) with radius 30 units is shown in Fig. 10.17.
6. Segmented image of brain MRI (Fig. 10.12) with radius 40 units is shown in Fig. 10.18

Comparisons of all segmented images of the brain MRI with different radii with the original image with respect to 21 image assessment parameters are shown in Table 10.10.

If we substitute the image assessment parameter matrix for six segmented images with the covariance

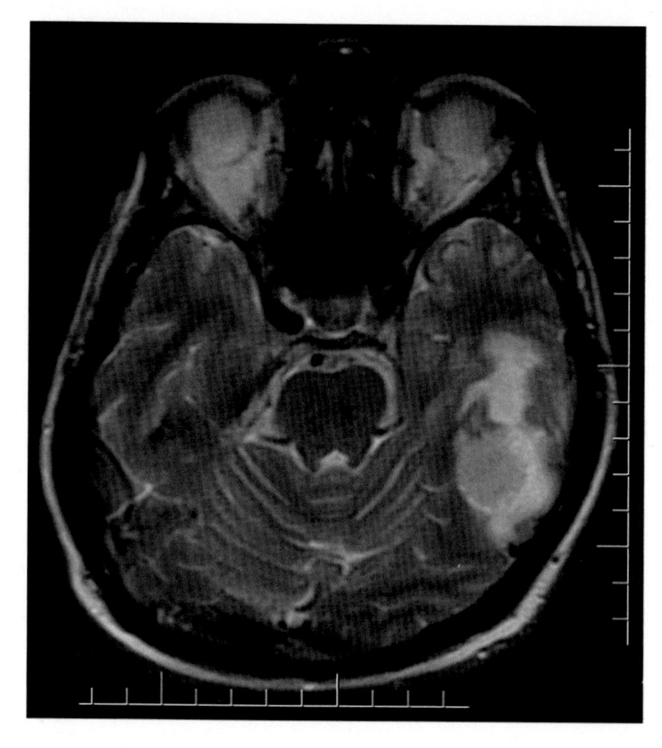

FIGURE 10.12 Brain MRI of suspected cancer. *MRI*, Magnetic resonance imaging.

FIGURE 10.14 Segmented image with radius 8 units.

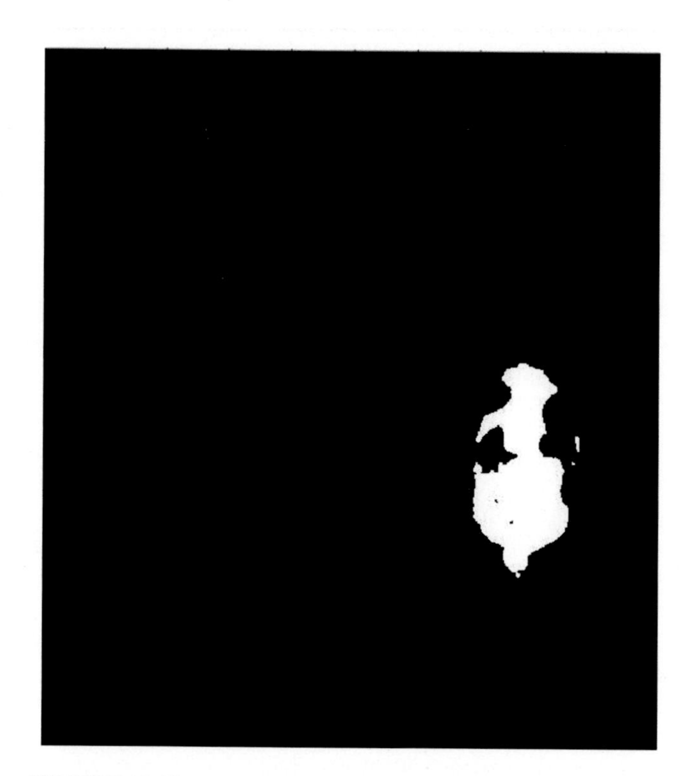

FIGURE 10.13 Segmented image with radius 1 unit.

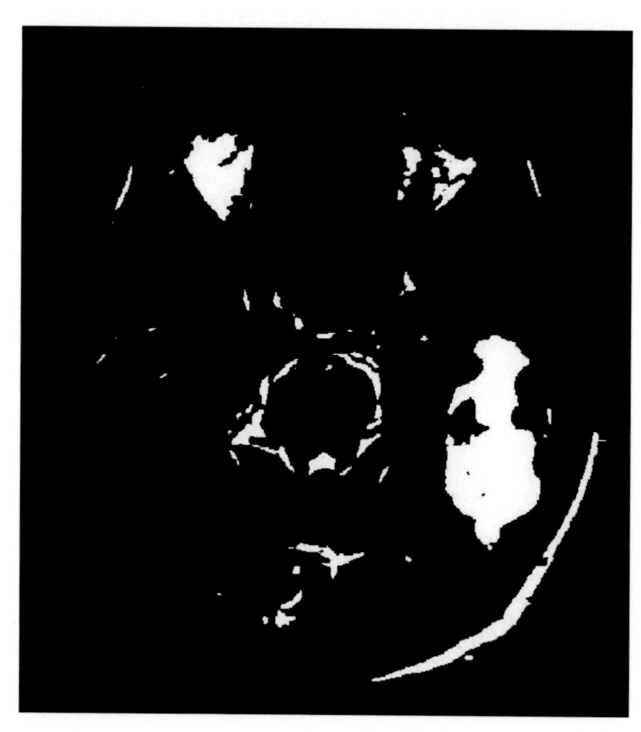

FIGURE 10.15 Segmented image with radius 15 units.

FIGURE 10.16 Segmented image with radius 22 units.

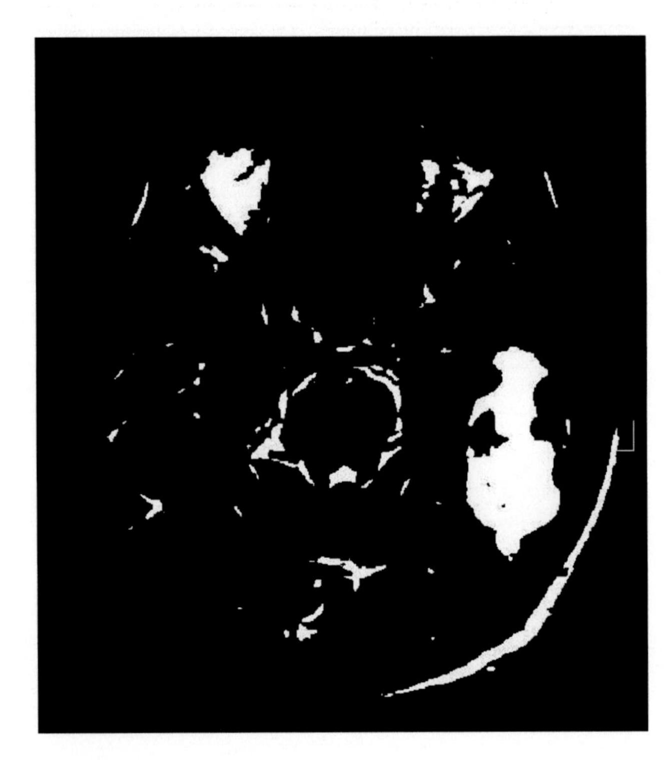

FIGURE 10.17 Segmented image with radius 30 units.

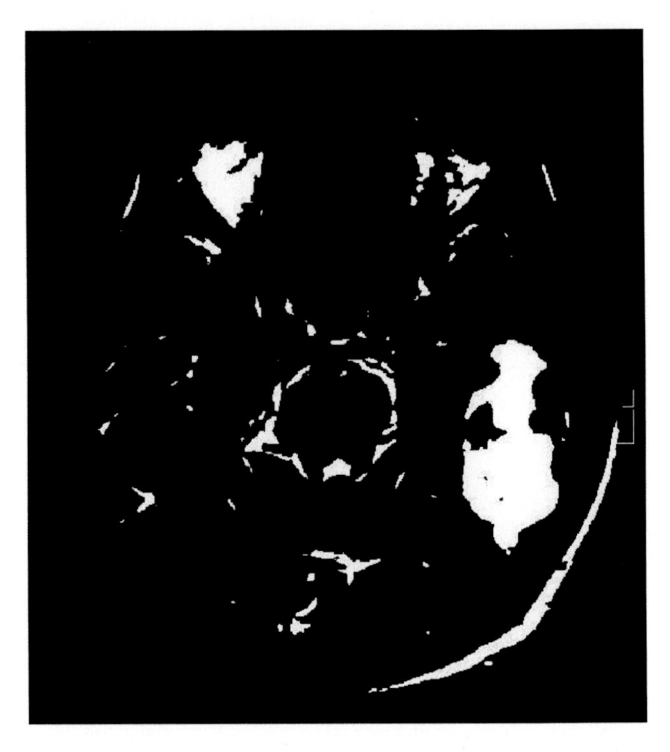

FIGURE 10.18 Segmented image with radius 40 units.

matrix of PCA, then the principal component parameters values are tabulated in sequence:

1. The principal component coefficient is shown in Table 10.11.
2. The principal component score is shown in Table 10.12.
3. The eigenvalue obtained from PCA calculation is shown in Table 10.13.
4. The percentage of total variance of each segmented image is shown in Table 10.14.
5. The centered value obtained from PCA calculation is shown in Table 10.15.
6. The probability of selection of each segmented image is shown in Table 10.16.
7. The recalculated probability of selection of each segmented image is shown in Table 10.17.

For the second brain MRI image shown in Fig. 10.12, a similar procedure is carried out. In this case, the highest eigenvalue is 1.45182×10^4 and the lowest eigenvalue is 0.000363361206870683. The corresponding segmented images order is obtained from the selection probability shown in Table 10.17.

The percentage of total variance experienced by each observation is tabulated in Table 10.18; the segmented image with radius 1 unit has the highest percentage of all (90.6259595754608) and the segmented image with radius 30 units has the lowest of all ($2.25837947378529 \times 10^{-7}$).

TABLE 10.10 Confusion matrix for the segmented image shown in Fig. 10.12 obtained for different radii.

Image assessment parameters	Segmented image with radius 1 unit	Segmented image with radius 8 units	Segmented image with radius 15 units	Segmented image with radius 22 units	Segmented image with radius 30 units	Segmented image with radius 40 units
True positive	23	23	23	23	23	23
True negative	44	207	339	371	374	381
False negative	0	0	0	0	0	0
False positive	389	196	92	56	56	55
Confusion value	19.58198381	19.19129555	18.98076923	18.90789474	18.90789474	18.90587045
True positive rate	44	125	159	176	181	181
True negative rate	504.6548074	505.0134827	505.1994593	505.26287	505.2629943	505.2672629
False negative rate	38.3451926	37.98651733	37.80054067	37.73713004	37.73700566	37.73273708
False positive rate	1	1	1	1	1	1
Accuracy	0.146929825	0.539906103	0.797356828	0.875555556	0.876379691	0.880174292
Null error rate	0.853070175	0.460093897	0.202643172	0.124444444	0.123620309	0.119825708
Sensitivity	44	125	159	176	181	181
Specificity	504.6548074	505.0134827	505.1994593	505.26287	505.2629943	505.2672629
Probability random index	104.46593	222.7384899	175.092081	144.2117864	140.9300184	133.014733
Positive predicted value	0.055825243	0.105022831	0.2	0.291139241	0.291139241	0.294871795
Negative predicted value	1	1	1	1	1	1
False discovery rate	0.944174757	0.894977169	0.8	0.708860759	0.708860759	0.705128205
False omission rate	0	0	0	0	0	0
F1 score	390	197	93	57	57	56
Mean square error	0.04341602	0.027624309	0.014449639	0.013193311	0.012388067	0.011974262
Peak signal-to-noise ratio	13.62349993	15.58708571	18.4014301	18.79646216	19.06996437	19.21751242

TABLE 10.11 Principal component coefficient of the segmented images of the brain MRI shown in Fig. 10.12.

Segmented image with different radii	Principal component 1	Principal component 2	Principal component 3	Principal component 4	Principal component 5	Principal component 6
Segmented image with radius = 1	0.3741	0.8422	−0.3841	0.0459	0.0194	0.0252
Segmented image with radius = 8	0.4002	0.2186	0.8222	−0.3229	−0.026	−0.1041
Segmented image with radius = 15	0.4155	−0.1473	0.1862	0.8513	−0.1486	0.1548
Segmented image with radius = 22	0.4184	−0.2641	−0.1471	−0.0351	0.8303	−0.2067
Segmented image with radius = 22	0.4191	−0.2708	−0.1898	−0.3731	−0.1624	0.7411
Segmented image with radius = 40	0.4198	−0.2793	−0.2895	−0.168	−0.5108	−0.6103

TABLE 10.12 Principal component score of the segmented images of the brain MRI shown in Fig. 10.12.

Image assessment parameters	Segmented image with radius 1 unit	Segmented image with radius 8 units	Segmented image with radius 15 units	Segmented image with radius 22 units	Segmented image with radius 30 units	Segmented image with radius 40 units
True positive	−190.9698	−9.2655	−2.9049	0.2242	0.45137	−0.0061
True negative	464.9368	−284.8999	−22.3498	7.3941	−1.8404	−0.0035
False negative	−247.2619	−11.547	−2.8522	0.2721	0.4084	−0.0065
False positive	84.9513	300.0506	−8.8047	1.06	−1.4851	−0.0013
Confusion value	−200.5895	−9.0519	−2.9073	0.2345	0.4396	−0.0062
TPR	110.8302	−116.6585	−0.0413	−6.8697	−1.3467	−0.0005
TNR	989.0066	38.0132	−3.9955	−0.7842	1.3514	0.0005
FNR	−154.5487	−7.2451	−2.9542	0.1956	0.4769	−0.004
FPR	−244.8138	−11.4478	−2.8545	0.27017	0.4103	−0.0064
Accuracy	−245.5555	−12.1372	−2.8663	0.2776	0.4137	−0.00423
Null error rate	−246.5195	−10.8576	−2.8403	0.2646	0.405	−0.0088
Sensitivity	110.8302	−116.6585	−0.04139	−6.8693	−1.3466	−0.0005
Specificity	989.0066	38.0132	−3.9955	−0.7842	1.3514	0.0005
PRI	129.0093	−14.0768	86.2747	2.1781	−0.4778	−6.2255
PPV	−246.7475	−11.7446	−2.9335	0.2426	0.4209	−0.0095
NPV	−244.8138	−11.4478	−2.8545	0.2701	0.4103	−0.0065
FDR	−245.3275	−11.2502	−2.7731	0.2996	0.3978	−0.0036
FOR	−247.2612	−11.547	−2.8522	0.2721	0.4084	−0.0065
F1 score	87.3988	300.1498	−8.807	1.0579	−1.4838	−0.0012
MSE	−247.2122	−11.5167	−2.8512	0.2704	0.4092	−0.0069
PSNR	−204.3498	−14.8745	−3.7943	0.5226	0.2254	0.082

TABLE 10.13 Eigenvalue obtained from PCA calculation of the segmented images of the brain MRI shown in Fig. 10.12.

Segmented image with different radii	Eigenvalues
Segmented image with radius = 1	145,812.3333
Segmented image with radius = 8	14,661.38061
Segmented image with radius = 15	412.1582996
Segmented image with radius = 22	7.917215679
Segmented image with radius = 30	0.87436882
Segmented image with radius = 40	0.000363361

TABLE 10.14 Percentage of total variance of each segmented image of the brain MRI shown in Fig. 10.12.

Segmented image with different radii	Percentage of total variance
Segmented image with radius = 1	90.62595958
Segmented image with radius = 40	9.112409469
Segmented image with radius = 15	0.256166543
Segmented image with radius = 8	0.004920745
Segmented image with radius = 22	0.000543442
Segmented image with radius = 30	$2.2583794737852 \times 10^{-7}$

TABLE 10.15 Centered value obtained from PCA calculation for the segmented images of the brain MRI shown in Fig. 10.12.

Image assessment parameters	Segmented image with radius 1 unit	Segmented image with radius 8 units	Segmented image with radius 15 units	Segmented image with radius 22 units	Segmented image with radius 30 units	Segmented image with radius 40 units
True positive	−78.1128	−80.9313	−78.4137	−76.6758	−77.1515	−77.0198
True negative	−57.1128	103.0686	237.5862	271.3244	273.8484	280.9801
False negative	−101.1128	−103.9313	−101.4137	−99.6758	−100.1515	−100.0198
False positive	287.8871	92.0686	−9.4137	−43.6758	−44.1515	−45.0198
Confusion value	−81.5308	−84.74	−82.4329	−80.7679	−81.2436	−81.114
True positive rate	−57.1128	21.0686	57.5862	76.3241	80.8484	80.9801
True negative rate	403.5419	401.0823	403.7857	405.587	405.1114	405.2473
False negative rate	−62.7676	−65.9448	−63.6131	−61.9386	−62.4145	−62.2871
False positive rate	−100.1128	−102.9313	−100.4137	−98.6758	−99.1515	−99.0198
Accuracy	−100.9659	−103.3914	−100.6163	−98.8002	−99.2752	−99.1399
Null error rate	−100.2597	−103.4712	−101.211	−99.5513	−100.0276	−99.9
Sensitivity	−57.1128	21.0686	57.5862	76.3241	80.8484	80.9801
Specificity	403.5419	401.0825	403.7857	405.587	405.1114	405.2473
Probability random index	3.353	118.8071	73.6783	44.5359	40.7784	32.9948
Positive predicted value	−101.057	−103.8263	−101.2131	−99.3846	−99.8604	−99.725
Negative predicted value	−100.1128	−102.9313	−100.4137	−98.6758	−99.1515	−99.0198
False discovery rate	−100.1686	−103.0363	−100.6137	−98.9669	−99.4427	−99.3147
False omission rate	−101.1128	−103.9313	−101.4137	−99.6758	−100.1517	−100.0198
F1 score	288.8871	93.0686	−8.4137	−42.6758	−43.1515	−44.0198
Mean square error	−101.0694	−103.9037	−101.3997	−99.6626	−100.1391	−100.0078
Peak signal-to-noise ratio	−87.4893	−88.3442	−83.0122	−80.8793	−81.0816	−80.8023

TABLE 10.16 Probability of selection of each segmented image of the brain MRI shown in Fig. 10.12.

Segmented image different radii	Probability of selection
Segmented image with radius = 1	$6.09036630651514 \times 10^{-15}$
Segmented image with radius = 8	$-2.43614652260606 \times 10^{-14}$
Segmented image with radius = 15	$-2.0301221021717 \times 10^{-14}$
Segmented image with radius = 22	$-2.90984167977946 \times 10^{-14}$
Segmented image with radius = 30	$-3.18052462673569 \times 10^{-14}$
Segmented image with radius = 40	$-1.15040252456397 \times 10^{-14}$

TABLE 10.17 Recalculated probability of selection of each segmented image of the brain MRI shown in Fig. 10.12.

Segmented image with different radii	Probability of selection (recalculated)
Segmented image with radius = 1	106.0903663
Segmented image with radius = 8	75.63853477
Segmented image with radius = 15	79.69877898
Segmented image with radius = 22	70.9015832
Segmented image with radius = 30	68.19475373
Segmented image with radius = 40	88.49597475

TABLE 10.18 Segmented images sequenced order in probability of selection.

Segmented image with different radii	Probability of selection sequentially
Segmented image with radius = 1	106.0903663
Segmented image with radius = 40	88.49597475
Segmented image with radius = 15	79.69877898
Segmented image with radius = 8	75.63853477
Segmented image with radius = 22	70.9015832
Segmented image with radius = 30	68.19475373

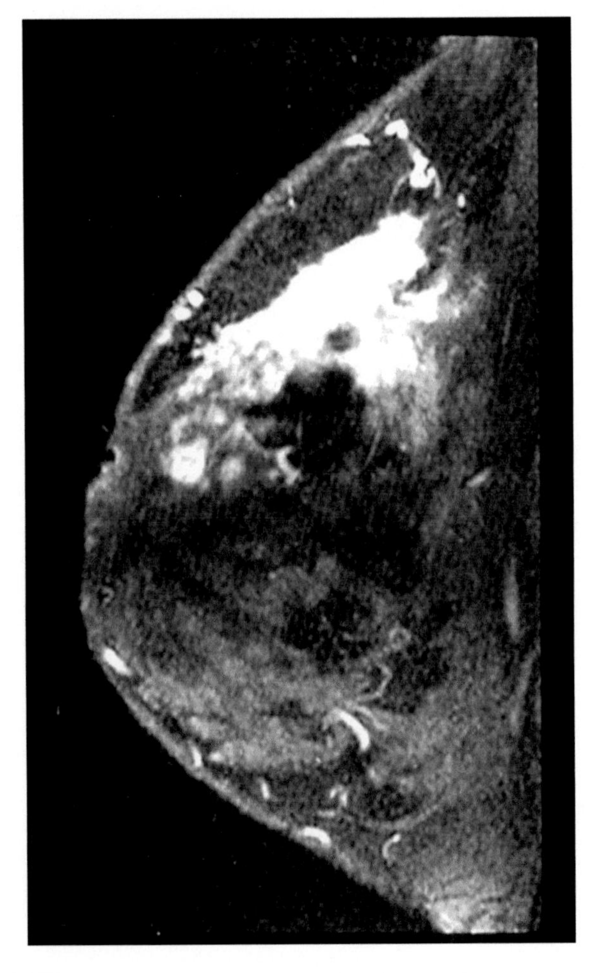

FIGURE 10.19 Breast mammogram of suspected cancer.

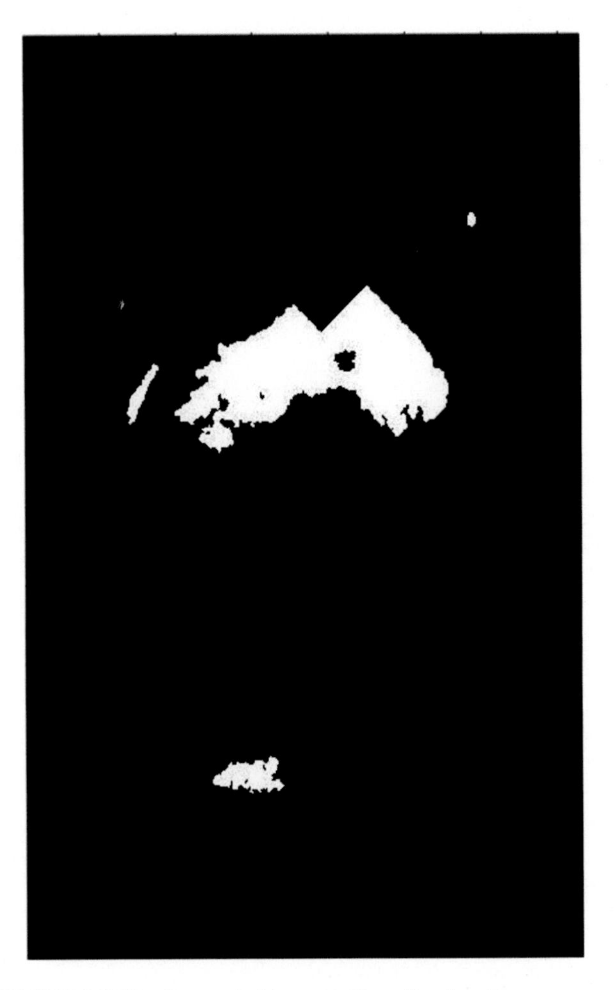

FIGURE 10.20 Segmented image with radius 1 unit.

Therefore, from all the above results. we can conclude that for this brain MRI, the segmented image with radius 1 unit will be selected from the entire segmented image. This means that the cancerous portion segmented by the segmented image with radius 1 unit may be malignant in future.

10.4.2 Detection of cancerous cells from a breast mammogram

In this subsection, we consider a breast mammogram image shown in Fig. 10.19, and a similar procedure is adopted for detection purposes.

The corresponding segmented images with different radii shown in this sequence are:

1. Segmented image of breast mammogram (Fig. 10.19) with radius 1 unit is shown in Fig. 10.20.
2. Segmented image of breast mammogram (Fig. 10.19) with radius 8 units is shown in Fig. 10.21.
3. Segmented image of breast mammogram (Fig. 10.19) with radius 15 units is shown in Fig. 10.22.
4. Segmented image of breast mammogram (Fig. 10.19) with radius 22 units is shown in Fig. 10.23.
5. Segmented image of breast mammogram (Fig. 10.19) with radius 30 units is shown in Fig. 10.24.
6. Segmented image of breast mammogram (Fig. 10.19) with radius 40 units is shown in Fig. 10.25.

Comparisons of all segmented images of the breast mammogram with different radii with the original image with respect to 21 image assessment parameters are shown in Table 10.19.

By substituting the image assessment parameter matrix for six segmented images with different radii with the covariance matrix of PCA, then seven principal component parameter values are tabulated in sequence:

FIGURE 10.21 Segmented image with radius 8 units.

FIGURE 10.22 Segmented image with radius 15 units.

FIGURE 10.23 Segmented image with radius 22 units.

FIGURE 10.24 Segmented image with radius 30 units.

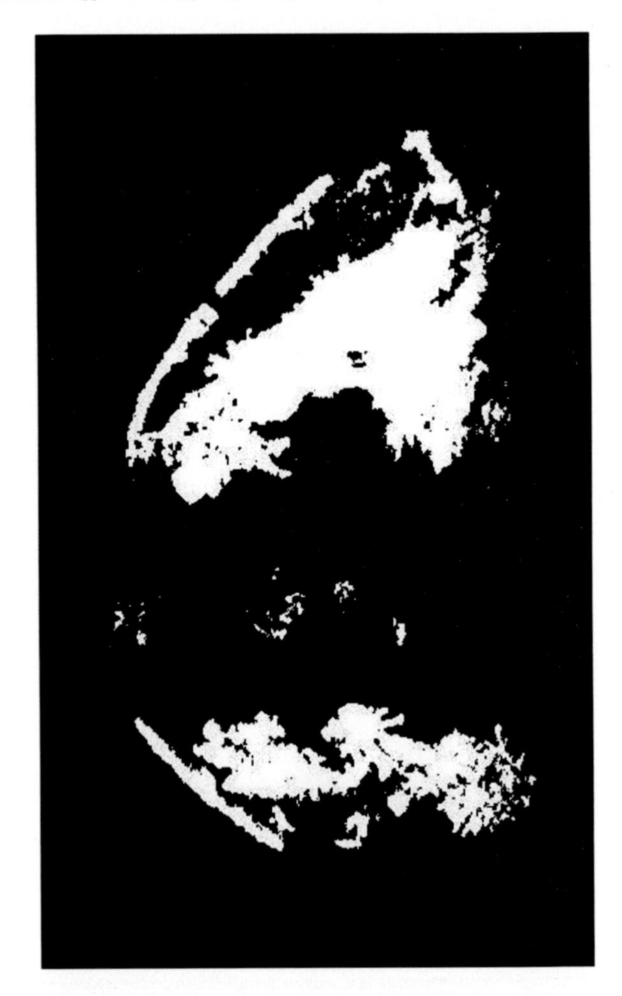

FIGURE 10.25 Segmented image with radius 40 units.

1. The principal component coefficient is shown in Table 10.20.
2. The principal component score is shown in Table 10.21.
3. The eigenvalue obtained from the PCA calculation is shown in Table 10.22.
4. The percentage of total variance of each segmented image is shown in Table 10.23.
5. The centered value obtained from PCA calculation is shown in Table 10.24.
6. The probability of selection of each segmented image is shown in Table 10.25.
7. The recalculated probability of selection of each segmented image is shown in Table 10.26.

In this case also, we found that the highest eigenvalue is 4.4×10^4 and the lowest eigenvalue is 0.0005209125819421. The percentage of total variance experienced by each observation is tabulated in Table 10.27; the segmented image with radius 22 units has the highest percentage of all (99.0670914097374)

TABLE 10.19 Confusion matrix for the segmented breast mammogram obtained for different radii.

Image assessment parameters	Segmented image with radius 1 unit	Segmented image with radius 8 units	Segmented image with radius 15 units	Segmented image with radius 22 units	Segmented image with radius 30 units	Segmented image with radius 40 units
True positive	116	116	116	116	116	116
True negative	1	1	4	14	84	234
False negative	0	0	0	0	0	0
False positive	205	161	139	127	114	77
Confusion value	130.8857143	130.8258503	130.7959184	130.7795918	130.7619048	130.7115646
True positive rate	148	191	218	203	239	264
True negative rate	930.4154739	930.4725754	930.5299334	930.5773496	930.6157373	930.6666449
False negative rate	261.5845261	261.5274246	261.4700666	261.4226504	261.3842627	261.3333551
False positive rate	1	1	1	1	1	1
Accuracy	0.363354037	0.420863309	0.463320463	0.505836576	0.636942675	0.819672131
Null error rate	0.636645963	0.579136691	0.536679537	0.494163424	0.363057325	0.180327869
Sensitivity	148	191	218	203	239	264
Specificity	930.4154739	930.4725754	930.5299334	930.5773496	930.6157373	930.6666449
Probability random index	120.7030201	120.7030201	123.2097315	131.3473154	178.9144295	225.4748322
Positive predicted value	0.361370717	0.418772563	0.454901961	0.477366255	0.504347826	0.601036269
Negative predicted value	1	1	1	1	1	1
False discovery rate	0.638629283	0.581227437	0.545098039	0.522633745	0.495652174	0.398963731
False omission rate	0	0	0	0	0	0
F1 score	206	162	140	128	115	78
Mean square error	0.174700954	0.163692188	0.151546592	0.134168835	0.106919143	0.075189472
Peak signal-to-noise ratio	7.577047229	7.859720455	8.194538263	8.723483502	9.709445289	11.23842966

TABLE 10.20 Principal component coefficient of segmented images of the breast mammogram shown in Fig. 10.19.

Segmented images with different radii	Principal component 1	Principal component 2	Principal component 3	Principal component 4	Principal component 5	Principal component 6
Segmented image with radius = 1	0.4072	−0.4722	0.7181	−0.0528	0.1149	−0.2816
Segmented image with radius = 8	0.409	−0.2701	−0.0475	−0.0648	−0.2714	0.8243
Segmented image with radius = 15	0.4099	−0.1486	−0.4578	−0.3285	−0.5168	−0.4745
Segmented image with radius = 22	0.4093	−0.1099	−0.3298	0.7987	0.2458	−0.1143
Segmented image with radius = 30	0.4085	0.2177	−0.217	−0.4803	0.7107	0.0524
Segmented image with radius = 40	0.4053	0.7889	0.3412	0.1281	−0.2834	−0.0062

TABLE 10.21 Principal component score of segmented images of the breast mammogram shown in Fig. 10.19.

Image assessment parameters	Segmented image with radius 1 unit	Segmented image with radius 8 units	Segmented image with radius 15 units	Segmented image with radius 22 units	Segmented image with radius 30 units	Segmented image with radius 40 units
True positive	−98.9963	−13.6569	−3.9725	2.3469	0.0123	0.00745
True negative	−245.7823	185.7031	51.0358	1.694	−5.3789	−4.151
False negative	−383.135	−14.3256	−4.8125	2.2959	0.0316	0.0066
False positive	−47.0375	−103.6728	30.7739	−8.0814	−1.5196	−0.0006
Confusion value	−62.76	−13.6942	−3.8183	2.3392	0.0078	0.0075
True positive rate	132.3825	69.7936	−36.1345	−8.3297	−2.5254	−0.0004
True negative rate	1896.2119	−8.7703	1.8591	2.7288	−0.0863	−0.0041
False negative rate	257.2887	−13.0091	−2.8519	2.3868	−0.048	0.0252
False positive rate	−380.6856	−14.3199	−4.8053	2.2963	0.0314	0.0066
Accuracy	−381.8255	−13.95	−4.809	2.3003	0.0644	0.00184
Null error rate	−381.9952	−14.6955	−4.8088	2.2918	−0.0013	0.0114
Sensitivity	132.3825	69.7936	−36.1345	−8.3297	−2.5254	−0.0004
Specificity	1896.2111	−8.7703	1.8591	2.7288	−0.0863	−0.0041
Probability random index	−15.8426	80.1632	14.5252	−4.5025	13.0071	0.0023
Positive predicted value	−381.985	−14.1455	−4.8429	2.3163	0.0298	0.0023
Negative predicted value	−380.6856	−14.3199	−4.8053	2.2963	0.0314	0.0066
False discovery rate	−381.8356	−14.5	−4.7748	2.2759	0.0332	0.011
False omission rate	−383.135	−14.3256	−4.8125	2.2959	0.0316	0.0066
F1 score	−44.588	−103.6674	30.7811	−8.0809	−1.5198	−0.0009
Mean square error	−382.8057	−14.407	−4.806	2.2917	0.0165	0.0102
Peak signal-to-noise ratio	−361.382	−11.2231	−4.6452	2.4388	0.394	−0.0953

TABLE 10.22 Eigenvalue obtained from the PCA calculation of segmented images of the breast mammogram shown in Fig. 10.19.

Segmented image with different radii	Eigenvalues
Segmented image with radius 22 units	440,753.7082
Segmented image with radius 8 units	3741.058938
Segmented image with radius 30 units	379.8331021
Segmented image with radius 40 units	18.87362558
Segmented image with radius 15 units	10.78385643
Segmented image with radius 1 unit	0.000520913

TABLE 10.23 Percentage of total variance of each segmented image of the breast mammogram shown in Fig. 10.19.

Segmented image with different radii	Percentage of total variance
Segmented image with radius 22 units	99.06709141
Segmented image with radius 8 units	0.840868315
Segmented image with radius 30 units	0.085374122
Segmented image with radius 40 units	0.004242177
Segmented image with radius 15 units	0.00242386
Segmented image with radius 1 unit	$1.1708419785014 \times 10^{-7}$

TABLE 10.24 Centered value obtained from PCA calculation for segmented images of the breast mammogram shown in Fig. 10.19.

Image assessment parameters	Segmented image with radius = 1	Segmented image with radius = 8	Segmented image with radius = 15	Segmented image with radius = 22	Segmented image with radius = 30	Segmented image with radius = 40
True positive	−36.8455	−36.763	−37.5181	−35.8362	−43.6718	−51.9603
True negative	−151.8455	−151.763	−149.5181	−137.8362	−75.6718	66.0396
False negative	−152.8455	−152.763	−153.5181	−151.8362	−159.6718	−167.9601
False positive	52.1544	8.2369	−14.5181	−24.8362	−45.6718	−90.9603
Confusion value	−21.9598	−21.9372	−22.7222	−21.0566	−28.9099	−37.2487
True positive rate	−4.8455	38.2369	64.4818	51.1637	79.3281	96.0396
True negative rate	777.5699	777.7094	777.0117	778.741	770.9439	762.7063
False negative rate	108.739	108.7643	107.9518	109.5863	101.7124	93.373
False positive rate	−151.8455	−151.763	−152.5181	−150.8362	−158.6718	−166.9603
Accuracy	−152.4821	−152.3422	−153.0548	−151.3304	−159.0348	−167.1406
Null error rate	−152.2088	−152.1839	−152.9814	−151.3421	−159.3087	−167.7799
Sensitivity	−4.8455	38.2369	64.4818	51.1637	79.3281	96.0396
Specificity	777.5699	777.7094	777.0117	778.741	770.9439	762.7063
Probability random index	−32.1425	−32.6006	−30.3084	−20.4889	19.2425	57.5145
Positive predicted value	−152.4841	−152.3443	−153.0632	−151.3589	−159.1674	−167.3592
Negative predicted value	−151.8455	−151.763	−152.5181	−150.8362	−158.6718	−166.9603
False discovery rate	−152.2068	−152.1818	−152.973	−151.3136	−159.1761	−167.5613
False omission rate	−152.8455	−152.763	−153.5181	−151.8362	−159.6718	−167.9603
F1 score	53.1544	9.2369	−13.5181	−23.8362	−44.6718	−-89.9603
Mean square error	−152.6708	−152.5993	−153.3666	−151.7021	−159.5649	−167.8851
Peak signal-to-noise ratio	−145.2684	−144.9033	−145.3236	−143.1127	−149.9623	−156.7218

TABLE 10.25 Probability of selection of each segmented image of the breast mammogram shown in Fig. 10.19.

Segmented image with different radii	Probability of selection
Segmented image with radius 1 unit	$-1.8947806286936 \times 10^{-14}$
Segmented image with radius 8 units	$4.06024420434343 \times 10^{-15}$
Segmented image with radius 15 units	$-8.12048840868686 \times 10^{-15}$
Segmented image with radius 22 units	$2.97751241651852 \times 10^{-14}$
Segmented image with radius 30 units	0
Segmented image with radius 40 units	$-2.70682946956229 \times 10^{-15}$

TABLE 10.26 Recalculated probability of selection of each segmented image of the breast mammogram shown in Fig. 10.19.

Segmented image with different radii	Probability of selection (recalculated)
Segmented image with radius 1 unit	81.05219371
Segmented image with radius 8 units	104.0602442
Segmented image with radius 15 units	91.87951159
Segmented image with radius 22 units	129.7751242
Segmented image with radius 30 units	100
Segmented image with radius 40 units	97.29317053

TABLE 10.27 Segmented image sequenced order for the probability of selection.

Segmented image with different radii	Probability of selection sequentially
Segmented image with radius 22 units	129.7751242
Segmented image with radius 8 units	104.0602442
Segmented image with radius 30 units	100
Segmented image with radius 40 units	97.29317053
Segmented image with radius 15 units	91.87951159
Segmented image with radius 1 unit	81.05219371

and the segmented image with radius 1 unit has the lowest ($1.1708419785014 \times 10^{-7}$).

Therefore, from all of the above results, we can conclude that for this breast mammogram, the segmented image with radius 22 units will be selected from all the segmented images. This means that the cancerous portion segmented by the segmented image with radius 22 units may be malignant in future.

10.5 Conclusion

Simulated findings reveal that the highest percentage of total variance is over 99%, whereas the maximum eigenvalue is of the order of 10^4 for a segmented image, for brain MRI, as well as for a breast mammogram. The main parameter taken into account for calculation of the probability of each segmented image is the centered value of each segmented image of this MRI suspected brain cancer. Based on the probability of selection, images are sequenced, which is required to detect the cancerous portion. The confusion matrix is calculated for different radii, and thereafter, the image assessment parameter matrix is substituted with the covariance matrix of PCA. A wider difference is observed for principal component coefficient, variance, and probability of selection for each segmented image; which significantly improves the accuracy of the proposed technique compared with the published data. From the data computed for PSNR, it is established that a higher PSNR can be achieved for an edge-detected image than the segmented image, which is better than that obtained using Otsu thresholding. Henceforth, the best results are achieved through a ML-based statistical algorithm applied in image processing, and the work can be justified for determination of the probability of a cell being cancerous.

References

Benjamin, D. J. (2014). The efficacy of surgical treatment of cancer—20 years later. *Medical Hypotheses*, *82*(4), 412–420.

Biemar, F., & Foti, M. (2013). Global progress against cancer—Challenges and opportunities. *Cancer Biology and Medicine*, *10*(4), 183–186.

Biji, C.L., Selvathi, D., & Panicker, A. (2011). Tumor detection in brain magnetic resonance images using modified thresholding techniques. In A. Abraham, J. L. Mauri, J. F. Buford, J. Suzuki, & S. M. Thampi (Eds.) *Advances in computing and communications: International Conference on Advances in Computing and Communications, Kochi, India, 193* (22–24 July), 300–308.

By Unknown Photographer - *This image was released by the National Cancer Institute, an agency part of the National Institutes of Health, with the ID 2703 (image) (next)., Public Domain*, Retrieved from https://commons.wikimedia.org/w/index.php?curid = 24052431

By © NevitDilmen, *CC BY-SA 3.0*. Retrieved from https://commons.wikimedia.org/w/index.php?curid = 18633668

By © NevitDilmen, *CC BY-SA 3.0*. Retrieved from https://commons.wikimedia.org/w/index.php?curid = 18633651

Dambreville, S., Rathi, Y., & Tannenbaum, A. (2006). Shape-based approach to robust image segmentation using Kernel PCA, *Proceeding of IEEE Computer Society Conference Computer Vis Pattern Recognition* (pp. 977–984).

Dimililer, K., & Ilhan, A. (2016). Effect of image enhancement on MRI brain images with neural networks. *Procedia Computer Science*, *102*, 39–44.

Han, Y., Feng, X. C., & Baciu, G. (2013). Variational and PCA based natural image segmentation. *Pattern Recognition*, *46*(7), 1971–1984.

Işın, A., Direkoğlu, C., & Şah, M. (2016). Review of MRI-based brain tumor image segmentation using deep learning methods. *Procedia Computer Science*, *102*, 317–324.

Jain, S., Jagtap, V., & Pise, N. (2015). Computer aided melanoma skin cancer detection using image processing. *Procedia Computer Science*, *48*, 735–740.

Kakde, O. G., Tandel, G. S., Biswas, M., Tiwari, A., Suri, H. S., Turk, M., ... Suri, J. S. (2019). A review on a deep learning perspective in brain cancer classification. *Cancers*, *11*(1), 111.

Kamencay, P., Jelšovka, D., & Zachariasova, M. (2011). The impact of segmentation on face recognition using the principal component analysis (PCA). In *IEEE Signal Processing Algorithms, Architectures, Arrangements, and Applications, Poznan, Poland*, 29–30 September.

Kourou, K., Exarchos, T. P., Exarchos, K. P., Karamouzis, M. V., & Fotiadis, D. I. (2015). Machine learning applications in cancer prognosis and prediction. *Computational and Structural Biotechnology Journal*, *13*, 8–17.

Kumar, K. S., Venkatalakshmi, K., & Karthikeyan, K. (2019). Lung cancer detection using image segmentation by means of various evolutionary algorithms. *Computational and Mathematical Methods in Medicine*, *2019*, 4909846.

Kumar, S., & Chong, I. (2018). Correlation analysis to identify the effective data in machine learning: Prediction of depressive disorder and emotion states. *International Journal of Environmental Research and Public Health*, *15*(12), 2907.

Nandi, A. (2015). Detection of human brain tumour using MRI image segmentation and morphological operators. In *IEEE International Conference on Computer Graphics, Vision and Information Security, Bhubaneswar, India*, 2–3 November.

Nasim, Z., Rajput, Q., & Haider, S. (2017) Sentiment analysis of student feedback using machine learning and lexicon based approaches. In: *International Conference on Research and Innovation in Information Systems, Langkawi, Malaysia*, 16–17 July.

Reddy, D., Dheeraj, Kiran, Bhavana, V., & Krishnappa, H.K. (2018). Brain tumor detection using image segmentation techniques. In: *IEEE International Conference on Communication and Signal Processing, Chennai, India*, 3–5 April.

Sadoddin, R., & Ghorbani, A.A. (2007). A comparative study of unsupervised machine learning and data mining techniques for intrusion detection. In: P. Perner (Ed.), *Machine learning and data mining in pattern recognition: international workshop on machine learning and data mining in pattern recognition, NY, USA*, 15–19 July, 4571 (pp. 404–418).

Samsuden, M.A., Diah, N.M., & Rahman, N.A. (2019). A review paper on implementing reinforcement learning technique in optimising games performance. In: *IEEE 9th International Conference on System Engineering and Technology, Shah Alam, Malaysia*, 7 October.

Sazzad, T.M.S., Ahmmed, K.M.T., Ul-hoque, M., & Rahman, M. (2019). Development of automated brain tumor identification using MRI images. In: *IEEE International Conference on Electrical, Computer and Communication Engineering, Cox'sBazar, Bangladesh*, 7–9 February.

Simeone, O., & Very, A. (2018). Brief introduction to machine learning with applications to communication systems. *IEEE Transactions on Cognitive Communications and Networking*, *4*(4), 648–664.

Win, K. Y., Choomchuay, S., Hamamoto, K., Raveesunthornkiat, M., Rangsirattanakul, L., & Pongsawat, S. (2018). Computer aided diagnosis system for detection of cancer cells on cytological pleural effusion images. *Pattern Recognition in Medical Decision Support*, *2018*, 6456724.

Wójcicka, A., Jędrusik, P., Stolarz, M., Kubina, R., & Wróbel, Z. (2014). Using analysis algorithms and image processing for quantitative description of colon cancer cells. *Information Technologies in Biomedicine*, *283*(3), 385–395.

Wu, Q., & Zhao, W. (2017). Small-cell lung cancer detection using a supervised machine learning algorithm. In: *International Symposium on Computer Science and Intelligent Controls, Budapest, Hungary*, 20–22 October.

CHAPTER

11

Classification of the operating spectrum for the RAMAN amplifier embedded optical communication system using soft computing techniques

Arup Kumar Bhattacharjee[1], *Soumen Mukherjee*[1], *Rajarshi Dhar*[2] and *Arpan Deyasi*[1]

[1]RCC Institute of Information Technology, Kolkata, India [2]IIEST Shibpur, Howrah, India

11.1 Introduction

After the pioneering work of Sir A. G. Bell in converting a voice signal into an electrical signal and transmitting through copper wires and reconverting back to a voice signal, the need for bandwidth has been increasing constantly for transmission of data in different forms. The trust of innovating new-generation communication system leads to present-day optical fibers associated with several boosters in the form of amplifiers to satisfy the demands of end users (Agrawal, 2010). Signal transmission in the optical domain is preferred because of the availability of a window frequency zone, and in order to eliminate the need for optical-to-electrical signal conversion again; optical amplifiers are proposed, which also remove the possibility of interference occurrence and the system has better immunity to noise (Ramaswami, Sivarajan, & Sasaki, 2009). Different types of amplifiers have been proposed in order to satisfy the requirements of low-loss transmission, among them, erbium-doped fiber amplifiers (EDFAs), RAMAN amplifiers (RAs), and semiconductor optical amplifiers (SOAs) are the choice of design engineers due to their potential advantages in different applications. Although EDFA is popular (Herbster & Romero, 2017) due to its lower cost, SOA (Agarwal & Agrawal, 2018) and RA (Mandelbaum & Bolshtyansky, 2003) have the advantages of operating in the system at 1330 nm and 1550 nm, the two major windows favored for minimum dispersion and minimum attenuation, respectively. RA has already been proved to be better than SOA in terms of noise reduction and lower cost, and therefore, present day fiber-optic systems are mostly researched with this device.

The Raman amplifier is one of the best choices in telecommunication systems owing to its characteristics of nearly zero dispersion, superior bit rate, reduced channel spacing, and better noise feature (Islam, 2002). Works are carried out primarily on the effective noise sources (Bromage, 2004), which can affect the gain performance of the system, and also on the stimulated Raman scattering. Four pumping lasers are proposed for designing a dense wavelength division multiplexing (DWDM) system, and low ripples are observed (Samra & Harb, 2009). Theoretical models are also proposed for noise analysis (Istianing, Heryana, & Syahriar, 2012), and simultaneously the effect of fiber length on the gain characteristics is measured. A backward RA with multipump facility is proposed with 64 channels for a WDM system (Pradhan & Mandloi, 2018) at 10 Gbps data rate. Reliability and safety issues also carry weight, as described by workers (Namiki, Seo, Tsukiji, & Shikii, 2006) in the domain of high-power operations. Crosstalk always has an effect in optical telecommunication systems, and its role in RA-based systems has been also investigated. The effect on bit error rate (BER) has been analytically estimated (Sultana & Majumder, 2012); later variation of pump power has been analyzed for a fixed channel length

Recent Trends in Computational Intelligence Enabled Research.
DOI: https://doi.org/10.1016/B978-0-12-822844-9.00022-0

(Tithi & Majumder, 2016). Henceforth, a lower channel length gives better performance in order to avoid crosstalk; however, it is not practically possible. Again, for a flatter gain curve, the role of Eye height and Q-factor are vital, but these two factors are not generally considered for simulation analysis as far as the authors are aware. Herein lies the need for optimization of performance analysis, and that parametric analysis is comprised of BER, gain, noise figure, EYE height, and OSNR for different data rates and lengths. This is the objective of the present proposal. The importance of soft computing techniques, therefore, will play a vital role, and are discussed in the next section.

11.2 Soft computing approaches in the optimization procedure

Soft computing techniques have been used for a long time to solve optimization problems. Various disciplines provide real-life problems which are difficult to solve, at least mathematically, in principle; therefore soft computing is excellent for relatively accurate prediction. Soft computing is a conglomerate of various techniques and methods which work together in a synergistic manner, and the outcome is flexible in terms of competence measurement for data processing when the situation is indefinite (Saridakis & Dentsoras, 2008). The main objective of this computational approach is to exploit the degree of tolerance for the sole purpose of precision measurement, where fairly accurate reasoning capability reduces the uncertainty from a solution (Wong, Gedeon, & Fung, 2002). The solution should be robust and cost-effective (Attarzadeh & Ow, 2010), and as accurate as possible.

Research is carried out to analyze the reliability optimization (Gen & Yun, 2006) using soft computing techniques in order to improve system performance. It is utilized to solve the real dynamic problems in agricultural sectors (Pentoś, Pieczarka, & Lejman, 2020); the scheduling problem is also solved (Silva, Sousa, Runkler, & Palm, 2005) when applied to a logistic process. Several works have been reported in the last few years for prediction analysis in different medical diagnostic cases (Gambhir, Malik, & Kumar, 2016; Ray & Pal, 2013), and bio-inspired soft computing takes a major role (Diwaker, Tomar, Poonia, & Singh, 2018) in this regard. When applied to different difficult NP problems it gives sustainable solutions (Pandian, Fernando, & Senjyu, 2019), as reported very recently. It is also chosen as the solution to a few real-time electronics engineering problems, as mentioned in the next paragraph.

According to Breiman (2001), the forest of random tree is an efficient method for predictor ensemble development with randomly selected decision trees. However, it should be noted that all the trees should be chosen from the selected data-subspaces (Biau, 2012) for achieving convergence. It is a fairly accurate prediction mechanism (Genuer, Poggi, & Tuleau-Malot, 2010), even for a very large number of inputs. Recently, this scheme has been utilized successfully in machine learning framework (Ren, Cheng, & Han, 2017) with a modification of Brieman's work; and the mode of classification determines the final output. The suboptimal classifier selection method (Bernard, Heutte, & Adam, 2009) is invoked to improve performance, whereas very recently, oblique decision trees with heterogeneous features are considered (Katuwal, Suganthan, & Zhang, 2020) which claim the best accuracy so far.

The soft computing technique is immensely popular in various branches of electronic engineering owing to its robustness and accuracy in prediction. Research works are available in optimizing antenna performance (Zhao, Zhang, Li, Wang, & He, 2012), very large scale integration (VLSI) architecture design (Mahdiani, Ahmadi, Fakhraie, & Lucas, 2010), and also in wireless sensor network (Kaur & Joshi, 2019). However, noteworthy works are yet to be published in the field of optical communication, to the best of the authors' knowledge. Some introspection reveals that the length of the channel and bit rate are two such crucial parameters in the field of optical communication, which controls the gain of the system, and also several other key parameters become complex interdependent functions of each other. Henceforth, it is the right place for incorporating soft computing techniques for parametric optimization in order to achieve the best possible performance. In the present problem, an optical communication system is considered with a RA at input, and optimization is carried out to obtain a flatter gain profile.

11.3 Objective of the present problem

Soft computing techniques are implemented to distinguish between the operating spectra of a RA-based optical communication system working at 1310 nm and 1550 nm, respectively. Four different bit rates are considered for each spectrum, and several optical characteristics like distance, gain, noise figure, input and output SNR, input and output OSNR, Q-factor, and Eye Height are considered for computation purposes. The problem therefore may be looked at as a two-class problem, or in more detail, an eight-class problem, where the neural network along with association analysis are the only techniques to identify the actual data rate for the system operating at a particular wavelength. The novelty of the proposed method lies in the features of the optical system, one can significantly predict the operating wavelength and corresponding bit rate which; it cannot be identified as no experimental system is available for the said purpose to date, to the best knowledge of the authors. Very costly OTDR can detect the loss, but from the obtained data, it becomes virtually impossible to find the actual input spectrum. This is a long-standing problem for communication system engineers, as inspection at the intermediate point of an optical fiber system cannot give the requisite operating spectrum and data rate very easily, and the proposed work may show some light in eliminating the problem. Once the operating spectrum and corresponding bit rate are obtained, one can also evaluate the changes required in the system for specific applications, and accordingly, the bit rate can be shifted. The sensitivity and specificity of the result are reported as justifying the claim.

11.4 Result analysis

Before discussing the classification and its visualization, some preprocessing to find the nature of the data is performed. The data set considered here is broadly divided into two parts based on wavelengths of 1310 nm and 1550 nm. A total run of 160 is done in total, and 18 different parameters are observed. Among all the parameters, the domains of wavelength (1310, 1550 nm), pump power (400 mW), and data rate (2.5, 5.0, 7.5, 10.0 Gbps), respectively, are considered as prime for computation. For the remaining 16 attributes the maximum, minimum, mean, and standard deviation are as described subsequently.

Visualizations of results shown in Tables 11.1 and 11.2 are given in Figs. 11.1 and 11.2.

Values of different parameters associated with the multilayer perceptron (MLP) for this problem are shown in Table 11.3 (Fig. 11.3). Here the data sets are classified using MLP that uses back-propagation to classify instances with three combination of training–testing pair which are (80%–20%), (85%–15%), and (90%–10%). The results for different split ratios are shown in Tables 11.4–11.7.

The meta-heuristic approach-based Bagging classifier was also used. This classifier performs classification and regression based on the base learner and its key objective is to reduce variance. Here the fast decision tree learner is used to generate the results. Values of different parameters associated with the Bagging classifier for this problem are shown in Table 11.8. As with the MLP, different training–testing pairs, which are (80%–20%), (85%–15%), and (90%–10%), are used to generate the results, which are shown in Tables 11.9 and 11.10 for 1310 nm and 1550 nm wavelengths, respectively. Similarly 5-, 10-, 20-folds cross-validations are also used for generating results, shown in Tables 11.11 and 11.12 for 1310 nm and 1550 nm wavelengths, respectively.

In this experimental setup, we used principal component analysis, a very popular and robust attribute selection technique. In this technique, the Ranker search technique is used to explore the search space for attribute selection. Top-ranked attributes with their associated properties are shown in Tables 11.13 and 11.14 for 1310 nm and 1550 nm, respectively. We have also generated top-ranked attributes using the ReliefF Attribute Evaluation Technique with Ranker Search Technique. Tables 11.15 and 11.16 depict the results of ReliefF Attribute Evaluation Technique for 1310 nm and 1550 nm respectively (Tables 11.17–11.25).

Another classification technique applied on the data sets is based on construction of the forest of random trees. The total number of instances considered for this random forest classifier is 80. Like other classification techniques used here, random forest classification also uses three different cross-validation approaches and three different split percentage techniques for generation of results for both data sets. Different parameters and their attributes used for the said classifier are shown below.

In this chapter, another rule-based classifier is used which generates a decision list for the data sets using the separate-and-conquer technique (Holmes, Hall, & Frank, 1999; Quinlan, 1992; Wang & Witten, 1997). In this approach, after each iteration the classifier builds a model tree using M5 and makes the "best" leaf into a rule. Here the batch size is considered as 100 and pruned rules are generated.

11.5 Practical implications

A closer inspection of simulated results has severe implications for practical fiber-optic system design. Once the key influential parameters are identified, it becomes very easy for the design engineers to analyze the performance of the system in terms of gain, and the position where a boosting section is required for long-haul transmission. Therefore total budget estimation is possible for a RA-based system, and has great importance from a practical point of view.

Another significant finding can be obtained from the simulation is that the key governing attributes are computed in both operating windows, namely 1310 nm and 1550 nm. This is very important from a practical perspective as under different constraints and requirements, both windows are utilized by communication engineers, and therefore, knowledge about common system parameters is extremely important in this regard. In this study, it has been found that both input

TABLE 11.1 Variation in all attributes for wavelength 1310 nm.

Attributes	Distance (km)	Gain (dB)	Noise figure (dB)	Input signal (dBm)	Input noise (dBm)	Input SNR (dB)	Input noise 0.1 nm (dBm)	Input OSNR (dB)	Output signal (dBm)	Output noise (dBm)	Output noise (W)	Output SNR (dB)	Output noise 0.1 nm(dBm)	Output OSNR (dB)	Q-factor	Eye height
Minimum	10	10.313465	−100	−3.4261899	−59.039493	43.900122	−61.080692	45.941322	−50.192411	−46.147278	2.43E-08	24.579583	−50.192411	26.620783	94.573	0.0105
Maximum	200	30.658818	27.893368	−2.6587813	55.613425	57.654625	7.4528474	57.654625	27.232664	1236.36	0.0124	55.748754	0.22065258	57.789954	9392.85	1.1974
Mean	105	23.02395125	15.04475383	−2.909766314	−52.99214554	51.54105556	−55.60983753	53.53110846	19.39361912	1.660597578	0.000485844	34.50997738	−16.43699241	36.55117724	2082.507715	0.41811125
StdDev	58.02661982	6.299427603	18.48359418	0.306944791	13.1999737	4.652981476	8.603555247	4.607192186	9.981136669	140.4469602	0.001417296	10.1841685	14.08677008	10.18416847	2608.060675	0.376190516

TABLE 11.2 Variation in all attributes for wavelength 1550 nm.

Attributes	Distance (km)	Gain (dB)	Noise figure (dB)	Input signal (dBm)	Input noise (dBm)	Input SNR (dB)	Input noise 0.1 nm(dBm)	Input OSNR (dB)	Output signal (dBm)	Output noise (dBm)	Output noise (W)	Output SNR (dB)	Output noise 0.1 nm(dBm)	Output OSNR (dB)	Q-factor	Eye height
Minimum	10	9.951066	−1.02715	−3.4262	−59.0395	43.9357	−61.0807	45.9769	7.05534	−36.7495	24.84473	−38.7907	26.88593	81.7369	0.0096	0.01
Maximum	200	30.58285	28.35864	−2.65872	−46.5944	55.61343	−48.6356	57.65463	27.15679	2.081225	51.26412	0.040026	53.30532	1009.11	1.1693	1.169
Mean	105	22.78841	17.63636	−2.90968	−54.4498	51.54012	−56.491	53.58132	19.87873	−15.062	34.94075	−17.1032	36.98195	414.4262	0.402301	0.402
StdDev	58.02662	6.391155	9.51974	0.306999	4.71897	4.515692	4.71897	4.515692	6.385738	12.68885	8.736438	12.68885	8.736438	288.71	0.367374	0.367

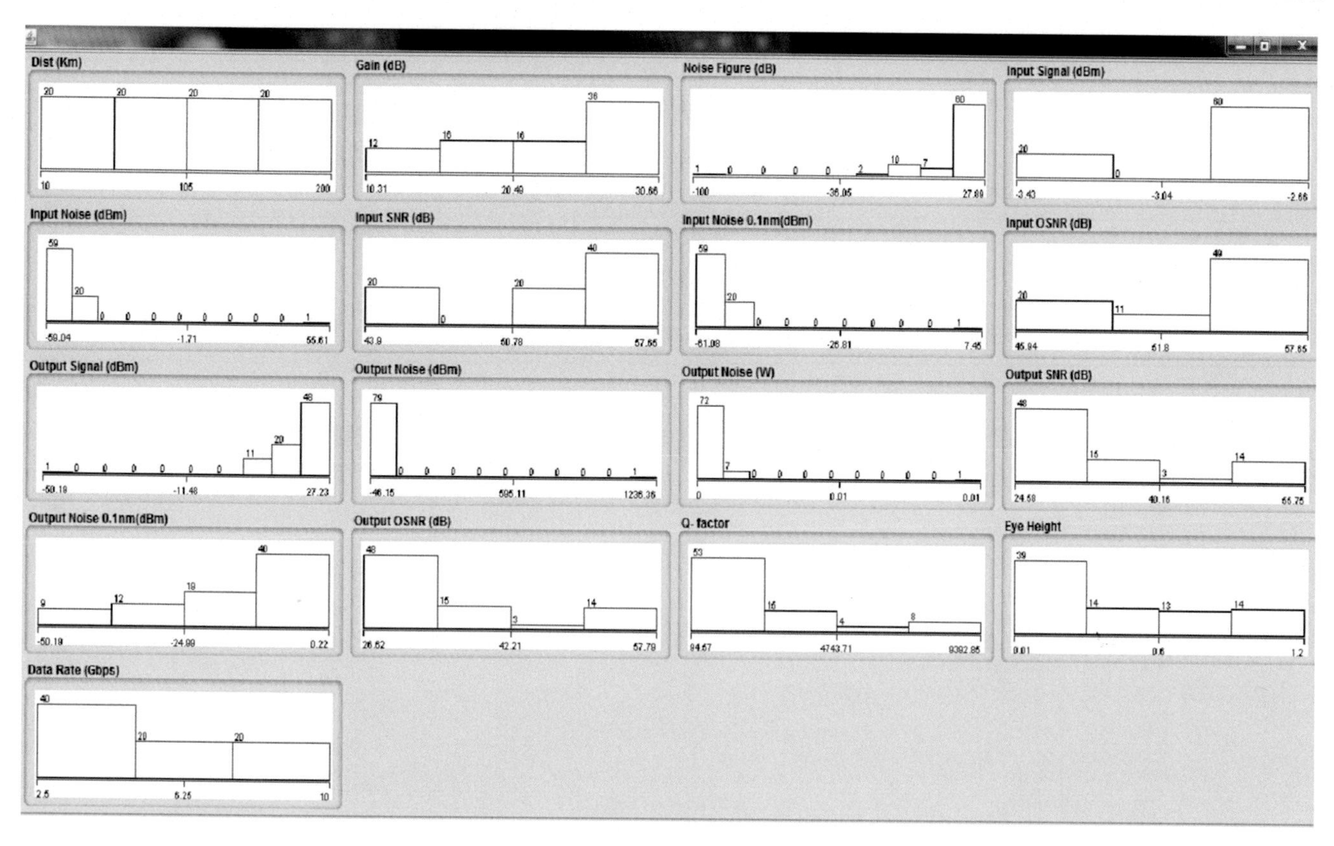

FIGURE 11.1 Variation in values of attributes for wavelength 1310 nm.

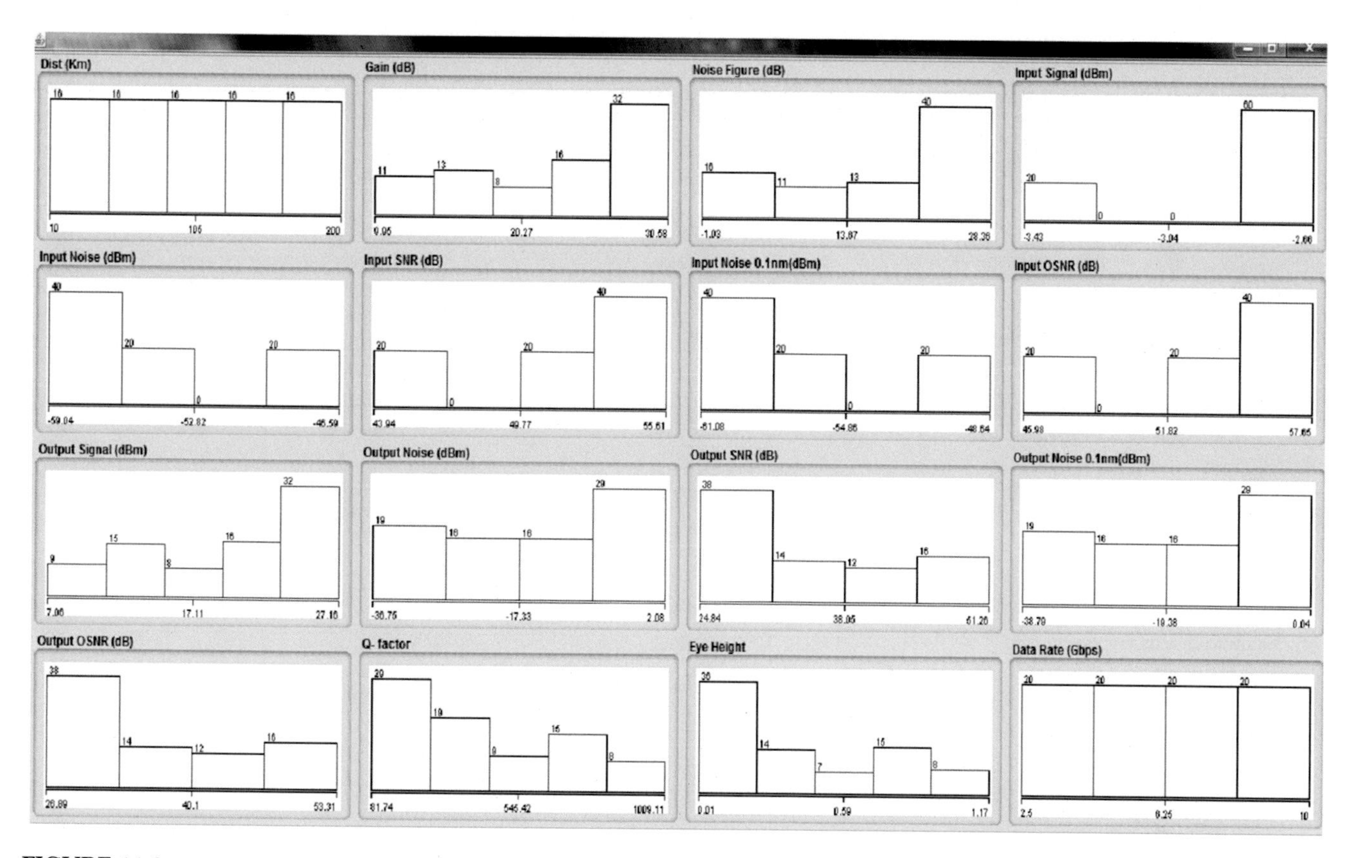

FIGURE 11.2 Variation in values of attributes for wavelength 1550 nm.

TABLE 11.3 Attributes and their values for multilayer perceptron.

Sl. no.	Attribute	Value
1.	Batch size	100
2.	Learning rate	0.3
3.	Momentum	0.2
4.	Auto build	True
5.	Normalized attributes	True
6.	Normalized numeric class	True

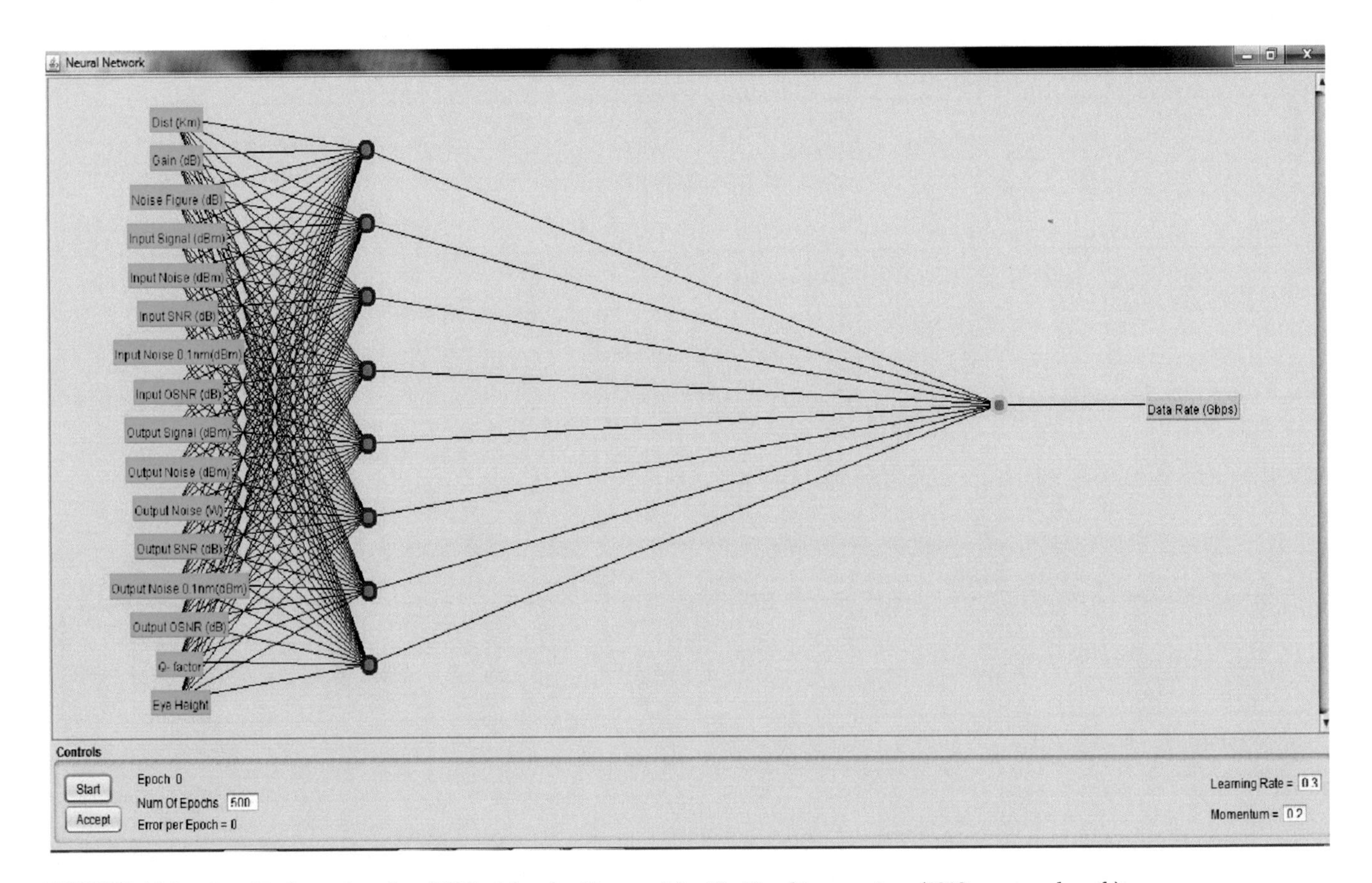

FIGURE 11.3 Graphical user interface (GUI) of the classifier used for 80–20 split percentage (1310 nm wavelength).

TABLE 11.4 Results of multilayer perceptron for different split percentages (1310 nm wavelength).

Parameter	Split percentage		
	80–20	85–15	90–10
Time taken to build model (seconds)	0.3	0.2	0.21
Time taken to test model (seconds)	0.01	0.0001	0.0001
Correlation coefficient	0.7455	0.6523	0.9997
Mean absolute error	0.6026	0.805	0.0432
Root mean squared error	2.2869	2.6689	0.0673
Relative absolute error (%)	21.4621	29.3263	1.7043
Root relative squared error (%)	74.6342	88.9424	2.3933

TABLE 11.5 Results of multilayer perceptron for different cross-validations (1310 nm wavelength).

Parameter	Cross-validation		
	Five-fold	10-fold	20-fold
Time taken to build model (seconds)	0.18	0.20	0.24
Correlation coefficient	0.9549	0.9453	0.9366
Mean absolute error	0.1423	0.1328	0.1533
Root mean squared error	0.8435	0.9328	1.0059
Relative absolute error (%)	5.6832	5.2694	6.0748
Root relative squared error (%)	30.1246	33.1103	35.6427

TABLE 11.6 Results of multilayer perceptron for different split percentages (1550 nm wavelength).

Parameter	Split percentage		
	80–20	85–15	90–10
Time taken to build model (seconds)	0.19	0.25	0.2
Time taken to test model (seconds)	0.0001	0.0001	0.0001
Correlation coefficient	0.9999	0.9999	0.9997
Mean absolute error	0.0377	0.0623	0.044
Root mean squared error	0.0485	0.076	0.0617
Relative absolute error (%)	1.4815	2.7382	2.0806
Root relative squared error (%)	1.7016	2.9276	2.5496

TABLE 11.7 Results of multilayer perceptron for different cross-validations (1550 nm wavelength).

Parameter	Cross-validation		
	Five-fold	10-fold	20-fold
Time taken to build model (seconds)	0.21	0.2	0.2
Correlation coefficient	0.9996	0.9998	0.9998
Mean absolute error	0.053	0.0402	0.0385
Root mean squared error	0.0831	0.0536	0.0497
Relative absolute error (%)	2.1041	1.595	1.5186
Root relative squared error (%)	2.947	1.8979	1.7504

TABLE 11.8 Attributes and values for the Bagging classifier.

Sl. no.	Attribute	Value
1.	Bag size percentage	100
2.	Batch size	100
3.	Number of iterations	10
4.	Random number of seed	1
5.	Calculated out-of-bag error	False
6.	Base classifier used	Fast decision tree learner
7.	Number of execution slots used constructing the ensemble	1

TABLE 11.9 Results of the Bagging classifier for different split percentages (1310 nm wavelength).

Parameter	Cross-validation		
	Five-fold	10-fold	20-fold
Time taken to build model (seconds)	0.0001	0.0001	0.01
Correlation coefficient	0.9999	0.9998	1.0
Mean absolute error	0.0141	0.0237	0.0011
Root mean squared error	0.0419	0.0635	0.0099
Relative absolute error (%)	0.5616	0.9386	0.0437
Root relative squared error (%)	1.4974	2.2548	0.3496

TABLE 11.10 Results of the Bagging classifier for different split percentages (1550 nm wavelength).

Parameter	Split percentage		
	80–20	85–15	90–10
Time taken to build model (seconds)	0.01	0.0001	0.02
Time taken to test model (seconds)	0.0001	0.0001	0.0001
Correlation coefficient	0.9562	0.9455	−0.0518
Mean absolute error	0.8584	1.4696	2.5916
Root mean squared error	1.0661	1.8221	2.9741
Relative absolute error (%)	33.232	56.0369	99.8504
Root relative squared error (%)	37.1382	60.3352	97.8715

TABLE 11.11 Results of the Bagging classifier for different cross-validations (1310 nm wavelength).

Parameter	Cross-validation		
	Five-fold	10-fold	20-fold
Time taken to build model (seconds)	0.0001	0.0001	0.01
Correlation coefficient	0.9999	0.9998	1.0
Mean absolute error	0.0141	0.0237	0.0011
Root mean squared error	0.0419	0.0635	0.0099
Relative absolute error (%)	0.5616	0.9386	0.0437
Root relative squared error (%)	1.4974	2.2548	0.3496

TABLE 11.12 Results of the Bagging classifier for different cross-validations (1550 nm wavelength).

Parameter	Cross-validation		
	Five-fold	10-fold	20-fold
Time taken to build model (seconds)	0.03	0.01	0.03
Correlation coefficient	0.9999	0.9990	0.9999
Mean absolute error	0.0094	0.0486	0.0082
Root mean squared error	0.0441	0.1256	0.0392
Relative absolute error (%)	0.372	1.9299	0.3216
Root relative squared error (%)	1.5645	4.4466	1.3787

TABLE 11.13 Top-ranked attributes for 1310 nm wavelength using the PCA technique.

Rank	Eigenvalue	Proportion	Cumulative	Attribute name
1	5.76692	0.36043	0.36043	Output noise (dBm)
2	4.85749	0.30359	0.66403	Input noise (dBm)
3	2.86499	0.17906	0.84309	Eye height
4	1.34596	0.08412	0.92721	Distance (km)
5	0.61776	0.03861	0.96582	Q-factor

TABLE 11.14 Top-ranked attributes for 1550 nm wavelength using the PCA technique.

Rank	Eigenvalue	Proportion	Cumulative	Attribute name
1	7.92305	0.5282	0.5282	Output OSNR
2	4.77314	0.31821	0.84641	Gain (dBm)
3	1.45162	0.09677	0.94319	Distance (km)
4	0.50026	0.03335	0.97654	Input signal (dBm)

TABLE 11.15 Top-ranked attributes for 1310 nm wavelength using the ReliefF technique.

Rank	Proportion	Attribute name
1	0.32624	Input signal (dBm)
2	0.20535	Input OSNR (dB)
3	0.17647	Input SNR (dB)
4	0.14102	Q-factor
5	0.04683	Input signal 0.1 nm (dBm)

TABLE 11.16 Top-ranked attributes for 1550 nm wavelength using the ReliefF technique.

Rank	Proportion	Attribute name
1	0.40775	Input signal (dBm)
2	0.19023	Q-factor
3	0.18162	Input noise 0.1 nm (dBm)
4	0.16833	Input noise (dBm)

TABLE 11.17 Attributes and their values for the random forest classifier.

Sl. no.	Attribute	Value
1.	Bag size percentage	100
2.	Batch size	100
3.	Number of iterations	100
4.	Random number of seed	1
5.	Maximum depth of the tree	Unlimited
6.	Number of execution slots used for constructing the ensemble	1

TABLE 11.18 Results of the random forest classifier for different cross-validations (1310 nm wavelength).

Parameter	Cross-validation		
	Five-fold	10-fold	20-fold
Time taken to build model (seconds)	0.18	0.15	0.06
Correlation coefficient	0.9942	0.9912	0.9936
Mean absolute error	0.0806	0.0884	0.07
Root mean squared error	0.3011	0.3721	0.3179
Relative absolute error (%)	3.22	3.5083	2.7744
Root relative squared error (%)	10.7542	13.2079	11.2647

TABLE 11.19 Results of the random forest classifier for different split percentages (1310 nm wavelength).

Parameter	Split percentage		
	80–20	85–15	90–10
Time taken to build model (seconds)	0.05	0.03	0.04
Time taken to test model (seconds)	0.0001	0.0001	0.0001
Correlation coefficient	0.9679	0.9522	0.998
Mean absolute error	0.2313	0.2958	0.0969
Root mean squared error	0.7908	0.9196	0.1885
Relative absolute error (%)	8.2365	10.7768	3.8219
Root relative squared error (%)	25.8091	30.6455	6.7062

TABLE 11.20 Results of the random forest classifier for different cross-validations (1550 nm wavelength).

Parameter	Cross-validation		
	Five-fold	10-fold	20-fold
Time taken to build model (seconds)	0.03	0.03	0.02
Correlation coefficient	0.998	0.9988	0.9984
Mean absolute error	0.0709	0.065	0.0703
Root mean squared error	0.1785	0.1437	0.1622
Relative absolute error (%)	2.8145	2.5797	2.7707
Root relative squared error (%)	6.3322	5.0847	5.7109

TABLE 11.21 Results of the random forest classifier for different split percentages (1550 nm wavelength).

Parameter	Split percentage		
	80–20	85–15	90–10
Time taken to build model (seconds)	0.04	0.02	0.04
Time taken to test model (seconds)	0.0001	0.0001	0.0001
Correlation coefficient	0.9979	0.9967	0.9983
Mean absolute error	0.0972	0.0833	0.0667
Root mean squared error	0.2058	0.2268	0.1837
Relative absolute error (%)	3.8204	3.6599	3.1556
Root relative squared error (%)	7.217	8.7357	7.5896

TABLE 11.22 Results of the M5 rule classifier for different cross-validations (1310 nm wavelength).

Parameter	Cross-validation		
	Five-fold	10-fold	20-fold
Time taken to build model (seconds)	0.36	0.09	0.04
Correlation coefficient	0.9977	0.9985	0.9996
Mean absolute error	0.09	0.0636	0.0357
Root mean squared error	0.1902	0.1545	0.0822
Relative absolute error (%)	3.5932	2.5244	1.4133
Root relative squared error (%)	6.793	5.4847	2.9131

TABLE 11.23 Results of theM5 rule for different split percentages (1310 nm wavelength).

Parameter	Split percentage		
	80–20	85–15	90–10
Time taken to build model (seconds)	0.01	0.08	0.01
Time taken to test model (seconds)	0.0001	0.0001	0.0001
Correlation coefficient	0.9999	0.999	0.9999
Mean absolute error	0.0369	0.1876	0.0329
Root mean squared error	0.0695	0.3469	0.0658
Relative absolute error (%)	1.3143	6.8331	1.2987
Root relative squared error (%)	2.2677	11.5591	2.3387

TABLE 11.24 Results of the M5 rule classifier for different cross-validations (1550 nm wavelength).

Parameter	Cross-validation		
	Five-fold	10-fold	20-fold
Time taken to build model (seconds)	0.02	0.01	0.04
Correlation coefficient	0.9963	0.9987	0.9997
Mean absolute error	0.1258	0.0639	0.0209
Root mean squared error	0.2596	0.145	0.063
Relative absolute error (%)	4.9907	2.5374	0.8227
Root relative squared error (%)	9.2078	5.1308	2.2192

TABLE 11.25 Results of the M5 rule classifier for different split percentages (1550 nm wavelength).

Parameter	Split percentage		
	80–20	85–15	90–10
Time taken to build model (seconds)	0.01	0.01	0.01
Time taken to test model (seconds)	0.0001	0.0001	0.0001
Correlation coefficient	0.9999	0.9999	0.9999
Mean absolute error	0.0503	0.0478	0.388
Root mean squared error	0.0868	0.0803	0.073
Relative absolute error (%)	1.9752	2.0973	1.8362
Root relative squared error (%)	3.0424	3.0923	3.0144

signal and quality factors are very influential in both operating windows as suggested by the ReliefF technique, and extreme importance should be attached from a design perspective. These factors are also present when PCA is invoked along with another common attribute called "distance." Henceforth, a soft computing method sets the priority of importance from a design stand-point.

11.6 Conclusion

Critical factors which affect the performance of a RA-based optical communication system are evaluated using PCA and ReliefF techniques, and similarity has been observed for the 1310 nm system. A better correlation coefficient is also obtained when the system is operated at the lower wavelength, in contrast to the conventional preference for a 1550 nm wavelength-based design. Multiple cross-validations are obtained to determine the correlation coefficient, and this also supports the earlier findings. the results speaks in favor of lower wavelength design of the system, which will lead to a flatter gain characteristic over a longer distance from the amplifier at the specified bit rate.

11.7 Limitations of research

The present research is primarily based on the simulation data available for a RA-based communication system, where the performance of the channel is considered under the presence of Gaussian noise only. However, several other important factors will come into play for a realistic system, for example, shot noise, thermal noise, and flicker noise. Thermal noise may not be very relevant for these types of systems, but in harsh environmental conditions it may affect the performance of the system. Flicker noise, a frequency-dependent parameter, has a great role in microwave and millimeter-wave communication systems; and therefore will have realistic interference as far as the practical system is concerned. Therefore analytical modeling is required along with the simulation to include these other interfering effects.

Bending of optical fiber can greatly reduce its signal strength and, more precisely, the radius of the curvature of the fiber. However, these factors can only be measured by introducing OTDR, and can henceforth can only be measured on a real-time basis. This effect cannot be incorporated into any simulation system, and is entirely relevant for a practical data set. This is another limitation of the present work, but this cannot be nullified by any other simulation, and therefore hindered the research.

With all these interpretations, however, the present work still has great significance, and can be explored further. This is briefly described in the next section.

11.8 Future research

The present simulation is carried out for a single pump-based system, and therefore may not be sufficiently efficient when several noise factors are incorporated. In order to reduce this, a dual-pump mechanism is proposed, although it has higher cost. This is very important for long-distance fiber-optic communication. Fibers placed under the sea require multiple pumping for efficient data transfer, and therefore dual-pumping analysis can greatly enhance the view of that system as far as performance is concerned. This is a great opportunity for researchers to estimate the critical parameters for a dual-pump system, which may help optical engineers to design a multipump system for optimum performance and cost function.

References

Agarwal, V., & Agrawal, M. (2018). Characterization and optimization of semiconductor optical amplifier for ultra high speed applications: A review. In *IEEE conference on signal processing and communication engineering systems*.

Agrawal, G. P. (2010). *Fiber-optic communication systems* (4th Ed.). Hoboken, NJ: Wiley.

Attarzadeh, I., & Ow, S.H. (2010). A novel soft computing model to increase the accuracy of software development cost estimation. In *2nd International conference on computer and automation engineering*, Singapore.

Bernard, S., Heutte, L., & Adam, S. (2009). On the selection of decision trees in Random Forests. In *International joint conference on neural networks*, 14–19 June, Atlanta, GA, USA.

Biau, G. (2012). Analysis of a random forests model. *Journal of Machine Learning Research*, *13*, 1063–1095.

Breiman, L. (2001). Random forests. *Machine Learning*, *45*, 5–32.

Bromage, J. (2004). Raman amplification for fibre communications systems. *Journal of Lightwave Technology*, *22*(1), 79–93.

Diwaker, C., Tomar, P., Poonia, R. C., & Singh, V. (2018). Prediction of software reliability using bio inspired soft computing techniques. *Journal of Medical Systems*, *42*(5), 93.

Gambhir, S., Malik, S. K., & Kumar, Y. (2016). Role of soft computing approaches in healthcare domain: A mini review. *Journal of Medical Systems*, *40*(12), 287.

Genuer, R., Poggi, J. M., & Tuleau-Malot, C. (2010). Variable selection using random forests. *Pattern Recognition Letters*, *31*, 2225–2236.

Gen, M., & Yun, Y. S. (2006). Soft computing approach for reliability optimization: State-of-the-art survey. *Reliability Engineering & System Safety*, *91*(9), 1008–1026.

Herbster, A. F., & Romero, M. A. (2017). EDFA design and analysis for WDM optical systems based on modal multiplexing. *Journal of Microwaves, Optoelectronics and Electromagnetic Applications*, *16*(1), 194–207.

Holmes, G., Hall, M., Frank, E. (1999). Generating rule sets from model trees. In *Twelfth Australian joint conference on artificial intelligence*, 1–12.

Islam, M. N. (2002). Raman amplifiers for telecommunications. *IEEE Journal of Selected Topics in Quantum Electronics, 8*(3), 548–559.

Istianing, D.K., Heryana, A., & Syahriar, A. (2012). Characteristics of Raman amplifiers in fiber optic communication systems. In *AIP conference proceedings*, 1454, 230.

Katuwal, R., Suganthan, P. N., & Zhang, L. (2020). Heterogeneous oblique random forest. *Pattern Recognition, 99*, 107078.

Kaur, S., & Joshi, V. K. (2019). A hybrid soft computing-based clustering protocol for wireless sensor networks. *International Journal of Modern Physics B, 33*(30), 1950356.

Mahdiani, H. R., Ahmadi, A., Fakhraie, S. M., & Lucas, C. (2010). Bio-inspired imprecise computational blocks for efficient vlsi implementation of soft-computing applications. *IEEE Transactions on Circuits and Systems I: Regular Papers, 57*(4), 850–862.

Mandelbaum, I., & Bolshtyansky, M. (2003). Raman amplifier model in single-mode optical fiber. *IEEE Photonics Technology Letters, 15* (12), 1704–1706.

Namiki, S., Seo, K., Tsukiji, N., & Shikii, S. (2006). Challenges of Raman amplification. *Proceedings of the IEEE, 94*(5), 1024–1035.

Pandian, P., Fernando, X., & Senjyu, T. (2019). Soft computing approaches for next-generation sustainable systems (SCNGS). *Soft Computing, 23*, 2483.

Pentoś, K., Pieczarka, K., & Lejman, K. (2020). Application of soft computing techniques for the analysis of tractive properties of a low-power agricultural tractor under various soil conditions. *Complexity, 2020*, 7607545.

Pradhan, D. D., & Mandloi, A. (2018). Performance analysis of flat gain wideband Raman amplifier for S + C and C + L Band DWDM system. *Advances in OptoElectronics*, 5703805.

Quinlan, R.J. (1992) Learning with continuous classes. In *Proceedings of the 5th Australian joint conference on artificial intelligence*, Singapore, 343–348.

Ramaswami, R., Sivarajan, K., & Sasaki, G. (2009). *Optical networks: A practical perspective* (3rd Ed.). Morgan Kaufmann.

Ray, S. S., & Pal, S. K. (2013). RNA secondary structure prediction using soft computing. *IEEE/ACM Transactions on Computational Biology and Bioinformatics, 10*(1), 2–17.

Ren, Q., Cheng, H., & Han, H. (2017). Research on machine learning framework based on random forest algorithm. *AIP Conference Proceedings, 1820*, 080020.

Samra, A.S., & Harb, H.A.M. (2009). Wide band flat gain Raman amplifier for DWDM communication systems. *In Proceedings of the 6th international conference on wireless and optical communications* networks, 212–216.

Saridakis, K. M., & Dentsoras, A. J. (2008). Soft computing in engineering design – a review. *Advanced Engineering Informatics, 22* (2), 202–221.

Silva, C. A., Sousa, M. C., Runkler, T., & Palm, R. (2005). Soft computing optimization methods applied to logistic processes. *International Journal of Approximate Reasoning, 40*(3), 280–301.

Sultana, H., & Majumder, S.P. (2012). Analytical evaluation of the effect of Raman amplifier induced crosstalk in a WDM system. In *14th international conference on advanced communication technology*, PyeongChang, South Korea.

Tithi, F.H., & Majumder, S.P. (2016). Performance limitations due to combined influence of ASE and Raman amplifier induced crosstalk in a WDM system with direct detection receiver. In *9th international conference on electrical and computer engineering*, Dhaka, Bangladesh.

Wang, Y., Witten, & Ian H. (1997) Induction of model trees for predicting continuous classes, In *Poster papers of the 9th European conference on machine learning*.

Wong, K. W., Gedeon, T. D., & Fung, C. C. (2002). The use of soft computing techniques as data preprocessing and postprocessing in permeability determination from well log data. *Studies in Fuzziness and Soft Computing: Soft Computing for Reservoir Characterization and Modeling, 80*, 243–271.

Zhao, X., Zhang, C., Li, Y., Wang, Z., & He, Y. (2012). Design of UHF RFID tag with on-chip antenna. *Advances in Intelligent and Soft Computing: Soft Computing in Information Communication Technology, 158*, 77–83.

CHAPTER

12

Random walk elephant swarm water search algorithm for identifying order-preserving submatrices in gene expression data: a new approach using elephant swarm water search algorithm

Joy Adhikary and Sriyankar Acharyya

Department of Computer Science and Engineering, Maulana Abul Kalam Azad University of Technology, Kolkata, India

12.1 Introduction

DNA microarray technologies provide an important facility to analyze the gene expression matrices, that is, to analyze the activity level of many genes under different conditions in an efficient manner (Heller, 2002; Khan, Michael, Yidong, Paul, & Jeffrey, 1999). Gene expression matrices are highly dimensional, where rows represent genes and columns represent conditions. These matrices are unbalanced because a large number of genes has been presented compared to the small number of conditions. Genes are situated in the chromosomes of every cell in an organism and the physiological and behavioral properties of the organisms are decided by them (Biswas & Acharyya, 2017). Each gene produces protein in its expression, which controls the different activities of the concerned organism. Due to some external effects, the protein production rate of a gene varies across different physiological stages or conditions (Biswas & Acharyya, 2017; Saha, Biswas, & Acharyya, 2016).

In gene expression analysis, the clustering technique is an important tool which partitions the elements (genes) into clusters based on their activities (Ben-Dor, Shamir, & Yakhini, 1999; Jiang, Tang, & Zhang, 2004). The clustering (Jiang et al., 2004; Getz, Levine, & Domany, 2000) techniques are classified into two classes: homogeneity and separation. The homogeneity model or similar cluster model shows genes having similar functions under the same conditions. But in some real situations, a group of genes (bicluster) is observed to show similar expression behavior even under different conditions (Maderia & Oliveira, 2004). The application of a standard local clustering approach in such cases is known as biclustering (Divina & Guilar-Ruiz, 2006; Maderia & Oliveira, 2004; Supper, Strauch, Wanke, Harter, & Zell, 2007; Tanay, Sharan, & Shamir, 2005, 2002). Order-preserving submatrices (OPSMs) are a special form of biclusters with coherence in values and they may not maintain the contiguous order (adjacent) in columns (Ben-Dor, Chor, Karp, & Yakhini, 2003; Gao et al., 2012; Xue et al., 2015; Yip et al., 2013).

The first proposed model for discovering significant OPSMs was based on a heuristic approach and it also established that this problem is non-deterministic polynomial time-hard (NP-hard) (Ben-Dor et al., 2003). Therefore it could not be assured to find all significant OPSMs. Another model was introduced to discover maximal OPSMs using head-trail tree hierarchical structure based on an a priori principle (Cheung, Cheung, Kao, Yip, & Ng, 2007). In Cheung et al. (2007) the number of maximal OPSMs was influenced by a supporting row threshold which increases with an increase in the database size. In Gao et al. (2012), a model was proposed called Deep OPSM, that is, based

Recent Trends in Computational Intelligence Enabled Research.
DOI: https://doi.org/10.1016/B978-0-12-822844-9.00037-2

on a KiWi framework. This OPSM model tries to find Deep OPSMs from large data sets. The Deep OPSM model is basically a heuristic method that fails to find all OPSMs (Gao et al., 2012). Another model for finding OPSMs with the help of repeated measurement techniques is not successful in the case of a large sequence of the real data set (Yip et al., 2013). In Xue et al. (2015), an algorithm is proposed to discover OPSMs with the help of the All Common Subsequence technique, prefix tree and a priori principle. The algorithm captures all OPSMs but must satisfy the minimum support threshold. The value of the threshold is predefined (Xue et al., 2015).

In this work, an attempt for the first time has been made to discover OPSMs using a metaheuristic algorithm. It is already mentioned that the OPSM problem is NP-hard and therefore metaheuristic algorithms are suitable to tackle such a problem (Beheshti & Shamsuddin, 2013; Mirjalili, Mirjalili, & Lewis, 2014). This type of algorithm is appropriate to find a near optimal solution in a real data set within a reasonable time. Metaheuristic (Das, Abraham, & Konar, 2009; Hussain, Salleh, Cheng, & Shi, 2019; Mirjalili et al., 2014) algorithms have been classified into two categories: single solution based and multiple solutions based (Beheshti & Shamsuddin, 2013). A single solution-based metaheuristic algorithm works with modifying and improving a single candidate solution. Simulated annealing (Bryan, Pádraig, & Nadia, 2005; Kirkpatrick, Gelatt & Vecchi, 1983), iterated local search (Lourenço, Martin, & Stützle, 2003), variable neighborhood search (Mladenović & Hansen, 1997), guided local search (Voudouris & Tsang, 2003) are some examples of single solution-based metaheuristic algorithms among others. Multiple solution-based algorithms works with modifying and improving multiple solutions. Some of the popular multiple solution-based algorithms are Genetic Algorithm (GA) (Holland, 1992), Particle Swarm Optimization (PSO) (Cecconi & Campenni, 2010; Jana, Mitra, & Acharyaa, 2019; Li, Yang, & Nguyen, 2012), Harmony Search (HS) (Mahdavi, Fesanghary, & Damangir, 2007), Elephant Swarm Water Search algorithm (ESWSA) (Mandal, Saha, & Paul, 2017), and many others. Multiple solution-based algorithms are more advantageous in many cases than single solution-based ones in the sense that they help a number of solutions to reach the promising region of the search space, which is very much needed to avoid local optima. They also assist to gather information about a huge search space (Beheshti & Shamsuddin, 2013; Lin & Gen, 2009; Mirjalili et al., 2014). Metaheuristic algorithms have three major classes depending on their basic properties. The classes are evolutionary type, physics based, and swarm intelligence (SI). Evolutionary algorithms are mainly inspired by evolution in nature. There are several popular evolutionary algorithms, such as GA (Holland, 1992; Horn, Nicholas, & Goldberg, 1994), Differential Evolution (DE) (Storn & Price, 1997), and Genetic Programming (Koza, 1992). Some physics-based algorithms are based on laws of physics like gravitation, black hole (BH), ray casting, and others. Gravitational Search Algorithm (Rashedi, Esmat, Nezamabadi-Pour, & Saryazdi, 2009), BH (Hatamlou, 2012) algorithm, Ray Optimization (Kaveh & Khayatazad, 2012) are remarkable among them. SI-based algorithms are the most popular metaheuristic algorithms, which consist of a group of intelligent search agents having fewer parameters than others. They preserve information about search space over the course of iterations and also save the best solutions obtained so far. These algorithms are mainly inspired by the social behavior of various creatures. Some popular SI-based algorithms include Marriage in Honey Bees Optimization Algorithm (Abbass, 2001), Cuckoo Search (Yang & Deb, 2009; Yang & Deb, 2014), Firefly Algorithm (FA) (Yang, 2010), Bird Mating Optimizer (Askarzadeh & Rezazadeh, 2012), PSO (Cecconi & Campenni, 2010; Jordehi, 2015; Li et al., 2012), and ESWSA (Mandal et al., 2017). In SI-based algorithms, movements of search agents are based on the social behavior of creatures. Implementation of this type of algorithm is easy as the number of operators used is less than in other approaches (Mirjalili et al., 2014).

This chapter applies the ESWSA (Mandal et al., 2017) to find OPSMs from a real-life data set. A new variant of ESWSA, namely, the Random Walk Elephant Swarm Water Search Algorithm (RW-ESWSA), is proposed here which has better exploration capability, incorporating randomized walk or movements in the search. A random inertia weight strategy (Bansal et al., 2011) is used here to improve the global search process of elephants. The step lengths of groups of elephants being randomized bring an opportunity for elephants to reach a better water source by diversifying their movements. The performance of the proposed method has been verified through application on benchmark functions followed by statistical testing (Derrac, García, Molina, & Herrera, 2011; Jordehi, 2015; Jana et al., 2019). Moreover, the proposed variant has been verified with five metaheuristic algorithms, which are PSO (Cecconi & Campenni, 2010), Firefly (Yang, 2010), DE (Guo, Yang, Hsu, & Tsai, 2015), Artificial Bee Colony (ABC) (Karaboga & Basturk, 2007), and HS (Geem, Km, & Loganathan, 2001). In the problem of finding OPSM (Ben-Dor et al., 2003), a comparison has been made between ESWSA (Mandal et al., 2017) and RW-ESWSA. In this comparison, the proposed variant RW-ESWSA has been able to recognize OPSMs of better quality compared to ESWSA (Mandal et al., 2017). The proposed variant RW-ESWSA brings enhancement to its exploration property by incorporating randomized movements or walks. It helps escape local minima to capture the best-quality OPSMs (Ben-Dor et al., 2003) with high biological relevance. The experiment has been conducted on two different real data sets and the biological relevance of the genes obtained from these OPSMs are tested based on Gene Ontology (GO), using Yeastract (Abdulrehman et al., 2010; Monteiro et al., 2007; Teixeira et al., 2006, 2018) and GOrilla (Eden, Roy, Israel, Doro, & Zohar, 2009; McManus et al., 2015; Supek, Matko, Nives, & Tomislav, 2011) tools. These tools identify only the relevant genes on the basis of p-value and GO. The OPSMs obtained contain the critical genes under different conditions of a disease.

The rest of the chapter is organized as follows. Section 12.2 briefly describes the problem, its general structure, and formulation. Section 12.3 describes the state-of-the-art method ESWSA and the proposed variant RW-ESWSA. Section 12.4 describes the experimental results, and Section 12.5 concludes the chapter and mentions some future works.

12.2 Problem description

Several heuristic approaches are available for discovering OPSMs (Ben-Dor et al., 2003; Cheung et al., 2007; Gao et al., 2012; Xue et al., 2015; Yip et al., 2013), but it is observed that there is no use of metaheuristic approaches. Discovering OPSMs is an NP-hard problem, so there is scope for applying metaheuristic approaches (Beheshti & Shamsuddin, 2013; Lin & Gen, 2009; Mirjalili et al., 2014). This section introduces the problem and also discusses the strategy of candidate solution generation. In this research, the formulation of the objective function is made to measure the quality of the candidate solutions (OPSMs).

12.2.1 Order-preserving submatrices

Order-preserving submatrix (OPSM) (Ben-Dor et al., 2003; Cheung et al., 2007; Xue et al., 2015; Yip et al., 2013) is a kind of clustering technique, which discovers from different pattern-based submatrices in the gene expression matrix, where rows imply a subset of genes and columns imply a subset of conditions (Ben-Dor et al., 2003). From this gene expression matrix, a submatrix is considered as OPSM if the entries of each row follow an increasing order in their values under different permutations of columns. The existence of this type of pattern indicates that significant biological relevance is present there. In OPSM, rows and columns do not need to be contiguous (Ben-Dor et al., 2003; Cheung et al., 2007). Let X be an OPSM consisting of a set of genes (G) and a set of conditions (C). Each element in X is represented by $x_{ij}(x_{ij} \in X)$, $i \in G$ and $j \in C$. For example, suppose $\boldsymbol{M}$ is a 5×6 data matrix, where rows imply a set of genes $\langle G_1, G_2, G_3, G_4, G_5 \rangle$ and columns imply a set of conditions $\langle C_1, C_2, C_3, C_4, C_5, C_6 \rangle$. From data matrix ($\boldsymbol{M}$), an OPSM $\boldsymbol{X}_1$ is selected, where the genes are $\langle G_2, G_3 \rangle$ and the conditions are $\langle C_1, C_2 \rangle$. It maintains an OPSM format it follows: $\{(G_2, C_1) < (G_2, C_2)\}$, $\{(G_3, C_1) < (G_3, C_2)\}$. In OPSM $\boldsymbol{X}_1$, rows and columns are contiguous. From data matrix ($\boldsymbol{M}$), another OPSM ($\boldsymbol{X}_2$) is selected, where the genes are $\langle G_1, G_3, G_5 \rangle$ and the conditions are $\langle C_1, C_3, C_6 \rangle$. It is maintaining the format of OPSM as $\{(G_1, C_1) < (G_1, C_3) < (G_1, C_6)\}$, $\{(G_3, C_1)) < (G_3, C_3) < (G_3, C_6)\}$, $\{(G_5, C_1) < (G_5, C_3) < (G_5, C_6)\}$. In OPSM $\boldsymbol{X}_2$, rows and columns are not contiguous.

$$\text{Data} - \text{matrix (M) is:}\quad \begin{array}{c} \\ G_1 \\ G_2 \\ G_3 \\ G_4 \\ G_5 \end{array} \begin{pmatrix} C_1 & C_2 & C_3 & C_4 & C_5 & C_6 \\ 4.05 & 2.09 & 5.02 & 3.25 & 1.98 & 6.77 \\ 1.32 & 2.02 & 5.11 & 3.33 & 6.45 & 1.33 \\ 1.34 & 2.04 & 5.98 & 5.67 & 3.56 & 7.44 \\ 1.25 & 2.98 & 5.76 & 3.33 & 2.87 & 6.77 \\ 2.99 & 3.87 & 3.23 & 5.21 & 14.28 & 6.99 \end{pmatrix}$$

Order Preserving Sub Matrix (OPSM),

$$\boldsymbol{X}_1: \begin{array}{c} \\ G_2 \\ G_3 \end{array} \begin{pmatrix} C_1 & C_2 \\ 1.32 & 2.02 \\ 1.34 & 2.04 \end{pmatrix}$$

Order Preserving Sub Matrix (OPSM),

$$\boldsymbol{X}_2: \begin{array}{c} \\ G_1 \\ G_3 \\ G_5 \end{array} \begin{pmatrix} C_1 & C_3 & C_6 \\ 4.05 & 5.02 & 6.77 \\ 1.34 & 5.98 & 7.44 \\ 2.99 & 3.23 & 6.99 \end{pmatrix}$$

12.2.2 Solution generation

In this chapter, each solution represents a submatrix and the length of each candidate solution is equal to the sum of the total number of rows and the total number of columns. Table 12.1 represents the structure of a candidate solution, where entry 0 indicates that the corresponding gene/condition is not selected in OPSM. The initial solution is designed in the following way. The bits 0's and 1's are randomly selected for

TABLE 12.1 Candidate solution structural form.

G_1	G_2	G_3	G_4	G_5	C_1	C_2	C_3	C_4	C_5	C_6
0	0	0	0	0	0	0	0	0	0	0

TABLE 12.2 Complete representation of candidate solution (order-preserving submatrices X_2).

G_1	G_2	G_3	G_4	G_5	C_1	C_2	C_3	C_4	C_5	C_6
1	0	1	0	1	1	0	1	0	0	1

positions in rows and columns. In this case, bit 1 indicates the corresponding gene/condition is selected and bit 0 indicates that the corresponding gene/condition is not selected in OPSM. This is presented in Table 12.2. After generating candidate solutions, the cost of each solution has been calculated and then sorted according to cost.

12.2.3 Cost function

Each candidate solution has a cost. There are different criteria in defining the cost function. Depending on the different criteria, the following cost types have been defined.

12.2.3.1 *Transposed virtual error* (VE^t)

Transposed virtual error (VE^t) is used as the cost function. It is used to measure the quality of an OPSM. It is used to identify the strength of relationship among genes. VE^t needs to be minimized satisfying $VE^t > 0$ (Pontes, Giráldez, & Aguilar-Ruiz, 2013, 2015; Pontes, Girldez, & Aguilar-Ruiz, 2010).

In the VE^t calculation, first one has to measure the virtual condition (a meaningful value for all the conditions of an OPSM, regarding each gene) for each gene of an OPSM (Pontes et al., 2010). The virtual condition for each gene is measured by the mean of expression values of every row or gene in an OPSM. It can be expressed by Eq. (12.1). Here, ρ_i represents the mean of expression values of the i-th row or gene of an OPSM. Eq. (12.2) defines $\widehat{\rho_i}$, and calculates the standardized values of virtual condition (for each ρ_i) in an OPSM. Here, μ_ρ and σ_ρ represent arithmetic mean and standard deviation for virtual condition, respectively (Pontes et al., 2013; Pontes et al., 2010). Eq. (12.3) defines $\widehat{x_{ij}}$, and calculates the standardized OPSM $(\widehat{x_{ij}})$ from an OPSM as a new OPSM. It is already proved in Pontes et al. (2010) that the value of mean and standard deviation of the obtained standardized OPSM $(\widehat{x_{ij}})$ will always be 0 and 1 (Pontes et al., 2013; Pontes et al., 2010). Here, σ_{c_j} and μ_{c_j} represent the standard deviation and arithmetic mean of all expression values for condition j, respectively. $VE^t(X)$ is used to calculate the cost of OPSM X, where I means the number of rows and J means the number of columns of an OPSM X. It can be defined as the numerical difference between the standardized value of OPSM $(\widehat{x_{ij}})$ and that of virtual condition $(\widehat{\rho_i})$, which is represented by Eq. (12.4) (Pontes et al., 2013, 2010).

$$\rho_i = \frac{1}{|J|}\sum_{j=1}^{|J|} x_{ij} \tag{12.1}$$

$$\widehat{\rho_i} = \frac{\rho_i - \mu_\rho}{\sigma_\rho} \tag{12.2}$$

$$\widehat{x_{ij}} = \frac{x_{ij} - \mu_{c_j}}{\sigma_{c_j}} \tag{12.3}$$

$$VE^t(X) = \frac{1}{|I|.|J|}\sum_{i=1}^{|I|}\sum_{j=1}^{|J|} abs\left(\widehat{x_{ij}} - \widehat{\rho_i}\right) \tag{12.4}$$

Order Preserving Sub Matrix (OPSM), X_1:

$$\begin{matrix} & \\ G_2 \\ G_3 \end{matrix}\begin{pmatrix} C_1 & C_2 \\ 1.32 & 2.02 \\ 1.34 & 2.04 \end{pmatrix}$$

Applying Eq. (12.1) to OPSM X_1, the virtual condition (mean of expression values of every row) is: $\rho_1 = 1.67$ and $\rho_2 = 1.69$.

Applying Eq. (12.2) on OPSM X_1, μ_ρ (arithmetic mean) $= \mu(\rho_1, \rho_2) = \mu(1.67, 1.69) = 1.68$ and σ_ρ(standard deviation) $= \sigma(\rho_1, \rho_2) = \sigma(1.67, 1.69) = 0.0141$. We get the standardized values of the virtual condition $(\widehat{\rho_i})$ as: $[-0.7092 \quad 0.7092]$.

After applying Eq. (12.3), μ_{c_j}(arithmetic mean): $(\mu_{c_1}, \mu_{c_2}) = (1.33, 2.03)$ and σ_{c_j}(standard deviation): $(\sigma_{c_1}, \sigma_{c_2}) = (0.0141, 0.0141)$. x_{ij} is the expression level of a gene, like $x_{2,1} = 1.32, x_{2,2} = 2.02, x_{3,1} = 1.34$ and $x_{3,2} = 2.04$. The standardized OPSM $(\widehat{x_{ij}})$ is: $\begin{bmatrix} -0.7092 & -0.7092 \\ 0.7092 & 0.7092 \end{bmatrix}$. Mean $(\widehat{x_{ij}}) = 0$ and Std $(\widehat{x_{ij}}) = 1$. This shows the validity of the VE^t.

$VE^t(X_1) = 7.85E - 15$. The minimization of VE^t indicates the quality of the order-preserving submatrix.

Order Preserving Sub Matrix (OPSM), X_2:

$$\begin{matrix} & \\ G_1 \\ G_3 \\ G_5 \end{matrix}\begin{pmatrix} C_1 & C_3 & C_6 \\ 4.05 & 5.02 & 6.77 \\ 1.34 & 5.98 & 7.44 \\ 2.99 & 3.23 & 6.99 \end{pmatrix}$$

$VE^t(X_2) = 0.8448$. $VE^t((X_2)$ is higher than $VE^t(X_1)$, so the quality of OPSM (X_2) is not better than OPSM (X_1).

12.3 Method

Metaheuristic optimization techniques are generalized, robust, and problem domain independent, that is, not problem specific like heuristics. These techniques are reliable and widely used. The limitations like confinement of search process into local minima and its early convergence that occur in heuristics are efficiently tackled here using a suitable exploration strategy (Beheshti & Shamsuddin, 2013; Lin & Gen, 2009). There is a balance between exploration and exploitation in metaheuristic search to make the method robust and reliable (Lin & Gen, 2009). They have the capacity of reproducibility of results. Here, a metaheuristic method called the ESWSA (Mandal et al., 2017) and its proposed variant the RW-ESWSA have been used to identify OPSMs.

12.3.1 Elephant swarm water search algorithm

The ESWSA (Mandal et al., 2017) is a nature-inspired algorithm based on SI. The main idea of this algorithm is inspired by water search techniques normally practiced by elephants. In times of drought, elephants move around and search for water divided into several swarms. A swarm consists of a collection of groups. Each group is a subset of elephants who work together to find the source of water. The guide of each group takes decisions for where to move next to find the water body. The algorithm considers that each elephant group has its own particular velocity and position and the group position is considered as a candidate solution to the problem. Whenever a water body is found by a group, its leader communicates the information to other groups of the swarm. They have two kinds of water search strategies: local and global. In local water search, each group of elephants discovers its so far best (nearest) location of the water source in its journey. This position of each group of elephants by which the so far best water source is discovered is considered and stored as the local best solution of the group. In global water search, there is a group of elephants whose position is the so far best among all the local best group positions in the swarm. This position of the corresponding best group of elephants in the swarm is considered and stored as the global best solution. The local and the global search movements of the groups are expressed by Eqs. (12.5) and (12.6), respectively. These searching strategies are controlled by a context-switching probability P (Mandal et al., 2017).

$$V_i = V_i * w + rand(1,d) \odot (Pbest_i - X_i); \tag{12.5}$$

$$V_i = V_i * w + rand(1,d) \odot (Gbest - X_i); \tag{12.6}$$

$$w = w_{max} - \left\{ \frac{w_{max} - w_{min}}{t_{max}} \right\} * t \tag{12.7}$$

$$X_i = V_i + X_i \tag{12.8}$$

ALGORITHM 1 Element Swarm Water Search Algorithm (ESWSA)

Input N /*the number of elephant groups*/;
Input p /*context switching probability*/; Input w_{max}, w_{min}, t, t_{max};
for $i = 1$ to N **do**
  Initialize positions X_i,velocity V_i;
  Set local best $Pbest_i = X_i$;
  Calculate cost (X_i);
end for
Global best $Gbest = Min(cost(X_i))$;
for $t = 1$ to t_{max} **do**
  Initialize $w = w_{max} - \left\{ \frac{w_{max} - w_{min}}{t_{max}} \right\} * t$;/* **LDIW** */
  for $i = 1$ to N **do**
    if (rand()$< P$) **then** /* **global search** */
      /* $\odot$ = **element wise product operator** */
      $V_i = V_i * w + rand(1,d) \odot (Gbest - X_i)$;
    else /* **local search** */
      $V_i = V_i * w + rand(1,d) \odot (Pbest_i - X_i)$;
    end if
    $X_i = V_i + X_i$; /* **Update position** */
    if (cost (X_i) $<$ cost $(Pbest_i)$) **then**
      $Pbest_i \leftarrow X_i$;
    end if
    if (cost $(Pbest_i)$ $<$ cost $(Gbest)$) **then**
      $Gbest \leftarrow Pbest_i$;
    end if
  end for
  $Y* \leftarrow Gbest$; /* Y^* **holds global best solution** */
end for
Return $Y*$;

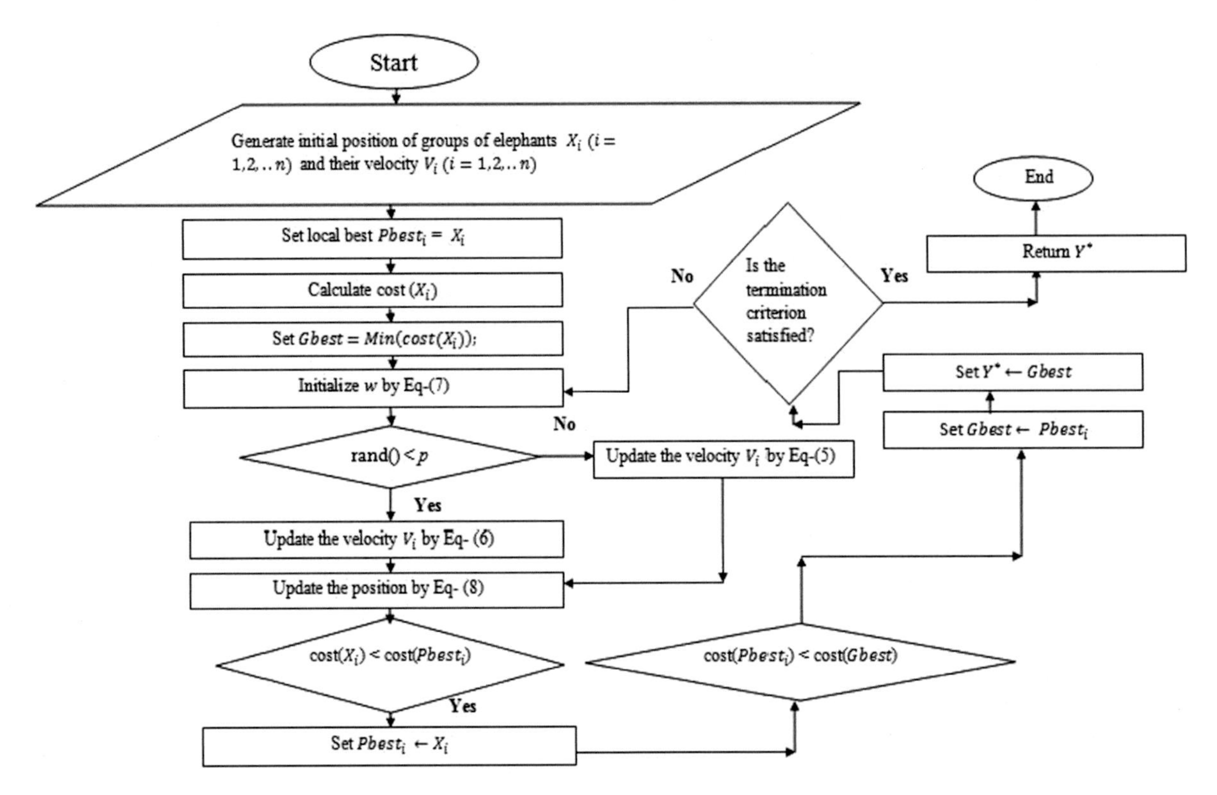

FIGURE 12.1 Flowchart of the Elephant swarm water search algorithm

In Eqs. (12.5) and (12.6),$rand(1, d)$ refers to a d-dimensional array of random values within [0, 1]. Here, w is an inertia weight strategy, called the linear decreasing inertia weight (LDIW) (Mandal et al., 2017), expressed by Eq. (12.7). w_{max} and w_{min} are two control parameters used here and the values of these parameters have been given in Section 12.4.1. t and t_{max} denote iteration and maximum number of iteration that have been used in Eq. (12.7). This strategy is used in both types of water search (local and global). In Eqs. (12.5), (12.6), and (12.8), V_i is the velocity of the i-th group of elephants and X_i is the current position of the i-th group of elephants. The best group finds water resource earlier than others. The local best solution of the i-th elephant group is defined by $Pbest_i$. The best solution among all local best solutions is defined by $Gbest$. $Gbest$ is the global best solution (Fig. 12.1).

12.3.2 Random walk elephant swarm water search algorithm

In ESWSA (Mandal et al., 2017), two major activities are local and global search. The LDIW strategy is used to improve the performance of water search capability of elephants in both local and global search processes. In the case of global water search, LDIW (w) has not been performed well because it (w) is decreased linearly from w_{max} to w_{min} in a systematic manner. It is responsible for causing premature convergence due to poor exploration capability of ESWSA. Therefore this research has proposed a random inertia weight strategy to improve the efficiency of the global search process. The modified global search process has been represented by Eq. (12.10). The random inertia weight strategy (Bansal et al., 2011) is represented by Eq. (12.9). In Eq. (12.9), c is a constant. Selecting the value of c has been analyzed in Section 12.4.1. Here, c is multiplied with $(rand()/2)$ and enhances the searching tactics with the effect of randomization. It also may increase the length of steps of elephants that brings the opportunity for them to find the water resource more effectively. In Bansal et al. (2011), the efficiency of random inertia weight strategy is already proved. The impact of random inertia weight strategy has been discussed in Section 12.4.7.

$$wt = c * (rand()/2) \tag{12.9}$$

$$V_i = V_i * wt + rand(1, d) \odot (Gbest - X_i); \tag{12.10}$$

First, the cost of the local best solution $(cost(Pbest_i))$ of the i-th elephant group is compared with the cost of its updated position of $(cost(X_i))$. In this comparison, if the cost of the updated position of $(cost(X_i))$ of the i-th elephant group is not less than the cost of the local best solution $(cost(Pbest_i))$, then it again updates the

ALGORITHM 2 Random Walk Element Swarm Water Search Algorithm (RW-ESWSA)

Input N /*the number of elephant groups*/;
Input p /*context switching probability*/; Input w_{max}, w_{min}, t, t_{max};
for $i = 1$ to N **do**
  Initialize positions X_i, velocity V_i;
  Set local best $Pbest_i = X_i$;
  Calculate cost (X_i)
end for
Global best $Gbest = Min(cost(X_i))$;
for $t = 1$ to t_{max} **do**
  Initialize $w = w_{max} - \{\frac{w_{max} - w_{min}}{t_{max}}\} * t$; /* **LDIW** */
  Initialize $wt = c^*(rand()/2)$; /* **Random Inertia Weight Strategy** */
  for $i = 1$ to N **do**
    if (rand() $< P$) **then** /* **global search** */
      /* $\odot$ = **element wise product operator** */
      $V_i = V_i * wt + rand(1, d) \odot (Gbest - X_i)$;
    else /* **local search** */
      $V_i = V_i * w + rand(1, d) \odot (Pbest_i - X_i)$;
    end if
    $X_i = V_i + X_i$; /* **Update position** */
    if (cost (X_i) $<$ cost $(Pbest_i)$) **then**
      $Pbest_i \leftarrow X_i$;
    else
    $X_i' = X_i + w * rand(0, 1)$;
    if(cost(X_i') $<$ cost$(Pbest_i)$) **then**
      $Pbest_i \leftarrow X_i'$;
    end if
    if (cost $(Pbest_i)$ $<$ cost $(Gbest)$) **then**
      $Gbest \leftarrow Pbest_i$;
    end if
  end for
  $Y* \leftarrow Gbest$; /* **Y* holds global best solution** */
end for
Return $Y*$;

position (X_i) of the i-th elephant group by Eq. (12.11). Otherwise, it stores X_i, as $Pbest_i$. The new position updating strategies helps elephants explore the search space more and more to reach the promising part in the search region. In Eq. (12.11), $X_i(i = 1, 2, ..n)$ is the existing position and $X_i'(i = 1, 2, ..n)$ is the updated position. This new strategy provides random movements for the elephants using the concept of randomization. It is one of the major contributions of this chapter to improve the exploring capability of the search process. The multiplier w is continuously adjusted by a linear decrease from w_{max} to w_{min} in a systematic way to control the explorative behavior of the search. The expression of w is given by $w = w_{max} - \{\frac{w_{max} - w_{min}}{t_{max}}\} * t$, where t denotes iteration number and control parameters are w_{max}, w_{min}. The values of these control parameters are analyzed in Section 12.4.1. w is multiplied with $rand(0, 1)$. The term $rand(0, 1)$ generates randomized explorative move and w controls these explorative movements by the linear decreasing property. Elephants update their positions using Eq. (12.11). The cost of recently updated solutions cost (X_i') and cost of the local best solution $(cost(Pbest_i))$ of the i-th elephant group are compared and the lower (better) one is stored into $Pbest_i$ (Fig. 12.2).

$$X_i' = X_i + w * rand(0, 1) \tag{12.11}$$

12.4 Numerical experiments

In this section, the performance of ESWSA (Mandal et al., 2017) and its proposed variant RW-ESWSA has been tested on benchmark functions using various experimental methods. The experiments were implemented in a machine with Pentium Dual-Core CPU and a 2 GB memory. The software environment was Microsoft Windows 7 and the platform was Matlab R2012b. Section 12.4.1 states the parameters setting and Section 12.4.2 briefly discusses the benchmark functions. Section 12.4.3 analyzes the convergence curves and Section 12.4.4 shows the convergence analysis of the proposed variant with the other meta-heuristic algorithms. Section 12.4.5 analyzes the performance of RW-ESWSA with the change in the objective function dimension. Section 12.4.6 describes the

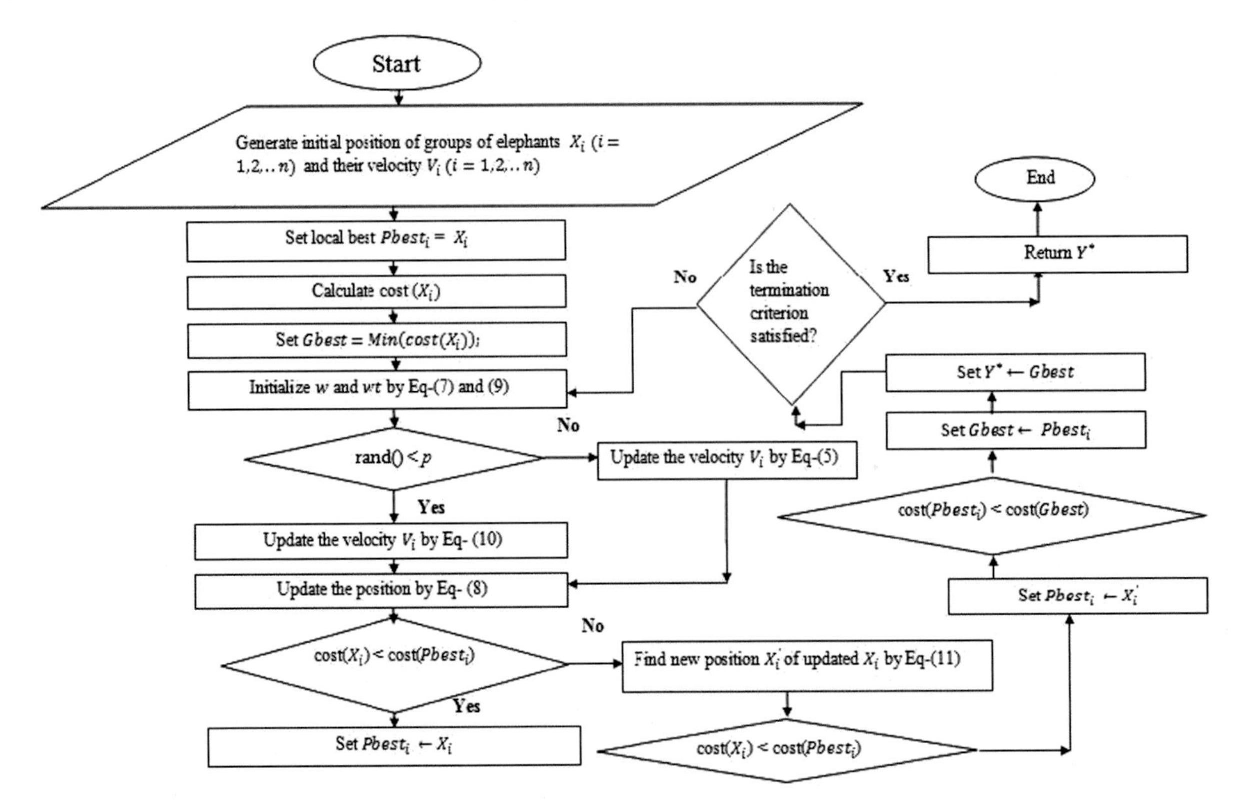

FIGURE 12.2 Flowchart of the Random walk elephant swarm water search algorithm.

TABLE 12.3 List of parameters with values.

Sl. no.	Parameter name	Parameter value
1.	w_{max}	0.9
2.	w_{min}	0.4
3.	P	0.6
4.	c	0.5

effectiveness of context switch probability, and Section 12.4.7 describes the impact of random inertia weight strategy. Section 12.4.8 shows the success rate of ESWSA and its proposed variant. Section 12.4.9 describes the experimental results of statistical testing. The experimental results on real-life gene expression data sets are given in Section 12.4.10. Finally, Section 12.4.11 describes the biological relevance.

12.4.1 Parameter settings

This section describes the various parameters which have been used in ESWSA (Mandal et al., 2017) and its proposed variant RW-ESWSA. The parameters and their values are given in Table 12.3. Parameters w_{max} and w_{min} have been used in the LDIW (Mandal et al., 2017) strategy. In Section 12.3, the importance of LDIW has been explained, and it is denoted by w (Mandal et al., 2017). The expression of w is given by $w = w_{max} - \{\frac{w_{max} - w_{min}}{t_{max}}\} * t$, where, w_{max} and w_{min} are two control parameters. This research has used the same values of control parameters as used in Mandal et al. (2017). The next parameter is context switching probability, denoted by P. This parameter helps take decisions as to whether the groups of elephants will search locally or globally. The value of P has been adjusted in Section 12.4.6. c is a constant, that is, used in random inertia weight strategy (Bansal et al., 2011). This strategy has been used in the proposed variant (RW-ESWSA). The value of c is already adjusted in Bansal et al. (2011) and the same value has been used in this research.

12.4.2 Benchmark functions

In this section, the performance of the proposed RW-ESWSA is compared with that of ESWSA. The size of the population is set to 10, the maximum number of iterations is set to 100, and 50 independent runs have been taken in the case of each benchmark function (Jamil & Yang, 2013; Jana et al., 2019; Jordehi, 2015). Here, 12 benchmark functions have been taken and each function is tested in different scalability (dimensions 5 and 10). The performance on benchmark functions shows the strengths and weaknesses of the methods used. The experiments have been conducted on four unimodal (one local optimum) and eight multimodal (more than one local optimum) benchmark functions. The four unimodal benchmark functions are: Sphere (F1), Zakharov (F2), Dixon-price (F3), and Shifted Sphere (F4). Among the four unimodal benchmark functions, three functions (F1, F2, and F3) are classical and one function (F4) has been taken from CEC 2005 (Suganthan et al., 2005) (special form of benchmark instances which are shifted, rotated forms of classical instances). The specifications of four unimodal benchmark functions (F1–F4) have been presented in Table 12.4. The eight multimodal functions are: Rastrigin (F5), Levy (F6), Ackley (F7), Rosenbrock (F8), Griewank (F9), Shifted Rotated Griewank's Function without Bounds (F10), Shifted Rastrigin's (F11), and Shifted Rosenbrock (F12). Among the eight multimodal benchmark functions, five functions (F5, F6, F7, F8, and F9) are classical and three functions (F10, F11, and F12) have been taken from CEC 2005 (Suganthan et al., 2005). The specifications of eight multimodal benchmark functions (F5, F6, F7, F8, F9, F10, and F12) have been represented in Table 12.5. The results for unimodal functions are represented in Tables 12.6 and 12.7, where the best value (minimum cost) has been made bold in each row. In Table 12.6, RW-ESWSA has outperformed ESWSA in all unimodal functions (F1, F2, F3, and F4) that reflects its strong exploitation strength. In Table 12.7, RW-ESWSA has performed the best on functions F1 and F2 among the four unimodal functions of dimension 10. RW-ESWSA shows its strong efficacy in multimodal function of dimensions 5 (Table 12.8) and 10 (Table 12.9). Among the eight multimodal functions, in Table 12.8, RW-ESWSA has outperformed its competitors on seven functions (F5, F6, F7, F8, F9, F11, and F12). In Table 12.9, RW-ESWSA has won the game for functions F5, F7, F8, F9, and F11. Therefore it is observed that the overall performance of RW-ESWSA is better in the case of multimodal benchmark functions also, which shows the strong exploration capability and ability of avoiding local optima of the variant.

TABLE 12.4 Specification of unimodal benchmark functions.

Function name	Formulation	Range
Sphere (F1)	$F2(X) = \sum_{t=1}^{n} X_t^2$	[− 5.12, +5.12]
Zakharov (F2)	$F2(X) = \sum_{t=1}^{n} X_t^2 + \left(\sum_{t=1}^{n} 0.5iX_t\right)^2 + \left(\sum_{t=1}^{n} 0.5iX_t\right)^4$	[− 5, +10]
Dixon-price (F3)	$F3(X) = (X_1 - 1)2 + \sum_{t=2}^{n}[i(2X_t^2 - X_{t-1})^2$	[− 10, +10]
Shifted Sphere (F4)	$F4(X) = \sum_{t=1}^{D} X_i^2 + f_{bias_1}$	[− 100, +100]

TABLE 12.5 Specification of multimodal benchmark functions.

Function name	Formulation	Range
Rastrigin (F5)	$F5(X) = 10n + \sum_{t=1}^{n}(X_t^2 - 10cos(2\pi X_t))$	[− 5.12, +5.12]
Levy (F6)	$F6(X) = sin^2(\pi X_t)\sum_{t=1}^{n-1}(Y_t - 1)^2[1 + 10sin^2(\pi Y_t + 1)^2] + (Y_t - 1)^2\left[1 + sin^2(2\pi Y_t)\right]\ where,\ Y_t = 1 + \frac{X_i - 1}{4}\ for\ i = 1, 23, ...n$	[− 10, +10]
Ackly (F7)	$F7(X) = 20 + e - 20\exp\left(-0.2\sqrt{1/n\sum_{t=1}^{n} X_t^2}\right) - exp\left(\sqrt{1/n\sum_{t=1}^{n} cos(2\pi X_t)}\right)$	[− 32, +32]
Rosenbrock (F8)	$F8(X) = \sum_{t=1}^{n-1}[100(X_t^2 - X_{t+1}^2)^2 + (X_t - 1)^2$	[− 5, +10]
Greiewank (F9)	$F9(X) = \sum_{t=1}^{n} X_{i/4000}^2 - \prod_{t=1}^{n} cos\left(\frac{X_i}{\sqrt{i}}\right) + 1$	[− 600, +600]
Shifted Rotated Griewank's Function without Bounds (F10)	$F10(Z) = \sum_{i=1}^{D}\frac{Z_i^2}{4000} - \prod_{i=1}^{D}\cos\left(\frac{Z_i}{\sqrt{i}}\right) + 1 + f_{bias4},$ $Z = (X - O) * M, X = [X_1, X_2, ..., X_D]\ where, D = dimensions,$ $M' = linear\ transformation\ mtrix,\ conditionn\ umber = 3$ $M = M'(1 + 0.3\lvert N(0, 1)\rvert)$ $O = [O_1, O_2, ..O_D]\ the\ shifted\ gloabal\ optimum$	[− 600, +600]
Shifted Rastrigin's Function (F11)	$F11(Z) = \sum_{i=1}^{D}(Z_i^2 - 10\cos(2\Pi Z_i) + 10) + f_{bias6}, Z = X - O,$ $X = [X_1, X_2, ..., X_D], O = [O_1, O_2, ..O_D]\ the\ shifted\ gloabal\ optimum$	[− 5, +5]
Shifted Rosenbrock (F12)	$F12(Z) = \sum_{i=1}^{D-1}(100(Z_i^2 - Z_{i+1})^2 + (Z_i - 1)^2) + f_{bias3},$ $Z = X - O + 1, X = [X_1, X_2, ..., X_D]\ where, D = dimensions,$ $O = [O_1, O_2, ..O_D]\ the\ shifted\ gloabal\ optimum$	[− 100, +100]

TABLE 12.6 Comparison of the results of elephant swarm water search algorithm and random walk elephant swarm water search algorithm on unimodal benchmark function for dimension 5 (best results are highlighted in bold).

	Mean	Std Dev	Median	Min	Max
Sphere (F1)					
ESWSA	6.53E-07	4.23E-06	2.74E-10	8.05E-15	2.99E-05
RW-ESWSA	**4.65E-09**	**1.22E-08**	2.83E-10	**6.90E-15**	**5.38E-08**
Zakharov (F2)					
ESWSA	3.055	12.142	3.00E-04	2.60E-11	70.312
RW-ESWSA	**0.794**	**2.7458**	**5.87E-07**	**6.45E-13**	**17.493**
Dixon-price (F3)					
ESWSA	0.1392	0.2854	0.0387	3.52E-05	1.904
RW-ESWSA	0.1485	**0.2709**	**0.0305**	**1.34E-05**	**1.634**
Shifted Sphere(F4)					
ESWSA	2.709	4.200	0.760	5.43E-04	17.008
RW-ESWSA	**1.553**	**2.255**	**0.595**	**1.50E-04**	**10.411**

ESWSA, Elephant Swarm Water Search Algorithm; *RW-ESWSA*, Random Walk Elephant Swarm Water Search Algorithm

TABLE 12.7 Comparison of the results of elephant swarm water search algorithm and random walk elephant swarm water search algorithm on unimodal benchmark function for dimension 10 (best results are highlighted in bold).

	Mean	Std Dev	Median	Min	Max
Sphere (F1)					
ESWSA	6.805E-04	0.0029	3.375E-06	**3.633E-10**	0.0184
RW-ESWSA	**2.942E-05**	**9.442E-05**	**1.077E-06**	1.201E-09	**4.733E-04**
Zakharov (F2)					
ESWSA	7.139	15.659	0.117	**4.140E-07**	**70.312**
RW-ESWSA	**6.271**	**15.043**	**0.025**	3.964E-06	**70.312**
Dixon-price (F3)					
ESWSA	**0.153**	**0.336**	**0.005**	3.100E-06	2.015
RW-ESWSA	0.196	0.439	0.014	**3.789E-07**	**2.001**
Shifted Sphere (F4)					
ESWSA	**1.577**	**2.904**	**0.219**	3.281E-04	**16.129**
RW-ESWSA	2.069	3.655	0.578	**5.689E-05**	17.064

ESWSA, Elephant Swarm Water Search Algorithm; *RW-ESWSA*, Random Walk Elephant Swarm Water Search Algorithm

TABLE 12.8 Comparison of the results of elephant swarm water search algorithm and random walk elephant swarm water search algorithm on multimodal benchmark function for dimension 5 (best results are highlighted in bold).

	Mean	Std Dev	Median	Min	Max
Rastrigin (F5)					
ESWSA	1.183	2.351	0.793	**1.732E-09**	13.266
RW-ESWSA	**0.990**	**1.475**	**0.334**	4.334E-09	**6.168**
Levy (F6)					
ESWSA	0.036	0.171	3.95E-07	4.26E-11	0.979
RW-ESWSA	**1.09E-05**	**6.60E-05**	**4.49E-08**	**1.35E-11**	**4.66E-04**
Ackley (F7)					
ESWSA	0.399	2.823	**7.655E-08**	**7.749E-10**	19.966
RW-ESWSA	**0.140**	**0.620**	5.260E-04	9.884E-06	**3.575**
Rosenbrock (F8)					
ESWSA	6.367E + 03	1.636E + 04	2.267E + 02	**9.412**	5.81E + 04
RW-ESWSA	**10.014**	**0**	**10.014**	10.014	**10.014**
Griewank (F9)					
ESWSA	0.0882	0.1692	**0.0237**	**9.12E-11**	1.012
RW-ESWSA	**0.0623**	**0.0935**	0.0242	3.94E-06	**0.402**
Shifted rotated griewank's function without bounds (F10)					
ESWSA	**0.0871**	0.1412	**0.0325**	2.28E-07	**0.6216**
RW-ESWSA	0.0941	**0.1382**	0.0452	**2.54E-08**	0.6636
Shifted rastrigin (F11)					
ESWSA	0.5106	**0.4641**	0.3925	0.0014	**1.3158**
RW-ESWSA	**0.4962**	0.7561	**0.1349**	**8.20E-06**	4.2895
Shifted rosenbrock (F12)					
ESWSA	2.22E + 05	4.162E + 05	2.68E + 02	**6.93E-04**	1.00E + 06
RW-ESWSA	**8.92E + 03**	**0**	**8.92E + 03**	8.92E + 03	**8.92E + 03**

ESWSA, Elephant Swarm Water Search Algorithm; *RW-ESWSA*, Random Walk Elephant Swarm Water Search Algorithm.

12.4.3 Convergence analysis

This section illustrates the convergence characteristics of ESWSA and RW-ESWSA for benchmark functions. Here, the X axis represents iterations (implies generation) and the Y axis represents cost values. The convergence graphs for Sphere (F1), Zakharov (F2), Dixon-Price (F3) Shifted Sphere (F4), Levy (F6), Ackley (F7), Shifted Rotated Griewank (F10), and Shifted Rastrigin (F11) are represented by Figs. 12.3–12.10. In convergence graphs for functions F1, F2, F3, F4, F6, F7, F10, and F11 (Figs. 12.3–12.10), the proposed variant (RW-ESWSA) has performed extremely well. In Figs. 12.3 and 12.6, ESWSA is closely competitive in exploration capability with RW-ESWSA. However, in Figs. 12.4 and 12.5, RW-ESWSA outperformed the other with its strong exploration ability. In Figs. 12.7–12.9, the cost of solution decreases slowly and steadily for RW-ESWSA. The performance of ESWSA is not good in the case of functions F6 and F7 (Figs. 12.7 and 12.8), because of poor exploration ability. RW-ESWSA performed very well in both the convergence curves (Figs. 12.7 and 12.8), because it has strong ability of local

TABLE 12.9 Comparison of the results of elephant swarm water search algorithm and random walk elephant swarm water search algorithm on multimodal benchmark function for dimension 10 (best results are highlighted in bold).

	Mean	Std Dev	Median	Min	Max
Rastrigin (F5)					
ESWSA	1.3207	2.0842	0.9950	**3.831E-08**	10.401
RW-ESWSA	**0.4705**	**0.4797**	**0.3001**	2.293E-04	**1.5095**
Levy (F6)					
ESWSA	**0.335**	**0.837**	0.0019	2.90E-08	**3.466**
RW-ESWSA	0.350	0.944	**3.54E-04**	**3.68E-09**	4.339
Ackley (F7)					
ESWSA	3.117	3.584	2.248	0.005	16.077
RW-ESWSA	**1.290**	**2.107**	**0.075**	**1.01E-04**	**9.211**
Rosenbrock (F8)					
ESWSA	5.44E + 03	1.51E + 04	**1.38E + 02**	**7.94E + 00**	5.55E + 02
RW-ESWSA	**1.88E + 02**	**0**	1.88E + 02	1.88E + 02	**1.88E + 02**
Griewank (F9)					
ESWSA	0.0609	0.1153	**0.0218**	1.196E-05	**0.6676**
RW-ESWSA	**0.0597**	**0.1137**	0.0239	**3.662E-06**	0.7457
Shifted rotated griewank's function without bounds (F10)					
ESWSA	1.9635	13.001	**0.0154**	2.211E-04	91.999
RW-ESWSA	**0.0799**	**0.2638**	0.0164	**6.372E-06**	**1.8543**
Shifted rastrigin (F11)					
ESWSA	0.6616	0.6937	0.5107	3.834E-05	3.9799
RW-ESWSA	**0.4378**	**0.5331**	**0.1837**	**2.203E-05**	**2.2194**
Shifted rosenbrock (F12)					
ESWSA	**4.98E + 05**	1.01E + 06	**1.23E + 05**	**7.73E + 01**	6.78E + 06
RW-ESWSA	1.01E + 06	**0**	1.01E + 06	1.01E + 06	**1.01E + 06**

ESWSA, Elephant Swarm Water Search Algorithm; *RW-ESWSA*, Random Walk Elephant Swarm Water Search Algorithm.

optima avoidance. In Fig. 12.10, the ESWSA converges earlier than RW-ESWSA to a minimum value of cost. It is observed that the overall performance of the proposed RW-ESWSA is far better than ESWSA.

12.4.4 Comparison with other metaheuristic algorithms

In this section, the performance of the proposed variant of ESWSA has been verified with other metaheuristic algorithms. In this comparison, five metaheuristic algorithms [PSO (Cecconi & Campenni, 2010), DE (Guo et al., 2015), ABC (Karaboga & Basturk, 2007), HS (Geem et al., 2001), and Firefly (Yang, 2010)] have been selected. The comparative analysis has been presented through Figs. 12.11–12.13. In each case, the proposed variant has shown better performance. In Figs. 12.11 and 12.12, ESWSA has become competitive with RW-ESWSA. In Fig. 12.13, FA's performance follows RW-ESWSA.

12.4.5 Performance of random walk elephant swarm water search algorithm with the change in the objective function dimension

In this section, the performance of RW-ESWSA is tested with different objective function dimensions (dimensions 5 and 10) on various benchmark functions. This section has represented some of the convergence curves (functions F1, F2, F4, and F6) among 12 functions. Each convergence curve shows (Figs. 12.14–12.17) that the solution is converging gradually toward the best solution. The convergence pattern is observed to be consistent irrespective of the dimension.

12.4.6 Effectiveness of context switch probability

The context switch probability (P) used in ESWSA is the most important parameter that controls the

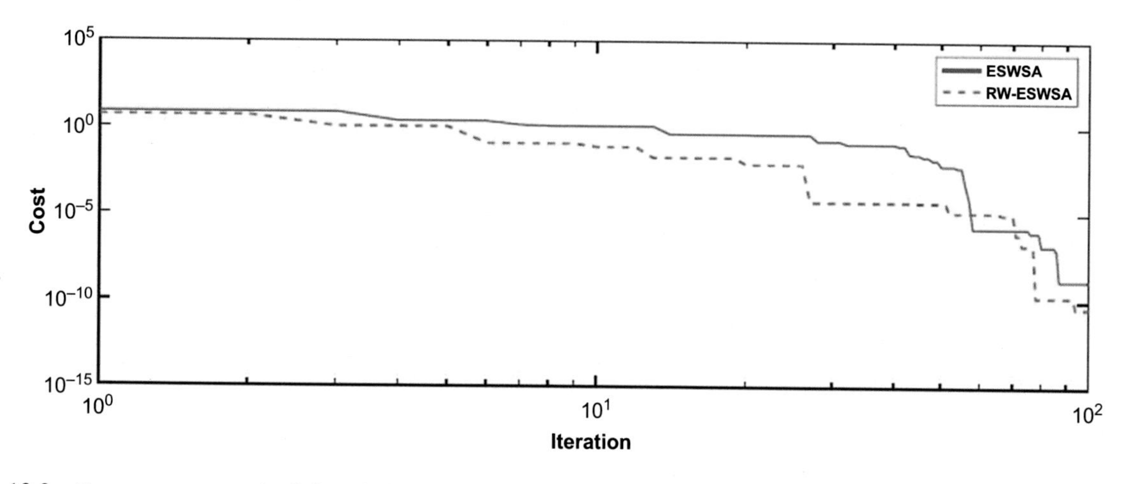

FIGURE 12.3 Convergence curve for Sphere (F1).

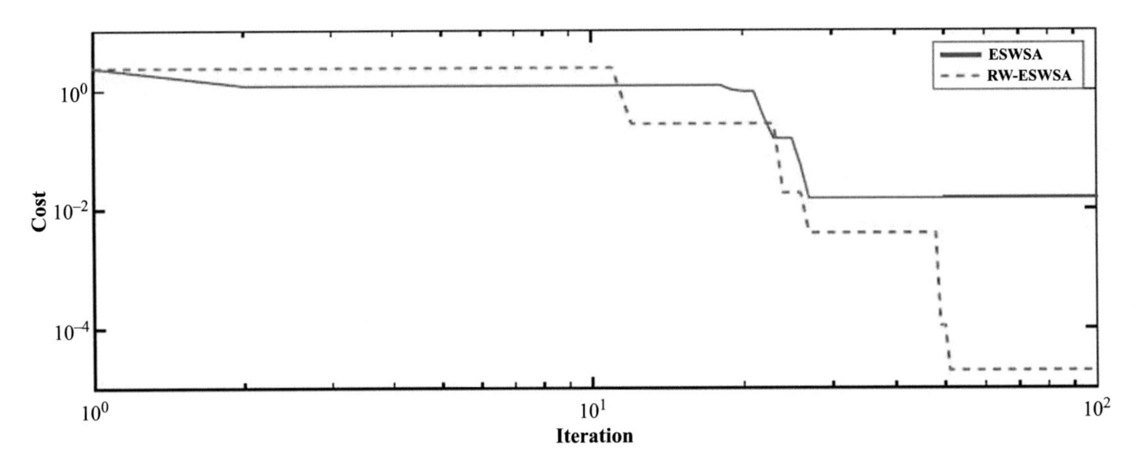

FIGURE 12.4 Convergence curve for Zakharov (F2).

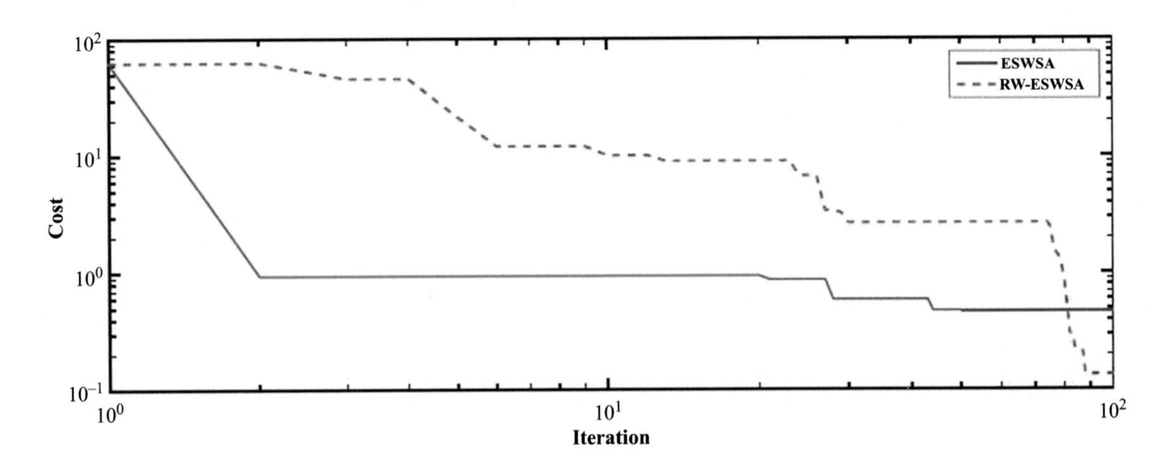

FIGURE 12.5 Convergence curve for Dixon Price (F3).

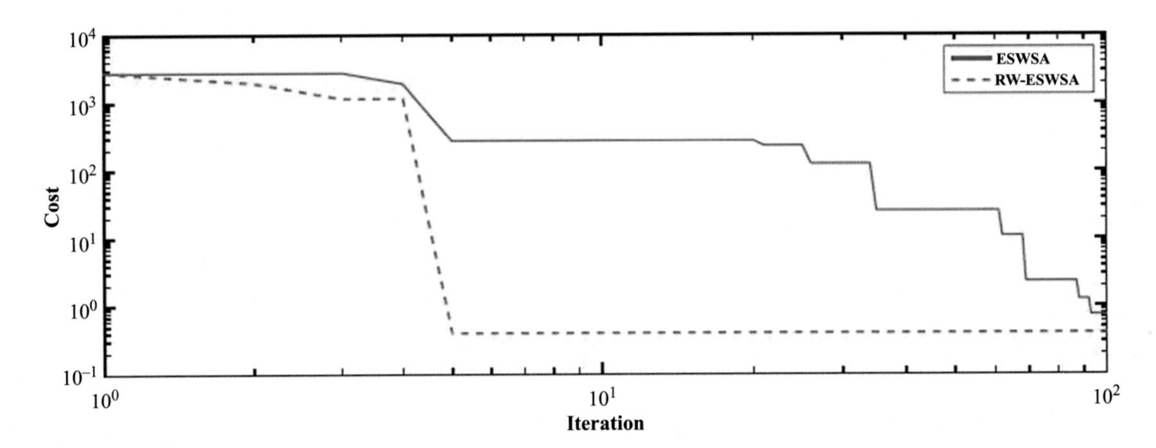

FIGURE 12.6 Convergence curve for Shifted Sphere (F4).

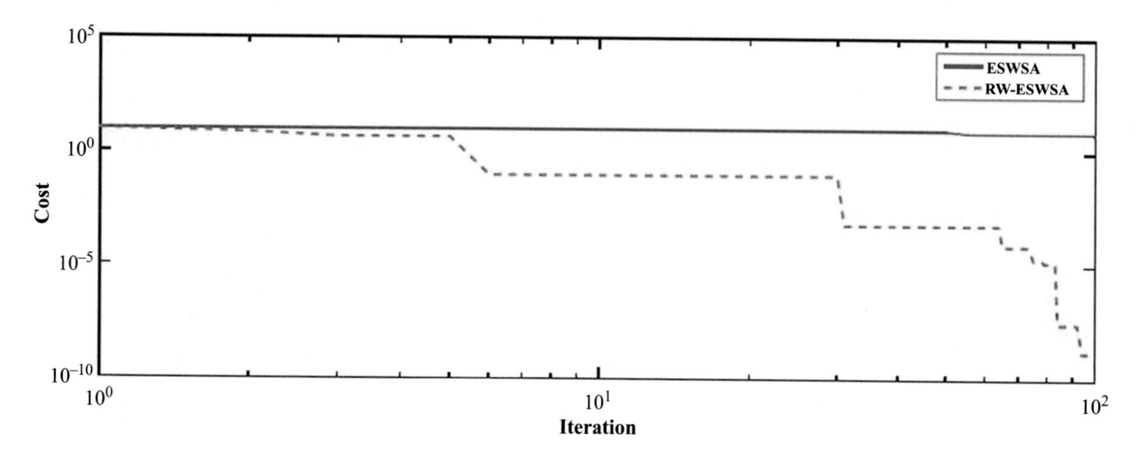

FIGURE 12.7 Convergence curve for Levy (F6)

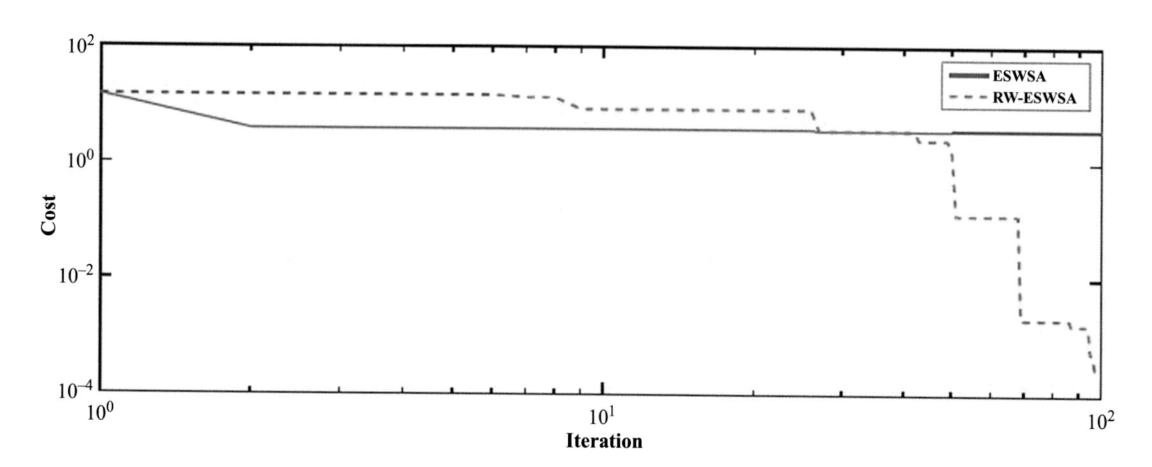

FIGURE 12.8 Convergence curve for Ackley (F7).

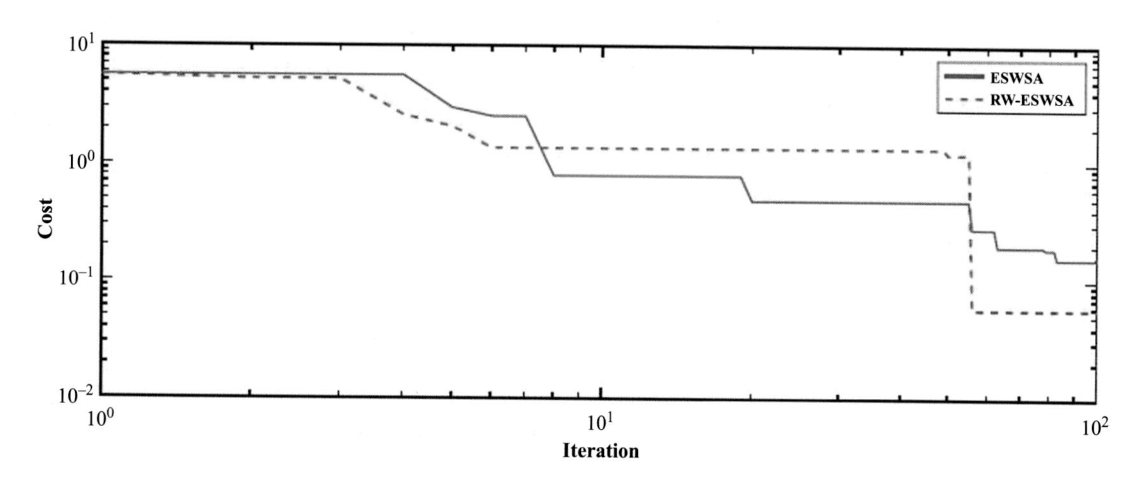

FIGURE 12.9 Convergence curve for Shifted Rotated Griewank's without Bounds (F10).

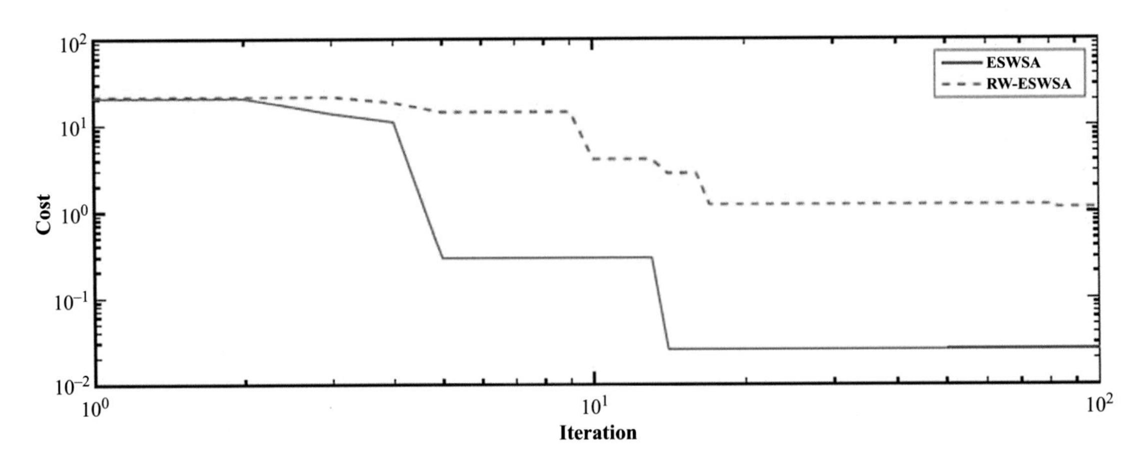

FIGURE 12.10 Convergence curve for Shifted Rastrigin (F11).

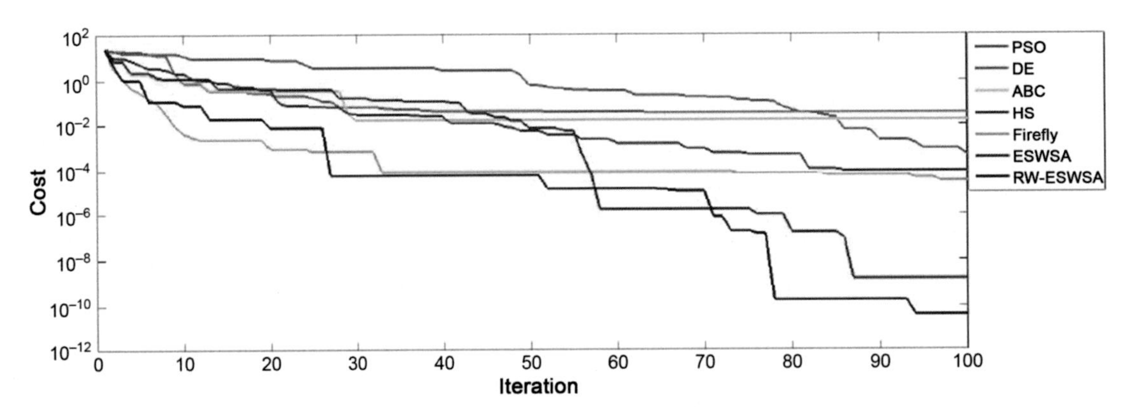

FIGURE 12.11 Convergence curve for Sphere (F1).

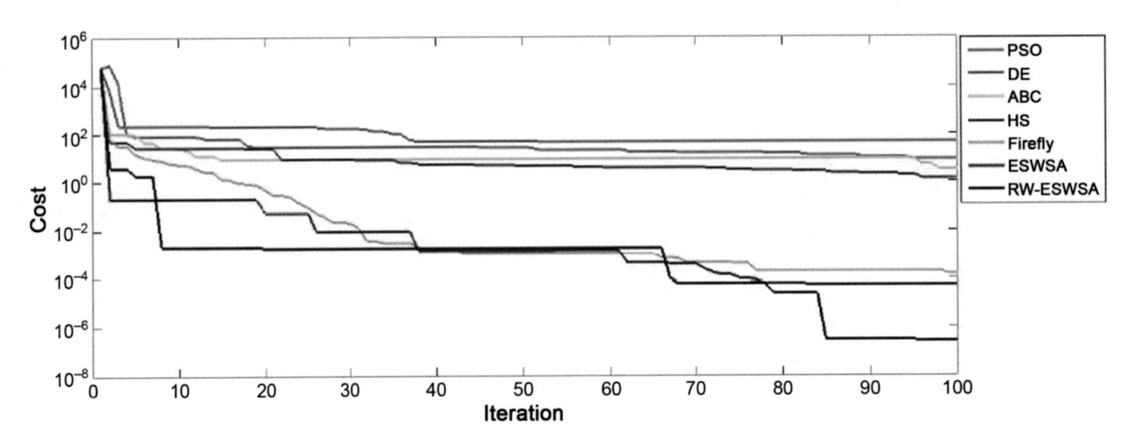

FIGURE 12.12 Convergence curve for Zakharov (F2).

searching strategies (local and global) of groups of elephants. The context switch probability is denoted by p (Mandal et al., 2017). The value of P belong to the set of values: {0.1, 0.2, 0.3, 0.4, 0.5, 0.6, 0.7, 0.8, 0.9}. The value of P has been tested for various benchmark functions in the case of using RW-ESWSA. In Tables 12.10 and 12.11, the value of P has been tested for sphere and levy benchmark function. The best cost value (minimized) has been achieved for $P=0.6$. The best cost value is bolded in Tables 12.10 and 12.11.

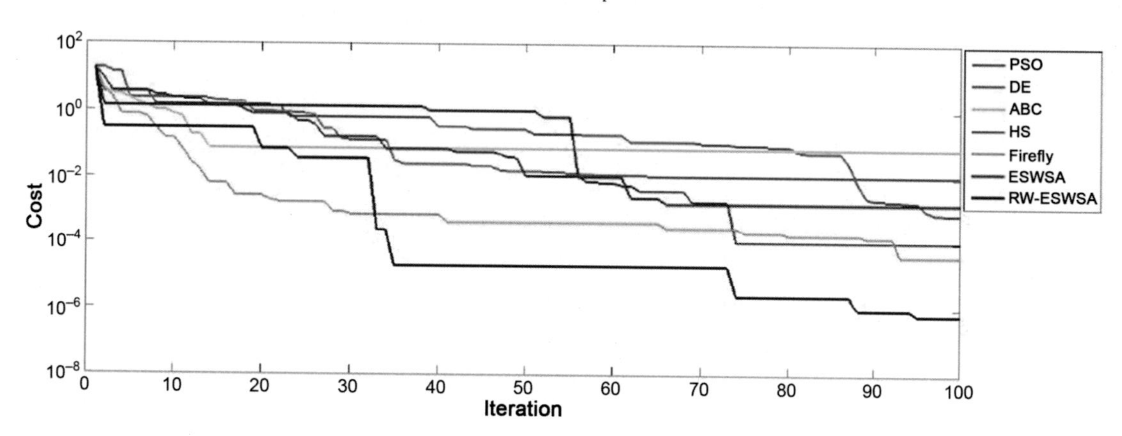

FIGURE 12.13 Convergence curve for Levy (F6).

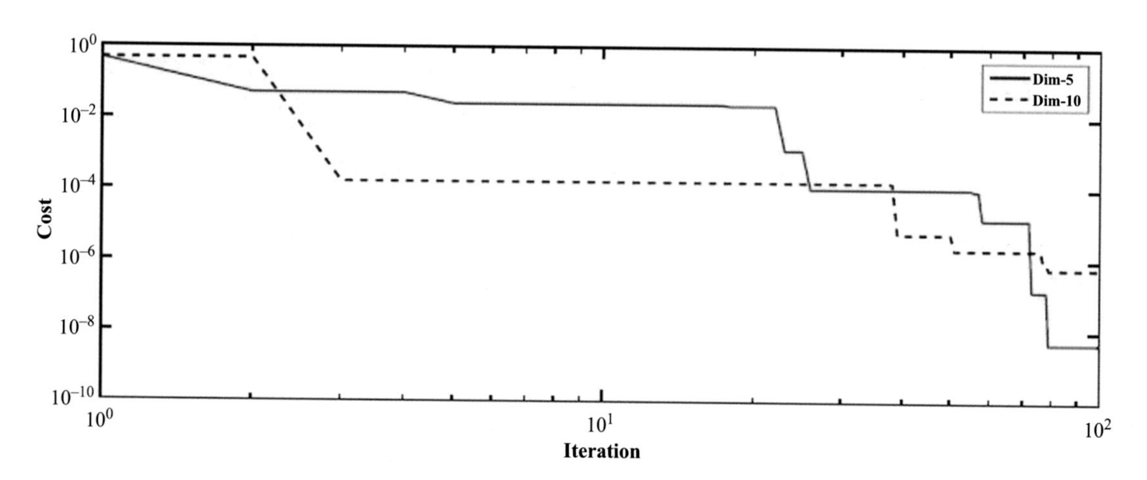

FIGURE 12.14 Convergence curve of random walk elephant swarm water search algorithm for Sphere (F1) benchmark function.

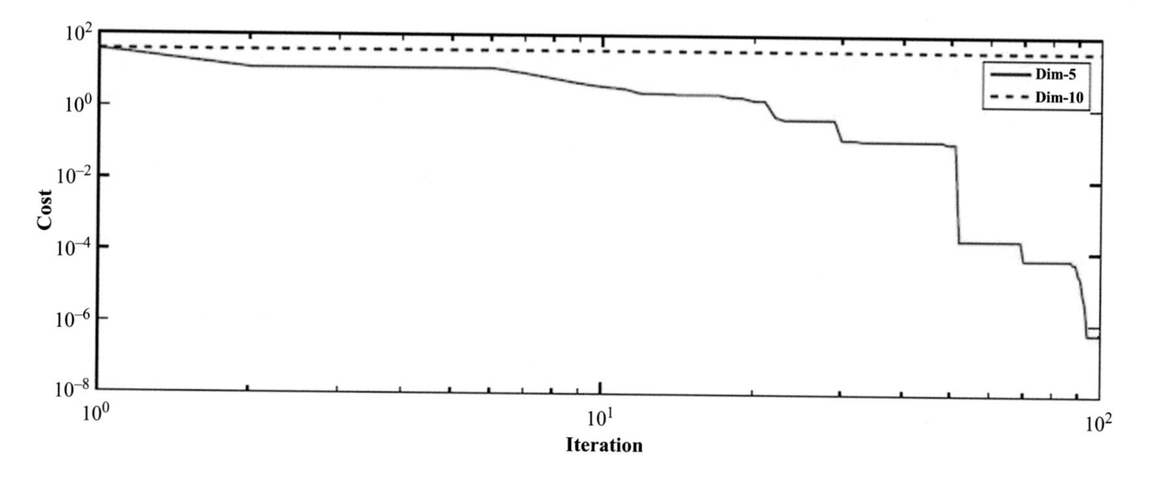

FIGURE 12.15 Convergence curve of random walk elephant swarm water search algorithm for Zakharov (F2) benchmark function.

12.4.7 Impact of random inertia weight strategy

This section describes the impact of the random inertia weight strategy (Bansal et al., 2011), which has been used in RW-ESWSA. The proposed variant has been tested with (1) random inertia weight strategy and (2) without random inertia strategy. This experiment has been done on two unimodal functions: Sphere (F1) and Shifted Sphere (F4) and two multimodal functions: Levy (F6) and Ackley (F7). It is represented by convergence curves shown in

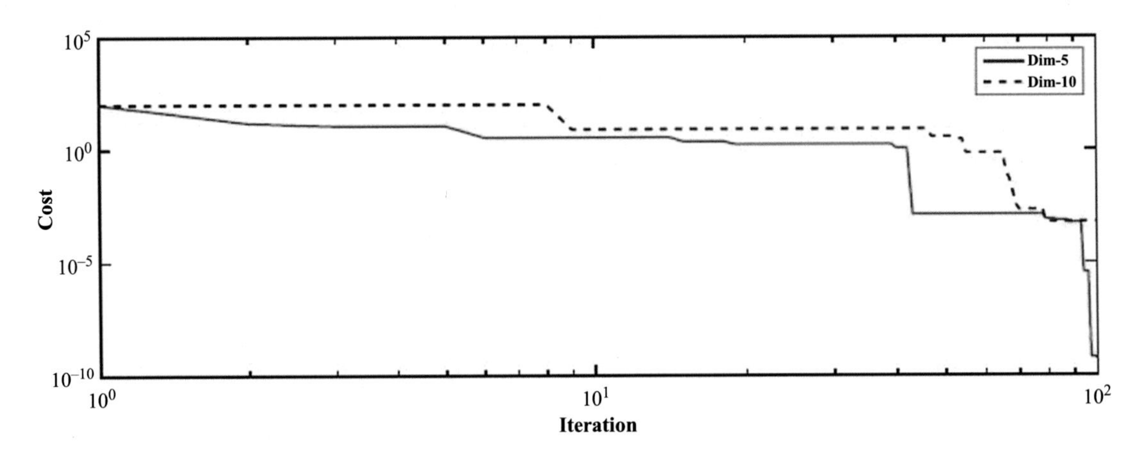

FIGURE 12.16 Convergence curve of random walk elephant swarm water search algorithm for Shifted Sphere (F4) benchmark function.

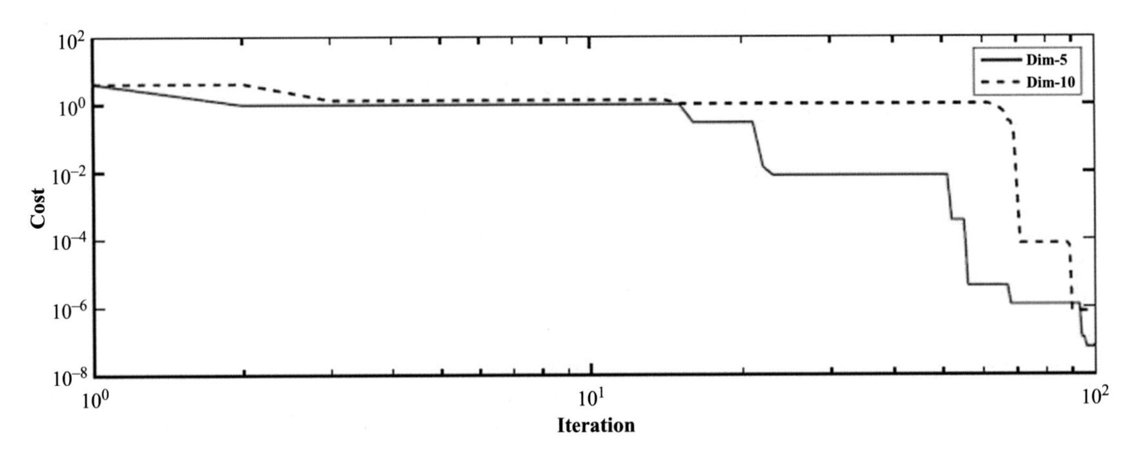

FIGURE 12.17 Convergence curve of random walk elephant swarm water search algorithm for Levy (F6) benchmark function.

TABLE 12.10 Cost for various values of P on sphere benchmark function in random walk elephant swarm water search algorithm (best results are highlighted in bold).

$P = 0.1$	$P = 0.2$	$P = 0.3$	$P = 0.4$	$P = 0.5$	$P = 0.6$	$P = 0.7$	$P = 0.8$	$P = 0.9$
3.19E-10	1.61E-10	6.55E-12	2.62E-13	1.44E-14	**6.90E-15**	8.39E-15	2.17E-13	3.40E-14

TABLE 12.11 Cost value for various values of P on levy benchmark function in random walk elephant swarm water search algorithm (best results are highlighted in bold).

$P = 0.1$	$P = 0.2$	$P = 0.3$	$P = 0.4$	$P = 0.5$	$P = 0.6$	$P = 0.7$	$P = 0.8$	$P = 0.9$
4.99E-10	2.85E-10	7.508E-11	1.048E-10	4.49E-11	**1.35E-11**	1.43E-11	1.24E-10	4.54E-11

Figs. 12.18–12.21. This shows that, if the random inertia weight strategy is used, then RW-ESWSA reaches gradually and steadily to the most promising part of the search region due to strong exploration capability.

12.4.8 Success rate

Table 12.12 illustrates the number of successful hits (Jana et al., 2019) for ESWSA and RW-ESWSA on 12 benchmark functions. These functions have been

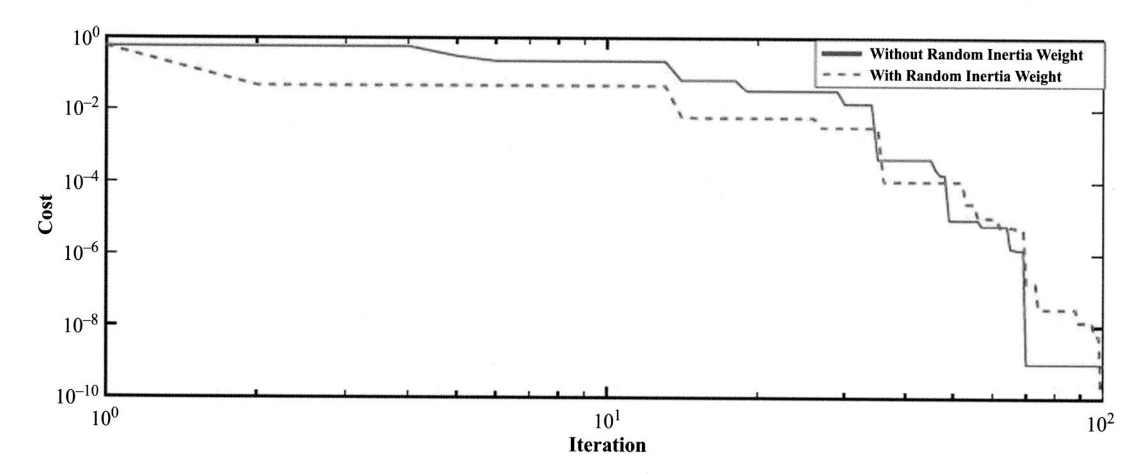

FIGURE 12.18 Convergence curve of random walk elephant swarm water search algorithm for Sphere benchmark function (F1).

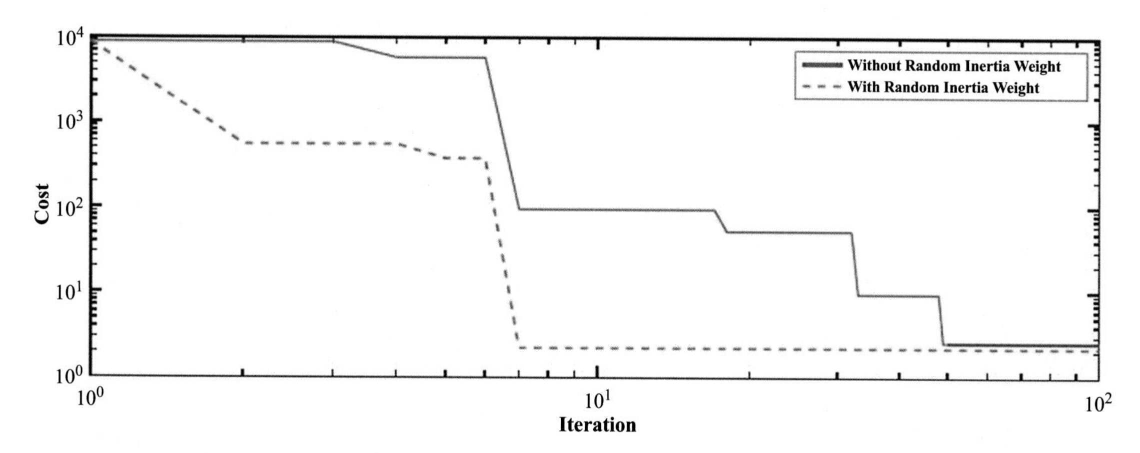

FIGURE 12.19 Convergence curve of random walk elephant swarm water search algorithm for Shifted Sphere benchmark function (F4).

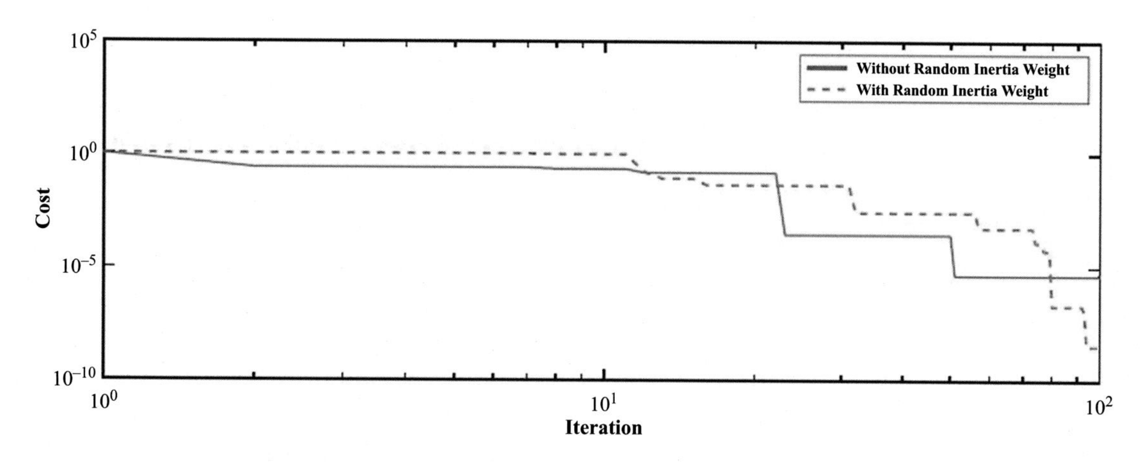

FIGURE 12.20 Convergence curve of random walk elephant swarm water search algorithm for Levy benchmark function (F6).

taken from CEC 2005 (Suganthan et al., 2005) benchmark set with dimension 5. A number of successful hits are denoted by the number of successful runs (out of 50) to reach a certain cost quality. In F1, the result shows that out of 50 runs, 42 runs have reached a certain cost quality in the case of RW-ESWSA. Therefore the percentage of successful hits is $(42/50) \times 100 = 84\%$. In the case of ESWSA, it shows that out of 50 runs, 33 runs have reached the same cost quality leading to the success rate [percentage of

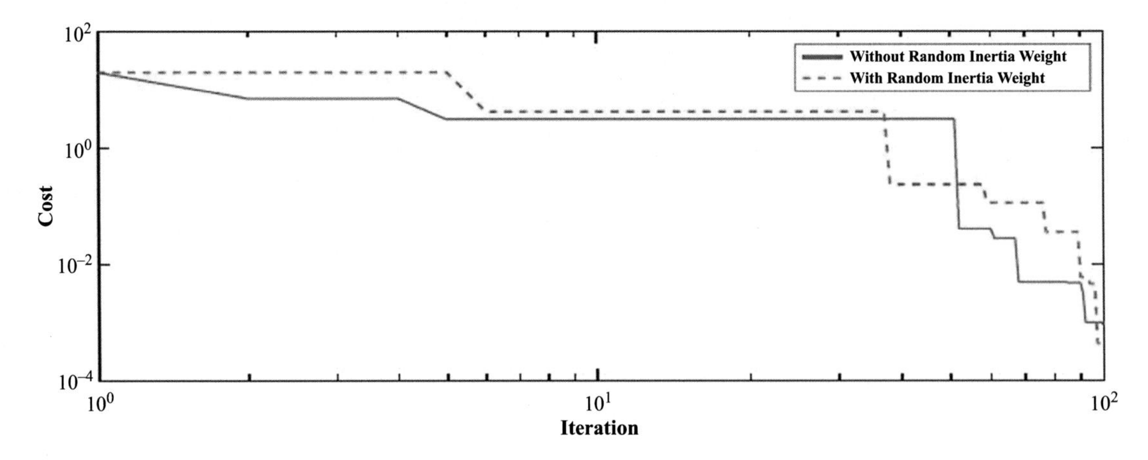

FIGURE 12.21 Convergence curve of random walk elephant swarm water search algorithm for Ackley benchmark function (F7).

TABLE 12.12 Comparison of random walk elephant swarm water search algorithm with elephant swarm water search algorithm on success rate for functions F1–F12 (best results are bolded).

	F1	F2	F3	F4	F5	F6	F7	F8	F9	F10	F11	F12
ESWSA	66	78	**92**	74	84.8	24	64	**100**	**84**	60	88.1	**100**
RW-ESWSA	**84**	**80.3**	88.3	**78.4**	**88**	**90.1**	**94.1**	**100**	72.8	**70.5**	**90**	**100**

ESWSA, Elephant Swarm Water Search Algorithm; *RW-ESWSA*, Random Walk Elephant Swarm Water Search Algorithm.

TABLE 12.13 Results of Wilcoxon pair-wise rank sum test on benchmark functions F1–F6.

	ESWSA vs RW-ESWSA					
Function	**F1**	**F2**	**F3**	**F4**	**F5**	**F6**
p-value	1.83E-15	0.0005	0.0323	0.5372	0.7266	1.287E-13

ESWSA, Elephant Swarm Water Search Algorithm; *RW-ESWSA*, Random Walk Elephant Swarm Water Search Algorithm.

TABLE 12.14 Results of Wilcoxon pair-wise rank sum test on benchmark functions F7–F12.

	ESWSA vs RW-ESWSA					
Function	**F7**	**F8**	**F9**	**F10**	**F11**	**F12**
p-value	7.44E-14	3.311E-20	0.006	0.0016	0.0412	0.0034

ESWSA, Elephant Swarm Water Search Algorithm; *RW-ESWSA*, Random Walk Elephant Swarm Water Search Algorithm.

successful hits (Jana et al., 2019)] of 66%. The best success rates are bolded in each function. RW-ESWSA has outperformed others in this respect in the maximum number of benchmark functions shown in Table 12.12. The functions are: F1, F2, F4, F5, F6, F7, F8, F10, F11, and F12. This clearly shows the strong efficacy of RW-ESWSA.

12.4.9 Statistical analysis

12.4.9.1 Wilcoxon's rank sum test between elephant swarm water search algorithm and random walk elephant swarm water search algorithm

Statistical testing plays an important role in establishing the significance of the newly proposed method. Here, a Wilcoxon's pair-wise (nonparametric) statistical test (Derrac et al., 2011; Jana et al., 2019; Jordehi, 2015) has been performed between the proposed method RW-ESWSA and the original version ESWSA. The results are analyzed based on the *p*-value. A p-value < 0.05 is accepted to have statistical significance. Tables 12.13 and 12.14 show that the newly proposed method is statistically significant subject to pair-wise comparison with ESWSA in different functions.

12.4.9.2 Wilcoxon's rank sum test between random walk elephant swarm water search algorithm and other metaheuristics

In this section, Wilcoxon's pair-wise statistical test has been performed between RW-ESWSA and five other metaheuristics algorithms [PSO (Cecconi & Campenni, 2010), HS (Geem et al., 2001), Firefly (Yang, 2010), ABC (Karaboga & Basturk, 2007), and DE (Guo et al., 2015)]. Comparison was carried out based on *p*-value and the result of this comparison has been represented in Table 12.15.

TABLE 12.15 Result of Wilcoxon pair-wise rank sum test between random walk elephant swarm water search algorithm and other metaheuristics algorithms.

Function	PSO vs RW-ESWSA (p-value)	HS vs RW-ESWSA (p-value)	Firefly vs RW-ESWSA (p-value)	ABC vs RW-ESWSA (p-value)	DE vs RW-ESWSA (p-value)
F1	7.504E-18	7.066E-18	1.212E-17	7.066E-18	6.719E-17
F2	3.932E-06	6.421E-06	0.9149	1.521E-06	8.117E-07
F3	9.144E-05	7.479E-05	3.321E-06	3.238eE-11	1.675E-08
F4	4.970E-05	0.0011	3.603E-04	5.743E-04	0.676
F5	0.5327	7.086E-12	3.797E-04	1.311E-07	6.470E-05
F6	0.0020	0.0014	0.0020	1.075E-06	7.550E-06
F7	1.225E-09	7.150E-09	4.157E-08	1.951E-17	1.101E-13
F8	0.248	0.8876	5.489E-07	3.305E-10	8.053E-06

ABC, Artificial Bee Colony; *DE*, Differential Evolution; *HS*, Harmony Search; *PSO*, Particle Swarm Optimization; *RW-ESWSA*, Random Walk Elephant Swarm Water Search Algorithm.

TABLE 12.16 Results of a real-life data set (best results are highlighted in bold).

Data set	Algorithm	No. of OPSMs	VE^t (Mean)
Yeast (Pontes et al., 2013)	ESWSA	100	1.37E-16
	RW-ESWSA	100	**3.98E-17**
Leukemia (Pontes et al., 2013)	ESWSA	100	1.75E-18
	RW-ESWSA	100	**5.87E-19**

ESWSA, Elephant Swarm Water Search Algorithm; *OPSM*, Order-Preserving Submatrices; *RW-ESWSA*, Random Walk Elephant Swarm Water Search Algorithm.

TABLE 12.17 Rank by gene ontology of 1 to 10 genes based on p-values using the yeastract tool.

Genes/ORF	RAD59	SUL1	MTE1	NEM1	JHD1	MRK1	S0A	RGA2	AGE1	TRP2
p-value	0.0000000	0.0000127	0.0000127	0.0000127	0.0000382	0.0000763	0.0001269	0.0001899	0.0001899	0.0000000

12.4.10 Results on a real-life problem

In this work, two data sets have been used: yeast (Pontes et al., 2013) and leukemia (Pontes et al., 2013). In the yeast data set: 2884 genes and 17 conditions are present, in the leukemia data set there are 7129 genes and 72 conditions. One hundred OPSMs have been extracted from each data set. The results of these data sets are presented in Table 12.16. The lower mean value of VE^t is considered as a better quality of OPSM. In each data set, RW-ESWSA discovered a better quality of OPSM compared to ESWSA. The results show the strong efficacy of RW-ESWSA.

12.4.11 Biological relevance

In this research, the biological significance of the best OPSM has been explored based on GO in the case of two data sets. The GO (Gene Ontology Consortium, 2019) is used to describe the functions and relationships of genes. It classifies the biological functions of genes based on three factors: molecular function, cellular component, and biological process. In the case of the yeast (Pontes et al., 2013) data set, the size of the best OPSM obtained is 28 × 14 (where, number of genes = 28 and number of conditions = 14). Here, the p-values have been provided for 20 biologically relevant genes of the 28 in Tables 12.17 and 12.18. This work is mainly based on GO terms (biological process) with the help of the YEASTRACT (**YEA**st **S**earch for **T**ranscriptional **R**egulators **A**nd **C**onsensus **T**racking) (Gene Ontology Consortium, 2019; Abdulrehman et al., 2010; Teixeira et al., 2006; Teixeira et al., 2018; Monteiro et al., 2007) tool. This tool provides a ranking list of biologically relevant genes based on GO. In case of the leukemia data set, the size of the best OPSM obtained is 8 × 32 (where number of genes = 8 and number of conditions = 32). These eight genes are:

TABLE 12.18 Rank by gene ontology of 11 to 20 genes based on p-values using yeastract tool.

Genes/ORF	PEX10	TLG1	PIB1	YOR1	AAD4	ERJ5	ISC10	BSC1	YDL086W	YHL041W
p-value	0.0000127	0.0000127	0.0000127	0.0000382	0.0000763	0.0001269	0.0001899	0.0001899	0.30366149	0.30366149

TABLE 12.19 Tested genes of best bicluster obtained from the leukemia data set using the GOrilla tool.

Name of genes	Associated GO term	Unresolved gene	Not existent in GO database
1. *NOP14-AS1*	RAB11A	*NOP14*	*NOP14-AS1*
2. *NOP14*	P2X4	*TRPC1A*	
3. *RAB11A*	PRRC2A		
4. *P2X4*	CEBPZ		
5. *PRRC2A*	CTLA4		
6. *CEBPZ*			
7. *CTLA4*			
8. *TRPC1A*			

GO, Gene Ontology.

NOP14-AS1, NOP14, RAB11A, P2X4, PRRC2A, CEBPZ, CTLA4, and *TRPC1A*. They have been tested with help of the GOrilla (Pomaznoy, Brendan, & Bjoern, 2018) tool based on GO ontology (biological process). Here, the threshold of p-value is set to 10^{-5}. Among these eight genes, unresolved genes are *NOP14* and *TRPC1A*. The *NOP14-AS1* gene is not present in the GO database. The remaining five genes (*RAB11A, P2X4, PRRC2A, CEBPZ*, and *CTLA4*) have biological relevance according to the associated GO term. This is presented in Table 12.19.

12.5 Conclusion

Identifying OPSMs is an important problem in computational genetics. It finds subgroups of genes in which the expression levels of genes follow an order in almost identical ways under some conditions. This type of OPSM pattern may help detect disease-critical genes responsible for causing disease. In these patterns, the expression levels of genes sometimes follows an increasing order indicating the hyperactivity property of genes. This information plays a significant role in gene therapy. This research has discovered OPSMs from two different datasets (yeast and leukemia) and explored the biological significance of these OPSMs. For this purpose, it has proposed a variant RW-ESWSA that performs better than ESWSA on various types of benchmark functions. The proposed variant has been tested along with other metaheuristic algorithms through convergence analysis. This shows that RW-ESWSA does not suffer from early convergence and at the same time it reaches a minimum which is better than ESWSA. To identify the best-quality OPSM, the proposed RW-ESWSA is applied to two different biological data sets (yeast and leukemia). In this observation, RW-ESWSA has outperformed ESWSA in finding better quality OPSMs. The quality of OPSM is determined by the lowest mean value of VE^t, which reflects the strong existence of biological relevance. For each data set, the analysis of the best OPSM is done to explore its biological relevance with the help of two online tools (Yeastract and GOrilla) based on GO. It concludes that the genes involved in these OPSMs are biologically relevant. The biological relevance is determined by the p-values obtained from applying Yeastract and GOrilla tools and is satisfactory.

References

Abbass, H. A. (2001). MBO: Marriage in honey bees optimization-a haplometrosis polygynous swarming approach. *Evolutionary Computation, Proceedings of the 2001 Congress*, 207–214.

Abdulrehman, D., Monteiro, P. T., Teixeira, M. C., Mira, N. P., Lourenco, A. B., Santos, S. C. D., ... Oliveira, A. L. (2010). YEASTRACT: Providing a programmatic access to curated transcriptional regulatory associations in *Saccharomyces cerevisiae* through a web services interface. *Nucleic Acids Research, 39*(1), D136–D140.

Askarzadeh, A., & Rezazadeh, A. (2012). A new heuristic optimization algorithm for modeling of proton exchange membrane fuel cell: Bird mating optimizer. *International Journal of Energy Research, 37*(10).

Bansal, J. C., Singh, P. K., Saraswat, M., Verma, A., Jadon, S. S., & Abraham, A. (2011). Inertia weight strategies in particle swarm optimization. In *Third world congress on nature and biologically inspired computing* (pp. 633–640), IEEE.

Beheshti, Z., & Shamsuddin, S. M. H. (2013). A review of population-based meta-heuristic. *International Journal of Advances in Soft Computing and Its Applications, 5*(1), 1–35.

Ben-Dor, A., Chor, B., Karp, R., & Yakhini, Z. (2003). Discovering local structure in gene expression data: The order-preserving sub-matrix problem. *Journal of Computational Biology, 10*(3–4), 373–384.

Ben-Dor, A., Shamir, R., & Yakhini, Z. (1999). Clustering gene expression patterns. *Journal of Computational Biology, 6*(3–4), 281–297.

Biswas, S., & Acharyya, S. (2017). Identification of disease critical genes causing Duchenne muscular dystrophy (DMD) using computational intelligence. *CSI Transaction on ICT, 5*(1), 3–8.

Bryan, K., Pádraig, C., & Nadia, B. (2005). Biclustering of expression data using simulated annealing. In *18th IEEE symposium on computer-based medical systems (CBMS'05)* (pp. 383–388), IEEE.

F. Cecconi, M. Campenni, PSO (Particle swarm optimization): One method, many possible application, In Agent-based evolutionary search, Springer (2010) 229-254.

Cheung, L., Cheung, D. W., Kao, B., Yip, K. Y., & Ng, M. K. (2007). On mining micro-array data by order-preserving submatrix. *International Journal of Bioinformatics Research and Applications*, *3*(1), 42–64.

Das, S., Abraham, A., & Konar, A. (2009). *Metaheuristic clustering* (178). Springer.

Derrac, J., García, S., Molina, D., & Herrera, F. (2011). A practical tutorial on the use of nonparametric statistical tests as a methodology for comparing evolutionary and swarm intelligence algorithms. *Swarm and Evolutionary Computation*, *1*(1), 3–18.

Divina, F., & Guilar-Ruiz, J. S. (2006). Biclustering of expression data with evolutionary computation. *IEEE Transactions on knowledge and Data Engineering*, *18*(5), 590–602.

Eden, E., Roy, N., Israel, S., Doro, L., & Zohar, Y. (2009). GOrilla: A tool for discovery and visualization of enriched GO terms in ranked gene lists. *BMC Bioinformatics*, *10*(1), 1–7.

Gao, B. J., Griffith, O. L., Ester, M., Xiong, H., Zhao, Q., & Jones, S. J. M. (2012). On the deep order-preserving submatrix problem: A best effort approach. *IEEE Transactions on Knowledge and Data Engineering*, *24*(2), 309–325.

Geem, Z. W., Km, J. H., & Loganathan, G. V. (2001). A new heuristic optimization algorithm: Harmony search. *Simulation*, *76*(2), 60–68.

Gene Ontology Consortium. (2019). The gene ontology resource: 20 years and still GOing strong. *Nucleic Acids Research*, *47*(D1), D330–D338.

Getz, G., Levine, E., & Domany, E. (2000). Coupled two-way clustering analysis of gene microarray data. *Proceedings of the National Academy of Sciences of the United States of America*, *97*(22), 12079–12084.

Guo, S. M., Yang, C. C., Hsu, P. H., & Tsai, J. S. H. (2015). Improving differential evolution with A successful-parent- selecting framework. *IEEE Transaction Evolutionary Computing*, *19*(5), 717–730.

Hatamlou, A. (2012). Black hole: A new heuristic optimization approach for data clustering. *Information Sciences*, *222*, 175–184.

Heller, M. J. (2002). DNA microarray technology: Devices, systems, and applications. *Annual Review of Biomedical Engineering*, *4*(1), 129–153.

Holland, J. H. (1992). Genetic algorithms. *Scientific American*, *267*, 66–72.

Horn, J., Nicholas, N., & Goldberg, D. E. (1994). A niched pareto genetic algorithm for multiobjective optimization. In *Proceedings of the first IEEE conference on evolutionary computation, IEEE world congress on computational intelligence* (pp. 82–87).

Hussain, K., Salleh, M. N. M., Cheng, S., & Shi, Y. (2019). Metaheuristic research: A comprehensive survey. *Artificial Intelligence Review*, *52*(4), 2191–2233.

Jamil, M., & Yang, X. S. (2013). A literature survey of benchmark functions for global optimization problems. *International Journal of Mathematical Modelling and Numerical Optimisation*, *4*(2), 150–194.

Jana, B., Mitra, S., & Acharyaa, S. (2019). Repository and mutation based particle swarm optimization (RMPSO): A new PSO variant applied to reconstruction of gene regulatory network. *Applied Soft Computing*, *74*, 330–355.

Jiang, J. D., Tang, C., & Zhang, A. (2004). Cluster analysis for gene expression data: A survey. *IEEE Transactions on Knowledge and Data Engineering*, *16*(11), 1370–1386.

Jordehi, A. R. (2015). Enhanced leader PSO (ELPSO): A new PSO variant for solving global optimisation problems. *Applied Soft Computing*, *26*, 401–417.

Karaboga, D., & Basturk, B. (2007). A powerful and efficient algorithm for numerical function optimization: Artificial Bee Colony (ABC) algorithm. *Journal of Global Optimization*, *39*(3), 459–471.

Kaveh, A., & Khayatazad, M. (2012). A new meta-heuristic method: Ray optimization. *Computers & Structures*, *112*, 283–294.

Khan, J., Michael, L. B., Yidong, C., Paul, S. M., & Jeffrey, M. T. (1999). DNA microarray technology: the anticipated impact on the study of human disease. *Biochimica et Biophysica Acta (BBA)-Reviews on Cancer*, *1423*(2), M17–M28.

Kirkpatrick, S., Gelatt, D. G., Jr., & Vecchi, M. P. (1983). Optimization by simulated annealing. *Science (New York, N.Y.)*, *220*, 671–680.

Koza, J. R. (1992). Evolution of subsumption using genetic programming. In *Proceedings of the first European conference on artificial life* (pp. 110–119).

Li, C., Yang, S., & Nguyen, T. T. (2012). A self-learning particle swarm optimizer for global optimization problems. *IEEE Transactions on Systems*, *42*(3), 627–646.

Lin, L., & Gen, M. (2009). Auto-tuning strategy for evolutionary algorithms: Balancing between exploration and exploitation. *Soft Computing*, *13*, 157–168.

Lourenço, H. R., Martin, O. C., & Stützle, T. (2003). *Iterated local search. Handbook of metaheuristics* (pp. 320–353). Boston, MA: Springer.

Maderia, S. C., & Oliveira, A. L. (2004). Biclustering algorithms for biological data analysis: A survey. *IEEE/ACM Transactions on Computational Biology and Bioinformatics*, *1*(1), 24–45.

Mahdavi, M., Fesanghary, M., & Damangir, E. (2007). An improved harmony search algorithm for solving optimization problems. *Applied Mathematics and Computation*, *188*, 1567–1579.

Mandal, S., Saha, G., & Paul, R. K. (2017). Recurrent neural network-based modeling of gene regulatory network using elephant swarm water search algorithm. *Journal of Bioinformatics and Computational Biology*, *15*(04), 1750016.

McManus, K. F., Kelley, J. L., Song, S., Veeramah, K. R., Woerner, A. E., Stevison, L. S., … Bustamante, C. D. (2015). Inference of gorilla demographic and selective history from whole-genome sequence data. *Molecular Biology and Evolution*, *32*(3), 600–612.

Mirjalili, S., Mirjalili, S. M., & Lewis, A. (2014). Grey wolf optimizer. *Advances in Engineering Software*, *69*, 46–61.

Mladenović, N., & Hansen, P. (1997). Variable neighborhood search. *Computers & Operations Research*, *24*(11), 1097–1100.

Monteiro, P. T., Nuno, D. M., Miguel, C. T., d'Orey, S., Tenreiro, S., Nuno, P. M., … Sa-Correia, I. (2007). YEASTRACT-DISCOVERER: New tools to improve the analysis of transcriptional regulatory associations in *Saccharomyces cerevisiae. Nucleic Acids Research*, *36*(1), D132–D136.

Pomaznoy, M., Brendan, H., & Bjoern, P. (2018). GOnet: A tool for interactive gene ontology analysis. *BMC Bioinformatics*, *19*(1), 470.

Pontes, B., Girldez, R., & Aguilar-Ruiz, J. S. (2010). Measuring the quality of shifting and scaling patterns in biclusters. In *IAPR international conference on pattern recognition in bioinformatics* (pp. 242–252).

Pontes, B., Giráldez, R., & Aguilar-Ruiz, J. S. (2013). Configurable pattern-based evolutionary biclustering of gene expression data. *Algorithms for Molecular Biology*, *8*(1), 4.

Pontes, B., Giráldez, R., & Aguilar-Ruiz, J. S. (2015). Biclustering on expression data: A review. *Journal of Biomedical Informatics*, *57*, 163–180.

Rashedi, E., Esmat., Nezamabadi-Pour, H., & Saryazdi, S. (2009). GSA: A gravitational search algorithm. *Information Sciences*, *179* (13), 2232–2248.

Saha, S., Biswas, S., & Acharyya, S. (2016). Gene selection by sample classification using k nearest neighbor and meta-heuristic algorithms. In *2016 IEEE 6th international conference on advanced computing (IACC)* (pp. 250–255).

Storn, R., & Price, K. (1997). Differential evolution: A simple and efficient heuristic for global optimization over continuous spaces. *Journal of Global Optimization*, *11*, 341–359.

Suganthan, P.N., Hansen, N., Liang, J.J., Deb, K., Chen, Y.P., Auger, A., & Tiwari, S. (2005). Problem definitions and evaluation criteria for the CEC 2005 special session on real-parameter optimization. KanGAL Report 2005005, 2005.

Supek, F., Matko, B., Nives, Š., & Tomislav, Š. (2011). REVIGO summarizes and visualizes long lists of gene ontology terms. *PLoS One*, *6*(7), e21800.

Supper, J., Strauch, M., Wanke, D., Harter, K., & Zell, A. (2007). EDISA: Extracting biclusters from multiple time-series of gene expression profiles. *BMC Bioinformatics*, *8*.

Tanay, A., Sharan, R., & Shamir, R. (2002). Discovering statistically significant biclustersin gene expression data. *Bioinformatics (Oxford, England)*, *18*(1), S136–S144.

Tanay, A., Sharan, R., & Shamir, R. (2005). Biclustering algorithms: A survey. *Handbook of Computational Molecular Biology*, *9*(1-20), 122–124.

Teixeira, C. M., Pedro, T. M., Margarida, P., Catarina, C., Cláudia, P. G., Pedro, P., & Mafalda, C. (2018). YEASTRACT: an upgraded database for the analysis of transcription regulatory networks in *Saccharomyces cerevisiae*. *Nucleic Acids Research*, *46*(D1), D348–D353.

Teixeira, M. C., Monteiro, P., Jain, P., Tenreiro, S., Alexandra, R. F., Nuno, P. M., … Sa-Correia, I. (2006). The YEASTRACT database: A tool for the analysis of transcription regulatory associations in *Saccharomyces cerevisiae*. *Nucleic Acids Research*, *34*(1), D446–D451.

Voudouris, C., & Tsang, E. P. (2003). *Guided local search. In Handbook of metaheuristics* (pp. 185–218). Boston, MA: Springer.

Xue, Y., Liao, Z., Luo, J., Kuang, Q., Hu, X., & Li, T. (2015). A new approach for mining order-preserving sub matrices based on all common subsequences computational and mathematical methods in medicine. *Computational and Mathematical Methods in Medicine*, *2015*.

Yang, X. (2010). Firefly algorithm, levy flights and global optimization. *Research and Development in Intelligent Systems*, *XXVI*, 209–218.

Yang, X. S., & Deb, S. (2009). Cuckoo search via Lévyflights, nature & biologically inspired computing. In *World congress on* (pp. 210–214).

Yang, X. S., & Deb, S. (2014). Cuckoo search: Recent advances and applications. *Neural Computing and Applications*, *24*(1), 169–174.

Yip, K. Y., Kao, B., Zhu, X., Chui, C., Lee, S. D., & Cheung, D. W. (2013). Mining order-preserving submatrices from data with repeated measurements. *IEEE Transactions on Knowledge and Data Engineering*, *25*(7), 1587–1600.

CHAPTER

13

Geopositioning of fog nodes based on user device location and framework for game theoretic applications in an fog to cloud network

Anjan Bandyopadhyay[1], *Utsav Datta*[1], *Antara Banik*[1], *Pratyay Biswas*[1] and *Vaskar Sarkar*[2]

[1]Department of Computer Science & Engineering, Amity University, Kolkata, India [2]Department of Mathematics, School of Science, Adamas University, Kolkata, India

13.1 Introduction

When it comes to interconnectivity of devices and sharing of data through the Internet, the cloud computing paradigm is the go-to solution. The NIST definition of cloud computing contains five characteristics: on-demand self-service, broad network access, resource pooling, rapid elasticity, and measured service (Mell & Grance, 2011). With the emergence of the Internet of Things (IoT), where there is a need for interconnectivity between singular devices, the cloud paradigm has proved to be an effective solution till date. It provides reliable services based on virtual storage for the realization of IoT vision (Gubbi, Buyya, Marusic, & Palaniswami, 2013). However, with the recent boom in the IoT trend, increasing numbers of devices are being interconnected with the help of cloud computing. By 2020, it was expected that the number of interconnected devices would reach 24 billion (Gubbi et al., 2013) and by 2025 the total installed base of IoT-connected devices is projected to reach 75 billion according to Statista (Statista Research Department, 2016).

With this ever-increasing number of devices and the limited capacity of the cloud, it is natural that performance would decrease. To overcome the limitations, the fog computing paradigm was put forward. Unlike the centralized cloud, the fog computing model is highly distributed through its large number of fog nodes which provides localization. Therefore fog nodes are able to achieve low latency and context awareness (Bonomi, Milito, Zhu, & Addepalli, 2012). Fog computing and cloud computing are not mutually exclusive, rather they are implemented together to achieve the desired properties. The fog model contains an intermediate layer between cloud and user devices. This "fog layer" is closer to the end users, due to which a lower latency is achieved. The elements which make up this layer are called fog nodes. Any device that has computing capabilities, storage, and the ability to be connected with a network can act as a fog node (Fog Computing & the Internet of Things, 2016).

There are various features that make fog computing a nontrivial extension of cloud computing (Osanaiye et al., 2017), but for our model we are interested in two of these features: geographical distribution and location awareness. It is a well understood fact that device–server geographical distance and latency are correlated as the greater the distance, the more time that is taken by data packets to reach the destination. Therefore it is of great interest that fog computing servers are located in an optimum geographical position such that the greatest number of devices benefit from it. In this chapter, we propose a model for computing the geographical positions of fog nodes in a two-fog layer (F2C) network based on significant location

Recent Trends in Computational Intelligence Enabled Research.
DOI: https://doi.org/10.1016/B978-0-12-822844-9.00030-X

points. Hence, the positions of the fog nodes are dependent on how the end-user devices are scattered in the region of concern.

After computing the positions, the two main applications of the F2C network are proposed. The first application is using the fog nodes as computational resources which provide computing services to the user devices and the second application is using the network as a physical layer for user-to-user data transmission.

13.2 System model

We consider the architecture with two fog layers and a single cloud. The fog nodes in layer 1 (FNL1) are in direct contact with the user devices, while fog layer 2 stands between layer 1 and the cloud (Tordera et al., 2016). FNL1 receives requests from the devices under it and is responsible for deciding whether the request is to be sent to the cloud or fog nodes in layer 2 (FNL2) for processing. Generally, highly time-sensitive requests are processed in the closest FNL2, while requests that are not time sensitive are sent to the cloud.

Fig. 13.1 shows a schematic representation of our vision for a two-layer fog paradigm. Devices send their requests to their assigned FNL1, which forwards the request to the cloud or FNL2 for processing. After processing, the processed data are sent back to the devices directly. This network architecture also provides us with an opportunity for transferring data from one device to another through the fog nodes while handling network congestion.

13.3 Literature review

With the recent boom in IoT, the focus on the fog computing paradigm has increased drastically. This is primarily because the fog computing methodology provides a fantastic base for incorporating and structuring IoT devices. This has led to the application of fog networks in various areas ranging from health care (Stantchev, Barnawi, Ghulam, Schubert, & Tamm, 2015; Kraemer, Alexander, Nattachart, and David, 2017) to smart cities (Perera, Yongrui, Julio, Stephan, & Athanasios, 2017). As "big data" is being described as the "new oil," companies and organizations are understanding the value and essential nature of data as a resource (Hirsch, 2013). As we generate huge amounts of data on a day- to-day basis, it is necessary to make sure that storing and retrieval of these "data" for usage is secure and as efficient as possible. This is again where the fog computing paradigm has come forward as a suitable candidate. With scope of scalability and the distributed nature of the network, it is widely preferred over the centralized cloud paradigm for resource allocation.

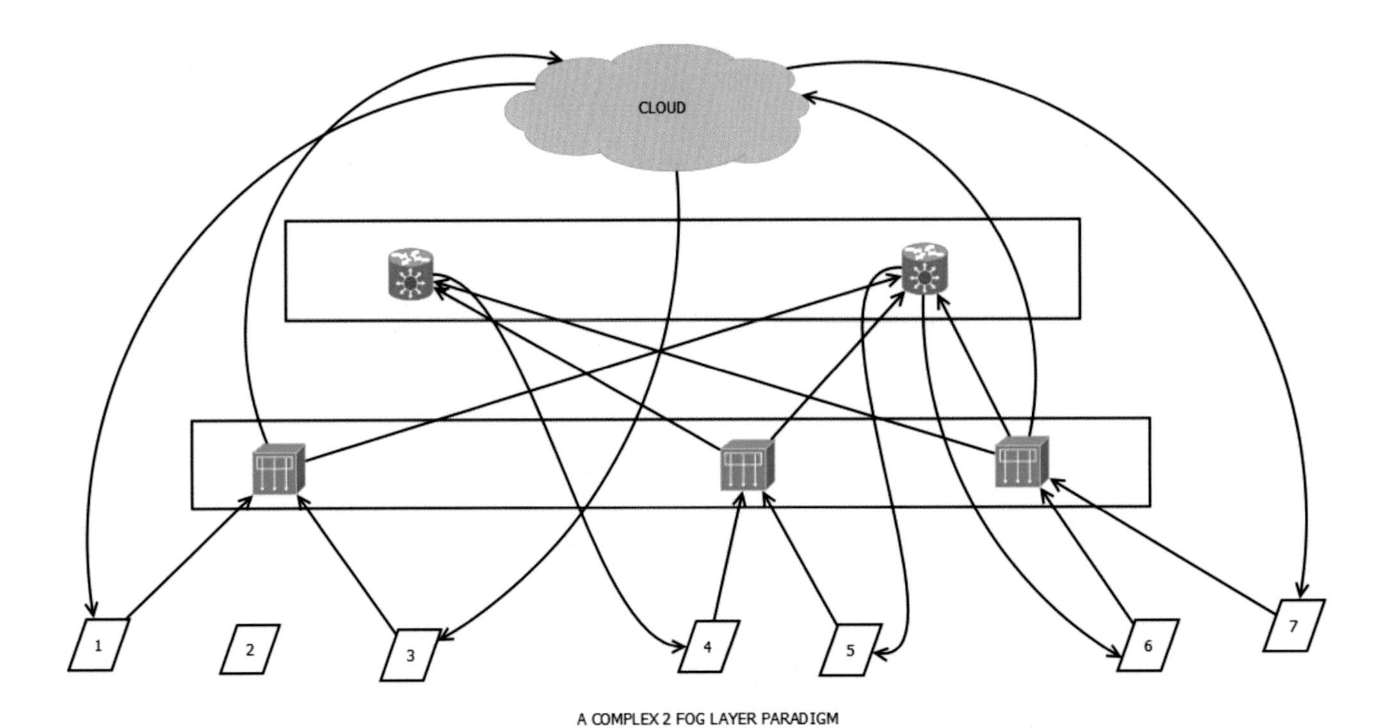

FIGURE 13.1 A complete two fog layer paradigm.

Both multilevel fog computing organization and auction theory for resource allocation in a network have been studied extensively as both are very powerful concepts. Mahmud, Srirama, Ramamohanarao, and Buyya (2019) maximize the quality of experience (QOE) by using a similar architecture to that described in Tordera et al. (2016), while Chang, Srirama, and Buyya (2017) used an extensive multilayer organization to develop a flexible fog paradigm called Indie Fog where the service providers do not need to deploy their own devices. Allocation of computational resources through an auction theory mechanism was proposed by Sutherland (1968). A. Bandyopadhyay et al. proposed an auction framework for data-as-a-service in cloud computing, where inside the auction framework collaboration an exchange of data takes place between smaller cloud subsets (Bandyopadhyay, Xhafa, Mukhopadhyay, Kumar Singh, & Sharma, 2019). Other allocation mechanisms such as T-SAM (Bandyopadhyay, Mukhopadhyay, & Ganguly, 2016) and P-SAM (Bandyopadhyay, Mukhopadhyay, & Ganguly, 2017) provide allocation models of resources under strict preferences in cloud computing.

13.4 Problem formulation

This study is divided into two parts, in the first part we propose a model for positioning of FNL1s and FNL2s based on user device density such that the nodes can benefit the greatest number of user devices by performing their respective functions which are mentioned in Section 13.2. We implement a combination of K-means clustering algorithm and mean shift clustering algorithm for finding the positions of FNL1s and FNL2s, respectively. In the second part of the proposed method, the two main applications of the network are proposed. The first application uses the FNL2s + cloud as computational resources where device requests requiring computational services are allotted to FNL2s or the cloud and computation is performed there. The second application uses the fog nodes and their interconnectivity nature to transfer data from one device to another using the network.

13.5 Proposed method

As stated earlier, this study is divided into two parts. In the first part, the geopositioning of the nodes is discussed, while in the second part, the mechanisms for the network applications are provided.

13.5.1 Geopositioning of fog nodes

For computing the positions of FNL1s and FNL2s, we first need to find significant points around which there is a high density of user devices. For stationary user devices, this is not a challenging task, but for devices that are not stationary such as mobile phones, etc. computing the significant points becomes a complex process. Several authors, including Kami, Enomoto, Baba, and Yoshikawa (2010) and Cao, Cong, and Jensen (2010), have proposed algorithms for determining such "significant locations" using raw GPS data (Cao et al., 2010; Kami et al., 2010). We assume that the extracted "significant locations" can be represented as points (X_s), therefore the points represent that there is a high density of devices situated around them. We use these points to compute the positions of the FNL1s. The K-means clustering algorithm (Hartigan & Wong, 1979) is implemented on the points (X_s). If there are k number of FNL1s present for installation then we group the points into k number of clusters, where the locations of the centroids of the clusters represent the positions for installing the FNL1s. Algorithm 1 depicts the K-means clustering algorithm.

ALGORITHM 1 K-means clustering

```
Select k ← no. of FNL1s
Place centroids at random points
Centroid (C1. C2...Ck)
Repeat:
1. Create k clusters by allotting X's to closest Ci
2. Update centroid position by Eq. (13.1).
Until: centroid position does not change
```

The closest centroid Ci from the point X_s is found on the basis of Euclidean distance between them. Let D be the Euclidean distance between the centroid and the point, then we find i which gives the argument of minimum for D:

$\arg\min_i D(X_s, C_i)$

We compute the new position of the centroids of the clusters by calculating the mean of all the points that lie in that cluster.

$$C_i = \frac{1}{n_i} \sum_{X_s \to Ci} X_s \quad (13.1)$$

New position of the centroid

In Eq. (13.1), n_i denotes the number of points that lie in cluster i.

Once the positions of the FNL1s are computed, the positions of the FNL2s are computed using the position of the FNL1s. We implement mean shift clustering algorithm on the computed FNL1 positions. Algorithm 2 depicts the algorithm used for positioning of FNL2s. The parameter passed in the algorithm is the range of the FNL2s. This essentially denotes the distance up to which the FNL2 can provide its service efficiently. In our proposed network design, all the FNL1s can establish connections to each FNL2, but the efficient range provides an area under which optimal connectivity can be assumed. After implementation of algorithm 2, we get a network hierarchy depicted in Fig. 13.1.

ALGORITHM 2 Mean shift clustering

```
r = radius of each FNL2 node
FL_list = list of FNL1 coordinate
n = number of FNL1 nodes

START
Repeat while n > 0
    h = abscissa of first element in FL_list
    k = ordinate of first element in FL_list
    flag = true
    repeat steps while flag == true
    count_list = NULL
    repeat steps while i< =n
        x = abscissa of ith element in FL_list
        y = ordinate of ith element in FL_list
        check if (x−h)^2 + (y−k)^2 < r^2
        then list ith element of FL_list in count_list
  new_h = mean of abscissa of elements in count_list
  new_k = mean of ordinate of elements in count_list
  check if (h == new_h && k == new_k)
  then list h & k in F2_list as abscissa & ordinate
        flag = false
        remove coordinate from FL_list matches
          count_list
  Else h = new_h and k = new_k
END
```

13.5.2 Applications of the proposed fog to cloud network

In the proposed network, the location points X_s denote that there is a large amount of user devices around them and the positions of the FNL1s are computed using the location points. Hence, the devices that contribute to the location point X_i can establish a connection with the FNL1 that contains the ith location point inside its cluster. The FNL1s can connect with every FNL2s and the cloud. The devices upload their requests to their respective FNL1s, and the FNL1s act as a buffer from where the requests are forwarded to the FNL2s or the cloud for processing after every time interval ΔT. From this point forward we refer to the FNL2s + cloud as processing resources (PRs).

13.5.3 Allocation of device requests to the processing resources

For allocation of device requests to the PRs, we use bid values (BV) to determine the priority of the requests. Each device submits a bid BV, along with the request. This BV is a virtual currency and represents the priority of the requests. Fig. 13.2 depicts the contents of a device request.

The device code "Di" references the device to which the processed request is to be sent back, the bid value BV depicts the priority and the time required T_r depicts the time that will be required by the request for complete processing.

For a resource allocation mechanism, a single FNL1 is selected which acts as the tracker. This FNL1 has access to the queues of all the FNL1s. Let us denote this FNL1 as L and the time required for data transfer from the ith element to the jth element as $t_{i \to j}$. These ith and jth elements can be FNL1, FNL2, or the cloud. The FNL1 "L" signals the other FNL1s where to forward the requests that are residing in their respective queues (Fig. 13.3).

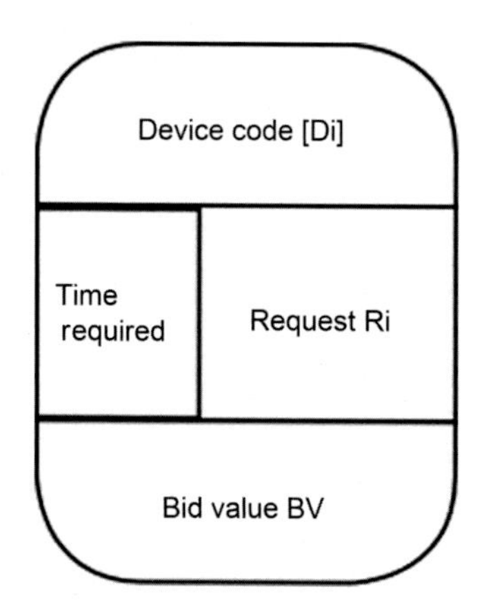

FIGURE 13.2 Computational request.

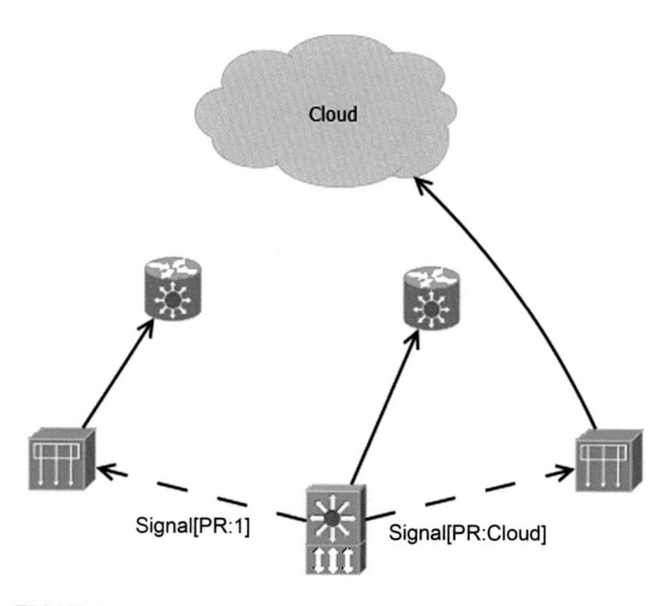

FIGURE 13.3 Tracker signaling other FNL1s.

By assigning a tracker, we make the resource allocation model a centralized mechanism. Let the total available processing capacity of the FNL2s in the time period ΔT_i be M_i and the space required by the pth request be S_{Rp}, then the first constraint we get in the mechanism is:

$$\sum_{p=1}^{n} S_{Rp} \leq M_i$$

Constraint 1: Available processing capacity

A device pays if and only if its request is allotted to a FNL2. No payment is made by the device if its request is allotted to the cloud for processing. We implement a general second price auction mechanism and hence, the payment made by device D_m on successful allocation of an FNL2 in the time period ΔT_i is the next highest bid made in the network.

$$\text{pay}_{(D_m)(\Delta T_i)} = \text{BV}_{\beta(\Delta T_i)} \tag{13.2}$$

In Eq. (13.2), $\text{BV}_{\beta(\Delta T_i)}$ is the next highest bid in the network in the time period ΔT_i.

Under constraint 1, we maximize the following objective by maximizing the total payment to be made by the devices in the time period ΔT_i.

$$\max \sum \text{pay}_{(D_m)(\Delta T_i)}$$

Objective 1: Maximize payment

Along with objective 1, the second objective in the mechanism is to select the jth element for the ith element in such a way that the summation of the time taken for data transfer from the ith element to the jth element is minimized.

$$\min \sum t_{i \to j}$$

Objective 2: Minimize time of data transfer

Since the proposed mechanism contains multiobjective optimization (Gunantara, 2018), there can be instances where more than one solution exists in the nondominated set. In such cases where there is the existence of more than one Pareto-optimal solution, we relax objective 2 to keep the mechanism time efficient.

To summarize the resource allocation mechanism, a tracker is selected from the pool of FNL1s which has access to the queues of all the FNL1s and signals the other FNL1s where to forward their user requests under the following conditions:

$$\max \sum \text{pay}_{(D_m)(\Delta T_i)} \tag{13.3}$$

$$\min \sum t_{i \to j} \tag{13.4}$$

$$\sum_{p=1}^{n} S_{Rp} \leq M_i \tag{13.5}$$

13.5.4 User-to-user data transfer using fog nodes

In modern computer networking, the exchange of data between systems takes place using the TCP/IP model. This model consists of four layers, which are the application layer, transport layer, Internet layer, and the network interface layer (Mundra and El Taeib).

The application layer is the topmost layer and is placed closest to the end users. The transport layer uses the transmission control protocol (TCP), which ensures that the data packets are correctly delivered between the devices. The Internet layer handles the movement of the packets through the network and makes sure that the packets reach the destination regardless of which path they take. Finally, the network interface layer describes how the packets are to be physically transferred through the network (Fig. 13.4).

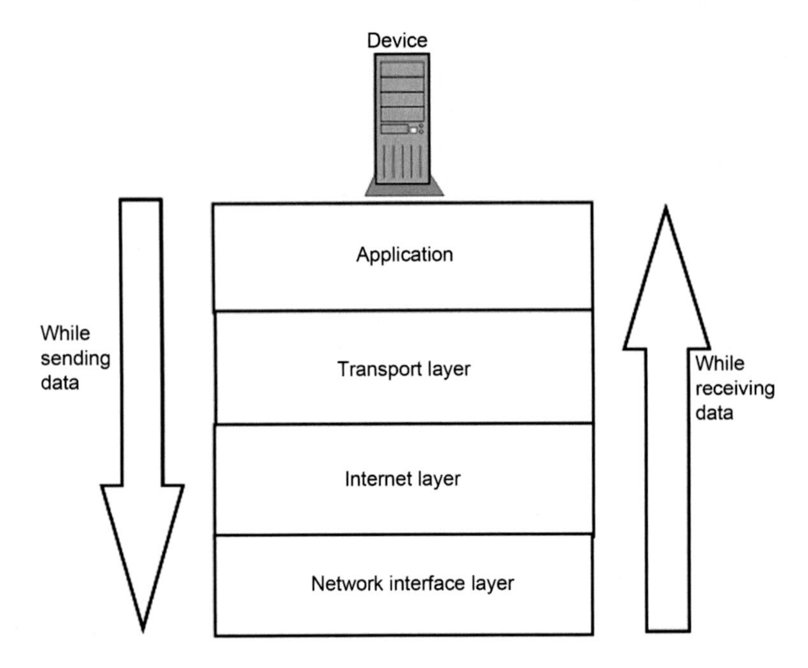

FIGURE 13.4 Typical four-layer network model.

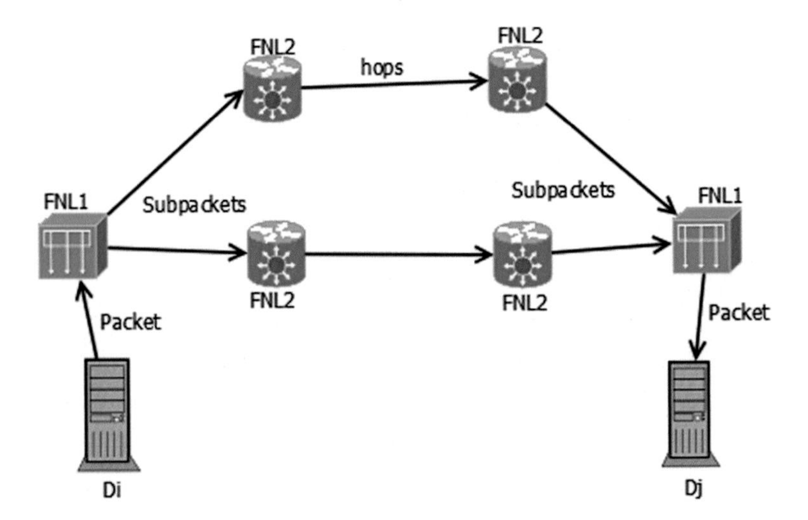

FIGURE 13.5 Data transmission through the network.

This type of data transmission protocol is implementable through the proposed fog network. Fig. 13.5 depicts the schema for data transmission from device D_i to device D_j through the F2C network.

The device D_i (sender) sends the data as a packet to its assigned FNL1, in the FNL1 the packet is divided into subpackets from where the subpackets are sent to the networks of FNL2s where they hop between them until the subpackets reach the FNL1 under which device D_j (receiver) resides. At the FNL1, the subpackets are reassembled to form the original packet and are forwarded to D_j.

13.5.5 Determining the cost of edges

Each edge is assigned a cost, C_e. We assume that the cost of edges $D_i \rightarrow \mathbf{FNL1}_i$ and $\mathrm{FNL1}_j \rightarrow D_j$ is 0. All other edges which connect $i \rightarrow j$ have a cost of:

$$C_e = \frac{\alpha_{(Fi)(\Delta T_i)}[l_{i \rightarrow j}]}{\mathbb{N}_e} \tag{13.6}$$

where

$$\alpha_{(Fi)(\Delta T_i)} = M_{\mathrm{TOT}(j)} / M_{\mathrm{TOT}(j)} - M_{\mathrm{oc}(FJ)(\Delta T_i)} \tag{13.7}$$

$M_{\mathrm{TOT}(j)}$ is the total capacity of the jth element and $M_{\mathrm{oc(FJ)}(\Delta T_i)}$ is the jth element's memory space that is occupied and hence is not available in the time period ΔT_i.

The cost of the edge C_e is directly proportional to the time taken for the data packet to reach element j from i using the edge e and is inversely proportional to the number of packets $\mathbb{N}_e$ using the edge at that instance. The variable $\alpha_{(Fi)(\Delta T_i)}$ is the ratio of total capacity of j to the available capacity of j. For the condition $M_{TOT(j)} = M_{oc(FJ)(\Delta T_i)}$, which implies that the element is full with no available space, the value of $\alpha_{(Fi)(\Delta T_i)}$ becomes infinity (∞), thus making the edge untraversable. Also, if $N_{e(max)}$ represents the maximum transfer capacity of the edge e, then for the condition $N_e > N_{e(max)}$, C_e is equal to ∞.

The total amount to be paid for the transmission of a single packet (μ) from the sender to the receiver through the network is the summation of the cost of the edges (e) that the packet used in the network.

$$Cost_{\mu} = \sum_{e \in E} C_e \tag{13.8}$$

cost of single packet transmission

The total payment to be done by the device D_i (sender) is the summation of the cost of its transferred packets.

$$Pay_{D_i} = \sum_{\mu=1}^{\omega} Cost_{\mu} \tag{13.9}$$

cost to device with ω transferred packets

It can be seen from Eq. (13.3) that the cost is shared among multiple devices (Nisan, Roughgarden, Tardos, & Vazirani) if packets from multiple devices use a common edge. This type of cost-sharing mechanism in a network was extensively discussed by Herzog, Shenker, and Estrin (1997).

13.5.6 Physical address of FNL2S

The FNL2 (j) (FII(j)), in the network is identified with an address: Address$[F_{II(j)}] \rightarrow (V(x)_j.V(y)_j)$. The $V(x)_j$ and $V(y)_j$ denotes the x and y coordinates, respectively, of the jth FNL2 with respect to a universal origin (0,0).

13.5.7 Packet flow inside the network

The sender device uploads the data to be transferred to its FNL1. The FNL1 breaks up the data into packets and forwards the packets to FNL2s such that the total cost of moving the packets to the respective FNL2s is minimized. Once the packet μ reaches the initial FNL2 [which acts as the sender FNL2, with the address $(V(x)_s.V(y)_s)$] the goal becomes to send μ to the receiving FNL2 with address $(V(x)_r.V(y)_r)$, via other intermediate FNL2s if necessary, such that the cost of packet transmission [Eq. (13.3)] is minimized. The receiving FNL2 is the layer 2 fog node that has the receiving device's (D_j) FNL1 inside its range.

Since the addresses of the FNL2s are determined by their geographical positions, to avoid redundant transfer of packets within the network the packets are transferred from the current FNL2 $(V(x)_C.V(y)_C)$ to the next FNL2 $(V(x)_{C+}.V(y)_{C+})$ if and only if the distance of $(V(x)_{C+}.V(y)_{C+})$ to $(V(x)_r.V(y)_r)$ is less than the distance of $(V(x)_C.V(y)_C)$ to $(V(x)_r.V(y)_r)$.

Algorithm 3 depicts the procedure for packet transfer from the sender FNL2 to the receiver FNL2.

ALGORITHM 3 Packet Transmission

$F_{II(C)} \leftarrow Current\ FNL2$
$T\{\} \leftarrow Set\ of\ previously\ traversed\ FNL2s$
$D_C = (V(y)_c - V(y)_r)^2 + (V(x)_c - V(x)_r)^2$
$D_{C+} = (V(y)_{c+} - V(y)_r)^2 + (V(x)_{c+} - V(x)_r)^2$
REPEAT:
$\mathscr{A}\{\} \leftarrow EmptySet$
$\forall\{\mathbf{FNL2s}\} - (\{F_{II(c)}\} \cup T\{\})$
Check IF: $D_{C+} < D_C$
Add $F_{II(C+)}$ to $\mathscr{A}\{\}$
ELSE: Reject $F_{II(C+)}$
$\forall$elements in $\mathscr{A}\{\}$
Compute C_e
$F_{II(Z)} \leftarrow \min(C_e(\mathscr{A}\{\}))$
Send packet μ to $F_{II(Z)}$
Add $F_{II(Z)}$ to $T\{\}$
$F_{II(c)} \leftarrow F_{II(Z)}$
UNTIL: $Address(F_{II(c)}) = (V(x)_r.V(y)_r)$

In the above algorithm, all the FNL2s in the network, except for the current FNL2 and the FNL2s that are already traversed by the packet are checked for the condition $D_{C+} < D_C$. All the FNL2s that satisfy the condition are added to the SET **A**{ }. Hence, the elements of set **A**{ } are the FNL2s that are closer to the receiver FNL2 than the current FNL2 is to the receiver. For all the elements in set **A**{}, the edge cost C_e is computed. Because of cost sharing $C_e \propto 1/N_e$, we want the maximum possible number of packets to use the same edge for transmission. The FNL2 providing the minimum cost is chosen as $F_{II(Z)}$. A network connection is established between $F_{II(c)}$ and $F_{II(Z)}$ and the packet is transferred to $F_{II(Z)}$. $F_{II(Z)}$ becomes the current node $F_{II(C)}$. This is repeated until the packets reach the receiver FNL2 whose address is $(V(x)_r.V(y)_r)$.

13.6 Simulation and discussion

13.6.1 Geopositioning of fog nodes

For simulation purposes, 100 random points are generated which represent significant location points X_s (Fig. 13.6). K-means clustering is implemented on the location points with $K = 10$. Fig. 13.7 depicts the positions of FNL1s. Using the positions of FNL1s, the positions of FNL2s are computed (Fig. 13.8). The range of FNL2s is assumed to be 40 units. With 40 units radius, three FNL2s are required for clustering the FNL1s. In the simulation, the cloud is assumed to be in a remote position.

13.6.2 Request allocation to processing resources

For simulating the resource allocation mechanism, we assume a network with three layer 1 fog nodes (FNL1s), two layer 2 fog nodes (FNL2s), and a single remote cloud.

The FNL1s are identified as $\Phi1, \Phi2$, and $\Phi3$. The FNL2s are $\varphi1$ and $\varphi2$. $\varphi1$ has a capacity of 10 u and $\varphi2$ has a capacity of 15 u. The cloud has a capacity of 30 u but is half as efficient compared to the fog nodes. We are using four requests with the characteristics shown in Table 13.1.

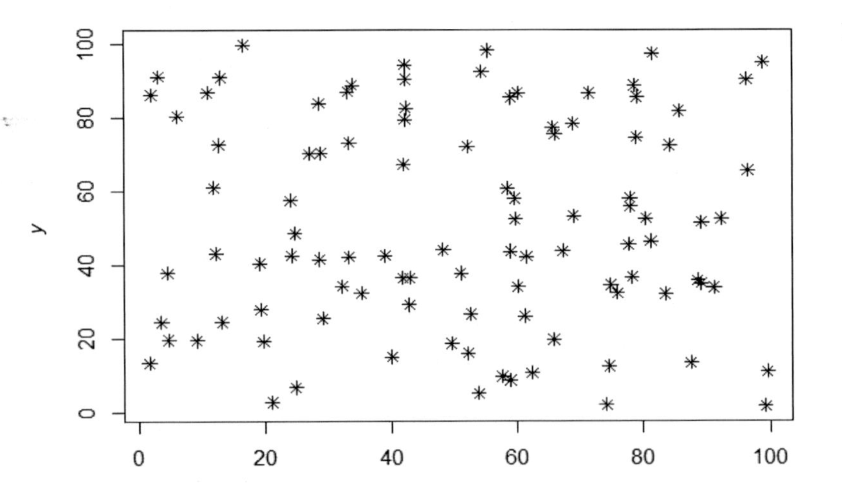

FIGURE 13.6 Significant location points.

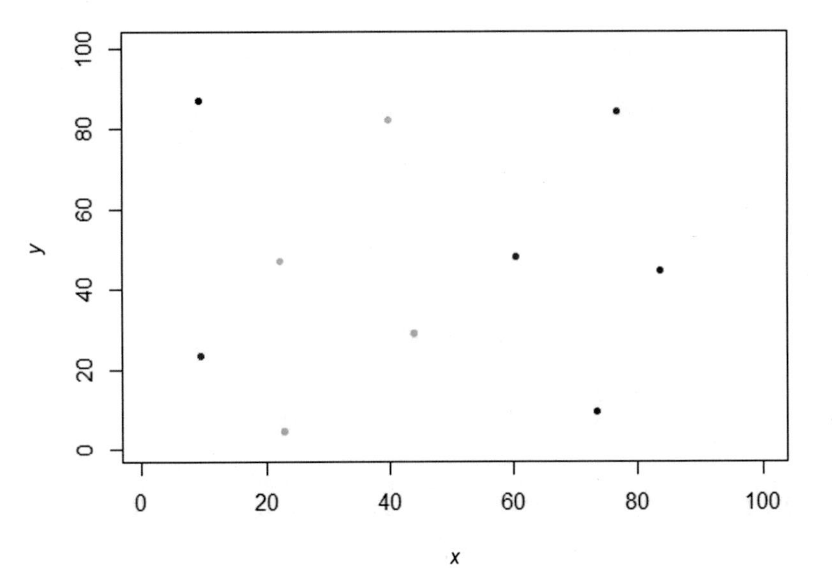

FIGURE 13.7 Position of layer 1 fog nodes.

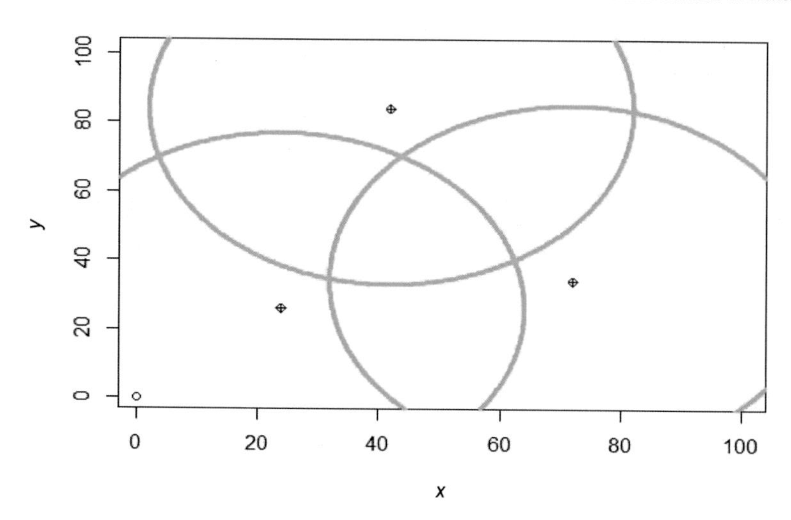

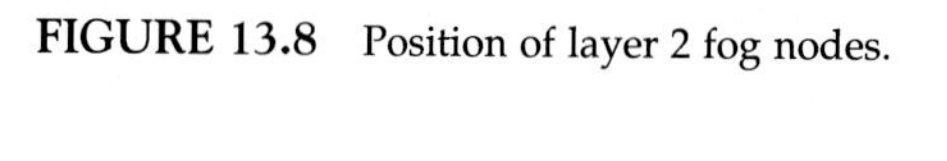
FIGURE 13.8 Position of layer 2 fog nodes.

TABLE 13.1 Four requests with the characteristics.

R_i	R_1	R_2	R_3	R_4
FNL1	Φ1	Φ2	Φ3	Φ3
BV_i	150	120	100	40
$T_{r(i)}$	$5\Delta T$	$10\Delta T$	$2\Delta T$	$4\Delta T$
S_{Rp}	10 u	8 u	12 u	8 u

TABLE 13.2 Required time for data transfer between the elements of the F2C network.

	Φ1	Φ2	Φ3	C_L
$\varphi 1$	30 ms	10 ms	20 ms	20 ms
$\varphi 2$	40 ms	30 ms	30 ms	30 ms
C_L	50 ms	70 ms	50 ms	–

TABLE 13.3 Bid value per unit time ΔT.

R_1	R_2	R_3	R_4
30	12	50	10

Table 13.2 shows the approximate time required for data transfer between the elements of the F2C network (cloud is denoted as C_L).

For request distribution, we first compute $\gamma_i = \mathrm{BV}_i/T_{r(i)}$. This is the bid value per unit time ΔT. The values are as given Table 13.3.

For the request distribution, we create a set of requests $\mathbf{W}\{R_i\}$ such that $\sum_{\mathrm{W}} S_{\mathrm{rp}} \leq M_{\varphi 1} + M_{\varphi 2}$ and $\max \sum_{\mathrm{W}} \gamma_i$. From the set, we allot the requests to the FNL2s such that summation of time taken for request transfer is minimized. This is handled by the tracker FNL1 "L." The following sequence diagram (Fig. 13.9) depicts the request processing in the PRs.

In Fig. 13.9, each request block represents that the request is being processed in the PR for a time period ΔT_i. The payments made by the devices are: $D_{R1} = 60$, $D_{R2} = 50$, $D_{R3} = 60$, and $D_{R4} = 0$. It can be seen from the illustration that not only is payment to be made only if the devices use the fog nodes, but also that the cost is dependent on demand. Another interesting property that arises due to the GSP auction mechanism is that the payment that is to be made will always be less than or equal to the bid value.

13.6.3 User-to-user data transfer

Fig. 13.10 shows a network mesh of 10 FNL2s in the Indian subcontinent area.

Two FNL1s ($F_{I(a)}$and $F_{I(b)}$) under the range of FNL2 {2} receive two data blocks ($m1$and$m2$) to be transferred from their respective devices. At the FNL1s, the blocks are broken down into packets (μ). $m1$ is broken down into 6μ and $m2$ into 5μ. The packets are forwarded to FNL2{2}. $m1$ is to be sent to FNL2{8} and $m2$ to FNL2{9}, which are the receiver FNL2s for the respective packets.$N_{e(\max)}$ is taken to be 8μ

In Fig. 13.11, the data block contains the data, the receiver FNL2's address, FNL1's address, and the receiving device's address. The block is broken into packets by FNL1. The packets are given a unique code (UC), which is the same for all the packets derived from a single block. It also contains a pointer to previous packet (AP), the subdata, address of receiving FNL2, the FNL1's address, and the pointer to the next packet (AS). The last data packet contains the receiving device's address instead of AS.

At the FNL2s where the packets currently reside, the next FNL2 which provides the minimum edge cost is selected for packet transfer. This repeats until the packets reach the destination FNL2. Fig. 13.12 shows the flow of packets from FNL2{2} to their respective destinations.

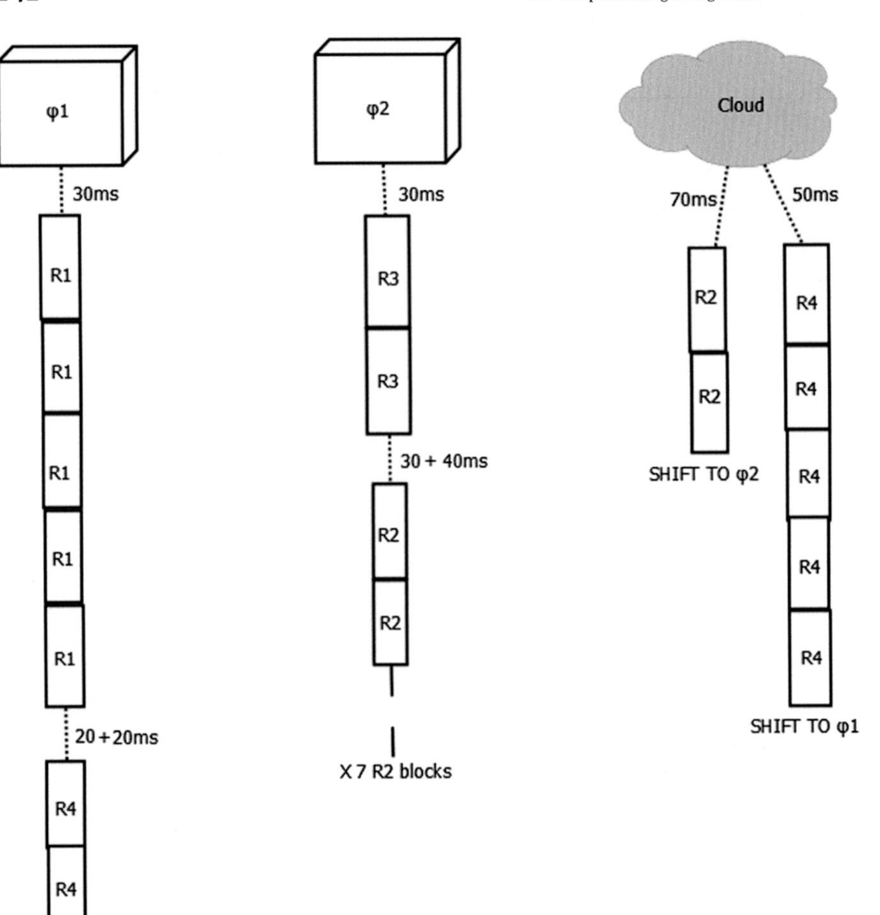

FIGURE 13.9 Sequence diagram for request processing in the PRs.

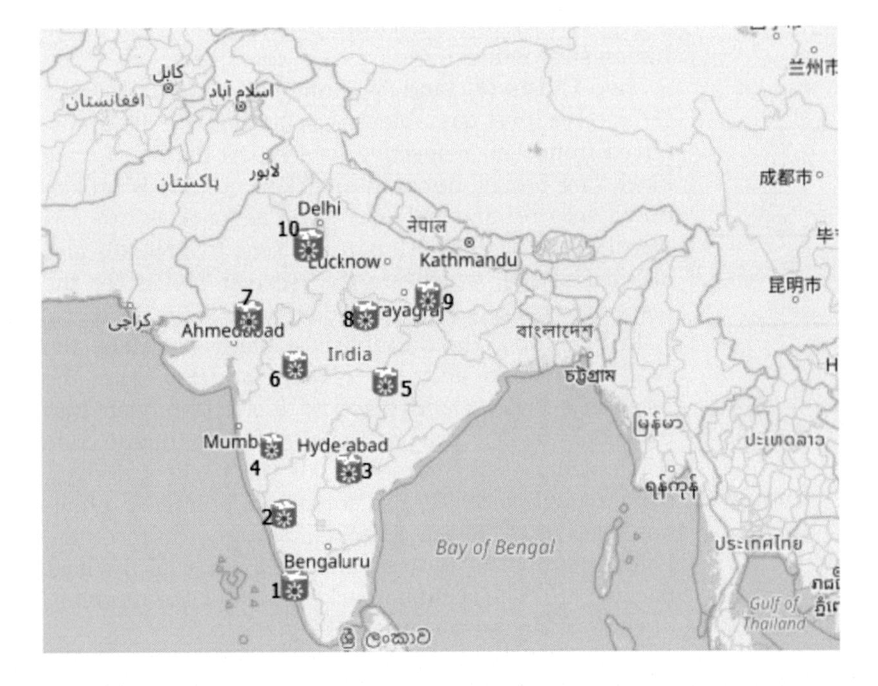

FIGURE 13.10 FNL2 network mesh.

In Fig. 13.12 the maximum capacity of the edges is eight packets and the packets are to be moved in a common direction till FNL2 {8}. Hence, the 11 packets (6 + 5) are grouped as eight and three and are transferred according to algorithm 3.

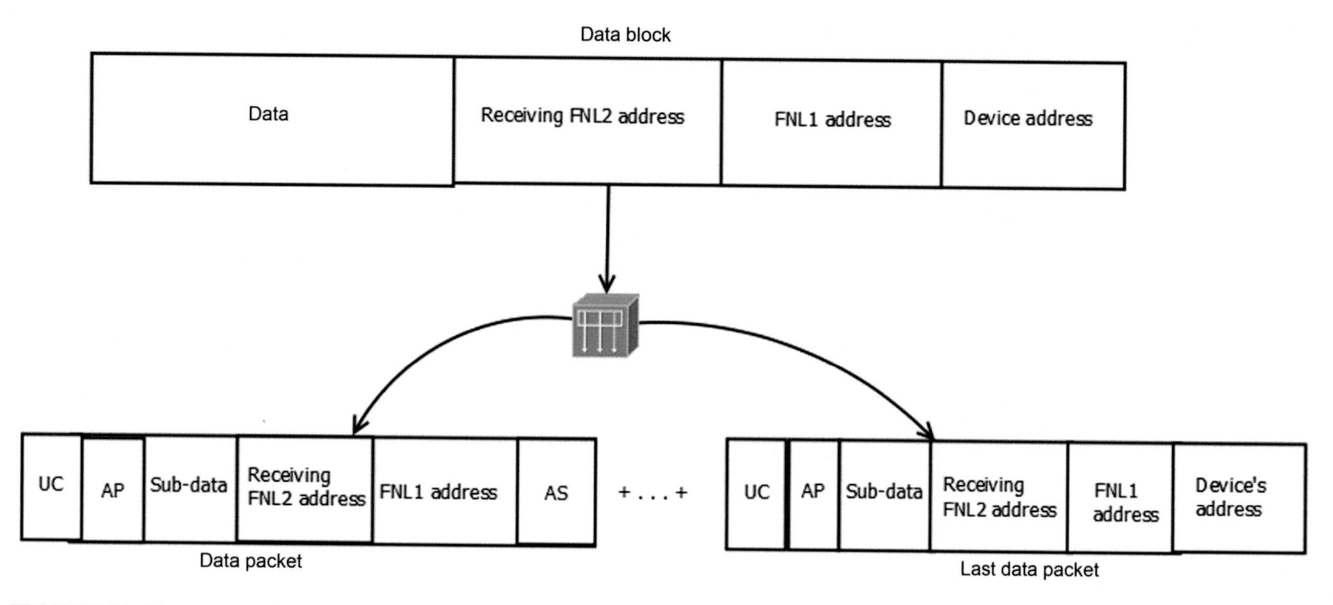

FIGURE 13.11 Data block, receiver FNL2's address, FNL1's address and the receiving device's address.

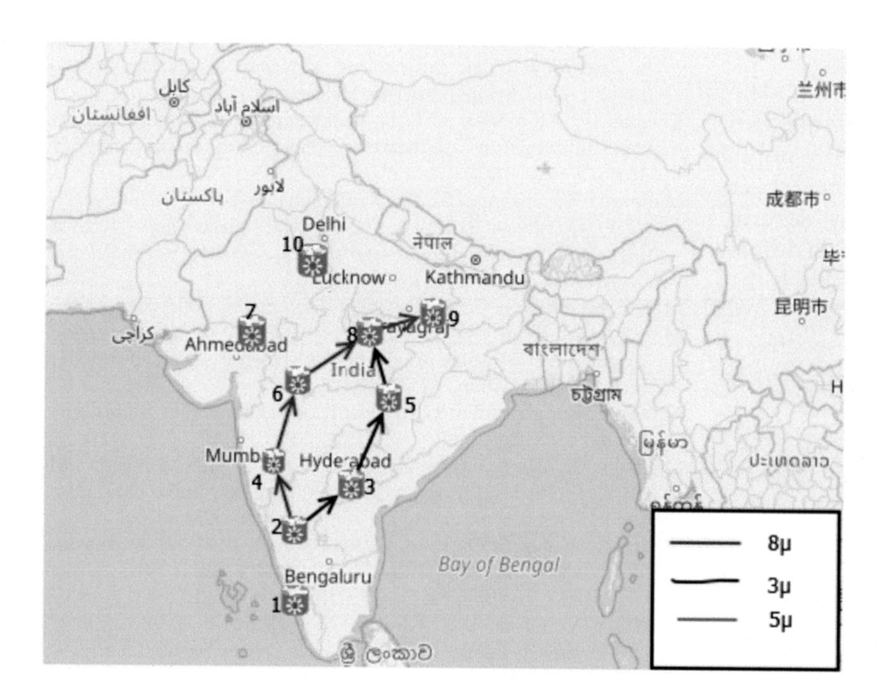

FIGURE 13.12 Maximum capacity of the edges and the movement of packets.

In Fig. 13.12, the red lines contain eight packets which are made of six $m1$ packets and two $m2$ packets, while violet lines depict the three remaining $m2$ packets. Assuming that simultaneous transmission occurs, the edge containing a lower number of packets is given the edge with the lowest cost. Hence, the value of $\alpha_{(Fi)(\Delta T_i)}[t_{i\to j}]$ for FNL2{2} to FNL2{3} is less than FNL2{2} to FNL2{4}. The packets reach FNL2{8}, which is the receiver FNL2 for $m1$. The six $m1$ packets are dropped off there and the remaining five $m2$ packets are transferred to FNL2{9}. The costs to be paid by the devices of $m1$ and $m2$ are:

$$D_{m1} = (C_{(2\to4)} \times 6) + (C_{(4\to6)} \times 6) + (C_{(6\to8)} \times 6)$$

$$D_{m2} = \left(C_{(2\to3)} \times 3\right) + \left(C_{(3\to5)} \times 3\right) + \left(C_{(5\to8)} \times 3\right) + \left(C_{(8\to9)} \times 5\right) + \left(C_{(2\to4)} \times 2\right) + \left(C_{(4\to6)} \times 2\right) + (C_{(6\to8)} \times 2)$$

where $C_{(i\to j)}$ is the cost of edge C_e between FNL2{i} and FNL2{j}.

13.7 Conclusions and future research

In this chapter we have proposed a method for computing the positions of installation of fog nodes in a double fog-layer fog to cloud network architecture based on user device locations. Although we have no claim of optimality of the said positions, the proposed method does fulfill the goal of taking the user devices' locations into account while deriving the positions of layer 1 and layer 2 fog nodes. Along with this, we proposed a framework for two applications of the network. The first application is using the layer 2 fog nodes along with the cloud as computational resources that provide computation services to the devices. The requests that need computational services are allotted on the basis of BV made by the devices. The second application is using the fog network for data transmission between devices. The data that need to be transferred are broken down into packets which are then transferred from the sender fog node to the receiver fog node via other fog nodes. The cost of the edges is shared among the devices that use the network at the same time for data transmission.

The framework proposed is inspired from a theoretic game concept which makes it ideal for implementation in a commercial network. Since it is assumed that the network is comprised of trusted users and servers, the framework does not contain any security mechanism. The immediate future work is to implement a security mechanism using encryption such that one party cannot access another party's data, as well as incorporating compression techniques so that a larger amount of data can be transferred through the network with minimum congestion.

References

Bandyopadhyay, A., Mukhopadhyay, S., & Ganguly, U. (2016, September). Allocating resources in cloud computing when users have strict preferences. In *Proceedings of the international conference on advances in computing, communications and informatics* (pp. 2324–2328). IEEE.

Bandyopadhyay, A., Mukhopadhyay, S., & Ganguly, U. (2017, September). On free of cost service distribution in cloud computing. In *Proceedings of the international conference on advances in computing, communications and informatics* (pp. 1974–1980). IEEE.

Bandyopadhyay, A., Xhafa, F., Mukhopadhyay, S., Kumar Singh, V., & Sharma, A. (2019). An auction framework for DaaS in cloud computing and its evaluation. *International Journal of Web and Grid Services (Online)*, *15*(2), 119–138.

Bonomi, F., Milito, R., Zhu, J., & Addepalli, S. (2012, August). Fog computing and its role in the internet of things. In *Proceedings of the first edition of the MCC workshop on mobile cloud computing* (pp. 13–16). ACM.

Cao, X., Cong, G., & Jensen, C. S. (2010). Mining significant semantic locations from GPS data. *Proceedings of the VLDB Endowment*, *3*(1–2), 1009–1020.

Chang, C., Srirama, S. N., & Buyya, R. (2017). Indie fog: An efficient fog-computing infrastructure for the internet of things. *Computer*, *50*(9), 92–98.

Fog Computing and the Internet of Things: Extend the cloud to where the things are. White paper. (2016). <https://www.cisco.com/c/dam/en_us/solutions/trends/iot/docs/computing-overview.pdf> Accessed 07.09.19.

Gubbi, J., Buyya, R., Marusic, S., & Palaniswami, M. (2013). Internet of Things (IoT): A vision, architectural elements, and future directions. *Future Generation Computer Systems*, *29*(7), 1645–1660.

Gunantara, N. (2018). A review of multi-objective optimization: Methods and its applications. *Cogent Engineering*, *5*(1), 1502242.

Hartigan, J. A., & Wong, M. A. (1979). Algorithm AS 136: A k-means clustering algorithm. *Journal of the Royal Statistical Society. Series C (Applied Statistics)*, *28*(1), 100–108.

Herzog, S., Shenker, S., & Estrin, D. (1997). Sharing the "cost" of multicast trees: an axiomatic analysis. *IEEE/ACM Transactions on Networking*, *5*(6), 847–860.

Hirsch, D. D. (2013). The glass house effect: Big Data, the new oil, and the power of analogy. *Maine Law Review*, *66*, 373.

Kami, N., Enomoto, N., Baba, T., & Yoshikawa, T. (2010, October). Algorithm for detecting significant locations from raw GPS data. In *Proceedings of the international conference on discovery science* (pp. 221–235). Springer, Berlin, Heidelberg.

Kraemer, F., Alexander, A. E. B., Nattachart, T., & David, P. (2017). Fog computing in healthcare–A review and discussion. *IEEE Access*, *5*, 9206–9222.

Mahmud, R., Srirama, S. N., Ramamohanarao, K., & Buyya, R. (2019). Quality of Experience (QoE)-aware placement of applications in Fog computing environments. *Journal of Parallel and Distributed Computing*, *132*, 190–203.

Mell, P., &Grance, T. (2011). The NIST definition of cloud computing.

Mundra, S., & El Taeib, T. (2015). TCP/IP protocol layering. International Journal of Computer Science and Information Technology Research, 3(1), 415–417.

Nisan, N., Roughgarden, T., Tardos, E., &Vazirani, V.V. Algorithmic game theory. Page- 495.

Osanaiye, O., Chen, S., Yan, Z., Lu, R., Choo, K. K. R., & Dlodlo, M. (2017). From cloud to fog computing: A review and a conceptual live VM migration framework. *IEEE Access*, *5*, 8284–8300.

Perera, C., Yongrui, Q., Julio, C. E., Stephan, R.-M., & Athanasios, V. V. (2017). Fog computing for sustainable smart cities: A survey. *ACM Computing Surveys (CSUR)*, *50*(3), 1–43.

Stantchev, V., Barnawi, A., Ghulam, M. S., Schubert, J., & Tamm, G. (2015). Smart items. *Fog and Cloud Computing as Enablers of Servitization in Healthcare. Sensors & Transducers*, *185*, 121–128.

Statista Research Department. (2016, November). <https://www.statista.com/statistics/471264/iot-number-of-connected-devices-worldwide/> Accessed 26.09.19.

Sutherland, I. E. (1968). A futures market in computer time. *Communications of the ACM*, *11*(6), 449–451.

Tordera, E.M., Masip-Bruin, X., Garcia-Alminana, J., Jukan, A., Ren, G.J., Zhu, J., &Farré, J. (2016). What is a fog node a tutorial on current concepts towards a common definition. *arXiv:1611.09193*.

CHAPTER

14

A wavelet-based low frequency prior for single-image dehazing

Subhadeep Koley[1], *Hiranmoy Roy*[2] *and Soumyadip Dhar*[2]

[1]Department of Electronics and Communication Engineering, RCC Institute of Information Technology, Kolkata, India
[2]Department of Information Technology, RCC Institute of Information Technology, Kolkata, India

14.1 Introduction

The source imaging device's image production quality greatly affects the overall efficiency of any machine vision application, for example, object tracking/detection, long-range photography, target-monitoring, and scene analysis, etc. (Koley, Sadhu, Roy, & Dhar, 2018). However, the perceptual clarity of the image often suffers substantial degradation due to scattering by atmospheric particles under harsh weather conditions like fog. The contrast and color-fidelity of images are noticeably impaired and must be restored. Therefore haze removal followed by contrast enhancement is a significant preprocessing step in various machine vision applications (Pallawi, 2016). Mathematically, image deterioration in the presence of haze is manifested by the image formation model, also known as Koschmeider's haze imaging model (Middleton, 1954).

$$I_{\text{hazy}}(i,j) = I_{\text{radiance}}(i,j)T(i,j) + A_{\text{global}}(1 - T(i,j)) \quad (14.1)$$

where $I_{\text{hazy}}(i,j)$ is a color image (with haze) acquired by an imaging device, and $I_{\text{radiance}}(i,j)$ is the original scene radiance or required haze-free image. The atmospheric light A_{global} delineates the intensity of the ambient light for a scene. The transmission map $T(i,j)$, such that $0 \leq T(i,j) \leq 1$, is a scalar value which denotes the percentage of scene radiance that reaches the imaging device directly instead of being scattered, and is supposedly constant for each color channel. This enables the haze-imaging model to treat each color channel independently. The transmission map is the most important factor for reconstruction of the haze-free image as it contains the major chunk of details that constitute the image. The term $I_{\text{radiance}}(i,j)T(i,j)$ is known as direct attenuation and describes the percentage of the scene radiance reaching the camera and is a multiplicative distortion. The term $A_{\text{global}}(1 - T(i,j))$ is called the air-light, which represents the reflected light from the object being captured that is scattered by atmospheric fog and aerosols and is additive by nature. The overall hazy image formation procedure is depicted in Fig. 14.1.

In this chapter, we utilize this model to obtain the scene radiance after estimating the transmission map and atmospheric light from the acquired hazy image. The fundamental idea here is to estimate the transmission map and air-light from the obtained hazy image and determine the unknown scene radiance by manipulating Eq. (14.1) (an equation with three known and one unknown variables). The remainder of the chapters consists of the literature survey details in Section 14.2, motivation and contribution in Section 14.3, proposed methodology in Section 14.4, followed by result analysis and conclusion in Sections 14.5 and 14.6, respectively.

14.2 Literature survey

To increase visibility in hazy images, early researchers used some elemental spatial and frequency domain filtering and histogram stretching methods (Pizer, Johnston, Ericksen, Yankaskas, & Muller, 1990), which were modest in terms of dehazing efficiency as well as the time complexity (Zhu, Mai, & Shao, 2015). The trade-off between dehazing efficiency and required processing time is the reason why dehazing remains an emerging area of research. Fattal (2008) delineated an image dehazing framework set up on surface-shading and scene

Recent Trends in Computational Intelligence Enabled Research.
DOI: https://doi.org/10.1016/B978-0-12-822844-9.00038-4

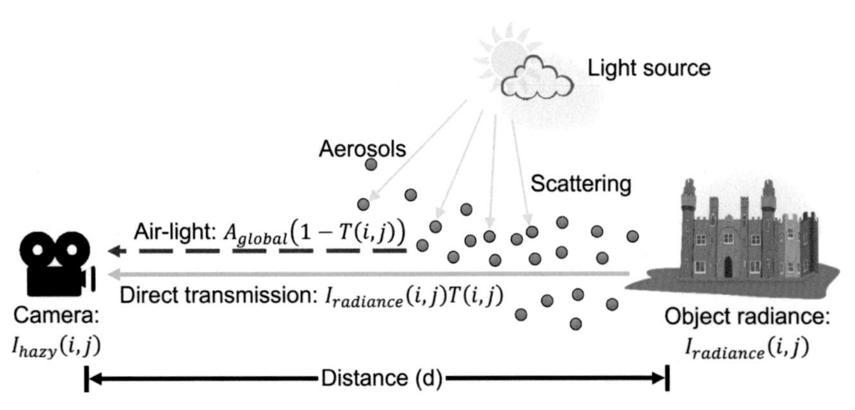

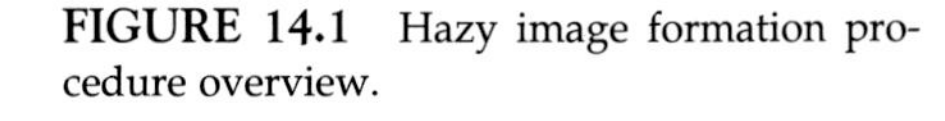
FIGURE 14.1 Hazy image formation procedure overview.

transmission theory (Fattal, 2008). Another image dehazing algorithm proposed by Tan (2008) achieved dehazing by cost function optimization in a Markov random field (Tan, 2008). Tarel and Hautiere (2009) presented a rapid framework, which preserves edges and corners using median filtering to accomplish dehazing (Tarel and Hautiere, 2009). This framework is set up on linear operation and multivariate optimization. Tripathi and Mukhopadhyay (2012) proposed another unsupervised single-image haze-removal framework based on anisotropic diffusion, which can deal with RGB as well as HVS color models (Tripathi and Mukhopadhyay, 2012). After observing numerous hazy and clear daylight images, Zhu et al. (2015) suggested a prior, namely the color attenuation prior. They designed a linear system for modeling the scene depth under this novel prior (Zhu et al., 2015). Ancuti and Ancuti (2013) gave a novel fusion-based approach for single-image dehazing. This method uses two images from the original input image by performing a white balance and a contrast-enhancing procedure (Ancuti and Ancuti, 2013). Jun and Rong (2013) were among the first, according to best of our knowledge, to use DWT for single-image dehazing. They first used histogram equalization, and afterwards adjusted the wavelet coefficients to achieve the desired effect (Jun and Rong, 2013). Kim, Jang, Sim, and Kim (2013) presented their method where they estimated the atmospheric light by using quad-tree subdivision, followed by a cost function optimization consisting of the contrast term and the information loss term to achieve dehazing (Kim et al., 2013). Set up on statistical data obtained from numerous hazy and atmospherically clear images, He, Sun, and Tang (2011) gave a ground-breaking prior, namely, the dark channel prior (DCP) (He et al., 2011). They stated that in the haze-free clear images, as a minimum, one color channel holds pixel values which tend to zero. With this supposition they assessed the fog thickness and achieved dehazing using an empirical hazy-image formation model. This framework has promised to be rewarding in a majority of the scenarios, but with the disadvantage of high time complexity of the soft matting (Zhu et al., 2015). Over the years, various modifications have been made extending the DCP method. Pallawi (2016) offered a scheme which aims at reducing the processing time of DCP scheme with guided filtering. Anwar and Khosla (2017) recommended another extension to DCP, where they used DCP and weighted least square filter along with high dynamic range tone mapping. Set up on DCP, Nair and Sankaran (2018) proposed another dehazing framework, where they employed one center-surrounded filter to improve the speed and memory requirement of the existing DCP algorithm. This method can work on all color models including RGB, Lab, and HSV. Set up on color channel transfer theory, Ancuti, Ancuti, Vleeschouwer, and Sbetr (2019) presented one dehazing algorithm, which works efficiently on different scenarios such as day- and night-time dehazing and underwater dehazing. Instead of the popular global air-light estimation, Ancuti, Ancuti, Vleeschouwer, and Bovik (2020) gave another dehazing algorithm based on local air-light estimation. This method performs better for night-time hazy scenes. Recently, deep-learning based methods have gained wide acceptance due to their superior performance. However, they often require huge training data with ground truths, which are often not available for the ill-posed image dehazing problem. Yu, Cherukuri, Guo, and Monga (2020) proposed an encoder–decoder dense convolutional network to image dehazing. This method performs efficiently on the nonhomogeneous NTIRE-2020 data set, but at the cost of a high training time. Based on nonlocal channel attention, Metwaly, Li, Guo, and Monga (2020) proposed another deep-learning framework for heterogeneous haze removal. However, this method also requires huge training data and time.

14.3 Motivation and contribution

The drawbacks of the scheme proposed by Fattal (2008) are the large processing time and low efficiency for dense haze. The method proposed by Tan (2008) does not require any in-scene structural details, although it does have a likelihood to oversaturation of image pixels (Zhu et al., 2015). The drawback of the scheme of Zhu et al. (2015) is that, like all other atmospheric scattering model-based algorithms, this one also uses a constant value of the scattering co-efficient (β). Ideally, β should vary with the scene depth to recover the exact scene radiance (Zhu et al., 2015). The serious limitation of the framework of Ancuti and Ancuti (2013) is that this fusion-based approach is capable of restoring only homogeneous fog. The method proposed by Jun and Rong (2013) is quite elementary and does not make use of any sort of state-of-the art haze imaging or atmospheric scattering models. On the other hand, among DCP-based methods, the resultant images from the Pallawi (2016) method contain traces of haze around the edges, resulting in an undesired halo effect. On the other hand, the scheme given by Anwar and Khosla (2017) tends to oversharpen and oversaturate the resultant dehazed image. Furthermore, there is no significant improvement in the time complexity. After studying various literatures on single-image dehazing we have been able to find a gap, which as far as we are aware none of the former researchers have exploited. The frequency domain behavior of the hazy images has been overlooked previously, and we tend to achieve better results by doing just that precisely. After observing numerous hazy and nonhazy images and their respective frequency spectrums, we have assumed that haze resides within the spatial low-frequency component of the hazy image. We call this low-frequency prior (LFP). Therefore removing haze with the DCP at only the low-frequency components will suffice. Here, DWT with the "sym4" filter bank is used to separate the low- and high-frequency components of the hazy image, following which a pre-trained convolutional neural network (CNN) has been utilized to remove the Gaussian noise and simultaneously enhance the finer details previously tarnished by the fog. Subsequently, both the modified high- and low-frequency components are merged together using inverse discrete wavelet transform to yield the desired haze-free image. The attained image finally undergoes a novel fuzzy image contrast enhancement algorithm to efficiently reinstate the color fidelity and richness of the image. Therefore, the novel contributions made in this chapter are:

1. An efficient and novel prior, namely LFP has been proposed;
2. The time complexity of the DCP method has been reduced to an accountable extent using LFP;
3. The frequency domain behavior of the "haze" is exploited and used for better dehazing efficiency.
4. A novel fuzzy contrast enhancement framework is proposed for contrast enhancement of the dehazed image to make it more visually appealing.

14.4 Proposed method

14.4.1 Low-frequency prior

The overview of the proposed algorithm has been summarized in Fig. 14.2.

In general, an image can be mathematically manifested as the product of the intensity of the incident light and the reflectivity of the imaged object (Gonzalez and Woods, 2011). In fact, the intensity term varies slowly in the spatial domain, therefore manifesting low-frequency (LF) behavior. On the other hand, the reflectivity term varies rapidly in the spatial domain, therefore contributes to High Frequency (HF) region. Since "Haze" or "Fog" occurs as a result of atmospheric light scattering, and it has a slow spatial variation throughout the image, therefore it is evident that haze will reside in the LF counterpart of the hazy image. From Fig. 14.3, it is clear that clear daylight haze-free images show a substantial amount of HF components in their corresponding 2-D Fourier magnitude spectrum. On the contrary in Fig. 14.4, the hazy, low-visibility images always constitute the LF. Similar observations can also be made with respect to the hazy and haze-free image pairs presented in Fig. 14.5.

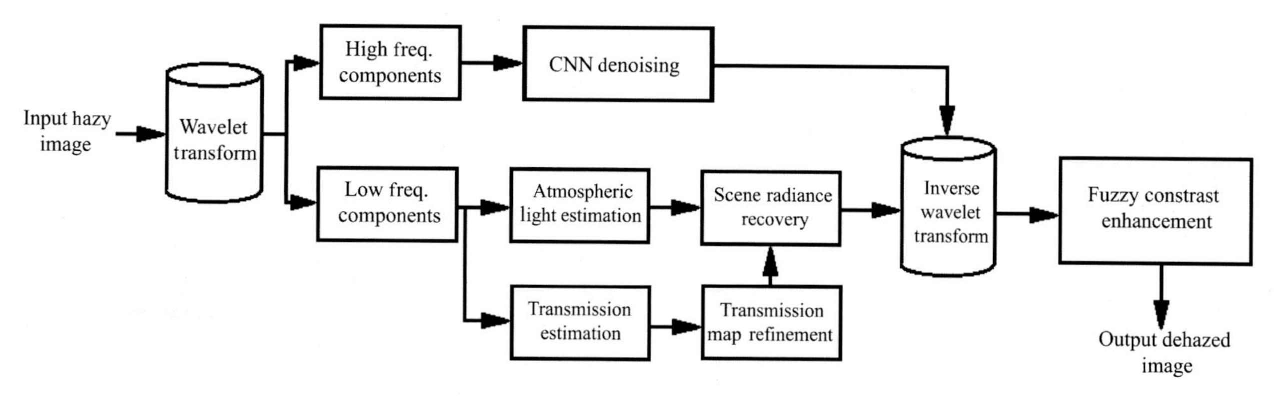

FIGURE 14.2 Overview of the proposed framework.

FIGURE 14.3 Clear daylight haze-free images (top row); corresponding 2-D Fourier magnitude plots (bottom row).

FIGURE 14.4 Hazy, low-visibility images (top row); corresponding 2-D Fourier magnitude plots (bottom row).

FIGURE 14.5 Hazy and haze-free image pairs (top row); corresponding 2-D Fourier magnitude plots (bottom row).

Therefore, after testing more than 200 hazy and dehazed images, we assume a prior that the "haze" always resides in the spatial low-frequency counterpart of a hazy image. We call this the low-frequency prior. As a result, we only perform the dehazing in the LF components of the hazy image to reduce computational complexity by a substantial amount.

Here, DWT has been used (Mallat, 1989) to segregate high- and low-frequency components. Fig. 14.6 depicts the one-level discrete wavelet analysis. In the case of 2D signals, DWT can be approximated by successive filtering followed by downsampling. First, low-pass and high-frequency filtering and downsampling processes are performed on image rows to generate the horizontal approximation and detail coefficients. Again low-pass and high-frequency filtering and downsampling processes are performed on the columns of horizontal approximation and detail to generate the four wavelet sub-bands (I_{LL}, I_{LH}, I_{HL}, I_{HH}). Here, I_{LL} represents the spatial low-frequency signal approximation and I_{LH}, I_{HL}, and I_{HH} denote the spatial HF detail components of the image. A more detailed mathematical explanation of DWT can be found in Mallat (1989).

14.4.2 Noise removal in high frequency

To the best of the authors' knowledge, all the previous dehazing algorithms suffer from the presence of Gaussian noise which, unlike "haze," resides in the spatial HF regions. Our proposed approach segregates the HF and LF components of the image and employs the denoising CNN presented by Zhang, Zuo, Chen, Meng, and Zhang (2017) on the HF components to reduce the Gaussian noise and to intensify the details. Since the invention of CNN, it has been exploited for various image-processing techniques, machine learning, and computer vision applications. Unlike a neural network where the input is a vector, CNN works on volume, that is, the input is a multichannel image (Zhang et al., 2017). The network architecture given in Zhang et al. (2017) consists of three types of layers, that is, (1) *Convolutional + Rectified Linear Units (Conv + ReLU):* these layers consists of a total of 64 filters each having the dimensions $3 \times 3 \times c$, used to generate a total of 64 distinct feature maps. Here, c represents the number of color channels present in the input image and ReLU is introduced for nonlinearity. (2) *Convolutional + Batch Normalization + Rectified Linear Units (Conv + BN + ReLU):* This combination is used in layer no. 2 to (D-1), employing a total of 64 filters of size $3 \times 3 \times 64$, and BN is used in between Conv and ReLU. (3) *Convolutional (Conv):* This last layer consists of a total of c filters each having a dimension of $3 \times 3 \times 64$. Using this CNN architecture, we have denoised the HF components of the hazy image (Fig. 14.7).

14.4.3 Dehazing in low frequency

It has been well established in LFP that haze resides in the low-frequency components of a hazy image and thus subjecting only the low-frequency components to the dehazing algorithm will serve the purpose of removing the haze from the image. The suggested dehazing scheme accommodates four steps, which are atmospheric and air-light estimation, transmission estimation, transmission map refinement, and scene radiance recovery. The dehazing framework concepts are set upon the atmospheric scattering model presented by Koschmieder. "Haze" can mathematically be manifested as (Middleton, 1954):

$$I(i,j) = I_{\text{faded}}(i,j) + L_{\text{air}}(i,j) \quad (14.2)$$

where the terms $I_{\text{faded}}(i,j)$ and $L_{\text{air}}(i,j)$ are the intensity of the attenuated image and atmospheric air-light, respectively. Both are functions of the distance from

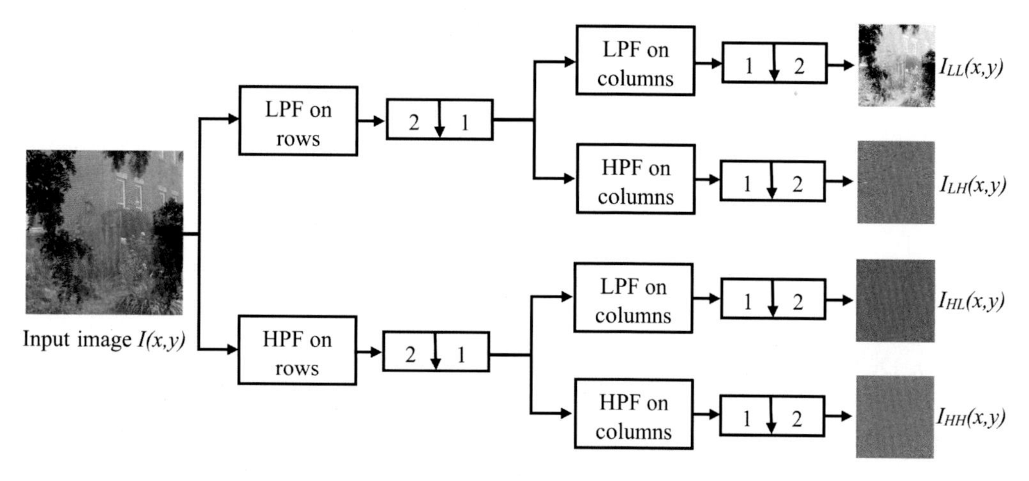

FIGURE 14.6 One-level discrete wavelet analysis of an image.

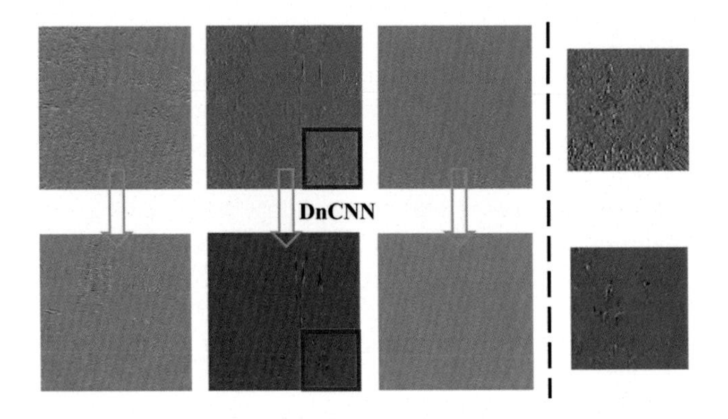

FIGURE 14.7 Original LH, HL, HH components (upper left), and denoised LH, HL, HH components (lower left). Zoomed portion of the original and denoised HL component (upper and lower right).

the object to the image-capturing device and can be depicted as

$$I_{\text{faded}}(i,j) = I_{\text{actual}}(i,j)e^{-\beta d(i,j)} \quad (14.3)$$

$$L_{\text{air}}(i,j) = A_{\text{global}}(1 - e^{-\beta d(i,j)}) \quad (14.4)$$

where $I_{\text{actual}}(i,j)$ is the scene radiance at point (i,j). β denotes the scattering coefficient, which specifies the aggregation of the haze in the image. $d(i,j)$ is the scene and camera distance and A_{global} is the global intensity of the sky region. He et al. described this framework in an abridged manner as

$$I_{\text{hazy}}(i,j) = I_{\text{radiance}}(i,j)T(i,j) + A_{\text{global}}(1 - T(i,j)) \quad (14.5)$$

where $I_{\text{hazy}}(i,j)$ and $I_{\text{radiance}}(i,j)$ are the hazy image and the scene radiance (desired dehazed image), respectively. $T(i,j)$ specifies the transmission estimation and can be delineated as

$$T(i,j) = e^{-\beta d(i,j)} \quad (14.6)$$

The expression $I_{\text{radiance}}(i,j)T(i,j)$ in Eq. (14.5) is recognized as direct attenuation, and the expression $A_{\text{global}}(1 - T(i,j))$ specifies the scattered air-light. Eq. (14.6) delineates the scene radiance, which is exponentially proportional with the distance $d(i,j)$. With all this information, the dehazed version can be restored as

$$I_{\text{radiance}}(i,j) = \frac{I_{\text{hazy}}(i,j) - A_{\text{global}}}{T(i,j)} + A_{\text{global}} \quad (14.7)$$

14.4.3.1 *Dark channel prior*

DCP is the most well-known prior used for dehazing (Zhu et al., 2015). DCP is the statistical assumption that in the non-sky regions an outdoor, clear color (R, G, B) image, at the minimum there will be one color channel with a pixel value tending to zero (He et al., 2011). This observation is most crucial in order to discriminate between hazy and haze-free images. In other words, a dark channel obtained from a clear daylight image would have a majority of black pixels, except for the sky regions and those obtained from a hazy image would have various intensities of gray pixels. The dark channel is expressed as

$$I_{\text{dark-channel}}(z) = \min_{c\in \text{R,G,B}}\left(\min_{(i,j)\in\delta(z)}\left(I_c(i,j)\right)\right) \quad (14.8)$$

$$I_{\text{dark-channel}}(z) \to 0 \quad (14.9)$$

where $I_c(i,j)$ is the color channels of the haze-free image $I(i,j)$. The outer "min" operation on $I_c(i,j)$ generates any one of the three color channels ($c \in \{R, G, B\}$) with the lowest pixel value. The inner "min" works over the local patch $\delta(z)$, centered at z to obtain the lowest intensity pixel. Contrasting with the originally proposed DCP algorithm with a patch size of 15×15, we suggest a patch size of 5×5 to warrant less accretion of haze around the edges to suppress the halo effect in the dehazed image. It is clear from Fig. 14.8 that a patch size of 5×5 generates a more detailed dark channel than a patch size of 15×15.

14.4.3.2 *Atmospheric light and transmission map estimation*

The expression A_{global} used in Eq. (14.5) indicates *air-light*, which is expressed as follows,

$$A_{\text{global}} = I_{\text{hazy}}\left(\operatorname{argmax}_z(I_{\text{dark}}(z))\right) \quad (14.10)$$

However, A_{global} is inaccurately determined when the input image carries regions with brightness higher than that of the sky-region patches. Hence, the top 0.1% dark-pixel values were chosen, and utilized to gage the A_{global}. The transmission map $T(i,j)$ is a portion of the total light reflected from the object, which is being acquired by an imaging device without dispersal. The transmission map is obtained using the "min" operator in local patch $\delta(z)$, centered at z. Dividing Eq. (14.5) with A_{global} we get

$$\min_{(i,j)\in\delta(z)}\left(\frac{I_{\text{hazy}}(i,j)}{A_{\text{global}}}\right) = \min_{(i,j)\in\delta(z)}\left(\frac{I_{\text{radiance}}(i,j)}{A_{\text{global}}}\right)T(i,j) + (1 - T(i,j)) \quad (14.11)$$

Taking, the minimum of the three color channels we get

$$\min_{(i,j)\in\delta(z)}\left(\frac{I_{\text{hazy}}(i,j)}{A_{\text{global}}}\right) = \min_{c\in\text{R,G,B}}\left(\min_{(i,j)\in\delta(z)}\left(\frac{I_{\text{radiance}}(i,j)}{A_{\text{global}}}\right)\right)T(i,j) + (1 - T(i,j)) \quad (14.12)$$

FIGURE 14.8 (A) Hazy house, (B) dark channel (15 × 15), (C) dark channel (5 × 5), (D) hazy forest, (E) dark channel (15 × 15), (F) dark channel (5 × 5).

In accordance with DCP, the dark channel of the haze-free image $I_{\text{radiance}}(i,j)$ tends to be zero. On the other hand, A_{global} is invariably greater than zero, hence

$$\min_{c\in\{R,G,B\}}\left(\min_{(i,j)\in\delta(z)}\left(\frac{I_{\text{radiance}}(i,j)}{A_{\text{global}}}\right)\right)\rightarrow 0 \tag{14.13}$$

Now, replacing Eq. (14.13) in Eq. (14.12) we get the $T(i,j)$ as

$$T(i,j)=1-\min_{c\in\{R,G,B\}}\left(\frac{I_{\text{hazy}}(i,j)}{A_{\text{global}}}\right)\forall 0\le T(i,j)\le 1 \tag{14.14}$$

$$T(i,j)=\begin{Bmatrix}0,\forall & \text{hazy regions}\\ 1,\forall & \text{haze}-\text{free regions}\end{Bmatrix}$$

As a matter of fact, on an atmospherically clear day with excellent visibility, a small amount of fog might be present at the depths of a natural image. Hence, during restoration of a hazy image, complete elimination of haze will impart an unnatural look to the image, as the perception of "field depth" might be lost. For the motive of preserving the natural look, a scanty haze is intentionally added in the image by employing a factor ξ $(0<\xi<1)$ in Eq. (14.14). Eq. (14.15) delineates the ultimate transmission map obtained. The value of ξ is highly image-dependent and in this chapter it has been put at 0.9.

$$T(i,j)=1-\left[\xi*\min_{c\in\{R,G,B\}}\left(\frac{I_{\text{foggy}}(i,j)}{A_{\text{global}}}\right)\right] \tag{14.15}$$

Fig. 14.9 depicts the dark channels, transmission maps, and recovered depth maps.

14.4.3.3 *Transmission map refinement*

Conserving image fidelity demands refinement of the computed transmission map. To rid an apparently dehazed image of minute traces of haze accumulated in the sharp edges or corners, fine-tuning of the coarse transmission map is quintessential. This eradicates the possible manifestation of the undesired halo effect. In accordance with He et al. (2011) the modified transmission map $\widetilde{T(i,j)}$ can be expressed as

$$\widetilde{T(i,j)}=T(i,j)*(L+\lambda U) \tag{14.16}$$

where L denotes the Laplacian matrix, λ indicates a normalization parameter (typically 0.0001), and U indicates a unit matrix having the same dimension as L. L can be calculated as

$$L(i,j)=\sum_{n|(i,j)\in W_n}\left(\delta_{ij}-\frac{1}{|W_n|}\left(1+(I_i-\mu_n)^T\left(\sum_n+\frac{\gamma}{|W_n|}\right)^{-1}(I_j-\mu_n)\right)\right) \tag{14.17}$$

where, $\sum_n$ delineates a 3×3 covariance matrix, δ_{ij} indicates the Kronecker delta function, μ_n is the color vector I_i and I_j in a window W_n. γ is the regularization parameter, usually at the range of 10^{-6}.

14.4.3.4 *Scene radiance restoration*

In accordance with Eq. (14.1) we can conclude that where $\widetilde{T(i,j)}$ tends to zero, the $I_{\text{radiance}}(i,j)$ calculation will be erroneous. Hence, for reduction of noise in images, we have restricted the $\widetilde{T(i,j)}$ value to a constant lower limit (t_{lower}) to deliberately conserve a

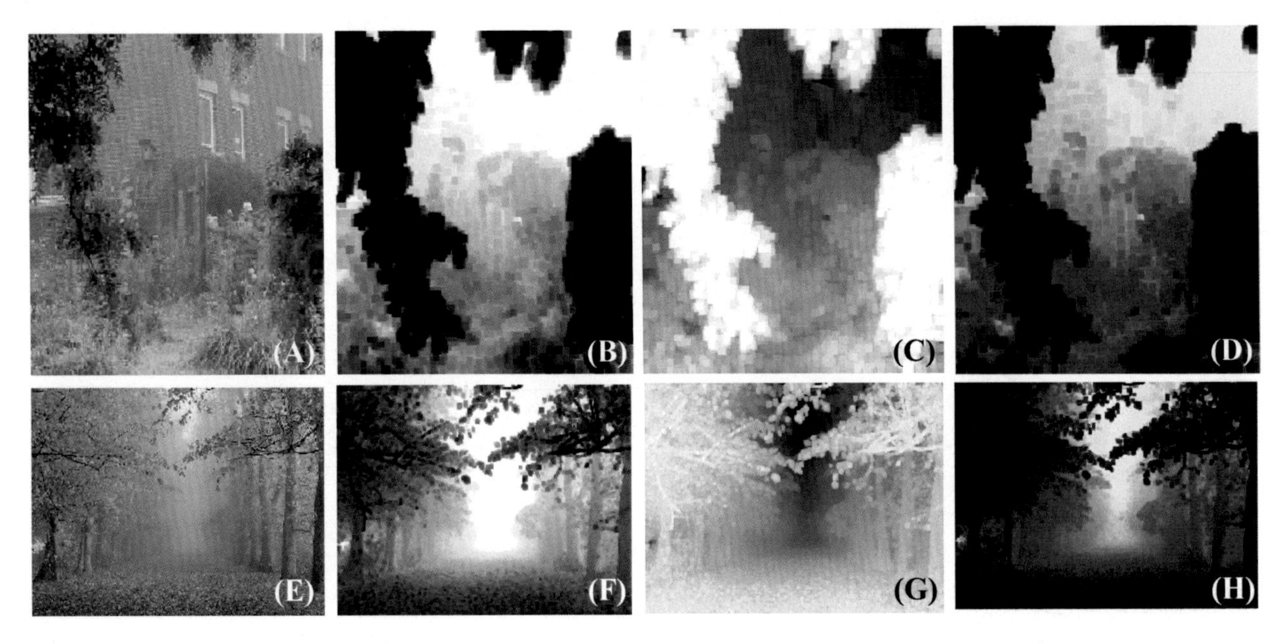

FIGURE 14.9 (A) Hazy house, (B) dark channel, (C) transmission map, (D) recovered depth map, (E) hazy forest, (F) dark channel, (G) transmission map, (H) recovered depth map.

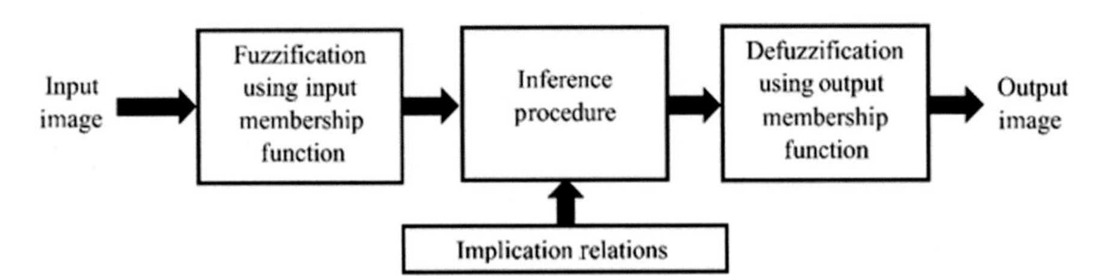

FIGURE 14.10 Overall architecture of the fuzzy contrast enhancement framework.

minute amount of haze in the densely fogged regions. Hence, the altered Eq. (14.5) can be expressed as

$$I_{\text{radiance}}(i,j) = \frac{I_{\text{hazy}}(i,j) - A_{\text{global}}}{\max\{T(i,j), t_{\text{lower}}\}} + A_{\text{global}} \quad (14.18)$$

Nevertheless, the recovered dehazed image will have poor contrast and color richness. Hence, a novel fuzzy contrast enhancement framework has been suggested in this chapter.

14.4.4 Fuzzy contrast enhancement

Boolean logic enables us to illustrate data that are either absolutely false (0) or true (1), but nothing in the middle. Nonetheless, this Boolean logic cannot realize complicated structures like the human visual system. Hence, frameworks must be devised which can work effectively with multivalued logic and permit effortless changeovers between "true" and "false," to constructively imitate the human nervous system. The complexities of real-world problems and their solutions arise as a result of constantly having to deal with the unknown. Proper evaluation of the element of uncertainty is thus of uttermost importance to effectively comprehend and resolve real-life problems. The uncertainty could arise from random or nonrandom events. The unpredictability or vagueness that cannot be characterized by probabilistic approaches can be efficiently demonstrated by means of fuzzy set theory. This is a mathematical tool that was introduced by Zedah (1965), and was one of the first methods to endow machines with the potentiality to handle indistinct or vague data effectively (Zedah, 1965). Under circumstances where we need to compute or define the degree to which an outcome belongs to an event, we turn to fuzzy or vague logic. In this chapter, we have used this fuzzy logic to augment the image by directly altering pixel intensities instead of modifying the probability of occurrence of pixel intensities. An overview of the proposed contrast enhancement framework is delineated in Fig. 14.10.

The steps can be elaborated as follows.

14.4.4.1 Fuzzification

The input dehazed image is mapped from existing "crisp set" to "fuzzy set" by establishing adequate linguistic variables and assigning appropriate membership functions to each of them. In this chapter, the pixel values have been fuzzified, by fitting Gaussian curves as

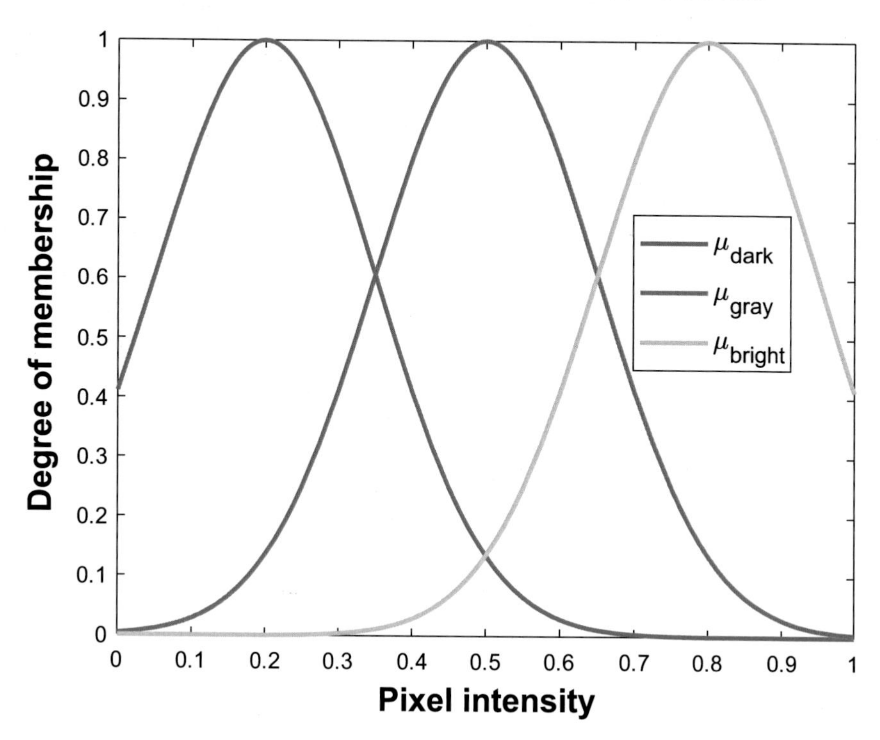

FIGURE 14.11 Input membership functions.

depicted in Fig. 14.11. Gaussian curves are nonconvex in nature. The standard deviation of the curves fitted should be moderate and optimum to only intensify pixel intensities and not concentrate or dilute them. In Fig. 14.11, μ_{dark} delineates the degree of membership of the dark pixels, μ_{gray} represents the degree of membership of the intermediate gray pixels, and μ_{bright} denotes the degree of membership of the bright pixels. Here, "dark," "gray," and "bright" are the atomic fuzzy linguistic variables.

14.4.4.2 Implication relations

Contrast enhancement depends on the pixel intensity modification principal, which can be achieved using the fuzzy if–then" rules as described below:

1. Output pixel value will be "darker," if the input pixel value is "dark";
2. Output pixel value will be "mid-gray," if the input pixel value is "gray";
3. Output pixel value will be "bright," if the input pixel value is "brighter."

Implication relations map the previously coined atomic terms to the compound linguistic terms like "darker," "mid-gray," and "brighter." Here, if–then conditional statements involving two linguistic terms have been employed. Several kinds of implication operators are available (Padhy and Simon, 2011). In this chapter, we have applied the "Mamdani Min" operator (Mamdani and Assilian, 1975). These relations enable us to modify pixel intensities for contrast enhancement. High-contrast images are identified by a significant difference among the maximum and minimum intensities of its constituent pixels. Hence, to perceivably augment the contrast, we need to expand the existing pixel difference.

14.4.4.3 Inference procedures

To ultimately evaluate linguistic descriptions and derive the desired goal, we employ suitable inference procedures. Here we have incorporated the Generalized Modus Ponens inference system, which says, if input (x) is "A" then output (y) will be "B." This physically means x is analytically known and y is analytically unknown (Padhy and Simon, 2011). Here A and B are fuzzy linguistic terms.

14.4.4.4 Defuzzification

In this finishing step, we reacquire the "crisp set" originating from the "fuzzy set" by employing output membership functions as depicted in Fig. 14.12 and aggregating them. Here, we have incorporated the Gaussian bell curves as our respective membership functions, where μ_{darker} specifies the degree of membership of darker pixels, μ_{midgray} delineates the degree of membership of the mid-gray pixels, and μ_{brighter} indicates the degree of membership of the brighter pixels. Here, membership functions are ultimately sampled to detect the respective membership grades used in fuzzy logic equations, to define resultant outcome region, thereby extrapolating the crisp output. This output is the union of all outputs of individual rule. In

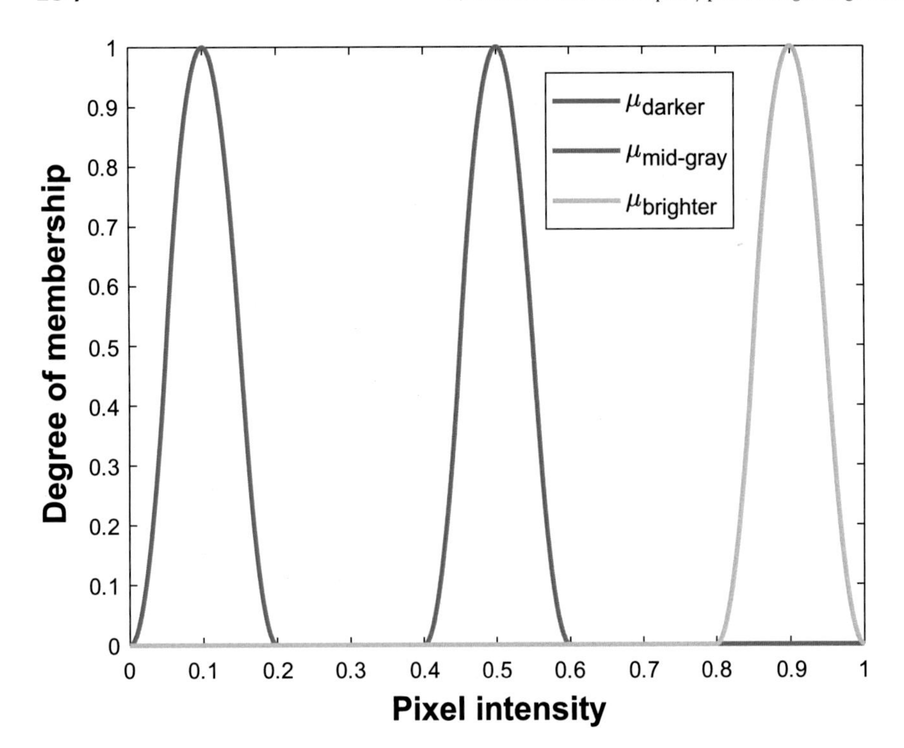

FIGURE 14.12 Output membership functions.

this chapter, we have exercised the mean-of-maxima approach which takes the crisp value with the highest degree of membership to generate output. However, when there exists more than one element in the universe of discourse with maximum value, the mean of the maximum is taken. The corresponding mathematical equation is,

$$u^* = \frac{1}{M}\sum_{k=1}^{M} u_k \tag{14.19}$$

where u_k is the k-th element and M is the overall number of such elements. This kind of approach is accurate as it deals with each individual pixel intensity and modifies them accordingly.

14.5 Analysis of results and discussion

All synthetic and natural hazy images presented here belong to FRIDA image database (Tarel, Hautière, Cord, Gruyer, & Halmaoui, 2010), D-HAZY data set (Ancuti, Ancuti, & Vleeschouwer, 2016), and websites of Raanan Fattal (Fattal, 2008) and Kaiming He (He et al., 2011), respectively.

14.5.1 Qualitative assessment

For qualitative performance evaluation, we have considered some state-of-the-art competing schemes namely, He et al. (2011), Fattal (2008), Tarel and Hautiere (2009), Zhu et al. (2015), Ren et al. (2018), Nishino, Kratz, and Lombardi (2012), Kim et al. (2013), Meng, Wang, Duan, Xiang, and Pan (2013), Nair and Sankaran (2018), Tan (2008), Kopf et al. (2008), and DehazeNet (Ren et al., 2016). All parameters are kept as originally defined by the respective authors.

Different juxtapositions with other state-of-the-art models have been depicted in Figs. 14.13, 14.14, and 14.15. In Fig. 14.13 it should be noted that the dehazing achieved by He et al. (2011) algorithm tends to make the image darker. Also, the algorithms presented by Tarel and Hautiere (2009) and Tan (2008) undersaturate and oversaturate the image, respectively. The schemes proposed by Zhu et al. (2015) and Kopf et al. (2008) also depict lesser dehazing efficiency as there is the visible presence of haze. Moreover, in contrast to the method of Fattal (2008), the proposed algorithm not only eliminates traces of visible haze but also enhances the contrast to a noteworthy extent. From Fig. 14.14 it is evident that the dehazing scheme adopted by Nair and Sankaran (2018) darkens the image, resulting in a loss of detail. Although the algorithm proposed by Ren et al. (2018) can eliminate haze up to an acceptable level, the output dehazed image lacks contrast fidelity. The context regularization-based scheme by Meng et al. (2013) completely distorts the color information in the output image. Also, the dehazing results presented in Fig. 14.15 delineate the primacy of the proposed scheme.

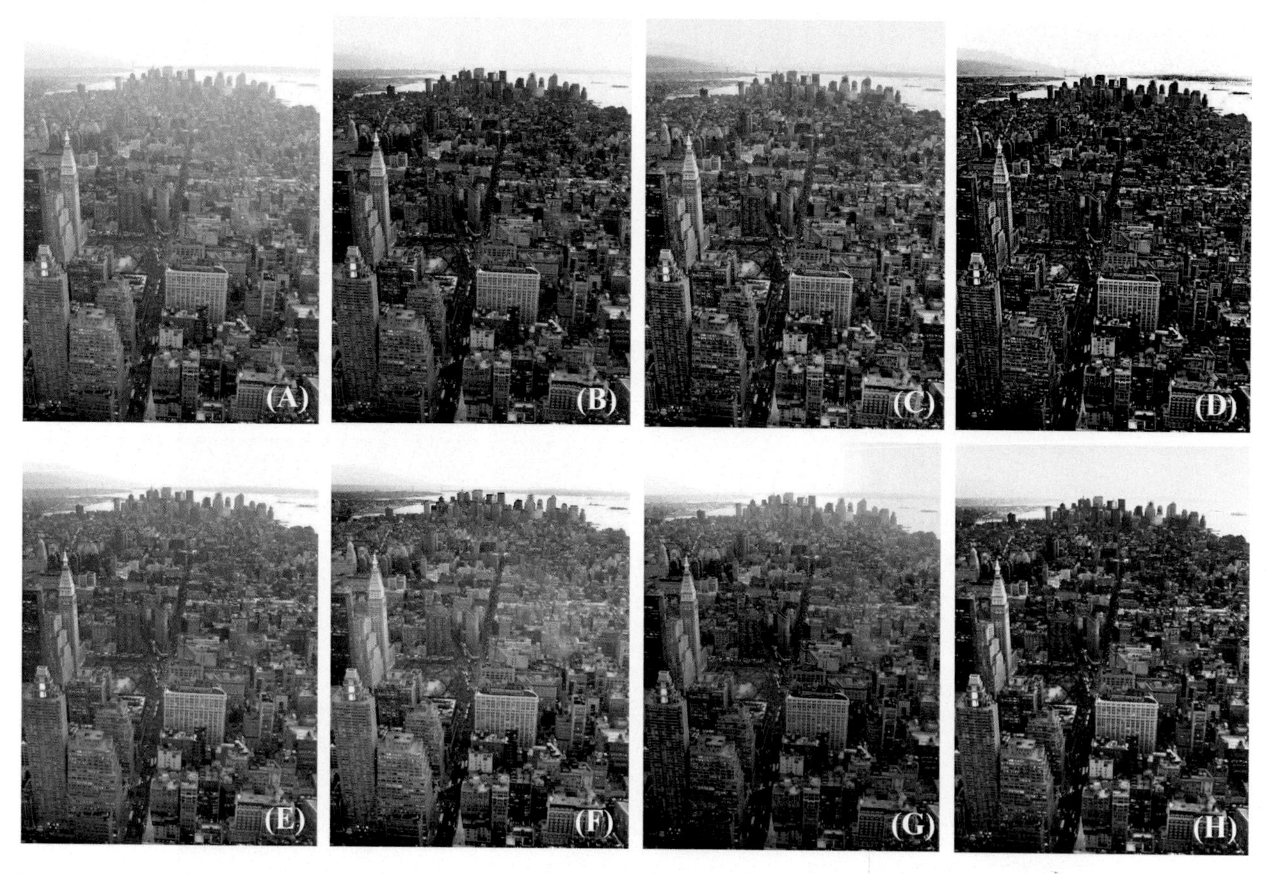

FIGURE 14.13 (A) Hazy "ny12," (B) He et al. (2011), (C) Tarel and Hautiere (2009), (D) Tan (2008), (E) Zhu et al. (2015), (F) Kopf et al. (2008), (G) Fattal (2008), (H) proposed.

FIGURE 14.14 (A) Hazy "ny17," (B), He et al. (2011), (C) Nair and Sankaran (2018), (D) DehazeNet, (E) Tan (2008), (F) Tarel and Hautiere (2009), (G) Fattal (2008), (H) Meng et al. (2013), (I) proposed.

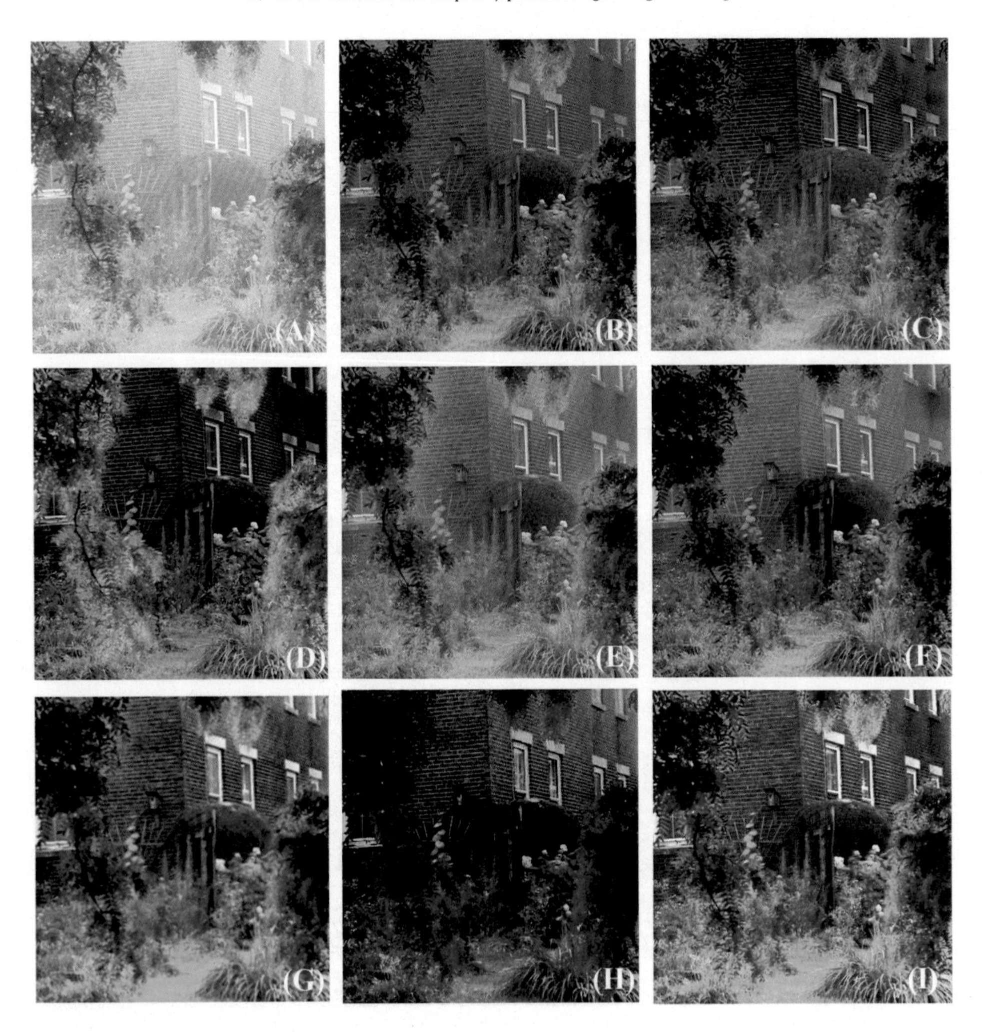

FIGURE 14.15 (A) Hazy "house," (B) He et al. (2011), (C) Fattal (2008), (D) Tarel and Hautiere (2009), (E) Zhu et al. (2015), (F) Ren et al. (2018), (G) Kim et al. (2013), (H) Nishino et al. (2012), (I) proposed.

Since the ground truth for natural hazy images might not always be at hand, for full reference objective evaluation we have added synthetic haze to some clear images and subjected them to our dehazing algorithm. Fig. 14.16 depicts two synthetically hazed images along with their dehazed output (by the proposed method), ground truth, and transmission map, respectively.

From Fig. 14.16 it is clear that the proposed approach not only eliminates haze from an image but also accurately restores the original color and contrast that were tarnished by the fog previously. Moreover, in Fig. 14.17 it is presented that the projected framework can effectively eliminate haze from areal, underwater, and synthetic images as well.

The reason behind specifying $\xi = 0.95$ and a patch size of 5×5 is well established in Fig. 14.18, where it is evident that the amount of haze visible increases with increasing patch size due to excessive approximation. Furthermore, for all three patch sizes, $\xi = 0.95$ eliminates haze much better than $\xi = 0.90$. A considerable amount of haze is present in He et al.'s (2011) method (red marked region) utilizing $\xi = 0.95$ and a patch size of 15×15. Hence, the choice of ξ as 0.95 and patch dimension of 5×5 is justified.

14.5.2 Quantitative assessment

Owing to the dearth of ground truths of natural hazy images, we have incorporated some no-reference quantitative evaluation descriptors for dehazing efficiency calculation. Visible edge ratio (e), mean gradient ratio ($\bar{r}$), number of saturated pixels in percent (σ), and perceptual fog density score (D) are the metrics selected for evaluating the dehazing efficiency of the projected framework (Choi, Youb, & Bovik, 2015; Hautière, Tarel, Aubert, & Dumont, 2008). Further mathematical description of e, $\bar{r}$, σ, and D can be

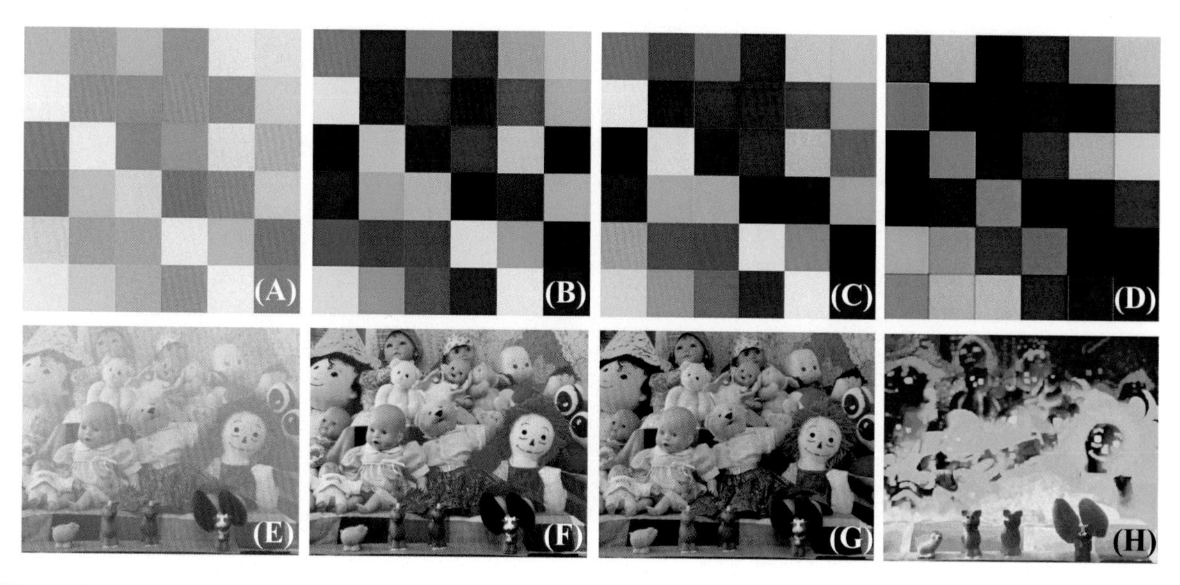

FIGURE 14.16 (A) Hazy "color grid," (B) dehazed "color grid," (C) true "color grid," (D) transmission map, (E) hazy "dolls," (F) dehazed "dolls," (G) true "dolls," (H) transmission map.

FIGURE 14.17 (A) Hazy "areal image," (B) hazy "synthetic image," (C) hazy "underwater image," (D) dehazed "areal image," (E) dehazed "synthetic image," (F) dehazed "underwater mage."

found in Choi et al. (2015) and Hautière et al. (2008). Physically e refers to the ratio of the number of edges visible in the corrected image to those not present in the original image (Hautière et al., 2008). On the other hand, $\bar{r}$ expresses the contrast enhancement ability of any proposed approach. It considers both visible and invisible edges present in the original hazy image (Hautière et al., 2008). σ signifies the percentage of the pixels that become totally white or back after restoration, but were neither prior to being subjected to dehazing algorithms (Hautière et al., 2008). Lastly, D gives us a score which indicates the presence of perceptual fog in the restored output (Choi et al., 2015). In fact, the higher the values of e and $\bar{r}$ indicate better texture and resolution, respectively, whereas lower values of σ and D represents greater dehazing efficiency (Choi et al., 2015; Hautière et al., 2008). It should be observed in the comparisons presented in Table 14.1 that, for the *"ny12"* image, the methods of He et al. (2011) and Fattal (2008) give negative values of e, which means some visible edges were lost during the restoration process. Moreover, the DehazeNet (Ren et al., 2016) method does not restore any visible edge, as $e = 0$. However, the proposed method yields the highest value of e compared to the other algorithms, indicating visible edge restoration of superior quality. Moreover, the proposed method also yields the highest values of $\bar{r}$ for all the test images except *"ny17."*

FIGURE 14.18 Simulation results with change of ξ and patch size: (A) output at $\xi = 0.95$ and patch size of 5×5 (proposed); (B) output at $\xi = 0.95$ and patch size of 10×10; (C) output at $\xi = 0.95$ and patch size of 15×15; (D) output at $\xi = 0.9$ and patch size of 5×5; (E) output at $\xi = 0.9$ and patch size of 10×10; (F) output at $\xi = 0.9$ and patch size of 15×15 (He et al., 2011).

Although DehazeNet (Ren et al., 2016) shows a superior $\bar{r}$ value than that of the proposed method in the case of "*ny17*," the output suffers from less visibility. Of them all, the methods of Tarel and Hautiere (2009) and Fattal (2008) exhibit the highest σ values, where over- or undersaturation is highly likely to occur. Although Zhu et al. (2015) achieved almost the lowest value of σ, it also shows a very high value of D for all the test images. Therefore, comparatively, the proposed approach has the highest value of $e, \bar{r}$ and the lowest value of D, σ, comprising of the highest dehazing capabilities without any significant loss of color, contrast, or texture fidelity. Another visual interpretation of the evaluation descriptor $\bar{r}$ is presented in Fig. 14.19, which shows the comparison of the *visual gradient ratio* of Hautière et al. (2008) for various competing approaches. In Fig. 14.19 it can be noted that none of the competing approaches, except the proposed one, can effectively restore the edges in the heavy fog regions (red marked). The schemes proposed by Nair and Sankaran (2018) and DehazeNet (Ren et al., 2016) have proven to be highly ineffective in the case of heavily foggy areas.

For a fair comparison, the proposed framework has also been benchmarked against the state-of-the-art D-HAZY data set (Ancuti et al., 2016). The D-HAZY data set contains more than 1400 images (from the Middleburry and NYU data sets) along with their depth maps and ground truths. Due to the availability of the ground truth images, we have used the full-reference Structural SIMilarity (SSIM) index and CIE color difference metric CIEDE2000 (Ancuti et al., 2016). SSIM measures the structural and geometric similarities between two images and returns a value in the range of [0, 1], where 0 represents no similarity and 1 represents high similarity. On the other hand, CIEDE2000 measures the changes in perceived colors between two images using the CIE2000 standard and returns a value between [0, 100], where a lower value indicates higher color similarity. We have compared the average (over all the D-HAZY dataset images) SSIM and CIEDE2000 values with other state-of-the-art methods in Table 14.2. There we can observe that the proposed method provides the highest SSIM and lowest CIEDE2000 values among other competing methods. Moreover, in Fig. 14.20 we have presented a few dehazed output images for qualitative comparison. In Fig. 14.20 we can observe how the proposed method preserves the original color and contrast fidelity.

14.5.3 Time complexity evaluation

All simulations presented here, have been performed in MATLAB R2018b environment in a 2.5 GHz Intel core i7 PC with 8 GB of RAM. All the processing times have been evaluated with an image dimension of 600×400, 5×5 patch size, and $\xi = 0.9$. The patch

TABLE 14.1 Qualitative metric value comparison.

Proposed	D	0.24	0.23	0.14	0.10
	Σ	0	0	0	0
	e	0.11	0.48	0.13	0.35
	$\bar{r}$	2.37	3.03	2.40	1.68
Zhu et al. (2015)	D	0.32	0.47	0.12	0.30
	σ	0	0	0.5	0
	e	0.06	0.03	0.09	0.10
	$\bar{r}$	1.11	1.12	1.14	1.04
Ren et al. (2016)	D	0.24	0.38	0.13	0.20
	σ	2.06	0.33	23.6	8.39
	e	0	−0.38	0.009	0.09
	$\bar{r}$	1.25	4.22	2.07	1.22
Fattal (2008)	D	0.25	0.35	0.12	0.14
	σ	7.79	4.88	14.8	18.6
	e	−0.05	−0.08	0.06	0.26
	$\bar{r}$	1.49	1.66	1.95	1.66
Tarel and Hautiere (2009)	D	0.24	0.24	0.12	0.33
	σ	0.15	0.01	0.06	0.11
	e	0.05	0.17	0.09	0.09
	$\bar{r}$	2.27	0.11	2.35	1.09
He et al. (2011)	D	0.42	0.28	0.13	0.20
	σ	0.85	0.86	13.3	0.77
	e	−0.08	0.008	0.05	0.22
	$\bar{r}$	1.53	1.95	1.68	1.18
Image		*ny12*	*ny17*	*house*	*forest*

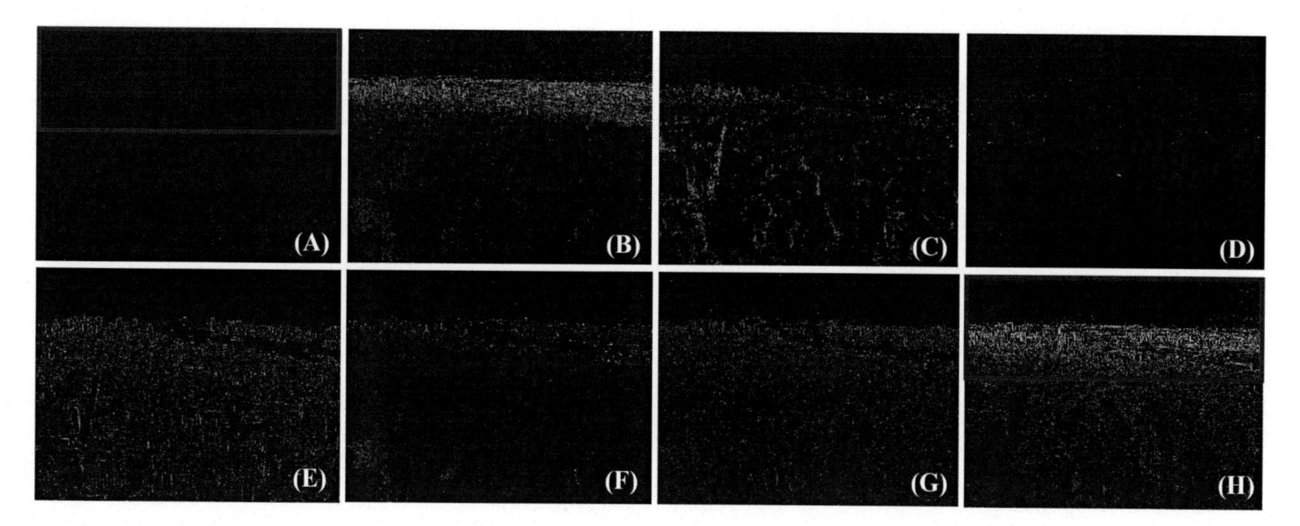

FIGURE 14.19 VGR comparison: (A) hazy "ny17," (B) He et al., (C) Fattal, (D) Kopf et al., (E) Nair et al., (F) Zhu et al., (G) DehazeNet, (H) proposed. *VGR*, Visual gradient ratio.

TABLE 14.2 Average SSIM and CIEDE2000 metric value comparison among different methods.

	Middleburry data set		NYU data set	
	SSIM	CIEDE2000	SSIM	CIEDE2000
Zuiderveld (1994)	0.665	15.252	0.622	18.054
Tarel and Hautiere (2009)	0.81	16.956	0.719	17.742
Fattal (2014)	0.796	18.418	0.747	14.656
Ancuti and Ancuti (2013)	0.829	14.431	0.771	14.136
He et al. (2011)	0.865	11.338	0.811	11.029
Meng et al. (2013)	0.831	14.429	0.773	12.216
Zhu et al. (2015)	0.865	12.542	0.801	12.087
Proposed	0.887	10.873	0.851	10.221

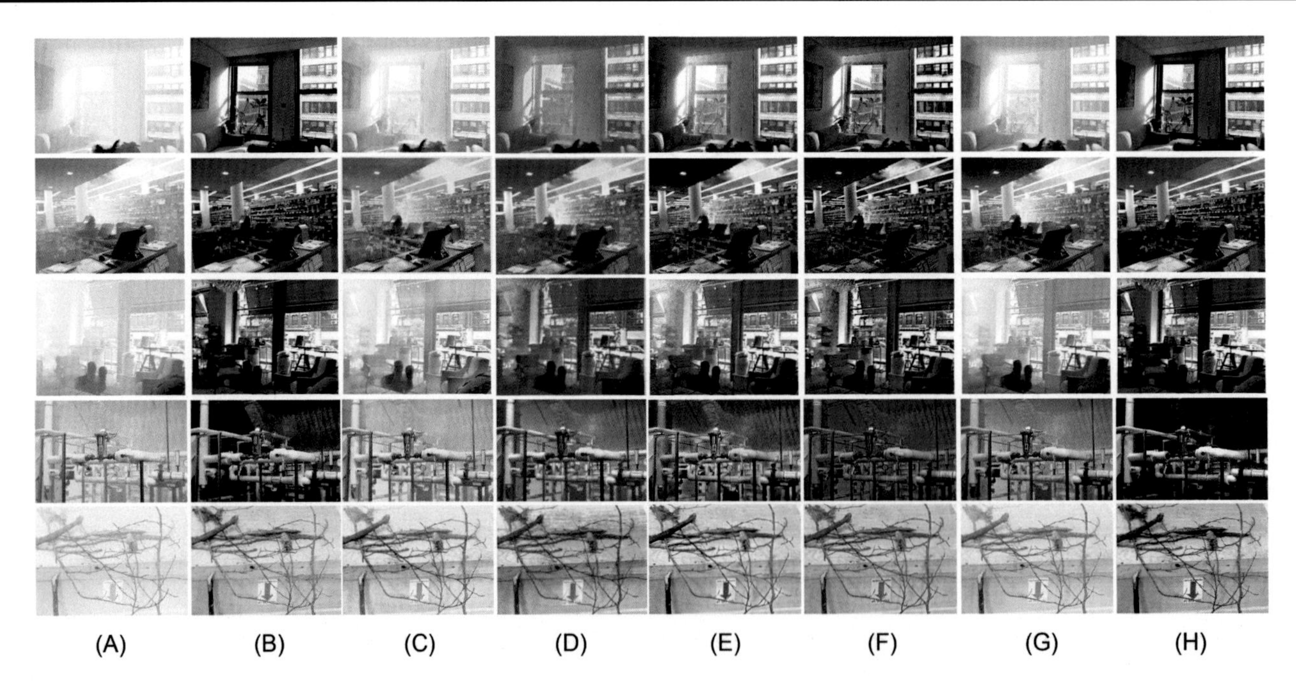

FIGURE 14.20 (A) Hazy images, (B) ground truth, (C) Zuiderveld (1994), (D) Ancuti and Ancuti (2013), (E) He et al. (2011), (F) Meng et al. (2013), (G) Zhu et al. (2015), (H) proposed.

size values and ξ also affect quantitative metrics like e, $\bar{r}$, σ, D. It is to be noted that the patch size and ξ values are distinct for a particular image, and the best solution was accomplished with the aforementioned numbers. The presented framework uses two-level wavelet decomposition to exploit the frequency domain behavior of the haze, and therefore the effective processing area of the low-frequency subimage is only $\frac{1}{16}$th of the original image. As a result, the processing time is reduced to a considerable extent. Table 14.3 collates the average processing time (seconds) of the projected framework with that of other competing methods.

Comparatively speaking, the proposed approach not only eliminates haze from the images efficiently but also has the least computational time complexity.

TABLE 14.3 Time complexity comparison.

Methods	Time complexity (s)
He et al. (2011)	14.35
Fattal (2008)	19.27
Tarel and Hautiere (2009)	4.12
Tripathi and Mukhopadhyay (2012)	3.26
Nair and Sankaran (2018)	2.23
Kim et al. (2013)	7.11
Meng et al. (2013)	13.07
Berman, Treibitz, and Avidan (2016)	2.23
Ren et al. (2016)	5.25
Proposed	0.89

14.6 Conclusions

Removal of haze from a single image is one of the most critical tasks in the domain of machine vision to assist object surveillance, tracking, and visibility restoration. In this chapter, a new LFP has been projected, which along with DCP achieves superefficient real-time dehazing. Also, a fuzzy contrast enhancement scheme is proposed alongside, which generates visually pleasing and texture-rich dehazed outputs, with faithful restoration of original colors. The objective of this chapter was to reduce the time complexity of the dehazing mechanism proposed by He et al. (2011), and it would suffice to say that it has been done considerably. The efficiency of the projected method has been assessed against various subjective and objective evaluations. Output results delineate that the resultant image is superior in terms of color, contrast, and fidelity to most of previously published methods. Albeit haze removal frameworks are difficult to realize for hazy video files, however, in the future we will focus on accelerating the framework for seamless hardware execution.

References

Ancuti, C., Ancuti, C.O., & Vleeschouwer, C.D. (2016). D-HAZY: A dataset to evaluate quantitatively dehazing algorithms. In *Proceedings of IEEE international conference on image processing (ICIP)* (pp. 2226–2230).

Ancuti, C., Ancuti, C. O., Vleeschouwer, C. D., & Bovik, A. C. (2020). Day and night-time dehazing by local airlight estimation. *IEEE Transactions on Image Processing, 29*, 6264–6275.

Ancuti, C. O., & Ancuti, C. (2013). Single image dehazing by multi-scale fusion. *IEEE Transactions on Image Processing, 22*(8), 3271–3282.

Ancuti, C. O., Ancuti, C., Vleeschouwer, C. D., & Sbetr, M. (2019). Color channel transfer for image dehazing. *IEEE Signal Processing Letters, 26*(9), 1413–1417.

Anwar, M. I., & Khosla, A. (2017). Vision enhancement through single image fog removal. *Engineering Science and Technology, 20*, 1075–1083.

Berman, D., Treibitz, T., & Avidan, S. (2016). Non-local image dehazing. In *Proceedings of IEEE international conference on computer vision and pattern recognition (CVPR)* (pp. 1674–1682).

Choi, L. K., Youb, J., & Bovik, A. C. (2015). Referenceless prediction of perceptual fog density and perceptual image dehazing. *IEEE Transactions on Image Processing, 4*(10), 3888–3901.

Fattal, R. (2008). Single image dehazing. *ACM Transactions on Graphics, 27*(3), 1–9.

Fattal, R. (2014). Dehazing using color-lines. *ACM Transactions on Graphics, 34*(1), 1–14.

Gonzalez, R. C., & Woods, R. E. (2011). *Digital image processing* (3rd ed.). Pearson Prentice Hall.

Hautière, N., Tarel, J. P., Aubert, D., & Dumont, É. (2008). Blind contrast enhancement assessment by gradient ratioing at visible edges. *Image Analysis and Stereology, 27*(2), 1–9.

He, K., Sun, J., & Tang, X. (2011). Single image haze removal using dark channel prior. *IEEE Transactions on Pattern Analysis and Machine Intelligence, 33*(12), 2341–2353.

Jun, W. L., & Rong, Z. (2013). Image defogging algorithm of single color image based on wavelet transform and histogram equalization. *Applied Mathematical Sciences, 7*(79), 3913–3921.

Kim, J. H., Jang, W. D., Sim, J. Y., & Kim, C. S. (2013). Optimized contrast enhancement for real-time image and video dehazing. *Journal Visual Communication Image Representation, 24*, 410–425.

Koley, S., Sadhu, A., Roy, H., & Dhar S. (2018). Single image visibility restoration using dark channel prior and fuzzy logic. In *Proceedings of IEEE second international conference on electronics, materials engineering and nano-technology (IEMENTech)*, Kolkata, India.

Kopf, J., Neubert, B., Chen, B., Cohen, M., Cohen-Or, D., Deussen, O., ... Lischinski, D. (2008). Deep photo: Model-based photograph enhancement and viewing. *ACM Transactions on Graphics, 27*(5), 1–10.

Mallat, S. G. (1989). A theory for multiresolution signal decomposition: The wavelet representation. *IEEE Trans. On Pattern Analysis and Machine Intelligence, 11*(7), 674–693.

Mamdani, E. H., & Assilian, S. (1975). An experiment in linguistic synthesis with a fuzzy logic controller. *International Journal of Man-Machine Studies, 7*(1), 1–13.

Meng, G., Wang, Y., Duan, J., Xiang, S., & Pan, C. (2013). Efficient image dehazing with boundary constraint and contextual regularization. In *Proceedings of IEEE international conference on computer vision (ICCV)* (pp. 617–624).

Metwaly, K., Li, X., Guo, T., & Monga, V. (2020). Nonlocal channel attention for nonhomogeneous image dehazing. In *Proceedings of IEEE/CVF conference on computer vision and pattern recognition workshops (CVPRW)* (pp. 1842–1851). Seattle, WA, USA.

Middleton, W.E.K. (1954). Vision through the atmosphere (Vol. 7). In J. Bartels (Ed.), Geophysik I.I./Geophysics I.I. (pp. 254–287.

Nair, D., & Sankaran, P. (2018). Color image dehazing using surround filter and dark channel prior. *Journal Visual Communication Image Representation, 24*, 9–15.

Nishino, K., Kratz, L., & Lombardi, S. (2012). Bayesian defogging. *International Journal of Computer Vision, 98*, 263–278.

Padhy, N. P., & Simon, S. P. (2011). *Soft Computing with MATLAB Programming* ((1st ed.). Oxford University Press.

Pallawi, N.V. (2016). Enhanced single image uniform and heterogeneous fog removal using guided filter. In *Proceedings of international conference of artificial intelligence and evolutionary computations in engineering systems (ICAIECES)* (pp. 453–463), India.

Pizer, S.M., Johnston, R.E., Ericksen, J.P., Yankaskas, B.C., & Muller, K.E. (1990). Contrast-limited adaptive histogram equalization: speed and effectiveness. In *Proceedings of the first conference on visualization in biomedical computing* (pp. 337–345).

Ren, W., Liu, S., Zhang, H., Pan, J., Cao, X., & Yang, M.H. (2016). Single image dehazing via multi-scale convolutional neural networks. In *Proceedings of European conference on computer vision*. 10.1007/978-3-319-46475-6_10.

Ren, W., Ma, L., Zhang, J., Pan, J., Cao, X., Liu, W., & Yang, M.H. (2018). Gated fusion network for single image dehazing. In *Proceedings of IEEE conference on computer vision and pattern recognition*.

Tan, R.T. (2008). Visibility in bad weather from a single image. In *Proceedings of IEEE 12th international conference on computer vision and pattern recognition (CVPR)* (pp. 1–8).

Tarel, J.P., & Hautiere, N. (2009). Fast visibility restoration from a single color or gray level image. In *Proceedings of IEEE 12th international conference on computer vision (ICCV)* (pp. 2201–2208).

Tarel, J.P., Hautière, N., Cord, A., Gruyer, D., & Halmaoui, H. (2010). Improved visibility of road scene images under heterogeneous fog. In *Proceedings of IEEE Intelligent Vehicles Symposium (IV'10)* (pp. 21–24), San Diego, CA, USA.

Tripathi, A. K., & Mukhopadhyay, S. (2012). Removal of fog from images: A review. *IETE Technical Review, 29*(2), 148–156.

Yu, M., Cherukuri, V., Guo, T., & Monga, V. (2020). Ensemble dehazing networks for non-homogeneous haze. In *Proceedings of IEEE/CVF conference on computer vision and pattern recognition workshops (CVPRW)* (pp. 1832–1841), Seattle, WA, USA.

Zedah, L. A. (1965). Fuzzy sets. *Information and Control*, *8*(3), 338–353.

Zhang, K., Zuo, W., Chen, Y., Meng, D., & Zhang, L. (2017). Beyond a Gaussian denoiser: Residual learning of deep CNN for image denoising. *IEEE Transactions on Image Processing*, *26*(7), 3142–3155.

Zhu, Q., Mai, J., & Shao, L. (2015). A fast single image haze removal algorithm using color attenuation prior. *IEEE Transaction on Image Processing*, *24*(11), 3522–3533.

Zuiderveld, K. (1994). *Contrast limited adaptive histogram equalization. Graphic Gems IV* (pp. 474–485). San Diego: Academic Press Professional.

CHAPTER

15

Segmentation of retinal blood vessel structure based on statistical distribution of the area of isolated objects

Rajat Suvra Nandy[1], *Rohit Kamal Chatterjee*[2] *and Abhishek Das*[3]

[1]Aliah University, Kolkata, India [2]Birla Institute of Technology, Mesra, Ranchi, India [3]Department of Computer Science and Engineering, Aliah University, Kolkata, India

15.1 Introduction

According to a global survey in 2019, about 9.3% of the total global population (463 million) has been affected by diabetes mellitus. The number of diabetic patients will increase to more than 10.2% of the world population (578 million) by 2030. Significantly, the number of adult diabetes patients, whose ages are between 20 to 79 years, has also increased (Saeedi et al., 2019). In 2019, the International Diabetic Federation estimated about 4.2 million death due to diabetes, and approximately USD 760 billion was spent on diabetic patients. The number of children and adolescents suffering from type I diabetes is also approximated at more than 1.1 million (https://www.idf.org/aboutdiabetes/what-is-diabetes/facts-figures.html). Most diabetic patients (about 80%) live in middle- and low-income countries (Dunachiea & Chamnand, 2019).

A considerable number of patients suffering from chronic diabetes mellitus have a very high chance of damaging the blood vessels of the retina, leading to diabetic retinopathy (DR). Every year, a significant number of adult patients aged between 20 and 74 years lose their vision due to DR (Cheung, Mitchell, & Wong, 2010). Therefore the early detection of DR can prevent vision loss for a considerable number of patients (Fig. 15.1) (Hoover & Goldbaum, 2003; Nandy, Chatterjee, & Das, 2020).

For the diagnosis of premature DR (Gelman, Martinez-Perez, & Vanderveen, 2005), observation of the anatomy of the blood vessel structure of the fundus is of utmost importance. The different types of deformity in the vessel structure indicate ophthalmic diseases. To prevent disease, regular monitoring of the blood vessel structure using a funduscopic image is essential, however the manual segmentation of the vessel's structure requires expert interventions, and is thus a costly and time-consuming process. A computer-aided diagnosis (CADx) system can alleviate this problem, but it needs a dependable and efficient algorithm. In the last two decades, a significant number of techniques in this domain are proposed (Fraz, Barman, & Remagnino, 2012). The existing algorithms can be broadly divided into two categories: (1) supervised (Korpusik, 2014; Lupascu, Tegolo, & Trucco, 2010; Xu & Luo, 2010; Marin, Aquino, Gegundez-Arias, & Bravo, 2011; Ricci & Perfetti, 2007; Jiang, Zhang, Wang, & Ko, 2018), where the different features of the retinal images input are trained to classify the vessel and nonvessel-like structures and (2) unsupervised (Florack, 1997; Al-Diri, Hunter, & Steel, 2009; Kundu & Chatterjee, 2012; Li, Bhalerao, & Wilson, 2007; Mondal, Chatterjee, & Kar, 2017; Jiang & Mojon, 2003; Nandy, Chatterjee, & Kar, 2017; Samanta, Saha, & Chanda, 2011), where no labels are present for the classes to train the system to segment the vessel and nonvessel structures, and so some thresholding and rule-based techniques are considered to be in this category.

The proposed method is an unsupervised technique that can isolate the blood vessel structure of the fundus image as accurately as possible. For the initial extraction of the vessel structure, a method proposed by Kundu and Chatterjee (2012) is used. According to this method, rotating locally adaptive line structuring element (LALSE) of different sizes are opened with the image to isolate the linear structures from the background,

Recent Trends in Computational Intelligence Enabled Research.
DOI: https://doi.org/10.1016/B978-0-12-822844-9.00004-9

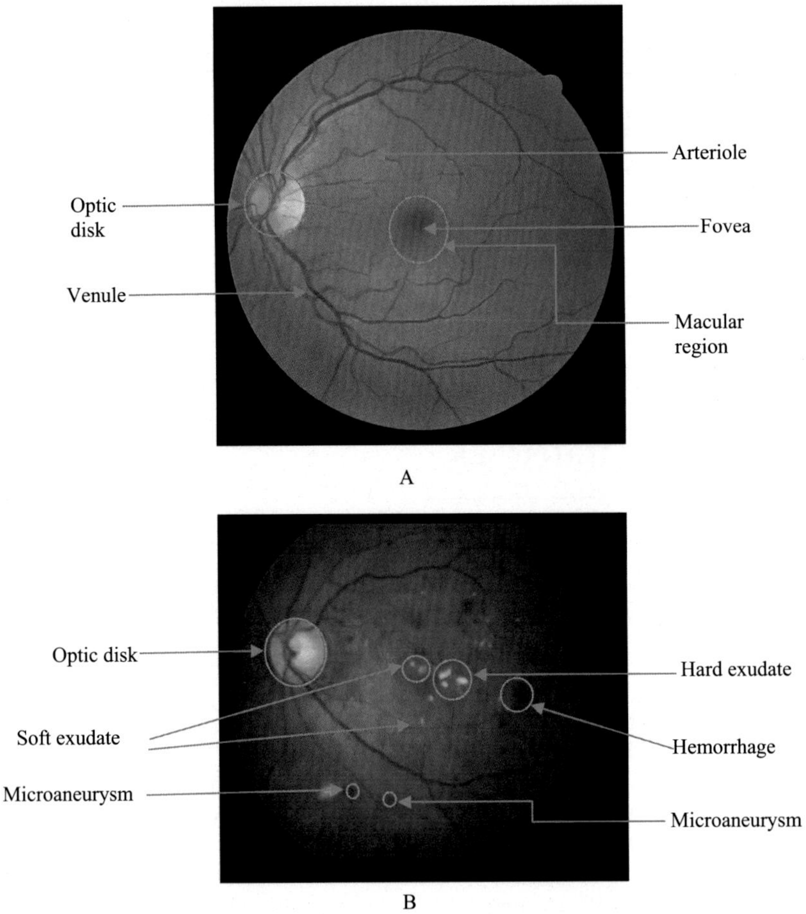

Optic disk
Venule
Arteriole
Fovea
Macular region

A

Optic disk
Soft exudate
Microaneurysm
Hard exudate
Hemorrhage
Microaneurysm

B

FIGURE 15.1 (A) Normal retinal image; (B) retinal image with pathologies.

followed by the application of a locally adaptive threshold to binarize the image. Here the assumption is that a small straight line could be used to approximate the shape of the curved segment and in turns the blood vessels present in the retina. This approach can effectively segment the fundus vessel structure but is confronted with two practical difficulties when applied for actual segmentation of blood vessels from funduscopic images. First, the curvatures of the blood vessels are lost as the length of the LSE (line structuring element) increases in size. Therefore the finer arterioles and venules are fragmented to create many linear artifacts. Second, as the fundus images are in general very noisy, and pathological objects close to the blood vessels are similar in contrast to the blood vessels, the ALSE (adaptive line structuring element) may fail to discriminate the retinal blood vessel from unwanted objects, and therefore the vessels are extracted along with other unwanted objects. This chapter aims to rectify the problems faced by the ALSE process and proposes a novel unsupervised algorithm that effectively eliminates noise and segments the retinal blood vessel structure from its background for different categories of retinal images, including pathological images.

Three important observations are useful for overcoming the shortcomings of the ALSE technique. (1) Restriction to the size of the LSE is essential to preserve the actual curvature, shape, and continuity of the vessel structure, because an increase in the size of the LSE could cause a deformity in the structure of the vessel. This observation entails keeping the size of the LSE small and restricting the number of iterations in the ALSE process. In effect, the small size of the line structuring element can preserve the retinal vessel's curvature, shape, and continuity, but is not able to remove the background noises and pathological objects present in the retinal image. To rectify this problem, a second observation is demanded. (2) In a restricted scale of observation, most noisy and pathological objects have isolated island-like structures detached from their neighborhood. Therefore all isolated objects could be securely removed from the fundus images without changing the actual vessel structure on a limited scale. (3) The third observation is an appropriate contrast stretching algorithm is required to separate the blood vessels from their neighboring isolated objects with very similar gray-level and contrast. These unwanted objects are eliminated using our second observation.

The above-mentioned observations demand the following steps for the implementation of the proposed algorithm:

1. Preprocessing: Using mathematical morphology operations small unwanted objects are eliminated and the minor breaks in the vessel structure are joined.

2. LALSE process: A LALSE process with a limited size of structuring element is applied to extract the full vessel structure with no deformation in shape or size, along with noise. The resultant image is converted into a binary image by a suitable adaptive thresholding algorithm.
3. Noise and background elimination: A statistical distribution of the areas of isolated objects in the resultant binary image is computed to discriminate the vessels from the noisy objects. The distribution is considered to be a mixture of two classes, namely, vessel area class and noise class. A histogram-based automatic thresholding algorithm is applied to discriminate the two classes. Depending on the shape and monotonicity of the histogram a threshold is identified to separate the blood vessels and noisy background objects class.

The output binary image of the proposed technique causes minimal distortion of the retinal blood vessel structure of the fundus image and does not contain any noisy or pathological objects.

The proposed technique contributes a different approach to discovering the threshold for the classification of the retinal blood vessel structure and noisy objects. This automatized histogram-based threshold detection technique is very fast and almost all the noisy objects (small or large) are eliminated from the fundus image. Another important aspect of this proposed technique is restricting the length of the LALSE, which can extract the vessel structure from the background without losing its curvature and shape.

The rest of this chapter is organized as follows: Section 15.2 describes the related works. In Section 15.3, some basic morphological operations are introduced, and Section 15.4 contains the proposed algorithm. Next, Section 15.5 describes the experiment, including the description of data, results, and performance evaluation. Finally, the conclusions are drawn in Section 15.6.

15.2 Related works

15.2.1 Matched filter method

Chaudhuri, Chatterjee, Katz, Nelson, and Goldbaum (1989) proposed an unsupervised match filter method where the cross-sectional retinal blood vessels (grayscale) are approximated by the Gaussian curve,

$$f(x,y) = I\left\{1 - re^{-(d^2/2\sigma^2)}\right\} \tag{15.1}$$

where d is calculated as a perpendicular distance from any point (x,y) to the straight line passing through the central part of retinal blood vessels along its length. The σ (variance) expresses the range of the intensity profile and the intensity (grayscale value) of the local background is defined by I. The reflectance (r) of the blood vessels is calculated in relation to its neighborhood. In this chapter, to detect the blood vessels, a two-dimensional matched filter method is used. The various orientations of the blood vessel structure have been detected by the convolution of 12 different matched filter kernels with the previously approximated image. Such a kernel is expressed as

$$K(x,y) = e^{-(x^2/2\sigma^2)} \quad \text{for } |y| \le L/2 \tag{15.2}$$

The length of the vessel segment is defined by L, where the expected permanent orientation is performed. Applying this method, the direction of the blood vessel is expected along the y-axis. The kernel $K(x,y)$ has to be rotated concerning the different orientations of vessels. For both abnormal and normal retinas, L is measured by analyzing blood vessels. This technique decreases the probability of false-positive (FP) recognition of the blood vessel in a noisy environment. This scheme can be compared with the Canny edge detector (Canny, 1986). The maximum response is taken after applying 12 convolutions by 12 different kernels with an angular rotation of 15 degrees. Finally, the resultant image is thresholded to convert into a binary retinal blood vessel structure. Hoover and Goldbaum (2003) noted that, in Chaudhuri et al. (1989), there was no satisfactory result found when a single global threshold was applied to the match filter's output for classification of the vessel structure, and they proposed a local region-based property for the classification of retinal vessels. In this paper (Hoover & Goldbaum, 2003), the pixels were classified into two groups, vessel and nonvessel. The final classification was found after applying a threshold probing technique.

15.2.2 Technique related to the region growing after the scale-space analysis

Martınez-Perez et al. (1999) proposed an unsupervised method where the region growing approaches were used after the scale-space analysis for segmentation of the retinal blood vessels. Here, the fundus blood vessels were described by two characteristics:

1. The image intensity (f) with its gradient $|\nabla f|$;
2. The value of the ridge-strengths (k) of the blood vessels.

These two characteristics are used in different scales. To determine the ridge-strengths of the blood vessels, the maximum eigenvalue $|\lambda_1|$ is calculated from the second-order differentiation of the given intensity matrix. For the measurement of the difference in the vessel's width of the fundus image, the aforementioned characteristics have been normalized using a scale "sl" on the given scale-space and the local maximum values are found. The local maximum values of the ridge-strength (k) and gradient magnitude (m) are calculated using Eqs. (15.3) and (15.4).

$$k = \underbrace{\max}_{sl} \frac{|\lambda_1(s)|}{sl} \tag{15.3}$$

$$m = \underbrace{\max}_{sl} \frac{|\nabla f(s)|}{sl} \tag{15.4}$$

In the next phase (region-growing), the histograms of the above-stated features are used to divide the pixels into two different classes. The first class is nonvessel objects and the second class is retinal blood vessel structure. This classification is made after changing the background of the given image and using the vessel's growing region. Here sinking of the characteristics can be achieved by thresholding of the resultant image after each iteration. The above-mentioned process is on-going until all the pixels are classified into the above classes.

15.2.3 Method related to the curvature estimation using mathematical morphology

Zana and Klein (2001) proposed an unsupervised method which is a general blood vessel segmentation technique based on mathematical morphology. This algorithm contains different types of mathematical morphology-based operations. The algorithm has several phases, which are described below.

1. The supremum of the morphological openings with a LSE at different orientations is taken to recognize the linear parts of the blood vessel. The morphological openings are used along with a class of different (LSEs and a sum of morphological top-hats along with each direction is calculated to enhance the blood vessels, irrespective of their direction.
2. The geodesic reconstruction is used on the supremum of the morphological openings over the retinal image (I_0) to suppress the noise. This method can be expressed as Eq. (15.5).

$$I_{op} = \gamma_{I_0}^{rec}\{Max_{1.......12}(\gamma_{L_i}(I_0))\} \tag{15.5}$$

where each LSE L_i (for every 15 degrees) is 1 pixel wide and $\gamma_{I_0}^{rec}$ is the geodesic reconstruction used on the supremum of the openings on I_0.

3. To eliminate the various types of unwanted objects, the Laplacian is computed to the resultant image.
4. Finally, the resultant image is calculated using a threshold for the segmentation of the desired vasculature.

In Kundu and Chatterjee (2012), an unsupervised adaptive mathematical morphology-based method is proposed. The technique is summarized in the following steps:

1. The RGB retinal image is converted into a grayscale image using Craig's formula.
2. A top-hat transformation is applied to the grayscale image to eliminate the smaller noisy artifacts.
3. A rotated LSE is applied to the output image of the previous step and the maximum response is taken. Iteratively increasing the length of the LSE makes a morphological angular scale-space (MASS) and helps to enhance the vessel structure and eliminate the optic disk.
4. Finally, a suitable threshold is applied to get the binary vessel structure.

Mondal et al. (2017) proposed an unsupervised automated vessel structure segmentation technique based on adaptive noise island detection (ANID). In this paper, the noise was found in a preprocessed retinal image, and is considered as an island, with the different type of noises categorized into the following three types:

1. A noise like a square island;
2. A noise like a vertical island;
3. A noise like a horizontal island.

This method is summarized in the following steps:

1. The RGB retinal image is converted into a grayscale image using Craig's formula.
2. A top-hat transformation is applied to the grayscale image to eliminate the smaller noisy artifacts.
3. The difference of Gaussian (DoG) filter (Davidson & Abramowitz, 2016) is used to enhance the vessel structure from the background. The DoG is shown in Eq. (15.6), where ρ_1 and ρ_2 are two different standard deviations.

$$G_{\rho_1,\rho_2}(x,y) = \text{Image} * \left(\frac{1}{2\pi\rho_1^2}e^{-(x^2+y^2)/2\rho_1^2} - \frac{1}{2\pi\,\rho_2^2}e^{-(x^2+y^2)/2\rho_2^2}\right) \tag{15.6}$$

where

$$G_{\rho_1,\rho_2}:\{X\subseteq\mathbb{R}^n\}\rightarrow\{Z\subseteq\mathbb{R}\}$$

4. The enhanced image contains huge amounts of noise, which are considered as an island. To inspect each isolated noise, a window filter is used whose boundary pixels are logical zeros, and the rest of the pixels are logical ones.

5. To eliminate the noise another window is used, whose boundary pixels are logical ones and the rest of the pixels are logical zeros. The size of the window filters is simultaneously increased until all noises are removed.

Nandy, Chatterjee, and Das (2020) published an unsupervised method to segment the retinal blood vessels using the morphological scaled grid (MSG) technique. This method efficiently can eliminate the noises from its neighborhoods. However, there is a problem when the size of the grid is increased, and some of the details of the vessel structure are lost. The algorithm is summarized as follows:

1. The RGB fundus image is converted into a grayscale image using Eq. (15.7).

$$I_{\text{grayscale}} = 0.31 \times \text{Re} + 0.69 \times \text{Gr} + 0 \times \text{Bl} \quad (15.7)$$

   where Gr is the green channel, which has maximum contrast, Bl is the blue channel, which contains maximum noise, and Re is the red channel.
2. Next, a top-hat transformation is applied to the grayscale image to eliminate the smaller (less than 3 pixels) noisy artifacts.
3. An ALSE is created to open (morphological) the output image, which is found in the previous step, and for a particular size of the ALSE, the maximum response is preserved. After the end of the iterations, an enhanced retinal vessel structure is found.
4. To separate the noise from the background a DoG filter is used.
5. Then, the enhanced grayscale image is converted into a binary image using Otsu's threshold (Otsu, 1979) to get the binary vessel structure.
6. Finally, the noises found in the binary vessel structure are eliminated using a scaled grid. This grid's dimension is similar to the fundus image and it is divided into several blocks or windows. If any block contains an isolated object, that does not contribute any part to the window boundary, it is considered as a noise and is eliminated. However, if any part of the object is continued through the common boundary of the two adjacent windows, this object is preserved as a vessel for that particular window size. After that, the window size is increased iteratively until all noises are eliminated.

In this algorithm, a significant problem is found when the noise and blood vessels are simultaneously present in the same window or block. At this juncture, the noise cannot be eliminated by this approach.

15.2.4 B-COSFIRE method

In Azzopardi, Strisciuglio, Vento, and Petkov (2015), an unsupervised automatic retinal blood vessel segmentation based on a combination of shifted filter responses (COSIRE) was proposed. This method is constructed using a computational model of combination of respective fields (CORF) (Azzopardi & Petkov, 2012) and a bar selective nonlinear COSFIRE filter, which can accurately detect the bar-shaped structures just like the blood vessels. This method is summarized in the following steps:

1. First, the green channel of the retinal image is extracted according to previously proposed works (Niemeijer, Staal, van Ginneken, Loog, & Abramoff, 2004; Mendonca & Campilho, 2006; Ricci & Perfetti, 2007; Soares, Leandro, Cesar, Jelinek, & Cree, 2006).
2. The nonlinear B-COSFIRE filter is configured by computing the WGM (weighted geometric mean) of the resultant of different DoG (difference of Gaussian) and its supports are aligned collinearly. Eq. (15.8) shows a structure of the B-COSFIRE filter. In this filter, there is a tuple of three parameters found, such as $(\sigma_{i,}\rho_{i,}\theta_{i,})$, where σ_i, is the standard deviation of DoG and ρ_i and θ_i stand for the polar coordinates of the supports of B-COSFIRE filter.

$$B = \{(\sigma_{i,}\ \rho_{i,}\theta_{i,}) \quad | i = 1, 2, 3, \ldots\ldots\ldots\ldots, n\} \quad (15.8)$$

   In Eq. (15.8), n represents the number of considered difference of Gaussian for the filter configuration. There are two types of B-COSFIRE filters, symmetric and asymmetric. The symmetric filters are selected for bars and the asymmetric filters are selected for bar-endings.
3. After applying a suitable threshold, blood vessel segmentation is achieved with the combination of the results of the two rotational invariant B-COSFIRE filters.

The B-COSFIRE filters are adaptable because their selection is dependent on the prototype pattern of the vessel-like structures. Therefore this is a trainable filter approach.

15.2.5 Supervised approach

There are several supervised methods found in the literature to segment the retinal vessel structure. Different types of classifiers have been proposed, such as support vector machine (SVM), neural networks, and Bayesian classifier.

In Xu and Luo (2010), a supervised retinal vessel segmentation method was proposed based on the SVM classifier. These authors attempted to overcome the problems found in the retinal image, due to the variation of contrast and they segmented the large as well as the thin blood vessels from the fundus images. The proposed method is summarized as follows:

1. First, to enhance the vessel structure and suppress the background normalization using a 25×25

median filter is applied on the converted green channel of the RGB image.

2. An adaptive threshold is applied to the enhanced image to convert it into a binary image and again a threshold T (T is the area of the connected component of 100 pixels wide) is used to extract the large component.
3. A large blood vessel always has a pair of local gradient maxima and minima on both sides throughout its structure. Therefore using this pair of gradients the large blood vessel structure is obtained. However, the residue parts of the image not only contain the noises but also some small vessels. Using the SVM classifier, small blood vessels can be extracted from the residual image.
4. Then, to remove the tiny vessel structure from the residue, wavelet and curvelet transformations (Emmanuel & David, 2005) are used first for feature extraction. Eq. (15.9) shows the wavelet function $\psi_{s,x}$, with scale s and location x and Eq. (15.10) shows curvelet function $\psi_{s,x,\theta}$, with scale s, location x, and direction θ.

$$Wf(s,x) = <\psi_{s,\,x}, f> \tag{15.9}$$

$$Cf(s,x) = <\psi_{s,\,x,\theta}, f> \tag{15.10}$$

5. The extracted features are used to estimate the hyper-plane of the binary SVM classifier and this plane can separate the tiny vessels from noises. In this paper, a Gaussian radial basis function (GRBF) is used as a kernel function of the SVM classifier. The GRBF ($K(u,v)$) is shown in Eq. (15.11).

$$K(u,v) = \exp\left\{-\frac{||u-v||^2}{2\sigma^2}\right\} \tag{15.11}$$

where u is the feature vector, σ is the width of the GRBF kernel, and v is the result found in the corresponding classification. If $v=1$, this implies that the corresponding pixel is a part of a tiny vessel, and if $v=-1$, this means that the corresponding pixel is not a part of a vessel. This is given in Eq. (15.12).

$$C = \begin{cases} C_1, & \text{when } v=1 \\ C_2, & \text{when } v=-1 \end{cases} \tag{15.12}$$

where C is assigned two different classes, C_1 (when $=1$) for tiny vessel structure and C_2 (when $v=-1$) for nonvessel structure.

6. A tracking growth approach using Hessian matrix has been applied to segment the tiny vessel structure and, ultimately, the whole vascular network is formed.

Another supervised method is that of Marin et al. (2011), where a grayscale moment invariant feature is used in a neural network for the classification. Korpusik (2014) proposed a vessel separation method using a multilayer perceptron neural network. In Jiang et al. (2018), an approach is presented based on the convolutional network (transfer learning approach) to segregate the vessel structure. Wang et al. (2015) suggested the two most commonly used classifiers as (1) convolutional neural network and (2) random forest, to segment the vasculature.

15.3 Basic morphological operations

This section includes the overview of the image, structuring element (SE), and some of the basic gray-level morphological operations (Gonzalez & Woods, 2008; Camps, Kanungo, & Haralick, 1996). The following operations and the notations are used in the proposed algorithm.

1. Image: A two-dimensional grayscale image (f) can be expressed as, $f(u,v) \in Z$ where $(u,v) \in D_f \subseteq Z^2$ and D_f is the domain of f.
2. SE: The SE (s) is a mask that is used to probe throughout the image f. The SE can be expressed as $s(u,v) \in Z$, where $(u,v) \in D_s \subseteq Z^2$ and D_s is the domain of s. For each SE (s), there is another corresponding SE (s^*) found, called the transposed or reflected SE, which can be expressed as $s^* = \{-x : x \in s\}$. In Fig. 15.2B, an E is shown. At this juncture, all the morphological operations are described using a flat SE (s_y), which corresponds to a structuring function $S_y(x)$ which can be expressed as in Eq. (15.13).

$$S_y(x) = \begin{cases} 0, & x \in S_y \\ -\infty, & x \notin S_y \end{cases} \tag{15.13}$$

3. Dilation: The dilation (δ_s) of the grayscale image can be defined as

$$\delta_s = [f \oplus s](u,v) = \max_{(u',v') \in D_{se}} [f(u-u', v-v') + s(u',v')] \tag{15.14}$$

4. Erosion: The erosion (ε_s) of the grayscale image can be defined as

$$\varepsilon_s = [f \ominus s](u,v) = \min_{(u',v') \in D_s} [f(u+u', v+v') - s(u',v')] \tag{15.15}$$

5. Opening: This is erosion followed by dilation, and can be expressed as

$$\gamma_s = \varepsilon_s[\delta_s] \tag{15.16}$$

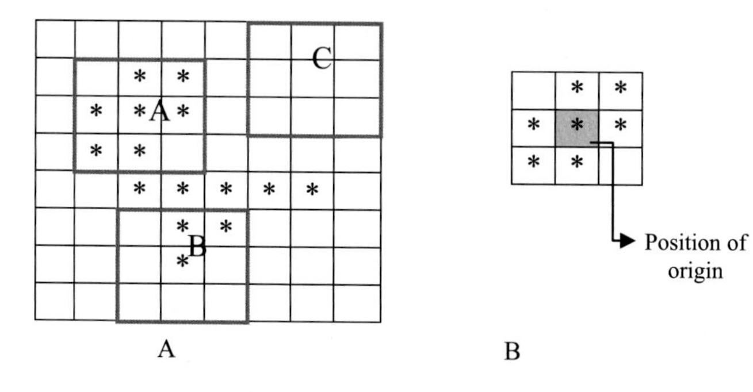

FIGURE 15.2 (A) Image (*f*), where the SE (*s*) fits at "A," hits at "B," and neither fits nor hits at "C." (B) Structuring element (*s*).

6. Closing: This is dilation followed by erosion, and can be expressed as

$$\varphi_s = \delta_s[\varepsilon_s] \tag{15.17}$$

7. Morphological gradient: The difference between the dilation (δ_s) and the erosion (ε_s) of an input image f is called the morphological gradient (g). It can be expressed as

$$g = \delta_s - \varepsilon_s = \{[f \oplus s](u,v) - [f \Theta s](u,v)\} \tag{15.18}$$

8. Top-hat transformation: The difference between a given image f and its opening (γ_s) is called the top-hat transformation (T_{hat}), which is expressed as

$$T_{\text{hat}}(f) = |f - \gamma_s(f)| \tag{15.19}$$

9. Bottom-hat: The difference between the closing (φ_s) of a given image and the image itself f is called the bottom-hat transformation (B_{hat}), which is expressed as

$$B_{\text{hat}}(f) = |\varphi_s(f) - f| \tag{15.20}$$

The above-mentioned morphological operations are used in our proposed algorithm with a different combination of structuring elements. The shape and size of the structuring element (*s*) are changed according to the requirement. To restore the vessel structure and remove the irrelevant objects from the fundus image, the size and shape of the structuring element are changed. In our proposed algorithm, two main types of structuring element are used to enhance the contrast: (1) disc-shaped and (2) line structuring elements (LAS).

15.4 Proposed algorithm

15.4.1 Preprocessing of the fundus image

At first, the color (RGB) fundus image is converted into a grayscale image (I_g) using Eq. (15.21), depending on the prominence of the vessel structure present in the red (R), green (G), and blue (B) channels (Kundu & Chatterjee, 2012). The green channel has maximum contrast and so it takes about 70%. In most of the supervised and unsupervised vessel segmentation methods (Chaudhuri et al., 1989; Florack, 1997; Martınez-Perez et al., 1999; Xu & Luo, 2010; Jiang & Mojon, 2003) only the green channel is considered for extraction of the vessel structure. The blue channel contains a maximum amount of noise and is darker (Salem & Nandi, 2008), therefore it is taken as 0%. The background of the fundus image is drenched with the red channel and has a spread intensity level, so it is taken at about 30%.

$$I_g = 0.30 \times R + 0.70 \times G + 0 \times B \tag{15.21}$$

15.4.2 Initial vessel-like structure determination

The width of the retinal blood vessels varies between 3 to 7 pixels (Samanta et al., 2011; Zana & Klein, 2001). Therefore to eliminate the objects with less than 3 pixels, a morphological opening ($\gamma_{\text{SE}_{d3}}$) is applied to the grayscale image I_g using a disk-shaped SE (SE_{d3}) with a diameter of 3 pixels. This morphological opening operation is shown in Eq. (15.22).

$$I_{\text{op}} = \gamma_{\text{SE}_{d3}}(I_g(x,y)) \tag{15.22}$$

Next, to join the small isthmuses and missing parts in a vessel, a morphological closing operation ($\varphi_{\text{SE}_{d8}}$) is employed with a disc-shaped SE (SE_{d8}) of 8 pixels in diameter, as shown in Eq. (15.23).

$$I_{\text{op-cl}} = \varphi_{\text{SE}_{d8}}(I_{\text{op}}) \tag{15.23}$$

The output image $I_{\text{op-cl}}$ is devoid of any noisy objects less than 3 pixels in size and small gaps in the vessels are repaired. To obtain the vessel-like structures from the background, a morphological top-hat transformation is applied to the $I_{\text{op-cl}}$. This morphological top-hat transformation is shown in Eq. (15.24). The output image I_{rs} contains the objects which are greater than 3 pixels.

$$I_{\text{rs}}(x,y) = |I_g(x,y) - I_{\text{op-cl}}| \tag{15.24}$$

15.4.3 Locally adaptive line structuring element generation and blood vessel segmentation

For segmentation of a vessel structure from the background, a LALSE is employed on I_{rs}. The LALSE ($\text{SE}^i_{\theta^\circ}$) is a one-dimensional flat line structuring element filled of 1 pixel and of length "i" and orientation angle "θ°." The LALSE rotates around its origin, which is present at the midpoint $(\lfloor i/2 \rfloor + 1)$th of the line structuring element. Fig. 15.2 shows an example of a LALSE with a length of 7 pixels.

Then, for a fixed length "i," on each iteration, $SE^i_{\theta^\circ}$ is rotated by an angle 10° going up to 180° and correspondingly a morphological opening is performed on each pixel of I_{rs}. After a full rotation, the maximum response $(G^i(x, y))$ for each pixel position is computed and preserved. After that, the length of the LALSE $(SE^i_{\theta^\circ})$ is increased by 1 pixel and the same procedure is repeated up to 7 pixels in length. It is observed that when the length (i) of the LALSE exceeds 7 pixels the retinal blood vessels are distorted. The above operations are shown in Eqs. (15.25) and (15.26) and are explained in Figs. 15.3 and 15.4.

$$G^i(x, y) = \max\left(\gamma_{SE^i_{180^\circ}}\left(\cdots\cdots\left(\gamma_{SE^i_{30^\circ}}\left(\gamma_{s^i_{20^\circ}}\left(\gamma_{SE^i_{10^\circ}}\left(\gamma_{SE^i_{0^\circ}}(I_{rs})\right)\right)\right)\right)\right)\right) \tag{15.25}$$

$$G^{i+1}(x, y) = \gamma_{SE^{i+1}_{\theta^\circ}}\left(G^i(x, y)\right) \tag{15.26}$$

15.4.4 Enhancement of vessel structure using difference of Gaussians

Now, to separate the low contrast noises present in the neighborhood to the vessel structure $(G^i(x, y))$, a DoG (difference of Gaussians,) is used. The DoG increases the contrast between the vessel structure of $G^i(x, y)$ and neighboring noisy objects. Using the DoG expeditiously, with proper selection of parameters, the noisy objects get separated from the boundary of the retinal vessel structure (Davidson & Abramowitz, 2016).

The Gaussian kernel is convolved with the image $G^i(x, y)$, having variances ρ_1^2 and ρ_2^2 $(\rho_1 > \rho_2)$, respectively. After that, the difference between two

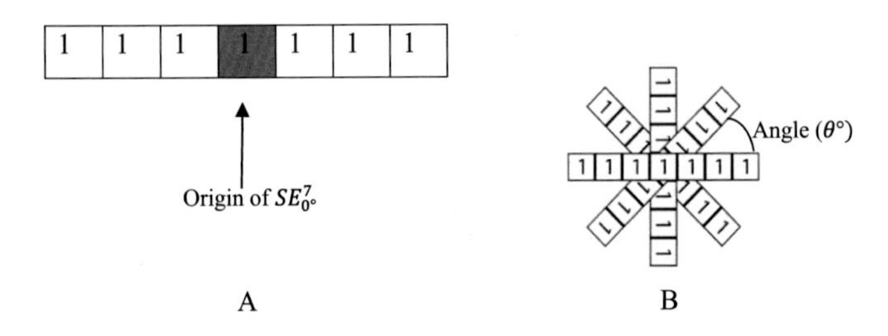

FIGURE 15.3 (A) Locally adaptive line structuring element $(SE^7_{0^\circ})$ with length 7 pixels where each pixel's value is one. (B) Rotation of $SE^7_{0^\circ}$ around its origin, located at $(\frac{7}{2} + 1) = 4$th pixel's position.

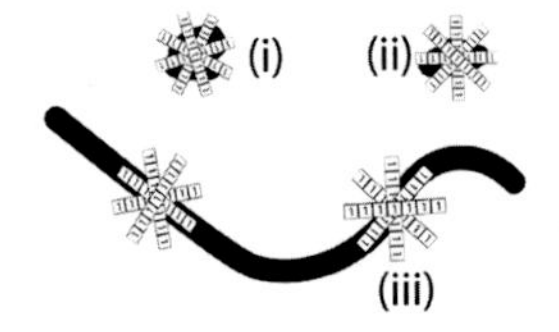

FIGURE 15.4 (i) and (ii) $SE^7_{\theta^\circ}$ does not match properly, considered as unwanted objects. (iii) $SE^7_{\theta^\circ}$ matches properly, so it is a vessel structure and hence it is stored.

convolved images is calculated (Marr & Hildreth, 1980), and the output image $\Psi_{\rho_1,\rho_2}(x, y)$ is found, as shown in Eq. (15.27).

$$\Psi_{\rho_1,\rho_2}(x, y) = G^i(x, y) * \left(\frac{1}{2\pi\,\rho_1^2} e^{-(x^2+y^2)/2\rho_1^2} - \frac{1}{2\pi\,\rho_2^2} e^{-(x^2+y^2)/2\rho_2^2}\right) \tag{15.27}$$

15.4.5 Binarization using local Otsu's threshold

At this juncture, the main problem is to extract the vessel structure from the retinal image, which contains a very similar contrast between the blood vessels and the noise. The variation, in contrast, is dependent on the corresponding position on the fundus image. Therefore an arbitrary global threshold cannot preserve the detailed vessel's information after binarization. Therefore a local Otsu's threshold (Otsu, 1979) is applied to Ψ_{ρ_1,ρ_2}, to extract the retinal blood vessel's anatomy from its background, to solve this problem. As a result, a binary image (I_{binary}), with the vessel structure, is extracted. Let, $\Psi_{\rho_1,\rho_2}(i, j)$ be the intensity at any point (i, j) of the image Ψ_{ρ_1,ρ_2}, then the thresholding can be expressed by Eq. (15.28), where T_{LOT}, is the locally selected Otsu's threshold. T_{LOT} varies with position (i, j) of the image Ψ_{ρ_1,ρ_2}.

$$\Psi_{\rho_1,\rho_2}(i, j) = \begin{cases} 0, & \text{if } \Psi_{\rho_1,\rho_2}(i, j) < T_{LOT} \\ 1, & \text{if } \Psi_{\rho_1,\rho_2}(i, j) \geq T_{LOT} \end{cases} \tag{15.28}$$

15.4.6 Elimination of noisy objects from a binary image

The resultant binary image I_{binary} contains numerous noisy objects along with vessel structure. Some important characteristics of these noisy objects are that they are isolated, relatively small in size compared to the vessels, scattered all over the image, and occurs more frequently. To separate those noisy artifacts, at first, all the connected areas are labeled with a unique integer to get a labeled binary image ($I_{labeled}$) and the areas of all labeled objects are calculated. As already stated, the area of the noisy artifacts is relatively small and their count is very high, and so, the frequencies of noisy objects are relatively higher than the vessels. Hence, area-wise frequencies (histogram) of $I_{labeled}$ are computed to identify the statistical mixture distribution of noise and vessel classes. A plot of such a histogram is shown in Fig. 15.6B for the image in Fig. 15.8E. This histogram shows that the frequencies of areas for the isolated objects are monotonically decreasing when the size of the objects increases. However, after a specific value of the object's size, the change in the statistical distribution is observed. A clear distinction of distribution

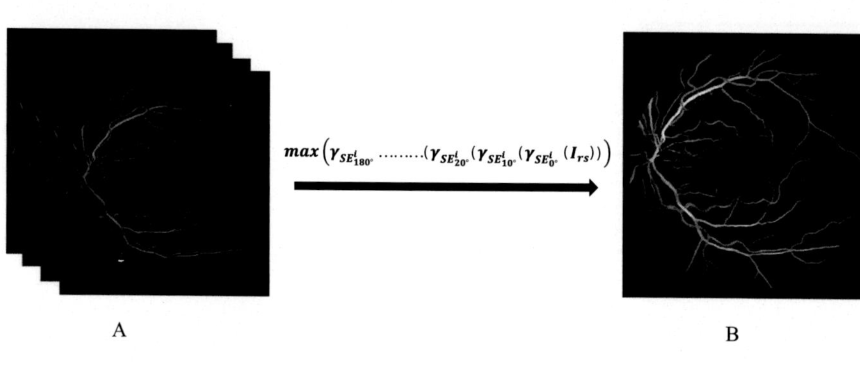

FIGURE 15.5 (A) A stack of retinal images is found after opening with different structuring elements ($SE^i_{\theta°}$). (B) After taking maximum response the image $G^i(x,y)$ is formed.

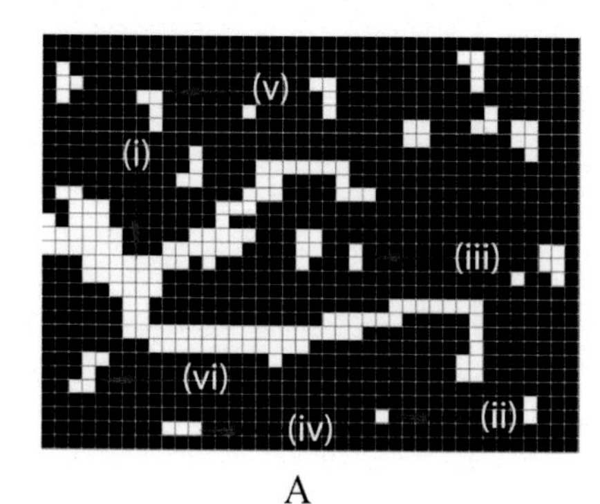

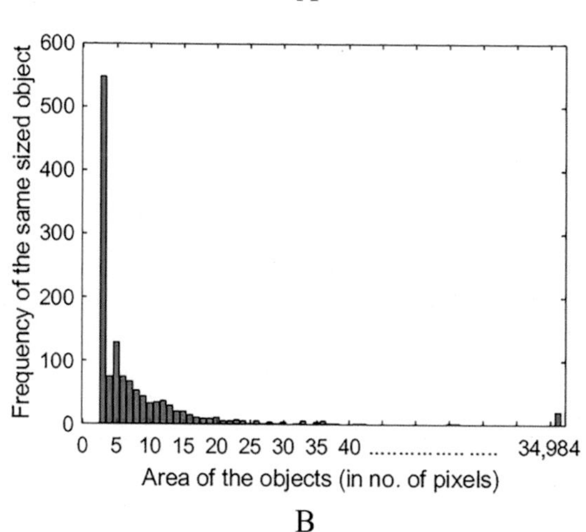

FIGURE 15.6 (A) A part of the retinal image, (i) the vessel's continuous part, and (ii)–(vi) the isolated noises. (B) The histogram shows the frequency of same-sized objects versus the unique size of the isolated object.

of noise and vessels can be observed from the histogram of binary objects.

A histogram-based automatic thresholding algorithm is applied to discriminate the two classes. The between-class variance is maximized to identify the threshold of noise and blood vessel class. The objects, whose area is less than the previously calculated threshold, is considered as noises and, using the corresponding labels, those small objects are filled with logical "0," and the resultant image is I_{vessel} is obtained. The image I_{vessel} gives a clear picture of the binary vessel structure. Fig. 15.7 shows the flowchart of the proposed algorithm.

15.5 Experiment

15.5.1 Database

The existing techniques and our proposed method are tested on the freely available databases such as DRIVE, CHASE_DB1, and STARE. The detailed information of these databases is given below:

1. DRIVE (https://drive.grand-challenge.org/): This database is found from a DR screening program held in the Netherlands. The images are captured by a Canon CR5 nonmydriatic 3CCD. In this program, about 400 people were tested (ages between 25 to 90 years) and 40 images are randomly selected to make the DRIVE database. This database is divided into two sets, the test set and the training set. Each set contains the original fundus image with its mask and the manually segmented ground truth images. The size of each image of the DRIVE database is 584 × 565 pixels.
2. CHASE_DB1 (https://blogs.kingston.ac.uk/retinal/chasedb1/): This database contains 28 fundus images with a pair of manually segmented ground truth vessel structures for each image. The original images are segmented by the two different human observers. For training and testing purposes, the first set of ground truths is commonly used and the second set of ground truths is used as a human baseline. The size of each image in this database is 999 × 960 pixels.

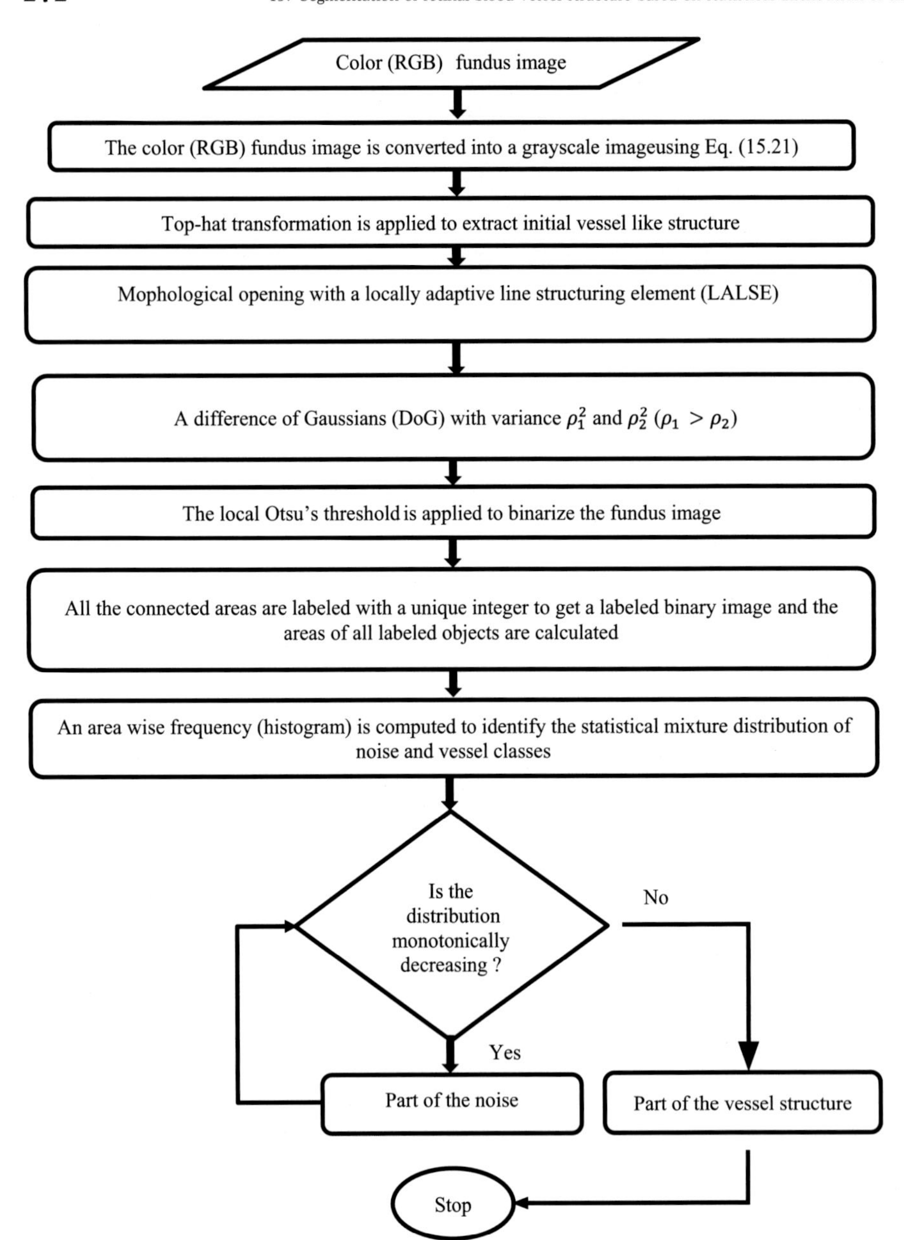

FIGURE 15.7 Flowchart of the proposed algorithm.

3. STARE (Hoover, Kouznetsova, & Goldbaum, 2000): This database contains about 20 color fundus images, captured by a TopCon TRV-50 camera. The size of each image in this database is 700 × 605 pixels. In this database 10 fundus images contain pathologies. There is a pair of manually segmented ground truth vessel structures present for each image. This manual segmentation is done by two different observers. The first set is annotated by A. Hoover and the second is annotated by V. Kouznetsova. For training and testing purposes, the first set of ground truths is commonly used and the second set of ground truths is used as a human baseline.

15.5.2 Experimental results

Fig. 15.8A shows the grayscale image I_g, which is formed using Eq. (15.21) on the original RGB image, where the contribution of the green channel is maximum (70%) because it has maximum contrast and minimum noise, and the contribution of the blue channel is nil (0%) because it contains a huge amount of noise.

Fig. 15.8B shows the image I_{rs}, which is formed after applying a morphological top-hat transformation, which is shown in Eq. (15.24) on the gray level image I_g. I_{rs} does not contain any object that has a diameter less than 3 pixels because the diameter of the vessel

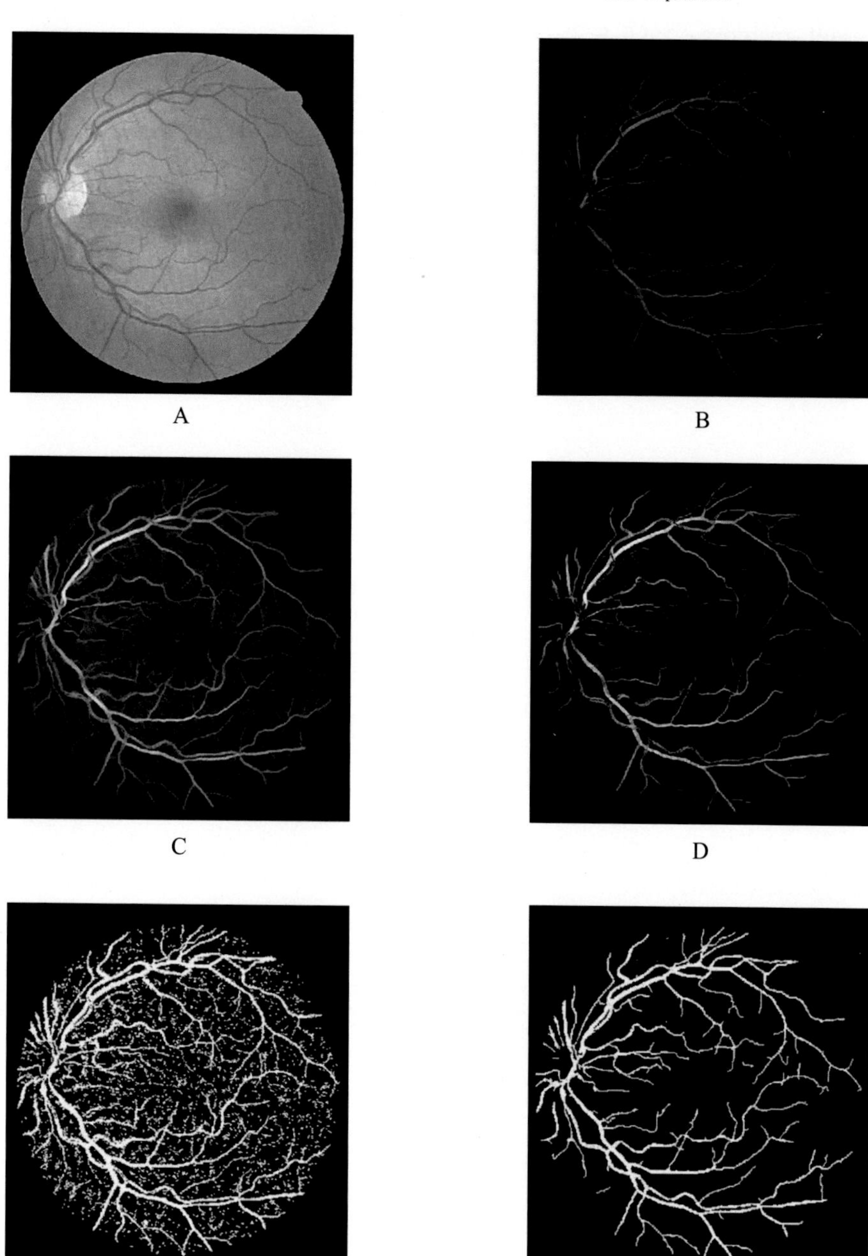

FIGURE 15.8 Retinal blood vessel detection phases, tested on the DRIVE database: (A) grayscale image I_g; (B) resultant image I_{rs}, after applying top-hat transformation on I_g; (C) output image G^i, after applying the LALSE $(SE^7_{\theta^\circ})$ on I_{rs}; (D) output image Ψ_{ρ_1,ρ_2}, after applying DoG on G; (E) output binary image I_{binary}, after using Otsu's threshold locally on Ψ_{ρ_1,ρ_2}; (F) final output image (I_{vessel}), after removing noises.

structure is greater than 3 and less than 8 pixels (Mondal et al., 2017).

To segment, the retinal vessel structure from the background the LALSE is applied on I_{rs}, using Eqs. (15.25) and (15.26) and the output image G^i is formed, as shown in Fig. 15.8C. Here the length of the LALSE $(SE^7_{\theta^\circ})$ is restricted to 7 pixels.

Fig. 15.8D shows the output image Ψ_{ρ_1,ρ_2}, after applying the DoG on G^i to increase the contrast between noises and the vessel structure using Eq. (15.27). The resultant image Ψ_{ρ_1,ρ_2} contains spatial information of the retinal vessel structure and the noises which are attached to the boundary wall of the vessels are suppressed.

The gray-level of the retinal image varies with location and these variations are not stable for fundus images. Therefore to convert into a binary retinal image a locally adaptive Otsu's threshold is applied on Ψ_{ρ_1,ρ_2} and the output binary image I_{binary} is formed, as shown in Fig. 15.8E. This binary image not only contains the retinal blood vessel structure but also a huge amount of noisy objects are distilled out.

To extract the vessel structure from the noisy binary image a threshold is determined from the histogram which contains the frequency of same-sized objects versus the unique size of the isolated object, and is shown in Fig. 15.6. Using this calculated threshold (area of the objects) the final output vessel structures (I_{vessel}) are formed, as shown in Fig. 15.8F. Other results are shown in Fig. 15.9, tested on CHASE_DB1 database.

15.5.3 Performance measurement

The performance of the given unsupervised method is measured using the pixel-wise comparison between the final output image and the given corresponding ground truth image in the DRIVE, CHASE_DB1, and STARE data sets, concerning the following measures of the confusion matrix: true positive (TP), FP, true negative (TN), and false negative (FN). The comparison with some recently published supervised and unsupervised methods is done using the following measures: sensitivity (Se), specificity (Sf), and accuracy

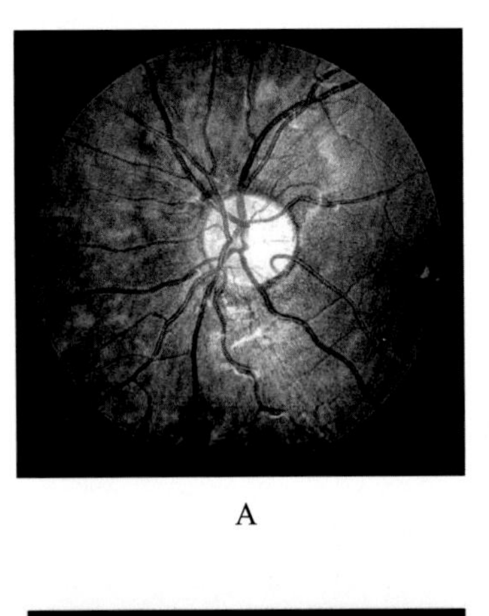

A

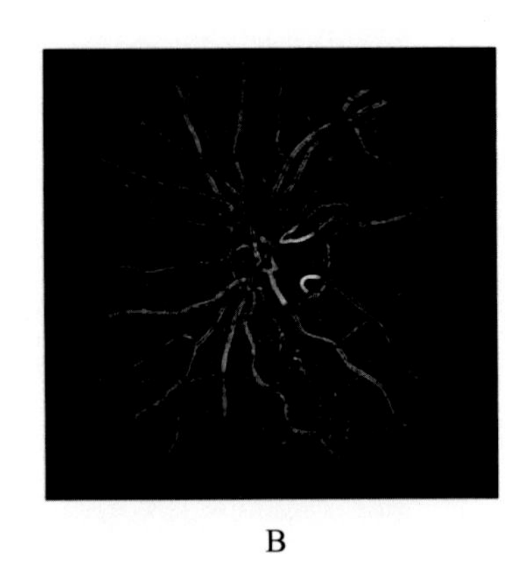

B

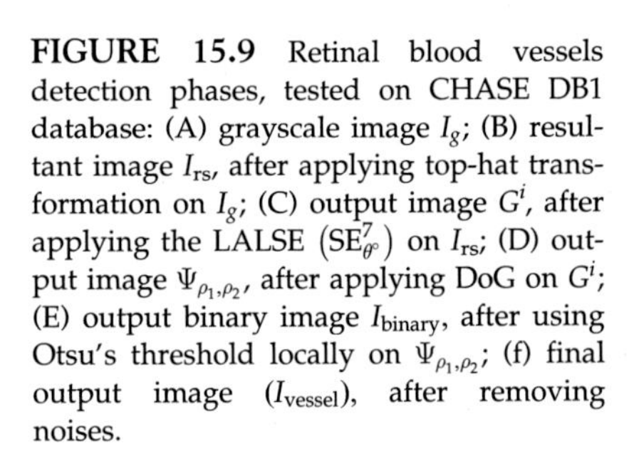

FIGURE 15.9 Retinal blood vessels detection phases, tested on CHASE DB1 database: (A) grayscale image I_g; (B) resultant image I_{rs}, after applying top-hat transformation on I_g; (C) output image G^i, after applying the LALSE $\left(SE^7_{\theta^\circ}\right)$ on I_{rs}; (D) output image Ψ_{ρ_1,ρ_2}, after applying DoG on G^i; (E) output binary image I_{binary}, after using Otsu's threshold locally on Ψ_{ρ_1,ρ_2}; (f) final output image (I_{vessel}), after removing noises.

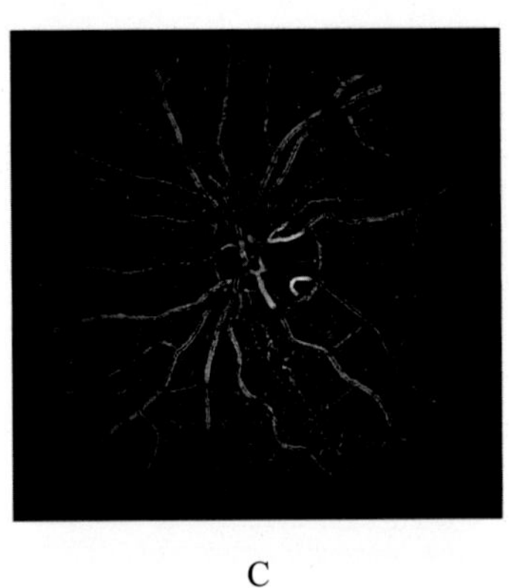

C

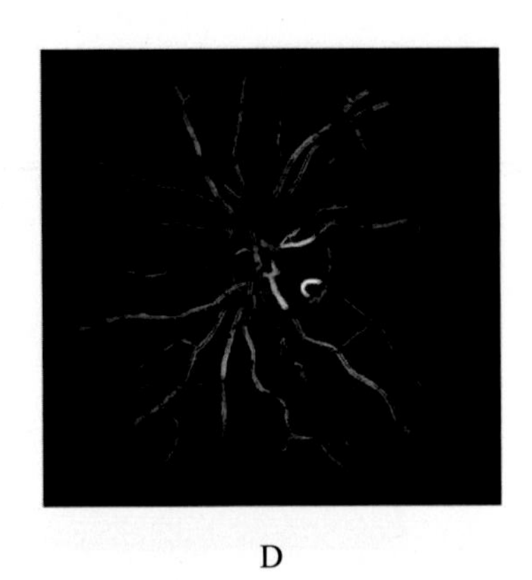

D

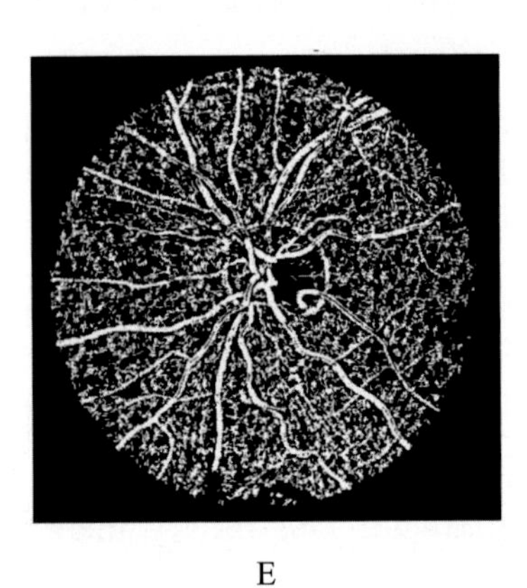

E

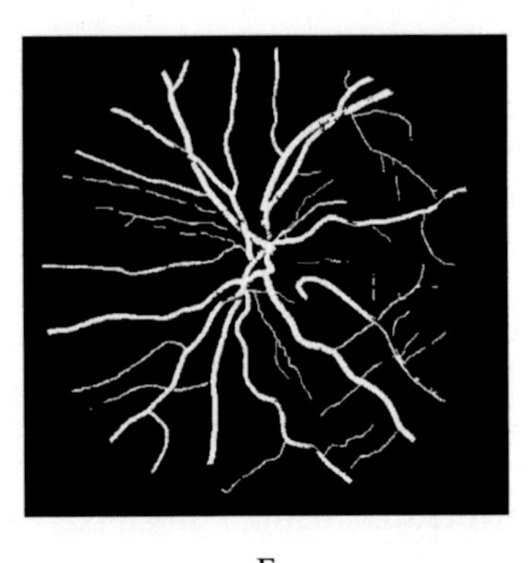

F

TABLE 15.1 Performance measures of our proposed method tested on the DRIVE database.

Serial no.	Name of the image	Sensitivity (%)	Specificity (%)	Accuracy (%)
01	01_test	76.42	97.28	95.82
02	02_test	74.21	97.64	95.60
03	03_test	75.85	96.47	95.43
04	04_test	78.42	97.65	95.98
05	05_test	78.63	97.86	96.26
06	06_test	76.26	97.21	95.79
07	07_test	75.52	97.45	96.32
08	08_test	76.96	98.24	96.65
09	09_test	74.61	97.46	95.27
10	10_test	75.31	96.82	94.97
11	11_test	76.35	98.17	96.85
12	12_test	75.92	98.25	96.63
13	13_test	76.81	97.72	96.42
14	14_test	76.53	97.35	97.73
15	15_test	75.80	98.27	96.43
16	16_test	74.69	97.46	96.07
17	17_test	74.86	96.87	95.79
18	18_test	73.93	97.43	95.47
19	19_test	75.58	98.24	96.85
20	20_test	74.78	97.45	96.41
Average		*75.87*	*97.56*	*96.14*

(Ac), as shown in Eqs. (15.29), (15.30), and (15.31). The sensitivity (Se), specificity (Sf), and accuracy (Ac) are measured on the DRIVE, CHASE_DB1, and STARE databases and the results are shown in Tables 15.1–15.3, respectively. Fig. 15.10 shows a comparison of the performance of our proposed algorithm tested on the above-mentioned databases. The performance of our proposed method with some of the existing techniques is shown in Table 15.4 and Fig. 15.11.

$$Se = \frac{TP}{TP + FN} \tag{15.29}$$

$$sf = \frac{TN}{TN + FP} \tag{15.30}$$

$$Ac = \frac{TP + TN}{TP + TN + FP + FN} \tag{15.31}$$

TABLE 15.2 Performance measures of our proposed method tested on the CHASE DB1 database.

Serial no.	Name of the image	Sensitivity (%)	Specificity (%)	Accuracy (%)
01	Image_01L	73.52	96.48	96.56
02	Image_02L	74.80	97.27	96.81
03	Image_03L	77.38	98.45	97.58
04	Image_04L	75.98	97.12	96.08
05	Image_05L	74.33	97.29	96.31
06	Image_06L	74.06	97.75	96.65
07	Image_07L	76.62	98.61	95.87
08	Image_08L	75.76	97.42	96.42
09	Image_09L	75.89	98.57	96.04
10	Image_10L	74.87	97.89	95.98
11	Image_11L	77.58	98.53	96.81
12	Image_12L	75.78	98.25	96.35
13	Image_13L	78.69	98.18	96.54
14	Image_14L	76.75	96.08	96.29
Average		*75.86*	*97.70*	*96.44*

TABLE 15.3 Performance measures of our proposed method tested on the normal (no pathology) fundus images (Mondal et al., 2017) of the STARE database.

Serial no.	Name of the image	Sensitivity (%)	Specificity (%)	Accuracy (%)
01	image 0081	74.43	95.52	97.53
02	image 0082	74.21	96.45	96.34
03	image 0162	75.58	97.75	96.02
04	image 0163	76.38	96.44	95.86
05	image 0235	76.02	95.79	96.63
06	image 0236	75.12	98.05	96.09
07	image 0239	74.81	96.52	97.13
08	image 0255	76.62	97.56	96.20
09	image 0319	76.49	95.92	97.19
10	image 0324	76.78	97.54	96.73
Average		*75.64*	*96.75*	*96.57*

15.6 Conclusions

This chapter proposes an efficient unsupervised method for the segmentation of blood vessels from the fundoscopic images. All the applied morphological

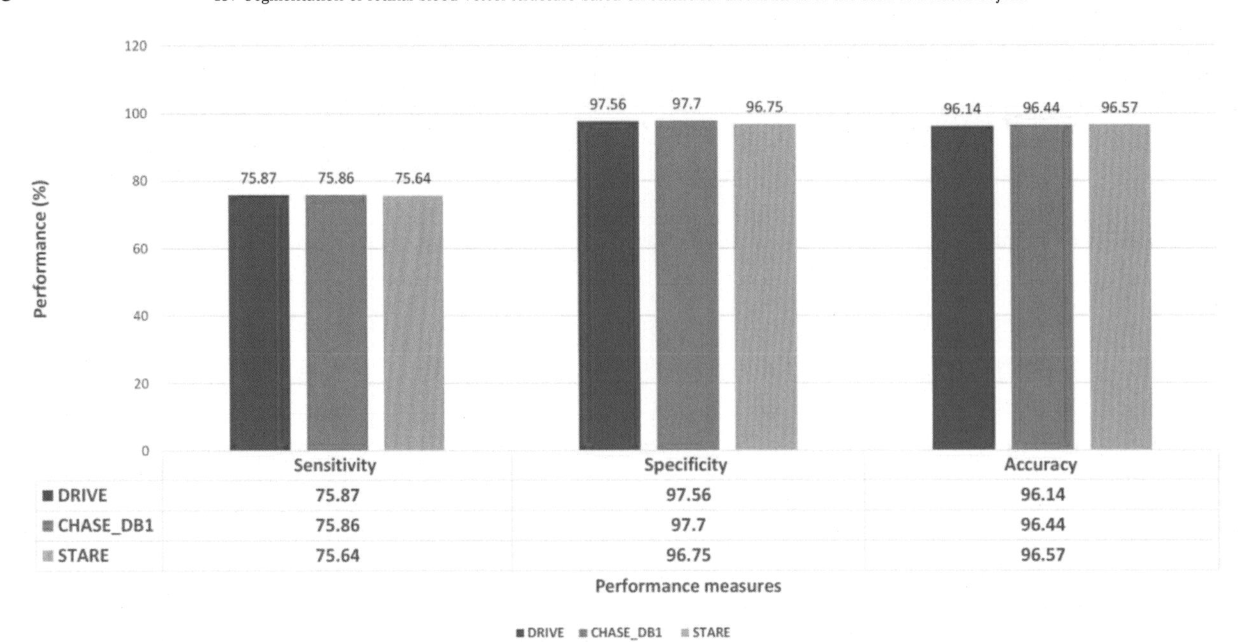

FIGURE 15.10 Comparison of the performance of our proposed algorithm tested on DRIVE, CHASE DB1, and STARE database.

TABLE 15.4 Evaluation of the performance of our proposed algorithm with some of the existing techniques.

Methodology	Classification	Image processing technique	Accuracy (%)	Sensitivity (%)	Specificity (%)
Ricci and Perfetti (2007)	Supervised	Line operators and support vector classification	95.95	–	–
Xu and Luo (2010)		Support vector machine, wavelets and Hessian matrix	93.28	77.60	–
Marin et al. (2011)		Neural network	94.52	70.67	98.01
Korpusik (2014)		Multilayer perceptron neural network	95.03	71.50	97.50
Jiang et al. (2018)		Convolutional network with transfer learning	96.24	75.40	98.25
Chaudhuri et al. (1989)	Unsupervised	Gaussian matched filter	87.73	–	–
Hoover and Goldbaum (2003)		Matched filter and threshold probing	92.19	68.28	95.89
Martınez-Perez et al. (1999)		Scale-space analysis and region growing	93.60	66.37	97.81
Zana and Klein (2001)		mathematical morphology and curvature evaluation	93.77	69.71	–
Kundu and Chatterjee (2012)		Adaptive mathematical morphology	92.73	67.48	95.66
Mondal et al. (2017)		Adaptive noise island detection	94.61	73.42	97.13
Azzopardi et al. (2015)		Combination of shifted filter responses	94.42	76.53	97.02
Nandy et al. (2020)		Morphological scaled grid	95.21	95.21	95.21
Samanta et al. (2011)		Mathematical morphology	82.53	89.26	76.98
Proposed technique		Statistical distribution of area of isolated objects	96.38	75.79	97.34

operations have antiextensive property, and so no new objects were introduced by the proposed algorithm. The average values of sensitivity (Se), specificity (Sf), and accuracy (Ac) of the proposed technique on the images found in the DRIVE, CHASE DB1, and STARE data set are 75.79%, 97.34%, and 96.38%, respectively, which indicates that the method is better than the recently published unsupervised methods concerning the accuracy and

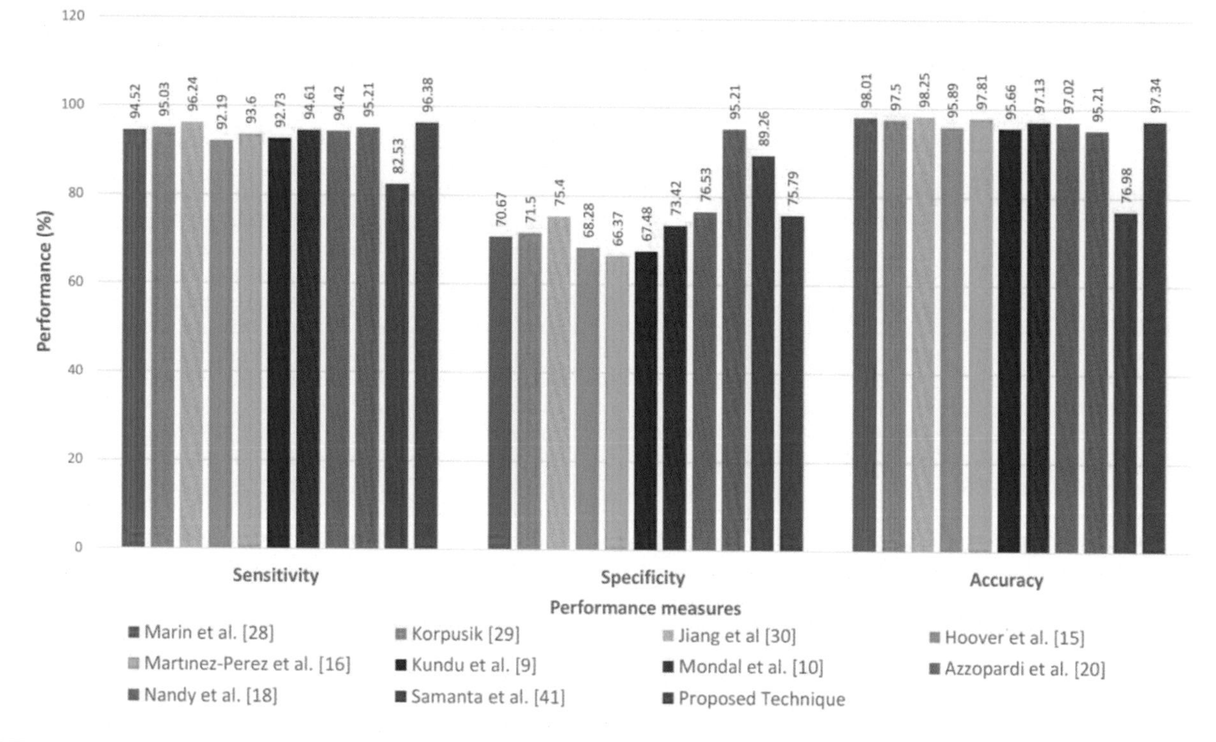

FIGURE 15.11 Evaluation of the performance of our proposed algorithm with some of the existing techniques tested on DRIVE database.

specificity. The comparison shows that the accuracy (Ac) of the proposed method is even better than some supervised techniques discussed in Section 15.2. The method can extract the vessel's structures from low- or high-contrast retinal images, even in presence of mild pathology, with a minimal amount of distortion or break in continuity. Thus, this method will be highly useful for the extraction and segmentation of blood vessels in retinal images.

References

Al-Diri, B., Hunter, A., & Steel, D. (2009). An active contour model for segmenting and measuring retinal vessels. *IEEE Transactions on Medical Imaging, 28*(9), 1488–1497.

Azzopardi, G., & Petkov, N. (2012). A CORF computational model of a simple cell that relies on LGN input outperforms the Gabor function model. *Biological Cybernetics, 106*, 177–189. Available from https://doi.org/10.1007/s00422-012-0486-6.

Azzopardi, G., Strisciuglio, N., Vento, M., & Petkov, N. (2015). Trainable COSFIRE filters for vessel delineation with application to retinal images. *Medical Image Analysis, 19*(1), 46–57.

Camps, O. I., Kanungo, T., & Haralick, R. M. (1996). Gray-scale structuring element decomposition. *IEEE Transactions on Image Processing, 5*(1), 111–120. Available from https://doi.org/10.1109/83.481675.

Canny, J. (1986). A computational approach to edge detection. *IEEE Transactions on Pattern Analysis and Machine Intelligence, PAMI-8*, 679–697.

Chaudhuri, S., Chatterjee, S., Katz, N., Nelson, M., & Goldbaum, M. (1989). Detection of blood vessels in retinal images using two-dimensional matched filters. *IEEE Transactions on Medical Imaging, 8*(3), 263–269.

Cheung, N., Mitchell, P., & Wong, T. Y. (2010). Diabetic retinopathy. *Lancet, 376*(9735), 124–136. Available from https://doi.org/10.1016/S0140-6736(09)62124-3, [PubMed].

Davidson, M. W., & Abramowitz, M. (2016). *Molecular expressions microscopy primer: Digital image processing – Difference of Gaussians edge enhancement algorithm*. Olympus America Inc., and Florida State University.

Dunachiea, S., & Chamnand, P. (2019). The double burden of diabetes and global infection in low-and middle-income countries, Advance Access publication 4 December 2018 *Transactions of the Royal Society of Tropical Medicine and Hygiene, 113*, 56–64.

Emmanuel, J. C., & David, L. D. (2005). Continuous curvelet transform I. Resolution of the wavefront set. *Applied and Computational Harmonic Analysis, 19*, 162–197. Available from https://doi.org/10.1016/j.acha.2005.02.003.

Florack, L. M. J. (1997). *Image structure*. Dordrecht, The Netherlands: Kluwer Academic.

Fraz, M. M., Barman, S. A., Remagnino, P., et al. (2012). Blood vessel segmentation methodologies in retinal images–A survey. *Computer Methods and Programs in Biomedicine, 108*, 407–433, In Press, Corrected Proof.

Gelman, R., Martinez-Perez, M. E., Vanderveen, D. K., et al. (2005). Diagnosis of plus disease in retinopathy of prematurity using retinal image multiscale analysis. *Investigative Ophthalmology & Visual Science, 46*(12), 4734–4738.

Gonzalez, R. C., & Woods, R. E. (2008). *Digital image processing* (3rd ed., pp. 627–687). Pearson Education.

Hoover, A., & Goldbaum, M. (2003). Locating the optic nerve in a retinal image using the fuzzy convergence of the blood vessels. *IEEE Transactions on Medical Imaging, 22*(8), 951–958.

Hoover, A., Kouznetsova, V., & Goldbaum, M. (2000). Locating blood vessels in retinal images by piece-wise threshold probing of a matched filter response. *IEEE Transactions on Medical Imaging, 19* (3), 203–210.

Jiang, X., & Mojon, D. (2003). Adaptive local thresholding by verification based multi-threshold probing with application to vessel detection in retinal images. *IEEE Transactions on Pattern Analysis and Machine Intelligence, 25*, 131–137.

Jiang, Z., Zhang, H., Wang, Y., & Ko, S. B. (2018). Retinal blood vessel segmentation using fully convolutional network with transfer learning. *Computerized Medical Imaging and Graphics, 68*, 1–15.

Korpusik, A. (2014). Hematopoietic stem cell based therapy of immunosuppressive viral infection numerical simulations. *Biocybernetics and Biomedical Engineering, 34*(2), 125–131.

Kundu, A. & Chatterjee, R.K. (2012). Morphological scale-space based vessel segmentation of retinal image. In: *Proceedings of the annual IEEE India conference*, (pp. 986–990).

Li, W., Bhalerao, A., & Wilson, R. (2007). Analysis of retinal vasculature using a multiresolution Hermite Model. *IEEE Transactions on Medical Imaging, 26*(2), 137–152.

Lupascu, C. A., Tegolo, D., & Trucco, E. (2010). FABC: Retinal vessel segmentation using AdaBoost. *IEEE Transactions on Information Technology in Biomedicine, 14*(5), 1267–1274.

Marin, D., Aquino, A., Gegundez-Arias, M. E., & Bravo, J. M. (2011). A new supervised method for blood vessel segmentation in retinal images by using gray-level and moment invariants-based features. *IEEE Transactions on Medical Imaging, 30*, 146–158.

Marr, D. & Hildreth, E. (1980). Theory of edge detection. Proceedings of the Royal Society of London, Series B, Biological Sciences. 207 (1167): 215–217.

Martınez-Perez, M., Hughes, A., Stanton, A., Thom, S., Bharath, A., & Parker, K. (1999). Scale-space analysis for the characterisation of retinal blood vessel. In C. Taylor, & A. Colchester (Eds.), *Medical image computing and computer-assisted intervention - MICCAI'99* (pp. 90–97).

Mendonca, A. M., & Campilho, A. (2006). Segmentation of retinal blood vessels by combining the detection of centerlines and morphological reconstruction. *IEEE Transactions on Medical Imaging, 25*(9), 1200–1213. Available from https://doi.org/10.1109/TMI.2006.879955.

Mondal, R., Chatterjee, R.K., & Kar, A. (2017). Segmentation of retinal blood vessels using adaptive noise island detection. In: *Proceedings of the fourth international conference on image information processing*.

Nandy, R. S., Chatterjee, R. K., & Das, A. (2020). Segmentation of blood vessels from fundus image using scaled grid. In A. Bhattacharjee, S. Borgohain, B. Soni, G. Verma, & X. Z. Gao (Eds.), *Machine learning, image processing* (vol 1240). Singapore: Springer, Network Security and Data Sciences. MIND 2020. Communications in Computer and Information Science.

Nandy, R. S., Chatterjee, R. K., & Kar, A. (2017). Extraction of blood vessels from retinal image using adaptive morphology. *International Journal of Computer Applications, 168*(11), 28–34.

Niemeijer, M., Staal, J., van Ginneken, B.; Loog, M., & Abramoff, M. (2004). Comparative study of retinal vessel segmentation methods on a new publicly available database. In: *Proceedinsg of the SPIE – the international society for optical engineering, medical imaging*, 16–19 February (Image Processing) (pp. 648–656), San Diego, CA, USA.

Otsu, N. (1979). A threshold selection method from gray-level histogram. *IEEE Transactions on System, Man, and Cybernetics, 9*(1), 62–66.

Ricci, E., & Perfetti, R. (2007). Retinal blood vessel segmentation using line operators and support vector classification. *IEEE Transactions on Medical Imaging, 26*(10), 1357–1365. Available from https://doi.org/10.1109/TMI.2007.898551.

Saeedi, P., Petersohn, I., Salpea, P., Malanda, B., Karuranga, S., Unwin, N., ... Williams, R., IDF Diabetes Atlas Committee. (2019). Global and regional diabetes prevalence estimates for 2019 and projections for 2030 and 2045: Results from the international diabetes federation diabetes atlas, 9th edition. Diabetes Research and Clinical Practice. 157, 107843. Available from https://doi.org/10.1016/j.diabres.2019.107843. Epub 2019 Sep 10. PMID: 31518657.

Salem, N.M. & Nandi, A.K. (2008). Unsupervised segmentation of retinal blood vessels using a single parameter vesselness measure. In: *Proceedings of the sixth Indian conference on computer vision, graphics & image processing* (pp. 528–534) IEEE Xplore.

Samanta, S., Saha, S.K., & Chanda, B. (2011). A simple and fast algorithm to detect the fovea region in fundus retinal image. In: *Proceedings of the second international conference on emerging applications of information technology* (pp. 206–209) IEEE Xplore.

Soares, J. V. B., Leandro, J. J. G., Cesar, R. M., Jelinek, H. F., & Cree, M. J. (2006). Retinal vessel segmentation using the 2-D Gabor wavelet and supervised classification. *IEEE Transactions on Medical Imaging, 25*(9), 1214–1222. Available from https://doi.org/10.1109/TMI.2006.879967.

Wang, S., Yin, Y., Cao, G., Wei, B., Zheng, Y., & Yang, G. (2015). Hierarchical retinal blood vessel segmentation based on feature and ensemble learning. *Neurocomputing, 149*, 708–717.

Xu, L., & Luo, S. (2010). A novel method for blood vessel detection from retinal images. *BioMedical Engineering OnLine, 9*, 14. Available from https://doi.org/10.1186/1475-925X-9-14.

Zana, F., & Klein, J. (2001). Segmentation of vessel-like patterns using mathematical morphology and curvature evaluation. *IEEE Transactions on Image Processing, 10*(7), 1010–1019.

CHAPTER

16

Energy efficient rendezvous point-based routing in wireless sensor network with mobile sink

Priyanjana Mitra[1], Sanjoy Mondal[1] and Khondekar Lutful Hassan[2]

[1]University of Calcutta, Kolkata, India [2]Aliah University, Kolkata, India

16.1 Introduction

The wireless sensor network (WSN)-assisted Internet of Things (IoT) (Wang, Qin, & Liu, 2018; Yetgin, Cheung, El-Hajjar, & Hanzo, 2017) consists of physical objects embedded with sensors, electronic circuits, software, and network connectivity to sense, gather, and exchange data over the network without any human intervention. Application of the IoT network has been drastically increased in several areas such as smart home infrastructure and appliances, smart road traffic management, smart security and surveillance, military and defense, healthcare, etc. Normally, IoT devices are scattered over the large areas and the embedded sensors monitor the surrounding environment, detect events, gather data, and forward the collected data to the others within a certain radio range (Lee & Kao, 2016). The individual sensor node in a WSN-assisted IoT network has resource constraints. It has limited processing speed, memory, energy, and communication bandwidth. However, the existing routing protocols of WSNs claim a significant amount of processing energy and memory that create uncertainty in the lifetime of the IoT network. Therefore productive usage of energy has been extensively explored to avoid disruption and extend the lifetime of the IoT network. Therefore there is a need for low device complexity and an energy-efficient protocol that ensures maximum devices will remain active for a prolonged amount of time. Clustering with multihop communication is a very common approach for researchers to increase the WSN lifetime. In this approach, nodes are grouped into clusters. Within each cluster, a node plays the role of the leader node called CH, and is responsible for collecting data from its member nodes (Abdulai, Adu-Manu, Banaseka, Katsriku, & Engmann, 2018). In addition, CH is responsible for aggregating the collected data and forwarding the aggregated data to the sink node. In this protocol, uneven distribution of processing load is clearly notable and, due to this uneven load, a subset of the nodes in the network consumes their energies rapidly and die out more quickly than the other nodes of the network, causing a hot-spot or sink-hole problem. An effective and well established solution to this hot-spot problem is a WSN with mobile sink (MS) (Kaswan, Singh, & Jana, 2018). This architecture consists of a large number of static sensor nodes (SNs) and one or more MS. The MS travels the network area accumulating data from the SNs. However, in the direct data collection method, collecting data from each device by the MS is a large challenge as devices are scattered over a wide area. Although it helps to decrease the number of multihop transmissions as well as to save the energy of the embedded SNs of each device, the drawback to this data collection method is that the MS has to travel a long path to collect data from each device. Sometimes this results in a buffer overflow problem as devices may have to wait a long time to deliver data. It also increases the latency in data delivery. In this chapter, we propose a solution to this problem by considering a few nodes as intermediate nodes, also known as RP (Praveen Kumar, Amgoth, & Annavarapu, 2018). The responsibilities of RP nodes are accumulating data from the nearest cluster head (CH) and aggregating the data. Once data are collected by the RP nodes, the MS visits only the RPs to collect data, which limits the traversing path of the MS. It is important to highlight that most of the total energy consumption by the SNs is caused by data transmission (DT). Energy consumption by the nodes due to DT is directly proportional to the distance between the sender and recipient. Another key cause of rapid energy loss is

Recent Trends in Computational Intelligence Enabled Research.
DOI: https://doi.org/10.1016/B978-0-12-822844-9.00014-1

intermediate data aggregation. Thus the life of the network can be extended by minimizing the transmission distance and selecting CHs and RPs carefully. In our proposed method we have employed the MultiObjective Optimization (MOO) technique to select RPs, while considering energy and distance as two selection parameters.

MOO is a field of multiple criteria decision-making that integrates multiple objective functions or goals to be optimized simultaneously. It is a useful methodology for sustainable system design and synthesis. One property of MOO is including possible conflicting objectives. The trade-off presence among all objectives mean that refinement of one objective is only possible by making a compromise with another objective (Li & Zhang, 2009). Therefore there is no optimum solution for all objective functions simultaneously, rather there are several Pareto optimal solutions or nondominated solutions (a feasible region of optimal solutions, Pareto front, PF). Different methods exist to solve the MOO problem. The simplest method is to convert the MOO problem into a single objective optimization (SOO) by giving weights to different objectives (the weighted objectives method). More often, MOO problems are solved by a bio-inspired metaheuristic evolutionary algorithm (Li, Deb, & Yao, 2018; Zitzler & Thiele, 1999). MultiObjective Genetic Algorithm (MOGA) (Zitzler & Thiele, 1999) and Nondominated Sorting Genetic Algorithm II (Deb, Pratap, Agarwal, & Meyarivan, 2002) are particularly widely accepted by researchers as solving techniques for MOO problems because they efficiently construct an approximate PF. This is because MOGA incorporates different types of bio-inspired operators to iteratively generate population and feasible solutions.

The contributions of this chapter are as follows:

- We present a clustering mechanism using K-means algorithm by considering all the homogeneous SNs.
- We propose an efficient CH selection mechanism based on the important parameter residual energy of the sensor node.
- A MOO-based efficient RP point selection mechanism is also proposed.

The remainder of this chapter is organized as follows: we explain the problem statement in Section 16.2. In Section 16.3 we give an overview of the related works in this field. The system model of this work is explained in Section 16.4. The general structure of the genetic algorithm (GA) is described in Section 16.5. Our proposed method is explained in Section 16.6. The simulation environment and performance analysis are described in Section 16.7. Section 16.8 gives a statistical analysis of our results, and Section 16.9 presents the conclusions and future scope.

16.2 Problem statement

In an IoT network all the physical devices installed with SNs accumulate data from different events from the outside world and transmit them to the base station by direct or multihop communication. Energy of SNs in WSN is consumed for data sensing, data processing (DP), and DTs, with the largest proportion of energy consumed by DT. Consequently, DT hinges on various important factors including the distance, packet size, amplification powers before the message transmission, etc. The aim of this research is to design a routing protocol which minimizes the power consumption of SN in order to extend the WSN-assisted network lifetime. For the issues discussed above, this research has focused on the following:

- In the case of DT, the long distance between the sender and receiver is the main cause of rapid energy depletion. Therefore by reducing the transmission distance we can extend the lifetime of the network.
- Cluster formation by grouping all SNs and selection of CH should be efficient. All members of a cluster can send their data to their CH, then the CH assembles the data and transmits them to its nearest RP. This protocol can reduce the transmission distance and extend the network's lifetime.
- To avoid latency of the data delivery and buffer overflow problem due to the long traveling path of MS, our next objective is optimally selecting intermediate nodes' RP by ensuring limited energy depletion of the network.

16.3 Literature survey

In recent years, a massive number of methodologies have been designed in order to ensure better survival of the SN. Most are based on static sinks and a few only are based on MSs. In this section we focus only on the clustering-based WSN protocol, RP-based protocol, and application of MOO-based algorithm in WSNs. We've done a survey of all existing routing techniques and presented it here in tabular format at Table 16.2.

16.3.1 Cluster-based routing protocol with static sink

Among all the existing WSN architectures, the clustering approach is very popular with researchers for extending the lifetime of WSNs. From a historical perspective, an energy-efficient approach Minimum Transmission Energy protocol (Ettus, 1998) has been proposed where data are sent through the nearest neighbor nodes but a problem arises when this protocol is used as the nearest nodes of the BS are overloaded by the routing processing load and results die out quickly. This uneven distribution of processing load has been reduced by several protocols including Low-Energy Adaptive Clustering Hierarchy (LEACH). The LEACH protocol (Heinzelman, Chandrakasan, & Balakrishnan, 2002) offers a distributed cluster generation technique by self-organizing a large number of nodes and selecting CHs periodically to overcome rapid depletion of the CH's energy. The CH collects data from its cluster members and transmits the aggregated data to the BS. However, a drawback of this protocol is that, as the selection of the CH is random, sometimes a low energy node may be elected as CH and it may not evenly be distributed. The improvised version of the LEACH algorithm is the LEACH-Centralized (LEACH-C) algorithm that considers the total residual energy as a parameter in the CH selection probability formula, so that nodes with high residual energy can be selected as CHs. Fuzzy C-Means Clustering Protocol (FCM) (Hoang, Kumar, & Panda, 2010) is another clustering-based routing protocol, where clusters are formed based on the Euclidean distance of the devices from the center of the cluster in which the devices belong. This cluster formation technique helps to create an energy balance among all the devices of the cluster. Initially, CHs are selected randomly as all nodes have the same energy. However, in the next round the node with the highest residual energy elects itself as CH. All the member nodes of the cluster transmit sensed data to their corresponding CH and the latter CH aggregates data and transmits them to the remote BS directly. At the time of cluster formation FCM does not consider the data generation capacity of the devices. If all the devices that generate lengthy messages are clubbed into one cluster then the assigned CH of this cluster consumes a large amount of energy more rapidly than other CHs of the network and, eventually, the network dies out earlier than others. Muruganathan et al. proposed a balanced cluster methodology called BCDP (Muruganathan, Ma, Bhasin, & Fapojuwo, 2005). In each CH, the number of member nodes is approximately equal, and the CH to CH routing protocol is used to transfer data to the BS. In HEED, Younis and Fahmy (2001), proposed a protocol where CH is selected based on SN's residual energy and adjacency to its neighbor. Therefore one CH gathers data from its large number of neighbors resulting rapid depletion of the energy of the CH. The Evaluate an Energy Efficient Clustering Scheme (EECS) (Ye, Li, Chen, & Wu, 2005) protocol is applicable for periodical data-gathering applications in WSNs. For CH selection, a constant number of candidate nodes are competing according to the node residual energy, and the winning node announces itself as the CH in its competition radius. However, the problem is in the dense networks as there are so many nodes competing for the CH designation, causing potential problems. The Topology Controlled Adaptive Clustering (Dahnil, Singh, & Ho, 2012) protocol (Anwit & Jana, 2019) ameliorates the performance of the EECS protocol. It gives the capability of CHs to balance their power level to achieve an optimal degree and maintain this value throughout their network lifetime, which results in a well-balanced clustering system that increases the network lifetime. The Hausdorff clustering method (Zhu, Shen, & Yum, 2009) forms clusters only once by following a greedy algorithm and selects CHs based on the location, communication efficiency, and network connectivity. As the clusters are formed only once, if the cluster formation is inefficient then it affects the lifetime of the network and nodes quickly die out. Local Energy Consumption Prediction-Based Clustering Protocol (LEACH-CP) selects CH by considering an intercluster communication-based routing tree. Algorithms predict the local energy consumption ratio of SNs. It provides an effective and realistic cluster radius to reduce the energy consumption of all WSNs. A CH selection algorithm based on fuzzy clustering and a PSO algorithm was proposed in Ni, Pan, Du, Cao, and Zhai (2017) where a fuzzy clustering algorithm was used to form an initial cluster according to geographical location and CHs in hierarchical topology are selected using an improved PSO algorithm where the fitness function is designed by taking into account both the energy consumption and distance factor. This algorithm reduces the mortality rate of the nodes and prolongs the lifetime of the network.

16.3.2 Cluster-based routing protocol with mobile sink

In the protocols discussed thus far, the BS is static and the transmission distance between CHs and the BS is an important factor regarding the depletion of power. As SNs are scattered in a large area, for some nodes the transmission distance becomes very high and also energy consumption is directly proportional to the transmission distance, this the architecture leads to high energy consumption and a data delivery delay (Ayaz, Ammad-uddin, Baig, & Aggoune, 2018). The next improved architecture is where the base station is mobile. In this case, the BS itself collects data from all member nodes. However, in the case of a large network area, MS has to travel a long distance to collect data from each device.

Some devices have to wait for a long time to deliver their data which causes a buffer overflow problem and increases in latency in data delivery (Wen, Wang, Zha, & Zhang, 2019). Banerjee and Ghosh (2015) proposed an algorithm called Mobile Collector Path Planning, which is used for controlling the movement of MS in WSNs. This algorithm ensures that MS covers the whole network and data are collected before buffer overflow. As MS collects data using single hop communication, a significant amount of energy is saved. Furthermore, this algorithm implements the duty-cycling schema among the SNs to preserve the energy of the network. However, this algorithm does not address finding a decent location for the cluster center so that the traveling path of MS becomes optimal. Energy-Aware Sink Relocation (Wang, Shih, Pan, & Wu, 2014) protocol was proposed as an idea to dynamically adjust the movement of MS and control the communication range of nodes based on the remaining energy of each sensor node. This protocol helps to solve the hot-spot problem. However, these adjustments lead a huge overhead that results in higher energy consumption of the network. Addressing the above problem, Yuan and Zhang (2011) proposed an effective method combining clustering and sink technology by dividing the sensor field into some equal-sized sectors and for each sector the highest weight member was selected as CH. Cluster members discover the optimal routing path to minimize energy consumption by transmitting data to their CHs. CHs make an intercluster communication chain by using a greedy algorithm. Now each CH only sends its collected data to the CH that is nearest to the sink in relation to itself. Then, to reduce the load of the CHs, researchers introduced a rendezvous-based model. Wang, Gao, Liu, Sangaiah, and Kim (2019) proposed a fixed RP(s)-based WSN network where a MS node collects data from RPs periodically. It can elongate the coverage area and reduce the energy consumption by the SNs, but the random movement of MS causes an additional communication delay in the network. A weight-based rendezvous planning algorithm (WRP) is proposed in Salarian, Chin, and Naghdy (2014) where each sensor node has weight based on its hop distance from the sink and number of neighbors. The highest weighted nodes are declared as RP(s). It selects the best set of RPs in the WSN to elongate the network's lifetime by balancing energy consumption, and a TSP algorithm is used to find a path between the RPs. However, here the problem is that the nodes near the RP may absorb a huge amount of energy at the time of DT in a multihop manner. Another RP selection technique (BI-DFAMDT), inspired by the firefly algorithm, is proposed in Yogarajan and Revathi (2018). This finds the optimal tour length among RPs. By minimizing the tour length it reduces energy consumption and hence extends the network lifetime. A cluster-based RP selection algorithm is proposed by Anagha and Binu (2015), where a weight is assigned to each sensor node by calculating the hop distance from the sink to the neighbor nodes and the highest weighted node becomes an RP. The remaining SNs send their data to the corresponding CH. The CH nodes gather data and forward them to the nearest RPs. Almi'ani, Viglas, and Libman (2010) offer an algorithm to discover the optimal number of RPs using a binary search approach so that the MS only has to visit a minimum number of nodes, but this algorithm does not consider the optimal location.

16.3.2.1 Rendezvous point-based routing protocol

Let us suppose there are n number of SNs and q number of RPs, then there are n^q possible ways for selecting n SNs from q RPs. In a brute force approach, the time complexity of this selection process is exponential. Clearly, it is an NP-hard problem. Hence researchers are motivated to applying optimization algorithms to design an optimal WSN routing protocol. Different bio-inspired heuristic algorithms give optimal results in the case of RP selection. An ACO-based path determination algorithm for the MS is proposed in Praveen Kumar et al. (2018). ACO is used to choose an optimal set of RPs and determined a tour using all the RPs. An MS visits all the RPs through the tour and collects data from each RP. In addition, a dynamic strategy for reselection of RPs is proposed which balanced the energy consumption of SNs. Another optimization algorithm-based RP selection methodology is proposed in Anwit and Jana (2019), where the GA is used to find the appropriate location of RPs and an optimal path for an MS is obtained. Wang, Cao, Li, Kim, and Lee (2017) proposed a technique to build a cluster using the particle swarm optimization (PSO) technique. The algorithm uses a virtual clustering technique to create an efficient route for the MS. For the election of RPs, two factors, namely remaining energy of the nodes and the node position, are taken into consideration. Such a SOO algorithm chooses the most salient performance metrics as the optimization objectives. However, it is unreasonable in a real WSN application to forcefully exaggerate one of the metrics over the others. Thus MOO algorithms which satisfy multiple objectives simultaneously can be adopted to design the optimization routing algorithm. Kaswan et al. (2018) proposed a PSO-based multiobjective algorithm that finds an energy-efficient route for the MS. Pareto dominance in MOPSO is used to obtain both local and global finest solutions for each particle. The result illustrates that the proposed algorithm performs better than other algorithms in terms of various performance metrics. Sengupta, Das, Nasir, & Panigrahi (2013) formulated sensor node deployment tasks using the

MOO algorithm where the goal was to find an arrangement of deployed SNs leading to enhancement of the network lifetime, coverage of the maximum area, and minimization of the energy consumption and the number of deployed SNs. Martins, Carrano, Wanner, Takahashi, and Mateus (2011) proposed a multiobjective hybrid approach by considering coverage, network lifetime, and required running time to get the desired solution. However, to the best of our knowledge, the selection of RP based on the optimized result of the average distance between CH and RP and remaining residual energy was not taken into account. Since energy dissipation is affected by DT distance the node of minimum distance with respective CH and with maximum residual energy is appropriate as an RP. As this selection procedure is an NP-hard problem, we are inspired to construct a MOGA-based scheme to design the CH- and RP-based trajectory of the MS.

16.4 System model

16.4.1 Network model

Here, we consider n number of homogeneous, stationary SNs deployed randomly throughout the region of interest (RoI) and an MS node. We assume continuous monitoring of the sensing field and every sensor node participates in every round. The SNs are divided into a predefined number of clusters and the clustering is fixed through all over the network lifetime shown in Fig. 16.1. Each sensor node has DP capabilities and a certain amount of energy that decreases due to data aggregation, transmission, and reception. We use the time division multiple access schedule for intracluster transmission and the carrier sense multiple access schedule for intercluster communication. Every cluster consists of a leader node known as CH. CH(s) collect data from their member nodes, aggregate the data and then transmit them to the nearest RP node. MS collects data from all the RP nodes. The notations and descriptions used in this chapter are depicted in Table 16.1.

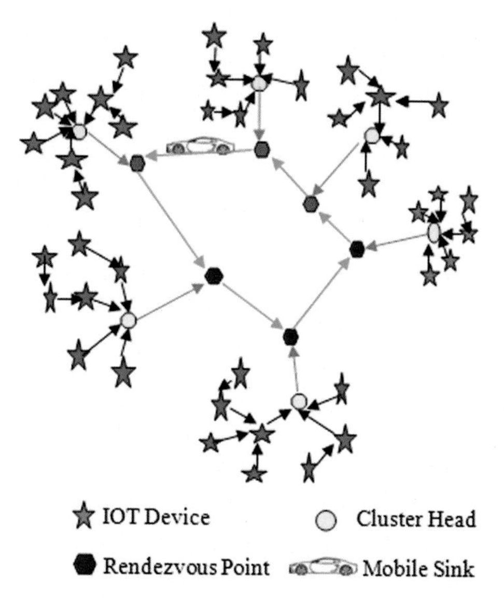

FIGURE 16.1 Network Model.

TABLE 16.1 List of notations.

Notation	Description
n	Number of sensor nodes
q	Number of rendezvous point
l	Length of each data packet in bits
d_0	Threshold distance
ε_{fs}	Amplification coefficient for free space
ε_{mp}	Amplification coefficient for multipath
E_{Tx}	Transmission energy
E_{Rx}	Receiving energy
N_{ij}	i-th node assigned to j-th cluster head
k	Number of cluster
$MaxAvgDis$	Maximum average distance between CH and member nodes
RP_i	i-th RP point
To_Res_En	Total residual energy of RP nodes
E_i	Residual energy of node i
E_0	Initial energy of node
EDA	Energy consumption for data aggregation
α	Constant
$d(CH_i, RP_j)$	Distance between i-th CH and j-th RP points
RE_{RP_j}	Residual energy of j-th RP node
Pkt_{drop}	Packet drop probability
$dist$	Distance between sender node and receiver node
H_0	Null hypothesis for E-TBD
H'_0	Null hypothesis for CBRP
H_1	Alternative hypothesis for E-TBD
H'_1	Alternative hypothesis for CBRP
t	Statistical test value
D_{avg}	Mean of sample value
S_d	Standard deviation of sample value
m	Number of sample for statistical test
NoA	Number of alive node
N_j	Number of RP nodes $\in$ j-th cluster

TABLE 16.2 Surveys relating to existing technique of clustering and RP selection algorithm.

Authors	Cluster based	RP-based model	Base station		Nature of algorithm
			Static	Mobile	
Matthew Ettus	No	No	Yes		Heuristic
Heinzelman et al. (2002)	Yes	No	Yes		Heuristic
Hoang et al. (2010)	Yes	No	Yes		Heuristic
Muruganathan et al. (2005)	Yes	No	Yes		Heuristic
Younis and Fahmy (2004)	Yes	No	Yes		Heuristic
Yu, Feng, Jia, Gu, and Yu (2014)	Yes	No	Yes		Heuristic
Banerjee and Ghosh (2015)	Yes	No		Yes	Heuristic
Wang et al. (2014)	Yes	No		Yes	Heuristic
Yuan and Zhang (2011)	Yes	No		Yes	Heuristic
Wang et al. (2019)	No	Yes		Yes	Heuristic
Salarian et al. (2014)	No	Yes		Yes	Heuristic
Anagha and Binu (2015)	Yes	Yes		Yes	Heuristic
Yogarajan and Revathi (2018)	No	Yes		Yes	SOO
Praveen Kumar et al. (2018)	Yes	Yes		Yes	SOO
Anwit and Jana (2019)	Yes	Yes		Yes	SOO
Wang et al. (2017)	Yes	Yes		Yes	SOO
Kaswan et al. (2018)	Yes	Yes		Yes	MOO
Martins et al. (2011)	Yes	Yes		Yes	MOO

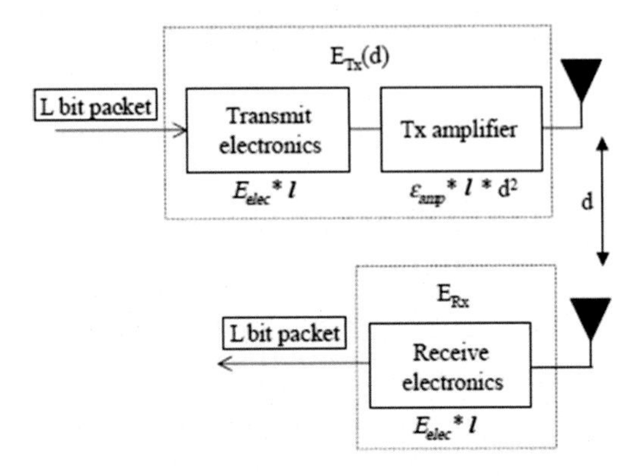

FIGURE 16.2 First-order radio energy model.

In this work, we employ the k-means clustering technique to form the clusters by grouping all the SNs, and it remains fixed until all nodes die. Within each cluster, CH(s) are selected depending on the average residual energy. Finally, a routing path is formed for the MS. An energy consumption model to account for the energy consumption is discussed below (Fig. 16.2).

16.4.2 Energy model

We consider a first-order radio model (Fig. 16.2) to account for the energy consumption. Energy exhaustion depends mainly on two parts: energy consumption due to DT and data reception. DT has two parts: signal generation and an increase in the strength of the signal. The amplifier utilizes two distinct powers to enhance the signal based on the transmission distance. That is why we have two separate energy models for DT: one is a free space model, which is for short-distance communication, the other one is a multipath fading model, which is for long-distance communication. The following equation shows the energy depletion due to transmission of l bit data packet over distance d. Based on transmission distance d, the free space model is implemented when d is lower than the threshold distance (d_0) otherwise the multipath fading (mp) model is used (Kaswan et al., 2018).

$$E_{Tx}(l,d) = \begin{cases} E_{elec} \times l + \varepsilon_{fs} \times l \times d^2 & d \leq d_0 \\ E_{elec} \times l + \varepsilon_{mp} \times l \times d^4 & d > d_0 \end{cases} \quad (16.1)$$

where E_{Tx} is the l bits data packet transmission energy. E_{elec} indicates the power consumption to run the transmitter. ε_{fs} and ε_{mp} are amplification coefficients of the free space model and the multipath fading model, respectively. d_0 represents the threshold value and can be calculated using:

$$d_0 = \sqrt{\frac{\varepsilon_{fs}}{\varepsilon_{mp}}}$$

Energy dissipation for receiving the l-bit data packet is given by,

$$E_{Rx}(l) = E_{Rx-elec} \times l = E_{elec} \times l \quad (16.2)$$

16.5 General structure of a genetic algorithm

The GA is an adaptive heuristic search algorithm that is an evolutionary algorithm. It is based on the idea of Charles Darwin's theory of natural evolution. This algorithm is often used to discover the optimal or near-optimal solution of optimization and search problems by depending on biologically inspired operators such as selection, crossover, mutation, etc. in the machine learning and research domain. Although this algorithm is randomized in nature, its execution is preferred to random local search (in which we find out different random solutions, and choose the best one), as it employ historical information also.

A GA consists of five phases: initial population, fitness function, selection, crossover, and mutation.

16.5.1 Encoding

Choosing the most suitable type of encoding schema is very important. Different types of encoding schema exist, such as binary encoding, decimal encoding, octal encoding, tree encoding, permutation encoding, etc. Depending on the types of problem, the encoding schema is selected.

16.5.2 Initial population

The algorithm begins by defining the population, which contains individuals, each with its own set of chromosomes. A solution to our problem is represented by each individual. An individual is formed by a set of parameters called genes. An array of genes forms a chromosome.

16.5.3 Fitness function

The fitness of each individual is defined by the fitness function. The ability of an individual to reproduce offspring is determined by the fitness score which is assigned by the fitness function. Individuals with better fitness scores have a higher chance of selection for the next phases.

16.5.4 Selection

This phase selects two pairs of individuals (parents) with high fitness scores, who can mate and produce offspring. Tournament selection, elitism selection, roulette wheel selection, and steady-state selection are popular selection operators.

16.5.5 Crossover

In biological science, the crossover is merely reproduction, and represents mating between two individuals. After the selection of two individuals, crossover points are chosen randomly. Then, the genes at these crossover points are exchanged and generate completely new individuals (offspring).

16.5.6 Mutation

The idea of this phase is to modify or insert random genes in newly generated individuals to support the diversity in the population.

The algorithm will continue until the population is converged, which means that the parents will not produce offspring which are notably different from the former generation, and then the algorithm will be terminated.

16.6 Proposed method

Here, we explain our proposed routing algorithm that can extend the lifetime of a WSN-assisted IoT network. The algorithm is centralized in nature and is executed in a central location. The first step in our algorithm is to form a predefined number of clusters by grouping the randomly distributed SNs over the RoI using k-means clustering methodology (Mondal, Ghosh, & Biswas, 2016). The clustering infrastructure remains the same throughout the network lifespan. After cluster formation, the next step is to select a CH of each cluster by observing the residual energy of all the member nodes. CH(s) collect data from their member nodes and aggregate the data. To reduce the long edge between the CH nodes and BS, some nodes are considered as RP(s) to accumulate data from the CH nodes. RP(s) are selected using MOGA (Nayak, Kavitha, & Khan, 2019). Among the RPs, a TSP like a tour is formed through which MS collects data from RPs. A flowchart of the proposed algorithm is given in Fig. 16.3. All the procedures are described in detail below.

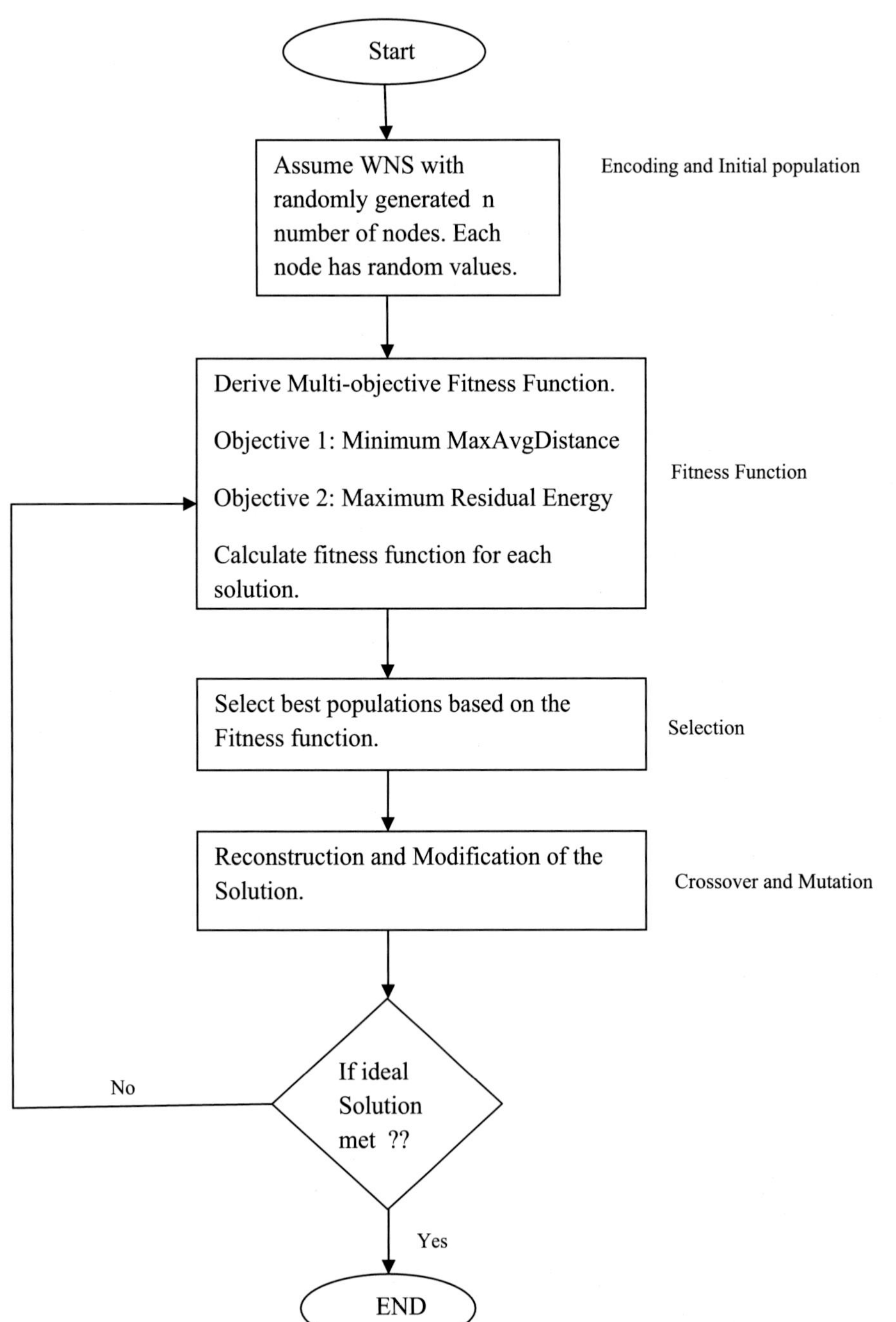

FIGURE 16.3 Flowchart of the proposed architecture.

16.6.1 Cluster head selection

We consider here n number of SNs $S = \{s_1, s_2, \ldots, s_n\}$ that are distributed randomly over the RoI. SNs are organized into K number of clusters. A set of CHs is defined by $CH = \{CH_1, CH_2, \ldots, CH_K\}$. Allocation of SNs to the particular cluster can be represented as N_{ij}, where

$$N_{ij} = \begin{cases} 1 & \text{if } i^{th} \text{ node assigned to } j^{th} \text{ CH} \\ 0 & \text{otherwise} \end{cases} \tag{16.3}$$

In this proposed method the CH is responsible for accumulating data from the member nodes, aggregating the data, and transmitting the whole data to the nearest RP. A node with maximum residual energy within the cluster is elected as the CH for that respective round. In each round the residual energy of SNs is updated and using the updated residual energy the CH for the next round is selected.

16.6.2 Rendezvous point selection

To reduce the energy dissipation by eliminating the concept of direct communication from CH to the BS, RP is introduced. A member node should be selected as the RP node if it satisfies two important factors, namely high residual energy and minimum distance from the CH. Firstly, like CH, an RP node consumes more energy compared to a common node, thus a node with higher residual energy is more suitable to be selected as RP. Secondly, the RP nodes receive data from CH nodes. Therefore the selection of RP node depends on the distance from the CH to RP. Since the communication distance between RP and CH is to be minimized, the RP selection procedure can be expressed as follows.

A set of rendezvous points (RPs) is defined as $RP = RP_1, RP_2, \ldots, RP_q$. By the selection of RP, our target is to reduce the overall energy consumption, resulting in the lifetime of the network being enhanced. It can be noted that the energy depletion is directly proportional to the transmission distance and hence an important parameter for the selection of RPs. For efficient RP selection, the following two factors are taken into consideration.

Maximum average distance between RP node and CH node: SNs are divided into K clusters.

The maximum average distance between the CH node and the corresponding member nodes can be defined as follows:

$$\text{MaxAvgDis} = \max_{j=1,2,\ldots,K} \left\{ \sum_{i=1}^{q} \frac{d(RP_i, CH_j) \times N_{ij}}{N_j} \right.$$

where, RP_i denotes i-th RP nodes, CH_j is the j-th cluster and N_j represents the number of RP nodes belong to the j-th cluster. $d(RP_i, CH_j)$ represents the Euclidean distance between the i-th RP and the j-th cluster.

Total residual energy of RPs:

$$To\_Res\_En = \sum_{j=1}^{q} (RE_{RPj}).$$

$$f_2 = \frac{1}{To\_Res\_En}$$

where q is the number of RP nodes, $RERP_j$ is the residual energy of the j-th RP. RPs are selected from all member nodes excluding CH nodes. *To_Res_En* represents the sum of residual energy of all RP nodes, that is, we need to minimize its reciprocal. Therefore we can formulate an optimization problem using the above two factors which can be expressed mathematically as

$$F = \alpha f1 + (1 - \alpha) f2 \quad (16.4)$$

A node with higher remaining energy and closer to the CH node is more likely to be selected as RP node. That means a lower value of F indicates a smaller transmission distance and higher residual energy. This problem is commonly known as an NP-hard problem. To optimize the objective function in this chapter, the MOGA is used. A flowchart of the MOGA algorithm is presented in Fig. 16.4.

An illustration: In our implementation we have considered 100 homogeneous SNs in a WSN area of size 100 × 100 m^2, deployed randomly throughout the network area. Using the K-means clustering algorithm we have formed 10 clusters by considering 100 nodes and throughout the duration of the network's lifetime the number of clusters and the infrastructure of the clusters will remain the same. The K-means clustering algorithm is an iterative algorithm that makes a predefined number

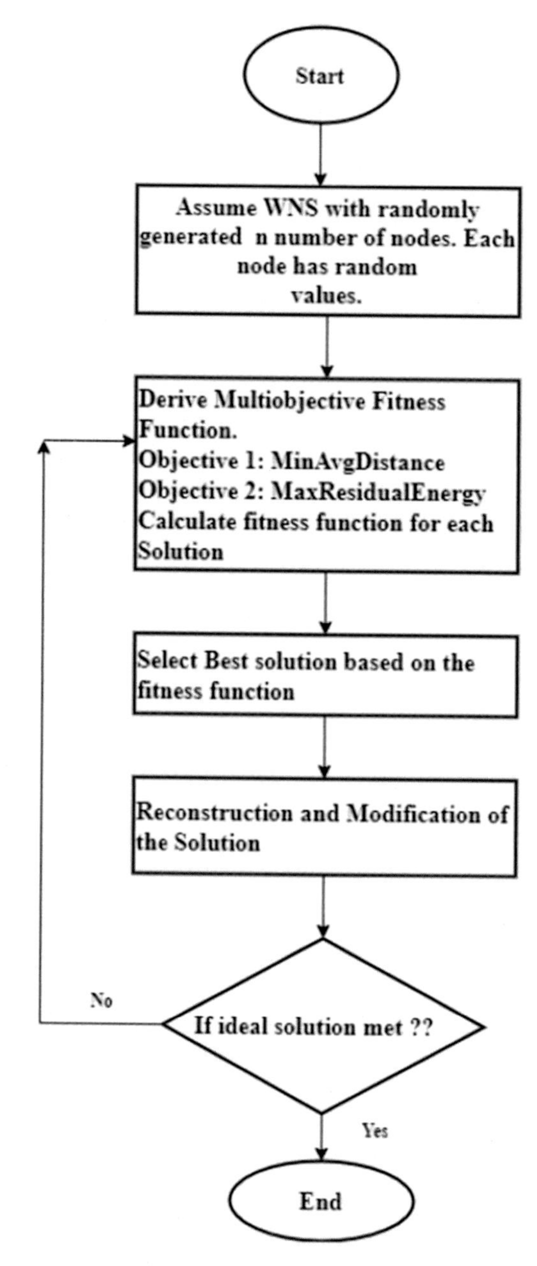

FIGURE 16.4 Flowchart of MOGA.

of nonoverlapping and almost similar partitions. It arranges data points for each cluster in such a way that the sum of the squared Euclidean distance between the data points and cluster's centroid is at the minimum. Next, in each cluster, the node with the highest residual energy is selected as the CH. The CH selection procedure is described in Section 16.6.1. After selecting the CH, our next step is RP selection using MOGA among all the nodes excluding the CHs. In our proposed algorithm the number of RPs is equal to the number of CHs (or the number of clusters). Hence in our implementation we have chosen 10 RP nodes. Our MOGA implementation for RP selection represents a chromosome by a string of genes and each gene represents an RP. Our goal is to prolong the network lifetime by minimizing energy depletion and this is done by selecting optimal RP nodes. To get the optimal RP nodes we design a fitness function using the MOO algorithm where we consider two objective functions, which are minimum average distance and maximum residual energy, as described in Section 16.6.2. The initial population is again enriched by the selection process. Each chromosome has a fitness value and chromosomes with lower fitness values have a higher chance of selection for further processing. Only the selected chromosomes participate in the crossover and mutation operations to generate new offspring. Here, two chromosomes *parent1* and *parent2* are randomly chosen to take participate in the crossover process. There are different types of crossover operations such as single-point crossover and multipoint crossover. In this case, we choose the single-point crossover for the sake of simplicity. A random position of the chromosome (here fourth position) is taken as a crossover point and generates new offspring (*child 1* and *child 2*). Next to apply the mutation process, we select two random positions (second and sixth). The values of these two positions are replaced by two randomly selected values in such a way that the same RP does not recur in an individual and does not hamper the acceptability of the individual. This reconstruction and modification process continue until we arrive at the ideal solution (as described in Fig. 16.4).

16.6.3 Tour formation for the mobile sink

A TSP like a tour is formed among all RPs using the MOGA. Once data are collected by the RP nodes from the nearest CH node the MS traverses through the path to collect data from the RPs.

After completion of each round of data collection our algorithm calculates and updates the remaining energy of the network. Depending on the updated energy, in each round a new CH is selected in each cluster and data collection and transmission are continued until the network dies out.

16.7 Simulation environment and results analysis

The proposed method is simulated by conducting a series of experiments using the MATLAB platform. The various parameters used in the GA and for other simulations are given in Tables 16.3 and 16.4, respectively. In this simulation, we have considered that the IoT devices are distributed randomly over the ROI $100 \times 100\ m^2$. To prove the scalability of our proposed algorithm, we varied the number of nodes from 100 to 300. Simulation results depicted in this part are to measure the performance of the proposed technique compared to state-of-the art E- TBD (Wen et al., 2019) and CBRP (Anagha & Binu, 2015). Experimental results are taken by aggregating multiple runs with various random deployment strategies. To measure the network lifetime we enumerated three metrics, namely the first node dies (FND), half of the nodes die (HND), and the last node dies (LND) (Fig. 16.5).

We inspect the performance of our proposed algorithm from various perspectives as described below.

16.7.1 Number of alive nodes

Our simulation is started with 100 SNs until all the SNs have died out. Fig. 16.6 illustrates that our proposed technique acts better in terms of all metrics,

TABLE 16.3 Genetic algorithm parameters.

Parameter	Value
Length of population	60
Dimension (dim)	$0.2 \times$ population size
Number of iterations	40
Crossover rate	$0.5 \times$ dim
Mutation rate	$0.5 \times$ dim

TABLE 16.4 Simulation parameters.

Parameter	Value
Node deployment	Random
Simulation area	100×100 m
Initial energy of node	0.05 J
Packet size	2000 bits
Antenna type	Omnidirectional
Eelec (in nano Joules/bit)	50
εfs (in pico Joules/bit/m^2)	10
εmp (in pico Joules/bit/m^2)	0.0013
EDA (in pico Joules/bit/signal)	5

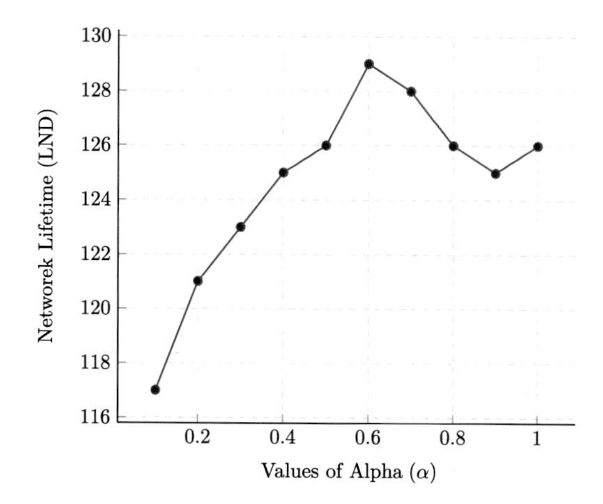

FIGURE 16.5 Network lifetime for different values of alpha (α).

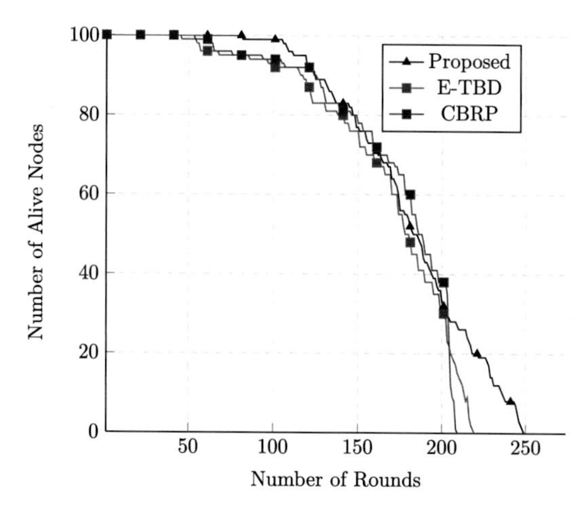

FIGURE 16.6 Number of rounds versus number of alive nodes.

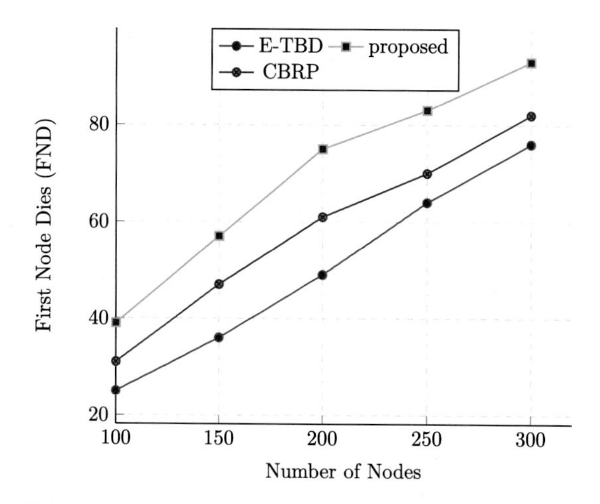

FIGURE 16.7 FND with varying number of nodes. *FND*, first node dies.

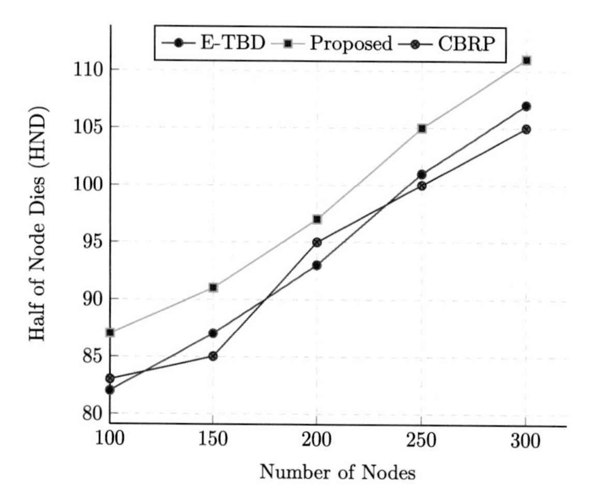

FIGURE 16.8 HND with varying number of nodes. *HND*, half of the nodes die.

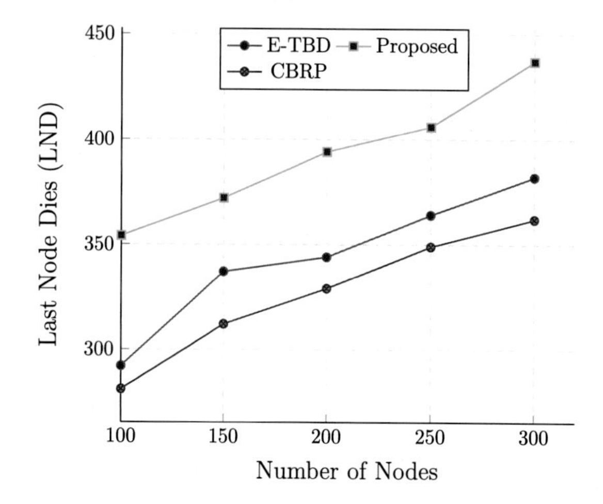

FIGURE 16.9 LND with varying number of nodes. *LND*, the last node dies.

namely FND, HND, and LND. This achievement is expected due to the proper selection of RPs. The efficient selection of RP points reduces the extra load of CH nodes, and also reduces the long-edge distance among the CHs and sink. The selection of RP is dependent on α [refer to Eq. (16.4)]. Therefore to set a proper value of α is very important. To choose the appropriate value of α we execute the proposed algorithm for different values of α varying from 0.1 to 1. Fig. 16.5 shows the network lifetime for different values of α. It can be noticed from this figure that, for the value $\alpha = 0.6$, the algorithm gives the maximum network lifetime. Therefore in this work we set $\alpha = 0.6$. Fig. 16.7 shows a comparison of FND by varying the number of nodes. Now we can conclude from the figure that FND increases according to the number of node increases but the performance of the proposed technique is better compared with E-TBD and CBRP. Figs. 16.8 and 16.9 present the performance of HND and LND, respectively, with varying numbers of nodes. We can draw a conclusion from the figures that like FND, HND and LND also follow the same trend while varying the number of nodes but the HNDs of both techniques are quite close compared to FND and LND.

16.7.2 Cumulative energy consumption

The network lifetime can be expanded by reducing energy depletion by SNs. Thus energy consumption over the round can be taken into consideration as a parameter to measure the network lifetime. Fig. 16.10 shows the cumulative energy consumption in rounds. We observe from this figure that the proposed algorithm outperforms E-TBD and CBRP. Energy consumed by the proposed technique is reduced due to efficient CH and RP node selection.

16.7.3 Cumulative data packet received at base station

The performance of the proposed technique can also be measured by the total number of data packet transmissions over a period of time. The number of data packet transmissions over the round is depicted in Fig. 16.11. We observe from this figure that the proposed algorithm gives better results compare with both E-TBD and CBRP.

16.7.4 Changing the base station location

In the proposed method, SNs transmit the collected data to the CH. Once the CH has received data from all of its member nodes, it aggregates the data and transmits them to the RP node and finally, the data are transmitted to the BS. Therefore the BS plays an important role in increasing the network lifetime. Since the energy consumption is directly proportional to the transmission distance, if the transmission distance is decreased, the network lifetime increases. Table 16.5 shows the impact of BS location on the network lifetime. It can be observed that, for all cases, as the BS moves toward the outside of the deployment region, the network lifetime decreases. This is because displacement of the BS toward the outside of the deployment region increases the transmission distance. It can also be observed from the table that for all cases both algorithms follow the same trend but the proposed algorithm performs better in each case. When the BS is located at the center of the deployment region, both algorithms give the maximum network lifetime. This is because, if the BS is in the center position, the transmission distance is at its minimum and hence network lifetime is increased.

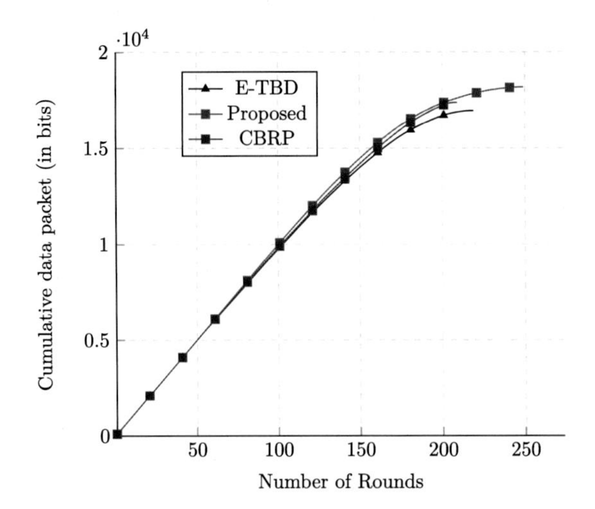

FIGURE 16.11 Cumulative data packets transmission to the BS.

TABLE 16.5 Network lifetime with varying BS positions.

Metric	Protocol	Base station positions				
		Center	(100,100)	(200,200)	(300,300)	(400,400)
FND	Proposed	41	35	29	13	9
	E-TBD	20	11	7	5	3
	CBRP	25	19	12	9	6
HND	Proposed	87	75	69	58	46
	E-TBD	82	69	52	39	23
	CBRP	84	64	55	41	21
LND	Proposed	350	321	287	236	211
	E-TBD	290	165	123	78	35
	CBRP	278	156	119	67	34

FND, First node dies; *HND*, half of the nodes die; *LND*, last node dies.

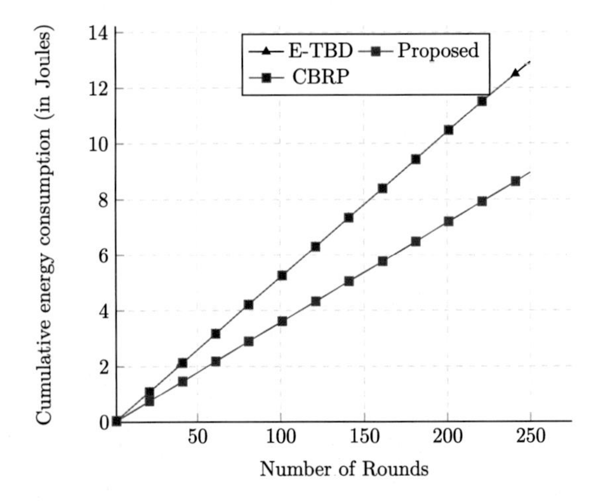

FIGURE 16.10 Cumulative energy consumptions.

16.7.5 Packet drop ratio and packet delay

In WSNs, DT packets are dropped for various reasons including noise, interference, and attenuation, with all

TABLE 16.6 Results for packet drop ratio and packet delay.

Protocol	Number of nodes				
	100	150	200	250	300
Packet drop ratio (%)					
E-TBD	2.43	2.98	3.02	3.24	3.56
CBRP	1.89	1.97	2.10	2.32	2.43
Proposed	0.78	0.89	0.93	1.01	1.23
Packet delay					
E-TBD	6.85	9.56	12.79	15.36	19.54
CBRP	5.92	8.51	10.17	12.07	13.56
Proposed	5.23	7.25	9.15	10.75	12.52

the reasons being very common in the WSN environment. Hence it is a salient property to measure the performance of the algorithm. In this chapter, we calculate the packet drop ratio (PDR) by following the uniform random distribution model proposed by Ahmad, Javaid, Khan, Qasim, and Alghamdi (2014). The distribution model can be derived as follows:

$$Pkt_{drop} = \begin{cases} 0 & 0 \le dist < 30 \quad (16.5a) \\ \frac{1}{70} \times (dist - 30) & (30 \le dist \le 100) \quad (16.5b) \\ 1 & (dist > 100) \quad (16.5c) \end{cases}$$

It is noted that the packet drop probability Pkt_{drop} is dependent on the transmission distance. From Eqs. (16.5a) and (16.5c) it can also be observed that when the transmission distance is less than 100 meters the packet drop probability is 0, whereas for a transmission distance greater than 100 meters it is 1. On the other hand, for the intermediate distance the probability is calculated based on Eq. (16.5b). Table 16.6 shows the PDR and packet delay (PD) for CBRP, E-TBD, and the proposed algorithm. It can be observed from the table that as the number of nodes increases, both PDR and PD increase for both algorithms. However, the proposed algorithm outperforms both as the CH and RPs are selected based on the average distance from the CH and member nodes and the average distance from the CH to RPs. With these important parameters, efficient selection of CH and RPs reduces the long-edge distances, thus refining the PDR and PD.

16.8 Statistical analysis

To draw a statistical inference between the existing and proposed algorithm, a pairwise t test is done. For this test, the number of alive nodes (NoA) is calculated

TABLE 16.7 Results of paired t-test.

Paired t-test	t value	P value	95% Confidence interval	
			Lower	Upper
E-TBD with proposed	16.56	$<10^{-5}$	5.77	7.32
CBRP with proposed	11.92	$<10^{-5}$	3.59	6.34

after each round for both algorithms and a pair (known as the observation pair) is formed for each round. Let $X = \{(x_1, y_1), (x_2, y_2), \ldots, (x_n, y_m)\}$ be a set of n observation pairs, where x_i and y_i denote the NoA for round i of E-TBD and the proposed algorithm, respectively. Thus the pair (x_i, y_i) forms a bivariate normal population which is correlated and can be called for a paired t-test (Sharma, 2010). The null hypothesis and alternative hypothesis are described below:

Null hypothesis (H_0): $NoA_{Proposed} = NoA_{E-TBD}$

Null Hypothesis (H'_0): $NoA_{Proposed} = NoA_{CBRP}$

Alternative Hypothesis (H_1): $NoA_{Proposed} > NoA_{E-TBD}$

Alternative Hypothesis (H'_1): $NoA_{Proposed} > NoA_{CBRP}$

Test statistic for $m - 1$ degrees of freedom t can be defined as

$$t = \frac{D_{avg}}{S_d/\sqrt{m-1}} \quad (16.6)$$

where D_{avg} denotes mean and S_d represents the standard deviation for the difference of NoA for the equal length correlated large sample. Here m represents the sample size. Then, for the 95% confidence interval

$$D_{avg} \pm t_{0.005} \times \left(S_d/\sqrt{m-1}\right) \quad (16.7)$$

where $t_{0.005}$ is the 5% t-distribution with $m - 1$ degrees of freedom. Table 16.7 shows the paired t-test results. It can be noted from this table that, for each case, p is less than 0.05, which indicates that the null hypotheses, that is, H_0 and H'_0 are rejected at a 5% significance level and consequently the alternative hypotheses $H1$ and H'_1 are accepted at a 95% significance level. All the upper and lower limits of the 95% confidence interval are also given in Table 16.7. Hence it can be inferred convincingly that our proposed method surpasses CBRP and E-TBD.

16.9 Conclusions and future work

Productive energy utilization is an important issue in the WSN-assisted IoT network. To enhance energy efficiency and network lifetime, in this chapter we propose an energy-efficient routing protocol for data collection which can be used for large-scale IoT networks. Efficient CH selection improves the network lifetime by reducing energy consumption. Furthermore, we introduce RP to reduce the long-edge distance. The RP is selected based on MOGA, which is a natural bio-inspired algorithm that gives optimal or near-optimal solutions when the search space is huge. This can lead to a prolonged network lifetime by minimizing energy consumption. An optimal path defined by the MOGA reduces the traveling distance of MS and data latency delay that helps to improve the utilization of energy and extend the network lifetime. Simulation results indicate that the proposed technique performs better than the existing technique in terms of energy efficiency and network lifetime. However, in this chapter, we consider a WSN with homogeneous SNs and a single MS. In future, we plan to develop a new algorithm for a heterogeneous network with multiple MSs. This work could be improved by analyzing other clustering architectures so that we can obtain better result in terms of energy conservation.

References

Abdulai, J.-D., Adu-Manu, K. S., Banaseka, F. K., Katsriku, F. A., & Engmann, F. (2018). Prolonging the lifetime of wireless sensor networks: A review of current techniques. *Wireless Communications and Mobile Computing*, *23*, 2018.

Ahmad, A., Javaid, N., Khan, Z. A., Qasim, U., & Alghamdi, T. A. (2014). $(ach)^2$: Routing scheme to maximize lifetime and throughput of wireless sensor networks. *IEEE Sensors Journal*, *14*(10), 3516–3532.

Almi'ani, K., Viglas, A., & Libman, L. (2010). Energy-efficient data gathering with tour length-constrained mobile elements in wireless sensor networks. In *Proceedings of the 2010 IEEE 35th conference on local computer networks*, LCN '10 (pp. 582–589). USA: IEEE Computer Society.

Anagha, K., & Binu, G. S. (2015). Rendezvous point based energy efficient data collection method for wireless sensor network. In *2015 International conference on control communication computing India (ICCC)*, (pp. 705–709).

Anwit, R., & Jana, P. (2019). An approximation algorithm to find optimal rendezvous points in wireless sensor networks. In *ICANI-2018* (pp. 193–204).

Ayaz, M., Ammad-uddin, M., Baig, I., & Aggoune, eM. (2018). Wireless sensor's civil applications, prototypes, and future integration possibilities: A review. *IEEE Sensors Journal*, *18*(1), 4–30.

Banerjee, I., & Ghosh, N. (2015). An energy-efficient path determination strategy for mobile data collectors in wireless sensor network. *Computers & Electrical Engineering*, *48*, 417–435.

Dahnil, D. P., Singh, Y. P., & Ho, C. K. (2012). Topology-controlled adaptive clustering for uniformity and increased lifetime in wireless sensor networks. *IET Wireless Sensor Systems*, *2*(4), 318–327.

Deb, K., Pratap, A., Agarwal, S., & Meyarivan, T. (2002). A fast and elitist multiobjective genetic algorithm: Nsga-II. *IEEE Transactions on Evolutionary Computation*, *6*(2), 182–197.

Ettus, M. (1998). System capacity, latency, and power consumption in multihop- routed ss-cdma wireless networks. In *Proceedings RAWCON 98. 1998 IEEE radio and wireless conference (Cat. No.98EX194)* (pp. 55–58).

Heinzelman, W. B., Chandrakasan, A. P., & Balakrishnan, H. (2002). An application- specific protocol architecture for wireless microsensor networks. *IEEE Transactions on Wireless Communications*, *1*(4), 660–670.

Hoang, D. C., Kumar, R., & Panda, S. K. (2010). Fuzzy c-means clustering protocol for wireless sensor networks.

Kaswan, A., Singh, V., & Jana, P. (2018). A multi-objective and pso based energy efficient path design for mobile sink in wireless sensor networks. *Pervasive and Mobile Computing*, *46*, 02.

Lee, J.-S., & Kao, T.-Y. (2016). An improved three-layer low-energy adaptive clustering hierarchy for wireless sensor networks. *IEEE Internet of Things Journal*, *3*, 951–958.

Li, H., & Zhang, Q. (2009). Multiobjective optimization problems with complicated pareto sets, MOEA/D and NSGA-II. *IEEE Transactions on Evolutionary Computation*, *13*(2), 284–302.

Li, K., Deb, K., & Yao, X. (2018). R-metric: Evaluating the performance of preference- based evolutionary multiobjective optimization using reference points. *IEEE Transactions on Evolutionary Computation*, *22*(6), 821–835.

Martins, F. V. C., Carrano, E. G., Wanner, E. F., Takahashi, R. H. C., & Mateus, G. R. (2011). A hybrid multiobjective evolutionary approach for improving the performance of wireless sensor networks. *IEEE Sensors Journal*, *11*(3), 545–554.

Mondal, S., Ghosh, S., & Biswas, U. (2016). ACOHC: Ant colony optimization based hierarchical clustering in wireless sensor network. In *2016 International conference on emerging technological trends (ICETT)* (pp. 1–7).

Muruganathan, S. D., Ma, D. C. F., Bhasin, R. I., & Fapojuwo, A. O. (2005). A centralized energy-efficient routing protocol for wireless sensor networks. *IEEE Communications Magazine*, *43*(3), S8–S13.

Nayak, P., Kavitha, K., & Khan, N. (2019). Cluster head selection in wireless sensor network using bio-inspired algorithm. In *TENCON 2019–2019 IEEE region 10 conference (TENCON)* (pp. 1690–1696).

Ni, Q., Pan, Q., Du, H., Cao, C., & Zhai, Y. (2017). A novel cluster head selection algorithm based on fuzzy clustering and particle swarm optimization. *IEEE/ACM Transactions on Computational Biology and Bioinformatics*, *14*(1), 76–84.

Praveen Kumar, D., Amgoth, T., & Annavarapu, C. S. R. (2018). Aco-based mobile sink path determination for wireless sensor networks under non-uniform data constraints. *Applied Soft Computing*, *69*, 528–540.

Salarian, H., Chin, K.-W., & Naghdy, F. (2014). An energy-efficient mobile-sink path selection strategy for wireless sensor networks. *Vehicular Technology, IEEE Transactions on*, *63*, 2407–2419, 06.

Sengupta, S., Das, S., Nasir, M. D., & Panigrahi, B. K. (2013). Multi-objective node deployment in wsns: In search of an optimal trade-off among coverage, lifetime, energy consumption, and connectivity. *Engineering Applications of Artificial Intelligence*, *26*(1), 405–416.

Sharma, J. K. (2010). *Fundamentals of business statistics* (2nd ed.). Dorling Kindersley.

Wang, C., Shih, J., Pan, B., & Wu, T. (2014). A network lifetime enhancement method for sink relocation and its analysis in wireless sensor networks. *IEEE Sensors Journal*, *14*(6), 1932–1943.

Wang, J., Cao, Y., Li, B., Kim, Hj, & Lee, S. (2017). Particle swarm optimization based clustering algorithm with mobile sink for wsns. *Future Generation Computer Systems*, *76*, 452–457.

Wang, J., Gao, Y., Liu, W., Sangaiah, A. K., & Kim, H. J. (2019). Energy efficient routing algorithm with mobile sink support for wireless sensor networks. *Sensors (Basel)*, *19*(7), 1494.

Wang, Z., Qin, X., & Liu, B. (2018). An energy-efficient clustering routing algorithm for wsn-assisted IoT (pp. 1–6).

Wen, H., Wang, T., Zha, D., & Zhang, B. (2019). *An energy-efficient distributed routing protocol for wireless sensor networks with mobile sinks. Ad Hoc Networks* (pp. 83–92). Springer International Publishing.

Ye, M., Li, C., Chen, G., & Wu, J. (2005). EECS: An energy efficient clustering scheme in wireless sensor networks. In *PCCC 2005.*

24th IEEE international performance, computing, and communications conference, 2005 (pp. 535–540).

Yetgin, H., Cheung, K. T. K., El-Hajjar, M., & Hanzo, L. H. (2017). A survey of network lifetime maximization techniques in wireless sensor networks. *IEEE Communications Surveys Tutorials, 19*(2), 828–854.

Yogarajan, G., & Revathi, T. (2018). Nature inspired discrete firefly algorithm for optimal mobile data gathering in wireless sensor networks. *Wireless Network, 24*, 2993–30007.

Younis, O., & Fahmy, S. (2004). Heed: A hybrid, energy-efficient, distributed clustering approach for ad hoc sensor networks. *IEEE Transactions on Mobile Computing, 3*(4), 366–379.

Yu, J., Feng, L., Jia, L., Gu, X., & Yu, D. (2014). A local energy consumption prediction-based clustering protocol for wireless sensor networks. *Sensors (Basel, Switzerland), 14*, 23017–23040, 12.

Yuan, X., & Zhang, R. (2011). An energy-efficient mobile sink routing algorithm for wireless sensor networks. In *2011 7th international conference on wireless communications, networking and mobile computing* (pp. 1–4).

Zhu, X., Shen, L., & Yum, T. P. (2009). Hausdorff clustering and minimum energy routing for wireless sensor networks. *IEEE Transactions on Vehicular Technology, 58*(2), 990–997.

Zitzler, E., & Thiele, L. (1999). Multiobjective evolutionary algorithms: a comparative case study and the strength pareto approach. *IEEE Transactions on Evolutionary Computation, 3*(4), 257–271.

CHAPTER

17

An integration of handcrafted features for violent event detection in videos

B.H. Lohithashva[1], V.N. Manjunath Aradhya[1] and D.S. Guru[2]

[1]Department of Computer Applications, JSS Science and Technology University, Mysuru, India [2]Department of Studies in Computer Science, University of Mysore, Mysuru, India

17.1 Introduction

Nowadays, we see plenty of surveillance cameras installed throughout private and public places. The reason behind this is the safety of humans and also the availability of the hardware equipment at reasonable prices. With the prior knowledge that visual information is generally accessible in surveillance systems, we focus on strategies using vision information (Lohithashva, Aradhya, Basavaraju, & Harish, 2019). An automatic surveillance system reduces the risk of security persons to prolonged videos. Local and global events are two different kinds of abnormal events. Local abnormal events that mainly focus on the region of interest are detected using low-level features in video, and global abnormal events extract entire information of the frame in the video. Spatiotemporal Interest Points (STIP) (Deniz, Serrano, Bueno, & Kim, 2014) are identified in the frames based on the extracted low-level features to depict human actions in a video. Conversely, it is possible to use global feature descriptors to extract motion features to detect abnormal activity (Hanson, Pnvr, Krishnagopal, & Davis, 2018). Recently, many researchers have published survey papers to detect violent events (Aradhya, Basavaraju, & Guru, 2019; Mabrouk & Zagrouba, 2018; Yu et al., 2020). The existing methods based on the segmentation (Imran, Raman, & Rajput, 2020), Optical Flow (OF) (Mabrouk & Zagrouba, 2017), subspace techniques (Amith & Aradhya, 2017; Krishna, Aradhya, Ravishankar, & Babu, 2012), STIP (Deniz et al., 2014; Mabrouk & Zagrouba, 2017), textures (Lloyd, Rosin, Marshall, & Moore, 2017; Lohithashva, Aradhya, & Guru, 2021), trajectories (Lamba & Nain, 2019), features fusion extraction (Febin, Jayasree, & Joy, 2019; Lohithashva, Aradhya, & Guru, 2020), deep learning (Accattoli, Sernani, Falcionelli, Mekuria, & Dragoni, 2020), and classifiers (Praskash, Ashoka, Aradhya, & Naveena, 2016) are used to detect violent events.

The Histograms of Oriented Gradients (HOG) feature descriptor was introduced by Dalal and Triggs (Dalal & Triggs, 2005) for human detection and object recognition. Subsequently, many researchers have been modifying the HOG descriptor for their research problems. Li, Zhong, Xie, and Pu (2019) used a texture-based feature descriptor, a method which uses spatiotemporal information with the coefficient of independent views to detect violent events. Ryan, Denman, Fookes, and Sridharan (2011) introduced the texture of OF to identify unusual events in video scenes. This method used spatial distribution information of the object, which can distinguish between normal and abnormal events. Deniz et al. (2014) introduced acceleration patterns to distinguish violent and nonviolent video scenes based on Radon transform to evaluate acceleration. Chen, Zhang, Lin, Xu, and Ren (2011) introduced the integration of magnitude and orientation, which is also called OF context histogram. The authors have used magnitude and orientation information to separate fight and nonfight scenes. Principal component analysis is used for dimension reduction of features. Finally, prominent features are fed to Support Vector Machine (SVM), random forest, and Bayes-net machine learning classifiers.

Similarly, Lloyd et al. (2017) presented a gray level cooccurrence matrix descriptor to detect unusual events. This method is based on the temporal distribution of spatial variation pixels in the frames. Mabrouk and Zagrouba (2017) introduced a local feature descriptor which extracts OF magnitude and orientation

Recent Trends in Computational Intelligence Enabled Research.
DOI: https://doi.org/10.1016/B978-0-12-822844-9.00039-6

prominent features using kernel density estimation which are fed to an SVM classifier to detect violent events. Febin et al. (2019) presented a combination of Motion Boundary Scale Invariant Features Transform (MoBSIFT) and movement filter algorithm. The movement filter algorithm extracts temporal information features of nonviolent events and avoids normal events. Furthermore, the combination of motion boundary, OF, and SIFT feature extracts prominent features to detect violent events. Recently, Accattoli et al. (2020) used 3D-CNN (Convolution Neural Network) features to detect fights, aggressive behavior, and violent scenes in video.

Violent event detection in real-time scenes in video based on CNN deep learning method was introduced by Imran et al. (2020). This method extracts short-term spatiotemporal information and is fed to a gated recurrent unit, which enables modeling the long-term dynamics of the video sequence. In addition, the authors also introduced a privacy protection scheme based on the randomization of pixel values. The local feature descriptor does not work well with lighting changes and many noisy features are detected in frames with complex backgrounds. Even global features may give unreliable feature information due to noise and complex backgrounds.

In order to overcome the above challenges and upgrade the performance of our proposed method, we fused gradient, OF, and texture feature descriptors to detect violent events. Many researchers have failed to detect automatic violent events because of a dramatic change in the background or abrupt entry of new objects further into the scene, unconstrained illumination, occlusion, and scale variation. Therefore in this chapter we propose an integration of handcrafted feature descriptors to distinguish violent and nonviolent video scenes.

The main contributions of the work are:

1. An integration of Global Histograms of Oriented Gradients (GHOG), Histogram of Optical Flow Orientation (HOFO), and GIST handcrafted features that are constructively extracted to distinguish between violent and nonviolent events.
2. Mean magnitude gradient features are surplus to inhibiting the motion correctly for a HOFO feature descriptor which uses spatiotemporal volume, where motion is present, and this process acts like a background subtraction technique.
3. The postprocessing technique is used to improve the accuracy of the proposed method.
4. Explored different evaluation metrics using the SVM classifier which demonstrate the efficacy of the proposed method needed to discriminate violent and nonviolent events.

This chapter is laid out as follows. In Section 17.2, the proposed method is illustrated. In Section 17.3, the experimentation results are demonstrated. Finally, we conclude the chapter in Section 17.4.

17.2 Proposed method

In this section, we illustrate the overview of the proposed method as can be seen in Fig. 17.1. There are three different methods of integration of handcrafted features, GHOG, HOFO, and GIST, which are based on gradient, OF, and texture features. The prominent features are extracted from a sequence of video frames. Finally, all the features are fed into SVM classifier to detect violent and nonviolent events.

17.2.1 Global histograms of oriented gradients feature descriptor

The GHOG descriptor is a well-known gradient feature extraction technique which is used to evaluate the edge information of the frame. Spatial object appearance and shape features can be identified by the projection of intensity gradient directions. Then the gradient orientation and magnitude can be calculated using a 1-dimensional gradient filter to measure horizontal and vertical intensity variations. It can be used horizontally p_x by convolving $(-1\ 0\ 1)$ and vertically q_y by convolving $(-1\ 0\ 1)^T$. Eq. (17.1) evaluates gradient magnitude M and Eq. (17.2) evaluates gradient orientation θ. Fig. 17.2 illustrates the GHOG feature extraction stages.

$$M = \sqrt{p_{x^2} + q_{y^2}} \tag{17.1}$$

$$\theta = \tan^{-1}\left(\frac{q_y}{p_x}\right) \tag{17.2}$$

Quantize the gradient orientation into eight bins ranging between 0 and 180 degrees, the gradient of the

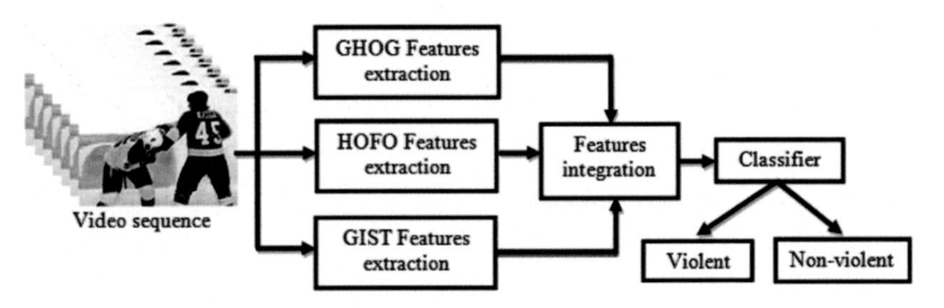

FIGURE 17.1 Overview of the proposed method.

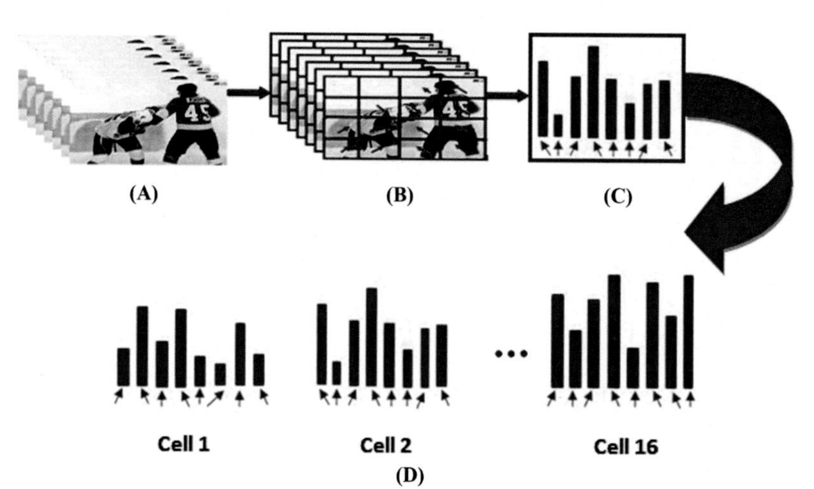

FIGURE 17.2 Extraction procedure of the global histograms of oriented gradients (GHOG) feature: (A) input sequences of video; (B) construction of histograms gradient in 4 × 4 block, (C) normalizing the gradient features into eight bins histogram, (D) the GHOG feature is determined.

amplitude of each direction is the weights. The frame is divided into a 4 × 4 block with no overlap. The overall histograms of oriented gradients for the entire frame are constructed by the concatenation of the whole histograms extracted from the window regions. The L_2 norm normalization is used to reduce the noise, illumination, and occlusion (Dalal & Triggs, 2005). Finally, concatenation of the whole block into the vector is performed to generate 128 (4×4×8) dimensional GHOG features.

17.2.2 Histogram of optical flow orientation feature descriptor

OF can be given a spatial arrangement as well as temporal changes information in a sequence of frames. Horn and Schunck (1981) for the very first time introduced the distribution of OFs. In this work, we have used Horn–Schunck (HS) OF, which can depict object motion information to detect violent events in a video. The entered sequence of frames in a video is worked through to present characteristics of motion at each pixel. OF can be employed to depict violent events by demonstrating differences in the motion from nonviolent events. The motion of an object is calculated from OF, which depicts motion characteristics. HS presented an OF by introducing global constraint about smoothness to calculate OF. An OF is formulated for a two-dimensional frame sequence as a global energy function, as can be seen in Eq. (17.3).

$$e=\int\left[(I_xp+I_yq+I_t)^2+\alpha(||p||^2+||q||^2)\right]dxdy \tag{17.3}$$

where I_x, I_y, and I_t, are the derived distribution of an intensity level of x, y, and time t directions, respectively, p stands for the horizontal component, and q stands for the vertical component of OF and α is a parameter comprising the angle regularization constant. The Lagrange equation is used to reduce the energy function e, as can be seen in Eqs. (17.4) and (17.5)

$$\begin{aligned}I_x(I_xp+I_yq+I_t)-\alpha^2\Delta p=0\\ I_y(I_xp+I_yq+I_t)-\alpha^2\Delta q=0\end{aligned} \tag{17.4}$$

submitted to,

$$\begin{aligned}\Delta p(x,y)=p'(x,y)-p(x,y)\\ \Delta q(x,y)=q'(x,y)-q(x,y)\end{aligned} \tag{17.5}$$

where p and q are calculated from the mean angle of p and q in a neighbor across the pixel location. The OF is calculated in an iterative system as can be seen in Eqs. (17.6) and (17.7):

$$p^{r+1}=p'^r-\frac{I_x(I_xp'^r+I_yq'^r+I_t)}{\alpha^2+I_x{}^2+I_y{}^2} \tag{17.6}$$

$$q^{r+1}=q'^r-\frac{I_x(I_xp'^r+I_yq'^r+I_t)}{\alpha^2+I_x{}^2+I_y{}^2} \tag{17.7}$$

where r is the concluding consequence. The computations depend on two adjoining sequences of frames by taking one occurrence. The magnitude and orientation at the individual pixel area (x, y) from the vector $[p, q]$ are selected. OF can enumerate low-level features to constitute motion magnitude distribution information. The proposed method can be seen in Fig. 17.3. The frame is split into a 4 × 4 block, the gradient orientation is quantized into eight bins and ranges from 0 to 180 degrees. The connection of the OF magnitude and orientation involves every cell in the block. Eventually, feature vectors are concatenated into a vector to generate 128 (4×4×8) dimensional HOFO features.

17.2.3 GIST feature descriptor

The GIST descriptor extracts global spatial structural information without segmentation of frames. In the first instance, the frame is partitioned into a 4×4 block size,

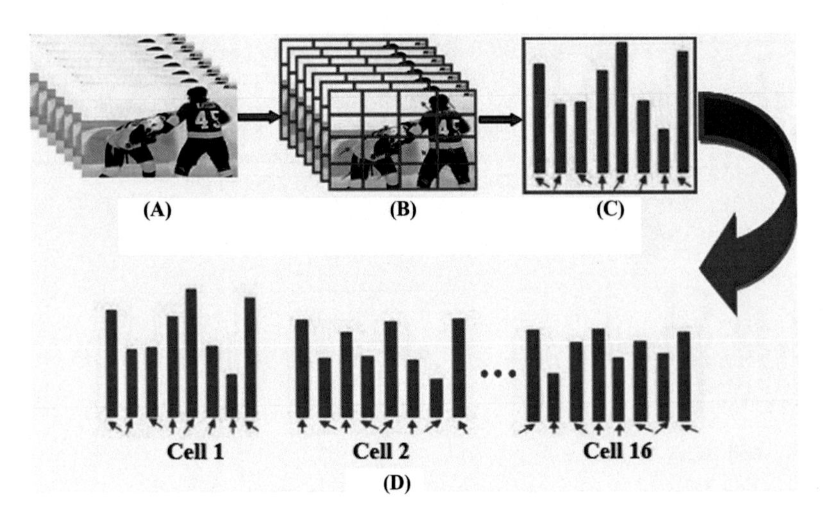

FIGURE 17.3 Extraction procedure of the histogram of optical flow orientation (HOFO) feature: (A) input sequences of video; (B) construction of optical flow (OF) histograms in a 4 × 4 block, (C) normalize the OF features into eight bins histograms, (D) HOFO feature is determined.

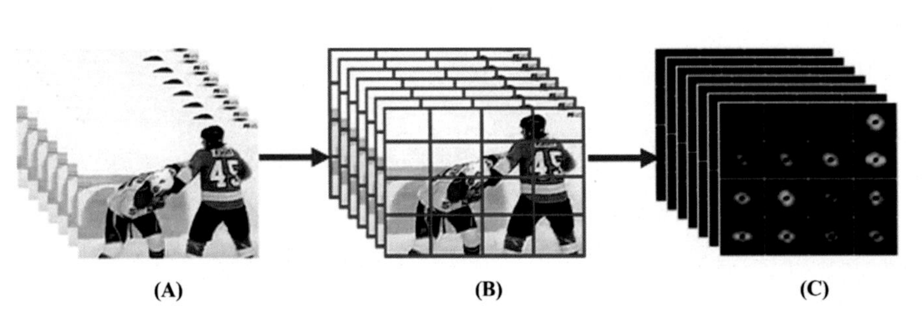

FIGURE 17.4 Extraction procedure of GIST feature: (A) sequences of input video, (B) structure of a 4 × 4 block, (C) GIST features are computed.

transformed into grayscale frames, and manipulated by a whitening filter. Therefore the presiding spatial information of the frames can be reserved. In this work, we have adjusted two scales (σ) and four orientations (θ) which gives eight features. The Gabor filter with a Gaussian kernel function is used to convolve the grayscale frames (Bovik, Clark, & Geisler, 1990), as can be seen in Eqs. (17.8)–(17.10). For each cell in the block, the mean intensity of the cell is computed. Eventually, the concatenation of each cell feature vector generates 128-dimensional GIST features.

$$G(p, q, \sigma, \theta) = \frac{1}{2\pi\sigma^2} e^{-\left(\frac{p'^2}{2\sigma^2} + \frac{q'^2}{2\sigma^2}\right)} e^{j\frac{\pi\alpha'}{\sigma}} \tag{17.8}$$

$$p' = p\ \cos\theta + q\ \sin\theta \tag{17.9}$$

$$q' = -p\ \sin\theta + q\ \cos\theta \tag{17.10}$$

where p constitutes the x and q constitutes the y axis of the frame, σ represents scale, and θ is the orientation. A set of spatial information with different scales and orientations is utilized to extract prominent features as can be seen in Fig. 17.4.

17.2.4 Fusion feature descriptors

In this section, GHOG, HOFO, and GIST integration feature descriptors are used to detect violent event in videos. The GHOG descriptor is used to extract gradient information of the events and 128 dimensions of feature vectors are obtained for each frame. The feature integration proposed method is capable of using multiframe features, complementing each other's advantages, and producing more reliable and consistent performance. GHOG is used to extract gradient or shape information, however, this method does not work well on complex backgrounds with noise. HOFO renders correct detection of temporal movement but it is slow and fails to extract sharp boundaries. However, the GIST descriptor works well even if it has a complex background and highly varied illumination. Therefore considering the advantages of each descriptor, and to improve the accuracy of our proposed method, we have integrated three handcrafted feature descriptors. We integrate GHOG, HOFO, and GIST descriptors in different combination as GHOG + HOFO, GHOG + GIST, HOFO + GIST, and GHOG + HOFO + GIST to enhance the results of the proposed method.

17.2.5 Classifier

SVM classifier is a supervised classification algorithm, which is based on the principle of structural risk minimization (SRM). Vladimir Vapnik (Cortes & Vapnik, 1995) introduced the SVM classifier, which initially was used for binary classification problem. Later, many researchers used multiclassification SVM for their applications. If the feature vectors are not separate linearly, nonparametric functions are used. It attempts to maximize the distance of the separating boundary between the violent and nonviolent events by maximizing the distance of the separated plane from each of the feature vectors. In this work, the coarse Gaussian kernel function is used to discriminate the features.

17.2.6 Postprocessing

The postprocessing technique significantly increases the accuracy and reduces the false-positive rate (FPR). Wang and Snoussi (2011) introduced the time postprocessing technique and Reddy, Sanderson, and Lovell (2011) introduced the space–time postprocessing method. In this work, for the postprocessing technique, we have taken 30 frames for detection, which significantly improves the performance.

17.3 Experimental results and discussion

In this section, we illustrate our proposed method to conduct experimentation on the Hockey Fight dataset and Violent-Flows dataset. Afterwards, the evaluation parameters are defined. Finally, the obtained results of our proposed method are compared with existing methods.

17.3.1 Datasets

To illustrate the efficiency of the proposed feature descriptors, experimentation is performed on the Hockey Fight dataset and Violent-Flows dataset and each dataset has complex background, varied illumination, scale changes, and occlusion.

17.3.1.1 Hockey Fight dataset

This dataset includes 1000 National Hockey League action videos (500 fight and 500 nonfight), specifically used for determining the violent event detection processes (Nievas, Suarez, García, & Sukthankar, 2011). There are conflicts between two or more players for each video. Each video clip is equivalent to 1.75 seconds. Different frame samples consisting of fight and nonfight scenes can be seen in Fig. 17.5.

17.3.1.2 Violent-Flows dataset

The Violent-Flows dataset consists of 246 action videos (123 violent and 123 nonviolent). Maximum violent video events took place in a football stadium during a match. This dataset is utilized to estimate the detection of crowded violent events (Hassner, Itcher, & Kliper-Gross, 2012). All the violent videos are in the aggressive events and each video is equivalent to 3.60 seconds. Samples of both violent and nonviolent frames are illustrated in Fig. 17.6.

17.3.2 Experimental setting

Currently, many existing methods ViF (Violent Flow), OViF (Oriented Violent Flow), combination of ViF and OViF (ViF + OViF), and DiMOLIF (Distribution of Magnitude Orientation Local Interest Frame) are used to detect violent events. We have illustrated our proposed method performance and compare it with four state-of-the-art methods on Hockey Fight and Violent-Flows datasets with a fivefold cross-validation technique as followed in Gao, Liu, Sun, Wang, and Liu (2016) and Hassner et al. (2012).

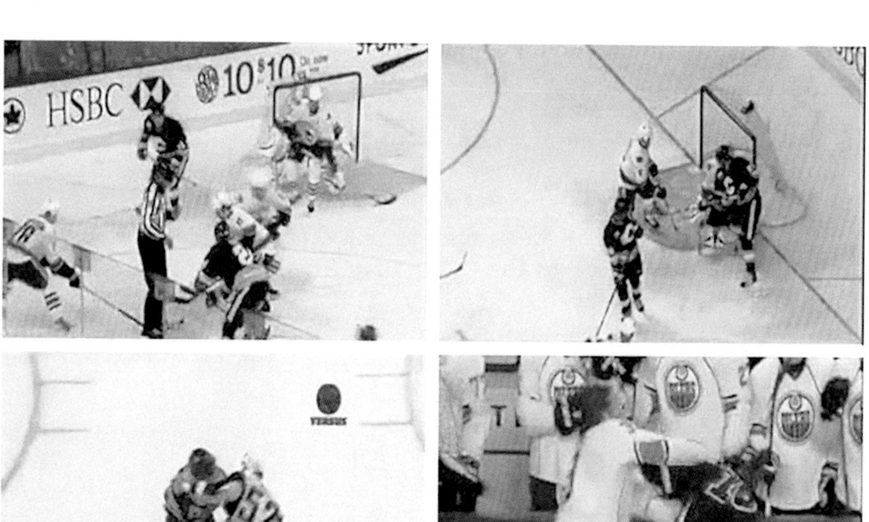

FIGURE 17.5 Hockey Fight dataset sample frames: nonfight scenes (*top row*), fight scenes (*bottom row*).

FIGURE 17.6 Violent-Flows dataset sample frames: nonviolent scenes (*top row*), violent scenes (*bottom row*).

17.3.3 Evaluation parameter

In this section we have used precision, recall, F-measure, accuracy, and area under the curve (AUC) evaluation metrics for the classification problem. The receiver operating characteristics (ROC) curve shows a graphical representation of the true positive rate (TPR) in contrast to the false-positive (f_p) rate. The AUC curve establishes how the classifier effectively distinguishes between violent and nonviolent events. These evaluation parameters are calculated in view of the following subsections:

1. true positive (*tp*): violent event rightly detected as violent;
2. true negative (*tn*): nonviolent event rightly detected as nonviolent;
3. false positive (*fp*): nonviolent event wrongly detected as violent;
4. false negative (*fn*): violent event wrongly detected as nonviolent.

17.3.3.1 *Precision*

Precision (*P*) is the proportion of positive observations predicted rightly to the positive observations predicted overall, as can be seen in Eq. (17.11).

$$P = \frac{t_p}{t_p + f_p} \tag{17.11}$$

17.3.3.2 *Recall*

Recall (*R*) is the proportion of rightly detected positive perceptions to all perceptions in the real class, as can be seen in Eq. (17.12).

$$R = \frac{t_p}{t_p + f_n} \tag{17.12}$$

17.3.3.3 *F-measure*

F-measure (*F*) examines both precision and recall. It is an average of both metrics. F-measure takes both (f_p) and (f_n) toward the result, as can be seen in Eq. (17.13).

$$F = \frac{2 \times (P \times R)}{P + R} \tag{17.13}$$

17.3.3.4 *Accuracy*

Accuracy (Acc) is used to test the rightly detected fight and nonfight events. To evaluate the accuracy test, we should compute the (t_p) rate and (t_n) rate in all evaluation instances. Accuracy is determined using Eq. (17.14).

$$\text{Acc} = \frac{t_p + t_n}{t_p + t_n + f_p + f_n} \tag{17.14}$$

17.3.3.5 *Area under the curve*

The area under the ROC curve is also known as the AUC. In the ROC curve, the *x*-axis shows a FPR and the *y*-axis shows a TPR. FPR and TPR evaluation metrics are used to detect the performance of the proposed method. FPR can be seen in Eq. (17.15) and TPR can be seen in Eq. (17.16).

$$\text{FPR} = \frac{f_p}{f_p + t_n} \tag{17.15}$$

$$\text{TPR} = \frac{t_p}{t_p + f_n} \tag{17.16}$$

TABLE 17.1 Performance evaluation metrics illustrated as a percentage using the Hockey Fight dataset.

Method	P	R	F	Acc	AUC
GHOG	93.08	92.82	91.41	91.25 ± 1.89	91.31
HOFO	92.71	92.39	90.90	90.77 ± 2.47	90.70
GIST	95.76	95.06	90.54	90.93 ± 3.19	90.46
GHOG + HOFO	96.93	96.65	93.50	93.26 ± 1.70	93.50
GHOG + GIST	97.98	97.82	94.65	94.46 ± 2.80	94.68
HOFO + GIST	96.37	96.69	93.90	93.80 ± 2.77	93.40
GHOG + HOFO + GIST	98.55	98.71	95.42	95.45 ± 2.05	96.93

AUC, area under the curve; *GHOG*, global histograms of oriented gradients; *HOFO*, histogram of optical flow orientation.

TABLE 17.2 Performance evaluation metrics illustrated as a percentage using the Violent-Flows dataset.

Method	P	R	F	Acc	AUC
GHOG	85.45	87.83	86.62	81.74 ± 3.67	82.27
HOFO	90.87	83.71	87.15	81.10 ± 2.53	82.74
GIST	92.61	85.59	88.96	86.21 ± 3.54	85.96
GHOG + HOFO	94.01	95.52	94.76	90.62 ± 1.04	91.92
GHOG + GIST	96.98	96.83	94.00	93.82 ± 2.62	94.88
HOFO + GIST	94.59	93.84	92.05	89.20 ± 3.11	90.10
GHOG + HOFO + GIST	98.12	95.45	96.77	95.21 ± 2.16	95.45

AUC, area under the curve; *GHOG*, global histograms of oriented gradients; *HOFO*, histogram of optical flow orientation.

17.3.4 Results and analysis

In this section, Hockey Fight and Violent-Flows datasets are separately used in the experimentation. In the Hockey Fight dataset videos are organized into two or more persons and Violent-Flows videos are organized into people willing to fight video circumstances. Both have complex backgrounds, unconstrained illumination, occlusion, and different scales. A single feature descriptor generally shows weaker performance, while GHOG achieves the best accuracy rate among the HOFO and GIST individual feature descriptors. Unsurprisingly, the integration feature descriptors show the best results by combining the advantages of the underlying features with accuracy. Experimentation results of the proposed method are shown in Tables 17.1 and 17.2. Feature integration descriptors extract the most dominating features from the original multiple feature sets involved in fusion and can remove redundant information. The combination of feature integration descriptors, for instance GHOG + HOFO, GHOG + GIST, HOFO + GIST, and GHOG + HOFO + GIST, demonstrated detection of a violent event. Fig. 17.7 shows the Hockey-Fight dataset ROC curve of the proposed handcrafted feature descriptors. The GHOG feature descriptor gives more satisfactory results than HOFO and GIST. This clearly illustrates that optical flow and texture feature differentiate violent and nonviolent events effectively. When the GHOG feature is integrated with HOFO and GIST, GHOG + GIST descriptor performance is better than GHOG + HOFO and HOFO + GIST. This demonstrates that an integration of gradient and texture features has more discriminative capability to classify the features. This motivated combination of the gradient, OF, and texture features. Consequently, the GHOG + HOFO + GIST fusion descriptor outperforms other individual and fusion descriptors.

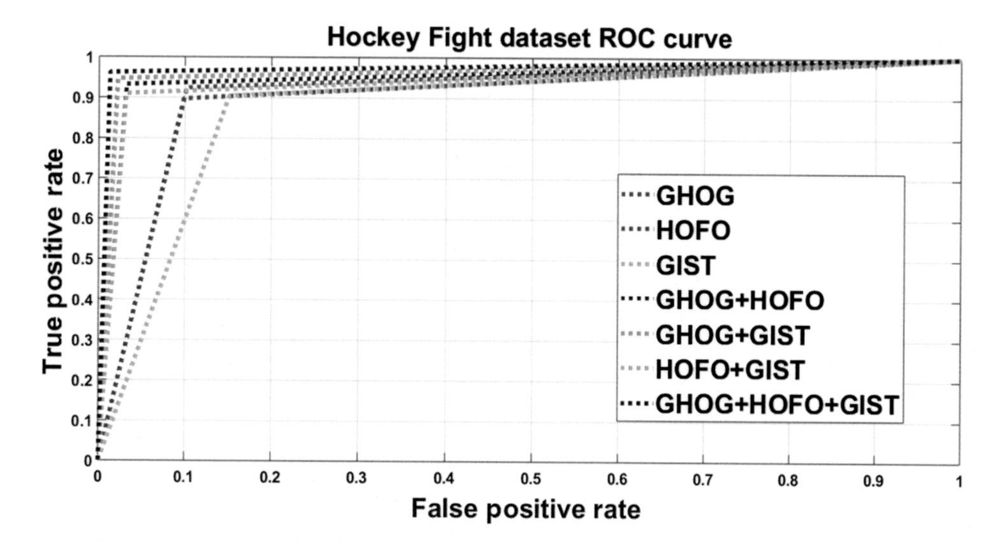

FIGURE 17.7 Hockey-Fight dataset receiver operating characteristics curves of the proposed feature descriptors.

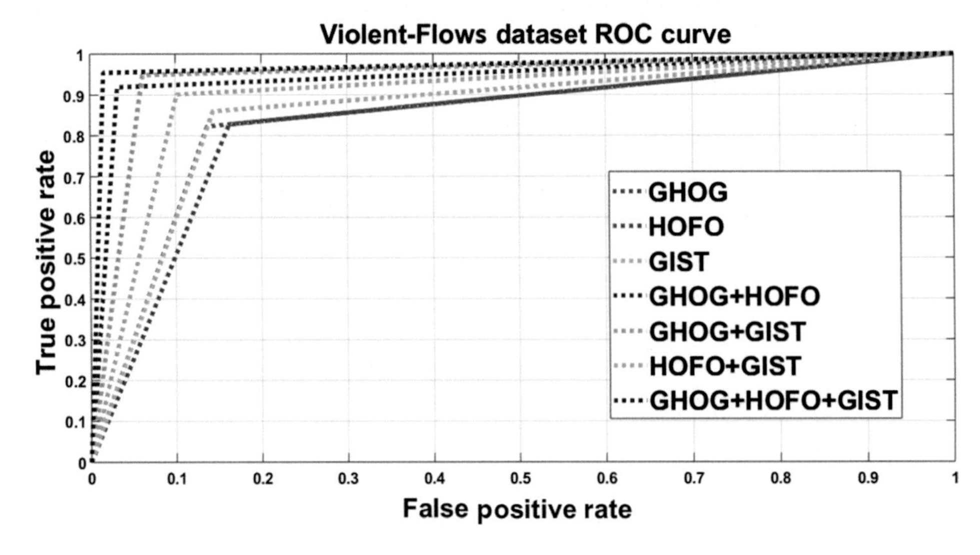

FIGURE 17.8 Violent-Flows dataset receiver operating characteristics curves of the proposed feature descriptors.

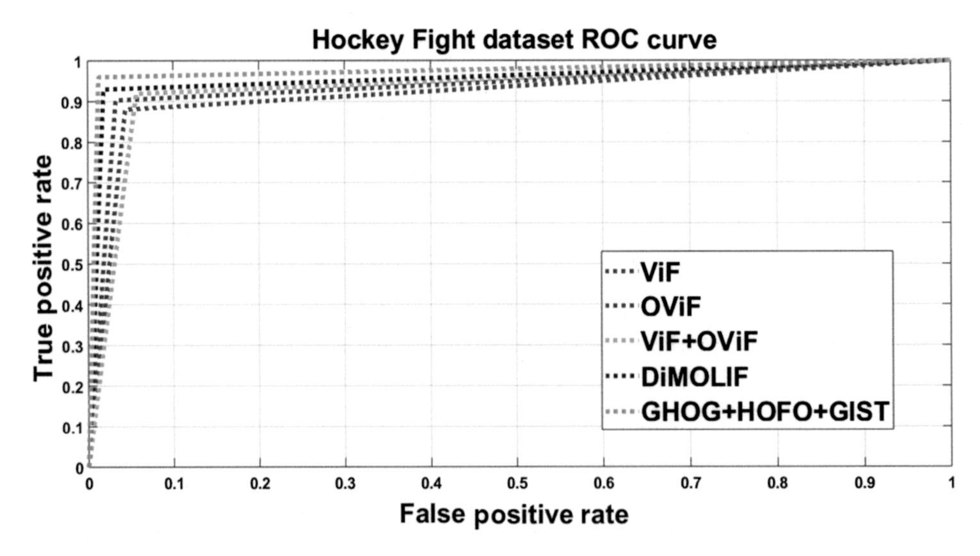

FIGURE 17.9 Proposed integrated feature fusion descriptor compared with existing methods using the Hockey Fight dataset.

A precision of 98.55%, recall of 98.71%, F-measure of 95.42%, accuracy of 95.45%, and AUC of 96.93% were obtained, as demonstrated in Table 17.1.

The results of the Violent-Flows dataset ROC curves with SVM classifier using our different feature descriptors are illustrated in Fig. 17.8. The GHOG + HOFO + GIST feature descriptor gives outstanding results compared with other feature descriptors. The GHOG + GIST descriptor accomplished substantially equal performance to the GHOG + HOFO + GIST descriptor. The GHOG + HOFO and HOFO + GIST descriptors gave acceptable results. The GHOG, HOFO, and GIST feature descriptors also gave adequate result. Furthermore, the comprehensive results can be seen in Table 17.2. The obtained precision, recall, F-measure, accuracy, and AUC results were, respectively, 98.12%, 95.45%, 96.77%, 95.21%, and 95.45% on the Violent-Flows dataset. Comparing Figs. 17.7 and 17.8, we deduced that the gradient and texture features accomplish an outstanding role in Hockey Fight and Violent-Flows datasets. Figs. 17.9 and 17.10 shows that the ROC curve illustration of our proposed integrated feature descriptor compared well with existing methods. It is distinctly clear that our proposed method outperforms other state-of-the-art methods. Tables 17.3 and 17.4 show our proposed feature integration descriptors in comparison with existing algorithms. The highest accuracy was 95.45% and AUC of 96.93% on the Hockey Fight dataset and the highest accuracy was 95.21% and AUC of 95.45% on Violent-Flows dataset. It is noted that our proposed method is capable of detecting violent events even if there is a cluttered background, varied illumination, little motion, and scale changes.

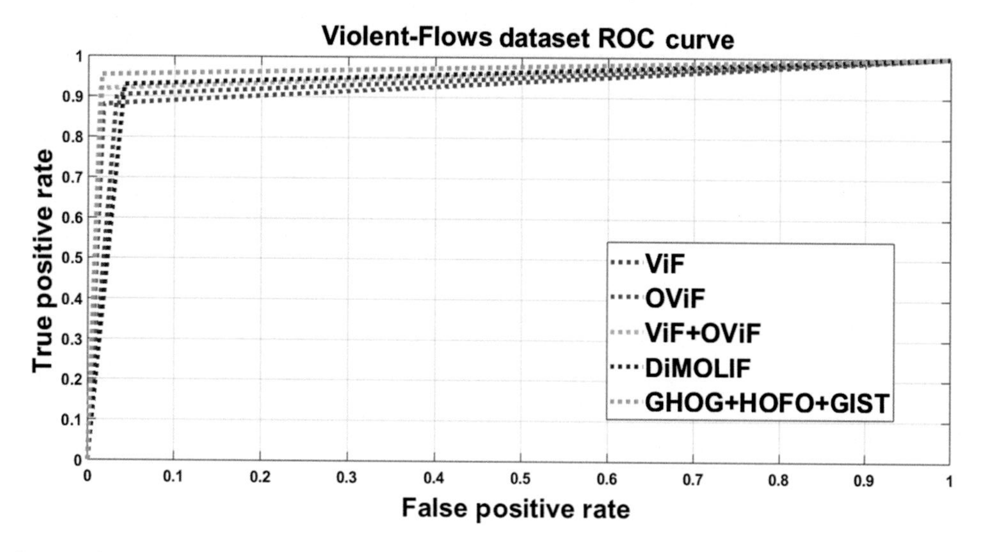

FIGURE 17.10 Proposed integrated feature fusion descriptor compared with existing methods using the Violent-Flows dataset.

TABLE 17.3 Performance comparison of results using the Hockey fight dataset.

Method	Hockey Fight dataset	
	Accuracy (SD)	AUC
ViF (Hassner et al., 2012)	81.60 ± 0.22	88.01
OViF (Gao et al., 2016)	84.20 ± 3.33	90.32
ViF + OViF (Gao et al., 2016)	86.30 ± 1.57	91.93
DiMOLIF (Mabrouk & Zagrouba, 2017)	88.60 ± 1.2	93.23
GHOG + HOFO + GIST	95.45 ± 2.05	96.93

AUC, area under the curve; *DiMOLIF*, distribution of magnitude orientation local interest frame; *GHOG*, global histograms of oriented gradients; *HOFO*, histogram of optical flow orientation; *OViF*, oriented violent flow; *ViF*, violent flow.

TABLE 17.4 Performance comparison of results using the Violent-Flows dataset.

Method	Violent-Flows dataset	
	Accuracy (SD)	AUC
ViF (Hassner et al., 2012)	81.20 ± 1.79	88.04
OViF (Gao et al., 2016)	76.80 ± 3.90	80.47
ViF + OViF (Gao et al., 2016)	86.00 ± 1.41	91.82
DiMOLIF (Mabrouk & Zagrouba, 2017)	85.83 ± 4.2	89.25
GHOG + HOFO + GIST	95.21 ± 2.16	95.45

AUC, area under the curve; *DiMOLIF*, distribution of magnitude orientation local interest frame; *GHOG*, global histograms of oriented gradients; *HOFO*, histogram of optical flow orientation; *OViF*, oriented violent flow; *ViF*, violent flow.

17.3.5 Space and time computation

In this section, ViF (Hassner et al., 2012), OViF (Gao et al., 2016), ViF + OViF (Gao et al., 2016), and DiMOLIF (Mabrouk & Zagrouba, 2017) baseline existing methods are compared with space and time evaluations with our proposed GHOG, HOFO, GIST, and fusion features descriptors. In our research work, we used eight histogram bins for each block. The ViF feature descriptor is another baseline method that can be used to detect violent events. In this method, two parameters are adjusted. Initially, the frame is partitioned into a 4×4 block size, later, the number of histogram bins is set to 20. Finally, the 320 ($4 \times 4 \times 20$) dimensions of the ViF feature vector are generated. The OViF descriptor also has two parameters to be set. The block size of OViF is the same as ViF and the histogram bins are set to nine. Consequently, 144 ($4 \times 4 \times 9$) dimensions of the OViF feature vector are generated. The ViF + OViF descriptor is a combination of ViF and OViF descriptors, which gives better violent event detection compared to individual ViF or OViF feature descriptors. It recommends that the fusion feature descriptor method is efficient for violent event detection. The combination of ViF and OViF feature descriptor generates 464 ($4 \times 4 \times 29$) dimensions of the feature vector. The DiMOLIF descriptor is based on the STIP to recognize significant frames that are used to extract substantial features using the nonparametric method. DiMOLIF will get 128 ($4 \times 4 \times 8$) features for each frame. Our proposed method used GHOG, that is, based on gradient features of 128 ($4 \times 4 \times 8$) dimensions, HOFO based on the OF features of 128 ($4 \times 4 \times 8$) dimensions, GIST based on the texture features of 128 ($4 \times 4 \times 8$) dimensions, and fusion descriptors are GHOG + HOFO, which is a combination of gradient and OF, the feature vector dimension of each frame is 256 ($4 \times 4 \times 16$). GHOG + GIST is a combination of gradient and texture, the feature vector dimension of each frame is 256 ($4 \times 4 \times 16$). HOFO + GIST is a combination of OF and texture, the feature vector dimension of each frame is 256 ($4 \times 4 \times 16$). GHOG + HOFO + GIST is a combination of gradient, OF, and texture, and the feature vector dimension of each frame is 384 ($4 \times 4 \times 24$).

TABLE 17.5 Time for computation for each frame.

Method	Duration (s/frame)	
	Violent	Nonviolent
BoF (STIP) (Chen & Hauptmann, 2009)	0.293	0.293
BoF (MoSIFT) (Chen & Hauptmann, 2009)	0.661	0.661
Deniz et al. (2014)	0.0419	0.0419
Serrano et al. Gracia et al. (2015)	0.0225	0.0225
BoF (MoBSIFT) (Febin et al., 2019)	0.257	0.257
BoF (MoBSIFT) + MF (Febin et al., 2019)	0.257	0.257
GHOG	0.0149	0.0149
HOFO	0.0197	0.0197
GIST	0.2858	0.2858

BoF, Bag of Features; *GHOG*, global histograms of oriented gradients; *HOFO*, histogram of optical flow orientation; *MoBSIFT*, motion boundary scale invariant features transform.

In this chapter, our proposed GHOG + HOFO + GIST feature descriptor combines gradient magnitude, OF, and texture distribution of the object perceptible motion using the extraction of distribution gradient in each frame. ViF is an OF-based feature descriptor, which extracts only gradient magnitude information, and does not work if the orientation changes. OViF is an extension of ViF, and extracts both magnitude and orientation of the OF, OViF performs well for the Hockey Fight dataset but performs poorly on the Violent-Flows dataset. Nevertheless, the DiMOLIF feature descriptor gives outstanding results compare with ViF and OViF descriptors because it takes advantage of local and global features. Actually, there are four attributes that need to be intimated for descriptors to detect a violent event. Some of the intimates are magnitude, orientation, spatial arrangement of the moving objects, number of objects moving in a video scene, mass, and acceleration. Our proposed method was based on gradient, optical, and texture features of object apparent motion using the extraction of GHOG + HOFO + GIST features to enhance the efficiency of the proposed method. We infer that for both the Hockey Fight and Violent-Flows datasets, our proposed method performs significantly well.

The performance of our proposed method is experimentally evaluated using an 8 GB RAM, Intel Core i7, Windows 10 operating system. The time computation of motion boundary scale invariant features transform (MoSIFT) (Chen & Hauptmann, 2009) is significantly high, the MoBSIFT (Febin et al., 2019) descriptor reduced the time computation using a movement filter technique. Deniz et al. (2014) took less time for computation compared to MoSIFT and MoBSIFT. Nevertheless, Gracia, Suarez, Garcia, and Kim (2015) also took less time for computation. Our proposed GHOG, HOFO, and GIST feature descriptors took 0.0149, 0.0197, and 0.2858 seconds per frame, respectively, to execute the proposed algorithm for both violent and nonviolent event detection with modest time computation, which demonstrates that our proposed GHOG and HOFO feature extraction methods have taken modest time for computation compared with existing methods. The GIST descriptor took less time for computation compared with MOSIFT and is approximately equal to time taken by the MoBSIFT descriptor. Table 17.5 illustrates a comparison between our proposed method's time for computation and that of state-of-the-art methods.

17.4 Conclusion

In this chapter, we have introduced feature integration descriptors for both crowded and uncrowded violent event detection in videos. Our proposed method has outperformed other methods in accuracy and time for computation. This chapter has also illustrated gradient, OF, texture features, and a combination of feature descriptors on the Hockey Fight and Violent-Flows dataset. Experimentation is conducted on different single descriptors and fusion feature descriptors. In the future, we aim to conduct experimentation on complex videos in an attempt to optimize the proposed method to improve its accuracy and reduce the computation time. Different feature selection methods are used to reduce the feature descriptor size and improve the performance of our proposed method.

Acknowledgment

The first author is financially supported by UGC under RGNF (Rajiv Gandhi National Fellowship), Letter no. F1-17.1/2014-15/RGNF-2014-15-SC-KAR-73791/(SA III/Website), SJCE, JSS Science and Technology University, Mysuru, Karnataka, India.

References

Accattoli, S., Sernani, P., Falcionelli, N., Mekuria, D. N., & Dragoni, A. F. (2020). Violence detection in videos by combining 3D convolutional neural networks and support vector machines. *Applied Artificial Intelligence*, *34*(4), 329–344.

Amith, R., & Aradhya, V. M. (2017). Linear projective approach for moving object detection in video (pp. 1–4).

Aradhya, V. M., Basavaraju, H., & Guru, D. (2019). Decade research on text detection in images/videos: A review. *Evolutionary Intelligence*, 1–27.

Bovik, A. C., Clark, M., & Geisler, W. S. (1990). Multichannel texture analysis using localized spatial filters. *IEEE Transactions on Pattern Analysis and Machine Intelligence*, *12*(1), 55–73.

Chen, M.-Y., & Hauptmann, A. (2009). *MoSIFT: Recognizing human actions in surveillance videos*. Citeseer.

Chen, Y., Zhang, L., Lin, B., Xu, Y., & Ren, X. (2011). Fighting detection based on optical flow context histogram. IEEE (pp. 95–98).

Cortes, C., & Vapnik, V. (1995). Support vector machine. *Machine Learning*, *20*(3), 273–297.

Dalal, N. & Triggs, B. (2005). Histograms of oriented gradients for human detection. IEEE, 1 (pp. 886–893).

Deniz, O., Serrano, I., Bueno, G., & Kim, T.-K. (2014). Fast violence detection in video. IEEE, 2 (pp. 478–485).

Febin, I., Jayasree, K., & Joy, P. T. (2019). Violence detection in videos for an intelligent surveillance system using mobsift and movement filtering algorithm. *Pattern Analysis and Applications*, *23*, 611–623.

Gao, Y., Liu, H., Sun, X., Wang, C., & Liu, Y. (2016). Violence detection using oriented violent flows. *Image and Vision Computing*, *48*, 37–41.

Gracia, I. S., Suarez, O. D., Garcia, G. B., & Kim, T.-K. (2015). Fast fight detection. *PLoS*, *10*(4), e0120448.

Hanson, A., Pnvr, K., Krishnagopal, S., & Davis, L. (2018). Bidirectional convolutional LSTM for the detection of violence in videos.

Hassner, T., Itcher, Y., & Kliper-Gross, O. (2012). Violent flows: Real-time detection of violent crowd behavior. IEEE (pp. 1–6).

Horn, B. K., & Schunck, B. G. (1981). Determining optical flow. *Artificial Intelligence*, *17*(1–3), 185–203.

Imran, J., Raman, B., & Rajput, A. (2020). Robust, efficient and privacy-preserving violent activity recognition in videos. In *Proceedings of the 35th annual ACM symposium on applied computing* (pp. 2081–2088).

Krishna, M. G., Aradhya, V. M., Ravishankar, M., & Babu, D. R. (2012). Lopp: Locality preserving projections for moving object detection. *Procedia Technology*, *4*, 624–628.

Lamba, S., & Nain, N. (2019). Detecting anomalous crowd scenes by oriented tracklets approach in active contour region. *Multimedia Tools and Applications*, *78*(22), 31101–31120.

Li, C., Zhong, Q., Xie, D., & Pu, S. (2019). Collaborative spatiotemporal feature learning for video action recognition. IEEE (pp. 7872–7881).

Lloyd, K., Rosin, P. L., Marshall, D., & Moore, S. C. (2017). Detecting violent and ab- normal crowd activity using temporal analysis of grey level co-occurrence matrix (GLCM)-based texture measures. *Machine Vision and Applications*, *28*(3–4), 361–371, Springer.

Lohithashva, B., Aradhya, V. M., & Guru, D. (2020a). Violent video event detection based on integrated LBP and GLCM texture features. *Revue d'Intelligence Artificielle*, *34*(2), 179–187.

Lohithashva, B., Aradhya, V. M., & Guru, D. (2021). Violent event detection: An approach using fusion GHOG-GIST descriptor. In *Advances in automation, signal processing, instrumentation, and control* (pp. 881–890). Springer.

Lohithashva, B., Aradhya, V. M., Basavaraju, H., & Harish, B. (2019). Unusual crowd event detection: An approach using probabilistic neural network. In *Information systems design and intelligent applications* (pp. 533–542). Springer.

Mabrouk, A. B., & Zagrouba, E. (2017). Spatio-temporal feature using optical flow based distribution for violence detection. *Pattern Recognition Letters*, *92*, 62–67.

Mabrouk, A. B., & Zagrouba, E. (2018). Abnormal behavior recognition for intelligent video surveillance systems: A review. *Expert Systems with Applications*, *91*, 480–491.

Nievas, E. B., Suarez, O. D., García, G. B., & Sukthankar, R. (2011). Violence detection in video using computer vision techniques. In *Computer Analysis of Images and Patterns* (pp. 332–339). Springer.

Praskash, B. A., Ashoka, D., Aradhya, V. M., & Naveena, C. (2016). Exploration of neural network models for defect detection and classification. *International Journal of Convergence Computing*, 2 (3–4), 220–234.

Reddy, V., Sanderson, C., & Lovell, B.C. (2011). Improved anomaly detection in crowded scenes via cell-based analysis of foreground speed, size and texture. IEEE (pp. 55–61).

Ryan, D., Denman, S., Fookes, C., & Sridharan, S. (2011). Textures of optical flow for real-time anomaly detection in crowds. IEEE (pp. 230–235).

Wang, T., & Snoussi, H. (2011). Detection of abnormal visual events via global optical flow orientation histogram. *IEEE Transactions on Information Forensics and Security*, *9*(6), 988–998.

Yu, M., Bambacus, M., Cervone, G., Clarke, K., Duffy, D., Huang, Q., … Liu, Q. (2020). *Spatiotemporal event detection: A review*. *International Journal of Digital Earth* (13, pp. 1–27).

CHAPTER

18

Deep learning-based diabetic retinopathy detection for multiclass imbalanced data

Shukla Mondal, Kaniz Fatima Mian and Abhishek Das

Department of Computer Science and Engineering, Aliah University, Kolkata, India

18.1 Introduction

Diabetic retinopathy (DR) causes blindness in humans due as a complication of diabetes. It is a common and progressive retinal disease that needs timely diagnosis according to medical experts (Aiello et al., 1998; Fong, Aiello, Ferris, & Klein, 2004). Because of the time-consuming manual diagnostics and lack of experienced medical experts and resources the diagnosis process is hampered for a large number of diabetic patients. Furthermore, if DR is not diagnosed in a timely fashion it leads to irreversible blindness. If DR is detected as early as possible and treated accordingly, the severity of the blindness can be reduced and further damage prevented (Grading, 1991).

The artificial neural network (ANN) uses the basic concept of deep learning, which has been a widespread machine learning technique since the 1980s. ANNs are used in various ways to develop machines by analyzing data such as texts, images, and speech to understand and gain the insights (Schmidhuber, 2014). Just like the structure of a human brain, an ANN consists of a large number of computational elements known as neurons. These neurons are interconnected with weights such that they can be updated according to the input.

Machine learning can power most aspects of the modern healthcare society to automated and increased efficiency to provide faster and more accurate treatments (LeCun, Bengio, & Hinton, 2015). Objects are identified by matching new patterns using these systems and then the search results are selected. With increasing computing power and resources, deep learning techniques are used to make such applications. The main motivation of this study is to propose a novel method to detect DR lesions and its associated biomarkers by using various deep learning techniques and choose the model which performs best among others (He et al., 2015).

In recent times deep learning architectures have made remarkable achievements in image classification tasks due to the availability of powerful computing resources and larger storage spaces. In order to achieve a fast and reliable automated DR detection system, convolutional neural network (CNN) models are useful and necessary to build such a system to analyze the DR retinal images. For this task a deep learning model is proposed where different CNN architectures, such as AlexNet (Krizhevsky, Sutskever, & Hinton, 2012), SqueezeNet (Iandola et al., 2016), DenseNet (Huang, Liu, van der Maaten, & Weinberger, 2018), ResNet (He, Zhang, Ren, & Sun, 2015), and VggNet (Simonyan & Zisserman, 2015) are considered to train with imbalanced multiclass data. Data imbalance in classes is a problem where the classification tasks in CNNs are greatly affected, leading to biased accuracy.

The remainder of this chapter is organized as follows. Related works in DR detection from retinal images with deep learning models are discussed in Section 18.2. Section 18.3 presents the data set description and preprocessing of DR images. The proposed model which detects DR from retinal images is described in Section 18.4. Section 18.5 describes an experimental analysis of the proposed DR detection model, and the conclusion and future work are outlined in Section 18.6.

18.2 Related works

Several pieces of research have been done to detect DR from retinal images using various deep learning

Recent Trends in Computational Intelligence Enabled Research.
DOI: https://doi.org/10.1016/B978-0-12-822844-9.00003-7

TABLE 18.1 Data set description.

Data set	Class 0 (no DR)	Class 1 (mild)	Class 2 (moderate)	Class 3 (severe)	Class 4 (proliferative DR)	Total samples
Original (Kaggle)	25,810	2443	5292	873	708	35,126
Betwixt (from original)	910	85	165	20	20	1200

DR, Diabetic retinopathy.

models. CNNs in particular have achieved great performances in image classification tasks. Wan, Liang, and Zhang (2018) proposed a model where transfer learning is used to classify the DR images and the method of learning the features automatically reduces the feature extraction process from DR images. Data normalization and augmentation are done at the same time to make up for the defects on the DR retinal images as well as the hyperparameter tuning and model selection. These results showed better accuracy on DR image classification.

Qummar et al. (2019) proposed an ensemble-based CNN framework to classify DR images, which used the largest available DR image data set from Kaggle to evaluate the model. The ensemble-based framework performed better than the other previously proposed models. It focused on classifying all the severity levels of DR, especially the detection of early levels of severity in DR, which is a major drawback of previously proposed models.

Quellec et al. introduced a model for binary classification and DR detection with three CNN architecture (Quellec, Charrière, Boudi, Cochener, & Lamard, 2017). The DR detection model was trained using a modified susceptibility analysis where the image-pixels played a role in the predictions. The performance of the model was enhanced by training with their proposed solution ConvNets model.

Zeng, Chen, Luo, and Ye (2019) presented a referable DR detection model where Inception V3 architecture along with a Siamese-like network structure are used to train the model. The results of the proposed model showed great potential to assist medical experts in diagnosing referable DR more efficiently and improved the screening rate.

Gargeya and Leng (2017) proposed a deep learning-based data-driven novel diagnostic tool for classifying and identifying DR from retinal images. The abnormal regions are visualized accurately for the DR detection problem in the input DR images, enabling automated diagnosis of the DR disease clinically.

Another CNN approach to detect DR from retinal images was proposed by Pratt et al. using a high-performance graphics processor unit (GPU) on DR images and demonstrated impressive outcomes in a DR image classification task (Pratt, Coenen, Broadbent, Harding, & Zheng, 2016). An associated issue indicated that over 10% of the images in their data set were considered ungradable. A certain level of DR was defined as a class on these images. The method produced better results and was comparable to previous works on DR detection using a more generalized data set and with no feature-specific detection.

18.3 Data set and preprocessing

The proposed DR detection model uses the publicly available data set from Kaggle competition[1] for the purpose of training and evaluating the system. In this chapter, 1200 betwixt images from the original data set were considered for training the proposed system, as shown in Table 18.1. The class labels in the data set considered for the proposed model were highly imbalanced, as illustrated in Table 18.1. The distribution of various DR stages and their counts are shown in Figs. 18.1 and 18.2, respectively.

After splitting the imbalanced data set into train data (80%) and test data (20%), it can be seen that the train data have 732 class 0 labels. To solve the imbalances in the train data the class labels other than class 0 are oversampled to 732 in the train data. Therefore the train data contain 732 of each class labels. The train data size is then 3660.

Various transformations for data augmentation on the train data are done to improve the training of the proposed model. The customized data bunch is used to do some custom tasks for splitting and oversampling. Fig. 18.3 shows the center cropping and data augmentation.

18.4 Methodology

In this work various CNNs such as AlexNet, DenseNet, ResNet, SqueezeNet, and VggNet have been considered to train the proposed model to detect DR from the test data. CNNs and the associated transfer learning and hyperparameter model tuning have made great advancements on image classification tasks.

[1]https://www.kaggle.com/c/diabetic-retinopathy-detection/data

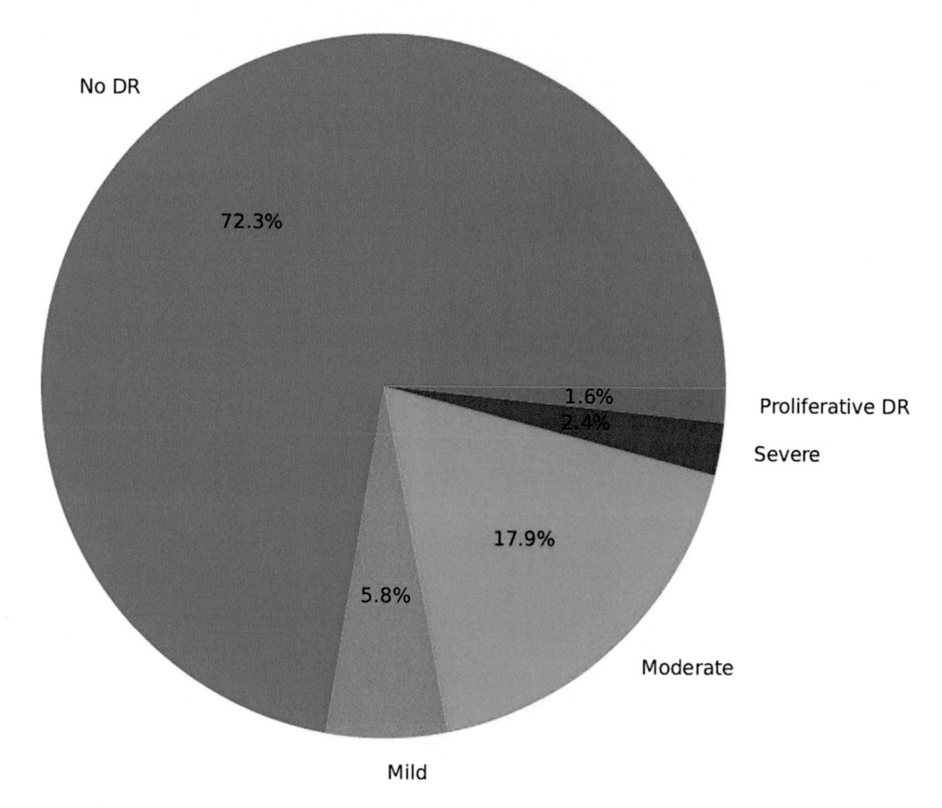

FIGURE 18.1 Distribution of DR fundus images at various stages. *DR*, Diabetic retinopathy.

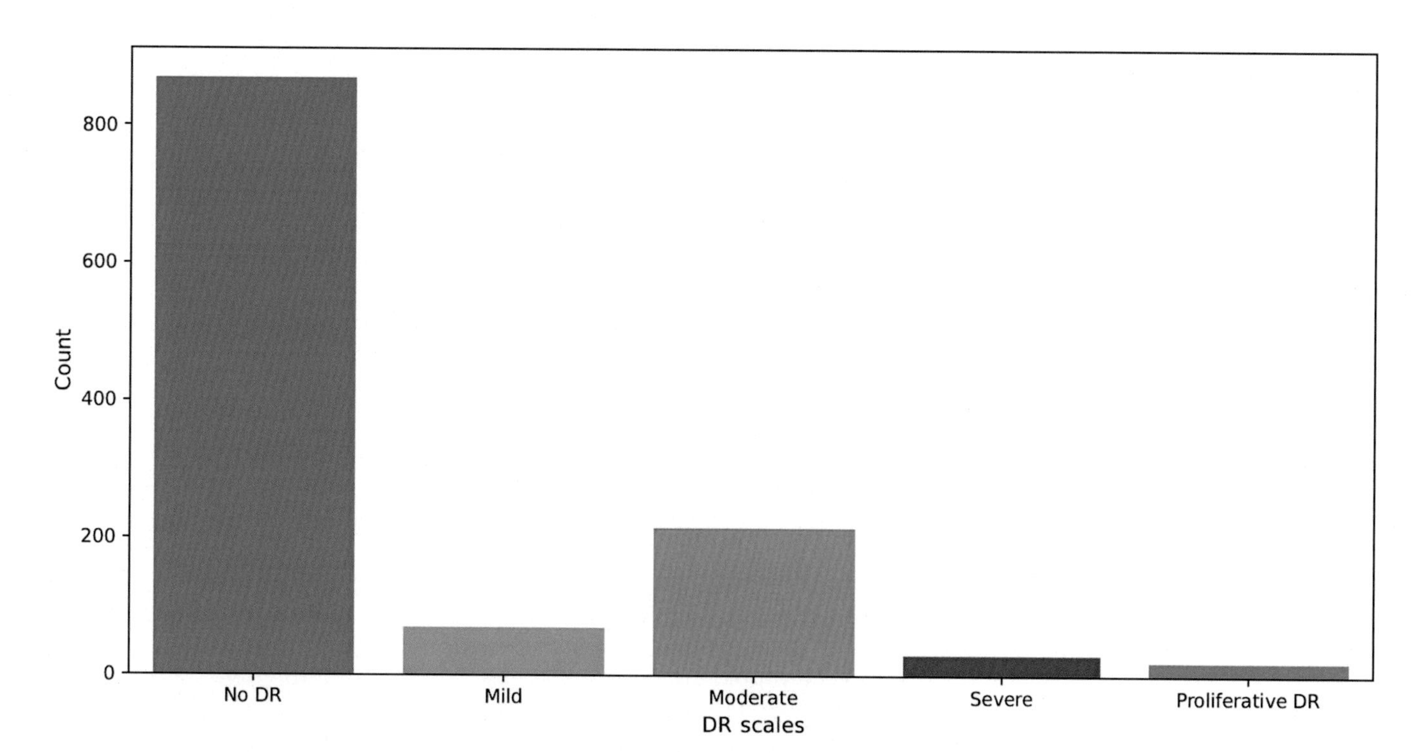

FIGURE 18.2 Count of DR fundus images at various stages. *DR*, Diabetic retinopathy.

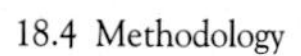

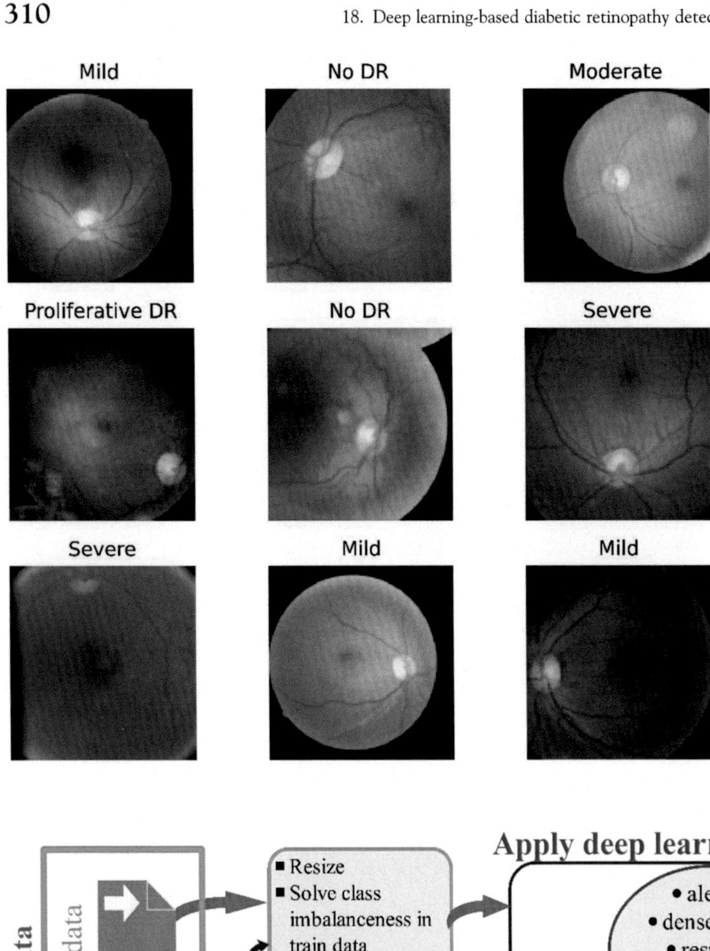

FIGURE 18.3 Sample preprocessed train data and corresponding class label.

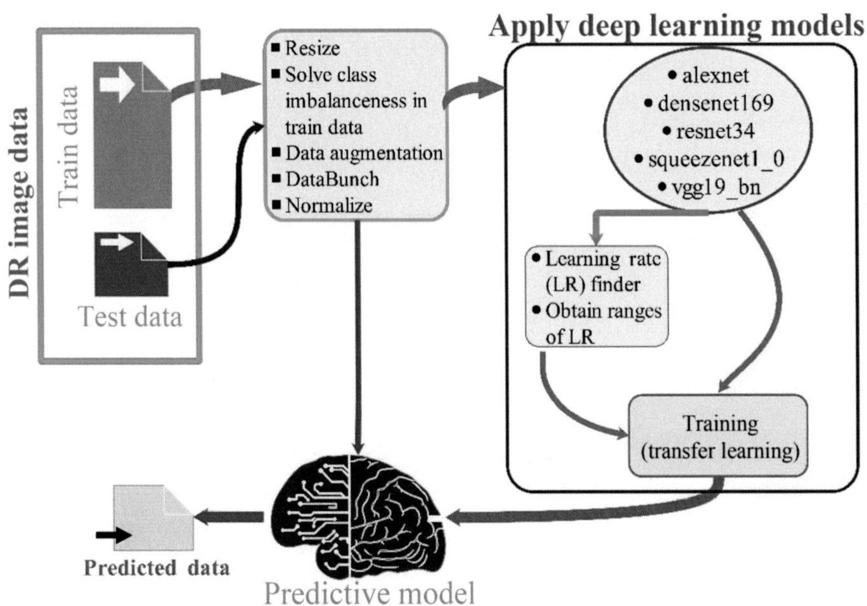

FIGURE 18.4 Proposed DR detection model. *DR*, Diabetic retinopathy.

18.4.1 Convolutional neural networks

CNN architecture consists of convolution layers, activation layers, and pooling. A deep, fully connected neural network (FCN) is then fed up from the output of the CNN, whose objective is to map for each input image to a set of 2D features into a class label. Various CNN architectures have evolved to accelerate the performance of image classification tasks by using high-performance computational tools like GPUs. AlexNet, DenseNet, ResNet, SqueezeNet, and VggNet are all such pretrained CNN architectures with different sizes of convolution, pooling, and output layers to enable faster classification for different sizes of image data sets. Fig. 18.4 shows the proposed DR detection model using the CNN architectures with transfer learning. Various CNN architectures mentioned earlier are introduced next.

AlexNet architecture consists of eight layers, which include three fully connected layers and five convolutional layers. Instead of using the tanh function it uses rectified linear units and allows multi-GPU training. In AlexNet overlap is introduced to "pool" outcomes of neurons of neighboring groups.

The residual block is introduced in the ResNet architecture where $y = F(x, W_i) + W_s x$ is used when x and $F(x)$ have dimensionality of different sizes such as 32×32 and 30×30. The term W_s is considered with 1×1 convolution, where the additional parameters are introduced to the model.

Each layer is connected to every other layer in the feedforward process in Dense Convolutional Network (DenseNet). Meanwhile, the classic convolutional networks with M layers have M connections like each and every other layer and its subsequent layers. Thus $M(M+1)/2$ direct connections are present in the network. Therefore inputs to each layer are the feature-maps of all the subsequent layers and the inputs to all the preceding layers are its own feature-maps. DenseNets has the most irresistible advantages such as reduced exploding-gradient problem, supports more feature reuse, strengthened propagation of features, and greatly reduces the parameter sizes.

VGGNet is the deep CNN model which succeeds the construction of deep layers of the neutral network with a convolution size of 16–19. It repeatedly stacks maximum pooling layers of size 2×2 and small convolution kernels of size 3×3. It ensures maximum performance, while decreasing the number of parameters.

SqueezeNet uses fire modules after a first standalone convolution layer and ends with a finishing convolution layer. Each fire module consists of filters and these filters are increased gradually from the start to the end of the network.

18.4.2 Training (transfer learning)

Transfer learning is used to retrain the last layers of a pretrained neural network. The learning rate (LR) finder developed by Smith is used to find the learning rate on the train data (Smith, 2017). By using pretrained CNN models and LR finder from the *fastai* library (fastai, 2020), it is seen that the loss decreases fastest around learning rate $\alpha = 0.01$, with the pretrained CNN architectures. Fig. 18.5 shows such the fastest decrease in loss around the learning rate $\alpha = 0.01$ on train data with pretrained AlexNet architecture.

It is also seen that the first layers are not changed as much with lower learning rates, while the last layers are changed more with higher learning rates. In this chapter, a range of learning rates $\alpha = [0.000001, 0.01]$ for different layers in the neural network is considered for training.

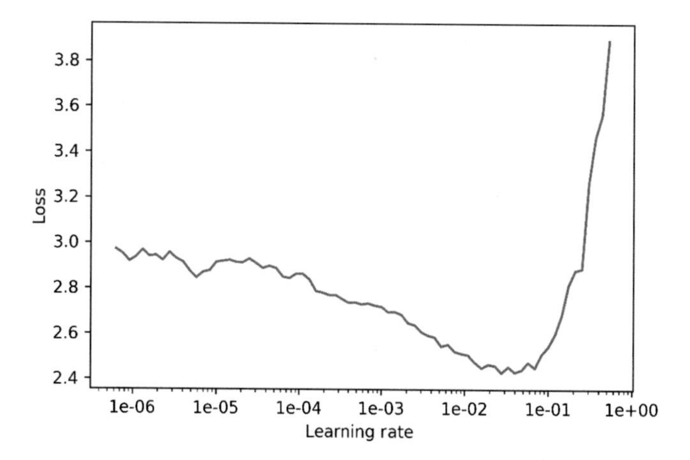

FIGURE 18.5 LR finder on train data with pretrained AlexNet architecture. *LR*, Learning rate.

18.4.3 Steps to train the proposed model

The proposed model uses five CNN architectures to train the model, as discussed earlier. Algorithm 18.1 discusses the training of the DR detection model for multiclass imbalanced data. After preprocessing the DR fundus images by resizing and cropping, data augmentation is performed during the training.

The pretrained CNN architectures are used to train the model in each epoch by using the range of learning rates, $\alpha = [0.000001, 0.01]$, as discussed earlier, instead of a single value of the learning rate. Then the performance is evaluated by the output from all the test samples.

18.5 Experimental results and discussion

In this section the proposed system is evaluated with the test data and the performance of the model discussed in terms of performance metrics such as model loss, model accuracy, precision, and recall. The configurations of the processing units used to train the proposed model are as follows:

- 32 GB of RAM;
- Intel Core i7 (4.27 GHz 8th Gen) processor; and
- NVIDIA Quadro P1000 (4 GB dedicated GPU, 16 GB shared GPU) with CUDA 10.1 driver package.

The model is also trained with progressive resizing using Google Colab (Bisong, 2019) Notebook, where the configurations provided are as follows:

- CPU: Intel(R) Xeon(R) CPU @ 2.00 GHz;
- GPU: Tesla T4/P4/PCIE;
- RAM: 12.74 GB.

ALGORITHM 18.1 Training DR detection model. *DR*, Diabetic retinopathy.

Input: train, test data

Output: predictive DR detection model

1: //Data pre-processing
Resize & data augmentation on train data:
//Cropping (224 × 224), batch size = 16, flipping (vertically),
Rotate (Max 360°), Zoom (0.1)Data bunch for splitting and oversampling to balance in classes of train dataNormalize each image.

2: //Import pretrained CNN architectures
M = {alexnet, densenet169, resnet34, squeezenet1_0, and vgg19_bn}

3: //Training (transfer learning)
while (pretrained CNN architectures M is completed) **do**
use range of learning rates, α = [0.000001, 0.01]
for each batch **in** train data **do**
if loss does not improve on subsequent five epochs **then**
update learning rate α
end if
end for
end while

4: //Evaluate test data
for each test sample in test data **do**
output from all trained models
end for

TABLE 18.2 Performance by the deep learning models.

CNN architectures	Train loss	Validation loss	Precision	Recall	Accuracy
AlexNet	0.577851	1.055273	0.310422	0.408492	0.551867
DenseNet	0.093581	0.740042	0.659377	0.622542	0.788382
ResNet	0.387945	0.938260	0.381484	0.415103	0.626556
SqueezeNet	0.445232	0.862627	0.458118	0.577702	0.622407
VggNet	0.219315	0.882297	0.515027	0.410715	0.746888

CNN, Convolutional neural network.

After performing an evaluation of test data, the performances of the CNN architectures as shown in Table 18.2 are compared with the performance evaluation metrics such as model loss, accuracy, precision, and recall. The confusion matrix, as shown in Fig. 18.6, shows the performance of the model on the test data for which the actual class label is known.

The model loss and accuracy define the effectiveness of the proposed model in DR detection. Accuracy is the most widely used metric to evaluate a model performance but in the case of imbalanced class of data the model performance can be dangerously misleading. The accuracy of the model is measured by $\text{Accuracy} = \frac{TP + TN}{TP + FP + FN + TN}$. Fig. 18.7

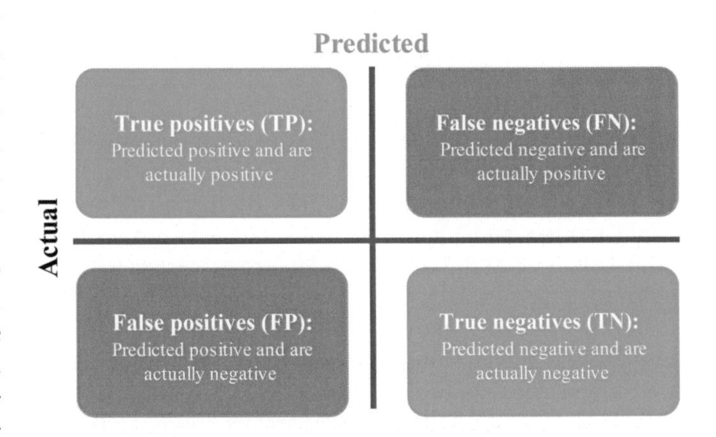

FIGURE 18.6 Basic representation of the confusion matrix.

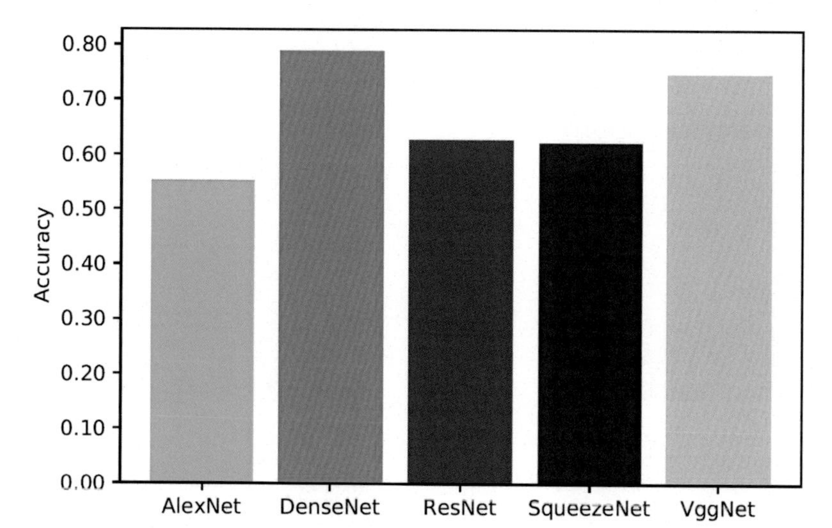

FIGURE 18.7 Accuracy comparison of the trained models.

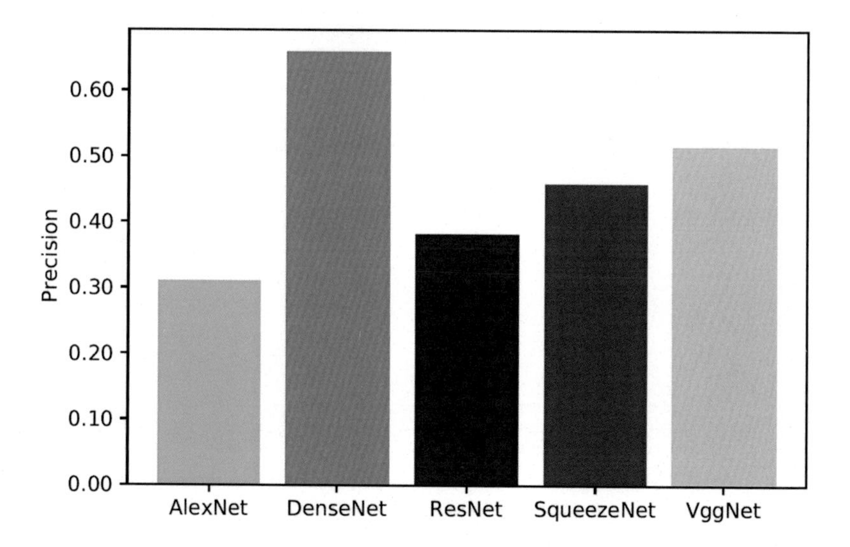

FIGURE 18.8 Precision comparison of the trained models.

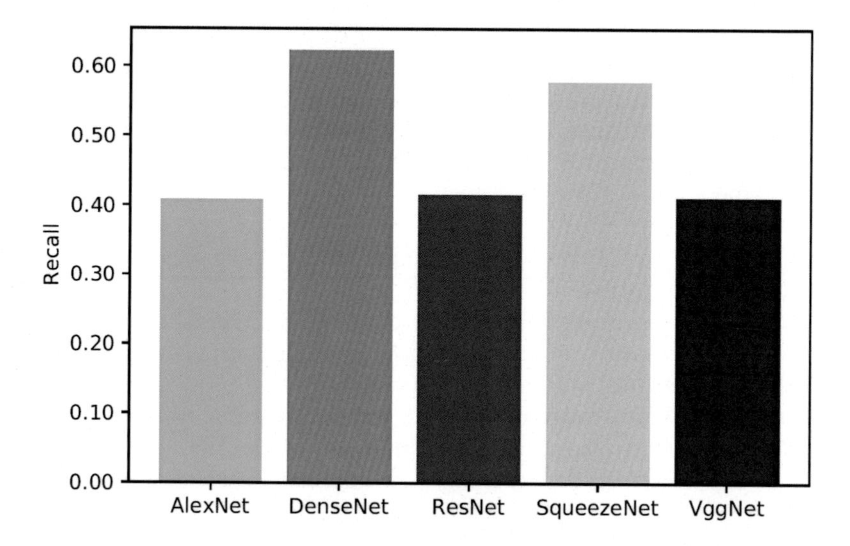

FIGURE 18.9 Recall comparison of the trained models.

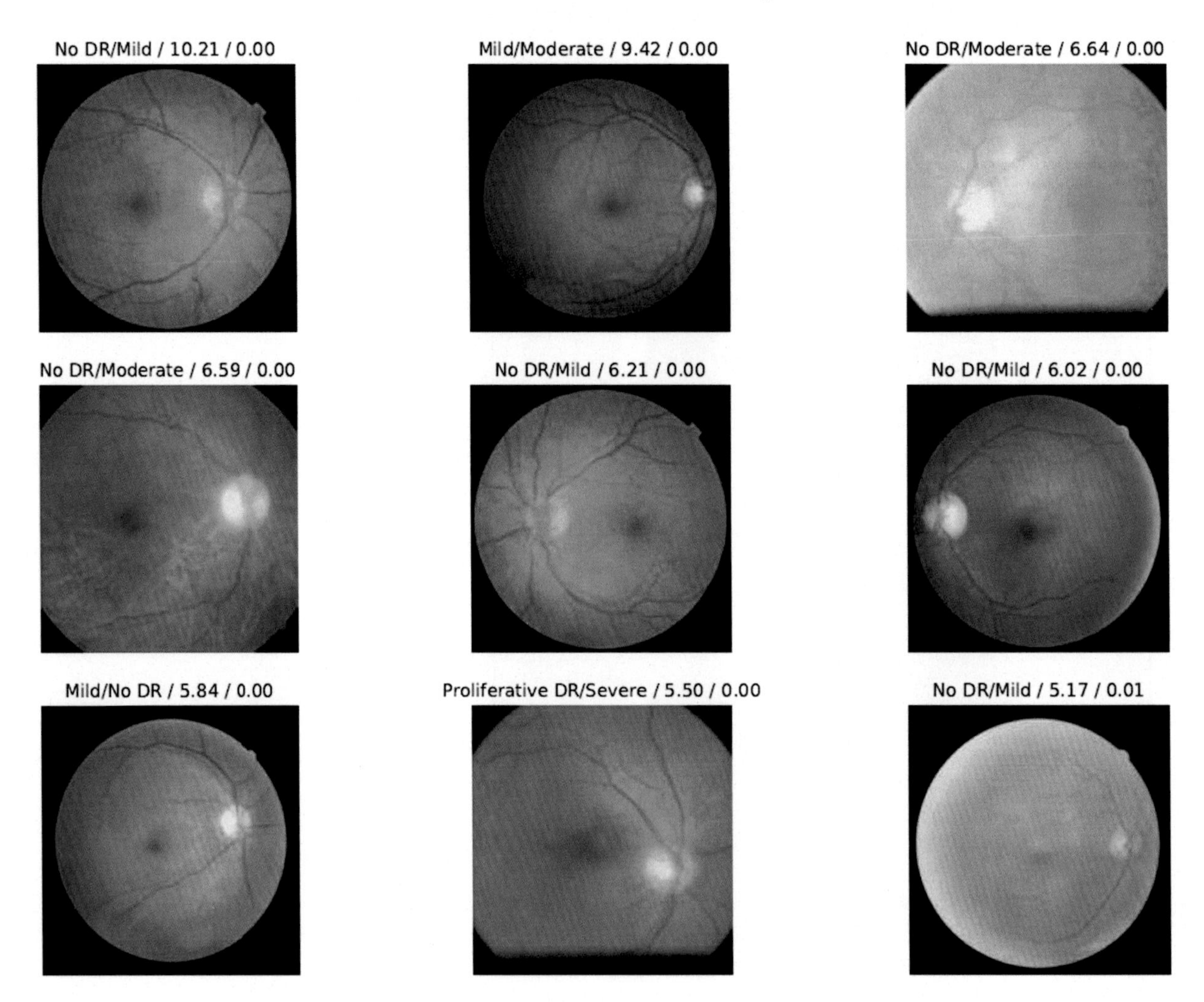

FIGURE 18.10 Top prediction losses in DenseNet architecture.

describes the comparative accuracy results of the trained models.

Precision and recall show the relevance of the result and correctness of the total relevant result, respectively, between 0 and 1. Precision is the proportion of positive samples out of the entire positive samples. Here the divisor is that the model prediction is positive from the entire given data set, so Precision $= \frac{TP}{TP + FP}$. Recall, sensitivity, or true positive rate is the percentage of positive samples out of the entire actual positive samples. Therefore Recall $= \frac{TP}{TP + FN}$, where the denominator is the actual positive samples present in the data set. The comparative results of the proposed trained models on precision and sensitivity are shown in Figs. 18.8 and 18.9, respectively.

Among all the CNN architectures it can be seen that the DenseNet model performs better on test data in DR detection. The top prediction losses are shown in Fig. 18.10 for the best performing model where the prediction on the test images is shown with corresponding prediction loss and their actual labels. The confusion matrix in DenseNet architecture with the sample test classes is shown in Fig. 18.11.

18.6 Conclusion and future work

Automatic detection of DR from the retinal images assists doctors to diagnose patients with DR efficiently. In this work, only 1200 images were used where they were oversampled and transfer learning was used to train the CNN architectures (AlexNet, DenseNet, ResNet, SqueezeNet, and VggNet) so that slight differences between the sample classes could be recognized for DR detection. The CNN architectures can learn features properly from a balanced data set, where the

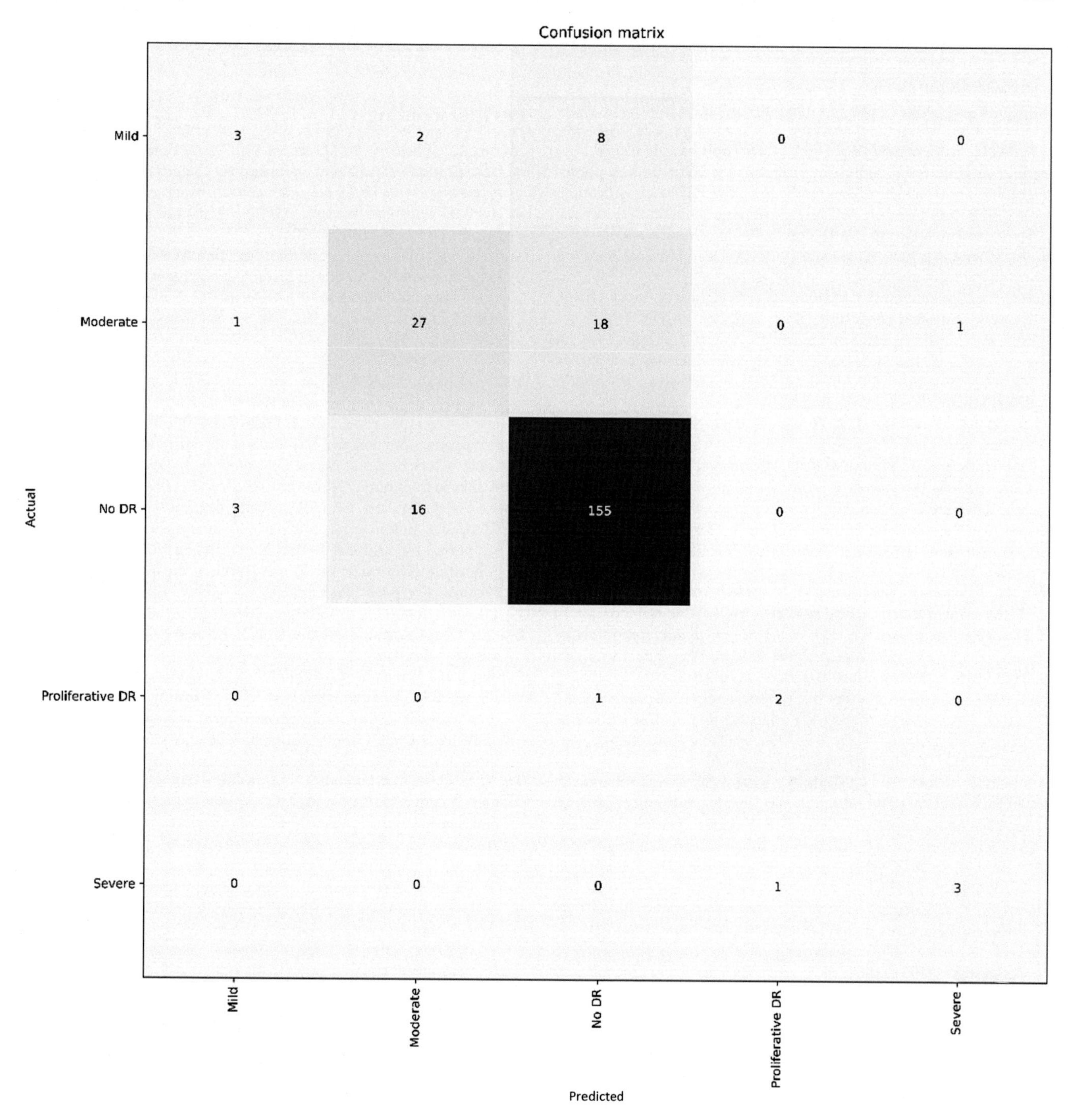

FIGURE 18.11 Confusion matrix in DenseNet architecture.

different classes of images are distributed equally. The CNN architectures lack effectiveness in the performance of the DR detection model in this work, although the oversampling method is applied to the highly imbalanced data classes. More image data, transfer learning, and hyperparameter tuning can be used to train the model. Other methods for dealing with imbalanced data sets can be used in future works.

References

Aiello, L. P., Gardner, T. W., King, G. L., Blankenship, G., Cavallerano, J. D., Ferris, F. L., et al. (1998). Diabetic retinopathy. *Diabetes Care, 21*, 143–156. Available from https://doi.org/10.2337/diacare.21.1.143.

Bisong, E. (2019). Google Colaboratory. In E. Bisong (Ed.), *Building machine learning and deep learning models on Google Cloud platform: A comprehensive guide for beginners* (pp. 59–64). Berkeley, CA: Apress, 10.1007/978-1-4842-4470-8_7.

Fong, D. S., Aiello, L. P., Ferris, F. L., & Klein, R. (2004). Diabetic retinopathy. *Diabetes Care*, *27*, 2540–2553. Available from https://doi.org/10.2337/diacare.27.10.2540.

fastai/fastai (2020). fast.ai.

Gargeya, R., & Leng, T. (2017). Automated identification of diabetic retinopathy using deep learning. *Ophthalmology*, *124*, 962–969. Available from https://doi.org/10.1016/j.ophtha.2017.02.008.

Grading diabetic retinopathy from stereoscopic color fundus photographs—an extension of the modified Airlie House classification. ETDRS report number 10. Early Treatment Diabetic Retinopathy Study Research Group (1991). Ophthalmology 98, 786–806.

He, K., Zhang, X., Ren, S., & Sun, J. (2015). Deep residual learning for image recognition. *arXiv*:1512.03385 [cs].

Huang, G., Liu, Z., van der Maaten, L., & Weinberger, K. Q. (2018). Densely connected convolutional networks. *arXiv*:1608.06993 [cs].

Iandola, F. N., Han, S., Moskewicz, M. W., Ashraf, K., Dally, W. J., & Keutzer, K. (2016). SqueezeNet: AlexNet-level accuracy with 50x fewer parameters and \textless0.5MB model size. *arXiv*:1602.07360 [cs].

Krizhevsky, A., Sutskever, I., & Hinton, G. E. (2012). ImageNet classification with deep convolutional neural networks. In F. Pereira, C. J. C. Burges, L. Bottou, & K. Q. Weinberger (Eds.), *Advances in neural information processing systems* (25, pp. 1097–1105). Curran Associates, Inc.

LeCun, Y., Bengio, Y., & Hinton, G. (2015). Deep learning. *Nature*, *521*, 436–444. Available from https://doi.org/10.1038/nature14539.

Pratt, H., Coenen, F., Broadbent, D. M., Harding, S. P., & Zheng, Y. (2016). Convolutional neural networks for diabetic retinopathy. In *Procedia computer science, 20th conference on medical image understanding and analysis (MIUA 2016)* 90 (pp. 200–205). Available from https://doi.org/10.1016/j.procs.2016.07.014

Quellec, G., Charrière, K., Boudi, Y., Cochener, B., & Lamard, M. (2017). Deep image mining for diabetic retinopathy screening. *Medical Image Analysis*, *39*, 178–193. Available from https://doi.org/10.1016/j.media.2017.04.012.

Qummar, S., Khan, F. G., Shah, S., Khan, A., Shamshirband, S., Rehman, Z. U., et al. (2019). A deep learning ensemble approach for diabetic retinopathy detection. *IEEE Access.*, *7*, 150530–150539. Available from https://doi.org/10.1109/ACCESS.2019.2947484.

Schmidhuber, J. (2014). *Deep learning in neural networks: An overview.* CoRR abs/1404.7828.

Simonyan, K. & Zisserman, A. (2015). Very deep convolutional networks for large-scale image recognition. *arXiv*:1409.1556 [cs].

Smith, L. N. (2017). Cyclical learning rates for training neural networks. *arXiv*:1506.01186 [cs].

Wan, S., Liang, Y., & Zhang, Y. (2018). Deep convolutional neural networks for diabetic retinopathy detection by image classification. *Computers & Electrical Engineering*, *72*, 274–282. Available from https://doi.org/10.1016/j.compeleceng.2018.07.042.

Zeng, X., Chen, H., Luo, Y., & Ye, W. (2019). Automated diabetic retinopathy detection based on binocular siamese-like convolutional neural network. *IEEE Access.*, *7*, 30744–30753. Available from https://doi.org/10.1109/ACCESS.2019.2903171.

Further reading

Ghosh, R., Ghosh, K., & Maitra, S. (2017). Automatic detection and classification of diabetic retinopathy stages using CNN. In *Proceedings of the 2017 4th international conference on signal processing and integrated networks (SPIN)*. Available from https://doi.org/10.1109/spin.2017.8050011

Gulshan, V., Peng, L., Coram, M., Stumpe, M. C., Wu, D., Narayanaswamy, A., et al. (2016). Development and validation of a deep learning algorithm for detection of diabetic retinopathy in retinal fundus photographs. *The Journal of the American Medical Association*, *316*, 2402–2410. Available from https://doi.org/10.1001/jama.2016.17216.

He, K., Zhang, X., Ren, S., & Sun, J. (2016). Identity mappings in deep residual networks. *arXiv*:1603.05027 [cs].

Hemanth, D. J., Deperlioglu, O., & Kose, U. (2020). An enhanced diabetic retinopathy detection and classification approach using deep convolutional neural network. *Neural Computing & Applications*, *32*, 707–721. Available from https://doi.org/10.1007/s00521-018-03974-0.

Kose, U., & Arslan, A. (2017). Optimization of self-learning in Computer Engineering courses: An intelligent software system supported by Artificial Neural Network and Vortex Optimization Algorithm: Optimization of self-learning: an intelligent software system. *Computer Applications in Engineering Education*, *25*, 142–156. Available from https://doi.org/10.1002/cae.21787.

lisa-lab/DeepLearningTutorials (2020). *Laboratoire d'Informatique des Systèmes Adaptatifs*.

Sutton, J. R., Mahajan, R., Akbilgic, O., & Kamaleswaran, R. (2019). PhysOnline: An open source machine learning pipeline for real-time analysis of streaming physiological waveform. *IEEE Journal of Biomedical and Health Informatics*, *23*, 59–65. Available from https://doi.org/10.1109/JBHI.2018.2832610.

Tu, J. V. (1996). Advantages and disadvantages of using artificial neural networks versus logistic regression for predicting medical outcomes. *Journal of Clinical Epidemiology*, *49*, 1225–1231. Available from https://doi.org/10.1016/S0895-4356(96)00002-9.

Usman, A., Muhammad, A., Martinez-Enriquez, A. M., & Muhammad, A. (2020). Classification of diabetic retinopathy and retinal vein occlusion in human eye fundus images by transfer learning. In K. Arai, S. Kapoor, & R. Bhatia (Eds.), *Advances in information and communication, advances in intelligent systems and computing* (pp. 642–653). Cham: Springer International Publishing. Available from https://doi.org/10.1007/978-3-030-39442-4_47.

Verma, S. (2020). *Multi-label image classification with neural network \textbar keras, medium.*

Wang, Z., Yin, Y., Shi, J., Fang, W., Li, H., & Wang, X. (2017). Zoom-in-Net: Deep mining lesions for diabetic retinopathy detection. *arXiv*:1706.04372 [cs].

CHAPTER

19

Internet of Things e-health revolution: secured transmission of homeopathic e-medicines through chaotic key formation

Joydeep Dey[1], Arindam Sarkar[2] and Sunil Karforma[3]

[1]Department of Computer Science, M.U.C. Women's College, Burdwan, India [2]Department of Computer Science & Electronics, Ramakrishna Mission Vidyamandira, Belur Math, India [3]Department of Computer Science, The University of Burdwan, Burdwan, India

19.1 Introduction

Dementia, schizophrenia, bipolar disorder, obsessive-compulsive disorder (OCD), insomnia, mood disorders, acute depression, major depressive disorder (MDD), anxiety, etc. are the most common and frequent psychiatric diseases. They constitute key aspects of societal developmental obstacles. For psychiatric treatments, it has been found that most of the patients are not willing to consult psychiatrists/physicians. To resolve this problem, the online communication of a homeopathic prescription has been proposed while ensuring patients' data security. To speed up the data processing in real time intelligent devices are used that are described as the Internet of Things (IoT). An e-Health system guided through the IoT has emerged as a new and effective tool to treat patients globally (Dey, Karforma, Sarkar, & Bhowmik, 2019). The objective of this proposed technique is to generate robust session keys on the basis of a chaotic sequence. This would be encrypted through a predefined key by a third party before transporting to users. Moreover, computational intelligence is involved in the secret sharing of homeopathic e-prescriptions through a public channel. Prior to that, a mask matrix would be generated and used for generating the encrypted forms of the partial shares. During the regeneration, the minimal numbers of threshold shares are used. A classical algorithm has been finally used to transmit the partial shares in encrypted form with the proposed session key. The psychiatric patients generally need noninvasive treatment, and so maybe treated through the proposed technique in a more secure way. Cryptography is the primary method to impose security on the medical data (Bhowmik, Sarkar, Karforma, & Dey, 2019). Shyness and feelings of inferiority of patients are addressed through this proposed e-health system. The primary objective of this proposed technique is to treat mentally challenged patients through the web-portal-based secured e-health system, in cases of noninvasive and nonemergency patients. The proposed system is based on chaotic symmetric key-based secret-sharing cryptography where the same key is used by all the doctors and patients. The key is obtained through an authenticated key distribution center (KDC). To neutralize man-in-the-middle attacks, this approach of generating keys is likely to be favorable.

Serotonin is a hormone produced by the brain, and sufficient amounts of this hormone result in better mood, while insufficient amounts result in depression. Genetic criteria are also significant contributors to psychiatric diseases. This chapter describes a system to enable patients to receive their homeopathic treatments from homes. Therefore data transmission is the primary focus of this chapter. Homeopathic treatment is focused on the philosophy of curing patients' mental and physical health problems. In fact, telemedicine is comprised of different categories of treatments through the online mode, such as allopathic treatments, homeopathic treatments, Ayurvedic treatments, and Unani treatments. In this chapter, the application of homeopathic treatments is described. Homeopathy treatments are feasible in the case of nonemergency and noninvasive patients, unlike allopathic treatments. Homeopathic medicines are

Recent Trends in Computational Intelligence Enabled Research.
DOI: https://doi.org/10.1016/B978-0-12-822844-9.00001-3

prescribed in very minute dosages to patients. Apparently, such doses are nontoxic to the human body, and produce no side effects, as compared with allopathic treatments. They also boost immunity against different viruses. This chapter deals with secured data transmission inside a public channel. With the help of the proposed homeopathic telemedicine, patients have convenient consultations with their doctors with more secured features. It deals with the symptoms and conditions of different patients. Traveling costs, nosocomial infections, waiting in queues, etc. are eradicated in such homeopathic telemedicine. Also, the treatment costs are very low and the wide availability of medicines is also an advantage of homeopathic telemedicine. It is more justified to treat patients remotely in this technology-friendly era using homeopathic medicines. Thus, hassle-free and flexible systems are preferred by patients in this technological era. Some homeopathic psychiatric medicines include the following (Viksveen et al., 2018). Calcarea carbonica and aconite are commonly prescribed for anxiety and stress with fast palpitations, dry mouth, dry skin, etc. Ignatia is given for grief, loss, mood swinger, etc. Kali phosphoricum is prescribed for overwhelming irrational desires that cause excessive stress. Lycopodium is given to treat a lack of self confidence. Sepia is used for menopausal female patients with fluctuating moods. *Hyoscyamus niger* is used to treat anxiety, irritability, brain restlessness, agitation, etc.

In this proposed technique, a mysterious secret-sharing concept has been implemented for the homeopathy telemedicine system. In a specified group of users of size n, there shall be a predefined threshold value k. Combinations of $K-1$ secret shares can't construct the original message if the predefined threshold value is K Das & Adhikari, 2010; Dautrich & Ravishankar, 2016). Each share contain the partial information about the plain text. Any combinations of K shares able to reconstruct the original text. However, for secure transmission it is essential that there is no part containing the total data. A concept of secret bytes should be combined, in which each share has a few missing bytes that can only be recovered from a group of exactly k number of threshold shares. In this way, a missing byte location for any k shares, but at the very least k, can be discovered. A secret can be shared among a large number of people by using data sharing, which means that all of the shares provide fractional information about the original data. That, as well as the concept of a favored recipient, should be familiarized with upgrading the patient's data protection. In these principles, if and only if $(k-1)$ legitimate shares, including the privileged share can construct the original information. Along with such a proposed encryption technique, psychiatric patients may use telemedicine services based on homeopathy treatments. Moreover, to observe the patients' body language, the proposed technique uses an IoT-based video recording system which is stored on the system. Thus, psychiatrists can view the neural motor actions and cognitive behavior of patients from very distant locations. Somatic expressions, hand–eye coordination, body language, mental reading ability, etc. are factors that can be perceived by the psychiatrists. Therefore the proposed technique illustrates the dynamic images of patients, while they upload their responses in a flexible manner.

19.2 Related works

Nien et al. (2007) showed in their research the realization of a chaotic-based map on some random sequences. They used this to create a sequence to encrypt images using an XOR operation. Jiménez-Serrano, Tortajada, and García-Gómez (2015) developed a mobile e-health app to detect postpartum depression with the help of machine learning. Mowery et al. (2017) showed different types of depression symptoms with psychological stressors in their paper. Ravichandran et al. (2017) designed a DNA-based chaos scheme to implement security for medical data/images. Sarkar, Dey, Bhowmik, Mandal, and Karforma (2018) computed a neural transmission/session key for the electronic health system. Rai et al. designed a mechanism to detect levels of depression by machine learning. Also, using machine learning, suitable treatments are suggested (Rai et al., 2019). However, they did not mention the data transmission security issues. Mdhaffar et al. proposed a technique of deep learning for depression detection using smartphones (Mdhaffar et al., 2019). Dey et al. described in their research work a meta-heuristic secured transmission of an e-prescription in the e-dental healthcare domain (Dey et al., 2019). Such encryption techniques were used on digital images of the IoT, and gained a good level of robustness. It is, however, better to use a session key transmitted through a third party called a KDC. To reduce the costs and improve the treatment facilities, the IoT concept has been adopted in the healthcare domain.

Khade and Narnaware (2012) proposed chaotic functions for different images to be encrypted. In their paper, the disorderly encryption calculation dependent on three-dimensional strategic guides, three-dimensional Chebyshev guide, and three-dimensional, two-dimensional Arnold's feline guide for shading the image as encryption was proposed. The two-dimensional Arnold's feline guide has been taken into consideration for the purpose of image pixel scrambling and the three-dimensional Arnold's feline guide has been considered for red, green, and blue segments replacement. The three-dimensional Chebyshev map has been used for the key age. The Chebyshev map has been considered as the public key cryptographic encryption and the subsequent dissipation of the designed private session keys. Arnold's feline guide plays out the double encryption, initially playing out rearranging and also playing out the replacement. Utilizing ACM, the connection among the contiguous pixels can be upset totally. However, the 3D feline guide can be used to replace dim/shading values. Exploration by Thampi and Jose (2013) was used through a 3D riotous guide. They incorporated a key sequence age measure, dispersion replacement, and concealing cycle. For dissemination purposes, an initial three-dimensional Chebyshev map was intelligently iterated multiple times and had yielded as a contribution to a three-dimensional strategic guide, and at that point replacement of S-boxes had been done and the final advancement of concealing was rearranging parts of the picture. For the period of chaotic directions' starting states, three hexadecimal current attributes and cruising point estimations were used. The primary stage comprises of the key sequence stage utilizing a 3D Chebyshev map and a 3D calculated guide. Initially, lots of irregular keys were produced by utilizing the 3D Chebyshev maps which are expressed as $f'n(y) = \cos n\theta$; where y equals $\cos\theta$ and thus such keys were utilized as the starting conditions for the 3D strategic guides. At that point the arbitrary qualities produced utilizing these guides were utilized for forward encryption. A converse encryption was then carried on. Moreover, in order to improve the security features and to prepare appropriate replacement, an S-box of AES is utilized. Yadava, Singh, Sinha, and Pandey (2013) proposed an encryption approach on the basis of Henon chaotic maps. Here, Henon is a tumultuous framework which changes to a one-dimensional disordered guide that is numerically characterized in terms of $Y_{n+2} = a \times Y_{2n+1} + b \times \mathrm{Sin}(wY_n)$. The shaded picture was changed into the RGB combination of three bits of a part network. A 1D Henon disorganized guide takes the red segment of the shaded picture to produce an arbitrary key sequence. The bit qualities acquired are a bitwise XOR operation with the first pixel estimation of the red segment of the unique change framework.

A new pattern has been seen for the methodology of encryption applied to telemedicine that was suitable for securing information transmission. Gritzalis and Lambrinoudakis (2004) carried out authentication tasks in the domain of online-based telemedicine. User authentication, granting of privilege, remote resource allocation, etc. were their main achievements. Krawczyk and Jain (2005) designed a method that has been developed as a blend of online digital signature and audible biometrics modalities. Online digital signatures were checked through a run-time pattern-matching and audio biometric program. Fewer errors were detected in their method. Wu, Lee, Lai, Lee, and Chung (2010) designed a secured mechanism that needed less time as compared to the existing methods. Their technique was based on a novel authentication that sorts the limitations of two-factor authentication methods. He, Chen, and Zhang (2011) developed the mime resistance against different types of opponents present in telemedicine networks. They used lower versatile calculation abilities. Al-Haj et al. developed a hybrid cryptographic engineering system on patients' medical data with the insuring of patient confidentiality and authenticity. Local tampering, robustness on data, imperceptibility, etc. were the tests used by them to enhance its performance (Al-Haj, Mohammad, & Amer, 2017). Madhusudhan and Nayak (2019) examined diverse cryptanalysis assaults such as mime attack, biometric attack, password attack, client/server compromisation attack, etc. on telemedicine systems. In fact, they tried to enhance the medical data security parameters using chaos authentication methods. Manojkumar, Karthigaikumar, and Ramachandran (2019) planned a low-force utilization circuit with better S-Box execution with low engendering delay. They confined the unapproved admittance to the clinical pictures. Rayachoti, Tirumalasetty, and Prathipati (2020) developed a technique for different types of biomedical imaging modalities guided through slantlet transformation. This identified the changed region of interest in the clinical reports carried out by programmers.

Exactness, versatility, information security, and data protection are the four essential issues that should be attended to. The Freeman chain code is utilized to distinguish the outside limits by methods for succession of more modest straight-line fragments in the predefined direction. Nayak, Subbanna Bhat, Acharya, and Sathish Kumar (2009) proposed a novel procedure to store scrambled data dependent on the advanced encryption standard and that were super-forced inside a retinal picture. Nandakumar and Jain (2004) proposed a calculation for coordinating details. They used the spatial domain to connect the interior points of interest around each of the finger impression information. This ensures a finer disposition of organized minute details in fingerprints. Music-motivated harmony search calculation has been utilized to locate the ideal arrangement in different genuine issues. Assad and Deep (2018) proposed a novel hybridized calculation of harmony search and recreated strengthening to generate better ideal solutions. Their numeric information demonstrated the advancements in their proposed methodology. Mathur et al. (2016) proposed AES-based content encryption utilizing dynamic key determination for upgrades. Murillo-Escobar, Cardoza-Avendaño, and López-Gutiérrez (2017) proposed a confused put-together encryption with respect to the ECG clinical signals in 2017 with logistic maps-based text encryption. Telemedicine frameworks have increased as a treatment device in this advanced computer-literate world. Wang, Gao, and Zenger (2015) looked into the utilization of harmony search calculation in designing the defined areas. Additionally, ideal issue plans dependent on metaheuristic harmony search were investigated by them. Dagadu, Li, and Aboagye (2019) created a session key dependent on disorganized capacity, which would be additionally diffused with the DNA over the clinical picture applications. Sarkar, Dey, Chatterjee, Bhowmik, and Karforma (2019) proposed a neural organization-based cryptography telehealth security framework. Biometrics has remarkable boundaries to set up the character standards of an individual through the underlying components.

Shamir's (1979) secret-sharing scheme depends on a (k, n) limit-based mystery-sharing strategy. A $(k-1)$ polynomial degree is most important here. The polynomial capacity of request $(k-1)$ is built as

$$f(x) = \left(p_0 + p_1x + p_2x^2 + p_3x^3 + \cdots + p_{k-1}x^{k-1}\right) \bmod m \ldots \quad (19.1)$$

where p_0 is the mystery, m is a prime number, and all different coefficients are chosen arbitrarily from mystery. Every one of the n shares is a couple (x_i, z_i) of numbers fulfilling $f(x_i) = z_i$ and $x_i > 0$, $1 \leq i \leq n$ and $0 < x_1 < x_2 < x_3 < \ldots < x_k \leq m-1$. When given the opportunity to opt for any k number of shares of the polynomial, it is interestingly merged together and then the mystery can be refigured only through Lagrange's addition. Blakley (1979) utilized this calculation to take care of the mystery-sharing issue. The mystery message is a point in a k-dimensional space and the n numbers of shares are relatively hyperplanes that cross in this point. The set of arrangement $y = (y_1, y_2, \ldots, y_k)$ in the following Eq. (19.2) structures a relative hyperplane.

$$p_1y^1 + p_2y^2 + \ldots + p_ky^k = b \ldots \quad (19.2)$$

The mystery of the point of convergence is obtained by getting the convergence of any k number of shares on these planes.

19.3 Complication statements

The following are the complications that can be identified in this domain:

- Fear of social popularization, felt by patients;
- Due to mental rigidness, nonparticipation and cooperation in the treatments by patients;
- Patients' data security in public channels;
- Intruder attacks on medical sensitive data;
- Key compromisation on telemedicine patients' terminal(s) and paths.

19.4 Proposed frame of work

If the patient (P) wants to communicate with the doctor (D) through an online web-portal, then P will request KDC for a session key. KDC will encrypt the session key generated though a chaotic sequence by the previously assigned permanent key to P and D, respectively. Through the online interface at the web-portal, different patients' inputs are captured, such as age, sex, blood pressure, periodical information, and mental status in terms of relationships or break-ups. Thus, after analyzing those symptoms, physicians may provide homeopathic medicines though online e-prescriptions. This can be done in a secured sharing manner. To mitigate the intruders, a key distribution center might use a logistic map of degree two (Dey et al., 2019; Mdhaffar et al., 2019) of degree two to diffuse the intruders. Thus, the same key based on a chaotic sequence will be passed to all the registered patients and doctors. The key received would be used for both encryption and decryption for the session. Once the session expires, the validity of the session key also expires. The meanings of the different terms used in the following proposed algorithm are given below.

C:

C: Floating Constant, n: Number of Users, $Mask[n_{C_{k-1}}][n]$ *: Mask Matrix, Y[128]: Proposed Session Key*

Proposed Algorithm.: IoT Homeopathy E-Prescription Transmission Based on Chaotic Key

*/*Chaotic key of 128 bits formation by the KDC */*

For $I = 0$ *to* 127

$Y_{n+1} = C \times (1 - Y_n)^2$

Sum (Y_{n+1}) *Mod* $2 = 0?\ Y_{n+1} = 1\text{: } Y_{n+1} = 0$ *//Filling of Session Key*

End for

Transfer of Y [128] *to users*

/*Secret Mask generation*/

(Continued)

C: (Continued)

```
For z = 1to nC_{k-1}
 For p = 1 to n
  Mask[nC_{k-1}][n] = GenerateSecretMask(z, p)
 End for
End for
/*Encryption of Open Shares with Chaotic Key*/
 For t = 1 to n
For s = 1 to nC_{n-k}
  EncryptedShare[t][s] = Share[t][s]XORY[s]
 End for
 Y[] = Y[] >> s
End for
/*AES Encryption of Encrypted shares with Session Key Y[128]*/
For Q = 1 to n
 FinalShare[Q] = AES(EncryptedShare[Q], Y[128])
End for
Transmit n transmittable partial encrypted shares
```

Here a novel technique has been proposed to generate transmission/session keys based on the chaos sequence that in turn is used for ciphering in homeopathy telemedicine. A mask matrix is designed for the subsequent XOR operations, which were carried on the session key and homeopathy e-prescription. This is the first round of ciphering done for the fragmentation. Furthermore, fusion between the blocks containing corresponding data and key fragments is done.

To treat mentally challenged patients remotely is the integral focus of this chapter. The medical data related to any patients are crucial and need to be protected from intruders. Thus, the proposed system may be considered as an important secured communication tool in homeopathic telemedicine.

19.5 Work flow diagram of the proposed technique

The work flow diagram of this proposed method is depicted in Fig. 19.1.

In this novel proposed methodology, the security mechanism has been used in the field of homeopathic telemedicine. The KDC is used to generate a session key of 128 bits. Using the chaotic sequence, a session key has been proposed for every transaction. Once generated, they are transmitted to the system users. A mask generation algorithm is run at the back end.

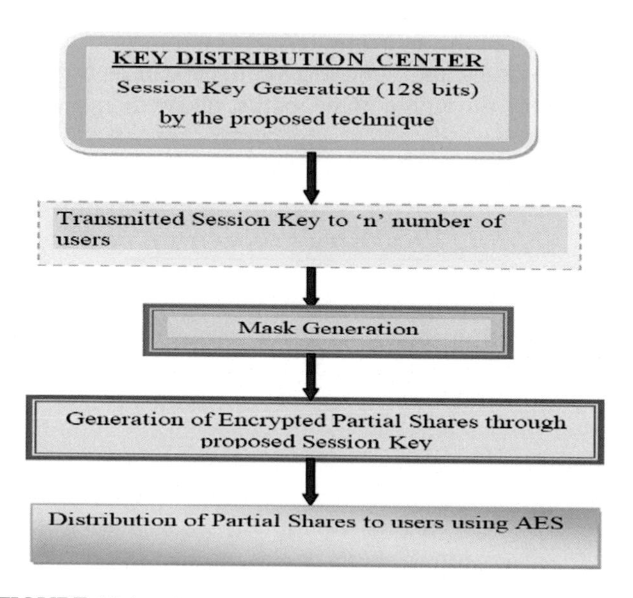

FIGURE 19.1 Flow diagram of the proposed technique.

The e-prescription is encrypted through the proposed session key to generate different shares. Finally, these are communicated to the system users by encrypting with AES. The beauty of this system is that the original data can only be restructured after the amalgamation of the needed threshold shares in the group. The proposed session key has been tested through different statistical tests which are explained in later sections.

The tests like NIST, histogram, entropy, autocorrelation, chi-square, session key analysis, etc. have shown efficacy in this proposed technique. The proposed technique has been compared with preexisting techniques.

19.6 Novelty of the proposed technique

Homeopathic medicines have no or few side effects. The following are the novelties of the proposed technique:

- Online secured transmission of homeopathic e-prescriptions with secret sharing;
- A KDC outsider has been utilized to produce a session key utilizing the chaotic sequence;
- A session key is communicated to both system users through a private channel;
- Moreover, using the mask generation methods, partial secret shares are generated and transmitted with n number of users;
- AES is used to transmit them in encrypted format with the proposed session key of 128 bits length;
- During the reconstruction phase, the minimum needful threshold shares only are eligible to restructure the actual e-prescriptions;
- Noninvasive and noncritical patients can be treated remotely through a homeopathic telemedicine system.

19.7 Result section

A session key generation mechanism has been implemented at the KDC server. Based on a constant value C for a single session, the chaotic random number is formed (Dey et al., 2019). This proposed key formation mechanism can be illustrated in the following example.

Example: An epoch of 128 to generate a random number, which is then multiplied by a floating constant C. The sum of digits of the product is calculated and checked with the following criteria.

$$If(Sum(product)Mod2)then$$

$$Session\_Key = Session\_Key||1$$

$$Else$$

$$Session\_Key = Session\_Key||0$$

$$Endif$$

The proposed technique generates a session key of length 128 bits using a chaotic sequence as defined above. Table 19.1 contains a description of such session keys.

TABLE 19.1 Proposed 128-bits session keys formed.

Key no.	Session key (in hexadecimal)	Fitness level	NIST test
1	cb c9 21 40 72 2e c5 0a 53 4d 7d f8 a9 f8 8f e9	Excellent	Passed
2	af df 19 82 1a ac 2f 7f 58 ac 6f 5b 22 fe 0a e4	Excellent	Passed
3	2d 58 5d ec 1f 77 7c b4 71 a5 bd 61 60 09 c3 25	Excellent	Passed
4	40 ef 2c 02 0c e2 30 9ffc e6 17 a6 df 7e 3e d4	Excellent	Passed
5	e1 c5 dd 79 a5 31 cf ff aa d1 91 b5 66 16 7b e4	Excellent	Passed
6	ee 87 5c d9 4d 0a 00 a3 67 f1 01 34 25 4c 0d 1f	Moderate	Passed
7	95 19 f6 10 7d f0 c9 db f6 e4 f7 3c d2 df 4c 7d	Moderate	Passed
8	c5 1b fb 33 f4 0d e2 d4 13 e4 84 56 dd 92 34 45	Excellent	Passed
9	63 7c b4 97 5b 0f 58 69 fb ce 76 5c 9e 20 97 a3	Moderate	Passed
10	50 d0 95 e1 0f 8c 64 85 2a 0e bf 8c e3 8d 21 1a	Excellent	Passed

Table 19.1 contains the table headers of Key no., Session key (in hexadecimal), Fitness level, and NIST test. It is clear that there is no correspondence between any pairs of keys generated by the KDC. Thus, by encrypting the homeopathic e-prescription using any of the proposed generated keys will be strong enough to prevent intruders from gaining access. Medical data thus will be preserved using this proposed approach (Wu et al., 2010).

19.7.1 Statistical key strength

The NIST test suite (Rukhin et al., 2001) is a complete statistics-related package comprised of 15 statistical tests. Its objective is to investigate the true randomness of chaotic session key sequences generated through the proposed technique. Different randomness checking was incorporated under this category. The following tables were obtained when using different session keys as given at Table 19.1 with favorable outputs. Ten different keys as stated in Table 19.1 are discussed here. Table 19.2 contains the index of the statistical tests that were conducted on our generated keys through the proposed technique.

Table 19.2 contains the table headers Sl. no., NIST statistical test name, and test ID. The test IDs given in the last column have been used in this chapter.

Tables 19.3–19.12 contain the table headers of Key no., Test ID, Sequence with P-value $\geq .05$, Proportion, and Result. In Tables 19.3–19.12, it has been found that the keys that were derived using the proposed technique have the characteristics of randomness. Thus this technique would be more efficient for encrypting the homeopathy e-prescriptions.

TABLE 19.2 Indexing on NIST tests.

Sl. no.	NIST statistical test name	Test ID (to be used here)
1	*Frequency*	ST#01
2	*Frequency(inBlock)*	ST#02
3	*Run*	ST#03
4	*LongestRunofOnesinBlock*	ST#04
5	*BinaryMatrixRun*	ST#05
6	*DiscreteFourierTransformation*	ST#06
7	*NonoverlappingTemplateMatching*	ST#07
8	*OverlappingTemplateMatching*	ST#08
9	*Maurer'sUniversalStatistical*	ST#09
10	*LinearComplexity*	ST#10
11	*Serial*	ST#11
12	*ApproximateEntropy*	ST#12
13	*CumulativeSum*	ST#13
14	*RandomExcursion*	ST#14
15	*RandomExcursionVariant*	ST#15

TABLE 19.3 NIST tests on key no. 1.

Key no.	Test ID	Sequence with P-value ≥ 05	Proportion	Result (1 denotes true, 0 denotes false)
1	ST#01	919	0.9190	1
1	ST#02	957	0.9570	1
1	ST#03	951	0.9510	1
1	ST#04	966	0.9660	1
1	ST#05	980	0.9800	1
1	ST#06	964	0.9640	1
1	ST#07	959	0.9590	1
1	ST#08	981	0.9810	1
1	ST#09	974	0.9740	1
1	ST#10	974	0.9740	1
1	ST#11	962	0.9620	1
1	ST#12	958	0.9580	1
1	ST#13	948	0.9480	1
1	ST#14	964	0.9640	1
1	ST#15	972	0.9720	1

TABLE 19.4 NIST tests on key no. 2.

Key no.	Test ID	Sequence with P-value ≥ .05	Proportion	Result (1 denotes true, 0 denotes false)
2	ST#01	919	0.9190	1
2	ST#02	957	0.9570	1
2	ST#03	951	0.9510	1
2	ST#04	966	0.9660	1
2	ST#05	980	0.9800	1
2	ST#06	964	0.9640	1
2	ST#07	959	0.9590	1
2	ST#08	981	0.9810	1
2	ST#09	974	0.9740	1
2	ST#10	974	0.9740	1
2	ST#11	962	0.9620	1
2	ST#12	958	0.9580	1
2	ST#13	948	0.9480	1
2	ST#14	964	0.9640	1
2	ST#15	972	0.9720	1

TABLE 19.5 NIST tests on key no. 3.

Key no.	Test ID	Sequence with P-value ≥ .05	Proportion	Result (1 denotes true, 0 denotes false)
3	ST#01	919	0.9190	1
3	ST#02	957	0.9570	1
3	ST#03	953	0.9530	1
3	ST#04	966	0.9660	1
3	ST#05	980	0.9800	1
3	ST#06	964	0.9640	1
3	ST#07	959	0.9590	1
3	ST#08	983	0.9830	1
3	ST#09	974	0.9740	1
3	ST#10	974	0.9740	1
3	ST#11	962	0.9620	1
3	ST#12	958	0.9580	1
3	ST#13	948	0.9480	1
3	ST#14	964	0.9640	1
3	ST#15	972	0.9720	1

19.7.2 Histogram and autocorrelation analysis

In Figs. 19.2 and 19.3, the histogram and autocorrelation of the homeopathic e-prescription prior to encryption without any proposed key are shown.

Non-uniformity has been observed at the spread of characters without encryption from Figs. 19.2 and 19.3. Those patterns were observed when the proposed technique was not applied to the homeopathic e-prescription.

TABLE 19.6 NIST tests on key no. 4.

Key no.	Test ID	Sequence with *P*-value ≥ .05	Proportion	Result (1 denotes true, 0 denotes false)
4	ST#01	949	0.9490	1
4	ST#02	957	0.9570	1
4	ST#03	954	0.9540	1
4	ST#04	966	0.9660	1
4	ST#05	980	0.9800	1
4	ST#06	964	0.9640	1
4	ST#07	959	0.9590	1
4	ST#08	984	0.9840	1
4	ST#09	974	0.9740	1
4	ST#10	974	0.9740	1
4	ST#11	962	0.9620	1
4	ST#12	958	0.9580	1
4	ST#13	948	0.9480	1
4	ST#14	964	0.9640	1
4	ST#15	972	0.9720	1

TABLE 19.7 NIST tests on key no. 5.

Key no.	Test ID	Sequence with *P*-value ≥ .05	Proportion	Result (1 denotes true, 0 denotes false)
5	ST#01	959	0.9590	1
5	ST#02	957	0.9570	1
5	ST#03	955	0.9550	1
5	ST#04	966	0.9660	1
5	ST#05	980	0.9800	1
5	ST#06	964	0.9640	1
5	ST#07	959	0.9590	1
5	ST#08	985	0.9850	1
5	ST#09	974	0.9740	1
5	ST#10	974	0.9740	1
5	ST#11	962	0.9620	1
5	ST#12	958	0.9580	1
5	ST#13	948	0.9480	1
5	ST#14	964	0.9640	1
5	ST#15	972	0.9720	1

In Fig. 19.4, the histogram and autocorrelation analysis of the proposed technique have been shown using the keys given in Table 19.1.

TABLE 19.8 NIST tests on key no. 6.

Key no.	Test ID	Sequence with *P*-value ≥ .05	Proportion	Result (1 denotes true, 0 denotes false)
6	ST#01	969	0.9690	1
6	ST#02	957	0.9570	1
6	ST#03	956	0.9560	1
6	ST#04	966	0.9660	1
6	ST#05	980	0.9800	1
6	ST#06	964	0.9640	1
6	ST#07	959	0.9590	1
6	ST#08	986	0.9860	1
6	ST#09	974	0.9740	1
6	ST#10	974	0.9740	1
6	ST#11	962	0.9620	1
6	ST#12	958	0.9580	1
6	ST#13	948	0.9480	1
6	ST#14	964	0.9640	1
6	ST#15	972	0.9720	1

TABLE 19.9 NIST tests on key no. 7.

Key no.	Test ID	Sequence with *P*-value ≥ .05	Proportion	Result (1 denotes true, 0 denotes false)
7	ST#01	979	0.9790	1
7	ST#02	957	0.9570	1
7	ST#03	957	0.9570	1
7	ST#04	966	0.9660	1
7	ST#05	980	0.9800	1
7	ST#06	964	0.9640	1
7	ST#07	959	0.9590	1
7	ST#08	987	0.9870	1
7	ST#09	974	0.9740	1
7	ST#10	974	0.9740	1
7	ST#11	962	0.9620	1
7	ST#12	958	0.9580	1
7	ST#13	948	0.9480	1
7	ST#14	964	0.9640	1
7	ST#15	972	0.9720	1

Therefore, from Fig. 19.4, it can be seen that the histogram and autocorrelation analysis charts are always better when encrypted through the proposed set of

TABLE 19.10 NIST tests on key no. 8.

Key no.	Test ID	Sequence with P-value ≥ .05	Proportion	Result (1 denotes true, 0 denotes false)
8	ST#01	989	0.9890	1
8	ST#02	957	0.9570	1
8	ST#03	958	0.9580	1
8	ST#04	966	0.9660	1
8	ST#05	980	0.9800	1
8	ST#06	964	0.9640	1
8	ST#07	959	0.9590	1
8	ST#08	988	0.9880	1
8	ST#09	974	0.9740	1
8	ST#10	974	0.9740	1
8	ST#11	962	0.9620	1
8	ST#12	958	0.9580	1
8	ST#13	948	0.9480	1
8	ST#14	964	0.9640	1
8	ST#15	972	0.9720	1

TABLE 19.11 NIST tests on key no. 9.

Key no.	Test ID	Sequence with P-value ≥ 0.05	Proportion	Result (1 denotes true, 0 denotes false)
9	ST#01	999	0.9990	1
9	ST#02	957	0.9570	1
9	ST#03	959	0.9590	1
9	ST#04	966	0.9660	1
9	ST#05	980	0.9800	1
9	ST#06	964	0.9640	1
9	ST#07	959	0.9590	1
9	ST#08	989	0.9890	1
9	ST#09	974	0.9740	1
9	ST#10	974	0.9740	1
9	ST#11	962	0.9620	1
9	ST#12	958	0.9580	1
9	ST#13	948	0.9480	1
9	ST#14	964	0.9640	1
9	ST#15	972	0.9720	1

keys on the homeopathic e-prescription. Thus, the intruders will not be in as good a position to detect the exact bits patterns of the session key of 128 bits. This validates the robustness of the proposed technique.

TABLE 19.12 NIST tests on key no. 10.

Key no.	Test ID	Sequence with P-value ≥ 0.05	Proportion	Result (1 denotes true, 0 denotes false)
10	ST#01	9109	0.91090	1
10	ST#02	957	0.9570	1
10	ST#03	9510	0.95100	1
10	ST#04	966	0.9660	1
10	ST#05	980	0.9800	1
10	ST#06	964	0.9640	1
10	ST#07	959	0.9590	1
10	ST#08	9810	0.98100	1
10	ST#09	974	0.9740	1
10	ST#10	974	0.9740	1
10	ST#11	962	0.9620	1
10	ST#12	958	0.9580	1
10	ST#13	948	0.9480	1
10	ST#14	964	0.9640	1
10	ST#15	972	0.9720	1

19.7.3 Chi-square comparison

In this section, the divergence between the observed character frequency and the actual character frequency has been done using the chi-square test. This was conducted using Eq. (19.3).

$$\chi^2 = \sum_{k=1}^{N} \frac{(\mathrm{OCH}_k - \mathrm{ECH}_k)^2}{\mathrm{ECH}_k} \quad \ldots \tag{19.3}$$

where OCH_k and ECH_k denote the existing distribution and the contemplated distribution of the k-th character frequency, respectively. A comparison of chi-square values between the AES and the proposed technique has been presented in Table 19.13.

Table 19.13 is comprised of the following table headers: Key no., Name of e-prescription, AES, and Proposed technique. From Table 19.13 it can be seen that the proposed technique of secret sharing-based transmission provides favorable quality of encryption in terms of the chi-square values obtained.

19.7.4 Differential attacks

Gatecrashers comprehensively endeavor to derive any piece of heuristics between the cipher text and unique homeopathy e-prescriptions. In the proposed technique, two different shares were selected, and related interpretations were formed based on the influenced number of shares. An example is given in Table 19.14.

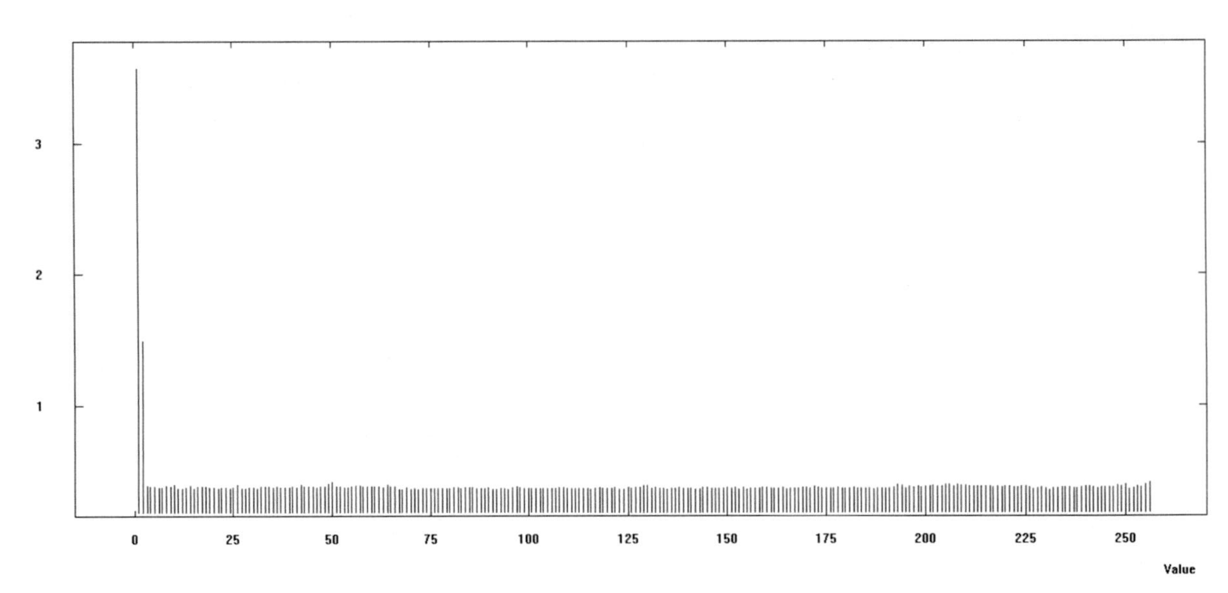

FIGURE 19.2 Histogram of the e-prescription prior to encryption.

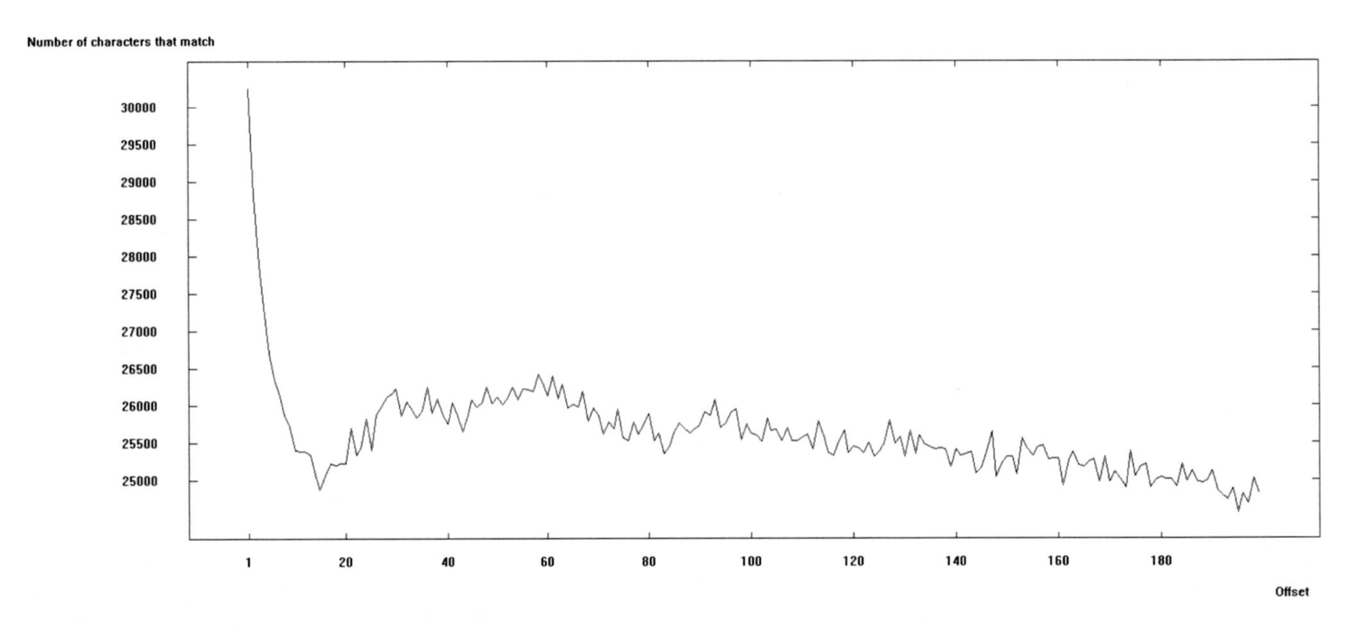

FIGURE 19.3 Autocorrelation of the e-prescription prior to encryption.

Table 19.14 is composed of the following table headers: Proposed key no. used, Complemented bits positions, and No. of bits altered in the new key. A negative correlation of -0.16534 has been found between the differences in the position of the flipped bits and the number of effective flipped bits. This value is close to zero, indicating that there is no symmetry in the pattern of the chaotic key formed. Thus, it would be a positive point for the proposed technique at the KDC.

Fig. 19.5 shows a bar graph when any two random bits are altered and the changes reflected in the total number of bits out of 128. In this connection, it can be concluded that no significant pattern in such changes occurred in the proposed technique. This can be expressed as another robustness parameter.

19.7.5 Security analysis

This section describes the security analysis carried out on the proposed homeopathy telemedicine system. Chaotic key were generated for the cryptographic transmission of the e-prescriptions over the public

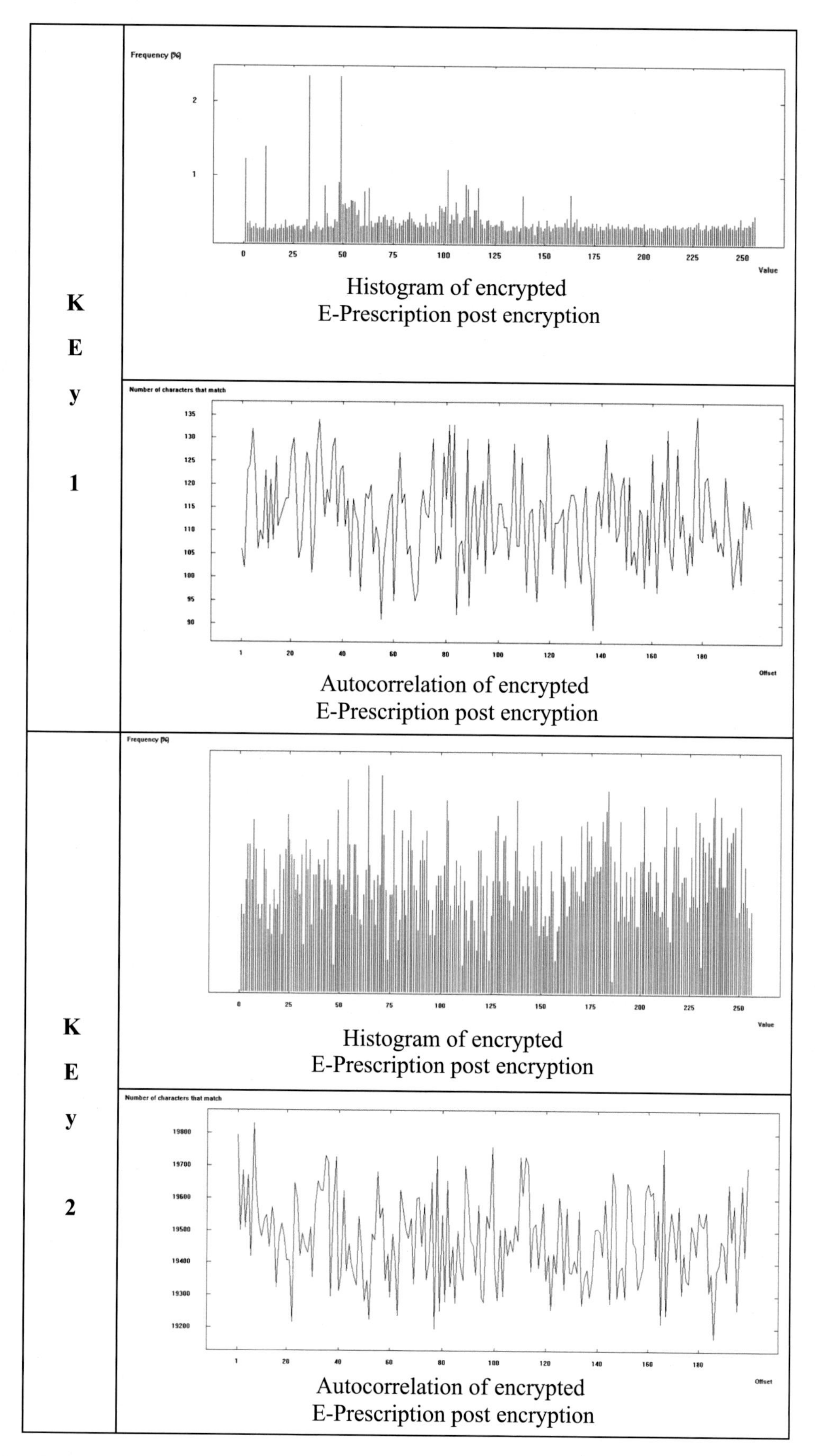

FIGURE 19.4 Histogram and autocorrelation of the e-prescription post encryption using the proposed keys.

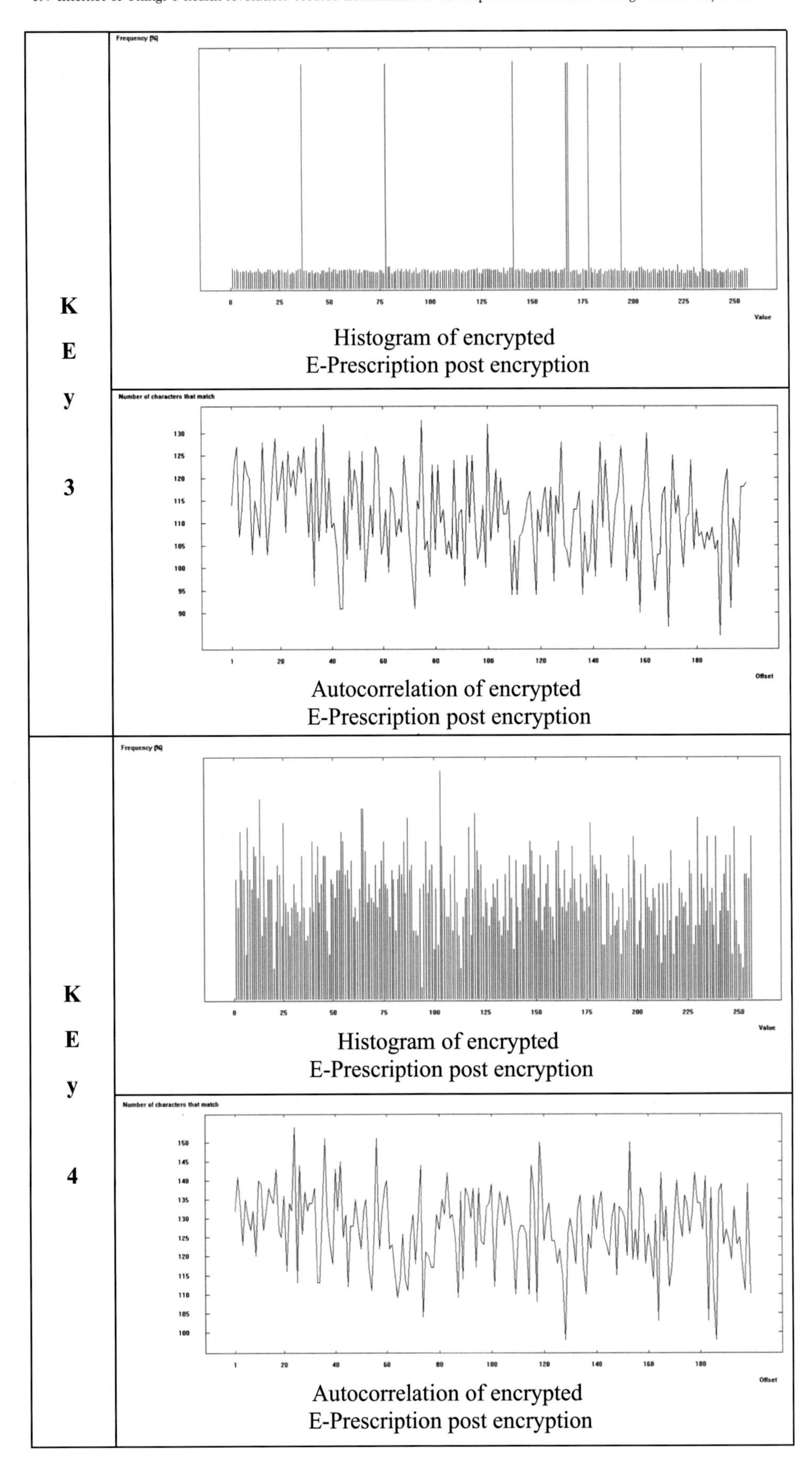

FIGURE 19.4 (continued)

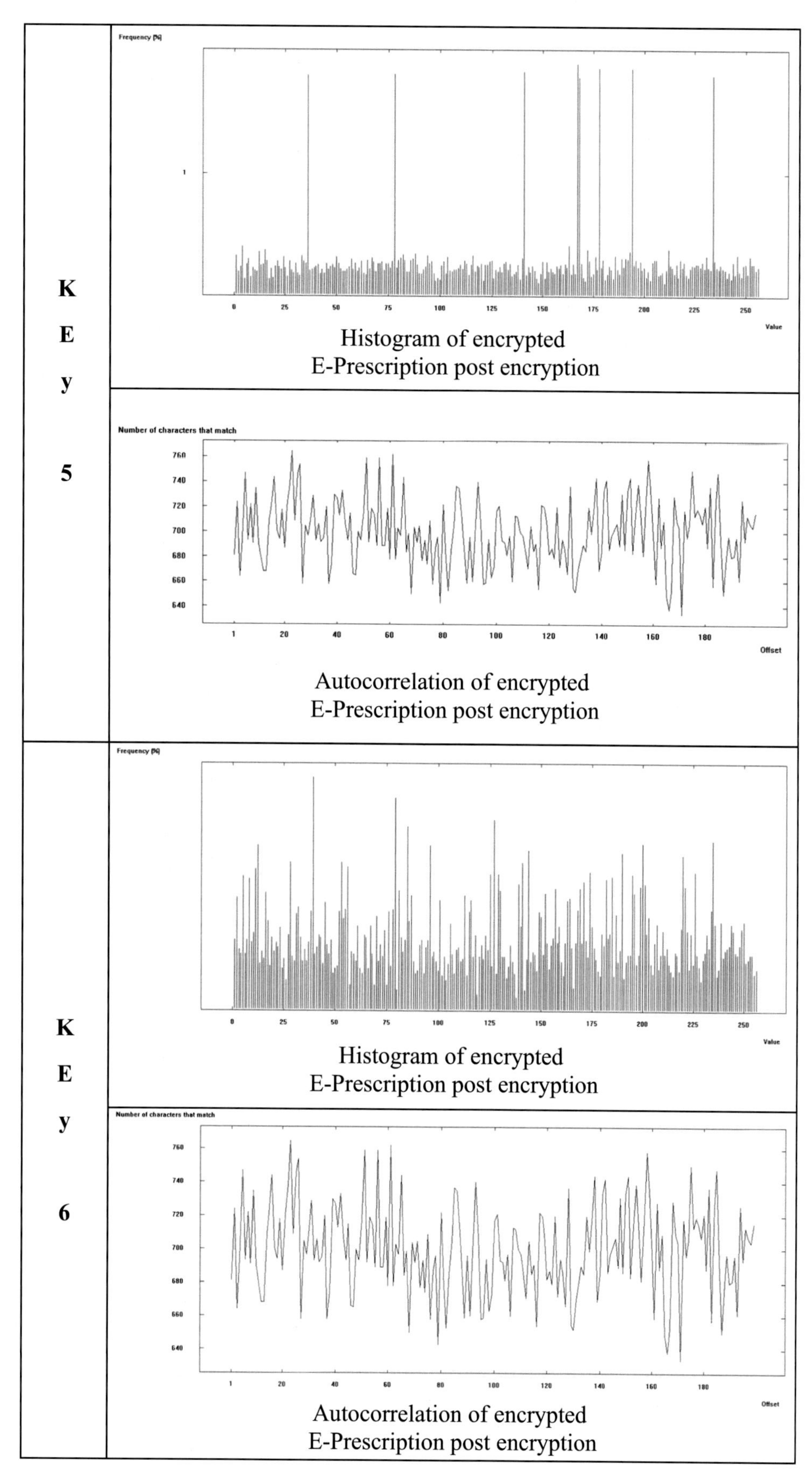

FIGURE 19.4 (continued)

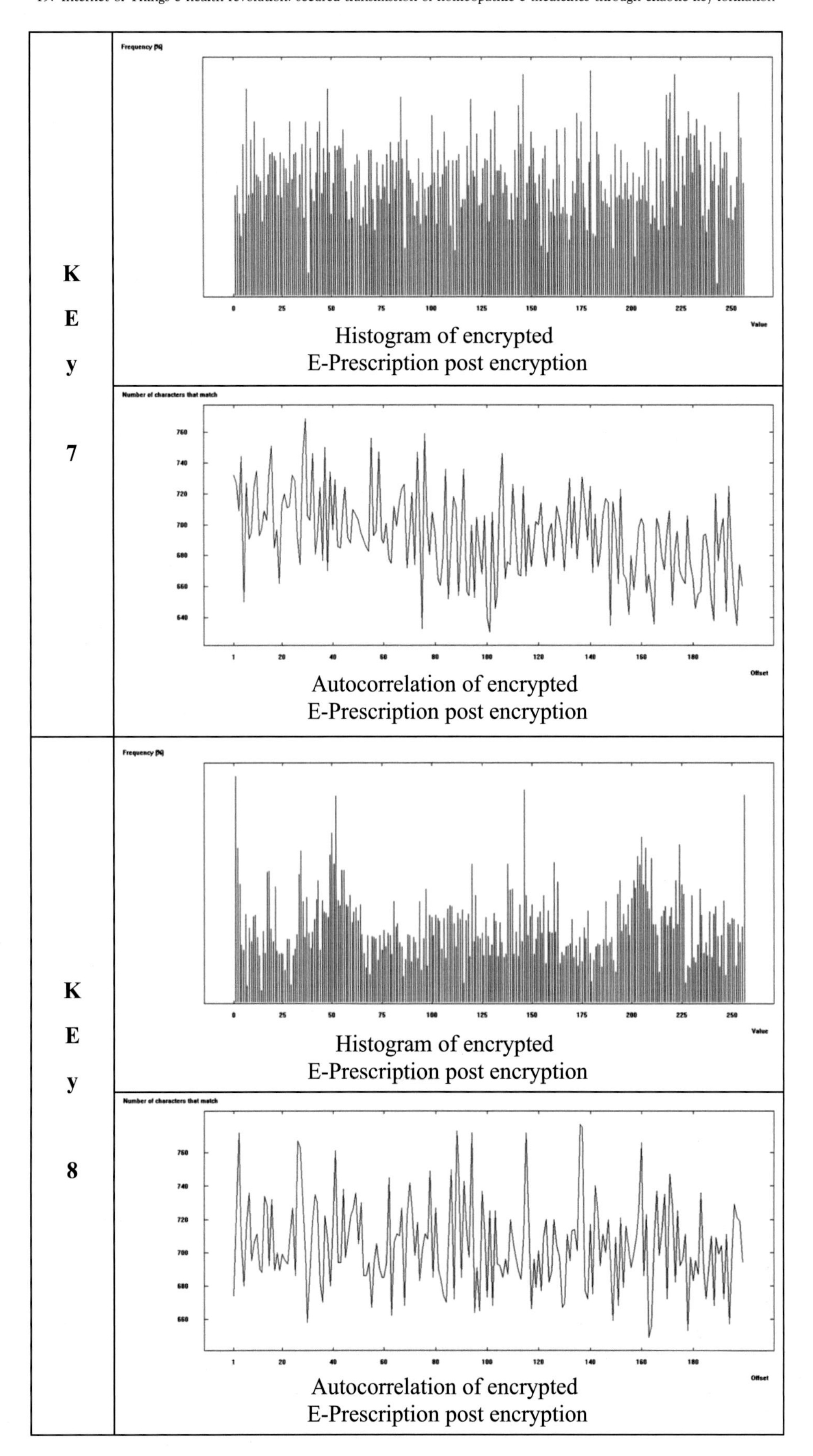

FIGURE 19.4 (continued)

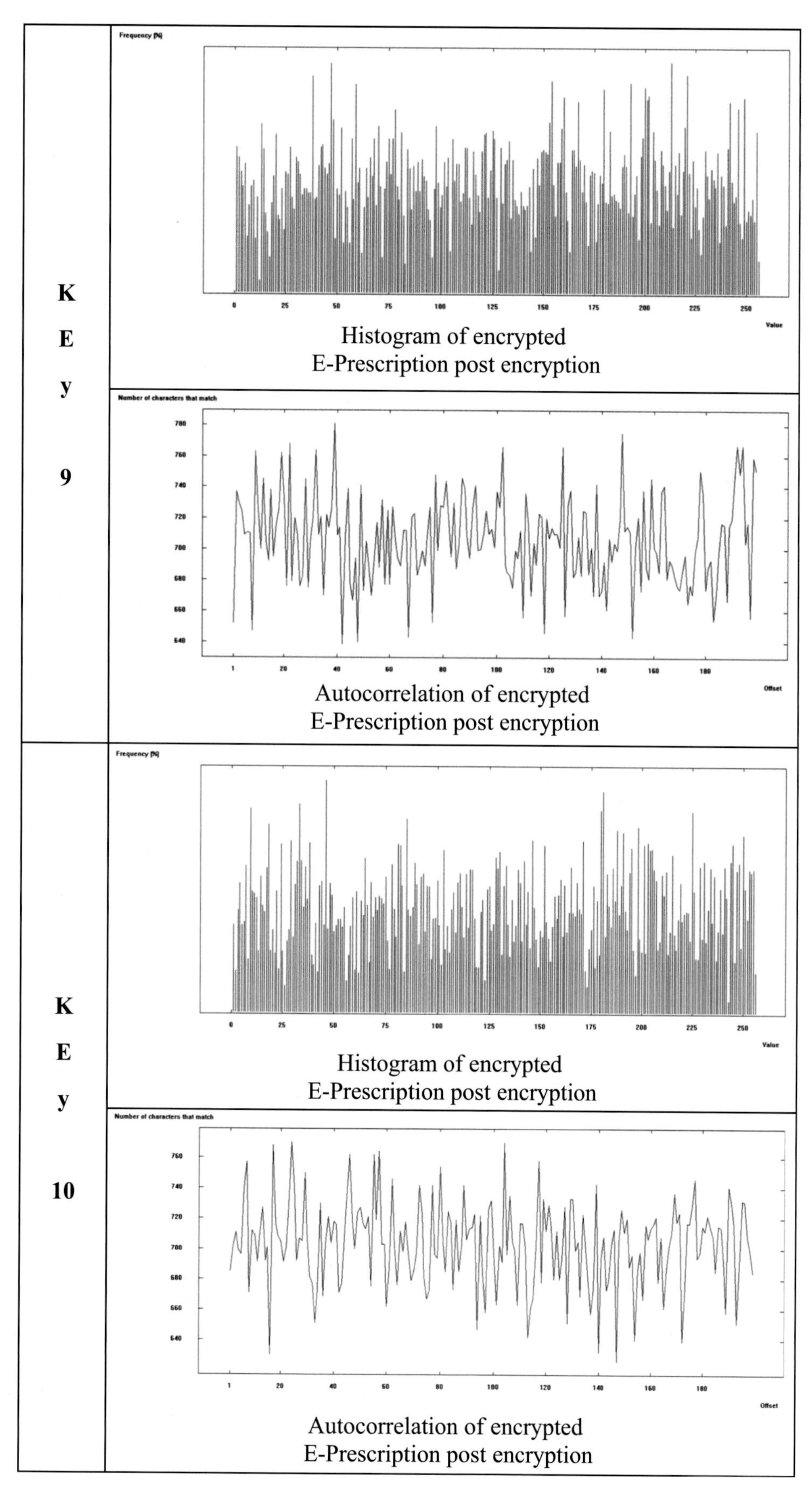

FIGURE 19.4 (continued)

TABLE 19.13 Comparison of chi-square values.

Key no.	Name of e-prescription	AES	Proposed technique
1	PRS#11	26197	31258
	PRS#12	14980	13968
	PRS#13	54789	68741
	PRS#14	12402	14789
	PRS#15	64715	65470
2	PRS#11	32578	29302
	PRS#12	14980	14720
	PRS#13	58909	69870
	PRS#14	22783	28771
	PRS#15	59700	64703
3	PRS#11	54713	31258
	PRS#12	19864	21700
	PRS#13	75680	85201
	PRS#14	24102	20123
	PRS#15	66055	65405
4	PRS#11	34101	39918
	PRS#12	19874	21058
	PRS#13	59820	69731
	PRS#14	19784	24669
	PRS#15	60124	65879
5	PRS#11	25472	30147
	PRS#12	17914	16589
	PRS#13	68742	80124
	PRS#14	19803	19879
	PRS#15	64561	65470
6	PRS#11	27451	36980
	PRS#12	25470	16978
	PRS#13	61202	78954
	PRS#14	19743	26541
	PRS#15	54787	60123
7	PRS#11	36587	34578
	PRS#12	31574	35601
	PRS#13	74878	68041
	PRS#14	21544	30089
	PRS#15	54780	53020
8	PRS#11	24187	39874
	PRS#12	20054	34801
	PRS#13	69032	67840
	PRS#14	14786	26547
	PRS#15	59806	69637
9	PRS#11	22697	31974

(Continued)

TABLE 19.13 (Continued)

Key no.	Name of e-prescription	AES	Proposed technique
	PRS#12	19140	33068
	PRS#13	65789	68521
	PRS#14	19871	29803
	PRS#15	59632	78410
10	PRS#11	30021	38987
	PRS#12	18740	22568
	PRS#13	51587	56481
	PRS#14	26580	36974
	PRS#15	68760	65877

TABLE 19.14 Changed bits position in the original key vs. No. of bits altered in the new key

Proposed key no. used	Complemented bits positions	No. of bits altered in the new key
1	(40,19)	65
2	(88,67)	106
3	(34,71)	108
4	(95,54)	71
5	(123,28)	25
6	(97,38)	41
7	(18,89)	56
8	(102,48)	66
9	(51,95)	12
10	(32,51)	38

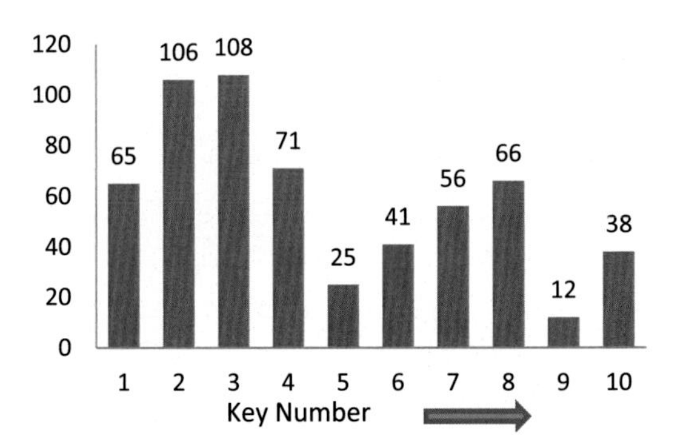

FIGURE 19.5 Any two bits flip in chaotic keys vs number of bits altered.

network. The use of a chaotic had redued the chances of intrudsions from different malicious attacks. Different types of attacks against the proposed system are briefly described.

1. *DoS attacks*: In this proposed technique, the partial secret shares of the homeopathy e-prescriptions were distributed to all the participating machines inside the group. An independent node has no privilege to reconstruct the data without cooperation from others. Thus, the workload of each node has been reduced. Therefore the proposed technique can efficiently withstand DoS attacks under such homeopathy telecare systems.
2. *Middle interference attacks*: Intelligent transportation mechanisms were deployed in this proposed technique. The transmitted data may be interfered with by external entities. The proposed homeopathy telemedicine system resists these interference attacks. The session key that was generated by the chaotic system was tested under different statistical properties (Wu & Huang, 2004).
3. *Replay attacks analysis*: This proposed technique can resist against a replay attack.

   Since the original homeopathy e-prescriptions were broken and encrypted into partial shares, it would not be possible to regenerate them unless the threshold shares were summed up. This means no single node contains all the data. In the case of a node being compromised, the loss due to data theft has been checked here.
4. *Man-in-the-middle attacks*: As an adversary component, intruders actively attempt to steal patients' relevant data inside the network. To decrypt the data, intruders need a minimum number of shares to reveal the information. However, this would not be feasible due to the number of participating and threshold shares that are kept hidden.
5. *Session key strength*: The KDC generates a session key and sends this to all the participating nodes in the same group. Before that it is checked by the NIST suite (Rukhin et al., 2001). Hence, this proposed technique ensures true randomness in the session key.

19.7.6 Analysis of the session key space

The key has been proposed in the area of homeopathy telemedicine. In 2018, IBM Summit, Oak Ridge, United States, discovered the quickest supercomputer with 123 PETAFLOPS. This implies that the supercomputer has the ability to function at 123×10^{15} floating point processing activities per second. We know that the total quantity of seconds present in a nonleap year may be tabulated as: $365 \times 24 \times 60 \times 60 = 31,536,000$ seconds. Table 19.15 contains the amount of time required (in years) to interpret the proposed session key by meddling. The most critical purpose of this proposed method is that it has no linkage regarding the session key combination. Subsequently, to figure out the exact combination of the true session key by gatecrashers would be an extremely cumbersome procedure. Consequently, the novel proposed strategy is adequate for data transmissions in homeopathy telemedicine systems. This approach will be decided to be a strong cryptographic system in the future.

TABLE 19.15 Time required to detect the key.

Serial number	Session key bits present	Number of possible combinations	Time needed to detect (years)
1	8bits	2^{8}	6.48×10^{20}
2	16bits	2^{16}	1.55×10^{17}
3	32bits	2^{32}	1.06×10^{12}
4	56bits	2^{56}	1.54×10^{5}
5	128bits	2^{132}	8.67×10^{52}

Table 19.15 contains the following table headers: Serial number, Session key bits present, Number of possible combinations, and Time needed to detect (years). Theoretically, 8.67×10^{52} years would be needed by the intruders to decipher the key.

19.7.7 Analysis of the information entropy

The entropy of data is evidence of its information content. Its novel illustration is based on the number of bits per character. On the off-case that a character has a poor chance of experiencing an occurrence, the character's information content is minimal. Characters are represented using ASCII from 0 to 255. The original plain homeopathy prescription is encoded utilizing the proposed strategy. Tables 19.15–19.19 contain an examination of the information entropy of the plain homeopathy prescription and its later proposed encryption. The acknowledgment of this data security proposed scheme may be legitimized by observing the excellent outcomes in Tables 19.16–19.20. Each session key has been tested on an individual homeopathy e-prescriptions one at a time. The summarized data are below in the tables.

Tables 19.16–19.20 contain the following table headers: Name of e-prescription, Key no. applied, Entropy of e-prescription, Entropy post encryption, and Maximum entropy. From the above tables, the outcomes obtained in this proposed technique has been proved to be satisfactory.

TABLE 19.16 Entropy values after encryption on PRS#11.

Name of e-prescription	Key no. applied	Entropy of e-prescription	Entropy post encryption	Maximum entropy
PRS#11	1	7.79	7.90	8.00
PRS#11	2	7.77	7.96	8.00
PRS#11	3	7.58	7.93	8.00
PRS#11	4	7.74	7.91	8.00
PRS#11	5	7.81	7.98	8.00
PRS#11	6	7.80	7.88	8.00
PRS#11	7	7.65	7.84	8.00
PRS#11	8	7.69	7.86	8.00
PRS#11	9	7.87	7.91	8.00
PRS#11	10	7.79	7.90	8.00

TABLE 19.17 Entropy values after encryption on PRS#12.

Name of e-prescription	Key no. applied	Entropy of e-prescription	Entropy post encryption	Maximum entropy
PRS#12	1	7.71	7.92	8.00
PRS#12	2	7.85	7.90	8.00
PRS#12	3	7.65	7.88	8.00
PRS#12	4	7.49	7.90	8.00
PRS#12	5	7.80	7.96	8.00
PRS#12	6	7.75	7.87	8.00
PRS#12	7	7.89	7.80	8.00
PRS#12	8	7.77	7.81	8.00
PRS#12	9	7.87	7.93	8.00
PRS#12	10	7.70	7.91	8.00

TABLE 19.18 Entropy values after encryption on PRS#13.

Name of e-prescription	Key no. applied	Entropy of e-prescription	Entropy post encryption	Maximum entropy
PRS#13	1	7.70	7.88	8.00
PRS#13	2	7.74	7.90	8.00
PRS#13	3	7.55	7.93	8.00
PRS#13	4	7.78	7.94	8.00
PRS#13	5	7.80	7.98	8.00
PRS#13	6	7.81	7.89	8.00
PRS#13	7	7.65	7.80	8.00
PRS#13	8	7.88	7.86	8.00
PRS#13	9	7.81	7.91	8.00
PRS#13	10	7.74	7.90	8.00

TABLE 19.19 Entropy values after encryption on PRS#14.

Name of e-prescription	Key no. applied	Entropy of e-prescription	Entropy post encryption	Maximum entropy
PRS#14	1	7.79	7.92	8.00
PRS#14	2	7.63	7.90	8.00
PRS#14	3	7.44	7.84	8.00
PRS#14	4	7.87	7.82	8.00
PRS#14	5	7.89	7.91	8.00
PRS#14	6	7.82	7.88	8.00
PRS#14	7	7.69	7.81	8.00
PRS#14	8	7.68	7.92	8.00
PRS#14	9	7.80	7.90	8.00
PRS#14	10	7.79	7.88	8.00

TABLE 19.20 Entropy values after encryption on PRS#15.

Name of e-prescription	Key no. applied	Entropy of e-prescription	Entropy post encryption	Maximum entropy
PRS#15	1	7.66	7.87	8.00
PRS#15	2	7.80	7.94	8.00
PRS#15	3	7.54	7.92	8.00
PRS#15	4	7.82	7.90	8.00
PRS#15	5	7.84	7.97	8.00
PRS#15	6	7.55	7.84	8.00
PRS#15	7	7.76	7.81	8.00
PRS#15	8	7.69	7.88	8.00
PRS#15	9	7.78	7.90	8.00
PRS#15	10	7.80	7.96	8.00

19.7.8 Encryption–decryption process time

The user interface of the proposed web-based homeopathy telemedicine system has been designed with flexibility. It enables noninvasive and noncritical patients to transmit their data and prescriptions to homeopathy physicians. The amount of transmission time needed is a vital aspect for its acceptance (Bhowmik, Dey, Sarkar, & Karforma, 2019; Dey, Sarkar, & Karforma, 2021; Sarkar, Dey, & Karforma, 2021). The time needed for the encryption and decryption phase must be optimal, as indicated in Table 19.21, on a daily basis.

Table 19.21 contains the following table headers: Data, Size, Type, Mean encryption time, and Mean decryption time.

TABLE 19.21 Proposed encryption and decryption duration.

Data	Size	Type	Mean encryption time	Mean decryption time
E-prescription	2.89 MB	PDF	3.8173 ms	2.3974 ms

TABLE 19.22 Encryption and decryption time needed on proposed keys 1–10.

Size of e-prescription (MB)	Name of e-prescription	Avg. encryption time (ms)	Avg. decryption time (ms)	Total avg. time (ms)
3.15	PRS#11	2575	1896	4444
2.64	PRS#12	2156	1765	3921
1.78	PRS#13	1845	1540	3385
2.85	PRS#14	1544	1600	3144
5.16	PRS#15	3183	2897	6080

Moreover, different homeopathy e-prescriptions of varying size were taken into consideration in this study. The secret keys, as mentioned in Table 19.1, are used one-by-one for the encryption and decryption method. Table 19.22 shows a summary of those parameters obtained when tested.

Table 19.22 contains the following table headers: Size of e-prescription, Name of e-prescription, Avg. encryption time, Avg. decryption time, and Total avg. time.

19.7.9 Time needed for an intrusion

The session key has been generated to encrypt the homeopathic e-prescription. Intruders are always attempting to anticipate the proposed session key. Here, a 128-bits session key has been generated using a chaotic sequence by the KDC. With the help of a supercomputer with 123×10^{15} floating point computing operations per second, to decrypt it requires $2^{128} = 3.40282 \times 10^{38}$ trials of different permutations. Each trial of permutation for decoding would consume 1000 PFLOPS to complete. The total number of seconds present in a year is calculated as: $365 \times 24 \times 60 \times 60 = 31,536,000$. Hence, 123×10^{12} trials are needed per second. Therefore the amount of time required to decrypt a single cipher text is calculated as: $(3.40282 \times 10^{38})/(123 \times 10^{12} \times 31,536,000) = 8.772 \times 10^{52}$ years. Such a huge unattainable amount of time required to decode the proposed session key is another positive factor of the technique proposed here.

TABLE 19.23 Comparative statement.

Criterion for comparison	Ref. no. 29	Ref. no. 30	Ref. no. 27	Ref. no. 28	Ref. no. 33	This chapter
Telemedicine system	Yes	No	No	No	No	Yes
Data encryption	Yes	Yes	Yes	Yes	Yes	Yes
Secret sharing	No	No	No	No	Yes	Yes
Information compression	Yes	No	Yes	No	No	No
Session key space	No	Yes	No	No	No	Yes
Histogram	No	Yes	No	No	No	Yes
Correlation	No	Yes	No	Yes	No	Yes
Autocorrelation	No	Yes	No	No	No	Yes
Entropy	No	Yes	No	No	No	Yes
Encryption–decryption time	Yes	Yes	No	No	Yes	Yes
Comparative statement	No	Yes	No	No	No	Yes

19.7.10 Comparative study with earlier works

This section shows a comparative study with existing earlier works in a tabular structure. The strengths and weaknesses of the proposed patients' data security technique may anonymously be viewed at a glance from Table 19.23.

Table 19.15 contains the following table headers: Criterion for comparison, and the remainder are some of the references cited in Section 19.2. From Table 19.23, the proposed methodology performs well when compared to previous works.

19.8 Conclusion

In this proposed technique, a session key generation mechanism based on secret-sharing cryptography was implemented on a homeopathy telemedicine system. According to the results related in the earlier sections, this proposed methodology of secured transmission through a public channel can be incorporated as an integral part on any online telemedicine system. The proposed technique is capable of dealing with man/woman-in-the-middle attacks. Reconstruction of original information can be possible after the ammalgamation of threshold number of shares including the privileged share from the specified user. Statistical tests were conducted to test its robustness. Moreover, the graphs obtained in the histogram and autocorrelation using the proposed set of session key achieved parity bench marks. The average encryption and decryption times in the proposed technique were calculated and found to be acceptable. Thus, through homeopathic medicines, mentally challenged persons (noninvasive and noncritical) can be remotely treated in a better and secure way. Today's IoT-based health security issues to preserve medical data may be enabled using the proposed technique (Islam, Kwak, Kabir, Hossain, & Kwak, 2015). In brief, societal development through better healthcare may be reached through this proposed technique, especially through a homeopathic telemedicine system.

Acknowledgments

The authors acknowledge the inspiration and moral support received from Dr. Sukriti Ghosal, Former Principal, M.U.C. Women's College, Burdwan, India. The authors also express their gratitude for homeopathy medical assistance received from Dr. Salim Ahmad (B.H.M.S., Kolkata, Consultant Homeopathic Practitioner), Assistant Teacher in Nutrition, Vidyasagar Uchcha Vidyalaya, Burdwan, and Former Guest Lecturer in the Department of Nutrition, M.U.C. Women's College, Burdwan, India.

References

Al-Haj, A., Mohammad, A., & Amer, A. (2017). Crypto-watermarking of transmitted medical images. *Journal of Digital Imaging, 30*, 26–38. Available from https://doi.org/10.1007/s10278-016-9901-1.

Assad, A., & Deep, K. (2018). A hybrid harmony search and simulated annealing algorithm for continuous optimization. *Journal Information Sciences—Informatics and Computer Science, Intelligent Systems, Applications, 450*(C), 246–266.

Bhowmik, A., Dey, J., Sarkar, A., & Karforma, S. (2019). Computational intelligence based lossless regeneration (CILR) of blocked gingivitis intraoral image transportation. *IAES International Journal of Artificial Intelligence (IJ-AI), 8*(3), 197–204.

Bhowmik, A., Sarkar, A., Karforma, S., & Dey, J. (2019). A symmetric key based secret data sharing scheme. *International Journal of Computer Sciences and Engineering, 07*(01), 188–192.

Blakley, G. R. (1979). Safeguarding cryptographic keys. In *Proceedings of the American Federation of information processing societies (AFIPS'79) national computer conference* (Vol. 48, pp. 313–317), CA, USA, February.

Dagadu, J. C., Li, J. P., & Aboagye, E. O. (2019). Medical image encryption based on hybrid chaotic DNA diffusion. *Wireless Personal Communications, 108*, 591.

Das, A., & Adhikari, A. (2010). An efficient multi-use multi-secret sharing scheme based on hash function. *Applied Mathematics Letters, 23*(9), 993–996.

Dautrich, J. L., & Ravishankar, C. V. (2016). Security limitations of using secret sharing for data outsourcing. In *IFIP annual conference on data and applications security and privacy (DBSec 2016)* (pp. 151–160), Trento, Italy.

Dey, J., Karforma, S., Sarkar, A., & Bhowmik, A. (2019). Metaheuristic guided secured transmission of e-prescription of dental disease. *International Journal of Computer Sciences and Engineering, 07*(01), 179–183.

Dey, J., Sarkar, A., & Karforma, S. (2021). Newer post-COVID perspective: Teledental encryption by de-multiplexed perceptrons. *International Journal of Information Technology*. Available from https://doi.org/10.1007/s41870-020-00562-1.

Gritzalis, D., & Lambrinoudakis, C. (2004). A security architecture for interconnecting health information systems. *International Journal of Medical Informatics, 73*(3), 305–309.

He, D. B., Chen, J. H., & Zhang, R. (2011). A more secure authentication scheme for telecare medicine information systems. *Journal of Medical Systems*. Available from https://doi.org/10.1007/s10916-011-9658-5.

Islam, S. M. R., Kwak, D., Kabir, M. H., Hossain, M., & Kwak, K.-S. (2015). The Internet of Things for health care: A comprehensive survey. *IEEE Access, 3*, 678–708.

Jiménez-Serrano, S., Tortajada, S., & García-Gómez, J. M. (2015). A mobile health application to predict postpartum depression based on machine learning. *Telemedicine Journal and e-Health: The Official Journal of the American Telemedicine Association, 21*(7), 567–574.

Khade, P. N., & Narnaware, P. M. (2012). 3D chaotic functions for image encryption. *IJCSI International Journal of Computer Science Issues, 9*(3), No 1.

Krawczyk, S., & Jain, A. K. (2005). Securing electronic medical records using biometric authentication. In T. Kanade, A. Jain, & N. K. Ratha (Eds.), *Audio-and video-based biometric person authentication. AVBPA 2005. Lecture notes in computer science* (3546). Berlin, Heidelberg: Springer. Available from https://doi.org/10.1007/11527923_115.

Madhusudhan, R., & Nayak, C. S. (2019). A robust authentication scheme for telecare medical information systems. *Multimedia Tools and Applications, 78*, 15255.

Manojkumar, T., Karthigaikumar, P., & Ramachandran, V. (2019). An optimized S-box circuit for high speed AES design with enhanced PPRM architecture to secure mammographic images. *Journal of Medical Systems, 43*, 31. Available from https://doi.org/10.1007/s10916-018-1145-9.

Mathur, N., et al. (2016). AES based text encryption using 12 rounds with dynamic key selection. *Procedia Computer Science (ELSEVIER), 79*, 1036–1043.

Mdhaffar, A., et al. (2019). DL4DED: Deep learning for depressive episode detection on mobile devices. In J. Pagán, M. Mokhtari, H. Aloulou, B. Abdulrazak, & M. Cabrera (Eds.), *How AI impacts urban living and public health. ICOST 2019. Lecture notes in computer science* (11862). Cham: Springer.

Mowery, D., Smith, H., Cheney, T., Stoddard, G., Coppersmith, G., Bryan, C., & Conway, M. (2017). Understanding depressive symptoms and psychosocial stressors on Twitter: A corpus-based study. *Journal of Medical Internet Research, 19*(2).

Murillo-Escobar, M. A., Cardoza-Avendaño, L., López-Gutiérrez, R. M., et al. (2017). A double chaotic layer encryption algorithm for clinical signals in telemedicine. *Journal of Medical Systems, 41*, 59.

Nandakumar, K., & Jain, A. K. (2004). Local correlation-based fingerprint matching. In *ICVGIP* (pp. 503–508), ICVGIP, Kolkata, December 2004.

Nayak, J., Subbanna Bhat, P., Acharya, U. R., & Sathish Kumar, M. (2009). Efficient storage and transmission of digital fundus images with patient information using reversible watermarking technique and error control codes. *Journal of Medical Systems, 33*, 163–171.

Nien, H. H., Huang, C. K., Changchien, S. K., Shieh, H. W., Chen, C. T., & Tuan, Y. Y. (2007). Digital color image encoding and decoding using a novel chaotic random generator. *Chaos, Solitons, and Fractals, 32*, 1070–1080.

Rai, S. C., et al. (2019). Mood mechanic. *International Journal of Innovative Technology and Exploring Engineering (IJITEE), 9*(2S).

Ravichandran, D., et al. (2017). DNA chaos blend to secure medical privacy. *IEEE Transactions on Nanobioscience, 16*(8).

Rayachoti, E., Tirumalasetty, S., & Prathipati, S. C. (2020). SLT based watermarking system for secure telemedicine. *Cluster Computing*. Available from https://doi.org/10.1007/s10586-020-03078-2.

Rukhin, A., Soto, J., Nechvatal, J., Smid, M., Barker, E., Leigh, S., ... Vo, S. (2001). A statistical test suite for random and pseudorandom number generators for cryptographic applications. *NIST Special Publication*, 800–822.

Sarkar, A., Dey, J., Bhowmik, A., Mandal, J. K., & Karforma, S. (2018). Computational intelligence based neural session key generation on e-health system for ischemic heart disease information sharing. In J. Mandal, D. Sinha, & J. Bandopadhyay (Eds.), *Contemporary advances in innovative and applicable information technology. Advances in intelligent systems and computing* (812). Singapore: Springer.

Sarkar, A., Dey, J., Chatterjee, M., Bhowmik, A., & Karforma, S. (2019). Neural soft computing based secured transmission of intraoral gingivitis image in e-health care. *Indonesian Journal of Electrical Engineering and Computer Science*, *14*(1), 178–184.

Sarkar, A., Dey, J., & Karforma, S. (2021). Musically modified substitution-box for clinical signals ciphering in wireless telecare medical communicating systems. *Wireless Personal Communications*. Available from https://doi.org/10.1007/s11277-020-07894-y.

Shamir, A. (1979). How to share a secret. *Communications of the ACM*, *22*(11), 612–613.

Thampi, C., & Jose, D. (2013). More secure color image encryption scheme based on 3D chaotic maps. *International Journal For Advance Research In Engineering And Technology*, *1*(IX).

Viksveen, P., et al. (2018). Homeopathy in the treatment of depression: A systematic review. *European Journal of Integrative Medicine*, *22*, 22–36.

Wang, X., Gao, X. Z., & Zenger, K. (2015). *The overview of harmony search. An introduction to harmony search optimization method. Springerbriefs in applied sciences and technology*. Cham: Springer, Print ISBN 978-3-319-08355-1.

Wu, Z., & Huang, N. E. (2004). A study of the characteristics of white noise using the empirical mode decomposition method. *Proceedings of the Royal Society of London, Series A: Mathematical, Physical and Engineering Sciences*, *460*(2046), 1597–1611.

Wu, Z. Y., Lee, Y. C., Lai, F., Lee, H. C., & Chung, Y. (2010). A secure authentication scheme for telecare medicine information systems. *Journal of Medical Systems*. Available from https://doi.org/10.1007/s10916-010-9614-9.

Yadava, R. K., Singh, B. K., Sinha, S. K., & Pandey, K. K. (2013). A new approach of colour image encryption based on Henon like chaotic map. *Journal of Information Engineering and Applications*, *3*(6).

CHAPTER

20

Smart farming and water saving-based intelligent irrigation system implementation using the Internet of Things

Sagnick Biswas[1], Labhvam Kumar Sharma[2], Ravi Ranjan[2], Sayak Saha[2], Arpita Chakraborty[1] and Jyoti Sekhar Banerjee[1]

[1]Department of ECE, Bengal Institute of Technology, Kolkata, India [2]Department of CSE, Bengal Institute of Technology, Kolkata, India

20.1 Introduction

Irrigation plays a key role in maintaining the economic balance of developing and underdeveloped agricultural-based countries like India, as agricultural is one of the most stable and important factors contributing to the nation's GDP. Agriculture (Dan, Xin, Chongwei, & Liangliang, 2015; Gondchawar & Kawitkar, 2016; Hari Ram, Vishal, Dhanalakshmi, & Vidya, 2015; Banerjee, Chakraborty, & Goswami, 2013) also plays a significant role in international imports and exports, and provides raw materials to industries on a national as well as on a global level. Thus, many countries are now focusing increasingly on agriculture to stabilize their economic growth. The major problems associated with agriculture, if not tackled correctly, can affect not only local consumers but, in a worst-case scenario, they can affect the nation's GDP also. In any type of cultivation, it is necessary to ensure that an adequate amount of water is supplied to the plants. Again, soil health also depends on the moisture level, humidity, temperature, etc. To tackle all these issues, modern research recommends two of the most promising tools of today's modern era, that is, the Internet of Things (IoT) and artificial intelligence-machine learning (AI-ML).

IoT (Bahga & Madisetti, 2014; Qiu et al., 2017) is the key empowering feature (Roy, Dutta, Biswas, & Banerjee, 2020) in most wireless applications (Banerjee, Chakraborty, & Karmakar, 2013; Banerjee & Karmakar, 2012; Banerjee, Chakraborty, & Chattopadhyay, 2017; Banerjee & Chakraborty, 2014; Banerjee & Chakraborty, 2015; Banerjee, Chakraborty, & Chattopadhyay, 2018a, b, c; Banerjee, Chakraborty, & Chattopadhyay, 2021), which are changing the world and making it ever smarter. An array of sensors (Pandey, Dutta, & Banerjee, 2019; Paul, Chakraborty, & Banerjee, 2019; Paul, Chakraborty, & Banerjee, 2017) or things connected to a microcontroller, and through the node MCU the sensed data are uploaded to the cloud. The system is designed in such a way that it can predict and interact (Banerjee, Goswami, & Nandi, 2014) without any human-to-machine or human-to-human communication being needed. The IoT can be described as an evolving technological innovation, through which things can be linked and controlled remotely without the use of any manual labor. It can optimize operations, boost productivity, provide security (Chakraborty, Banerjee, & Chattopadhyay, 2020), participate in decision-making (Saha, Chakraborty, & Banerjee, 2017; Saha, Chakraborty, & Banerjee, 2019), and save resources and costs in agriculture (Putjaika, Phusae, Chen-Im, Phunchongharn, & Akkarajitsakul, 2016). Automation (Chakraborty, Banerjee, & Chattopadhyay, 2017; Chakraborty, Banerjee, & Chattopadhyay, 2019; Chakraborty & Banerjee, 2013; Das, Pandey, Chakraborty, & Banerjee, 2017; Das, Pandey, & Banerjee, 2016), at the same time, can play a major role in reducing the human effort to as little as possible. However, one thing we need to remember is that an array of sensors uploads the sensed values that are required for further computation. The development

Recent Trends in Computational Intelligence Enabled Research.
DOI: https://doi.org/10.1016/B978-0-12-822844-9.00043-8

of agriculture has much to do with the economic welfare of India. Every year a huge population of India suffers due to lack of rainfall, and the reduced amount of groundwater is another very important area of concern. We need to conserve groundwater and use it with efficient and effective technologies, such as the IoT and AI-ML, to face the challenging conditions and increase the productivity of agriculture (Shenoy & Pingle, 2016), so that it can reach the needy and satisfy the growing demand. In today's modern era, many problems can be solved with the use of automation. The same principle can be applied toward agriculture, to make the complex process of agriculture operate in a smart way which involves fertilizing, watering, harvesting, etc. which is simpler and more efficient with the help of the IoT and AI-ML tools.

In this respect, we have used an array of sensors to estimate the soil moisture content, temperature, humidity, and water usage. All the collected data are stored in the server-side cloud, which is processed using an ML algorithm (Banerjee et al., 2019; Chattopadhyay et al., 2020; Guhathakurata, Kundu, Chakraborty, & Banerjee, 2021; Guhathakurata, Saha, Kundu, Chakraborty, & Banerjee, 2020a, 2020b; Saha, Guhathakurata, Saha, Chakraborty, & Banerjee, 2021) to estimate the optimum amount of water required by all subgrids with the help of the IoT. In this way, the important components of farming, that is, soil moisture content identification, temperature measurement, and humidity determination, are automated and visualized through the Web and mobile applications to achieve smart farming. The key aspects of this chapter are explained as follows. First, determination of different essential elements of farming, as mentioned earlier, are programmed, and are also visualized through the Web and mobile applications to obtain smart farming. Another contribution of this chapter is to identify the predicted amount of water that is required for a particular field for a particular time duration, as all the water consumption details of the field are stored in the cloud, and hence it is possible to find out using an AI-ML tool and can be accessed through the Web and mobile applications for the daily, monthly, or seasonal water consumption requirements of a particular field. Finally, the moisture content of the soil is measured by a soil moisture sensor which triggers a pump via a microcontroller when the moisture content in the soil goes below a certain threshold. Thus, water usage is optimized as, nowadays, groundwater conservation is a primary responsibility because water is also considered a priced commodity.

The chapter has been framed as follows. The related studies are defined in Section 20.2. Section 20.3 presents the system model of the proposed solution. Section 20.4 includes the functions and applications of the machine learning model in this chapter. A step-by-step outline of the proposed methodology is briefly discussed in Section 20.5. Section 20.6 outlines the results and discussions and is accompanied by a comparative study and conclusions in Sections 20.7 and 20.8, respectively.

20.2 Related studies

Due to the dominant growth of the IoT, all sectors is in the process of upgrading to the next level using IoT, and agriculture is not an exception. To make procedures more intelligent and smarter, many researchers are working to integrate traditional farming with IoT applications. A brief review is presented here.

Managing water in an agricultural area can be done using an IoT system, as suggested by Hari Ram et al. (2015). Excluding surplus water from the field and, when the field is dry, providing water, are the key issues described in the paper. Two pipes are used in their system, one for removing water and another for pumping water based on the water level of the field which is indicated through a sensor. Soil hygrometer-based moisture sensing and solar panel operated systems are two significant characteristics of the proposed system.

Monitoring the necessary parameters of farming, that is, nutrient levels, humidity, pH, and temperature, etc. and analyzing the cultivation ecosystem can be performed using the IoT-based system AgriSys in Abdullah, Al Enazi, and Damaj (2016). Labview is used in programming and controller complexity is reduced by fuzzy control in this system. Sensors are integrated with PhidgetInterfaceKit 8/8/8 to control different sensor data for maintaining greenhouses. The fuzzy inference system is used here to reduce the number of components and system complexity. Multiple sensor data can be accessed at any time in the multiple input multiple output-based AgriSys as it is also deployed in a Web server.

The authors applied IoT technology to monitor the greenhouse atmosphere. They only considered the temperature inside the greenhouse, and did not considered sunlight and humidity (Dan et al., 2015). A wireless sensor network (WSN) and Zig-bee technology are jointly used to control climatic data. An intermediate node accepts the processed data and transfers them to a personal computer, which can be viewed remotely. This system offers medium reliability at a low cost.

Shenoy and Pingle (2016) authors proposed an Arduino-based polyhouse, which enhances productivity, controlling soil moisture, soil pH, the rate of soil nutrients, humidity temperature, etc. The system consists of an array of sensors, RFID tags, and GPS module. The system performance depends on the image recognition phases and precision of the robotic arms, as the crop health is determined through the image recognition algorithm and a robotic arm is used to harvest the crop. All the sensors perform their responsibilities in the polyhouse. The authors claimed a success rate using this IoT system of approximately 60%.

An ARM processor-based IoT system was suggested by Nagothu (2016) for watering a field automatically. A weather-predicting website was used to forecast whether water was required or not in the coming days. If the soil moisture reveals a lack of water in the soil, the system immediately checks for the occurrence of rainfall, and if there is no chance of this happening then water is sprayed onto the field. The main disadvantage of this system is that it depends on the accuracy of weather forecasting.

A WSN and IoT-based smart farming system is proposed in Gondchawar and Kawitkar (2016), where water spraying, weeding, alarming animals and birds, monitoring of the field, soil moisture sensing, etc. are performed by a GPS-enabled robot. Raspberry PI, high-resolution image catching equipment, interfacing sensors, actuators combined with microcontrollers, and Zig-bee or Wi-Fi-based systems are used to perform all the activities. An external power source is provided to the robot and attached to the Raspberry PI module and microcontrollers.

Putjaika et al. (2016) proposed an intelligent farming technique where a control system was used which consists of a Wi-Fi module attached to a centralized server. The central server updates all the sensed data and using wireless communication instructions all the required actions are taken. The main disadvantage of the proposed system is that Wi-Fi demands higher power consumption, which is a major constraint for any IoT system.

To observe the crops and plant health in an agricultural field, an image-processing technique is used in an IoT-based system (Kapoor, Bhat, Shidnal, & Mehra, 2016). In the suggested approach, the accuracy of both, that is, the IoT and image processing, are combined. The weather information for the field is provided by humidity and temperature sensors. The moisture level of the soil is provided by the soil moisture sensors. Processing through the captured images, plant health is determined using MATLAB. The key disadvantage of this system is the performance of the image-processing algorithms for the different data sets.

Agrawal and Singhal (2015) proposed a unique IoT system which was comprised of Arduino, Raspberry PI, and Zig-bee modules. Their suggestion was to provide water directly at the roots of the plants. The solenoid valves- and ultrasonic sensors-based proposed irrigation system does not sense the moisture level of the soil which surrounds the plant, hence, manual monitoring is required.

20.3 System model

The proposed idea of smart irrigation works first by dividing the field into a grid pattern where the entire field is considered as a grid and it is further subdivided into four subgrids. In this way, if a user wants to expand the area which needs to be monitored or, in simple terms, wants to scale up it will be very easy to do so, also, this grid pattern approach allows flexibility and scalability.

The subgrids are then monitored with several sensors to measure the moisture, humidity, temperature, etc. along with a pair of microcontrollers (Arduino) and a pair of node MCUs at each of the subgrids (see Fig. 20.1). Here one pair of Arduino and node MCUs is used for collecting the sensor data and sending them to the server-side cloud storage. On the other hand, the second pair of Arduino and node MCUs is used to fetch data from the server-side cloud, and watering the subgrid as predicted by the machine learning model. The amount of water that is consumed by a certain grid or subgrid will be measured with the help of a water flow meter that will be installed at the main water supply as well as each of the individual subgrids in order to get the real-time data of how much water has been consumed by a certain grid or subgrid. The microcontroller (Arduino-I) collects data from the soil moisture sensor along with the rest of the sensors and the water flow meter, and stores the data in its buffer space. These data are then transferred to the node MCU-I to send the respective data to the server-side cloud via RESTful APIs. The necessary data collected from all the sensors help the machine learning model to be able to predict the amount of water required by a subgrid of the area being monitored as well as the entire grid's water requirement.

Fig. 20.1 is a block diagram representation of a particular subgrid. The diagram shows the collection of different sensor data by the Arduino-I and data communication through the node MCU-I, which is bound by IIC protocol. Simultaneously it also shows the node MCU-II receiving data from the server and communicating the same with the Arduino-II to perform the subgrid watering as predicted by the machine learning model. It can also be seen how the user interface retrieves data from the cloud for better visualization in the Web and mobile applications. To achieve smart irrigation, we have designed a system that has both parts, that is, hardware and software. The system works in the following manner.

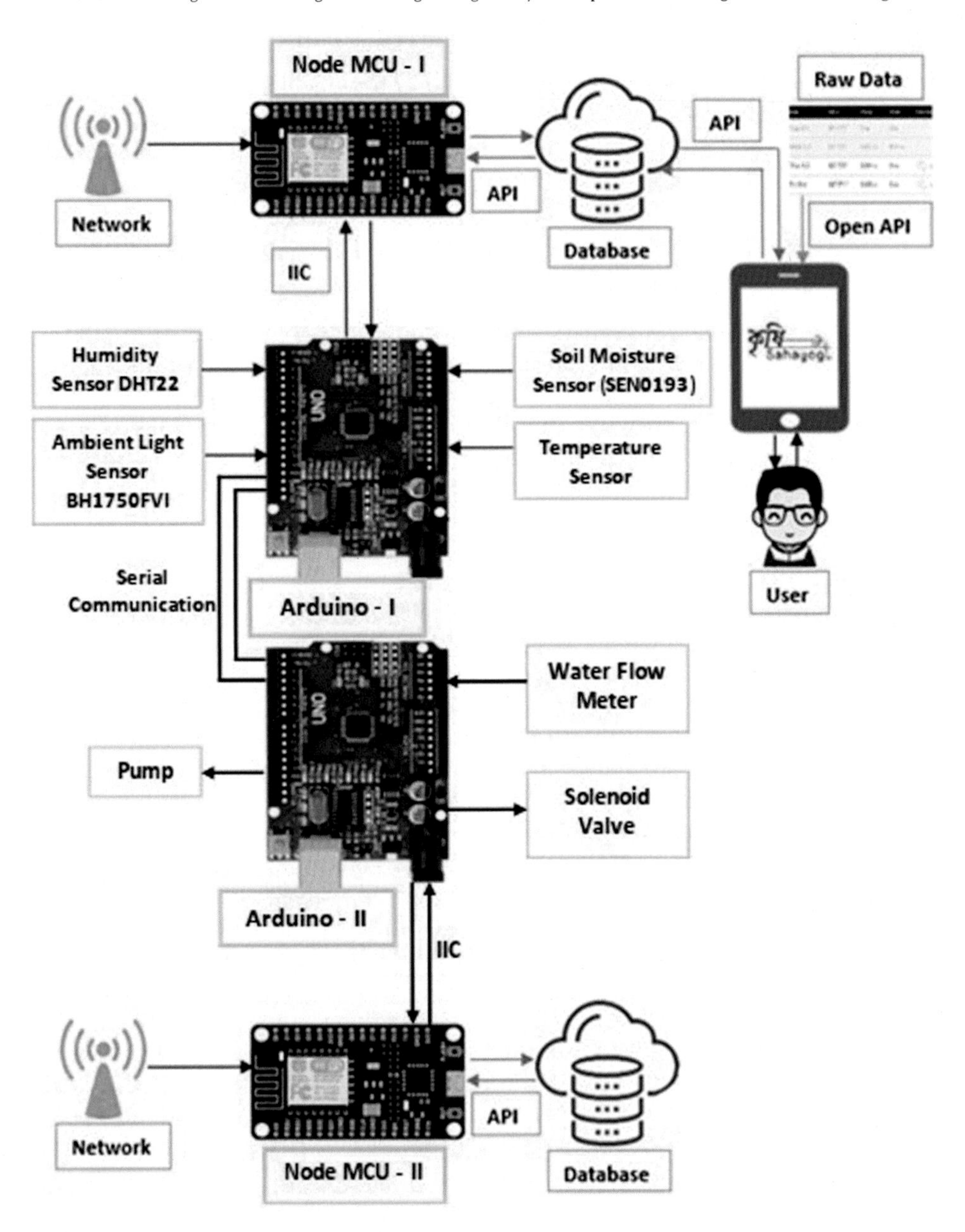

FIGURE 20.1 Block diagram of a particular subgrid.

20.3.1 Hardware operation

We have already mentioned that we divided the area of the field that we are going to monitor using an array of sensors in a grid pattern, where the entire area is considered a grid and it is further divided into subgrids that are monitored (see Fig. 20.2). First and foremost, the entire field area is divided into four subgrids, and each grid is equipped with an array of soil moisture sensors, solenoid valve, water flow meters, and water sprinklers. The node MCU-I collects the sensor data from the Arduino-I for transmitting to the cloud with the water consumption details from the respective grid and then the machine learning model computes using these data to predict the water usage for each grid. Then node MCU-II receives the predicted data from the server and communicates the same with the Arduino-II to perform the subgrid watering. For simplicity, other sensors are not illustrated in Fig. 20.2, and subgrid watering is only shown to subgrid 1.

For achieving a smart irrigation system, our approach is more scalable because if the size of the field is increased then the process of subdividing the field into subgrids is carried out in the same fashion. At the same time, for the water distribution we use the same approach where the main water supply for the area is a node and it is further divided into child nodes for each of the subgrids and water flow meters are

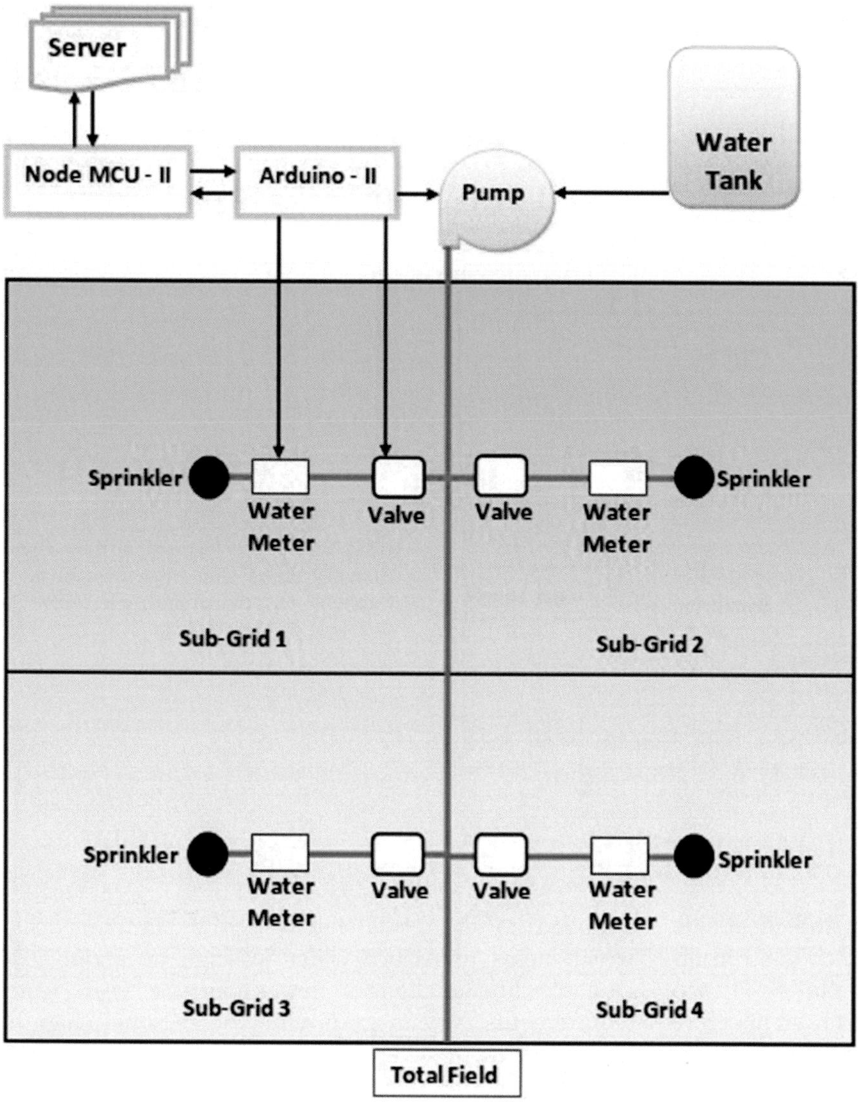

FIGURE 20.2 The proposed grid pattern architecture with the watering in a subgrid.

installed on each of the nodes to monitor the water consumption for the main supply node as well as the child nodes, that is, the subgrids. The array of sensors comprises soil moisture, sunlight, humidity, temperature, and water flow meters/sensors.

All these sensors feed the data to Arduino-I, that is, the microcontroller used in our proposed idea (see Fig. 20.3). The Arduino microcontroller consists of the main controller chipset ATMEGA-328P, which is an 8-bit controller. The microcontroller is bound with the Wi-Fi module using an interintegrated circuit (I2C or IIC protocol). The data collected by the microcontrollers are stored in the buffer space. The Wi-Fi module (node MCU-I) reads the data from the buffer space and then sends them to the server and they are then stored in the database. The stored data are then used for further computation by using the machine learning model for predicting the value of water consumption for the following days. In this way our system can predict the water requirement for a field on a particular day, giving an understanding of a day's water demand. Based on sensed data of soil moisture level for any subgrid going below the threshold, then the pump goes to the ON state and the sprinkler distributes water to the subgrids (see Fig. 20.4).

Fig. 20.4 depicts the instruction flow from the server side when the soil moisture level for any subgrid goes below the threshold. The microcontroller (Arduino-II) fetches the data from the server-side cloud, and accordingly performs the desired tasks and waters the particular subgird in need of water.

20.3.2 Software operation

We have developed a cross-platform for users, that is, the Web as well as a mobile application. The

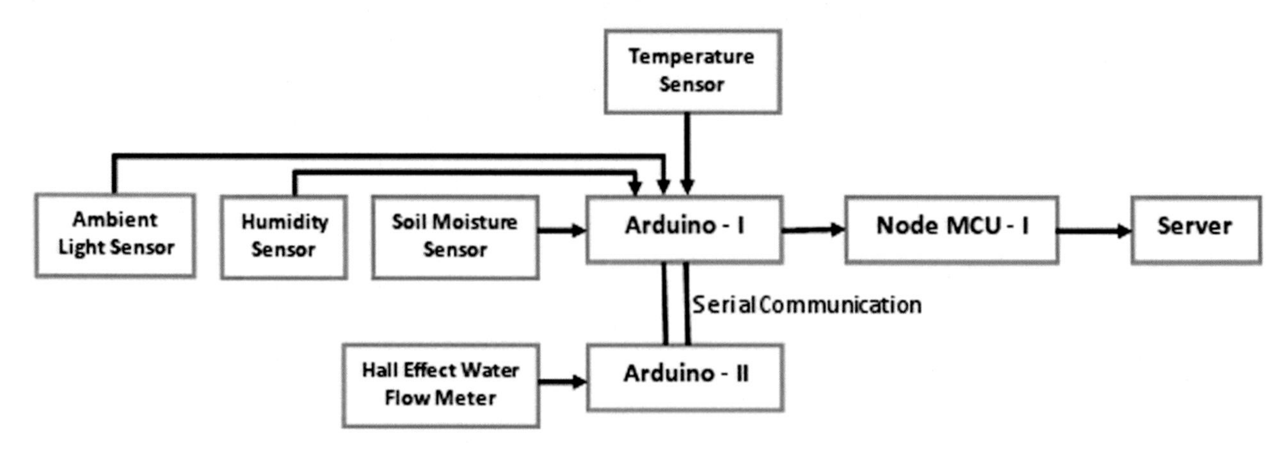

FIGURE 20.3 Sensed information flow goes to the server side.

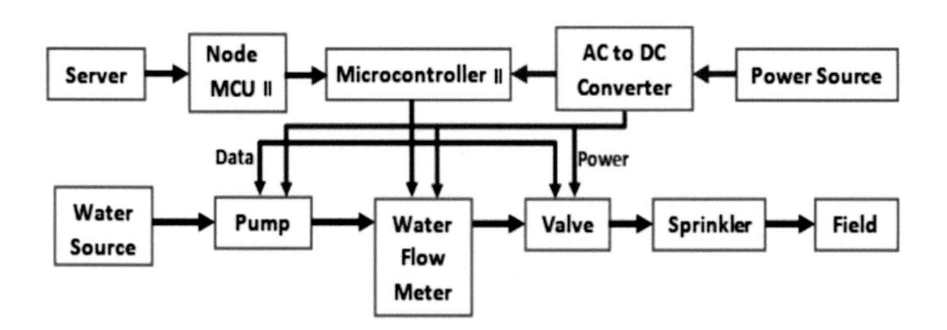

FIGURE 20.4 Instruction flow comes from the server side when the soil moisture level for any subgrid goes below the threshold.

software end consists of server-side logic and client-side logic, more commonly known as the backend and frontend. We have developed the server-side part on Django frameworks, which is built on the MVT architecture (Model-View-Template) along with a relational database that stores all the sensor data and retrieves the amount of water required by a certain part of the area that is being monitored. In order to connect the hardware part with the software part, we use Representational State Transfer (REST) APIs to wirelessly send and receive data from and to the sensors and database. The server receives the moisture level from the various parts of the field via the moisture sensors. Similarly, the water being consumed by the subgrids of the area being monitored by the water flow meters is sent to the cloud also. The data received from the sensors are stored in the database and simultaneously processed in real time. If the moisture level goes below a certain level at any part of the field then a request to turn the pump ON is initiated by the system and simultaneously a request to turn the valve ON is also initiated for the respective subgrid of the field. The water consumption, as well as other parameters that are being stored on the server, allows the artificial intelligence of the system to efficiently calculate the water requirement for the following day and the same is supplied to the grids and subgrids simultaneously, which helps to reduce water wastage by about 20%. Due to climate changes throughout the year, water requirements vary in grids with the seasonal changes. Hence, our approach not only conserves water but also electricity at the same time as the electricity is being used to unnecessarily pump water, and in this way groundwater can be preserved. For the client-side, we have provided the user with all the necessary weather details, all the parameters that are being monitored grid wise, along with the pump status that indicates whether the pump is ON or OFF and also the valve status is displayed to indicate which grids are currently consuming water and which are not. This allows the user to keep an easy track of everything that is happening in the field in real time. All the parameters that are being monitored can be visualized through different graphs in the mobile application. This allows the user to monitor all the previous data that are stored on the database and to see how parameters are changing.

20.4 Application of machine learning model

The system proposed in this chapter deals with automating the traditional process of farming. As is known, the biggest reason for automating the age-old irrigation system is for utilizing water in the proper way and avoiding water wastage. The proposed system comes with a machine-learning (Boursianis et al., 2020; Mahbub, 2020; Muniasamy, 2020; Sheikh et al., 2020; Guhathakurata, Saha, Kundu, Chakraborty, & Banerjee, 2020c; Navarro, Costa, & Pereira, 2020; Rezk, Hemdan, & Attia, 2020) model that can effectively determine the exact amount of water needed for the proper growth of plants.

The field is divided into multiple grids. Each grid has a source of the water inlet. In this chapter, we have applied the multiple-linear regression (MLR) model for predicting water usage. The authors have considered multiple parameters for predicting water usage for each grid; these parameters are grid area, soil moisture level of every grid, temperature, and water consumed by the subgrid on different days (see Table 20.1). It is clearly visible from Table 20.1 how the water requirement of the same subgrid changes with changing soil moisture and temperature on different dates.

As we are going to predict the quantity of water, we need to use a regression algorithm, and as there are multiple parameters, we have used MLR. MLR, also known simply as multiple regression, is a statistical technique that uses several explanatory variables to predict the outcome of a response variable. Table 20.1 shows the sample data set of a subgrid, which is used to train the MLR-based machine learning model. The accuracy of our prediction model is 77.9%.

TABLE 20.1 Sample data set of a particular subgrid.

Date	Subgrid area (m^2)	Soil moisture level of the subgrid (%)	Temperature of the subgrid (°C)	Water consumed by the subgrid (L)
Day 1	100	25	42	107
Day 2	100	40	38	79
Day 3	100	65	34	67
Day 4	100	30	27	70
Day 5	100	70	28	55
Day 6	100	50	18	46

Our proposed system (see Fig. 20.5) can predict grid-level water consumption requirements after successful training of the data set by the machine learning algorithm. This approach ensures the minimum wastage of water. Due to climate changes throughout the year, water requirements vary in grids with the seasonal changes. Thus, our system can efficiently calculate the amount of water required for a particular field for a particular season. Our system is smart enough to identify any sort of leakage in the water pipelines at any node, and in this way wastage of water can be prevented.

Fig. 20.5 shows how the machine learning model works and computes data based on its precision algorithms. As a case study, we have considered a field with multiple grids. Fig. 20.6 shows the total amount of water used versus the number of days for a particular field using ML and without using ML. It is observed that using the ML algorithm the water required is 424 L, whereas without using the ML algorithm the water required for the same field is 540 L. From this case study, it is clear that a 21.48% water saving is possible using the ML algorithm, which is also supported by Fig. 20.6.

20.5 Step-by-step procedure of the proposed methodology

The step-by-step procedure of the proposed methodology is described below (see Fig. 20.7).

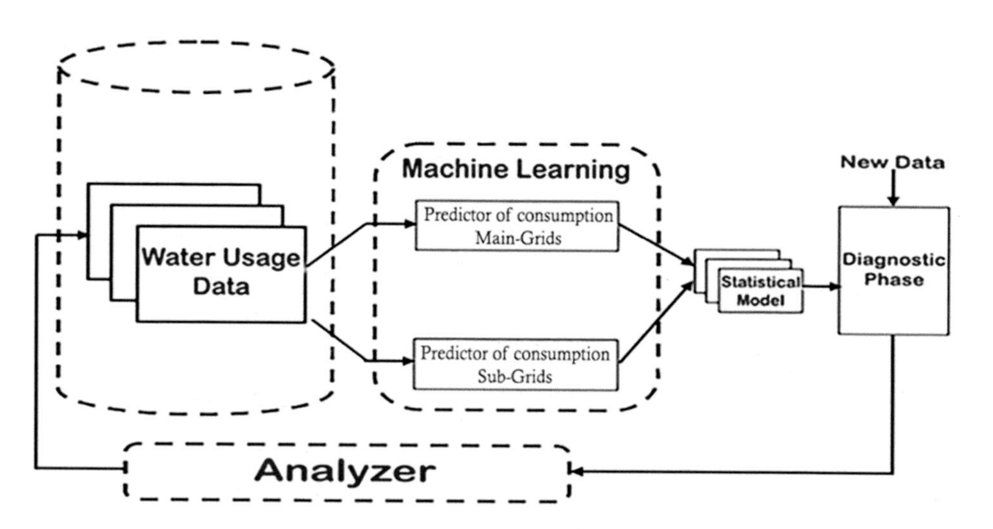

FIGURE 20.5 Machine learning model.

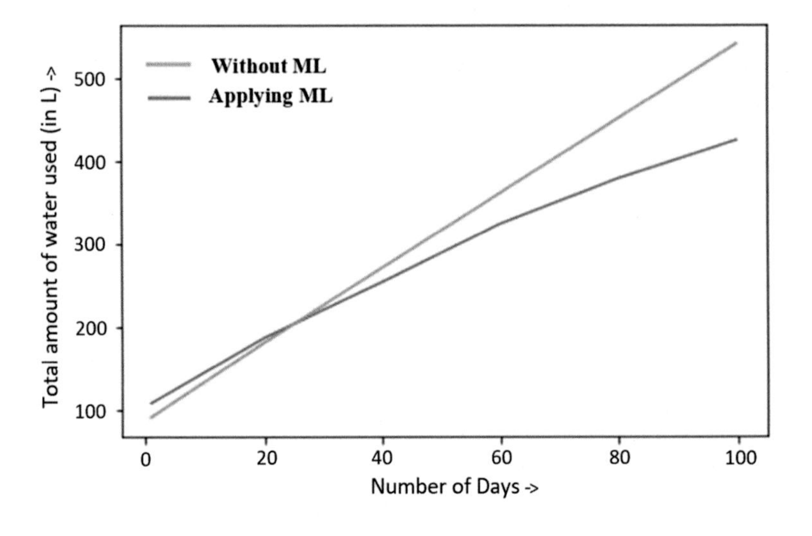

FIGURE 20.6 Total amount of water used versus number of days.

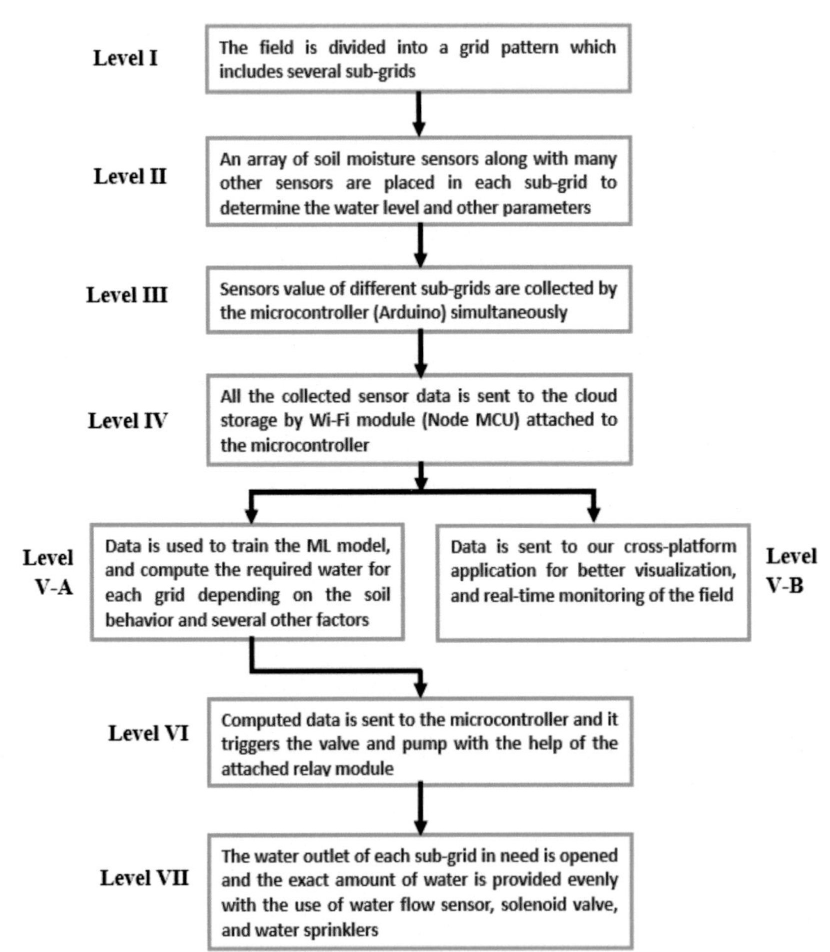

FIGURE 20.7 Step-by-step procedure of the proposed methodology.

Level I: First and foremost, the entire land for irrigation is divided into several small subgrids to gain greater accuracy and scalability. This way, it makes it easy to monitor the entire agricultural field in a simplified manner.

Level II: In the second step, we place an array of capacitive soil moisture sensors (SEN0193) in each subgrid to determine the moisture or water content of the soil. In parallel with the soil moisture sensors, many other sensors (atmospheric humidity, temperature, sunlight, etc.) are attached to record all other essential parameters.

Level III: In this level, when we have completed setting-up all hardware components, the microcontroller

(Arduino) starts collecting data from the sensors of individual subgrids simultaneously. All the data are collected in a fixed interval of time and are stored in the buffer space until the microcontroller establishes the connection and transmits data to the Wi-Fi module (node MCU).

Level IV: This step involves the transfer of data to the server-side cloud by REST APIs. The working in this step requires the availability of a decent Internet connection. The ESP8266 attached to the node MCU connects with the Internet via a Wi-Fi network and transfers the desired data to the cloud storage.

Level V-A: In this level, the data stored in the server-side cloud are provided to the machine learning model. The modern ML model predicts the water requirement of every subgrid based on the soil behavior and many other factors.

Level V-B: In this step, the client-side cloud fetches the data from the server-side cloud. The fetched data are processed and used for better visualization purposes and real-time monitoring of the field through our cross-platform application.

Level VI: At this stage, the computed data and instruction are collected by the microcontroller from the server-side cloud through RESTful API. According to the instruction and data, the MCU triggers the pump and the solenoid valve of the respective subgrid in real time.

Level VII: In this level, the water outlet of each subgrid in need of water is opened, and the exact amount of required water is spread evenly by the use of a water pump, water flow meter, and water sprinkler attached to the water outlet of every subgird.

The subgrid watering procedure can be explained through the flowchart in Fig. 20.8.

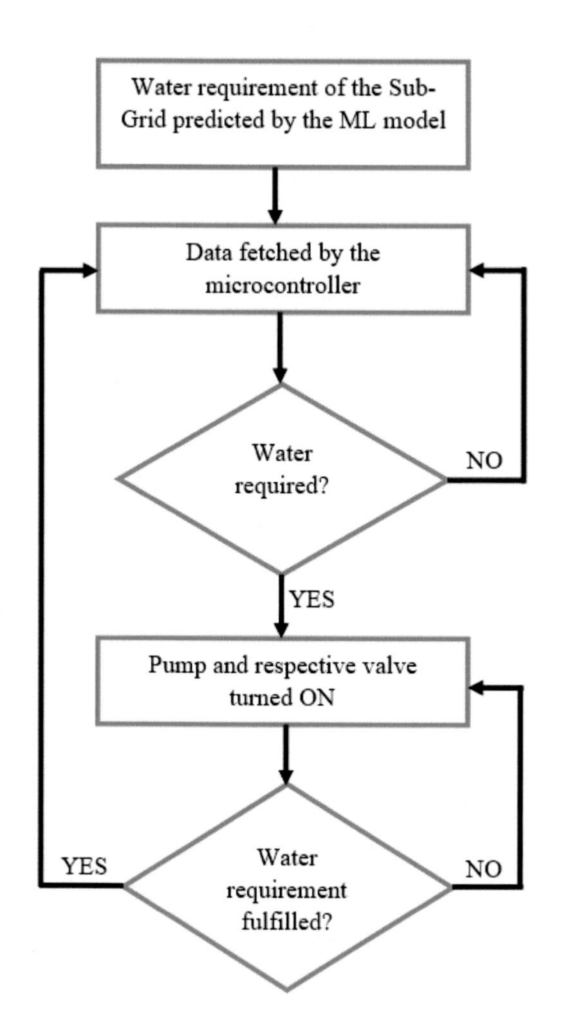

FIGURE 20.8 Flowchart of the subgrid watering procedure.

The water requirement of each subgrid is predicted by the modern machine learning model and stored in the server-side cloud storage. The microcontroller collects this value and desired instruction and the necessary action is taken in real time. If there is a requirement for water, then the MCU turns "ON" the pump and the respective solenoid valve otherwise returns to the previous step. Then the water flow meter keeps a check on the water flow output, and as soon as the requirement is fulfilled the pump and the valves are turned "OFF," and the cycle continues from the beginning.

20.6 Results and discussion

We implemented a cross-platform Web as well as a mobile application (Biswas, Sharma, Ranjan, & Banerjee, 2020) for the ease of the user (see Fig. 20.9). The Web application is based on vue.js framework and the android application is built on an android studio using java as the primary language. The fetching and updating of data are done using representational state transfer (Rest API) which is done using python on the Django framework. Our application has a user-end as well as an admin-end. The admin-end is used to monitor the entire user and all their activities and to make sure that all the users are receiving the correct data in real time. For the user, we store all the data gathered from the sensors to train with the machine-learning algorithm and provide the user with the current weather status, that is, moisture, temperature, humidity, etc. in a grid-level manner along with the valve status (see Figs. 20.10–20.16). In case of any leakage or overusage, we also alert the user. Also, for the ease of the user, we provide an array of graphs for the user to monitor the various parameters. In case the user has any problems and wants to notify the admin about

FIGURE 20.9 Login screen of the Web and mobile application.

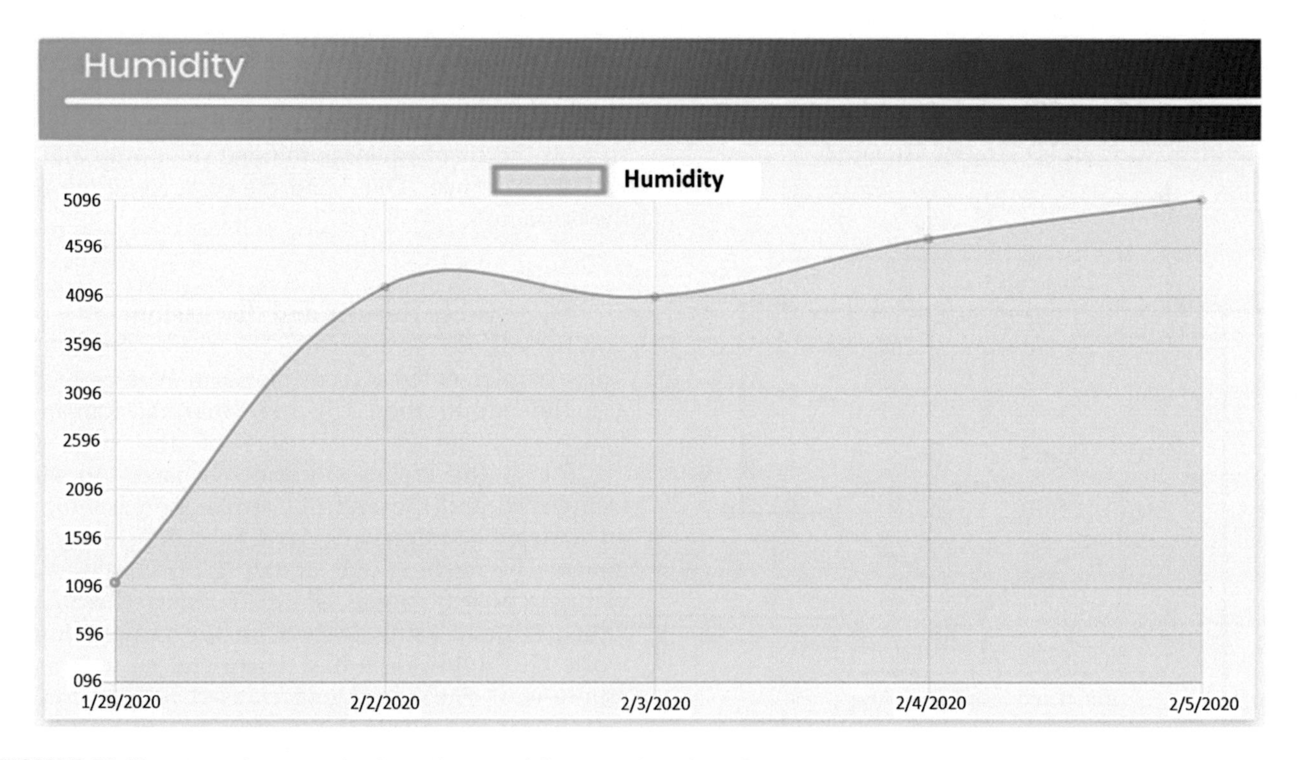

FIGURE 20.10 The real-time graphical visualization of the atmospheric humidity versus time.

any problem, they also can submit a complaint with a description. The diagrams are given below.

The user, that is, the farmer, can create their respective accounts and obtain the desired visuals through the Web and mobile application login (see Fig. 20.9).

Another strength of our system is that if for any reason sensors are not able to work and the data cannot be uploaded to the cloud, prediction and decision-making are not possible, however, our system at that moment also works smoothly using the weather APIs, capturing online related information for that location (see Fig. 20.16). Using weather APIs, rainfall, and wind speed can also be visualized in Figs. 20.14 and 20.15.

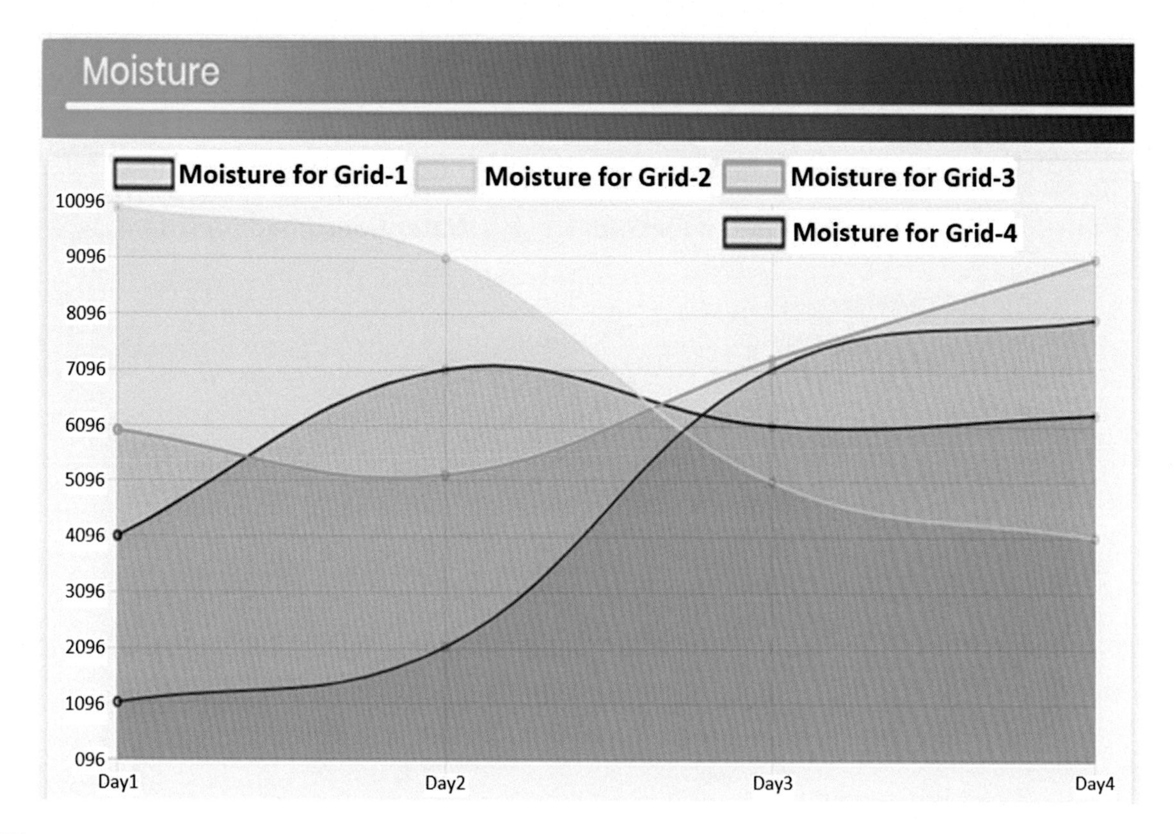

FIGURE 20.11 The real-time graphical visualization of the soil moisture of the individual grids versus time.

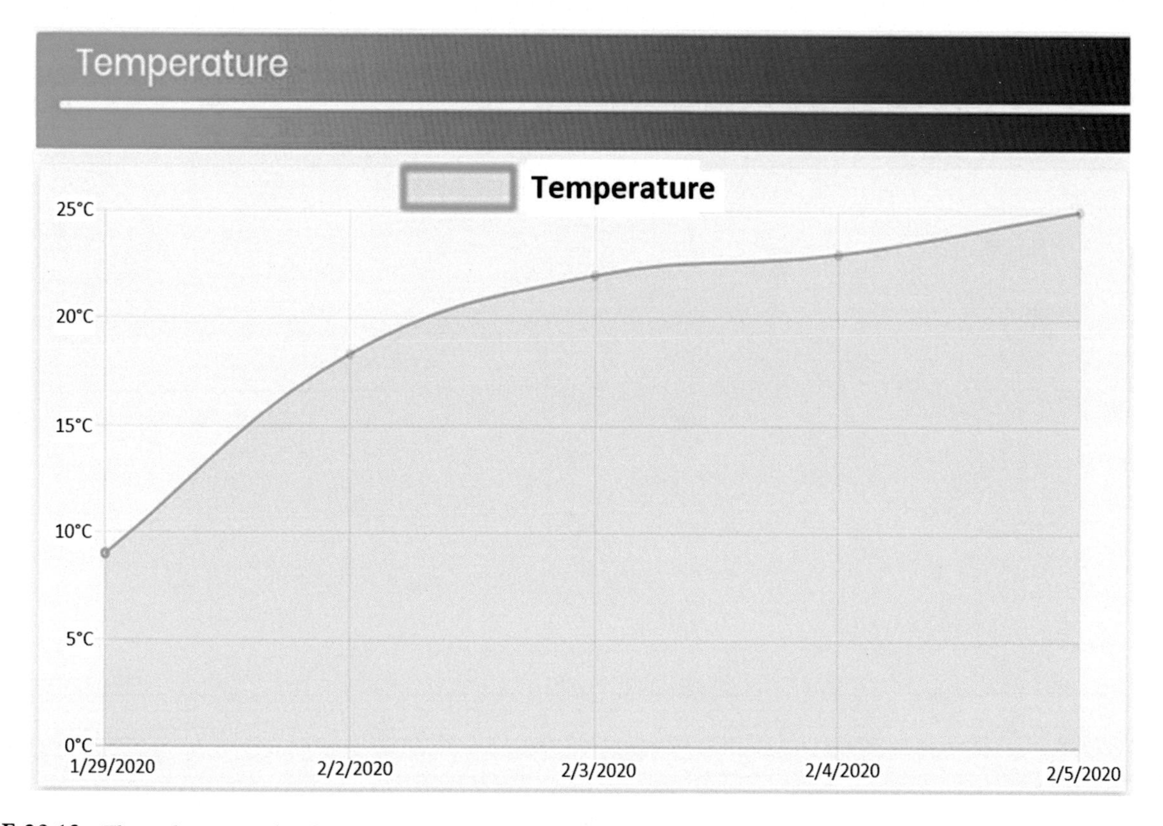

FIGURE 20.12 The real-time graphical visualization of the atmospheric temperature versus time.

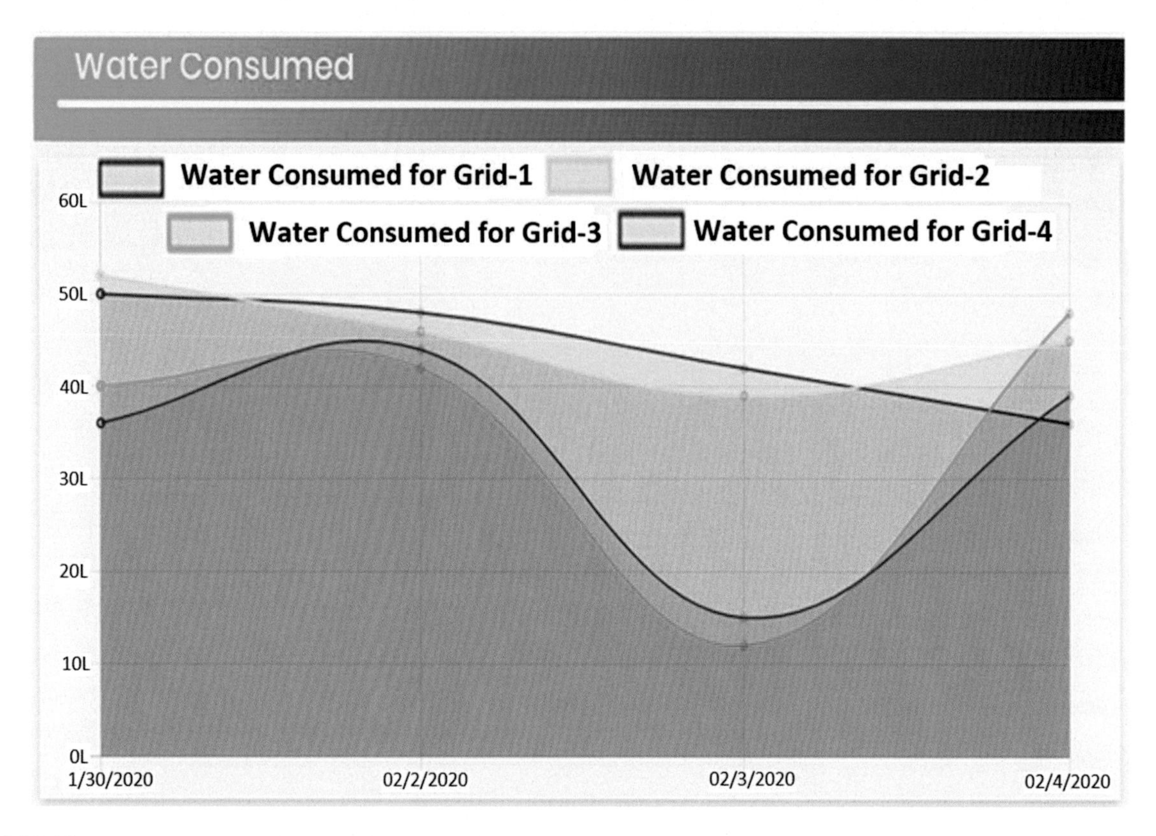

FIGURE 20.13 The real-time graphical visualization of the water consumed by the individual grids versus time.

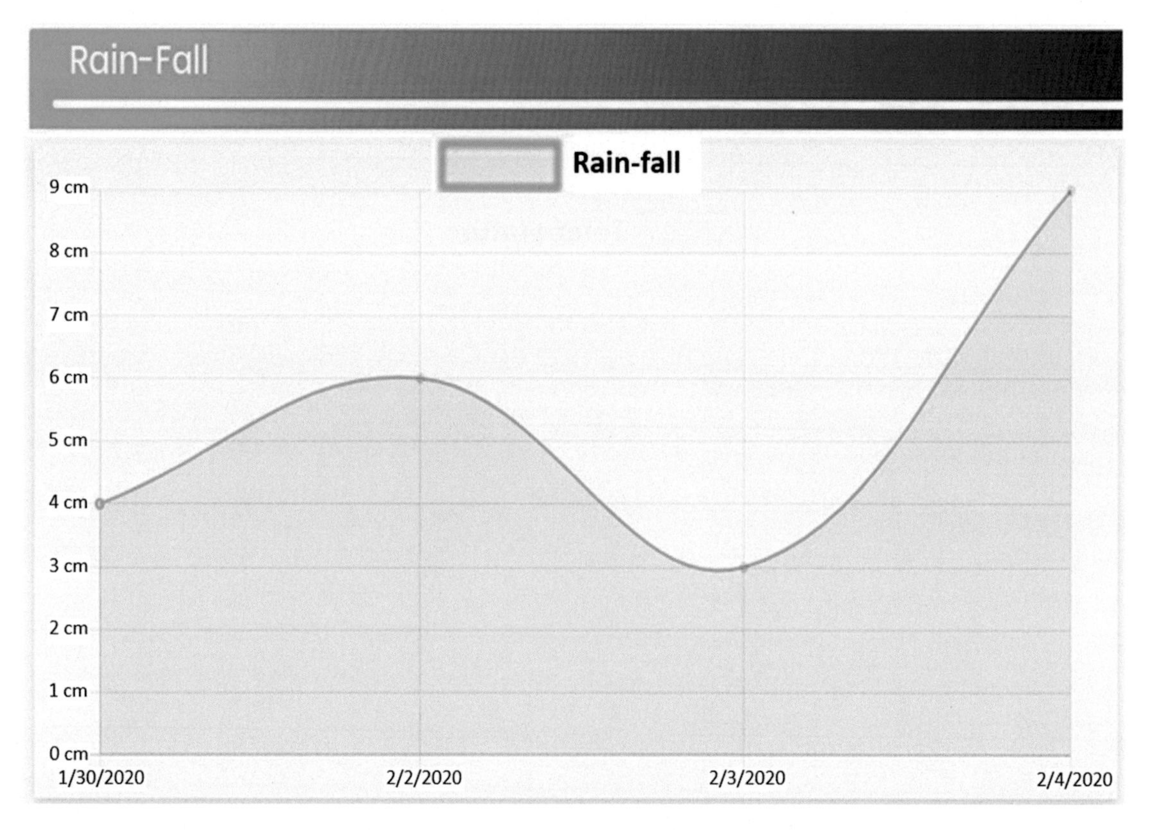

FIGURE 20.14 The real-time graphical visualization of the atmospheric rainfall versus time using weather APIs. *APIs*, Application programming interfaces.

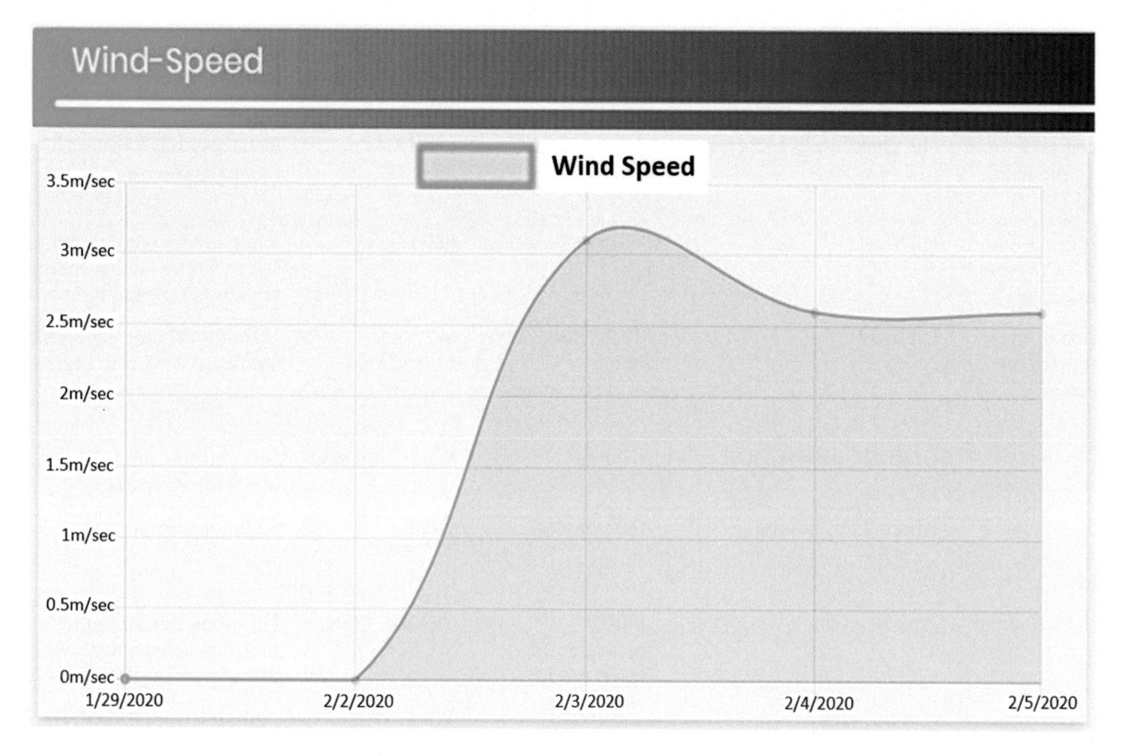

FIGURE 20.15 The real-time graphical visualization of the atmospheric wind speed versus time using weather APIs. *APIs*, Application programming interfaces.

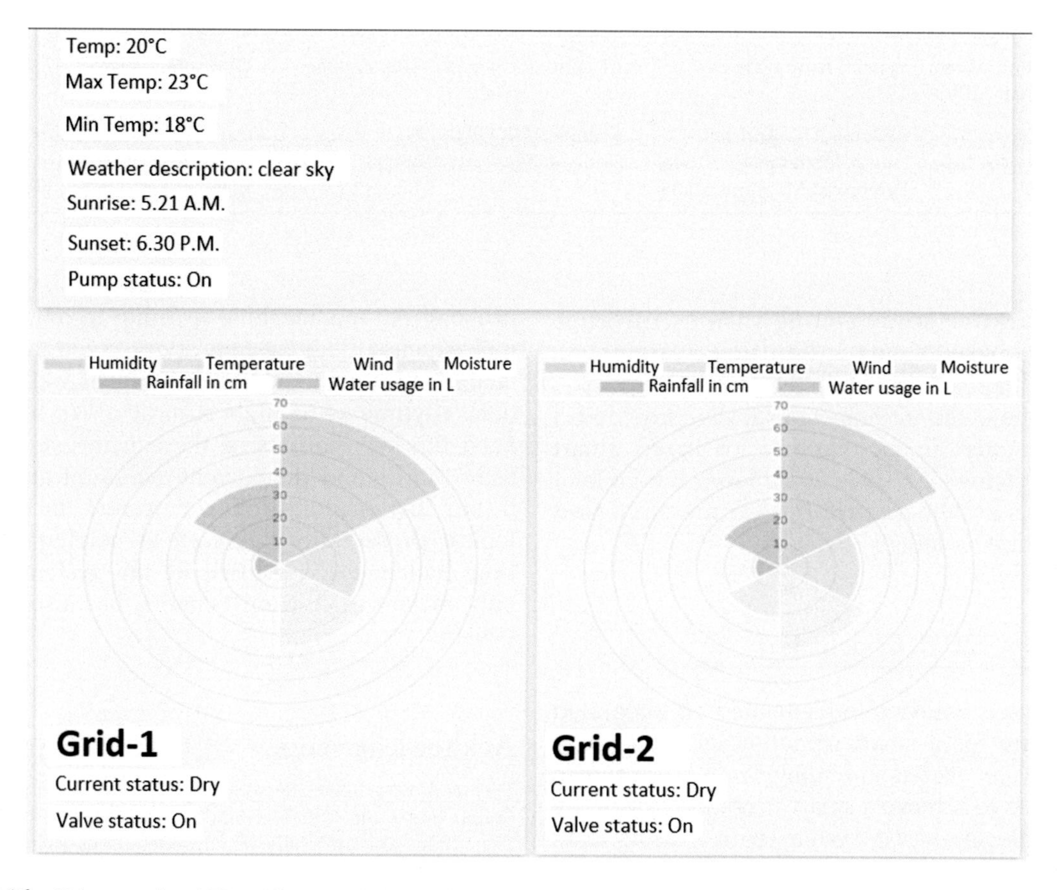

FIGURE 20.16 Using weather APIs grid status. *APIs*, Application programming interfaces.

TABLE 20.2 Comparative study.

Suggested IoT applications	Software tool applied	MCU used	Communication protocol applied	Sensors applied
Using IoT water management in the field (Hari Ram et al., 2015)	Not given	Not given	GSM	RFID, soil hygrometer, SDI-12 VRS-20 radar stage sensor
AgriSys—ubiquitous and smart agricultural process (Abdullah et al., 2016)	LabView	PhidgetInterfaceKit 8/8/8	GSM	Temperature sensor, humidity sensor, soil moisture sensor, thermocouple sensor, pH sensor, light sensor
Greenhouse monitoring system using intelligent agriculture (Dan et al., 2015)	LabView	STM8S103F3 chip 8051 microcontroller, CC2530 chip	802.15.4/ 6LowPAN, Zig-bee, GPRS,	Humidity sensor, light sensor, temperature sensor, pressure sensor
Agriculture using IoT (Shenoy & Pingle, 2016)	Open CV, Arduino IDE,	Arduino	Wi-Fi, Bluetooth	Soil moisture sensor, humidity sensor, temperature sensor
Smart watering system based on weather (Nagothu, 2016)	Android application	ARM processor	GPRS	Soil moisture sensor
Using WSN and IoT smart agriculture (Gondchawar & Kawitkar, 2016)	Raspbian OS	AVR microcontroller, Raspberry PI	Zig-bee, WSN, Wi-FI, GPS	Ultrasonic sensor, humidity sensor, soil moisture sensor, temperature sensor, PIR motion sensor
Intelligent farming by a control system (Putjaika et al., 2016)	Arduino IDE	Arduino	Wi- Fi	Light intensity sensor, Humidity sensor, Soil moisture sensor, Temperature sensor
Image processing and IoT-based smart agriculture (Kapoor et al., 2016)	Arduino IDE, MATLAB	Arduino	Wi-Fi	Serial JPEG camera module, temperature sensor, soil moisture sensor, humidity sensor
Smart drip irrigation system (Agrawal & Singhal, 2015)	Python, Arduino IDE	Arduino, Raspberry PI	GPS, Zig-bee	Ultrasonic sensor
Our proposed system	Arduino IDE, Android Studio, Visual Studio Code, Python, AI-ML applications	Arduino UNO-R3, Node MCU	Wi-Fi, NFC, RFID	Capacitive soil moisture sensor, humidity and moisture, temperature, LDR sunlight sensor, water flow meter

20.7 Comparative study among various Internet of Things based smart agriculture systems

In this section, the authors holistically provided a comparative study among various IoT-based smart agriculture systems (see Table 20.2). From the table, it is clear that our system outperforms existing IoT-based smart agriculture systems.

20.8 Conclusion

In this chapter, we have implemented an integrated IoT architecture for a smart irrigation system, where the sensors, water meters are "things" on the Internet. We have aimed to achieve a smart irrigation system by developing this IoT-based system with sensors, that can provide high data processing functionality utilizing AI and machine learning techniques at minimal expense. This system adopted automation which enables all users to access real-time as well as historical data anytime with high accuracy. We have also utilized the key features of the existing smart irrigation technologies and the current communication protocols in our implemented IoT architecture. In terms of ecological preservation, as well as solving several real-time challenges, we anticipate this system to have not only major agricultural benefits, but also many social benefits.

Acknowledgments

This work was financially supported by The Institution of Engineers (India) under the R & D Grant-in-Aid scheme (UG2020026; 2019). The authors also gratefully acknowledge the assistance of the Bengal Institute of Technology, Kolkata.

References

Abdullah, A., Al Enazi, S., & Damaj, I. (2016). AgriSys: A smart and ubiquitous controlled-environment agriculture system. In *2016 3rd MEC international conference on big data and smart city (ICBDSC)* (pp. 1–6). IEEE.

Agrawal, N., & Singhal, S. (2015). Smart drip irrigation system using raspberry pi and arduino. In *International conference on computing, communication & automation* (pp. 928–932). IEEE.

Bahga, A., & Madisetti, V. (2014). Internet of Things: A hands-on approach. *VPT*.

Banerjee, J., Maiti, S., Chakraborty, S., Dutta, S., Chakraborty, A., & Banerjee, J.S. (2019). Impact of machine learning in various network security applications. In *2019 3rd international conference on computing methodologies and communication (ICCMC)* (pp. 276–281). IEEE.

Banerjee, J. S., & Chakraborty, A. (2014). Modeling of software defined radio architecture and cognitive radio: The next generation dynamic and smart spectrum access technology. In *Cognitive radio sensor networks: Applications, architectures, and challenges* (pp. 127–158). IGI Global.

Banerjee, J. S., & Chakraborty, A. (2015). Fundamentals of software defined radio and cooperative spectrum sensing: A step ahead of cognitive radio networks. In *Handbook of research on software-defined and cognitive radio technologies for dynamic spectrum management* (pp. 499–543). IGI Global.

Banerjee, J. S., Chakraborty, A., & Chattopadhyay, A. (2017). Fuzzy based relay selection for secondary transmission in cooperative cognitive radio networks. In *Advances in optical science and engineering* (pp. 279–287). Singapore: Springer.

Banerjee, J. S., Chakraborty, A., & Chattopadhyay, A. (2018a). A novel best relay selection protocol for cooperative cognitive radio systems using fuzzy AHP. *Journal of Mechanics of Continua and Mathematical Science, 13*(2), 72–87.

Banerjee, J. S., Chakraborty, A., & Chattopadhyay, A. (2018b). Relay node selection using analytical hierarchy process (AHP) for secondary transmission in multi-user cooperative cognitive radio systems. In *Advances in electronics, communication and computing* (pp. 745–754). Singapore: Springer.

Banerjee, J. S., Chakraborty, A., & Chattopadhyay, A. (2018c). Reliable best-relay selection for secondary transmission in co-operation based cognitive radio systems: A multi-criteria approach. *Journal of Mechanics of Continua and Mathematical Science, 13*(2), 24–42.

Banerjee, J. S., Chakraborty, A., & Chattopadhyay, A. (2021). A decision model for selecting best reliable relay queue for cooperative relaying in cooperative cognitive radio networks: the extent analysis based fuzzy AHP solution. *Wireless Networks*. Available from https://doi.org/10.1007/s11276-021-02597-z.

Banerjee, J. S., Chakraborty, A., & Goswami, D. (2013). A survey on agri-crisis in India based on engineering aspects. *International Journal of Data Modelling and Knowledge Management, 3*(1–2), 71–76.

Banerjee, J. S., Chakraborty, A., & Karmakar, K. (2013). Architecture of cognitive radio networks. In *Cognitive radio technology applications for wireless and mobile ad hoc networks* (pp. 125–152). IGI Global.

Banerjee, J.S., Goswami, D., & Nandi, S. (2014). OPNET: A new paradigm for simulation of advanced communication systems. In *Proceedings of international conference on contemporary challenges in management, technology & social sciences, SEMS* (pp. 319–328).

Banerjee, J. S., & Karmakar, K. (2012). A comparative study on cognitive radio implementation issues. *International Journal of Computer Applications, 45*(15), 44–51.

Biswas, S., Sharma, L. K., Ranjan, R., & Banerjee, J. S. (2020). GO-COVID: An interactive cross-platform based dashboard for real-time tracking of COVID-19 using data analytics. *Journal of Mechanics of Continua and Mathematical Science, 15*(6), 1–15.

Boursianis, A.D., Papadopoulou, M.S., Diamantoulakis, P., Liopa-Tsakalidi, A., Barouchas, P., Salahas, G., George Karagiannidis, Shaohua Wan, Sotirios K. Goudos (2020). Internet of Things (IoT) and agricultural unmanned aerial vehicles (UAVs) in smart farming: A comprehensive review. Internet Things, 2020, 100187.

Chakraborty, A., & Banerjee, J. S. (2013). An advance Q learning (AQL) approach for path planning and obstacle avoidance of a mobile robot. *International Journal of Intelligent Mechatronics and Robotics (IJIMR), 3*(1), 53–73.

Chakraborty, A., Banerjee, J.S., & Chattopadhyay, A. (2017). Non-uniform quantized data fusion rule alleviating control channel overhead for cooperative spectrum sensing in cognitive radio networks. In *2017 IEEE 7th international advance computing conference (IACC)* (pp. 210–215). IEEE.

Chakraborty, A., Banerjee, J. S., & Chattopadhyay, A. (2019). Non-uniform quantized data fusion rule for data rate saving and reducing control channel overhead for cooperative spectrum sensing in cognitive radio networks. *Wireless Personal Communications, 104*(2), 837–851.

Chakraborty, A., Banerjee, J. S., & Chattopadhyay, A. (2020). Malicious node restricted quantized data fusion scheme for trustworthy spectrum sensing in cognitive radio networks. *Journal of Mechanics of Continua and Mathematical Science, 15*(1), 39–56.

Chattopadhyay, J., Kundu, S., Chakraborty, A., & Banerjee, J.S. (2020). Facial expression recognition for human computer interaction. In *International conference on computational vision and bio inspired computing* (pp. 1181–1192). Springer, Cham.

Dan, L.I., Xin, C., Chongwei, H., & Liangliang, J. (2015). Intelligent agriculture greenhouse environment monitoring system based on IOT technology. In *2015 International conference on intelligent transportation, big data and smart city* (pp. 487–490). IEEE.

Das, D., Pandey, I., & Banerjee, J.S. (2016). An in-depth study of implementation issues of 3D printer. In *Proceedings of MICRO 2016 conference on microelectronics, circuits and systems* (pp. 45–49).

Das, D., Pandey, I., Chakraborty, A., & Banerjee, J. S. (2017). Analysis of implementation factors of 3D printer: The key enabling technology for making prototypes of the engineering design and manufacturing. *International Journal of Computer Applications*, 8–14, ISSN:975-8887.

Gondchawar, N., & Kawitkar, R. S. (2016). Smart agriculture using IoT and WSN based modern technologies. *International Journal of Innovative Research in Computer and Communication Engineering*.

Guhathakurata, S., Kundu, S., Chakraborty, A., & Banerjee, J. S. (2021). A novel approach to predict COVID-19 using support vector machine. In *Data science for COVID-19*. Elsevier, In press.

Guhathakurata, S., Saha, S., Kundu, S., Chakraborty, A., & Banerjee, J.S. (2020). South Asian Countries are less fatal concerning COVID-19: A fact-finding procedure integrating machine learning & multiple criteria decision making (MCDM) technique. Journal of the Institution of Engineers (India): Series B, Springer. https://doi.org/10.1007/s40031-021-00547-z.

Guhathakurata, S., Saha, S., Kundu, S., Chakraborty, A., & Banerjee, J. S. (2021a). South Asian Countries are less fatal concerning COVID-19: A hybrid spproach using machine learning and M-AHP. In *Computational intelligence techniques for combating COVID-19*. Springer (Press).

Guhathakurata, S., Saha, S., Kundu, S., Chakraborty, A., & Banerjee, J. S. (2021b). A new approach to predict COVID-19 using artificial neural networks. In *Cyber-physical systems: AI and COVID-19*. Elsevier (Press).

Hari Ram, V. V., Vishal, H., Dhanalakshmi, S., & Vidya, P. M. (2015). Regulation of water in agriculture field using Internet Of Things. In *2015 IEEE technological innovation in ICT for agriculture and rural development (TIAR)* (pp. 112–115). IEEE.

Kapoor, A., Bhat, S.I., Shidnal, S., & Mehra, A. (2016). Implementation of IoT (Internet of Things) and image processing in smart agriculture. In *2016 international conference on computation system and information technology for sustainable solutions (CSITSS)* (pp. 21–26). IEEE.

Mahbub, M. (2020). A smart farming concept based on smart embedded electronics, internet of things and wireless sensor network. In *Internet of Things* (9). Elsevier100161.

Muniasamy, A. (2020). Machine learning for smart farming: A focus on desert agriculture. In *2020 international conference on computing and information technology (ICCIT-1441)* (pp. 1–5). IEEE.

Nagothu, S.K. (2016). Weather based smart watering system using soil sensor and GSM. In *2016 World conference on futuristic trends in research and innovation for social welfare (Startup Conclave)* (pp. 1–3). IEEE.

Navarro, E., Costa, N., & Pereira, A. (2020). A systematic review of IoT solutions for smart farming. *Sensors (Basel, Switzerland)*, *20*(15), 4231.

Pandey, I., Dutta, H.S., & Banerjee, J.S. (2019). WBAN: A smart approach to next generation e-healthcare system. In *2019 3rd international conference on computing methodologies and communication (ICCMC)* (pp. 344–349). IEEE.

Paul, S., Chakraborty, A., & Banerjee, J.S. (2017). A fuzzy AHP-based relay node selection protocol for wireless body area networks (WBAN). In *2017 4th international conference on opto-electronics and applied optics (Optronix)* (pp. 1–6). IEEE.

Paul, S., Chakraborty, A., & Banerjee, J. S. (2019). The extent analysis based fuzzy AHP approach for relay selection in WBAN. In *Cognitive informatics and soft computing* (pp. 331–341). Singapore: Springer.

Putjaika, N., Phusae, S., Chen-Im, A., Phunchongharn, P., & Akkarajitsakul, K. (2016). A control system in an intelligent farming by using arduino technology. In *2016 fifth ICT international student project conference (ICT-ISPC)* (pp. 53–56). IEEE.

Qiu, T., Liu, J., Si, W., Han, M., Ning, H., & Atiquzzaman, M. (2017). A data-driven robustness algorithm for the internet of things in smart cities. *IEEE Communications Magazine*, *55*(12), 18–23.

Rezk, N. G., Hemdan, E. E. D., Attia, A. F., El-Sayed, Ayman, & El-Rashidy, Mohamed A. (2020). An efficient IoT based smart farming system using machine learning algorithms. In *Multimedia Tools and Applications*. Springer.

Roy, R., Dutta, S., Biswas, S., & Banerjee, J. S. (2020). Android things: A comprehensive solution from things to smart display and speaker. In Proceedings of international conference on IoT inclusive life (ICIIL 2019), NITTTR Chandigarh, India (pp. 339–352). Singapore: Springer.

Saha, O., Chakraborty, A., & Banerjee, J.S. (2017). A decision framework of IT-based stream selection using analytical hierarchy process (AHP) for admission in technical institutions. In *2017 4th international conference on opto-electronics and applied optics (Optronix)* (pp. 1–6). IEEE.

Saha, O., Chakraborty, A., & Banerjee, J. S. (2019). A fuzzy AHP approach to IT-based stream selection for admission in technical institutions in India. In *Emerging technologies in data mining and information security* (pp. 847–858). Singapore: Springer.

Saha, P., Guhathakurata, S., Saha, S., Chakraborty, A., & Banerjee, J. S. (2021). Application of machine learning in app-based cab booking system: A survey on Indian scenario. In *Applications of Artificial Intelligence in Engineering, Proceedings of First Global Conference on Artificial Intelligence and Applications (GCAIA 2020)*, Springer, In press.

Sheikh, J.A., Cheema, S.M., Ali, M., Amjad, Z., Tariq, J.Z., & Naz, A. (2020). IoT and AI in precision agriculture: Designing smart system to support illiterate farmers. In *International conference on applied human factors and ergonomics* (pp. 490–496). Springer, Cham.

Shenoy, J., & Pingle, Y. (2016). IOT in agriculture. In *2016 3rd international conference on computing for sustainable global development (INDIACom)* (pp. 1456–1458). IEEE.

Further reading

Albright, L.D., & Langhans, R.W. (1996). *Controlled environment agriculture scoping study*. Electric Power Research Institute.

Arduino, Arduino. Retrieved from https://www.arduino.cc/. (Accessed 20 September 2020).

Bo, Y., & Wang, H. (2011). The application of cloud computing and the internet of things in agriculture and forestry. In *2011 international joint conference on service sciences* (pp. 168–172). IEEE.

Kadage, A.D., & Gawade, J.D. (2009). Wireless control system for agricultural motor. In *2009 second international conference on emerging trends in engineering & technology* (pp. 722–725). IEEE.

Kim, Y., Evans, R. G., & Iversen, W. M. (2008). Remote sensing and control of an irrigation system using a distributed wireless sensor network. *IEEE Transactions on Instrumentation and Measurement*, *57*(7), 1379–1387.

Latte, M.V., & Shidnal, S. (2016). Multiple nutrient deficiency detection in paddy leaf images using color and pattern analysis. In *2016 international conference on communication and signal processing (ICCSP)* (pp. 1247–1250). IEEE.

Lee, M., Hwang, J., & Yoe, H. (2013). Agricultural production system based on IoT. In *2013 IEEE 16Th international conference on computational science and engineering* (pp. 833–837). IEEE.

Li, R.H., Yu, J.X., Huang, X., Cheng, H., & Shang, Z. (2012). Measuring robustness of complex networks under MVC attack. In *Proceedings of the 21st ACM international conference on information and knowledge management* (pp. 1512–1516).

Li, S. (2012). Application of the internet of things technology in precision agriculture irrigation systems. In *2012 international conference on computer science and service system* (pp. 1009–1013). IEEE.

Ma, J., Zhou, X., Li, S., & Li, Z. (2011). Connecting agriculture to the internet of things through sensor networks. In *2011 international conference on internet of things and 4th international conference on cyber, physical and social computing* (pp. 184–187). IEEE.

Python (programming language), Wikipedia, Retrieved from https://en.wikipedia.org/wiki/Python_(programming_language). (Accessed 20 September 2020).

Qiu, T., Chen, N., Li, K., Qiao, D., & Fu, Z. (2017). Heterogeneous ad hoc networks: Architectures, advances and challenges. *Ad Hoc Networks*, *55*, 143–152.

Rui, J., & Danpeng, S. (2015). Architecture design of the Internet of Things based on cloud computing. In *2015 seventh international conference on measuring technology and mechatronics automation* (pp. 206–209). IEEE.

Sarma, A. C., & Girão, J. (2009). Identities in the future internet of things. *Wireless Personal Communications*, *49*(3), 353–363.

Soil pH, Wikipedia, Retrieved from https://en.wikipedia.org/wiki/Soil_pH. (Accessed 20 September 2020).

Stankovic, J. A. (2014). Research directions for the internet of things. *IEEE Internet of Things Journal*, *1*(1), 3–9.

Sun, B., Jao, J., & Wu, K. (2013). Wirless sensor based crop montoring system for agriculture using Wi-Fi network dissertation. *IEEE Computer Science*, 280–285.

Tsai, C. W., Cho, H. H., Shih, T. K., Pan, J. S., & Rodrigues, J. J. (2015). Metaheuristics for the deployment of 5G. *IEEE Wireless Communications*, *22*(6), 40–46.

Wang, N., Zhang, N., & Wang, M. (2006). Wireless sensors in agriculture and food industry—Recent development and future perspective. *Computers and Electronics in Agriculture*, *50*(1), 1–4.

Yan-e, D. (2011). Design of intelligent agriculture management information system based on IoT. In *2011 fourth international conference on intelligent computation technology and automation* (Vol. 1, pp. 1045–1049). IEEE.

Zhou, Z., & Zhou, Z. (2012). Application of internet of things in agriculture products supply chain management. In *2012 international conference on control engineering and communication technology* (pp. 259–261). IEEE.

CHAPTER

21

Intelligent and smart enabling technologies in advanced applications: recent trends

Mayurakshi Jana[1] *and Suparna Biswas*[2]

[1]Department of Computer Science, Bijoy Krishna Girls' College, Howrah, India [2]Computer Science and Engineering, Maulana Abul Kalam Azad University of Technology, Kolkata, India

21.1 Introduction

In the era of the Internet of Things (IoT) (Adi, Anwar, Baig, & Zeadally, 2020) and big data, intelligent computing of data is necessary. With the growing population it is very difficult to manage our day-to-day lives without using intelligent computing. There are several fields where intelligent computing has become a necessary feature. From healthcare to industry it can handle multidimensional heterogeneous data. It can generate results based on existing resources. Therefore resource consumption is manageable. Intelligent computing consists of artificial intelligence, natural language processing, cybersecurity, deep learning, wireless sensor networks, etc. (Fig. 21.1).

21.2 Enabling intelligent technologies used in recent research problems

21.2.1 Internet of Things

IoT is an interconnected network of smart devices. This interconnected network is used in various domains like smart healthcare, smart transport, smart parking, smart home, and smart agriculture. The IoT generally consists of sensors, which are basically used to collect information from various devices or the human body. For the human body sensors can be both wearable and implantable. Some common examples of sensors are given in Table 21.1.

The sensory data are transferred to the cloud via some transmission media protocol that can be wired or wireless. Some transmission media protocols are shown in Table 21.2.

Further, the data are stored in a cloud server. Some popular cloud services are:

- Amazon Web Services (AWS);
- Microsoft Azure;
- Google cloud platform (GCP);
- IBM Watson.

Cloud is basically used for the operations described in Table 21.3.

After doing necessary computations the results are displayed into edge devices such as smartphones or laptops. Users can easily access these data through software applications.

21.2.2 Machine learning

One of the most important applications of artificial intelligence (AI) is machine learning (ML). This is used to enhance the capability of the system to learn from the experience. Traditional ML algorithms depend on the given data. Also, they take decisions of a particular problem based on real-world knowledge. ML is used in detecting false alarms, drug discovery, pattern recognition, text-to-speech or speech-to-text recognition, entertainment recommendations, soil moisture prediction, video surveillance, etc.

The advantages of ML algorithms include:

- ML algorithms do not need human intervention to write a program. They can make predictions based upon a given data set and real world knowledge.
- ML algorithms can easily recognize patterns. That is why the prediction of diseases or recommendations for e-commerce websites are done straightforwardly.

Recent Trends in Computational Intelligence Enabled Research.
DOI: https://doi.org/10.1016/B978-0-12-822844-9.00045-1

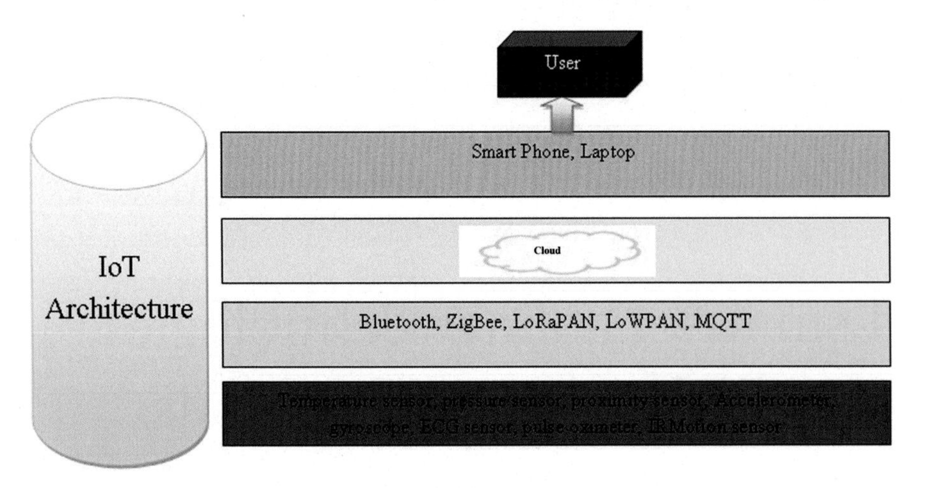

FIGURE 21.1 Classical diagram of Internet of Things architecture.

TABLE 21.1 Various types of sensors.

Sensor	Function	Example
Temperature sensor	Mostly used to measure the temperature of the human body. Also used to detect temperature of the environment or soil	LM35
Pressure sensor	Measures the blood pressure of human body. Also used for measuring environmental pressure	E8PC
Proximity sensor	Used to detect nearby objects without physical contact	Si114x, Si1102
Accelerometer and gyroscope	Accelerometer is used to detect the linear motion and gyroscope determines the angular position of that particular device	ADXL345
ECG sensor	Records the electrical impulses through heart muscles	AD8232
Pulse oximeter sensor	Used to monitor the saturation percentage of oxygen in blood	MAX32664
IRMotion sensor	Detects movement of a person using temperature differences	SN-AIRS06

TABLE 21.2 Protocols related to various layers of the Internet of Things architecture

Data link layer						
Protocol	**Wired**	**Wireless**	**Range**	**Bandwidth**	**Data rate**	**Cost**
Bluetooth	×	✓	10–100 m	2.4 GHz	1–3 Mbps	Low
Zigbee	×	✓	30–100 m	2.4 GHz	20–250 kbps	Low
802.11	×	✓	50–100 m	5 GHz	1–450 Mbps	Low
GSM 3G, 4G, LTE	×	✓	Long distance	5–20 MHz	100 Mbps–1 Gbps	Low
LoRaWAN	×	✓	2–7 km	125 kHz or 500 kHz	250 bps–11 kbps	High
Optical fiber, coaxial cable	✓	×	500 m (optical fiber) 185 m (coaxial cable)	1 GHz (optical fiber) 750 MHz (coaxial cable)	1600 Gbps (optical fiber) 10 Mbps (coaxial cable)	High (optical fiber) Low (coaxial cable)
Network layer						
Encapsulation	6LoWPAN					
Routing	RPL, CORPL, CARP					
Application layer						
TCP	XMPP, MQTT and REST/HTTP					
UDP	DDS					

- They can handle high-volume multidimensional "big data."
- The evaluation parameters including accuracy, sensitivity, specificity, etc. are high as the algorithms are continuously improving with experience gained from acquired data.

The disadvantages of ML algorithms include:

- ML algorithms need a large number of resources to carry out prediction.
- Choosing of an accurate ML algorithm is a difficult task. Therefore applying all ML algorithms to find the one with the highest accuracy is a difficult and time-consuming task.

Sometimes the training data set used in the ML algorithm is biased; therefore the predicted result will be biased (Fig. 21.2).

TABLE 21.3 Cloud services and functionalities.

SaaS (Software as a Service)	Software is used over Internet without installing in a computer system
PaaS (Platform as a Service)	Both hardware and software platforms of a third party are used over the Internet
IaaS (Infrastructure as a Service)	Provides computational virtualized resources to work over the Internet

21.2.3 Deep learning

Deep learning is another application of AI and a subset of ML. It takes raw data as input and represents patterns as output. A number of hidden layers are used to extract features from the input data set. A layer with more abstract features is created. Therefore fewer resources are needed and an unbiased data set is generated.

What is the difference between ML and deep learning?

ML algorithms need human interventions but deep learning algorithms do not need any human intervention to make features for the training model (Fig. 21.3).

21.2.4 Metaheuristics

The metaheuristics approach is an optimization approach which produces good result for optimization problems where some of the data in the data set are missing or incomplete. Some popular metaheuristics algorithms are:

- Ant Colony Optimization (Tsai, Chiang, Ksentini, & Chen, 2016): In this technique, software agents, that is, ants are used to find the best possible path on a weighted graph. Each ant selects a vertex and moves to another vertex while keeping the memory of the path just like an ant in a real-life scenario.
- Bat Algorithm (BA) (Pereira, Pereira, Papa, Rosa, & Yang, 2016): The BA uses the idea of a virtual bat

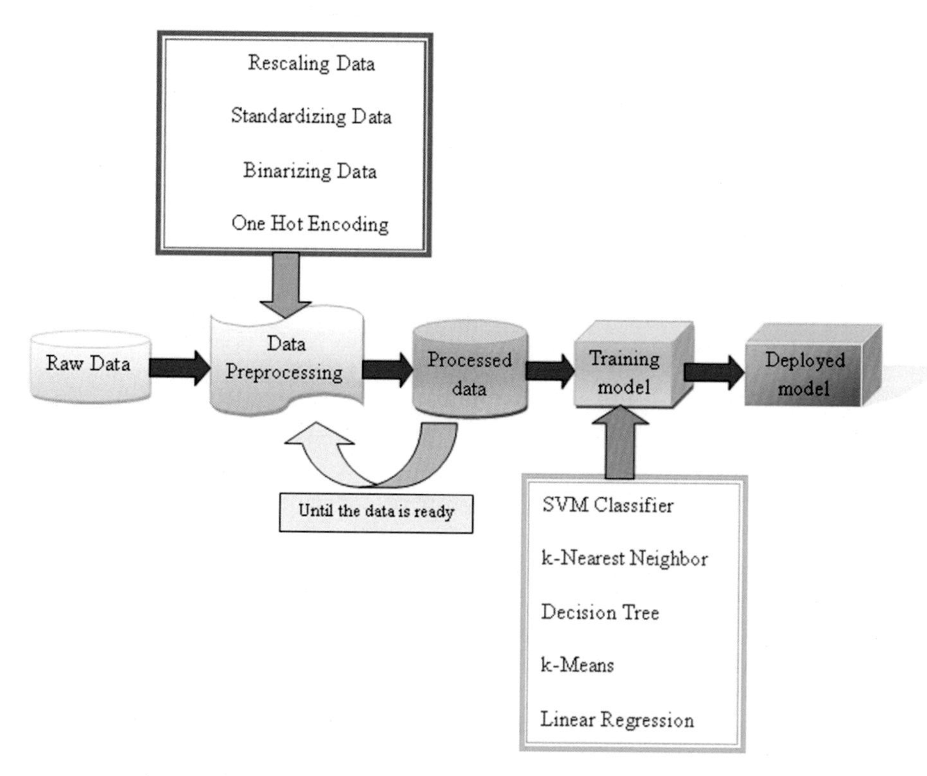

FIGURE 21.2 Process of machine learning algorithm.

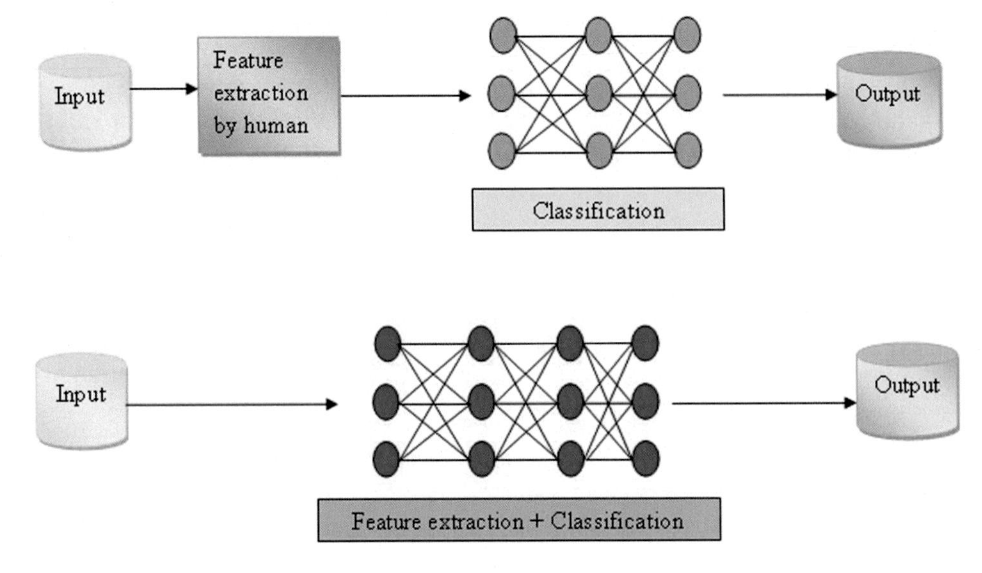

FIGURE 21.3 Difference between machine learning and deep learning.

which has a velocity, varying frequency, and wavelength. In the searching process the final destination is reached when certain criteria are met.

- Firefly algorithm (FA) (Pereira et al., 2016): Fireflies are bioluminescent and attract each other. This concept is used in this algorithm where two terms are attracted to each other using Gaussian or other distribution.
- Genetic algorithm (Tsai et al., 2016): The genetic algorithm is based on natural selection. This algorithm chooses the best individual from a pool of data.
- Particle swarm optimization (Pereira et al., 2016; Tsai et al., 2016): Particle swarm optimization is similar to the genetic algorithm but it cannot select the best individual. The particles are iteratively improved to solve a particular problem.

21.2.5 Classification of various smart applications

21.2.5.1 *Smart healthcare*

There are various subdomains where IoT along with ML, deep learning, and metaheuristics algorithms are employed to solve complex problems.

21.2.5.2 *Monitoring of patients*

With the increasing popularity of IoT-based smart domains, researchers have found smart healthcare to be the most important paradigm among them. The global population is growing daily and therefore providing medical facilities to patients has become a difficult task. In developing countries, it is infeasible to provide the existing medical facilities to all citizens. To cover a large section of people, a low-cost, highly reliable health monitoring system (Garbhapu & Gopalan, 2017) can be used. A pulse oximeter and a temperature sensor are employed in a wrist band for collection of patient data. The data are transmitted over IEEE 802.15.4 to a Raspberry Pi3 circuit which further transmits the data to healthcare professionals using its in-built Wi-Fi module. The whole system can provide 98% and 95% accuracies for temperature and pulse monitoring, respectively, with a significantly low-cost budget of $8.4. Along with the temperature sensor and pulse oximeter many other sensors like an electrocardiogram (ECG) sensor can be used to measure heart rate and rhythms, an accelerometer is used to capture a fall, and a light detector detects patient movement. In Bansal and Gandhi (2017), the collected sensory information were sent to the cloud using a Raspberry Pi microcontroller unit. Further information is processed in the cloud and if any abnormality is detected this low-cost system can generate an alert to the healthcare providers. ECG sensors are used to monitor the heart continuously. In Catarinucci et al. (2015), an intelligent system was built to monitor heart signals to detect heart-related diseases. Generally, a metallic nanomaterial dry electrode-based ECG sensor is placed in a T-shirt which is biocompatible and can be used for a longer duration. These sensors collect heart information and if any abnormality is found they send information to healthcare personnel via the Ethernet, Wi-Fi, wireless sensor network, etc. In Hossain (2016), a smart hospital system (SHS) is proposed where patients' real-time health data as well as environmental conditions are collected through a hybrid sensing network (HSN). The HSN is composed of several RFID-enabled devices which can collect patients' physiological data and also collect information from the environment such as temperature and pressure. The local area network (LAN) is used to connect the network and remote users. Further, these data are conveyed to the doctors. For better understanding of patients' health, ML techniques are used. In an IoT-based environment (Ganesan & Sivakumar, 2019), patients' speech and facial data are collected to check patients' physical state of health. The collected data are stored in the cloud where data preprocessing is done and required features are extracted. Finally, the Gaussian mixture model (GMM) is applied which generates an accuracy of 99.9% for normal state, 99.5% for pain state, and 98.8% for tensed state, respectively.

21.2.5.3 Disease detection and diagnosis

ML algorithms can be used for heart disease prediction. In Kumar, Lokesh, Varatharajan, Gokulnath, and Parthasarathy (2018), the UCI repository data set is used for the diagnosis of heart diseases. Also, patients' health data are obtained from some wearable sensor devices. Therefore the data set, sensory data, and patients' medical health records are the inputs of the cloud server. The dataset is used for training purposes and sensory data, and the patients' medical health records are used for testing purposes. Different ML algorithms with varied accuracy, f-score, precision, recall, and kappa values are compared. The J48 classifier algorithm gives better results than other ML algorithms, with 91.48%, 91.50%, 91.50%, 91.50%, and 82.68% values for accuracy, f-score, precision, recall, and kappa, respectively, for the J48 classifier. Diabetes is a lifestyle disease whose early detection is necessary. Again, in Abdelgawad, Yelamarthi, and Khattab (2016), UCI repository data are used for continuous monitoring and diagnosis of diabetes. Generally, patients' physiological parameters from various hospitals are taken by wearable and implantable sensor devices which are further transmitted to a cloud server via a mobile network. In the cloud server, the UCI data and real health data are compared using ML algorithms. The evaluation parameters of sensitivity, specificity, and accuracy are measured where a fuzzy rule-based neural classifier can give the highest values of any ML algorithm-based classifiers. For heart disease diagnosis, Manogaran, Varatharajan, and Priyan (2018) recommended a hybrid system working on multiple kernel learning with an adaptive neuro-fuzzy inference system. Features are collected from a healthy person and a person with heart-related problems in a reduced dimensional way. ANFIS is a multilayer artificial neural network (ANN) which is used to identify blood pressure and cholesterol. A total of 250 observations are taken including age, blood pressure level, blood sugar level, heart rate variability, body temperature, and cholesterol and chest pain type. The evaluation parameters give results of sensitivity at 98%, specificity 99%, and mean square error of 0.01, which are better than any ML algorithms. Alzheimer disease is a critical illness and is increasingly common. In most cases, it is found on elderly people. Varatharajan, Manogaran, Priyan, and Sundarasekar (2018) introduced a dynamic time wrapping (DTW) algorithm to compare the foot movements of patients. The wearable sensor devices are used in an IoT environment which is used to collect gait signals of patients over time. To identify the disorder, the authors collected both normal and Alzheimer patients' foot movements. The performance of the model results are sensitivity 95.9% and specificity 94%, with respect to other ML models. Therefore the early detection of Alzheimer disease is possible. Parkinson disease (PD) can cause severe movement disorders. Also, it cannot be detected at an early stage. In Pereira et al. (2016), researchers have shown that handwritten or drawing materials can be used to detect PD using deep learning algorithms. A data set, HandPD, was taken for 35 individuals, including 14 patients and 21 healthy persons. The convolution neural network (CNN) was used for feature extraction and classification based on parameters like base learning rate η, penalty parameter (momentum) α, and weight decay λ. The different metaheuristics algorithms like BA, Particle Swarm Algorithm (PSO), FA, and Random Search (RS) were employed to adjust the CNN. A total of 264 images from the data set were taken, from which 124 were PD patients' and 140 were healthy persons' samples. The CNN consisted of: convolution layers = 5, pooling layers = 5, normalization layers = 2, ReLU layers = 7, inner product layers = 3, dropout layers = 2, accuracy layer = 1, and softmax loss layer = 1. The training data set was 30%, validation data set 20%, and testing data set 50%. Therefore, CNN with metaheuristics can determine the best results. One of the most challenging tasks lies with big data from the healthcare sector which is sometimes found to be incomplete or missing. To solve this problem. a latent factor model has been proposed (Chen et al., 2017). The real-life data set are collected from hospitals which include the patients' electronic health records (EHRs), medical images, and vital body parameters. The data set is further classified into structured data and unstructured text data based on disease risk prediction. This is done by using ML and deep learning algorithms like naïve Bayesian (NB), k-nearest neighbor (KNN), and decision tree (DT) algorithm for structured data. For text data, the CNN-based unimodal disease risk prediction (CNN-UDRP) algorithm is used to detect the risk of cerebral infarction. For structured and text data, CNN-MDRP is used. A feature extraction mechanism is used. CNN-UDRP extracted 79 features from S-data and 100 from T-data which were further fused. The stochastic gradient method was used to train the parameters. Finally, prediction with 94.8% accuracy was made using CNN-MDRP.

21.2.5.4 Outbreak prediction and prevention

Sareen, Sood, and Gupta (2018) have illustrated the accurate prediction of the deadly Ebola virus. Ebola is a dangerous virus that spreads through human-to-human interaction. In an IoT environment, vital data are collected, that is, patients' information, symptoms, social interactions etc. This information is transferred to the cloud via the Internet for classification. The J48 decision tree is used to divide patients' into categories such as exposed and infected, with an accuracy of 94%. Another harmful virus of the Indian subcontinent is dengue virus that is spread by mosquitoes. The fog and cloud environment would be effective for detection and prevention of dengue outbreaks, as suggested in Pravin, Prem Jacob, and Nagarajan (2020). Patients' information is collected via sensor devices and transferred to the fog environment. Depending on the severity the fog environment generates an alert to an infected locality and further sends this information to the cloud storage. The cloud is responsible for sending alert signals to doctors or healthcare workers. The proposed model works on the principle of the fog and cloud environments generating less delay than the individual fog or cloud environments. The SVM classifier generates a shorter response time than other ML classifiers to obtain the required information. Another contagious disease, MARS-CoV, is an airborne virus that has a high mortality rate. It is necessary to detect which areas will have outbreaks of this disease (Sandhu, Sood, & Kaur, 2016). The health attributes are collected and stored in a database. The Bayesian belief network (BBN) classifier is used for various dependencies related to the MARS-CoV virus. A GPS-based risk analysis is done to identify risk-prone zones. A total of 0.2 million users' data was analyzed in this paper and they generated 80% accuracy in classification and appropriate GPS rerouting.

21.2.5.5 Personalized treatments and recommendations

It is sometimes necessary to monitor patients continuously. At the same time, it should be effective enough to advice personalized treatments. Not only patients, but also others could receive recommendations based on their health parameters, diet, and personal information using some recognized health apps.

To get personalized treatments or recommendations (Mulani et al., 2020) patients' electronic health records, nutrition data, and survey data from various sources are required. This "big data" is analyzed by deep reinforcement learning techniques. Data can be stored in structured, semistructured, or unstructured formats. Missing data are preceded or followed by a value or replaced by a constant. Then the data are converted into a particular format and normalized. Based on these data, various machine and deep learning algorithms are applied and include diseases like obesity, heart diseases, diabetes, liver diseases, asthma, and many more. The incorporated information is implemented on an "Actor-Critic Model." This model is able to predict diseases early and can generate recommendations for individuals (Table 21.4).

21.2.6 Smart home

In an IoT-based network, a smart home is an environment of connected wireless intelligent sensor devices. The devices include smart home hubs and controllers, smart home surveillance cameras, smart locks and home security tools, smart heating and cooling machines, smart lighting systems, smart kitchen appliances, and smart health and fitness devices. Basically, the smart home environment is needed to enhance the security system, with remote monitoring, activity recognition, and unnatural event detection.

In Cicirelli et al. (2016), activity recognition is done using a three-layer "CASE" architecture. The first layer consists of all types of sensors. The second layer is responsible for the interface between the sensor and cloud layer. The cloud layer gathers all sensory data which are heterogeneous in nature and uses data-mining algorithms to analyze these data. All collected sensory data are gathered and certain features are extracted from them. Depending on the features activity, discovery and activity recognition are possible. The CASE tool can collect data from both the environment and human body. Therefore body posture recognition is made possible. For this, the K-NN classifier is used as a real-time monitoring system. In a smart home environment, various smart devices are employed to facilitate a comfortable life. However, the security issue of smart devices should be maintained, otherwise it can lead to malicious attacks. In Nobakht, Sivaraman, and Boreli (2016), an IoT-based intrusion detection and mitigation framework is developed to recognize intrusion events and block them. The database is well maintained to store smart devices with their known attacks. Sensor devices that are present in networks are used to detect these attacks based on features of network traffic, and a mitigation unit is used to take action against known attacks. Therefore the prediction precision is 98.53% and the prediction recall is 95.94% for a nonlinear classification model. In a smart home scenario, energy management, particularly, electricity cost should be efficiently managed. In Khan et al. (2019), smart appliances based in a residential area were chosen where the power of each appliance, load factor, time used, and cost were measured. The hybridization of two basic metaheuristic approaches, that is, harmony search algorithm and enhanced differential evolution, was used. This technique is good for reducing the peak-to-average ratio

TABLE 21.4 Classification of various domains of smart healthcare.

Sl. no.	Healthcare domain	Sensor used	Learning approach	Dataset		Evaluation results
				Existing	Proposed	
1.	Patient monitoring (Bansal & Gandhi, 2017; Catarinucci et al., 2015; Garbhapu & Gopalan, 2017; Hossain, 2016)	Pulse oximeter, temperature sensor, ECG sensor, RFID	Not used	Not used		Accuracy = 98% for temperature sensor 95% for pulse monitoring
2.	Patient monitoring (Ganesan & Sivakumar, 2019)	Audio-video capturing devices	GMM		✓	Accuracy = 99.9% for normal state, 99.5% for pain state and 98.8% for tensed state, respectively
3.	Disease diagnosis (Kumar et al., 2018)	ECG sensor	J48 decision tree	✓		Accuracy = 91.48 F-score = 91.50 Precision = 91.50 Recall = 91.50 Kappa = 82.68
4.	Disease diagnosis (Abdelgawad et al., 2016)	Wearable sensors	Fuzzy rule-based neural classifier	✓		Higher than any other classifier
5.	Disease diagnosis (Manogaran et al., 2018)	Blood pressure, blood sugar, heart rate, temperature, and cholesterol	Artificial neural network	✓		Sensitivity = 98% Specificity = 99% Mean square error = 0.01
6.	Disease detection and diagnosis (Varatharajan et al., 2018)	EEG, PPG	Dynamic time wrapping		✓	Sensitivity = 95.9% Specificity = 94%
7.	Disease detection and diagnosis (Pereira et al., 2016)	Not used	Convolution neural network with Bat Algorithm (BA), Particle Swarm Optimization (PSO), Firefly Algorithm (FA)	✓		Accuracy for meander data set, overall = 79.62% spiral data set, overall = 89.55%
8.	Disease detection and diagnosis (Chen et al., 2017)		CNN-based unimodal disease risk prediction	✓		Accuracy = 94.8%
9.	Outbreak prediction (Chen et al., 2017)	RFID, wearable sensor	J48 Classifier		✓	Accuracy = 94% Resource utilization = 92%
10.	Outbreak prediction (Sareen et al., 2018)	Location sensor	SVM classifier		✓	SVM produces result in shorter response time
11.	Outbreak prediction (Sandhu et al., 2016)	GPS-sensor	Bayesian belief network	✓		Accuracy = 80%
12.	Personalized treatment and recommendations (Mulani et al., 2020)	Wearable devices	SVM, naïve Bayes, k-means clustering, decision tree, adaptive Bayesian network, artificial neural network, back propagation neural network, deep neural network		✓	Deep reinforcement learning gives recommendation for every age group

and cost reduction. A binary cuckoo search algorithm is better than many ML algorithms for human activity recognition in a smart home (Kaur, Kaur, Sharma, Jolfaei, & Singh, 2020). The human activity data are gathered from various sensors and these are analyzed using ML algorithms. The evaluation parameters cannot give the highest value for any one classifier, whereas a metaheuristic-based classifier can give an accuracy of 93.7% for human behavior recognition.

21.2.7 Smart transport

In a smart city environment, a smart transportation system is a necessity. It is used to enhance safety and mobility, and to reduce environmental pollution.

User- and environment-friendly as well as energy-efficient IoT-based bus stops are proposed in Kamal et al. (2019). The environmental parameters like humidity, temperature, and various gases are measured using sensors employed with microcontrollers in bus stops. Also, the occupancy is checked. Therefore energy consumption can be reduced based on lower occupancy and also measurement of the above-mentioned environmental parameters is informed through a mobile app. In Lin, Wang, and Ma (2017), an intelligent transportation system was built to enhance sustainability. This architecture was divided into four layers: the first layer is responsible for collecting data from various sensors employed in vehicles, the second layer is used for communication between vehicles and the transportation system, the third layer is responsible for overall control of the system, and the fourth layer is a user interface layer.

21.2.8 Smart parking

It can be difficult to find a suitable parking space in a busy city, sometimes causing significant time costs and high charges to the driver. In a smart city environment, it is possible to predict nearby free parking spaces using only an IoT-based application or some IoT-based ML techniques. Tsai, Kiong, and Sinn (2018) proposed an arduino-based system which is used to detect cars in a parking space. Basically it has a navigation system both for indoors and outdoors. It uses the user's position and RFID reader to check the occupancy. iBeacon is used to implement this navigation system, and enhances the average pre-reaction time by 43%. The deployment of sensors and other devices to check for a vacant place in parking areas is costly. Therefore advanced deep learning technology is used in an IoT-based network to reduce the cost and enhance the capability (Bura et al., 2018). Both the ground-level and top-view cameras are used to capture the license plate and occupancy in parking areas, respectively. These data are stored in the cloud. The proposed model can detect objects and can store license numbers of cars using deep learning methods. AlexNet, AlexNet with two convolution layers, and a custom-designed network model (one convolution layer) are used where the accuracy is 99.8584, 99.70, and 99.51, respectively. The time taken for inference in the proposed model is 7.11 milliseconds, which is much less than with the other two data sets. In Camero, Toutouh, Stolfi, and Alba (2018), the deep learning technique with a recurrent neural network is used to predict the occupancy rate of cars. RNN has large computational resources, therefore two metaheuristic approaches are needed to find the optimal RNN; one is genetic algorithm based and the other is evolutionary strategy based. Both strategies are useful for RNN optimization. Another two metaheuristic algorithms are used for optimized search time for parking space, that is, FA and Feed Forward Back Propagation Neural Network (NN) approach (Singh, Dutta, Singhal, & Choudhury, 2020). FA is responsible for determining the best route for a vehicle. Therefore the output of the FA algorithm is the shortest route which is input to the neural network. A neural network is used to determine the occupied space, unoccupied slots, and wrongly occupied slots. The search time is reduced to 12.23 from 22.84 seconds using these two algorithms.

21.2.9 Smart agriculture

The IoT expands its revolution in the field of agriculture. It is very efficient in soil moisture prediction, precision farming, livestock monitoring, land optimization, etc. using the ML techniques. Further metaheuristic approaches have been taken to optimize resources.

In the field of agriculture, the most important task is to determine which soil is suitable for which crop (Kumar, Sharma, Sharma, & Poonia, 2018). Therefore, metaheuristic approaches are used in the soil data set to predict the appropriate soil. Soil images are taken from data set and features are extracted using speeded up robust features (SURF). The bag-of-words technique is used to convert images to codeword. Finally the chaotic spider monkey optimization (CSMO) algorithm is used to obtain the best result. CSMO shows better evaluation parameter values than metaheuristic approaches. In Singh et al. (2019), ML techniques are used in the IoT-based agriculture sector to predict the soil moisture in smart irrigation system. Various sensor devices are employed like soil moisture sensors, environment temperature sensors, soil temperature sensors, humidity and UV radiation sensors in a Raspberry Pi. The collected information is stored in a database with weather forecast data. ML techniques are compared using these data and gradient boosting regression trees (GBRT) gives the maximum accuracy that is 0.94 and 0.93 for soil moisture prediction while considering soil temperature and without considering sol temperature, respectively. Therefore fresh water consumption is optimized. For crop production, low-resolution satellites are used for monitoring. However, for the prediction of crop production it is necessary to take environmental and satellite data with a metaheuristic approach (Saranya and Nagarajan, 2020). The collected satellite images from http://redhook.gsfc.nasa.gov/ are classified using multiple linear regression model (MLR), ANN, and a proposed model that is ANN optimized with population-based incremental learning (PBIL). The proposed model has a lower average difference, correlation coefficient, and RMSE than the other two methods for crops like corn and soybean. However, no noise-handling mechanism for the images is used.

21.3 Issues and challenges

IoT-based smart domains remain limited in their ability to provide a low-cost, highly secure, big data-handling model. Every domain has its own particular problems (Al-Qaseemi, Almulhim, Almulhim, & Chaudhry, 2016). Many researchers have proposed solutions for these problems. The following are some of the common problems related to IoT-based architecture.

- Challenges related to sensors:
  - Sensors are highly affected by humidity and temperature. They can take wrong input from patients.
  - The sensors are self-heating. They can cause skin irritation also, therefore long-term usage is not recommended.
  - The proximity sensor has a limited area to work compared with an inductive or capacitive sensor.
  - The ECG sensor can record values after a certain time gap. If an arrhythmia occurs during the time gap it will not be detected.
  - Smart sensors have higher complexity, and also design is very costly.
  - The sensors require constant operational power to work.
  - Expertise is needed to install and handle the sensors.
- Challenges related to the data set:
  - A huge volume of data is expected to be handled. These data can be heterogeneous and multidimensional.
  - Sometimes, the data in the data set are missing. Data preprocessing operations are used to deal with missing or inappropriate data. This takes a huge amount of time for preparation of data.
  - For a proposed data set, it is very difficult to interoperate between data taken from sensor devices and data taken from software applications.
  - Many challenges lie within the volume, velocity, and variety of unstructured data.
- Challenges related to security:
  - In an IoT environment, the security of data is a big issue. There are potential security threats related to the IoT network.
  - The identification and authentication of a large number of edge devices increases the complexity.
  - The IoT is vulnerable to cyberattacks. It may cause virus attacks and theft of credentials.
- Challenges related to proper data analysis: It is very difficult to choose the best ML algorithm for a particular problem.
- Challenges related to connectivity: An IoT network always needs connectivity between all the components. This may be with LAN, MAN, or WAN, therefore networking devices with a continuous connection facility are required.

21.4 Case study

See Table 21.5.

TABLE 21.5 Case studies related to various domains.

Domain	Function
Smart healthcare (Gupta, Agrawal, Chhabra, & Dhir, 2016)	Collects, records, analyzes, and shares real-time health data
Smart healthcare (Rahmani et al., 2015)	Implements data mining, machine intelligence in a local server in an energy-efficient and secure way
Smart healthcare (Fan, Yin, Xu, Zeng, & Wu, 2014)	Creates a patient-centric rehabilitation system
Smart healthcare (Wan et al., 2018)	Monitors real-time health data using wearable IoT and cloud-based architecture
Smart healthcare (De & Chakraborty, 2020)	Detects diseases like liver disorders, hepatitis, heart disease, diabetes, and chronic kidney disease
Smart home (Batalla & Gonciarz, 2019)	Implements security measures
Smart home (Ghayvat, Mukhopadhyay, Gui, & Suryadevara, 2015)	Deploys the project in different houses to detect wellness of inhabitant
Smart home (Kang, Moon, & Park, 2017)	Security framework for smart home appliances
Smart transportation (Rajak, Mallick, & Kushwaha, 2019)	To create "green corridor" for emergency basis
Smart transportation (Krishna & Tyagi, 2020)	Detects security attacks in transportation systems
Smart parking (Roman, Liao, Ball, Ou, & de Heaver, 2018)	To find roadside parking occupancy
Smart parking (Aydin, Karakose, & Karakose, 2017)	Finds a closed free parking space based on genetic algorithm
Smart agriculture (Zareiforoush, Minaei, Alizadeh, & Banakar, 2016)	Automated classification and sorting of milled rice grains based on images

21.5 Open research issues

Future research opportunities lie in following sectors:

1. *Security*: ML and deep learning algorithms are heavily dependent on IoT networks. However, the IoT layers are vulnerable to cyberattacks (Noor & Hassan, 2019), such as the physical layer being affected by a denial of service attack, tampering, jamming, eavesdropping; the network layer can be affected by a man-in-the-middle attack, spoofing, flooding; the transport layer can affected by Trojan horses; and the application layer can be affected by malicious code attacks, cross site scripting, etc. Therefore IoT layers need improved mechanisms to deal with these attacks.
2. *Edge devices*: In an IoT environment, a lot of edge devices are used. The problems related to edge devices are authentication issues, latency problems, bandwidth mismatching, and disturbances in real-time data health monitoring. Therefore the entire system needs improvement to solve these issues.
3. *Learning algorithms*: We have seen that the machine and deep learning algorithms are needed in an IoT framework for faster computation and detection of various solutions. However, finding the best algorithm for a problem as well as data preparations are very important and time-consuming tasks. Also, feature extraction or selections are complex tasks, and so reduced computation time and an energy-efficient algorithm are needed.

21.6 Conclusion

This chapter highlights some of the recent trends of popular IoT-based smart domains. This survey aims to provide some basic and intelligent technologies based on deep learning or metaheuristics algorithms. For healthcare, patient monitoring, disease identification, outbreak prediction, and personalized treatments are discussed. In the future, a smart model in this domain will be developed. Other domains such as smart home, smart transportation, smart parking, and smart agriculture-related intelligent models have been discussed also.

References

Abdelgawad, A., Yelamarthi, K. & Khattab, A. (2016). IoT-based health monitoring system for active and assisted living. Available from https://doi:10.1007/978-3-319-61949-1_2.

Adi, E., Anwar, A., Baig, Z., & Zeadally, S. (2020). Machine learning and data analytics for the IoT. *Neural Computing & Applications*, *32*, 16205–16233. Available from https://doi.org/10.1007/s00521-020-04874-y.

Al-Qaseemi, S. A., Almulhim, H. A., Almulhim, M. F., & Chaudhry, S.R. (2016). IoT architecture challenges and issues: Lack of standardization. Available from https://doi.org/10.1109/FTC.2016.7821686.

Aydin, I., Karakose, M., & Karakose, E. (2017). A navigation and reservation based smart parking platform using genetic optimization for smart cities. Available from https://doi.org/10.1109/SGCF.2017.7947615.

Bansal, M., & Gandhi, B. (2017). IoT based smart health care system using CNT electrodes (for continuous ECG monitoring), ISBN: 978-1-5090-6471-7/17/$31.00 © 2017. IEEE.

Batalla, J. M., & Gonciarz, F. (2019). Deployment of smart home management system at the edge: Mechanisms and protocols. *Neural Computing & Applications*, *31*, 1301–1315. Available from https://doi.org/10.1007/s00521-018-3545-7.

Bura, H., Lin, N., Kumar, N., Malekar, S., Nagaraj, S. & Liu, K. (2018). An edge based smart parking solution using camera networks and deep learning. Available from https://doi:10.1109/ICCC.2018.00010.

Camero, A., Toutouh, J., Stolfi, D. H., & Alba, E. (2018). Evolutionary deep learning for car park occupancy prediction in smart cities. In R. Battiti, M. Brunato, I. Kotsireas, & P. Pardalos (Eds.), *Learning and intelligent optimization. LION 12 2018. Lecture notes in computer science* (11353). Cham: Springer. Available from https://doi.org/10.1007/978-3-030-05348-2_32.

Catarinucci, L., De Donno, D., Mainetti, L., Palano, L., Patrono, L., Stefanizzi, M. L., & Tarricone, L. (2015). An IoT-aware architecture for smart healthcare systems. *IEEE Internet of Things Journal*, 2(6), 515–526. Available from https://doi.org/10.1109/JIOT.2015.2417684.

Chen, M., Hao, Y., Hwang, K., Fellow, L., & Wang, L. (2017). *Disease prediction by machine learning over big data from healthcare communities.* IEEE Access. Available from https://doi:10.1109/ACCESS.2017.2694446.

Cicirelli, F., Fortino, G., Giordano, A., Guerrier, A., Spezzano, G., & Vinci, A. (2016). On the design of smart homes: A framework for activity recognition in home environment. *Journal of Medical Systems*, *40*, 200. Available from https://doi.org/10.1007/s10916-016-0549-7.

De, S., & Chakraborty, B. (2020). Disease detection system (DDS) using machine learning technique. In V. Jain, & J. Chatterjee (Eds.), *Machine learning with health care perspective. Learning and analytics in intelligent systems* (Vol. 13)). Cham: Springer. Available from https://doi.org/10.1007/978-3-030-40850-3_6.

Fan, Y. J., Yin, Y. H., Xu, L. D., Zeng, Y., & Wu, F. (2014). IoT-based smart rehabilitation system. *IEEE Transactions on Industrial Informatics*, *10*(2).

Ganesan, M., & Sivakumar, N. (2019). IoT based heart disease prediction and diagnosis model for healthcare using machine learning models. Available from https://doi:10.1109@ICSCAN.2019.8878850.

Garbhapu, V. V., & Gopalan, S. (2017). IoT based low cost single sensor node remote health monitoring system. *Procedia Computer Science*, *113*, 408–415.

Ghayvat, H., Mukhopadhyay, S., Gui, X., & Suryadevara, N. (2015). WSN- and IOT-based smart homes and their extension to smart buildings. *Sensors (Basel)*, *15*(5), 10350–10379. Available from https://doi.org/10.3390/s15051035.

Gupta, P., Agrawal, D., Chhabra, J., & Dhir, P.K. (2016). IoT based Smart HealthCare Kit. In *International conference on computational techniques in information and communication technologies (ICCTICT)*.

Hossain, M. S. (2016). Patient state recognition system for healthcare using speech and facial expressions. *Journal of Medical Systems*, *40*(12), 272. Available from https://doi.org/10.1007/s10916-016-0627-x.

Kamal, M., Atif, M., Mujahid, H., Shanableh, T., Al-Ali, A. R., & Nabulsi, A. A. (2019). IoT based smart bus stops. Available from https://doi:10.1109/ICSGSC.2019.00-27.

Kang, W. M., Moon, S. Y., & Park, J. H. (2017). An enhanced security framework for home appliances in smart home. *Human Centric Computing and Information Science*, *7*, 6. Available from https://doi.org/10.1186/s13673-017-0087-4.

Kaur, M., Kaur, G., Sharma, P. K., Jolfaei, A., & Singh, D. (2020). Binary cuckoo search metaheuristic-based supercomputing framework for human behavior analysis in smart home. *Journal of Supercomputer, 76*, 2479–2502. Available from https://doi.org/10.1007/s11227-019-02998-0.

Khan, Z. A., Zafar, A., Javaid, S., Aslam, S., Rahim, M. H., & Javaid, N. (2019). Hybrid meta-heuristic optimization based home energy management system in smart grid. *Journal of Ambient Intelligence and Humanized Computing, 10*, 4837–4853. Available from https://doi.org/10.1007/s12652-018-01169-y.

Krishna, A. M., & Tyagi, A. K. (2020). Intrusion detection in intelligent transportation system and its applications using blockchain technology. In *International conference on emerging trends in information technology and engineering (IC-ETITE)* 978-1-7281-4142-8/20/$31.00 ©2020 IEEE. Available from https://doi:10.1109/ic-ETITE47903.2020.332.

Kumar, P. M., Lokesh, S., Varatharajan, R., Gokulnath, C., & Parthasarathy, P. (2018). Cloud and IoT based disease prediction and diagnosis system for healthcare using fuzzy neural classifier. *Future Generation Computer Systems, 86*, 527–534. Available from https://doi.org/10.1016/j.future.2018.04.036.

Kumar, S., Sharma, B., Sharma, V. K., & Poonia, R. C. (2018). Automated soil prediction using bag-of-features and chaotic spider monkey optimization algorithm. *Evolution Intelligent*. Available from https://doi.org/10.1007/s12065-018-0186-9.

Lin, Y., Wang, P., & Ma, M. (2017). Intelligent transportation system (ITS): Concept, challenge and opportunity. Available from https://doi:10.1109/BigDataSecurity.2017.50.

Manogaran, G., Varatharajan, R., & Priyan, M. K. (2018). Hybrid recommendation system for heart disease diagnosis based on multiple Kernel learning with adaptive neuro-fuzzy inference system. *Multimedia Tools and Applications, 77*, 4379–4399. Available from https://doi.org/10.1007/s11042-017-5515-y.

Mulani, J., Heda, S., Tumdi, K., Patel, J., Chhinkaniwala, H., & Patel, J. (2020). Deep reinforcement learning based personalized health recommendations. In S. Dash, B. Acharya, M. Mittal, A. Abraham, & A. Kelemen (Eds.), *Deep learning techniques for biomedical and health informatics. Studies in big data* (68)). Cham: Springer. Available from https://doi.org/10.1007/978-3-030-33966-1_12.

Nobakht, M., Sivaraman, V., & Boreli, R. (2016). A host-based intrusion detection and mitigation framework for smart home IoT using OpenFlow. Available from https://doi:10.1109/ARES.2016.64.

Noor, Mb. M., & Hassan, W. H. (2019). Current research on Internet of Things (IoT) security: A survey. *Computer Networks, 148*, 283–294. Available from https://doi.org/10.1016/j.comnet.2018.11.025.

Pereira, C. R., Pereira, D. R., Papa, J. P., Rosa, G. H., & Yang, X.-S. (2016). Convolutional neural networks applied for Parkinson's disease identification. In A. Holzinger (Ed.), *Machine learning for health informatics. Lecture notes in computer science* (9605). Springer International Publishing AG. Available from https://doi:10.1007/978-3-319-50478-019.

Pravin, A., Prem Jacob, T., & Nagarajan, G. (2020). An intelligent and secure healthcare framework for the prediction and prevention of Dengue virus outbreak using fog computing. *Health Technology, 10*, 303–311. Available from https://doi.org/10.1007/s12553-019-00308-5.

Rahmani, A.-M., Thanigaivelan, N. K., Gia, T.N., Granados, J., Negash, B., Liljeberg, P., & Tenhunen, H. (2015). Smart e-Health gateway: Bringing intelligence to Internet-of-Things based ubiquitous healthcare systems, 15/$31.00 ©2015. *IEEE 12th annual IEEE consumer communications and networking conference (CCNC)*.

Rajak, B., Mallick, S., & Kushwaha, D. S. (2019). An efficient emergency vehicle clearance mechanism for smart cities. *Journal of Mechanics of Continua & Mathematical Science, 14*(5)), 78–97. Available from http://doi.org/10.26782/jmcms.2019.10.00007.

Roman, C., Liao, R., Ball, P., Ou, S., & de Heaver, M. (2018). Detecting on-street parking spaces in smart cities: Performance evaluation of fixed and mobile sensing systems. *IEEE Transactions on Intelligent Transportation Systems, 19*(7), 2234–2245. Available from https://doi.org/10.1109/TITS.2018.2804169.

Sandhu, R., Sood, S. K., & Kaur, G. (2016). An intelligent system for predicting and preventing MERS-CoV infection outbreak. *Journal of Supercomputer, 72*, 3033–3056. Available from https://doi.org/10.1007/s11227-015-1474-0.

Saranya, C. P., & Nagarajan, N. (2020). Efficient agricultural yield prediction using metaheuristic optimized artificial neural network using Hadoop framework. *Soft Computing, 24*, 12659–12669. Available from https://doi.org/10.1007/s00500-020-04707-z.

Sareen, S., Sood, S. K., & Gupta, S. K. (2018). IoT-based cloud framework to control Ebola virus outbreak. *Journal of Ambient Intelligence and Humanized Computing, 9*, 459–476. Available from https://doi.org/10.1007/s12652-016-0427-7.

Singh, G., Sharma, D., Goap, A, Sehgal, S., Shukla, A. K., & Kumar, S. (2019). Machine learning based soil moisture prediction for Internet of Things based Smart Irrigation System, 978-1-7281-3988-3/19/$31.00 ©2019 IEEE.

Singh, R., Dutta, C., Singhal, N., & Choudhury, T. (2020). An improved vehicle parking mechanism to reduce parking space searching time using firefly algorithm and feed forward back propagation method. *Procedia Computer Science, 167*, 952–961. Available from https://doi.org/10.1016/j.procs.2020.03.394.

Tsai, C.-W., Chiang, M.-C., Ksentini, A., & Chen, M. (2016). Metaheuristic algorithms for healthcare: Open issues and challenges. *Computers & Electrical Engineering, 53*, 421–434. Available from http://doi.org/10.1016/j.compeleceng.2016.03.005.

Tsai, M.-F., Kiong, Y. C., & Sinn, A. (2018). Smart service relying on Internet of Things technology in parking systems. *Journal of Supercomputer, 74*, 4315–4338. Available from https://doi.org/10.1007/s11227-016-1875-8.

Varatharajan, R., Manogaran, G., Priyan, M. K., & Sundarasekar, R. (2018). Wearable sensor devices for early detection of Alzheimer disease using dynamic time warping algorithm. *Cluster Computing, 21*, 681–690. Available from https://doi.org/10.1007/s10586-017-0977-2.

Wan, J., Al-awlaqi, M. A. A. H., Li, M. S., O'Grady, M., Gu, X., Wang, J., & Cao, N. (2018). Wearable IoT enabled real-time health monitoring system. *Journal of Wireless Communication Network, 2018*, 298. Available from https://doi.org/10.1186/s13638-018-1308-x.

Zareiforoush, H., Minaei, S., Alizadeh, M. R., & Banakar, A. (2016). Qualitative classification of milled rice grains using computer vision and metaheuristic techniques. *Journal of Food Science and Technology, 53*, 118–131. Available from https://doi.org/10.1007/s13197-015-1947-4.

CHAPTER

22

Leveraging technology for healthcare and retaining access to personal health data to enhance personal health and well-being

Ayan Chatterjee[1], *Ali Shahaab*[2], *Martin W. Gerdes*[1], *Santiago Martinez*[3] *and Pankaj Khatiwada*[1]

[1]Department of Information and Communication Technology, Centre for e-Health, University of Agder, Kristiansand, Norway [2]Cardiff School of Technologies, Cardiff Metropolitan University, Cardiff, United Kingdom [3]Department of Health and Nursing Science, Centre for e-Health, University of Agder, Kristiansand, Norway

22.1 Introduction

Securing computerized information and infrastructure has become one of the essential parts of information technology in digital assaults. We transfer immense quantities of confidential data electronically and store even more, creating real gold mines for hackers who want to steal valuable information following illegal access and denial-of-service attacks. In general, information security assurance is high for access control techniques, fortification of data over networks, and data security within the enterprise. Secrecy and information assurance are significant global rights.

Effective management of personal and person-generated data (PGD) in a highly specialized healthcare system requires digital data sharing to achieve coordinated care. Specific PGD are very sensitive and controlled by policies, such as "General Data Protection Regulation" (Voigt & Von dem Bussche, 2017), "Normen" (Normen Guidelines, 2020), and "Health Insurance Portability and Accountability Act" (Ness, 2007). Signed consent is required before collection of PGD from patients/participants to maintain its security and accessibility. If anyone tries to access it for another purpose, such as curiosity, then he/she will be violating general security guidelines (Ness, 2007). Protected health information is health data linked to information that identifies a "subject."[1] "Deidentification" (Neamatullah et al., 2008) techniques are used in eHealth technology to remove the direct or indirect link to reidentify a subject. Health data security policies provide guidelines on how to protect electronic health data (EHR) and share it among legitimate users. This sharing must be approved by the legal designates. Patient engagement (Domecq et al., 2014) is an interaction with the health providers and is a key strategy to manage and prevent health risks by accessing their personal and health records (know more about health, feel connected, and act accordingly). However, most subjects are concerned about the privacy and misuse of their personal health record (PHR) in digital platforms. Digital health data protection (Rumbold & Pierscionek, 2017) distributes data protection strategies into the following three subareas: privacy, security, and trust. Privacy means that people/entities only authorized by the subjects can access EHR. Security protects EHR from external, unauthorized access. Trust ensures authorized sharing of EHR between the agreed parties. Security and trust are interrelated. Healthcare-specific security standards are depicted in Fig. 22.1. The following are some well-established methods to ensure health data privacy in digital infrastructure (Chen, Yang, Chiang, & Shih, 2014; Centers for Disease Control & Prevention, 2003;

[1]Subject signifies a patient/participant.

Recent Trends in Computational Intelligence Enabled Research.
DOI: https://doi.org/10.1016/B978-0-12-822844-9.00044-X

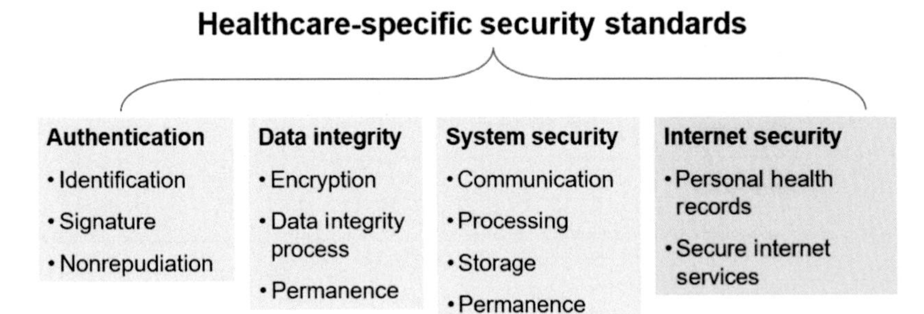

FIGURE 22.1 Healthcare-specific security standards.

Mohammed, Fung, Hung, & Lee, 2009; Patil & Seshadri, 2014; Yawn, Yawn, Geier, Xia, & Jacobsen, 1998): authentication (e.g., transport layer security, secure sockets layer, and AuthO), encryption (e.g., Rivest, Shamir, Adleman, data encryption standard, and advanced encryption standard), data masking, access control, deidentification, HybrEx, and identity-based anonymization.

Public key infrastructure (PKI) (Hu, Chen, & Hou, 2010) and blockchain (Ekblaw, Azaria, Halamka, & Lippman, 2016) are two popular methods for digital data sharing, maintaining the privacy of data. PKI includes the following three components for sharing digital health data among authorized parties: (1) public and private keys, (2) message/data and digital signature, and (3) key organizations (registration authority and certificate authority). The recipient uses the sender's public key to decrypt the digital signature, verifying that the sender sent it. Once the message is encrypted with the recipient's public key, only they will be able to read it since only they have the matching private key.

22.1.1 Blockchain technology: a brief overview

Blockchain, the cryptocurrency Bitcoin's underlying technology, is a peer-to-peer, distributed, append-only (P2P) asset transfer network (Nakamoto, 2019). Blockchain is a type of distributed ledger supported by a group of geographically distributed nodes through different consensus protocols. It democratizes the power through decentralization and prevents information tampering by distributed archiving of information, using multiple encryptions and hashing techniques. Essentially, blockchain is an ordered list of blocks of data where transactions by users are grouped in the form of blocks, and each block has a cryptographic pointer to the previous block, forming a chain-like structure in which anomalies can be easily detected. Each node supporting the blockchain network maintains a copy of the blockchain and synchronizes it with the rest of the network via different consensus protocols. Unlike distributed databases, the nodes supporting the blockchain network do not inherently trust each other and independently verify every transaction component on the blockchain network, providing a distributed log of events. Since no central authorities manage the blockchain networks, they are highly resistant to censorship and a single point of failure.

Blockchains also allow users to create smart contracts, which are self-executing contracts containing legal prose of agreements between parties. Since blockchains are distributed, and the data are replicated thousands of times, in most cases, only a commitment or cryptographic proof of the data is added to the blockchain while underlying data are stored in file storage systems such as cloud or interplanetary file system (IPFS) (Benet, 2014). The data integrity on the blockchain is guaranteed if most nodes in the network are honest. Once a block has been created and appended to the chain, it is computationally costly to change the block's data, and the difficulty increases exponentially as new blocks are appended to the blockchain, making the history immutable. A blockchain system (as depicted in Fig. 22.2) can be (1) decentralized: a public system where anyone can participate in the network and all records are visible to the public; (2) centralized: a private system where participation is limited and only authorized personnel from a company can view the records; or (3) partially decentralized: consortium among multiple organizations where privileges are managed between multiple organizations. Blockchain technology allows us to record, share, and sync data across geographically distributed parties so that all parties can achieve consensus about the "truth" and the data cannot be altered in the future. This immutability property of the blockchain makes it a suitable candidate for applications requiring accurate history and data sharing among multiple parties, such as medical records and health data (Shahaab, Lidgey, Hewage, & Khan, 2019).

22.1.1 The work summary

The entire study is inspired by a workshop held at the "Not Equal" summer school on digital society for social justice on August 27–30, 2019, organized by

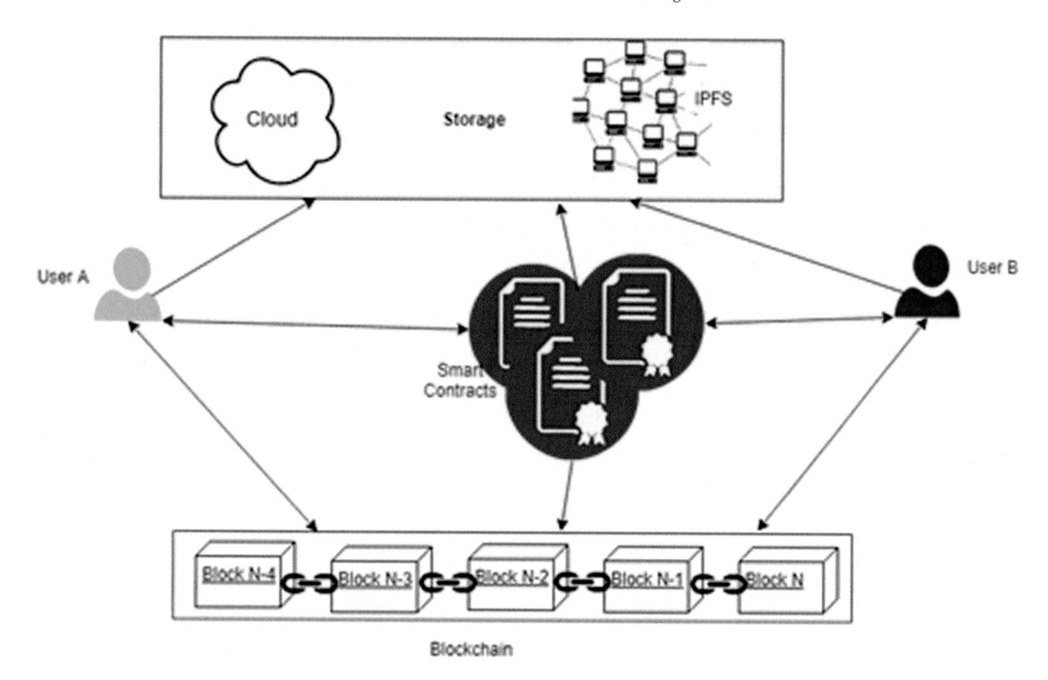

FIGURE 22.2 An abstract diagram of a blockchain ecosystem. Each block contains cryptographically secured transactions and is appended to the predecessor block. Data are stored in a file storage system and cryptographic proof is posted on the blockchain. Smart contracts can govern the access control and terms and conditions of exchange between user A and user B.

the University of Swansea, United Kingdom, in collaboration with other universities and research groups, such as Newcastle University, UK Research and Innovation, University of Sussex, Royal Holloway University, and Engineering and Physical Sciences Research Council, relating to the "algorithmic social justice and digital security" (Crivellaro, Coles-Kemp, Dix, & Light, 2019; Not Equal page, 2020). In this 4-day workshop, 20 participants were divided into five different groups to explore ways to extend collaborative engagement using creative practices. In the collaborative sessions, participants were asked to write down potential research questions related to automated decision making, social justice, fairness, and society intersect on day 1. On day 2, groups were formed based on a similar set of research questions. On day 3, LEGO bricks and supporting materials were provided to individual groups to formulate a respective set of research questions and their potential approach for a solution. On day 4, groups were asked to present their views with a group presentation. In the discussion and idea exchange session on day 4, we identified potential challenges related to (1) security algorithm design following ethics, and (2) EHR data security, personal access, and portability issues.

In this study, we have focused on the EHR data security. This chapter's most important contributions or novelty are as follows: (1) *Can we have a global healthcare data portability system with blockchain technology?* and (2) *How can we ensure the security and privacy of EHR?* The rest of the chapter is structured as follows: Section 22.2 elaborates EHR-related challenges in healthcare based on different patient stories. In Section 22.3, we discuss methods for digital security in healthcare. Section 22.4 covers a general discussion. The chapter is concluded in Section 22.5. For security and portability challenges of EHR data, we have identified the potential of blockchain technology in Section 22.3.

22.2 Patient stories and identified challenges

The leading four stories collected from the "Not Equal" summer school workshop (Not Equal page, 2020), are described in the following subsections portraying PGD (Chatterjee & Prinz, 2018; Chatterjee & Roy, 2018a,b,c,d,e,f; Chatterjee, Gerdes, & Martinez, 2020; Chatterjee, Gerdes, Prinz, Martinez, & Medin, 2020; Cretikos et al., 2008; Crivellaro et al., 2019; Dias & Paulo Silva Cunha, 2018; Groff & Mulvaney, 2000; Menachemi & Collum, 2011; Money, Caldwell, & Sciarra, 1999; Weiss et al., 2005) and their security challenges.

22.2.1 Patient story 1

Anna Kalb (AK) is a 70-year-old lady who lives in a small Scandinavian village. She was widowed 2 years ago. AK has a daughter who lives approximately 600 kms away. She is suffering from a chronic illness. She needs to take care of her health condition. Her general physician (GP) is located far from her house (approximately 90 min drive). Her home is also far from the nearest hospital. AK has recently been diagnosed with chronic obstructive pulmonary disease, obesity, and she is a potential diabetes risk. AK also has sporadic episodes of mild depression. Therefore she needs daily health monitoring and recommendations/suggestion/feedback based on her health conditions. She needs to go through day-to-day analysis of her physiological and behavioral (activity level, dietary habit, and sleeping pattern) data for personalized recommendations generation, followed by a goal evaluation. AK cannot visit her GP daily. She visits her GP once a month, and hospital once a year. AK's health status will deteriorate steadily unless monitored well on a timely basis. AK has received a suggestion to assess her health with remote monitoring. She is now worried as she is very new to the digital e-health monitoring system. AK has to learn how to check her health parameters, such as glucose, oxygen saturation level (SPO_2), and wear necessary wearable BLE (Bluetooth low-energy) devices, and handle them so that data can be appropriately streamed to a centralized decision support system (DSS).

Now she is worried about her personal data (EHR) security and its privacy regarding: (1) *Who will be the owner of the collected data?* (2) *Who will own the generated information related to the subject?* (3) *What will be the access control rules to access person-generated electronic records?* and (4) *Will the research group reuse/sell the data without any personal consent?*

22.2.2 Patient story 2

Ahmed is an 80-year-old male from Pakistan and is one of several billion people around the world who do not have the benefit of clinical information security and its instant availability. He fled his home country because of strict oppression and guaranteed asylum in the United Kingdom. Ahmed's child, who was at that point a UK inhabitant, employed attorneys for his case. Back in Pakistan, Ahmed was determined to have stage 3 cancer, yet the lawyer in the United Kingdom disclosed to Ahmed's child that Ahmed ought not disclose about his ailment as it would affect his asylum case. Therefore Ahmed concealed his complete medical history and treatment plans. Upon reaching the United Kingdom, and reaching asylum, he was diagnosed with health problems and it was later found that he had cancer. Due to a specific gap in the ongoing treatment, his health condition deteriorated further, and without proper care and medication plan, Ahmed died 3 weeks later. Ahmed's life could have been saved if he had revealed his medical history after crossing the border with supporting medical documents (EHR).

This story can be narrated with another viewpoint. Ahmed carried all his paper-based medical details with him, but on the way, he lost them. He persuaded the government of his homeland to share his medical history by sending a digital copy. However, access to digital health records is blocked outside of that country. Then the question arises *how could Ahmed have had his medical records protected and ported with him across the border?* He wished his medical records to be secured, portable, and persistent.

22.2.3 Patient story 3

Martina is a 40-year-old lady. She has been living in the United Kingdom for 5 years with her daughter Layla who is 6 years old. They are registered with a GP at the "XYZ Hospital" where Martina has been working. The GP asked Martina to go for some medical tests as she was suffering from chronic illness. The GP also informed her about the importance of an EHR system (central storage) to store personal medical records safely in electronic format so that authorized GPs can have access to them when required. In addition, she had been asked to wear wearable BLE devices for continuous health monitoring (BP, HR, SPO_2, GSR, activities) to sustain a healthy lifestyle. She was worried about the following thoughts (1) *How much has the medical technology developed for personal monitoring health and giving decision support?* and (2) *Is her EHR in safe hands?*

She consulted again with the GP closest to her home. The GP assured her about the positive aspects of the wearable secured BLE devices for health monitoring (SPO_2, heart rate, BP, step count, sedentary bouts, sleeping time, diet planning, and GSR response), and explained to her about EHR data security. She was delighted. The mom and daughter planned to travel to Hawaii. One beautiful morning, Martina discovered some rashes on Layla's face and hands. The local hospital could not access the Layla's EHR. They tested Layla separately, and she was found to be allergic to pollen. The family is now worried about the portability issues of EHR across the geographical border.

22.2.4 Patient story 4

Ruth Jones, who lives in the United Kingdom, is 86 years old and has chronic health conditions. She used

to work as a technologist and researcher. She needs to consult with her GP on a biweekly basis. She has an in-depth interest in technological revolutions and ubiquitous health monitoring. She is inclined to use digital health-monitoring systems to keep herself fit. She uses trusted wearable sensor devices and health applications for daily monitoring of physiological (SPO_2, BP, HR, and GSR) and behavioral patterns (activity, diet, gait, and sleep) to attain a healthy lifestyle. She is looking for a health management system with personalized recommendations generation capability to manage her health goals following the health-risk prediction. However, she is concerned about
personal and health data security in a digital system.

She believes that EHR is better than paper-based health record management, and she has heard about "blockchain" technology, a distributed, scalable, ledger-based technology that has considerable potential to secure personal health data with distributed keys. She is now struggling to understand: (1) *How does the blockchain-based authentication process work?* (2) *How is ownership of keys distributed in a blockchain-based authentication process?* (3) *Will the blockchain help cross-border EHR data portability?* and (4) *Will the blockchain create any personal burden to manage the assigned key?*

We have identified the following open challenges as defined in Table 22.1, from all the stories described above.

22.3 Electronic health record, its security, and portability

In this section, we discuss the importance of blockchain technology to protect EHR and ensure its secure sharing across international borders.

22.3.1 Electronic health record

EHR is the systematic collection of patient and population health information in digital format. It helps secure communication of patient's healthcare data between different healthcare professionals, such as GPs, specialists, care teams, and pharmacies. It plays a vital role in telemedicine, where patients and physicians need not be at the same location. Digital health data can be collected in different ways, such as appointments with GPs, hospitals, laboratories, pharmacy, specialists, wearable Bluetooth-enabled (BLE) sensors, smartphone applications, self-reported data, digital questionnaires, and feedback forms (Chatterjee, Gerdes, & Martinez, 2019; Soceanu, Vasylenko, Egner, & Muntean, 2015). Data collected from heterogeneous sources are massive, unintuitive, and raw. Therefore they must be annotated with semantic metadata for more expressive representation, standardization, and creation of rational abstraction. Semantic data (Peckham & Maryanski, 1988) help to create a knowledge base for formal analysis of stored data with reasoning. Reasoning reveals hidden knowledge inside data, either with the rules [semantic web rule language (Horrocks et al., 2004)] or with machine intelligence [DSS (Chatterjee et al., 2019)]. Ontology (Smith, 2012) provides a framework for data interoperability and describes healthcare data collected from heterogeneous sources with proper annotation. DSS analyses healthcare data to generate alerts, reminders, personalized recommendations, and real-time decision aids. HAPI-fast healthcare interoperability resources (FHIR) (Boussadi & Zapletal, 2017) is another platform to overcome EHR interoperability with JSON (Nurseitov, Paulson, Reynolds, & Izurieta, 2009) annotation. It is a complete implementation of the HL7 FHIR (Bender & Sartipi, 2013) standard for healthcare interoperability.

TABLE 22.1 Identified challenges from the patient stories.

Story no.	Challenges
1	Importance of privacy and protection during handling of personal and person-generated health-related data
	Aspects of ethics during electronic monitoring
	Potential of a health-monitoring system to maintain privacy
	Secure portability of electronic health record
2, 3	The possibility to make patients as data owners to avoid data exploitation
	Leveraging technology to assist the patients in redefining the data ownership
	How to make the patients aware of needs and outcomes?
4	Trust, gender bias, and ethical aspects of digital healthcare system
	Better portability and accessibility of personal health data with blockchain technology

Healthcare data collected from heterogeneous sources must be stored at a centralized repository in a secure way to protect against illegitimate access, ensuring health data protection, security, data ownership, and privacy. EHR is more advantageous than the traditional paper-based medical record-keeping system (Chatterjee et al., 2019), in terms of time [faster access, International Classification Of Diseases (ICD) ready coding (Reed, 2010), reduced human errors and readability issues], cost (reduces labor costs, and operational costs), security (password protection, standardization, encryption, policies, protection against loss and destruction), and eligibility (data ownership, access protection, federal regulations, secure sharing).

22.3.2 Electronic health record data-sharing challenges and opportunities

Jian et al. noticed that no single EHR system provides interoperability since EHR data are generated across different information systems using different schemas (Jian et al., 2011). Even though there is a consensus on the advantages of sharing health data, addressing challenges around privacy, trust, and transparency is vital (Jian et al., 2011). An EHR system is only considered "trustworthy" when it can demonstrate the ability to maintain confidentiality, privacy, accuracy, and data security (Jian et al., 2011). Different techniques to preserve the traits mentioned above are used in EHR systems. Aleman et al. conducted a systematic literature review of 49 articles and reported encryption techniques (symmetric and asymmetric key schemes) and login/password to be the most common methods (13 articles each) of preserving security and privacy of EHR data, followed by PKI-based digital signature schemes (11 articles). The role-based access control model was also identified as the preferred choice (Fernández-Alemán, Señor, Lozoya, & Toval, 2013).

Hutchings et al. reported a consistent desire to maintain some control over the health data, based on the results from 6859 responses gathered from 35 studies (Hutchings, Loomes, Butow, & Boyle, 2020). Some respondents also wanted to know where and when their data were being used, suggesting that access without the patient's consent is a violation of their privacy and concerns about unauthorized access (theft, hacking, or sharing without consent) to the data were also reported (Hutchings et al., 2020).

Blockchain technology has been recently recognized as a promising suite of technologies that use some of the best practices in EHR data security and privacy, while simultaneously addressing critical data ownership and access concerns.

22.3.3 Blockchain and electronic health record

Medrec (Azaria, Ekblaw, Vieira, & Lippman, 2016) utilizes a blockchain network to manage and share Electronic medical records (EMRs) and provide an immutable log and access to medical data owners. No personal data are added to the blockchain. The only hash of the data is stored on the blockchain for data integrity purposes, and "smart contracts"[2] are utilized to access the patient's data. Wang and Song proposed a consortium blockchain-based system for the traceability and integrity of cloud-based EHR data, using attribute- and identity-based encryption for data security and authorization (Wang & Song, 2018). Cao et al. identified critical issues with the existing cloud-based EHR outsourcing solutions and proposed a public blockchain (Ethereum) integrated EHR management solution for records integrity and suitability (Cao, Zhang, Liu, Zhang, & Neri, 2019). The authors propose recording each operation on the EHR as a transaction on the public blockchain not to be illegally modified in the future, and integrity can be verified. Omar et al. analyze the challenges in centralized EMR solutions and highlighted the potential of blockchain-based solutions (El Rifai et al., 2020). The authors further highlighted implementation challenges in French PHR and provided potential remedies to the highlighted challenges (El Rifai et al., 2020). Zyskind et al. proposed a general decentralized access-control system for personal data. Personal data are kept off-chain with the blockchain's pointers and access control managed by smart contracts (Zyskind & Nathan, 2015). FHIRChain proposed storing metadata of medical data on the blockchain while storing the data off-chain and utilizing smart contracts to exchange data. MedChain proposed a blockchain network, focusing on data sharing between medical stakeholders such as patients, hospitals, and pharmacies (Gordon & Landman, 2016).

22.4 Discussion

GPs generally have access to the EHR, which is not portable. If a person moves from their own country to another, he/she loses their medical data, and they need to collect lost medical records from the start. Here, we have discussed a system where people can port their medical data with them when they wish to cross international borders and can interact with the GPs of a new

[2]Smart contract is a computer program or a transaction protocol which is aimed at involuntarily executing, controlling, or documenting legally appropriate events and actions permitted in the terms of a contract or agreement.

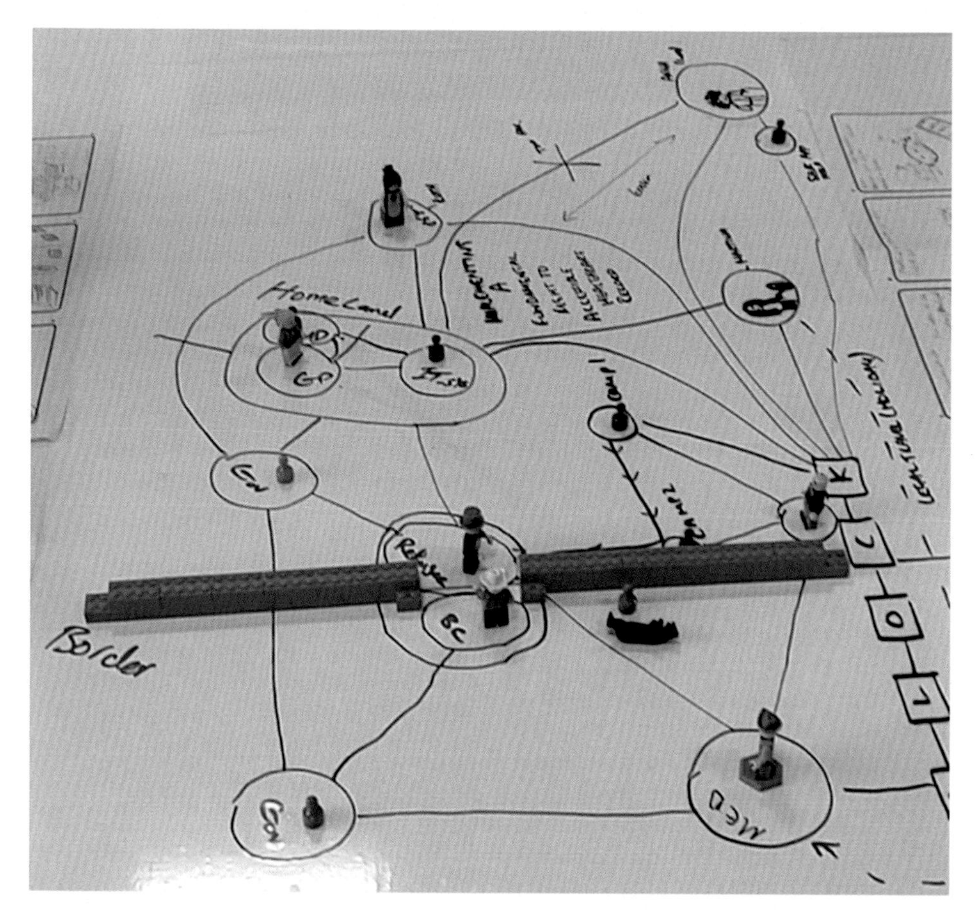

FIGURE 22.3 Data portability across the international border.

country if the situation demands. The scenario is well depicted in Fig. 22.3, where the orange barrier prepared with LEGO bricks signifies an international border. Our assessed blockchain-inspired system can securely carry personal medical records or EHR cross-border.

According to a 2018 report of the World Health Organization, 214 million people have been forcefully displaced and are on the move internationally (Kuruvilla et al., 2016). When people are forced to leave their homes, they seldom have the opportunity to secure their medical records, identities, or other belongings. The Norwegian Refugee Council found that 70% of Syrian refugees lacked essential identification documents. Having a person's medical history available in a reasonable time can be a matter of life and death, especially for those living in extreme conditions. As a part of the study, health data portability issues for disaster-struck people who are displaced due to sociopolitical crises, wars, or violence were debated. Specific potential sociotechnical solutions as a part of the mind-mapping process were considered, and systems' traits were identified with the aim of potentially creating a global healthcare system, accessible by anyone at any time.

The identified key traits are:

1. the solution must be censorship resistant;
2. it must hold the integrity of the medical records;
3. it must protect the identity of the vulnerable and the patient should have ownership of the data and access control;
4. it should allow data aggregation as the displaced person moves from one place to another;
5. it could potentially serve as an identity basis for the individual; and
6. the infrastructure should be easy to deploy and maintain.

22.4.1 Censorship resistance

A traditional centralized EHR system owned by a state or for-profit organization is inherently prone to censorship. Global politics and macroevents can result in the censorship of states or their citizens, giving monopolies enormous power through a global EHR system. Furthermore, users will not trust a system, that is, owned by a centralized stakeholder as they will fear the misuse of their data. Blockchain technology's inherent decentralization properties, immutability, auditability, provenance, and availability make it a suitable candidate to act as a backbone for the global health system. Public blockchains, such as Ethereum, can be used as a globally available infrastructure to deploy a cryptographically enhanced solution to preserve EHR data.

22.4.2 Enhanced integrity and security

The medical data of a patient can be encrypted using a Shamir n-1 shared key algorithm (Shamir, 1979), where a few stakeholders can participate in the data's decryption. These encrypted data can be hosted on distributed storage such as IPFS or file coin (Benet & Greco, 2018). The hash pointer of the data can be posted on the blockchain to preserve the data's integrity. We recommend using hierarchical keys for transacting on the blockchain so that the patient's complete history can be protected in case of a compromise of a single transaction. Although the identity on the blockchain is only the public key, users' identities can be further protected by routing the transactions through mixers and using zero-knowledge proofs (EY Blockchain GitHub, 2020; Hopwood, Bowe, Hornby, & Wilcox, 2016).

22.4.3 Data aggregation and identity basis

Since the patient owns the hierarchical wallet's root key, the patient will own all the medical history and aggregate medical history. Furthermore, the immutable transactions on the blockchain can prove the refugee's identity and provide evidence of their journey as they moved from one place to the next.

22.4.4 Ownership and access control

Blockchain technology ensures data security at storage and helps cross-border downloading of digital medical records safely without disclosing the patient's identity. As part of the patient engagement policy, in the blockchain-based EHR security mechanisms, keys are handed over to the trusted parties (such as GPs) and the patient. In the blockchain-based new system, patients must manage their assigned keys to care for their medical data. This might lead to added responsibility or burden to some patients and can be frustrating for them.

22.5 Conclusion

Health data are not easily portable. It takes weeks for the data to be ported from one GP to another. Cross-border portability is almost impossible. People from developing nations still rely on carrying their medical records, mostly hard copies. It would be promising if a global healthcare data portability system could be built to port, download, and access a patient's complete medical history legitimately. In our discussed blockchain-based system, patients are encouraged to port their medical records across international boundaries in a legal, secure, and anonymized way. The study has helped us to understand how different data points and agents interact and the importance of EHR cross-border portability.

Acknowledgments

The authors express their thanks to University of Agder, Department of Information and Communication Technology, Centre for eHealth for providing the infrastructure to carry out this study. Additional thanks are also due to Professor Alan Dix [British author, researcher, and professor at University of Swansea, United Kingdom, specializing in human–computer interaction (HCI)] for organizing the "Not Equal" summer school, 2019.

References

Azaria, A., Ekblaw, A., Vieira, T., & Lippman, A. (2016). Medrec: Using blockchain for medical data access and permission management. In *Proceedings of the second international conference on open and big data (OBD)*, August 22. (pp. 25–30) IEEE.

Bender, D. & Sartipi, K. (2013). HL7 FHIR: An agile and restful approach to healthcare information exchange. In *Proceedings of the twenty-sixth IEEE international symposium on computer-based medical systems*, June 20. (pp. 326–331). IEEE.

Benet, J. (2014). IPFS-content addressed, versioned, P2P file system, July 14. *arXiv:1407.3561*.

Benet, J., & Greco, N. (2018). Filecoin: A decentralized storage network. *Protocol Labs* (pp. 1–36).

Boussadi, A., & Zapletal, E. (2017). A fast healthcare interoperability resources (FHIR) layer implemented over i2b2. *BMC Medical Informatics and Decision Making*, *17*(1), 120.

Cao, S., Zhang, G., Liu, P., Zhang, X., & Neri, F. (2019). Cloud-assisted secure eHealth systems for tamper-proofing EHR via blockchain. *Information Sciences*, *485*, 427–440.

Centers for Disease Control and Prevention. (2003). HIPAA privacy rule and public health. Guidance from CDC and the US Department of Health and Human Services. *MMWR: Morbidity and Mortality Weekly Report*, *52*(Suppl. 1), 1–7.

Chatterjee, A., Gerdes, M. W., & Martinez, S. (2019). eHealth initiatives for the promotion of healthy lifestyle and allied implementation difficulties. In *Proceedings of the international conference on wireless and mobile computing, networking and communications (WiMob)*, October 21. (pp. 1–8). IEEE.

Chatterjee, A., Gerdes, M. W., & Martinez, S. G. (2020). Identification of risk factors associated with obesity and overweight—A machine learning overview. *Sensors*, *20*(9), 2734.

Chatterjee, A., Gerdes, M. W., Prinz, A., Martinez, S. G., & Medin, A. C. (2020). Reference design model for a smart e-coach recommendation system for lifestyle support based on ICT technologies. In

Proceedings of the twelfth international conference on ehealth, telemedicine, and social medicine (eTELEMED). (pp. 52–58).

Chatterjee, A., & Prinz, A. (2018). Image analysis on fingertip video to obtain PPG. *Biomedical and Pharmacology Journal, 11*(4), 1811–1827.

Chatterjee, A., & Roy, U. K. (2018a). Algorithm to calculate heart rate & comparison of butterworth IIR and Savitzky-Golay FIR filter. *Journal of Computer Science and Systems Biology, 11*, 171–177.

Chatterjee, A. & Roy, U. K. (2018b). Algorithm to calculate heart rate by removing touch errors and algorithm analysis. In *Proceedings of the international conference on circuits and systems in digital enterprise technology (ICCSDET)*, December 21. (pp. 1–5). IEEE.

Chatterjee, A., & Roy, U. K. (2018c). Non-invasive cardiovascular monitoring. *Journal of Electronics and Communication Engineering & Technology, 7*(1), 033–047.

Chatterjee, A., & Roy, U. K. (2018d). Non-invasive cardiovascular monitoring-a review article on latest PPG signal based on computer science researches. *International Journal of Engineering and Management Research, 3*, 1–7.

Chatterjee, A., & Roy, U. K. (2018e). Non-invasive heart state monitoring an article on latest PPG processing. *Biomedical and Pharmacology Journal, 11*(4), 1885–1893.

Chatterjee, A. & Roy, U. K. (2018f). PPG based heart rate algorithm improvement with butterworth IIR filter and Savitzky-Golay FIR filter. In *Proceedings of the second international conference on electronics, materials engineering & nano-technology (IEMENTech)*, May 4. (pp. 1–6). IEEE.

Chen, C. L., Yang, T. T., Chiang, M. L., & Shih, T. F. (2014). A privacy authentication scheme based on cloud for medical environment. *Journal of Medical Systems, 38*(11), 143.

Cretikos, M. A., Bellomo, R., Hillman, K., Chen, J., Finfer, S., & Flabouris, A. (2008). Respiratory rate: The neglected vital sign. *Medical Journal of Australia, 188*(11), 657–659.

Crivellaro, C., Coles-Kemp, L., Dix, A., & Light, A. (2019). Not-equal: Democratizing research in digital innovation for social justice. *Interactions, 26*(2), 70–73.

Dias, D., & Paulo Silva Cunha, J. (2018). Wearable health devices—Vital sign monitoring, systems and technologies. *Sensors, 18*(8), 2414.

Domecq, J. P., Prutsky, G., Elraiyah, T., Wang, Z., Nabhan, M., Shippee, N., ... Erwin, P. (2014). Patient engagement in research: A systematic review. *BMC Health Services Research, 14*(1), 1–9.

Ekblaw, A., Azaria, A., Halamka, J. D., & Lippman, A. (2016). A case study for blockchain in healthcare: "MedRec" prototype for electronic health records and medical research data. In *Proceedings of IEEE open & big data conference*, August 13 (Vol. 13, p. 13).

El Rifai, O., Biotteau, M., de Boissezon, X., Megdiche, I., Ravat, F., & Teste, O. (2020). Blockchain-based personal health records for patients' empowerment. In *Proceedings of the international conference on research challenges in information science*, September 23 (pp. 455–471). Springer, Cham.

EY Blockchain GitHub. <https://github.com/eyblockchain/> Accessed 07.07.20.

Fernández-Alemán, J. L., Señor, I. C., Lozoya, P. Á., & Toval, A. (2013). Security and privacy in electronic health records: A systematic literature review. *Journal of Biomedical Informatics, 46*(3), 541–562.

Gordon, W. J. & Landman, A. (2016). *Secure, decentralized, interoperable medication reconciliation using the blockchain*. NIST/ONC.

Groff C.P., Mulvaney P.L. inventors and assignee. (2000). Wearable vital sign monitoring system. United States patent US 6,102,856. August 15.

Hopwood, D., Bowe, S., Hornby, T., & Wilcox, N. (2016). :, . *Zcash protocol specification* (4). San Francisco, CA: GitHub.

Horrocks, I., Patel-Schneider, P. F., Boley, H., Tabet, S., Grosof, B., & Dean, M. (2004). SWRL: A semantic web rule language combining OWL and RuleML. *W3C Member Submission, 21*(79), 1–31.

Hu, J., Chen, H. H., & Hou, T. W. (2010). A hybrid public key infrastructure solution (HPKI) for HIPAA privacy/security regulations. *Computer Standards & Interfaces, 32*(5-6), 274–280.

Hutchings, E., Loomes, M., Butow, P., & Boyle, F. M. (2020). A systematic literature review of health consumer attitudes towards secondary use and sharing of health administrative and clinical trial data: A focus on privacy, trust, and transparency. *Systematic Reviews, 9*(1), 1–41.

Jian, W. S., Wen, H. C., Scholl, J., Shabbir, S. A., Lee, P., Hsu, C. Y., & Li, Y. C. (2011). The Taiwanese method for providing patients data from multiple hospital EHR systems. *Journal of Biomedical Informatics, 44*(2), 326–332.

Kuruvilla, S., Bustreo, F., Kuo, T., Mishra, C. K., Taylor, K., Fogstad, H., ... Rasanathan, K. (2016). The Global strategy for women's, children's and adolescents' health (2016–2030): A roadmap based on evidence and country experience. *Bulletin of the World Health Organization, 94*(5), 398.

LEGO, https://en.wikipedia.org/wiki/Lego

Menachemi, N., & Collum, T. H. (2011). Benefits and drawbacks of electronic health record systems. *Risk Management and Healthcare Policy, 4*, 47.

Mohammed, N., Fung, B. C., Hung, P. C., & Lee, C. K. (2009). Anonymizing healthcare data: A case study on the blood transfusion service. In *Proceedings of the fifteenth ACM SIGKDD international conference on knowledge discovery and data mining*, June 28. (pp. 1285–1294).

Money, E.W., Caldwell, R., & Sciarra. M., inventors; Life Sensing Instrument Co Inc, assignee. (1999). Vital sign remote monitoring device. United States patent US 5,919,141. July 6.

Nakamoto, S. (2019). *Bitcoin: A peer-to-peer electronic cash system*. Manubot.

Neamatullah, I., Douglass, M. M., Li-wei, H. L., Reisner, A., Villarroel, M., Long, W. J., ... Clifford, G. D. (2008). Automated de-identification of free-text medical records. *BMC Medical Informatics and Decision Making, 8*(1), 32.

Ness, R. B. (2007). Joint Policy Committee. Influence of the HIPAA privacy rule on health research. *JAMA, 298*(18), 2164–2170.

Normen Guidelines. <https://ehelse.no/normen> Accessed 09.07.20.

Not Equal page. <https://not-equal.tech/not-equal-summer-school/> Accessed 07.07.20.

Nurseitov, N., Paulson, M., Reynolds, R., & Izurieta, C. (2009). Comparison of JSON and XML data interchange formats: A case study. *Caine, 9*, 157–162.

Patil, H. K., & Seshadri, R. (2014). Big data security and privacy issues in healthcare. In *Proceedings of the IEEE international congress on big data*, June 27. (pp. 762–765). IEEE.

Peckham, J., & Maryanski, F. (1988). Semantic data models. *ACM Computing Surveys (CSUR), 20*(3), 153–189.

Reed, G. M. (2010). Toward ICD-11: Improving the clinical utility of WHO's International Classification of mental disorders. *Professional Psychology: Research and Practice, 41*(6), 457.

Rumbold, J. M., & Pierscionek, B. (2017). The effect of the general data protection regulation on medical research. *Journal of medical Internet Research, 19*(2), e47.

Shahaab, A., Lidgey, B., Hewage, C., & Khan, I. (2019). Applicability and appropriateness of distributed ledgers consensus protocols in public and private sectors: A systematic review. *IEEE Access, 7*, 43622–43636.

Shamir, A. (1979). How to share a secret. *Communications of the ACM, 22*(11), 612–613.

Smith, B. (2012). *Ontology. The furniture of the world* (pp. 47–68). Brill Rodopi.

Soceanu, A., Vasylenko, M., Egner, A., & Muntean, T. (2015). Managing the privacy and security of ehealth data. In *Proceedings of the twentieth international conference on control systems and computer science*, May 27. (pp. 439–446). IEEE.

Voigt, P., & Von dem Bussche, A. (2017). *The EU general data protection regulation (GDPR). A practical guide* (1st ed.). Cham: Springer International Publishing.

Wang, H., & Song, Y. (2018). Secure cloud-based EHR system using attribute-based cryptosystem and blockchain. *Journal of Medical Systems, 42*(8), 152.

Weiss, B. D., Mays, M. Z., Martz, W., Castro, K. M., DeWalt, D. A., Pignone, M. P., ... Hale, F. A. (2005). Quick assessment of literacy in primary care: The newest vital sign. *The Annals of Family Medicine, 3*(6), 514–522.

Yawn, B. P., Yawn, R. A., Geier, G. R., Xia, Z., & Jacobsen, S. J. (1998). The impact of requiring patient authorization for use of data in medical records research. *Journal of Family Practice, 47*, 361–365.

Zyskind, G. & Nathan, O. (2015). Decentralizing privacy: Using blockchain to protect personal data. In *Proceedings of the IEEE security and privacy workshops*, May 21. (pp. 180–184). IEEE.

CHAPTER

23

Enhancement of foveolar architectural changes in gastric endoscopic biopsies

Mousumi Gupta[1], *Om Prakash Dhakal*[2] *and Amlan Gupta*[3]

[1]Department of Computer Applications, Sikkim Manipal Institute of Technology, Majitar, India [2]Department of Medicine, Sikkim Manipal Institute of Medical Sciences, Gangtok, India [3]Department of Pathology, Sikkim Manipal Institute of Medical Sciences, Gangtok, India

23.1 Introduction

Gland formation and architecture is one of the key criteria for determination of malignant grading in gastric cancers. The gastric glands are responsible for mucus secretion and this mucus protects the epithelium from hostile chemicals (Gibson, Anderson, Mariadason, & Wilson, 1996). Histopathology involves analysis of gland tissue which is observed using various colored stains. In clinical practice, pathologists manually try to segment the glands by observing their morphology. The morphological appearances of nuclei and glands are highly correlated for determining the severity of disease. Pathologists try to quantify the gland morphology to reach conclusions about the cancer grade.

Before we delve into the niche area of the application of automated image analysis in histology for cancer detection of the stomach we introduce the reader to some of the nuances of the microscopic features of the stomach. This would be followed by alterations recognizable by pathologists as disease in small pieces of tissue taken from the surface lining of the stomach by a gastroenterologist using an endoscope. These tissue pieces are usually 0.1–0.3 cm and are fixed in formalin to preserve the tissue architecture (arrangement of cells) as in the living and they are embedded with molten wax into solid blocks which makes it possible for them to be cut into very thin slices 4 μm. These thin slices are stained with hematoxylin and eosin to color the cells; that is, the cytoplasm becomes pink and the nuclei purple. Pathologists use a number of criteria to determine whether these cells in a given arrangement have properties that point to a certain disease pattern.

The stomach is a part of the digestive system and can be irritated by many things that are ingested as part of food or otherwise. This irritation can lead to diseases ranging from gastritis to cancer of the stomach. One of the common modalities of diagnosis is looking at the surface lining of the stomach with an endoscope. In the case there is a lesion, the physician takes a tiny (2 mm) fragment of this surface lining called the gastric mucosa. This gastric mucosal fragment undergoes processing so that it can be cut into thin slices of 4-micron thickness, before being cleaned and stained. With various stain colors these slides are visualized under a microscope.

The surface lining is called the epithelium and is lined by tall columnar cells called foveolar cells. This lining is undulating with pits known as foveolar pits. The entire lining is composed of these cells, and is called the surface foveolar epithelium (Fig. 23.1). These cells when irritated cause so-called foveolar-type lesions which are very distinct with dark nuclei (known as dysplasia). Occasionally these foveolar cells change to another type of cell with clear cytoplasm (giving a goblet-like appearance) surrounded with light boundaries. This is known as metaplasia, but these metaplastic changes are highly variable. The risk of gastric cancer increases with this metaplasia change occurring frequently in the gastric mucosa. Pathologists attempt to detect these metaplastic glands and assess the cancer's presence or absence.

A gastritis or gastric cancer diagnosis involves endoscopy with biopsy and histology. A gastric tumor involves not only the mucosa and submucosa but also the muscularis propria layer (Nakayoshi et al., 2004).

Recent Trends in Computational Intelligence Enabled Research.
DOI: https://doi.org/10.1016/B978-0-12-822844-9.00046-3

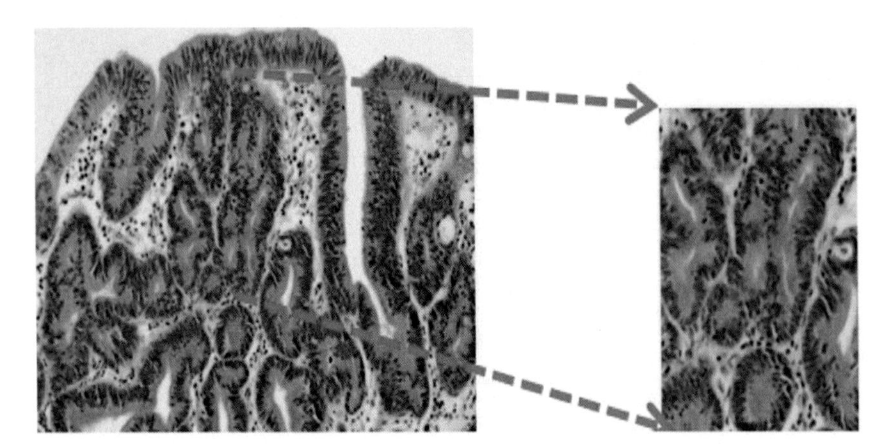

FIGURE 23.1 Digitized version of a gastric histology image and the portion highlighting the foveolar-type dysplasia.

However, these endoscopic biopsies are so small that they do not reach very deep into the wall to show invasion into the muscularis layer. The dysplastic changes seen in histology point toward malignancy and are used to diagnose with the help of certain criteria used by the pathologist when they visually survey the slides under a microscope (Veta, Pluim, Van Diest, & Viergever, 2014). These morphological features form the criteria to determine the lesions at risk. Recent advancements in digital histopathology have made it possible to visualize the dysplasia through an effective segmentation algorithm. There is several software available for computer-aided diagnosis of histopathology images.

Image segmentation on histopathology images carries an important role in dysplasia detection (Bennett et al., 2005). Recently, full slide images can be captured by a whole slide scanner (WSI). Virtual analyses for these WSI images were made possible through machine learning algorithms (Madabhushi & Lee, 2016). A machine learning algorithm is more effective if one can accurately extract the features from the tissue texture. The initial phase for extraction of tissue texture involves image segmentation. Segmentation is an image analysis procedure to segregate various textures based on statistical differences. This chapter presents an algorithm to segment the foveolar dysplastic region from gastric biopsy images. The main aim of this development is to help pathologists, so that early detection of dysplasia is possible from this distinguishable visualization. The watershed transformation technique may be able to differentiate lesions. A gastric biopsy image may contain several lesions that are analyzed by pathologists to determine the different grades of gastric carcinoma (de Vries et al., 2008). The most common identification by pathologists is estimating the nature of gland architecture and the nuclear density, which determines the malignancy and its grade (Sakurai, Sakashita, Honjo, Kasyu, & Manabe, 2005). An accurate visualization of these lesions will help in the early detection of metaplasia and/or dysplasia.

There are two main contributions in this chapter. First, foveolar dysplasia detection is a new research field. Second, the proposed watershed transformation has been proven to provide better segmentation for gastric glands.

23.1.1 Importance of gland and nuclei segmentation on clinical diagnosis

Histologic image processing has been tried when there is involvement of multiple organ systems. These have been well documented in the review paper by Madabhushi (Madabhushi & Lee, 2016). The literature indicates that these targeted tissues mainly include the breast and prostate. In breast, the Nottingham score and grade are well defined as the percentage of gland formation or solid formation and nuclear features. Meanwhile in the prostate the morphologic criteria have been well defined by Gleason (Ren, Sadimin, & Wang, 2015) in terms of scores. Gleason (Ren et al., 2015) looks only at the architecture, that is, sheets versus glands. No such ordinal values exist for stomach cancers. However, such criteria could be developed for gastric cancer, but would require high precision to be widely accepted.

The structure of the histopathology images consists of a multidimensional pattern. These images represent a not so well organized stromal tissue of lamina propria and organized glandular structure. Geometrically, these structures form points of cloud with d-dimensional space but all these points do not form a single normal distribution. Therefore revealing the structural information requires more assumptions on the sample data set. Histopathology images consist of various hyperellipsoidal-shaped clouds of various sizes. An assumption can be made as these samples form a mixture of c-normal distribution, and then this assumption can lead to a larger variety of situations. Segmentation yields data description in terms of group of data points which possess strong structural similarities. Each cluster of data points is assigned a meaningful label after segmentation. In medical images these labels are validated by clinicians. An optimum labeling occurs if each cluster is well segmented.

Gland and nuclei segmentation is the key step for analyzing histopathology images. Gland and nuclei patterns become highly correlated with disease growth. Pathologists try to visually examine the morphological differences between these glands and nuclei, and sometimes this results in a high error rate while defining the grading. Automated segmentation for gland morphology will produce an initial diagnostic observation for the pathologists.

23.1.2 Traditional gland segmentation computational models

Gland segmentation is a recently emerging research area in digital pathology. Segmentation for the gland region is challenging as this area is mostly occluded by other tissues. Evaluation for gland formation is the main criterion for the grading of gastric cancer. Scientists have been trying to quantify and automate this procedure.

23.1.2.1 Region-growing method model

Wu, Xu, Harpaz, Burstein, and Gil (2005) proposed a region-growing algorithm for separating nuclei. Quantification of nuclei is required for decision-making on gastric carcinoma. Wu et al. used large empty points as the seed point for region growing. One of the advantages of this algorithm is that it is controlled by regional feature analysis and no prior knowledge of the input image is required. This algorithm does not work well for complex histology textures. Among the other computational models used for segmenting glands is the graph partitioning method of Gunduz-Demir, Kandemir, Tosun, and Sokmensuer (2010). They applied graph-based techniques with a region-growing algorithm. Another modification of the region-growing algorithm includes the polar coordinate method. In the polar coordinate method a seed point is selected from the middle of the gland image and neighborhoods are collected using a rotating ray with optimum length from the seed point in the 2π counterclockwise direction. Fu, Qiu, Shu, and Ilyas (2014) applied region growing with a polar coordinate method for gland segmentation.

23.1.2.2 Watershed transform model

The watershed transform introduced by Beucher (Beucher, 1979; Beucher & Meyer, 1993) has been used for various image segmentations. It retains a number of advantages in histological image segmentation. The primary models have been well described by Gonzalez et al. in their classic text "Digital Image processing using MATLAB." The watershed model includes three variations: (1) watershed with distance; (2) watershed with gradient; and (3) watershed with marker. Among these the marker-based and gradient-based ones are mostly used in gland segmentation.

23.2 Current state of the art

Specialized metaplasia of the intestinal type is a risk factor for adenocarcinoma. Conventionally, the surface of the stomach scanned using endoscopy, which is used for mucosal visualization. Ultimately, identifying the nature of epithelial changes requires meticulous study by pathologists.

Fig. 23.2 shows the stages of gastric cancer progression analyzed by pathologists. During the inflammation process, there is a reduction in gland tissues and fibrous tissues replace these. Metaplasia involves a change in mucosa architecture and forms dysplasia. Dysplasia is morphologically categorized as low grade or high grade depending upon the changes seen in foveolar architecture and foveolar cell changes.

Gastric foveolar dysplasia was traditionally defined as gastric mucosal irritation with morphologic alteration.

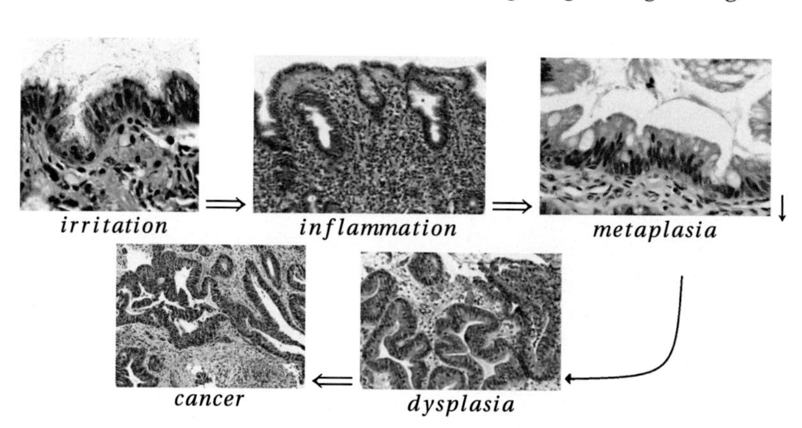

FIGURE 23.2 Stages of gastric cancer progression. [Note: microphotography of irritation is stained with giemsa (*H. pylori* infection stain) hence it is blue in appearance, all the rest are hematoxylin and eosin stain. Regular stain is used for initial screening and diagnosis by all histopathologists.]

Pathologists regularly observe this irregular branching pattern as part of the morphologic features from histopathology images. Pathologists have defined these dysplastic features as a precursor of malignant lesions.

Pathologists try to identify individuals who are at great risk. Repeat endoscopy and extensive biopsy are required for nonvisible high-grade dysplasia (Larghi, 2007). A suitable image segmentation algorithm helps to highlight this dysplasia and the foveolar architecture and is a diagnostic help for pathologists.

Recent advancements in digital pathology demand automated computerized algorithm development for analyzing digital histopathology images to assist pathologists in making a quantitative decision. There were 132 articles on Medline in February 2020 identified by searching "Histology [mesh] AND Image processing computer assisted [mesh] AND segmentation." This means that computer-aided segmentation has been conducted in histopathology images for cancer detection. However, a similar search with "Histology [mesh] AND Image processing computer assisted [mesh] AND segmentation AND stomach [Mesh]" yielded no publications in Medline-indexed peer-reviewed journals. Thus, the authors believe that the work on gastric histology image segmentation remains extremely limited. This may be because in intestinal metaplasia it is difficult to obtain definitive data (Guelrud, Herrera, Essenfeld, & Castro, 2001).

In this work, hematoxylin and eosin (H&E)-stained slides for gastric samples were carried out and an image-processing segmentation algorithm applied to study various organ systems. In digital gastric histopathology, solid organs and organelles such as lymph nodes have two cell populations and are homogeneous in texture. Glandular and stromal elements sometimes present together in solids, for example, prostate, and also viscous organs such as the large intestine with glandular elements. In the colon and prostate, most glands are of one type, mucin-secreting tall columnar cells, and so are easier to segment. This is not true for glandular cells in the stomach which are of many different textures and color intensities. Similarly, stroma in which the glands are embedded in prostatic tissue are colonic tissues that are predominantly homogeneous, while this is not always true with gastric mucosal fragments. This too creates inappropriate segmentation of the images. In such cases, modification of existing segmentation algorithms usually suffices and will help clinicians to make an accurate decision at an early stage.

The stomach has varying histologic features from the initial gastroesophageal junction where cardiac type mucosa is seen, subsequently the body has fundic type of mucosal architecture and finally in the pylorus it has antral type of mucosal architecture. Thus, it is pertinent that the segmentation methodology captures the glandular architecture appropriately. Most histology image segmentation entails finding the edges of the nucleus versus the cytoplasm. In gastric histopathology, highlighting the portion of prostate or colon may require finding the outline of near-circular glands from the stroma. Various histopathology digital image segmentation algorithms have already been proposed in the literature (Chao, Cen, Huan, Yazhu, & Su, 2015).

Histopathology image segmentation is mostly based on three spatial domain approaches. These are: (1) thresholding using histogram analysis; (2) evaluating the gradient; and (3) spatial neighborhood evaluation. Based on these three approaches the most common and prominent segmentation algorithms include Otsu's thresholding (He, Long, Antani, & Thoma, 2017), active contour model (Xu, Janowczyk, Chandran, & Madabhushi, 2010), and k-means (Xu et al., 2014). These three algorithms have been individually tested on a gastric mucosal biopsy digital histopathology image.

Fig. 23.3 depicts a gastric histopathology image with surface epithelium, foveolar pits, deep mucin-secreting glands, and connective tissue stroma. The Otsu threshold technique was applied to the given image to suppress the background. Threshold is the simplest and most effective method for segmentation. Otsu produces fine lines between the regions, but this threshold will not work for noisy images. Otsu is able to discriminate

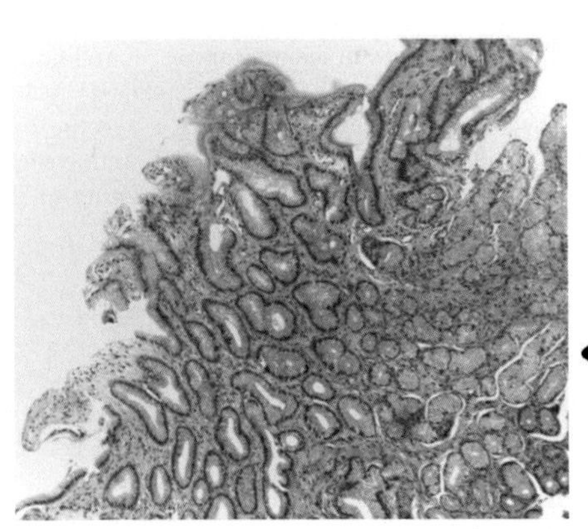

FIGURE 23.3 (*Left*) Gastric histopathology image with surface epithelium and foveolar pits. (*Right*) Threshold image where the glandular architecture is missing.

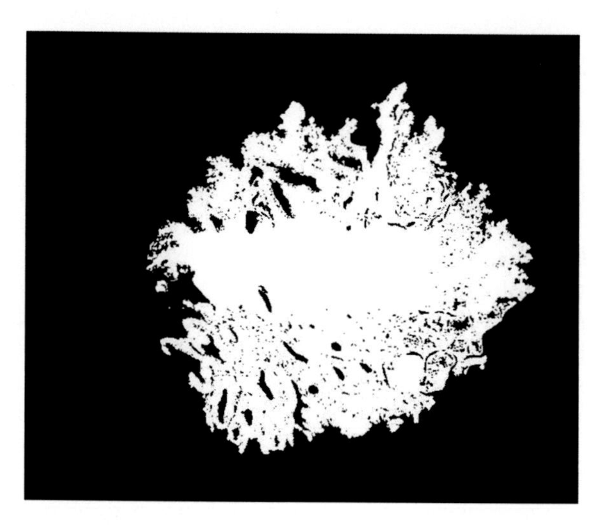

FIGURE 23.4 Result of an active contour model applied on the gastric histopathology digital image shown in Fig. 23.3 (*left*).

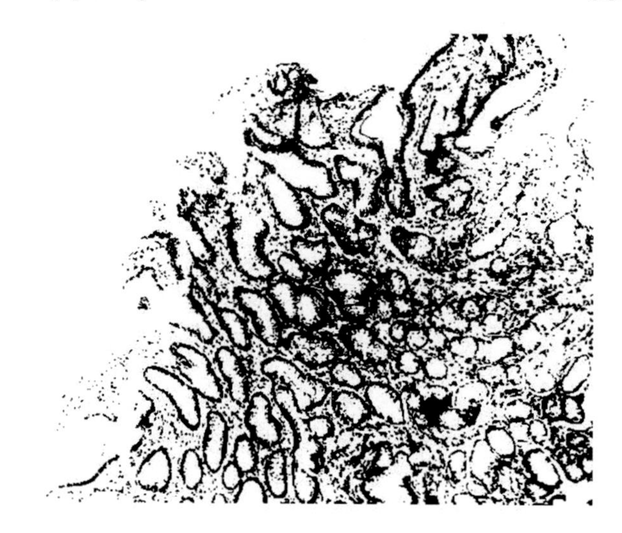

FIGURE 23.5 Result of k-means clustering applied to a gastric histopathology image.

interclass variance and suppress the background after highlighting the required features. A gastric mucosal biopsy image is tested with Otsu's threshold. The results of the threshold using the Otsu method yields the results shown in Fig. 23.3. As the tissue area and gland region on histopathology images are mostly occluded with each other this is complicated for segregation.

After applying Otsu's threshold the tissue areas were highlighted but the glandular structure was missing (depicted in Fig. 23.3).

A gradient-based active contour model (ACM) approach is tested on the same gastric mucosal biopsy image. Evaluation of the ACM model includes local minima and requires initializing the control points. ACM evaluates edge function and relies on the image gradient. ACM only highlights the area with edges defined by the gradient. Fig. 23.4 shows the result of an ACM model. This result does not include the glandular structure as a limitation of ACM is that it extracts only close objects. A gastric biopsy image with heterogeneous object structure using ACM does not produce significant results.

A neighborhood-based cluster application, the k-means algorithm, is applied on the same gastric mucosal histopathology image. k-Means is suited to segmentation of many histopathology images (Xu & Mandal, 2015). However in gastric histopathology images, k-means does not produce a significant result. K means algorithm cannot be used for gland segmentation because K-means method selects an initial point and due to this initial point selection the image plot tends to converge to a local minima. Though the outline of glands could be obtained with k-means clustering the glands comprising foveolar cells could not be separated from other mucin-secreting deeper glands. Fig. 23.5 shows the result of segmentation after applying k-means.

During gastric histopathology image segmentation, one of the most significant issues is segregating and distinguishing the variations in cellular architecture. This variation needs either to be eliminated or to be separated from the other components for accurate diagnosis. Therefore modifications to existing segmentation algorithms may suffice. With these in mind, image histograms have large areas of intersection pixel values between different forms of glands and hence inappropriate segmentation results have been obtained.

There is some merit in merging segmented patches by different exciting methods. However, the precedence of segmenting methods needs to be determined for such hybrid systems. Again, there is some merit in double threshold-based watersheds. However, this analysis used for the test image given above, resulted in poor discrimination between the foveolar glands and other mucinous glands. Graph-based methods and level set methods were also not found to be useful when segmenting the closely apposed gland linings if the pixel values were within a narrow range.

Thus, segmentation experiments were conducted using microscopic images from anonymized clinical cases, whose findings and follow-up results were available in archives and could be confirmed by the pathologist and endoscopist.

23.3 Source of images and image processing

The most common preliminary screening for gastric carcinoma is endoscopy, and a pathologic diagnosis is an important component of the strategy for therapy, which may be endoscopic mucosal resection for low-grade well-differentiated tumors, but on the other hand poorly differentiated tumors or high-grade tumors may get additional therapy, such as adjuvant external-beam radiation therapy with chemotherapy before surgery. This major decision-making is based on histologic evaluation by endoscopic biopsy.

23.3.1 Description of the data set

The Pathology Department of Central Referral Hospital, Gangtok, Sikkim, has a regular inflow of gastric endoscopic biopsies due to a high incidence of gastric cancer in the state of Sikkim (Verma et al., 2012). Initially, slides with known nondysplastic nonmetaplastic samples were taken and a library of digital images was created using a Leica microscope and LAS imaging software. This was followed by a similar selection of slides with known dysplastic cases. An image library was created for known samples. An anonymized random selection of slide numbers (using random number tables) was blinded. These images were tested using the proposed algorithm. For validation of the developed algorithm, a comparison was carried out to see the correlation with human examination for the same slides. This chapter presents the initial segmentation results of the first set of images with a small number of samples ($n = 12$).

23.3.2 Segmentation approach

Techniques applied for image segmentation differ based on image properties. Image properties are traditionally evaluated through gray-level statistics. This includes histogram specification (Willenbockel et al., 2010), co-occurrence (Gupta, Bhaskar, Bera, & Biswas, 2012), and correlation (Hild & Roux, 2006) analysis. Medical image segmentation plays a crucial role in automated medical image analysis. A large volume of medical images necessitates the use of automation through digital tools. Except radiology applications, other recent research fields on biomedical images include: (1) decisions on treatment; (2) quantification on tissue analysis; and (3) computer-assisted surgery. Image segmentation is the elementary step in biomedical image analysis as it provides information about the textures, shape, and spatial location of an object. In the literature, existing algorithms for medical image segmentation incorporate uncertainty in object recognition and boundary detection. However, there remains a large gap in this field of research. Perfect image segmentation algorithms for medical images are necessary for clinicians to make early decisions. The algorithms developed for medical image segmentation are purely based on specific applications and image-capturing devices. The main concern in medical image segmentation is finding every homogeneous region with some specific characteristics and distinguishing each region significantly with its adjacent region.

Pathology labs recently went through a digital transformation. This chapter deals with digital histopathology segmentation on gastric biopsy images. A light microscope (optical microscope) is the basic tool for pathologists to visualize slides. The main concerns for the pathologist are to see the texture of tissues and interpret the growth of diseases. During gastric histopathology pathologists manually observe the gastric cells through a microscope and interpret the abnormality using tissue texture analysis. This interpretation is qualitative and opinions vary with the experience of different pathologists. The observation can be tedious and time consuming. In the digital era, a light microscope is attached to a computer monitor which makes it possible to view the slides in a larger version. Image processing software make it possible to analyze the tissue sections precisely. A significant boundary depiction for every tissue makes possible computational automation in tissue segmentation.

This chapter presents a segmentation approach to gastric histopathology. Gastric cancer is one of the prominent malignancies as stated by the WHO (Stewart et al., 2003). Because of its hostile nature, gastric cancer is considered as among the deadliest of all cancers. Therefore diagnosis at early stage is very important. Gastric histopathology images are mixed with complex nuclei, gland, and tissue textures. These images have heterogeneous and diverse texture features, which make them complex in automated segmentation. The proposed approach is an improvement over watershed segmentation.

Pathological slides are traditionally prepared using H&E stains. Clinicians visualize the color variation between the tissue region and manually quantify the disease aggressiveness. Therefore the primary aim for automated segmentation is to evaluate this color variation. The overall flow for the proposed segmentation approach is shown in Fig. 23.6. The same flow is shown in Fig. 23.7 for an example histopathology image.

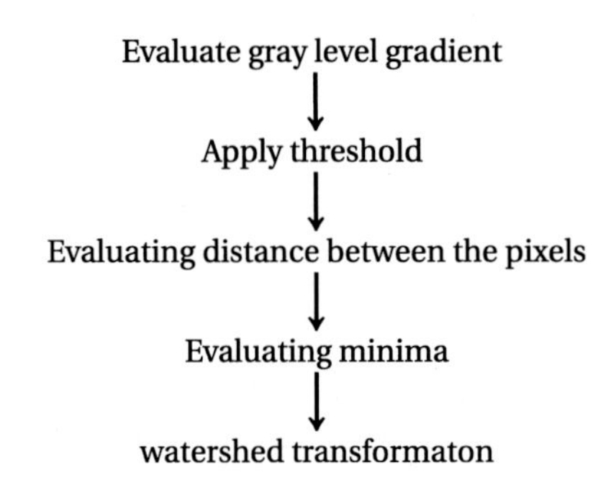

FIGURE 23.6 Flow for the proposed approach.

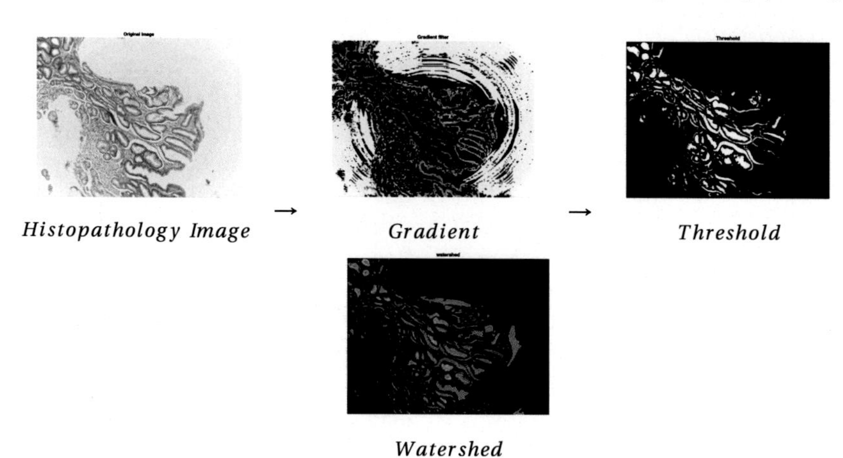

FIGURE 23.7 Flow of the proposed approach with an example histopathology image.

Watershed is an important concept for image segmentation. In watershed segmentation the object marker is of vital concern. At the initial step the original image is transformed to a gradient image and this helps to generate the shapes of foveolar tissue. Gland and nuclei textures in histopathology possess a spatial heterogeneous property. The morphology gradient technique is applied at the first stage. This approach smoothens the texture irregularities between the high-intensity background and low-intensity foreground. The morphology gradient acts as a highlighting operation between the gland and nuclei texture. From the literature it has been observed that watershed segmentation always performs well for a high gradient. Major drawbacks of this transformation are: (1) it reject those edges with low gradient values and (2) over-segmentation. In this proposed approach the first drawback of watershed segmentation is overcome by evaluating the gradient at the initial stage. Gradient application is able to create discrimination between the color variation.

Application of the threshold on the gradient image aims at reducing false edges. This threshold (Bernsen, 1986) is applied to overcome over-segmentation, which is one of the major drawbacks of watershed transformation. Instead of taking a single value as threshold for the whole image, the 'adaptive threshold process' selects a pixel value from 3 X 3 window for threshold value. This process continues for neighbouring 3 x3 windows. The threshold is evaluated using the mean of maximum and minimum as depicted in Eq. (23.1).

$$\text{Threshold}_{\text{pixel}} = \frac{\text{Maximum}(x,y)_{\text{nhd}_{3\times 3}} + \text{Minimum}(x,y)_{\text{nhd}_{3\times 3}}}{2} \tag{23.1}$$

The advantage for thresholding is that it provides a refinement on the lesion contour. In watershed segmentation, two pixels are said to be connected if there are regional similarities. The distance matrix is evaluated using the Euclidean distance (Danielsson, 1980) measurement. Finally, the watershed seed point is taken from the evaluated minima. The minima corresponds to the collection of pixels with the lowest regional elevation on the image histogram.

All minimas are a collection of pixels whose intensities are less than their neighborhood pixels. Watershed transform starts with a seed pixel and gradually increases its region by selecting each neighborhood pixel. This creates a catchment basin (Roerdink & Meijster, 2000). The catchment basin is a set of points which have topographically local minimas. The catchment basin creates a path with connected pixels and these pixels converge to a common minima. The watershed is that elevated area which divides each region through the catchment basin. The watershed can be defined as the set of points which do not belong to any catchment basin (Veta, Pluim, Van Diest, & Viergever, 2014).

Gastric histopathology images are sometime overcrowded with nuclei. Another gradient mask with [3 × 3] size is provided with watershed transformation. Through this technique the nuclei are separately visible. The gradient mask first segregates the image into different parts and then the watershed transform finds the boundaries for different lesions. It has been noticed that the algorithm is able to distinguish foveolar and glandular architecture from gastric histopathology images, which is the main objective.

23.3.3 Numerical definitions

Any image can be considered as a digital grid and an assumption can be made that this as a square grid D where vertices are pixels. For a digital image, D is finite. A set of pixels in D forms a graph-like structure that resembles $G = (V, E)$, where E can be considered as a subset of connectivity, whether four-connected or eight-connected.

The gradient image is evaluated to enhance the foveolar lines from gastric histopathology images. The gradient is the difference between the highest and lowest pixels within a neighborhood set. A mathematical representation for evaluating the gradient is:

$$\Delta(f) = \sqrt{(\partial f + \partial x)^2 + (\partial f + \partial y)^2}$$

Let X denote the set of points neighboring the pixel (x, y). The distance between two pixels x, y on a given image is denoted as *Dist* (x, y). Then, the distance of the pixel point to the complementary set X^c can be represented as:

$$\forall (x,y) \in X \delta(x,y) = Dist(x,y), X^c)$$

The minima is the shortest distance and represents the steepest slope. The minima can be defined as:

- If there are two points a and b existing in a surface S then a path is a sequence of points between a and b.
- A minima is the sinking point of the given surface S. There is a set of minima in a given topographic surface.

The watershed is the set of points and is represented by:

$$\text{Watershed}(f) = D \cap (\cup_{i \in I} \text{minima}_i)^c$$

where (minima_i) is the minima for some index set i.

The watershed transform of the digital image assigns a unique label to the pixels of D.

Through this technique the asymmetric foveolar lesion lines are well extracted. Fig. 23.8 provides the schema for watershed transformation. The nuclei of small lymphocytes are labeled as "**A**" shown in the peak. These cells are denser than nuclei. Foveolar cells labeled as "**B**" are just below the peak in the given schema. From the schematic diagram it can be seen that the descent is not as steep in the graph, and instead there is a gradual descent. During segmentation, smaller peaks detected and encountered on the path of downward descent are labeled together.

However, the descent from any nuclear pixel values, for example "**A**" or "**B**," to the surrounding cytoplasm is denoted by "**C**." It is noticeable that the descent to "**C**" is steeper and forms a significant watershed. Thus maximum hits are labeled. Again, the inflection points are associated with certain transition in the glandular/cellular architecture with a possibility of labelling them. There is a plateau but it is noted as the empty spaces in the microphotograph labeled as "**D**" in the schema. In the histopathology image of gastric biopsy, the cytoplasmic border to empty space is steep but lesser than for the nuclei to cytoplasm. Therefore to determine the architectural pattern of glands rather than nuclei to cytoplasm a watershed model is needed. This can separate the different gradients of descent and accordingly highlight the area of interest. The image histogram around the cytoplasmic edges shows small peaks before the descent to clear space "**D**." In the watershed algorithm it is not captured. This is an area for further extended work.

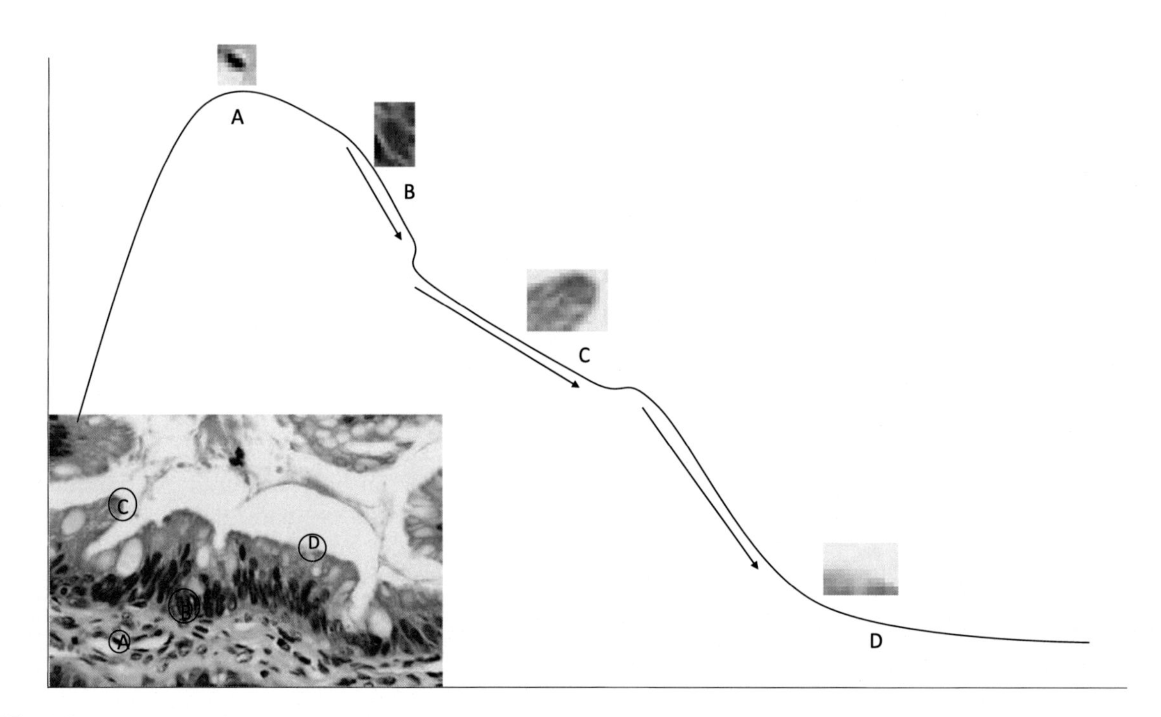

FIGURE 23.8 Application of watershed in histology using hematoxylin and eosin (constructed by Amlan Gupta).

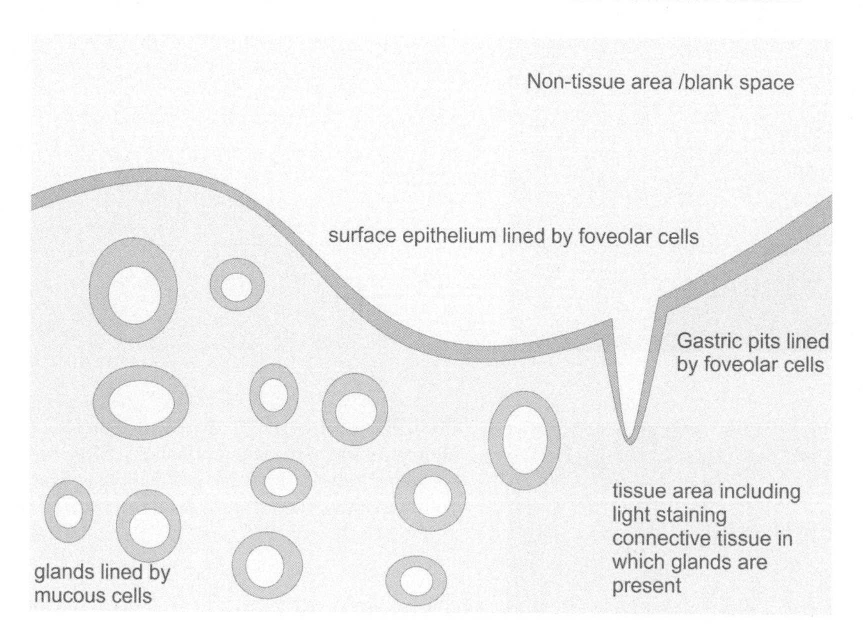

FIGURE 23.9 Representation of the glandular mucous cell in gastric histopathology image (drawn by Amlan Gupta).

23.4 Outcomes and discussion

Before we delve into the segmentation result, we need some operational definitions used in diagnostic histopathology, and we have tried to provide the meaning for each medical terminology in simple language for the nonspecialist. The schematic diagram shown in Fig. 23.9 provides the images for basic histology components.

The glandular epithelial cells and the foveolar epithelial cells in the surface and pit lining show alterations with disease. Fig. 23.9 shows some changes in the lightly shaded area, which is termed the stroma. When the cells multiply it is called hyperplasia. Hyperplasia produces crowding of the glands. When the cells show abnormal multiplication and irregularity, rather than just crowding, then it is described as dysplasia. Dysplasia areas appear darker than their surroundings. When there is dysplasia and some epithelial cells in groups come out of the confines of the gland outline, then the term "invasion" is used. One of the implications for invasion is usually carcinoma (in common parlance, cancer).

The novelty of the proposed approach lies in that it can significantly distinguish glandular tissue from other tissues. Here four gastric biopsy images with different textures and diagnosis are represented. These four samples are examples from the original clinical cases. Microphotographs of gastric histopathology in Figs. 23.10 and 23.11 includes foveolar pits. These foveolar pits are combined with other tissue textures. After watershed transformation these pits are distinguishable and visible. During validation, pathologists can correlate them with the original images. Figs. 23.12 and 23.13 shows glandular dysplasia. The proposed methodology appropriately segmented these glandular structures.

Tissue preparation and staining have a large impact on visualization as well as on making the diagnosis from digital histopathology images (Gheorghe, 2006). Figs. 23.10 and 23.11 depict two microphotographs (histologic images) from gastric endoscopic biopsy sections. Both images show longitudinal foveolar pits.

In a gastric biopsy sample, lesions are identified through color variation. The proposed modified watershed transform is applied. The segmentation result highlights the nonadenomatous pattern and emphasizes the foveolar dysplasia architecture. Watershed transformation is applied on the gradient image and the glandular boundary is obtained. The rough regions of lesions are marked by masking and thresholding.

Figs. 23.12 and 23.13 shows glandular hyperplasia in gastric biopsy images. The segmentation result in Fig. 23.13 shows the prominence of tubular architectures on gastric biopsy images. During gastric biopsy examination, pathologists visualize the tubular architecture under a microscope. This tubular architecture is one of the determinants for the absence or presence of cancerous changes on gastric biopsy. Table 23.1 shows the differentiation of gland patterns present for watershed segmentation concordance with the pathologists' impressions. However, there are a few cases where malignancy inconsistency is reported by pathologists.

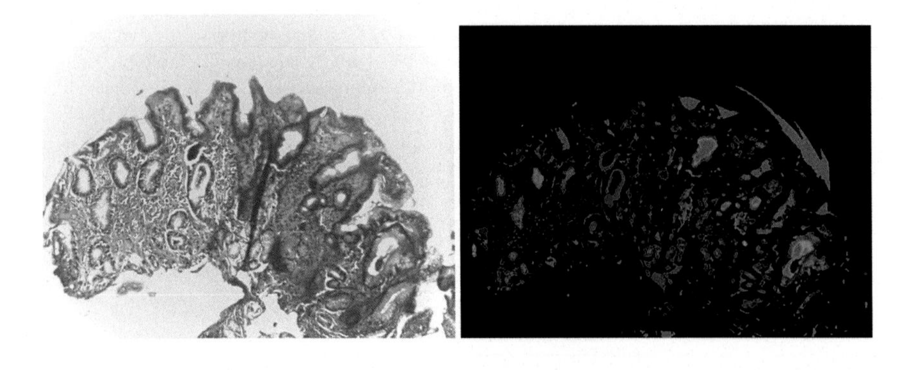

FIGURE 23.10 (*Left*) Microscopic image of nondysplastic foveolar epithelium showing separated tubular foveolar pits (empty spaces within glands). (*Right*) Segmentation result.

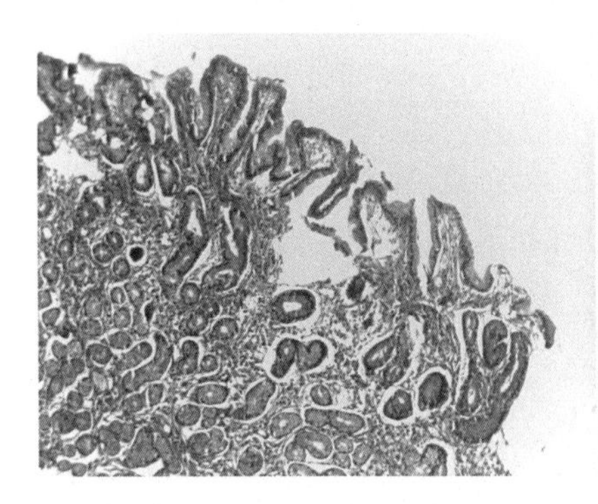

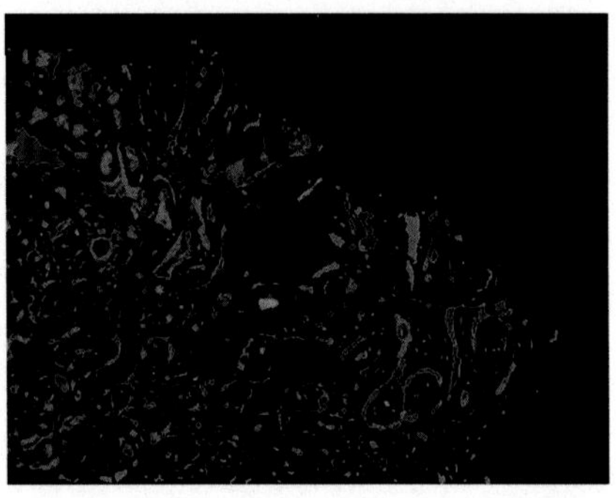

FIGURE 23.11 (*Left*) Microscopic image of nondysplastic foveolar epithelium showing separated tubular foveolar pits (empty spaces within glands). (*Right*) Segmentation result.

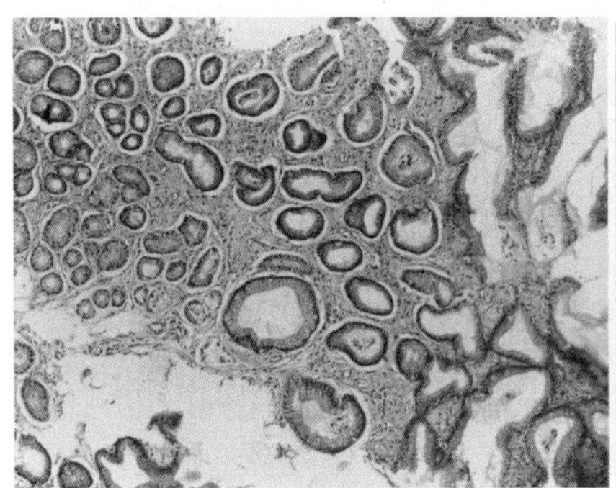

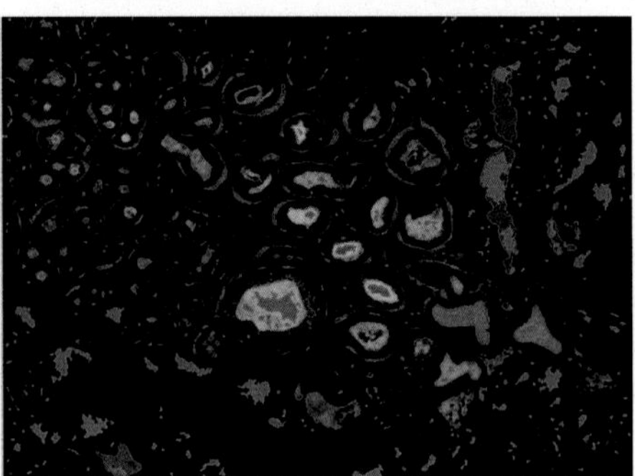

FIGURE 23.12 (*Left*) Microphotograph of gastric mucosa crowded with nondysplastic tubular foveolar pits without a filter. (*Right*) Segmentation result.

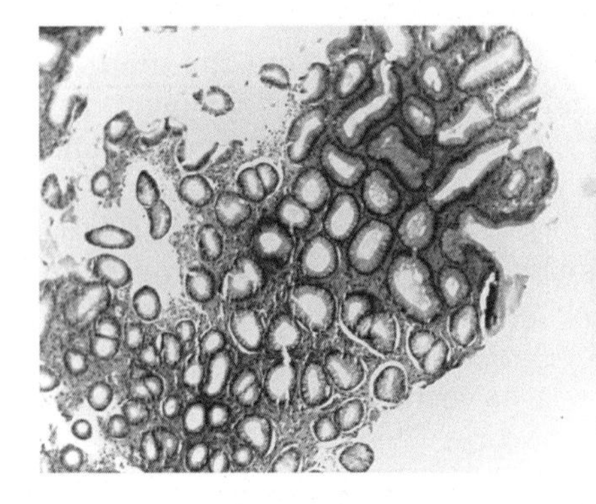

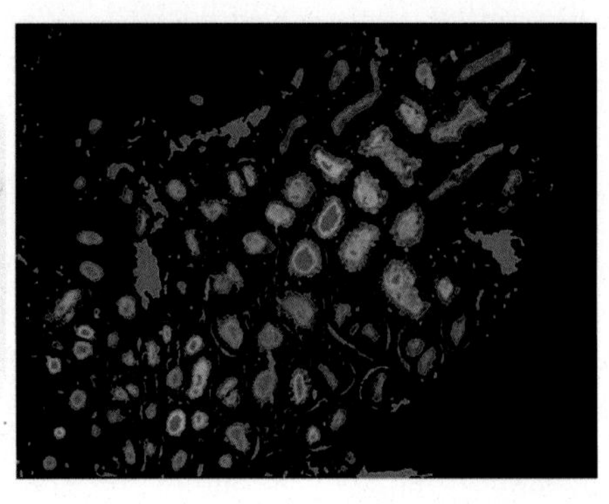

FIGURE 23.13 (*Left*) Gastric histopathology image with glandular hyperplasia. (*Right*) The glandular architecture is visible after applying the proposed approach.

23.5 Future possibilities and challenges

Whole-slide image scanning is now commercially available in lower and middle income countries. They are already being used in education pioneered by the Juan Rosai collection of seminar slides to telepathology for second opinions. The untapped potential is in the big data that each of these slides and a conglomerate of slides from gastric endoscopic

TABLE 23.1 Pathologist concordance.

Histologic type	Number of images	Segmentation	Pathologists concur
Normal	2	2	2
Hyperplasia	2	2	2
Dysplasia	2	2	2
Malignant	2	2	Equivocal

biopsies may provide. Segmentation by algorithms, such as watershed, have the advantage of removing redundant data points that can create unnecessary computational complexity.

Automated histological classification of disease has a long way to go. Even in specific tumor pathologies, discriminating between bipolar decisions also needs multiple steps. These steps include image acquisition, digitization, segmentation, feature extraction, and usage a set of discriminant rules which act either in tandem or simultaneously. When the discriminants have to compartmentalize between three units which are ordinal, for example, benign→ borderline→ malignant, the approach becomes significantly more complex. When the sets are nominal, for example, inflammatory, metabolic, genetic, and neoplastic, then feature extraction issues become very complex. In this area, discriminating rules have many gray zones and hazy areas. To be able to discriminate among multiple organs with varied normal histology appearances involves extreme complexity. An image repository for recall and matching would require enormous memory and computational resources. We believe that, for a long time, human intervention will be required for most histology diagnosis. Automation will help in the finer discrimination in specific areas where there are issues of nonconcordance between different pathologists in decision-making or classification.

With the advent of whole-slide imaging equipment, the acquisition of entire slide images has numerous possibilities for future works. For example, to transmit these whole slide images which are in gigapixel to pathologists are tedious and time consuming (Tellez, Litjens, van der Laak, & Ciompi, 2021). However, if, for example, gastric mucosal endoscopic biopsies are mounted onto slides, the area covered by the tissue section is a very small fraction of the entire slide imaged. Segmentation would lead to reducing the sparse areas. In gastric mucosa, the major component of interest is the glands, that is, their structure, their pattern of arrangement, and the hyperchromasia of the nuclear staining. The glands are embedded in a connective tissue stroma which has a lighter appearance than the glands. Occasionally, this stromal tissue is extensively infiltrated by cells like lymphocytes, which have hyperchromatic nuclei, as in cases of gastritis. This may interfere with the segmentation if it is purely threshold-based segmentation. There has been dramatic progress in the computational aspect of large data images in the recent past, with segmentation using extraction of features, such as morphological characteristics, allowing for a fresh look at image information quantity, for example, the area ratio of foveolar cell cytoplasm and nuclei, and nuclear irregularity in dysplastic glandular cells.

23.6 Conclusion

Highlighting foveolar arrangements from a gastric biopsy image is the first stage in the classification of suspicious regions. Not all image segmentation techniques can be utilized in segmentation of microscopy of tissue, and also different methodologies may be needed for different tissues. In this chapter we focus on a narrow area of one specific tissue (the mucosal lining tissue of the stomach) to highlight this fact. As illustrated in this chapter, histopathology of the stomach foveolar architecture is optimally distinguished by modified watershed transformations. Irregular lesion markers are enhanced by combining thresholding, masking, and watershed transformation. Thus, a simultaneous multiple approach may open a new avenue for developing a fully automated image analysis system for the diagnosis of tissue-specific lesions, such as gastric carcinomas and other gastric lesions.

Acknowledgment

Mousumi Gupta and Amlan Gupta acknowledge the Indian Council of Medical Research for approval for funding by ICMR grant ID number 2020-5638, entitled "Feasibility study of using whole slide histopathology image acquisition system for diagnosis and development of machine learning approach for grading of gastric cancer."

References

Bennett, G. L., Krinsky, G. A., Abitbol, R. J., Kim, S. Y., Theise, N. D., & Teperman, L. W. (2005). Sonographic detection of hepatocellular carcinoma and dysplastic nodules in cirrhosis: Correlation of pretransplantation sonography and liver explant pathology in 200 patients. *American Journal of Roentgenology*, *179*, 75–80.

Bernsen, J. (1986). Dynamic thresholding of gray-level images. In *Proceedings of the eighth International conference on pattern recognition*, Paris.

Beucher, S. (1979). Use of watersheds in contour detection. In *Proceedings of the international workshop on image processing*. CCETT.

Beucher, S., & Meyer, F. (1993). Mathematical morphology in image processing. In *Proceedings of the international workshop on image processing*, vol. 34, 433–481.

Chao, L., Cen, S., Huan, Z., Yazhu, C., & Su, Z. (2015). Multiple instance learning for computer aided detection and diagnosis of gastric cancer with dual-energy CT imaging. *Journal of Biomedical Informatics*, *57*, 358–368.

Danielsson, P. E. (1980). Euclidean distance mapping. *Computer Graphics and Image Processing*, *14*(3), 227–248.

de Vries, A. C., van Grieken, N. C., Looman, C. W., Casparie, M. K., de Vries, E., Meijer, G. A., & Kuipers, E. J. (2008). Gastric cancer risk in patients with premalignant gastric lesions: A nationwide cohort study in the Netherlands. *Gastroenterology*, *134*, 945–947.

Fu, H., Qiu, G., Shu, J., & Ilyas, M. (2014). A novel polar space random field model for the detection of glandular structures. *IEEE Transactions on Medical Imaging*, *33*(3), 764–776.

Gheorghe, C. (2006). Narrow-band imaging endoscopy for diagnosis of malignant and premalignant gastrointestinal lesions. *Journal of Gastrointestinal and Liver Diseases*, *15*, 77.

Gibson, P. R., Anderson, R. P., Mariadason, J. M., & Wilson, A. J. (1996). Protective role of the epithelium of the small intestine and colon. *Inflammatory Bowel Diseases*, *2*(4), 279–302.

Guelrud, M., Herrera, I., Essenfeld, H., & Castro, J. (2001). Enhanced magnification endoscopy: A new technique to identify specialized intestinal metaplasia in Barrett's esophagus. *Gastrointestinal Endoscopy*, *53*, 559–595.

Gunduz-Demir, C., Kandemir, M., Tosun, A. B., & Sokmensuer, C. (2010). Automatic segmentation of colon glands using object-graphs. *Medical Image Analysis*, *14*(1), 1–12.

Gupta, M., Bhaskar, D., Bera, R., & Biswas, S. (2012). Target detection of ISAR data by principal component transform on co-occurrence matrix. *Pattern Recognition Letters*, *33*(13), 1682–1688.

He, L., Long, L. R., Antani, S., & Thoma, G. R. (2017). Histology image analysis for carcinoma detection and grading. *Computer Methods and Programs in Biomedicine*, *107*, 538–556.

Hild, F., & Roux, S. (2006). Digital image correlation: From displacement measurement to identification of elastic properties–A review. *Strain*, *42*(2), 69–80.

Larghi, A. (2007). Long-term follow-up of complete Barrett's eradication endoscopic mucosal resection (CBE-EMR) for the treatment of high grade dysplasia and intramucosal carcinoma. *Endoscopy*, *39*, 1086–1091.

Madabhushi, A., & Lee, G. (2016). Image analysis and machine learning in digital pathology: Challenges and opportunities. *IEEE Transactions*, 170–175.

Nakayoshi, T., Tajiri, H., Matsuda, K., Kaise, M., Ikegami, M., & Sasaki, H. (2004). Magnifying endoscopy combined with narrow band imaging system for early gastric cancer: Correlation of vascular pattern with histopathology. *Endoscopy*, *36*, 1080–1084.

Ren, J., Sadimin, E.T., & Wang, D.E. (2015). Computer aided analysis of prostate histopathology images Gleason grading especially for Gleason score 7. In *2015 37th annual international conference of the IEEE engineering in medicine and biology society (EMBC)*. IEEE, p. 3013–3016.

Roerdink, J. B. T. M., & Meijster, A. (2000). The watershed transform: Definitions, algorithms and parallelization strategies. *Fundamenta Informaticae*, *41*, 187–228.

Sakurai, T., Sakashita, H., Honjo, G., Kasyu, I., & Manabe, T. (2005). Gastric foveolar metaplasia with dysplastic changes in Brunner gland hyperplasia: Possible precursor lesions for Brunner gland adenocarcinoma. *The American Journal of Surgical Pathology*, *29*, 1442–1448.

Stewart, B.W., & Kleihues, P. (2003). *World cancer report*.

Tellez, D, Litjens, G, van der Laak, J, & Ciompi, F (2021). *Neural Image Compression for Gigapixel Histopathology Image Analysis. IEEE Transactions on Pattern Analysis and Machine Intelligence, 1–1., 43* (2), 567–578. Available from https://doi.org/10.1109/TPAMI.2019.2936841.

Verma, Y., Pradhan, P. K., Gurung, N., Sapkota, S. D., Giri, P., Sundas, P., ... Nandakumar, A. (2012). Population-based cancer incidence in Sikkim, India: Report on ethnic variation. *British Journal of Cancer*, *106*, 962–965.

Veta, M., Pluim, J. P., Van Diest, P. J., & Viergever, M. A. (2014). Breast cancer histopathology image analysis: A review. *IEEE Transactions on Biomedical Engineering*, *61*, 1400–1411.

Veta, M., Pluim, J. P. W., Van Diest, P. J., & Viergever, M. A. (2014). Breast cancer histopathology image analysis: A review. *IEEE Transactions on Biomedical Engineering*, *61*, 1400–1411.

Willenbockel, V., Sadr, J., Fiset, D., Horne, G. O., Gosselin, F., & Tanaka, J. W. (2010). Controlling low-level image properties: The SHINE toolbox. *Behavior Research Methods*, *42*(3), 671–684.

Wu, H. S., Xu, R., Harpaz, N., Burstein, D., & Gil, J. (2005). Segmentation of intestinal gland images with iterative region growing. *Journal of Microscopy*, *220*(3), 190–204.

Xu, H., & Mandal, M. (2015). Epidermis segmentation in skin histopathological images based on thickness measurement and k-means algorithm. *EURASIP Journal on Image and Video Processing*, *2015*(1), 18.

Xu, J., Janowczyk, A., Chandran, S., & Madabhushi, A. (2010). A weighted mean shift, normalized cuts initialized color gradient based geodesic active contour model: Applications to histopathology image segmentation. *Medical Imaging 2010: Image Processing*, *7623*, 76230y.

Xu, Y., Zhu, J.-Y., Eric, I., Chang, C., Lai, M., & Tu, Z. (2014). Weakly supervised histopathology cancer image segmentation and classification. *Medical Image Analysis*, *18*, 591–604.

Index

Note: Page numbers followed by "*f*" and "*t*" refer to figures and tables, respectively.

T